Handbook of Methods in Cultural Anthropology

Handbook of Methods in Cultural Anthropology

EDITOR:

H. Russell Bernard, *University of Florida*

EDITORIAL BOARD

Handbook of Methods in Cultural Anthropology

H. Russell Bernard
editor

PRESS

A Division of Sage Publications, Inc.
Walnut Creek ■ *London* ■ *New Delhi*

For information address:

AltaMira Press
A Division of Sage Publications, Inc.
1630 North Main Street, Suite 367
Walnut Creek, California 94596 USA
explore@altamira.sagepub.com
http://www.altamirapress.com

Sage Publications, Ltd.
6 Bonhill Street
London, EC2A 4PU
United Kingdom

Sage Publications India Pvt. Ltd.
M-32 Market
Greater Kailash I
New Delhi 100 048
India

LIBRARY OF CONGRESS CATALOGING-IN-PUBLICATIONS DATA

Handbook of methods in cultural anthropology / H. Russell Bernard,
editor.
     p. cm.
   Includes bibliographical references and index.
   ISBN 0–7619–9151–4 (cloth)
   1. Ethnology—Methodology. I. H. Russell (Harvey
Russell), 1940–
GN345 .H37 1998
305.8'001–ddc21   98–25423
                                                            CIP

PRINTED IN THE UNITED STATES OF AMERICA

                98 99 00 01 02 03 04   7 6 5 4 3 2 1

Editorial Production: Carole Bernard/ECS
Cover Design: Joanna Ebenstein

Contents

Preface   7
H. RUSSELL BERNARD

1 ■ Introduction: On Method and Methods in Anthropology   9
H. RUSSELL BERNARD

Part I: Perspectives

2 ■ Epistemology: The Nature and Validation of   39
Anthropological Knowledge
THOMAS SCHWEIZER

3 ■ In Search of Meaningful Methods   89
JAMES FERNANDEZ and MICHAEL HERZFELD

4 ■ Research Design and Research Strategies   131
JEFFREY C. JOHNSON

5 ■ Ethics   173
CAROLYN FLUEHR-LOBBAN

6 ■ Feminist Methods   203
CHRISTINE WARD GAILEY

7 ■ Transnational Research   235
ULF HANNERZ

Part II: Acquiring Information

8 ■ Participant Observation   259
KATHLEEN M. DEWALT and BILLIE R. DEWALT,
with CORAL B. WAYLAND

9 ■ Direct Systematic Observation of Behavior   301
ALLEN JOHNSON and ROSS SACKETT

10 ■ Person-Centered Interviewing and Observation   333
ROBERT I. LEVY and DOUGLAS W. HOLLAN

11 ■ Structured Interviewing and Questionnaire Construction   365
SUSAN C. WELLER

12 ■ Discourse-Centered Methods   411
BRENDA FARNELL and LAURA R. GRAHAM

13 ■ From Pictorializing to Visual Anthropology   459
FADWA EL GUINDI

14 ■ Fieldwork in the Archives: Methods and Sources   513
in Historical Anthropology
CAROLINE B. BRETTELL

Part III: Interpreting Information

15 ■ Reasoning with Numbers   549
W. PENN HANDWERKER and STEPHEN P. BORGATTI

16 ■ Text Analysis: Qualitative and Quantitative Methods   595
H. RUSSELL BERNARD and GERY W. RYAN

17 ■ Cross-Cultural Research   647
CAROL R. EMBER and MELVIN EMBER

Part IV: Applying and Presenting Anthropology

18 ■ Methods in Applied Anthropology   691
ROBERT T. TROTTER, II and JEAN J. SCHENSUL

19 ■ Presenting Anthropology to Diverse Audiences   737
CONRAD PHILLIP KOTTAK

About the Authors   763
Author Index   775
Subject Index   795

Preface

Carole Bernard and I lived in Cologne, Germany, for a year in 1994–1995. Thomas Schweizer, director of the Institute for Ethnology at the University of Cologne, had invited me to be an Alexander von Humboldt research scholar there. It was the sort of opportunity scholars dream about: the chance to do nothing but read, write, and reflect, and to do all this while interacting with graduate students and colleagues. No classes. No committee work. Paradise.

This handbook is partly a product of that year. I have been interested in social research methods for as long as I can remember, so I took the opportunity in Cologne to read and read, and then read some more. My goal was to become better grounded in the range of methods used by scholars across the social sciences and to understand the role that anthropologists had played in the development of social research methods.

The idea for this handbook emerged in conversations about all this by e-mail, with Mitch Allen, editor of AltaMira Press. It seemed like a good time to take stock. The last handbook, edited by Raoul Naroll and Ronald Cohen, had been published in 1970. The content of the discipline of cultural anthropology and the demography of the profession had gone through big changes since then. In 1970, most anthropologists went into academic jobs. Today, most are in nonacademic jobs. Fewer graduate students do fieldwork in small, isolated communities now. They couldn't, even if they wanted to, for such communities are an endangered social species. In 1972, women received just 32% of the Ph.D. degrees in anthropology in the U.S. In 1995, women received 59% of the doctorates.

There was also the resurgence of the great epistemology debate that has so long pervaded the social sciences. Each side claims support from an indisputable observation: On the one hand, people construct their own realities, and the process

7

is dynamic, ever-changing; on the other, there are regularities in human behavior and human thought. While rhetorical energy is spent arguing that (a) the first fact renders impossible the pursuit of the second or that (b) the second fact renders irrelevant our worrying about the first, working scholars of all persuasions are out there doing empirical research. The core of the discipline, it seemed to me, was in the fact that nearly all cultural anthropologists choose from the same awesomely large kit of tools.

My goal, then, from the beginning has been to put together a handbook that would be useful to academic anthropologists and practicing anthropologists; to interpretivists and positivists; to idealists and materialists.

No project of this magnitude can be managed alone. Six colleagues graciously agreed to join this project and serve as a board of editors: Carol Ember (HRAF), Michael Herzfeld (Harvard), Jane Hill (Arizona), Roy ("Skip") Rappaport (Michigan; deceased), Nancy Scheper-Hughes (UC-Berkeley), and Thomas Schweizer (Cologne). When I thought about senior people whose work was respected by colleagues across the field, Rappaport's name came immediately to mind. Tragically, he didn't live to see the end of the project.

Right from the beginning, the members of the editorial board contributed ideas about chapters that needed to be included in the handbook and about who might write those chapters. They read the chapters and offered critical advice and support. Three of them (Ember, Herzfeld, and Schweizer) contributed chapters themselves. I am grateful to all.

Over the years, I have come to expect nothing less than the best of editorial guidance from Mitch Allen. He never disappoints, never holds back, never pulls punches. I am also grateful to the following colleagues (in alphabetical order) who read various chapters of the handbook in draft and provided detailed reviews: Devon Brewer, Karen Brodkin, Edward Bruner, Douglas Caulkins, Garry Chick, Victor De Munck, William Dressler, Darna Dufour, Robert V. Kemper, David Kertzer, Maxine Margolis, and Alvin Wolfe.

Special thanks go to Ronald Cohen, my colleague at the University of Florida. His was a pioneering effort in 1970 when he and Naroll put together that first handbook of methods in cultural anthropology.

My thanks also go to the Alexander von Humboldt Stiftung, Bonn, and to the College of Liberal Arts and Sciences at the University of Florida for support during 1994–95.

I know that I cannot thank sufficiently my partner, Carole Bernard, for her support all along the way and specifically for her work copyediting and producing the final product. But I can try.

H. Russell Bernard
Gainesville, FL
July 20, 1998

Introduction
On Method and Methods
in Anthropology

This introduction has two parts. In Part 1, I offer some remarks about the history and scope of methods in cultural anthropology. Later, in Part 2, I describe in some detail what is in the various chapters.

Part 1: On Methods in Anthropology

Method is about choice—the choice of taking a *verstehen* or a positivist approach; the choice of collecting data by participant observation or in the archives, by direct observation or by interviewing; the choice of making quantitative measurements or collecting oral, written, or visual text. The authors in this handbook deal with all these choices, and more.

I will have a lot more to say later about the content of the chapters in this handbook. In this first part of the introduction, though, I want to make clear why this book is important—for all social scientists, not just for anthropologists. Conventional wisdom notwithstanding, anthropology has always been about methods, from the earliest days of the discipline right up to the present. Anthropologists have been prodigious consumers and adapters of research methods, and they have made important contributions to the big social science toolkit as well. I am going to document this and put it in perspective here.

There has always been a certain tension between those who would make anthropology a quantitative science and those whose goal it is to produce documents that convey the richness—indeed, the uniqueness—of human thought and experience. Eric Wolf captured this in his wonderful aphorism that "Anthropology is the most humanistic of the sciences and the most scientific of the humanities" (1964:88). Students of cultural anthropology may be asked early in their training to take a stand for interpretivism *or* positivism, humanism *or* science, qualitative *or* quantitative research.

Readers of this handbook will find no support for this polarized vision of method. Instead, they will find scholars laying out the methods they use in practicing their craft—a craft rooted, for every author in this book, in one of the most essentially empirical traditions in all of science: participant observation fieldwork. Some authors are identified with interpretivist methods, some with quantitative methods for the collection and analysis of data, but none dismiss humanism or science and none ask their readers to choose once and for all between expressing their findings in words or in numbers.

Romancing the Methods

John Whiting and some of his fellow graduate students at Yale during the 1930s asked about having a seminar on methods. "Leslie Spier informed us disdainfully," recalls Whiting, "that this was a subject to discuss casually at breakfast and was not worthy subject matter for a seminar" (Whiting 1982:156). Try quoting Whiting at a convention of anthropologists. Chances are, you will discover that everyone chimes in with a favorite story of the same ilk.

It's all well and good for anthropologists to romanticize fieldwork—vulcanologists do it, too—particularly for fieldwork in places that take several days to get to, where the local language has no literary tradition, and where the chances of coming down with a serious illness are nontrivial. Social research really is harder to do in some places than in others. But the fact is, there is a long, noble tradition of concern with research methods in anthropology—quantitative and nonquantitative, humanistic and scientific.

Kathleen and Billie DeWalt quote at length in Chapter 8 what is surely one of the most-cited early discussions of methods in anthropology: Malinowski's introduction to *Argonauts of the Western Pacific* (1922). It is justly famous because, as the DeWalts say, it established the importance of long-term participant observation as a strategic method for field research on other cultures. No peering off the veranda at the natives for Malinowski.

Participant observation is an important method in anthropology but, as the DeWalts point out, it is one of many methods used in fieldwork. By the time Malinowski went to the Trobriands, *Notes and Queries on Anthropology*—the fieldwork manual produced by the Royal Anthropological Institute (RAI) of Great Britain and Ireland—was in its fourth edition (the first came out in 1874). The sixth (and last) edition was published in 1951 and was reprinted five times until 1971. That final edition was edited by Brenda Seligmann and "a committee of the Royal Anthropological Institute" that included the likes of E. E. Evans-Pritchard, Daryl Forde, Raymond Firth, Meyer Fortes, and W. E. Le Gros Clark—and is must reading for anyone interested in learning about field methods. Strip away the quaint language and the vestiges of colonialism—"a sporting rifle and a shotgun are . . . of great assistance in many districts where the natives may welcome extra meat in the shape of game killed by their visitor" (RAI 1951:29)—and the book is still full of useful, late-model advice about how to conduct a census, how to handle photographic negatives in the field, what questions to ask about sexual orientation, infanticide, food production, warfare, art . . . The book is just a treasure.

In the 1920s, leading sociologists were concerned with moving their discipline away from an emphasis on social reform—away from the study of what ought to be and toward the study of what is. If the public were ever to trust social science, said Carl Taylor, then the emphasis had to be on "exact and quantitative expressions and measurements" (Taylor 1920:735). This, he said, required "technologies which will reduce observations to a comparative basis" (p. 753). The technology of choice, said Taylor, was the social survey, a method dating at least to John Howard's monumental, comparative study of prisons (1792).

Taylor's idea of what a survey should be was much broader than just question-naires. "The survey method," he said, "is nothing whatever but the recognized and accepted comparative method of all science," and he concluded that "what . . . surveys can do and have done in the field of anthropology and ethnology, they can do and probably are destined to do for any body of knowledge or field of research to which they are applied (1920:752–753).

Taylor singled out the systematic study of vision, hearing, and pain that Charles and Brenda Seligmann (1911) had done on the Veddas of Sri Lanka. (Charles Seligmann was an ethnologist and physician.) Their 422-page ethnographic account covered family life, religion, the arts, property, and inheritance—and an 18-page report of the results of some psychological tests that they had used in their study of Vedda senses. Some of those tests had been devised by W.H.R. Rivers, an experimental psychologist who became interested in anthropology in 1899 when he was invited to join the Torres Straits expedition and saw the opportunity to do comparative studies of non-Western people (Tooker 1997:xiv).

Rivers, of course, developed the genealogical method—highly detailed, ego-centered graphs for organizing kinship data. The genealogical tables he produced in his study of the Murray Islanders were singled out by Taylor as an example of "as perfect a scientific compilation as could well be imagined" (Taylor 1920:753. See Rivers's work in Volume VI of Haddon 1901–1935). These works by anthro-pologists, said Taylor, were examples of research to which all social science could aspire. Anthropologists continue to this day to work on improved methods for representing complex kinship structures (see White and Jorion 1992).

Rivers continued his work in anthropology and his development of the genealogical method with his research on the Todas of India (Rivers 1906). He developed what he called the "method of indirect corroboration." This method involves "obtaining the same information first in an abstract form and then by means of a number of concrete instances" (p. 11). Here is Rivers explaining the method with reference to his study of the laws of property inheritance:

> I first obtained an account of what was done in the abstract—of the laws governing the inheritance of houses, the division of the buffaloes and other property among the children, etc. Next I gave a number of hypothetical concrete instances; I took cases of men with so many children and so many buffaloes, and repeating the cases I found that my informant gave answers which were consistent not only with one another but also with the abstract regulations previously given. Finally I took real persons and inquired into what had actually happened when A or B died, and again obtained a body of information consistent in itself and agreeing with that already obtained. (p. 11)

Rivers discussed his selection of informants, how he came to know that one of his informants had lied to him, the pros and cons of paying informants for their time, the need for getting information from many informants rather than just from a trusted few, and the importance of using the native language in field research.

Taylor must also have known about Lewis Henry Morgan's study, *Systems of Consanguinity and Affinity of the Human Family* (1870). It was a massive, cross-cultural survey of kinship systems. Morgan collected a lot of the data on various Indian tribes himself, but he also sent questionnaires to missionaries and Indian agents. And Taylor surely also knew about Edward Burnett Tylor's key contribution to the literature on cross-cultural surveys (see Tylor 1889).

Contrary to popular wisdom, then, anthropologists have been keen survey methodologists from the earliest days of the discipline. Unlike sociologists, however, anthropologists studied small, remote groups of people. "These groups," observed Robert Lynd in 1939, "were 'primitive,' according to Western European standards, and therefore the older social sciences did not much care what anthropology did with them" (p. 14).

The point is, that by the time *A Handbook of Method in Cultural Anthropology* was published in 1970, the concern for methods in anthropology was already quite venerable. That volume, edited by Raoul Naroll and Ronald Cohen, was an enormous compilation—1,000 pages and 49 chapters by 46 authors (Naroll and Cohen wrote 6 of the chapters and participated in several others), including 5 that were reprinted from journal articles. The chapters in that handbook, as well as all the chapters on methods in *Anthropology Today* (Kroeber 1953), and in the *Handbook of Social and Cultural Anthropology* (Honigmann 1973), are as useful today as they were when they first appeared. The pioneering textbooks by Pertti

Pelto (1970; and Pelto and Pelto 1978), by John Brim and David Spain (1974), by Allen Johnson (1978) and by Michael Agar (1996 [1980]) contain a wealth of information and wisdom. In writing my own textbook (Bernard 1994 [1988]) I depended heavily on the work of all these predecessors and on the work of colleagues across the social sciences.

Methods, in fact, are us, and the book you are reading—this 1998 handbook—replaces nothing. It adds to a growing body of work about methods of inquiry in cultural anthropology and to methods in the social sciences in general. That is one of the really nice things about research methods: There are more and more of them as time goes on.

Methods Belong to All of Us

Another nice thing about methods is that disciplines cannot own them. Just as it was never true that only sociologists did surveys, it was never true that only anthropologists did participant observation fieldwork. Of course, these days, everybody knows that everybody does everything. Methods really do belong to everyone and this does not just go for methods-as-techniques. It goes just as much for methods-as-approach, methods-as-commitment, and methods-as-epistemology. Neither quantitative nor qualitative researchers have the exclusive right to strive for objectivity; neither humanists nor scientists have a patent on compassion; and empiricism is as much the legacy of interpretivists and idealists as it is of positivists and materialists.

Of course, new methods *develop* within particular disciplines, but any method that seems useful will get picked up and tried out, sooner or later, across the disciplines. Projective tests, like the Rorschach and the TAT, were used by anthropologists in the 1940s (Du Bois 1944; Gladwin and Sarason 1953; Henry and Spiro 1953), were quite popular for a while (see Lindzey [1961] and Hsu [1972] for reviews) and continue to be used by some anthropologists to this day (see Paul 1989; Tsatoulis-Bonnekessen 1993; Boyer at al. 1994). The consensus model of culture was developed in the 1980s by two anthropologists and a psychologist (Romney et al. 1986) and has already started showing up in psychology journals (Johnson et al. 1992; Van Raalte et al. 1992). A solution to the ecological inference problem (inferring individual behavior from aggregate data) was worked out recently by a political scientist (King 1997) and will have wide application in sociology, criminology, and demography. Field experiments were developed by social and educational psychologists (see the classic volume by Cook and Campbell [1979] and Boruch [1997] for a review of more recent work) but some anthropologists also do field experiments (see, for example, Harris et al. 1993).

And of course, participant observation—the *sine qua non* of anthropological fieldwork—is no one's property. I've heard talk at anthropology conventions about how the discipline somehow "lost" the method of participant observation. I could not disagree more. Anthropologists continue to make consistent use of participant observation fieldwork, but we did not invent that method by ourselves. Sociologist Beatrice Webb was doing participant observation—complete with real note taking and informant interviewing—in the 1880s and she wrote at length about the method in her 1926 memoire (Webb 1926). Just about then, the long tradition in sociology of urban ethnography began at the University of Chicago under the direction of Robert Park (one of the many participant observers trained by Park was his son-in-law, Robert Redfield). That tradition continues today in the pages of the *Journal of Contemporary Ethnography*, which began in 1972 under the title *Urban Life and Culture*.

Participant observation today is absolutely ubiquitous in the social sciences. It has been used in recent years by political scientists (Fenno 1990; Glaser 1996), social psychologists (Weisfield and de Olivares 1992; Smith and Inder 1993), psycho-analysts (Perry 1985; Hirsch 1990; Hegeman 1995), students of management (Gummeson 1991; Weick 1995; Watson 1996), researchers in nursing (De Valck and Van de Woestijne 1996; Woodgate and Kristjanson 1996), education (Woods 1986; Rovegno and Bandhauer 1997), social work (Lawler and Hearn 1997) and expert systems engineering (Meyer 1992), as well as by legions of sociologists (see Denzin and Lincoln 1994).

Among the salutary results of all this is a continually growing body of literature, including a lot by anthropologists, about participant observation itself. There are highly focused studies, full of practical advice, and there are poignant discussions of the overall *experience* of fieldwork (Agar 1996, Wolcott 1995, Smith and Kornblum 1996).

The boundaries between the disciplines remain strong, but those boundaries are no longer about methods—if they ever were—or even about content. Anthropologists today are more likely to study army platoons (Killworth 1997) or consumer behavior (Sherry 1995) or the mean streets of big cities (Bourgois 1995; Fleisher 1998) than they are to study isolated tribal peoples. Today, the differences *within* anthropology and sociology with regard to methods are more important than the differences *between* the social sciences. There is an irreducible difference, for example, between those of us for whom the first principle of inquiry is that reality is constructed uniquely by each person and those of us who start from the principle that external reality awaits our discovery through a series of approximations. There is also an important (though not incompatible) difference between those of us who seek to *understand* human phenomena in relation to differences in beliefs and values and those of us who seek to *explain* human thought and behavior as the consequence of external forces.

Whatever our epistemological differences, however, the actual methods by which we collect and analyze our data belong to everyone across the social sciences.

Anthropology: The Humanistic, Positivistic, Interpretive Science, Etc.

Anthropology was built by empiricists, including many who understood that reducing people to words was no better than reducing them to numbers and who did both with aplomb. Franz Boas took his Ph.D. in physics from the University of Kiel, with mathematics and geography as his minors. When he turned his attention to anthropology, he advocated a historical, particularizing approach, but he did not abandon numbers. Nor did most of his students. Alfred Kroeber, for example, analyzed measurements on 300 years of data on skirt length, waist height, and depth of décolletage to look for long-term patterns in style (Richardson and Kroeber 1940).

Robert Lowie, Clark Wissler, Edward Sapir, Margaret Mead, Ruth Benedict, and Elsie Clews Parsons considered themselves scientists. One of Boas's students, Paul Radin, famously rejected his mentor's scientific bent. He accused Boas of being *naturwissenschaftlich eingestellt*, or science minded, of treating ethnology as a branch of natural science and named his cofrêres—Sapir, Kroeber, Mead—as examples of the bad things that happen to cultural anthropologists who follow the path of quantification (Radin 1933:10).

But even Radin was an arch empiricist. His passion against quantification was surpassed by his commitment to the continual collection of texts. It was Radin who made it clear for all time that, while theories come and go, original texts, in our informants' own languages, are available for every generation to analyze anew. Inspired by Boas's efforts with George Hunt (a Kwakiutl), Radin handed Sam Blowsnake (a Winnebago) a pad and a pencil—an act that produced one of anthropology's most famous texts, *Crashing Thunder: The Autobiography of a Winnebago Indian*—and established a model for emically oriented ethnography (Blowsnake 1920).[1]

Above all, the distinction between quantitative and nonquantitative must never be used as cover for talking about the difference between science and humanism. Lots of scientists do their work without numbers; and many scientists whose work is highly quantitative consider themselves to be humanists. Humanism is often used as a synonym for humanitarian or compassionate values and a commitment to the amelioration of suffering. The myth that science is the absence of these values is truly pernicious. Jane Goodall said recently that part of her work these days is not to watch chimps, but to correct the mistaken idea that science has to be dispassionate. "I am often asked to talk about the softer kind of science," she says, "as a way of bringing children back into realizing that [science] is not about chopping things up and being totally objective and cold" (Holloway 1997:44).

We must reject a culture that equates objectivity with being cold. Counting the dead accurately in Rwanda is one way—not the only way—to preserve outrage. We need more, not less, science, lots and lots more, and more humanistically informed science, to contribute more to the amelioration of suffering and the weakening of false ideologies—racism, sexism, ethnic nationalism—in the world.

Humanism sometimes means a commitment to subjectivity—that is, to using our own feelings, values, and beliefs to achieve insight into the nature of human experience. This kind of humanism is, of course, the foundation of many clinical disciplines as well as the foundation of participant observation ethnography (see Berg and Smith [1985] for a review of clinical methods in social research). It is not something apart from social science. It is a method used by idealists and materialists alike.

Humanism sometimes means an abiding appreciation of and search for the unique—the unique in human experience and the unique in culture. If the rest of social science was the search for regularities, then anthropology was the search for exceptions. It is a truism that one cannot fully know someone else's life without living that person's life. Giving birth, surviving hand-to-hand combat, living with AIDS . . . in some way, all experience is surely unique. But just as surely, there are commonalities of experience. To write a story about the thrill or the pain of a successful or failed border crossing, a successful or failed job hunt, a winning or losing struggle with illness—or to write someone else's story for them, as an ethnographer might do—these are not activities *opposed* to a natural science of experience. They *are* the activities of a natural science of experience, whether or not they are done in service to explanation or understanding, to nomothetic or idiographic goals.

Humanism is sometimes pitted against positivism, which is said to be linked to support for whatever power relations happen to be in place. Historically, though, positivism was linked to the most critical stance. *The Subjection of Women* (1869) by John Stuart Mill was a radical work in its day, advocating full equality for women. Adolphe Quételet, the Belgian astronomer whose study of demography and criminology carried the audacious title *Social Physics* (1969[1835]), was a committed social reformer. The legacy of positivism as a vehicle for social activism is clear in Jane Addams's work with destitute immigrants at Chicago's Hull House (1926), in Sidney and Beatrice Webb's attack on the British medical system (1910), in Charles Booth's account of the conditions under which the poor lived in London (1902), and in Florence Nightingale's (1871) assessment of death rates in maternity hospitals.[2]

The central position of positivism as a philosophy of knowledge is that experience is the foundation of knowledge. We record what we experience visually, auditorily, and emotionally. The quality of the recording, then, becomes the key to knowledge. Can we, in fact, record what others experience? Yes, of course we can. Are there pitfalls in doing so? Yes, of course there are. For some social researchers these pitfalls are evidence for natural limits to social science, while for others they are a challenge to extend the current limits by improving measurement. Whether they rally to the idealist or the materialist flag, all social scientists can be humanists by any or all of these definitions. When insight and understanding are achieved, we may call it knowledge. The fact that knowledge is tentative is something we all learn to live with.

The practice that we associate today with the positivist perspective in social science, however, is not the positivism of Auguste Comte, of Adolphe Quételet, of John Stuart Mill; nor is it even the logical positivism of the Vienna Circle. None of these is the tradition that so many today love to hate.

That honor belongs to what Christopher Bryant (1985:137) calls "instrumental positivism." In his 1929 presidential address to the American Sociological Society, William F. Ogburn laid out the rules. In turning sociology into a science, he said, "it will be necessary to crush out emotion." Further, "it will be desirable to taboo ethics and values (except in choosing problems); and it will be inevitable that we shall have to spend most of our time doing hard, dull, tedious, and routine tasks" (1930:10). Eventually, he said, there would be no need for a separate field of statistics because "all sociologists will be statisticians" (p. 6). This kind of rhetoric just begged to be reviled. There were challenges to Ogburn's prescription, but, as Oberschall (1972:244) concluded, it was Ogburn's commitment to value-free science and to statistics that won the day.

"It is certainly desirable to be precise," said Robert Redfield (1948:148), "but it is quite as needful to be precise about something worth knowing." We are all free, of course, to identify ourselves as humanists or as positivists, but it's much more fun to be both. The scientific component of anthropology demands that we ask whether our measurements are meaningful, but the humanistic component forces us to ask if we are pursuing worthwhile ends and doing so with worthwhile means.

In the end, the tension between science and humanism is wrought by the need to answer practical questions with evidence and the need to understand ourselves—that is, the need to measure carefully and the need to listen hard.

Permanent Methodological Eclecticism

While anthropology has always been an eclectic discipline with regard to methods, the adoption by anthropologists of the full range of social research methods has accelerated since 1970. This was not a random event: In 1970, most anthropologists went into academic jobs; by 1975, most did not.

A generation earlier, in 1950, just 22 Ph.D. degrees were awarded by U.S. universities in anthropology. In 1957, the Soviet Union launched the first orbiting satellite—Sputnik. The arms race that followed, with its MAD (mutually assured destruction) strategy, produced billions of dollars for expansion of U.S. universities. And this growth wasn't just for math and the natural sciences. All those engineers and physicists needed courses in English, philosophy, history, and the social sciences. Combined departments of sociology and anthropology separated, and

Ph.D.-granting anthropology programs proliferated. When I began graduate study at the University of Illinois in 1961, it had recently separated from sociology. Four years later, the department awarded its first Ph.D. degree.

The expansion was irrepressible. By 1970, the number of anthropology Ph.D.s had jumped to a heady 195, but that was just the beginning. By 1974, all those new Ph.D.-granting departments were filled with assistant professors training thousands of graduate students—and awarding over 400 Ph.D. degrees per year (Givens and Jablonski 1996). With the expansion complete, all those assistant professors were in place and there were no new jobs in the academy (D'Andrade et al. 1975).

The attraction of anthropology for new students, however, remained undiminished. The number of Ph.D. degrees awarded annually by institutions that participate in the survey of the American Anthropological Association has remained, on average, 413 since 1974. In total, about 11,000 Ph.D. anthropologists were produced from 1970–1998 (Givens and Jablonski 1996).

Demography being more-or-less destiny, those who had participated in the great 1960s expansion began to retire in the mid-1980s. From 1985–1994, an average of 331 academic jobs were listed in the *Anthropology Newsletter* (Givens and Jablonski 1996). But with all those anthropologists from previous years still applying for academic jobs, the openings were (and remain) far fewer than the number of available candidates.

Not that all those Ph.D.s were out of work. The jobless rate for anthropologists was 1.6% in 1993, the last time the NSF looked (Givens and Jablonski 1996). During all the tough years of the 1970s and 1980s, young anthropologists knocked on, and eventually opened, many doors (Koons et al. 1989). They rewrote their résumés and competed successfully for jobs in medical schools and other parts of the university. But most importantly, they competed for jobs in industry and government. They joined consulting firms and opened their *own* firms, specializing in international market research, in training executives for overseas assignments, in rapid rural assessment for health care delivery programs, in developing ecotourism —the list is as big as the hunger and imagination of the pioneers themselves. By 1986, for the first time in the history of the discipline, more anthropologists were employed in nonacademic jobs than in academe (see Fluehr-Lobban 1991:5).

This same thing happened, of course, in sociology, but the effects were quite different. As anthropologists competed for nonacademic jobs, they were forced to be more explicit about their methods. Program administrators were accustomed to hiring social scientists whose methods and products were known commodities. It was the anthropologists who had to make the adjustment, not the sociologists, psychologists, and economists.

By and large, the result was a synthesis of qualitative and quantitative approaches—a synthesis that we see today coming into academe from many directions. In the absence of, say, a few thousand new academic jobs for anthropologists, the continued move toward sophisticated methodological eclecticism is permanent.

Part 2: What's in the Handbook?

This handbook has 19 chapters by a total of 27 active researchers. Chapters 2–7 cover epistemology, methods in the search for meaning, research design, ethics, feminist approaches, and approaches for transnational research. Chapters 8–14 cover specific strategies and techniques of data collection including participant observation, direct observation, person-centered interviewing, structured interviewing, methods for the collection and analysis of natural discourse, methods for the collection and analysis of visual data, and methods of historical anthropology. Chapters 15–17 describe methods of data analysis including numerical methods, methods for the systematic analysis of text, and methods for testing cross-cultural hypotheses. Chapter 18 deals with the range of methods used in applied anthropology, and Chapter 19 is a discussion of methods for presenting anthropology to various audiences.

Readers should come away from this book with a sense of the richness in the methods available to all of us because of the diversity in perspective that we bring to the research craft.

Thomas Schweizer sets the tone for the book in Chapter 2, tracing the "centrifugal and centripetal tendencies" that emerge from anthropology's special location between the humanities and the sciences. The method of empathic reasoning and the method of display, through prose, of that reasoning is as strong as ever in the humanistically oriented segment of our discipline. It plays well for all of us because we can all resonate to a good story about how people experience their lives, their bodies, their illnesses, their children.

On the other hand, as Schweizer makes clear, our discipline is equally rooted in positivism—in the "method of hypothesis testing as a general procedure for generating and validating scientific knowledge." In the end, says Schweizer, "the difference in kind between the presence of the hermeneutic circle in the humanities at one extreme and the lack of it in the natural sciences on the other becomes a mere difference in degree."

Recently, as Schweizer points out, two approaches—postmodernism and radical constructivism—have developed as alternatives to both classical positivism and classical hermeneutics. Postmodernism, says Schweizer, "questions systematic approaches to the production of cumulative knowledge (which radical constructivism does not reject), and postmodernism and radical constructivism both adopt a relativistic stance that stresses the creative power of scientists to invent 'reality'." Schweizer sorts through these epistemological alternatives—positivism, hermeneutics, postmodernism, and radical constructivism—pointing out where they converge and diverge. The search for convergences, says Schweizer, "shouldn't silence the real differences or lead to shallow, false compromises. Instead, it should open up the possibility that there are overlapping concerns and rational procedures in each framework that can be cross-fertilized and even combined."

Chapter 3, by James Fernandez and Michael Herzfeld, continues the theme of building a bridge across the interpretivist-positivist divide. The "fashionable distinction between positivistic and interpretive styles of analysis," say Fernandez and Herzfeld, is "itself caught up in an identifiable, describable social rhetoric." What is needed is "not a contemptuous dismissal of methodology as scientistic nonsense, but a determinedly empirical insistence on the constant calibration of the methods we use to elicit data with our informants' understanding of what constitutes appropriate discourse, social interaction, and intellectual activity." This chapter, then, is at once a statement about epistemology and a description of methods for studying meaning.

And how to find meaning? Look, say Fernandez and Herzfeld, for the ways that meaning plays out in expressive culture—in the architectonics of buildings and village layout, in dance, in games, in dyadic interactions, and in work. Herzfeld, for example, has videotaped interactions between artisans and their apprentices. He has been playing the tapes, with the sound turned off, for other knowledgeable people in the culture, and asking them to comment on the interaction. The men, he says, tend to sympathize with the artisans, while women tend to sympathize with the apprentice, "thereby demonstrating the replication of ideologies of hierarchy in adjacent but discrete contexts of social life." In other words, just as buildings and games reflect features of our culture, so do our reactions to the actions of others reflect our deepest understandings of our culture.

Fernandez and Herzfeld also advise us to take part in physical activities. "Anthropology," they say, "is often conducted in circumstances in which to talk a good game is not really to play it at all. . . . Claims to cultural knowledge through purely verbal operations may be a black-box-opening operation of the most problematic kind. The more secure method of approximation is to have learned by apprenticeship how to do . . . to operationalize by bodily activity, what others know how to do in the world." Learn, in other words, to walk the walk, not just talk the talk to understand the meaning of activities, objects, and words to our informants. We may never get it all right, since there may be many ways to get anything right in a given culture, but corporeal understanding is critical to understanding. Fernandez, for example, acquired an agricultural plot among the Fang and apprenticed himself to some elders in order to understand agricultural practices. Among the Bwiti, he danced dances in all-night sessions, among Asturian villagers he did an apprenticeship learning to manage the scythe, and he followed workers into the mines.

The position taken by Fernandez and Herzfeld—what they call the "militant middle ground"—accepts neither the militantly positivistic orientation of some colleagues nor the militantly antipositivistic position of others. I share their enthusiasm for taking part physically in the lives of those whom we would understand and their enthusiasm for making cultural anthropology the enterprise in which we all participate to understand and explain human experience and behavior.

In Chapter 4, Jeffrey Johnson surveys the broad range of research designs and strategies in cultural anthropology. Once again, we see that the history of our discipline is one of tension between two essentially different approaches to research design. Each approach has its advantages and disadvantages, but selecting between them can be excruciating. "While early British and U.S. anthropologists advocated the scientific method in ethnographic research," says Johnson, "there is little evidence that they considered appropriate design issues when they actually did the research."

This may have been because it was just too difficult to make reliable, accurate, and valid measurements of variables in human thought and behavior under tough field conditions. Or it may have been the result of simply being torn between the Scylla of precision and the Charybdis of verisimilitude, between the desire to explain and the joy of understanding. Like all the authors in this handbook, Johnson stresses the importance of the ethnographic approach. The strength of this approach, he says, "is its ability to incorporate a wide range of methods, strategies, and designs within a single enterprise, all combining in ways to improve the chances for credible results." Johnson shows, with a series of concrete examples, the differences between exploratory and explanatory research. He lays out the varieties of experimental and nonexperimental research designs and discusses issues of sampling. "It is critical," says Johnson, "to remember the connection between theory, design (including sampling), and data analysis from the beginning, because how the data were collected, both in terms of measurement and sampling, is directly related to how they can be analyzed."

In Chapter 5, Carolyn Fluehr-Lobban seeks to make ethical considerations "an ordinary, not extraordinary, part of anthropological practice." She traces the history of ethical issues in the discipline, from Franz Boas's public excoriation in 1919 of anthropologists who worked as intelligence agents for the American military, to the ethical debates during the Vietnam War era, to the promulgation of the latest PPR—the Principles of Professional Responsibility—by the American Anthropological Association.

The principles that guide ethical conduct in any research, says Fluehr-Lobban, are openness and disclosure. This is what makes it possible for the people with whom we interact in our research to choose whether to provide us with information or not. Since 1971, every code of ethics promulgated by the American Anthropological Association has taken a firm stand against secret research. Fluehr-Lobban points out that "secret" is not the same as "proprietary." The World Bank, for example, may contract for proprietary research, but the research is not conducted clandestinely nor are the results secret. Thus, one key question to ask about any research project, says Fluehr-Lobban, is: "Would I be willing to disclose the source(s) of my funding to the people I'm studying?"

Disclosure and openness have been forced on researchers with the implementation of the principle of informed consent. Informed consent, however, is not as easy to ensure as one might think. Fluehr-Lobban advises anthropologists against asking students to fill out research questionnaires in classes that students are taking for credit. To do this, she says, is a coercive act—one that violates the spirit, if not the letter, of the principle of informed consent. Nor, she says, should anthropologists take an "exceptionalist view" of the principle of informed consent. "The rights of research participants," she says, "don't vary whether they're studied by psychologists, cardiologists, or anthropologists." There are, of course, some special issues associated with informed consent in fieldwork settings. Anthropologists, says Fluehr-Lobban, should not be "shy or intimidated about educating members of institutional review boards about the nature of anthropological research and the methods we use" but we cannot simply walk away as if the rules don't apply. "Developing awareness of the fundamental importance of ethics as a key component of professionalism," she says, "and as a necessary adjunct to science and research is an essential task of the next generation of anthropologists."

Christine Gailey follows in Chapter 6 with a discussion of feminist methods. We must, says, Gailey, acknowledge that "scientific inquiry, takes place in a social world and is conducted by people who have cultural frameworks that shape their thinking." But, she warns, this "should not translate into a rejection of quantitative techniques—that somehow these are inherently masculinist or antifeminist. . . . Indeed," she says, "techniques can be viewed as neutral, and our goal may be to reduce bias by making our assumptions and epistemological claims clear to our audiences." Thus, she says, abandoning claims to perfect objectivity does not mean pursuing bias. Researchers can become aware of their own biases and can communicate those biases to their audiences. "Cross-checking for bias, for feminist anthropologists," says Gailey, "lies in reflexivity, in critically examining the links that we make or do not make between our assumptions, how our research is designed and conducted, and the conclusions we draw."

Gailey traces how feminist thinking has influenced and is influenced by other approaches. She advocates an approach that calls for "integrating feminism into one's relations in daily life" and notes that this is what distinguishes feminism from other critical approaches. This may create a tension that comes with responsibility to various audiences and interlocutors, but, says Gailey, "The creative discomfort or tension that results from the adoption of such responsibility is part of one's state of being, because ethics are part of the methodology."

Chapter 7, by Ulf Hannerz, is about a new field in cultural anthropology—transnational research. The history of method in our discipline, says Hannerz, is marked by the study of populations that have more and more fluid borders—from isolated, preliterate people, to more-or-less self-contained peasant communities, to migrants from villages to cities, to localized ethnic groups, and now to cultural groups that have no borders at all. "With studies of the transnational and the global," says Hannerz, anthropology "may face the final test of its tools."

Transnational studies pose unique methodological problems. For one thing, they may require fieldwork at both ends and a knowledge of the language of two or more countries. Ethnographers need command of French and English, Hindi and English, or Chinese and English in order to conduct transnational studies in say, Québec, Bombay, or Hong Kong. A field worker must know both Spanish and English in any study of the fast-developing U.S.-Mexico border culture.

Hannerz points out that network analysis was prominent in anthropology during the 1960s and 1970s but that it became unattractive to anthropologists as it became more focused on itself, as method. With the development of transnational studies, however, Hannerz says, "network analysis may again offer ways of thinking about how units of study are constituted and about the social spaces occupied by varied actors."

Another feature of contemporary anthropology, says Hannerz, and particularly of transnational studies, is that "fieldwork goes on in some ways, even as the ethnographers have absented themselves physically from their fields." Anthropologists have always kept in touch with their friends and consultants from field sites, but today some of us maintain contact by e-mail in places where electricity has only recently arrived. "As transnational fields are constituted," says Hannerz, "with their own internal patterns of long-distance cohesion, such ways of keeping in touch on the part of the researcher will not necessarily appear as strikingly deviant." Will this contact itself forge a transnational cultural environment?

Chapters 8–13 on specific methods of data collection begins with Kathleen and Billie DeWalt's discussion of participant observation. They observe that the descriptions by Malinowski in 1922 and Bourgois in 1995 of their fieldwork are strikingly similar. This suggests, say the Dewalts, "that the method . . . is so closely tied to a relatively unchanging theoretical core in anthropology as to provide the basis for a wide range of theoretical development around that core."

The DeWalts lay out the goals of participant observation and many of the techniques that comprise this strategic method. The goals include: (1) creating self-conscious empathy for the lived experience of people in another culture; (2) developing an articulate, intellectualized understanding of the causes and consequences of this lived experience; (3) gaining the kind of rapport with people that comes only from a genuine interest in their experience; and (4) using that rapport to engage in all kinds of research activities, from unstructured conversational interviews to pile sorts and survey questionnaires.

Ultimately, the objective of ethnography, they say, "should not be to learn more about ourselves as individuals (although that will happen), but to learn more about others." They call for "systematic study of the effects of biases, predilections, and personal characteristics on the research enterprise," noting that, "being a man or woman may be the most significant social fact concerning an individual and obviously should have an impact on participant observation." Few ethnographers can speak to this issue as authoritatively as can the DeWalts.

Chapter 9, by Allen Johnson and Ross Sackett, deals with direct observation. "In ethnography," they say "what people *do* matters." They recognize the importance of using multiple methods in the field, including participant observation and interviewing, but that these methods are, by themselves, "inadequate to the task of constructing trustworthy accounts of activity patterns." Studying behavior under field conditions, however, is no easy task. I can say from my own experience that the temptation to study talk rather than action can really be irresistible. Most of us, in other words, record *reports* of behavior. For some behaviors, knowledgeable informants can report accurately on the mean—what people generally do. But, as Johnson and Sackett's chapter makes clear, if you really need to know, for example, what a series of individuals eat, or how much time women in a society have for leisure, there is no substitute, despite the difficulties, for direct observation. The challenge, they say, is to focus more attention on human behavior, not as a substitute for the study of culture, but as a vital complement to our understanding of culture itself.

Johnson and Sackett address the key questions involved in studying behavior under field conditions: "What does it mean to describe an activity? Whom should we observe, when, and where? At what level of detail? How can we sample from the stream of behavior in a community to generate a fair representation of people of differing age, gender, and status, in all the relevant contexts of their lives?" They describe the problems of sampling, selecting units of analysis, and choosing between spot observation and continuous monitoring of behavior, and they offer guidance on several options for recording behavioral observations.

The next two chapters are about two quite different approaches to interviewing. In Chapter 10, Robert Levy and Douglas Hollan discuss person-centered interviews, and this is followed in Chapter 11 by Susan Weller's discussion of structured interviewing.

Person-centered interviewing, according to Levy and Hollan, is the study of the interrelations of private and public worlds of people in a community—that is, the study of how people's minds and selves are affected by and, in turn, affect the culture and society of the communities in which they live. A person-centered interview, say Levy and Hollan, "moves back and forth" between treating people as *informants* who report on their society—"asking a Tahitian interviewee something like 'Please describe for me exactly how and why supercision . . . (a penis-mutilating rite of passage) is done by Tahitians"—or as *respondents* who report on themselves—"asking him 'Can you tell me about *your* supercision? What did you think and feel about it then? What do you think and feel about it now?'"

Some topics that are particularly suited to open-ended, person-centered interviewing, according to Levy and Hollan, are personal identity; personal morality, sexuality, fantasy, and dreams; reactions to illness and stress; responses to death, to religion, to children; and so on. The exploration of private experience (for example, the feelings, thoughts, and experiences of a Hindu Untouchable in response to his or her public role and behavior) is important for anthropology's humanistic aims. But, argue Levy and Hollan, personal data also help us understand social change and stability and a community's responses to internal and external forces.

The person-centered, open-ended interview becomes more than just culturally standardized discourse, more than a report of culturally and socially important facts. It is also a sample of behavior. This allows us, say Levy and Hollan, to pay close attention not only to what people say, but to how and when they say it. We can also examine the interaction between the interviewer and the interviewee, looking for examples of how the interviewer may be distorting and biasing the interview process.

Person-centered interviewing requires excellent rapport, and fluency in the local language. "It is deeply distorting," say Levy and Hollan, "not to work primarily in the respondent's core language." It also requires time. "The depth, significance, and honesty of respondent responses tends to grow over the course of a series of interviews. Inexperienced interviewers fear that they will run out of questions, that the interviews will become sterile, that the respondent will become annoyed. This is not what happens in well-conducted interviews where understanding deepens and where . . . the respondent usually regrets having the series discontinued."

From the sort of interviewing that requires learning to say "uh-huh" and "tell me more about that" in just the right places, we move to a discussion of highly structured interviewing. "In general," says Weller, in Chapter 11, "the less that is known about an area, the more appropriate are unstructured, open-ended methods." She describes what she calls a "bottom-up" approach, in which the initial goal is exploration and the development of "a set of items relevant to the area of interest and to the people to be interviewed." The results of this approach can be incorporated into more systematic interviews. This combination of exploratory and systematic methods, she says, "produces a study superior to one based on either method alone, although it involves a greater commitment of time and energy."

Weller notes that a "top-down" approach can also be valid. That is, "one might begin with survey results collected by someone else (a national survey, the census, etc.) and supplement their findings with more detailed, open-ended work on the same topic." Kempton et al. (1995) used this approach in their study of U.S. environmental values, and Baer (1996) used results from the U.S. Census to develop in-depth interviews with Mexican migrant workers in Florida. "Survey results," says Weller, "are good at providing a representative picture of what the population may be doing or thinking, but are limited in the depth with which they may explore a topic."

Weller describes the variety of methods available for in-depth studies of cultural domains, including free-recall listing, pile sorts, triad tests, sentence substitution, and the cultural consensus model. She lays out the methods for constructing questionnaire items, including scales and indices. Many anthropologists will want to use a scaling device at some time in their fieldwork, but scales develped for one population might not transfer to another. Weller describes in detail some methods for translating and adapting scales to new environments, and she outlines the steps for creating and testing new scales in the field.

In Chapter 12, Laura Graham and Brenda Farnell discuss discourse-centered methods. One of the key concepts in this linguistic anthropological tradition is that culture is visible in actual discourse between and among persons—an emergent phenomenon that is "constantly open to new associations and interpretive moves." These moves are not random, but are guided by rules for coding social phenomena in language. The rules, say Graham and Farnell, "are discovered through fieldwork and data collection and involve the interaction of such things as the ethnographer, the individuals with whom she or he works, and the community as well as formal elements of texts themselves."

This work requires taping and accurate transcribing and close attention to detail. Like Levy and Hollan, Graham and Farnell insist that field notes aren't nearly enough to capture the verbal data on which close analysis depends. With a corpus of transcribed discourse, however, a researcher can look for features and patterns that, say Graham and Farnell, are "implicated in broader social and cultural phenomena, such as relations of power, kinship, identity, gender relations, aesthetics, and affect." It is the analysis and interpretation of these texts, say Graham and Farnell, "together with interpretation of their connections to broader social phenomena [that] distinguish discourse-centered research from other anthropological methodologies."

For example, Graham used two tape recorders in her work with the Xavante. As one recorder played back specific instances of discourse, the other recorder captured her consultant's responses to questions that Graham asked about how the language was being used and about interactions between speakers. Using that method, Graham discovered "features associated with the speech of elders and alternative patterns of person marking and verb morphology used in speech to, or about, certain kin and affines." These features were not found in elicitations—in the speech of informants who responded to questions from the ethnographer.

In Chapter 13, Fadwa El Guindi describes the development of methods in visual anthropology—from Félix-Louis Regnault film in 1888 of a Wolof woman making pots at the Exposition Ethnographique de l'Afrique Occidentale; to Margaret Mead and Gregory Bateson's work of 1936–1938 that produced 22,000 feet of 16mm film and 25,000 still shots in Bali and New Guinea (which, says El Guindi, showed how film could be used to record the details of bodily movement and nonverbal behavior); to Sol Worth and John Adair's 1966 "native film experiment" in which

Navajos were asked to shoot film records of their own culture; and to El Guindi's own explorations of method in her shooting of a feature on an Egyptian birth ritual.

Worth and Adair, says El Guindi, based their project on the idea that "motion picture film—conceived, photographed, and sequentially arranged by a people, in this case, the Navajo—would reveal aspects of coding, cognition, and values that may be inhibited, not observable, or not analyzable when the investigation is totally dependent on verbal exchange—especially when such research must be done in the language of the investigator." That, says El Guindi, turned out to be an important idea, one that has been modified and replicated in projects in other cultures.

In describing her own experience in filming *El Sebou': Egyptian Birth Ritual*, El Guindi shows the ethnographic filmmaker at work, devising new methods during the shooting itself to deal with issues and questions she had raised in developing the project. In a method called "layering," for example, El Guindi uses several techniques "all layered within the film itself" to translate and communicate a culture to a foreign audience. These techniques include "bottom-of-screen English subtitling of Arabic statements made by the people in the film, segment-by-segment English titling of Arabic songs, subjective voice (English rendition of voices faithful in diction and mannerism), and objective voice (analytic narrative)."

In recent years, many anthropologists have adopted the standards of historical methods for studies in family history, demographic history, oral history, life history, and political-economic history. In Chapter 14, Caroline Brettell assesses the methods of historical anthropology, or what she calls "fieldwork in the archives." For some historical anthropologists, she says, the object is to capture the emic view of history—how local people understand their own history—while for others, the object is more global and comparative, to understand "the social, political, economic, and cultural processes that characterize human behavior in the past as well as in the present."

According to Brettell, the documents that anthropologists use in the study of historical problems include tax records, church and civil archives of births and deaths, police and judicial records, wills, property transactions, diaries, and many secondary sources as well—even photographs. Still, because anthropologists use historical methods to link the past with the present—because they "enter the archives through the back door of ethnography"—their work remains different from the work of historians. Anthropologists, says Brettell, often make leaps of interpretation that "might make the historian wince."

Brettell discusses the recent case of disagreement between Gananath Obeyeskere (1992) and Marshall Sahlins (1995) regarding the interpretation by Hawaiians of the death of Captain James Cook in 1799. The disagreement between these two scholars is profound, but, says Brettell, they would probably agree on two things: "(1) Historical documents should be read with a sensitivity to the social, political, and cultural context within which they were produced; and (2) We must work not only to identify the ethnocentrism of the writer of a document but our own ethnocentrism as evaluators of that document."

Chapter 15, by W. Penn Handwerker and Stephen Borgatti, describes the numerical methods of data analysis that are used most often by cultural anthropologists. In ethnographic research, say Handwerker and Borgatti, we begin by collecting data from one person. "When we go to the next person, "we always find something different, as well as something much the same. And so it goes." We continue this process until we feel that we can "construct a story . . . about the people we worked with: about their lives and the circumstances in which they have lived; about what those people now think, feel, and do."

Ethnographers, say Handwerker and Borgatti, collect two quite different kinds of data: cultural data—data on the "systems of mental constructions [that] people use to interpret themselves and the world around them and of the behavior isomorphic with those systems of meaning"—and data on the individual characteristics—things like age and gender, years spent in school, or how much, if any, violence people experienced as children. The goal for many ethnographers, say Handwerker and Borgatti, is to learn what is typical—How do most people conceptualize an event? At what age do most people become parents?—and many ethnographers also hope that their field research work will allow them to generalize beyond the few informants whom they can interview.

Some ethnographers also want to go beyond description and explain how patterns and observed variability in cultural and individual data emerge and persist or change. "We aim," say Handwerker and Borgatti, "to explain variability in culture and behavior as a function of variability in experience, and search for concrete events and circumstances that shape those experiences." In the end, numerical methods are thus "nothing more than explicit tools of data collection and analysis that address core research questions: 'Did we get it right?' and 'To whom, if anyone, can we validly generalize?'" In addition, "explicit reasoning with numbers . . . lets us see things in and about people's lives we'd otherwise miss and answer questions in ways that help us pinpoint those errors in judgment that make us quintessentially human."

In Chapter 16, Gery Ryan and I discuss methods of text analysis. Anthropologists have always had a strong tie to texts. Debates about materialism and postmodernism and functionalism come and go, but the texts collected by Franz Boas (from the Kwakiutl) and Edward Sapir (from the Wishram), and the films shot by Margaret Mead and Gregory Bateson (of the Samoans and the Balinese) remain for new generations of scholars to interpret. In fact, most of the recoverable data about human thought and human behavior is text of one kind or another. With new technologies coming along (voice recognition software, high-speed scanners, etc.), it will become easier and easier to examine subtleties of text that were invisible to us before.

Ryan and I describe developments in grounded theory (a qualitatively oriented approach to text analysis) and classical content analysis (a quantitative approach).

Both approaches involve identifying themes and testing hypotheses. Other methods that involve the analysis of text include analytic induction (also known as Boolean analysis), schema analysis, the comparison of texts across and within cultures, and the comparison of stories across and within cultures. Intracultural comparison involves collecting many examples of the same story (like asking 200 Americans to tell the story of "George Washington and the cherry tree") in order to examine variation in how culture heroes are portrayed. Cultural schema analysis involves understanding statements like: "Blanche lost her data because she forgot to save her work." We know that Blanche's forgetting to save her work did not actually *cause* her to lose her data. A whole set of links are left out, but they are easily filled in by any listeners who have the background to do so.

Many cultural anthropologists try to understand *a culture*. For others, the goal is to derive and test hypotheses about *culture* itself from the systematic comparison of *cultures* as units of analysis. The methods for doing this—deriving hypotheses, selecting a sample, coding the variables, and doing appropriate statistical tests—are the focus of Chapter 17 by Carol and Melvin Ember.

Cross-cultural researchers, say the Embers, ask descriptive questions and questions about the causes and consequences of cultural variation. It is one thing, for example, to ask "What proportion of societies have dowry?" and quite another to ask "Why do 3% of the world's societies have dowry?" It is one thing to ask "What proportion of societies practice polygyny?" and another to ask "What is the effect of polygyny on total fertility?"

Testing hypotheses across cultures presents interesting challenges of measurement and sampling because ethnographies—the fundamental data for comparative research—are not based on a standardized set of questions to begin with. For example, "If an ethnographer says 'extended family households are typical,' we don't know if that means 50% or 100%." On the other hand, say the Embers, "we can be very confident it doesn't mean 0–40%. And we can be fairly sure it doesn't mean 40–49%." If you want to know whether the frequency of extended families is related to, say, the practice of agriculture, "then we should be able to see the relationship even though we can't use a percentage measure based on numerical information."

Cross-cultural research has deep roots in our discipline. One of Edward Burnett Tylor's best-known papers, published in 1889, was on a method for showing the association of customs across cultures. But it was George Peter Murdock at Yale in the 1930s who is most responsible for the development of cross-cultural research today. Murdock's goal, say the Embers, was to establish a database of ethnography so that scholars could make systematic comparisons of cultures. This led, in 1949, to the Human Relations Area Files (HRAF). Today, HRAF is a consortium of 20 sponsoring universities (and hundreds of others) that support the collection and coding of a continually growing archive of ethnographies (currently about a million pages) on 365 cultures (and counting) around the world. The collection is used by researchers across the social and biological sciences. Since 1994, the annual increments to the collection (about 40,000 pages a year) have been electronic (CD-ROM, Internet). The Embers anticipate that this will encourage even more comparative research as time goes on.

In Chapter 18, Robert Trotter and Jean Schensul survey the methods used in and developed by applied anthropologists. The filling and closing of the academic market for anthropologists in the early 1970s left a generation of new Ph.D.s to fend for themselves. And fend they did, opening thousands of new jobs in industry, commerce, and government. Applied anthropologists use all the methods of anthropology—in fact, all the methods of social research—and this means that they require very broad training in research methods. The role of the anthropologist in a research project, the speed with which research often must be done, and the ethical responsibilities implied by the conduct of research that can have direct impact on people's lives are some key differences in applications research.

In traditional ethnography, say Trotter and Schensul, the role of the anthropologist and the informant can be reversed. "Applied anthropology calls for reciprocal learning and sharing of expertise in identifying a problem, defining a researchable question, conducting research, and using results." Also, much of the research done by applied anthropologists is done as part of a multidisciplinary team.

Another difference between applied and basic anthropology is the speed with which results have to be delivered. It used to be part of the anthropological canon that ethnography took a year. We are learning better. The method of rapid rural assessment, developed jointly by agricultural economists and anthropologists, has become generalized to rapid ethnographic assessment.

Finally, all anthropologists are obliged to consider the ethical implications of their work, but, say Trotter and Schensul, applied anthropologists have an even greater burden of responsibility because "the human, social, and ecological consequences of applied research are immediate, potentially significant, and sometimes critical to the life and survival of communities."

In Chapter 19, on presenting anthropology to diverse audiences—to our colleagues, students, government bureaucrats, the general public, and our own informants—Conrad Kottak describes the breadth of writing in the discipline. "Cultural anthropology," says Kottak, "is a book field." By contrast, the most important form of communication in biological anthropology is scholarly articles in peer-reviewed journals. Cultural anthropologists are also expected to write articles, but the distinction Kottak draws is a mirror for the scientific and humanistic emphases that characterize anthropology.

"In general," says Kottak, "it isn't possible to write a book for more than one audience." He draws on his personal experience, and the experience of others, in writing monographs, contract reports, grant proposals, textbooks, tradebooks, scholarly articles, and articles for the popular press. He offers practical advice on using these various literary forms, learning to write for particular audiences, responding to reviews, dealing with the media, and so on.

Kottak shows that content and style changes in academic writing, just as it does in popular writing. He compares, for example, the titles of the first three articles in an issue of the *American Ethnologist* from 1984 and those from an issue in 1997. The titles in the earlier issue are more straightforward—there were no colons in the titles and little jargon—while titles from the more recent issue are more playful and more literary. Away from the academy, in team research on applications projects, where so much anthropology goes on, "the discourse, behavior, and modus operandi of the mix of professionals making up a team tend to converge toward an organizational norm." Anthropologists, says Kottak, should be ever mindful of the special potential contribution of their field.

And Finally

This handbook is the latest and most complete compilation of the current state of the art in anthropological methods. Readers will be introduced to the full range of methods used in empirical anthropological research. Just as anthropologists are eclectic users of methods from psychology and sociology, our colleagues in those disciplines will find in this handbook contributions to the development of the methodological toolkit. All of us across the social sciences today are making far greater demands on our methods than we ever did before. These demands are for accuracy, validity, precision, reliability, and, above all, credibility. We all want our research to make a difference. Some of us want to contribute to the widespread understanding of humanity's diversity of experience. Some of us want to contribute to the prediction, explanation, and, yes, control, of the phenomena we study.

This handbook leaves no doubt that the humanistic and scientific methods for doing these things are improving all the time. It leaves no doubt about the need for constant vigilance regarding ethical conduct of research. It leaves no doubt that anthropology has fully joined—as a consumer and as a contributor—the discussion and development of methods in the social sciences.

NOTES

1. The first edition of Blowsnake's autobiography was published in 1920 as part of the University of California's series on archaeology and ethnology. The book titled *Crashing Thunder: Autobiography of a Winnebago Indian* was published in 1926 by D. Appleton and Co. and was reprinted in 1983 by the University of Nebraska Press.

2. I am indebted to McDonald (1993, 1994) for pointing me to Nightingale's long-ignored work.

REFERENCES

Addams, Jane. 1926. *Twenty Years at Hull-House*. New York: Macmillan.

Agar, Michael. 1996 [1980]. *The Professional Stranger: An Informal Introduction to Ethnography*, 2d ed. San Diego: Academic Press.

Baer, R. D. 1996. Health and Mental Health among Mexican American Migrants: Implications for Survey Research. *Human Organization 55*(1):58–66.

Berg, David N., and K. K. Smith, eds. 1985. *Exploring Clinical Methods for Social Research*. Beverly Hills, CA: Sage Publications.

Bernard, H. Russell. 1994 [1988]. *Research Methods in Anthropology: Qualitative and Quantitative Approaches*, 2d ed. Walnut Creek, CA: AltaMira Press.

Blowsnake, Sam. 1920. The Autobiography of a Winnebago Indian. Paul Radin, ed and tr. Berkeley: University of California Press. (*University of California Publications in American Archaeology and Ethnology 1*[7]).

Booth, Charles, ed. 1902. *Life and Labor of the People of London*. New York: Macmillan.

Boruch, Robert F. 1997. *Randomized Experiments for Planning and Evaluation: A Practical Guide*. Thousand Oaks, CA: Sage Publications.

Bourgois, Philippe I. 1995. *In Search of Respect: Selling Crack in El Barrio*. New York: Cambridge University Press.

Boyer, L. Bryce, R. M. Boyer, and H. F. Stein, eds. 1994. *Essays in Honor of George A. De Vos*. Hillsdale, NJ: Analytic Press.

Brim, John A., and D. H. Spain. 1974. *Research Design in Anthropology: Paradigms and Pragmatics in the Testing of Hypotheses*. New York: Holt, Rinehart and Winston.

Bryant, Christopher. 1985. *Positivism in Social Theory and Research*. New York: St. Martin's Press.

Cook, Thomas D., and D. T. Campbell. 1979. *Quasi-Experimentation: Design and Analysis Issues for Field Settings*. Boston: Houghton Mifflin.

D'Andrade, Roy G., E. A. Hammel, D. L. Adkins, and C. K. McDaniel. 1975. Academic Opportunity in Anthropology 1974–90. *American Anthropologist 77*:753–773.

Denzin, Norman K., and Yvonna S. Lincoln, eds. 1994. *Handbook of Qualitative Research*. Thousand Oaks, CA: Sage Publications.

De Valck, C., and K. P. Van de Woestijne. 1996. Communication Problems on an Oncology Ward. *Patient Education & Counseling 29*:131–136.

Du Bois, Cora Alice. 1944. *The People of Alor: A Social-Psychological Study of an East Indian Island*. Minneapolis: University of Minnesota Press.

Fenno, Richard F. 1990. *Watching Politicians: Essays on Participant Observation*. Berkeley: Institute of Governmental Studies, University of California.

Fleisher, Mark 1998. *Dead End Kids: Gang Girls and the Boys They Know*. Madison: University of Wisconsin Press.

Fluehr-Lobban, Carolyn. 1991. Professional Ethics and Anthropology: Tensions Between Its Academic and Applied Branches. *Business and Professional Ethics 10*(4):57–68.

Givens, David, and T. Jablonski. 1996. 1996 AAA Survey of Departments. In *The AAA Guide*. Pp. 304–315. Arlington, VA: American Anthropological Association.

Gladwin, Thomas, and Seymour B. Sarason. 1953. *Truk: Man in Paradise*. New York: Wenner-Gren Foundation for Anthropological Research.

Glaser, James M. 1996. The Challenge of Campaign Watching: Seven Lessons of Participant-Observation Research. *PS: Political Science & Politics* 29:533–537.

Gummesson, Evert. 1991. *Qualitative Methods in Management Research*. Thousand Oaks, CA: Sage Publications.

Haddon, Alfred C., ed. 1901–1935. *Reports of the Cambridge Anthropological Expedition to Torres Straits*. Cambridge, England: The University Press.

Harris, Marvin, J. G. Consorte, J. Lang, and B. Byrne. 1993. Who Are the Whites? Imposed Census Categories and the Racial Demography of Brazil. *Social Forces* 72:451–462.

Hegeman, Elizabeth B. 1995. *Cross-Cultural Issues in Interpersonal Psychoanalysis*. Hillsdale, NJ: Analytic Press.

Henry, Jules, and Melford Spiro. 1953. Psychological Techniques: Projective Tests in Field Work. In *Anthropology Today*. A. L. Kroeber (and others), eds. Pp. 417–429. Chicago: University of Chicago Press.

Holloway, Marguerite. 1997. Profile: Jane Goodall. *Scientific American* (October):42–44.

Honigmann, John, ed. 1973. *Handbook of Social and Cultural Anthropology*. Chicago: Rand McNally.

Howard, John. 1973 [1792]. *Prisons and Lazarettos*. Vol. 1. *The State of the Prisons in England and Wales: With Preliminary Observations, and an Account of Some Foreign Prisons and Hospitals*. Montclair, NJ: Patterson Smith.

Hsu, Francis L. K., ed. 1972. *Psychological Anthropology*. Cambridge: Schenkman.

Johnson, Allen W. 1978. *Quantification in Cultural Anthropology: An Introduction to Research Design*. Stanford: Stanford University Press.

Johnson, Kathy E., Carolyn B. Mervis, and James S. Boster. 1992. Developmental Changes Within the Structure of the Mammal Domain. *Developmental Psychology* 28:74–83.

Kempton, Willett, J. S. Boster, and J. A. Hartley. 1995. *Environmental Values in American Culture*. Cambridge: M.I.T. Press.

Killworth, Paul R. P. 1997. Culture and Power in the British Army: Hierarchies, Boundaries and Construction. Ph.D. diss., University of Cambridge.

King, Gary. 1997. *A Solution to the Ecological Inference Problem: Reconstructing Individual Behavior from Aggregate Data*. Princeton: Princeton University Press.

Koons, Adam, Beatrice Hackett, and John P. Mason. 1989. *Stalking Employment in the Nation's Capitol: A Guide for Anthropologists*. Washington, DC: The Washington Association of Professional Anthropologists.

Kroeber, Alfred, ed. 1953. *Anthropology Today*. Chicago: University of Chicago Press.

Lawler, John, and J. Hearn. 1997. The Managers of Social Work: The Experiences and Identifications of Third Tier Social Services Managers and the Implications for Future Practice. *British Journal of Social Work 27*:191–218.

Lindzey, Gardner. 1961. *Projective Techniques and Cross-Cultural Research*. New York: Appleton-Century-Crofts.

Lynd, Robert. 1939. *Knowledge for What? The Place of Social Science in American Culture*. Princeton: Princeton University Press.

Malinowski, Bronislaw. 1922. *Argonauts of the Western Pacific: An Account of Native Enterprise and Adventure in the Archipelagoes of Melanesian New Guinea*. New York: E. P. Dutton.

Malinowski, Bronislaw. 1927a. *The Father in Primitive Psychology*. New York: Norton.

Malinowski, Bronislaw. 1927b. *Sex and Repression in Savage Society*. New York: Harcourt, Brace.

McDonald, Lynn. 1993. *The Early Origins of the Social Sciences*. Montreal: McGill-Queen's University Press.

McDonald, Lynn 1994. *The Women Founders of the Social Sciences*. Ottawa: Carleton University Press.

Meyer, Mary A. 1992. How to Apply the Anthropological Technique of Participant Observation to Knowledge Acquisition for Expert Systems. *IEEE Transactions on Systems, Man, and Cybernetics 22*(5):983–991.

Mill, John Stuart. 1869. *The Subjection of Women*. New York: D. Appleton.

Morgan, Lewis Henry. 1870. *Systems of Consanguinity and Affinity of the Human Family*. Washington, DC: Smithsonian Institution.

Naroll, Raoull, and Ronald Cohen, eds. 1970. *A Handbook of Method in Cultural Anthropology*. New York: Natural History Press.

Nightingale, Florence. 1871. *Introductory Notes on Lying-In Institutions. Together With a Proposal for Organising an Institution for Training Midwives and Midwifery Nurses*. London: Longmans, Green.

Oberschall, Anthony. 1972. The Institutionalization of American Sociology. In *The Establishment of Empirical Sociology*. A. Oberschall, ed. Pp. 187–251. New York: Harper & Row.

Obeyesekere, Gananath. 1992. *The Apotheosis of Captain Cook: European Mythmaking in the Pacific*. Princeton: Princeton University Press.

Ogburn, William F. 1930. The Folk-Ways of a Scientific Sociology. *Publication of the American Sociological Society 25*:1–10.

Paul, Robert A. 1989. Psychoanalytic Anthropology. *Annual Review of Anthropology 18*: 177–202.

Pelto, Pertti J. 1970. *Anthropological Research: The Structure of Inquiry*. New York: Harper & Row.

Pelto, Pertti, and G. Pelto 1973. Ethnography: The Fieldwork Enterprise. In *Handbook of Social and Cultural Anthropology*. John Honigmann, ed. Pp. 241–288. Chicago: Rand McNally.

Pelto, Pertti, and G. Pelto. 1978. *Anthropological Research: The Structure of Inquiry*, 2d ed. New York: Cambridge University Press.

Perry, Helen Swick. 1985. Using Participant Observation to Construct a Life History. In *Exploring Clinical Methods for Social Research*. D. N. Berg and K. K. Smith, eds. Pp. 319–332. Beverly Hills, CA: Sage Publications.

Quételet, Adolphe. 1969 [1835]. *Physique sociale, ou, essai sur le développement des facultés de l'lomme*. Paris: J.-B. Bailliere et fils. Originally published in 1835. Reprinted in translation in 1969 from the 1842 edition as: *A Treatise on Man and the Development of His Faculties*. Gainesville, FL: Scholars' Facsimiles and Reprints.

Radin, P. 1933. *The Method and Theory of Ethnology*. New York: McGraw-Hill.

Redfield, Robert. 1948. The Art of Social Science. *American Journal of Sociology* 54(3):181–190.

Richardson, J., and A. L. Kroeber 1940. Three Centuries of Women's Dress Fashions: A Quantitative Analysis. *Anthropological Records* 5(2):111–153.

Rivers, W. H. R. 1906. *The Todas*. New York: Macmillan.

Romney, A. K., S. C. Weller, and W. H. Batchelder. 1986. Culture as Consensus. *American Anthropologist* 88:313–338.

Rovegno, Inex, and Dianna Bandhauer. 1997. Norms of the School Culture that Facilitated Teacher Adoption and Learning of a Constructivist Approach to Physical Education. *Journal of Teaching in Physical Education* 16:401–425.

Royal Anthropological Institute of Great Britain and Ireland. 1951. *Notes and Queries on Anthropology*, 6th ed. London: Routledge and Kegan Paul.

Sahlins, Marshall. 1995. *How Natives Think: About Captain Cook For Example*. Chicago: University of Chicago Press.

Seligmann, Charles Gabriel, B.Z.S. Seligmann, with C. S. Myers, and A. M. Gunesekara. 1911. *The Veddas*. Cambridge, England: The University Press.

Sherry, John F., Jr. 1995. *Contemporary Marketing and Consumer Behavior: An Anthropological Sourcebook*. Thousand Oaks, CA: Sage Publications.

Smith, Anne B., and Patricia M. Inder. 1993. Social Interaction in Same and Cross Gender Pre-School Peer Groups: A Participant Observation Study. *Educational Psychology 13*: 29–42.

Smith, Carolyn D., and W. Kornblum 1996. *In the Field: Readings on the Field Research Experience*, 2d ed. Westport, CT: Praeger.

Taylor, Carl C. 1920. The Social Survey and the Science of Sociology. *American Journal of Sociology 25*(1919–1920):731–756.

Tooker, Elizabeth. 1997. *Introduction. Systems of Consanguinity and Affinity of the Human Family. Lewis Henry Morgan.* Lincoln: University of Nebraska Press.

Tsatsoulis-Bonnekessen, Barbara. 1993. Exploring Ethnic Contact with Stories and Stereotypes: The Thematic Apperception Technique and the Adjective Checklist as Supporting Interview Tools. *Cultural Anthropology Methods* 5(2):1–3.

Tylor, Edward B. 1889. On a Method of Investigating the Development of Institutions Applied to the Laws of Marriage and Descent. *Journal of the Royal Anthropological Institute of Great Britain and Ireland 18*:245–272.

Van Raalte, Judy L., B. W. Brewer, D. D. Brewer, and D. E. Linder. 1992. NCAA Division II College Football Players Perceptions of an Athlete Who Consults a Sport Psychologist. *Journal of Sport and Exercise Psychology 14*:273–282.

Watson, Tony J. 1996. How Do Managers Think? Identity, Morality and Pragmatism in Managerial Theory and Practice. *Management Learning 27*:323–341.

Webb, Beatrice 1926. *My Apprenticeship*. London: Longmans, Green.

Webb, Beatrice. 1963. *American Diary, 1898*. Madison: University of Wisconsin Press.

Webb, Sidney, and Beatrice P. Webb. 1910. *The State and the Doctor*. New York: Longmans, Green.

Weick, Karl E. 1995. *Sensemaking in Organizations*. Thousand Oaks, CA: Sage Publications.

Weisfeld, Glenn E., and Karen de Olivares, 1992. A Participant-Observation Course in Applied Adolescent Development. *Teaching of Psychology 19*:180–182.

White, Douglas R., and Paul Jorion. 1992. Representing and Computing Kinship: A New Approach. *Current Anthropology 33*:454–453.

Whiting, J.W.M. 1982. Standards for Psychocultural Research. In *Crisis in Anthropology. View from Spring Hill, 1980*. E. A. Hoebel, R. Currier, and S. Kaiser, eds. Pp. 155–164. New York: Garland.

Wolcott, Harry F. 1995. *The Art of Fieldwork*. Walnut Creek: AltaMira Press.

Wolf, E. R. 1964. *Anthropology*. Englewood Cliffs, NJ: Prentice-Hall.

Woodgate, Roberta, and Linda J. Kristjanson. 1996. A Young Child's Pain: How Parents and Nurses "Take Care." *International Journal of Nursing Studies 33*:271–284.

Woods, Peter. 1986. *Inside Schools: Ethnography in Educational Research*. London: Routledge & Keegan Paul.

PART I
PERSPECTIVES

THOMAS SCHWEIZER

Two

Epistemology
The Nature and Validation of Anthropological Knowledge

In this chapter I discuss the nature and justification of anthropological knowledge. The core methodological problems of anthropological research are: (1) how to produce valid descriptions of other people/societies/cultures; and (2) how to establish comparative and theoretical syntheses of these descriptions. These core problems are broken down and translated into lower-level methodological problems in debates within and across different methodological frameworks.

I introduce the positivist framework as a representative of the scientific approach and present hermeneutics and postmodernism/radical constructivism as exemplars of the humanist approach in the social sciences. I present the developments, main tenets, and some strengths and weaknesses of these methodological frameworks. Then I address three key problems of anthropological research: (1) the problem of reality, relativism, and truth; (2) the relationship between interpretation (including empathic *verstehen*) and explanation; and (3) the problem of theory construction and theoretical progress.

Epistemology and Methodology in Anthropology

Epistemology is a subdiscipline of philosophy concerened with the nature and validation of knowledge (that is, "reasoned, true belief") in general. In cultural anthropology, epistemology addresses the scope and justification of factual knowledge that anthropologists have established through fieldwork (Werner and Schoepfle 1987:Vol. 1, Ch. 1), historical reconstruction, and comparative studies on human cultures past and present. This quest for empirical knowledge can be applied to any society and culture, including the anthropologist's. Generating valid anthropological knowledge becomes more difficult in practice, when anthropologists investigate what some call the "Other"—people who speak a different language and belong to different historical and cultural traditions. In such cases, researchers and researched can't easily take for granted a common cultural background, and this creates special problems for generating valid knowledge. Still, anthropologists like Melford Spiro (1986, 1990) argue that our belonging to one species, humankind, produces some minimum commonality of understanding; as examples, see the evidence for emotional universals in Ekman (1980), and, for the universal logical forms by which humans reason, in D'Andrade (1995:194–199).

In debates about the aims and conduct of research in human, social, and behavioral sciences, the most agreed-on point is that researchers in a particular field lack a uniform methodological and theoretical framework. Epistemology discusses the general problems of how we can know something and what knowledge is, whereas methodology is a more specific discussion of the goals and procedures of inquiry in particular disciplines.

In discussing methods and theories, empirical disciplines like anthropology, sociology, and psychology shift the focus from very general, epistemological reasoning at the core of philosophy to the more concrete methodological level of how to conduct research and what the goals of inquiry are. Epistemological questions become translated into more manageable methodological ones that can guide empirical research. Most debates on theory and method in anthropology are methodological, postulating different goals for the research agenda and favoring different strategies on how to achieve the goals (for example, hermeneutic understanding versus scientific explanation, thick description versus establishment of societal laws). As used here, *method* refers to the procedures of acquiring knowledge on a subject matter, while *theory* refers to substantive results of a more general nature on the state and structure of the subject matter.

Methodology includes discussion of method—How shall we proceed?—and of the principles of theory construction—What are the goals of inquiry? What shall the knowledge that we want to produce on our subject matter be like? What does the concept of theory mean? A methodological framework, then, is a particular school of thought that makes some claims and sets up prescriptions on how to conduct research in a discipline. The most basic distinction in the methodology of the social and behavioral sciences and the humanities is the split between scientific and humanist methodologies (Bohman 1991; Hollis 1994; Lang 1994; Kuznar 1997). The scientific method involves the claim that there is no difference in principle between the goals (description and explanation) and the conduct of research in all disciplines; the humanistic method involves the claim for special goals and procedures of research in the humanities that take meaning and history into account.

Positivism, on the one hand, and hermeneutics (including postmodernism and radical constructivism as recent currents), on the other, are the main representatives of scientific versus humanist methodologies respectively. In the United States, the four-field orientation connects cultural anthropology, prehistory, biological anthropology, and linguistics in departments and with a common history, so the clash of scientific versus humanist methodologies has been most intense in anthropology. The centrifugal and centripetal tendencies emerging from this special location between the sciences and the humanities and the ensuing propensity to adopt the different science or humanist agendas has been captured by Eric Wolf (1964:88), who observed that anthropology is "the most humanist of the sciences and the most scientific of the humanities."

In cultural anthropology, adherents of the different agendas debate the goals of inquiry and draw different rules for empirical research. But fieldwork practices—how ethnographers collect data by participant observation, open-ended interviews, and systematic techniques (Agar 1980, 1986; Werner and Schoepfle 1987; Bernard 1994) and how they write ethnographic reports—had been unifying bonds across rival methodological currents. Depending on their adherence to various methodological frameworks, anthropologists disagreed about specific procedures, but there was general consensus on the value and conduct of gathering ethnographic knowledge on the ground and presenting data on actors in their local and regional context in reports. Further, all competing anthropological schools were in some way interested in comparison of ethnographic cases, although they disagreed about the systematics of comparison.

At first, recent postmodernist challenges of ethnographic authority and writing seemed to end anthropological consensus on fieldwork practices and the monographic tradition of ethnographic writing (Clifford and Marcus 1986; Marcus and Fischer 1986; Clifford 1988). However, after intense programmatic debate, even practitioners of this critical school adhered to fieldwork and now produce ethnographic descriptions that differ in focus, but not in principle, from monographs of the past or from descriptions produced by anthropologists following other methodological frameworks (for example, Kondo 1990; Lindstrom 1990; Gewertz and Errington 1991; Dumont 1992; Steedly 1993; Tsing 1993; Yang 1994; Gupta and Ferguson 1997 in general). Note the similarity to the methodological and theoretical debates on formalism versus substantivism in economic anthropology in the 1960s. This tended to separate economic anthropologists at the level of programmatic statements, while at the empirical level of monographic description, the theoretical splits had only slight consequences. A current assessment of the subdiscipline shows that substantivist concerns and formalist models have become blended even at the theoretical level (Netting 1993; Plattner 1989; Wilk 1996). The problem of comparative synthesis, however, is still there.

I conclude this introductory discussion of anthropological epistemology by pointing out that there are two main problems of methodological debate in anthropology: (1) At the ethnographic, more observational level, we must consider how to produce valid descriptions of the Other (person, culture, society). (2) At a more theoretical level of anthropological synthesis, we must answer the question of how to compare ethnographic cases across time and space and how to arrive at valid theoretical generalizations.

In methodological discussions, these fundamental problems are split into lower-level problems, like the contrast between *verstehen* and explanation (see below). In the following, I outline the different methodological approaches used in anthropology to address these issues and some related lower-level problems encountered in pursuing valid ethnographic descriptions and producing sound theoretical syntheses. I take into account the broader epistemological and methodological reasoning in the philosophy of science and the neighboring human, social, and behavioral disciplines. I draw on analytic philosophy of science as a metatheory (Kutschera 1982; Stegmüller 1969, 1973, 1979a, 1979b; Bunnin and Tsui-James 1996, among others; readers should be aware of this possible bias).

I discuss the differences in the frameworks as well as the similarities, describing them as rational procedures for acquiring anthropological knowledge. More specifically, I would like to make the point that positivism is less homogeneous than is sometimes thought and that scientific and humanist approaches are different in focus, but complementary (as are *verstehen* and explanation). In the theory section, I propose the new structuralist theory concept as a rich and precise framework for describing and analyzing the structure of generalizations and their change in the discipline. Thus, my goal is to assess methodological frameworks and methodological problems in anthropology and to sketch a proposal for solving these problems. First, I introduce the different methodological frameworks as background traditions of research. Second, I discuss some key problems of ethnographic description and theoretical generalizations that have been put forward by the different methodological schools.

Divergent Methodological Frameworks

Below the basic split between scientific and humanist approaches, two, three, or four—depending on one's standpoint—main schools frame specific discussions of epistemological and methodological issues in anthropology and related disciplines.

1. *Positivism* proposes a unified methodology for different branches of the sciences and the humanities. It poses the discovery of general laws as the ultimate goal of scientific inquiry and advocates the scientific method of hypothesis testing as a general procedure for generating and validating scientific knowledge. The growth of cumulative knowledge in the natural sciences is the model for this framework. However, positivists disagree on the specifics of their methodology (and many dislike the term "positivism" as well).

2. *Hermeneutics* (the more general term, or *interpretivism* as a more narrow term), the rival framework to positivism, is rooted in the humanities. It tries to establish a special methodology for understanding meaning in the human and social sciences. The model case of hermeneutics is the interpretation of texts, and its objective is the exploration of common understandings in historically based cultural traditions.

3. *Postmodernism* and (4) *radical constructivism* are relatively new approaches. Some consider them radical versions of hermeneutics, whereas others claim that these approaches are true methodological alternatives to both positivism and hermeneutics. Postmodernism questions systematic approaches to the production of cumulative knowledge (which radical constructivism does not reject), and postmodernism and radical constructivism both adopt a relativistic stance that stresses the creative power of scientists to invent "reality."

In the following, I characterize the main tenets of these frameworks. Positivist and hermeneutic ideas have been developing for two centuries. So, I concentrate discussion on these approaches rather than on postmodernism and radical constructivism whose new ideas are still shifting and progressing. Since methodological frameworks are complex belief systems allowing for internal variation, there is no simple and deterministic connection between a particular framework and the historical/political context in which it is embedded.

Thus, I focus on ideas as the more enduring and interesting parts of these frameworks and put less emphasis on the historical, political, and biographical contingences of their creators and supporters.[1] Since every framework tends to conceive the world in its own terms, I look for convergences across frameworks in a quest for a more general methodological agenda. This shouldn't silence the real differences or lead to shallow, false compromises. Instead, it should open up the possibility that there are overlapping concerns and rational procedures in each framework that can be cross-fertilized and even combined.

The Science Approach: Varieties of Positivism

Today, the term "positivism" is often associated negatively with narrow-minded data collection, number crunching, and acceptance of the status quo. This wasn't its meaning in the nineteenth century, when it was established by European social scientists and social reformers. A variety of sometimes very different meanings are associated with positivism.

When Auguste Comte and his disciples coined the concept of *positivism* in the nineteenth century, it had an enlightenment and antimetaphysical spirit. "Positive" meant collecting and validating *factual* knowledge by scientific methods. In the classic, positivist stance, true knowledge had been obscured by the traditional powers of the state and the church and their metaphysical agents. Thus, classic positivism was not at all a politically neutral or conservative doctrine. Eventually, it fell into disrepute when it turned out that its antimetaphysics were based on a rather metaphysical creed of progress. But the positivist movement, along with related currents like evolutionary theory, provided the foundation for several social and behavioral science disciplines. It also led to the recognition and better practice of scientific principles, not the least being respect for the erudite collection of empirically based "social facts."

The second meaning of positivism relates to the ideas of *logical positivism* as developed in Vienna during the 1920s and '30s by scholars in philosophy and some related disciplines (see Carnap [1963] for a personal account, Geier [1993] for a historical one of the "Vienna Circle"; Janik and Toulmin [1973] on the *zeitgeist*; and Achinstein and Barker [1969] on logical-positivist ideas). As with earlier positivists, these people wanted to free philosophy and the empirical sciences of any metaphysical, speculative assumptions not founded on observation or confirmed by empirical tests. The newly invented methods of formal logic were applied to philosophical and other scientific statements to clarify language, to detect and refute metaphysical claims, and to create better science. The ideas of the logical positivists spread to other parts of Europe (Berlin, Prague, Oxford, Cambridge) and the Americas before and after World War II. The clarity of rational debate and critical spirit among its adherents were outstanding. In fact, some of the movement's key early ideas were refuted from within. The strict empiricist doctrine, for example, demanding that all theoretical statements be based on observation couldn't be maintained because the universal truth claims of theoretical statements always transcend the limited observational evidence available from tests.

Viennese philosopher Karl Popper (1969a, 1969b, 1972) regarded himself a critic of logical positivism. Nevertheless, he developed *critical rationalism* (a third variety of positivism) in opposition to but connected with logical positivism. Popper concluded that positive evidence ("confirmation") and the inductive method (the search for rules that lead from limited observations to the establishment of valid generalizations) are not at the heart of science. Rather, negative evidence ("falsification") and deduction are at the core. Because our tests are limited, we can never be sure that a (universal) theoretical statement is true. Even if all present evidence is confirmatory, there could always be a refutation in the future. Failure of prediction inevitably leads to a refutation of the generalizing statement, because, according to rules of logic, a wrong consequence disproves the truth of the premise. In the spirit of critical rationalism, when choosing between rival hypotheses, we should always select the one that has a higher information content by being more general and thus more challenging due to its wider range of application. And we should keep the one that has survived serious attempts at falsification and therefore has proven less false than its rival.

Against this falsificationist view, some philosophers of science, most notably Willard Quine (1961:Ch. 2) pointed out that the test situation is always more complex: a wrong conclusion could imply that the hypothesis at hand is wrong, but it could also falsify any other statements in the premise, including measurement theories and observational statements. Hence, the use and test of hypotheses is always based on a holistic understanding of the whole test situation and is guided by inductivist (probabilistic) judgments of the development potential of theoretical statements in future applications (Papineau 1996). So, the one-sided critical view of falsificationism has to be supplemented by a more positive heuristic of hypothesis construction and theory development.

The fourth variant of positivism is *analytic philosophy*, which became the dominant mode of philosophical thinking in the Americas and some parts of Europe and Asia. Some of the ideas of logical positivism, critical rationalism, and early as well as later positivist ideas were taken into analytic philosophy. Formal analysis as a tool of rational reconstruction and criticism are the main pillars of this framework that leaves a lot of room for internal debates and theoretical diversity. "Analytic philosophy of science" (a better general term than positivism) has had a significant impact on some social and behavioral sciences and has furnished methodological self-reflection in these disciplines. Economics has seen the most grounded and intense debate of methodological issues regarding the different currents of positivism (Albert 1967; Latsis 1976; Marchi 1988, 1992; Blaug 1992; Backhouse 1994, among others).

The Positivist Thrust

There are three main points to remember from this short sketch.

1. Positivism in the past has never been as narrow-minded as is sometimes depicted today by its critics. There is considerable *diversity* within positivism/analytic philosophy of science.
2. In the positivist view, the scientific method rests on some minimum and therefore necessary standards: *clarity of language* (definitions and concepts are tools for communication) and *validation of truth claims by rational means* of logic and empirical inquiry (including a concern to lay open the assumptions of arguments and tests so that other members of the scientific community can check the evidence). For all adherents of analytic methodology, these standards apply to any discipline. In principle, at least, there's no difference among the natural, social, and behavioral sciences and the humanities, because they all depend on the rules of logic and empirical validation and use the method of "conjectures and refutations" (Popper 1969b—or a similar approach of the invention of hypotheses, logical proof, and empirical testing, also called "the hypothetico-deductive method"; Hempel 1966; Kuipers 1996).

3. Scientific, research-oriented positivism seeks to establish *laws* (logically sound theoretical generalizations that have survived serious attempts at refutation). In the analytic perspective, such laws rule nature, society, and culture and can be used in scientific explanations. Some analytic philosophers of science have attempted to demonstrate that even in the humanities historians, for instance, implicitly use laws of human nature or quasi-laws (claiming validity for certain areas and epochs only) in explaining historical events and processes (Hempel 1965—this view is not accepted by all historians and philosophers of history; see the discussion in Brodbeck [1968:Sect. 5]; Bohman [1991:Ch. 1]).

Positivist Impact on Anthropology

Within anthropology, at least implicitly, nineteenth-century and logical positivism informed the methodological outlook of earlier leaders like Franz Boas (1961: 260–269), Robert Lowie (1959:279–291), Alfred Kroeber (1948:Sect.1, 7), George Peter Murdock (1949), A. R. Radcliffe-Brown (1957, 1968), and others. Their successors adopted some ideas of analytic philosophy of science, and most anthropologists adhered to a positivist methodology up to the 1960s, when hermeneutics provided many with a new challenge and reorientation. Siegfried F. Nadel's (1951) almost philosophical treatise on "The Foundations of Social Anthropology" is exceptional in its explicitness of adopting a logical positivist stance, as a result of his training as a philosopher in the Vienna Circle before becoming an anthropologist. And Radcliffe-Brown's (1957) general ideas on comparative anthropology as a "natural science of society" were influenced by positivist thinking, although he never actually established societal laws.

Thus, positivism mainly had an impact at the level of general methodological orientation of anthropologists. It also informed discussions of observational techniques: Many anthropologists adopted the empiricist part of the positivist agenda by enhancing the quality of data collection in the field. The search for laws, however—the crucial theoretical agenda of the more recent and more sophisticated brands of positivism—was never the prime goal of "positivist anthropology" in the past (perhaps with the exception of Murdock [1949]), and then the tide turned to interpretive and postmodernist methodologies. So, when critics debunk positivism as an infertile perspective in anthropology, we should remember that this framework has never been really tested with regard to theory building (compared to its successful application in economics and some parts of sociology and psychology, among others). Currently, a refined positivist agenda—including the search for generalizations—is being pursued mainly in the subfields of demographic, ecological, economic, cognitive, and some parts of social anthropology and in neighboring fields like biological anthropology and archaeology.

The Humanist Approach

Hermeneutics

Hermeneutics (from Greek *hermeneutike*, meaning the art of interpretation) has its roots in the classical tradition of Greek antiquity. It originally flourished in the humanities, which were preoccupied with the exegesis of historical texts like the Bible, philosophical and jurisdictional treatises, historical documents, and literature of the past, often written in foreign languages and stemming from distant epochs (Geldsetzer 1989). A major problem for philologists has been to understand and unravel the meaning of ancient terms and to grasp the meaning of whole texts. Thus, hermeneutics was first a valuable collection of heuristic rules and interpretive hints on how to read and interpret historical texts.[2]

Beginning in the late nineteenth and early twentieth centuries, some mostly German philosophers and associated humanist methodologists developed the larger vision that hermeneutic rules of text interpretation could be extended to become general guidelines for research in the humanities. In this view, all humanities were conceived as being preoccupied with the study of meaning created by human beings in particular historical settings. In addition, as hermeneutic methodologists noted, the interpretive activity itself is embedded in and dependent on historical traditions, because interpretation rests on historically framed preconceptions.

The notion of the "hermeneutic circle" is invoked to describe the constant dialogue between preconceived background knowledge on the text as a whole and newly acquired insights into the meaning of its parts. The key features of meaning and historical situatedness were considered to be in sharp contrast to those of the natural sciences whose objects do not produce meaning and whose researchers can neglect history. In the hermeneutic perspective, natural scientists are only interested in the unchanging, invariant aspects of their subject matter. Therefore, hermeneutics adherents drew the methodological conclusion that the search for general laws in nature is the goal of the natural sciences (using experiments and observations from the outside). In contrast, the study of humans and their meaningful products in special historical circumstances should describe the particular and proceed along the lines of text interpretation and empathic understanding (*verstehen*, in the sense of adopting the actor's point of view).

Sometimes these contrasting goals of inquiry are described by the opposition of *nomothetic* (law seeking) versus *ideographic* (describing the particular). In accordance with these ideas, the humanities shouldn't try to establish general laws. To do so would miss the subjective, meaningful, and historically specific nature of human subjects and lead only to trivial results. As Wilhelm Dilthey, an influential proponent of the humanities framework, put it (1900:144): "We explain nature, [but] we understand the living of the mind." Philosophers like Edmund Husserl, using an approach called phenomenology, attempted to show how everyday life is structured by rules of meaning. This line of thinking had a major impact on the work of Alfred Schutz (1964) in sociology. In philosophy, Martin Heidegger, Husserl's successor, developed a radical version of hermeneutics that tried to eliminate any remnants of scientific/technocratic rationality. By reconsidering Greek hermeneutical traditions, Heidegger attempted to reach a deeper level of insight into the essential nature of things and human existence. His thinking was influential in the human and moral sciences, but less so in the social sciences (on Heidegger in his time, see Safranski [1994]).

Building on the hermeneutic model of text interpretation, Heidegger's pupil Hans Georg Gadamer (1965) expanded hermeneutics into a general theory of interpretation for the humanities, stressing that interpretation has to bridge different traditions: that of the past to which a text belongs and the tradition of the interpreter that entails assumptions on which meanings to expect. Understanding results in a dialogue between these different traditions. Paul Ricoeur (1981) and other continental philosophers worked on projects similar to Gadamer's to extend hermeneutics to cover any understanding of meaning in the perspective of text analysis.

Hermeneutic Impact on Anthropology

In contemporary anthropology, hermeneutical ideas were taken up by Clifford Geertz (1975, 1983, 1988, 1995) and his followers in attempts to establish an interpretive anthropology. Geertz's (1975:5) programmatic statement on "thick description" as the goal of interpretive ethnography echoes Dilthey's separation between interpretation and explanation: "Believing, with Max Weber, that man is an animal suspended in webs of significance he himself has spun, I take culture to be those webs, and the analysis of it to be therefore not an experimental science in search of law but an interpretive one in search of meaning."

Geertz sometimes uses the text model in a narrow sense: ethnographers have to rely on field notes and transcripts of the stories told by informants to arrive at an ethnographic interpretation and synthesis (as in the Moroccan merchant's story analyzed in Geertz [1975:7–9]). But its main use is in the wider, metaphorical sense of "culture as an assemblage of texts" (Geertz 1975:448, 1983:30–33), when a whole culture or society is seen as a collection of texts—that is, an ensemble of socially produced and shared meanings. The task of the anthropologist is not only to unravel the meaning of written and verbal messages she or he has collected in the field, but also to understand what whole cultural scenes and the whole culture are all about semantically (Geertz 1983:Ch. 3).[3]

In his model of ethnographic understanding, Michael Agar (1986:Ch. 2) has explored insights from Gadamer and Schutz on bridging different traditions to arrive at an in-depth methodology of the unfolding of knowledge in fieldwork. Ethnographic knowledge grows through a series of cognitive breakdowns, when expectations fail, and following attempts at resolution by ethnographers who try to solve the puzzles. Cognitive coherence is finally achieved or reachieved by fitting together different pieces of tradition. Hermeneutics played a prominent role in ethnographies portraying senses of self, emotions, religious, and secular systems of beliefs in different societies. Ideas of philosophical hermeneutics strongly influenced interpretive and symbolic anthropology (for example, Dolgin et al. 1977).

Hermeneutics as text interpretation is less prominent now than it was in the 1970s. Since the mid-1980s it has given way to postmodernist thinking, which questioned interpretive accounts of the Other and found classic interpretive ethnographies wanting (Marcus and Fischer 1986:Ch. 2; Clifford 1988:Ch. 1): In their writings, interpretivists like Geertz silence the voices of the Other, which are part of heteroglossic fieldwork, and homogenize the partial ethnographic experiences by producing abstract, totalizing monologues. The contrast between understanding and explanation is still debated by different methodological frameworks and will be addressed below.

Postmodernism and Radical Constructivism

There are varieties of postmodernism, too (see Derrida [1967]; Lyotard [1984]; Rosenau [1992]; Seidman and Wagner [1992]; Seidman [1994], Dirks et al. [1994]; and Welsch [1996] for appraisals of different positions in an evolving literature), but it has been drawing mainly on hermeneutics as a springboard for establishing a conceptually less constrained and more open and pluralistic framework of thought.

Postmodernist thinking in philosophy and the humanities argues against universal visions of science and systematic approaches to knowledge. On the contrary, it stresses the historical embeddedness, the incompleteness, and the limited validity of any system of knowledge in general, and Western rationality in particular. In this respect, it is a continuation of hermeneutic concerns with meaning and historical situatedness. It is interesting that the postmodernist proposition of the historical limits of knowledge is a generalizing statement at the metalevel, that is itself a claim for a universal truth and thus contradicts its own premise.

The relativistic stance of postmodern philosophy has been adopted by post-modernist anthropology (see Clifford and Marcus [1986]; Marcus and Fischer [1986]; and Clifford [1988] as classic expositions; Fox [1991] and Marcus [1994] as newer discussions). Ironically, in anthropology the postmodernist view is often combined with a dismissal of positivism (see, however, Friedrich 1992). Strictly speaking, there can be no argument against positivism as one of many traditions if we hold to the idea that there is no metatheory, only multiple and partial visions of reality. If "anything goes" is the metarule for the pursuit of knowledge as some postmodernists hold, then there must also be room for the positivist game of science. In this chapter I won't go into further details of present postmodernist methodology. I focus instead on the more developed hermeneutic ideas as examples of the humanist approach and thereby use the hermeneutic insight (Gadamer 1965:281) that it's hard to judge events of the present compared to distant events of the past.

"Radical constructivism" has emerged recently as a new methodological framework that makes claims similar to postmodernism (Glasersfeld 1995). It questions the existence of a world out there and conveys the instrumentalist view that all scientific knowledge is just the imagination of a scientific community and has no relation to objective reality at all. The focus on subjectivity of experience is a common thread with hermeneutics. While radical constructivists emphasize sound observation (and thereby establish some common ground with positivism) this respect for received scientific procedures does not imply a tacit belief in reality. It should be interpreted instead as adherence to the norms of scientific communities irrespective of whether reality exists or not. Given the commitment of radical constructivists to established scientific procedures, their dismissal of realism has few consequences for research and can be neglected to a certain degree. Later, in the section on key methodological problems, I tackle the reality and relativism issue addressed by all methodological frameworks, but debated most intensely by postmodernists and radical contructivists.

The Challenge of History and the Rise of Sophisticated Methodologies

In the last part of this assessment of methodological frameworks, I sketch some recent developments, mostly within the analytic philosophy of science, that arrive at syntheses of former debates and lead to solutions that I later propose. In particular, in the theory section of this chapter I follow the structuralist concept of theory that overcomes some of the difficulties older, including positivist methodologies encountered when they were confronted with and challenged by the history of science. First, I introduce the background and basic ideas of these current developments.

History of Science and the New Structuralist Theory of Science

In recent years history, sociology, and anthropology of science have become important correctives of a normative philosophy of science (see Franklin [1995] for an anthropological overview). Historians of science like Thomas Kuhn (1962) showed that some of the best natural scientists didn't always follow the strict methodological rules prescribed in positivist textbooks of scientific method. Periods of "normal science," when hypotheses are tested and falsified in the framework of a dominant theory (paradigm) are punctuated by periods of revolutionary change in dominant theory—the so-called paradigm shifts—periods when research practices are changing and don't conform to the strict rules of scientific method.

After Kuhn's work, some of the more naive methodological prescriptions of positivism had to be modified or abandoned entirely. More complex methodologies have been proposed, shifting the focus from the test of isolated hypotheses to the development of whole theoretical networks (Lakatos and Musgrave 1970). A *structuralist theory of science* has emerged as the main (and powerful) approach for rationally reconstructing what scientists do. (See Stegmüller [1976, 1979a]; Balzer, Moulines, and Sneed [1987]; Kim [1991]; Balzer and Moulines [1996]; and Balzer [1997] for critical appraisals; this structuralist theory has no relation to anthropological structuralism). This framework integrates many of the earlier insights of analytic philosophy of science and of history of science in a new synthesis (including Lakatos [1970] as a less formalized forerunner). Applying a set-theoretic formalization of the theoretical core of any science, this new structuralism attempts to integrate conceptually the "normal" development and testing of hypotheses within a leading theory (paradigm) with the overthrow and succession of scientific theories during times of scientific revolution. I will elaborate on this below.

General Versus Specific Philosophy of Science

The conclusion to be drawn from this on-going research is that the precise concepts and results of analytic philosophy of science (and of any other epistemological/methodological framework) can be used as guidelines and critical yardsticks to discuss methodological questions in any discipline. But the significance of the methodological distinctions and the value of the rules of method laid down in these treatises must be judged against the specific background of the questions and answers established by a particular scientific community. It has been most productive to combine general, systematic methodological analysis that specifies the *necessary* conditions of scientific concepts with the reconstruction of specific pieces of research to gain a deeper, *sufficient* understanding of what scientific research is all about. This has been emphasized in a conclusion to the Kuhn debate reached by Wolfgang Stegmüller (1979a:79).

Key Problems in Anthropological Epistemology and Methodology

Three issues have figured prominently in discussions within and between the scientific and the humanist methodologies in anthropology: (1) the problem of realism, relativism, and truth; (2) the problem of understanding and explanation and their relationship; and (3) the problem of theory construction and theoretical progress. The first problem is epistemological and asks whether it is possible to have true knowledge of the world: Is there a world out there and how can we know anything about it? The second problem is methodological and addresses the goals (description/explanation) and procedures of empirical inquiry: What do we mean by *verstehen* and explanation and what are their consequences for the pursuit of empirical knowledge? The third problem is methodological, too, and has special relevance for law-seeking approaches: How can we construe a concept of theory that's productive for empirical, generalizing research?

There is no solution to these problems on which all the methodological frameworks agree—in fact, their position toward these problems establishes their methodological differences. But, there's some consensus that these points are indeed key problems of contemporary anthropological and social science methodology. Most adherents of the scientific approach adopt the stance that there is a real world out there. However, one could still conduct positivist-style research (as a solution to problems two and three) without accepting a realist position in problem one, as radical constructivists do. On the other hand, if we confine anthropology's task to describing particular cultures and societies (in essence, the humanist approach), then we don't need an elaborate theory suitable for producing generalizations across different cultures, societies, and times.

A fourth problem, the problem of value judgments and applied knowledge, centerered on Max Weber's plea in the first part of this century (1904, 1917) for value-free social science. The problem was a focus of intense debate in the past (Brodbeck 1968:Sect. II), but there is less controversy today about ethical principles than about the practical applications of ethical norms. Even Weber recognized in his work that scholarship is embedded in and depends on a *background* of ethics and normative judgments. Furthermore, he included norms and values as part of the *subject matter* of the social sciences and knew that research is guided by *normative rules of method*. He didn't consider these points problematic, but wanted to keep separate the language of facts, on the one hand, and the language of values and norms, on the other, in the pursuit of scientific research.

In Weber's view, factual statements ("What is the case?" and "Why is some-thing the case?") that can be *checked* by logic and empirical validation shouldn't be confused with normative statements ("What should be the case?") that can only be *decided* according to religious, political, or other dogmas beyond rational reasoning. However, the wish to do good necessitates the ability to do good, and the factual knowledge that enables our successful moral intervention has to rest on sound logic and true facts. Weber seems to have held the pragmatic view that when we put too much emphasis on normative commitments, we might leave scientific "objectivity" (or intersubjectivity, see below) aside and thereby fall victim to wishful thinking and distort "reality." If we're too committed, Weber feared, we might disregard logic and factual evidence that work against our normative convictions (see, for example, Sahlins [1995:191–198] critiquing Obeyesekere [1992], blaming the latter for distorting the historical record for emotional reasons; on the debate in general, see Borofsky [1997]). Therefore (and this is the core of Weber's doctrine of value-free social science), in the analysis part of a scientific investigation, factual and normative statements should be kept distinct and should never be confused.

In my view, the kernels of truth in Weber's position are (1) that normative and factual statements are different; and (2) that moral commitments that aren't rationally controlled can distort one's analysis. But there are many more links of reasoning between factual and normative statements possible than Weber could know, and we can engage in a much deeper rational discussion of normative and ethical issues than he had envisioned in his decision-making approach to ethics. (Rawls's [1971] theory of justice is an example; Stegmüller [1973:46–64] is both a rational reconstruction and a devastating critique of this and other aspects of Weber's thinking on value judgments.)

Whether we follow Weber's advice to separate factual and normative statements analytically (as I would do for the reasons he gives, but without agreeing to his extreme, almost nonrational decisionist approach to ethical questions) or whether we strive for a closer connection between both types of arguments (as adherents of advocacy would do, see Scheper-Hughes [1994]), we still have to solve the reality problem, the *verstehen*/explanation problem, and the problem of theory construction. These problems pose factual questions, and even if we let our normative commitments guide empirical research closely, these questions have to be answered first. To be sure, the better our factual knowledge, the better we can change reality in principle by manipulating the causes producing the undesired or desired effects. However, changing causes can still be difficult to achieve in practice and can also raise further, unintended and unwished-for consequences. Still, there's no question that a theoretically informed social and political practice is better than practice without theory—which raises the question of what a good theory is and leads to a key problem of method.

Realism, Relativism, and Truth (Key Problem 1)

Is there any objective reality? Can there be objective knowledge? If so, in what sense? How do we establish truth?—these are the leading questions of this section. In the discussion, I move from discussion of the realist position to procedures of empirical validation. Then I address radical alterity as an extreme example of relativism and a possible obstacle to cross-cultural understanding.

Realism

The so-called *realist claim* that there is a world out there that exists irrespective of our imaginations and subjectivities is a metaphysical, but nonetheless compelling, doctrine. Since all our knowledge is fallible and depends on observations that can be ultimately false, we can't *prove* the truth of this claim and convince a skeptical relativist who thinks that everything "out there" is just a product of our imagination. However, common sense and shared experiences tell us that there's something objective besides our individual experiences.

In everyday life, we routinely evaluate statements to determine whether they're purely subjective or point to something shared or real. We also have to make decisions and act *as if* there is a world out there. Although we can't *prove* the realist hypothesis, belief in it is backed by pragmatism: it's a simpler, more parsimonious hypothesis, and it makes life easier to assume an objective reality that accounts for intersubjectively shared experiences. But, we must be cautious and understand that our experience of the world is (1) framed by learned cultural conceptions; and (2) is therefore not a direct, one-to-one representation of the world (as the "fax" model of socialization assumes, see Strauss [1992:9]). Human beings seem to make a difference between individual experience (inner states) and something objective out there as the trigger or object of experience (Kutschera 1982:401–405).

In addition to this universal distinction rooted in the common nature of all humans, individually and culturally variable preconceptions (concepts, hypotheses, theories) are part of our experience of the world and structure our expectations (see D'Andrade [1984] on culturally constructed things). So, the real and the ideal are mixed in human perception and representation (Putnam 1981; Lenk 1995:Ch. 6). Neither naturalistic descriptions of ethnographic experiences grounded in open-ended interviewing and participant observation nor the results of systematic interviewing based on pile sorts or triads tests, for example, capture reality in raw condition. Some selection, some reactivity, and some interpretation based on previous preconceptions are always part and parcel of data collection and analysis.

This does not mean, however, that all experiences and ensuing data are of equal value and that we can't improve our knowledge. We can compare the information content of different statements, test them as to their truth, and thereby increase our understanding of the world. In this respect, falsification is crucial. As Popper points out: "Theories are our own inventions, our own ideas; they are not forced upon us, but are our self-made instruments of thought: this has been clearly seen by the idealist. But some of these theories of ours can clash with reality; and when they do, we know that there is a reality; that there is something to remind us of the fact that our ideas may be mistaken. And that is why the realist is right" (1969b:117).

Empirical Validation

How can we *validate empirical statements*? The scientific approach was invented in the West as a rational means for systematically generating validated knowledge. Although it's a particular cultural tradition of rational discourse, its standards have diffused to other cultures and its use isn't limited to Westerners. The diffusion of science and the public support it has achieved is due mainly to its efficiency for producing sound knowledge. The scientific approach is designed to provide strong tests of empirical hypotheses and theories and thereby to increase the correspondence of our preconceptions with reality.

Two methodological standards are minimal and thus necessary for reaching this objective: (1) *Clarity of language* is meritorious because it enhances analysis and criticism of the claims of truth and the logical structure of arguments. (2) Procedures of validation, like empirical tests, must be established in scientific communities as *controls* of the validity of empirical statements. This entails the idea that in science, as a rational discourse, truth claims must be justified by logic and empirical evidence and can't be finessed by recourse to intuition and higher authorities (although intuition may be important in the discovery of scientific ideas). *Intersubjectivity* means that the concepts and procedures applied by a researcher should be public so that other members of the scientific community can understand and control the logic of arguments and the weight of the empirical evidence. In principle, at least, the information given should enable others to replicate the study.

Empirical procedures for checking and validating scientific knowledge are specific for each discipline (see, Werner and Schoepfle's minimum standards for ethnography [1987,Vol. 2:Ch. 11]). But it's hard to think of a rational (that is, scientific) approach to knowledge that does not adhere to these minimum standards of clarity and empirical validation. The objectivity (read: intersubjectivity) of scientific knowledge rests on these standards. While these ideas have been given prominence in the analytic tradition of the philosophy of science, there is some recognition of these standards in the other methodological frameworks. Thus, radical constructivists do not accept the realist background theory but adhere to strict methodological procedures of logic and observation. Some hermeneutic and postmodernist texts are difficult to comprehend due to the metaphorical language and imagery preferred by their authors, but no doubt they use rational arguments to convince others, and, when it comes to interpretation of texts or discourses, logic and evidence count.

The Impossibility of Radical Alterity

Radical alterity (Keesing 1994:301), the ultimate impossibility of understanding the Other (person, culture, society) is sometimes mentioned as an obstacle to the growth of systematic knowledge in anthropology. However, the relativist claim that due to our different socialization and different individual experiences we can *never, in principle,* understand the Other has to be rejected as logically unsound.[4] True, interpersonal and cross-cultural communication can be difficult. But difficulty should not be made an obstacle in principle. The statement that I can't, in principle, understand the Other (say, some utterance or text) presupposes that I know the meaning of all the terms that the Other uses. If I don't, I can't tell that their meaning is totally different from the meaning of comparable terms that I can use to express his or her ideas. This tacitly presupposes that I first have to completely understand the Other's words to make the outrageous claim that I can never understand him or her. The argument is self-defeating, because I've just managed to understand the radical Other, which is the claim that this argument denies.

What we must do is try to interpret and translate what the Other says and writes in a sympathetic, charitable way. We can never be sure that we capture the meaning of strange words in the right sense (the principle of the indeterminacy of translation, Quine [1960:Ch. II]), but the principle of charity is the only practical way out (p. 59]; see the lucid discussion of the term "hippopotamous" used in a strange sense, in Davidson [1984:100–101]). Charitable translation is, in fact, the ordinary and only feasible strategy used by ethnographers in the field. According to Donald Davidson (1989:159–160), to whom I owe these fundamental insights on the impossibility of radical alterity (which he calls "radical conceptual relativism"),

> If by radical conceptual relativism we mean the idea that conceptual schemes and moral systems, or the languages associated with them, can differ massively—to the extent of being mutually unintelligible or incommensurable, or forever beyond rational resolve—then I reject conceptual radicalism. Of course there are contrasts from epoch to epoch, from culture to culture, and person to person of kinds which we all recognize and struggle with; but these are contrasts which, with sympathy and effort, we can explain and understand. Trouble comes when we try to embrace the idea that there might be more comprehensive differences, for this seems (absurdly) to ask us to take up a stance outside our own ways of thought.

The construal of radical alterity is an extreme position. But once it's refuted, this principled reason against systematic research in the humanities is gone. (The relevance of Davidson's philosophical ideas on anthropological debates has been further explored by Bowlin and Stromberg [1997]; on relativism in general, see Krausz [1989], Searle [1995], and Harre and Krausz [1996]). The next key methodological problem tackles more concrete issues of how to conduct research.

Interpretation or Explanation? (Key Problem 2)

Interpretation—in the sense of empathic understanding (*verstehen*)—has been proposed by hermeneutics as *the* method of the humanities. Positivists in the social and behavioral sciences pursue the search for laws in culture and society and try to explain cultural and social phenomena by recourse to laws. The first task is to unravel the meaning of the concepts of *verstehen* and *explanation* to better understand the kind of methodological procedures and theoretical objectives underlying both. The second task is to discuss the relationship between both approaches and to problematize the idea that the distinction of interpretation versus explanation is congruent with the distinction between the human and the natural sciences.

When reading Dilthey or Geertz, who stress massive methodological differences between both kinds of disciplines and claim *verstehen* as an exclusive method for the study of culture and society (see the quotes above), it might seem absurd to look for *relationships* between interpretation and explanation. However, Weber for one, the chief witness cited by Geertz in the quote above, didn't see a stark contrast between these concepts. He envisioned an integration of both, when he wrote about "scientific understanding" and characterized sociology (1972:1) as "a discipline that tries to understand social action interpretively and thereby attempts to explain its process and consequences causally."

Varieties of Verstehen/Understanding

The meaning of the German word *verstehen* (translated as "understanding" in English) is less clear than often thought (Kutschera 1982:ch.2; Stegmüller 1979b). It opens up a range of different, partially related concepts that need to be distinguished. Against this background, I can clarify the more complex concept of *empathic understanding* (*verstehen* in a strong and special sense) that interpretivists advocate as *the* method of *verstehen* in the humanities. In hermeneutic methodological treatises (for example, Dilthey 1900; Gadamer 1965), the different senses of *verstehen*/understanding aren't always distinguished. So these texts often have a rather opaque quality, making it difficult to assess their specific claims. *Verstehen*/understanding can refer to the following (Kutschera 1982: 80–84):

1. *Understanding of meanings:* knowing the significance of terms or gestures (for example, when one knows the content of specific words used by a speaker in a particular context or a writer in a text).
2. *Determinative understanding:* knowing the meaning of an event or process by referring to its aim or the pattern that it belongs to (for instance, when one observes a sequence of actions in a particular culture and knows that it is performed by the actors as an initiation ritual).
3. *Causal understanding:* knowing why an event happens, because one knows its causes (for example, explaining a certain relaxation of behavior as the consequence of alcohol consumption).

4. *Rational understanding:* knowing the reasons why an actor chooses a certain behavior given his or her preferences and his or her knowledge of the probability of outcome (for example, why an actor buys or sells shares in the stock market depending on his/her calculation of profit and risk).

5. *Intentional understanding:* knowing why an actor chooses a certain behavior (for instance, why an actor engages in physical education in order to achieve better health). In contrast to rational understanding, intentional understanding does not invoke the idea of an efficient means/ends scheme—any purpose will do.

6. *Functional understanding:* knowing what something contributes to the working of a larger system (for example, what role a certain job plays in a production scheme).

7. *Genetic understanding*: knowing how an event has become transmitted as an outcome of a temporal sequence (for example, how the custom of decorating Christmas trees in the present goes back to traditions of the North European past).

These different usages of *verstehen*/understanding don't exhaust the whole semantic field. In fact, many of these different concepts can co-occur in research, and they are not restricted to the humanities, as we will see later. Also, some of these concepts are process/product-words that refer both to the sequence of generating knowledge and to the results of this process.

Verstehen *as Empathic Understanding*

What does "the operation called *verstehen*" (Abel 1948) really mean, as proposed by hermeneutic philosophy (Gadamer 1965; Ricoeur 1981) and interpretive social science (Geertz 1975)? (In this discussion, I am informed by the rational reconstructions of Abel [1948]; Stegmüller [1969:360–375, 1979b]; and Kutschera [1982:132–149].) Basically, *empathic understanding* is invoked when we want to know the reasons or purposes underlying the meaningful behavior (including speech) of other people in the present or past. In this case, interpretivists propose that the researcher engage in a thought experiment and try to grasp the actor's point of view by acting as though he or she were in that situation. To be sound, this thought experiment has to rest on validated ethnographic or historical background knowledge or risk distorting the decision situation of the actor and mistakenly take the self for the Other. More concretely, let's look at ethnographic research and break down the task of reaching empathic understanding into three parts:

1. *The discovery process.* In fieldwork, empathic understanding means that the researcher starts with certain events or behaviors of actors and tries to elicit and document the "subjective" definition of the situation the actors (and the ethnographer, as participant observer) are in. She or he would capture the thinkings/feelings actors associate with the whole situation and the particular

actions taken. Gaining this knowledge would enable the ethnographer to comprehend and adopt the native standpoint to a certain degree. She or he can then describe a particular situation "through native eyes"—although this knowledge will always be incomplete and fallible.

This characterization follows Geertz's (1983:56–57) discussion of what it means to "understand the native's point of view." He emphasizes the *verstehen* part more than the *einfühlen* (empathy) part of empathic understanding and reconstructs the whole task by distinguishing between experience-near and experience-distant concepts. In his view, interpretive ethnographers search for a description in terms of concepts that are close to observation (including native, emic concepts). Goodenough (1994:264) states the goals of such an emic description as the correct prediction of what the actors do and the ability to act as the natives do in a particular situation: "We record what we see people do and what they say about what they do and then try to infer from this record what it is that we need to know in order to participate, ourselves, in what is going on and do so in ways that those people accept as showing we are knowledgeable."

Several of the senses of understanding explained above are part and precondition of gaining empathic understanding: one would need to learn and know (1) the meaning of utterances (the numberings here refer to the classification of the different meanings of *verstehen* in the previous section), (2) the kind of situation, (3) the reasons, and (4) the intentions of actors as a minimum. Thus, understanding the meaning of words and rules governing particular cultural scenes is at the heart of the *verstehen* approach in ethnography.

The goals of interpretive anthropology, however, are bigger and not restricted to understanding meaningful action in particular events. The goals include understanding the whole fabric of society and the whole ensemble of cultural texts along the lines of hermeneutic text interpretation. This calls for a larger synthesis of the data on meaningful action across different types of events and would contain empathic understanding of particular events only as a step in a larger hermeneutic project (see 3, below).

2. *Description of results.* Interpretive ethnographic writers mostly adopt a naturalistic style and try to convey "the native's point of view" as closely as possible by giving information on concrete cases. This type of report is also called phenomenological, because it favors observation-near language (the experience-near concepts mentioned by Geertz [1983:56]) and tries to depict the decision situation faced by actors as closely as possible. In these descriptions, ethnographers usually sketch the larger context as a stage for individual action. Then they draw on the background of actors, their senses of the situation they're in, their thoughts and feelings, and their strategic choices. Lastly, they trace the actions taken by the dramatis personae and the collective outcome of often divergent strategies of actors guided by different interests.

Use of native terms and quotes from key actors creates a sense of authenticity in these reports. William Whyte's (1943) snapshots on the life of a street gang in Boston; Clyde Mitchell's (1956) analysis of the Kalela dance in an urban, multiethnic context in Sambia; Victor Turner's (1957) descriptions of social dramas as sequences of conflict and conflict resolution among the matrilineal Ndembu in the same country; and Clifford Geertz's (1975:Ch. 6) study of a ritual in a Javanese town at the apex of political conflicts are classic and convincing examples of a case-centered *verstehen* approach. Many recent interpretivist/postmodernist monographs quoted above (most notably Kondo [1990] and Dumont [1992]) contain ethnographic vignettes that serve the same purpose of demonstrating by concrete examples how the Other acts and reacts in natural situations. Philippe Bourgois's (1995) in-depth study of crack dealers in East Harlem, New York, is justly praised for its combination of actors' verbatim quotes and ethnographic observation of actions and events these people are involved in.

3. *Generalization.* Most researchers who adopt this naturalistic strategy of describing others in concrete situations are not content simply to describe individual cases. The stories they tell are selected as examples of some cultural or social tendency and offered to the reader as typical of the larger system described and as revealing of salient and/or contested issues in the society or (sub)culture studied. Thus, the point of Geertz's notion of thick description (1975:Ch. 1) is that a concrete case should reveal some general cultural truth —how, for example, the Javanese think, feel, and act. As Geertz notes (1995: Ch. 3, pp. 49–51), the problem of generalization looms large in ethnographic case studies and is not easily solved—but it must be.

Recently, Lila Abu-Lughod (1991:149–157, 1993:Introduction) has argued against generalizations in anthropology and has launched a project of writing "ethnographies of the particular." She is right in criticizing the flat and abstract generalizations apparent in much of interpretive ethnographies (for example, Geertz's shortschrifts on the Javanese or the Balinese). At the descriptive level, it's interesting and complementary to generalizing approaches to portray the particularities of lived experiences of concrete actors at particular times. However, it's hard to believe how she can depict the individuality of particular Others without rendering information on the general ethnographic and historical context that gives each selected persona her or his particularity. Some sort of generalization is unavoidable; otherwise, the difference between the particular and the general does not become revealing.

Furthermore, explicit generalizations can be conducted as controlled, multilevel procedures that, apart from rendering information on central tendencies, can display dispersion at the different levels of societal integration and observation (family, neighborhood, local community, region, class, ethnic group, state, world) in a sensitive way. The value of such investigations would be enhanced if we could engage in generalizations across different time frames and detect stability as well as change at each point in time. In this sophisticated way, ethnographic generalization could capture the general and the particular and need not homogenize and reify the different persons and units studied. I conclude this section on empathic understanding with the following points:

1. Trying to grasp the native standpoint is the gist of the *verstehen* approach. In most ethnographic research this is a useful starting point, but it's not necessarily the only technique of data gathering and the end of analysis.
2. *Empathic understanding* is mainly a powerful heuristic strategy for detecting patterns of meaning in texts and discourses. It belongs to the context of discovery of (interpretive) hypotheses. In ethnographic applications, it's basically a procedure for finding out what other people think and feel and how their subjective (but to a certain extent shared) beliefs structure meaningful action. In ethnographic reports, case material illustrates some general point the interpretivist has discovered by empathic understanding. In text interpretation, empathic *verstehen* arrives at ideas as to how the different parts of a text hang together and exhibit some coherence.
3. In the context of justification of results, the products of empathic understanding have to conform to ordinary standards of scientific validation. Thus, the interpretive statements should be logically consistent and in accord with the facts. When there are rival interpretations (see the example of dissent in text interpretation presented in Stegmüller [1979b:46–53]), both should be logical and, in the text, the one that makes sense in more instances is preferred over the other (Ricoeur 1981:210–215) or, in discourse analysis, the one that better predicts what the actors do in a particular situation is preferred. In ethnographic descriptions, control of the adequacy of interpretations is often difficult. But, as fieldwork methods texts point out, we can enhance the validity of ethnographic knowledge and better assess the typicality of interpretive statements by combining qualitative case material with 1) verbatim recording and transcriptions of native consultants; 2) text analysis of transcriptions; and 3) numerical data on the frequency of ideas, behaviors, and observed events (Agar 1980:Chs. 6, 7; Romney et al. 1986; Werner and Schoepfle 1987:I, 139–162; Bernard 1994:Ch. 4).

The Hermeneutic Circle

Along with empathic understanding, methodologists of the humanist approach often mention the so-called hermeneutic circle as a special precondition for acquiring knowledge on humans. What is a hermeneutic circle? Gadamer (1965: 250–283) and other proponents of hermeneutics point to a special methodological dilemma on which each understanding of a text (or utterance) depends. We have to know the meaning of the parts (say, words in a text) to understand the meaning of the whole. But, to understand the meaning of the parts, we also need to know the whole of the text as background knowledge. Hermeneutic work on texts or discourse, then, has to shift between these two opposite sides of one interpretive undertaking.

Critics of hermeneutics (Stegmüller 1979b; Albert 1994) make two points. First, this isn't a vicious circle that we cannot evade or even a principal problem that we cannot solve since we must always distinguish between background knowledge (assumptions) and claims that can be checked. In principle, every element of background knowledge can be criticized (but not all at the same time). Second, this dilemma is not exclusive to the humanities. It applies to any knowledge-making situation, including hypothesis testing in the natural sciences. Stegmüller (1979b) demonstrates this by comparing an interpretive debate on a medieval poem, on the one hand, to an astrophysical explanation, on the other. The social sciences fall between these extremes or belong to either the humanities or the sciences depending on one's methodological standpoint.

Stegmüller's (1979b:58–68) main finding is that the distinction between background knowledge and interpretive hypotheses can be drawn sharply in the natural sciences, whereas this distinction is often blurred in the humanities. So, with a closer look, the difference in kind between the presence of the hermeneutic circle in the humanities at one extreme and the lack of it in the natural sciences on the other becomes a mere difference in degree.

Understanding as a Special Method of the Humanities

Now we can pose the related and larger question: *Is understanding peculiar to the humanities?* The general answer is no, but there's a qualification. The different senses of *verstehen*/understanding outlined above aren't restricted to the humanities. Some also apply to the natural sciences. Thus, a student of nature has to understand the meaning of words in scientific texts (sense 1, above); he or she has to classify events (sense 2); causal (sense 3) and functional understanding (sense 6) are definitely part and even genetic understanding (sense 7) (for example, evolution) is often part of ordinary work in the natural sciences. However, and in this respect hermeneutics is right, the meaning dimension is unique to human studies. And the fact that human subjects can reflect and purposefully change their behavior must also be considered. The next question is whether meaning and reflexivity exclude the search for laws in the human, social, and behavioral sciences, as some leaders of hermeneutics claim. Before we look at this, I have to clarify the meaning of explanation itself.

The Concept of Scientific Explanation

How can we explain explanation? Like *verstehen*/understanding, the word explanation has different meanings, some overlapping with the senses of *verstehen* discussed above (Hempel 1965; Stegmüller 1969; Kutschera 1982:Ch. 2; Pitt 1988; Bartelborth 1996). Here, I confine the discussion to scientific explanation. More specifically, I focus on DN (deductive nomological) explanation (also called the HO schema of explanation after Carl Hempel and Paul Oppenheim who first reconstructed it in 1948 [Hempel 1965:Ch. 10]).

DN explanation is the prototype of scientific explanation. It answers the *explanation-seeking why-question* that asks for the occurrence or some feature of a certain phenomenon X. Let p be the descriptive statement specifying that this phenomenon X is the case. Since we are looking for an explanation of p, it's called the *explanandum* (Latin, what is to be explained). The answer, called the *explanans* (the thing doing the explaining), is represented by two types of statements: at least one lawlike sentence of the conditional form "if q, then p" and one (or more) descriptive statement(s) specifying that the antecedent condition q of the lawlike statement is the case. The lawlike statement can be much more complex than the one presented here that postulates only one condition, q. Given the lawlike statement(s) and the statement(s) on the antecedent condition(s) as premises of an explanatory argument, one can then logically conclude that p is true. In formal terms: $(q \land (q \rightarrow p)) \rightarrow p$. In words: if q and (q implies p), then p.

Here's a simple example. We might wonder why there is social stratification in the Javanese community of Sawahan that I observed in 1979. The descriptive statement: "The village Sawahan is a stratified community" is the explanandum p. We could use the lawlike statement from cross-cultural research: "If a community has intensive agriculture, then it has social stratification" $(q \rightarrow p)$ in conjunction with the descriptive statement on the truth of the antecedent condition "Sawahan has intensive agriculture" (q) to deduce the explanandum p, that Sawahan is stratified. A valid explanation presupposes that the lawlike statement and accompanying descriptive statements are true or at least well confirmed. The pragmatic distinction between laws that are well confirmed and lawlike statements that are formally similar, but not as validated as laws, rests on this fact. We needn't make too much of this distinction. The gist of laws and lawlike statements as scientific generalizations is that they claim conditional truth for an unlimited set of phenomena—that is, all cases that fulfill the antecedent condition. They aren't restricted in their truth claim to specific places and times (although one could use quasi-laws that are restricted to certain regions or epochs to explain phenomena within these boundaries).[5] The conditional form of deterministic laws rules out historical inevitability, because the consequence is only predicted to happen *if* the antecedent is true.

The conditions specified in a law or lawlike statement of the *deterministic* form shown above are sometimes called "real reasons" for the occurrence of the phenomenon that is to be explained. Deterministic laws or lawlike statements claim that the consequence happens without exception if the antecedent condition is fulfilled. As an example of a deterministic law, take the basic demographic equation: *population change in a certain time period = births—deaths +*

immigration—emigration (the population change as dependent variable is explained by the conditions in the right-hand part of the equation). We could argue that there is always some error or chance fluctuation in empirical data and that therefore empirical data only *approximate* deterministic laws (on approximation in general, see Moulines [1996:7], Kuipers [1996], and Balzer [1997:200–232]). Over time, research efforts could lead to better approximations by reducing measurement errors and by including additional conditions that enhance causal understanding and prediction.

However, in social sciences there are frequently so many exceptions to a lawlike statement that we have to give up the whole idea of a deterministic relationship and can only claim a statistical connection. (Note that this is a pragmatic statement, depending on the current state of knowledge in a domain. It does not rule out the possibility that in the future we could establish deterministic laws on the same subject matter). Hence, we can only posit that if the antecedent is given, then the consequence happens in most cases. Weakening deterministic laws to statistical ones leads to a different type of reasoning and leaves the standard model of DN explanation. Then we're no longer answering explanation-seeking why questions by giving real reasons and using deductive logic. Instead, we're switching to *reason-seeking* or *epistemic why-questions* that ask for good reasons to believe that the phenomenon specified in the why-question is the case. Such questions are answered by *epistemic reasons*. Whereas real reasons are reasons *of* phenomena, epistemic reasons are reasons *for* phenomena. As an example, take the well-established statistical law on the sex ratio at birth: this backs the expectation that there will be slightly more males than females at birth. But this statistical law does not allow us to predict *for individual cases* whether a boy or girl will be born.

Lawlike statements and laws of a statistical form that postulate a high probability to expect p when q is the case, belong to epistemic reasoning. In social science methodology, "causal analysis" covers both types of reasoning, while the antecedent conditions are often called "causes" and the consequences "effects." In contrast, philosophers of science hold to the distinction between real reasons and epistemic ones. They use the term "cause" in a much more restricted sense for real reasons in laws of succession (when there is temporal asymmetry between earlier causes and later effects in deterministic laws). Anthropology need not adopt this special terminology, but the difference between epistemic and real reasons can be revealing.

A lot of research in analytic philosophy of science attempts to extend the scope of DN explanation and cover more deviant cases in more encompassing rational reconstructions of explanation (Pitt 1988; Bartelborth 1996). The necessary minimum conditions for adequate scientific explanations have been specified as a result of these general inquiries, and DN explanation is considered a special case of a broader concept of explanation. In this broader view, "explanations are essentially unifications of our knowledge [and] we should conceive them as embeddings of an explanandum E in a model M. At first we take 'model' in an informal sense meaning a representation of something. In this sense it includes . . . mechanical or analogical models . . . as well as theoretical models. . ." (Bartelborth 1996:30).

The theoretical models include laws as elucidated above (see Bartelborth [1996] for an extended discussion). The philosophical thinking on DN explanation, statistical reasoning, and the minimum standards of scientific explanation in conjunction with the the search for laws in the natural, social, and behavioral sciences have had an impact on empirical research in anthropology. Even if one were skeptical of the positivist agenda in the humanities, there is a growing body of lawlike statements in anthropology and the other social and behavioral sciences. As examples, take the well-established findings from comparative research on the causal links between population growth, economic intensification, social stratification, and political integration in human societies (Johnson and Earle 1987; Netting 1993) or the cognitive anthropological finding on the pervasiveness of schemata as organizing devices in human thought (D'Andrade 1995:Ch. 6). The crucial methodological question now is how to integrate the goals and procedures of understanding and explanation. Above, I tried to show that both approaches rely on rational procedures and have merits. Can we combine them?

Understanding and Explanation: From Opposition to Integration

How are understanding and explanation related? (1) Conceptually, both procedures aren't polar opposites (Stegmüller 1973, 1979b). A valid contrast to explanation (embedding a case in a larger, generalizing model, typically using laws or lawlike statements) is description (singular statements specifying what the case is in particular entities). (2) The dichotomy of *verstehen*/explanation doesn't lead to a fertile classification. Explanation is possible in the medical sciences, psychology, economics, and other social and behavioral sciences, including anthropology; interpretation, in several of the senses distinguished above, also plays a role in the natural sciences. In addition, not all the natural sciences can conduct experiments (astronomy, for example), and they are not confined to the invariant aspects of their subject matter (as Dilthey had it), but take history into account as well (for example, natural history in biology or astronomy). So the simple distinction between the natural and the human sciences according to explanation and *verstehen* disappears. (3) A more productive methodology in social sciences attempts to integrate *verstehen* and explanation. In this new perspective, we can first use (empathic) *understanding* to discover hypotheses on the subjective meanings of actors and then consider meanings as well as the conditions of the larger context in which actors are embedded in more encompassing *explanations* of social and cultural phenomena.

In this respect, some interesting methodological ideas have been put forward by rational choice theorists in sociology (most notably Esser [1991, 1993, 1996]; Lindenberg [1989, 1990, 1992, 1996]; Lindenberg and Frey [1993]; on rational choice theory in general, see Coleman [1990]; Coleman and Fararo [1992]; and Bohman [1991:67–76] for its logic of explanation). Following some of Weber's early concerns, these analysts begin with the "logic of the situation" at the level of individual actors: using *verstehen*, they investigate the actor's view of his or her situation, including cultural preferences. This leads to information on actors' goals and expectations. Then analysts study the economic, political, and social restrictions of the context that enables and constrains individual action. Finally, they use a refined rational actor model (as a law or lawlike statement) to explain the actors' strategic actions. They also trace the purposeful and unintended collective outcomes of individual choices on the larger system.

The refinement of the rational actor model refers mainly to the fact that the economizing scheme has to incorporate social constraints to avoid the flaw of the undersocialized actor and has to include social approval in addition to material well-being as maximizing goals (Lindenberg 1990, 1996). In a diachronic perspective, one can study the embeddedness of actors in previous institutional and cultural arrangements and, contrastingly, the emergence of new norms and institutions as an effect of present actions. This embeddness and emergence is borne out, too, by anthropological applications of rational choice theory (see, for example, Cashdan [1990], Ensminger [1992], and Ensminger and Knight [1997] on how actors use and change institutions; Netting [1993] on the rational core of small-scale agriculture). Thus, in a major reconstruction, sociologist Hartmut Esser (1991) demonstrates how the *verstehen*-oriented social theory of Alfred Schutz (1964) corresponds with rational choice theory and can be incorporated in rational choice explanations.

These social theories use empathic *verstehen* as a bridge between a very general and abstract economic and social theory, on the one hand, and information on the concrete decision situation of actors, on the other. Siegwart Lindenberg discusses heuristic strategies on how to cross-fertilize these two approaches to arrive at more precise and more realistic, but still sufficiently general explanations (1992, 1996). We needn't accept economic theory in full or at all, although it's very powerful and challenging. It's also clear that anthropological applications of rational choice theory have to draw a lot more on cultural background traditions molding goals and actions in variable cultural and social contexts (Schweizer 1996:Chs. 2, 3; Görlich 1998). But this is a promising attempt to integrate *verstehen* and explanation in a more encompassing explanatory theory. This theoretical approach challenges the older, false distinction between *verstehen* and explanation and the accompanying idea that both procedures exclude each other. Better theories capture subjective meanings (the actors' views) *and* objective constraints (the institutional context and shared beliefs prevailing in society at a certain time). By integrating both kinds of information, they arrive at more grounded, in-depth explanations.

Theory Construction and Theoretical Progress
(Key Problem 3)

Here, I discuss how to construct theory and in what sense there can be theoretical progress—that is, systematic growth of knowledge. First, I look at theory in hermeneutics, which contains some preliminary insights and is useful for generalizing in case studies. Then I present the established view of theories in analytic philosophy of science that has framed positivist discussion about what a theory is. The main point of this section, though, is to introduce the structuralist theory concept, which is a new development in analytic philosophy of science. In my view, this concept has great potential for rational reconstructions of theoretical work in any science. I will propose this new theory concept that could guide explanatory research in anthropology and solve some of the methodological problems generated by cross-societal, cross-cultural, and cross-historical generalizations.

Theory in Hermeneutics

In a paper entitled "In praise of theory," the philosopher Gadamer (1983:43) tells us that the root of theory is "[t]o see that what is." He remarks that this isn't meant to be the mere description of factual occurrences, but of something deeper, a pattern that we can only "see" when we try to get rid of our prejudices (p. 44). Gadamer (1965:11) also points out that theory looks for the general. The stipulations that theory aims to represent something general, not just the surface description of a particular case, and that the general can thus be abstract, hidden, are elements of other concepts of theory (see below, and think of Lévi-Strauss's [1963] similar idea of "structure").

Working in the spirit of hermeneutics, interpretive anthropology seems content to *describe* particular cultures. Nevertheless, some generalization is involved at the level of individual cultures when interpretive ethnographers try to capture the essential qualities of a culture. This general, theoretical aspect comes to the fore when interpretivists try to tell us what it means "to be Javanese," etc. Then they try to capture common symbolic understandings shared by members of a culture. When hermeneutic anthropologists compare cultures (mainly comparisons between the ethnographer's "I" and the culturally distant Other; see, however, Geertz [1995:Chs. 2, 3] on Morocco and Java), they don't seek universal characteristics of all cultures or humans per se. Again, they use contrasts to discover the essential features of the unique cultures that are compared.

This search for the essential quality of cultures is equivalent to the search for a comprehensive interpretation that gives clues to the different parts of a text in hermeneutic text interpretation. The more parts of a text that can be covered by a particular interpretive hypothesis, the better the interpretation is, compared to rival ones. I never heard much about competing interpretations in interpretive ethnography, but the same idea should hold: An interpretation that makes sense of more cultural data should be the better, culture-specific generalization. Thus, hermeneutic anthropology is informed by the general expectation and key hermeneutic insight that meanings and historical traditions are of prime importance in every cultural and social setting. Aside from the idea that ethnographers should derive interpretations of cultures that challenge factual evidence and that a more encompassing interpretation that makes sense of a bigger part of textual evidence is preferred, there is no well-developed theory or growth of systematic knowledge in hermeneutics. Abu-Lughod's (1991, 1993) pleas for ethnographies of the particular (see the section on empathic understanding, above) open up the possibility that even at the level of particular cultures, explicit generalizations will become less important in hermeneutic anthropology.

Theory Concepts in Analytic Philosophy of Science

The concepts of theory established by the different currents of analytic philosophy of science share the common idea that *theories should be generalizing devices aimed at illuminating the particular by reference to some broader principles*. Positivist philosophers of science set themselves the task to arrive at a more precise and comprehensive concept of theory, taking the explanatory schemata of physics (among others) as exemplary cases of elaborate theories. Basically, they hold that theories are complex structures that pose difficult problems of logical deduction and empirical validation. Hence, the formal structure of theories should be distinguished from their substantive interpretation. Rules of correspondence work as bridges between the formal structure and the empirical applications. Theories are conceived as networks of laws. They differ in generality and contain observable as well as abstract, theoretical concepts. The latter are called "T-theoretical" when they can only be determined by applying the theory in question (for example, the general concept of utility in economic theory whose significance depends on and is established by applying some kind of maximization hypothesis), whereas the "T-nontheoretical" concepts can be measured independently of the theory (Stegmüller 1979a:Sect. 3; Moulines 1996:7).

How does a theory come into contact with empirical data and how, if ever, can it be refuted or confirmed? Different adherents of the analytic framework dissent about this. The general positivist vision of the integrative role of scientific theories is underlined by Carl Hempel (1966):

Theories are usually introduced when previous study of a class of phenomena has revealed a system of uniformities that can be expressed in the form of empirical laws. Theories then seek to explain those regularities and, generally, to afford a deeper and more accurate understanding of the phenomena in question. To this end, a theory construes those phenomena as manifestations of entities and processes that lie behind or beneath them, as it were. These are assumed to be governed by characteristic theoretical laws, or theoretical principles, by means of which the theory then explains the empirical uniformities that have been previously discovered, and usually also predicts 'new' regularities of similar kinds. (p. 70)

The main difference among concepts of theory established by rival analytic philosophies of science relates to whether theories are logically connected sets of *statements*—that is, as statements can they be true or false, or not. The first alternative is the received *statement view of theories* as proposed by Carl Hempel (1965, 1966) and Karl Popper (1969a, 1969b), among others. This version turned out to be very clumsy when philosophers of science tried to rationally reconstruct particular theories. It became more awkward when it had to cope with theory change in a diachronic perspective. Hence, a *nonstatement, so-called structuralist view of theories* has been proposed as an alternative (Stegmüller 1976, 1979a; Balzer et al. 1987; Balzer and Moulines 1996; Balzer 1997:Ch. 2). Ulises Moulines (1996) explains the logic:

According to structuralism, theories are not sets of statements. But, of course, this is not to deny that it is very important for science to make statements—things that can be true or false, that can be verified, falsified or somehow checked. What structuralism maintains is that theories are not statements but are *used* to make statements—which, of course, have then to be checked. The statements made by means of scientific theories are, intuitively speaking, of the following kind: that a given domain of intended applications may actually be subsumed under the theory's principles (laws, constraints, and links). (p. 9)

Elements of Theories in the New Structuralist View

Within the structuralist theory perspective, general methodological work and detailed reconstructions of specific theories in different branches of science have led to the discovery of subtle and precise concepts for describing theories and yielded new insights on the use of theories in the empirical sciences (Balzer et al. 1987; Balzer and Moulines 1996; their formal approach builds on Suppes's set-theoretical axiomatization of scientific theories [1957:Ch. 12]). An in-depth introduction to the structuralist theory concept would require the reconstruction of particular anthropological theories. I cannot discuss this in detail here, but I will introduce some of the structuralist concepts and suggest how these concepts relate to anthropological generalizations. So far, Franklin Tjon Sie Fat (1990) has used a preliminary version of the structuralist theory concept in his formal reconstruction of kinship alliance theory, while Alexander Bierstedt (1997) introduces structuralist concepts in his assessment of evolutionary theory in anthropology.

The basic idea of structuralism is that theories are conceptual structures, not statements. They contain general principles, formal models, empirical applications, and methodological prescriptons on data structures and measurement. As concepts, theories can't be true or false, only more or less productive. They induce empirical statements on intended applications and lower-level laws that can be refuted.

Basically, structuralists distinguish a *formal core K* and an open set of *intended applications I* as two essential facets of any theory. Members of a scientific community *having or holding a theory* (Stegmüller's pragmatic concept for the use of a common theory [1979a:29–32]) share the formal structure—including the principal laws expressed in this formalism and a set of paradigmatic, successful empirical applications—of the theory (as a subset of the set of intended applications). "Normal work" consists of specializing the principles to cover new domains, and to expand the set of true, intended applications. We can (following Stegmüller [1979a:33]) "distinguish between three kinds of 'normal scientific' progress: (1) *theoretical progress*, consisting of a refinement of the net of theory-element cores [work on K mentioned above, TS], (2) *empirical progress*, consisting of a successive increase in the set of intended applications: $I_t \subset I_{t+1}$, and (3) *progress in confirmation* by which assumed elements are transformed into firm elements of I."

Scientific revolutions can be reconstructed as intertheoretic relations, whereby there is overlap of the set of intended applications of rival theories that enables transfer of the successful applications from one theory to the other in case of theory dislodgement with reduction (Diederich 1996:77–78). But reconstruction of theory change with and without reduction is still a thorny issue (Stegmüller 1979a:Sect. 11; Diederich 1996; Balzer and Moulines 1996). The received concept of theory in analytic philosophy of science had already revealed the insight that scientific theories are hierarchical systems that differ widely in their generality.

At the lowest level of theoretical abstraction, structuralism defines a *theory-element T* as an ordered pair of the form $T = <K,I>$ whereby K is the formal core and I is the set of intended applications of the theory-element (introduced above as the most basic distinction). The empirical claim of a theory element is, roughly, that a particular phenomenon can be characterized as behaving according to the theoretical principles contained in K and thus belongs to the set of intended applications I—which has to be checked. This claim can be falsified, it can be true, or it can turn out to be approximately true. When the general theoretical principles of the formal core are extended to and *specialized for different domains*, we get a *theory-net* that links several theory-elements in a more complex theoretical pattern. As Moulines (1996) elucidates:

Some "real-life" examples of scientific theories can actually be reconstructed as one theory-element. However, this is true only for the simplest kinds of theories we encounter in scientific literature. More often, single theories in the intuitive sense have to be viewed as aggregates of several (sometimes a great number of) theory-elements. These aggregates are called *"theory-nets."* This reflects the fact that most scientific theories have laws of very different degrees of generality within the same conceptual setting. We may say that all axioms of a theory are axiomatic but some are more axiomatic than others. A theory is not a "democratic" sort of entity. Rather, it is a strongly hierarchical system. Usually, there is a single fundamental law "on the top" of the hierarchy and a vast array of more special laws (and constraints) with different degrees of specialization. Each special law . . . determines a new theory-element. What holds together the whole array of laws in the hierarchy is, first, the common conceptual framework, second, the common distinction between the T-theoretical and the T-nontheoretical layer, and third, the fact that they are all specializations of the same fundamental law. (pp. 10–11)

The structuralist literature contains formal definitions, examples, and extended discussion of these concepts of theory-elements or theory-nets, and it has detected even more elaborate theoretical structures (Balzer et al. 1987; Balzer and Moulines 1996). In his recent textbook, Wolfgang Balzer (1997:48–49) draws the main contrast between "little theories" (theory-elements plus characteristic data structures and test procedures) on the one hand and more comprehensive "big theories" (theory-nets) that integrate several little theories on the other.

The Uses of Theories

When researchers holding a theory (in the sense of common theory-element or theory-net) embark on the specialization of theoretical principles and when they are checking intended applications there is falsification and confirmation, whereas the formal core of a theory is not subject to falsification (Diederich 1996:76):

The claim that the paradigm's theoretical structure is extendable to further cases is, of course, subject to possible failure: the scientific community may not be able to actually apply the theory to certain cases and thus may be urged (by resistance of "reality") to remove these cases from the domain of intended applications. . . . The failure to apply the theory in a certain situation does not falsify the respective claim of the theory (since it may be applied to this situation later on), let alone the theory itself; strictly speaking, the latter is not even possibly subject to falsification, since it is, in itself, no statement at all, but a certain structure (and a heuristic to generate claims about phenomena of a certain domain).

Critical rationalists (Popper 1969b; Kim 1991; Schmid 1996:238–240) who hold the statement view of theories wouldn't accept this "instrumentalist view" of theories as tools for producing generalizing statements. For them, even top-level theoretical principles are falsifiable. However, structuralist rational reconstruction of the role of theories comes closer to scientific practice and thus seems a more valid description of what scientists actually do. We should remember that in the structuralist perspective, theories are not immunized against criticism. Theories can be more or less productive, and one that doesn't lead to successful applications will eventually be abandoned. And there is always refutation at the level of intended applications and lower-level laws. So, empirical applications and testing are crucial for research, but a successful theory won't be overthrown by a few failed applications.

The new structuralist view doesn't lead to totally different empirical research in the discipline, but it changes the perspective on what a theory is and what it's useful for. In this chapter, I've introduced this new perspective on theory and theory building, because structuralist research on theories contains formally precise and rich concepts for dissecting empirical theories and their evolution. It has led to a much more detailed and realistic view of theory and theory change than its predecessors. In addition, the structuralist concept of theory as a combination of theoretical principles, an open set of intended applications, including exemplary cases, and methodological prescriptions on data and measurement, makes a lot of intuitive sense in anthropological theory building.

Typically, in anthropology theories are introduced, rendered plausible, and challenged by rival theories via fitting or resisting ethnographic cases. There has been a lot of reanalysis of renowned cases in the light of alternative theoretical frameworks. Some examples include the Kula (Malinowski 1922; Leach and Leach 1973), Nuer segmentary lineages (Evans-Pritchard 1940), political systems of highland Burma (Leach 1954), the ritual cycle among the Tsembaga of Papua New Guinea (Rappaport 1968), and the historical events connected with Captain Cook's stay at Hawaii as the most recent controversy (Sahlins 1981; 1995 versus Obeyesekere 1992; critically assessed in Borofsky 1997). So a theory concept that stresses theoretical principles *and* empirical applications as necessary and equally important components and that highlights the important role creativity plays in connecting theoretical concepts and empirical examples is closer to actual research practice and thus more revealing than earlier and alternate concepts. What remains to be clarified is what kind of theories are used in anthropological research.

Theories in Anthropology

What is *the state of theory construction* in anthropology? Generally, the discipline is still in a natural history stage of theory building. Anthropologists are primarily devoted to carefully observing and classifying their objects/subjects of study and establishing empirical generalizations (if they're interested in generalizations). There aren't many deep theoretical principles (but see below), and there is more explanatory success about some parts of culture and society (for example, economy and ecology) than others (for example, religion; social organization and cognition being intermediate). But this is due more to pragmatic circumstancs than to the instrinsic nature of "social and cultural reality," in general, or to the nature of the special subfields. When a scientific community doesn't engage in a systematic search for regularities, there won't be much discovery of empirical generalizations and theoretical principles. In the classification below, the first two types of generalizations wouldn't qualify as theory building in the strong sense of structuralist philosophy of science discussed above, whereas the last two types of generalization are devoted to the construction of anthropological theories in the proper sense.

1. *Generalizations as part of a case study.* At the most elementary level, "describing a culture (or society)" necessitates discovering cultural leitmotifs —shared patterns of behavior and thought—that give some coherence to the empirical systems anthropologists study. Human collectives would break down if there weren't some shared expectations and cooperation. Ethnography attempts to detect such patterns. Describing these patterns doesn't rule out intracultural or intrasocietal variation (which can be systematic). And the prevalent rules or activity patterns needn't be very fixed and rigid. As I argued above, even *verstehen* approaches in ethnography aim at generalizations at the level of particular cultures. Sometimes an ethnography leads to the discovery of hypotheses that claim to be true and are, in fact, valid for a lot of other ethnographic cases.

2. *Hypothesis construction as part of comparative research.* At a higher level of generalization, cross-cultural research aims at discovering and testing hypotheses that are true for many cultures. However, theoretical progress is often hindered because many of these hypotheses stick closely to the observational level and they're isolated, ad hoc. Since most anthropologists are more interested in finding differences than similarities, the generalization task is even more aggravated. A higher level of synthesis is achieved when comparativists work on establishing whole explanatory schemes, thereby arriving at structures that qualify as theories in the strong sense. This is the next type.

3. *Cultural and social types as theory-elements.* A lot of explanatory schemes in anthropology are generalizations at the middle level that are informed by some theoretical idea (say, how human nature, the environment, economic forces, social and political structures, and patterns of thought are linked and how they mold society). These ideas lead to testable hypotheses that are checked in the ethnographic record and are illustrated by exemplary cases. When researchers systematically compare ethnographic and historical cases of the past and present to arrive at cross-cultural, cross-societal, and cross-historical syntheses, they establish cultural and social types (for example, Johnson and Earle 1987; Maryanski and Turner 1992).

These typologies are much more than mere schematic descriptions of different types of societies, and they're much more integrative than the testing of isolated hypotheses. These authors attempt theoretical reductions of the massive ethnographic record investigated and they try to integrate lower-level hypotheses. The theoretical agenda underlying these typologies is that the different types represent nonrandom, fundamental configurations of demographic, social, ecological, economic, political, and cognitive/emotive phenomena that relate to and are valid in a lot of ethnographic cases belonging to a certain type (for example foragers, chiefdoms, agrarian communities, etc.). Furthermore, a certain configuration specifies constraining as well as enabling conditions that influence the historical trajectory of certain types (How does a Big Man collectivity become a local group or chiefdom? What happens to hunter/gatherers when they become sedentary? How can we explain the move from foraging to agrarian modes of subsistence?).

To a degree, the types are theoretical idealizations that can be illustrated by empirical cases and that are approximated by other cases belonging to a given type. The typology is refined in light of new empirical and theoretical evidence obtained by research. Theoretical progress in constructing these typologies is difficult insofar as the intended theoretical statements are often diachronic, postulating causal developments like the transformation or emergence of types in an evolutionary framework, whereas the majority of ethnographic descriptions are static, cross-sectional investigations. For this generalizing task, anthropology would need more longitudinal datasets describing cases at different points in time, and it should carefully analyze the available record on historical junctions when one type changes to another one to establish more validated, in-depth empirical generalizations.

4. *Anthropological theory-nets.* Some theoretical structures in anthropology (and related disciplines) qualify as theory-nets in the structuralist sense. Think of rational choice theory (Coleman 1990; Coleman and Fararo 1992; Ensminger 1992; Ensminger and Knight 1997; Görlich 1998), evolutionary ecology (Smith and Winterhalder 1992), social network analysis (Wasserman and Faust 1994; Wasserman and Galaskiewicz 1994; Wellman and Berkowitz 1997), and cognitive anthropology (Holland and Quinn 1987; D'Andrade and Strauss 1994; Strauss and Quinn 1994; D'Andrade 1995), among others, as examples of contemporary theories. We could also reconstruct other theoretical currents including those of the past, like evolutionism, structural-functionalism, structuralism (see Tjon Sie Fat [1990] on structuralist kinship theory as an attempt in this direction), cultural ecology, cultural materialism, symbolic anthropology, etc., as theory-elements or theory-nets in the structuralist view.

The core of the theory in anthropological theory-nets are general principles that guide research and formal models for deducing statements that can be checked empirically. On the empirical side are intended applications, including paradigmatic examples. Both would yield a theory-element. When there are specializations of the principles at the top for different domains of application, we have theory-nets. In addition to the models and intended applications, every theory includes characteristic data structures and testing devices. I won't go into details, but let me offer some hints how the structuralist theory concepts apply to the four theoretical currents mentioned above.

For (1) *rational choice theory*, the model of "economic man" (not the bogus version dismissed in earlier anthropological discourses, but a more realistic version presented in Coleman [1990:Chs. 1, 2]; Lindenberg and Frey [1993]; Lindenberg [1990, 1996], Esser [1993, 1996]) belongs to the core. Mathematical game theory, although different in history and scope, represents some additional theoretical principles on strategic action. Some economic applications of the theory of prices can be considered as exemplary applications of rational choice theory, while a lot of work now concerns the extension of the economic model to noneconomic phenomena and the specialization of the basic premises to account for new domains (for example, Becker 1976; Coleman 1990). Taken together, this establishes a theory-net. Using theoretical principles and reworking them so that they can be applied to a particular domain is nicely illustrated in Lindenberg's exposition on how to explain social action with the help of rational choice principles (1996):

> A core theory of action is isolated by taking the five most relevant aspects of human nature to be found in the literature. The attributes are: resourceful, restricted, expecting, evaluating, maximizing (RREEM). For each aspect, bridge assumptions have to be made before the core can be used as a theory of action. For example, if we interpret "resourcefulness" and "expecting" as being completely informed about alternatives and prices, if we take "evaluating" as preference functions for consumer goods, if "restricted" refers to somebody's budget, and "maximizing" refers to the technical meaning of choosing the package of goods that maximizes utility given price and budget constraints, then we have *homo economicus* as most often encountered in economics textbooks. In most contexts, however, there would be reason to make the model more complex, for example by at first letting go the assumption of market transparency in favour of subjective probabilities and by introducing social goods, such as "social approval," with shadow prices under the heading of "evaluating." (p. 306)

Similarly, in the theory of *evolutionary ecology* (2), natural selection would establish the topmost principles at the theoretical core. Specialization of these principles to patterns of food acquisition among hunter-gatherers, and reproductive behavior set up domains of intended applications of the theory covering a lot of empirical cases and containing a lot of specialized theoretical principles (Betzig 1997).

Social network analysis (3) can also be reconstructed as a theory-net. There are theoretical principles establishing an overall relational perspective (Wellman and Berkowitz 1997) and specific hypotheses on the patterning of strong and weak ties and their impact on an actor's strategies (Wasserman and Galaskiewicz 1994; Schweizer 1996:Ch. 4). Graph theory, algebra, and statistics lend formal representations of social structure (Wasserman and Faust 1994). The set of intended applications includes the classic case studies of this approach, while adherents of the paradigm are expanding the set of intended applications (Hage and Harary 1991, 1996; Schweizer and White 1998).

At the theoretical core, *cognitive anthropology* (4) is characterized as a mix of principles and procedures from linguistics, cognitive psychology, anthropology, and computer science (Strauss and Quinn 1994, 1997; D'Andrade 1995). The set of intended applications includes native taxonomies, cognitive schemata, and cultural consensus, among others.

What is most revealing is that these evolving anthropological theory-nets are cross-cutting disciplinary boundaries by integrating parts from different disciplines for the sake of better explanations. Thus, evolutionary ecology is connecting biology and anthropology; rational choice theory has been used in economics, sociology, political science, and anthropology. Social network analysis is an interdisciplinary brand of structural thinking in several social science disciplines (sociology, psychology, anthropology, communications, organizational studies, geography, history, marketing, etc.), and cognitive anthropology has reemerged in the 1990s as an anthropological variety of the broad cognitive sciences field. It seems to me, then, that the best of our current theories must transcend narrow disciplinary boundaries.

I conclude by pointing out some crucial features of theory construction in anthropology. (1) There are some explanatory schemes that qualify as theory-elements and theory-nets. Research should attempt to refine the understanding of theoretical principles of these theories and to expand the set of intended applications. (2) There are empirical generalizations and isolated hypotheses that should be integrated into more encompassing explanatory schemes. (3) Generalization at the level of single cultures and societies is often the first step of theory building, but theoretical work shouldn't stop at this level. Theoretical integration is the crucial task ahead of us. We need not integrate all our hypotheses, but we should try hard to establish networks of validated hypotheses that lead to theory-elements and theory-nets.

Conclusion: Toward an Integrative Agenda

I consider the *methodological frameworks* to be partial and rationally grounded routes to the generation of systematic empirical knowledge on human societies and cultures. (1) In discussing *positivism*, I've stressed the internal diversity of this analytic framework and the fact that the theoretical part of the positivist agenda is still underdeveloped in the discipline. Anthropologists should embark on theoretical syntheses of the ethnographic record, producing better theories that enhance causal understanding of and orientation in the world and that lead to better, theoretically informed applied research. (2) My discussion of *hermeneutics* as the main exponent of the humanist approach focused on the importance of meaning, reflexivity, and historical embeddedness among humans, captured and represented by hermeneutic case studies of texts and discourses. Grasping the actor's point of view and rendering rich descriptions of natural settings are the main strengths of the hermeneutic approach. However, neither framework rules out the possibility of the other and the two can even be cross-fertilized as the examination of the relationship between *verstehen* and explanation shows (see below).

Regarding the *key problems of anthropological method*, I introduced a revised realist perspective as background tradition. It assumes that there's a real world out there, that it's conceptually construed in part, that it's difficult to establish hypotheses on the world. There is no way out except to engage in empirical validation and to eliminate false hypotheses by repeated checking. As to the ultimate impossibility of understanding the Other, I've shown this doctrine of radical alterity to be logically flawed. Thus, we have to rely on charitable translation of what other people say and do.

The term "understanding" covers a whole set of different and related concepts that aren't specific for humanist research. Interpretation (meaning of words, actions, etc.) in a general sense is pervasive and present in all fields of scholarship, including the social and natural sciences. The hermeneutic circle (an on-going dialogue between understanding the parts and the whole of a text or discourse) is not specific to investigations in the humanities. In the natural (and social) sciences, this distinction parallels the difference between background knowledge and tested hypotheses. This distinction is not a serious problem, however, because any element of the background knowledge can be checked in principle at least.

Empathic understanding (*verstehen* in the special sense of grasping the actor's point of view) is a useful heuristic approach in anthropological and social science research. It uncovers patterns of meaning and leads to the discovery of interpretive hypotheses on purposeful action, but it has to solve the usual problems of logic and empirical truth by ordinary means of scientific validation. This is apparent when we consider that the stories and cases produced by *verstehen* should somehow be typical for the larger setting that is investigated, and this often implicit claim has to be proven. Scientific explanation is elucidated next as embedding of a phenomenon in some theoretical model, usually containing laws. The drawing of polar opposites between empathic understanding and explanation is rejected as a misplaced contrast. Both procedures are complementary and can be combined in more encompassing explanatory schemes that integrate subjective meanings and objective constraints.

The concept of *theory in hermeneutics* is depicted as the uncovering of a hidden message in a text or discourse and the search for some general pattern underlying concrete cases. This quest then leads to a focus on salient patterns of thinking, feeling, and activity in particular cultures or texts, while the concept of *theory in the science ("positivist") framework* aims at larger syntheses, generalizing across different cases, places, and epochs. The established positivist view of *theories as statements* is contrasted with *the new structuralist nonstatement view of theories*. In this perspective, theories are conceptual structures containing general principles, formal models, and an open set of intended empirical applications.[6] Members of a scientific community holding a theory are striving to refine the principles and to extend the set of intended applications. While the theoretical core cannot be falsified, intended applications and special laws can be false. *Theory-elements* (cores and applications only) and *theory-nets* (that in addition to the theoretical core and applications include specializations of the theoretical principles to different domains) are distinguished as important elements of scientific theories. In anthropology, cultural and social types can be conceptualized as theory-elements, while some explanatory schemes that cross-cut disciplinary boundaries in the social and behavioral sciences (like evolutionary ecology, rational choice theory, social network analysis, cognitive anthropology) achieve the status of theory-nets. The crucial theoretical task ahead is to integrate generalizations from case studies, ad hoc hypotheses from cross-cultural research, and the available theory-elements and theory-nets into more encompassing theoretical structures.

These theoretical structures can still be partial and selective. Integration will never cover everything, but a more integrative approach is possible and advisable. In the past, methodological debates in anthropology and related subjects overly emphasized the differences between theoretical and methodological schools. Too much effort has gone into critiques and not enough into constructive efforts (the next step after necessary criticism). It is time to stress that the fieldwork tradition and a concern for comparative synthesis are common issues to all anthropologists, leading to convergences at least of problems and sometimes even of solutions across different frameworks.

Furthermore, close inspection of methodological problems and solutions reveals that some of the differences in kind of past debates (most notably empathic understanding versus explanation; culture-specific thick description versus the search for laws) only establish differences of degree. They can even be considered supplementary and can be incorporated as useful steps in larger and richer theoretical projects. Rereading the writings of previous anthropologists clearly reveals that there has been a refinement of methodological and epistemological thinking, that the standards of ethnographic description have become much more sophisticated, and that the discipline has gained a real increase in causal understanding. Standing on the shoulders of these scholars, anthropologists today can conduct constructive, theoretical syntheses of the massive data and selective theoretical ideas that have accumulated in the discipline.

NOTES

I thank the editor and the following people for valuable advice: Joachim Görlich, Peter Kappelhoff, Hartmut Lang, members of my colloquium on anthropological theory and method, in particular Michael Bollig, Christoph Brumann, Clarence Gravlee, Michael Schnegg, Thomas Widlok, and Barbara Zschoch.

1. Useful background information on the philosophical currents discussed in the text can be found in Bunnin and Tsui-James (1996) and in the *Encyclopedia Britannica* (see the entries on the keywords philosophy of science, [logical] positivism, analytic philosophy, and leading figures like Auguste Comte, Rudolf Carnap, Karl Popper, and Martin Heidegger, among others). The focus on ideas in my presentation can also be grounded in Popper's (1972:154) pluralist philosophy (although we needn't draw on his conception): "In this pluralistic philosophy the world consists of at least three ontologically distinct sub-worlds; or, as I shall say, there are three worlds: the first is the physical world or the world of physical states; the second is the mental world or the world of mental states; and the third is the world of intelligibles, or of *ideas in the objective sense*; it is the world of possible objects of thought: the world of theories in themselves, and their logical relations; of arguments in themselves; and of problem situations in themselves."

2. In an interesting study, Dovring (1954) points to the beginning of quantitative text analysis in the hermeneutic tradition when rival schools of Protestant biblical exegesis turned to word frequency counts to settle a theological dispute at the courts in Sweden in the eighteenth century.

3. To keep the terminology concise, I use the term "text" only for documents produced for storing information in a written form (like letters, field notes, transcripts of interviews, observational records, reports, fiction, etc.) and "discourse" for verbal interactions. This doesn't question the legitimacy of studying "culture as a text" in a metaphorical sense.

4. The gist of the thesis of radical alterity is the claim of a universal impossibility to understand other people, and this leads to a logical flaw. One reader of a previous version of this chapter related this claim to another cognitive limitation—the almost impossibility of any humans to understand how cruel humans can be, thinking of the Holocaust, the recent massacres in Rwanda, or even individual cruelties. Although one can try to causally understand how such events come about, I concede that there is a point in these instances where rational understanding ends and where it's impossible to grasp how humans could act like that. This, however, is not a logical matter (as the thesis of radical alterity discussed in the text), but a serious practical limitation to understand the cruel Other.

5. I use the word "hypothesis" as a general term for unvalidated, conditional statements, whereas laws and lawlike statements are hypotheses that have been tested and confirmed. Hypotheses can postulate deterministic or statistical relationships between antecedent conditions and consequences; they can also have different and more elaborate forms than the logical implications (deterministic if/then statements) connecting two phenomena that are mentioned in the text. On the different logical forms see, for instance, Suppes (1957:Ch.1).

6. In his recent exposition of the theory concept, Balzer (1997:48–60) includes data structures and approximation in his definition of "theory," which is much in accord with actual research practices in empirical disciplines. This empirical turn (compared to the more

theoretical core interests of structuralist philosophy of science in general) comes with an attempt to include the social sciences and applied natural sciences in the consideration of an appropriate theory concept.

REFERENCES

Abel, Theodore F. 1948. The Operation Called Verstehen. *American Journal of Sociology* *54*:211–218.

Abu-Lughod, Lila. 1991.Writing Against Culture. In *Recapturing Anthropology*. Richard G. Fox, ed. Pp. 137–162. Santa Fe: School of American Research Press.

Abu-Lughod, Lila. 1993. *Writing Women's Worlds*. Berkeley: University of California Press.

Achinstein, Peter, and Stephen F. Barker, eds. 1969. *The Legacy of Logical Positivism*. Baltimore: Johns Hopkins Press.

Agar, Michael H. 1980. *The Professional Stranger*. New York: Academic Press.

Agar, Michael H. 1986. *Speaking of Ethnography*. Qualitative Research Methods Series, Vol 2. Thousand Oaks, CA: Sage Publications.

Albert, Hans. 1967. *Marktsoziologie und Entscheidungslogik*. Neuwied, Germany: Luchterhand.

Albert, Hans. 1994. *Kritik der reinen Hermeneutik*. Tübingen, Germany: Mohr.

Backhouse, Roger E., ed. 1994. *New Directions in Economic Methodology*. London: Routledge.

Balzer, Wolfgang. 1997. *Die Wissenschaft und ihre Methoden*. Freiburg: Alber.

Balzer, Wolfgang, and C. Ulises Moulines, eds. 1996. *Structuralist Theory of Science*. Berlin: de Gruyter.

Balzer, Wolfgang, C. Ulises Moulines, and Joseph D. Sneed. 1987. *An Architectonic for Science*. Dordrecht, Netherlands: Reidel.

Bartelborth, Thomas. 1996. Scientific Explanation. In *Structuralist Theory of Science*. Wolfgang Balzer and C. Ulises Moulines, eds. Pp. 23–43. Berlin: de Gruyter.

Becker, Gary. 1976. *The Economic Approach to Human Behavior*. Chicago: University of Chicago Press.

Bernard, H. Russell. 1994. *Research Methods in Anthropology: Qualitative and Quantitative Approaches*, 2d ed. Walnut Creek, CA: AltaMira Press.

Betzig, Laura, ed. 1997. *Human Nature*. Oxford: Oxford University Press.

Bierstedt, Alexander. 1997. *Darwins Erben und die Vielfalt der Kultur*. Frankfurt: Peter Lang Verlag.

Blaug, Mark. 1992. *The Methodology of Economics or How Economists Explain*, 2d ed. Cambridge: Cambridge University Press.

Boas, Franz. 1961 [1940]. *Race, Language and Culture*. New York: MacMillan.

Bohman, James. 1991. *New Philosophy of Social Science*. Oxford: Polity Press.

Borofsky, Robert. 1997. Cook, Lono, Obeyesekere, and Sahlins. *Current Anthropology* 38:255–282.

Bourgois, Philippe. 1995. *In Search of Respect*. Cambridge: Cambridge University Press.

Bowlin, John R., and Peter G. Stromberg. 1997. Representation and Reality in the Study of Culture. *American Anthropologist* 99:123–134.

Brodbeck, May, ed. 1968. *Readings in the Philosophy of the Social Sciences*. London: Macmillan.

Bunnin, Nicholas, and E. P. Tsui-James, eds. 1996. *The Blackwell Companion to Philosophy*. Oxford: Blackwell.

Carnap, Rudolf. 1963. Intellectual Autobiography. In *The Philosophy of Rudolf Carnap*. Paul A. Schilpp, ed. Pp. 1–84. La Salle, IL: Open Court.

Cashdan, Elizabeth. 1990. Information Costs and Customary Prices. In *Risk and Uncertainty in Tribal and Peasant Economies*. Pp. 259–278. Boulder: Westview Press.

Clifford, James. 1988. *The Predicament of Culture*. Cambridge: Harvard University Press.

Clifford, James, and George E. Marcus, eds. 1986. *Writing Culture*. Berkeley: University of California Press.

Coleman, James S. 1990. *Foundations of Social Theory*. Cambridge: Belknap Press.

Coleman, James S., and Thomas J. Fararo, eds. 1992. *Rational Choice Theory*. Thousand Oaks, CA: Sage Publications.

D'Andrade, Roy. 1984. Cultural Meaning Systems. In *Culture Theory*. Richard A. Shweder and Robert A. LeVine, eds. Pp. 88–119. Cambridge: Cambridge University Press.

D'Andrade, Roy. 1995. *The Development of Cognitive Anthropology*. Cambridge: Cambridge University Press.

D'Andrade, Roy, and Claudia Strauss, eds. 1994. *Human Motives and Cultural Models*. Cambridge: Cambridge University Press.

Davidson, Donald. 1984. *Inquiries into Truth and Interpretation*. Oxford: Clarendon Press.

Davidson, Donald. 1989. The Myth of the Subjective. In *Relativism*. Michael Krausz, ed. Pp. 159–172. Notre Dame: University of Notre Dame Press.

Derrida, Jacques. 1967. *L'écriture et la différence*. Paris: Editions du Seuil.

Diederich, Werner. 1996. Pragmatic and Diachronic Aspects of Structuralism. In *Structuralist Theory of Science*. Wolfgang Balzer and C. Ulises Moulines, eds. Pp. 75–82. Berlin: de Gruyter.

Dilthey, Wilhelm. 1900(1894). Ideen über eine beschreibende und zergliedernde Psychologie. In his *Gesammelte Schriften*, Vol. 5. Bernhard Groethuysen, ed. Pp. 139–240. Stuttgart: Teubner.

Dirks, Nicholas B., Geoff Eley, Sherry B. Ortner, eds. 1994. *Culture/Power/History*. Princeton: Princeton University Press.

Dolgin, Janet L., David S. Kemnitzer, and David M. Schneider, eds. 1977. *Symbolic Anthropology*. New York: Columbia University Press.

Dovring, Karin. 1954. Quantitative Semantics in 18th-Century Sweden. *Public Opinion Quarterly 18*:389–394.

Dumont, Jean-Paul. 1992. *Visayan Vignettes.* Chicago: University of Chicago Press.

Ekman, Paul. 1980. *The Face of Man.* New York: Garland STPM Press.

Ensminger, Jean. 1992. *Making a Market.* Cambridge: Cambridge University Press.

Ensminger, Jean, and Jack Knight. 1997. Changing Social Norms: Common Property, Bridewealth, and Clan Exogamy. *Current Anthropology* 38:1–24.

Esser, Hartmut. 1991. *Alltagshandeln und Verstehen.* Tübingen, Germany: Mohr.

Esser, Hartmut. 1993. The Rationality of Everyday Behavior. A Rational Choice Reconstruction of the Theory of Action. *Rationality and Society 5*:7–31.

Esser, Hartmut. 1996. Die Definition der Situation. *Kölner Zeitschrift für Soziologie und Sozialpsychologie* 48:1–34.

Evans-Pritchard, E. E. 1940. *The Nuer.* Oxford: Clarendon Press.

Fox, Richard G., ed. 1991. *Recapturing Anthropology.* Santa Fe: School of American Research Press.

Franklin, Sarah. 1995. Science as Culture, Cultures of Science. *Annual Review of Anthropology 24*:163–184.

Friedrich, Paul. 1992. Interpretation and Vision: A Critique of Cryptopositivism. *Cultural Anthropology 7*:211–231.

Gadamer, Hans-Georg. 1965 [1960]. *Wahrheit und Methode.* Tübingen, Germany: Mohr.

Gadamer, Hans-Georg. 1983. *Lob der Theorie.* Frankfurt: Suhrkamp.

Geertz, Clifford. 1975. *The Interpretation of Cultures.* London: Hutchinson.

Geertz, Clifford. 1983. *Local Knowledge.* New York: Basic Books.

Geertz, Clifford. 1988. *Works and Lives.* Stanford: Stanford University Press.

Geertz, Clifford. 1995. *After the Fact.* Cambridge: Harvard University Press.

Geier, Manfred. 1993. *Der Wiener Kreis.* Reinbek, Germany: Rowohlt.

Geldsetzer, Lutz. 1989. Hermeneutik. In *Handlexikon zur Wissenschaftstheorie.* Helmut Seiffert and Gerard Radnitzky, eds. Pp. 127–139. Munich: Ehrenwirth.

Gewertz, Deborah B., and Frederick K. Errington. 1991. *Twisted Histories, Altered Contexts.* Cambridge: Cambridge University Press.

Glasersfeld, Ernst von. 1995. *Radical Constructivism.* London: Falmer Press.

Goodenough, Ward H. 1994. Toward a Working Theory of Culture. In *Assessing Cultural Anthropology.* Robert Borofsky, ed. Pp. 262–275. New York: McGraw-Hill.

Görlich, Joachim. 1998. Between War and Peace: Gift Exchange and Commodity Barter in the Central and Fringe Highlands of Papua New Guinea. In *Kinship, Networks, and Exchange.* Thomas Schweizer and Douglas R. White, eds. Pp. 303–331. Cambridge: Cambridge University Press.

Gupta, Akhil, and James Ferguson, eds. 1997. *Anthropological Locations.* Berkeley: University of California Press.

Hage, Per, and Frank Harary. 1991. *Exchange in Oceania.* Oxford. Clarendon Press.

Hage, Per, and Frank Harary. 1996. *Island Networks.* Cambridge: Cambridge University Press.

Harre, Rom, and Michael Krausz. 1996. *Varieties of Relativism.* Oxford: Blackwell.

Hempel, Carl G. 1965. *Aspects of Scientific Explanation and Other Essays in the Philosophy of Science.* New York: Free Press.

Hempel, Carl G. 1966. *Philosophy of Natural Science.* Englewood Cliffs, NJ: Prentice-Hall.

Holland, Dorothy, and Naomi Quinn, eds. 1987. *Cultural Models in Language and Thought.* Cambridge: Cambridge University Press.

Hollis, Martin. 1994. *The Philosophy of Social Science.* Cambridge: Cambridge University Press.

Janik, Allan, and Stephen Toulmin. 1973. *Wittgenstein's Vienna.* New York: Simon and Schuster.

Johnson, Allen W., and Timothy Earle. 1987. *The Evolution of Human Societies.* Stanford: Stanford University Press.

Keesing, Roger M. 1994. Theories of Culture Revisited. In *Assessing Cultural Anthropology.* Robert Borofsky, ed. Pp. 301–312. New York: McGraw-Hill.

Kim, Bo-Hyun. 1991. *Kritik des Strukturalismus.* Amsterdam: Radopi.

Kondo, Dorinne K. 1990. *Crafting Selves.* Chicago: University of Chicago Press.

Krausz, Michael, ed. 1989. *Relativism.* Notre Dame: University of Notre Dame Press.

Kroeber, Alfred L. 1948. *Anthropology.* New York: Harcourt Brace.

Kuhn, Thomas S. 1970 [1962]. *The Structure of Scientific Revolutions.* Chicago: University of Chicago Press.

Kuipers, Theo A. F. 1996. Truth Approximation by the Hypothetico-Deductive Method. In *Structuralist Theory of Science.* Wolfgang Balzer and C. Ulises Moulines, eds. Pp. 83–113. Berlin: de Gruyter.

Kutschera, Franz von. 1982. *Grundfragen der Erkenntnistheorie.* Berlin: de Gruyter.

Kuznar, Lawrence A. 1997. *Reclaiming a Scientific Anthropology.* Walnut Creek, CA: AltaMira Press.

Lakatos, Imre. 1970. Falsification and the Methodology of Scientific Research Programmes. In *Criticism and the Growth of Knowledge.* Imre Lakatos and Alan Musgrave, eds. Pp. 91–195. Cambridge: Cambridge University Press.

Lakatos, Imre, and Alan Musgrave, eds. 1970. *Criticism and the Growth of Knowledge.* Cambridge: Cambridge University Press.

Lang, Hartmut. 1994. *Wissenschaftstheorie für die ethnologische Praxis.* Berlin: Reimer.

Latsis, Spiro, ed. 1976. *Method and Appraisal in Economics.* Cambridge: Cambridge University Press.

Leach, Edmund R. 1954. *Political Systems of Highland Burma.* London: Athlone Press.

Leach, Jerry W., and Edmund R. Leach, eds. *The Kula.* Cambridge: Cambridge University Press.

Lenk, Hans. 1995. *Interpretation und Realität.* Frankfurt: Suhrkamp.

Lévi-Strauss, Claude. 1963. *Structural Anthropology.* New York: Basic Books.

Lindenberg, Siegwart. 1989. Social Production Functions, Deficits, and Social Revolutions: Prerevolutionary France and Russia. *Rationality and Society* 1:51–77.

Lindenberg, Siegwart. 1990. Homo Socio-oeconomicus: The Emergence of a General Model of Man in the Social Sciences. *Journal of Institutional and Theoretical Economics* 146:727-748.

Lindenberg, Siegwart. 1992. The Method of Decreasing Abstraction. In *Rational Choice Theory.* James S. Coleman and Thomas J. Fararo, eds. Pp. 3–20. Thousand Oaks, CA: Sage Publications.

Lindenberg, Siegwart. 1996. Constitutionalism Versus Relationalism: Two Versions of Rational Choice Sociology. In *James S. Coleman.* Jon Clark, ed. Pp. 299–312. London: Falmer Press.

Lindenberg, Siegwart, and Bruno S. Frey. 1993. Alternatives, Frames, and Relative Prices: A Broader View of Rational Choice Theory. *Acta Sociologica 36*:191–205.

Lindstrom, Lamont. 1990. *Knowledge and Power in a South Pacific Society.* Washington, DC: Smithsonian Institution Press.

Lowie, Robert H. 1959 [1937]. *The History of Ethnological Theory.* New York: Rinehart & Company.

Lyotard, Jean-François. 1984. *The Post-Modern Condition: A Report on Knowledge.* Minneapolis: University of Minnesota Press.

Malinowski, Bronislaw. 1922. *Argonauts of the Western Pacific.* London: Routledge & Kegan Paul.

Marchi, Neil de, ed. 1988. *The Popperian Legacy in Economics.* Cambridge: Cambridge University Press.

Marchi, Neil de, ed. 1992. *Post-Popperian Methodology of Economics.* Boston: Kluwer.

Marcus, George E. 1994. After the Critique of Ethnography: Faith, Hope, and Charity, but the Greatest of These Is Charity. In *Assessing Cultural Anthropology.* Robert Borofsky, ed. Pp. 40–54. New York: McGraw-Hill.

Marcus, George E., and Michael M. J. Fischer. 1986. *Anthropology as Cultural Critique.* Chicago: University of Chicago Press.

Maryanski, Alexandra, and Jonathan H. Turner. 1992. *The Social Cage.* Stanford: Stanford University Press.

Mitchell, J. Clyde. 1956. *The Kalela Dance.* Rhodes-Livingstone Papers 27. Manchester: Manchester University Press.

Moulines, C. Ulises. 1996. Structuralism: The Basic Ideas. In *Structuralist Theory of Science.* Wolfgang Balzer and C. Ulises Moulines, eds. Pp. 1–13. Berlin: de Gruyter.

Murdock, George Peter. 1949. *Social Structure.* Glencoe, IL: Free Press.

Nadel, S. F. 1963 [1951]. *The Foundations of Social Anthropology.* London: Cohen & West.

Netting, Robert McC. 1993. *Smallholders, Householders.* Stanford: Stanford University Press.

Obeyesekere, Gananath. 1992. *The Apotheosis of Captain Cook.* Princeton: Princeton University Press.

Papineau, David. 1996. Philosophy of Science. In *The Blackwell Companion to Philosophy.* Nicholas Bunnin and E. P. Tsui-James, eds. Pp. 290–324. Oxford: Blackwell.

Pitt, Joseph C., ed. 1988. *Theories of Explanation.* Oxford: Oxford University Press.

Plattner, Stuart, ed. 1989. *Economic Anthropology.* Stanford: Stanford University Press.

Popper, Karl. 1969a [1934]. *Logik der Forschung.* Tübingen, Germany: Mohr [Engl. transl. *The Logic of Scientific Discovery.* New York 1959: Basic Books].

Popper, Karl. 1969b. *Conjectures and Refutations.* London: Routledge & Kegan Paul.

Popper, Karl. 1972. *Objective Knowledge.* Oxford: Clarendon Press.

Putnam, Hilary. 1981. *Reason, Truth, and History.* Cambridge: Cambridge University Press.

Quine, Willard Van Orman. 1960. *Word and Object.* Cambridge: M.I.T. Press.

Quine, Willard Van Orman. 1961. *From a Logical Point of View.* Cambridge: Harvard University Press.

Radcliffe-Brown, A. R. 1957 [1948]. *A Natural Science of Society.* Glencoe: Free Press.

Radcliffe-Brown, A. R. 1968 [1952]. *Structure and Function in Primitive Society.* New York: Free Press.

Rappaport, Roy A. 1968. *Pigs for the Ancestors.* New Haven: Yale University Press.

Rawls, John. 1971. *A Theory of Justice.* Cambridge: Harvard University Press.

Romney, A. Kimball, Susan C. Weller, and William H. Batchelder. 1986. Culture as Consensus: A Theory of Culture and Informant Accuracy. *American Anthropologist 88*: 313–338.

Rosenau, Pauline Marie. 1992. *Postmodernism and the Social Sciences.* Princeton: Princeton University Press.

Ricoeur, Paul. 1981. *Hermeneutics and the Human Sciences.* John B. Thompson, ed. and transl. Cambridge: Cambridge University Press.

Safranski, Rüdiger. 1994. *Ein Meister aus Deutschland: Heidegger und seine Zeit.* Munich: Hanser.

Sahlins, Marshall. 1995. *How Natives Think.* Chicago: University of Chicago Press.

Scheper-Hughes, Nancy. 1994. Embodied Knowledge: Thinking with the Body in Critical Medical Anthropology. In *Assessing Cultural Anthropology.* Robert Borofsky, ed. Pp. 229–242. New York: McGraw-Hill.

Schmid, Michael. 1996. *Rationalität und Theoriebildung.* Amsterdam: Radopi.

Schutz, Alfred. 1964. *Collected Papers II: Studies in Social Theory.* The Hague: Nijhoff.

Schweizer, Thomas. 1996. *Muster sozialer Ordnung.* Berlin: Reimer.

Schweizer, Thomas, and Douglas R. White, eds. 1998. *Kinship, Networks, and Exchange.* Cambridge: Cambridge University Press.

Searle, John R. 1995. The *Construction of Social Reality*. New York: Free Press.

Seidman, Steven, ed. 1994. *The Postmodern Turn*. Cambridge: Cambridge University Press.

Seidman, Steven, and David G. Wagner, eds. 1992. *Postmodernisn and Social Theory*. Oxford: Blackwell.

Smith, Eric Alden, and Bruce Winterhalder, eds. 1992. *Evolutionary Ecology and Human Behavior*. New York: Aldine de Gruyter.

Spiro, Melford E. 1986. Cultural Relativism and the Future of Anthropology. *Cultural Anthropology 1*:259–286.

Spiro, Melford E. 1990. On the Strange and the Familiar in Recent Anthropological Thought. In *Cultural Psychology*. James W. Stigler, Richard A. Shweder, Gilbert Herdt, eds. Pp. 47–61. Cambridge: Cambridge University Press.

Steedly, Mary Margaret. 1993. *Hanging Without a Rope*. Princeton: Princeton University Press.

Stegmüller, Wolfgang. 1969. *Probleme und Resultate der Wissenschaftstheorie und Analytischen Philosophie*. Vol. 1: *Wissenschaftliche Erklärung und Begründung*. Berlin: Springer.

Stegmüller, Wolfgang. 1973. Neue Betrachtungen über Aufgaben und Ziele der Wissenschaftstheorie. In *Probleme und Resultate der Wissenschaftstheorie und Analytischen Philosophie*, Vol. 4. Pp. 1–64. Berlin: Springer.

Stegmüller, Wolfgang. 1976. *The Structure and Dynamics of Theories*. Berlin: Springer.

Stegmüller, Wolfgang. 1979a. *The Structuralist View of Theories*. Berlin: Springer.

Stegmüller, Wolfgang. 1979b. Walther von der Vogelweides Lied von der Traumliebe und Quasar 3 C 273: Betrachtungen zum sogenannten Zirkel des Verstehens und zur sogenannten Theoriegeladenheit von Beobachtungen. In *Rationale Rekonstruktion von Wissenschaft und ihrem Wandel*. Wolfgang Stegmüller, ed. Pp. 27–86. Stuttgart: Reclam.

Strauss, Claudia. 1992. Models and Motives. In *Human Motives and Cultural Models*. Roy D'Andrade and Claudia Strauss, eds. Pp. 1–20. Cambridge: Cambridge University Press.

Strauss, Claudia, and Naomi Quinn. 1994. A Cognitive/Cultural Anthropology. In *Assessing Cultural Anthropology*. Robert Borofsky, ed. Pp. 284–300. New York: McGraw-Hill.

Strauss, Claudia, and Naomi Quinn. 1997. *A Cognitive Theory of Cultural Meaning*. Cambridge: Cambridge University Press.

Suppes, Patrick. 1957. *Introduction to Logic*. Princeton: Van Nostrand.

Tjon Sie Fat, Franklin E. 1990. Representing Kinship: Simple Models of Elementary Structures. Ph.D. thesis. Leiden: Faculty of Social Sciences.

Tsing, Anna Lowenhaupt. 1993. *In the Realm of the Diamond Queen*. Princeton: Princeton University Press.

Turner, Victor W. 1957. *Schism and Continuity in an African Society*. Manchester: Manchester University Press.

Wasserman, Stanley, and Katherine Faust. 1994. *Social Network Analysis: Methods and Applications*. Cambridge: Cambridge University Press.

Wasserman, Stanley, and Joseph Galaskiewicz, eds. 1994. *Advances in Social Network Analysis*. Thousand Oaks, CA: Sage Publications.

Weber, Max. 1904 [1968]. Die Objektivität sozialwissenschaftlicher und sozialpolitischer Erkenntnis. In his *Methodologische Schriften. Johannes Winckelmann, ed.* Pp. 1–64. Frankfurt: Fischer.

Weber, Max. 1917 [1968]. Der Sinn der Wertfreiheit der soziologischen und ökonomischen Wissenschaften. In his *Methodologische Schriften. Johannes Winckelmann,* ed. Pp. 229–277. Frankfurt: Fischer.

Weber, Max. 1972. *Wirtschaft und Gesellschaft*. Tübingen, Germany: Mohr.

Wellman, Barry, and S. D. Berkowitz, eds. 1997. *Social Structures: A Network Approach*, 2d rev. ed. Greenwich, CT: JAI Press.

Welsch, Wolfgang. 1996. *Vernunft*. Frankfurt: Suhrkamp.

Werner, Oswald, and G. Mark Schoepfle. 1987. *Systematic Fieldwork*. 2 vols. Thousand Oaks, CA: Sage Publications.

Wilk, Richard R. 1996. *Economies and Cultures*. Boulder: Westview Press.

Wolf, Eric. 1964. *Anthropology*. Englewood Cliffs, NJ: Prentice-Hall.

Whyte, William Foote. 1943. *Street Corner Society*. Chicago: University of Chicago Press.

Yang, Mayfair Mei-hui. 1994. *Gifts, Favors, and Banquets*. Ithaca: Cornell University Press.

JAMES FERNANDEZ
MICHAEL HERZFELD

Three

In Search of Meaningful Methods

Fieldpaths: On the Meaning of Method

Lost as a dead metaphor in the word "method" is the Greek *hodos,* "way, path, road." Webster's dictionary (1959:1548) tells us that method is following some systematic course (Latin *cursus,* from *currere,* "to run") of action. Why, given the contingencies and uncertainties of life's constant negotiations of meaning, we should hope to follow any systematic course of action is not clear in the dictionary definition. This is an epistemological question requiring resolution for particular cases, and the very contingency of choice—imposed by the varying needs of different disciplines—belies the common assumption that methodology is necessarily dictated by a logic that stands outside culture and history.

The problem is compounded in the analysis of meaning by the fact that the very *object* of analysis is also the *medium* for the exercise of the method. While much has been written about the virtues of various metalanguages of method, none—certainly in the fields of semiotics and semantics—has been plausibly upheld as context independent

For these reasons, methodological specificity will, in most cases, be a clarification of the goal to which the path is thought to lead and of what is to be revealed in achieving that goal We begin here by etymological reflections on some of the tropes buried in the central terms under discussion.[1] In a theoretical phase in which anthropology is still recovering from the determined resistance of classic structuralism to both historical specificity and textual philology, there are nevertheless good reasons for using etymology—which is both historical and, at least traditionally, philological—as a reflexive methodological instrument.

Attention to etymology also shows that the anthropological study of meaning cannot rest on assumptions of pure reference, for these ignore the temporal instability of semantics: Meanings rarely stay the same for long. The critical term is *use*, and the primary methodological challenge is to assemble as full an account as possible of the *contexts of use* for each item to which local commentators attribute referential meaning. In this way, the anthropologist treats the claims of referentiality (and other forms of pragmatic essentializing) as themselves elements of the social universe of symbol-production, empirically identifiable precisely because they have been disaggregated from the processes of routinization that protect them from challenge in everyday life. In this approach, the object of empirical investigation is not *semantic accuracy*, in some absolute sense, but the *use that informants make* of symbols and models.

For example, arguments used to center on whether lineage segmentation was an accurate description of social reality or "merely" a folk model (Peters 1967; Salzman 1978). Once it became possible to treat it instead as a metaphor for political uncertainty (Meeker 1979:222), it could also be asked who used it, under what conditions, and for what purposes (according to their own or others' attributions of motive), and this made it possible to see segmentation as a pragmatic resource in the marshalling of historical memory for political purposes (Dresch 1986; Shryock 1997). This also made it possible to recognize the constitutive role given to metaphor by effective and interested social actors, rather than by literal-mindedly rejecting the model it represented as "inaccurate" and as divorced from the empirical domain. As a result, instead of worrying about whether a social group "really" practices lineage segmentation, we can see how individuals manage the observed pattern of political alliances by *using* the idea of segmentation as a legitimation for intended or already accomplished acts of violence, loyalty, and factionalism.

Perhaps the most obvious locus for this kind of distinction between literalist and symbolic understandings of fact lies in the management of history, where any critique of factuality must appear to be corrosive of power—precisely the point that Vico was at pains to make in his *New Science* (see below). This is especially true for the interpretation of material remains, notably archeological sites, because these physically imposing cultural objects force us to confront the fallacy of misplaced concreteness head-on. Thus, rather than asking which narratives about a historical site are "correct," we can learn a great deal more by examining how the various interpretations of that site are *used* by interested factions and individuals (Bruner and Gorfain 1984; Herzfeld 1991; Gable et al. 1992; Bond and Gilliam 1994; El-Haj In press). The literal content attributed to the narratives and the symbols deployed in their perpetuation (see Handelman 1990) are interesting primarily for the uses to which they are put (see Roberts 1997).

Much in such analyses will not be reducible to a verbal account of "what these symbols mean." There are many intangibles. To take a particularly salient example, does the echo of an etymological root that *we* can recognize mean that our informants recognize it, too? Or, more significantly, does their puzzlement when we ask them about this mean that the connection is, in some absolute sense, "not there"? Here we are particularly invoking what J. L. Austin (1971), writing of excuses, called "trailing clouds of etymology"—a motif to which we shall return. Without necessarily reviving Lévi-Strauss's (1963) unfortunate distinction between "conscious" and "unconscious" models—in which the former were impoverished because the "natives" supposedly did not have "our" capacity to detach their immediate interpretations to the real, full significance of the social phenomena in question—we may certainly assume that much of what we acknowledge as poetic "resonance" in speech, visual and olfactory signs, and indeed virtually every semiotic domain of culture would lose its evocative power, like an Aristophanes joke painstakingly dissected in the *apparatus criticus*, once people became too directly conscious of "how it worked."

To be sure, there are obvious aspects of meaning (Rappaport 1979:173–221), or at least there seem to be some, but obviousness is itself culturally contingent (Douglas 1975; Miceli 1982). Moreover, much that is meaningful in social interaction and its attendant cultural configurations, shaped by and shaping of personal understandings, is not at all obvious even to the actors.

Second, while pointing out the obvious is—obviously?—a primary task, providing paths by which inquiry can proceed in order to discover and understand that which is not so obvious is crucial to method in the study of meaning. In the most reductionist of terms, meaning is not exhausted by a listing of referential correspondences or denotations, and it would be a poor ethnography that failed to grapple with the innuendoes, ironies, and other connotative meanings by which people construed the intimacies of everyday existence. Indeed, avoiding these cloudy issues, however discomfitting they may be and however deeply they offend our own methodological desire for order, would be an open invitation to engage in linguistic and other forms of cultural incompetence.

Third, the study of meaning is also, as a consequence of its dependence on being able to respond to such indefinable but undeniable problems, pronouncedly reflexive. The inquiry compels reflection on its own organizing tropes so as not to fall prey to unrecognized and unanalyzed path dependencies—that is, to teleological expectations that are concealed within the presuppostions of the methodology itself. Thus, any method for the study of meaning will entail reflecting on the tropes that appear to frame its argument in an interesting and intelligible way. (A good example is the significance of our own cultural and "rational" distaste for the kinds of analytic disorder just mentioned: They are violations of a categorical order, and, as such, represent the irruption of an awkward reality into the symbolic order of science—an instructive irony, given that symbolism is so often conceptually opposed to science.)

The "frames of intelligibility" (Geertz 1973:36) that we use are thus not to be taken for granted as inevitable and universally self-evident. And the particular tropes on which they depend and their difference from the tropes characteristic of other frames of intelligibility can be readily demonstrated, as in Salmond's (1982:82–86) comparison of European and Maori framing of knowledge claims in territorial terms (European), on the one hand, and sacred wealth terms (Maori), on the other.

What is involved here is what in his *New Science* (1984 [1744]), the eighteenth-century Neapolitan philosopher Giambattista Vico called "poetic wisdom"—wisdom about the experiential sources of our understanding and about the ways in which our knowledge is represented and organized by various devices of the imagination so as both to frame and, by performance, to fulfill what is taken and received as intelligible. This wisdom, for Vico (and, more recently, for Bourdieu [1977] and Jackson [1989]), is often lost in the mesmerizing abstractionism of intellectual life and has to be rescued from it. In particular, Vico, who deployed etymology against its normativizing uses by the official establishment to develop a critical, defamiliarizing, and consequently subversive method, argued that when thinkers lose sight of the material, social, and corporeal metaphors out of which their abstract ideas arise, they also lose a sense of the experiential grounding of their knowledge. Superficial intellectual enthusiasms and actual loss of knowledge are the effective outcomes.

Vico argued that "in all languages the majority of expressions for inanimate things are made by means of allusions to the human body and its parts and to human sensations and human passions" (Vico II:2,2,2 [1984:248] in Herzfeld [1987:13, 169–170]). The probing of these allusions is basic to Vico's notion of poetic wisdom. He argued that we must remember these crude origins of abstract reason if we are to avoid the ignorant and ultimately degrading conviction that our thought, with its claims to transcendence and sophistication, has escaped our corporeal historical selves. This old point about poetic wisdom has been more recently developed in the cognitive theory of metaphor, which anchors the dynamic of the tropes in the *prototypical* corporeal and sensation-anchored domains of human experience (the *experiential gestalts* of life) (Lakoff and Johnson 1980; Johnson 1987; Lakoff 1987).

Arguments like this—whether of Vico or in the latter-day cognitive approach to metaphor—should be particularly congenial to anthropologists, for it enables them to lodge the sources of academic abstractions—the scaffolding of learned theorizing with all its attendant, often arrogant narcissism and solipsism—in the tropes of entirely local and embodied sensations and experiences as these are understood and articulated by the people we study. By juxtaposing our interlocutors' wisdom and theoretical capacity with the formal knowledge of academic writers, we may actually be able to develop more useful tools of analysis to decipher local meanings: The similarities and differences that emerge may help us understand the range of what people "mean by meaning" (see, for example, Herzfeld [1985], for a juxtaposition of Jakobson's [1960] "poetic function" with local concepts of meaning). In place of vague generalizations about meaning, we recast our theoretical frameworks as ethnographic data in a comparative project engaged by both our informants (who are usually, after all, trying to make sense of us) and ourselves.

Recognizing, then, that the concept of "method" is itself enmeshed in a complex history of shifting signification permits a determinedly empirical insistence on the constant calibration of the methods we use to elicit data with our informants' understanding of what constitutes appropriate discourse, social interaction, and intellectual activity. At the same time, and for the reasons that Vico was the first to recognize, any method must be in some sense both a path and the project of following that path. Thus, it is dynamic and actively adaptive to circumstances rather than preordained and given; and, in the sense that method constitutes the criteria of relevance for its own objects of discovery, it is also constitutively performative. Following a path of investigation is a methodological performance in this active (or "performative") sense: The choice of the path we follow determines and in some sense guarantees the "truth" that can be asserted as a consequence of following that particular path.

Indeed, anthropologists have argued in recent years that good ethnographic field methods must provide a clear account of the field paths followed to obtain the data out of which the local knowledge and the eventual ethnography built on it are constructed (Sanjek 1990:398–400; see also Fernandez 1993, 1996)—a position that exposes the fashionable distinction between positivistic and interpretive styles of analysis as itself caught up in an identifiable, describable social rhetoric. It has been similarly argued that historical method must be critically aware of its path dependency, and, at the same time, of the degree to which it may be overly influenced by a teleological dynamic which overcommits it to final causes and a priori endpoints of pathlike reasoning (Goldstein 1976; Sewell 1996; Tilly 1997).

There is a delicate balance here by which a method must be purposive without being deterministic—that is, allegedly immanent in what it is used to investigate and thus self-fulfilling. Thus, while we seek to condition and control through pathlike procedures, the presence of pure randomness and contingency in the undertaking of inquiry through the use of method, we do not thereby dispose of the ever-present possibility of contingency in the actual working out of human interaction. When method appears to have that effect, often indexed in English by passive-voice constructions indicating an avoidance of scholarly *agency* and *accountability*, it has clearly strayed from the path of empirical inquiry and fallen into the trap of pure self-reference—the very danger against which Vico's etymological subversions were intended to provide a provocative and persistent warning.[2] Method implies systematization of procedure usually leading to the goal of greater clarity or parsimony in the explanation of human affairs. Method is itself a project that recognizes the presence and influence of projects in the social and cultural affairs of those studied (Sartre 1963), including the presence of goals as immanent in these projects. But it entails caution about the a priori presence of final causes in its own procedures and its empirical claims depend on its remaining open to contingency—the combination of predictability and improvisation that characterizesthe social interaction it studies. It remains answerable to what Marx, here perhaps following Vico (Tagliacozzo 1983), said in *The Eighteenth Brumaire* (1978 [1852]:Section 1) that, while "men make their own history, they do not make it just as they please."

Social and Cultural Poetics as a Method for the Study of Meaning in Performance

We noted above that method *most usually* works toward greater parsimony (powerful simplicity) of explanation, with the caveat that frequently enough, as far as the study of meaning is concerned, what is produced is an understanding of the greater complexity in the processes by which meaning is configured. The notion of poetic wisdom is sensitive to that complexity and thereby challenges parsimonious accounts, so to speak, to account for their parsimony—for their reductiveness, as it often turns out to be. For poetic wisdom is not the study of meaning in the abstract. Instead, it attends to the dynamic of meaning in actual performance—the means by which significance is conveyed in actual social life. In this it anticipates historically the development of use or action theories of meaning as opposed to an empirically indefensible reliance on the notion of pure reference.

Our view is that poetic principles guide all *effective* and *affective* social interaction. By this we mean that the mind engaged in action in the social world is as much if not more a poetic instrument as it is an abstracting and concept-forming instrument (Gibbs 1994). Indeed, to the extent that there can be a poetics of precision, these are not necessarily separate or even distinguishable entities, and only an antiempirical, preemptive logic would allow us to presuppose that they were. Conversely, affectations of numerical or monetary imprecision—such as when a merchant pretends not to weigh produce carefully, or when a customer ostentatiously avoids looking at the scale—demonstrate disdain for calculation, which is considered socially disruptive. In fact, effective performances of such careful imprecision, especially by the economically disadvantaged, may be a way of creating social solidarity (for example, within a social class or a profession) on the basis of which people can help each other—a form of social capital that also reduces their dependence on often hostile market mechanisms in obtaining cheaper goods and services (Herzfeld 1991:168–174).

The conveying of *sign*ificance in action is the heart of the matter that should concern us. And this requires us to focus on signs themselves, that is, on the wisdom that the various traditions of semiotic and symbolic inquiry in anthropology provide. Here we are obliged to recognize distinct but interrelated traditions of understanding: semantic anthropology, on the one hand (Crick 1976; Parkin 1982) (or "semiotic ethnography" [Herzfeld 1983]), and symbolic anthropology, on the other (Peacock 1975; Dolgin et al. 1977; Colby et al. 1981). We also must recognize that there have also been two distinct but also interrelated deployments of poetic wisdom: social poetics and cultural poetics. The first, social poetics, is grounded in a recognition of the role of cultural form in social life. Building on several strands—the recognition of cultural form (for example, modes of hierarchy or of inclusion and exclusion) in interaction (Fernandez 1977a), the traditions of "use" or "action" theory in semantics (analogous to practice theory in social anthropology and largely derived from the work of J. L. Austin [1962, 1971]), Jakobson's concept of "poetic function" (1960), and a long and complex tradition of rhetorical analysis in several semiotic domains and intellectual traditions—social poetics (Herzfeld 1985, 1997a) is the study of how social actors play on their societies' conventions in ways that, if successful, increase their power or status, while also sometimes contributing to cultural change.

Some critics have charged that this approach can only work in agonistic societies where the competition over the control of good form is palpable. But we answer that it is possible to perform nonperformance, to be boastfully modest and demure, and to make an extravagance out of restraint (whether social or aesthetic). It is vital, in pursuing a social poetics, to detach our methodology from assumptions (such as those that have dogged studies of "Mediterranean" or "Melanesian cultures") about some cultures being "more agonistic" than others. Such assumptions too easily reflect the social norms of our own cultural milieu and thereby illustrate perfectly what we have just said about the dangers of solipsistic methodology. And, of course, there may be no actual competition present in a given situation. But the creative deformation of norms—what, in another context, Boon (1982) has called "the exaggeration of culture"—must always be a response to people's understanding of what Bourdieu (1984) has theorized as the value of "cultural capital." Contestation thus lies at the root of the *realization* of human existence, even when we live in societies where the dominant ideology is a denial of any such thing.

The term "cultural poetics" surely does not deny the contestatory and agonistic politics of everyday life. That dimension is evoked in the subtitle of the collection that has stimulated so much recent inquiry into cultural poetics in anthropology, *Writing Culture: The Poetics and Politics of Ethnography* (Clifford and Marcus 1986). And notable recent instances of the cultural poetics approach (Crain 1989; Limón 1994) seek to keep the practical politics of everyday life, the war of position as Limón calls it (evoking Gramsci), in focus. But the practitioners of cultural poetics desire in their interpretations to focus, to quote Limón again, "on the aesthetically salient and culturally embedded textualities and enactments" (p. 14) of social life, which is to say the cultural preoccupations of that life. They seek to probe the "political unconscious"—in Jameson's phrasing, the "socially produced, narratively mediated and relatively unconscious ideological responses of people" to recurrent problematics and challenges to their situation (1981:Ch.1). The unconscious may be analytically opaque, to say the least, but failing to recognize its existence, however we label it, is equally unjustified methodologically and may lead to false assumptions about the very nature of knowledge.

The apparent concreteness of language is a major source of this fallacy (misplaced concreteness), and this overdetermination is nowhere more evident than in discussions of (or, worse, careless uses of the term) "poetics." Cultural poetics has been so heavily associated with textuality, for example, that its practitioners have often felt obliged to add the words "and politics," where a clearer definition of poetics itself should have made that phrase redundant, for, inasmuch as poetics is about creativity, it is inherently also about power.[3]

This last point requires some elaboration. Taken together, the approaches of social poetics and cultural poetics constitute a contemporary and comprehensive program—constellation of paths of inquiry—for the study of meaning. From the first, however, they have faced two criticisms: that they are too language based or logocentric and that they either neglect or ignore the dynamic interdependence between meaningfulness—the significance present in symbolic activity we might say—and power relations. We tried to make clear above that poetics and politics have been mutually complementary from the first. Still, the lingering association of poetics with a purely textual reading of the Aristotelian discussion of rhetoric and dramatic statement has tended to confine the term to the verbal and to exclude it from the raw, as opposed to the rhetorical, exercise of power. Meaning is never reducible to verbal form or restricted to language itself. We nevertheless wish to emphasize that the *reflexive* and *recursive* nature of language are main challenges to the complexity through which we must find our way and that, pragmatically, the medium of language must often be our principal guide; we should not forget that even the most determined (and determinist) materialists gain access to the majority of their data through conversation and archival consultation.

We further argue that political dynamics, the play of power, even raw power, has its inescapable rhetorical or poetic component. The writings of F. G. Bailey are suggestive in this regard, for they show that an inadequate performance can be constitutive of major shifts in the balance of power (Bailey 1973, 1983, 1994; see also Paine 1981): We "do things with words" (Austin 1962) and all manner of other signs. Yet both narratives and carefully observed sequences of events can, at the least, allow us to track probable causalities, which become significant especially as they are recognized by the social actors in question.

The transgressive move of using poetics as fundamental to a social science in a sense explicitly separated from that of poetry is, in part, intended to animate if not shock practitioners into recognizing the technical features by which we grasp the place of the rhetorical and the expressive in human affairs. The common, restrictive, and usually logocentric sense by which the term poetics is commonly understood should not obscure the deeper and more general semiotic properties and processes of human interaction that a social and cultural poetics seeks to evoke and appraise.

Such an approach illuminates the way that the main entities of social life, the bodily beings logocentrically denoted by the social pronouns, inchoate in their base natures, obtain social identity and the possibilities of extrabodily social experience by poetic processes of predicating physically sensate signs on themselves. (Fernandez 1974). We speak of a "body politic," and we can trace its vicissitudes in the disciplines and constraints imposed on individual bodies in its name (Cowan 1990). We can also approach physical monuments as ornaments of the body politic, analogous to those of the body personal, thereby treating the most obviously material manifestations—architecture, for example—as tropes of collective identity that is also personal and familial. Indeed, we would argue, this approach ironically speaks more directly to the materiality of experience than do many of the approaches that are styled "materialist." This is especially applicable in the sense that the embodied nature of human knowledge is embedded in relations of causality—especially as performativity—that are often channeled precisely through those phenomena that self-styled materialists dismiss as merely symbolic and therefore epiphenomenal (for example, Bloch [1975] and, in curiously similar terms, Harris [1974]).

Poetic Function

A social poetics, and by extension a cultural poetics, can usefully begin from the concept of "poetic function," as originally formulated by Jakobson (1960). His definition was ostensibly a purely linguistic one and all the material adduced to explore it was taken from the verbal domain (Waugh 1976), but the underlying principles—as must follow from Jakobson's communicative model—were unequivocally social. Methodologically, this alerts us to the possibility of a Jakobsonian classification of the uses of metaphors and other tropes, defined in terms of social actors (sender, destination, audience), that would be sufficient to ground the inchoateness and ambiguity of so much figurative language in the observed details of social interaction. It also suggests that similar principles might obtain for the entire range of human semiotic domains.

Moreover, formal properties emerge more from the social relationships among actors than from the sometimes "fuzzy" semantics of their language itself (see also Bourdieu 1977:113). Jakobson (1985), for example, was much concerned with the poetic uses of symmetry, chiasmus, parallelism, and opposition—idioms ideally suited to, and perhaps originating in, the oppositional aspects of social life, and powerfully iconic of that life, but—by the same logic—often also conducive to a *loss* of referential meaning. (This consideration also undoubtedly undergirded his occasional collaboration with Lévi-Strauss, in whom it generated a more abstract understanding of the concept of complementary opposition.)

Parallels between social relations and aesthetic elaborations, as in architecture (or, better, architectonics) (Fernandez 1977b, 1992b; Preziosi 1979; Blier 1994) are perhaps the more obvious "diagrams" of the poetic resonances between bodily experiences and living structures. In Newfoundland, for example, Pocius (1979) showed how the distribution of more and less hierarchically organized rug designs in formal front-room and familial kitchen spaces, respectively, reproduced the contrast in the social uses to which these two types of room were put. Another example is provided by rhyming couplings that reproduce sexual couplings (Dundes et al. 1972; Herzfeld 1985) in a manner sometimes explicitly recognized in the associated terminology. Here, the apparently superficial play on notions of sexuality offers an arena for playing on and contesting conventional expectations about other social relationships. Poetics is particularly attuned to the playfulness of social life—indeed, is about that playfulness: how people master the rules to demonstrate that the rules have not mastered them.

The Play of Meaning

At this point, we especially wish to focus attention on the notion of play. Vico himself exhibits a certain playfulness in his subversive use of etymology—his tracing of semiotic and tropological origins. Note that we say "semiotic and tropological origins" rather than merely "the origin of words." This expansion of etymology enables us to expand the notion of poetics to a more technical sense than originally suggested by Vico and is more consistent with the thoughts of Jakobson, namely, to the *play on the conventions of form*. We thus evoke the theme of play and playfulness (as opposed to planfulness) (Fernandez 1994) as central to meaning creation and as diagnostic of it.

This is, in turn, consistent with our view that meaningful knowledge of the constantly changing world is found not in classification itself and the planfulness that it represents (and that may be indeed a suppression of active knowing in favor of an imposed conformism), but in the act of reclassifying and of challenging or reconstituting existing classifications. In other words, play reveals form as it revels in it—sometimes in the moment of recasting or destroying it.

In this sense, etymology is a kind of diachronic pun: It undercuts received and conventional meanings. Often used by the powerful to legitimate their power, it may also be used subversively or playfully to undercut that power. This was Vico's understanding of etymology—a device through which the discovery of the instability of the term-referent relationship suggested the "civic disability" (Struever 1983) inherent in all human institutions rather than their capacity to resist forever the erosion of time.

By noting the instability of meaning in all symbols—including, but by no means confined to, linguistic elements—Vico provided both a method for analyzing the role of meaning creation in the construction and maintenance of political authority and an illustration of the subversive activity by which cultural dynamics and change in that authority occur. A complaisant view of meaning privileging reference over use would have been of no practical use in understanding how social actors playfully manipulate the truth claims of seemingly fixed symbols to satisfy their own interests. Vico's perspective, although conceived for very different ideological reasons and under conditions very different from those of modern anthropology, thus anticipated the present-day interest of anthropologists in action- or use-oriented theories of meaning and the constant social and cultural transformations for which they attempt to account.

The Elicitation of Nonverbal Meanings in Symbolic Interaction

There is always the tendency for discussion of methods, particularly when etymological method is invoked, to become logocentric. But we must recognize that nonverbal signs are important in the flow of meaning—that they may, indeed, play a far larger role in the constitution of sense than will ever be possible to recuperate from the data available to us. We might argue that their relative absence from the literature has been diagnostic of their very success at insinuating themselves into the realm of what Mary Douglas has called "self-evidence" (1975)—the common-sense, taken-for-granted aspects of a culture that are precisely what anthropology should defamiliarize and bring into focus.

When linguistic models predominate, methods usually entail the elicitation of taxonomies and the systematic recording of violations of those taxonomies—"matter out of place," in Douglas's formulation (1966). When we turn away from language, the question of elicitation becomes vastly more difficult. Gesture and posture can't be reduced to verbal equivalents and must be indicated by notational systems of various kinds; these are often cumbersome or recondite and pose a practical challenge to comprehension and interdigitation with the verbal (see Farnell and Williams 1990; Farnell 1994).

One approach, recently attempted by Herzfeld, entails videotaping sequences of dyadic interactions (in this case, between artisans and their apprenticeships), then playing them *with the sound turned off* to other culturally knowledgeable actors and asking the latter to comment on the interaction, supply the words being used, and answer some specific questions about the nature of the interaction. This avoids facile equations of bodily movement with segmental speech units and permits greater access to ideological presuppositions entertained by the actors themselves. Preliminary inspection of Herzfeld's material from Crete shows that male commentators tend to sympathize with the artisans and female with the apprentices, thereby demonstrating the replication of ideologies of hierarchy in adjacent but discrete contexts of social life. Note, too, that the "diagramming" of social relations in the Jakobsonian sense allows us to recognize homologies of political relationship across two or more spheres (here, labor and gender).

While such elicitation is to some extent intrusive, it fits increasingly with a worldwide familarity with the technology that makes it feasible, thereby reducing the effects of shyness and embarrassment (on which, moreover, some social actors are willing to provide their own glosses). The method requires a set of dyads that can eliminate random effects. For example, given that the local term for apprentice in Herzfeld's Cretan field site means "foster son" as well, the inclusion of a father-son dyad—in which the relationship was significantly warmer—helps to "materialize" the significance of kinship in affective terms. The repetition of the same scene with different voiceover and subtitle instructions to the viewer-respondents also accommodated a variety of sensibilities (for example, visual as well as verbal, attention to eye contact as well as gesture), and respondents were invited to put their own words into the actors' mouths as a means of determining conventional expectations about such relationships. Some sessions induced elaborate reminiscences, which could then be compared with longer-term testimonies by former apprentices and artisans, and this helped establish ways in which informants could conceptually square their long-term recollections of ideal-typical relationships with the immediacy of experiences that were often very different. Especially through this comparison of the elicited responses with the verbal commentaries from a rich series of artisans' oral work autobiographies, language moved the analysis beyond a purely referential and language-based model of meaning.[4]

Returning to diachronic aspects, the origins of nonverbal signs have usually proved harder to trace than verbal etymologies, in the absence of notational systems analogous to writing. Their very evanescence makes them ideal vehicles for indirection, ambiguity, irony, and other nonreferential modes of meaning. But the adequacy of the lexicographic model of referentiality is brought even more into question by the flows of nonverbal meaning often tied up in symbols in which the absence of lexicographic methods challenges (or should challenge) the illusion of analytically reducible reference.

Difficult as it is to specify methods for the study of nonverbal meaning, it would be an impoverished anthropology that excluded from the domain of culture everything not reducible to verbal equivalents. Symbolic analysis has sought to escape the purely verbal. The difficulty is that it has tended to rest on contested claims of ethnographic authority (Sperber 1975, 1985; Clifford 1983) or on putting forth formalized systems that often enough, in circular fashion, justified their own logic, a criticism made of Lévi-Straussian structuralism (see Leach 1970, 1976). Such circularity of argument weakens the claims of symbolic analysis to have escaped solipsism (Schwimmer 1978).

Recovering Meaning in Use and Emergence

Openness to nonverbal meanings brings with it a host of problems. However, since all contemporary human communities whose symbolic universes we attempt to enter are composed of language-using subjects, we emphasize that the Vichian notion of *poetic knowledge/wisdom* suggests the outline of an appropriate methodology. Vico's own use of etymology was notoriously unreliable, but if we recast his phylogeny of human semiosis as an ontogeny of semiotic forms—if, in other words, we suppose that all meaningful acts have a history and that the process of their formation can be reconstructed—we have propositional paths that enable us to appeal to at least two central foci: *use* and *change over time*.

The first of these two operations concerns the recovery of simple image-schemata as these repose in primary experience or process. This is the "argument of images" (Fernandez 1986; see Stark 1996). Although anchored in the concept of the image (which has usually been taken to be visual but need not necessarily be so—we shall briefly explore other iconicities below), it works primarily with verbalized tropes invoked as the basis of claims to local knowledge. But if this kind of interpretation is to be applied to tropes and symbols not expressed in language or supported by verbal exegesis, the basis of interpretation must become one of observed use. This assumption of ethnographic presence and direct observation of actual use undergirds inspired studies of tropes and symbols, of which an early and extended example comprises Turner's studies of Ndembu symbolism (Turner 1967). Unless this observational anchorage is made explicit, as it was not in Turner's case, the regrettable appearance of arbitrariness or invention—a projection of referentiality onto an analysis that is not intended to convey it—becomes the basis of criticism (Sperber 1985).

The second operation is analogous to the pragmatic turn to observations of actual change in use in ongoing action. Stimulated by the etymological impulse, it is above all historical. It is the restoration of the centrality of time in all interpretation by following the paths that particular usages follow over long periods of time. Such study gives substance to the idea that cultural form is always in a state of emergence (Bauman 1984; Bruner 1994). Our reconstructions of meaning thus starts from the recognition that before we can say what the meaning of a given action or object situation might be, we must first establish the range of acceptable alteration in the form of the act both at present and over time. In this context, we may even conclude that meaning is itself an inappropriate term and that "meaningfulness" is the more significant and appropriate form because it implies an ongoing temporal and emergent process of successive usages that themselves have a range of acceptability.

This move, which protects us from the tendency to essentialize our own categories by invoking as explicitly as possible the primacy of *use* and *action*, both complicates and strengthens description. It does so by keeping reification at bay, for it reminds us that the empirical task, both etymologically and pragmatically, is the grounded inspection of lived experience (Greek *empeiria*) rather than an exercise in abstract classification far removed from the social contexts in which we gather our data.

Indeterminacy: Tapping the Historical Consciousness of Permissible Variation

Tracking variation over time in the uses of signs makes us aware not only of emergence of meaning but of a considerable degree of variation (Fernandez 1965) and even indeterminacy (Giddens 1984) in the meaning of common practices and their accompanying and associated symbolic components. In the anthropological literature there has long been awareness of ranges of permissible variation, from culture to culture and time to time, in dress or performance styles, for example (Kroeber and Richardson 1952 [1940]), or in the graphing of the differential distribution of normative behaviors generally (LeVine 1973). But the study of the meanings attached to or promoted by these differences is usually lacking. Empirical observation shows, moreover, that there is a temporal dimension here in relation to which meaningfulness in action can be derived. As a modest example, a too-sudden change in the way of doing things with respect to table manners may provoke anger or contempt and thus very significant social meaning. So it is vital to link the tempo of performance (Bourdieu 1977:6–7) to the rate of change in the prior form of the act: Some acts are much more resistant to change than others, and variations have greater potentiality for meaning production both for the participants as well as the observer.

Analysis may thus, at a crude level, entail listing *conventions* and mapping them onto a social grid or a temporal chart in order to establish empirically the range, context, and character of permissible *invention*. This is clearly a complicated matter—but only the most determined Cartesian would claim that it was less empirical than the summing-up of such complex matters in the form of a referential taxonomy devoid of the ambiguity that lies at the heart of all experienced social life. Moreover, it can be checked against informant responses, both openly elicited and supposedly "natural" (a revealing term in itself; see, for example, Boehm [1980], in which the methodological and cultural artifice entailed in such invocations of nature is clearly exposed). When a single action appears to constitute a solecism in certain actors but not in others, the difference indexes the other factors that contribute to the shifting, but often identifiable, flux of interpretation and meaning. We may thereby, for example, infer what factors influence informants' judgments of each other and how predictable their effects are thought to be.

Some of these ranges are codified for us. Etiquette books register, for example, both the rigidity or permissible range of behaviors and reflect the acceptable rate of long-term change. But only long-term participant observation can effectively reveal the significance of different tempos. Sudden variation or acceleration of behavior excites the search, in gossip for example, for meaningful explanations such as "foreign influence" or "degeneration of morality." Actors teeter between social boorishness or approbation for social daring: Their attribution to either categorization depends not only on what they do and what relationship they have with those who are judging, but also on ever-shifting perceptions of what constitutes a permissible distortion of convention—an appraisal often influenced by the actors' own mastery of play. There is some evidence that abrupt variation attests to superficial rigidity of norms and that a challenge to such norms can constitute status-gaining acts of daring, particularly in societies in which an ideology of opposition to authority is explicit. Cretan artisans, for example, deny that they encourage insubordination in their apprentices. The evidence suggests, however, that they usually retain for long periods of time only those apprentices who have shown sufficient daring and resourcefulness to undermine the artisans' formal authority—a paradox that exemplifies the role of ethical and political ambiguity in many societies where agonistic relations are prominent.

In a truly Vichian mode, then, observation of the shifting relationship between "etymological cognates" among modes of social comportment becomes an investigation of the kinds of semiotic stability necessary, in a given culture or society, to the effective maintenance, negotiation, or usurpation of power. The converse also holds true. "Time servers," "hacks," "wimps," "bureaucrats" are labels reserved in many societies for those who, precisely because they follow social norms too rigidly, marginalize themselves from the fellowship of ordinary social interchange and thus from its manifold possibilities for inventive meaning creation. Etiquette books have their modern equivalent in the transnational world in the form of handbooks designed to help entrepreneurs negotiate their way through foreign cultures, but only by following their evolution through several editions (see, for example, Mole 1990, 1992, 1995) can we trace both the authors' learning path and the deeply hidden flexibility of the culture itself. The proliferation of such books and the telegraphic instructions travelers find in guidebooks often occasion mirth from local people precisely because such formalization usually leads to the excessively literal observance of rules: True mastery can only be shown by bending those rules within the shifting limits understood, supposedly, only by those who inhabit the culture's intimate spaces.

A historical awareness of what has transpired may provide actors with quite flexible templates for present action as the range of ways that Turner's (1972, 1974) "social dramas" can be played out indicate. The use of historical consciousness in understanding the range of possibly meaningful action and the scope of the indeterminate is always problematic. In societies with no recorded history of symbolic forms such analyses are hardly feasible, as neither informant nor analyst will have the knowledge of the relevant antecedent events in a form that can easily be matched to the sense of documentary facts available—albeit from differing perspectives—to both. It is all too easy to reduce that knowledge to dismissive remarks about formulaic representation, as was customary in folkorists' accounts of songs and tales about historical events, but this overlooks the fact that modern journalism is equally subject to formulaic design, as in the clichés from which most headlines are built. Academic discourse, similarly, often has a reductive effect on the information its users seek to convey. Of course, the reenactment of mythological events is a kind of collective remembering. But even here, the problems of translation and the establishing of "coevalness" (Fabian 1983) are so great that they may defeat the best of intentions, and they certainly leave enormous areas of ambiguity unresolved.

Most famously perhaps, or at least most recently, the Sahlins-Obeyesekere debate (Obeyesekere 1992; Sahlins 1995) about the Hawaiian understanding of Captain Cook's murder centers on just such a question of recovering and assessing interpretations from indigenous myth and ritual practice. The debate suggests the magnitude of the problem in recovering just what occurred in the events surrounding Cook's death. There were for the Hawaiians, to be sure, ritual precedents for such a death, but the intractable problem of deducing what these precedents meant and what behaviors they might provoke or determine remains, and interpretations made of them are inevitably subject to present interests (see also Borofsky 1997; Parmentier 1996; Roberts 1997).

Modern nationalism is another arena in which, with extraordinary rapidity, "the facts" become inextricably entangled with constructions of the past necessarily derived from present concerns and leading to a serious questioning of the very distinction between the supposedly analytic categories of history and myth (see Hill 1988, 1996; Steedly 1993; J. Rappaport 1994). Recording the ways in which even such "fixed" relations as those of kinship can be renegotiated in the course of political realignment (for example, Shryock 1997) also sheds valuable light on the ways in which the meaning of the past may be calibrated, for social actors, to the political exigencies of the present; in such cases, context-free assertions of the truth or falsehood of historical assertions are not so much untrue in themselves as simply unhelpful and uninformative.

What is involved is an etymology of forms that are not necessarily or invariably verbal: The attempt here is to discover essentialized meaning in the past. Standard etymology was indeed precisely a form of essentialism in action, an effort to establish a past for words, the denotata of which, through the common error of misplaced concreteness, were represented as equivalent to essentialized objects—institutions, nations, values. Its proponents sought "the truth" (*to etumon*)—the goal that made Vico's intentionally subversive use of etymology so dangerous, since any threat to the order of words logically entailed an equivalent threat to the order of things. Nonverbal etymologies are a special case of the more general rhetorical phenomenon of self-backgrounding or self-evidence that typifies all signification based on resemblance, especially one claimed to be timeless—iconicities, the seeming "naturalness" of which provides a refuge from analytic scrutiny and makes them ideal tools of political propaganda and especially to claims of racial, cultural, or linguistic continuity with a supposedly fixed point in the past (Herzfeld 1997a:56–73). Such iconicities are truly constitutive of cultural capital and the claims of power. In the case of linguistic etymologies, it may sometimes suffice to record who asserts them and under what peculiar circumstances, as well as to note the terms in which challenges—including claims of unscholarliness!—are mounted in turn.

The idea of an etymology beyond language may strike some as a contradiction in terms, but this offers a peculiarly ironic illustration of the problem. Only a prior assumption that facticity can only be established through language and that language is capable of pure referentiality—that the relations among words are "like," "icons of," the things they supposedly denote—would logically make the notion of etymology exclusively verbal. We argue, to the contrary, that—as with poetics—challenging that long-cherished assumption of a self-proclaimed common sense must be part of a critical anthropology's methodological commitment to meaning.

Truth to tell, notions of nonverbal etymology have been around for a long time. De Jorio (1832) provides a minor instance of the attempt to connect the visual rhetoric of modern Neapolitan gesture with the forms of gesticulation represented in ancient statuary (see especially Kendon 1995). Art historians recognize the rhetorical intentions in the making of such links easily. Gombrich's (1979) well-known studies of *visual* "rhetoric" (his term), in pointing up implications of class and status, are perhaps a more useful illustration of what underlies our insistence that a social poetics is inevitably political, a point that was realized in an important way by the anthropologist E. W. Ardener (1971), when he pointed to the "blank banners" of resistance. These represent the outer edges of iconicty. Only the faintest traces connect them to each other and to the explicit configurations that hesitantly begin to emerge in what Scott (1990) has called the "hidden transcripts" of peasant resistance; they may be engaged in configuring the sociopolitical landscape long before they are translated into verbally explicit forms of protest and revolt. When we move to the etymologies of art, architecture, and space, and still more of gesture (to name just a few examples), the traces are more clearly marked, and the aura of antiquity and deep knowledge surrounding such etymological linkages may be also clear enough.[5]

Synchronically, such nonverbal etymologies may be accessible by a kind of triangulation of linkages in one area of culture: architectonics. Among the Fang of Gabon, for example, we can identify parallel structures in the architectonics of dwellings, village layout, games, and dance forms (Fernandez 1982:Ch. 4). This is a replication of structures (Vogt 1965) that suggest investment of persistent common thematic meanings in the deployment of bodies in multiple ways through space. Herzfeld (1991) has argued that architecture represents the clothing of the body politic and suggests in that architectonic metaphor the linkages and tensions between external display in its various forms and interior familiarities. These tensions are likely to be especially acute in societies where the physical body is itself notably an object of strong, socially organized sentiments of embarrassment (such as in southern Europe). This insight may also help archaeologists overcome the absence of explicit verbal information. Concentricities between the deployment of specific decorative motifs in domestic house plans paralleling their distribution in the territories of dominant and subaltern populations, for example, may—if ethnographic parallels are any basis for judgment—be highly suggestive for deciphering the management of cultural capital and thus for the relationship between domestic and civic power (Herzfeld in Gardin and Peebles 1992; see also Leone [1988], Gardin [1980], Gero [1991], and Watson [1994], in which meaning is reviewed in many contexts, including those of class, susbsistence conditions, gender, and technology).

The tension between what is observed and the specificities of informant exegesis is a constant in fieldwork, particularly in such complex matters as the interpretation of meaning, but we also insist that the ideal—as, at the very least, a model-for (Geertz 1973) action, and thus as consequential—is no less real than what is conventionally assigned to the latter category. Again, the turn to practice-oriented theories has fatally undercut the old division of labor between the symbolic and the material. Verbal exegesis is unquestionably beset by ambiguity. But it's also anchored in indexical relationships to significant parallelisms, so that variations among different exegetical texts may provide, not greater or lesser approximations to the truth, but a means of access to the ways in which seemingly rigid codes provide protection and justification for a wide range of cultural invention.

Systematic Aspects and Limits of Meaning Acquisition

In informant exegesis, it is difficult to escape the tense relationship between politics and meaning, a relationship sketched out in a pioneering way in Abner Cohen's *Two-Dimensional Man* (1974). But this tension, the messy suspension between a desire for sincere and accurate description, on the one hand, and political commitment to the established privileges of always-already body-based, ingroup-oriented and ingroup-adapted biases, on the other, is a condition of social life, and its presence in field observation as a supposed inadequacy is, in fact, the source of its claim to produce knowledge.

This struggle of *social subjectivism,* as we might call it—the struggle *for* objectivism, on the one hand, and the out-and-out self-assertion and consequent rejection of objectivism, on the other—is a condition of both informant exegesis and testimony and eventual anthropological interpretation. This tension in the subject may appear in testimony to or exegesis in everyday life. For the ethnographer, it represents the difficulty of escaping social subjectivity and to be in some ultimately unattainable sense objective, can be, as Jenkins argues (1994), a source of knowledge. For it is in this tension and struggle for objectivity in the pursuit of meaning that anthropological knowledge most closely models the politics of its object of study. There is a reflexive interrelationship in the two systems of meaning. Fieldwork, Jenkins argues, is a form of apprenticeship in which the body, or the "body in the mind"), is trained by a combination of frustration and example to expose the inadequacy and thereby enrich a purely intellectualist approach. But it is the *comparison* of anthropological method with observed local practices that, for Jenkins, rescues this phenomenological insight from a crass subjectivism—or from a thinly disguised objectivism (see Reed-Danahay's [1995] critique of Bourdieu [1977, 1984], for example).

Apprenticeship, not childhood socialization, is the operative model here, although anthropological research has long been characterized as a process of socialization to another culture. This distinction is methodologically useful and important, since the forms of apprenticeship in a given society can be studied to contextualize the ethnographer's own learning processes (Delbos and Jorion 1984; Coy 1989; Kondo 1990). The model of socialization, by contrast, implies both a passivity and an absence of intentionality that do not correspond to the actual experience and maturity of intention of ethnographers, however infantilized they may be made to feel; it is thus epistemologically unsound (Karp and Kendall 1982). The metaphor of apprenticeship and the accession to artisanal excellence with its attendant implications of situated learning (Lave and Wenger 1991) can be compared with local methods of inculcation and experienced as such. It also has the advantage of forcing anthropologists—who are rather wordy creatures on the whole—to be attentive to, if not to adopt, a set of practices in which verbality is actively discounted or even disapproved in favor of handiness, artisanship, real-world know-how (*savoir faire*) rather than academic know-say or say-how (see Pirsig 1974; Bourdieu 1977; Willis 1977; Dougherty 1985; Jackson 1989). Anthropology is often conducted in circumstances in which to talk a good game is not really to play it at all.

This circumstance, in turn, brings the ethnographer's frustration with the often inarticulate imponderables of the ethnographic experience more directly into line with those of repressed craft apprentices who must not only suppress their questions and backchat, but must also, because of that situation, find practical ways of overcoming the dearth of verbal communication to learn anything at all—in short, they must learn by seeing and doing and not by saying. What they seem to learn, in many cases, is the kind of cunning or better craft needed to abstract practical knowledge from observation and hands on participation very much like that described by Jenkins (1994) for the day-to-day business of fieldwork. Claims to cultural knowledge through purely verbal operations may be a black-box-opening operation of the most problematic kind. The more secure method of approximation is to have learned by apprenticeship how to do (the essence, be it noted, of *poiesis*, the proper subject-matter of poetics), to operationalize by bodily activity, what others know how to do in the world (Fernandez 1992a).

In several different field situations, we have found it useful not only for rapport but simply for ethnographic learning to try and apprentice our bodily selves, we might say, to local masters. Among Fang villagers, Fernandez acquired an agricultural plot and sought not only advice on agricultural practice from elders but participation and direction of his physical efforts in his apprentice practice. When working on the religious movement of Bwiti, he sought help in learning the bodily discipline necessary for participation in some of the easier dances in the complex dance cycle and, as a consequence, danced at times in the all-night cycle. In his work among Asturian villagers (Spain), Fernandez also sought physical participation in agricultural activity, apprenticing himself as a mower learning to manage the scythe, and he sought to relive the miner's experience in its most corporeal terms by entering into the mine with the various *officios* and following them to their various work sites.

Herzfeld was less successful at persuading a sheep-thief to take him along on a raid. But the way in which Herzfeld's verbalized enthusiasm for the project so disgusted the shepherd—who declared that while *he* had made a *nóïma* (a *non*verbal gesture) Herzfeld had inappropriately responded with speech, thereby demonstrating his ineptness—was a valuable object-lesson, perhaps more useful even than the participation in communal house-building work parties through which Herzfeld did nevertheless come to acquire a more physically engaged sense of community. Coy (1989) and others have documented the advantages and limits of actual apprenticeship as a source of descriptive insight (see above). But it's important not to romanticize one's own experiences, common though the ground and moment may be, as a realization of those of the local informants: There is a real risk of trivializing the latter. Examination of the *discourse* about that experience (for example, popular and critical responses to fictional accounts) may at least furnish information about the culturally acceptable *representation* of such experiences. This should not be confused with direct knowledge of the representation itself, though, unless we are also prepared—as we must—to assume a degree of commonality in all human experience under conditions of strong *physical* engagement. We come to experience that engagement, not necessarily as a conscious act of self-apprenticeship aimed at gathering data (which is not, after all, our informants' usual primary concern), but through relatively disinterested forms of emulation (see Jackson 1989:134–135).

The Corporeal Locus of Meaningful Activity

We wish here to pinpoint what is, in effect, a method of attentiveness to bodily meaning or embodied meaning (or "body-in-the mind meaning"). This is surely appropriate to social and cultural anthropology, for much meaningfulness in social life is so embodied and implicit and is not cerebralized according to academic preferences. Indeed, one of the most cerebral descriptions of the fieldwork experience, Evans-Pritchard's (1940:13) celebrated account of "Nuer-osis," clearly betrays the frustration of trying to formulate verbally unarticulated knowledge, as, more generically, does Lévi-Strauss's (1963) equally intellectually problematic comment on conscious models.

The absence of verbalization in the learning process is not a complete barrier to understanding, however, for by working alongside our informants we can partially—and sometimes only inchoately—perceive the grounds of their social experience across differences of culture, political hierarchy, and gender, as Jackson (1989) has noted in his own attempts to grapple with the life worlds of African peasant women (although this account presupposes a somewhat problematic concept of empathy). Such an approach works through what Fernandez (1974) identified as the basis of the social role of metaphor: It predicates a sign of known selfhood on a necessarily inchoate other.

As Rapport (1993) remarks, however, even within one's own culture (hardly an unproblematic concept), there are severe limitations. The possibilities through participation of reading the mostly unarticulated and also diverse and only partially intermeshing world views of English villagers (1993:Part I) are necessarily limited by social conventions of silence and introversion, even though they may also, in their very closedness, be revelatory of what those world views mean for social actors as they try to decipher each other's intentions and inner lives. We would do incalculable violence to the reality of social life if we insisted on perfect representations of social experience as the criterion of admissibility (see also Leavitt 1996). For actors who may be thought to share a range of cultural experiences, responses to literary form may also be a valuable source of insight, especially when critics can be viewed as registering a cultural model of the plausibility of fictional accounts of psychological inner states (Cohen 1994; Herzfeld 1997b).

It is in this reaching back or below language that we can most critically understand Vico's "poetic wisdom"—not, that is, as an origin tale, complete with a culture-hero, to explain (in the manner of an "etiological myth") the mundane practices of our workaday world, but as an empirical recovery of the ways in which the body registers all knowledge before it is processed as increasingly abstract "disembodied" representation. All human knowledge of the world beyond immediate sensory experience is mediated by signifying processes located as Vico noted, and as both phenomenologists (Merleau-Ponty 1962; Csordas 1994) and the cognitive linguists (Lakoff and Johnson 1980; Johnson, 1987; Lakoff 1987) have attempted to demonstrate in more formal ways, in the body's preobjective placement from which the self negotiates its life world.

We are taking a militantly middle-ground position here (see Herzfeld 1997a), emphasizing a mode of fieldwork that focuses on the mediations of corporeal experience and that locates what has been called "the mind" where Vico located it—in the body. The rejection of such fieldwork as unempirical merely because we presently lack a full conceptual apparatus for describing such processes we regard as a refusal to engage descriptively with the imponderabilia of meaning. But to leave matters there would be a poor excuse *for* and a poor contribution *to* meaningful methodology. We can provide—indeed, we have indicated—some paths to follow and techniques to use in the project of recovering the meaningfulness of expressive forms.

Paths to and Techniques of Meaningful Inquiry into the Agonies of Everyday Life

A central form by which life is made meaningful is narrative emplotment—the characterization of human interaction and of the persons involved therein in dramatic terms. Characters are ensnared in various mixtures of tragic or comic expectations vis-à-vis themselves and others, and they are consequently involved in interactions that lead, by their agonistic interaction, to various states of more or less enduring resolution, requitement, or denouement of their affairs. In the process of the denouement, they obtain confirmation, denial, or significant transformation. This theatrical trope—basically the idea of social role playing—has long been persuasive as a plausible formulation for grasping the essentials of human interaction. In starkest form, social interaction is seen as the struggle for desired or feared characterization as heroes, villains, and fools (Klapp 1972). Less dramatically, Turner (1974) has taken this dramatic trope and made it into a phased method of social analysis, linking the short-term performance of ritual time in Van Gennep's celebrated tripartite schema to the *longue durée* of historical event structures.

But this dramatic or narrative trope of social science understanding, or at least its teleological implications of ultimate denouement or resolution, can be found in much less explicit form in models of human or social or cultural development. In one form or another, these all imply what can be called progressive transformations of character, denouements of a kind. It has been noted for Western literary culture that male autobiographies tend to be more deterministically teleological than female (Jelinek 1980); given the new interest in "auto-ethnography"—the comparison of "their" constructions of their cultures with "ours" of our own and theirs (Reed-Danahay 1997)—this kind of generalization should be distinctly susceptible to cross-cultural comparison and to sensitivity to changes across time and between contrasted contexts.

The master trope of teleology has certainly been a major element in anthropology's own self-construction, which is perhaps one thing that makes it hard to recognize as distinctive or worthy of comment when we encounter it in the field. This was most obvious in classical evolutionism in its dramatic developments from savagery to civilization. Even Vico, whose views we regard here as classic and informative in any discussion of meaningful methods, narrated a developmental model of progressive transformation over historical time of consciousness in successive social formations. He pointed up not only the key tropes of a given sociocultural stage of development but the tropological phases, metaphoric, metonymic, synechdochic, and ironic, through which these successive stages might be expected to pass. Vico's awareness of the tropological in the study of meaning rests on notions of the tropes as part and parcel of a society's narrative sense of its place in space and time.

We may not necessarily buy into the developmental narratives themselves, either of particular analysts such as Vico or of particular societies (see Hodgen 1964; Nisbet 1965), but they raise questions of reconstructing or deconstructing the taxonomies that constitute the local idiom of common sense in respect to both societal division and societal progression. It makes clear our obligation in the study of meaning to be alert to and describe such taxonomies in their context of use (Douglas 1966, 1975, 1992). These tropes and taxonomies are plainly central to the meaningfulness of social life. However, they do not exhaust either the semantic universe or the range of concepts and emotions to which social actors wish to give expression. Even the linguistic modeling of *emotives* with no verbal equivalents, "gustemes," or the formal analysis of gesture and the like does not dispose of what is left, for clearly there are many areas of expression not easily captured by linguistic models.

Take the matter of spatial communication and the meaning of space. Spatial idioms in language are plentifully available for class, status, and power analysis. The feudally derived upper town, lower town in Europe, and the co-occurent railroad extension and western town settlement in the United States produce the distinction between this side of the tracks and the other side—or even a "space on the side of the road" (Stewart 1996) that is altogether marginal. Spatial figuration rather easily maps on social formation and can be analyzed taxonomically. This teleological mapping of spatial arrangements on society and vice versa is Durkheimian in the sense that they are reconstructions of the working out of the ritual space/social space teleology found in *The Elementary Forms of the Religious Life* (Durkeim 1976), as found in other oppositional taxonomies. Bourdieu (1973), Douglas (1970), and Needham (1962), for example, have all shown how the physical layout of domestic and public space may express the key complementary oppositions (notably but not exclusively those of gender) obtaining in a given society. Bourdieu (1977) has expressed dissatisfaction with such a reductionist formalism and has posited a much more complex temporal-spatial posture or readiness for inteaction in the world, the *habitus* (although this, a concept ultimately derived from Mauss, appears to be no less deterministic in important respects).

In more recent work on landscape (Rapport 1993:Part I; Schama 1995) and on the organization of public space, both these explicit oppositions lodged in the lexicon as well as deeper lying, less explicit meanings lodged in history, personal and social, and the complexities of corporeal experience in the world are explored (Lawrence and Low 1995). This work shows us methods for the study of the meaning of space much more responsive to a *poetics of space*—and more grounded (indeed, literally so)—than that intended by Gaston Bachelard (1964). Uses of space tie architectonics to political and other immediate interests, and thus also provide an especially useful perspective on the dynamic interplay between state ideologies and the politics of everyday life, as we saw earlier in the discussion of narratives about historic sites.

Ordinary people only attribute meaning to ideology when it impinges on their everyday experiences, and the calibration of ideal-typical models of space (for example, sacred enclosures and the *haram* of the home, tensions between external and internal domestic ornament as expressions of conflicting ideologies of national culture) provides an accessible arena for examining contestations of meaning between the state (or religious community) and the domestic sphere. These may be recovered through narrative: Bahloul (1996), comparing the memories of Jewish refugees from Algeria with those of the remaining Muslim inhabitants of a once-shared domestic compound, has effectively shown how to elicit the shifting meanings of space in a highly politicized context. Here, it is the comparative perspective, grounded in a common physical space, that permits a clearer understanding of how meaning organizes the perception of space.

An opening up to the poetics method propounded here is seen in the relatively recent willingness of anthropologists to use modern urban-industrial societies, not as pale or distorted sites for the fragmentation of Maussian total social facts (supposedly found in their pristine oppositional perfection in the "exotic" societies), but as contexts in which we can examine our own subjective embodied knowledge about supposedly necessary equivalences between spatial forms and linguistic meanings. Here we can explore embodiments in all their complexity. In such settings, we can more explicitly investigate the lack of fit between prescriptive ideologies of meaning and actual practice or use, thereby also obviating earlier and ethnocentric distinctions between "complex" and "simple" societies that may have been the result of our own classificatory desire for closure than of the realities experienced by the members of supposedly simple societies. The argument of Mary Douglas's *Purity and Danger* is as applicable to the self-protectiveness of national or international bureaucracy (Herzfeld 1992; Malkki 1995; Barnett 1997) or to the "untouchability" factor in urban ghettoization dynamics as it is to local ritual. Conversely, agency and practice complicate local and nonliterate social relations as much as they do the life of highly industrialized, geographically extensive social formations.

Postures of Poetic Wisdom in Ethnographic Inquiry and Interpretation

Revitalizing Moments

The suggestiveness of the trope of path orientation in meaningful inquiry should not determine method altogether. As Vico showed, claims to open-endedness themselves contain the seeds of their own disproof: Even ambiguity can be reified as dogma. Social life oscillates, on the one hand, between established and more-or-less inflexible routines that, once learned, tend to lose their ability to convey meaning with any real immediacy and, on the other hand, moments of much more intense—because more palpably exceptional—meaning. Their intensity arises from increased uncertainty and unresolved complexity—from an increase in ambiguity, *not* of referential stability. Indeed, informants' inability to provide a clear gloss on some symbolic form may index a moment of important—if temporarily unfathomable—conceptual change.[6]

In addition, such concerns highlight the inadequacy of Durkheim's reified dichotomy of sacred and profane. This is not to downplay the importance in anthropology of ethnography enriched by long-term observation and attention to the intimate details of everyday routines (thick description [Geertz 1973]), or the identification of particular events as diagnostic of systemic changes (Moore 1987). But we wish to emphasize the importance of particularly heightened moments of meaningfulness seeking to understand the special vitality that they embody. Such events may serve as moments of social revitalization or devitalization (Wallace 1956). This is an organic trope (Nisbet 1965)—of vitality in social life—that focuses our attention, again, on the bodily experiences entailed in that life. Here the methodological challenge is to recognize through its external signs or narrative realization the embodiment by the social subject of social experience—the translation of social suffering, for example, into bodily disease (Kleinman et al. 1997) or the translation of social celebrations into a heightened sense of bodily well-being—and to relate such correspondences to larger patterns of social change or stability.

Meaningfulness derives from the special reinforcement or abatement of the intensity or transformation of social relations. On transformation there exists a significant literature, an important segment of which addresses the "structure of the conjuncture" or transformative event in history (Braudel 1980; Sahlins 1981). This approach suggests a method of tracking the changes in accustomed (normative) structures of behavior as a consequence of such events. Our emphasis here is less on the structures involved than on the corporeal resonances arising from the reinforcement or weakening of old associations or the emergence of new ones. This interest in surprising or arrested moments or events in culture in respect of embodied experience contrasts with other approaches to meaning that engage primarily with routine, and that seem to emphasize path dependency without regard to the associational structures involved. The study of meaning is bound to have to consider the nature of *surprise-fulness*, not only with respect to the conjunction of the prevailing and changing systems of structure, but also with respect to the associated corporeal commonplaces of social interaction and the confirmation or challenges to these presuppositions. These surprise-full moments, at any rate, account for differences in the quality of life from moment to moment and phase to phase, differences that constitute an important part of life's changing meaningfulness.

Qualitative Inquiry and the Quality Space of Life

The trope of quality space for the temporal complexities of corporeal-mental life has long been recognized as a basic time-space conversion and is used in social sciences to plot the vectors of judgment by which the body in the mind weighs and asssesses its experiences and, consequently, decides to act in the world (Osgood et al. 1957). And the notion of quality space has long been given by philosophers a special place as a fundamental tool of understanding of how the mind places its experiences in corporeal terms (Quine 1981). This trope, indeed, has assumed the status of a kind of elementary form of reference (Fernandez 1973) in seeking to understand in a methodological way the motivations of metaphoric predication itself. It can be understood as a trope anchored in the primordial gestalts of human experience as this takes place in our gravitationally anchored three-dimensioned world (see Lakoff and Johnson 1980). It is as a means by which to grasp those displacements *from* unacceptable experiences *to* more satisfactory experiences that metaphoric predications are often used (Fernandez 1974, 1986).

A social poetics must consider method itself under this rubric, as a form of understanding that uses a choice of tropes to organize its clarifying activity in the world. Of equal interest are other tropes of utility in the rhetoric of methodological argument, tropes of thickness, as in "thick description" (Geertz 1973), or of depth, as in deep or penetrating analysis and of movement (as in "social movements"). All these "figurations of social thought," like the tropes of game, drama, and text (Geertz 1983), are fundamental in the arguments of methodology and methodologists, and it is their presence and evocative associations that a poetic approach takes into particular account. Even culinary tropes organize assessments of data: "thin" or "meaty" ethnography, "raw" and "cooked" data (the latter being somewhat suspect), and "processed" analysis. It would be hard to claim that such assessments lay outside the criteria of cultural value, although the device of labeling them as "merely" metaphorical sometimes indexes the attempt to do so.

A poetics approach is not limited to analyses of the figuration of methodological argument but, as we have said, brings under scrutiny the associated commonplaces of the tropes of everyday life (including, but not privileging, that of the methodologist). Relevant here, in terms of both their cultural history and their role in everyday understanding, are analyses of tree (Fernandez 1998) and bird imagery (Friedrich 1996, 1997).

We find the tree trope in a wide variety of social and intellectual circumstances, from family trees and roots and other specimens from the genealogical arboretum to tree diagrams in logic and linguistics and the quasi-totemic identification of social groups with trees—a set of associations worked out extensively in *The Golden Bough* (Frazer 1890). The presence of birds as figurations of the human condition has deep classical antecedents and is a widespread trope of power in other cultures, such as, for example, those so vividly presented in mythological form in Robert Gardner's (1983) New Guinea ethnographic film, *Dead Birds*. It is hardly possible to understand the New Guinea people's sense of the qualities and perimeters of their lives, their quality space, and their life world generally without taking into account this master trope (see also Feld 1982). But then birds in many cultures, whether in the bush or in the hand, are prime figurative references that many men and women may grasp as they reach to understand the complexities, the fulfillment and the fatalities of their lives. The question "What is it like to be a human?" corresponds to the widespread attempt to *figure out* what it is like to be a tree or a bird or a bat (Nagel 1974). Often this *figuring out* takes the form of anthropomorphisms of various kinds (Guthrie 1993). But the poetic possibilities of cultural self-understanding of what it is to be human—to be, that is, a human *animal*—are seemingly without limit.

Conclusion

> It is the mark of a man experienced in the world and interested in studying it to look for no more precision than the subject matter allows.
>
> Aristotle, *The Nichomachean Ethics*

Why end on an exclusively reflexive and recursive note, by concluding with a poetics of methodology itself? An honest methodology located almost anywhere between Popper and Foucault (if not at the solipsistic extremes beyond these authors and their followers) must recognize its own entailment in figuration and metaphor, as Max Black (1962) noted. When we say that a method is meaningful, we are assessing its significance; this is not a confusion of meaning *qua* semantics and meaning *qua* social importance. That distinction is itself contingent and culturally specific; there are cultures in which it is either unrecognized or explicitly dismissed as untenable. Thus, to say that a method is meaningful presupposes a social and cultural context; any methodology that claims to be supracultural—that is, context-independent—is an exercise in circularity and self-deception. A method is a kind of practice in the immediate, as open to reflexive analyses as any other practice. Its elaborations of procedures of discovery are hardly *sui generis* and cannot be satisfied with the pursuit of reputation and esteem among methodologists alone (Taylor 1985).

An honest method must inevitably reflect on the material and social metaphors on which its practices and its ideas about its practices are based (Herzfeld 1987). Moreover, it must take account of the relation between the commitment to formal procedure, which is characteristic of the practice of any methodology, and the facts of the contingency and open-endedness of much of life as it is lived—an inchoateness that motivates much figuration in thought and practice (Fernandez 1974). Methodology is itself motivated by contingency; it can be viewed as a coping response to the inchoate in the sense that it seeks explicit procedures and practices as free as possible from the conditions of the life that motivates it. We say "as free *as possible*" because we recognize that such freedom is always relative, indeterminate, and subject to empirical denial ("falsification," in a sense expanded to a greater degree of provisionality than that intended by Popper).

The view we take here, however, is that any methodology, to be judged an adequate approach to the human condition, should embrace the actuality of the contingency that besets that condition and should recognize the often necessarily unpredictable ways in which people cope with such contingencies. Methodology in anthropology, if not always in the human sciences generally, should itself be a *coping* practice—a way of coping with human copings with the inchoate, not denial of this rich actuality. In other words, methodology in anthropology, which is, in effect, method in ethnographic practice and in ethnographic interpretation and explanation, shares something fundamental with the human condition that constitutes its own subject. Method does not escape the human condition, and it should not mystify itself with the hope of such platonic transcendence, which is a version of the logical error, as we have already noted, of misplaced concreteness. This point has been made with some insistence by Bourdieu (for example, 1990:Book 1). He and others have repeatedly shown how highly structured theories of theorists and methodologists are themselves artifactual effects of a lack of practical mastery (Bourdieu 1977) and a negligence of the social conditions that make social science possible (Jenkins 1994).

These concerns notwithstanding, we have tried to identify some explicit procedures and processes here. Precisely *because* we view methodology as a form of socially embedded practice, our "middle ground" posture requires us to acknowledge *both* the importance of establishing some norms *and* the virtual impossibility of stabilizing them against the corrosion of time and doubt. Now that ethnographers no longer confine themselves to reputedly isolated communities but work in bureaucracies, science laboratories, and international organizations, they have been forced to confront the inevitable partiality of their research and to turn it to practical advantage.

As Stacia Zabusky, one of the few anthropologists to have commented explicitly on this methodological issue in the context of analyzing large-scale international organizations, remarks of her work in the European Space Agency: "To be inside practice . . . is to be situated somewhere and somewhen in particular; but to be inside practice is also the only way to come to know, ethnographically, the social system, since the system is replicated and reproduced through agents' everyday actions, evasions, and enunciations of value" (1995:42). For her own work, she chose a "crossroads" department, in which the partiality of her sample was itself made explicit and, consequently, accessible to analysis as a tangible aspect of the indeterminacy as well as the cultural values and conflicts that characterized her chosen ethnographic situation. (We should also note that the intensity and intimacy of even the most unstructured ethnographic work represent an implicitly statistical assessment as much as any numerical sampling device. And see the discussion by Jeffrey Johnson [this volume] of Zabusky [1995].

Given that her focus was on cooperation, choosing a site where the limits of that value in practice would become palpable precisely because of the intermediary position of that site was methodologically appropriate and, in any event, highly productive. It is also worth noting that fieldwork is itself always, and nowhere more clearly than in Zabusky's methodological statement, a synecdochical activity, a sampling that local actors can always accuse of unrepresentativeness—thereby, perhaps, confirming the accuracy of its perceptions beneath the surfaces of propriety and cultural defensiveness. In this respect, it's worth emphasizing that methods are enmeshed in what one of us has called "the politics of significance," in which objections to non-Cartesian methods are often linked with surprising fixity of purpose to nationalistic and other political ideologies (Herzfeld 1997c).

Inchoateness may not seem a promising target for methodology. On the other hand, to ignore it would be decidedly nonempirical. It is often the condition of the very possibility of method, and it certainly corresponds in its refusal of arbitrary closure to such natural-science understandings as complementarity (Bohr) and uncertainty (Heisenberg). The practical issue—and methodology is about (indeed, *is*) practice—is simply that an accurate and empirically sound representation of social life requires some means of recognizing the "fuzzy" and "indeterminate" social matrix out of which emerge graspable and explicit meanings. Vico, whose path we have followed so assiduously here, certainly recognized a contingent sense in which truth claims could be established, for his assertion of the necessary imperfection of human knowledge, ultimately grounded though it was in theological preoccupations, does not depart radically from positivistic models of falsifiability *except in its anticipation of Foucault's explorations of the relationship between discourse and power*—and this is the crucial, enabling condition for the emergence of a methodologically explicit social and cultural poetics such as we have sketched here. Ever attentive to the provisionality of our acts and deeds, then, we now propose the following stages in the research process as a plausible path for the attainment of poetic wisdom:

1. Elicitation and ethnographic learning on a model of apprenticeship, in which the ethnographer both internalizes and attempts to render explicit formal norms of social practices and interactions of the more routine kinds.
2. Recording commentaries on conformity and deviance in these norms synchronically and diacronically, with careful attention paid to the social relationships obtaining between commentators and their subjects and anthropologists and informants.
3. Probing, through imagined reconstruction and other techniques, for the images and organizing tropes that define specific norms as practical projects in the world and on which they may depend for their realization.
4. Through participant observation, relating this "poetic function" (the "play of meaning") to political norms and practices, defined as the maintenance and contestation of systems of privilege, differential qualities of life, and hierarchized rights of choice and decision.
5. Anchoring these images and tropes in bodily experience and its vicissitudes, the corporeal locus from which embodiment they derive their meaning and exploring the system of entailments which constitutes the cultural logic present in social interaction and the qualitative anchor of meaningfulness. (We add parenthetically that, in addition to the well-tried resources of narrative analysis, new recording devices such as video permit the exposure of field materials to multiple observation, making it possible to establish systematic features of interpretive differences by class, gender, age, cultural identity, and so forth.)
6. Tracing the more obvious narrative emplotments of social life, the social dramas, with their oppositional or agonistic workings-out and denouements and their sometimes discomfitting entailment in encompassing tropes of revitalization, quality space, and so on.

These stages in the research process permit evaluation of what once were called the "expressive aspects" of mundane activity. For some time, anthropologists spoke of "expressive culture," but we might now more reasonably ask, "When is culture *not* expressive?" In a semiotic anthropology of partially Peircean derivation (see, for example, Fernandez 1965; Herzfeld 1983; Singer 1984; Parmentier 1994) the *symbolic* aspect is recognized only as the most explicitly meaning-conveying, in contrast to the relational meanings of indexicality and the seemingly natural meanings of iconicity. In a sense, the shift from local social relations to national and ethnic identities on the grand scale is a shift from primarily indexical ("we are all related") to primarily iconic ("we are all alike") claims, in which the symbolic provides the grounds for contesting this view or interpreting it for specific advantages and goals (Herzfeld 1997a). Thus, we can say that the emphasis falls quite variably and in differing proportions on these three aspects of meaning, and we can only get a purchase on this slippery shape-shifting (Fernandez 1974) by remembering that they are indeed aspects—not icons, indexes, and symbols, but iconicity, indexicality, and symbolism (see also Eco 1976). This move both resists the reification demanded by normativity in both reductive social science and equally reductive bureaucratic institutions. Concomitantly, it recognizes the shiftiness of human interaction and experience.

But there is also an epistemological consequence. For such a perspective requires us to dispense with similar reifications of the meaningful in our own self-classification. Anthropologists have indeed long been engaged in replacing the old-fashioned segmentation of the discipline into separate fields of study, one of which is called symbolism, with a more integrative view. In this less-fragmented perspective, religious, economic, symbolic, and many other aspects of social activity are not reduced to the demarcation of separate functions that is held—often unconvincingly, we would add—to typify modern, industrial, Western society. In pursuing that approach, our goal in this essay has been to suggest ways, not of figuring out the symbolism of a given population as a finite subset of its cultural equipment, but of finding the semiotic implications, the figurations, of all social interaction.

NOTES

1. Herzfeld was once challenged at a conference about his use of unnecessarily long words. The key offender turned out to be "trope"! Ironically, it would be hard to find a more eloquent demonstration of the inadequacy of referentiality as a model of the socially recognizable. There is, in fact, a technical reason for preferring trope to the loose use of "metaphor," and it is doubly ironic that those who display the most passionate allergy to trope are usually those who demand a more numerate form of precision in other areas of the discipline!

2. As editor of *American Ethnologist* (1994–98), Herzfeld has often been struck by the effects of passive-voice constructions as a means of evading responsibility for analysis and data, and in most cases he asked authors to switch to a first-person mode.

3. It is our view that the distinction in anthropology between the two approaches, that of a social and cultural poetics as indicated, frames the fundamental dynamic of the poetics approach in anthropology. The journal *Poetics* (Amsterdam), which has appeared since the early 1970s, although casting a wide net, is largely devoted to the work of sociologists, social psychologists, and psychologists; only occasionally do anthropologists publish there. These scholars are interested in narrative processes and narrative devices and in measuring by

various technical methods their consequences in the maintenance of social order and in the formation of public opinion. At the other extreme, *Poetics Today* (Tel Aviv), also only occasionally a locus for anthropological work, is predominantly engaged in semiotic and literary criticism of verbal texts. Both journals thus share a basic concern with language, although their epistemological orientations are radically divergent.

4. This research, conducted in 1993–95, was supported by Award #9307421 of the National Science Foundation.

5. If Vico was right to suggest that all verbal expression was grounded in the immediacy of bodily experience, this grants the body a primacy emphasized in a recent cognitive linguistics work (Johnson [1987] and see also, for a rather different approach, Farnell [1994, 1995] and Farnell and Graham in this volume). Vico's own method was strictly etymological: He traced political abstractions back to terms denoting physical images, arguing that vision itself was "immured in the body" and that, for this reason, intellectual activity could not be separated analytically from bodily sensation.

6. What the linkages mean for social actors is quite another matter—Austin's phrase "trailing clouds of etymology" nicely captures the problem: The fact that *we* know that "having an accident" suggests the impersonal forces implied by the Latin verb *accidit* tells us absolutely nothing about the degree to which the social actors are themselves conscious of any such linkage, even though their actions may suggest it—and few anthropologists have bothered, or are adequately equipped to seek, the evidence for links of this sort. The problem is philological and psychological as well as social and cultural.

REFERENCES

Ardener, Edwin. 1971. Introduction. In *Social Anthropology and Language*. E. W. Ardener, ed. A.S.A. Monographs, 10. London and New York: Tavistock Publications.

Austin, J. L. 1965. *How to Do Things with Words. The William James Lectures*. Cambridge: Harvard University Press.

Austin, J. L. 1971. A Plea for Excuses. In *Philosophy and Linguistics*. Colin Lyas, ed. Pp. 79–101 London: Macmillan.

Bachelard, Gaston. 1964. *The Poetics of Space*. New York: Orion Press.

Bahloul, Joëlle. 1996. *The Architecture of Memory: A Jewish-Muslim Household in Colonial Algeria, 1937–1962*. Cambridge: Cambridge University Press.

Bailey, F. G. 1973. *Debate and Compromise; The Politics of Innovation*. Oxford: Blackwell.

Bailey, F. G. 1983. *The Tactical Uses of Passion: An Essay on Power, Reason, and Reality*. Ithaca: Cornell University Press.

Bailey, F. G 1994. *The Witch-Hunt, or, The Triumph of Morality*. Ithaca: Cornell University Press.

Barnett, Michael N. 1997. The UN Security Council, Indifference, and Genocide in Rwanda. *Cultural Anthropology 12*:551–578.

Bauman, Richard. 1984 [1977]. *Verbal Art as Performance*. Prospect Heights, IL: Waveland.

Black, Max. 1962. *Models and Metaphors: Studies in Language and Philosophy*. Ithaca: Cornell University Press.

Blier, Suzanne Preston. 1994. *The Anatomy of Architecture: Ontology and Metaphor in Batammaliba Architectural Expression*. Chicago: University of Chicago Press.

Bloch, Maurice, ed. 1975. *Political Language and Oratory in Traditional Society*. London and New York: Academic Press.

Boehm, Christopher. 1980. Exposing the Moral Self in Montenegro: The Use of Natural Definitions to Keep Ethnography Descriptive. *American Ethnologist* 7:1–26.

Bond, George C., and Angela Gilliam, eds. 1994. *Social Construction of the Past: Representation as Power*. New York: Routledge.

Boon, James A. 1982. *Other Tribes, Other Scribes: Symbolic Anthropology in the Comparative Study of Cultures, Histories, Religions, and Texts*. Cambridge and New York: Cambridge University Press.

Borofsky, Robert. 1997. Cook, Lono, Obeyesekere, and Sahlins. *Current Anthropology* 38:255–282.

Bourdieu, Pierre. 1973. The Kabyle House. In *Rules and Meanings*. Mary Douglas, ed. Harmondsworth, England: Penguin.

Bourdieu, Pierre. 1977. *Outline of a Theory of Practice*. Cambridge and New York: Cambridge University Press.

Bourdieu, Pierre. 1984. *Distinction: A Social Critique of the Judgement of Taste*. Cambridge: Harvard University Press.

Bourdieu, Pierre. 1990. *In Other Words: Essays Towards a Reflexive Sociology*. Cambridge, England: Polity.

Braudel, Fernand. 1980. *On History*. Chicago: University of Chicago Press.

Bruner, Edward M. 1994. Abraham Lincoln as Authentic Reproduction: A Critique of Post-Modernism. *American Anthropologist* 96:397–415.

Bruner, Edward M., and Phyllis Gorfain. 1984. Dialogue Narration and the Paradoxes of Masada. In *Text, Play, and Story*. Stuart Plattner, ed. Pp. 56–79. Washington, DC: American Ethnological Society.

Clifford, James. 1983. On Ethnographic Authority. *Representations* 1(12):118–146.

Clifford, James, and George E. Marcus, eds. 1986. *Writing Culture: The Poetics and Politics of Ethnography*. Berkeley: University of California Press.

Cohen, Abner. 1974. *Two-Dimensional Man: An Essay on the Anthropology of Power and Symbolism in Complex Society*. Berkeley: University of California Press.

Cohen, Anthony P. 1994. *Self-Consciousness: An Alternative Anthropology of Identity*. London and New York: Routledge.

Colby, Benjamin N., James W. Fernandez, and David Kronenfeld. 1981. Toward a Convergence of Cognitive and Symbolic Anthropology. *American Ethnologist* 8:442–450.

Cowan, Jane K. 1990. *Dance and the Body Politic in Northern Greece*. Princeton: Princeton University Press.

Coy, Michael, ed. 1989. *Apprenticeship: From Theory to Method and Back Again.* Albany: State University of New York Press.

Crain, Mary M. 1989. *Ritual, memoria popular y proceso político en la sierra ecuatoriana.* Quito: Corporación Editora Nacional: Ediciones Abya-Yala.

Crick, Malcolm. 1976. *Explorations in Language and Meaning: Towards a Semantic Anthropology.* New York: John Wiley.

Csordas, Thomas J. 1994. *Embodiment and Experience: The Existential Ground of Culture and Self.* Cambridge: Cambridge University Press.

de Jorio, Andrea. 1832. *La mimica degli antichi investigata nel gestire napoletano.* Naples: Fibreno.

Delbos, Genevieve, and Paul Jorion. 1984. *La transmission des savoirs. Collection ethnologie de la France.* Paris: Editions de la Maison des Sciences de l'Homme.

Dolgin, Janet D., D. S. Kemnitzer, and David Schneider, eds. 1977. *Symbolic Anthropology: A Reader in the Study of Symbols and Meanings.* New York: Columbia University Press.

Dougherty, Janet W. D. 1985. *Directions in Cognitive Anthropology.* Urbana: University of Illinois Press.

Douglas, Mary. 1966. *Purity and Danger: An Analysis of Concepts of Pollution and Taboo.* London: Routledge & Kegan Paul.

Douglas, Mary. 1975. *Implicit Meanings: Essays in Anthropology.* London and Boston: Routledge & Kegan Paul.

Douglas, Mary. 1992. *How Classification Works: Nelson Goodman among the Social Sciences.* Edinburgh: Edinburgh University Press.

Dresch, Paul. 1986. The Significance of the Course Events Take in Segmentary Systems. *American Ethnologist 13*:309–324.

Dundes, Alan, Jerry W. Leach, and B. Özkök. 1972. The Strategy of Turkish Boys' Verbal Dueling Rhymes. In *Directions in Sociolinguistics: The Ethnography of Communication.* John J. Gumperz and Dell Hymes, eds. Pp. 130–160. New York: Holt, Rinehart and Winston.

Durkheim, Emile. 1976. *The Elementary Forms of the Religious Life,* 2d ed. London: Allen and Unwin.

Eco, Umberto. 1976. *A Theory of Semiotics.* Bloomington: Indiana University Press.

El-Haj, Nadia Abu. In press. Translating Truths: Nationalism, the Practice of Archaeology, and the Re-making of Past and Present in Contemporary Jerusalem. *American Ethnologist.*

Evans-Pritchard, E. E. 1940. *The Nuer: A Description of the Modes of Livelihood and Political Institutions of a Nilotic People.* Oxford: Clarendon Press.

Fabian, Johannes. 1983. *Time and the Other: How Anthropology Makes Its Object.* New York: Columbia University Press.

Farnell, Brenda M. 1994. Ethno-graphics and the Moving Body. *Man (n.s.) 29*:929–974.

Farnell, Brenda M. 1995. *Do You See What I Mean?: Plains Indian Sign Talk and the Embodiment of Action.* Austin: University of Texas Press.

Farnell, Brenda M., and Drid Williams. 1990. *The Laban Script*. Canberra: Australian Institute of Aboriginal and Torres Strait Islander Studies.

Feld, Steven. 1982. *Sound and Sentiment: Birds, Weeping, Poetics, and Song in Kaluli Expression*. Philadelphia: University of Pennsylvania Press.

Fernandez, James W. 1965. Symbolic Consensus in a Fang Reformative Cult. *American Anthropologist 67*: 902–927.

Fernandez, James W. 1974. The Mission of Metaphor in Expressive Culture. *Current Anthropology 15*:119–145.

Fernandez, James W. 1977a. Poetry in Motion: Being Moved by Amusement, by Mockery, and by Mortality in the Asturian Countryside. *New Literary History 8*:459–483.

Fernandez, James W. 1977b. *Fang Architectonics. Working Papers in the Traditional Arts*, No. 1. Philadelphia: Institute for the Study of Human Issues.

Fernandez, James W. 1982. *Bwiti: An Ethnography of the Religious Imagination in Africa*. Princeton: Princeton University Press.

Fernandez, James W. 1986. *Persuasions and Performances: The Play of Tropes in Culture*. Bloomington: Indiana University Press.

Fernandez, James W. 1992a. What I Learned from *The Parrot's Egg* and *The Bull Who Crashes in the Kraal*: The Senses of Time Binding and Turn Taking in Being with the Other. In *Dialectical Anthropology: Essays in Honor of Stanley Diamond*. Christine Gailey, ed. Pp. 209–216. Gainesville: University of Florida Press.

Fernandez, James W. 1992b. Architectonic Inquiry: Review Article. *Semiotica 89*(1–3): 215–226.

Fernandez, James W. 1993. Advice to the Perplexed Ethnographer in an Age of Soundbites. *American Ethnologist 20*:179–184.

Fernandez, James W. 1994. Spielerisch un Planvoll: Zur Theorie der Tropen in der Anthropologie. *Historische Anthropologie 2*(1):1–19.

Fernandez, James W. 1996. Path-ologies of Iberianist Thought. Unpublished ms.

Fernandez, James W. 1998. On Trees of Knowledge of Self and Other in Culture: Models for the Moral Imagination. In *The Social Life of Trees*. Laura Rival and Maurice Bloch, eds. Pp. 81–110. London: Berg.

Frazer, James George, Sir. 1890. *The Golden Bough: A Study in Comparative Religion*. London: Macmillan.

Friedrich, Paul. 1996. Culture in Poetry and the Poetry in Culture. In *Culture/Contexture: Explorations in Anthropology and Literary Studies*. E. Valentine Daniel and J. N. Peck, eds. Pp. 37–38. Berkeley: University of California Press.

Friedrich, Paul. 1997. An Avian and Aphrodisian Reading of the Odyssey. *American Anthropologist 99*:306–320.

Gable, Eric, Richard Handler, and Anna Lawson. 1992. On the Uses of Relativism: Facts, Conjecture, and Black and White Histories at Colonial Williamsburg. *American Ethnologist 19*:791–805.

Gardin, Jean-Claude. 1980. *Archaeological Constructs: An Aspect of Theoretical Archaeology*. Cambridge: Cambridge University Press.

Gardin, Jean-Claude, and Christopher S. Peebles, eds. 1992. *Representations in Archaeology*. Bloomington: Indiana University Press.

Gardner, Robert. 1983. *Dead Birds*. New York: McGraw-Hill Films.

Geertz, Clifford. 1973. *The Interpretation of Cultures*: Selected Essays. New York: Basic Books.

Geertz, Clifford. 1983. Blurred Genres: The Refiguration of Social Thought. In *Local Knowledge: Further Essays in Interpretive Anthropology*. Clifford Geertz, ed. Pp. 20–35. New York: Basic Books.

Gero, Joan. 1991. *Engendering Archaeology: Women and Prehistory. Social Archaeology*. Oxford: Basil Blackwell.

Gibbs, Raymond W. 1994. *The Poetics of Mind: Figurative Thought, Language, and Understanding*. Cambridge: Cambridge University Press.

Giddens, Anthony. 1984. *The Constitution of Society: Outline of the Theory of Structuration*. Cambridge, England: Polity Press.

Goldstein, Leon J. 1976. *Historical Knowing*. Austin: University of Texas Press.

Gombrich, E. H. 1979. *The Sense of Order: A Study in the Psychology of Decorative Art. The Wrightsman Lectures*, No. 9. Ithaca: Cornell University Press.

Guthrie, Stewart. 1993. *Faces in the Clouds: A New Theory of Religion*. New York: Oxford University Press.

Handelman, Don. 1990. *Models and Mirrors: Towards an Anthropology of Public Events*. Cambridge: Cambridge University Press.

Harris, Marvin. 1974. *Cows, Pigs, Wars and Witches: The Riddles of Culture*. New York: Random House.

Herzfeld, Michael. 1983. Looking Both Ways: The Ethnographer in the Text. *Semiotica* *46*:151–166.

Herzfeld, Michael. 1985. *The Poetics of Manhood: Contest and Identity in a Cretan Mountain Village*. Princeton: Princeton University Press.

Herzfeld, Michael. 1987. *Anthropology Through the Looking-Glass: Critical Ethnography in the Margins of Europe*. Cambridge: Cambridge University Press.

Herzfeld, Michael. 1991. *A Place in History: Social and Monumental Time in a Cretan Town*. Princeton: Princeton University Press.

Herzfeld, Michael. 1992. *The Social Production of Indifference: Exploring the Symbolic Roots of Western Bureaucracy*. Oxford: Berg.

Herzfeld, Michael. 1997a. *Cultural Intimacy: Social Poetics in the Nation-State*. New York: Routledge.

Herzfeld, Michael. 1997b. *Portrait of a Greek Imagination: An Ethnographic Biography of Andreas Nenedakis*. Chicago: University of Chicago Press.

Herzfeld, Michael. 1997c. Anthropology and the Politics of Significance. *Social Analysis* 41:107–138.

Hill, Jonathan. 1988. *Rethinking History and Myth: Indigenous South American Perspectives on the Past.* Urbana: University of Illinois Press.

Hill, Jonathan. 1996. *History, Power, and Identity: Ethnogenesis in the Americas, 1492–1992.* Iowa City: University of Iowa Press.

Hodgen, Margaret T. 1964. *Early Anthropology in the Sixteenth and Seventeenth Centuries.* Philadelphia: University of Pennsylvania Press.

Jackson, Michael. 1989. *Paths Toward a Clearing: Radical Empiricism and Ethnographic Inquiry.* Bloomington: Indiana University Press.

Jakobson, Roman. 1960. Linguistics and Poetics. In *Style in Language.* Thomas A. Sebeok, ed. Pp. 350–377. Cambridge: M.I.T. Press.

Jakobson, Roman. 1985. Verbal Art, Verbal Sign, Verbal Time. In *Collected Essays of Roman Jakobson.* Krystyna Pomorska and Stephen Rudy, eds., assisted by Brent Vine. Minneapolis: University of Minnesota Press.

Jameson, Fredric. 1981. *The Political Unconscious: Narrative as a Socially Symbolic Act.* Ithaca: Cornell University Press.

Jelinek, C. Estelle, ed. 1980. *Women's Autobiography: Essays in Criticism.* Bloomington: Indiana University Press.

Jenkins, Timothy. 1994. Fieldwork and the Perception of Everyday Life. *Man (n.s.)* 29:433–455.

Johnson, Mark. 1987. *The Body in the Mind: The Bodily Basis of Meaning, Imagination, and Reason.* Chicago: University of Chicago Press.

Karp, Ivan, and Martha B. Kendall. 1982. Reflexivity and Fieldwork. In *Explaining Human Behavior.* Paul Secord, ed. Pp. 249–273. Beverly Hills, CA: Sage Publications.

Kendon, Adam. 1995. Andrea De Jorio: The First Ethnographer of Gesture? *Visual Anthropology* 7:371–390.

Klapp, O. E. 1972. *Heroes, Villains, and Fools: Reflections of the American Character.* San Diego: Aegis.

Kleinman, Arthur M., Veena Das, and Margaret Lock, eds. 1997. *Social Suffering.* Berkeley: University of California Press.

Kondo, Dorinne K. 1990. *Crafting Selves: Power, Gender, and Discourses of Identity in a Japanese Workplace.* Chicago: University of Chicago Press.

Kroeber, A. L., and Jane Richardson. 1952 [1940]. Three Centuries of Women's Dress Fashions, a Quantitative Analysis. *Anthropological Records* 5(2):111–154. Berkeley and Los Angeles: University of California Press. Reprinted in *The Nature of Culture.* Pp. 358–372. Chicago: University of Chicago Press.

Lakoff, George, and Mark Johnson. 1980. *Metaphors We Live By.* Chicago: University of Chicago Press.

Lakoff, George. 1987. *Women, Fire, and Dangerous Things: What Categories Reveal about the Mind.* Chicago: University of Chicago Press.

Lave, Jean, and Etienne Wenger. 1991. *Situated Learning: Legitimate Peripheral Participation. Learning in Doing.* Cambridge: Cambridge University Press.

Lawrence, Denise, and Setha M. Low 1995. Built Environment and Spatial Form. *Annual Review of Anthropology 19*:453–505.

Leach, Edmund Ronald. 1970. *Claude Lévi-Strauss. Modern Masters.* New York: Viking Press.

Leach, Edmund Ronald. 1976. *Culture and Communication: The Logic by which Symbols are Connected: An Introduction to the Use of Structuralist Analysis in Social Anthropology.* Cambridge: Cambridge University Press.

Leavitt, John. 1996. Meaning and Feeling in the Anthropology of Emotions. *American Ethnologist 23*:514–539.

Leone, Mark P. 1988. *The Recovery of Meaning: Historical Archaeology in the Eastern United States.* Anthropological Society of Washington Series. Washington, DC: Smithsonian Institution Press.

LeVine, Robert A. 1973. *Culture, Behavior, and Personality.* Chicago: Aldine.

Lévi-Strauss, Claude. 1963. *Structural Anthropology.* New York: Basic Books.

Limon, José Eduardo. 1994. *Dancing with the Devil: Society and Cultural Poetics in Mexican-American South Texas.* Madison: University of Wisconsin Press.

Malkki, Liisa H. 1995. *Purity and Exile: Violence, Memory, and National Cosmology among Hutu Refugees in Tanzania.* Chicago: University of Chicago Press.

Marx, Karl. 1978 [1852]. *The Eighteenth Brumaire of Louis Bonaparte,* 1st ed. Beijing: Foreign Languages Press.

Meeker, Michael E. 1979. *Literature and Violence in North Arabia.* Cambridge: Cambridge University Press.

Merleau-Ponty, Maurice. 1962. *Phenomenology of Perception.* New York: Humanities Press.

Miceli, Silvana. 1982. *In nome del segno: Introduzione alla semiotica della cultura.* Palermo: Sellerio.

Mole, John. 1990. *Mind Your Manners: Culture Clash in the European Single Market.* London: Industrial Society.

Mole, John. 1992. *Mind Your Manners: Managing Culture Clash in the European Single Market.* London: Nicholas Brealey.

Mole, John. 1995. *Mind Your Manners: Managing Business Cultures in Europe,* new ed. London: Nicholas Brealey.

Moore, Sally Falk. 1987. Explaining the Present: Theoretical Dilemmas in Processual Ethnography. *American Ethnologist 14*:727–736.

Nagel, Thomas. 1974. What It Is Like to Be a Bat. *The Journal of Philosophy 34*:435–450.

Needham, Rodney. 1962. *Structure and Sentiment: A Test Case in Social Anthropology.* Chicago: University of Chicago Press.

Needham, Rodney. 1972. *Belief, Language, and Experience*. Oxford: Basil Blackwell.

Nisbet, Robert A. 1965. *Social Change and History: Aspects of the Western Theory of Development*. New York: Oxford University Press.

Obeyesekere, Gananath. 1992. *The Apotheosis of Captain Cook: European Mythmaking in the Pacific*. Princeton: Princeton University Press; Honolulu: Bishop Museum Press.

Osgood, Charles Egerton, George J. Suci, and Percy H. Tannenbaum. 1957. *The Measurement of Meaning*. Urbana: University of Illinois Press.

Paine, Robert. 1981. *Politically Speaking: Cross-Cultural Studies of Rhetoric*. Philadelphia: Institute for the Study of Human Issues.

Parkin, David, ed. 1982. *Semantic Anthropology. A.S.A. Monographs*, No. 22. London and New York: Academic Press.

Parmentier, Richard J. 1994. *Signs in Society: Studies in Semiotic Anthropology*. Bloomington: Indiana University Press.

Parmentier, Richard J. 1996. Haole-ing in the Wind: On the Rhetoric of Identity Anthropology. *Anthropological Quarterly* 69:220–230.

Peacock, James L. 1975. *Consciousness and Change: Symbolic Anthropology in Evolutionary Perspective*. New York: John Wiley.

Peters, Emrys. 1967. Some Structural Aspects of the Feud among the Camel-Herding Bedouin of Cyrenaica. *Africa* 37:261–282.

Pirsig, Robert M. 1974. *Zen and the Art of Motorcycle Maintenance: An Inquiry into Values*. New York: Morrow.

Pocius, Gerlad L. 1979. Hooked Rugs in Newfoundland: The Representation of Social Structure in Design. *Journal of American Folklore* 92:273–284.

Preziosi, Donald. 1979. *Architecture, Language and Meaning: The Origins of the Built World and Its Semiotic Organization. Approaches to Semiotics*, No. 49. The Hague and Paris: Mouton.

Quine, W. V. 1981. *Theories and Things*. Cambridge: Harvard University Press.

Rappaport, Joanne. 1994. *Cumbe Reborn: An Andean Ethnography of History*. Chicago: University of Chicago Press.

Rappaport, Roy A. 1979. *Ecology, Meaning, and Religion*. Richmond, CA: North Atlantic Books.

Rapport, Nigel. 1993. *Diverse World-Views in an English Village*. Edinburgh: Edinburgh University Press.

Reed-Danahay, Deborah. 1995. The Kabyle and the French: Occidentalism in Bourdieu's Theory of Practice. In *Occidentalism: Images of the West*. James G. Carrier, ed. Pp. 61–84. Oxford: Oxford University Press.

Reed-Danahay, Deborah E., ed. 1997. *Auto/ethnography: Rewriting the Self and the Social*. Oxford: Berg.

Roberts, Michael. 1997. Histories. *International Social Science Journal* 49:373–385.

Sahlins, Marshall. 1981. *Historical Metaphors and Mythical Realities: Structure in the Early History of the Sandwich Islands Kingdom. ASAO Special Publications*, No. 1. Ann Arbor: University of Michigan Press.

Sahlins, Marshall. 1995. *How "Natives" Think: About Captain Cook, For Example*. Chicago: University of Chicago Press.

Salmond, Anne. 1982. Theoretical Landscapes: On Cross-Cultural Conceptions of Knowledge. In *Semantic Anthropology. A.S.A. Monographs*. No. 22. David Parkin, ed. Pp. 65–87. London and New York: Academic Press.

Salzman, Philip Carl. 1978. Does Complementary Opposition Exist? *American Anthropologist 80*: 53–70.

Sanjek, Roger. 1990. *Fieldnotes: The Makings of Anthropology*. Ithaca: Cornell University Press.

Sartre, Jean-Paul. 1963. *Search for a Method*. Trans. and with an introduction by Hazel Barnes. New York: Knopf.

Schama, Simon. 1995. *Landscape and Memory*. New York: Knopf.

Schwimmer, Eric, ed. 1978. *The Yearbook of Symbolic Anthropology*, Vol. 1. London, C. Hurst & Co.; Montreal: McGill-Queen's University Press.

Scott, James C. 1990. *Domination and the Arts of Resistance: Hidden Transcripts*. New Haven: Yale University Press.

Sewell, William Hamilton. 1996. Three Temporalities: Towards an Eventful Sociology. In *The Historic Turn in the Human Sciences*. T. J. McDonald, ed. Pp. 245–280. Ann Arbor: University of Michigan Press.

Shryock, Andrew. 1997. *Nationalism and the Genealogical Imagination: Oral History and Textual Authority in Tribal Jordan*. Berkeley: University of California Press.

Singer, Milton B. 1984. *Man's Glassy Essence: Explorations in Semiotic Anthropology*. Bloomington: Indiana University Press.

Sperber, Dan. 1975. *Rethinking Symbolism*. Cambridge: Cambridge University Press.

Sperber, Dan. 1985. *On Anthropological Knowledge: Three Essays*. Cambridge: Cambridge University Press; Paris: Editions de la Maison des Sciences de l'Homme.

Stark, F. 1996. *Communicative Interaction, Power and the State: A Method*. Toronto: University of Toronto Press.

Steedly, Mary Margaret. 1993. *Hanging Without a Rope: Narrative Experience in Colonial and Postcolonial Karoland*. Princeton: Princeton University Press.

Stewart, Kathleen. 1996. *A Space on the Side of the Road: Cultural Poetics in an "Other" America*. Princeton: Princeton University Press.

Struever, Nancy. 1983. Fables of Power. *Representations 4*:108–127.

Tagliacozzo, Giorgio, ed. 1983. *Vico and Marx: Affinities and Contrasts*. Atlantic Highlands, NJ: Humanities Press.

Taylor, Charles. 1985. *Philosophy of the Human Sciences*. New York: Cambridge University Press.

Tilly, Charles, ed. 1997. *Roads from Past to Future*. Lanham, MD: Rowman and Littlefield.

Turner, Victor. 1967. *The Forest of Symbols: Aspects of Ndembu Ritual*. Ithaca: Cornell University Press.

Turner, Victor. 1972 (1958). *Schism and Continuity in an African Society*. Atlantic Highlands, NJ: Humanities.

Turner, Victor. 1974. *Dramas, Fields, and Metaphors; Symbolic Action in Human Society*. Ithaca: Cornell University Press.

Vico, Giambattista. 1984 [1744]. *The New Science of Giambattista Vico*. Thomas G. Bergin and Max H. Fisch, trans. Ithaca: Cornell University Press.

Vogt, Evon Z. 1965. Structural and Conceptual Replication in Zinacantan Culture. *American Anthropologist* 58:264–281.

Wallace, Anthony F. C. 1956. Revitalization Movements: Some Theoretical Considerations. *American Anthropologist* 58:264–281.

Watson, Rubie S., ed. 1994. *Memory, History, and Opposition under State Socialism*. Santa Fe: School of American Research Press.

Waugh, Linda R. 1976. *Roman Jakobson's Science of Language*. The Hague: Peter de Ridder Press.

Webster's New International Dictionary of the English Language, 2d ed. 1959. Springfield, MA: G. and C. Merriam.

Willis, Paul E. 1977. *Learning to Labour: How Working Class Kids Get Working Class Jobs*. Farnborough, England: Saxon House.

Zabusky, Stacia E. 1995. *Launching Europe: An Ethnography of European Cooperation in Space Science*. Princeton: Princeton University Press.

JEFFREY C. JOHNSON

Four

Research Design and Research Strategies

We need a powerful mode of argumentation, a mode that ensures we can represent our representations in credible ways. In such worlds, a systematic argument enjoys a star-spangled legitimacy. We need a way to argue what we know based on the process by which we came to know it. That's what I seek, not as the only possible representation that our field can offer, but as an essential lever to try and move the world.

Michael A. Agar (1996:13)

Introduction

In a complex world of competing arguments, who is to be believed or trusted? Are data themselves, independently of how they were conceived and collected, proper evidence for making a case? Although some may be swayed by the elegance of a well-written essay, for many it's crucial to know something about the author, his or her motivations, experiences, skills, methods of investigation, and so on before passing judgment on the conclusions. In Agar's statement above, we get the impression that a credible argument should be systematic and based on a process that informs us about how researchers came to know what they know.

It is the articulation of this "process by which we came to know it" that reflects the elements of research design. For Stinchcombe (1987:23), the observations produced by how a study was designed are fundamental to the proper assessment of empirical evidence: "We always want to reject evidence if it can be explained by the design of the research or by a large number of small, unorganized causes." Some things, like perceptual errors, that hinder our observation may be beyond our control. Some things, like site selection, sampling, measurement, and recording are at least partly within our control. The value of empirical evidence can only be properly evaluated by understanding the details of how the research was conducted.

According to Pelto and Pelto (1978:291): "Research design involves combining the essentials of investigation into an effective problem-solving sequence. Thus the plan of research is a statement that concentrates on the components that *must be present* in order for the objectives of the study to be realized." This statement illustrates at least two important elements of research design.

First, research design involves an a priori plan or strategy for all phases of the research (such as data collection and analysis) including, for some researchers, the production of the final product (like an ethnography). By definition, a plan cannot deal with the unanticipated or unknown realities of research, such as tragedies or acts of nature that disrupt fieldwork. A good understanding of the research problem and the research site allows us to plan for some contingencies, but there is no research design crystal ball. In fact, chance factors often lead to great discoveries or unexpected findings. Still, while luck plays a role in research, planning for such luck is not within the realm of research design (Kirk and Miller 1986).

Second, an idealized plan gives guidelines for linking theory to the methods of data collection and analysis that yield either valid or "defensible" results. I use "defensible" in addition to "valid," which I normally use, to make readers aware that I am broadening the traditional application of research design to include the variety of research strategies found in anthropology today. Interpretive, hermeneutic, and postmodern approaches make little explicit reference to ethnographic design issues, but well-written examples from ethnography may provide "moral evidence" to deal with current social problems, moving people (including politicians) in ways that numerical facts can't (Seidman 1994:134). Nevertheless, a well-articulated project design helps "to promote the effective conduct of research," whether one starts from a positivist or humanist perspective (Ellen 1984:158).

On a practical level, good research design is essential in the competition for research grants and contracts. There is much variation in what funding agencies and foundations expect regarding research design. One agency may require a detailed description of the proposed project paying attention to the research design logic of science (for example, validity, reliability, hypotheses, etc., see also Plattner [In press]); others may require a description of the research problem and site but require less detail about the methods of data collection and analysis. All funding agencies expect a well-organized outline of the proposed project—one that meets the design expectations of peer reviewers and agency personnel.

A distinction needs to be made between what's sometimes called the laundry-list component of research and research *design*. The laundry-list component is important. It involves details about getting into and out of the field situation, travel arrangements, getting proper government permissions, making contacts at the field site, arranging for living accommodations, and so on. *Design*, on the other hand, involves the methodological and analytical details that contribute to the credibility, validity, believability, or plausibility of any study. In this chapter I concentrate on elements of design related to the production of valid results or a believable ethnographic account.

The Need for Design

Evidence for the power of research design is all around us. The invention of the simple control/treatment design of clinical trials allowed researchers in this century to evaluate competing therapies and to select the ones that worked best. One result is that infectious childhood diseases that killed thousands of young people a century ago are today only a memory in industrialized countries. The lessons learned from controlled experimentation are applied today to the policy arena where groups are in conflict over resources or because of social inequalities (Johnson and Pollnac 1989; Porter 1995). Members of such competing groups—such as large-scale commercial producers, commodity producers, environmental groups, and real estate developers—believe strongly in their positions. They have evidence, often anecdotal, that their positions are credible. Without some unbiased means for assessing the evidence, the truth is only be a matter of who has the most political clout.

The outcry for a ban on nets in tuna fishing is a famous recent example. Environmental organizations launched campaigns to ban nets in tuna fishing because dolphins are often caught incidentally in that fishery. Media campaigns in the U.S. showing pictures of dolphins being caught in nets (generally not in U.S. waters), contributed to Florida's totally banning fishing nets—even though no marine mammals were threatened by the use of nets in Florida waters. Thus, policy emerges from interactions between groups of differing political, ideological, social, and economic backgrounds.

There has been similar concern over the incidental catch of harbor porpoises by net fishers in New England (Schneider 1996). This case led to a systematic test of a technology that might ameliorate the problem. Wildlife conservationists petitioned the U.S. federal government in 1991 to declare harbor porpoises a threatened species. In response, the fishing industry proposed the voluntary use of "pingers"—an underwater acoustic device—to keep porpoises from their nets. The effectiveness of the device, however, was in question, and there was no firm evidence in the literature about it. Fishers petitioned the federal government to fund a study of pinger effectiveness. The study used the classic control/treatment design in which catch rates for a set of nets with pingers were compared to catch rates for set of nets without pingers.

In the first experiment, the control net caught 10 porpoises while the treatment net caught none. Some conservationist groups claimed the study was biased in that the treatment nets were placed in areas known not to have large numbers of porpoises. So another study was conducted placing experimental treatment and control nets in the same proximity. This time, the treatment net caught only 1 porpoise while the control net caught 32. Some environmental groups were still concerned that evidence with more statistical power was needed. Lobbying efforts by fishers yielded more funds for a larger, more comprehensive study involving more than 10,000 fishing nets. Both control and treatment nets were outfitted with pingers, but only the pingers on treatment nets would activate once placed in the water. Thus, fishers were blind as to which nets were control and which were treatment—a classic double-blind experimental design. Again the evidence was impressive: The treatment nets caught 2 porpoises (1 was thought to be deaf), while the control nets caught 25.

The issue is still under debate, but this series of studies illustrates how the elements of research design help muster evidence in light of competing beliefs and philosophies. In each successive study, investigators tried to control for as many extraneous variables as possible so that the hypothesized effect could be assessed (that is, the effectiveness of pingers compared to not using pingers). The logic of the research design contributed to the production of credible results.

Although the power of experimental design is evident, concern for its application in anthropology—particularly cultural anthropology—has been limited. Some early exceptions include Brim and Spain's (1974) book on hypothesis-testing designs, Pelto and Pelto's (1978) book on research methodology in cultural anthropology, and Naroll and Cohen's (1973) *A Handbook of Method in Cultural Anthropology*, which has several chapters that address issues in research design (LeVine 1973; Sechrest 1973; Spindler and Goldschmidt 1973). Bernard (1994) has elaborated in more detail on issues of design, but his treatment is necessarily limited, given his task of describing the range of methods available to anthropologists.

If research design gets relatively little attention from anthropologists, other social scientists have written volumes about it. What should we make of this apparent dearth of specific treatments of research design in cultural anthropology? I don't think we should make too much of it because the important elements of research design—reliability, informant accuracy, validity, objectivity, and operationalization of theoretical concepts—have been present in the writings of cultural anthropologists even before Boas.

Boas, Malinowski, and Research Design in the Scientific Tradition

Boas and most of his students advocated a natural science logic in the collection of ethnographic materials and a true concern for the collection of reliable data that could lead to the production of valid theory. Yet, despite his concern for scientific method, Boas was more explicit about his methods of data analysis than about his methods of fieldwork and data collection (Ellen 1984; Boas 1920). Malinowski was also concerned with the aims of science and with methodological rigor. His earliest contributions, however, were more a demonstration of the value of ethnographic writing—his "unusual literary sense" (Lowie 1937:231)—rather than of methodological details of proper ethnographic fieldwork (Ellen 1984).

A good example of this tension between the stated early concerns for the methods of science and the actual use of such methods in ethnography comes from correspondence between Boas and his student Margaret Mead during her first fieldwork in Samoa. As Orans (1996) describes it, Mead wrote to Boas with her concerns about possible violations of scientific principles in the data she had collected to that point. She wrote of her doubts about the comparability of cases and about her ability, or even the need, to do a quantitative comparison of the similarity of attitudes among the adolescent girls in her study. She had concerns—and I believe she thought her mentor, Boas, would feel similarly—as to whether a valid comparison of this type could be made given the selection process for her sample of girls.

The constraints of field research may lead one to stray from the idealized prescriptions of a research design, but Mead was attempting to exert her authority without necessarily following the research procedures advocated by Boas and others. Orans says: "What she wants is permission to present data simply as 'illustrative material' for the representativeness of which one will simply have to take her word" (p. 127). What is most surprising is Boas's response to Mead. He writes:

> I am very decidedly of the opinion that a statistical treatment of such intricate behavior as the one that you are studying, will not have very much meaning and that the characterization of a selected number of cases must necessarily be the material with which you operate. Statistical work will require the tearing out of its natural setting, some particular aspects of behavior which, without that setting may have no meaning whatever. A complete elimination of the subjective use of the investigator is of course quite impossible in a matter of this kind but undoubtedly you will try to overcome this so far as that is all possible. (from Orans 1996:128)

This response is important for at least two reasons. First, it demonstrates the differences between the stated scientific objectives of ethnographic work as advocated by Boas and the actual practice of ethnographic research. There appears to be a perception that a systematic treatment of the data will have to be abandoned to preserve context and meaning. Ironically, this concern for context and meaning over methodological rigor, particularly for those in search of theoretical foundations (that is, the Boasian idea of data leading to the construction of theory), would ultimately hinder the comparability of data from different ethnographic sources (see Moran [1995] for a recent discussion of this issue and see Ember and Ember, this volume).

Second, Boas's concern for contextual meaning over the statistical analysis of data was prophetic. Rightly or wrongly, the preeminence of contextualization has been a consistent issue in ethnographic research and has often clouded issues in research design. The idea that quantification detracts from context and meaning in the ethnographic endeavor—evident even in the time of Boas—and a failure to understand that systematic methods—whether quantitative or qualitative—help minimize the subjectivity of the investigator have impeded the development of well-delineated research strategies in anthropology.

It's tempting to explain this as the consequence of the intensely personal nature of fieldwork, and the complexity of a holistic approach. However, this debate has its parallel in sociology where schools such as ethnomethodology and symbolic interactionism developed in response to the largely quantitative macro-level focus of the discipline. These micro-level approaches are attempts to get at a better understanding of meaning in everyday life (Cook 1994).

Boas's final sentence in his response to Mead illustrates that even at this early stage the issue of the subjectivity of ethnographic research was of concern. There was a faith, however, that awareness of the potential biases associated with the subjectivity of the investigator could be dealt with in some reasonable way. A further irony is that the one thing that might have lessened potential subjectivity biases—the use of standardized methods—was rejected outright because meaning might be compromised. Mead's position on these various elements of research design provided fuel for the continuing discussions about the validity of her original findings (Brim and Spain 1974; Freeman 1983; Orans 1996).

Thus, while early British and U.S. anthropologists advocated the scientific method in ethnographic research, there is little evidence that they considered appropriate design issues when they actually did the research. As Urry (1984) sees it:

> In Britain the claims that anthropology not only studied a distinctive body of data but also that it possessed a sophisticated methodology to collect these data, was an important factor in the establishment of anthropology as a discipline. This was less necessary in America where, by the late nineteenth century, anthropology was already established in universities, museums and government agencies. But in spite of claims to scientific methodology, particularly in the British tradition, there are surprisingly few details about actual methods anthropologists used in the field, beyond a few first principles and illustrative anecdotes. There was a wide belief among British anthropologists that fieldwork could not be taught to new recruits, but could only be experienced by individuals in the field. In the American tradition texts provided what was regarded as an objective body of data, whereas the British tradition was more a matter of subjective experience. It is a strange paradox in the development of field methods that the scientific study of other cultures has been built upon such a foundation. (p. 61)

There is much anecdotal evidence for a belief, across the British and U.S. traditions, in a trial-by-fire method of training for ethnographers. This belief supports the current lack of formal training in methods and research design in anthropology. Agar (1980) and Bernard (1994) relate stories about Kroeber's recommendations regarding the teaching and conduct of ethnographic research. In the stories, one concerning Wagley's teaching of a field methods course and one concerning a graduate student at Berkeley asking for advice before going to the field, Kroeber's response was a terse, one liner that reflected the attitude of the times. Even in the late 1960s, when concern for methodological rigor was probably at its peak in anthropology, many treatments of research methods and design in the literature played down the need for more systematic methods and design detail, particularly with respect to hypothesis-testing approaches (LeVine 1973). A good example of this is a book by Thomas Rhys Williams (1967) published in the Spindlers's series on field methods. Williams writes:

> I believe that only someone wholly involved and fully immersed in fieldwork can really communicate the essence of cultural anthropology to students or general readers. And since I have indicated here that research in culture involves a great deal of unique personal experience for the anthropologist, I have taken the position that it is probably unlikely there can be a rigorous, systematic, and formal presentation of methods in the study of culture like those of the natural sciences and that there are overriding concerns among many sociologists, psychologists, and economists. I find this stance comfortable, for it is my conviction that so long as prime theoretical concerns in the study of culture are an attempt to record and understand the native's view of his culture and the objective and historical realities of culture, then methods for field study will have to reflect the end purpose of making a whole account of a part of the human experience. (pp. 64–65)

LeVine (1973) and others (Johnson 1990) make the point that the nature of fieldwork, in terms of its requisite huge investments in time and geographical focus, has often limited the attractiveness of more formal research designs because of its commitment to studying specific problems in a specific way. The realities of fieldwork often dictate the need to change the problem focus or, finding that the proposed hypotheses are inappropriate to the cultural setting under study, the need to somehow salvage the research.

Laboratory and survey researchers have some flexibility to change the problem focus and study populations in light of emerging problems, but field workers are limited in their ability to do so. Thus, the idea of researchers "putting all their eggs in one basket" may have limited the a priori formulation of problems in fieldwork (LeVine 1973:184). Further, the huge investment in time and resources limited another important goal of science, that of replication, since an ethnographer couldn't realistically be expected to replicate someone else's work. The "my natives" or "my village" mentality of some and the fact that careers were made by discovering new theories or describing exotic less well-known cultures has certainly inhibited replication efforts (Johnson 1990).

Contemporary Design Issues in Cultural Anthropology

There is an ongoing debate in cultural anthropology concerning science and its role in contemporary research. A discussion of the basic arguments as related to epistemology, objectivity, reality, authority, and the like are beyond the scope of this chapter (see Schweizer in this volume). Suffice to say that traditionally, research design and its logic have been associated with science and an underlying belief in objectivity and explanation. The historical tension between interpretive and scientific approaches in anthropology has given way to an outright rejection by some anthropologists of science and its logic of design. To say that the research design logic of science has been replaced by something that is recognizable as the research design logic of, say, postmodernism would, I think, be misleading. It is not that interpretive approaches lack some form of research plan; but the term "design" itself smacks of the very formalism that is being rejected. A more appropriate term that would encompass the diversity currently found in cultural anthropology might be "research strategy."

Figure 1 is a taxonomic characterization of the different types of research strategies found in contemporary cultural anthropology. The figure distinguishes between strategies within the realm of interpretive studies and those using systematic strategies that have more of the elements of science. This is a highly simplified representation. Many examples of research in anthropology fall within the two extremes of the continuum. Under the systematic distinction are the two primary categories of exploratory and explanatory approaches, each entailing a specific design strategy. The light line connecting the two categories indicates their complementarity and interrelatedness in that a design may include both within an overall research design framework. These approaches are by no means mutually exclusive in approaching a research problem (see section on Research Design in Systematic Research, below).

In its most extreme form, systematic strategies tend to involve the search for explanations of phenomena and the pursuit of theoretical foundations. In searching for such foundations, there is a need for objectivity, replication, and control over possible sources of error leading to a valid assessment of a given theory. Epistemologically, systematic work is objectivist. Its practitioners are ultimately interested in research findings that approximate an external truth. As a result, the assessment of any theory involves research designs more heavily concerned with the means—the research process, rather than simply the way the study was written or argued—since the validity of study results depends on the scientific soundness of the research design. For any given research problem, it is the purpose of research design to ward off as many threats to validity as possible. This leads to designs that involve concern for a higher degree of methodological and analytical detail, whether quantitative or qualitative. In this line of thinking, the researcher is a field-worker-as-writer.

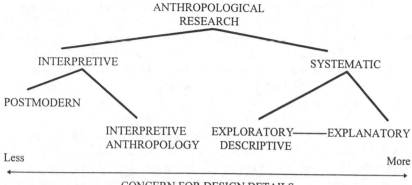

IN SEARCH OF:
UNDERSTANDING
MORAL TALES
LOCAL RATIONALES

IN SEARCH OF:
RULING OUT RIVAL HYPOTHESES
OBJECTIVITY
POSSIBLE SOURCES OF ERROR
REPLICATION
THEORETICAL FOUNDATIONS

PURPOSE:
A BELIEVABLE ACCOUNT OR STORY

PURPOSE:
VALID ASSESSMENT

EPISTEMOLOGY:
SUBJECTIVIST
VALUE MEDIATED FINDINGS
OR CREATED FINDINGS

EPISTEMOLOGY:
OBJECTIVIST
FINDINGS APPROX. THE TRUTH

CONCERN FOR:
THREATS TO BELIEVABILITY

CONCERN FOR:
THREATS TO VALIDITY

MEANS FOR DIMINISHING THREATS:
LITERARY

MEANS FOR DIMINISHING THREATS:
METHODOLOGICAL

Exploratory: Exploratory approaches are used to develop hypotheses and more generally to make probes for circumscription, description, and interpretation of less well-understood topics. This is similar to the grounded theory ideas of Glaser and Strauss (1967), where exploratory descriptive research leads to the development of more meaningful theory and measures. Exploratory research can be the primary focus of a given design or just one of many components.

Explanatory: Explanatory approaches generally involve testing elements of theory that may already have been proposed in the literature or that have been informed by exploratory research. Research designs in this mode are determined a priori and their primary purpose is to eliminate threats to validity, where validity is concerned with whether things are what they appear to be or are the best approximation to the truth (Cook and Campbell 1979). In this enterprise, explanation can involve a general search for causality or prediction.

Figure 1. Types of anthropological research strategies and their features.

Interpretive strategies, on the other hand, differ from systematic approaches in that they question a researcher's ability to maintain objectivity, particularly in the ethnographic context where the ethnographer is often the instrument of measurement. A variety of names are used in the lexicon of social scientists that can be associated to varying degrees with an interpretive strategy. Phenomenology, hermeneutics, symbolic anthropology, interpretive anthropology, interpretive interactionism, deconstructionism, postmodernism, and constructivism, to name a few, question, in one way or another, some or all of the ontology, epistemology, and methodology of systematic approaches. Although some of the older interpretive strategies that emerged from the scientific tradition in the social sciences, such as early interpretive anthropology, still adhered to some logical empiricist methodology and maintained a degree of belief in ethnographic authority, more recent approaches, such as postmodernism and constructivism, are more radical in their sweeping rejection of scientific method and design logic (see Schwandt 1994). In contrasting Geertz and early interpretive anthropology with some of the later postmodern turns of such ethnographic writers as James Clifford, Rabinow (1986) observes:

> At first glance James Clifford's work, like that of others in this volume, seems to follow naturally in the wake of Geertz's interpretive turn. There is, however, a major difference. Geertz (like the other anthropologists) is still directing his efforts to reinvent an anthropological science with the help of textual mediations. The core activity is still social description of the other, however modified by new conceptions of discourse, author, or text. The other for Clifford is the anthropological representation of the other. This means that Clifford is simultaneously more firmly in control of his project and more parasitical. He can invent his questions with few constraints; he must constantly feed off others' texts. (p. 242)

There is a fundamental belief that the intersubjective, everyday meanings and how they are produced, maintained, and changed in any given context often defy objective study and explanation. Practitioners of almost all interpretive paradigms are searching in one way or another for some understanding (*verstehen*) rather than for some explanation of social phenomena. However, some interpretive work is more similar in nature to the exploratory or descriptive strategies found under the systematic side of Figure 1 than to some of the more radical forays into, for example, postmodernism. Thus, the rather simple characterization of research strategies found in Figure 1 attempts to recognize the variation inherent in the range of work found in contemporary anthropology by placing "interpretive anthropology" adjacent to "exploratory/descriptive" (see, for example, the work of Zabusky 1995). Discussions about this debate can be found in Seidman (1994), on the one hand, and Faia (1993), on the other, and, more specifically for anthropology, by Kuznar (1997).

An important implication here is that scholars who follow this line of inquiry are searching for local rationales rather than nomothetic theory or universal foundations and may be more interested in conveying a moral tale of some type rather than a value-free account (Seidman 1994). Further, the purpose of research strategies under these interpretive paradigms is more focused on the production of a believable or plausible account or story rather than a single depiction of the truth, since it is thought that there are a multitude of plausible accounts rather than just a single true story. Epistemologically, interpretive paradigms are subjective, with findings that are value mediated or even created. Thus, there is less focus on the means of research, such as methods of data collection and analysis as found in the systematic strategies, and more on the ends of research—the ethnographic or literary product. In contrast to the field-worker-as-writer, we find the writer-as-field-worker (Denzin and Lincoln 1994).

For scholars like Geertz, analysis of ethnography has less to do with the methods of observation and description than the inscriptions and writings concerning the meaning of human action. In many ways, this blurs the distinction between what is anthropological and what is literary. More extreme forays into experimental ethnography have blurred this distinction even further, and there is more of a focus on writing strategies that include such approaches as montages, evocative representations, polyvocal texts, and even ethnographic fictions (Denzin and Lincoln 1994). While systematic analytical paradigms are primarily concerned with threats to validity, recent interpretive paradigms are focused more on threats to believability —as in "Do you believe my story?" (Tyler 1991:85)—or, in critical theory, threats to trustworthiness (Kincheloe and McLaren 1994). If we talk of an interpretive method, particularly with regard to postmodernism, it more than likely involves both the researcher's immersion into the cultural context of the actor(s) and some means, usually literary, for conveying the understanding gained from such an immersion.

As stated, many interpretive studies are closer in character to exploratory and descriptive research in the systematic mode than to some of the more extreme postmodern studies. A good example of this is Zabusky's (1995) ethnographic study of cooperation in European space science that she admits "took the form of mutual exploration rather than unidirectional examination" (p. 46). She contrasts her study with research on cooperation by "experimental" psychologists, emphasizing the cultural and social orientation of her work and the importance of considering context (social, cultural, political, etc.) in her analysis. Following in the "thick description" tradition of Geertz, Zabusky clearly believes in some kind of ethnographic authority. In a short methodology section, she discusses the challenge of conducting participant observation research in this rather complex, geographically dispersed, cross-cultural setting. She also discusses the rationales for selecting the site and the group she studied, problems of working in a linguistically and technically diverse social milieu, the use of semistructured and unstructured interviews, and the effect of her role as ethnographer on informant relations and data quality. Although Zabusky doesn't talk specifically about design or about concerns for potential threats to validity, there is implicit concern for such issues throughout the ethnography.

In contrast to Zabusky, there is a body of interpretive work in anthropology that is more extreme in its rejection of systematic design issues. Ramos (1995), for example, has recently published an ethnography based on a rewrite of her 1972 dissertation, with additional ethnographic insights. She rejects the "anthropological austerity" of her original work in favor of an "intersubjective understanding" that captures the "flavor" of her ethnographic encounter with the Yanomami. To her, the original work was "old-fashioned and theoretically unsophisticated" and had to be replaced by a more reflexive work. This contrast between the old and the new reflects the increased variation in epistemological emphasis in the field that has developed over the last 30 years. As Ramos sees it, "I found myself making forays into the self-conscious meanderings of reflexive anthropology in order to shift the axis of analysis from the skeletonlike dissertation to the flesh and blood of ethnography" (p. 6).

Along with this shift came the freedom not to be concerned with issues of bias and validity or with the need for working systematically, thus allowing for a less restrictive ethnographic narrative. Although Ramos discusses informant interviewing and various sources of data, her introduction is largely devoted to discussions of her reliance on her own memory in writing the ethnography and the shift in the narrative between synchrony and diachrony. Thus, there is little discussion of research design and methods of data collection as might be found in work in the systematic tradition. Instead, Ramos emphasizes the emergent and reflexive nature of data and the literary strategies used in producing the ethnographic product. Other examples in this vein include Panourgia's (1995) use of *we* and *they* in her "Athenian Anthropography" and Behar's (1993) use of montage in her collaboration with a single woman in the telling of that woman's life story. Behar discusses the multiplexity of roles, in that she was variously involved as "priest, interviewer, collector, transcriber, translator, analyst, academic, connoisseur, editor, and peddler" (p. 12).

The idea of a montage as an organizing principle was also central to Taussig's (1987) historical and ethnographic account of shamanism, colonialism, and terror in South America. This work is important in at least two ways. First, it is representative of the genre that rejects explanation in favor of conveying a moral tale. Its purpose is not a traditional attempt at explanation where facts are considered real, but political interpretation and representation of facts, independent of their "realness." Second, Taussig uses the "principle of montage" as a means, at least in his view, for better relating the lessons of history. As he states:

> As against the magic of academic rituals of explanation which, their alchemical promise of yielding system from chaos, do nothing to ruffle the placid surface of this natural order, I choose to work with a different conflation of modernism and the primitivism it conjures into life—namely the carrying over into history of the principle of montage, as I learned that principle not only from terror, but from Putumayo shamanism with its adroit, albeit unconscious, use of the magic of history and its healing power. (p. xiv)

These examples offer only a brief glimpse of the range of possible strategies in use by interpretivists in anthropology. For some, interpretive work is an exploratory enterprise with an implicit concern for methodological issues. For others, interpretive work is concerned more with the strategies and methods of ethnographic presentation and with the reflexive character of the ethnographic enterprise. Thus, traditional methods sections are replaced by discussions on how to read the work or on the particular methods used in writing the ethnography itself (see, for example, Panourgia's discussion on the use of the *parerga*).

In the following pages, I focus primarily on research designs in systematic research. For further discussion of research strategies in the interpretive mode, see Fernandez and Herzfeld (this volume).

Research Design in Systematic Research: The Challenge of Making a Case

In some social science disciplines, like psychology, the design of research is driven by features of the analysis. Analysis-of-variance models and multigroup comparisons (factorial designs) may dictate the whos, whats, and wheres of a given project. In sociology, multiple regression models, structural equation models, and path analytic models (all related analytical techniques) have influenced the design of survey research. Ethnography, referred to as the anthropological method by William Foote Whyte (1984), has influenced the nature of design in anthropology, but in profoundly different ways.

Whereas the analytical techniques most often used in psychology, sociology, and economics often led to rather standard designs, in anthropology the eclectic nature of ethnography leaves the design of research more open ended. There are generally no ethnographic "analytical techniques" driving the design, although ethnography has been variously associated with a number of qualitative methods. The good news is that ethnographic research is amenable to a wide range of research designs, including the use of multiple designs within a single ethnographic context. This allows for flexibility, multiple tests of a theory, increased chances for various types of validity, triangulation, and the potential for high levels of innovation and creativity. The bad news is that the open-ended character of ethnography contributes to a less well-focused discussion of research design issues in ethnographic approaches.

Part of the confusion stems from a lack of consensus on what ethnography really is (Johnson 1990). To some, it is both a process and a product (Van Maanen 1988). Although this process might be equated to a method, it's better to think of ethnography as a strategy in which a variety of methods can be used in the quest for knowledge (Pelto and Pelto 1978). Thus, ethnography should involve multiple methods, both qualitative and quantitative, and may involve applying more than one research design. This is particularly true today, given the large number of computer analytical packages available for analyzing text (see Bernard and Ryan, this volume). Currently, the qualitative analysis of text and discourse is no longer restricted to either interpretive or exploratory approaches, but can also be used in hypothesis testing and explanatory research.

Figure 2 illustrates the relationship between exploratory and explanatory approaches within the ethnographic context. This contrast between explanatory and descriptive or exploratory approaches is commonly made in nonexperimental disciplines in both the natural and social sciences. Community ecologists, for example, similarly distinguish between exploratory or descriptive studies that seek to describe and determine patterns in ecological data and those studies that specifically seek to predict or test hypotheses. As with research in community ecology, ethnographic research can be purely exploratory or descriptive—involving a research process focused on producing better theory—or purely explanatory, although this is usually not the case. Rather, the most common model has exploratory research informing and complementing explanatory research. As we will see in the examples to come, exploratory research is often an essential component of the explanatory research process. Exploratory research may contribute to the production of reliable and valid measures, provide information essential for constructing comparison groups, facilitate construction of structured questions or questionnaires, or provide information necessary for producing a sound probability or nonprobability sample.

The figure shows that the overall research process is more than just a matter of study design. There is no substitute for a good theory, and there is a critical need to link theory, design, data collection, analysis, and interpretation in a coherent fashion. Design, however, is the foundation of good research. No amount of sophisticated statistics, computer intensive text analysis, or elegant writing can salvage a poorly designed study. Hurlbert (1984) emphasizes this in a classic paper on the design of field experiments in ecology. "Statistical analysis and interpretation," he says, "are the least critical aspects of experimentation, in that if purely statistical or interpretive errors are made, the data can be reanalyzed. On the other hand, the only complete remedy for design or execution errors is repetition of the experiment" (p. 189). Redoing an experiment because of fundamental design errors is one matter; redoing a year-long ethnographic field study because of such errors is quite another.

Figure 2 shows that the research process involves a simultaneous concern for the development of empirical statements from theory (for example, hypotheses), the operationalization of theoretical concepts (for example, meaningful and reliable measures), design (for example, groups to be studied), data collection (for example, qualitative versus quantitative), and data analysis (for example, multiple regression and text analysis). Theoretical knowledge is derived either from earlier studies or from exploratory work. The levels at which theoretical concepts are measured (for example, nominal or ordinal), the types of sampling strategies used, and the application of appropriate types of analysis must all be considered as a part of the design. For example, the particular structure of an empirical statement or hypothesis will partially determine the manner in which theoretical concepts are operationalized and eventually analyzed. (Stinchcombe [1987] provides an excellent discussion of how empirical statements are derived from theory.)

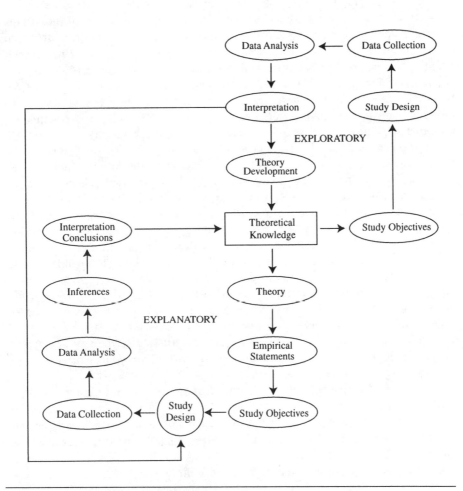

Figure 2. Relationship between exploratory and explanatory approaches within the overall ethnographic research process.

Thus, research design is more than just methods of data collection and analysis. It involves constructing a logical plan that links all the elements of research together so as to produce the most valid assessment possible of some theory, given some set of realistic constraints (for example, cost, scope, geographical setting, etc.). The purpose of research design is to ward off as many threats to validity as possible and to help one eliminate competing hypotheses. It requires careful attention to detail and, often, an admission concerning the potential weakness of a given design. Outside the laboratory, a multitude of influences can threaten the validity of any conclusions. In natural settings, particularly fieldwork, there is no perfect design that can control for all possible extraneous effects at once. A recognition of limitations doesn't invalidate a study's results. Rather it creates an open forum that can contribute much to important theoretical and methodological debates. Without such attention to good design and methodological detail, researchers leave themselves open to one of the worst criticisms of all—of being "not even wrong" (Orans 1996). In other words, a lack of design and methodological detail makes it next to impossible to fairly and adequately assess the validity of any study's conclusions such that "rightness" or "wrongness" may not even be debatable.

True experiments involve random assignment and afford the best chances for controlling for things like: the effects of extraneous factors (that is, unmeasured variables that might affect the dependent variable); the effects of selection (that is, comparison groups differ because of the way they were selected and not due to the treatment); the effects of reactive measurement (that is, the measurement procedure itself caused a change in the dependent variable); or interaction effects involving selection (that is, when selection interacts with other factors to create erroneous findings). These and other sources of error are all potential rival hypotheses and randomized experiments are best at eliminating the threats of rival explanations. Designs of this type, however, are often impossible in anthropological fieldwork. Nevertheless, the principles of experimentation are instructive and are a guide for understanding potential sources of error, even in a nonlaboratory setting. I borrow terminology from Kleinbaum et al. (1982) in constructing a typology of research designs. Included are *experiments, quasi-experiments, observational study designs,* and what I refer to as *natural experiments.*

Experiments involve the random allocation of subjects to groups and afford the most control over distorting effects from extraneous factors. Random allocation produces equivalent comparison groups, and artificial manipulation of independent variables (also known as explanatory variables or study factors), with all other variables or factors controlled for, allows for the most valid assessment of the causal relationship between the independent and dependent variables or response variables. What separates quasi-experiments from true experiments is the lack of random assignment of group members. Random assignment maximizes the probability that experimental groups are equivalent on key variables prior to the introduction of an intervention. Nonrandom assignment lays an experiment open to validity threats and reduces our ability to make causal inferences. Observational studies involve neither random assignment of members to comparison groups nor the manipulation by the observer of independent variables.

This distinction between experimental and observational approaches is similar to one in ecological field studies. Hurlbert (1984) distinguishes between two classes of experiments. He terms the first *manipulative experiments*. These are basically true experiments involving random assignment, multiple comparisons (for example, treatment versus control), and the manipulation of independent variables. He refers to the second as *mensurative experiments*, which involve simply the measurement of variables in space and time and among a number of comparison groups, without random allocation and the manipulation of experimental factors.

The primary distinction lies between that of *sampling* versus *allocation*. In manipulative experiments, analytical units are randomly allocated to comparative groups, whereas in mensurative experiments selection of units is based on some probability or nonprobability sampling scheme. While random assignment aids in controlling for confounding variables by producing homogeneous comparative groups, random sampling of units produces comparison groups that are representative of such groups. Random sampling meets the restrictions of some statistical tests, but it does not afford the same protection as does random assignment of group members against the potential effects of extraneous factors. Mensurative designs, then, are observational and characteristic of the types of comparative designs found in field studies in anthropology.

Finally, natural experiments are similar to quasi-experiments except that the manipulation of independent variables occurs naturally or is unplanned rather than artificial or directed. Thus, comparison groups may be chosen on the basis of different levels of exposure to some naturally occurring or human-induced phenomena (for example, natural disaster, war, or the building of a dam). Cook and Campbell (1979) make a similar distinction but refer to these kinds of natural experiments as "passive-observational studies." Anthropologists involved in development and evaluation research are most likely to use this design.

True experiments are, of course, rare in anthropology (but see Harris et al. [1993] for an example of a true experiment in a field setting). Even in quasi-experiments, it's often difficult to manipulate independent variables directly. Howevert, with careful attention to design and ethnographic context, quasi-experimental and natural experimental designs can be applied to anthropological field settings, particularly in evaluation research and development research. Johnson and Murray (1997), for example, used a quasi-experimental design to evaluate the use of fish aggregation devices (FADS) in small-scale fisheries development projects. Two fixed fishing structures (piers) were pretested for differences in catch rates. Then, FADS, umbrella-like units suspended in the water column, were alternately placed at the piers and individual fishers were interviewed simultaneously during randomly selected times at both the treatment (the pier with the FADS) and the control (the pier without the FADS) piers. Johnson and Murray compared and determined catch rates.

From a statistical standpoint, designs that don't involve random assignment—including quasi-experiments—are considered observational (Cook and Campbell 1979). It is important, though, to contrast quasi-experiments to what Kleinbaum et al. (1982) refer to as observational studies. The most common designs used traditionally by anthropologists have been observational in nature. Designs of this type lack direct control over independent variables and, thus, have more potential problems with various types of internal validity and with the ability to assess time order effects and causality. However, if done properly, such designs can have increased external validity and generalizability.

Due to their predominance in anthropology, the examples that follow are comparative observational designs. Most research designs in the explanatory mode, like true experimental designs, are comparative (for example, control versus treatment). Table 1 describes examples from observational and quasi-experimental study designs discussed by Kleinbaum et al. (1982) and Cook and Campbell (1979). More details can be found in these and other sources (for example, Robson 1993). In anthropological fieldwork, these designs and others can be used in tandem to test or explore components of a theory (such as combinations of time series and repeated measures designs particularly applicable to long-term fieldwork). For example, in their study of preschool children, Johnson et al. (1997) used a *cross-sequential design*, which involved cross-sectional research on a cohort of children carried out over time.

When one is interested in explanation, the importance of comparative thinking in ethnographic work cannot be overemphasized. Discussing "common sense knowing" in evaluation research, Campbell (1988) gives an important critique of ethnography. His idea is that "to know is to compare" is fundamental to explanatory work in anthropology:

> The anthropologists have never studied a school system before. They have been hired after (or just as) the experimental program has got under way, and are inevitably studying a mixture of the old and the new under conditions in which it is easy to make the mistake of attributing to the program results which would have been there anyway. It would help in this if the anthropologists were to spend half of their time studying another school that was similar, except for the new experimental program. This has apparently not been considered. It would also help if the anthropologists were to study the school for a year or two prior to the program evaluation. (This would be hard to schedule, but we might regard the current school ethnographies as prestudies for new innovations still to come.)
>
> *All knowing is comparative*, however phenomenally absolute it appears, and an anthropologist is usually in a very poor position for valid comparison, as their own student experience and their secondhand knowledge of schools involve such different perspectives as to be of little comparative use. (p. 372; emphasis added)

While the purpose of experimental design is to ward off as threats to validity, there are several types of validity—face, construct, statistical conclusion, internal,

TABLE 1

Examples of Basic Research Designs Relevant to Anthropologists

Observational Designs

Cohort Study

    Design: Often referred to as a panel study, this is a longitudinal design where individuals are followed through time. May involve comparison groups subjected to different treatments or exposed to different conditions.

Cross-Sectional Study

    Design: Often referred to as a survey study, it generally involves a random sample of a target population. Stratified sampling is often used to ensure adequate sampling of comparison groups. Although study factors are not controlled directly, designs of this type allow for the statistical control of variables during analysis.

Case-Control Study

    Design: For some study factor (like an outcome variable), compares a group of cases in which members have some characteristic of interest with one or more groups in which the characteristic of interest is absent. It is assumed that both groups come from the same underlying population. Often, members of the groups are matched on one or more variables.

Static-Group Comparison

    Design: A variant of the cross-sectional design in which a treatment group(s) (that is, members exposed to some variable of interest) is compared with a comparison or control group whose members are not exposed to the variable of interest.

Quasi-Experimental Designs

    One group posttest only design

        Design: Pretest observations are made on a single group. The group receives a treatment of some type and posttest observations are made.

    Posttest only nonequivalent groups design

        Design: Experimental and comparison or control group are determined without random allocation of group members. Experimental group receives treatment while the control group does not. Posttest observations are made and groups are compared.

    Pretest/posttest nonequivalent groups design

        Design: Experimental and comparison or control group is determined without random allocation of group members. Pretest observations are made on both groups. Experimental group gets the treatment while control group does not. Posttest observations are made and groups are compared.

    Interrupted time series design

        Design: One experimental group in which a series of observations is made both prior to some treatment and after the treatment.

external, etc. In one way or another, various study designs, in combination with other considerations such as the operationalization of theoretical constructs and sampling, are better or worse at dealing with each. Here, I stress the importance of thinking through how validity threats have influenced and will influence observations or data (for a more in-depth discussion of how these types of validity can impact study conclusions, see Cook and Campbell 1979). Potential errors and bias creep in at various steps in the research process. It's your job to contain these errors. In research design, forewarned is forearmed.

Tables 2 and 3 give examples of threats to internal and external validity as discussed in Cook and Campbell (1979) for quasi-experimental designs. Internal validity is concerned with the approximation to the truth within the research setting. External validity is concerned with the approximation to the truth as expanded to other settings—that is, with the generalizability of research findings. The threats in Table 2 deal with extraneous factors that may account for the presence or absence of a hypothesized effect (that is, contrast validity with invalidity). In the quasi-experimental case, this means changes between pre- and posttest, but this way of thinking can be expanded to include hypothesized effects dealing with differences, similarities, or associations whether diachronic or synchronic.

TABLE 2

Threats to Internal Validity in Quasi-Experimental Designs

History—Change due to unmeasured or unobserved factors
Testing—Change resulting from experience gained by subjects as a consequence of measurement
Instrumentation—Change resulting from varying the way study participants are tested
Regression—When selection of participants are atypical or extreme on a given measure, subsequent measures will become less extreme and there will be regression toward the mean
Mortality—Changes due to participants dropping out of the study
Maturation—Change in study participants over time due to factors unrelated to expected effects
Selection—Observed effects due to nonrandom assignment of members and nonequivalence of groups
Selection by Maturation Interaction—Predisposition of selected group members to grow apart
Ambiguity about Causal Direction—When time-order and causal direction is ambiguous
Diffusion of Treatment—Change due to one group receiving all or a portion of treatment meant for another group
Compensatory Equalization of Treatments—Tendency toward giving all groups the same treatment
Compensatory Rivalry—Participants' perceptions (for example, threats) that affects performance not a part of the treatment

TABLE 3

Threats to External Validity

Selection—Problems with generalizing due to the selection process for study subjects (e.g., nonrepresentative)
Setting—Problems with generalizing due to the nature of the study setting (e.g., setting atypical)
History—Problems with generalizing to either the past or the future

Cook and Cambell (1979) detail how each of the quasi-experimental designs in Table 1 are better or worse at dealing with each of the threats to validity that are found in Tables 2 and 3. For example, the pretest/posttest nonequivalent groups design controls for some internal threats to validity, but it's problematic with respect to controlling for changes due to how groups members were selected (selection maturation), changes due to how individuals were tested (instrumentation), changes due to the selection of individuals with extreme pretest measures leading to regression toward the mean (regression), and changes due to local events not a part of the study (history). Each of these threats may hamper a researcher's ability to assess the contribution of a hypothesized effect to any changes observed. Similarly, threats to external validity, such as problems stemming from biased samples or research in atypical or unique settings, can hamper the generalizability of one's findings. Kleinbaum et al. (1982) offer a similar discussion of the strengths and weaknesses of observational designs in terms of controlling for threats to both internal and external validity.

Other sources of potential bias include sampling error (that is, chance), non-response, the use of imprecise measures, data recording errors, informant inaccuracies, and interviewer effects (see Pelto and Pelto 1978; Bernard 1994). Careful attention to sampling, whether probabilistic (Babbie 1990) or nonprobabilistic (Johnson 1990), is essential. Measurement, operationalization of theoretical concepts, and type of analysis used are other important factors. How reliable are your measures in terms of precision, sensitivity, resolution, and consistency? Are they valid, particularly with respect to accuracy and specificity, in that they are actually measuring what they are intended to measure? Attention and concern with all the potential sources of error, whether stemming from how the study was designed, how the data were collected (for example, face-to-face interviews or mail-out surveys), or how the data were analyzed (for example, statistical conclusion validity), will help lead to the production of solid evidence.

Some Comments on Sampling

Many probability and nonprobability sampling designs are available for any given research problem. These include systematic sampling, stratified random sampling, cluster sampling, and multistage sampling. The selection of any of these designs or the development of some hybrid design depends on the overall design of the research itself. The nature of the groups or characteristics to be compared—in terms of such things as the size of the comparison groups in the overall population, the frequency of characteristics of interest in the population, the availability of a sampling frame, the ability to identify members of the population (for example, hidden or clandestine populations)—all influence the choice of a sample design. But it's not always easy to know who or what you want to sample and to know enough about these sampling units to derive a valid sample.

The selection of units of analysis, whether settings, events, times, households, or people, is important for understanding a variety of internal and external threats to validity, but it is particularly important for increasing external validity. We mostly think of selection in terms of some type of sample units. To generalize to a target population, the sample has to be representative of the population of interest. This is essential if we are to generalize to a whole population and is generally, though not always, a requirement for classical statistical tests.

When generalization to a target population is the objective, you should strive to define a sampling universe or frame using a selection procedure with known error limits and one that represents the population of interest. This usually entails a random sample of some kind. There is a vast literature on sampling theory and random sampling procedures, including discussions of sample sizes (see, for example, Bernard [1994] for a summary and Babbie [1990] for detailed discussion of sampling issues).

Cook and Campbell (1979) discuss two sampling models for increasing external validity in quasi-experiments. These models don't necessarily involve random selection and are consequently less powerful than are random samples. In one approach, the *model of deliberate sampling for heterogeneity,* target classes of units, whether classes or categories of persons, places, times, or events, are deliberately chosen to represent the range of such classes found in the population. Thus, testing for a treatment effect across a wide range of classes in the set of all possible classes (including both extremes and the modal class) in the population allows the researcher to say something about how the effect holds in a variety of settings. While this might not be generalized to the population as a whole, it does inform the researcher if an effect holds across wide ranging classes within the population. The logic behind this model can be extended beyond the quasi-experimental case to observational studies. Kempton et al. (1996) used a static-group comparative design sampling across a range of groups that varied with respect to their values on environmental issues. Kempton et al. interviewed members of Earth First (a radical environmentalist group) and dry cleaning shop owners (who depend on toxic chemicals for their business).

For some populations, it may be impossible to develop a sampling frame from which to draw a sample. In these cases, there are a variety of solutions, including intercept sampling, snowball sampling, random walks, quota sampling, and purposive sampling. Each of these approaches has potential problems, and most do not allow for generalizations about a population since they involve elements of unknown error even if the method involves some form of random selection criteria (for example, random selection of locations in which to intercept respondents).

Nonprobability sampling methods have come to be associated with qualitative approaches or for the selection of ethnographic informants, particularly key informants or consultants (Werner and Schoepfle 1987; Johnson 1990; Miles and

Huberman 1994). In some cases, a researcher may not be interested in generalizing to a population but may just want to know whether two subgroups obtained from a snowball sample differ with respect to some variable of interest. In that case, much of the bias in the sample is a matter of the logic used in the original selection of sample seeds and any statistical analysis of the data must be concerned about violations of assumptions for the particular statistical test to be employed (for example, independence of observations or random sample from a population). Such matters are particularly germane for observational designs using various social network approaches (see Johnson [1994] for a review).

How samples are chosen is an important element of any research design. If you are interested in generalizing to a given population, random sampling of some kind is essential. If generalization is not a primary goal, then sampling requirements may be relaxed. In most cases, if you can use a random sample, do it! No matter what the sampling method, you should be *explicit* about how you chose the sampling units. This increases the chances of detecting potential bias and also makes replication feasible. Replication is extremely important to external and other types of validity, such as construct validity. Random sampling has been a primary requirement in the proper application of parametric statistics. If you don't use random sampling, pay careful consideration to possible violations of assumptions for a given statistical test.

Recent developments in randomization and computer-intensive methods of statistical analysis involve less restrictive assumptions concerning the data (for example, assumption of a random sample from a population or skewed, sparse, or small sample sizes), opening the way for the development of new test statistics particularly suited for the problem at hand (Noreen 1989; Johnson and Murray 1997). These new approaches seem particularly well suited for the imperfect world of ethnographic research, where the rather restrictive assumptions of parametric analysis are often difficult to meet. But it is critical to remember the connection between theory, design (including sampling), and data analysis from the beginning, because how the data were collected, both in terms of measurement and sampling, is directly related to how they can be analyzed. The next section shows how concern for the elimination of potential errors and bias through design and attention to methodological detail applies to discussions about the findings of Margaret Mead and Derek Freeman in Samoa.

Mead Versus Freeman: Research Design as Mediator

Derek Freeman's (1983) criticism of Margaret Mead's work and her findings in Samoa has led to reactions from anthropologists who come from different epistemological traditions. Some have defended Mead (Shankman 1996); others have pointed to the biases and flaws in Freeman's argument (Marcus 1983; Ember 1985).

The criticisms and counter-criticisms are difficult to assess, given the time between Mead's and Freeman's studies, the differences in locations of their work, and the differences in their ideological positions (Ember 1985). Freeman contended that some of Mead's informants lied to her and that Mead's commitment to a particular ideological position caused her to evaluate evidence incorrectly. We certainly cannot hold Mead to the design standards available today. Still, it is instructive to review her work through a contemporary design lens, noting how slight modifications in design and method could have thwarted later criticisms.

Mead used what can be referred to as a static group comparison design with a conjectural treatment group. The comparison group, Samoan adolescent girls, was compared to a conjectural treatment group, American adolescent girls, to test the proposition that exposure to Western civilization increases adolescent trauma. Implicit in this proposition is the overall theoretical notion that culture is the major factor contributing to human behavior. Brim and Spain (1974) recognized several problems in the design that could have affected Mead's ability to draw valid conclusions.

- There were no equivalent measurement procedures for the two groups. In her use of a conjectural treatment group, Mead assumed some things about American adolescents without collecting comparable data. Mead relied mostly on herself as an instrument to measure the variables of interest.
- There were possible problems with interaction between selection and the effects of extraneous variables. That is, any observed difference between the two groups with respect to the dependent variable, adolescent trauma, might have been due to one or several extraneous (unmeasured) factors and might have had nothing to do with the independent variable, exposure to Western culture.
- In lieu of the between-culture comparisons, Mead could have made a within-case comparison that would have suffered less from problems with possible sources of error. She could have chosen comparison groups that were as similar as possible in order to rule out the effects of unmeasured variables as much as possible. For example, Mead could have compared girls living in the households of native pastors to those who did not. She could then have tested the proposition that exposure to competing standards of sexual morality leads to higher levels of emotional distress in adolescents.

More recently, Martin Orans did fieldwork in Samoa. Some of his experiences were incongruent with Mead's descriptions. Orans (1996) reanalyzed Mead's field notes and correspondence and once again found that her depiction of Samoa as a halcyon society was at odds with his own impression of Samoa as much more agonistic. If Samoa was not, during Mead's day, a halcyon society, then her conclusions might have been flawed. Orans's work was, of course, many years after Mead's, and he worked at different field sites than did Mead. But, in common with Brim and Spain, Orans found itemized problems with Mead's research design.

- There was a lack of comparisons between various sources of data that were crucial to Mead's argument. For example, Mead made an assertion concerning the relationship between the size of residential units and adolescent troubles. She did not, however, make any systematic comparisons among the different units. Similar to the observation by Brim and Spain, Orans points out that Mead made no comparison of sexual behavior between girls living in a native pastor's household and girls living with their own family.
- There is a lack of well-defined samples for both people and events. Mead makes assertions about the rarity of events without any knowledge of the frequency distribution of all such events. In addition, she had a tendency to understate the population and overstate the proportion of girls in her study.
- There is a lack of specificity in the development and operationalization of key concepts. For example, there was no measurement on which to compare differences in stress experienced by adolescents in Samoa and the United States.

For Brim and Spain, and for Orans, Mead's research design limited her ability to draw the conclusions she did. More attention to issues of research design and methods would have improved her chances to make valid claims and possibly limited later criticism of her work. In ethnographic research, no matter the mix of methods, the design of the study should allow for an ethnographers' hypotheses or hunches to be rejected as well as confirmed (Campbell 1975).

Research Design in Anthropological Practice: Systematic Research Strategies

The following examples illustrate some of the issues discussed so far. Several examples are reviews of studies that incorporate comparative designs of various types in which nonequivalent groups are constructed in order to control for as many extraneous factors as possible, and the manipulation of independent variables is a function of how comparative groups were chosen. These examples show how, even for less powerful designs, the interplay of exploratory and explanatory approaches can aid in guarding against threats to validity (Robson 1993).

Field Experiments

In field experiments, the experimenter has little control over all possible extraneous factors and the experiment may not involve random assignment of subjects to groups. Nevertheless, field experiments can be quite informative and, if carefully constructed, can provide formal tests of hypotheses derived from and complementary with ethnography. In his work on "colonizing the night," Melbin (1987) theorized that the night was a frontier, not unlike the western United States in the nineteenth century. Frontiers have certain features in common. Among other things, they provide escape and opportunity, tolerate a wider range of behaviors, consist of isolated settlements, have fewer status distinctions, involve novel hardships, have decentralized authority, involve lawlessness and peril, have a reputation for helpfulness and sociability, lag in the development of policies to exploit and regulate, and involve a variety of interest group conflicts.

Melbin conducted four tests of the feature relating to helpfulness and sociability. He designed a clever experiment in which keys were placed at similar locations during each two-hour field visit over a 24-hour period covering day and night. The idea was to see if there were a difference in key-returning behaviors among the different times. According to Melbin, "To find a key is to come across an implied need for help" (p. 75). The hypothesis was that residents of the night would return keys on average more often than those of the day. The keys had the request to "Please Return," with an address encased in plastic (keys dropped in the mailbox were delivered by the U.S. Postal Service to the address on the keys with postage due). Each of the keys were coded so they could be identified as to what time of day they were picked up and from what location.

In all, 326 keys were picked up, of which 220 were returned. Returned keys were also scored for the manner in which they were sent. One point was given for keys dropped unwrapped in the mail, two points for keys returned wrapped in an envelope, and three points if the envelope contained a personal note. Contrary to expectations, night-timers were not more amiable than day-timers in their key-returning behaviors; in fact, they were the least "helpful." However, Melbin's three other tests supported the hypothesis of more sociability and helpfulness at night.

Melbin speculates that the variation in results may have been due to the fact that the other three experiments involved direct personal contact among the subjects, while the key experiment involved no such interactions. This example illustrates nicely the importance of not relying on a single test, but having multiple tests and measures (Stinchcombe 1987). Had Melbin conducted only the key experiment, he may have come to very different conclusions regarding the helpfulness and sociability of night-timers. This example also shows how readily multiple tests can be incorporated into a research design within a field setting.

In all research, but particularly in field experiments like the one described above, there should be a concern for ethics and the well-being of experimental participants. Unlike studies where informed consent is obtained prior to participation, in experiments like Melbin's, individuals often participate without knowing about it. The ramifications and consequences of experimental outcomes must be considered thoroughly before any experimental design is implemented.

Control and Treatment in a Two-Community Comparative Design

One of the central concerns of medical anthropologists has been to better understand the relationship between health-related behaviors and native perceptions about illness. Young and Garro's (1982) investigation of treatment choice in two Mexican communities is an example of a static-group comparison where the presence or absence of the treatment is based on selection criteria not directly under the control of the researchers. One of the primary purposes of the research design was the elimination of competing hypotheses—the hallmark of good research design—and the testing of the primary hypothesis is an example of descriptive inference, as opposed to statistical inference. Descriptive inference is an approach highly suited for much anthropological research.

An important issue in this area of research concerns the factors influencing the use of Western treatments among non-Western populations. One explanation views use tied to congruence between a client's medical beliefs and scientific medical theory: the higher the congruence, the more likely the client will choose a physician's treatment. Termed the "conceptual-incompatibility" hypothesis, a number of studies have suggested that such a congruence was the primary determinant of treatment choice among Third World peoples. Young and Garro took a different stance, stressing physician accessibility as the most important determinant of physician use. An important element of this position is that traditional medical beliefs are not a barrier to choice of physician treatment.

The research design included the comparison of two Mexican communities that were similar in terms of cultural traditions and economies but varied in terms of access to Western medical services. The town of Pichátaro had restricted access (a 20-minute bus ride from Uricho), while the town of Uricho had easy access. From a random sample of approximately 10% of the households in each of the towns, Young and Garro collected data on the number of illnesses that had occurred during the previous two months and the treatment each had received. Later, the researchers collected triads data and what they call term-frame data on informants' perceived similarity of illnesses.

Young and Garro tested the two main hypotheses in sequence. They had to establish differences in treatment choice behavior in the two communities before they could assess any hypotheses concerning differences in beliefs. Using a standard chi-square test, the authors found a significant difference in the frequency distribution of treatment alternatives between the two towns, with the exception of folk curers. Thus, the two communities seemed to differ in their use of Western medical services. This established, Young and Garro could then test the second hypothesis relating to the similarity in beliefs between the two communities. Ironically, in statistical terms, the authors have more interest in the null hypothesis of no difference in beliefs than in the alternative hypothesis of a difference in beliefs between the two communities. Using multidimensional scaling, Young and Garro (1982) compared the belief data and found striking similarities in the medical beliefs of communities. They conclude:

> On the basis of the data from the triads study and the term-frame interviews, we see little reason to reject the "null hypothesis" of no significant differences between the responses of the two groups of informants. This leads us to the conclusion that the substantial variation apparent in the use of a physician's treatment between the two samples, a consequence of differential access to such treatment, occurs without corresponding degrees of variation in resident's attitudes and beliefs about illness. (p. 1462)

The authors' careful attention to research design and analytical issues contributed to the production of impressive evidence that casts doubt on the validity of the "conceptual-incompatibility" hypothesis. Note that the analysis used to test the hypothesis concerning similarities in beliefs involved descriptive inference, not statistical inference. Despite the authors' claims of finding no "significant difference," there was no real way, at least when the study was conducted, to assess the extent to which any differences were significant in the sense of statistical probability. Recent developments in statistical procedures allow us to assess the similarities in aggregated judged-similarity matrices between the two communities (see Handwerker and Borgatti, this volume, and Hubert 1987). In Young and Garro's case, a visual inspection of the graphical representations of the data could lead to no other conclusion than that there was little or no difference in beliefs between the two communities (see Figure 3). This distinction is important, particularly with regard to anthropological research, in that hypothesis-testing research can be done without narrowly restricting it to analytical methods using statistical inference.

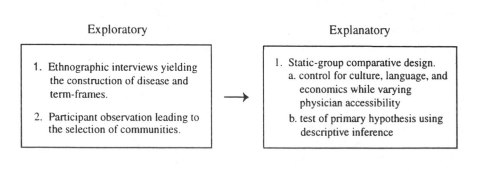

Figure 3. Overall design framework for the Young and Garro study.

There are, of course, threats to validity in this study. Because respondents weren't randomly assigned into comparison groups, it's difficult to know the influences of confounding variables on physician utilization and beliefs about illness. It is unrealistic to suppose that Young and Garro could have randomly assigned community members to the different comparison groups in order to control for confounding variables and then subject their informants to the treatments of interest. Given a lack of pretest observations, we can only assume that beliefs were similar prior to the availability of physicians in Uricho. In lieu of equalization through randomization, Young and Garro, through extensive ethnographic background research, produced groups that, although nonequivalent in the quasi-experimental sense, shared similarities with regard to a number of important characteristics. This isn't perfect, but a greater in-depth exploratory understanding and an explicit discussion of design can enhance our chances for the production of valid explanations.

Comparative Design and Ethnobiology

Ethnobiologists have long debated whether folk biological classifiers are natural historians who compare animals on the basis of their morphological characteristics or pragmatists who compare on the basis of the utility of organisms. Boster and Johnson (1989) explored this issue in an ethnobiological study of fish. Were individual informants classifying organisms on the basis of form or function? Boster and Johnson used a static group comparison design to compare several groups of expert fishermen with a group of novice fishermen. This is analogous to treatment and control groups without the random assignment of subjects to experimental units and where the treatment is implied rather than researcher directed (that is, natural differences in experience with fish). In the comparison, both culture and language were held constant while experience with fish was varied. Four groups—from North Carolina, East Florida, West Florida, and Texas—were sampled to examine the effects of different kinds of experience since there are regional variation in species abundance.

To ensure that experts were, in fact, experienced recreational fishermen, the rosters of sport fishing clubs in each region were sampled at random. The selection of control group subjects, by contrast, involved a purposeful selection procedure in which potential subjects were screened for recreational fishing experience. Using a questionnaire to gain background information, 15 college undergraduates who had the least amount of recreational fishing experience were selected from two introductory anthropology classes. These students were the control group. Each of the four expert groups comprised 15 subjects chosen at random from a larger sample of recreational fishermen. Thus the groups to be compared consisted of five groups of 15 subjects, four consisting of experts and one of novices.

All the groups were shown cards with artists' renderings and the common names of 43 marine species commonly found from North Carolina to Texas. Individuals were asked to perform an unconstrained judged similarity of the fish—a free pile sort (see Weller, this volume, and Weller and Romney 1988). Further, beliefs about the use and functional characteristics of the fish obtained from extensive ethnographic interviews were turned into a sentence-frame completion task described by Weller and Romney (1988). Finally, a measure of morphological similarities was determined, using taxonomic distances between pairs of fish. Boster and Johnson used statistical and graphical methods to evaluate whether experts' and novices' judgments of fish, at the aggregate and individual levels, were closer to the morphological characteristics of fish (taxonomic distance) or the uses of fish (beliefs about use). Using statistical and descriptive inference, the authors concluded that whether informants use form or function for classification depends on the knowledge base of the informants and the methods used to test their knowledge (see Figure 4).

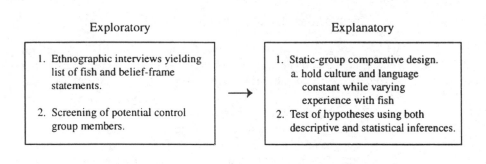

Figure 4. Overall design framework for the Boster and Johnson study.

Some of the criticisms of the Young and Garro study apply to this example as well. Lack of random assignment of subjects to treatment and control groups and pretest observations limit the ability to make causal inferences. But the in-depth ethnographic background research, the particular structure of the hypothesis, and the overwhelming reliability of informant responses make for more confidence in the possible validity of the study's conclusions.

Exploratory Research and the Development of Cultural Models

Often the primary objective of research design is more a matter of discovery and exploration than the testing of hypotheses. Although such designs are less driven by an established theoretical framework, there still is need to pay careful attention to a number of design details in the proper development of new theories and models.

An example of research in this mode is Naomi Quinn's (1996) development of Americans' cultural models concerning marriage.

There is a body of literature that views the interaction of culture with the individual as so deeply unique and personal as to not be researchable in terms of cultural universals, coherence, or even sharing. In contrast, Quinn views culture as being shared—that there are cultural models for a variety of domains that are widely held in common, and that these models can be developed from the discourses of cultural members.

Based on in-depth interviews with 22 informants, Quinn (1996) attempted to build a cultural model of Americans' reasoning about marriage. Because she was interested in a model that was shared, it was crucial to interview a wide range of couples who, although of the same culture, were not just from one region of the country or of only one ethnicity, religion, or social class. As she puts it:

> All of my interviewees were residents of the same middle-sized southeastern city or its immediate environs; all were native-born Americans who spoke English as a first language; and all were married during the period of their interviews, all in first marriages. Beyond these constancies of cultural and marital experience, they were selected to maximize diversity with regard to such obvious differences as their occupations and educational backgrounds, religious affiliations and ethnic and racial identities, their neighborhoods and social networks, and the duration of their marriages. (p. 399)

Although not generally representative of either the regional population or of the population of the United States, Quinn claims that her sample of informants represents the regions' population in terms of the high degree of recent in-migration to the area from regions outside the South. Her sample is an attempt to capture the range of diversity found in the region. In my view, the consistency of her findings in this diverse sample of informants makes her case stronger (see Johnson 1990). That is, finding commonality in the face of diversity provides stronger evidence of a shared cultural model (Johnson and Griffith 1996). In principle, this is similar to Cook and Campbell's (1979) model of deliberate sampling for heterogeneity as one of several means for warding off threats to external validity.

Based on an in-depth analysis of informants' discourse about marriage, Quinn produced a cultural model incorporating a number of causal links in informants' reasoning as to a "lasting marriage" (see Figure 5). Although the model appeared to be widely shared among informants from Quinn's sample and data collected from other studies on marriage, research still has to be designed to test this model across settings and researchers.

Issues of validity in this case are not as overriding as they would be in a purely explanatory study. Quinn was careful and diligent in her selection of informants, and her diligence certainly contributes to the potential validity of her model. However, further research in the explanatory mode is now warranted.

Exploratory

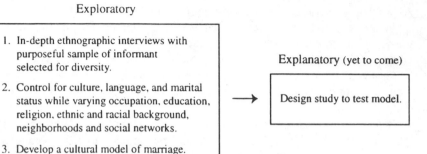

1. In-depth ethnographic interviews with purposeful sample of informant selected for diversity.

2. Control for culture, language, and marital status while varying occupation, education, religion, ethnic and racial background, neighborhoods and social networks.

3. Develop a cultural model of marriage.

Explanatory (yet to come)

Design study to test model.

Figure 5. Overall design framework for the Quinn study.

Participant Observation and the Search for Validity

As seen in Figure 2, exploratory and descriptive research are often essential components of an overall explanatory research design. In a series of papers, Koester (1996) and his colleagues (Koester et al. 1996) offer excellent examples of the role of participant observation in more clearly defining the set of HIV risk behaviors surrounding injection drug use. In most earlier research on injection drug users (IDUs) and HIV risk, the primary risk factor was viewed in terms of direct needle sharing. Thus, most large epidemiological studies of IDUs focused mainly on direct sharing behaviors in attempts to understand seroconversion rates and other risk factors.

Based on participant observation among IDUs, Koester (1996) identified nine other behaviors that were outside the realm of the direct sharing of a single syringe by two or more IDUs. Termed "indirect sharing," these nine behaviors can promote the transmission of HIV among IDUs who, although not sharing needles directly, often share water for mixing of drugs or for rinsing syringes, share drug-mixing containers (cookers and spoons), share cottons for filtering, and share the actual drug solution itself. These findings are undeniably important for larger epidemiological work that examines elements of IDUs' behaviors and such things as producing valid models of seroconversion.

In a subsequent study, Koester et al. (1996) used these additional distinctions in sharing to look at the prevalence of injection-related HIV risk behaviors among several subpopulations of injection drug users (see Figure 6). A major component of the study was the comparison of IDUs who engaged in both direct sharing and indirect sharing with IDUs who engaged in indirect sharing only and those who several subpopulations of injection drug users (see Figure 6). A major component of the study was the comparison of IDUs who engaged in both direct sharing and indirect sharing with IDUs who engaged in indirect sharing only and those who neither shared directly nor indirectly. Statistical tests of group differences provided a greater understanding of the risk factors associated with the different types of behavior. This is a good example of the application of exploratory research in the production of better measures of potentially important explanatory variables.

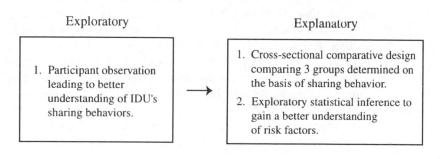

Figure 6. Overall design framework for the Koester and Koester et al. studies.

Case-Control Study Design: *Susto*, A Folk Illness

Here we look at an example of a study design used to investigate the extent to which disease is molded by culture. Rubel et al. (1985) report on a study of a folk illness known as *susto*, found in many cultural groups throughout North and South America. Folk beliefs surrounding *susto* attribute loss of a critical substance or force due to a frightening experience. The authors were interested in three primary hypotheses relating to role performance and the presence of the illness, psychiatric impairment and *susto*, and relationship between organic disease and *susto*. The ultimate aim of the study was to show the relationship between various social forces and *susto* susceptibility.

The design involved three communities that differed in history, language, and culture but had similarities in social, demographic, and economic factors. Rubel et al. carefully selected communities that were as similar as possible in terms of forms of government and gender-specific role expectations. The proposed design could have been conducted in a single community, but the authors felt that the generalizability of the results would be enhanced with a multiple case-control study design.

One subsample was of individuals who complained of *susto* during the fieldwork or who had admitted their condition to relatives or curers. Selection depended on the condition by men in the community and may also have affected the reporting of the condition by women. Another problem involved the existence of more social stratification in one community than expected, leading to a lower incidence of reported cases of the illness (higher-income people recognized the condition but felt that belief in it was more superstitious than real). However, Rubel et al. felt comfortable with the comparability among the *susto* subsamples from the communities. These groups will be referred to as the *asustados* groups.

The researchers were careful to make the control group as comparable to the *asustados* groups as possible. Because the *asustados* were "sick," control group members must also be sick. Thus, sick people were compared to sick people and control group members were selected from the pool of patients at the project clinics in each of the communities. Patient records provided the information on which to make the final selection. In addition to the control group being sick, males were matched with males and females with females and *asustados* and controls were matched in terms of age. Matched pairs were made within communities only. This design allowed for a variety of comparisons, including comparisons by controls and *asustados*, by gender, and by matched pairs both within and between cultural groups (see Figure 7).

Symptomology and health problems were operationalized using a panel of physicians. Psychiatric impairment was operationalized using the 22-item Screening Score for Psychiatric Impairment. Based on earlier ethnographic research, social stress, an important component for understanding an individual's inability to perform social roles, was operationalized using the Social Stress Gauge developed by one of the researchers.

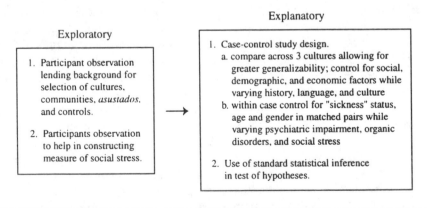

Figure 7. Overall design framework for the Rubel et al. study.

Using standard methods of statistical inference, Rubel et al. found that there was, in fact, an association between *susto* and an individual's perception of the adequacy of his or her performance of critical social roles. Although there was no association between *susto* and psychiatric impairment, there was a relationship between *susto* and the suffering of more organic disease signs.

This study is important because of the authors' candor about the potential threats to validity they encountered in conducting the research. The stigma of *susto* among males and the greater social stratification encountered in one of the communities are possible threats to the validity of their conclusions. But the researchers' awareness of the problems, combined with the strength of their multiple case-control study design, increases our confidence in their conclusions. This is an excellent example of a study design that incorporates within-study replication or multiple tests of a theory. Multiple tests are always much more convincing than a single test (Stinchcombe 1987).

Multimethod Ethnography and the Comparison of Models

Many peasant societies in Central America are experiencing dramatic economic and cultural change. One consequence of these changes is increasing economic differentiation. Parallel to these economic changes, there has been a shift in religious preference over the last 70 years. For some researchers, the shift from Catholicism to Protestantism helps account for economic change, as Protestantism is more compatible with capitalist ideology and the accumulation of wealth. Goldin (1996) wanted to understand the relationships among religious affiliation, economic ideology, occupation, and economic status in a Guatemalan township (Almolonga). Her study design incorporates quantitative and qualitative methods in the overall ethnographic enterprise.

Based on extensive participant observation, Goldin constructed four plausible models that might account for what she observed while in the field. Using her experience as a participant observer, Goldin developed a survey which she applied to a random sample of 10% of the heads of households in the township (n = 57). She made an earnest attempt to control for as many biases as possible and, using the data collected during the survey, conducted statistical tests of the four competing models. This provided for an evaluation of the explanatory power of each. Her selection of variables allowed a comparison of different levels (for example, Catholic versus Protestant) across the four variables. Using path analytic modeling, she applied different statistical controls in each of the competing models. As she describes the process leading to the selection of the best model:

> The results of my study, of course, must be interpreted within the constraints of the data collection methods. First, qualitative approaches were used to suggest different mechanisms and relationships that might be operating within Almolonga. Then, a

survey approach was used to evaluate the viability of these mechanisms in terms of characterizing general trends within Almolonga. My conclusions must be interpreted in terms of these general trends. I don't doubt that there are exceptions to them. Indeed, I interacted with several individuals who had life histories that were inconsistent with my general characterization and who were the basis for suggesting the competing models discussed above. However, when a large representative sample of the township was aggressively pursued, the different data sets tended to support model C as the one that characterizes the general tendencies within the township. (p. 72)

This study is an example of multimethod ethnography in which there was a combination of exploratory and explanatory approaches—that is, qualitative data and tests of models with data collected using a cross-sectional design. The combination helped Goldin in the specification of appropriate variables, in the development of a sound survey instrument, and in the specification and assessment of the four competing models. The study shows how the use of multiple methods fosters triangulation that contributes to the production of valid conclusions (see Figure 8). Her research design illustrates the danger in relying on a single method without attention to sampling. Had Goldin relied exclusively on, say, the life histories of a nonprobabilistic sample of informants without specified selection criteria (Johnson 1990), she might have arrived at a very different, and possibly erroneous, conclusion.

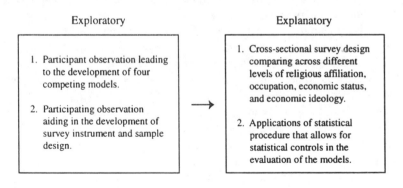

Figure 8. Overall design framework for the Goldin study.

Summary

This review of research design and strategies in cultural anthropology only scratches the surface of the research designs, hybrid designs, and combinations of designs possible within an ethnographic context. The newer forays into experimental and other ethnographic forms of presentation are more reflexive in character and more concerned with believable and moving representations rather than the production of valid accounts or conclusions.

With advances in computer technology, qualitative data analysis can now be a powerful mode to test theories. Similarly, advances in computer-intensive methods for testing hypotheses have the potential to expand the range of designs possible, particularly in the imperfect world of fieldwork (Johnson and Murray 1997). The strength of the ethnographic approach is its ability to incorporate a wide range of methods, strategies, and designs within a single enterprise, all combining in ways to improve the chances for credible results.

As anthropologists, we should take full advantage of both our current understanding of research design and these new developments to produce a "powerful mode of argumentation." It is mostly through attention to these concerns that anthropology and anthropologists will have the opportunity to, as Agar says, "move the world."

REFERENCES

Agar, M. 1980. *The Professional Stranger: An Informal Introduction to Ethnography.* New York: Academic Press.

Agar, M. 1996. *AAA Newsletter.* January.

Babbie, E. 1990. *Survey Research Methods*, 2d ed. Belmont, CA: Wadsworth.

Behar, R. 1993. *Translated Woman.* Boston: Beacon Press.

Bernard, H. R. 1994. *Research Methods in Anthropology: Qualitative and Quantitative Approaches*, 2d ed. Walnut Creek, CA: AltaMira Press.

Boas, F. 1920. The Methods of Ethnology. *American Anthropologist 22*(4):311–321.

Boster, J. S., and J. C. Johnson. 1989. Form or Function: A Comparison of Expert and Novice Judgments of Similarity Among Fish. *American Anthropologist 91*(4): 866–889.

Brim, J. A., and D. H. Spain. 1974. *Research Design in Anthropology: Paradigms and Pragmatics in the Testing of Hypotheses.* New York: Holt, Rinehart and Winston.

Campbell, D. T. 1975. "Degrees of Freedom" in the Case Study. *Comparative Political Studies 8*(2):178–213.

Campbell, D. T. 1988. Qualitative Knowing in Action Research. In *Methodology and Epistomology for Social Science: Selected Papers* E. S. Overman, ed. Pp. 360–376. Chicago: University of Chicago Press.

Cook, T. D. 1994. *Criteria of Social Scientific Knowledge: Interpretation, Prediction, Praxis.* Lanham, MD: Rowman and Littlefield.

Cook, T. D., and D. T. Campbell. 1979. *Quasi-Experimentation: Design and Analysis for Field Settings.* Chicago: Rand McNally.

Denzin, N. K., and Y. S. Lincoln. 1994. Entering the Field of Qualitative Research. In *Handbook of Qualitative Research*. N. K. Denzin and Y. S. Lincoln, eds. Pp. 1–19. Thousand Oaks, CA: Sage Publications.

Ellen, R. F. 1984. Introduction. In *Ethnographic Research: A Guide to General Conduct*. R. F. Ellen, ed. Pp. 1–12. London: Academic Press.

Ember, M. 1985. Evidence and Science in Ethnography: Reflections on the Mead-Freeman Controversy. *American Anthropologist* 87(4):906–910.

Faia, M. A. 1993. *What's Wrong with the Social Sciences? The Perils of the Postmodern*. Lanham, MD: University Press of America.

Freeman, D. 1983. *Margaret Mead and Samoa: The Making and Unmaking of an Anthropological Myth*. Cambridge: Harvard University Press.

Glaser, B. G., and A. L. Strauss. 1967. *The Discovery of Grounded Theory: Strategies for Qualitative Research*. Chicago: Aldine.

Goldin, L. R. 1996. Models of Economic Differentiation and Cultural Change. *Journal of Quantitative Anthropology* 1–2(6):49–74.

Harris, M., J. G. Consorte, J. Lang, and B. Byrne. 1993. Who Are the Whites: Imposed Census Categories and the Racial Demography of Brazil. *Social Forces* 72(2): 451–462.

Hubert, L. J. 1987. *Assignment Methods in Combinational Data Analysis*. New York: Marcel Dekker.

Hurlbert, S. H. 1984. Pseudoreplication and Design of Ecological Field Experiments. *Ecological Monographs* 54(2):187–211.

Johnson, J. C. 1990. *Selecting Ethnographic Informants*. Qualitative Research Methods Series, Vol. 22. Thousand Oaks, CA: Sage Publications.

Johnson J. C. 1994. Anthropological Contributions to the Study of Social Networks: A Review. In *Advances in Social Network Analysis*. S. Wasserman and J. Galaskiewicz, eds. Pp. 113–151. Thousand Oaks, CA: Sage Publications.

Johnson, J. C., and D. C. Griffith. 1996. Pollution, Food Safety, and the Distribution of Knowledge. *Human Ecology* 24(1):87–110.

Johnson, J. C., M. Ironsmith, A. L. Whitcher, G. M. Poteat, and C. W. Snow. 1997. The Development of Social Networks in Preschool Children. *Early Education and Development* 8(4):389–406.

Johnson, J. C., and J. D. Murray. 1997. Evaluating FAD Effectiveness in Development Projects: Theory and Praxis. In *Fish Aggregation Devices in Developing Fisheries: Potential and Pitfalls*. R. Pollnac and J. Poggie, eds. Pp. 143–158. Kingston: ICMRD.

Johnson, J. C., and R. Pollnac, eds. 1989. *Managing Marine Conflicts*. Special issue of *Ocean and Shoreline Management* 12(3).

Kempton, W., J. S. Boster, and J. A. Hartley. 1996. *Environmental Values in American Culture*. Cambridge: M.I.T. Press.

Kincheloe, J. L., and P. L. McLaren. 1994. Rethinking Critical Theory and Qualitative Research. In *Handbook of Qualitative Research*. N. K. Denzin and Y. S. Lincoln, eds. Pp. 138–158. Thousand Oaks, CA: Sage Publications.

Kirk, J., and M. L. Miller. 1986. *Reliability and Validity in Quantitative Research*. Qualitative Research Methods Series, Vol. 1. Thousand Oaks, CA: Sage Publications.

Kleinbaum, D. G., L. L. Kupper, and H. Morgenstern. 1982. *Epidemiologic Research: Principles and Quantitative Methods*. Belmont, CA: Lifetime Learning Publications.

Koester, S. 1996. The Process of Drug Injection: Applying Ethnography to the Study of HIV Risk Among IDU's. In *AIDS, Drugs and Prevention: Perspectives on Individual and Community Action*. T. Rhodes and R. Hartnoll, eds. Pp. 133–148. London: Routledge Press.

Koester, S., R. E. Booth, and Y. Zhang. 1996. The Prevalence of Additional Injection-Relation HIV Risk Behaviors Among Injection Drug Users. *Journal of Acquired Immune Deficiency Syndromes and Human Retrovirology 12*:202–207.

Kruskal, J. B., and M. Wish. 1978. *Multidimensional Scaling*. Beverly Hills, CA: Sage Publications.

Kuznar, L. A. 1997. *Reclaiming a Scientific Anthropology*. Walnut Creek, CA: AltaMira Press.

LeVine, R. A. 1973. Research Design in Anthropological Field Work. In *A Handbook of Methods in Cultural Anthropology*. R. Naroll and R. Cohen, eds. Pp. 183–195. New York: Columbia University Press.

Lowie, R. H. 1937. *The History of Ethnological Theory*. New York: Rinehart.

Marcus, G. 1983. One Man's Head. *New York Times Book Review, March 27*:3, 22–23.

Melbin, M. 1987. *Night as Frontier: Colonizing the World After Dark*. New York: The Free Press.

Miles, M. B., and A. M. Huberman. 1994. *Qualitative Data Analysis*, 2d ed. Thousand Oaks, CA: Sage Publications.

Moran, E. F., ed. 1995. *The Comparative Analysis of Human Societies: Toward Common Standards for Data Collection and Reporting*. Boulder: Lynne Rienner.

Naroll, R., and R. Cohen, eds. 1973. *A Handbook of Method in Cultural Anthropology*. New York: Columbia University Press.

Noreen, E. W. 1989. *Computer-Intensive Methods for Testing Hypotheses*. New York: John Wiley.

Orans, M. 1996. *Not Even Wrong: Margaret Mead, Derek Freeman, and the Samoans*. Novato, CA: Chandler and Sharp.

Panourgia, N. 1995. *Fragments of Death, Fables of Identity*. Madison: University of Wisconsin Press.

Pelto, P. J., and G. H. Pelto. 1978. *Anthropological Research: The Structure of Inquiry*, 2d ed. Cambridge: Cambridge University Press.

Plattner, S. In press. Scientific Anthropology at the National Science Foundation. In *Anthropology Between Science and the Humanities*. C. Furlow, ed. Walnut Creek, CA: AltaMira Press.

Porter, T. M. 1995. *Trust in Numbers*. Princeton: Princeton University Press.

Quinn, N. 1996. Culture Contradictions: The Case of America's Reasoning about Marriage. *Ethos 24*(3):391–425.

Rabinow, P. 1986. Representations are Social Facts: Modernity and Post-Modernity in Anthropology. In *Writing Culture: The Poetics and Politics of Ethnography*. J. Clifford and G. E. Marcus, eds. Pp. 234–262. Berkeley: University of California Press.

Ramos, A. R. 1995. *Sanuma Memories*. Madison: University of Wisconsin Press.

Robson, C. 1993. *Real World Research: A Resource for Social Scientists and Practitioner-Researchers*. Oxford: Blackwell Publishers.

Rubel, A. J., C. W. O'Nell, and R. Collado-Ardon. 1985. *Susto, A Folk Illness*. Berkeley: University of California Press.

Schneider, D. 1996. Alarming Nets. *Scientific American (September)*:40–42.

Schwandt, T. A. 1994. Constructivist, Interpretivist Approaches to Human Inquiry. In *Handbook of Qualitative Research*. N. K. Denzin and Y. S. Lincoln, eds. Pp. 118–138. Thousand Oaks, CA: Sage Publications.

Sechrest, L. 1973. Experiments in the Field. In *A Handbook of Methods in Cultural Anthropology*. R. Naroll and R. Cohen, eds. Pp. 196–209. New York: Columbia University Press.

Seidman, S. 1994. *The Postmodern Turn: New Perspectives on Social Theory*. Cambridge: Cambridge University Press.

Shankman, P. 1996. The History of Samoan Sexual Conduct and the Mead-Freeman Controversy. *American Anthropologist 98*(3):555–567.

Spindler, G., and W. Goldschmidt. 1973. An Example of Research Design: Experimental Design in the Study of Culture Change. In *A Handbook of Method in Cultural Anthropology*. R. Naroll and R. Cohen, eds. Pp. 210–219. New York: Columbia University Press.

Stinchcombe, A. L. 1987. *Constructing Social Theories*. Chicago: University of Chicago Press.

Taussig, M. 1987. *Shamanism, Colonialism, and the Wild Man: A Study in Terra and Healing*. Chicago: University of Chicago Press.

Tyler, S. A. 1991. A Post-modern In-stance. In *Constructing Knowledge: Authority and Critique in Social Science*. L. Nencel and P. Pels, eds. Pp. 78–95. London: Sage Publications.

Urry, J. 1984. A History of Field Methods. In *Ethnographic Research: A Guide to General Conduct*. R. F. Ellen ed. Pp. 35–62. London: Academic Press.

Van Maanen, J. 1988. *Tales of the Field: On Writing Ethnography*. Chicago: University of Chicago Press.

Weller, S. C., and A. K. Romney. 1988. *Systematic Data Collection*. Qualitative Research Methods Series, Vol. 10. Thousand Oaks, CA: Sage Publications.

Werner O., and G. M. Schoepfle. 1987. *Systematic Fieldwork*, Vol. 2. Thousand Oaks, CA: Sage Publications.

Whyte, W. F. 1984. *Learning from the Field: A Guide from Experience*. Newbury Park, CA: Sage Publications.

Williams, T. R. 1967. *Field Methods in the Study of Culture*. In the series *Studies in Anthropological Method*, George Spindler and Louise Spindler, eds. New York: Holt, Rinehart and Winston.

Young, J. C., and L. Y. Garro. 1982. Variation in the Choice of Treatment in Two Mexican Communities. *Social Science and Medicine 16*:1453–1465.

Zabusky, S. E. 1995. *Launching Europe: An Ethnography of European Cooperation in Space Science*. Princeton: Princeton University Press.

Five

Ethics

Introduction

Considerations of ethics are often raised after some incident has occurred or when an anthropologist feels discomfort about the conduct or progress of fieldwork. The anthropologist's methods may be questioned or his or her position in the social group may be challenged. Access to resource persons may have changed dramatically, or even been denied. Research goals may appear suddenly unattainable and, confused or desperate, the anthropologist may wonder what has gone wrong and why.

When the anthropological researcher and persons studied respect and trust one another, there are positive feelings and outcomes on both sides. However, if an anthropologist has had little or poor training for the field, it will be difficult for him or her to resolve the everyday dilemmas that are part of the practice of the discipline. For example, the anthropologist may not have been well prepared as to the social and political environments of the people to be studied. Or the anthropologist may receive funding from a private or public foundation without having fully considered the conflicting demands and responsibilities between the funder and the people studied. During the research, when the field situation changes and the anthropologist's position becomes ambiguous, the art of negotiating and repositioning oneself resolves to ethical principles and choices.

Matters of ethics are an ordinary, not extraordinary, part of anthropological practice. However, there have been some celebrated cases of alleged ethical misconduct involving major political events of the day. These occurred in Latin America in 1960s, in Vietnam in the 1960s and 1970s, and in the People's Republic of China in the 1980s. So, ethics and professional responsibilities have been

173

sensitive and controversial topics. Moreover, because ethical conduct may be perceived as overlapping with morality or personal principles, anthropologists, like other human beings, may be reluctant to talk about it for fear of "having done something wrong." Sometimes, just raising the issue of ethics in fieldwork causes a defensive reaction. The person being queried feels that he or she is being accused of wrongdoing rather than just being asked whether ethics have been considered in the fieldwork plan. In this chapter on ethics and methods in anthropological research, I want to focus on how to make ethical considerations an integral part of the ordinary, day-to-day practice of our craft.

History of Ethics in Anthropology

The history of ethical discourse in cultural anthropology intersects with national and international politics and the changing contexts and paradigms of fieldwork. Various incidents have precipitated crises that have forced anthropologists to hold a mirror up to ourselves and to be reflective about the consequences of our actions. Until recently, historical concern with matters of ethics has been more reactive than proactive, more defensive maneuvering than an affirmative tackling of ethical issues. However, significant changes have taken place since 1994, and I shall try to balance the broad historical picture of crises about ethics and anthropology with recent developments in the profession.

The first formal statement on ethics was developed by applied anthropologists in 1949, after discussions that began in the immediate post–World War II era. The Society for Applied Anthropology (SfAA) Committee was chaired by Margaret Mead, and saw its role as creating a document for general use by applied anthropologists. Since that time, the SfAA has amended its guidelines twice, in 1963 and 1983 (see, Statement on Ethics of the Society for Applied Anthropology 1963; and Proposed Statement on Professional and Ethical Responsibilities 1983). Nevertheless, fundamental issues of research—such as the relationship between anthropologist and research collaborators, employers, nongovernmental, or voluntary organizations, and the protection of informant confidentiality—are all significantly present in the statement. The American Anthropological Association (AAA) produced its first statement on ethics nearly two decades later, in 1967.

The first ethics "incident" took place in World War I. It involved Franz Boas, one of the most famous American anthropologists, indeed, perhaps the founder and designer of the unique holistic brand of American anthropology. A prolific writer and experienced ethnographer, Boas also had a strong civic sensibility and was a frequent contributor to numerous nonanthropological periodicals. In a letter published in *The Nation*, Boas, widely known as a pacifist, objected to the wartime activities of four anthropologists who had combined intelligence gathering with their research.

By accident incontrovertible proof has come to my hands that at least four men who carry on anthropological work, while employed as government agents, introduced themselves to foreign governments as representatives of scientific institutions in the United States, and as sent for the purpose of carrying on scientific research. They have not only shaken the truthfulness of science, but have also done the greatest possible disservice to scientific inquiry. (Boas 1919)

For this letter of protest, Boas was censured formally by the Anthropology Society of Washington and isolated in general by the anthropological establishment for having drawn the general public's attention to the activities of several anthropologists working as government intelligence gatherers. The issue eventually subsided, and Boas's career was not adversely affected, but sensitivities may have persisted for Boas did not resurrect the subject even though the same situation might have arisen during the years of World War II while he was still alive.

Throughout this century, the issue of anthropologists in the employ of government has retained its potency and significance. Indeed, the AAA drafted the first formal statement on ethics in 1967. This was in the wake of the U.S. Department of the Army's Project Camelot, after revelations that counterinsurgency research in Latin America was a major focus of the proposed social science research. The AAA's first statement on ethics makes explicit reference to the avoidance of the use of the name of anthropology, or the title of anthropologist, as a cover for intelligence activities (Statement 1967:sect. II.6).

A more recent example is that of federal funds made available through the Department of Defense's National Security Education Program (NSEP) for training in foreign language and international studies. The NSEP was established through legislation sponsored by Senator David Boren in 1991. The NSEP provides funds for undergraduate study abroad and fellowships for graduate students to strengthen the national capacity in international education in critical world areas (Preliminary Guidelines 1994–95 Pilot Grants Program, National Security Education Program).

Although funding for international studies had been declining and the Department of Defense monies were tempting, the NSEP was criticized by virtually every major area studies association—including the African Studies Association, the Middle East Studies Association, the Latin American Studies Association, and the Asian Studies Association. Further, their members and potential student applicants were cautioned about the risks of the relationship of foreign area studies scholars with military and intelligence-gathering organizations and priorities. The following resolution of the Middle East Studies Association conveys the types of concerns that the area studies associations had:

The Board of Directors of the Middle East Studies Association joins the African Studies Association and the Latin American Studies Association in expressing appreciation to Senator Boren for his leadership in developing the national Security Education Act. We also share their serious concerns about the administration of the act, in particular its location in the Department of Defense, and the involvement of the CIA on the National Security Education Board. [The MESA Board] deplores the location of responsibility in the U.S. Defense and intelligence community for a major foreign area research, education and training program of students and specialists. This connection can only increase the existing difficulties of gaining foreign governmental permissions to carry out research and to develop overseas instructional programs. It also can create danger for students and scholars by fostering the perception of involvement in military or intelligence activities, and may limit academic freedom. (Partial text of resolution adopted by MESA Board, 1992; the resolution was revised and passed by referendum vote of MESA membership in 1993; published in *Mesa Newsletter* 1994.)

The AAA, while it cautioned its members to negotiate and understand clearly their relationship to their own and host governments, did not take any specific action nor pass any resolution regarding the creation of NSEP. Perhaps the AAA took no direct action in the National Security Education Program because it was mindful of the need for the funding of international research, governmental or not, and aware of the more direct action and interest of the area studies associations. However, the broadly based reaction to the recent Department of Defense's NSEP is a reminder of the seriousness of the issue of the use or appearance of the use of anthropology or any discipline as a cover for intelligence gathering. It demonstrates the continuing relevance of Boas's admonition of 1919 to avoid such ties to defense, military, and intelligence agencies.

The Vietnam War era was the most important turning point for anthropology and other social sciences. It caused us to take matters of professional ethics seriously, to develop a code of conduct, and to provide a mechanism for enforcement. Once again, allegations that anthropologists had engaged in counterinsurgency research, this time in Thailand and Southeast Asia, precipitated a crisis in the field. Anthropologist was pitted against anthropologist, just as the entire American society was torn asunder by issues of politics and morality in the Vietnam war. The end result, after heated confrontations in print and in public meetings, was the formation of a Committee on Ethics and the drafting and promulgation of the first code of ethics by the AAA in 1971 (see Statement on Ethics: Principles of Professional Responsibility 1971). In this code, a strong first principle was enunciated that lasted for a generation: "In research the anthropologist's paramount responsibility is to those he studies. When there is a conflict of interest, these individuals must come first."

Today, even if more than half of anthropologists weren't female, the reference to "he" would be unacceptable, but this language illustrates that much has changed in ethics as well as gender since 1971. Other strong principles reflected the tenor of the times.

(1) that no secret or clandestine research be carried out; that even the appearance of conducting clandestine research hurts the good reputation of anthropology and its

practitioners; (2) that in relations with one's own and host governments anthropologists should not be required to compromise ethics as a condition for the conduct of research (3) when an anthropologist by his[her] actions jeopardizes peoples studied, colleagues, students or others the Association may inquire into the propriety of these actions and take appropriate measures. (Principles of Professional Responsibility 1971)

Tension Between Applied and Academic Anthropologists

In the decades after the end of the Vietnam War, the immediacy and intensity of these selected core principles faded dramatically as contract or proprietary research for governmental and nongovernmental agencies became more common and tended to neutralize the issue of secret/clandestine research for governments. This coincided with the post–Vietnam War economic downturn. Many professionally trained anthropologists were unable to secure academic employment, and some turned to professional work in the applied fields. This demographic transformation meant that in 1986, for the first time since the founding of the AAA in 1902, more anthropologists (51%) were employed outside of academia than within it (Fluehr-Lobban 1991a:5).

Throughout the 1980s, practicing anthropologists increased in such numbers so as to constitute something of a lobbying force within the AAA, and some formed a new professional organization, the National Association of Practicing Anthropologists (NAPA). It sought to revise the PPR to make it more accommodating to the interests and needs of professional, nonacademic anthropologists. In particular, the practicing anthropologists were concerned that the "first responsibility of the anthropologist to the people studied could not always be met under the terms of contract research." They attempted unsuccessfully to revise the PPR in 1984, again precipitating charged debates within the profession. They eventually created their own set of ethical guidelines that were more suited to the complexities of contract and proprietary research.

Many academic anthropologists, recalling the heady days in which the PPR was created, were reluctant to see any modification of the principle that the first responsibility in research is to the people studied. I have summarized some of the tensions between academic and applied anthropologists expressed during this time (Fluehr-Lobban 1991b), suggesting that the differences were significant enough to challenge the traditional holism of anthropology itself. Discussions of differences, real and imagined, between academic and practicing anthropologists, continued throughout the 1980s. They were carried out in various forums, including symposia at the annual AAA meetings, several of which I organized and chaired. These debates and discussions evoked the subtitle of my 1991 edited volume on ethics and the profession of anthropology, "dialogue for a new era" (Fluehr-Lobban 1991a).

Some subjective sources of tension between practicing anthropologists and academic anthropologists also surfaced during the the 1980s, when jobs for anthropologists were scarce. Academic anthropologists may have not have fully understood or were skeptical about the types of contract-based research with which practicing anthropologists were involved. And applied anthropologists may have experienced some isolation from the traditionally academically oriented discipline as they pioneered new venues for applying and using anthropological research. Some academic anthropologists asserted that their research was "pure," whereas applied research is compromised by the client-researcher relationship. These tensions have eased at present, as the job market has improved somewhat. The present revised code of ethics makes no distinction whatsoever between so-called pure and so-called applied research. Practicing anthropologists have contributed ideas and their perspective to the new code. In the end, research is research, period.

Call for Revision of the PPR, A Code for All of Anthropology

Beyond the tension between academic and practicing anthropologists, other weaknesses in the PPR were revealed. For example, a complex grievance procedure was provided for the AAA Committee on Ethics (COE). The procedure included receiving and screening cases, with the Executive Board being responsible for the final judgment and any action taken. However, not a single anthropologist has been censured since this function of the COE was adopted in 1976. What has happened was that the COE was primarily called on, time after time, to mediate disputes between colleagues over matters of plagiarism, employment, and personal differences. Based on her experience as former member and chair of the AAA COE, Janet Levy concluded that the grievance mechanism should be reviewed and possibly eliminated because of the complex procedures involving multiple levels of review and the slowness and general lack of resolution of intraprofessional disputes (Levy 1994).

In 1994, the AAA decided to reexamine systematically the underlying principles and practice of professional ethics within the discipline. A Commission to Review the AAA Statements on Ethics was formed in 1994 and continued its work through 1997. It was initiated by John Cornman, then executive director of AAA, and chaired by James Peacock, then president of AAA, and included AAA members from archaeology and physical anthropology, as well as applied and cultural anthropologists who have traditionally been at the center of ethics discourse. I was a member of this commission.[1]

The commission discussed changes in the PPR and reached consensus on a number of fundamental issues. After 2 years, the PPR was revised and a new code of ethics was drafted (see Fluehr-Lobban 1996). The most important procedural change is that the code shifts from one that has a grievance procedure with ability to sanction individual anthropologists to one that emphasizes ethics education. As mentioned above, over the nearly 25 years that the PPR had been in effect no anthropologist had been censured, so the "teeth" of the professional code had not been applied. Ethics education is preferred so that an ongoing discussion of ethical issues can take place as the profession develops and adapts to changing circumstances for anthropological research.

A major development is that, for the first time, the new code of the AAA speaks to ethical issues we confront in the four-field definition of American anthropology. "Anthropological researchers have primary ethical responsibility to the people, species, and materials they study and to the people with whom they work." This is a modification of the former "first responsibility" of the anthropologist to the people studied, a cornerstone principle of the 1971 PPR. Thus, the anthropologist is now enjoined to do no harm, to respect the well-being of humans and nonhuman primates, and to conserve the archaeological, fossil, and historical record.

Without being explicit, the new code reinforces and may even reinvigorate the integrative, holistic approach that has been the hallmark of American anthropology. It also reflects a reaction to the proliferation of codes of different anthropological groups. These codes had been developed in response to the realization or complaint that the AAA code didn't address their subgroup's concerns. For example, by 1995, when the new code was drafted, there were codes of professional ethics for the AAA (the PPR), the Society for Applied Anthropology, the NAPA, the Society of Professional Archaeologists, and the Archaeological Institute of America.[2]

The general admonition in the new code to "do no harm" is a basic principle in many professional codes and is purposefully broad. But in commenting on the draft code, NAPA judged this phrasing to be too simplistic. Practicing anthropologists, they argue, are involved in many types of research, frequently affecting individuals and groups with diverse and sometimes conflicting interests. In such cases of potential conflict, no absolute rule can be observed, but the individual practitioner must make carefully considered ethical choices and be prepared to make clear the assumptions, facts, and issues on which those choices are based (Jordan 1996:18).

The issue of secret or clandestine research, which has evoked such passion in the past, has gradually evolved to concerns over proprietary research, where anthropologists contract their services to an agency for a specified period of time and amount of funding. Clandestine research has been consistently criticized in previous codes and statements on ethics; proprietary research has been an area where applied and practicing anthropologists have urged their colleagues to be aware of possible conflicts between the interests of funders of research and the people studied. Presumably, anthropologists conducting pure research (probably more mythology than fact) were not constrained by their funders in the same ways that anthropologists conducting proprietary research are. The revised code extinguishes distinctions between pure and applied research—quite simply, research is research, and standards of ethical conduct in research are the same, irrespective of private or public funding. The new code does call for the open and accessible publication of research results within a reasonable period of time, which might be negotiated in advance, in order to ensure that secret research is not sanctioned.

The new code contains specific language regarding informed consent, which means that anthropology has situated itself within the broader scientific and professional community of scholars and scientists in the United States and increasingly in the world. The informed consent language is intended to encompass both the ethical and legal intent of this broad principle. This will be discussed in detail below.

Finally, the new code addresses the issue of advocacy in anthropology and whether this is an ethical responsibility. It was agreed that advocacy is very much a moral choice that may be made by individual anthropologists, but it is not a professional duty. When anthropologists choose advocacy, they should be cautious about the selective use of their data for whatever good cause is being advocated.

An Ethically Conscious Model of Anthropological Research

The foregoing discussion of the history of ethical discourse and concern within anthropology should demonstrate to the relative newcomer to the field that anthropologists and their professional associations take ethics seriously. Ethics should be considered first, not last, in anthropological fieldwork. Thinking about ethics should be a part of every research plan from beginning to end, from initial design, to pursuit of funding, through actual research, to eventual publication of results. There are many regulations that students and researchers become aware of only when conducting research, but a little advance preparation might allow them to make more informed and better decisions. The basic guidelines for the ethical conduct of research in anthropology, or any field, are openness and disclosure. The present draft code of the AAA is clear and unambiguous on this fundamental idea: "In both proposing and carrying out research, anthropologists must be open about the purpose(s), potential impacts, and source(s) of support for research projects with funders, colleagues, persons studied or providing information, and with relevant parties affected by the research" (Draft Code 1995:A.41).

Consideration of Ethics at Every Stage of Research and Publication

Anthropologists, and probably other researchers, like to think that they have complete freedom in the conduct of their research. "Just come up with a good idea and go and study it," might have been the advice of anthropologist-mentors in past generations. However, the complexities and sensitivities of conducting research in the postcolonial, non-Western world, not to mention studying American populations, make this absolutist position untenable today.

Potential Research Projects

From the initial concept of a research project, an anthropologist should ask him- or herself the following: Can I carry out the project without violating ethical standards or compromising professional standards? If there are questions about this—for example, concerning Native American rights to cultural and material property—can I modify the research to accommodate the legitimate interests of the group to be studied? Is negotiating the terms of research a possibility or, among some groups, a necessity? Have I discussed the ethical issues or questions with other anthropologists and mentors, with members of the ethics committee of my institution, with some representatives of the group I plan to study, if possible? Have I acquainted myself with the existence, guidelines, procedures of tribal, ethnic, or national review boards? If ethical considerations are sufficiently serious, should I consider abandoning the project?

Sources of Funding

In the next phase, the anthropologist should ask the following questions of him- or herself. Have I considered various sources of funding appropriate to the research and their potential regulatory role over the conduct of my research? Have I thought about the conditions that certain funding sources may impose upon my research? Have I answered the question in the affirmative, that I would be willing to disclose the source(s) of my funding to the people/group(s) studied? If the research is being funded by a nongovernmental organization, or if the funding is slated for very specific proprietary research, have I discussed with the funder the degree to which the research results will remain private, or eventually become a part of the public domain? Have I satisfied myself that the research is proprietary and not secret?

Using Data from Research

In the last phase, the anthropologist should think about the following: Have I considered the potential use(s) to which my research will be put? Have I resolved, to my own satisfaction, potential conflicts of interest between the client-funder and the people-culture researched?

The questions raised here are not simple ones, but if you ask and answer them satisfactorily *before* you begin your research, you will save yourself a good deal of anxiety and discomfort in the field. Such questions and answers might also be the proper doses of prevention that avoid disaster when communication and trust break down because openness and disclosure weren't practiced. Most people, irrespective of cultural difference, operate in good faith when they have the necessary information to make informed choices. If you're open with "informants," you give them the right to say no to your requests for information.

Proprietary and Secret Research

Students and researchers may be confused by the difference between proprietary and secret research. This is an especially sensitive subject for anthropology since it was allegations that secret research had been conducted in Southeast Asia that led to the crisis that produced the first AAA code of ethics.

Proprietary research is normally negotiated between client and researcher for a specific project, length of research, and terms of publication. Proprietary research is normally not "owned" by the researcher, but is research conducted for the client. Often, proprietary research is conducted for nongovernmental organizations, such as the World Bank, or nonprofit groups, such as "Save the Children." Usually, access to the published results of the research is not restricted.

In secret research, openness and disclosure of research intentions, funding, and outcome of research is normally not practiced with the people studied. Further, publication of research results is usually restricted and not available to the general public through usual avenues of distribution. Professional codes of ethics within the AAA, from 1971 to the present revisions, have stood firmly and consistently against anthropologists engaging in secret research of any kind. The present code says: "The researchers must have the intention and expectation to disseminate publicly results of the research within a reasonable period of time" (Draft Revised Code 1995).

Research Review Boards

All universities and colleges are mandated by federal guidelines to have Institutional Review Boards (IRBs) that are charged with the responsibility to review all research proposals that involve the conduct of research with human subjects.[3] The guidelines were originally established for research in the biomedical fields, but anthropologists are also bound by these regulations. Some anthropological research may be evaluated as being of minimal risk to research participants, such as the observation of public behavior.

Little anthropological research remains solely in the public domain. It often moves to a personal, closer relationship with human beings. Physical anthropology research may be classified as a type of biomedical research requiring informed consent. Archaeologists, though they work primarily with material culture, are nonetheless responsible to various "stakeholders," who may be representatives of indigenous peoples, state or national historic commissions, and/or their sponsors, each of whom has a special and sometimes conflicting interest with the other. Ideally in this situation, or a like one for cultural research, the anthropologist can play a constructive role as broker, negotiating and achieving compromise among the various interested parties. There is no subfield of anthropology, nor any part of the practice of anthropology, that is free of ethical responsibility.

There has been some resistance by anthropologists to being called before review boards, thereby having what we may view as our special field methods subjected to scrutiny. Perhaps because our research is comparative and most often conducted outside of the United States, we tend to believe that the rules don't apply to us. A parallel tendency sees anthropological research as unique and therefore not related to ideas or ethical practices that developed outside of our discipline. This view mistakenly adopts an exceptionalist view of anthropological research as being fundamentally different from other kinds of research. Again, research is research, and the rights of research participants don't vary whether they're studied by psychologists, cardiologists, or anthropologists. Nor do the responsibilities of the researchers vary substantially. Indeed, today much anthropological research is conducted in an interdisciplinary environment where ethical standards must be uniform.

Review boards themselves vary considerably. Some may take a strict or narrow interpretation of informed consent, requiring explanations of why anthropological research does not lend itself to the use of consent forms. IRBs may be sensitive or insensitive to issues in cross-cultural research, depending on the experiences of board members. Anthropologists would do well to consult with their IRB and perhaps open a dialogue with members about the nature and extent of federal and institutional regulation of their proposed research; an initial informal inquiry might make the formal request go more smoothly. The researcher might inquire how the research proposal would best address the expected standards of research practice while bringing up some of the particular cultural or linguistic issues that are a usual part of anthropological research.

A large amount of anthropological research today is carried out in the United States, and federal guidelines apply because the anthropologists are recipients of federal funding. These guidelines have been enacted since the publication of the last general *Handbook of Research Method in Cultural Anthropology* (Naroll and Cohen 1973). Researchers from outside the United States should acquaint themselves with comparable national or institutional review boards.

My own experience as a member and later chair of my home institution's Committee on Research with Human Participants is that review boards are user-friendly places that act more in an advisory capacity than as "courts of law," where researchers are given a thumbs up or down approval or rejection. Usually, in my experience, a research design that is flawed or insufficiently addresses issues of ethics can be discussed, negotiated, redesigned, improved, and eventually approved. The dialogue is what is important, all part of taking a proactive approach to ethics, not one based on the fear of alleged misconduct or wrongdoing. Don't be shy or intimidated about educating members of IRBs, or their equivalents, about the nature of anthropological research and the methods we use, and do negotiate issues or areas of possible disagreement with committee members.

Low-Risk, Unobtrusive Research

Much of anthropological or social scientific research may appear to be of low or minimal risk, with insignificant or no potential harm to participants. As such, federal regulations and institutional review may be exempt in cases of low or nil risk to those studied. The President's Commission for the Study of Ethical Problems in Medical, Biomedical and Behavioral Research (1980–83) adopted the view that consent need not be obtained for research characterized by the following conditions:

1. the observation of behavior on public places where questions of privacy do not exist;
2. review of publicly available information, including personal identity information;
3. research using low-risk methods, such as questionnaires, interviews, or tests in which agreement to participate effectively constitutes consent.

The first two might be considered unobtrusive research, where no observable risk to those studied can be shown. In the latter case, however, anthropologists should not exempt themselves from practicing full disclosure simply because they are using low-risk methods, such as using questionnaires or interviews. In administering tests, the potentially coercive relationship between test-giver and test-taker should be recognized as one where a power differential exists. Using students to fill out questionnaires within the classroom setting, for example, has a coercive dimension, and anthropologists should instead look for venues for research outside of the classroom.

Informed Consent

One of the areas where there may be disagreement about research methods and ethics is the subject of informed consent. This has become a virtual canon of ethics and research in all fields, whether the research is biomedical, behavioral, or social scientific (see Fluehr-Lobban 1994). The legal doctrine of informed consent grew out of the post–World War II world that was shaken to its moral and ethical core, not only by the revelation of Nazi atrocities, but by the collaboration of science with immoral and unethical practices. Originally developed for medical research, informed consent has expanded to include research with humans across the scientific-social scientific spectrum, with psychology having provided the historic bridge between the two. In 1995, the principle of informed consent was added to the new code of ethics of the American Anthropological Association.

Few anthropologists know this history or appreciate its relevance to their own research. Some may view informed consent in a rather mechanistic fashion because, frankly, in medical research, much of it has devolved to signing a form for legal purposes. This is unfortunate, because the genesis of informed consent and its guiding spirit is that of openness and disclosure in research practice. By extension, in social science research, using the spirit of informed consent means that the researcher actually discusses the methods and likely research outcome with the participant, thus the studier and the studied develop an open relationship. Ideally, informed consent opens up a two-way channel of communication that, once opened, allows for a continuous flow of information and ideas. This is the spirit of informed consent, rather than the mechanistic application of a form designed more to protect the researcher than the research participant.

In an article in *Human Organization,* I argued for the acceptance of the spirit of informed consent, combined with behavior that is appropriate to our methods and our traditionally close relationship with the peoples we research (Fluchr Lobban 1994). For purposes of federal regulation and enforcement, informed consent has been defined as "the knowing consent of an individual, or a legally authorized representative, able to exercise free power of choice without undue inducement or any element of force, fraud, deceit, duress, or other form of constraint or coercion" (Rules and Regulations, *Federal Register* 1994).

For federally regulated agencies that sponsor research, the documentation of informed consent must be demonstrated in one of the following ways: (1) written consent document, to be signed by the subject or authorized agent; (2) a "short form" summary document ensuring that informed consent requirements have been met; (3) modification of 1 and 2, where minimal risk is demonstrated or where obtaining informed consent would invalidate the objectives of research. In the latter case, the responsibility of the external review committee or IRB increases proportionately to the diminished informed consent requirement.

The present revised code of the AAA makes significant reference to informed consent for the first time. It is worth excerpting here:

> Anthropological researchers must obtain in advance the informed consent of persons being studied, providing information, owning or controlling access to material being studied or otherwise identified as having interests which might be impacted by the research. It is understood that the degree and breadth of informed consent will depend upon the nature of the project. . . . Further it is understood that the informed consent

process may be dynamic. . . . Informed consent does not necessarily imply or require a particular written or signed form. It is the quality of the consent, not the format, that is relevant (Draft Code 1995:B.3).

Much anthropological research has escaped federal regulation because it is small scale (in other words, few anthropologists have been funded by the National Science Foundation or National Institute of Health). Also, as noted, many anthropologists viewed their own research as relatively benign, posing little risk to research informants, and, perhaps, they believed they could protect their subjects from harm. However, much contemporary anthropological research is occurring in complex areas of applied social science and in public sector, community-based projects with protected Americans. The contemporary reality is that the anthropological researcher is often a part of a multidisciplinary team working in U.S. alcohol and drug abuse research projects, for example, or in development-related projects overseas.

Questions of the universality of informed consent can be posed at this point. In fact, many who oppose the application of informed consent in anthropology bring up its cultural and legal history in the United States. European social anthropologists may be reluctant to apply informed consent as an ethical or legal concept because of its perceived specific connection to the United States. However, the intent of informed consent, without the mechanistic use of forms and legalistic implications of its application, is becoming more universally recognized as a significant ethical principle that transcends culture and language.

Working with this historical tie to U.S. postwar history, we may legitimately ask whether non-American research participants are entitled to the same protections afforded by informed consent as are Americans. I hope that the answer would be that humans, irrespective of culture or nation, are entitled to the same rights and protections, but I fear that there may be, in practice, a double standard.

Does the concept of informed consent translate across languages and cultures? Arguments against using informed consent in anthropology have drawn on the cultural relativist theme. J. A. Barnes (1979) argued that informed consent is a U.S. or Western concept that cannot be fully explained in cross-cultural research. Honesty about one's research methods, goals, and sources of funding, however, is not a Western concept. Although cultures vary in their modes of communication, no culture endorses dishonesty or deception. Experienced anthropological researchers know of the benefits of an open, mutual relationship with research participants. Some even think in terms of a "covenantal" relationship that anthropologists have with their research collaborators (Wax 1995).

I will draw on my own 6 years of anthropological research, spanning 25 years and three different African countries, to inform this discussion. I began my doctoral research when the first code of anthropological ethics was promulgated, and those heated debates among anthropologists over the politics of research were my training ground. In the Sudan in 1970, people were suspicious as to why two American researchers had come all that way to learn Arabic and study their culture. The CIA was mentioned as the agent behind us, rather than an American university fellowship, and my husband (a fellow anthropologist) and I felt awkward and untrusted. The only antidote to this public perception was honesty, openness, and full disclosure of who we were and what we intended to do during our 18 months in the country.

We waited six months for our visas in the United States and three more months for permission by the National Research Board to conduct research. The waiting, patience, and openness were beneficial as we made friends with the members of the research board, learned basic colloquial Arabic, and word spread that we were actually decent, honorable Americans, not CIA agents.

During subsequent research in the Sudan (1979–80), in Egypt (1982–84), in and Tunisia (1990), we developed greater familiarity with the language, with research participants, and cultural sensibilities about research and privacy issues. I came to understand that being open about research is a way to keep open the lines of communication throughout the course of research, to allow negotiation of terms of research as it progresses through its various stages. Informed consent doesn't translate literally and directly into Arabic, or I suspect, many other languages. But making honest attempts to talk about the nature, course, and research funding and allowing a relationship to unfold that may even permit a participant's withdrawal from research is more ethical and probably results in better research. In my fieldwork, once people understood the nature of my inquiry into some, admittedly, sensitive family law cases and issues, they asked that certain information not be used or published. Sometimes they withheld information, understanding that certain individuals or families might be compromised by public knowledge of their personal conflicts.

In retrospect, this selected review of my fieldwork experiences is not without its own dose of self-criticism. I am acutely aware that higher-class families were more sensitive about protecting their respectability and privacy than were lower-class, less well-educated families, and I may have exerted a double standard in this respect. In another vein, I became increasingly cognizant of highly sensitive research subject matter, such as the rise of Islamist movements in Egypt, Sudan, and Tunisia during later stages of my research career. I struggled with the ethical dilemma of being open with national research boards, disguising my interest in fundamentalist Islam with other research objectives, or resolving the dilemma by not conducting research. In the end, I decided not to carry out the research on the subject and to postpone or altogether avoid research in the country I had chosen.

For my generation of anthropologists trained in the 1960s and 1970s, and those who preceded awareness of the importance of theoretical and practical ethics, the training we received in graduate school was inadequate to carry out informed and balanced ethical decision making. With the shift from an adjudicative code to an educational one, the hope is that professional ethics and active discussion of ethical dilemmas will become an integral part of undergraduate and graduate education in anthropology.

Informed Consent Without Forms: Acknowledging the Risk of Paternalism

Almost invariably, when the subject of informed consent is brought up with anthropologists, the first objection they raise is the use of a consent form. However, informed consent does not require forms. Indeed, much of anthropological research, utilizing methods of participant observation, would mitigate against using forms. However, researchers should be aware that they may be required by their funding agency or home institution to use informed consent forms. Most, if not all, medical-biological research that interfaces with physical or cultural anthropology requires informed consent forms. I fear that informed consent, when mechanically applied using a form or some verbal formula, becomes more of a protection for the researcher than the researched. Informed consent obtained in this way is unilateral rather than bilateral and protects the researcher against charges from participants that they did not understand fully the intent or outcome of research.

In a research relationship with non-Western, often relatively powerless participants, the Western researcher may feel awkward asking for a signature on a consent form. The person being studied may not be literate or the official appearance of the form may be intimidating. A psychologist conducting cross-cultural research with Guatemalan women (Lykes 1989) concluded that the informed consent form had become a barrier between researcher and researched. The researcher regarded resistance to signing the form as a positive demonstration of assertion of control over the research environment. Our "subjects" are not necessarily passive. The value of conducting research in an open, collaborative manner is that informed consent becomes a natural part of the development of the research project and relationship with those you study. You can obtain informed consent without using forms by raising relevant issues that inform and thereby empower the participant.

It is true that anthropological research can be highly personal, with intimate relations of confidence and trust developing as a result of long-term residence with people; it is also true that research is often conducted in the local language, which conveys a greater intimacy than would occur in translation. That intimacy is a powerful instrument that you must use with care so as not to violate the trust established, nor abuse the confidence that has been given to you.

An unconscious or unspoken paternalism may have kept some of these issues from being fully aired in anthropological discourse. This is what used to be called the "My Tribe" syndrome, where anthropologists might have felt that they did what was best for "their" people. In social or cultural anthropology, under historical conditions of actual colonialism or perceived colonial-like agencies like the American Bureau of Indian Affairs, paternalism was not uncommon and may have characterized human relations between anthropologist and subject (Asad 1973:16).

The era of colonialism has passed, and indigenous peoples of America, indeed the postcolonial world, are actively restructuring their relationships with states and all manner of external institutions that impact their lives, including the activities of researchers. Most U.S. and Canadian Tribal Councils have autonomous research review boards to which anthropologists and other researchers must apply before receiving approval to carry out their projects. Typically, through the process of requesting permission to conduct research, the terms and conditions of the research plan are negotiated, in effect an official airing of the proposal where the required openness and disclosure amount to informed consent.

Controversy over ethical and legal issues arising from the Human Genome Diversity Project has centered on the potential abuse of relationships between powerful Western scientific bodies and relatively powerless indigenous populations about who owns and controls human genetic materials, including cell lines that can be developed from DNA samples taken by researchers. I suspect that the proper communication amounting to informed consent was lacking in the celebrated case where "theft" or appropriation of human genetic material was alleged. The obvious solution is to engage in a open dialogue of the risks and benefits of the proposed research with the research participants themselves and, ideally, to engage with them as collaborators. This is a clear and positive trend in anthropological research, which is increasingly recognized as constituting not only better ethics in research, but as producing better research results.

Much of the history of informed consent has been linked to protecting the rights of individuals, reflective of the norms of American life. However, anthropologists and non-Western scholars have been the leading spokespersons asserting the difference between Western and other cultures in the matter of the greater value placed on collective rights in non-Western societies. This should not present any insurmountable obstacle to obtaining informed consent, for negotiations with representative and responsible agents of tribal and ethnic groups can be combined with individual consent. In some cases, where large community-based studies are proposed and negotiated, public meetings of potential participants are scheduled, where opposing viewpoints can be openly expressed. These can and should be regularized as an ongoing part of the course of research, ensuring active community involvement and monitoring. Some potential researchers may feel uncomfortable with the degree of openness that is being discussed here, but we must acknowledge that retreating from openness may result in some form of deception. This is why we must carefully consider the ethical implications of every phase of our research project.

The purposes of this rather lengthy discussion of informed consent are twofold. First, the application of the ethical and legal principle of informed consent has been a recent development, relatively late for the biomedical, physical dimensions of anthropological research, and in conformity with recent developments in sociocultural research. Therefore, the utility of informed consent may need some explanation and justification. Second, the spirit of informed consent has a certain potency as a summary concept for research, irrespective of discipline or sub-discipline. Informed consent, in its fullest interpretation, means openness and disclosure with participants, and models of research that are collaborative, rather than hierarchical and relatively nonparticipatory. This may be reflected in a detectable change in terminology of social research, with fewer references to "informants" and "subjects" and more reference to "collaborators" and "participants." When the spirit of informed consent is implemented, it results in better researchers and better research.

Concluding Remarks

The Preamble to the revised AAA code of ethics states that the anthropological researcher, scholar, or teacher is a member of many different communities, each with its own set of contextual obligations, for example, as a member of a family, a community, a public or private employee, and a host of other roles and statuses (see Appendix to this chapter [p. 195]). Anthropological research can place the researcher/scholar in complex situations, where competing but legitimate ethical claims can arise.

The informed and ethically conscious researcher will recognize the multiple layers of responsibility that can obtain in research. These might include ethical responsibility to the people studied in their complex relations with one another and to their state and other communities and institutions that impact their lives; responsibility to those into whose confidence you were taken; responsibility to the truth, to science, and to one's discipline; and responsibility to the client or funder of research.

With these complexities in mind, the AAA Commission, charged with reviewing the statements on ethics, modified the original code. In the Principles of Professional Responsibilities, the anthropologist's "first responsibility" was to the "people studied." The modified version said, "Anthropological researchers have primary ethical obligations to the people, species, and materials they study and to the people with whom they work" (Final Draft, Code of Ethics of the American Anthropological Association, 1997). In the context of this assessment, the anthropologist must be guided by the following general ethical principles of conduct:

1. To do no harm or wrong, understanding that the development of knowledge can lead to change which may be positive or negative for some people. Weighing the kinds, degrees, duration, and probability of goods to be gained and harms to be avoided is the task of the informed and ethically conscious researcher.

2. Avoiding deception or knowing misrepresentation of one's research goals, methods, or funding with the persons/communities studied is a sine qua non of social research. This extends, naturally, to any fabrication of evidence, falsification of data, or plagiarism in the processing and publication of the results of research.
3. Acting impartially, such that all persons affected by our research are treated in the same manner, insofar as this is possible under the conditions of research. (Final Report of the Commission, AAA Draft Code of Ethics, *Anthropology Newsletter* 1996)

These are general principles that should guide all research, including the social research of cultural anthropologists. Studying these principles and discussing their application in various research settings should be part of undergraduate and graduate education and training in anthropology; reference to them should be a part of every research proposal. Developing awareness of the fundamental importance of ethics as a key component of professionalism and as a necessary adjunct to science and research is an essential task of the next generation of anthropologists. Ethics education, and more importantly, constructive and engaged dialogue about the ethics of social research, should be more central to our work and our profession than it is at the moment.

The dialogue about ethics and research extends to the international arena. In 1996, I was invited to the 4th Biennial Conference of the European Association of Social Anthropologists in Barcelona to discuss the recent changes in the AAA code of ethics and to consider international perspectives in anthropology and ethics. An international Ethics Network was created to facilitate discussion of ethics and anthropology across national borders at the suggestion of Peter Pels of the University of Amsterdam. This meeting acknowledged the major changes that have taken place worldwide in the practice of anthropology and in the conduct of anthropological research.

Anthropologists, irrespective of national origin or country of research, face common challenges and similar responsibilities when they conduct research in our ever-shrinking global context. Whether as academic researchers, development workers in governmental or nongovernmental agencies, or one of a myriad of new applications of anthropology, researchers need to consider their ethical choices and professional responsibilities in ever more complex social environments. AIDS-related studies in cross-cultural research, participation in development projects, and the study of ethnic minorities in nation-states are just a few examples of contemporary research projects that raise ethical dilemmas and require dialogue—and possibly, negotiation of the terms and conditions of research within funding agencies and the nation-states where the research is to be carried out. Already, a study of how anthropologists make ethical decisions in research is being carried out by George Ulrich of the University of Copenhagen. An international discussion of cases and comparison of research experiences would be a welcome addition to broadening the discourse about ethics in anthropology.

NOTES

1. Other members of the Commission to Review the AAA Statements on Ethics included James Peacock, Barbara Frankel, Janet Levy, Murray Wax, and Kathleen Gibson.

2. All of these codes, through the 1990 AAA revision, are reprinted in my edited volume, *Ethics and the Profession of Anthropology: Dialogue for a New Era* (1991). The most recent Code of Ethics is reprinted here as an Appendix by permission of the American Anthropological Association. Not for further reproduction.

3. Historically, research participants have been referred to as "subjects" in biomedical and psychological research. Anthropologists-sociologists have used the term "informants." However, "participants" or "collaborators" is gradually replacing "subjects" and "informants" as more egalitarian ideals of the relationship between researcher and researched are evolving.

REFERENCES

Asad, Talal, ed. 1973. *Anthropology and the Colonial Encounter*. London: Ithaca Press.

Barnes, J. A. 1979. *Who Should Know What: Social Science, Privacy and Ethics*. Cambridge: Cambridge University Press.

Boas, Franz. 1919. Correspondence: Scientists as Spies. *The Nation 109*:279.

Final Report of the Commission to Review the AAA Statements on Ethics; Draft AAA Code of Ethics. 1996. *Anthropology Newsletter (April)*:13–16.

Fluehr-Lobban, Carolyn. 1991a. Professional Ethics and Anthropology: Tensions Between Its Academic and Applied Branches. *Business and Professional Ethics 10*(4):57–68.

Fluehr-Lobban, Carolyn, ed. 1991b. *Ethics and the Profession of Anthropology: Dialogue for a New Era*. Philadelphia: University of Pennsylvania Press.

Fluehr-Lobban, Carolyn. 1994. Informed Consent in Anthropological Research: We Are Not Exempt. *Human Organization 53*(1):1–9.

Fluehr-Lobban, Carolyn. 1996. Developing the New Code of Ethics. *Anthropology Newsletter (April)*:17–18.

Jordan, Ann. 1996. Review of the AAA Code of Ethics. *Anthropology Newsletter (April)*:17–18.

Levy, Janet. 1994. Report to the American Anthropological Association. *Anthropology Newsletter (February)*:1, 5.

Lykes, M. Brinton. 1989. Dialogue with Guatemalan Indian Women: Critical Perspectives on Constructing Collaborative Research. In *Representations: Social Constructions of Gender*. Rhoda K. Unger, ed. Pp. 167–185. Amityville, NY: Baywood Publishing.

MESA Newsletter 16:1, May 1994. Tucson: University of Arizona.

Naroll, Raoul, and Ronald Cohen, eds. 1973. *A Handbook of Method in Cultural Anthropology*. New York: Columbia University Press.

Proposed Statement on Professional and Ethical Responsibilities. 1983. *Human Organization 42*:367.

Protection of Human Subjects. 1990. Part 1028, *Code of Federal Regulations*. Ch. 11 (1–1–90) ed. p. 1028.1. Washington, DC: U.S. Government Printing Office.

Rules and Regulations. May 19, 1994. *Federal Register 59*(96):26116–26119.

Statement on Ethics of the Society for Applied Anthropology. 1963. *Human Organization 23*:237.

Statement on Ethics: Principles of Professional Responsibility. Adopted by the Council of the American Anthropological Association, May 1971 (as amended through November 1976).

Statement on Problems of Anthropological Research and Ethics, Adopted by the Council of the American Anthropological Association. 1967. Reprinted in *Ethics and the Profession of Anthropology: Dialogue for a New Era*, Carolyn Fluehr-Lobban, ed. Pp. 243–246. Philadelphia: University of Pennsylvania Press.

Wax, Murray. 1995. Informed Consent in Applied Research: A Comment. *Human Organization 54*(3):330–331.

WORKS RELEVANT TO ETHICS AND CULTURAL ANTHROPOLOGY

AAA Newsletter, monthly column, Ethical Dilemmas (this is a good way to keep current with ethical discourse in the United States).

Appell, G. N. 1978. *Ethical Dilemmas in Anthropological Inquiry: A Case Book*. Waltham, MA: Crossroads Press.

Beauchamp, Tom L., and Terry P. Pinkard, eds. 1983. *Ethics and Public Policy: An Introduction to Ethics*. Englewood Cliffs, NJ: Prentice-Hall.

Bulmer, Martin, ed. 1982. *Social Research Ethics*. London: Allen and Unwin.

Cassell, Joan, and Sue-Ellen Jacobs, eds. 1987. *Handbook on Ethical Issues in Anthropology*. Special publication, No. 23. Washington, DC: American Anthropological Association.

Chambers, Erve. 1980. Fieldwork and the Law. *Social Problems 27*:330–341.

Chambers, Erve, and M. G. Trend. 1981. Fieldwork Ethics in Policy-Oriented Research. *American Anthropologist 83*:626–628.

Clinton, C. A. 1976. The Anthropologist as Hired Hand. *Human Organization 34*:197–204.

Code of Ethics of the American Anthropological Association. Final Draft, March 1, 1997; published in *Anthropology Newsletter 39*(3):10–11, March 1998.

Deloria, Vine. 1980. Our New Research Society: Some Warnings to Social Scientists. *Social Problems 27*(3):265–271.

Faden, Ruth R., and T. L. Beauchamp, in collaboration with Nancy M. P. King. 1986. *A History and Theory of Informed Consent*. New York: Oxford University Press.

Galliher, John F. 1980. Social Scientists' Ethical Responsibility to Superordinates. *Social Problems 27*(3):298–308.

Gert, Bernard. 1995. Universal Values and Professional Codes of Ethics. *AAA Newsletter (October)*:30–31.

Green, Edward C., ed. 1984. *Practicing Developmental Anthropology*. Boulder and London: Westview Press.

Johnson, Rebecca Lynn, and the students of the University of South Carolina's Ethics and Anthropology class. 1995. Ethics for the Future. *AAA Newsletter (September)*:67.

Jorgensen, Joseph. 1971. On Ethics and Anthropology. *Current Anthropology 12*:321–334.

MacIntyre, Alasdair. 1993. Ethical Dilemmas: Notes from Outside the Field. *Anthropology Newsletter 34*(7):5–6.

Mead, Margaret. 1969. Research with Human Beings: A Model Derived from Anthropological Field Practice. *Daedalus 98*:361–386.

Messenger, Phyllis Mauch, ed. 1989. *The Ethics of Collecting Cultural Property: Whose Culture? Whose Property?* Albuquerque: University of New Mexico Press.

Pels, Peter. 1994. National Codes of Ethics and European Anthropology: A Call for Cooperation and Exchange. *European Association of Social Anthropology Newsletter (September)*:9–10.

Pelto, Perti, and Gretel Pelto. 1978. *Anthropological Research*. Cambridge: Cambridge University Press.

Professional Ethics, a multidisciplinary journal (formerly *Business and Professional Ethics*), PO Box 15017, Gainesville, FL 32604.

Punch, Maurice. 1986. *The Politics and Ethics of Fieldwork*. Qualitative Research Methods Series, Vol. 3. Thousand Oaks, CA: Sage Publications.

Reynolds, Paul Davidson. 1982. *Ethics and Social Science Research*. Englewood Cliffs, NJ: Prentice-Hall.

Rynkiewich, Michael A., and James P. Spradley, eds. 1976. *Ethics and Anthropology: Dilemmas in Fieldwork*. New York: Wiley.

Shore, Cris, and A. Ahmed, eds. 1995. *The Future of Anthropology: Its Relevance to the Contemporary World*. London: Athlone.

Skomal, Susan. 1994. Lessons for the Field—Ethics in Fieldwork. *Anthropology Newsletter 35*(5):1, 4.

Washburn, Wilcomb E. 1989. Anthropological Advocacy in the Hopi–Navajo Land Dispute. *American Anthropologist 91*:738–743.

Wax, M. L. and J. Cassell, eds. 1979. *Federal Regulations: Ethical Issues and Social Research*. Boulder: Westview Press.

Whyte, William F. 1958. Freedom and Responsibility in Research: The Springdale Case. *Human Organization 17*:1–2.

Appendix
Code of Ethics of the American Anthropological Association

I. Preamble

Anthropological researchers, teachers and practitioners are members of many different communities, each with its own moral rules or codes of ethics. Anthropologists have moral obligations as members of other groups, such as the family, religion, and community, as well as the profession. They also have obligations to the scholarly discipline, to the wider society and culture, and to the human species, other species, and the environment. Furthermore, fieldworkers may develop close relationships with persons or animals with whom they work, generating an additional level of ethical considerations.

In a field of such complex involvements and obligations, it is inevitable that misunderstandings, conflicts, and the need to make choices among apparently incompatible values will arise. Anthropologists are responsible for grappling with such difficulties and struggling to resolve them in ways compatible with the principles stated here. The purpose of this Code is to foster discussion and education. The American Anthropological Association (AAA) does not adjudicate claims for unethical behavior.

The principles and guidelines in this Code provide the anthropologist with tools to engage in developing and maintaining an ethical framework for all anthropological work.

II. Introduction

Anthropology is a multidisciplinary field of science and scholarship, which includes the study of all aspects of humankind—archaeological, biological, linguistic, and sociocultural. Anthropology has roots in the natural and social sciences and in the humanities, ranging in approach from basic to applied research and to scholarly interpretation.

As the principal organization representing the breadth of anthropology, the American Anthropological Association (AAA) starts from the position that generating and appropriately utilizing knowledge (i.e., publishing, teaching, developing programs, and informing policy) of the peoples of the world, past and present, is a worthy goal; that the generation of anthropological knowledge is a dynamic process using many different and ever-evolving approaches; and that for moral and practical reasons, the generation and utilization of knowledge should be achieved in an ethical manner.

The mission of American Anthropological Association is to advance all aspects of anthropological research and to foster dissemination of anthropological knowledge through publications, teaching, public education, and application. An important part of that mission is to help educate AAA members about ethical obligations and challenges involved in the generation, dissemination, and utilization of anthropological knowledge.

The purpose of this Code is to provide AAA members and other interested persons with guidelines for making ethical choices in the conduct of their anthropological work. Because anthropologists can find themselves in complex situations and subject to more than one code of ethics, the AAA Code of Ethics provides a framework, not an ironclad formula, for making decisions.

Persons using the Code as a guideline for making ethical choices or for teaching are encouraged to seek out illustrative examples and appropriate case studies to enrich their knowledge base.

Anthropologists have a duty to be informed about ethical codes relating to their work, and ought periodically to receive training on current research activities and ethical issues. In addition, departments offering anthropology degrees should include and require ethical training in their curriculums.

No code or set of guidelines can anticipate unique circumstances or direct actions in specific situations. The individual anthropologist must be willing to make carefully considered ethical choices and be prepared to make clear the assumptions, facts and issues on which those choices are based. These guidelines therefore address general contexts, priorities and relationships which should be considered in ethical decision making in anthropological work.

III. Research

In both proposing and carrying out research, anthropological researchers must be open about the purpose(s), potential impacts, and source(s) of support for research projects with funders, colleagues, persons studied or providing information, and with relevant parties affected by the research. Researchers must expect to utilize the results of their work in an appropriate fashion and disseminate the results through appropriate and timely activities. Research fulfilling these expectations is ethical, regardless of the source of funding (public or private) or purpose (i.e., "applied," "basic," "pure," or "proprietary").

Anthropological researchers should be alert to the danger of compromising anthropological ethics as a condition to engage in research, yet also be alert to proper demands of good citizenship or host-guest relations. Active contribution and leadership in seeking to shape public or private sector actions and policies may be as ethically justifiable as inaction, detachment, or noncooperation, depending on circumstances. Similar principles hold for anthropological researchers employed or otherwise affiliated with nonanthropological institutions, public institutions, or private enterprises.

A. Responsibility to people and animals with whom anthropological researchers work and whose lives and cultures they study.

  1. Anthropological researchers have primary ethical obligations to the people, species, and materials they study and to the people with whom they work. These obligations can supersede the goal of seeking new knowledge, and can lead to decisions not to undertake or to discontinue a research project when the primary obligation conflicts

with other responsibilities, such as those owed to sponsors or clients. These ethical obligations include:

* To avoid harm or wrong, understanding that the development of knowledge can lead to change which may be positive or negative for the people or animals worked with or studied
* To respect the well-being of humans and nonhuman primates
* To work for the long-term conservation of the archaeological, fossil, and historical records
* To consult actively with the affected individuals or group(s), with the goal of establishing a working relationship that can be beneficial to all parties involved

2. Anthropological researchers must do everything in their power to ensure that their research does not harm the safety, dignity, or privacy of the people with whom they work, conduct research, or perform other professional activities. Anthropological researchers working with animals must do everything in their power to ensure that the research does not harm the safety, psychological well-being or survival of the animals or species with which they work.

3. Anthropological researchers must determine in advance whether their hosts/ providers of information wish to remain anonymous or receive recognition, and make every effort to comply with those wishes. Researchers must present to their research participants the possible impacts of the choices, and make clear that despite their best efforts, anonymity may be compromised or recognition fail to materialize.

4. Anthropological researchers should obtain in advance the informed consent of persons being studied, providing information, owning or controlling access to material being studied, or otherwise identified as having interests which might be impacted by the research. It is understood that the degree and breadth of informed consent required will depend on the nature of the project and may be affected by requirements of other codes, laws, and ethics of the country or community in which the research is pursued. Further, it is understood that the informed consent process is dynamic and continuous; the process should be initiated in the project design and continue through implementation by way of dialogue and negotiation with those studied. Researchers are responsible for identifying and complying with the various informed consent codes, laws and regulations affecting their projects. Informed consent, for the purposes of this code, does not necessarily imply or require a particular written or signed form.

It is the quality of the consent, not the format, that is relevant.

5. Anthropological researchers who have developed close and enduring relationships (i.e., covenantal relationships) with either individual persons providing information or with hosts must adhere to the obligations of openness and informed consent, while carefully and respectfully negotiating the limits of the relationship.

6. While anthropologists may gain personally from their work, they must not exploit individuals, groups, animals, or cultural or biological materials. They should recognize their debt to the societies in which they work and their obligation to reciprocate with people studied in appropriate ways.

B. Responsibility to scholarship and science

1. Anthropological researchers must expect to encounter ethical dilemmas at every stage of their work, and must make good-faith efforts to identify potential ethical claims and conflicts in advance when preparing proposals and as projects proceed. A section raising and responding to potential ethical issues should be part of every research proposal.

2. Anthropological researchers bear responsibility for the integrity and reputation of their discipline, of scholarship, and of science. Thus, anthropological researchers are subject to the general moral rules of scientific and scholarly conduct: they should not deceive or knowingly misrepresent (i.e., fabricate evidence, falsify, plagiarize), or attempt to prevent reporting of misconduct, or obstruct the scientific/scholarly research of others.

3. Anthropological researchers should do all they can to preserve opportunities for future fieldworkers to follow them to the field.

4. Anthropological researchers should utilize the results of their work in an appropriate fashion, and whenever possible disseminate their findings to the scientific and scholarly community.

5. Anthropological researchers should seriously consider all reasonable requests for access to their data and other research materials for purposes of research. They should also make every effort to insure preservation of their fieldwork data for use by posterity.

C. Responsibility to the public

1. Anthropological researchers should make the results of their research appropriately available to sponsors, students, decision makers, and other nonanthropologists. In so doing, they must be truthful; they are not only responsible for the factual content of their statements but also must consider carefully the social and political implications of the information they disseminate. They must do everything in their power to insure that such information is well understood, properly contextualized, and responsibly utilized. They should make clear the empirical bases upon which their reports stand, be candid about their qualifications and philosophical or political biases, and recognize and make clear the limits of anthropological expertise. At the same time, they must be alert to possible harm their information may cause people with whom they work or colleagues.

2. Anthropologists may choose to move beyond disseminating research results to a position of advocacy. This is an individual decision, but not an ethical responsibility.

IV. Teaching

Responsibility to students and trainees

While adhering to ethical and legal codes governing relations between teachers/mentors and students/trainees at their educational institutions or as members of wider organizations, anthropological teachers should be particularly sensitive to the ways such codes apply in their discipline (for example, when teaching involves close contact with students/trainees in field situations). Among the widely recognized precepts which anthropological teachers, like other teachers/mentors, should follow are:

1. Teachers/mentors should conduct their programs in ways that preclude discrimination on the basis of sex, marital status, " race," social class, political convictions, disability, religion, ethnic background, national origin, sexual orientation, age, or other criteria irrelevant to academic performance.

2. Teachers'/mentors' duties include continually striving to improve their teaching/training techniques; being available and responsive to student/trainee interests; counseling students/trainees realistically regarding career opportunities; conscientiously supervising, encouraging, and supporting students'/trainees' studies; being fair, prompt, and reliable in communicating evaluations; assisting students/trainees in securing research support; and helping students/trainees when they seek professional placement.

3. Teachers/mentors should impress upon students/trainees the ethical challenges involved in every phase of anthropological work; encourage them to reflect upon this and other codes; encourage dialogue with colleagues on ethical issues; and discourage participation in ethically questionable projects.

4. Teachers/mentors should publicly acknowledge student/trainee assistance in research and preparation of their work; give appropriate credit for coauthorship to students/trainees; encourage publication of worthy student/trainee papers; and compensate students/trainees justly for their participation in all professional activities.

5. Teachers/mentors should beware of the exploitation and serious conflicts of interest which may result if they engage in sexual relations with students/trainees. They must avoid sexual liaisons with students/trainees for whose education and professional training they are in any way responsible.

V. Application

1. The same ethical guidelines apply to all anthropological work. That is, in both proposing and carrying out research, anthropologists must be open with funders,

colleagues, persons studied or providing information, and relevant parties affected by the work about the purpose(s), potential impacts, and source(s) of support for the work. Applied anthropologists must intend and expect to utilize the results of their work appropriately (i.e., publication, teaching, program and policy development) within a reasonable time. In situations in which anthropological knowledge is applied, anthropologists bear the same responsibility to be open and candid about their skills and intentions, and monitor the effects of their work on all persons affected. Anthropologists may be involved in many types of work, frequently affecting individuals and groups with diverse and sometimes conflicting interests. The individual anthropologist must make carefully considered ethical choices and be prepared to make clear the assumptions, facts and issues on which those choices are based.

2. In all dealings with employers, persons hired to pursue anthropological research or apply anthropological knowledge should be honest about their qualifications, capabilities, and aims. Prior to making any professional commitments, they must review the purposes of prospective employers, taking into consideration the employer's past activities and future goals. In working for governmental agencies or private businesses, they should be especially careful not to promise or imply acceptance of conditions contrary to professional ethics or competing commitments.

3. Applied anthropologists, as any anthropologist, should be alert to the danger of compromising anthropological ethics as a condition for engaging in research or practice. They should also be alert to proper demands of hospitality, good citizenship and guest status. Proactive contribution and leadership in shaping public or private sector actions and policies may be as ethically justifiable as inaction, detachment, or noncooperation, depending on circumstances.

VI. Epilogue

Anthropological research, teaching, and application, like any human actions, pose choices for which anthropologists individually and collectively bear ethical responsibility. Since anthropologists are members of a variety of groups and subject to a variety of ethical codes, choices must sometimes be made not only between the varied obligations presented in this code but also between those of this code and those incurred in other statuses or roles. This statement does not dictate choice or propose sanctions. Rather, it is designed to promote discussion and provide general guidelines for ethically responsible decisions.

VII. Acknowledgments

This Code was drafted by the Commission to Review the AAA Statements on Ethics during the period January 1995-March 1997. The Commission members were James Peacock (Chair), Carolyn Fluehr-Lobban, Barbara Frankel, Kathleen Gibson, Janet Levy, and Murray Wax. In addition, the following individuals participated in the Commission meetings: philosopher Bernard Gert, anthropologists Cathleen Crain, Shirley Fiske, David Freyer, Felix Moos, Yolanda Moses, and Niel Tashima; and members of the American Sociological

Association Committee on Ethics. Open hearings on the Code were held at the 1995 and 1996 annual meetings of the American Anthropological Association. The Commission solicited comments from all AAA Sections. The first draft of the AAA Code of Ethics was discussed at the May 1995 AAA Section Assembly meeting; the second draft was briefly discussed at the November 1996 meeting of the AAA Section Assembly.

The Final Report of the Commission was published in the September 1995 edition of the Anthropology Newsletter and on the AAA web site (http://www.ameranthassn.org). Drafts of the Code were published in the April 1996 and 1996 annual meeting edition of the Anthropology Newsletter and the AAA web site, and comments were solicited from the membership. The Commission considered all comments from the membership in formulating the final draft in February 1997. The Commission gratefully acknowledge the use of some language from the codes of ethics of the National Association for the Practice of Anthropology and the Society for American Archaeology.

VIII. Other Relevant Codes of Ethics

The following list of other Codes of Ethics may be useful to anthropological researchers, teachers and practitioners:

Animal Behavior Society 1991. Guidelines for the Use of Animals in Research. *Animal Behavior 41*:183–186.

American Board of Forensic Examiners n.d. Code of Ethical Conduct. (American Board of Forensic Examiners, 300 South Jefferson Avenue, Suite 411, Springfield, MO 65806).

Archaeological Institute of America
1991 Code of Ethics. *American Journal of Archaeology 95*:285.
1994 Code of Professional Standards. (Archaeological Institute of America, 675 Commonwealth Ave, Boston, MA 02215–1401. Supplements and expands but does not replace the earlier Code of Ethics).

National Academy of Sciences
1995 *On Being a Scientist: Responsible Conduct in Research*, 2d ed. Washington, DC: National Academy Press (2121 Constitution Avenue, NW, Washington, DC 20418).

National Association for the Practice of Anthropology
1988 Ethical Guidelines for Practitioners.

Sigma Xi
1992 Sigma Xi Statement on the Use of Animals in Research. *American Scientist 80*:73–76.

Society for American Archaeology
1996 Principles of Archaeological Ethics. (Society for American Archaeology, 900 Second Street, NE, Suite 12, Washington, DC 20002–3557).

Society for Applied Anthropology
1983 Professional and Ethical Responsibilities. (Revised 1983.)

Society of Professional Archaeologists
   1976 Code of Ethics, Standards of Research Performance and Institutional Standards.
   (Society of Professional Archaeologists, PO Box 60911, Oklahoma City, OK
   73146–0911).
United Nations
   1948 Universal Declaration of Human Rights.
   1983 United Nations Convention on the Elimination of All Forms of Discrimination
   Against Women.
   1987 United Nations Convention on the Rights of the Child.
   Forthcoming United Nations Declaration on Rights of Indigenous Peoples.

Six

Feminist Methods

Introduction

Anthropology as a field lends itself to feminist methods. First, at least in its North American version, because of the core concern with cultural dynamics and shifting terrains of meaning, it flourishes on the borderland between the social sciences and humanities. This interdisciplinary space is one valued in feminist research in general. Second, anthropology is comparative and historical in scope, permitting those who wish to seek patterns to do so, while remaining skeptical of unified theories based on nationalist assumptions or images of human nature rooted in particular societies. Third, there is a historical tendency in anthropology to focus on the local, the everyday, or the marginal.

At its worst, anthropology can ignore global structures of meaning or transform peoples into exotic objects for consumption by more powerful audiences. At its best, it becomes the witness for human practices that resonate with but are not mere reflexes of, the processes of global capitalism or earlier colonialism, worlds of meaning in the making. Anthropology can value the local, the subordinated, the creation of meaning among those who are not powerful in the reductive sense of wealth or political control or even social prestige. Perhaps it is this tendency that contributed to the formative influence that anthropologists in the early 1970s had in the development of what have become international or transnational feminisms.

Taken narrowly as techniques of investigation, the methods of feminist anthropology—its use of fieldwork, interviews, surveys, and quantitative data collection—aren't distinct from those of other critical methods in anthropology.

Even the coupling of theory and method found in this paper, while typical of feminist methods in anthropology, can be found in other forms of critical anthropology: Theory informs method and method shapes theory. What is distinctive is how theory and method are related: The bridges between the two are ontology (the set of assumptions that underlies one's research design) and epistemology (how one knows what one thinks one knows, the basis for knowledge claims).

Feminist anthropology, then, is distinguished by the ontological and epistemological dimensions of method. We shall see that there is no one feminist method in anthropology (or in any other discipline). Instead, epistemological and ontological debates within feminism—what we want to know, what we can assume, and what ends our produced knowledge serves—unite the diverse research efforts.

The Feminism of Eleanor Leacock

Before delving into the general questions of ontology and epistemology in feminist anthropology, let us ground ourselves in one feminist anthropologist's work, to see how feminism informs her range of writing and activism. Eleanor Leacock's work, stretching from 1954–1985, shows a unity of concern and a diversity of techniques of inquiry.

Leacock's overarching concern—linking a wide range of ethnohistorical and ethnographic accounts and analyses of social and cultural theory—was with the dynamics of social hierarchies, including gender hierarchies, and how resistance and whatever emancipatory practices may exist are grounded in everyday practice. Her research reflected the various terrains in which these struggles ensued: serving Innu activists in Labrador who were trying to stop NATO overflights that disturbed animal life; publishing one of the first accounts of racism and resistance in inner-city education; birthing a generation of feminist anthropologists through her introduction to Engels's *The Origin of the Family, Private Property, and the State* (1972); pointing out the limitations of structuralist formulations regarding gender (Leacock 1977a; Leacock and Nash 1977); and the methodological and epistemological problems associated with assertions of universal male dominance (Leacock 1981, 1983). Leacock collaborated in producing anthologies on women and colonization (Etienne and Leacock 1980) and women's work viewed through place and time (Leacock and Safa 1986).

Leacock posed questions tackling different aspects of these unifying concerns. Depending on what questions were asked, Leacock used participant observation, textual analysis, archival research, direct observation, interviewing, and various types of surveys. At the suggestion of Gene Weltfish, Leacock once did a ground survey of fur-trapping lines among the Innu of Labrador and used these data in a political-economic analysis. Her work is clearly and unapologetically situated as advocacy, but she did not flinch from criticizing those for whom she advocated. One gets a sense of her respect for the people who facilitate the research, a keen sense of dynamics and structure, and wide and careful reading in the social sciences. What some have criticized as evolutionary thinking (Silverblatt 1988), I think was instead a tailoring of writing to disparate audiences. Leacock's dialectical sense of causation made historical transformation a matter of structural disjunctures and contingencies that were shaped by human agency. The only "evolution" was one of chronology, not destiny or inevitability (Leacock 1983).

Leacock, in fact, had an unusually disparate set of audiences to address: her undergraduate and graduate students, her international anthropology colleagues, feminist and antiracist social activists in the United States and in other countries, and mechanical evolutionists within the Marxist tradition. Her feminist claims were always grounded in comparative and historical research; only in her autobiography does she situate herself socially in the nested contexts of race, city, country, and beyond. Her work as a whole is feminist in the sense that gender is always a central dimension of analysis, but what constitutes "women" is complicated by concerns with kin roles, generation, class, and race or ethnicity, as well as historical context. There is no "woman"—essentialized, timeless, and passively defined by others—in her texts.

With the example of Leacock in mind, we can consider the distinctive features of feminist methodologies in anthropology.

Feminist Ontology

The bedrock assumption in feminist research is that gender is a key dimension of human societies and cultures. Correlatively, studies that ignore gender or that subsume it without investigation into "family life" or "sex roles" do serious disservice to our understanding of social and cultural dynamics. Feminists disagree whether gender is always constructed as a hierarchy, but there is agreement that gender is generally associated with differential social power or authority.

Feminists in anthropology share a concern that power inherently shapes the kinds of understanding we develop of our own and other societies and cultures. But we differ in how we conceptualize power and whether we see it as grounded—or "located" in current parlance—in social relations and structures or as more amorphously associated with conceptual schemas and language practices. Some of us see these as dialectically related. Despite such theoretical differences, feminist anthropologists probably concur that: (1) power differences shape the lived experiences of people and the meanings that people attribute to those experiences; (2) in state societies, gender is one of several intersecting variables that together produce differences in power among sets of people; and (3) gender is a major organizing principle that shapes the reproduction of culture and, consequently, the transformation of cultural practices.

Feminist anthropology is distinguished as well by the vantage point taken in inquiry. Sometimes, gender in general is the lens through which the researcher views a society, but more commonly the viewpoint is from the perspective of *a woman* or of *some category of* women (for example, middle-class women, professional women, battered women, and so on). This perspective is necessarily partial and doesn't claim to encompass all possible perspectives on a particular society or cultural setting.

It also is not politically neutral—it is a stance or standpoint (see Harding 1987). Because we are cultured beings, objectivity is impossible; claims of objectivity gird a set of research approaches and policies that support the status quo. Researchers can situate themselves within acknowledged perspectives or scholarly traditions. We have an obligation to let our audiences know why we think we can claim what we claim. Abandoning claims to objectivity, however, doesn't mean bias. Bias differs from situating oneself. A biased researcher merely makes assumptions that remain implicit or that are not even recognized as assumptions. Bias can be avoided to the extent that researchers can work to be aware of their own assumptions and can convey those to audiences. Such self-reflection and intellectual forthrightness helps the audience situate and evaluate claims within a wider field of argument. Cross-checking for bias, for feminist anthropologists, lies in reflexivity, in critically examining the links that we make or do not make between our assumptions, how our research is designed and conducted, and the conclusions we draw.

Acknowledging that inquiry, including scientific inquiry, takes place in a social world and is conducted by people who have cultural frameworks that shape their thinking should not translate into a rejection of quantitative techniques—that somehow these are inherently masculinist or antifeminist (see, for example, Reinharz 1992). Indeed, techniques can be viewed as neutral, and our goal may be to reduce bias by making our assumptions and epistemological claims clear to our audiences. Some feminist anthropologists are also empiricists, deeply committed to the goals of positivist science. In the larger frame of feminist anthropology, the claims of positivism are held up to scrutiny in the same way as are the ontological and epistemological claims of other traditions (structuralist, poststructuralist, Marxist-feminist, etc.): What is the context for these claims? Who is the audience? How is expertise established and for whom? What is truth in this framework and how does the author claim it? Most notably, how does this understanding further feminist practice?

Feminist researchers argue that research should inform our own social engagement. Feminist research, as distinct from research on women, seeks to link theoretical understandings with practical activity, human agency as a matter of course. The knowledge we produce regarding gender configurations and women's struggles in whatever contexts should, routinely, guide our own efforts, our own everyday lives (see Lamphere et al. 1997). Feminist ontology thus produces a reflexive methodology, one that sees the researcher's own social engagement as deeply implicated in and by the research.

Another assumption now made by feminist anthropologists is that gender is socially constructed. Gender is distinct from sex differences, although gender categories may be isomorphic with the categories of sex difference in particular societies. Feminist anthropologists also assume that gender varies culturally and across time periods and social strata. Indeed, one of the hallmarks of feminist theory in the late twentieth century is a mistrust of the assertion that there is a concept of "woman" apart from or independent of national and cultural agendas. Gender ideologies and hierarchies are cross-cut by other hierarchies and ideologies. The intersection of these hierarchies, whether mutually constraining or synergistic, produces different experiences of gender and other dimensions of identity—age, ethnicity, class, race, sexual orientation, religion—that may operate in a society. Listening to the words and observing the actions of people whose everyday lives are riven by conflicting stresses of race, gender, and class helps us dismantle widely held notions that there is an essential nature to women or men (see Stack 1997).

The call for integrating feminism into one's relations in daily life also distinguishes feminism from other critical methodologies. As Kaufman (1996:165) writes, feminist methodology is "not just a reconceptualization of a way of 'doing research,' but also a way of living in the world. It openly advocates a decentered nonauthoritarian approach to all human relationships and to thinking about those relationships."

Other critical methodologies don't insist on such efforts. Typically, calls for action and engagement are at the public-domain level—addressing national or international policies, clearly defining one's research agenda to one's informants, helping shape the policies of one's professional organizations, universities, or local communities. The activist aspect usually stops at arenas deemed private, particularly family and personal relationships of one's colleagues. The feminist rubric that "the personal is political" disallows such compartmentalization. The problem, always, is setting priorities.

More than other critical methodologies, then, feminist anthropology makes research and the researcher—no matter how elaborately theorized the research or how seemingly abstract or microlevel the concerns of the researcher herself— accountable to a range of audiences. The audiences to whom the researcher is accountable include not only colleagues in the social sciences and the humanities or informed lay readers, but also the subjects of the research and the researcher's family and community members. The connecting thread in this myriad of audiences is the call to engage in helping reduce gender inequities wherever these occur. It would not be acceptable, for instance, for anyone calling themselves a feminist anthropologist to investigate the intricacies of how gender hierarchies operate in society X while expecting a pregnant or new mother colleague to carry on as if the new state of being had no effect on her everyday workload. It isn't sufficient to investigate the relationship between gender and sexuality in society Y while reproducing gender stereotypes or practicing homophobia in one's own milieu. It isn't enough to teach about gender difference while ignoring student complaints about sexual harassment by one's departmental colleague; or shrugging off a teacher's gender stereotyping in the classroom because your son benefits from it in terms of attention time. The creative discomfort or tension that results from the adoption of such responsibility is part of one's state of being, because ethics are part of the methodology (Jaggar 1991).

Now that these ethical, practical, and theoretical issues are outlined, I turn to the epistemological dimensions of feminist methodologies in anthropology.

Feminist Epistemologies

How do feminist researchers know what they know? On what basis are knowledge claims made? What are data in feminist research? What is the relationship of observed reality to evidence? What constitutes proof? Within feminism there are debates regarding each of these issues. These debates provide a wider latitude for what is considered feminist research than detractors might think. There is no orthodoxy, but there are types of feminist research that mark periods in feminist scholarship in the second half of the twentieth century. These can be characterized as: gynocentrism, standpoint theory, and intersection analysis. They represent different degrees, depths, and facets of an overarching feminist critique of science, even as many feminist researchers remain committed to scientific inquiry (Harding 1991).

Beginnings: How Does Focusing on Women
Change Anthropological Inquiry?

While always useful as a research strategy, feminist empiricism or gynocentrism was most prevalent in the earliest phase of feminist anthropology, roughly 1970–1980. Whatever the disagreements among feminists in this period, most shared an underlying commitment to positivism. The first step in the process of creating a feminist anthropology was uncovering male bias in the discipline. How did the central questions of anthropology embody assumptions that what men did was more important than what women did? How were women's sources of authority, dignity, and value ignored or denied in the way research was conducted (see Rosaldo and Lamphere 1974; Rapp [Reiter] 1975)? In retrospect, it has been called the "add women and mix" period (Harding 1987). What does placing women at the center of analysis—or even including them—do to the questions we can imagine, the ways research can be conducted, the conclusions that can be drawn? What difference does it make to have research done by women?

In this form of feminist research, the researcher first reviews existing literature on the topic, being attentive to indications of masculinist bias in assumptions made, research design, development of evidence, data analysis, and conclusions. Retrieval of earlier studies, ignored or merely forgotten in the academy, is necessary in this phase. Contributions by earlier generations of women anthropologists or ethnographers should be reexamined and given the value they warrant (see Lurie 1966; Golde 1970; Gacs et al. 1988).

Appreciating the efforts made by pioneers gives us a better sense of why feminist anthropology came to be shaped the way it is. Anthropological literature in and before the 1950s presented marriage as the central institution of kinship, and kinship studies were where references to women were clustered. So we can expect that feminist critiques of anthropology would begin, on the one hand, by integrating women's work and sources of authority through kin connections into the analysis, as Eleanor Leacock's (1954) research on the Innu of Labrador did, and, on the other hand, by reconsidering how marriage was defined. Kathleen Gough's (1959) research on the Nayars of Kerala, India, challenged the ways that anthropologists had defined marriage. While not read as feminist at the time, this early work would inspire later, more explicitly feminist research.

The next step was to design research that would correct these distortions, usually within the same theoretical tradition. Researchers corrected the biases inherent in: (1) selecting only male informants; (2) assuming that whatever men did was more important that what women did; (3) analytically demeaning the contributions of women; (4) discounting research topics that would be associated with women in the researcher's own culture; and (5) assuming that women did the same things as men. The basic questions most research designs posed were: "What does this topic look like when women are included?" and "How do portrayals of this society change when women are the focus or are included in the analysis?"

Based on these early investigations, questions emerged regarding how one establishes what "women's status" is; whether women were universally subordinated, whether sex differences were the same as gender differences between people labeled "women" and those labeled "men" in various societies; why women would have more or less power in different types of societies, and so on. Approaches to feminist anthropological research were diverse, following major theoretical orientations in the discipline among functionalists, structuralists, and Marxists. These approaches can be seen in early anthologies, which stimulated cross-cultural analyses of gender roles and of women's authority patterns through time and place (see Jacobs [1971]; Paulme [1971]; Rosaldo and Lamphere [1974]; [Reiter] Rapp [1975]; Schlegel [1977]). Alongside the anthologies came a series of theoretical and ethnographic studies, such as Leacock's commentaries (1972) and Friedl's (1975) and Sanday's (1981) comparative research, among others. By the mid-1970s, the proliferation of research on women within anthropology was examined in a series of review essays (Lamphere 1977; Quinn 1977; Rapp 1978).

By focusing on what women were doing, and designing research that required observing and talking with women as well as with men (Strathern 1972), researchers provided insights into cultural dynamics that had been assumed before to exclude women from important social decision-making. In a series of historical and contemporary case studies, researchers identified diverse sources of authority available to women at various stages in their life, arenas where some women could become authoritative, and ways in which vital contributions made by women were accorded social recognition and value or were rendered invisible (see, for example, Van Allen 1972).

On a practical level, the effort led to important changes in state policies toward local ethnic groups (Stack 1974), shifts in how development was conceptualized and how projects were implemented (Leacock 1977b; Okeyo 1980), and sometimes to local women organizing to ameliorate their own conditions (Omvedt 1977; Bell and Ditton 1980). Within the academy, these approaches led to a profound reevaluation of kinship studies, economic anthropology, and political anthropology (Vincent 1990), among other subfields. The concomitant push for affirmative action by the ongoing women's movement saw important changes in hiring and, to a lesser extent, tenuring and promotion of women (Sanjek 1978).

Most of the early studies (1970–1980) assumed that gender differences paralleled sex differences or uncritically accepted sex differences as unmediated by cultural perception of naturalness. Yet even in this early period, there were those who understood that sex differences were not the same as gender (Oboler 1980), and that gendering changed historically and in relation to racial stratification, even if the term gender was used only rarely at the time (see Stack 1974; Leacock and Nash 1977).

The effort to retrieve earlier, submerged ethnographies that did deal with women in important ways, such as Krige and Krige's *The Realm of a Rain Queen* (1943), challenged assumptions about the presumed parallel of sex and gender: Prominent Lovedu females could be simultaneously wives and mothers and husbands and fathers, for example. Other women scholars, reflecting on field experiences, noted their being situated locally as categorical men, so the contention that this first spate of feminist anthropology didn't distinguish sex and gender isn't accurate: some did, even if the terms used then weren't the same as the distinctions used now. Many researchers, however, identified gender roles as sex roles; later feminist scholars would point out the limitations inherent in such analyses, particularly when claims were being made about "women's status" (Amadiume 1987).

Focusing on "what the women are doing" is still a viable research strategy in arenas of social research that retain a masculinist set of assumptions and social relations. In those arenas, it is still unknown what women contribute in terms of productive and reproductive activities and how this work and, indeed, women's lives have cultural and social value. It generally remains a starting point for ethnographic research, although focusing on gendering will often change initial impressions and including other dimensions of social hierarchy (class, ethnicity or race, sometimes regional or religious affiliation) will prevent "women" from becoming a monolithic category. Most feminist researchers now appreciate the importance of analyzing how gendering occurs in a specific setting and how it might be changing in relation to local, national, and international political and economic processes, as well as in relation to life cycle and kin dynamics.

A more radical departure from the early studies entails questioning the "natural-ness" of sex differences, some arguing that the split between sex and gender is itself a Cartesian dichotomy. While at first blush this may seem absurd, the argument is not that there are not physiological distinctions between females and males related to reproduction, but that, on the one hand, what constitutes sex difference has changed with new technologies and, on the other hand, a person's perception of what "counts" as a natural difference is culturally shaped.

Conducting this kind of corrective research raised three other sets of issues for feminist anthropologists: (1) how funding for field research is granted and con-sequently how research topics are valued; (2) how the audience and discipline values research and researchers; and (3) how the social category of the researcher shapes the relationship of researcher and those studied. The first two sets of issues exposed key areas of male bias in anthropology and related disciplines: Research by or about women was not comparably valued. These issues became painfully obvious when the first round of tenure decisions of newly included women scholars publishing their research on gender saw a flurry of rejections.

Here the social engagement relationship of theory and practice came into play. As researchers were uncovering dynamics in other societies that valued women's work, or how women's contributions were structurally eclipsed in more hierarchical settings, researchers came to realize how similar dynamics operated or did not exist in their own milieus. The sharing of research results in the emerging cohort of feminist anthropologists led to national campaigns to redress male bias, including orchestrated action to affect university policies and funding priorities in private and public foundations.

Alongside a large number of individual researchers' case studies, Friedl's (1975), Leacock's (1972), and Sack's (Brodkin [Sacks] 1979) comparative studies suggested that women in less-stratified settings enjoyed greater social authority. Researchers differed, however, about whether gender hierarchies existed in societies not encom-passed by states. Debates ensued regarding: variations in the meaning of marriage (Etienne 1980); how to assess women's status (Ortner 1974; Brodkin [Sacks] 1976; Edholm et al. 1978); whether public/private realms existed in all societies (Lamphere 1974, 1977; see also Lamphere 1993); whether a division of labor by gender meant gender hierarchy (Leacock 1972; Brown 1975); and whether state formation involved the historical development of consistent gender hierarchy (Rapp 1977; Silverblatt 1978; Gailey 1980, 1987a, 1987b; Ortner 1981).

Feminist anthropology in the 1970s problematized the study of women in a number of dimensions and legitimated the line of inquiry, at least as a "ghetto" that most departments should have represented in some manner. The works were mostly empirically grounded—that is, based on field or archival research. Some were empiricist—presuming a tangible, measurable real world existing independently of interpretation. Some were also positivist, aiming at general social laws and the achievement of a gradually perfected truth. The influence of the flood of field studies and theoretical writings led researchers to question whether it was accurate to talk about women as if they were a homogeneous group in stratified societies. This realization helped move the discourse of feminist anthropology to discussions of gender as a configuration of cultural expectations of people, a script that might not be isomorphic with the categories of sex difference.

1980s–Early 1990s: Problematizing Gender, Complicating Women's Identities and Oppressions

By the early 1980s, researchers who had not already done so were moving away from discussing "women" or assuming that writers could present women as having a modal experience even in one culture. Correlatively, feminist anthropologists concerned with peasant communities eroded notions that "the household" was a monolithic unit vis-à-vis outside power relations, presenting kin networks and housing arrangements as fraught with internal, gendered power dynamics. The 1980s also saw demands for inclusion and diversification within feminism by women of color, which brought new concerns on both practice and research fronts to feminist anthropology. The differential effects of race, class, ethnicity, nationality and, sexual orientation on the lives of women and men made feminist anthropologists move toward analyzing settings as "intersections" of social hierarchies that produced distinctive perceptions of the world (see, for example, Mullings 1986; Morgen 1989). The evolutionism that marked much of the earlier work was replaced by researchers focusing on configurations of political economy and sociocultural dynamics that shaped diverse sources of oppression and authority within societies at any given point in time.

Moreover, the 1980s saw the emergence of a series of studies that complicated the category "women" with both historical and comparative variation and that began to examine the gendering of analytical categories commonplace in anthropology (MacCormack and Strathern 1980 [1987]). Others analyzed the transformation of gender through imposed political and economic processes and resistance to those processes as a vehicle for understanding the range of feminist practices in the world. Etienne and Leacock's *Women and Colonization* (1980) was a series of case studies analyzing dimensions of colonization (conquest, economic domination, state formation, ethnic and class formation, racism, religious conversion) as each involved efforts to impose new notions of gender or to ordain aspects of local gender systems that "fit" the colonizing agents' notions of propriety. The case studies also investigate how these colonial agendas were sometimes as cross-purposes and often triggered profound (sometimes successful) local resistance.

The argument was that gender was a historical, changing set of beliefs that were related to political and economic changes but not reducible to them. Gendering was a process that articulated disparate structures of racial, ethnic, and religious domination in colonialism, but depended also on women's and men's actions, or agency (a point explored later in Stoler 1991). It also introduced ways of documenting historical and contemporary resistance to the imposition of gender hierarchies and the uneven development of gender hierarchies even under conditions of capitalist development (Nash 1985; see also Gailey 1987b).

The activism of gays and lesbians within the United States opened a new terrain for scholarly inquiry, legitimating the study of sexuality that long had been limited, with very few exceptions, to heterosexual and clinical studies. Gayle Rubin's early contribution (1975) led the way by challenging the "naturalness" of heterosexuality in sex-gender systems and calling attention to the heterosexual bias in the anthropological study of kinship. An anthology by Whitehead and Ortner (1981) sought to discuss the relationship between sexuality and gender as cultural constructs. Some of the contributors approached the issue of sexuality in a cultural context that included historical change. In keeping with the overall structuralist perspective of the volume, however, gender was assumed to be inherently hierarchical, although taking different forms in different circumstances. The volume's linkage of sexuality with gender systems anticipated the move among many feminist anthropologists in the 1980s toward Foucault's version of poststructuralism (Yanagisako and Delaney 1995), particularly the assumption that difference is rooted in conceptual schemas where the terms may shift as part of a configuration of cultural practices, including the ways in which the issues are framed by those considered as experts or powerful.

Because of the examination of feminist movements that these previously submerged or ignored voices demanded, researchers had to abandon more naive assumptions that "being a woman" alone gave a privileged lens through which to view power relations in a setting. This led to feminist anthropologists critically examining the relationship of structural oppression to the types of women's activities and activism. Women's identities were more complex—cross-cut and embedded in other kinds of sociocultural hierarchies—and this complexity required careful investigation. The forms of social hierarchy that interwove and collided, producing multiple identities for women and men, also created arenas where action was possible, where agency mattered. This growing complexity moved most of the terrain of debate from positivism toward what became known as standpoint theory.

Standpoint Approaches

The early feminist approaches raised another set of methodological issues, namely, how does the social category and position of the researcher influence her or his relationship with those who make the study possible, the subjects? In early studies, it was thought that because the researcher was in a marginalized category, women, and so were the people among whom the researcher lived and observed, there would be a kinship that might even provide a privileged lens for analysis (see, for example, Rohrlich-Leavitt et al. 1975). This position was consciously parallel to that of cultural nationalism within the black power movement in the United States: The researcher from a disempowered category has an edge in conducting research on other disempowered people. Even though she is privileged in being able to conduct the research at all (national privilege), she carried with her the consciousness of her own oppression within her home society. Thus, the researcher in the marginalized category develops a kind of "double consciousness" that permits insight into the kinds of power relations that might be oppressing the people whom she studies. They might relate to her better, because on some level she is one of them, too. The position raised two questions: On what basis do we make claims to which audiences? How do we reduce the chasm of power between anthropologist and informants/subjects?

This argument was controversial in the 1970s and remains so today. A number of strategies were developed for addressing the problem of power in anthropological field research: advocacy, witnessing, conducting research on those more powerful, and so on. The nature of one central technique of field research, participant observation, was criticized for its inherent evasion of the question of commitment and its reproduction of "othering," that is, rendering the subjects of research into objects, voyeurism by the more powerful.

Demands from oppressed groups—primarily women of color—within industrial capitalist countries and the postcolonial world for inclusion, for being heard, and for shaping the research agenda, made the pretense of "shared fate" in feminist fieldwork seem another form of imperial arrogance (Narayan 1995). Some called for research to be done only by women from the same culture, but as many pointed out, the class, ethnicity, race, and religion of outsiders might make them better witnesses than someone whose gender or national identity was the same (see Whitehead and Conaway 1986; Bell et al. 1993). What emerged from this ongoing controversy are different feminist strategies, on the one hand, for developing ongoing patterns of sharing and collaboration with informants versus focusing on fieldwork as a place and the relationship with informants as a lens to explore the conundrums of the complex identities of the researcher in her own society, on the other.

Some proposed a kind of resolution to this by having the researcher's configuration of social categories be somewhat aligned with those of the subjects. The problem is, of course, which categories matter more for the research in question.

The researcher might consider that because there is a "match" with informants in one or two dimensions there is privileged access or understanding. But other dimensions could be more important to the subjects of research, possibly alienating them from the researcher who is unable or unwilling to recognize these other dimensions. Indeed, for U.S. feminists, class differences within a shared ethnicity pose particular problems, as class analysis isn't encouraged within the social sciences. Acknowledging power differences is necessary in feminist research, but how to integrate one's knowledge of them into the research design and process is a matter of contention. An early life history/ethnography that investigated the problems of "translating" for a different audience and the consequences of that translation, was Shostak's *Nisa: The Life and Words of a !Kung Woman* (1981).

The 1990s: Translation, Testimonies, and Transnational Questions of Power

Creating "situated knowledges"—a series of clearly interested arguments—has been suggested by others as a means of making clear that knowledge is socially produced and a historically shifting terrain of contentious meanings. Situated knowledge, based on the meanings created by the encounter between people who are different in various ways, depends on understanding that social hierarchies make shared meanings unlikely. It is a logical outgrowth from what is called "standpoint theory" and a resolution of some of its problems. Harding (1987) characterized *standpoint* as feminist analysis that "insists the inquirer him/herself be placed on the same critical plane as the overt subject matter, thereby recovering the entire research process for scrutiny in the results of research" (p. 9).

She elaborates that standpoint entails explicitly acknowledging for the audience/reader the role played by the researcher's "class, race, culture, and gender assumptions, beliefs, and behavior" in shaping the research design, process, and results. The researcher in this stance can't remain the anonymous expert, the hidden authoritative voice. It is sometimes seen as a vehicle for achieving authorial responsibility and for insisting that the audience has a right to know that knowledge is socially produced. This concern with empowering the reader to join the evaluation process by making the author accountable for the text has become widespread in the 1990s.

The question of accountability enters into feminist anthropology in the mid-1980s and articulates in an important way with an implicit contradiction between feminist practice and cultural relativism. One of the major debates continuing to the present day challenges cultural relativism where violence against women is concerned. A number of researchers have argued that the particular expertise of feminist anthropology can help stop violence against women and can facilitate recovery from violation (Hoff 1990). Studies of gang and acquaintance rape (Sanday 1990, 1995, 1996), wife battering (Counts et al. 1992), female genital mutilation (Gruenbaum

1982 [1993]), and legal outcomes of women seeking redress or protection from violent partners call into question anthropology's historical commitment to relativism where the health and safety of marginalized people are involved. But the issues involved also underscore the relationship of the researcher's relative social power to the kind of research we undertake. Let's consider an early and controversial example.

Beginning in the 1980s, there was an outcry among several anthropologists from the United States and other Euro American countries calling for an international ban on female circumcision, clitoridectomy, and infibulation in a range of countries in Africa. (See Walley [1997] for a fine discussion of the issues involved.) Feminist anthropologists and feminists in general from countries where female circumcision and infibulation are routine responded to this call in ways that rocked feminist circles across the globe. Feminists from Egypt, Nigeria, Sudan, and other relevant countries had denounced the practices and called for their abandonment before feminists from other parts of the world became involved (for example, El Saadawi 1980; Thiam 1986 [1978]).

These African activist scholars and public health workers have called the activists from the United States—both white and black—to task for reinforcing colonial images of Africa and for focusing more on claiming leadership of some kind of "global feminism" than on showing needed international solidarity. The question was not whether female genital mutilation was tolerable— no one involved in the debates defended the practice. But local activists insisted that others consider: (1) What happens to girls—ranging from sexual harassment to sexual assault and prostitution—if the practice is legally banned without providing alternative ways to establish respectability; (2) What venues for activism might be more appropriate for activists from other countries—such as placing pressure on their own countries to grant asylum or addressing the murders and mutilations of women on a daily basis within the activists' own countries; and (3) What happens to the effectiveness of local feminist interventions when perceived leadership is too closely identified with intellectuals from former or present colonial powers?

The ensuing discussions have revealed the power dynamics inherent in cultural relativism: The notion of a homogeneous culture does not fit the realities lived by women and men in societies riven by class, gender, ethnic, racial, or religious hierarchies. Whose version of the culture is privileged when researchers argue that a particular practice is "traditional" and, therefore, inviolate? Whose interests are served by recourse to legal rather than community-based actions? Does a top-down strategy necessarily mimic masculinist models of social action?

At the same time, the debate has challenged feminist researchers within more powerful countries to examine the responsibility of outside investigators to local women and national-level activists. The power dynamics in the range of international feminisms are intricate, complicated by lines of national status, class, and color (see Bolles 1996). They demand that the researcher examine how collaborative the planned project is and how it articulates with work being done by local feminist activists and organizations (Stephen 1997). One positive result of the debates has been the proliferation of research on the role of U.S. medical, legal-judicial, and social institutions in facilitating violence against women (for example, Sanday 1995) or in addressing the multiple needs of women who have been violated, particularly where these women come from diverse backgrounds (Connell 1997; Richie and Kanuha 1997). Many of these recent studies situate the anthropologist more clearly and involve collaboration with the subjects of the research in a more forefronted way.

Calls for arguing from a stated position are efforts to make inquiry accountable. While clearly articulated standpoints make evaluation easier and place debates on a straightforward footing, the power problem remains: Some knowledges are better situated for inclusion in global debates and policy than others. How do we situate ourselves as ethnographers, for instance, without either overwhelming the voices and perspectives of local people or irritating the readers with self-indulgent forms of reflection? The strategies taken to address the question of feminist solidarity versus intersecting hierarchies that create power differences depend largely on the political stance of the researchers in relation to the women who make the research possible (Brodkin [Sacks] 1988).

The concern with standpoint approaches in feminist anthropology continues. It also has given rise to an offshoot, born of the efforts to make standpoints clear and to produce an anthropology that forefronts the unequal negotiating process inherent in field research. Feminist anthropologists engaged in field research where the anthropologist's identity overlaps those of her informants in key ways have emphasized that shared dimensions of identity are no guarantor of either access or resolution of questions of expertise or power. For example, Weston's (1997) research in lesbian and gay communities in the United States and Lewin's (1993) work on the implications of lesbian mothering for American kinship have stressed the need for negotiating and developing consensual strategies for communication between the ethnographer and her informants where both are aware of the implications of the research for an entire community, even as the author remains accountable to both community and wider audiences for her arguments. Field research involving vulnerable populations, such as battered women or breast cancer activists, highlights the need to not revictimize as well as the vagaries of participant observation where empathy, power, deployment of data, and confidentiality are so clearly implicated in women's safety and well-being (Hoff 1990; Anglin 1997; Connell 1997).

As the new global division of labor that draws on women and men differently and intensifies conditions leading to international migration (Nash and Fernandez-Kelley 1983), a condition of transnationalism has been created. On an unprecedented scale, people's identities and affiliations are being constructed from experiences of migration, living "in between" as well as in two or more countries (and gender systems), and tapping cultural resources from a variety of sources. Transnationalism has made concerns about feminist practice in field research even more important. The shift in communications technology, literacy, and migration have meant that informants are better informed, more skeptical of outside expertise, and are not invisibly and silently ensconced far from the researcher's home. Feminist anthropologists tackling the thorny issue of how not to impose a form of feminism embedded in a particular configuration of gender, race, class, and cultural tradition have begun to explore what methodology means in these new transnational, linked but power-laden spaces (see Grewal and Caplan 1994).

Reflexive approaches are one response to the problems raised (see Enslin 1994). In these approaches, the researcher assumes that the entire research process—from design to audience—reveals as much, if not more, about the society sending the researcher and the researcher's own concerns as it does about the people who are the subjects of inquiry. Most feminist anthropologists would argue that the problems they research are, to a degree at least, sparked, shaped, or informed by issues in their own society and/or the concerns of the people with whom they work. The degree to which reflexivity characterizes a feminist text varies, but all seek to make the act of writing and filtering experience—of creating knowledge claims—apparent to the reader. For those most committed to the approach, the task of the author is as much to unmask and lay bare the artificiality, the edifice, of the text as it is to make any other claims (Behar 1993; Behar and Gordon 1995).

Some go so far as to write about experience as if it and the production of knowledge were the same. The multiplicity and often amorphous swirl of perceptions, meanings, and emotions accompanying a significant event or process must be related to an audience, a problem, a reference to become knowledge; the form of writing and sense of audience shape the knowledge produced (Wolf 1992). Experiential knowledge is possible, but it is not given. Writing about experience without these intervening concerns is memoir. Some feminist ethnographies done in the name of reflexivity convert the researcher into the main, or a main, object of research. While this is not a problem for memoir as a genre, it is a problem for ethnography (see Wagner-Martin 1994). Politically, the field memoir can create a new form of silencing. In the interest of redressing the imbalance of power that originally makes translation of one people's experiences for an audience in another culture, according to the Latin American saying, into betrayal (Alarcon 1994), the researcher uses the words of the informant as a foil for her own exploration of self. The risk here is collapsing the certainly problematic anthropological encounter into a kind of psychological memoir or, at worst, a travelogue. As Mascia-Lees et al. (1989) point out, research in this vein risks audience alienation.

In the testimonial of Maria Teresa Tula (1994), done in association with Lynn Stephen, Stephen argues that collaborative encounters are necessarily flawed in a global setting where power accrues to the researcher, but that this is no excuse to withdraw from feminist practice. She argues that feminist ethnographers can have witnessing and facilitating roles, furthering the agendas of the informants and adding to the subjects' sense of their own experiences her privileged lens onto global capitalist processes, state dynamics, and the like. This kind of collaboration involves sharing lessons from both parties' efforts and bringing the collective wisdom to bear on issues in each society, informing both collaborators' practices. In another volume on women-centered social movements in Latin America, Stephen (1997) argues that working-women's movements often develop out of concerns for the well-being of family and community. In addressing these issues, participants come to define what can be seen as a feminist agenda and adopt strategies of empowerment that define a distinctively indigenous feminist practice.

As discussed above, a range of techniques of investigation can be used in feminist anthropological research. The techniques used depend largely on the questions posed and what can be developed as data in the research context. Also relevant are the audiences for whom the research is intended. If feminist ethnographers are trying to influence policy, for example, the research conducted has to make sense to policy makers: Quantitative techniques may be necessary in such circles. The same researchers could use the same research project to reach decidedly different audiences as well—social scientists or undergraduate students, for example. They would therefore develop data and communicate it in different ways to relate to those people. What marks the project as feminist is (1) the focus on gender as a salient analytical category, and (2) the purpose in contributing to an overall effort to dismantle gendered forms of oppression and exploitation. Generally, these twin aspects make the research interdisciplinary as well.

Impact on Archaeology, Physical/Biological, and Linguistic Subfields

Today, for instance, American anthropology's canonical "four fields" are disputed and defended arenas where addressing questions about humans is seen as meaningful—our symboling capacity, our sense of our own physiological make-up, our sociocultural structures and universes of meaning, and our sense of our past. Feminist anthropology both merges some of those terrains and operates within them. Yet feminist anthropology has developed unevenly in the subfields of anthropology, a fact that reflects in large measure the different proportions of women to men in the subfields. Wylie argues, for instance, that feminist methods in archaeology have been later to develop than those within ethnology (Wylie 1991). Patterson (1995) holds that this is due to both social exclusion and hermetic concerns with empiricism (for example, Flannery and Marcus 1994). Indeed, the first feminist anthology in ethnology was published 20 years before the first one in archaeology (Gero and Conkey 1991), and the uneven development of the concept of gender in these initial articles reflects some of the scholars' discomfort with the notion of gender rather than simply women. But there are excellent examples of how gendering archaeology can provide vital new insights into sociocultural dynamics (see Wright 1996).

Brumfiel's research (1996) shows how gender can be central to the analysis of state dynamics, a concern that has dominated the subfield since its inception. Using standard field techniques and a theoretical orientation informed by debates regarding gender from a number of disciplines, Brumfiel challenges the prevailing ideology in the archaeology of state formation that attention to gender is best limited to the division of labor and the succession disputes or alliance strategies of ruling elites. This is not to say that gender doesn't matter in these arenas, only that women are more than producers and vehicles of political alliance among the "real" movers and shakers, that is, men (see Wright 1996). Brumfiel's work also shows that archaeological data need not limit the extent to which sex can be analytically separated from gender, but that theorizing gender can help us develop new data (see Conkey and Williams 1991). Using stylistic variations from central and more marginalized areas of the empire, Brumfiel constructs an argument that local material culture can literally embody through gendered symbols, resistance to a dominant state ideology of gender. This moves the argument beyond the gender division of labor, although that is also important, to mark and provide the contours of cultural struggle.

In biological anthropology, pioneering examinations in the 1970s by Lancaster (1973) and Leibowitz (1983 [1975]) of male bias in primate studies and in human origins work produced novel theorizations that changed the "story" of human origins permanently. It was one of the most important contributions during the more disciplinary, "corrective" phase of feminist anthropology. During the 1970s, widely accepted "man the hunter" arguments that stressed the centrality of purportedly all-male hunting groups in the development of language, food sharing, and cooperation were countered by "woman the gatherer" ones, which stressed the centrality of gathering and mother-infant bonding (Slocum 1975; Zihlman and Tanner 1978). Only Leibowitz questioned why feminists would assume that any gender division of labor existed from the outset of humanity and offered a revisionist interpretation of the fossil and material culture remains that proposed an initial age-based technical division of labor; a gender division of labor, she argued, only emerged during *Homo erectus* times (Leibowitz 1983).

In the following decades, new ethological studies have refined or challenged these views of human evolution (for example, Hrdy 1981). Critiques of basic assumptions that gender is derived from sex differences, however, are slower to emerge in physical anthropology circles (see Zihlman 1985), given the marginalization of women whose work does not fit into the dominant paradigms in the field (see Lancaster [1991] for an extensive review of these issues). Haraway's *Primate Visions* was pathbreaking in its exposé of the gendering of primatology and human origins research (Haraway 1989). Most of the analyses of how science has objectified women's bodies and biological processes and how women's diverse experiences can lead us to revise such iconographic visions of physiology, however, have come from cultural anthropologists (Gottlieb 1988; Martin 1992; Franklin 1993a; Ginsburg and Rapp 1995).

Since linguistics is itself a discipline, justice can hardly be done to the exciting work on gender and language in this small space. Feminist linguistics has focused from the outset on analyzing how various languages are gendered and how that gendering, in turn, shapes ways of thinking about the social world and ordering social relationships (Bonvillain 1993; Tannen 1994). In the 1980s, feminist linguists investigated gendered languages of specific workplaces and their implications for how technology, warfare, and so on, enter into societal discourse (for example, Cohn 1988). Exciting research today is going on into the ways that gender affects classroom discourse and the marginalization of girls and women (Tannen 1996). Others have analyzed gender dynamics in primary and secondary language acquisition (for example, Pica et al. 1991) and how gender bias enters classrooms through language use in naming, claiming, and distancing (for example, Wellhouse and Yin 1997). Feminist linguistic anthropologists also have been active in documenting the ways that creoles and pidgins, born of colonial encounters, are gendered in ways that may hamper women's actions in postcolonial and decolonization efforts. Related research focuses on how in linguistically diverse postcolonial settings, women's access to learning national languages may be blocked by educational structures and local practices. Other arenas include the gendering of nationalist discourses or the deployment of gendered languages in the shaping or dissolution of community in transnational settings (see Urciuoli 1995).

Feminist Methods in Action

By the 1990s, feminist anthropology had become a legitimate, even ensconced, specialization. But despite efforts to integrate gender and feminist epistemologies in the anthropology curriculum (Morgen 1989; Ewick 1994), canonical texts in anthropology—including the so-called new ethnography that discusses the power dynamics of fieldwork and representing other people through writing (for example Clifford and Marcus 1986)—continue to ignore or give short shrift to the influences of feminist anthropologists (Lutz 1990). The exclusion has not stopped the methodological and theoretical debates in feminism and feminist anthropology (see Folbre 1993). The 1990s have seen feminist anthropologists reexamining central anthropological concepts, such as kinship, whenever gender is deployed as a lens (Collier and Yanagisako 1987; Collier et al. 1993). Similarly, new studies explore the ways that gender, race, and class are mutually constructive (Brodkin 1996), and how gender provides a novel way of understanding the dynamics within ethnic and working-class communities (Lamphere 1987; Brodkin 1993). But even without these exciting new ventures onto classic anthropological terrains, we can see from the discussion above that there is little in the concerns of the "new ethnography" that hasn't been discussed over the past 20 years in feminist anthropology's methodological debates.

Indeed, the interdisciplinarity of feminist anthropology marks it as a model for the debates regarding textuality, the writer as expert, and the question of reflexivity in social science inquiry, and the relationship of theory and practice. Perhaps because women—and women of color in particular—in the industrial capitalist societies that produce most anthropologists are barraged with naturalizing and reductive images of their being, feminist anthropologists have been more critical and earlier in their criticism of the objectifying and reductive tendencies in social research. Let us examine some actual studies to see how the methods work in practice and how theoretical inquiry and practice can be mutually instructive.

Research on gender and power proceeds apace in this decade, in an effort to call attention to and change policies directed at women, but with new attention to ways that other vectors of social power affect the research process and new strategies for redressing the imbalance and producing participatory research (see Jarrett 1994; Wang et al. 1996). For example, Ida Susser's ongoing work with Denise Oliver, Maritza Williams, and a team of other anthropologists on homeless families in New York City in the 1990s shows keen attention to intersections of identities in the development of research strategies and in outreach work. In a series of articles Susser examines, through narratives from homeless women "talking to" social workers, how dire poverty shapes women's lives as mothers, wives, sexual partners, and intermittent workers (Susser 1991, 1993, 1996; Susser and Gonzalez 1992).

The work is unusual in how that agency is portrayed. Women are both active on behalf of themselves and their children, yet also structurally and therefore personally vulnerable. Men and children are considered actors as well because the work seeks to present a comprehensive view of gender relations across generations and in relation to the agencies and gatekeepers the people must engage to survive. The research itself was team constructed, with interviewers whose racial and ethnic backgrounds would provide useful differences in how people interviewed might deploy information—the perception of relative power between interviewer and interviewee.

Although difficult to conduct, given the transience of the interviewees, multiple interviews were conducted. Social workers were included because, as Susser explains, they often are the only outsiders with any sustained connection to these families and because they simultaneously hold power over them but also can get resources no one else can (Susser 1998). The multiple predicaments faced by these women and their families are placed in a political-economic and historic context of a rapidly restructuring New York City (1996). The research has clearly drawn implications for health care, social welfare, and domestic violence services. Thus, the study addresses the power relations of anthropologists and informants structurally by diversifying the team and making policy arguments at key public events in the city without agonizing about the personal identity of the researchers. In tandem with this research into the relationship of gender to the political and economic aspects of oppression in late capitalism within the United States, internationally, and transnationally (di Leonardo 1993), two other arenas are of growing importance in feminist anthropology today: the politics of sexuality and its relationship to gender and other aspects of social hierarchy and the cultural and political-economic aspects of reproduction.

The research being conducted on sexuality and culture demands that we reconsider how closely or obliquely sexual orientation and practices are linked with gender systems and identities. Works such as Riley's and Weston's different treatments of American kinship when focused on lesbian families (Riley 1988; Weston 1991), and Lewin's (1993) argument about reproduction and parenting in lesbian communities encouraged reexamination of what kinship means and how kinship is forged. Today, because of the intervention of technologies permitting transsexuality, new questions are being discussed. Researchers are called on to evaluate whether people involved are also transgendered. More fundamentally, these studies ask what shapes commitment or orientation of persons to gender identities. In doing so, the problematic between the social construction of gender, on the one hand, and what are presented usually as natural sex differences, on the other, is made more complicated (Franklin 1993a). Such technologies challenge the naturalness of sex difference and make apparent that what is received as nature is actually a cultural encoding of physicality. For example, female-to-male transsexual operations in the United States make a strong claim that maleness in the United States is conceived of as having a penis and more testosterone than estrogen production, but is not necessarily related to ejaculation or sperm production. This arena of inquiry pushes the frontiers of feminist anthropology past the dichotomies of earlier eras to a more fully social constructionist appreciation of both sex and gender.

Research on the gendering of reproduction, similarly, draws on the technologies invented and deployed in metropolitan centers of late capitalism to reexamine what is meant by sex differences, on the one hand, and familial kin roles, on the other (Franklin 1988). The class, race, and gender issues surrounding surrogacy, in-vitro fertilization, egg transplantation, sperm donation, and even cloning demand that we evaluate what kinship categories mean in this new social setting (Ginsburg and Rapp 1991, 1995; Strathern 1992; Franklin 1993b, 1997). Correlatively, the expansion of transnational and transracial adoption in many industrialized capitalist countries, particularly where these adoptions tend to favor one gender or the other, creates new arenas of complicated gender and racial as well as class and national identities (Gailey 1998) and call on anthropologists to develop new models of kin formation (Modell 1994). This work on reproduction in the new world order articulates with research on cultural variations in how human status and social personhood accrue to fetuses and infants (Morgan 1993), research that can help readers approach debates over reproductive rights in a different way, one that side-steps the polemics. Feminist anthropologists, by engaging in research that demands that they problematize the participation end of participant observation and develop more explicitly collaborative studies, are at the forefront of these new studies.

Conclusion

A range of feminist anthropologists are operationalizing the often-invoked need to understand how class and race, ethnicity, or nationality shape the experience of gender and our strategies for transforming oppressive relations and structures within our own societies and elsewhere (Brodkin [Sacks] 1988; Harrison 1991). This concern with "intersections" cannot be dismissed as a genuflection in the direction of political correctness at home, for if we make claims about ourselves through the inevitably partial knowing gleaned from others, we must understand how these important aspects of social differentiation (if not always hierarchy) shape the lives of the people who make our studies possible (see Morgen 1989). Moreover, we need to see how shifting and intersecting social and cultural identities affect the questions we can imagine and pose and how we are perceived in our research settings and among our audiences.

Feminist anthropology can't escape the inherent production of Others so long as difference is reproduced through the normal operations of our political economies and attendant ideological practices, but the process of Othering can be held up to scrutiny. One of the consequences of its becoming institutionalized as a specialization is the defense of boundaries signaled by the recent efforts to produce canonical feminist texts (Behar and Gordon 1995) and to inscribe canonical histories (Viswesrayan 1997). The view of feminist methodologies presented in this handbook is in part a response to those efforts, a warning and a claim for appreciating the insights and diversity of approaches and theories that informed feminist practices in anthropology from the outset. The vitality of feminist methodologies lies in the linkage of practice and social engagement with theorizing and collaborating with others to produce useful knowledges. As the specialization becomes entrenched, there will be a tendency, which we can resist, toward methodological orthodoxy and toward theorizing estranged from our own social involvements. We need to guard against viewing our own scholarship and engagement as inherently feminist simply because we define ourselves as feminist or are seen that way.

By keeping linkage of theory and practice vigorous, however, exciting research prospects can be envisioned—ways of helping understand and project voices of those who have been disenfranchised, marginalized, or silenced because of their gender, race, class, and other social positioning. The global impact of industrial capitalism and the upheavals that accompany its normal operations call on us to listen, to engage, and to convey to our own communities and other audiences, the gendering of struggles throughout the world. Local variations in what constitutes gendering, the relative importance of gender in social structures and cultural practices, and how gendering shapes people's perceptions of possible pasts, presents, and futures matter more now than ever before if we are not to be consumed and fragmented beyond all ability to construct meaningful lives. Such an anthropology—by speaking from our various and shifting standpoints, and mostly by standing alongside and opening audiences for previously silenced or muted voices—offers much to the development of feminist agendas and practices throughout the world.

ACKNOWLEDGMENTS

I am grateful to Karen Brodkin and H. Russell Bernard for very helpful criticisms and suggestions regarding the paper. I also thank Mary Anglin, Thomas Patterson, and an anonymous reviewer for their comments on an earlier draft.

REFERENCES

Alarcon, Norma. 1994. Traddutora, Traditora: A Paradigmatic Figure of Chicana Feminism. In *Scattered Hegemonies*. Inderpal Grewal and Pat Caplan, eds. Pp. 110–133. Minneapolis: University of Minnesota Press.

Amadiume, Ifi. 1987. *Male Daughters, Female Husbands: Gender and Sex in an African Society*. London: Zed.

Anglin, Mary. 1997. Working from the Inside Out: Implications of Breast Cancer Activism for Biomedical Policies and Practices. *Social Science and Medicine* 44(9):1403–1415.

Behar, Ruth. 1993. *Translated Woman*. Boston: Beacon Press.

Behar, Ruth, and Deborah Gordon, eds. 1995. *Women Writing Culture*. Berkeley: University of California Press.

Bell, Diane, Pat Caplan, and Wazir Jahan Karim. 1993. *Gendered Fields: Women, Men, and Ethnography*. London: Routledge.

Bell, Diane, and Pam Ditton. 1980. *Law: The Old and the New: Aboriginal Women in Central Australia Speak Out*. Canberra: Aboriginal History.

Bolles, A. Lynn. 1996. *Sister Jamaica: A Study of Women, Work, and Home in Kingston*. Lanham, MD: University Press of America.

Bonvillain, Nancy. 1993. *Language, Culture, and Communication: The Meaning of Messages*. Englewood Cliffs, NJ: Prentice Hall.

Brodkin [Sacks], Karen. 1976. State Bias and Women's Status. *American Anthropologist* 78(3):565–569.

Brodkin [Sacks], Karen. 1979. *Sisters and Wives: The Past and Future of Sexual Equality*. Westport, CT: Greenwood Press.

Brodkin [Sacks], Karen. 1988. Toward a Unified Theory of Class, Race, and Gender. *American Ethnologist 16*(3):534–550.

Brodkin [Sacks], Karen. 1993. Euro-Ethnic Working-Class Women's Community Culture. *Frontiers 14*(1):1ff.

Brodkin [Sacks], Karen. 1996. Race and Gender in the Construction of Class. *Science and Society 60*(4):471–478.

Brown, Judith K. 1975. Iroquois Women: An Ethnohistoric Note. In *Toward an Anthropology of Women*. Rayna Reiter [Rapp], ed. Pp. 235–251. New York: Monthly Review.

Brumfiel, Elizabeth. 1996. Figurines and the Aztec State: Testing the Effectiveness of Ideological Domination. In *Gender and Archaeology*. Rita Wright, ed. Pp. 143–166. Philadelphia: University of Pennsylvania Press.

Clifford, James, and George Marcus. 1986. *Writing Culture: The Poetics and Politics of Ethnography*. Berkeley: University of California Press.

Cohn, Carol. 1988. Sex and Death and the Rational World of Defense Intellectuals. In *Women on War*. Daniela Gioseffi, ed. Pp. 84–99. New York: Simon and Schuster.

Collier, Jane, Michelle Rosaldo, and Sylvia Yanagisako. 1993. Is There a Family? New Anthropological Views. In *Talking about People: Readings in Contemporary Anthropology*. William Haviland and Robert Gordon, eds. Pp. 151–158. Mountain View, CA: Mayfield.

Collier, Jane, and Sylvia Yanagisako. 1987. Toward a Unified Analysis of Gender and Kinship. In *Gender and Kinship*. Jane Collier and Sylvia Yanagisako, eds. Pp. 14–50. Stanford: Stanford University Press.

Connell, Patricia. 1997. Understanding Victimization and Agency: Considerations of Race, Class, and Gender. Special Issue: Gender, Violence, and the Law. *Political and Legal Anthropology Review 20*(2):115–143.

Conkey, Margaret, and Sarah Williams. 1991. Original Narratives: The Political Economy of Gender in Archaeology. In *Gender at the Crossroads of Knowledge*. Micaela di Leonardo, ed. Pp. 102–139. Berkeley: University of California Press.

Counts, Dorothy, Judith K. Brown, and Jacqueline Campbell, eds. 1992. *Sanctions and Sanctuaries: Cultural Perspectives on the Beating of Wives*. Boulder: Westview.

di Leonardo, Micaela. 1993. What a Difference Political Economy Makes: Feminist Anthropology in the Postmodern Era. *Anthropological Quarterly 66*(2):76–81.

Edholm, Felicity, Olivia Harris, and Kate Young. 1978. Conceptualising Women. *Critique of Anthropology 3*(9–10):103–114.

El Saadawi, Nawal. 1980. *The Hidden Face of Eve: Women in the Arab World*. London: Zed.

Enslin, Elizabeth. 1994. Beyond Writing: Feminist Practice and the Limitations of Ethnography. *Cultural Anthropology 9*:537–568.

Etienne, Mona. 1980. Women, Men, Cloth and Colonization: The Transformation of Production-Distribution Relations among the Baule (Ivory Coast). In *Women and Colonization*. Mona Etienne and Eleanor B. Leacock, eds. Pp. 214–238. New York: Praeger.

Etienne, Mona, and Eleanor B. Leacock. 1980. Introduction: Women and Anthropology, Conceptual Problems. In *Women and Colonization*. Mona Etienne and Eleanor B. Leacock, eds. Pp. 1–23. New York: Praeger.

Ewick, Patricia. 1994. Integrating Feminist Epistemologies in Undergraduate Research Methods. *Gender and Society 2*(1):92–108.

Flannery, Kent, and Joyce Marcus. 1994. On the Perils of "Politically Correct" Archeology. *Current Anthropology 35*:441–442.

Folbre, Nancy. 1993. How Does She Know? Feminist Theories of Gender Bias. *History of Political Economy 25*(1):167ff.

Franklin, Sarah. 1988. Reproductive Futures: Recent Literature and Current Feminist Debates on Reproductive Technologies. *Feminist Studies 14*(3):545–561.

Franklin, Sarah. 1993a. Essentialism, Which Essentialism? Some Implications of Reproductive and Genetic Techno-Science. *Journal of Homosexuality 3*(4):27ff.

Franklin, Sarah. 1993b. Postmodern Procreation. *Science as Culture 17*:522–542.

Franklin, Sarah. 1997. Dolly: A New Form of Transgenic Breedwealth. *Environmental Values 6*(4):427ff.

Friedl, Ernestine. 1975. *Women and Men: An Anthropologist's View*. New York: Holt, Rinehart and Winston.

Gacs, Uta, Aisha Khan, Jerrie McIntyre, and Ruth Weinberg, eds. 1988. *Women Anthropologists*. Westport, CT: Greenwood Press.

Gailey, Christine Ward. 1980. Putting Down Sisters and Wives: Tongan Women and Colonization. In *Women and Colonization*. Mona Etienne and Eleanor B. Leacock, eds. Pp. 294–322. New York: Praeger.

Gailey, Christine Ward. 1987a. *Kinship to Kingship: Gender Hierarchy and State Formation in the Tongan Islands*. Austin: University of Texas Press.

Gailey, Christine Ward. 1987b. Evolutionary Perspectives on Gender Hierarchy. In *Analyzing Gender*. Beth Hess and Myra Ferree, eds. Pp. 32–67. Thousand Oaks, CA: Sage Publications.

Gailey, Christine Ward. 1998. Making Kinship in the Wake of History: Gendered Violence in U.S. Older Child Adoption. *Identities: Global Studies in Culture and Power 5*, forthcoming.

Gero, Joan, and Margaret Conkey, eds. 1991. *Engendering Archaeology*. Cambridge: Basil Blackwell.

Ginsburg, Faye, and Rayna Rapp. 1991. The Politics of Reproduction. *Annual Review in Anthropology 20*:311–343.

Ginsburg, Faye, and Rayna Rapp, eds. 1995. *Conceiving the New World Order*. Berkeley: University of California Press.

Golde, Peggy, ed. 1970. *Women in the Field: Anthropological Experiences*. Chicago: Aldine.

Gottlieb, Alma. 1988. *Blood Magic: The Anthropology of Menstruation*. Berkeley: University of California Press.

Gough, Kathleen. 1959. The Nayars and the Definition of Marriage. *Journal of the Royal Anthropological Institute 89*:23–34.

Gruenbaum, Ellen. 1982 [1993]. The Movement Against Clitoridectomy and Infibulation in Sudan: Public Health Policy and the Women's Movement. *Medical Anthropology Newsletter 13*(2). Reprinted in 1993 in *Gender in Cross-Cultural Perspective.* Caroline Brettell and Carolyn Sargent, eds. Pp. 411–422. Englewood Cliffs, NJ: Prentice Hall.

Grewal, Inderpal, and Pat Caplan, eds. 1994. *Scattered Hegemonies*. Minneapolis: University of Minnesota Press.

Haraway, Donna. 1989. *Primate Visions: Gender, Race, and Nature in the World of Modern Science*. New York: Routledge.

Harding, Sandra. 1987. Is There a Feminist Method? In *Feminism and Methodology*. Sandra Harding, ed. Pp. 1–14. Bloomington: Indiana University Press.

Harding, Sandra. 1991. *Whose Science? Whose Knowledge?* Ithaca: Cornell University Press.

Harrison, Faye. 1991. *Decolonizing Anthropology*. Washington, DC: Association of Black Anthropologists/American Anthropological Association.

Hoff, Lee Ann. 1990. Theoretical and Methodological Issues. In *Battered Women as Survivors*. Pp. 243–255. New York: Routledge.

Hrdy, Sarah Blaffer. 1981. *The Woman That Never Evolved*. Cambridge: Harvard University Press.

Jacobs, Sue-Ellen, ed. 1971. *Women in Perspective*. Urbana: University of Illinois Press.

Jaggar, Alison. 1991. Feminist Ethics: Projects, Problems, Prospects. In *Feminist Ethics*. Claudia Card, ed. Lawrence: University Press of Kansas.

Jarrett, Robin. 1994. Living Poor: Family Life Among Single Parent, African-American Women. *Social Problems 41*(1):30–49.

Kaufman, Debra Renee. 1996. Rethinking, Reflecting, Rewriting: Teaching Feminist Methodology. *The Review of Education/Pedagogy/Cultural Studies 18*(2):165–174.

Krige, Eileen Jenson, and J. D. Krige. 1943. *The Realm of a Rain Queen*. London: Oxford University Press.

Lamphere, Louise. 1974. Strategies, Cooperation, and Conflict among Women in Domestic Groups. In *Women, Culture, and Society*. Michelle Rosaldo and Louise Lamphere, eds. Pp. 97–112. Stanford: Stanford University Press.

Lamphere, Louise. 1977. Review Essay: Anthropology. *Signs 2*(3):612–627.

Lamphere, Louise. 1987. *From Working Daughters to Working Mothers: Women in a New England Industrial Community*. Ithaca: Cornell University Press.

Lamphere, Louise. 1993. The Domestic Sphere of Women and the Public World of Men: The Strengths and Limitations of an Anthropological Dichotomy. In *Gender in Cross-Cultural Perspective*. C. Brettell and C. Sargent, eds. Pp. 67–76. Englewood Cliffs, NJ: Prentice Hall.

Lamphere, Louise, Helen Ragone, and Patricia Zavella, eds. 1997. *Situated Lives*. New York: Routledge.

Lancaster, Jane. 1973. In Praise of the Achieving Female Monkey. *Psychology Today* 7(4):30–36ff.

Lancaster, Jane. 1991. A Feminist and Evolutionary Biologist Takes a Look at Women. *Yearbook of Physical Anthropology 43*:1–11.

Leacock, Eleanor B. 1954. *The Montagnais "Hunting Territory" and the Fur Trade*. Washington, DC: American Anthropological Association Memoirs 78.

Leacock, Eleanor B. 1972. Introduction. In *Frederick Engels: The Origins of the Family, Private Property, and the State*. Eleanor B. Leacock, ed. Pp. 7–67. New York: International Publishers.

Leacock, Eleanor B. 1977a. The Changing Family and Lévi-Strauss, or Whatever Happened to Fathers? *Social Research 44*(2):235–259.

Leacock, Eleanor B. 1977b. Women, Development, and Anthropological Facts and Fictions. *Latin American Perspectives 4*(1–2):8–17.

Leacock, Eleanor B. 1981. *Myths of Male Dominance*. New York: Monthly Review.

Leacock, Eleanor B. 1983. Interpreting the Origins of Gender Inequality: Conceptual and Historical Problems. *Dialectical Anthropology 7*(4):263–284.

Leacock, Eleanor B., and June Nash. 1977. *Ideologies of Sex: Archetypes and Stereotypes*. Annals of the New York Academy of Sciences 285: Issues in Cross-Cultural Research. Leonore Adler, ed. Pp. 618–645. New York: New York Academy of Sciences.

Leacock, Eleanor B. and Helen Safa, eds. 1986. *Women's Work*. South Hadley, MA: Bergin and Garvey.

Leibowitz, Lila. 1983 [1975]. Origins of the Sexual Division of Labor. In *Woman's Nature*. Marian Lowe and Ruth Hubbard, eds. Pp. 123–147. Elmsford, NY: Pergamon Press.

Lewin, Ellen. 1993. *Lesbian Mothers: Accounts of Gender in America*. Ithaca: Cornell University Press.

Lurie, Nancy. 1966. Women in Early American Anthropology. In *Pioneers of American Anthropology: The Uses of Biography*. June Helm, ed. Pp. 29–83. Seattle: University of Washington Press.

Lutz, Catherine. 1990. The Erasure of Women's Writing in Sociocultural Anthropology. *American Ethnologist 17*(4):611–627.

MacCormack, Carol, and Marilyn Strathern, eds. [1980] 1987. *Nature, Culture, and Gender*. Cambridge: Cambridge University Press.

Martin, Emily. 1992. *The Woman in the Body*. Boston: Beacon Press.

Mascia-Lees, Frances, Patricia Sharpe, and Colleen Ballerino Cohen. 1989. The Postmodernist Turn in Anthropology: Cautions from a Feminist Perspective. *Signs 15*(1):7–33.

Modell, Judith. 1994. *Kinship with Strangers: Adoption and Interpretations of Kinship in American Culture*. Berkeley: University of California Press.

Morgan, Lynn. 1993 [1989]. When Does Life Begin? A Cross-Cultural Perspective on the Personhood of Fetuses and Young Children. In *Talking about People: Readings in Contemporary Anthropology.* William Haviland and Robert Gordon, eds. Pp. 28–38. Mountain View, CA: Mayfield.

Morgen, Sandra. 1989. Introduction. In *Gender and Anthropology: Critical Reviews for Research and Teaching.* Sandra Morgen, ed. Pp. 1–20. Washington, DC: American Anthropological Association.

Mullings, Leith. 1986. Uneven Development: Class, Race, and Gender in the United States before 1900. In *Women's Work.* Eleanor B. Leacock and Helen Safa, eds. Pp. 41–56. South Hadley, MA: Bergin and Garvey.

Narayan, Kirin. 1995. Participant Observation. In *Women Writing Culture.* Ruth Behar and Deborah Gordon, eds. Pp. 33–48. Berkeley: University of California Press.

Nash, June, ed. 1985. *Women and Change in Latin America.* South Hadley, MA: Bergin and Garvey.

Nash, June, and Maria Patricia Fernandez-Kelley, eds. 1983. *Women and Men and the International Division of Labor.* Albany: State University of New York Press.

Oboler, Regina Smith. 1980. Is the Female Husband a Man? Woman/Woman Marriage among the Nandi of Kenya. *Ethnology 19*(1):69–88.

Okeyo, Achola Pala. 1980. Daughters of the Lakes and Rivers: Colonization and the Land Rights of Luo Women. In *Women and Colonization.* Mona Etienne and Eleanor B. Leacock, eds. Pp. 186–213. New York: Praeger.

Omvedt, Gail. 1977. On the Participant Study of Women's Movements: Methodological, Definitional, and Action Considerations. In *The Politics of Anthropology: From Colonialism and Sexism Toward a View from Below.* Gail Huizer and Bruce Mannheim, eds. Pp. 373–393. The Hague and Paris: Mouton.

Ortner, Sherry. 1974. Is Female to Male as Nature Is to Culture? In *Woman, Culture, and Society.* M. Rosaldo and Louise Lamphere, eds. Pp. 67–88. Stanford: Stanford University Press.

Ortner, Sherry. 1981. Gender and Sexuality in Hierarchical Societies. In *Sexual Meanings: The Cultural Construction of Gender and Sexuality.* Harriet Whitehead and Sherry Ortner, eds. Pp. 359–409. Cambridge: Cambridge University Press.

Patterson, Thomas. 1995. *Toward a Social History of Archaeology in the United States.* Fort Worth: Harcourt Brace.

Paulme, Denise, ed. 1971. *Women of Tropical Africa.* Berkeley: University of California Press.

Pica, Teresa, Lloyd Holliday, and Nora Lewis. 1991. Language Learning Through Interaction: What Role Does Gender Play? *Studies in Second Language Acquisition 13*(3): 343–361.

Quinn, Naomi. 1977. Anthropological Studies on the Status of Women. *Annual Review in Anthropology 6*:181–225.

Rapp, Rayna [Reiter], ed. 1975. *Toward an Anthropology of Women.* New York: Monthly Review.

Rapp, Rayna [Reiter]. 1977. The Search for Origins: Unraveling the Threads of Gender Hierarchy. *Critique of Anthropology* 3(9–10):5–24.

Rapp, Rayna [Reiter]. 1978. Review Essay: Anthropology. *Signs* 4(3):497–513.

Reinharz, Shulamit, ed. 1992. *Feminist Methods in Social Research*. New York: Oxford University Press.

Reiter, Rayna. See Rapp, Rayna.

Richie, Beth, and Valli Kanuha. 1997. Battered Women of Color in Public Health Care Systems: Racism, Sexism, and Violence. In *Through the Prism of Difference*. Maxine Baca Zinn, Pierette Hondagneu-Sotelo, and Michael Messner, eds. Pp. 121–129. Boston: Allyn and Bacon.

Riley, Claire. 1988. American Kinship: A Lesbian Account. *Feminist Issues* (Fall): 75–94.

Rohrlich Leavitt, Ruby, Barbara Sykes, and Elizabeth Weatherford. 1975. Aboriginal Woman: Male and Female Perspectives. In *Toward an Anthropology of Women*. Rayna Reiter (Rapp), ed. Pp. 110–126. New York: Monthly Review.

Rosaldo, Michelle, and Louise Lamphere, eds. 1974. *Women, Culture, and Society*. Stanford: Stanford University Press.

Rubin, Gayle. 1975. The Traffic in Women. In *Toward an Anthropology of Women*. Rayna Reiter (Rapp), ed. Pp. 157–210. New York: Monthly Review.

Sacks, Karen. See Brodkin, Karen.

Sanday, Peggy Reeves. 1981. *Female Power and Male Dominance: On the Origins of Inequality*. Cambridge: Cambridge University Press.

Sanday, Peggy Reeves. 1990. *Fraternity Gang Rape*. New York: New York University Press.

Sanday, Peggy Reeves. 1995. Pulling Train. In *Race, Class, and Gender in the United States*. Paula Rothenberg, ed. Pp. 396–402. New York: St. Martin's Press.

Sanday, Peggy Reeves. 1996. *A Woman Scorned: Acquaintance Rape on Trial*. New York: Doubleday.

Sanjek, Roger. 1978. The Position of Women in the Major Departments of Anthropology, 1967–1976. *American Anthropologist* 80:894–904.

Schlegel, Alice, ed. 1977. *Sexual Stratification: A Cross-Cultural View*. New York: Columbia University Press.

Shostak, Marjorie. 1981. *Nisa: The Life and Words of a !Kung Woman*. New York: Random House/Vintage.

Silverblatt, Irene. 1978. Andean Women in the Inca Empire. *Feminist Studies* 4(3):37–61.

Silverblatt, Irene. 1988. Women in States. *Annual Reviews in Anthropology* 17:427–460.

Slocum, Sally. 1975. Woman the Gatherer: Male Bias in Anthropology. In *Toward an Anthropology of Women*. Rayna Reiter (Rapp), ed. Pp. 36–50. New York: Monthly Review.

Stack, Carol. 1974. *All Our Kin*. New York: Harper and Row.

Stack, Carol. 1997. Different Voices, Different Visions: Gender, Culture, and Moral Reasoning. In *Through the Prism of Difference*. Maxine Baca Zinn, Pierette Hondagneu-Sotelo, and Michael Messner, eds. Pp. 51–57. Boston: Allyn and Bacon.

Stephen, Lynn. 1997. *Women and Social Movements in Latin America: Power from Below*. Austin: University of Texas Press.

Stoler, Ann. 1991. Carnal Knowledge and Imperial Power: Gender, Race, and Morality in Colonial Asia. In *Gender at the Crossroads of Knowledge*. Micaela di Leonardo, ed. Pp. 51–102. Berkeley: University of California Press.

Strathern, Marilyn. 1972. *Women in Between: Female Roles in a Male World, Mt. Hagen, New Guinea*. London: Seminar Press.

Strathern, Marilyn. 1992. *Reproducing the Future: Essays on Anthropology and the New Reproductive Technologies*. New York: Routledge.

Susser, Ida. 1991. The Separation of Mothers and Children. In *The Dual City*. J. Mollenkopf and M. Castells, eds. Pp. 207–225. New York: Russell Sage Foundation.

Susser, Ida. 1993. Creating Family Forms: The Exclusion of Men and Teenage Boys from Families in the New York City Shelter System, 1987–91. *Critique of Anthropology* 3(3):267–285.

Susser, Ida. 1996. The Construction of Poverty and Homelessness in U.S. Cities. *Annual Review in Anthropology* 25:411–435.

Susser, Ida. 1998. Inequality, Violence, and Gender Relations in a Global City: New York, 1986–1996. *Identities: Global Studies in Culture and Power 5*, forthcoming.

Susser, Ida, and M. Gonzalez. 1992. Sex, Drugs, and Videotape: The Prevention of AIDS in a New York City Shelter for Homeless Men. *Medical Anthropology 14*: 307–232.

Tannen, Deborah. 1994. *Gender and Discourse*. New York: Oxford University Press.

Tannen, Deborah. 1996. Gender in Research on Language: Researching Gender Patterns in Classroom Discourse. *Tesol Quarterly 30*(2):341ff.

Thiam, Awa. 1986 [1978]. Clitoridectomy and Infibulation. In *Speak Out, Black Sisters: Feminism and Oppression in Black Africa*. Dorothy Blair, trans. Pp. 57–87. London: Pluto Press.

Tula, Maria Teresa, and Lynn Stephen. 1994. *Hear My Testimony: Maria Teresa Tula, Human Rights Activist from El Salvador*. Austin: University of Texas Press.

Urciuoli, Bonnie. 1995. Language and Borders. *Annual Reviews in Anthropology 24*: 525–547.

Van Allen, Judith. 1972. "Sitting on a Man": Colonialism and the Lost Political Institutions of Igbo Women. *Canadian Journal of African Studies 6*:165–181.

Vincent, Joan. 1990. *Politics and Anthropology*. Tucson: University of Arizona Press.

Visweswaran, Kamala. 1997. Feminist Ethnographies. *Annual Review in Anthropology 26*:591–621.

Wagner-Martin, Linda. 1994. *Telling Women's Lives: The New Biography*. New Brunswick, NJ: Rutgers University Press.

Walley, Christine. 1997. Searching for "Voices": Feminism, Anthropology, and the Debate Over Female Genital Mutilation. *Cultural Anthropology 12*:405–438.

Wang, Caroline, Mary Ann Burris, and Xiuang Yue Ping. 1996. Chinese Village Women as Visual Anthropologists: A Participatory Approach to Reaching Policymakers. *Social Science and Medicine 42*:1391–1400.

Wellhouse, Karyn, and Zenong Yin. 1997. "Peter Pan Isn't a Girl's Part": An Investigation of Bias in a Kindergarten Classroom. *Women and Language 20*(2):35ff.

Weston, Kath. 1991. *Families We Choose. Lesbians, Gays, Kinship*. New York: Columbia University Press.

Weston, Kath. 1997. Fieldwork in Gay and Lesbian Communities. In *Through the Prism of Difference*. Maxine Baca Zinn, Pierette Hondagneu-Sotelo, and Michael Messner, eds. Pp. 79–85. Boston: Allyn and Bacon.

Whitehead, Tony, and Mary Ellen Conaway, eds. 1986. *Self, Sex and Gender in Cross-Cultural Fieldwork*. Urbana and Champaign: University of Illinois Press.

Whitehead, Harriet, and Sherry Ortner, eds. 1981. *Sexual Meanings: The Cultural Construction of Gender and Sexuality*. Cambridge: Cambridge University Press.

Wolf, Marjorie. 1992. *A Thrice-Told Tale: Feminism, Postmodernism, and Ethnographic Responsibility*. Stanford: Stanford University Press.

Wright, Rita, ed. 1996. *Gender and Archaeology*. Philadelphia: University of Pennsylvania Press.

Wylie, Alison. 1991. Gender Theory and the Archaeological Record: Why There Is No Archaeology of Gender. In *Engendering Archaeology*. Joan Gero and Margaret Conkey, eds. Pp. 31–56. Cambridge: Basil Blackwell.

Yanagisako, Sylvia, and Carol Delaney, eds. 1995. *Naturalizing Power*. New York: Routledge.

Zihlman, Adrienne. 1985. Gathering Stories for Hunting Human Nature. *Feminist Studies 11*:364–377.

Zihlman, Adrienne, and Nancy Tanner. 1978. Gathering and the Hominid Adaptation. In *Female Hierarchies*. Lionel Tiger and Heather Fowler, eds. Pp. 163–194. Chicago: Beresford.

Seven

Transnational Research

Transnationality and globalization have become increasingly prominent in anthropology since the late 1980s. They are recurrent foci at professional meetings, and new journals such as *Public Culture* (since 1988) and *Identities* (since 1994) are devoted, to a large degree, to issues and phenomena relating to them. Older, mainstream journals likewise pay frequent attention to them. Moreover, this is an area where different research orientations and objectives overlap, and engagement with global and the transnational issues often becomes linked with general theoretical issues of modernity and postmodernity.

In this chapter, I comment briefly on conceptions of globalization and transnationality and their place in the development of anthropology. I also map the main genres of transnational research, concentrating on contributions by anthropologists. Then I present some practical and methodological concerns that may become particularly important in transnational anthropology, although I emphasize the considerable methodological continuity between it and other kinds of social and cultural anthropology.

Transnational Anthropology Past and Present

Reactions to the recent wave of transnational interests in anthropology have varied. Some suspect that it's all a fad that (they hope) will soon disappear or that will take a more modest place in the wide array of possible research interests. Others argue that it presents a major challenge to rethink radically some central assumptions in anthropological and other social science research traditions. Some are wary of it on political grounds; one commentator proposes that it may be "the ideological partner of expanding international markets and the delocalization of industrial production, trends that can proceed only if cultural islands are broken up and rendered compatible with the flow of ideas, commodities and labor through them" (Shryock 1996:30). Others, with long memories, comment that this is "reinventing anthropology"—in the same sense as reinventing the wheel. The global and transnational, they argue, have been anthropological concerns for a long time, and only ignorance or cultivated intellectual amnesia, perhaps combined with a new generation's anxiety to carve out its own niche in the academic marketplace, will turn them into something altogether new.

The suggestion that the anthropology of globalization and transnationality in its recent form has been merely an acquiescent scholarly annex to expansive Western financial, commercial, and industrial enterprise is hardly fair. More often than not, it has rather been a variety of critical anthropology, with "resistance" to alien influence and domination as a key idea. Global or transnational interconnectedness, now or in other periods, is rather too complex and multifaceted for any simple moral or intellectual stance of being for or against it.

We can recognize transational and global themes in anthropology's past in the preoccupation with diffusion early in the twentieth century, or with acculturation, "culture contact," "social change," or modernization in the decades around midcentury. Obviously, these aren't all the same, yet the recognition that the world is not a mosaic of bounded entities, existing in isolation from one another, is a common denominator. We could construct an intellectual history of transnational anthropology, but not everything that is part of it may contribute very much to a usable past.[1]

This also implies that transnational events, structures, processes, and products did not appear all of a sudden in the twentieth century, or even its last few decades. In some ways, the global ecumene of connections and cultural flows may be a very old thing. However, its characteristics need to be specified with reference to time as well as place. It is now widely recognized that globalization need not mean global homogenization. This is one reason why one recurrent theme in anthropology and related fields has been the opposition and interplay between "the global" and "the local." It is equally true that globalization may have varied through history, in form and intensity.[2] Long-distance social and cultural interconnectedness may, indeed, have intensified and broadened its scope during the twentieth century, due in large part to new technologies of transportation and communication, but in some ways it's as old as humanity itself.

If we prefer to limit the use of the term "globalization" to processes with a literally world-encompassing or at least transcontinental scope, then the term "transnational" need not always be equally inclusive. Some comments on the range of conditions and phenomena it refers to may be useful.

One tendency is to contrast transnational and international, in an attempt to restrict the use of the latter term to contexts where states appear as corporate actors vis-à-vis one another. The term transnational is thus meant to draw attention to the growing involvement of other kinds of actors—individuals, kinship groups, ethnic groups, firms, social movements, etc.—in activities and relationships that transcend national boundaries. Such a formulation, however, may draw attention to a certain ambiguity inherent in both terms. What they actually refer to may be states—political units—rather than nations—communities defined on the basis of common culture and history. The tendency to conflate these two, and to assume that every state (and, for that matter, every nation) is a nation-state, is again apparent here.[3] Consequently, and paradoxically, we may find entities like "transnational nations," consisting of ethnic diasporas—nations extending across many state boundaries.

Different disciplines may handle these kinds of ambiguities in their own ways. In anthropology, there are three main ingredients, of varying strength, in transnational studies. One is that the transnational is something that crosses the boundaries between politically defined autonomous units. The second emphasis is on a spatial dimension: The transnational tends to relate to what is somehow "long-distance." The third is also more a matter of cultural implications: The transnational is expected to encompass diversity of meanings and meaningful forms in some way.

Transnational studies are not by definition comparative, although explicit or implicit comparisons are often involved. What matters is that some phenomenon or complex of phenomena can be seen as transnationally distributed in a manner that also involves ongoing interconnectedness, interaction, exchange, or mobility. Frequently, an interest in such phenomena includes a concern with contrasting local or national adaptations and contextualizations, and so comparison is a prominent aspect of transnational research. On the other hand, the classic idea of comparative anthropology—that units are independent of one another—is clearly not present.

Some Genres of Transnational Anthropology

Anthropological research that may be described as transnational in one sense or another takes many forms. A large part of it has, in fact, been of a theoretical, conceptual, and programmatic nature, but for more empirical work we can identify certain genres as being particularly important, although they frequently shade into each other.[4] Without reviewing the variety of existing research, I will comment on each of these genres here and point to a few studies that can serve as examples.

Communities Open to the World

In an older tradition of anthropology, we were intent on portraying and analyzing local life, often in the framework of the "global mosaic" and perhaps oriented toward "the ethnographic present." In that context, we may have been inclined to disregard the presence of the district officer and the missionary and the availability of imported matches, zinc buckets, and radio batteries in the village market.

Departing somewhat from this stance, there are accounts of what we may describe as "communities open to the world"—a fairly continuous concern of anthropologists going back to the times of acculturation and modernization studies at midcentury. Robert Redfield's *A Village that Chose Progress* (1950) or Margaret Mead's *New Lives for Old* (1956) come to mind as classic examples. More recently, such studies have also drawn inspiration from Immanuel Wallerstein's (1974) world-system theory, centering on domination and conflict between core and periphery, largely in the terms of political economy. Eric Wolf's magisterial overview *Europe and the People Without History* (1982), coming closer to ethnographic concerns, similarly insists that the study of local life cannot ignore the development of the global political economy over the past 500 years or so; however, it does not quite bring the study or long-distance interconnections into the recent past and the present.

One theme in the ethnography of communities open to the world has been that of resistance: While influences reaching in from the outside appear massively powerful, local people respond through confrontation, evasion, subversive interpretation, satire, or sheer misunderstanding so as to blunt their effectiveness. No doubt a great deal of rich and illuminating ethnography has been generated here, although the word "resistance" is used to refer to so many practices that it risks losing some of its potency.[5]

Another recurrent theme can be described as "cultural creativity," not necessarily totally separate from that of resistance. This has often been a response to the tendency, already mentioned, to assume that globalization equals global cultural homogenization. This theme suggests that as previously separate cultural items (ideas, aesthetic forms, organizational forms, technologies, and so on) come into contact through greater transnational interconnectedness, new inventions and syntheses of various kinds are generated. Terms such as "hybridity" and "creolization" have come to the fore in these writings, where globalization is viewed in terms of a continued production of new diversity.[6] Studies in popular culture have made important contributions to such understandings of transnational cultural process; Waterman's (1990) ethnography of Nigerian *jùjú* music is one example.

Research on the openness of communities to the world can obviously remain quite close to time-tested anthropological field practices. There can still be a single local, or at least intranational, concentration of concrete research activities, even as we watch for foreign social, political, economic, or cultural influences. In the working perspective toward the interrelations of "the local and the global," too, there has been a tendency to take both categories somewhat for granted, allowing "the local" to take on a quality of primordiality. Under the influence of recent theorizing about modernity and postmodernity, the variable constructions of locality through social and cultural action have come under more active scrutiny, as have the discipline's traditional conceptions of "the field" (see, for example, Appadurai 1995; Hannerz 1996:25ff.; Gupta and Ferguson 1997; Olwig and Hastrup 1997).

Translocalities

Most studies of communities open to the world deal with places where most people are, after all, sedentary, and the places are somewhat peripheral within the global order. There are sites, though, that are intensely involved in mobility and in the encounters of varied kinds of mobile people and where this is quite central to their organizational characteristics. These communities also tend to be nodes within transnational social and cultural processes. Arjun Appadurai (1995:216) has described them as "translocalities," suggesting that "many such locations create complex conditions for the production and reproduction of locality, in which ties of marriage, work, business and leisure weave together various circulating populations with kinds of 'locals'. . . ."

There is little ethnography of translocalities yet, but the idea comes up often that hotels, airports, and similar institutions deserve more attention. I have tried to outline the characteristics of world cities and their cultural processes in related terms (Hannerz 1996:127ff.), and Sulayman Khalaf (1992) has discussed Arabian Gulf societies as sites with a lot of transiency. An interest in world's fairs, recently exemplified in several disciplines, may have had a start in anthropology with Burton Benedict's (1982) historical study of the San Francisco Exposition of 1915.

Border Studies

Research on border communities and border areas might be seen as special cases of communities open to the world—there is a concern with local life in a single place, but with its particular quality of facing in at least two different directions and being shaped by differences between the respective national contexts. The border between Mexico and the United States—with its highly diverse cross-border linkages and contrasts between countries in different stages of development—has been the most prominent, even exemplary, site of such studies in anthropology and other human sciences, as Robert Alvarez (1995) has observed in a recent review. There is, of course, also a related tendency to use border and borderland concepts more metaphorically, to refer to culturally and socially liminal, marginal, or interstitial conditions.

Migration

Anthropological studies of migration in the 1950s and 1960s were mostly concerned with intranational (or intracolonial) mobility—in large part with African, Asian, or Latin American villagers becoming townspeople. In later decades, however, migration has increasingly become transnational: Pakistanis and West Indians to England; Turks to Germany; North Africans to France; Mexicans, Indians, Koreans, and more West Indians to the United States; and so on.

In considerable part, the studies of migrants have been matters of single-site research, mostly at the receiving end, of immigrant communities and their involvement with the surrounding society. Yet, increasingly, it is regarded as both desirable and practicable to do such research at both ends, sending and receiving. In *Between Two Cultures* (1977), James L. Watson described it as a unique feature of the book that "all contributors have had field experience at *both* ends of the migration chain, in the migrants' own country of origin and in Britain." He suggested that, according to his own experience (in studying a Hong Kong Chinese lineage), "it is impossible to gain a true picture of immigration as a *process* without investigating the people and their families on both sides."

Since then, this has become rather more of a standard operating procedure. I suspect that it's not only a matter of anthropologists demanding more of themselves and each other, but that it's also related to the fact that transnational migration has somewhat changed character. There was certainly always some return migration and circular migration, but more often now, migrants and those who remained home can stay in rather close touch through return trips and visits from home, not to mention via telephone calls, faxes, and exchanges of consumer goods. Increasingly, the people at home and those abroad (perhaps somewhat problematic categories) thus come to form a single coherent, although spatially dispersed, social field.

Schiller et al. (1992:1) refer to those migrants "whose networks, activities and patterns of life encompass both their host and home societies" and whose "lives cut across national boundaries" as "transmigrants." They draw on their own research experiences in Southeast Asia, the Caribbean, and the United States to formulate a more general research perspective (see also Basch et al. 1994). The work of Roger Rouse (1992) on what he terms a "transnational migrant circuit" including, in particular, the *municipio* of Aguililla in Michoacán, Mexico, and Redwood City in California's Silicon Valley, also illuminates this tendency. A prominent aspect is the concern with the embeddedness of the relationships among the transmigrants themselves in a wider setting, involving, for instance, class structure, media, and state agencies (not least those regulating immigration).[7]

A large proportion of work on transnational migrants centers on working-class migrants, involved mostly in industrial or service occupations. These certainly make up a large proportion of the entire migrant population, but there is likewise considerable transnational mobility among highly skilled, higher-income people involving "brain drain" as well as considerable capital movements. Johanna Lessinger (1992a, 1992b) and Aihwa Ong (1992), among others, have paid some ethnographic attention to such groups. Yet another large, internally very heterogeneous, category of migrants in the late twentieth-century world are refugees—often with a very different relationship to their areas of origin than that of the typical transmigrant. Liisa Malkki (1995) has recently reviewed refugee studies as a field of growing anthropological concern, where there is particular reason to attend closely to the institutionalization of the refugee category through the activities of national and international agencies.

Diasporas

There are some very old diasporas, such as those of Jews and Armenians. In the twentieth century, dispersed ethnic or national communities are being continuously generated anew, often by labor migration and exile. There is hardly a sharply defined conceptual boundary between diasporas and transmigrant communities, especially as the former term has grown in popularity and come into expanding use, also of a more metaphorical nature. But we may think of the typical diaspora as one where generations have already lived away from the old homeland and where the relationship to that homeland is somehow problematic. It may be, or may have been, inaccessible. On the other hand, there may be more coming and going, and interactions and exchanges of various kinds, between the various outposts in other countries. James Clifford (1994) has recently explored the diaspora concept and its place in the contemporary landscape of ideas. Michael Fischer and Mehdi Abedi (1990:253ff.) exemplify current diaspora ethnography with their account of ritual life among Iranians in North America.

Transnational Corporations and Occupations

Much of the growth of transnational structures and relationships in this century has taken place in the realm of work. Anthropologists have devoted some attention to the activities and the impact of transnational (or multinational) corporations. Alvin Wolfe (1963, 1977) was one of the earliest commentators within anthropology, drawing on his understanding of Central African mining companies. June Nash (1979), in another early publication, discussed the corporations in general terms and reported on some exploratory fieldwork at a site, she says, "within a few yards of my office and a ten-minute subway ride from my apartment." Since then, there has been one attempt at historical and theoretical overview (Hunt 1987) as well as more intense ethnography, many involving corporations' Third World manufacturing sites (see, for example, Ong 1987).

It is, of course, possible to do such studies in a single site, somewhat in line with the communities-open-to-the-world genre. One study that involves fieldwork in several places is Christina Garsten's (1994), on the organizational culture of Apple, the computer company. Garsten did research at the company headquarters in Silicon Valley, at the European head office in Paris, and at the Swedish branch office in Stockholm. She was able to follow the interpenetration of local life with long-distance communication and visits and to see how the California-inspired, deliberately constructed corporate culture of the company's management was modified by employees in offices elsewhere.

The transnational anthropology of work, however, doesn't necessarily deal with large corporations. It's also about occupations, occupational communities, and occupational life-styles that are smaller in scale and more individualized but involve contacts and mobility across national boundaries—experiences that have become common for at least some practitioners. Tommy Dahlén (1997) has described the emergent profession of interculturalists: trainers and consultants working mostly in the marketplace, teaching awareness of cultural differences and thus sharing some of the ideas and concerns of anthropologists.

Another Swedish anthropologist, Helena Wulff, has recently been studying the transnational occupational culture of ballet dancers. The dancers' careers often take them through companies in several countries (so that a company, conversely, is often made up of dancers of many nationalities). Going on tour or training in other countries is part of the round of work, and a transnational circulation of videos has become important for instruction as well as for promotion (Wulff 1998). The transnational integration of the ballet world is aided, clearly, by the presence of explicit, homogeneous standards and the relative marginality of language in instruction and performance. Yet here, too, the contrast between the global and the local enters the picture through differences in styles and working conditions.

Yet another obviously transnational occupational grouping for which an ethnography is available is that of media foreign correspondents. Mark Pedelty (1995) concentrated his study on war correspondents in El Salvador in the early 1990s, toward the end of the war there. With a somewhat different range of interests, I have also considered this group, mostly on the basis of biographical and autobiographical accounts (Hannerz 1996:112ff.).

Finally, anthropologists themselves make up a transnational occupational grouping. A large proportion of them does much of its work abroad, and even those engaged in "anthropology at home" tend to be continuously and consciously involved with colleagues in other countries, at least by way of reading matter. The ongoing debate about outsider and insider anthropologies—for one enlightening contribution, see Kirin Narayan (1993)—may be viewed against this background.

Tourism

If there is a globalization of work, there is also a globalization of leisure: The anthropology of tourism has been an expanding field for some time and much of it involves travel between countries. The volume edited by Valene Smith (1977) was an early contribution to this genre; Nelson Graburn (1983) offered a general perspective soon thereafter, and the journal *Annals of Tourism Research* has been an important outlet for anthropological writings on tourism. Deborah Gewertz and Frederick Errington's (1991) study of the Chambri of Papua New Guinea is an example of an ethnography, somewhat in a communities-open-to-the-world style, in which tourism figures importantly.

A contrast is often made between two kinds of tourists. On the one hand, there is tourism of individuals or small groups, seeking to adapt to local facilities and ways of life and looking for more "authentic" experiences. On the other, there is mass tourism, which, to some extent, creates its own institutions and environments. By so doing, it isolates itself from the host society in some ways and in other ways it shapes the latter to fit the requirements of the visitors and those of the industry that handles them. Orvar Löfgren's (forthcoming) study of European charter tourism in the Mediterranean area offers a view of the latter type of leisure travel.

Cyberspace

Classic ethnography involves people in physically present, face-to-face relationships. In many kinds of transnational anthropology, this remains the dominant relational form. Increasingly, though, people cross boundaries without carrying their bodies along. While the anthropological exploration of cyberspace has hardly more than begun, there is a quickly growing interest in the possibilities of new information technology. Since that technology has such a great capacity to transcend physical distances and national boundaries, it is unlikely that this will *not* become a significant genre in transnational studies (unless it is simply absorbed as an aspect of other genres). Arturo Escobar (1994) and Gustavo Lins Ribeiro (1997) suggest general visions of an anthropology of cyberculture. In an essay by David Edwards (1994) on the nature of "fieldwork" on (rather than "in," perhaps) Afghanistan, we glimpse the author monitoring the news groups "Soc.Cul.Afghanistan" and "Soc.Religion.Islam" on the Internet and worrying somewhat about the ethics of being an anonymous reader of other people's messages.

Media

As media technology diversifies, the dividing line between cyberspace and media studies as types of transnational anthropology may become rather blurred. We can think of "media studies," however, as centering more often on those communication technologies that tend to involve more asymmetrical relationships between specialized producers/senders and relatively large audiences. The assumption that media are "mass media" may be becoming obsolete in several ways, but the tendency to have separate bodies of research for the producing and consuming sides of mediated relationships continues to be strong. And ethnographic methods have recently grown increasingly important at the consuming end.

But the point here is that consuming is itself a kind of producing—interpretation is an active engagement with media content, and may lead to further action. It's not to be taken for granted in the way it frequently has been, especially in some earlier styles of mass communication research.

The argument is relevant across a range of written, print, and electronic media. Laura Bohannan's (1966) well-known essay, "Shakespeare in the Bush," about the way Tiv villagers in midcentury central Nigeria responded to Hamlet, is surely a progenitor of later transnational media studies. Most often, however, the point has recently been made with reference to film and television programs. In transnational studies, this becomes part of a critical response to the scenario of global cultural homogenization: even if the same programming becomes available and perhaps popular everywhere, it cannot be taken for granted that it is understood in precisely the same way everywhere. The study by Israeli media researchers Tamar Liebes and Elihu Katz (1990), of the varying interpretations of the TV series *Dallas* by groups of different national origin in Israel, offers striking evidence of this.

Interest in the actual audience handling of media has made ethnography a popular notion in media studies outside anthropology, too. Here, anthropologists may at times be skeptical with regard to what passes for ethnography in some research contexts. The amount, intensity, and breadth of actual observation of audiences and their daily rounds is sometimes very limited. Anthropologists may prefer to integrate an understanding of media use into a more wide-ranging ethnographic study where the interactions between media experiences and other experiences, relationships, and interests can be better grasped. Minou Fuglesang (1994) used such an approach. She studied how young Muslim women in a town on the Swahili coast of East Africa view Bombay-produced Indian movies on video and integrate such viewing and their own related commentary with their educational experience, local religious debate, observations of foreign tourists, family roles, and life-career prospects.

Transnational media studies need not be limited to studies of how particular media products of one country are received by audiences elsewhere. Often technologies and media genres diffuse transnationally, but a local production, adapted to local contexts, takes place. In a competitive market situation, such a production doesn't necessarily lose out to imported counterparts. This, then, may be another example of cultural creativity generated by transnational interconnectedness; of hybridity, or creolization. The interest in "indigenous media," operated, for example, by Australian Aborigines and other ethnic minority groups—see Ginsburg (1991)—may be considered as part of transnational anthropology.

Appadurai (1991:198ff.) has suggested that especially via the media, the balance between lived experience and imagination may have shifted in many human lives in recent times. Fantasy turns into a major form of social practice as an increasing variety of alternative ways of living are vividly presented. Although Appadurai may be thinking primarily of alternatives that could seem attractive, the media may also make available scenes of disaster, war, and suffering for our imagined worlds. There is some possibility of a transnational, "electronic empathy" here, a sense that those far-away strangers can be understood by our own emotional resources, once such pictures are effectively distributed throughout the world. Another view, suggested by Arthur and Joan Kleinman (1996), is that suffering, broadcast on a daily basis as "infotainment," is distorted and thinned out, turned into another commodity. Probably, depending on the wider context of audience interpretations, responses could go either way.

To repeat, media ethnography has developed mostly at the receiving end of the message flow. The engagement with the production end of transnational media structures has so far been limited in anthropology, although Pedelty's study of war correspondents in El Salvador, mentioned above, is an example. Yet media anthropology is undoubtedly here to stay and to grow.[8] Its bases and its development to date have been extensively and illuminatingly reviewed by Debra Spitulnik (1993).

Commodities

Studying the transnational mobility of material things is perhaps the oldest genre of transnational anthropology—this, after all, was what diffusionism was in large part about, around the last turn of the century. At present, such study is mostly part of that anthropology of commodities and consumption that has developed quickly since the 1980s.[9] (Commodities are not always material, of course, although they often are.)

As commodities move over distances and across national boundaries, they are carried through a more or less intricate network of relationships between producers, intermediaries, and consumers, and the activities of these various actors may themselves become one focus of study. A major research interest would also be to learn what these categories of people think of the objects themselves, their origins, and their paths of travel. Because these movements in space and through varied contexts are often far from transparent to participants, dramatic shifts in interpretations may occur along the way—as, for example, in stories of cargo cults in Oceania.[10]

A number of studies of this type deal with art objects—or with objects that sooner or later come to be understood and evaluated in esthetic terms. June Nash (1993) has edited a volume of studies that concentrate mostly on the production side, among Middle American artisans who supply crafts to the world market. Christopher Steiner (1994) has followed "African art in transit" all the way—from villages of the Ivory Coast, through marketplaces in towns and cities, and through the hands of West African transnational traders, to galleries in New York.[11]

Other studies cast light on the global passages of foodstuffs—as does Sidney Mintz's (1985) historical study of sugar, or Jonathan Friedman's (1994:105) remarks on Coca Cola and the Congolese. Advertising is a conspicuous part of commodity imagery that operates transnationally as well, and consequently William O'Barr (1989) has interviewed the man in charge of shaping the idea of Coke in Brazil, Malaysia, South Africa, and elsewhere. Karen Tranberg Hansen (1994) has investigated the sale and identity-constructing consumption of European and American used clothing in towns of Zambia. And, as acceptance of commodities often coheres into larger patterns, Nancy Rosenberger (1992) discusses how Western home styles are presented in Japanese magazines, while Steven Sampson (1994) offers a glimpse of how the newly rich in eastern Europe acquire understandings of life in affluence from the West.

Doing Transnational Studies

One conclusion that can be drawn from this overview of important genres of transnational anthropology is that the latter entails considerable internal diversity. Methodologically, it can hardly be characterized by any one set of approaches that would distinguish it from other anthropology. Observation (more or less participant), informant work, life histories, surveys, textual analyses—all the usual ingredients of the anthropologist's craft—are as relevant to transnational studies as elsewhere in the discipline. At the same time, some tools and techniques may take on a relatively greater centrality. For instance, since transnational units of study are less often fully carried by face-to-face contacts, attention to media almost always plays some part. (Although they can now rarely be disregarded in local or national research contexts either.)

Yet a series of methodological issues seems particularly prominent in transnational research. These may involve some characteristic anxieties and significant challenges that need to be identified, at least as areas of further work and debate.

Units of Study

How to delineate the field often appears less obvious in transnational studies than in classical local ethnography. There may be no more or less bounded territory here; a village, town, or neighborhood with a reasonably settled population, available to acceptably comfortable ethnographic surveillance. (Of course, there can be exceptions in this respect, for example, in what was described above as communities open to the world.) How do transnational ethnographers conceive of their units of study?

The units may, indeed, be spatially dispersed. In discussing this, there has been a tendency to speak of "multilocale" or "multisited" fieldwork, and this points to a significant aspect of what is involved.[12] The practice of ethnography may have to be distributed over several places.

We can expect that in such cases the topic, the sense of problem, will often suggest fairly strongly how a field may be demarcated and where research should be carried out: Migrants are to be studied at home and abroad, the transnational corporation perhaps at headquarters and at branch sites. But there are choices to be confronted here and constraints to be taken into account, more varied and complicated than in the selection of a single site. Would it be desirable (and if so, why) in media anthropology to study CNN or the Bombay movie industry, both at its production and consumption ends? Are all potential sites implied by a research topic accessible? Given that a diaspora or an occupational community may be spread over not two or three, but dozens or hundreds of locations in the world, how does one decide on a manageable selection, one that can yield the most desirable combined ethnography?

In one way, the formulation multisited ethnography somewhat obscures an important fact: The research may need to be not merely multilocal but also trans-local. The unit, perhaps, is (in most cases) a *network* of sites, and parts of one's ethnography may have to be *between* these sites, somehow deterritorialized. Serious effort must thus be devoted to an adequate conceptualization and description of the translocal linkages and the interconnections between these and the localized social traffic.

It would be helpful here to have a developed sense of structure (and of the room for maneuver within it), and we may argue that such a sense has not been particularly strong in much of recent transnational research. The anthropological tradition is strongest in the study of more intimate relationships, face-to-face interactions, smaller-scale structures—*Gemeinschaft* rather than *Gesellschaft*. Yet a relational point of view toward the cohesion of translocal, transnational units seems to require a more varied vocabulary of kinds of connections.

When network analysis drew most attention in anthropology in the 1960s and 1970s, it showed tendencies toward conceptual and methodological involution that limited its attractiveness. But in transnational and other translocal studies, network analysis may again offer ways of thinking about how units of study are constituted and about the social spaces occupied by varied actors (see Hannerz 1992b).

Such a research perspective could also include some sensitivity to the range of kinds of relationships that occur in modern societies, and not least in transnational contexts. In a formulation close enough to a social anthropological tradition, sociologist Craig Calhoun (1991, 1992) contrasts "direct" and "indirect" social relationships and distinguishes two types in each of these. Direct relationships are those of physical copresence: "primary" and "secondary" relationships, according to a familiar vocabulary.[13] (The former are seen as linking whole persons, the latter enactors of specific roles.) Of the two kinds of indirect relationships, "tertiary" ones are mediated by technology and/or large-scale organization. We can be aware of these as at least potentially relationships between persons, although usually they are mediated by markets or bureaucracies. "Quaternary" relationships, on the other hand, are one-sided; surveillance relationships, of which one party is not entirely aware. Information technology plays a large part here, as, for example, census data and credit card records may allow one party to keep track of another more or less unobtrusively.

When transnational research deals with the fact that states, and passages across borders between states, are involved in a study, an ethnography that disregards tertiary and quaternary relationships may seem quite incomplete. As indicated above, however, studies of transmigrants are among those that have recently taken such linkages increasingly into account (see Hannerz 1996:91ff.).

Dispersion Versus Intensity

A study that is spread out over a number of sites, at considerable distances from one another, also involves certain practical problems. Is it possible to meet normal ethnographic standards and to have the expected sense of deep involvement if (assuming that only the normal amount of research time is at one's disposal) one has to scatter one's attention over many sites?

This is certainly a serious question that has to be confronted (see Marcus 1995:99ff.). We may at times have to accept some tradeoff between depth and breadth. It will perhaps not be possible to follow the shifts between seasons, to learn through the everyday redundancies of social life, equally fully in every site.

A number of points must be considered here, however. Insisting on carrying out an entirely local study in a site strongly marked by translocal and transnational connections would surely not result in satisfactorily complete, deep ethnography either. Unless we limit anthropological work to autonomous local units (of which there are not so many these days), we need to experiment with the distribution of attention. In any case, the notion of a "complete ethnography" now seems rather dubious. Whether in local or translocal research, the definition of the research problem may imply more focused attention on some phenomena than on others.

It's also important to recognize that transnational research is not by definition research on large-scale units. Even as such research is extended in space, it sometimes involves relatively limited populations. One could study transnational families and kin groups; and in a study of high-energy physicists, Sharon Traweek

(1988:3) notes that the most active researchers in the field make up a community of no more than 800 or 1,000 members worldwide. They may have other interaction patterns among themselves, and are no doubt embedded differently in a wider social context, but in sheer numbers they are comparable to a largish village.

In some cases, the relationship between the temporalities of the researcher and the field also works out differently in transnational and multisited studies than it does in classical ethnography. In the latter, the anthropologist is a transient in a community where most members are life-time residents, and even a one-year stay is short compared to the involvement of these natives. This may be true in transnational fields as well, but a combination of sites can include some where the ethnographer is not alone in being more or less footloose. They are translocalities, as sketched above. Some such sites are perhaps durable, although the inhabitants pass through. In other instances, they may themselves be short-term phenomena—sports events, conventions, trade fairs, etc. Here, the ethnographer may even be around for as long as the site lasts, and perhaps there is no sense of loss of cumulativity and repetition at all.

Finally, it's increasingly true in contemporary anthropology, whether single- or multisited, that fieldwork goes on in some ways, even as the ethnographers have absented themselves physically from their fields. Many anthropologists maintain more or less continuous contact with one or some handful of informants by way of letter, telephone, or e-mail. As transnational fields are constituted, with their own internal patterns of long-distance cohesion, such ways of keeping in touch on the part of the researcher will not necessarily appear as strikingly deviant. What Gusterson (1997) has described as "polymorphous engagement" may well be the natural adaptation to these fields.

Cultural Competence

Ethnographers' unease about the risk of overextending themselves across too many sites in too little time is likely to be further increased if they feel that they also have to cope with more cultural variation. Does each additional site imply starting more or less anew in acquiring knowledge of another culture, or at least a different set of preparations?

For several kinds of transnational study this may not be altogether necessary. Some anthropologists focus on ethnic or national groups distributed over several countries. Others deal with specialized occupational communities that share knowledge, orientations, and practices across borders. Yet, there are certainly occasions where the ethnographer's competences face more serious challenges, as may be the case with language skills. In an ethnic diaspora, for example, a whole series of different bilingual combinations can be involved, and no single ethnographer can be expected to master all the languages involved. Marcus (1995:101) concludes that so far, most multisited field studies have, in fact, been carried out in monolingual, mostly English-speaking settings.

Perhaps when studies are conducted in sites and combinations of sites that involve more cultural and linguistic diversity, we will have to accept that ethnographies will be more partial and in some ways more superficial. Perhaps we must also conclude that whether carried out in one place or many, ethnography is the art of the possible and that it may be better to have some of it than none at all. Yet it would then be desirable for researchers to acknowledge the constraints on their work. It is also possible that due to personal background or interests, some researchers are better equipped to function as scholarly cosmopolitans, in a variety of contexts.

One additional solution should be identified. Ethnography has tended to be a lone-wolf enterprise (with teams of spouses as the occasional exception). In transnational research, however, there's a particular reason to consider the alternative of collaborative work, drawing on the complementary backgrounds and competences of several scholars. This could also be a way of dealing with other issues identified above. Each member of a small team of scholars might, for example, be able to spend more time, indeed all the research time available, in one of the sites of a multisite study, thus decreasing the risks of thinness and superficiality.

Certainly such a team might be recruited in its entirety in one country or even in a single academic institution. But it seems to be in the nature of transnational research that collaborations between anthropologists from different countries would be another alternative. There are now anthropologists in and from nearly all countries. One consequence of this has been an increasing frequency of adversary relationships between expatriate anthropologists and those who do their "anthropology at home" in the same place. At least some projects of transnational research could instead involve more cooperative research between scholars in different locations, with shared intellectual concerns so that confrontations over ethnographic authority and informal ethnographic property claims are less likely to occur than in locally or nationally focused projects. There could be problems of scholarly compatibility within such teams, but there are networks of transnational collegial friendship and trust that could be a fundamental resource here. Such collaborative work is now facilitated by new information and communication technology (even in the write-up phase).

Prospect/Retrospect

It is hardly time yet to offer a more conclusive view of transnational anthropology and its methods. Some problems have not been solved; some have perhaps not been clearly formulated or even identified. As new cohorts of anthropologists formulate their projects, more new ethnographic genres may emerge and old ones may be recombined. And, as the kinds of relationships that cross boundaries proliferate, there could seem to be forever more research possibilities.

But with transnational research, in one particular way, anthropology may also come to a resting point. The ultimate natural unit for anthropologists, Alfred Kroeber (1945:9) argued more than half a century ago, must be "the culture of all humanity." If, at that time, the discipline was still mostly preoccupied with the people of bands, tribes, and villages, it later continued its journey of exploration into peasant societies and cities. Now, with studies of the transnational and the global, it may face the final test of its tools.

NOTES

This chapter is based on studies carried out within the framework of the "National and Transnational Cultural Processes" project based at the Department of Social Anthropology, Stockholm University, and the Department of Ethnology, University of Lund, and supported by the Swedish Resesearch Council for the Humanities and Social Sciences. I wish to acknowledge the valuable exchanges about questions of research practice that I have had in that context with several colleagues in Stockholm: Ulf Björklund, Bengt-Erik Borgström, Tommy Dahlén, Minou Fuglesang, Christina Garsten, Hasse Huss, Enrique Rodriguez Larreta, Galina Lindquist, Ronald Stade, Britt-Marie Thurén, and Helena Wulff.

1. In a discussion of keywords in transnational anthropology, I have tried to identify some of the ingredients of such a history (Hannerz 1997).

2. For one sociologist's attempt to periodize globalization, see Robertson (1992:58–59).

3. For a critique along such lines, see Verdery (1994).

4. Marcus (1995), in a review of "multisited" ethnography, has suggested six strategies: follow the people; follow the thing; follow the metaphor; follow the plot, story, or allegory; follow the life or biography; and follow the conflict. Apart from these strategies of mobility, he notes the strategically situated, single-site ethnography. While not all multisited research is necessarily transnational, there is a partial overlap between this classification and the one which follows. Appadurai's (1990) distinction between ethnoscapes, mediascapes, technoscapes, finanscapes, and ideoscapes as dimensions of global cultural flow (see also Appadurai 1991) may also be seen to relate, although perhaps somewhat problematically, to the rather concrete genre classification here.

5. For an illuminating discussion of resistance conceptions in recent anthropology, see Ortner (1995); and on "resistance and accommodation," Marcus (1989, 1992).

6. "Creolization" seems to be the term that has drawn more conceptual and theoretical comment in anthropology; see, for example, Fabian (1978:317), Drummond (1980), Graburn (1984:402ff.), Hannerz (1987, 1992a:261ff., 1996:65ff.), and Friedman (1994:208ff.). García Canclini (1995) offers a discussion of hybridity in relation to modernity.

7. On the latter, see also, for example, Garrison and Weiss (1987), Colen (1990), and Margolis (1994:21ff.).

8. For some prominent examples apart from the work mentioned here, see, for example, Abu-Lughod (1993, 1995) and Das (1995).

9. See, for example, Miller (1987) and Friedman (1995).

10. Appadurai's (1986:41) discussion of "knowledge and commodities" is central here.

11. In a somewhat similar vein, Myers (1991) and Morphy (1995) have discussed the journey of Australian Aboriginal art into metropolitan art galleries.

12. See, for example, Marcus and Fischer (1986:90ff.) and Marcus (1989:24ff., 1992:315ff., 1995).

13. In the present context, it should perhaps be noted that primary and secondary relationships need not always be characterized by physical copresence. More interpersonal kinds of information technology (ranging from letter writing and telephone calls to e-mail and exchanges of home videos) allow such relationships to be carried on at least partly outside the face-to-face situation, and this is certainly of great importance in transnational contexts.

REFERENCES

Abu-Lughod, Lila, ed. 1993. Screening Politics in a World of Nations. *Public Culture* 5:465–604.

Abu-Lughod, Lila. 1995. The Objects of Soap Opera: Egyptian Television and the Cultural Politics of Modernity. In *Worlds Apart*. Daniel Miller, ed. Pp. 190–210. London: Routledge.

Alvarez, Robert R., Jr. 1995. The Mexican-U.S. Border: The Making of an Anthropology of Borderlands. *Annual Review of Anthropology* 24:447–470.

Appadurai, Arjun. 1986. Introduction: Commodities and the Politics of Value. In *The Social Life of Things*. Arjun Appadurai, ed. Pp. 3–63. Cambridge: Cambridge University Press.

Appadurai, Arjun. 1990. Disjuncture and Difference in the Global Cultural Economy. *Public Culture* 2(2):1–24.

Appadurai, Arjun. 1991. Global Ethnoscapes: Notes and Queries for a Transnational Anthropology. In *Recapturing Anthropology*. Richard G. Fox, ed. Pp. 191–210. Santa Fe: School of American Research Press.

Appadurai, Arjun. 1995. The Production of Locality. In *Counterworks*. Richard Fardon, ed. Pp. 204–225. London: Routledge.

Basch, Linda, Nina Glick Schiller, and Cristina Szanton Blanc. 1994. *Nations Unbound.* Langhorne, PA: Gordon and Breach.

Benedict, Burton. 1982. *The Anthropology of World's Fairs*. Berkeley: Scolar Press.

Bohannan, Laura. 1966. Shakespeare in the Bush. *Natural History* 7575(7):28–33.

Calhoun, Craig. 1991. Indirect Relationships and Imagined Communities: Large-Scale Social Integration and the Transformation of Everyday Life. In *Social Theory for a Changing Society*. Pierre Bourdieu and James S. Coleman, eds. Pp. 95–121. Boulder: Westview Press/Russell Sage Foundation.

Calhoun, Craig. 1992. The Infrastructure of Modernity: Indirect Social Relationships, Information Technology, and Social Integration. In *Social Change and Modernity*. Hans Haferkamp and Neil J. Smelser, eds. Pp. 205–236. Berkeley: University of California Press.

Clifford, James. 1994. Diasporas. *Cultural Anthropology 9*:302–338.

Colen, Shellee. 1990. 'Housekeeping' for the Green Card: West Indian Household Workers, the State, and Stratified Reproduction in New York. In *At Work in Homes: Household Workers in World Perspective*. Roger Sanjek and Shellee Colen, eds. Pp. 89–118. Washington, DC: American Anthropological Association.

Dahlén, Tommy. 1997. *Among the Interculturalists*. Stockholm Studies in Social Anthropology, 38. Stockholm: Almqvist and Wiksell International.

Das, Veena. 1995. On Soap Opera: What Kind of Anthropological Object Is It? In *Worlds Apart*. Daniel Miller, ed. Pp. 169–189. London: Routledge.

Drummond, Lee. 1980. The Cultural Continuum: A Theory of Intersystems. *Man 15*: 352–374.

Edwards, David B. 1994. Afghanistan, Ethnography, and the New World Order. *Cultural Anthropology 9*:345–360.

Escobar, Arturo. 1994. Welcome to Cyberia: Notes on the Anthropology of Cyberculture. *Current Anthropology 35*:211–223.

Fabian, Johannes. 1978. Popular Culture in Africa: Findings and Conjectures. *Africa 48*:315–334.

Fischer, Michael M. J., and Mehdi Abedi. 1990. *Debating Muslims*. Madison: University of Wisconsin Press.

Friedman, Jonathan. 1994. *Cultural Identity and Global Process*. London: Sage Publications.

Friedman, Jonathan, ed. 1995. *Consumption and Identity*. Reading, England: Harwood.

Fuglesang, Minou. 1994. *Veils and Videos*. Stockholm Studies in Social Anthropology, 32. Stockholm: Almqvist and Wiksell International.

García Canclini, Néstor. 1995. *Hybrid Cultures*. Chicago: University of Chicago Press.

Garrison, Vivian, and Carol I. Weiss. 1987. Dominican Family Networks and United States Immigration Policy: A Case Study. In *Caribbean Life in New York City*. Constance R. Sutton and Elsa M. Chaney, eds. Pp. 235–254. New York: Center for Migration Studies.

Garsten, Christina. 1994. *Apple World*. Stockholm Studies in Social Anthropology, 33. Stockholm: Almqvist and Wiksell International.

Gewertz, Deborah B., and Frederick K. Errington. 1991. *Twisted Histories, Altered Contexts*. Cambridge: Cambridge University Press.

Ginsburg, Faye. 1991. Indigenous Media: Faustian Contract or Global Village? *Cultural Anthropology 6*:92–112.

Graburn, Nelson H. H. 1983. The Anthropology of Tourism. *Annals of Tourism Research 10*:9–33.

Graburn, Nelson H. H. 1984. The Evolution of Tourist Arts. *Annals of Tourism Research 11*:393–419.

Gusterson, Hugh. 1997. Studying Up Revisited. *Political and Legal Anthropology Review* *20*(1):114–119.

Gupta, Akhil, and James Ferguson, eds. 1997. *Anthropological Locations*. Berkeley: University of California Press.

Hannerz, Ulf. 1987. The World in Creolisation. *Africa 57*:546–559.

Hannerz, Ulf. 1992a. *Cultural Complexity*. New York: Columbia University Press.

Hannerz, Ulf. 1992b. The Global Ecumene as a Network of Networks. In *Conceptualizing Society.* Adam Kuper, ed. Pp. 34–56. London: Routledge.

Hannerz, Ulf. 1996. *Transnational Connections*. London: Routledge.

Hannerz, Ulf. 1997. Fluxos, fronteiras, híbridos: Palavras-chave da antropologia transnacional. *Mana* (Rio de Janeiro) *3*:7–39.

Hansen, Karen Tranberg. 1994. Dealing with Used Clothing: *Salaula* and the Construction of Identity. *Public Culture 6*:503–523.

Hunt, Edwin S. 1987. Multinational Corporations: Their Origin, Development, and Present Forms. In *Research in Economic Anthropology*, Vol. 8. Barry L. Isaac, ed. Pp. 317–375. Greenwich, CT: JAI Press.

Khalaf, Sulayman N. 1992. Gulf Societies and the Image of the Unlimited Good. *Dialectical Anthropology 17*:53–84.

Kleinman, Arthur, and Joan Kleinman. 1996. The Appeal of Experience; The Dismay of Images: Cultural Appropriations of Suffering in Our Times. *Daedalus 125*(1): 1–23.

Kroeber, Alfred L. 1945. The Ancient *Oikoumenê* as an Historic Culture Aggregate. *Journal of the Royal Anthropological Institute 75*:9–20.

Lessinger, Johanna. 1992a. Investing or Going Home? A Transnational Strategy among Indian Immigrants in the United States. In *Towards a Transnational Perspective on Migration*, Vol. 645. Nina Glick Schiller, Linda Basch, and Cristina Blanc-Szanton, eds. Pp. 53–80. New York: Annals of the New York Academy of Sciences.

Lessinger, Johanna. 1992b. Nonresident-Indian Investment and India's Drive for Industrial Modernization. In *Anthropology and the Global Factory*. Frances Abrahamer Rothstein and Michael L. Blim, eds. Pp. 62–82. New York: Bergin and Garvey.

Liebes, Tamar, and Elihu Katz. 1990. *The Export of Meaning*. New York: Oxford University Press.

Lins Ribeiro, Gustavo. 1997. In Search of the Virtual-Imagined Transnational Community. *Anthropology Newsletter 38*(5):80–78.

Löfgren, Orvar. Forthcoming. *Making Holidays.* Berkeley: University of California Press.

Malkki, Liisa H. 1995. Refugees and Exile: From "Refugee Studies" to the National Order of Things. *Annual Review of Anthropology 24*:495–523.

Marcus, George E. 1989. Imagining the Whole: Ethnography's Contemporary Efforts to Situate Itself. *Critique of Anthropology 9*(3):7–30.

Marcus, George E. 1992. Past, Present and Emergent Identities: Requirements for Ethnographies of Late Twentieth-Century Modernity Worldwide. In *Modernity and Identity*. Scott Lash and Jonathan Friedman, eds. Pp. 309–330. Oxford: Blackwell.

Marcus, George E. 1995. Ethnography in/of the World System: The Emergence of Multi-Sited Ethnography. *Annual Review of Anthropology 24*:95–117.

Marcus, George E., and Michael M. J. Fischer. 1986. *Anthropology as Cultural Critique*. Chicago: University of Chicago Press.

Margolis, Maxine L. 1994. *Little Brazil*. Princeton: Princeton University Press.

Mead, Margaret. 1956. *New Lives for Old*. New York: Morrow.

Miller, Daniel. 1987. *Material Culture and Mass Consumption*. Oxford: Blackwell.

Mintz, Sidney W. 1985. *Sweetness and Power*. New York: Viking Press.

Morphy, Howard. 1995. Aboriginal Art in a Global Context. In *Worlds Apart*. Daniel Miller, ed. Pp. 211–239. London: Routledge.

Myers, Fred. 1991. Representing Culture: The Production of Discourse(s) for Aboriginal Acrylic Paintings. *Cultural Anthropology 6*:26–62.

Narayan, Kirin. 1993. How Native is a "Native" Anthropologist? *American Anthropologist 95*:671–686.

Nash, June. 1979. Anthropology of the Multinational Corporation. In *The Politics of Anthropology*. Gerrit Huizer and Bruce Mannheim, eds. Pp. 421–446. The Hague and Paris: Mouton.

Nash, June, ed. 1993. *Crafts in the World Market*. Albany: State University of New York Press.

O'Barr, William M. 1989. The Airbrushing of Culture: An Insider Looks at Global Advertising. *Public Culture 2*:1–19.

Olwig, Karen Fog, and Kirsten Hastrup, eds. 1997. *Siting Culture*. Routledge: London.

Ong, Aihwa. 1987. *Spirits of Resistance and Capitalist Discipline*. Albany: State University of New York Press.

Ong, Aihwa. 1992. Limits to Cultural Accumulation: Chinese Capitalists on the American Pacific Rim. In *Towards a Transnational Perspective on Migration*, Vol. 645. Nina Glick Schiller, Linda Basch, and Cristina Blanc-Szanton, eds. Pp. 125–143. New York: Annals of the New York Academy of Sciences.

Ortner, Sherry. 1995. Resistance and the Problem of Ethnographic Refusal. *Comparative Studies in Society and History 37*:173–193.

Pedelty, Mark. 1995. *War Stories*. New York: Routledge.

Redfield, Robert. 1950. *A Village that Chose Progress*. Chicago: University of Chicago Press.

Robertson, Roland. 1992. *Globalization*. London: Sage Publications.

Rosenberger, Nancy. 1992. Images of the West: Home Style in Japanese Magazines. In *Re-made in Japan*. Joseph J. Tobin, ed. Pp. 106–125. New Haven: Yale University Press.

Rouse, Roger. 1992. Making Sense of Settlement: Class Transformation, Cultural Struggle, and Transnationalism among Mexican Migrants in the United States. In *Towards a Transnational Perspective on Migration*, Vol. 645. Nina Glick Schiller, Linda Basch, and Cristina Blanc-Szanton, eds. Pp. 25–52. New York Annals of the New York Academy of Sciences.

Sampson, Steven L. 1994. Money Without Culture, Culture Without Money: Eastern Europe's Nouveaux Riches. *Anthropological Journal on European Cultures 3*:7–30.

Schiller, Nina Glick, Linda Basch, and Cristina Blanc-Szanton, eds. 1992. *Towards a Transnational Perspective on Migration*, Vol. 645. New York: Annals of the New York Academy of Sciences.

Shryock, Andrew. 1996. Tribes and the Print Trade: Notes from the Margins of Literate Culture in Jordan. *American Anthropologist 98*:26–40.

Smith, Valene, ed. 1977. *Hosts and Guests*. Oxford: Blackwell.

Spitulnik, Debra. 1993. Anthropology and Mass Media. *Annual Review of Anthropology 22*:293–315.

Steiner, Christopher B. 1994. *African Art in Transit*. Cambridge: Cambridge University Press.

Traweek, Sharon. 1988. *Beamtimes and Lifetimes*. Cambridge: Harvard University Press.

Verdery, Katherine. 1994. Beyond the Nation in Eastern Europe. *Social Text 38*:1–19.

Wallerstein, Immanuel. 1974. *The Modern World-System*. New York: Academic Press.

Waterman, Christopher A. 1990. *Jùjú*. Chicago: University of Chicago Press.

Watson, James L., ed. 1977. *Between Two Cultures*. Oxford: Blackwell.

Wolf, Eric. 1982. *Europe and the People Without History*. Berkeley: University of California Press.

Wolfe, Alvin W. 1963. The African Mineral Industry: Evolution of a Supranational Level of Integration. *Social Problems 3*:153–164.

Wolfe, Alvin W. 1977. The Supranational Organization of Production: An Evolutionary Perspective. *Current Anthropology 18*:615–620.

Wulff, Helena. 1998. *Ballet across Borders*. Oxford: Berg.

PART II
ACQUIRING INFORMATION

KATHLEEN M. DEWALT
BILLIE R. DEWALT
with CORAL B. WAYLAND

Eight

Participant Observation

Introduction

Participant observation is accepted almost universally as the central and defining method of research in cultural anthropology. Despite this, there is no single agreed-on definition for what constitutes participant observation. For writers such as Spradley (1980), Van Maanen (1988), and Agar (1996), participant observation subsumes the bulk of what we call fieldwork. Spradley (1980) used the term "participant observation" to refer to the general approach of fieldwork in ethnographic research, and Agar (1996) used it as a cover term for all of the observation and formal and informal interviewing in which anthropologists engage.[1]

We take a narrower view here. For us, participant observation is one among a number of methods that are used in anthropological fieldwork. We take this position because, while much of what we call fieldwork includes participating and observing the people and communities with whom we are working, the *method* of participant observation includes the explicit use in behavioral analysis and recording of the information gained from participating and observing. That is, all humans are participants and observers in all of their everyday interactions, but few individuals actually engage in the systematic use of this information for social scientific purposes. We argue below that the method of participant observation requires a particular approach to recording observations (in field notes), and that the information the ethnographer gains through participation is as critical to social scientific analysis as more formal research techniques like interviewing, structured observation, and the use of questionnaires and formal elicitation techniques.

Here, participant observation is a method in which an observer takes part in the daily activities, rituals, interactions, and events of the people being studied as one of the means of learning the explicit and tacit aspects of their culture. "Explicit culture makes up part of what we know, a level of knowledge people can communicate about with relative ease" (Spradley 1980:7). Tacit aspects of culture largely remain outside our awareness or consciousness. It is the feeling of discomfort we have, for example, when someone stands too close to us or touches us in a way that seems too familiar.[2] Participant observation is a way to collect data in a relatively unstructured manner in naturalistic settings by ethnographers who observe and/or take part in the common and uncommon activities of the people being studied.

While anthropologists had done ethnographic fieldwork before him, Malinowski (1922, 1935) is usually credited with developing "something novel" (Stocking 1983; Sanjek 1990b)—an approach to fieldwork that gradually became known as the method of participant observation. Malinowski's discussion of his approach is still the fundamental description of the method of participant observation:

> Soon after I had established myself in Omarkana Trobriand Islands, I began to take part, in a way, in the village life, to look forward to the important or festive events, to take personal interest in the gossip and the developments of the village occurrences; to wake up every morning to a new day, presenting itself to me more or less as it does to the natives. I would get out from under my mosquito net, to find around me the village life beginning to stir, or the people well advanced in their working day according to the hour or also the season, for they get up and begin their labors early or late, as work presses. As I went on my morning walk through the village, I could see intimate details of family life, of toilet, cooking, taking of meals; I could see the arrangements for the day's work, people starting on their errands, or groups of men and women busy at some manufacturing tasks. Quarrels, jokes, family scenes, events usually trivial, sometimes dramatic but always significant, form the atmosphere of my daily life, as well as of theirs. It must be remembered that the natives saw me constantly every day, they ceased to be interested or alarmed, or made self-conscious by my presence, and I ceased to be a disturbing element in the tribal life which I was to study, altering it by my very approach, as always happens with a newcomer to every savage community. In fact, as they knew that I would thrust my nose into everything, even where a well-mannered native would not dream of intruding, they finished by regarding me as a part and parcel of their life, a necessary evil or nuisance, mitigated by donations of tobacco. (1922:7–8)[3]

Malinowski's approach was distinguished from earlier forms of fieldwork in that it included an emphasis on everyday interactions and observations rather than on using directed inquiries into specific behaviors. And, Sanjek notes, following others (Fortes 1957; Leach 1957), "As he observed, he also listened" (1990b:211).

Writing more than 70 years later, Bourgois, who lived for more than 4 years in the neighborhoods in which he worked, described his approach to research in a more contemporary context in similar terms:

I spent hundreds of nights on the street and in crack houses observing dealers and addicts. I regularly tape recorded their conversations and life histories. Perhaps more important, I also visited their families, attending parties and intimate reunions—from Thanksgiving dinners to New Years Eve celebrations. I interviewed, and in many cases befriended, the spouses, lovers, siblings, mothers, grandmothers, and—when possible—the fathers and stepfathers of the crack dealers featured in these pages. (1995:13)

To differing extents, each of these ethnographers practiced the method by living in the community, taking part in usual and unusual activities, "hanging out," and conversing (as compared with interviewing) while consciously observing and ultimately recording what was observed. The participating observer seeks opportunities to spend time with and carry out activities with members of communities in which she or he is working. Because enculturation takes place at the same time (it is hard to avoid), we believe that tacit understanding is also being developed. It is an understanding that is not easily articulated or recorded, but that can be mobilized in subsequent analysis.

In addition to one of the first explicit descriptions of participant observation, another of Malinowski's major contributions to anthropology was the development of the functionalist theoretical perspective that assumed "that the total field of data under the observation of the field worker must somehow fit together and make sense. . . " (Leach 1957:120). Whether one feels that Malinowski's particular approach to fieldwork resulted in the development of a particular theoretical perspective (Sanjek 1990b), or that his theoretical perspective influenced his method of collecting information (Holy 1984), at its beginning, participant observation was linked with functionalist theory.

While linked historically with functionalist theory, the method of participant observation is certainly not tied to it any longer. Participant observation has, in fact, been the catalyst for the development of a number of theoretical perspectives. What seems common across theories, however, are the expectations that: (1) We can learn from observation (keeping in mind that the observer becomes a part of what is being observed); (2) Being actively engaged in the lives of people brings the ethnographer closer to understanding the participants' point of view; and (3) Achieving understanding of people and their behaviors is possible. As Picchi (1992) points out: "Participant observation . . . disallows selective learning about a people. Adjusting to a new culture provides on a daily basis many different types of experiences that prevent anthropologists from concentrating too assiduously on any one aspect of people's traditions" (p. 44).

The approach that ethnographers use in their field research and in participant observation is highly individualistic. Their field research is affected by a complex mix of their personal characteristics, their theoretical approach, and the context within which they work. But we can use the experiences of other ethnographers to learn more systematically how to craft our own individual approaches. Because participant observation is one of the key techniques anthropologists use for learning substantial amounts about the people they study, as well as themselves, it is our view that a much more systematic examination of this method may be the best means of improving anthropological field research. In this chapter, we examine the method of participant observation and how it has been used by a variety of ethnographers. Our purpose is to show how we can learn from and build on the experiences of others in order to improve this most essential of anthropological methods.

Participation and Observation

Recent years have seen a much more self-reflexive examination of participant observation among anthropologists, and it is to issues raised in these examinations to which we now turn. The first issue relates to the degree of "participation" and of "observation" that are utilized. Benjamin Paul anticipated some of the current debates when he noted that: "Participation implies emotional involvement; observation requires detachment. It is a strain to try to sympathize with others and at the same time strive for scientific objectivity (1953:69)." Bernard (1995) distinguished participant observation from both pure observation and from pure participation. Pure observation, as used by some sociologists and psychologists (see Tonkin 1984; Adler and Adler 1994), seeks, to the maximum extent possible, to remove the researcher from the actions and behaviors so that they are unable to influence them.[4] Pure participation has been described as "going native" and "becoming the phenomenon" (see Jorgenson 1989:62).

Spradley identified what he described as a continuum in the "degree of participation" (1980:58–62), although his categories confound degree of participation with the degree of an ethnographer's emotional *involvement* in the community. We believe that these two dimensions require separation so that we have modified his categories to focus only on the aspect of participation.

"Nonparticipation" is when cultural knowledge is acquired by watching television, reading newspapers, or reading diaries or novels. Much information can be acquired in this way even though no active interaction with people is required.[5] "Moderate participation" is when the ethnographer is present at the scene of the action but doesn't actively participate or interact, or only occasionally interacts, with people in it. Many anthropologists, for example, will live in their own house or perhaps even in a larger community. They essentially "commute" to the field to question informants or to participate in only certain of the everyday activities of the community.[6]

"Active participation" is when the ethnographer actually engages in almost everything that other people are doing as a means of trying to learn the cultural rules for behavior. Good, for example, talks about his decision to move into the *shapono* (large, circular communal houses) of the Yanomama as an important step in learning about them. He reports: "Yanomama nights were an event, that first night and every night afterward. It wasn't as if the community just went to sleep, then woke up the next morning. No, a Yanomama night was like another day. All sorts of things went on" (Good 1991:67). In a house in which 75 people were sleeping together, babies cried, men laid plans for a hunt, shaman took drugs and chanted, Big Men made speeches, all without regard to the others who were sleeping. At first, this was difficult for Good: "When something got me up, I was up. I'd lie in the hammock for an hour trying to get back to sleep among all the nighttime noises of the *shapono*. Eventually I got used to this, too. Like the Yanomama, I'd spend eleven hours in my hammock at night to get seven or eight hours of actual sleep" (Good 1991:68–69).[7] Good has no doubt that the insight derived from living in the *shapono* was superior.

Finally, in "complete participation," the ethnographer is or becomes a member of the group that is being studied. Examples of this include ethnographers who are and study jazz musicians or anthropologists who become hobos or cab drivers for a time (see Riemer 1977).

Other researchers have focused more on the dimension of emotional involvement in participant observation. Geertz (1995) commented about the process of learning through participant observation in this way: "You don't exactly penetrate another culture, as the masculinist image would have it. You put yourself in its way and it bodies forth and enmeshes you." Behar drew on this metaphor to note: "Yes, indeed. But just how far do you let that other culture enmesh you?" (1996:5). Behar noted that participant observation is an oxymoron, a paradox (see Tonkin 1984). While the focus on a term that is, at its root, paradoxical can be seen as adding to the mystification of the work of ethnography, it also highlights what we believe to be the creative tension between the goal of documented observation and the critical goal of understanding the situated observer. *Participant* observation is a paradox because the ethnographer seeks to understand the native's viewpoint, but NOT "go native."[8] When the grant runs out, we go back to our desks. But, as Behar argues, the ethnographer as researcher and writer must be a "vulnerable observer," ready to include all of her pain and wounds in research and writing, because it's part of what he or she brings to the relationship.

While not all of us are ready to adopt the path of vulnerable observation, participating allows the ethnographer to "know" in a unique way because the observer becomes a participant in what is observed. At the same time, however, our attempts to remain observers of actions and behaviors maintains a certain distance between us and the people we want to "know."

Barbara Tedlock has argued that exploring the dynamic tension between participation and observation is critically important. She noted that, in the past, many ethnographers wrote personalistic accounts of their field research under pseudonyms so as to maintain their reputations as professional ethnographers. From her perspective, however, these accounts should be part of the data of anthropology. She argues that we should engage in the "observation of participation," an approach that she terms *narrative ethnography*. Narrative ethnography combines the approaches of writing a standard monograph about the people being studied (the Other) with an ethnographic memoir centering on the anthropologist (the Self) (Tedlock 1991:69). What is most valuable in the kinds of accounts that she is advocating is that they go a long way toward demystifying the process of doing ethnography. That is, by examining how other anthropologists have dealt with the "degree of participation" problem and with their emotional involvement, students can better appreciate the circumstances, emotions, and reactions they are likely to experience when they begin their own field research.

Why Participant Observation Is Important

We believe that, irrespective of the degree of involvement or of participation, the practice of participant observation provides two main advantages to research. First, it enhances the quality of the data obtained during fieldwork. Second, it enhances the quality of the interpretation of data. Participant observation is thus both a data collection and an analytic tool.

What does attempting to participate in the events and lives around one mean to data collection and analysis? Living with, working with, laughing with the people that one is trying to understand provides a sense of the self and the Other that isn't easily put into words. It is a tacit understanding that informs both the form of research, the specific techniques of data collection, the recording of information. and the subsequent interpretation of materials collected.

In studying Yolmo healing, Robert Desjarlais (1992) trained to become an apprentice shaman. To do so, he found it necessary to learn how to move and to experience his body as a Yolmo. He argues that much of the learning regarding peoples' lives is tacit and at the level of the body. He notes that as he gained cultural knowledge, learned how to sip tea, caught the meaning of jokes, participated in the practice of everyday life, these interactions shaped his "understanding of local values, patterns of actions, ways of being, moving, feeling" (Desjarlais 1992:26). Desjarlais argues that his body incorporated the meanings and gave a greater understanding of the images he experienced in trances as part of his training as a shaman.

> Through time, experiencing the body in this manner (including the residual, intermingling effect it had on how I stepped through a village, climbed a hill, or approached others) influenced my understanding of Yolmo experiences; it hinted at

new styles of behavior, ways of being and moving through space that I did not previously have access to. By using the body in different ways, I stumbled on (but never fully assimilated) practices distinct from my own. Touching head to heart merged thinking and feeling (two acts unsegregated in Yolmo society); a sense of the body as a vessel dynamically compact led me to see Yolmo forms as vital plenums of organ and icon; and my loose assemblage of bent knees and jointed bones contributed to the springboard technology that gradually brought some force and ease to my shamanic "shaking." (1992:27)

The process by which this might take place, while difficult to convey in words, comes as the result of sharing the lives of people over a significant amount of time. Part of what we know about life in rural Mexico is tacit. It is embodied in the way we walk, move and talk (imperfectly translated, of course, because everyone still knows we aren't Mexicans). We note that the timbre of our voices changes in Spanish to approximate that of Temascalcingo voices and that we are much more animated in our speech and bodily gestures. This embodiment of tacit cultural form also informs interpretation of meaning. Most obviously, it allows us to understand nonverbal communication, to anticipate and understand responses. It shapes how we interact with others and, more fundamentally, it shapes how we interpret what we observe.

Desjarlais is one of many ethnographers who have apprenticed themselves in the field in order to gain new perspectives. Coy (1989) argued that the apprenticeship experience results in "ways of knowing" and "learning to see" that are distinct from less participatory approaches. He argues, like Desjarlais, that these ways of knowing are connected to the physical performance of the duties required in the role being examined. Tedlock (1991:71) argues that successful formal and informal apprentice-ships are ways of undergoing intensive enculturation. The field worker who doesn't try to experience the world of the observed through participant observation will find it much harder to critically examine research assumptions and beliefs and themselves (see Clifford 1997:91).

Now that we have considered these definitional issues concerning participation, observation, and the like, we would like to turn to a discussion of how one actually does participant observation. This isn't a mystical procedure; it's one with which all of us have had experience.

Doing Participant Observation

Children learn their own culture through participant observation. As infants and toddlers, we learned a great deal by observing parents, relatives, and others. As our ability to communicate through language improved, this learning process was enhanced. Observing the behavior of others around us and participating in our society led to our knowledge of correct and incorrect behavior; the forms that we are to use to express or hide emotions; appropriate facial, hand, and bodily gestures; and all the other tacit and explicit aspects of our culture.

As ethnographers, we are, in a sense, returning to those awkward first attempts to learn a culture—but with some advantages and disadvantages. In terms of advantages, we are adults and have gone through the process of learning a culture and have acquired a lifetime of experience living within a culture. These are also disadvantages because we bring a series of preconceptions, biases, and developed personal characteristics to the enterprise. Being ethnographers, we also expect more of our participant observation. That is, we are not just interested in how we can "get by" in the culture we are learning, we also want to develop a more systematic understanding of that other culture—an understanding that we can analyze and interpret for our colleagues and students.

An additional advantage is that we should have profited from the experiences of other ethnographers. Unfortunately, the method of doing participant observation—indeed, of doing anthropological field research—has for too long been shrouded in mystery. Many anthropologists have sent students to the field to "see if they can survive." The implication here is that some individuals are constitutionally suited to become ethnographers; those who can't will discover that during their first field experience and presumably choose another profession. Aside from being a somewhat barbaric approach to teaching, we reject this attitude because we believe that good ethnographers are not born that way; most reasonable, sensitive and intelligent individuals can be trained and educated to be good participant observers and field researchers.

Having been involved in a variety of field research projects during the past three decades, and having read many accounts of hundreds of other experiences, we believe that the following are the basic elements and attitudes that are required to do participant observation.

1. The ethnographer has to approach participating and observing any particular situation with an open mind and a nonjudgmental attitude. That is, while the activities in which the ethnographer is taking part may be extraordinarily exotic or mundane, a good field researcher must react to the goings-on with sensitivity and discretion.

2. Almost all people love to tell their story and to share their experiences with those who take an interest in them. While we should be sensitive about intruding into situations where we are not wanted or welcome, if an ethnographer shows genuine interest in learning more about behaviors, thoughts, and feelings, he or she will be a welcome guest at most activities.

3. It is normal to feel awkward and unsure when observing and participating in a new situation. The feeling of "culture shock" (Bock 1970) when you are confronted with a wide variety of new behaviors and stimuli is something almost all ethnographers have experienced. Both of us have often felt very intimidated and anxious about what we were *supposed* to do on many occasions,

but these are probably the times in which we were learning the most about the people and places we were studying. As one learns more, they also begin to feel much more comfortable and confident.

4. Everyone will make mistakes, but most of these can be overcome with time and patience. As Whyte has emphasized: "It is important to recognize that explorations in the field are bound to confront one with confusing situations and conflicting pressures, so that some errors are almost inevitable, but few errors are serious enough to abort a project" (1984:11). Bourgois (1995:19–20) makes a similar point.

5. It's important to be a careful observer. This is a skill that can be enhanced through practice. We remember our first experience in the field in Temascalcingo, Mexico when we only had a rudimentary knowledge of Spanish. One of our mentors, Pertti J. Pelto, suggested that we could still learn a lot by doing a census of the different kinds of stalls in the open-air Sunday market, by counting the numbers of people at the market with bare feet and the number wearing shoes or boots, by making maps of the houses in the villages, and by making charts of where people sat in meetings. These tasks served the purpose of attuning us to nonverbal cues, got us out and about in the community where we began interacting with people, and taught us that a lot can be learned just by being careful observers.

6. It's important to be a good listener (Leach 1957; Sanjek 1990b:211). Through language we rapidly acquire a substantial amount of information in a short time. If we listen, we will learn much more quickly.[9]

7. We should be open to being surprised and to learning the unexpected. This is perhaps the strength of participant observation as a method. In contrast to social science research that uses structured techniques in order to test hypotheses (Picchi calls this selective learning [1992:144]), participant observation puts the researcher into situations in which he or she is acquiring information in an open-ended fashion. The insights gained from this method often can and should be used later on to be verified and substantiated through more structured techniques.

These general attitudes and elements are guidelines for those who are beginning to use participant observation as one of the tools in conducting ethnographic research. Those individuals who develop or use these attributes can generally expect to achieve sufficient rapport with people to make participant observation a useful ethnographic tool.

Establishing Rapport/Becoming a Participant as Well as an Observer

The establishment of "rapport " is often talked about as both an essential element in using participant observation as a tool as well as the goal of participant observation. Villa Rojas (1979), writing about his and his collaborators' field research in the Mayan region of Mexico says, "Our close contact with local people has always led to excellent rapport, the only basis on which really reliable information can be obtained" (p. 59). The definition of what constitutes rapport, however, is an elusive one. In our own thinking, we have often used a definition for which we can no longer find the citation. In this formulation, rapport is achieved when the participants come to share the same goals, at least to some extent—that is, when both the "informant" and the researcher come to the point when each is committed to help the other achieve his or her goal, when informants participate in providing information for "the book" or the study, and when the researcher approaches the interaction in a respectful and thoughtful way that allows the informant to tell his or her story. Nader (1986) suggested a more one-sided view. She (1986) wrote: "Rapport, pure and simple, consists of establishing lines of communication between the anthropologist and his informants in order for the former to collect data that then allows him to understand the culture under study" (p. 113).[10]

Many field workers find that they can point to a single event or moment when the groundwork for the development of true rapport and participation in the setting was established (for example, Whyte and Whyte 1984; Nader 1986; Stack 1996; Sterk 1996:89; Whyte 1996). Clifford Geertz (1973) elegantly describes the event that allowed him and his wife to begin to establish rapport in the Balinese village in which they worked. The Geertzes had been in the village for about a month, during which time the villagers treated them as though they were not there. They were rarely greeted, people seemed to look right through them, some people would move away when they approached. It was truly an anthropologist's nightmare.

Their breakthrough came as a result of a police raid on an illegal cockfight they were observing. Although the Geertzes could have stood their ground and presented the police with their credentials and permissions, they chose to run away with the rest of the villagers when the cockfight was raided. In Geertz's words:

> On the established anthropological principle, "When in Rome," my wife and I decided, only slightly less instantaneously than everyone else, that the thing to do was run too. We ran down the main village street, northward, away from where we were living. . . . About halfway down another fugitive ducked suddenly into a compound—his own it turned out—and we, seeing nothing ahead of us but rice fields, open country and a very high volcano, followed him. As the three of us came tumbling into the courtyard, his wife, who had apparently been through this sort of thing before, whipped out a table, a tablecloth, three chairs, and three cups of tea, and we all, without any explicit communication whatsoever, sat down, commenced to sip tea and sought to compose ourselves. (p. 415)

When moments later the police arrived, the Geertzes' adopted host was able to provide a lengthy and accurate description of who they were, what they were doing in the village, and what permissions they had. In addition, he noted, the Geertzes had been in this compound all afternoon sipping tea and knew nothing about the cockfight. The bewildered police left. After that, the Geertzes were enthusiastically incorporated into the community.

An even more dramatic account of a single event that lead to the establishment of rapport is provided by Kornblum (1996), who was called on to stand with "his" gypsy family when they were attacked by Serbians in their camp outside Paris. In a moment of crisis, he became one of them. He relates that it resulted in a subtle change in his relationship with the Gypsies. He was then viewed with respect rather than with disdain.

We found in our work in Temascalcingo that the quality of the information we were receiving improved after our return from a three-week trip to the United States to renew our visas and take a break from fieldwork. Until that point, people seemed to be unsure of our interest in them and their lives. The fact that we had visited our own culture and families, but had returned to renew our stay in Mexico, demonstrated our commitment to the people in this Mexican community. Everywhere we went, people said "*Que milagro*" (what a miracle) and greeted us with greater warmth and affection than they had previous to our break. Suddenly, our previous questions about sensitive subjects like witchcraft were answered in great detail rather than tossed off and evaded.

In a number of these cases, the breakthrough in rapport was achieved when the anthropologists showed that their relationship with the community was important and serious; when they demonstrated a more-than-passing commitment to a community. We returned to Puerto de las Piedras against the expectations of community members who had assumed we would not. Clifford and Hillary Geertz acted like Balinese villagers when they could have acted like privileged foreigners. Kornblum risked violence to stand with the people with whom he was working. While these dramatic examples are more vivid, rapport generally is established slowly, simply by continuing to live with and interact with a group of people.

This discussion of the process of developing rapport and coming to be accepted in a community begs the question of how long it takes to achieve. In reality, a lot depends on the ability, characteristics, and experience of the ethnographer, the circumstances and characteristics of the group being studied, and the kinds of information that one wants to obtain. We have often, for example, participated in rapid appraisals (Kumar 1993) in which the objective is to obtain a quick impression of farming techniques, agricultural problems, or significant kinds of illnesses in a community. In these situations, the ethnographer has to achieve "instant rapport" that is sufficient to put informants at ease to answer the questions being asked. On the other hand, in our initial fieldwork in Temascalcingo (B. DeWalt 1979; K. DeWalt 1983), we were unable to obtain much information at all on topics such as witchcraft or traditional curing practices until we had spent over six months in the field (see discussion below on ethnographer bias). In some situations in which the people being studied are for some reason (for example, harsh exploitation by outsiders, situations of violence or deprivation, extreme isolation) very suspicious, it may never be possible to achieve a substantial amount of rapport. It has become relatively standard in ethnographic inquiries to think of a minimum of a year of fieldwork as necessary to gain sufficient insight from participant observation, but this is only a general guideline.

A Note on Notes

A whole chapter should be devoted to discussing strategies for writing, managing, and analyzing field notes. Space limitations make this impossible, but several important issues about field notes should be addressed here. Field notes are the primary method of capturing data from participant observation. Researchers can audio- or videotape more formal interviews and events to record words and behaviors for later analysis and record more formally the results of response to formal elicitation, time allocation, input and output of energy, etc., but writing field notes is virtually the only way for researchers to record the observation of day-to-day events and behavior, overheard conversations, and casual interviews that are the primary materials of participant observation. A useful maxim that we have always used in training students is that: "If you didn't write it down in your field notes, then it didn't happen" (at least so far as being data for analysis).

Until recently, relatively little had been written about the nature of field notes and how anthropologists record observation. The sixth edition of *Notes and Queries* (Seligman 1951), for example, devotes only 1.5 pages to a discussion of "descriptive notes" as one of four essential types of documentation. (The other three are: maps, plans and diagrams; texts; and genealogical and census data.)

Notes and Queries suggests three kinds of notes, which are still relevant today: (1) records of events observed and information given (in which the researcher takes time to interview or converse with participants as events take place); (2) records of prolonged activities and ceremonies (in which interview is not feasible); and (3) following the practice of contemporary ethnographers, a set of chronological, daily notes, which the committee called a journal, (but that is distinct from the personal diary which a number of ethnographers keep [for example, Malinowski 1967]). Pelto (1970) and Pelto and Pelto (1978) provide approximately two pages of discussion of field notes in each edition of their book on *Anthropological Research*. Most of this space is devoted to examples of the level of detail (high) that they see as desirable in recording field notes. More books about field notes are coming out all the time (for example, Sanjek 1990c; Bernard 1994).

Sanjek (1990c) addresses issues about field notes in more detail. In this volume, Jean Jackson (1990) summarizes the responses of a sample of 70 field workers, mostly anthropologists, to a series of questions about their relationships with their field notes. Sanjek (1990a) reviews the historical changes in the nature of participant observation and field notes.

Experience and the literature suggest that there are several important points about field notes and their relationship to the participant observation method. The first is that *observations are not data* unless they are recorded in some fashion for further analysis. Even though it seems after a few months in the field that common events and their variations will remain indelibly etched in the researchers mind for all time, memory is unfortunately more fleeting and less trustworthy than that. We lose the fine detail of observations and conversation all too quickly. The admonition in *Notes and Queries* that "It is unwise to trust to memory; notes should be written as soon as possible" (Seligman 1951:45) is still relevant today.

Participant observation is an iterative process, and, as we have noted, part of what occurs is the development of a tacit understanding of meanings, events and contexts by the researcher. Sanjek (1990b) notes that pioneering researchers like Malinowski and Mead knew this. They continually read and reread field notes, searching for things they did not understand, or on which they felt they had incomplete information (what Agar refers to as "breakdowns" [1986]), so as to direct the flow of subsequent conversations or interviews. Mead and Malinowski recorded both observations and reflections on their fieldwork experience in field notes and personal diaries. If the researcher's daily reactions to events and contexts are not recorded, it will be virtually impossible to reconstruct the development of understanding, and to be able to review the growing relationship between the researcher and study participants in a manner that allows for reflexivity at the end of the process.

The second point is that field notes are simultaneously data and analysis. By this we mean that they should be the careful record of observation, conversation, and informal interview carried out on a day-by-day basis by the researcher. At the same time, field notes are a product, constructed by the researcher. This inherent contradiction embodied in field notes is part of the continuing discussions about the nature of anthropological inquiry and of ethnography. We believe that few anthropologists really ever believed that their observations were unbiased, or that eliminating bias was even possible or desirable in research. However, debates over the last two decades have made this point even more salient. Field notes are at least one more step removed from objective observation than the nonobjective observation itself and are a construction of the ethnographer and part of the process of analysis. As one of Jackson's (1990) respondents said about field notes: "Each anthropologist knows it is a dialectic. The informant creates it; you create it together. There must be a tremendous sense of responsibility in it, that is, a sense of political history, one version" (p. 14). According to Clifford (1990), the view of the field note as "pure inscription"—that is, pure recording—cannot be sustained. Speaking of description (thick or otherwise), he writes: "Ethnography cannot, in practice, maintain a constant descriptive relationship to cultural phenomena. It can maintain such a relationship only to what is produced in field notes. . ." (p. 68). Although anthropologists once deposited copies of their field notes in libraries for other researchers to consult, this practice is unfortunately being lost.

Whether public note taking, either of "scratch notes" (Sanjek 1990c) and "jottings" (Bernard 1994) or longer more transcriptual notes, has an impact on the flow of participant observation is a question that has been answered in a number of different ways by researchers. With respect to the impact of note taking during events, *Notes and Queries on Anthropology* suggests: "The investigator must sense the native attitude to note taking in public. Many peoples do not object to it, simply regarding it as one of the European's unaccountable habits" (Seligman 1951:45).

On the other hand, they note that some people may become suspicious when the ethnographer takes notes, and a few people who are "otherwise friendly may never tolerate the practice." Jackson (1990) reports that a number of the ethnographers she interviewed found that taking field notes in front of participants was uncomfortable and objectifying. Others found that participants were insulted when notes were not taken, suggesting that what they had to say was not important enough to record.

Whyte (Whyte and Whyte 1984) went to relatively great lengths to avoid taking notes in front of participants in his research in Cornerville. To gain accurate maps of interaction in a men's club, he went home or to the bathroom in order to record events. Bourgois (1995, 1996), on the other hand, openly taped both interviews and conversations as he hung out with crack dealers in El Barrio in East Harlem. Participants in his study even joked about "how the book was coming" (1995:27), an experience many of us have had with participants, who may even be anxious to see the finished work.

A final note on field notes: Participant observation can be a very stressful experience (we often call this culture shock). It's sometimes comforting and helpful in assuaging guilt on days when we just need to be out of the scene to say to ourselves: "Well, today I MUST stay in and catch up on my field notes." And, as it is almost always true, it is the perfect excuse. However, it is for just this reason that Agar (1996) is critical of time spent in recording field notes, which he sees as more profitably spent in interviewing.

Ethical Concerns

Of all the methods usually applied in the field by anthropologists, participant observation raises the greatest number of ethical questions. When individuals are being interviewed by structured interview schedules or when their interviews are being recorded in some way, most understand that the information resulting from these activities will be used in the research carried out by the field worker. However, the activities carried out during participant observation are less clearly so.

The field worker is traveling alongside community members, participating in events, work, leisure activities, hanging out. Community companions will probably not be aware that the field worker will faithfully record an account of these events as soon as possible, and that this will form a data core for analysis. Even if field workers make it clear that they will "write a book" or report on their experiences, informants may not realize that what they share as "gossip" during informal conversations will form part of this report. Field workers rarely recite their informed consent script during afternoon conversations carried out while swinging in hammocks, while drinking a beer in the bar after a day's work, or while in bed with a lover. In fact, if informants were always consciously aware of our activities as ethnographers, the information we acquire would be less rich. We want them to forget, for a time at least, that we are outsiders. We want to develop sufficient rapport and to have them become so comfortable with us as community participants that they will share insights and information that only insiders would know. We regard this as the strength of our method.

Therefore, as Punch (1994) points out, quoting Ditton (1977), participant observation is *inevitably* unethical "by virtue of being interactionally deceitful" (Ditton 1977:10). That is, it is by its nature deceptive. We have all been impressed by the degree to which our informants will suspend a conversation or interaction to remind us that the topic about which they are speaking is important, and to make sure that we will put it "in the book." But it is more often the case that the informants "forget" that casual interactions may form part of the data to be used in analysis.

What are our responsibilities under these circumstances? We have often taken the position that providing anonymity for communities and individuals is sufficient to protect our informants. However, in the modern world, it is increasingly difficult to even suggest that the identities of communities will remain hidden. Punch recommends that we carry out research with this powerful method, but "think a bit first" (1994:95). While this is probably good advice, the responsibility "to do no harm to our informants" (AAA 1997) is great. It is the ethnographer's responsibility not only to think a bit first, but to make conscious decisions on what to report and what to decline to report, based on careful consideration of the ethical dimensions of the impact of information on those who provide it, and the goals of research. Whyte (Whyte and Whyte 1984) reminds us that much of our work can be put to unintended use.

It's important to emphasize that ethical questions surround not only the published information we provide but also relate to our field notes. We would like to comment on two issues.

The first is the ethical question about taking notes publicly. Doing so, at least part of the time, reinforces for participants that what is being done is research. The participants in Bourgois's crack research knew he was writing a book, and when he openly taped interviews and conversations on the street, it was clear to participants what was on the record and off. In fact, they sometimes suggested that he turn on his recorder when he turned it off. For us, taking notes or taping events openly alleviates some of the concern that participants lose awareness that they are participating in research.

The second issue has to do with preserving anonymity for participants identified in field notes. Not only is there the potential that field notes can be subpoenaed; governmental funding organizations such as NSF and NIH are becoming increasingly concerned with research integrity and falsification of data in funded research. They are demanding that primary data be available for review by others. Universities are developing policies concerning research integrity of nonfunded and funded research in which data, including field notes, would be available for inspection by review boards should allegations of a breach of research integrity be alleged.

On occasion, anthropologists have gone to jail to protect the identities of their informants. However, some concern with the protection of the identity of informants in field notes can help alleviate these problems. While most internal review boards for the use of human subjects require that all questionnaires and transcribed interview data be stored without names, field notes have always constituted a gray area. With computerization, however, it becomes relatively easy to assign code names or numbers to participants and use these from the outset or use the global search and replace facilities of word processing programs to expurgate real names from field notes. The research integrity policy statement for the University of Pittsburgh, for example, now suggests that real names be expurgated from field notes against the possibility that they will be requested by others.

Another important ethical issue is about maintaining relationships developed in the field. Ethnographers actively try to develop close relationships and to identify with the group they are studying. These relationships, though, are almost always transient (Punch 1994). While many informants become true friends, such friendships are difficult to maintain when the anthropologist is thousands of miles away.

Anthropologists need to be aware of the implications of relationships and obligations that they incur in the field. Two field researchers we knew joined ritual dance groups in a Mexican village in which they were doing research. The commitments into which they entered were for several years. Both ethnographers danced for two years during which they were in the field, but were unable to fulfill their commitments for the full terms of their appointments. Fortunately for them, because there was a lot of out-migration, the community was used to individuals who could not get back in time for key festivals in which dancing was required. It was possible for them to send money to the community to fulfill their commitments in those years when they could not get to the field to dance but this could have caused substantial problems.

Many anthropologists enter into fictive kinship relationships in order to find a place in a community. Catherine Lutz (1988) became a "daughter" to fit into Ifaluk society. She discussed the benefits and costs to her research of this relationship.

Assuming this kind of relationship has a number of implications and adds a series of responsibilities for the anthropologists that should be carefully considered before the identity is accepted. Becky Ross, whose story forms one of the ethical case studies published by the AAA (Cassell and Jacobs 1997), was "adopted" into a family as a daughter and granddaughter. When it became necessary to assume the responsibilities of a true granddaughter and care for an elderly "grandfather" she did it, at personal expense (loss of precious field time), until the biological grand-children were available to take over.

Even when the relationship is not intimate or familial, it may present ethical dilemmas. As part of research with older adults in rural settings in Kentucky, one of the places Kathleen and her collaborators "hung out" to get a better under-standing of the problems facing older adults was the Senior Citizens' Centers. Here they chatted with the program participants, rode the transportation vans, and ate the meals provided by the centers. All the participants and the program staff knew that the researchers were studying food and nutrition problems in the communities.

When the regional senior picnic was planned for a recreation area near Central County, the researchers were invited to attend and arrived with the participants from the Central County Senior Center. They ate box lunches, participated in the auction for such goodies as fried apple pies and home-canned vegetables and pickles. Much of the afternoon was spent in competitions among senior citizens, including walking races, baking contests, etc. One of the contests was an extemporaneous speaking contest. Judging was to focus on originality and eloquence of individuals who were given a topic on which to speak. However, there were no obviously unbiased potential judges. Most of the people at the picnic were participants or staff of individual centers.

Kathleen and one of her collaborators were asked to be judges. Although protesting that they might be biased toward the contestant from Central County, they agreed. During the introduction of judges, the Central County Senior Center Director introduced Kathleen and her co-researcher by saying: "I would like to introduce two people to whom we have become very close over the past few months." Kathleen's heart sank because she realized that the project was nearing its end and that she was not prepared to maintain a long-term relationship with the center and participants after the project was over. Realizing the implied commitment to the community in the director's words, she began to develop a plan to put more distance between herself and the residents of the center.

Over the years, we have developed strong personal relationships in different places and with different people. While we have tried to return as often as possible to communities we have studied to let individuals know we still think of them, this has not always been possible. Good intentions to correspond have rarely been possible to maintain. The message is that while the field worker is almost always transient, we must recognize that this transience may not be the expectation of those individuals who become our informants.

A final ethical issue relates to what we might call "limits to participation." Because this is one of the most important questions with which most ethnographers eventually have to contend, we dedicate a special section to it.

Limits to Participation?

There are some dramatic cases of the need to establish limits to participation because engaging in these behaviors may be illegal, dangerous to the personal health of the ethnographer, or both. Obvious examples include situations in which ethnographers study shamanistic use of hallucinogens or other drugs (for example, Castañeda 1972), drug cultures, prisons, or high-risk sexual practices. Bourgois (1995, 1996), for example, became quite involved with the drug dealers with whom he was working, although he abhorred the violence and other activities in which they engaged. There are also many accounts of ethnographers being confronted with whether to engage in romantic and/or sexual involvements with members of communities they study (see below).

On a less dramatic level, there are experiences like those of Bill in Temascalcingo. When we began research there, Bill decided the town cantina would be a good place to find out what was going on in the community. All was going well until one of the increasingly inebriated patrons asked Bill what we were doing there. Bill's explanation that we were there to study the local culture led his new companion to pull a very large pistol out of his belt and to state: "The Indians around here only understand one thing and that's this. I'll help you find out about the culture of those fucking Indians. Tomorrow we'll go up in the hills to talk to them." The next morning (not very early), the man showed up at our house, pistol at the ready, to assume the role of research assistant to the anthropologist. Bill faced a very difficult situation in getting rid of his new-found friend without insulting him, patiently explaining that we were not there to study only "Indians" and that we would feel much better about using our own methods for getting people to talk with us. Bill decided that, in the future, there were probably better venues than the cantina for finding out what was going on in the community.

Deciding how much to participate or not to participate in the life of the people being studied is not easy to decide. There are also often occasions during which the ethnographer faces a difficult decision about whether or not to *intervene* in a situation. Kenneth Good gave a particularly wrenching example of this. During his research with the Yanomama of South America, he came across a situation in which a group of teenage boys and three older women were engaged in a tug of war. A woman whom he had befriended earlier was in the middle. Good ascertained that the teenagers were trying to drag the woman off to rape her while the old women were trying to protect her. He described his dilemma as the young boys succeeded in pulling her off into the bushes:

I stood there, my heart pounding. I had no doubt I could scare these kids away. They were half-afraid of me anyway, and if I picked up a stick and gave a good loud, threatening yell, they'd scatter like the wind. On the other hand, I was an anthropologist, not a policeman. I wasn't supposed to take sides and make value judgments and direct their behavior. This kind of thing went on. If a woman left her village and showed up somewhere else unattached, chances were she'd be raped. She knew it, they knew it. It was expected behavior. What was I supposed to do, I thought, try to inject my own standards of morality? I hadn't come down here to change these people or because I thought I'd love everything they did; I'd come to study them. (1991:102–103)

Good decided to do nothing but wrote that this was a turning point in his integration into the community. A month later, he did intervene in a similar situation (1991:104–105).

Every ethnographer sooner or later faces dilemmas like these that become difficult ethical issues (see Rynkiewich and Spradley [1976] for a useful compilation). We may appeal to "cultural relativism" or to the role of "objective observer" to avoid intervention in situations like those faced by Good. However, when we see the people with whom we are working being exploited, subject to violence or damaged in some other way, it's increasingly difficult to justify not intervening.

Nash concluded that the world should not be seen as simply a laboratory in which we carry out our observations but rather a community in which we are "coparticipants with our informants" (1976:164). She used this as an argument for working to try to help the tin miners she was studying in Bolivia fight for their rights. Scheper-Hughes (1996) argues even more strongly that the role of the ethnographer includes activism. She describes how she chose to intervene in the punishment of several young boys caught stealing in a South African village. She intervened to take an accused boy to the hospital to save his life after his punishment at the hands of villagers, even though her research was, in part, one outcome of popular justice.

To a large extent, the establishment of our own limits to participation depends greatly on our own background and the circumstances of the people we study. Our personal characteristics as individuals—our ethnic identity, class, sex, religion, and family status—will determine how we interact with and report on the people we are studying. In the following sections, we discuss some of the most important ways in which the personal characteristics of the ethnographer affect participant observation—and how these personal characteristics often results in limits to participation.

Gender Issues in Participant Observation

One of the important contributions of theoretical discussions over the past two decades has been the axiomatic acceptance of the ethnographer as a gendered, raced, classed, etc. individual, rather than as a neutral research tool. Being a man or woman may be the most significant social fact concerning an individual and obviously should have an impact on participant observation.

The gender of the ethnographer has an impact on several areas of the ethnographic enterprise. A quite important influence relates to the experiences of the ethnographer during the field research. Women in the field have often been harassed and have become victims of violence in ways different from men (Warren 1988). Just as men are often barred from situations in which they can know the intimate worlds of women, women ethnographers are sometimes barred from important parts of the worlds of men.

The reports of ethnographers, however, suggest that women may find it easier to gain access to some aspects of men's lives than male ethnographers find it to gain access to the worlds of women (Nader 1986). Other researchers have argued that, in general, women make naturally better field workers because they are more sensitive and open than are men (Nader 1986; Warren 1988). Some feminist and ethnic writers argue that true rapport and accurate portrayal of the voice of the participant can only be achieved by researchers who come close to matching the informants in gender, race, and class (hooks 1989, 1990).

Differential access to the lives of women has resulted in generations of predominantly male-biased ethnography, which has often paid little heed to the lives and concerns of women. Several classic ethnographic debates are at least partly the result of the different vantage point of the ethnographer. For example, the view of economic exchange in the Trobriand Islands that Malinowski (1922) presented is enlarged and enhanced by the work of Weiner (1988), who focused more of her work on exchanges involving women. (A contrasting case, however, is that of the discrepancies in the reports of Mead [1923] and Freeman [1983] concerning the sexual lives of Samoan girls. Freeman, a male, claims that his data about premarital sexual behavior are more detailed and accurate than Mead's because he spoke Samoan fluently and she did not.)

Catherine Lutz (1988) has written about the experience of being a woman in Ifaluk. She noted that the lives of men and women on Ifaluk are sharply divided. Men and women, husbands and wives may spend very little time together. This is not to say that women do not have high social status in many domains of life on Ifaluk. It is a matrilineal society, in which women contribute strongly to the economy through control of agricultural production, but that world is highly gendered. Lutz, however, had anticipated that she would be able to achieve the "genderless" or "generalized gender" status that a number of women ethnographers reported in other settings (see Fluehr-Lobban 1986; Jackson 1986; Lederman 1986; Warren 1988). In fact, she found that she could not achieve this, but was required to conform to the gender expectations of the community around her. Lutz recorded the event that finally convinced her to abandon the hope that she could create a role outside of the Ifaluk system of expectations. She wrote:

On the first evening, Tamalkar [her fictive "father"] and my "mother," Ilefagomar, gave me a first elementary primer on what I should and should not do; I should say *siro* (respect or excuse me) when passing a group of seated people; I should use the tag *mawesh* (sweetheart) when addressing someone; I should crouch down rather than remain standing if others were sitting; and, Tamalekar emphasized, I should not go into the island store if there were more than two men inside. I was to consider myself their daughter, they said, and Tamelakar would from then on refer to me before others as his daughter. A week later, a *toi*, or "mass meeting," of the island's men was called; on hearing this, I said that I would like to see it and was brought over to the meeting site by a middle-aged man from the village. Tamelakar was already there. Seeing me, he anxiously asked, "Where are you going?" and looked both uncomfortable and displeased when he heard I was interested in observing the meeting. As direct requests are rarely refused, he did not respond, but waved me to sit off to the side by his relatives. With this and subsequent encounters, such all-male occasions soon lost their interest for me, and I spent the great majority of my time with women in cook huts, gardens and birth houses. (1988:36–37)

Lutz expected to be able to choose the role that she would adopt in Ifaluk and anticipated that she would "allow" (1988:33) herself to be socialized in arenas in which she was interested. If one is to be successful as a participant observer, however, that is not always possible.

Jean Briggs (1986) was never able to adopt the role of *kapluna* (white) daughter to the satisfaction of her fictive Utkuhiksalingmiut "family." As a result, she reports months of stymied research in which community members essentially shunned her because she couldn't keep her temper and act like an Utkuhiksalingmiut woman.

A number of women, however, have successfully stepped outside the prescribed roles for women within a particular cultural setting. Women have been involved with research on agricultural production, or other economic activities in which both men and women might work, but the spheres of men and women are different. Allen (1988), for example, was able to study the tasks of both men and women in her Peruvian research, although she notes that her original entrance into the community was eased because she was accompanied by a male colleague.

Some of the most successful and fascinating fieldwork is done by teams of men and women. Murphy and Murphy (1974) showed a view of Mundurucu society that was almost unique for its time in the way it placed in counterpoint the perspectives of men and women. The Murphys could do this because they had simultaneous access to different events and to different informants during the same events.

Having the perspective and/or assistance of a member of the opposite sex can often be quite important. In research in rural Kentucky, Sara Quandt, Beverly Morris, and Kathleen DeWalt were investigating the nutritional strategies of older adults (Quandt et al. 1997). After a number of months of in-depth interviewing with samples of key informants in each of two counties, they had heard virtually nothing about alcohol use or production of moonshine. Even carefully worded and rather oblique interviewing about alcohol, however, was met with flat denials.

One day the research team traveled to Central County with Jorge Uquillas, an Ecuadorian sociologist who had expressed an interest in visiting the Kentucky field sites. One of the informants they visited was Mr. B, a natural storyteller who had spoken at length about life of the poor during the past 60 years. Although he had been a great source of information about use of wild foods and recipes for cooking game he had never spoken of drinking or moonshine production. Within a few minutes of entering his home on this day, he looked at Uquillas, and said "Are you a drinking man?" (Beverly whipped out the tape recorder and switched it on.[11]) Over the next hour or so, Mr. B talked about community values concerning alcohol use, the problems of drunks and how they were dealt with in the community, and provided a number of stories about moonshine in Central County. The presence of another man gave Mr. B the opportunity to talk about issues he found interesting, but felt would have been inappropriate to discuss with women.

Men and women have access to different settings, people, and bodies of knowledge. Our own experience has been that having a man and woman involved in fieldwork at the same time has provided a more balanced view of community life, of key relationships, and of the interaction of households and families than we would have had if we had worked alone. We base this on not only our experience in working with one another in a number of projects, but also on other projects in which we have worked with larger teams involving men and women. Fortunately, for many decades, men and women have been about equally represented among students entering cultural anthropology programs. For this reason, it is much more likely that collaboration by males and females in field research can occur.

At the same time, we would not claim that working as a couple has given us any "special" insight into the communities and people we have studied. Any ethnographer brings their own special perspective to the field. Single ethnographers with characteristics that differ from our own would not have discovered some things that we noted, but at the same time, there are other behaviors that our own perspective did not allow us to see. Kathleen's interests in medical and nutritional topics, and Bill's interests in economic and agricultural issues, resulted in rich data on those aspects of life (B. DeWalt 1979; K. DeWalt 1983). On the other hand, we have much less data on issues like kinship, sexuality, symbolism, and ethnohistory.

Up Close and Personal: Sex in the Field

As several recent writers have noted (Caplan 1993; Kulick 1995; Lewin and Leap 1996a), even in the climate of reflexivity, the sexuality of the field worker hasn't been much discussed by ethnographers, either in their monographs or methodological notes. Nor was a discussion of sex in the field part of the methodological or theoretical training of many anthropologists. Esther Newton (1996) has written that she learned in graduate school "because it was never mentioned—that erotic interest between field worker and informant didn't exist; would be inappropriate; or couldn't be mentioned. . ." (p. 213). She had no idea which.

Kulick and Willson (1995) find the taboo on discussing sex and the sexuality of the ethnographers somewhat curious, as ethnographers haven't hesitated to discuss the sexuality of the people they have studied. Some well-known exceptions to the long silence about sex and sexuality in the field include references in Malinowski's diaries (1967), Rabinow's (1977) discussion of an affair in Morocco, Turnbull's (1986) mention of his Mbuti lover, and from one of the very few women to speak of this, Cesara's (1982) reflections on her fieldwork experience among the Lenda.

Good's account is less about sex and sexuality, but describes his relationship with a Yamomama woman. He first agreed to become betrothed to Yarima when she was less than 12 years old. Although his initial agreement to this arrangement was made almost casually in a conversation with a village headman, Good became more attached to Yarima during several years of returning to South America. He describes his increasing emotional involvement, the eventual consummation of their relationship after she began menstruating, how he dealt with his rage and jealousy after Yarima was raped by another Yanomama, and their eventual marriage and moving to the United States. The book also includes observations from Yarima's perspective (Good 1991). An engaging and personal account, Good makes no claims that this relationship enhanced or hindered his understanding of the Yanomama.

Jean Gearing (1995), however, describes how she became attracted to her "best informant" on the island of St. Vincent, became his "girlfriend" and eventually married him. She argues persuasively that her romantic relationship with a Vincentian, which was viewed as appropriate by the community, not only increased her acceptance in the community, but opened up the opportunity to gain significant insight into Vincentian life, both through a shifting in her relationships with others and with her husband as an informant.

In the introduction to one of several recent volumes on sex and sexuality in the field, Kulick (1995) reviews some of the factors implicated in the lack of discussion of sex and sexuality in fieldwork. He includes among these: the supposed objectivity of the observer (Dwyer 1982), that sexuality should not make a difference in the objective recording and analysis of the customs and habits of other people; the general disdain (until recently) in the discipline for personal narratives (Pratt 1986); and more general cultural taboos about discussing sex, or at least our own sexuality (Kulick 1995:3). Kulick suggests as well, following Newton (1993), that silence about sexuality has served the purpose of "fortifying male heterosexuality by keeping above the bounds of critical inquiry and of silencing women and gays" (1995:4).

In recent years, several volumes of essays have been published that deal more directly with the issues of sex and sexuality in the field (Whitehead and Conaway 1986; Bell et al. 1993; Kulick and Willson 1995; Lewin and Leap 1996a). Several factors have contributed to this increased attention. The first is the contemporary emphasis on reflexivity which suggests that the ethnographer is situated sexually as well as with respect to, gender, class, race, etc. (Caplan 1993; Altork 1995; Kulick 1995; Lewin and Leap 1996). Discussions of sexuality, then, become part of the process of reflexivity. A second trend is the increase in research on gay and lesbian communities by gay and lesbian ethnographers; this has resulted in a number of accounts of the experience of being a "native ethnographer." Finally, there is increasing acceptance of the discussions concerning sexual relationships in the field for all researchers.

Several ethnographers have written about the impact on their research of a fuller participatory involvement in the community itself, both the effect of being accepted as a "native" and the information they gain as a result of sexual activity (Cesara 1982; Bolton 1995, 1996; Gearing 1995; Leap 1996; Murray 1996; Lewin and Leap 1996b; Newton 1996). Bolton (1995, 1996), for example, discusses not only the ways in which his homosexuality influenced his examination of gay communities in the "years of the plague" [AIDS] but also how his sexual activity became "data."

Murray (1991, 1996) has written several thoughtful essays on the use of information gained during sexual activity as data in research. For Murray, having sexual relationships with other gay men in Guatemala became fieldwork on eliciting terms relating to homosexuality in Central America only in retrospect. His primary motivation for having sex with Guatemalans was not to recruit informants, although he admits to having thought about the "representativeness" of his "sample" at one point. In the one instance in which he reports that he went with a man out of curiosity, rather than attraction, they ended up not having sex. However, Murray argues that "Having sex with the natives is not a royal road to insight about alien sexualities" (1996:250). Further, he is concerned that "conclusions based on sexual participation are distorted by confusing the intimacies possible with strangers with native's everyday intimate lives" (p. 242). Coming from a more textually oriented theoretical and methodological approach, he suspects that even behavior under these circumstances is adjusted to fit what the participants believe the researchers want to know. He prefers "native documents not elicited by foreigners" as data (p. 250). Even this conclusion, however, is, in part, the result of his juxtaposing "experience near" data from participant observation with interviews and other research materials.

To summarize, then, sexual relationships in the field raise two issues that are quite important to review here. One has to do with observation. Increased attention to reflexivity suggests that sexuality is a key characteristic of the observer, apart from gender (although obviously these two cannot be separated). As Kulick (1995) puts it, it is time to ask: "What are the implications of the anthropologist as a sexually cognizant knower?" (p. 6). The answer to this question, provided by a number of contributors to his and several other volumes, is that there are a number of implications and recognizing the observer as a sexually situated observer is important both in the writing of ethnography and the reading of the ethnography.

The second issue has to do with participation. As several writers have noted, participation in sexual relationships may be important to acceptance in a community and the development of rapport (Turnbull 1986). More commonly, ethnographers who discuss these issues argue that intimate relationships provide access to information that might not have been available otherwise (Gearing 1995; Murray 1996).

Intimate relationships, however, raise several ethical questions. What is the potential for sexual exploitation of research participants, especially when the ethnographer is a white, heterosexual male from a developed country? Despite the feeling of many ethnographers (especially new researchers) that they are dazed, confused, and relatively powerless, differences in race, class, and gender put most ethnographers in a more powerful position than the citizens of the communities in which they work. Gender differences may not be at issue for gay and lesbian researchers, but class and ethnic differences are still likely to be important.

What are the implications for the use of information gained during sexual encounters as "data"? As we noted earlier, participant observation raises a number of ethical questions, principally because it's not always clear when the ethnographer is conducting research. It would seem that this potential would be magnified in the context of intimate relationships.

In this vein, the matter of informed consent, which is becoming more important in research involving human subjects, becomes extremely relevant. Should we be developing informed consent scripts that can be whispered at an appropriate moment? This is not an idle question. We have developed elaborate guidelines for ensuring that the people we study are given a full explanation of the purposes of the research, and we stress that we should always ask permission when making sound or photographic recordings. It seems apparent that much greater discussion is required concerning the ethics of sexuality as a research tool or as a component of doing field research.

Another disturbing question that arises for us is: What will be the impact of sexual relationships on the experiences of subsequent researchers in doing ethnography? Several women researchers we know, Kathleen included, have experienced reluctance and even hostility from potential women informants as a result of their expectation that "U.S. women" were out after their husbands. Several of our female graduate students have found themselves in awkward situations because of the perception among some Latin American men that all U.S. women are "loose." In part, these problems were the results of previous experience with researchers who did have intimate relationships with men (including married individuals) in the community.

Finally, to what extent does sexual activity place researchers, especially women, at risk for sexual assault? Both women and men may be at risk for sexual assault in the field, but the risk for women is higher (Warren 1988; Lee 1995). Rape of the researcher in the field is not often talked about, but several cases are personally known to us. In the literature, Eva Moreno (1995) discusses how a combination of ambivalence and inattention to sexual cues resulted in her rape by a male research assistant. Howell (1990) reports that 7% of a sample of women anthropologists reported rape or attempted rape in the field, noting at the same time that this probably is a significant underreporting of rape.

Some women attempt to assume a "sexless" identity to help protect against assault. Others have, or invent, burly husbands and boyfriends, who, even in their absence, can serve as male protectors. An interesting byproduct of the discussion of sex in the field provided by Murray (1996) is his suggestion that his beginning sexual activity with other men in Guatemala may have compromised the position of his woman companion. She had been using him as a foil against other men, a strategy that became much less effective when he became sexually active.

Like many other anthropologists, we have always strongly advised students that sexual relationships with informants or other individuals in communities in which we were working should be avoided. Bernard (1995) notes this advice as common for beginning anthropologists. The risks—ethical, personal, and to the research enterprise—have always seemed too high to us. The narratives of researchers who have developed intimate relationships in the field, though, suggest that the risks are not always great and a "blanket prohibition" is not only impossible (ethnographers are, after all, human) but perhaps not even desirable. Our own advice to graduate students has often been ignored, although the results of these encounters has further reinforced our contention that sex and fieldwork is not a good combination.

Participating and Parenting: Children and Field Research[12]

Fieldwork is traditionally portrayed as a solitary endeavor, but, in reality, many anthropologists bring their families, including their children, to the field with them. The presence of children in the field shapes the research experience in a number of distinct ways. Children can help ease the loneliness and isolation characteristic of fieldwork in foreign cultures. However, they also present a number of challenges to anthropologists in the field. As part of the trend to demystify anthropological fieldwork, a number of anthropologists have written about their experiences with children in the field. While each fieldwork experience is unique, a number of themes emerge regarding the effect of children on participant observation.

Many anthropologists report that their children had a positive impact on participant observation. Bringing children to a field site can lead to increased rapport with the research community. A solitary anthropologist showing up in a remote area to live alone for a period of a year or more may seem extremely bizarre in many cultures. In most cases, the people who are being studied are able to relate more easily to an anthropologist living with his or her family. Mimi and Mark Nichter (Nichter and Nichter 1987) believed that the presence of their young son made it easier for villagers to relate to them during their research in a rural Indian village. Bourgois (1995) describes how his son's cerebral palsy was diagnosed in a clinic in *El Barrio*, and that his son's ability to negotiate the neighborhood, rolling his walker over trash and crack vials in the streets of *El Barrio* helped establish Bourgois as a community member.

Also, the presence of children accompanying a researcher can signify his or her adult status. In many cultures a childless adult, especially a married childless adult, may be viewed as strange, dangerous, or the object of pity. During our first field experience in Temascalcingo, it was a concern for many people that we had been married for more than a year without having a child and without signs of Kathleen being pregnant (see also, Klass and Solomon Klass 1987). During their first field experience in the Sudan, Carolyn Fluehr-Lobban and Richard Lobban (Fluehr-Lobban and Lobban 1986, 1987) reported that people had trouble accepting their status as a married couple because they had no children. Many Sudanese doubted that they were truly married, but their return to the field ten years later with their daughter Josina reassured their friends and acquaintances.

Bringing children into the field can also open up new areas of information to the anthropologist. Most researchers who bring young children in the field often receive a constant stream of advice about child care from friends and neighbors. While an overabundance of friendly advice can be exasperating, it can also teach anthropologists about the culture they are working in. Mimi and Mark Nichter reported that they gained valuable insights into rural Indian ideas about child development from villagers' comments made about their son's "constitution" (Nichter and Nichter 1987). This advice can also challenge the anthropologist's unexamined cultural biases and assumptions. Renate Fernandez (1987) learned that children sleeping alone in their own room was viewed as a type of social deprivation in rural Spain.

Anthropologists can also learn about a culture from the way people react to their children. When informants are enculturating children, they are also teaching the anthropologist about their culture. During Diane Michalski Turner's (1987) fieldwork in Fiji, the villagers with whom she lived devoted a lot of time teaching her two-year-old daughter to become Fijian. By watching how villagers interacted with her daughter, Michalski Turner was able to learn not only how one becomes Fijian, but also about Western/Fijian power relationships.

And children can help gather data that is inaccessible to adults. G. E. Huntington (1987) reports that her nine-year-old daughter was an invaluable source of information about Hutterite children's informal culture. As a result, Huntington learned how Hutterite children engage in very different behaviors when they are in front of adults and when they are among other children participating in their own culture.

Bringing children into the field, however, has its disadvantages. Some anthropologists report that the responsibilities of child care forced them to miss out on certain opportunities. Reflecting on her research in Jamaica, Joan Cassell (1987) relates how she frequently missed nighttime events because she felt compelled to stay home with her two children. Young, unruly children can also disrupt meetings and interviews. Perhaps the biggest disadvantage of bringing children to the field is the amount of time that researchers devote to child care (and hence lose to the fieldwork). Many anthropologists, especially those solely responsible for child care, report that the presence of children severely curtailed the amount of time they could devote to fieldwork. Melanie Dreher, who brought three children to rural Jamaica to conduct postdoctoral research with her, states,"I suspect it took me twice the time to accomplish half the work that I would have normally accomplished" (Dreher 1987:165). During fieldwork among an indigenous tribe in the northwest Amazon, Christine and Stephen Hugh-Jones (Hugh-Jones 1987) had to devise alternating fieldwork schedules so that one of them would always be available to supervise their two children.

Our personal experiences with children in the field have been generally quite positive. Our two fair-haired children were an instant magnet everywhere we have traveled in Latin America and opened many doors for us. We also found that, early in our careers when we were relatively poor graduate students or assistant professors, we could more easily afford child care in Mexico or Honduras than we could in the United States. As our children moved into their teens and began to have obligations and wishes of their own, it became more difficult for us to take them to the field. During these years, we began to schedule our time in the field separately so that one of us stayed in the United States with the children, while the other was engaged in doing field research.

Whether children help or hinder participant observation depends on a number of factors. It seems that there is a significant effect depending on whether the anthropologist is returning to a site or arriving for the first time. Most anthropologists who arrive at a field site for the first time with their children seem to experience more problems than veteran field workers (Cassell 1987; Michalski Turner 1987). The age of the children also shapes the field experience. Very young children, while needing more care, adapt more readily and experience less severe culture shock (Fluehr-Lobban and Lobban 1987; Nichter and Nichter 1987). Older children seem to have a more difficult time adapting to new and foreign cultures (Scheper-Hughes 1987). The field situation itself also shapes the experience with the children. Bringing children to a field site where they already speak the language is easier on both the children and the parent than introducing them to a culture where they are only able to communicate with their family (Cassell 1987; Hugh-Jones 1987). The presence of another parent to share child care responsibilities certainly facilitates a field worker's time in the field with his or her children (Fluehr-Lobban and Lobban 1987; Scheper-Hughes 1987).

Ethnographer Bias

Because participant observation is perhaps the quintessential qualitative method, the question of reliability is critically important. As the above discussions of the effects of gender, sexuality, and the field worker's family situation suggest, it's quite apparent that these personal attributes can substantially affect participant observation in field research. Postmodernist writers particularly emphasize that the observer and his or her circumstances and biases cannot be separated from the accounts that they write.

In addition, ethnographers surely differ in terms of their abilities and qualifications. Until recently, however, it has been rare for the accuracy of field reports to be questioned. This is so despite an increasing number of controversies coming to light in which the data collected by different anthropologists who have worked in the same area differ substantially (for example, Redfield [1930] and Lewis [1951] concerning Tepoztlán in Mexico; Mead [1923] and Freeman [1983] on Samoa; and Benedict [1934] and Barnouw [1963] on the Zuni). This acceptance of the reliability of data contrasts markedly with the controversies embroiling anthropology and other social science disciplines concerning the interpretation or theory built with the data.

Building theory, of course, depends on having reliable data, so it's lamentable that so little attention has been given to the issues of reliability and validity of the information collected. The relatively small amount of formal examination of ethnographer bias in anthropology is evidence that these issues merit much more attention than they have previously received.

The pioneering work on ethnographer bias was done by Raoul Naroll (1962; 1970), who became concerned that his cross-cultural research results may have been affected by systematic errors in ethnographic reporting. In the most striking finding, Naroll (1962:88–89) found that the incidence of witchcraft reported in particular societies was related to the amount of time the ethnographer spent in the field. He showed that ethnographers who spent more than a year in the field were significantly more likely to report the presence of witchcraft beliefs among the societies they studied than those who spent shorter amounts of time in the field.

Our own research in Temascalcingo provided a striking personal confirmation of Naroll's finding. Above we referred to leaving the field for three weeks after our first six months in the field. Before our brief hiatus, we had asked people many times about magical and witchcraft beliefs, particularly because these topics were so relevant to Kathleen's medical anthropological research. Everyone had denied that there were any such beliefs in the community. Almost the very day of our return, however, one of our key informants began regaling us with a recounting of a conflict that had occurred during our absence. The conflict included accusations by one of the parties that witchcraft was being used against them. During the remaining months in the field, witchcraft was a common theme of our conversations with people who had denied its existence before. We are convinced that the willingness of people to talk with us about such themes reflected a breakthrough in their level of confidence and comfort with us. Thus, as Naroll (1962) and we can attest, the length of time that a person spends engaged in participant observation does make a very large difference in the kind of findings that may be reported.

Controlling for sources of ethnographer bias has become increasingly common in cross-cultural research since Naroll's early work. Another example of the importance of ethnographer bias comes from the work of Rohner et al. (1973). Their work focused on the effects of bias in reporting about parental acceptance-rejection and its importance in personality development in children and adults. One striking finding of these analyses was that ethnographers who use multiple verification efforts report more parental rejection and other "negative" personality traits among the people they study. Rohner et al. reported that this seems to be linked to a "bias of romanticism" among anthropologists. Unless ethnographers use methods other than just participant observation, they are unlikely to report the negative aspects of their subjects' personalities and lives. They quoted Lévi-Strauss (1961:381), who observed that "At home the anthropologist may be a natural subversive, a convinced opponent of traditional usage; but no sooner has he in focus a society different from his own than he becomes respectful of even the most conservative practices." This argues for a mix of methods in which participant observation is just one of the tools that anthropologists use to find out the behavior of the people they study.

The "quality" of participant observation will vary depending on the personal characteristics of ethnographers (for example, gender, age, sexual orientation, ethnic affiliation), their training and experience (for example, language ability, quality of training, etc.), and perhaps their theoretical orientation. As interpretive anthropology makes clear, all of us bring biases, predispositions, and hang-ups to the field with us, and we cannot completely escape these as we view other cultures. Our reporting, however, should attempt to make these biases as explicit as possible so that others may use these in judging our work. What is also apparent, however, is that by utilizing more formal methods of data collection in conjunction with participant observation, we may improve the quality and consistency of our reporting.

Much of the recent trend in postmodernist writing in anthropology explicitly aims toward presenting both "the Self and Other . . . within a single narrative ethnography" (Tedlock 1991:69). The point is often made that "objectivity" is not possible in the study of human behavior. While we can agree with this position, we don't accept the corollary that is often drawn that therefore we should not strive to improve our observational skills or search for explanatory theories concerning human behavior. Understanding ourselves and our reactions to field research and the individuals we study should be a beginning point, not the final product of ethnography. Indeed, psychoanalysis was commonly used by anthropologists like Cora DuBois, Abram Kardiner, Ruth Benedict, and others both as a method of studying other cultures as well as a personal means for coming to terms with their own reactions to their research. They then went about the business of trying to construct social scientific explanations of peoples' behavior through ethnography. Our perspective is that we should go beyond the individual postmodern musings that are too common in contemporary anthropology to more *systematically* examine how the anthropologist's race, gender, sexual preferences, and other factors affect their observations. The work of Naroll and others who followed his lead are suggestive of how informative such studies can be.

Beyond the Reflexivity Frontier

Participant observation as a technique of fieldwork has been a hallmark of anthropological research since the beginning of the twentieth century and has been a distinguishing characteristic for anthropology compared with other social sciences. It may be constitutive—that is, it may be essential to anthropology. Although tied to functionalist theoretical approaches early in the century, the reliance on participant observation and the recording of chronologically oriented descriptive field notes, which also include the incorporation of the ethnographer's thoughts and reactions, laid the groundwork for much of the theoretical development autochthonous to anthropology. That the descriptions of the research enterprise provided by Malinowski in 1922 and Bourgois (among many others) in 1995 can appear so similar, suggests that the method, while not atheoretical (no method is) is so closely tied to a relatively unchanging theoretical core in anthropology as to provide the basis for a wide range of theoretical development around that core.

The movement into more reflexive ethnographic writing has resulted in a quantum increase in the number of accounts of the fieldwork experience presented by ethnographers from a number of different theoretical approaches. The result, we believe, is a continuing demystification of the process of fieldwork and ethnographic writing. Making explicit the process of participant observation allows the reader to better understand the information presented by the ethnographer. Narrative ethnography (Tedlock 1991) and personal accounts of field experience also provide the opportunity for new researchers to begin to anticipate problems, identify alternative strategies and begin to craft their personal approaches to participant observation early in the fieldwork experience. The approach to training in ethnography common a generation ago held that each new ethnographer should go out and reinvent anthropology methodologically and sink or swim on their own ability to do so. We believe that this is a form of intellectual elitism. And, although we still occasionally hear similar sentiments from some of our colleagues in anthropology, the increasing number of monographs and textbooks addressing issues in ethnographic methods and the number of formal courses in methods available in our universities suggest that we have gone beyond that time.

Approaches that emphasize the "observation of participation" are quite useful and important (especially for training budding anthropologists), but we see these as complementary to the use of participant observation as a means of collecting verifiable, reliable data concerning human behavior. We accept that none of us can become completely objective measuring devices. We can, however, use participant observation in conjunction with other methods to serve anthropology as a scientific pursuit.

That is, we see reflexivity as a beginning point rather than as an end to ethnography. We need to be aware of who we are, understand our biases as much as we can, and to understand and interpret our interactions with the people we study. Once we have done that, we can strive to determine whether there are regularities in human behavior.

From a personal point of view, what is heartening to us is that much previous anthropological and other social scientific research can be quite useful in building generalizations. Both of us have engaged in comparative work in which we have utilized the work of other anthropologists and other social scientists. An example of Kathleen's work is her evaluation of research on the relationship between cash cropping and human nutrition. One hypothesis that was very common in the literature was that as people switched from semisubsistence crops to cash crops their nutritional status became worse. Summarizing studies from around the world, she was able to show that there is not a simple relationship between these two phenomena. When people switched from semisubsistence crops to cash cropping, there has not been a necessary improvement or decline in human nutrition. Other factors, some of which are specified in her work, are also involved and must be studied (DeWalt 1993).

In a similar vein, Bill has looked at the literature on agrarian reform communities in Mexico (DeWalt and Rees 1994) and on development in indigenous communities in Latin America (Roper et al. 1996). In both cases, he and his collaborators were able to find common patterns in the data presented by individuals working at many different times, places, and with different theoretical perspectives. It was possible, on the basis of comparative analysis of the ethnographic materials, to draw important policy conclusions.

Our experience has been that, despite differences in theoretical perspectives, gender, ethnicity, and other personal factors, the broad-brush observations of individual researchers concerning human behavior are relatively consistent. Certainly, if we look at the fine detail or if we look for consonance in theoretical conclusions, we will find many differences. Rather than using the latter as justification for giving up on making participant observation and other anthropological methods more verifiable and reliable, we believe it's more productive to focus on the generalizations that can be derived from such data. The aim should then be to improve our methodological skills to work toward building generalizations that are even stronger.

Conclusions

Participant observation is the hallmark of anthropological methods. The active engagement of an ethnographer in the lives of the people being studied—whether they are a group from halfway around the world, an exotic subculture of our own society, or people who don't look or act much differently from ourselves—is an essential tool. There is no substitute for gaining tacit and implicit knowledge of cultural behavior than living among people and sharing their lives. We believe that the practice of participant observation has been one of the catalysts for theoretical development in anthropology.

Participant observation raises many important ethical issues for ethnographers. These issues include the problem of establishing "limits to participation"—should ethnographers engage in illegal behaviors, should they establish sexual relationships with informants, and should they take up the causes held dear by the people we study? Another ethical issue on which we touched was finding the proper mix between participation and observation. In addition, there is the problem of maintaining the anonymity of the people whom we study, often for their own protection. There are no easy answers to these ethical issues; like the processes of doing participant observation and fieldwork, these problems require discussion in methods classes. Our own view is that, as a starting point, our responsibility as ethnographers is to try to ensure that the people we study are not harmed by our personal involvements with them and are not negatively affected by the information we collect and write about them.

Finally, we acknowledge that every one who chooses to use this method will bring his or her own biases, predilections, and personal characteristics with him or her and will face a number of challenges and choices. In this chapter, we have focused on the most important of these and have tried to convey what we have learned from our own personal experiences and those of other anthropologists. The primary message is that, while we should be aware of our own identities and how these may affect our field research, we should continue to work toward scientific observations of people and their cultures. The objective of ethnography should not be to learn more about ourselves as individuals (although that will happen), but to learn more about others. Systematic study of the effects of biases, predilections, and personal characteristics on the research enterprise is a valid social scientific endeavor and requires further development.

NOTES

1. For Agar, the interview is more important than the participation, and observation serves as source of questions about which to interview. However, he sees participant observation as providing the context for the rest of the enterprise.

2. We may find it difficult to articulate what it is that makes us feel uncomfortable because these aspects of cultural knowledge remain outside of our general consciousness. It is participation in the context around us that allows us to gain insight into the tacit.

3. Malinowski further cautions against living in compounds apart from the people under investigation like other "white men" do and insists on the need to live in the community.

4. Most anthropologists, however, would argue that the range of behaviors that are susceptible to pure observation or can be understood through pure observation is small.

5. Postmodern anthropologists may base their analyses on "texts" that can be written or spoken materials. In the former case, no face-to-face interaction with informants is required.

6. We have carried out fieldwork in an essentially "commuting" situation and as residents of communities. There is no doubt for us that greater understanding comes from living in the community.

7. Good reports that it was this experience that contributed to his increasing divergence from his then-adviser's portrayal of the Yanomama as "the fierce people" (Chagnon 1983). Although Good saw the violence in their culture, he also saw a substantial amount of harmony and group cohesion.

8. Tedlock discusses a number of cases of anthropologists who are candidates for having "gone native." As she points out, however, in each case the individual continued to publish ethnographic accounts (1991:70).

9. This brings to mind a well-known joke in anthropological circles about a "postmodern anthropologist." Postmodern anthropologists are very concerned about documenting their own personal responses to what the people they study are telling them. This ethnographer is conducting an interview with a "native" that stretches on for many hours. Finally, the native becomes restless and says to the ethnographer: "Excuse me, but we've talked enough about you. Can we now talk about me for a while!"

10. Nader also quotes Robin Fox as commenting after a trip to the Southwest: "There were all the anthropologists, and there were all the tourists. The tourists were asking the Indians all the questions that the anthropologists wanted to ask, but didn't because they were afraid of ruining rapport (Nader 1986:113)." Building rapport often involves not directly addressing certain issues or asking pointed questions, but allowing these to emerge out of the flow of everyday conversation.

11. During this research project, the ethnographers had asked permission and recorded many of their conversations with informants. In terms of ethics, it is important that ethnographers always explain how recordings will be used and ask permission before taping or videotaping any interview or conversation.

12. This section was prepared with the assistance of Coral B. Wayland.

REFERENCES

Adler, Patricia, and Peter Adler. 1994. Observational Techniques. In *Handbook of Qualitative Research*. Norman Denzin and Yvonna Lincoln, eds. Pp. 377–392. Thousand Oaks, CA: Sage Publications.

Agar, Michael. 1986. *Speaking of Ethnography*. Qualitative Research Methods Series, Vol. 2. Thousand Oaks, CA: Sage Publications.

Agar, Michael. 1996. *The Professional Stranger: An Informal Introduction to Ethnography*, 2d ed. San Diego: Academic Press.

Allen, Katherine. 1988. *The Hold Life Has: Coca and Cultural Identity in an Andean Community*. Washington, DC: Smithsonian Institution Press.

Altork, Kate. 1995. Walking the Fire Line: The Erotic Dimension of the Fieldwork Experience. In *Taboo: Sex, Identity, and Erotic Subjectivity in Anthropological Fieldwork*. Don Kulick and Margaret Willson, eds. Pp. 107–139. London: Routledge.

American Anthropological Association (AAA). 1997. *Code of Ethics of the American Anthropological Association*. http://www.ameranthassn.org/ethcode.htm.

Barnouw, Victor. 1963. *Culture and Personality*. Homewood, IL: Dorsey.

Behar, Ruth. 1996. *The Vulnerable Observer: Anthropology that Breaks Your Heart*. Boston: Beacon Press.

Bell, Diane, Pat Caplan, and Wazir Jahan Karim. 1993. *Gendered Fields: Women, Men and Ethnography*. London: Routledge.

Benedict, Ruth. 1934. *Patterns of Culture*. New York: Houghton Mifflin.

Bernard, H. Russell. 1994. *Research Methods in Anthropology: Qualitative and Quantitative Approaches*, 2d ed. Walnut Creek, CA: AltaMira Press.

Bock, Philip K. 1970. *Culture Shock: A Reader in Modern Cultural Anthropology*. New York: Knopf.

Bolton, Ralph. 1995. Tricks, Friends and Lovers: Erotic Encounters in the Field. In *Taboo: Sex, Identity, and Erotic Subjectivity in Anthropological Fieldwork*. Don Kulick and Margaret Willson, eds. Pp. 140–167. London: Routledge.

Bolton, Ralph. 1996. Coming Home: Confessions of a Gay Ethnographer in the Years of the Plague. In *Out in the Field: Reflections of Lesbian and Gay Anthropologists*. Ellen Lewin and William Leap, eds. Pp. 147–170. Urbana: University of Illinois Press.

Bourgois, Philippe. 1995. *In Search of Respect: Selling Crack in El Barrio*. Cambridge: Cambridge University Press.

Bourgois, Philippe. 1996. Confronting Anthropology, Education and Inner-City Apartheid. *American Anthropologist* 98(2):249–265.

Briggs, Jean. 1986. Kapluna Daughter. In *Women in the Field: Anthropological Experiences*, 2d ed. Peggy Golde, ed. Pp. 19–44. Berkeley: University of California Press.

Caplan, Pat. 1993. Introduction. In *Gendered Fields: Women, Men and Ethnography*. Diane Bell, Pat Caplan, and Wazir Jahan Karim, eds. Pp. 19–27. London: Routledge.

Cassell, Joan. 1987. "Oh No, They're Not My Shoes!": Fieldwork in the Blue Mountains of Jamaica. In *Children in the Field*. Joan Cassell, ed. Pp. 1–26. Philadelphia: Temple University Press.

Cassell, Joan, and Sue Ellen Jacobs. 1997. *Handbook on Ethical Issues in Anthropology*. A special publication of the American Anthropological Association, Number 23. http://www.ameranthassn.org/sp23.htm

Castaneda, Carlos. 1972. *Journey to Ixtlan: The Lessons of Don Juan*. New York: Simon and Schuster.

Cesara, Manda. 1982. *Reflections of a Woman Anthropologist: No Hiding Place*. New York: Academic Press.

Chagnon, Napoleon. 1983. *Yanomamo: The Fierce People*, 3rd ed. New York: Holt, Rinehart and Winston.

Clifford, James. 1990. Notes on (Field)notes. In *Fieldnotes: The Makings of Anthropology*. Roger Sanjek, ed. Pp. 47–70. Ithaca: Cornell University Press.

Clifford, James. 1997. *Routes: Travel and Translation in the Late Twentieth Century*. Cambridge: Harvard University Press.

Coy, Michael. 1989. Introduction. In *Apprenticeship: From Theory to Method and Back Again*. Michael Coy, ed. Pp. x–xv. Albany: State University of New York Press.

Desjarlais, Robert. 1992. *Body and Emotion: The Aesthetics of Illness and Healing in the Nepal Himalayas*. Philadelphia: The University of Pennsylvania Press.

DeWalt, Billie R. 1979. *Modernization in a Mexican Ejido: A Study in Economic Adaptation*. New York and Cambridge: Cambridge University Press.

DeWalt, Billie R., and Martha W. Rees. 1994. *The End of the Agrarian Reform in Mexico: Past Lessons, Future Prospects*. San Diego: Center for U.S.–Mexican Studies.

DeWalt, Kathleen M. 1983. *Nutritional Strategies and Agricultural Change in a Mexican Community*. Ann Arbor: UMI Research Press.

DeWalt, Kathleen M. 1993. Nutrition and the Commercialization of Agriculture: Ten Years Later. *Social Science and Medicine* 36:1407–1416.

Ditton, J. 1977. *Part-Time Crime*. London: MacMillan.

Dreher, Melanie. 1987. Three Children in Rural Jamaica. In *Children in the Field*. Joan Cassell, ed. Pp. 149–171. Philadelphia: Temple University Press.

Dwyer, Kevin. 1982. *Moroccan Dialogues: Anthropology in Question*. Prospect Heights, IL: Waveland Press.

Fernandez, Renate. 1987. Children and Parents in the Field: Reciprocal Interests. In *Children in the Field*. Joan Cassell, ed. Pp. 185–215. Philadelphia: Temple University Press.

Firth, Raymond, ed. 1957. *Man and Culture: An Evaluation of the Work of Bronislaw Malinowski*. New York: Harper Torchbooks.

Fluehr-Lobban, Carolyn, and Richard Lobban. 1986. Families, Gender and Methodology in the Sudan. In *Self, Sex and Gender in Cross-Cultural Fieldwork*. T. L. Whitehead and M. E. Conaway, eds. Pp. 182–193. Urbana: University of Illinois Press.

Fluehr-Lobban, Carolyn, and Richard Lobban. 1987. Drink from the Nile. In *Children in the Field*. Joan Cassell, ed. Pp. 237–255. Philadelphia: Temple University Press.

Freeman, Derek. 1983. *Margaret Mead in Samoa: The Making and Unmaking of an Anthropological Myth*. Cambridge: Harvard University Press.

Fortes, Meyer. 1957. Malinowski and the Study of Kinship. In *Man and Culture: An Evaluation of the Work of Bronislaw Malinowski*. Raymond Firth, ed. Pp. 157–188. New York: Harper Torchbooks.

Gearing, Jean. 1995. Fear and Loving in the West Indies: Research from the Heart. In *Taboo: Sex, Identity, and Erotic Subjectivity in Anthropological Fieldwork*. Don Kulick and Margaret Willson, eds. Pp. 186–218. London: Routledge.

Geertz, Clifford. 1973. Deep Play: Notes on the Balinese Cockfight. In *The Interpretation of Cultures: Selected Essays*. Clifford Geertz, ed. Pp. 412–435. New York: Basic Books.

Geertz, Clifford. 1995. *After the Fact: Two Countries, Four Decades, One Anthropologist*. Cambridge: Harvard University Press.

Good, Kenneth, with David Chanoff. 1991. *Into the Heart: One Man's Pursuit of Love and Knowledge among the Yanomama*. New York: Simon and Schuster.

Holy, Ladislav. 1984. Theory Methodology and the Research Process. In *Ethnographic Research: A Guide to General Conduct*. R. F. Ellen, ed. Pp. 13–34. London: Academic Press.

hooks, bell. 1989. *Talking Back: Thinking Feminist, Thinking Black*. Boston: South End.

hooks, bell. 1990. *Yearning: Race, Gender, and Cultural Politics*. Boston: South End.

Howell, Nancy. 1990. *Surviving Fieldwork, A Report of the Advisory Panel on Health and Saftey in Fieldwork*. Special Publication of the AAA #26. Washington, DC: American Anthropological Association.

Hugh-Jones, Christine. 1987. Children in the Amazon. In *Children in the Field*. Joan Cassell, ed. Pp. 27–63. Philadelphia: Temple University Press.

Hunt, Jennifer. 1984. The Development of Rapport Through the Negotiation of Gender in Fieldwork among Police. *Human Organization* 43:16–34.

Huntington, G. E. 1987. Order Rules the World: Our Children in the Communal Society of the Hutterites. In *Children and Anthropological Research*. Barbara Butler and Diane Michalski Turner, eds. Pp. 53–71. New York: Plenum Press.

Jackson, Jean. 1986. On Trying to Be an Amazon. In *Self, Sex and Gender in Cross-Cultural Fieldwork*. T. L. Whitehead and M. E. Conaway, eds. Pp. 263–274. Urbana: University of Illinois Press.

Jackson, Jean. 1990. "I Am a Fieldnote": Fieldnotes as a Symbol of Professional Identity. In *Fieldnotes: The Makings of Anthropology*. Roger Sanjek, ed. Pp. 3–33. Ithaca: Cornell University Press.

Jorgensen, D. 1989. *Participant Observation*. Thousand Oaks, CA: Sage Publications.

Klass, Morton, and Sheila Solomon Klass. 1987. Birthing in the Bush. In *Children in the Field*. Joan Cassell, ed. Pp. 121–147. Philadelphia: Temple University Press.

Kornblum, William. 1996. Introduction. In *In the Field: Readings on the Field Research Experience*, 2d ed. Carolyn D. Smith and William Kornblum, eds. Pp. 1–7. Westport, CT: Praeger.

Kulick, Don. 1995. Introduction. In *Taboo: Sex, Identity, and Erotic Subjectivity in Anthropological Fieldwork*. Don Kulick and Margaret Willson, eds. Pp. 1–28. London: Routledge.

Kulick, Don, and Margaret Willson, eds. 1995. *Taboo: Sex, Identity, and Erotic Subjectivity in Anthropological Fieldwork*. London: Routledge.

Kumar, Krishna. 1993. *Rapid Appraisal Methods*. Washington, DC: World Bank.

Leach, Edmund. 1957. The Epistemological Background to Malinowski's Empiricism. In *Man and Culture: An Evaluation of the Work of Bronislaw Malinowski*. Raymond Firth, ed. Pp. 119–137. New York: Harper Torchbooks.

Leap, William. 1996. Studying Gay English: How I Got Here from There. In *Out in the Field: Reflections of Lesbian and Gay Anthropologists*. Ellen Lewin and William Leap, eds. Pp. 128–146. Urbana: University of Illinois Press.

Lederman, R. 1986. The Return of Redwoman: Fieldwork in Highland New Guinea. In *Women in the Field: Anthropological Experiences*, 2d ed. Peggy Golde, ed. Pp. 359–387. Berkeley: University of California Press.

Lee, Raymond. 1995. *Dangerous Fieldwork*. Qualitative Research Methods Series, Vol. 34. Thousand Oaks, CA: Sage Publications.

Lévi-Strauss, Claude. 1961. *Tristes tropiques*. New York: Criterion Books.

Lewin, Ellen, and William Leap. 1996a. Introduction. In *Out in the Field: Reflections of Lesbian and Gay Anthropologists*. Ellen Lewin and William Leap, eds. Pp. 1–28. Urbana: University of Illinois Press.

Lewin, Ellen, and William Leap, eds. 1996b. *Out in the Field: Reflections of Lesbian and Gay Anthropologists*. Urbana: University of Illinois Press.

Lewis, Oscar. 1951. *Life in a Mexican Village: Tepoztlán Restudied*. Urbana: University of Illinois Press.

Lutz, Katherine. 1988. *Unnatural Emotions: Everyday Sentiments in a Micronesian Atoll, Their Challenges to Western Theory*. Chicago: University of Chicago Press.

Malinowski, Bronislaw. 1922 [1961]. *Argonauts of the Western Pacific*. New York: Dutton.

Malinowski, Bronsilaw. 1935 [1978]. *Coral Gardens and Their Magic*. New York: Dover.

Malinowski, Bronislaw. 1967. *A Diary in the Strict Sense of the Word*. New York: Harcourt, Brace and World.

Mead, Margaret. 1923. *Coming of Age in Samoa*. New York: William Morrow.

Michalski Turner, Diane. 1987. What Happened When My Daughter Became Fijian. In *Children and Anthropological Research*. Barbara Butler and Diane Michalski Turner, eds. Pp. 97–114. New York: Plenum Press.

Moreno, Eva. 1995. Rape in the Field: Reflections from a Survivor. In *Taboo: Sex, Identity, and Erotic Subjectivity in Anthropological Fieldwork*. Don Kulick and Margaret Wilson, eds. Pp. 219–250. London: Routledge.

Murphy, Yolanda, and Robert F. Murphy. 1974. *Women of the Forest*. New York: Columbia University Press.

Murray, Stephen O. 1991. Sleeping with the Natives as a Source of Data. *Society of Gay and Lesbian Anthropologists Newsletter 13*:49–51.

Murray, Stephen O. 1996. Male Homosexuality in Guatemala: Possible Insights and Certain Confusions from Sleeping with the Natives. In *Out in the Field: Reflections of Lesbian and Gay Anthropologists*. Ellen Lewin and William Leap, eds. Pp. 236–261. Urbana: University of Illinois Press.

Nader, Laura. 1986. From Anguish to Exultation. In *Women in the Field: Anthropological Experiences*, 2d ed. Peggy Golde, ed. Pp. 97–116. Berkeley: University of California Press.

Naroll, Raoul. 1962. *Data Quality Control: A New Research Technique*. New York: Free Press.

Naroll, Raoul. 1970. Data Quality Control in Cross-Cultural Surveys. In *A Handbook of Method in Cultural Anthropology*. Raoul Naroll and Ronald Cohen, eds. Pp. 927–945. Garden City, NY: Natural History Press.

Nash, June. 1976. Ethnology in a Revolutionary Setting. In *Ethics and Anthropology: Dilemmas in Fieldwork*. Michael A. Rynkiewich and James P. Spradley, eds. Pp. 148–166. New York: John Wiley.

Newton, Esther. 1993. My Best Informant's Dress: The Erotic Equation in Fieldwork. *Cultural Anthropology 8*(1):3–23.

Newton, Esther. 1996. My Best Informant's Dress: The Erotic Equation in Fieldwork. In *Out in the Field: Reflections of Lesbian and Gay Anthropologists*. Ellen Lewin and William Leap, eds. Pp. 212–235. Urbana: University of Illinois Press.

Nichter, Mimi, and Mark Nichter. 1987. A Tale of Simeon: Reflections on Raising a Child while Conducting Fieldwork in Rural South India. In *Children in the Field: Anthropological Experiences*. Joan Cassell, ed. Pp. 65–90. Philadelphia: Temple University Press.

Paul, Benjamin. 1953. Interview Techniques and Field Relationships. In *Anthropology Today*. A. L. Kroeber, ed. Pp. 430–451. Chicago: University of Chicago Press.

Pelto, Pertti J. 1970. *Anthropological Research: The Structure of Inquiry*. New York: Harper and Row.

Pelto, Pertti J., and Gretel H. Pelto. 1978. *Anthropological Research: The Structure of Inquiry*, 2d ed. New York: Harper and Row.

Picchi, Debra S. 1992. Lessons in Introductory Anthropology from the Bakairi Indians. In *The Naked Anthropologist: Tales from Around the World*. Philip R. DeVita, ed. Pp. 144–155. Belmont, CA: Wadsworth Publishing.

Pratt, Mary Louise. 1986. Fieldwork in Common Places. In *Writing Culture: The Poetics and Politics of Ethnography*. James Clifford and George Marcus, eds. Pp. 27–50. Berkeley: University of California Press.

Punch, Maurice. 1994. Politics and Ethics in Qualitative Research. In *Handbook of Qualitative Research*. Norman Denzin and Yvonna Lincoln, eds. Pp. 83–98. Thousand Oaks, CA: Sage Publications.

Quandt, Sara, Mara Z. Vitolins, Kathleen M. DeWalt, and Gun Roos. 1997. Meal Patterns of Older Adults in Rural Communities: Life Course Analysis and Implications for Undernutrition. *Journal of Applied Gerontology 16*(2):152–171.

Rabinow, Paul. 1977. *Reflections on Fieldwork in Morocco.* Berkeley: University of California Press.

Redfield, Robert. 1930. *Tepoztlán.* Chicago: University of Chicago Press.

Riemer, Jeffrey W. 1977. Varieties of Opportunistic Research. *Urban Life and Culture 5*:467–478.

Rohner, Ronald, Billie R. DeWalt, and Robert C. Ness. 1973. Ethnographer Bias in Cross-Cultural Research: An Empirical Study. *Behavior Science Notes 8*:275–317.

Roper, J. Montgomery, John Frechione, and Billie R. DeWalt. 1996. *Indigenous People and Development in Latin America: A Literature Survey and Recommendations.* Latin American Monograph and Document Series, No. 12. World Bank and Center for Latin American Studies, Pittsburgh: University of Pittsburgh.

Rynkiewich, Michael A., and James P. Spradley. 1976. *Ethics and Anthropology: Dilemmas in Fieldwork.* New York: John Wiley.

Sanjek, Roger. 1990a. The Secret Life of Fieldnotes. In *Fieldnotes: The Makings of Anthropology*. Roger Sanjek, ed. Pp. 187–270. Ithaca: Cornell University Press.

Sanjek, Roger. 1990b. A Vocabulary for Fieldnotes. In *Fieldnotes: The Makings of Anthropology*. Roger Sanjek, ed. Pp. 92–121. Ithaca: Cornell University Press.

Sanjek, Roger, ed. 1990c. *Fieldnotes: The Makings of Anthropology.* Ithaca: Cornell University Press.

Scheper-Hughes, Nancy. 1987. A Child's Diary in the Strict Sense of the Term: Managing Culture Shocked Children in the Field. In *Children in the Field*. Joan Cassell, ed. Pp. 217–236. Philadelphia: Temple University Press.

Seligman, Brenda Z. 1951. *Notes and Queries on Anthropology*, 6th ed. London: Routledge & Kegan Paul.

Spradley, James P. 1980. *Participant Observation.* New York: Holt, Rinehart and Winston.

Stack, Carol. 1996. Doing Research in the Flats. In *In the Field: Readings on the Field Research Experience*, 2d ed. Carolyn D. Smith and William Kornblum, eds. Pp. 21–25. Westport, CT: Praeger.

Sterk, Claire. 1996. Prostitution, Drug Use and AIDS. In *In the Field: Readings on the Field Research Experience*, 2d ed. Carolyn D. Smith and William Kornblum, eds. Pp. 87–95. Westport, CT: Praeger.

Stocking, George. 1983. The Ethnographer's Magic: Fieldwork in British Anthropology from Tylor to Malinowski. In *Observers Observed: Essays on Ethnographic Fieldwork*. George Stocking, ed. Pp. 70–120. Madison: University of Wisconsin Press.

Tedlock, Barbara. 1991. From Participant Observation to the Observation of Participation: The Emergence of Narrative Ethnography. *Journal of Anthropological Research 47*(1): 69–94.

Tonkin, Elizabeth. 1984. Participant Observation. In *Ethnographic Research: A Guide to General Conduct*. R. F. Ellen, ed. Pp. 216–223. London: Academic Press.

Turnbull, Colin. 1986. Sex and Gender: The Role of Subjectivity in Field Research. In *Self, Sex and Gender in Cross-Cultural Research*. T. L. Whitehead and M. E. Conaway, eds. Pp. 17–27. Urbana: University of Illinois Press.

Van Maanen, John. 1988. *Tales of the Field: On Writing Ethnography*. Chicago: University of Chicago Press.

Villa Rojas, Alfonso. 1979. Fieldwork in the Mayan Region of Mexico. In *Long-Term Field Research in Social Anthropology*. George Foster, Thayer Scudder, Elizabeth Colson, and Robert Kemper eds. Pp. 45–64. New York: Academic Press.

Warren, Carol A. B. 1988. *Gender Issues in Field Research*. Thousand Oaks, CA: Sage Publications.

Weiner, Annette B. 1988. *The Trobrianders of Papua New Guinea*. New York: Holt, Rinehart and Winston.

Whitehead, T. L., and M. E. Conaway, eds. 1986. *Self, Sex and Gender in Cross-Cultural Research*. Urbana: University of Illinois Press.

Whyte, William Foote. 1996. Doing Research in Cornerville. In *In the Field: Readings on the Field Research Experience*, 2d ed. Carolyn D. Smith and William Kornblum, eds. Pp. 73–85. Westport, CT: Praeger.

Whyte, William Foote, and Katherine King Whyte. 1984. *Learning from the Field: A Guide from Experience*. Beverly Hills, CA: Sage Publications.

Willson, Margaret. 1995. Afterward: Perspective and Difference: Sexualization, the Field and the Ethnographer. In *Taboo: Sex, Identity, and Erotic Subjectivity in Anthropological Fieldwork*. Don Kulick and Margaret Willson, eds. Pp. 251–275. London: Routledge.

ALLEN JOHNSON
ROSS SACKETT

Nine

Direct Systematic Observation of Behavior

Introduction

Behavior—what people *do*—is a fundamental dimension of cultural diversity. Whether we think of behavior as customs, habits, practices, lifeways, or activity patterns, an important task of all ethnographic inquiry is to illuminate the patterns of action and interaction of the people we study. The central thesis of this chapter is that direct systematic observation is our best approach to developing trustworthy accounts of people's behavior. As such, it deserves a more prominent place in the ethnographic toolkit than most anthropologists seem to appreciate.

Systematic observation is structured by explicit rules about who we observe, when and where we observe them, what we observe, and how we record our observations. These entail selection among options, each with associated tradeoffs. Here we guide the newcomer to systematic observation through the maze of choices from project conceptualization to the sampling and recording of behavior patterns.

Why Do Direct Systematic Observation?

We distinguish three broad methods of ethnographic field research: interview, participant observation, and direct systematic observation. Interview research, an eclectic category that includes a large and diverse array of specific methods, relies entirely on research subjects as sources of ethnographic knowledge. Participant observation places the ethnographer at the scene, where a combination of direct observation and interview provide the evidence from which rich ethnographic accounts may be constructed. By direct systematic observation, we mean those ethnographic methods that—in contrast to interviews—rely primarily on the researcher's first-hand observations and that—in contrast to participant observation —are seriously attentive to problems of sampling and measurement.

Rather than study behavior for its own sake, anthropologists commonly undertake behavioral description as one component in more holistic ethnographic investigations that include people's attitudes, discourse, and organization. In these holistic efforts, interviewing and participant observation—the traditional mainstays of ethnography —are often the methods used for describing behavior as well as for describing what people think, how they are organized, and so on. We endorse multiple methods and recognize the complementarity between them. We argue here, however, in the strongest terms that interviews and participant observation are, by themselves, inadequate to the task of constructing trustworthy accounts of activity patterns. There is an irreducible need for other, more rigorous observational methods.

Interviews Versus Direct Systematic Observation

The methodological distinction between interviews and direct systematic observation is related (but not identical) to the emic/etic distinction in the sense that to obtain emic data—which requires an interpretation by a research subject—it is usually necessary to conduct some sort of interview, whereas the data of direct observation are usually classified as etic. What confounds this neat dichotomy is that interview data may also be classified as etic to the degree that our research subjects are regarded as reporters of events they have witnessed first hand (Harris 1990:53). The general distinction between interview and direct observation, therefore, is most properly that between interview methods that emphasize meaning, interpretation, and subjective experience as against research methods (including some interviews) that emphasize accurate reporting of observed scenes and activities—ideally, without interpretation. This last caveat is fundamental and raises methodological problems that are too often swept under the rug by researchers unwilling to face the painful implications.

The fact is that humans (including both trained field workers and untrained research subjects) are surprisingly incapable of accurately describing scenes they have observed with their own eyes (and ears and other senses). Abundant evidence shows that when research subjects are asked to report on their own behavior, and these reports are compared to researchers' records of the subjects' behavior based on direct observation, the research subjects' accounts of their own behavior are substantially "wrong"—that is, they show errors of from 50%–80% when compared to the observational data (Bernard et al. 1986:388; Engle and Lumpkin 1991). This means, to put it bluntly, that anthropologists who rely uncritically on their research subjects for descriptions of behavior are more likely to be wrong than right. Certainly, this is a methodological issue worthy of the most serious attention.

Where does the problem lie? It is most serious for researchers who treat their informants' descriptions of the past as accurate descriptions of *behavior*. For example, for years the University of California asked faculty to report annually on their use of time for the previous year, the information to be used in helping set public policy on such issues as how much time professors were expected to spend in teaching and supervising students as opposed to research, conferences, and outside consulting. Routinely, professors reported their average work week to be more than 60 hours, with abundant time devoted to teaching. The question skeptics are entitled to ask is, "Are these self-reports to be believed?" Or, more generically, are our research subjects the "videotape-like creatures with near-perfect retrieval systems" that our research methods sometimes assume (D'Andrade 1974:124)?

The methodological issue is clarified by the distinction between short- and long-term memory (D'Andrade 1995:42–44). Roughly speaking, directly observed events are first stored in short-term memory, which appears to be relatively objective and accurate about recording what actually transpired, but which has a very limited storage capacity. Quickly, therefore, knowledge stored in short-term memory is transferred elsewhere in the brain—to long-term memory. How quickly this happens is debated, but it is generally thought to take a matter of seconds.

Long-term memory has the advantage over short-term memory in that its storage capacity is far greater, but it has a serious defect from the standpoint of research methods: The correlation between records made immediately on observation (depending on short-term memory) and records based on later recall (long-term memory) is extremely low—generally around $r = .25$ (Shweder 1982). What happens to information in long-term memory? The answer is not surprising to cultural anthropologists: The direct observations that were stored in short-term memory are systematically distorted to conform to cultural expectations. In particular:

> What people remember as going together are the kinds of behavior they judge to be similar. Humans show a systematic distortion in their memories. They falsely recall "what goes with what" based on "what is like what." This effect has been demonstrated across a wide range of kinds of materials, not just behavior frequencies. . . . Overall, these results throw doubt on a broad class of retrospectively based research data.
>   . . . The results [however] are much happier for the study of the organization of *culture*. . . . Cognitively shared salient features are an interesting part of a society's culture. (D'Andrade 1995:84)

We can expect, then, that when anyone is asked to report on his or her own behavior in the past, or on the observed behavior of others, systematic distortions—selective remembering and forgetting—will shape the memory so strongly as to make it largely irrelevant as a description of the detailed behavior in question.

The silver lining of this cloud is that, if in fact people's cultural models of behavior more or less accurately reflect *average* behavior in their communities, then their long-term memories will not be far off as reports of what people usually do (Romney et al. 1986). What the reports of UC professors tell us, therefore, is most likely some combination of their implicit, shared views of how professors typically behave, with the addition of some more-or-less deliberate distortion based on their perceived self-interest: After all, professors know quite well that the activity questionnaires play a role in the political process of university funding. The compiled data almost certainly exaggerate the length of the faculty work week and likely also the proportions of time spent in teaching. They are, of course, entirely useless as records of such potentially interesting behaviors as socializing in the hallways or staring out the window.

Anthropologists and other behavioral scientists should be more distressed by this problem than they appear to be. Although there are certainly times during ethnographic research when long-term memory must be relied on for behavioral descriptions, field workers should refrain from doing so casually. Although direct observation is sometimes difficult or awkward, informant recall—or even the researcher's write-up of fieldnotes at day's end—is no substitute. Recall data, based on long-term memory, are about cultural pattern (the informant's or the researcher's), not about observed behavior.

Participant Observation Versus Direct Systematic Observation

The problem of erroneous descriptions arising from cultural distortion also weakens participant observation as a method of behavioral research. One problem is that anthropologists don't naturally or automatically gather *representative* data on behavior. On the contrary, like all people, they are driven by their interests and cultural models to privilege certain behaviors over others as "relevant" or "interesting." To demonstrate this, Sackett (1996) examined the spectrum of activities described in a number of anthropological accounts drawn from textbooks, ethnographies, and five years of articles from the *American Anthropologist*. He took a random sample of descriptions of behavior found in these publications, which resulted in 750 activity descriptions divided equally from these three kinds of anthropological writings. He then compared these activity descriptions with the actual frequency of those activities in people's behavior as reported in time allocation studies from around the world (Table 1).

Two features of Table 1 are especially noteworthy. First, the relative conspicuousness of activities reported is quite similar across the three modes of anthropological writing (for example, the frequency of discussion of political and religious behaviors hovers around 36%). This suggests that writers in the various anthropological modes share a view of which activities are important and worth attention and which can safely be ignored.

TABLE 1

Comparison of Anthropological Activity Descriptions with Actual Time Allocation

| | % of Behavior Descriptions | | | | |
Activity	Textbooks (n = 250)	Ethnographies (n = 250)	*Amer. Anth.* (n = 250)	Overall (n = 750)	Global Adult Time Allocation
political/religious	38.4	36.4	34.0	36.3	2.8
food production	22.0	18.4	26.4	22.3	11.0
eating, rest, sleep	14.0	18.4	12.8	15.1	62.0
commercial	12.0	9.6	10.0	10.5	8.8
family care	9.2	11.2	8.8	9.7	12.0
making/fixing things	4.4	6.0	8.0	6.1	3.4

SOURCE: Sackett 1996.

Second, there is *no consistent relationship* between the conspicuousness of a behavior in our professional discourse and the amount of time people around the world actually spend engaged in that behavior. In fact, political and religious practice—mainly, public ceremonials like rituals and rallies—commands the greatest proportion of anthropological attention (36%) yet actually occupies the least amount of people's time (<3%). Self-absorbed activities like eating, sleeping, and relaxing occupy by far the greatest proportion of people's lives (over 60% of their time), yet constitute only 15% of published descriptions.

Sackett's research also reveals a strong gender bias in activity descriptions (Table 2). Far more anthropological attention is being paid, at least in professional writings, to activities cross-culturally associated with men rather than women. Men's activities are *eight times more likely* to be described in these writings than are women's activities, although the actual frequencies with which these activities are performed by the men and women of the world are not greatly different (12.3% for predominantly women's activities, 18.6% for predominantly men's).

Tables 1 and 2 provide evidence of strong shared biases in how anthropologists describe behavior. Our point here does not concern whether or not these biases are appropriate, only that they exist and carry important implications for behavioral measurement. As long as participant observation alone stands as the main method of behavioral description, we can expect these biases to shape the way observations are recorded during fieldwork and later reported in scholarly publications. The same kinds of biases that shape long-term memory also direct the field worker's attention and colleagues' and editors' judgments regarding what is deserving of description, analysis, and publication.

The methodological solution to this problem is to take the researcher's attention off auto-pilot, so to speak, by introducing rigorous procedures for sampling and

TABLE 2
*Comparison of Anthropological Attention to
Women's and Men's Activities*

Cross-cultural division of labor	% of Behavior Descriptions				Global adult time allocation
	Textbooks (n = 250)	Ethnographies (n = 250)	*Amer. Anth.* (n = 250)	Overall (n = 750)	
Activities performed predominantly by women	6.8	8.8	6.4	7.3	12.3
Activities showing little cross-cultural gender bias	29.6	34.4	32.8	32.3	69.1
Activities performed predominantly by men	63.9	56.8	60.8	60.4	18.6

SOURCE: Sackett 1996.

recording behavior—in effect requiring field workers to observe and report behaviors they might otherwise neglect. Such neglect is virtually inevitable unless addressed. Over time, field workers become so familiar with their subjects' behavior that they begin to stop noticing quotidian commonplaces. Field workers fall into comfortable field routines that make some scenes and locations much more likely to be observed than others; and they find it easier to remember cases that confirm their own understandings of what is going on and to forget the negative cases that defy their understandings.

Hence, there is much in anthropological method—indeed, in human nature—to make it highly improbable that routine descriptions of behavior based on participant observation research will validly describe actual behavior. For example, we can't make sense of an ethnographer's report that child care is predominantly women's work unless we are told precisely what child care is: Does it include producing the food the child eats, or having socially recognized responsibility for its well-being, or is it limited to directly handling the child? And what is the quantitative basis for the report: Is it the relative frequency of care, total time spent, the amount of physical exertion, or some combination of all of these?

The current state of anthropological fieldwork is such that ethnographers are generally inconsistent in the ways they describe activities, differing substantially in their definitions of such basic categories as labor, housework, and child care. It is now a commonplace in activity studies that how much "work" people do depends sensitively on just which activities we consider work. Even a small shift in definitions can lead to radically different conclusions (Johnson 1975). Some differences between ethnographies are inevitable given the difference in social and cultural contexts in which research is done, but lack of explicit attention to definitions makes it impossible to distinguish real cultural diversity from differences in ethnographers' arbitrary and idiosyncratic conventions. Although the solutions to these difficulties come from scientific methodology, the broad goal, of value to scientists and humanists alike, is *verisimilitude*—a recognizable similarity to the actual lives of the people we study.

The Challenge of Behavior Measurement

A commitment to include behavioral measurement in fieldwork immediately brings us to a dilemma: Measuring the ongoing stream of behavior in its natural detail, complexity, and context is so daunting as to be a practical impossibility. Behavior —somebody doing something—refers in phenomenological terms to observable changes in location, posture, expression, and vocalization. Simply describing a subject's location requires at least six pieces of information (latitude, longitude, altitude, compass azimuth, orientation to the horizon, and time). Posture is far more complicated: Given the human body's 206 bones and their articulation at joints, we would have to recreate 218 joint angles precisely in order to reproduce a subject's posture at any given instant (Alexander 1992). Add to this a minimum of 58 facial muscle groups involved in expression, and we would have to record a total of 282 pieces of information (6 location measures, plus 218 degrees of postural freedom, plus 58 facial muscle groups) simply to describe someone's behavior at a moment in time.

And these 282 pieces of information allow us to dip only once into the stream of behavior. To animate our description with the verisimilitude of a motion picture (which itself is only a sampling of the stream of behavior), we would have to update all these variables 24 times each second. At this frame speed, we would have to make 406,080 measurements per minute of observation, amounting to over 24 million measurements to describe just one hour of spontaneous behavior. And we haven't even addressed the problem of describing a subject's speech or the setting in which the behavior is happening.

This dilemma is real for every behavioral researcher and has long attracted serious methodological discussion (for example, Chapple and Arensberg 1940; Harris 1964). A large part of the solution is beyond the scope of this chapter: In the process of research design, clarifying the purposes of the research allows the field worker to select and distill from all the possible ways of describing behavior those that most efficiently answer the key questions of the research project (Martin and Bateson 1993; Bernard 1994). Hence, flexing the shoulder, extending the elbow, pronating the hand, and flexing the fingers around a piece of fruit become "grasping an orange," and that, in turn, becomes part of an act of food procurement, food preparation, gift exchange, theft, or eating (as the case may be). Any of these higher-order categories of activity may or may not be of interest to any given research project.

Once we have a clear sense of the subject and goals of the research, we need to address several questions that have profound implications for how we conduct our behavioral study: Is observation an appropriate technique? How does systematic observation integrate with other activities? What information do we need to collect?

Is Observation Appropriate?

Whiting and Whiting (1973) have argued that behavior observation is more expensive in field and analysis time than other ethnographic activities and should only be used when other techniques are less effective. To justify this investment, first and foremost the study must be about behavior. That is, activity descriptions must be able to help answer the key questions posed by the research proposal. When those questions ask what activities are like, who performs them, and in what contexts they occur, observation is appropriate. Questions about the consequences of activities for individual well-being, alteration of the environment, genetic fitness, and so on, can also be answered by observations carefully supported by other ethnographic evidence.

Practical concerns limit the appropriateness of behavioral observations. Will research subjects tolerate the presence of the observer? Will they act in the observer's presence as they would if the observer were not there? Are some kinds of observation less acceptable to subjects than others? Can the behaviors of interest be observed without violating subjects' sense of decency and privacy? Is the observer likely to witness illegal or stigmatizing behaviors and, if so, are the consequences of reporting or not reporting them morally and ethically acceptable?

Experienced field workers will agree, however, that these practical concerns arise in any participant observation research. Perhaps the methodological rigor of systematic observation highlights the problems, for the option of quietly putting away one's notebook, turning away, or leaving the scene is available to the participant observer more so than to the systematic observer. And, given the serious problems associated with using informant recall to answer behavioral questions, we must be prepared to make the investment in direct systematic observation where it is the only appropriate method for answering key research questions.

How Does Systematic Observation Integrate with Other Ethnographic Activities?

Participant observation, interview, and systematic observation compete for our limited field time and attention. The inflexible scheduling often required of systematic observation highlights the conflict: Most sampling strategies require us to be present at particular times and places, when we might prefer to pursue interesting events elsewhere in the community—to interview an unexpectedly cooperative informant or to escape the community in private contemplation. Furthermore, systematic observation is sometimes a less comfortable role for the researcher, owing to its requirements of detachment and objectivity. It creates a distance, in contrast to the essentially friendly, mutually attentive, and empathetic relationship fostered by interviews and participant observation.

But it's best to recognize and embrace the synergy between systematic observation and both interviewing and participant observation. On the one hand, systematic observation keeps participant observation honest by explicitly confronting the implicit biases of long-term memory, variations in contemporary research fashions, and inconsistent definitions. On the other hand, it addresses the potential biases and ambiguities of an interview, helping identify conscious and unconscious deceptions and distortions. Reciprocally, both interview and participant observation increase our confidence in the validity of the results of systematic observation by helping us understand the consequences of behavior for subjects' well-being, motivations, and emic conceptions of activity.

What Information Do We Need to Collect?

Actors, Actions, and Settings

We find it helpful to distinguish three broad categories of variables common in activity studies: actors (including both the focal subject(s) and the social others with whom she or he interacts), actions (the behaviors we want to study, whether specific acts and activities, the content of speech, or the consequences of behavior) and settings (including the location of action, details of the physical space in which the actors act and interact, and the "props" which they manipulate and use, such as furniture, implements, foods, etc.).

For ethnographic research, the most common and most useful focus is on actors, a sample of whom are selected for observation such that their actions and the settings in which they act are the content of the observations. More rarely, it is an action (for example, political speeches) or a setting (for example, a public speaking space) that is the focus.

Level of Behavior Measurement

Different research questions require different levels of behavior measurement. Since higher levels of measurement usually cost more (in various ways), we should be clear about the minimal data quality needed to answer a question before settling on a suitable method (Martin and Bateson 1993). In general, actions can be measured as nominal variables or as quantitative variables.

1. Nominal variables. Some issues can be resolved with nominal-level data—that is, as presence or absence of particular behaviors. We might, for example, ask whether a particular behavior is in the repertoire of the population we study (for example, does anyone in the community fish, or make pottery, or observe Hindu food restrictions?). Alternatively, we may want to know whether a certain behavior occurred during a given time interval (for example, does anyone fish in winter, or make pottery on Sunday?). Such questions are relatively easy to answer and may even be reliably addressed through informant recall.

    The chief disadvantage of nominal data is that they are poor indicators of how much of a behavior people do or of a behavior's relative importance in their lives. For example, two subjects could have fished on the same day, but the actual time they spent fishing and the number of fish they caught could have differed greatly.

2. Quantitative variables. Some questions require data on the actual amount of behavior. Measuring the actual amount of behavior performed increases our capacity to evaluate the importance of the behavior. Behavior researchers commonly distinguish four quantitative measures of behavior:

    Frequency refers to the number of occurrences of a behavior during a given time interval, most conveniently expressed as a rate (instances per unit time).

    Duration is the length of time for which a single occurrence of a behavior lasts, measured in time units.

    Total duration is the total amount of time spent performing the activity during a particular interval of time, numerically equivalent to the frequency of the behavior multiplied by the average duration. It is the measure most commonly used in time allocation studies, expressed either in time units (for example, hours per day) or as a percentage of time.

    Intensity refers to the pace at which the behavior is performed. It may be measured by a local rate such as elemental acts per unit of time (ax swings per minute) or rate of production (meters of cloth woven per day), or by a more generally comparative measure like energy expenditure (Montoye et al. 1996).

Behavior Flow

In addition to measuring the presence or amount of a behavior, we might also be interested in behavior flow. The flow of behavior is the sequence of behaviors from one activity to another. We may be interested in the flow of behavior in the short term, such as the component actions in weaving a basket, or in longer term sequences like the daily round or annual cycle.

Measuring the amount and flow of activities increases the power of our data but it generally entails more fieldwork and greater risk of influencing the behavior of our subjects (reactivity). Measuring behavior also places greater constraints on the kinds of sampling and recording methods we use. Below, we examine further the tradeoffs among alternative methods.

Temporal Resolution

The focus of behavioral observation may be on short episodes (events) or long ones (states), each with different methodological implications. An example of an event is a schoolyard fight: A glare is met by a challenge, prompting a shove in response, erupting in a brief skirmish that is quickly stopped by schoolyard monitors; within seconds the event is over.

The interesting feature of behavioral events tends to be their *frequency*: How often do schoolyard fights occur and are they frequent in relation to other behaviors on the schoolyard or elsewhere? Since events last such a short time, they require a deliberate sampling strategy, such as *continuous monitoring* for periods of time.

By contrast, the daily commute to work has the qualities of a behavioral state: It is extended in duration, often rather repetitive, and possibly monotonous. The salient features of states are usually their *total duration* over some period of time and the *duration* of each occurrence.

For example, the duration of the daily commute between home and workplace, and the total time spent commuting as a part of the working day are much more revealing about how we spend our lives than the fact that we do it twice a day. Because states are of longer duration than events, they are easier to encounter during research and can be observed either by continuous monitoring, or by sampling the behavior stream at discrete moments, a strategy called *instantaneous time-sampling*.

Descriptive Resolution

We have discussed the overwhelming amount of detail possible in behavioral observation. A simple activity like grasping an orange could potentially require thousands of points of measurement. The more detailed the resolution of behavioral study, the more costly the research in time, technology, and, probably, the good will of the research subjects. Detailed description of the discrete *acts* that go into making up the generalized sequences we call *activities*, therefore, must be justified by the theoretical and practical goals of the research project.

In our experience, even those observers who collect data on specific acts tend, in the long run, to abstract and generalize these into descriptions of activities anyway. For example, the act of "walking down the trail while carrying a rifle" is detailed and specific, but the most useful form of description usually ends up being "hunting deer." Why not save a step and record the activity "hunting deer" in the first place? If we collect too much detail in the field, we waste field time and then require additional time later—probably after the field site is long behind us and far away—trying to infer meaningful activity from data sheets full of incremental acts.

Sampling

All field workers interested in fair and accurate descriptions of what people do have wished at one time or another to be a fly on the wall or an omnipresent (and invisible) observer—gifted with the oft-mentioned "god's-eye view." The only realistic option is, of course, a compromise in the form of sampling. Sampling for systematic behavioral observation requires several steps:

Step 1: Establishing the Limits of the Study

We first need to establish the *sampling universe*, the envelope of people, places and times from which we will select entities for observation.

Social Boundaries

Although it is typical in ethnographic research for many practical issues to influence the selection of a population for study—such as access to the population, the investigator's language facility, the research budget—it is still the case that the best research population is one that is most appropriate for answering the key research questions identified in the research proposal. The size of the targeted social universe may vary greatly, from a single Yanomami family (Lhermillier and Lhermillier 1983) to entire national (Niemi, Kiiski, and Liikkanan 1981) and multinational (Szalai 1972) communities.

In large-scale studies (and even some smaller ones), the temptation is great to reduce the scope of the research by selecting specific categories of individuals for focus, using criteria like age, sex, social class, or ethnicity. While attractive as a way of conserving resources, we urge researchers to resist this temptation. In our experience, it leads to no end of lamentation once the research is over, primarily because the most important "context" for individuals' activities is the activities of the others around them. Researchers who study only the women in a community regret the absence of information on men; those who study only children wish they had included adults; those who study only the Hindus of some village wish they had data on neighboring Muslims for comparison; and so on. It is far more satisfying to develop sampling methods that include the whole range of kinds of people in research populations.

Geographical Boundaries

Once a research population has been identified and a sample drawn, it often happens that individuals in that sample leave the field site and are beyond the limits to which the researcher can travel to observe them. This is true when subjects leave to work in distant cities or go on trek. Field workers must impose a distance rule on observations, such as the *day-range* of common activities, limited by the time it takes to travel to a site and back in a single day (Carlstein 1982). A common strategy in such cases is to define a category of activity coded "Away," to indicate that subjects are temporarily resident elsewhere (see, for example, Paolisso and Sackett 1988). It is possible to add information to this code by spelling out what the purpose of the trip was stated to be, such as working for wages, shopping, or visiting relatives. But these data are not comparable to the data of direct observation and should be treated separately in later analyses.

Temporal Boundaries

The major issues of temporal sampling concern how long a period of study is required to get a good sample of ordinary behavior and how to handle the problem of nighttime activity. The convention in ethnographic research is to study a community for at least a full year, to observe the variations of the seasons and the full annual cycle: This rule applies as well to behavioral observation. Arguments for shorter time frames can be made in some cases, where seasonal variations can be demonstrated not to be very important (perhaps in some cities or with respect to key activities like infant care).

Regarding the daily "observation window," the ideal is to make observations throughout the 24-hour cycle, but such research is rare because it is intrusive and making night visits is often culturally prohibited and dangerous. Therefore, "dawn-to-dusk" studies are often a practical necessity, but they are problematic because they systematically overestimate time use in some activities and underestimate it in others (Gross 1984; Scaglion 1986). When systematic observations are limited to daytime, some other technique such as participant observation or interview should be used to establish in a general way what goes on at night.

Step 2: Choosing the Units to Observe

Having chosen a sample for observation, we must decide what to target for observation. As we have said, most behavior studies concern some combination of three variables: actors, activities, and settings. Usually, we focus on one of these and observe how the others vary in relation to it.

Targeting People

Most commonly, research focuses on individuals, who should be selected for their *representativeness*. In a small community, it may be possible to include all individuals for observation, as is often done in time allocation studies of neighborhoods or villages. In a larger community, samples of individuals may be drawn for observation. The best sample in such cases is always a random sample, drawn using a lottery or table of random numbers. It may be tempting to build an opportunity sample in such cases, using people with whom the researcher is already familiar (and, by implication, avoiding those who are unfamiliar or with whom the researcher doesn't get along). This should be avoided because it will compromise the reliability of the sample as being representative of the population and thus threaten the study's overall validity. By the same token, all aspects of the observation routine should be randomized as far as possible. For example, if the schedule of observations is such that individual X is always observed on Tuesday, even though X was chosen at random for inclusion in the study, the observations on X will not be representative of her or his general activity patterns.

Targeting Activities or Settings

Occasionally, the research questions call for targeting certain activities. For example, Lee (1979) observed the time his !Kung (Botswana) informants took to make ostrich eggshell canteens (360 minutes), arrow poison (300 minutes), and shelters (900 minutes). By determining who made each type of artifact, its unit labor cost, its useful lifetime, and the number of such objects maintained by a family, Lee could estimate the total time men and women devoted to manufacturing and repair each day (men, 64 minutes; women, 45 minutes).

Another possibility is to target settings, like houses, meeting places, schoolyards, etc. In the 1970s, psychologists Bornstein and Bornstein (1976) examined spontaneous walking speed in 15 communities ranging in size from 365 people (Psychro, Crete) to over 2,600,000 (Brooklyn, New York). In the downtown of each community they marked a 50-foot stretch of walkway along a main street and recorded the time passers-by took to cover the distance. They found a remarkably strong correlation ($r = 0.91$) between the size of the community and walking speed: The larger the community, the faster people walked. Later research established this as a general and robust cross-cultural pattern and even related it to the incidence of heart disease (Levine 1990).

Scans or Follows?

Whatever the focus on actor, activity, or setting, researchers generally have the choice of concentrating on a single individual (*follows*) or tracking the activities of members of a group (*scans*). In *focal-individual follows*, we select one subject and monitor her or his behavior over time, to the exclusion of others, as the Bornsteins did in their research. In *group scans*, we record either sequentially or synchronously the behaviors of a number of associating individuals (Altmann 1974; Dunbar 1976). A common strategy in time allocation studies is *household scan sampling*, which targets whole households and records the activities of all the members present at the moment of contact (Johnson 1975; Baksh 1989–90). In some ethnographic situations it may be practical to scan an entire community sequentially by walking a circuit from house to house (for example, Hames 1979; Betzig and Turke 1985; Flinn 1988).

Step 3: Scheduling Observations

A strategy for scheduling observations should be developed at the beginning of behavioral research to ensure that the study period is sampled evenly. The main issues are: when to begin each observing session, how long the session should last, and how to sample time within the session (Gross 1984; Bernard 1994).

Scheduling Observing Sessions

Behavior patterns are usually structured by the time of day, day of the week and month, weather patterns, and season. Unless we use a strategy to ensure representative sampling, these habitual activity rhythms will confound the patterns we think we see in the data. For example, in contemporary society if behavior observations were made only on weekdays, the absence of weekend behaviors would strongly distort our data as a description of the full range of behavior patterns. The best solution is to schedule observing sessions at random, since with a large enough sample the habitual activity rhythms will be fairly captured in the data, rather than distorting it. Under some circumstances (not holistic ethnographic research), it may be acceptable to limit observations to a single time or circumstance: For example, Borenstein and Borenstein (1976) limited their observations of walking speed in all cases to sunny days of moderate temperature, to eliminate weather as a confounding factor in their study.

Sampling Strategies

How long do we keep the target individual or group under observation? The answer depends on which of four main sampling strategies we choose: continuous monitoring, fixed-interval instantaneous sampling, random-interval instantaneous sampling, and one-zero sampling,

Continuous Monitoring

For the fullest account we may choose to target a single individual and follow her or him throughout the day (for example, Dufour 1984; Hill et al. 1985) or for several days in succession (Szalai 1972). Continuous monitoring is Bernard's (1994) term, synonymous with focal-animal sampling (Altmann 1974), continuous recording (Martin and Bateson 1993), systematic observation (Whiting and Whiting 1973), continuous scan/focal follow (Hames 1992, for groups and individuals), and continuous observation (Gross 1984). With its goal of producing a detailed description of the subject's stream of behavior over the observation session, this is the most intuitive of the sampling strategies, a kind of ethnographic narrative structured by operational rules for sampling and description.

The most common method is to note the onset of each activity and the time at which it began. Whenever the subject changes activities, therefore, a new notation is made. The resulting record is a *list of behavioral events* that can be analyzed for duration and sequence. Of all the systematic observation strategies, continuous monitoring results in the most comprehensive and flexible descriptions. It provides narratives of scenes and processes that can provide illustrative anecdotes; it chronicles both brief events and protracted states; it can provide levels of measurement from nominal lists of behaviors to quantitative behavior frequencies, durations, and even intensities. One of its great attractions is maintaining a record of the sequencing of behavior ("flow"), including the sequences of verbal or nonverbal exchange between subjects that are indispensable in studies of interaction.

> Example: Panter-Brick (1989), Tamang (Nepal). In farming communities, pregnant women commonly work through much of their pregnancy and nursing periods, yet little in detail is known about how pregnancy and lactation affect women's behavior. In a remote Tamang farming community, Panter-Brick found she could not use spot checks because people dispersed too much during daily work, so she selected focal-subject follows. For a whole annual cycle (1982–83) and all daylight hours (11 in winter, 13.5 in summer) she used local assistant pairs to keep two people each day under continual direct observation, recording their activities minute-by-minute, resulting in 7,678 hours of observations on 297 woman days, with 24 women who were either pregnant or lactating, and 19 who were neither. Among her key findings: pregnant and lactating women work significantly less than others during slack seasons (1.5 to 2.5 hours less per day), but work nearly as much as others during heavy work seasons (under 0.5 hours less per day), when their labor input is decisive for their household food supply.

As with all systematic observation methods, there are tradeoffs to be considered with continuous monitoring. If its chief advantages are its detail, faithful rendering of sequences, and an intuitive storylike record, its costs are nonetheless significant. For one thing, it imposes heavy demands on observers, making errors and reduced levels of detail more likely the longer the session goes on. Whiting and Whiting (1975) found in their comparative study of child socialization that after only a few minutes even trained observers became increasingly telegraphic, selective, and unreliable in their descriptions.

For another, it raises the likelihood of subject reactivity, since it is difficult to act normally in the presence of a foreigner (or even a fellow community member working as a field assistant) following closely behind making continuous notations on a clipboard. Continuous monitoring is subject to statistical problems that result from the lack of independence of observations. It is subject to difficulties in determining exactly where activities begin and end (Gross 1984:539), and to problems associated with diverting too much field time away from other important ethnographic activities.

For these reasons, continuous monitoring is most appropriate when behavior measurement is the primary goal of the research and the powerful data that the method provides are essential to answering key research questions. Otherwise, it is a useful adjunct to other ethnographic methods as a way to document in great detail specific cultural practices. Other strategies are available that produce the same kinds of data at lower cost and often at greater reliability.

Fixed-Interval Instantaneous Sampling

This is also known as time-point sampling (Martin and Bateson 1993), instantaneous and scan sampling (Altmann 1974), and fixed-interval sampling (Gross 1984), and is but one level of abstraction from continuous monitoring. Instead of recording the continuous flow of behavior, fixed-interval sampling divides the observing session into discrete equal-length time intervals and makes observations on the instant marking the transition from one interval to the next. Typically, observations are made once a minute on the minute, but intervals from once every 15 seconds to every 5 minutes are common. Less demanding on observers, and less precise, it results in a *list of intervals*, each characterized by a particular behavior. The resulting record is much like a motion picture, with each observation representing a brief frame in a sequence of data points over the observing session. In longer intervals, such as the 5-minute intervals in Whiting and Whiting (1975), behavior in the interval is described in narrative fashion, a kind of minicontinous monitoring.

The primary use of fixed-interval sampling is to measure the total duration of activities. If we are making one observation per minute for a 60-minute session, for example, and find that, say, "resting" has been described for 22 of those observations, then we may calculate that 22/60, or 37% of that subject's time during that hour was spent resting. By scheduling observations over a full day (either "daylight" or around the clock), total daily time spent in each activity can be estimated.

Example: Bailey, R. C. and Peacock, N. (1988), Efe (Zaire). The Efe pygmies are tropical forest foragers who live in close symbiosis with settled Lese horticulturalists, a relationship of considerable theoretical interest in cultural anthropology. Bailey following the men and Peacock the women, they used 1-hour focal follows, wherein every minute on the minute (as indicated by a digital watch with count-down functions) the observer recorded the subject's activity using a verb-object code, their posture, location, and the nearest neighbor within 10 meters. Where appropriate, they also recorded the type of food being eaten, the weight of the load carried, responsibility for tending a cooking pot, type of weapon carried, and social interactions (who interacted, what type of interaction, verbal exchanges, child care, etc.). Subjects were always aware that they were being observed but rarely interacted with the observers; when the observer's presence had an obvious impact on their behaviors, this was noted and the observation was omitted from the data in the sample. Results showed these "foragers" spending surprising amounts of time tending Lese gardens (Efe women spent 111 minutes per day in swiddens as compared to only 40 minutes per day for Efe men), and much of their "foraging" activity is spent obtaining honey and meat for trade to Lese villagers.

The advantages of fixed-interval sampling over continuous monitoring are that field workers experience less fatigue and can collect much more information at each sampling interval than they could on a continuous observation routine. When subjects remain in one place, the field worker can also monitor the activities of more than one person, but this advantage evaporates when individuals separate during the observation, forcing the observer to do a focal-follow on an individual or subgroup that remains together.

Some of the disadvantages of continuous monitoring remain true for fixed-interval sampling: the continuous presence of the field worker increases the risk of subject reactivity, and the successive observations within a session are not statistically independent. In contrast to continuous monitoring, it is debatable whether estimates of frequency, duration, and sequence are entirely trustworthy when derived solely from fixed-interval sampling. As a rule, such estimates are reliable only if the sampling interval is shorter than the duration of each instance of a given behavior. *But we cannot know this unless we already have information on activity duration.* Since behaviors differ in their typical duration (for example, events versus states), a given sampling interval may give stable estimates of frequency for some behaviors but not others. Techniques for choosing the appropriate sample interval are discussed by Martin and Bateson (1993:93).

Perhaps because of these potential drawbacks, fixed-interval sampling is less often used than other techniques of systematic observation. If the goal is data on activity frequencies, durations and sequences, then continuous monitoring is more trustworthy and has greater face validity. If all we need are total durations of activities, then random-interval sampling is cheaper, more compatible with other ethnographic activities, and perhaps more reliable.

Random-Interval Instantaneous Sampling

Also known as spot observations, spot checks, or simply as the time allocation technique, this is a highly preferred method for certain purposes. Behavior, like time, flows seamlessly from moment to moment. Continuous monitoring records the flow, abstracted only by restricting observation to sessions with clearly marked start and end points. Fixed-interval observation abstracts further from the behavior flow by sampling the observation session itself at a series of evenly spaced discrete moments. Random-interval sampling takes this process of abstraction to its logical extreme: The *entire observing session* is reduced to a single instantaneous observation. If the record of fixed-interval sampling is analogous to a motion picture, spot observation is analogous to an album of random photographs: A few might seem scattershot and unrepresentative, but a large number of truly random snapshots provide an *overall* summary of how people spend their time. But also like such a photo album, and unlike either continuous monitoring or fixed-interval sampling, the order of images carries little or no information about the sequence of activities that precede and follow each observation.

Spot observation begins with an observing schedule that specifies the day and time of each observation and the target individual(s) whose behavior is to be described. Target individuals and observation times should be selected at random, although compromises for practical reasons—such as targeting whole households at random rather than individuals, or following a circuit through the community—are often acceptable. Ideally, the observer finds the target individual at the selected time and records the activity at the instant the target was first seen (or, if the target saw the observer first, the activity she or he was doing *just before* she or he paused to greet the observer). Context data (location, weather, tools being used, etc.) can also be recorded at this moment. If the research subject is absent, interviews can be used to fill in the description, although this should be kept as a separate kind of data to be distinguished in later analysis.

Since each observing session is only a moment, the field worker is left with ample time for detailed descriptions of setting, informal *ad libitum* observations, and ethnographic interviews. This almost seamless integration with other ethnographic activities makes the method appealing even in research where behavioral measurement is secondary to other ethnographic goals. In a sense, spot observation is only a formalized (and randomized) version of common ethnographic visiting practices.

Example: Johnson, A. and O. Johnson (1988), Machiguenga (Peru). Wanting a description of how tropical forest forager-horticulturalists spend time, but not wanting to commit large amounts of field time to continuous monitoring, the researchers applied the spot observation technique (Johnson 1975). Between July 1972 and August 1973, they visited all households in a scattered settlement of 13 households at random during daylight hours (6 am to 7 pm) only, "because travel after dark is hazardous and visiting at night is not encouraged." Households and visiting times were specified in advance using a table of random numbers. Visits were not made every day, because of other demands on the researchers' time, but over the research year visits were made on 135 days totaling 3,495 spot observations of individuals. Activities were coded into a hierarchical coding scheme based on eleven major activity categories (with subcategories in each): eating, food preparation, child rearing, manufacture, wild food collection, garden labor, idleness, hygiene, visiting, school, and wage labor. "The brief time spent in recording activities took only a small fraction of the total field time. In fact, the visits brought us into contact with community members who could be interviewed for other purposes" (Johnson 1975:304). Among the findings of the study was the sensitivity of conclusions about "work" to differences in definition: If "work" is garden labor, then men work 16% of the daytime, women only 7%; if work includes all food production, the percentage climbs to 34% for men, 13% for women; add food preparation and manufacture, 46% for men, 47% for women; add child care and the men's figure remains the same but women's rises to 56%. Not only does the absolute amount of work change, but also our evaluation of whether men or women work longer hours (see Baksh 1990).

Gross (1984:540–541) writes, "Random spot checks are in fact very economical of observer time. . . . [Compared to other techniques] in terms of sampling validity and level of detail . . . there is little question that random spot checks is the method of choice in time allocation studies." The method also improves the ethnographic enterprise by requiring researchers to be present at places and times they might not ordinarily choose, broadening exposure to local scenes and bringing serendipitous insights. Because each observation is statistically independent, some statistical problems disappear.

On the other hand, tradeoffs exist here as well. Researchers have noted the difficulty of observing an instant of behavior. In reality, field workers tend to watch during a brief "observation window" before they come to a judgment about which behavior the subject is performing: even here, without the benefit of long-term memory, the researcher is still making a choice about which aspects of the stream of behavior to code into "activity" (Altmann 1974; Martin and Bateson 1993). Cross-cultural psychologists have found evidence that individuals in a variety of cultures integrate successive events over a period of about three seconds to construct a subjectively experienced "present" (Feldhutter et al. 1990). Perhaps we should acknowledge that "instantaneous" behavior sampling actually involves a three-second observation window during which the observer constructs the observed activity in ways that have not yet been explored.

Furthermore, if spot observers did consistently record the behavior that occurred the instant they first spotted the target, the most prominent activity would likely be "greeting anthropologist" (Scaglion 1986). Hence, the rule: Record the activity in progress before the presence of the observer became known to the target. But, to the degree to which we use context to decide what the person was doing, we collapse context and behavior where ideally they would be separate data points that we could compare later, confounding efforts to use observational data to understand how environment (context) influences behavior.

Another problem with spot checks is that as a practical reality we end up relying on informant reports and recall to describe a significant amount of behavior, namely, that of individuals not locatable during the spot check. On the one hand, this opens us up to the same problems of memory distortion and biased attention as any other interview data. On the other hand, it introduces other biases, since activities conducted away from the observing eye of the field worker are often certain kinds of activities, including activities at a distance (hunting, wage labor) and those done in private (sex, defecation, violence). Spot checks of readily visible activities will underestimate these activities, and are also liable to overestimate social activities (Hawkes et al. 1987), and household activities (Borgerhoff Mulder and Caro 1985).

In common with other methods of direct observation, another bias of spot observations concerns nighttime activities (Bernard 1994:325–327). Confining the observations to daytime, typical of spot observations, has the obvious result of over-representing daytime activities. Scaglion's (1986) study of 24-hour time allocation in an Abelam community (New Guinea) makes clear that many interesting activities occur at night, including ritual, socializing, food preparation, and even such food production as hunting and gardening.

Spot observations will give a rough picture of time allocation within a small community with a surprisingly small number of observations, perhaps as low as 1,000. That is, in a community of 200, as few as five observations on each individual, if conducted strictly at random, would allow for a broadly accurate picture of how people spend time (Baksh 1989–90). But the more detailed a description needs to be, the more observations must be made. Rare activities, for example, will be missed or inaccurately estimated by small numbers of spot observations. Bernard and Killworth (1993) have estimated the number of observations needed to achieve varying levels of accuracy depending on how rare or common a given activity is (see Bernard 1994:325–326).

One-Zero or Activity Presence Sampling

One-zero sampling is useful when all we need to know is whether a particular behavior of interest—say, hunting or wage labor—occurred during some specified interval of time, but we don't care how much of the activity was performed. Several techniques are commonly used in one-zero sampling, including person-day records, leave-and-return logs, and the in-out diary. The person-day diary is a running account of who performed a particular activity each day of the study, based either on direct observation or interview. The leave-and-return log is a refinement that records the time the subject leaves to perform an activity and the time she or he returns. It is analogous to an industrial worker's time card in that it gives a list of the tasks performed and the window of time within which they occurred, but does not tell just how much of the time window was actually spent in the specified activity as opposed to rest, socializing, eating, and so forth.

In practice, activity-presence recording is most useful when applied to general activity categories of considerable duration, such as labor patterns. Since each subject can be surveyed quickly, it allows the researcher to keep track of a large number of subjects each day. It gives a semiquantitative assessment of activity by measuring the *number of intervals* in which the target activity occurs, sometimes called a "Hansen frequency" (Martin and Bateson 1993). The label "frequency" is misleading, however, since the method doesn't provide true frequencies and systematically underestimates activity frequencies (since some activites are missed) while overestimating durations (since uncounted activities also helped fill the time window).

> Example: Hurtado and Hill (1987), Cuiva (Venezuela). Scholars had disputed whether Cuiva still lived as foragers or had now become settled agriculturalists. Fieldwork in 1985 used a battery of methods to document subsistence ecology. During one 25-day field visit, the authors used an "in-out notebook" to record departure and return times of all individuals leaving the settlement, noting food resources brought back and the composition of foraging parties (n=921 person-days, 517 for men and 404 for women). Unlike other foragers, this study shows that Cuiva men produce more food than the women do, and do so more efficiently; it also established that the bulk of their food still comes from wild game and roots, confirming their status as foragers.

The chief advantages of activity-presence recording are that it is cheap in observer time, nontechnical, objective, and reliable within the limits of what it seeks to measure. Minimal observer judgment is required to score behavior, and recall data can be used with perhaps less error than in other forms of behavioral observation. It gives valuable data about labor variation among individuals, age-sex groups, days of the week, and seasons. Because the observer doesn't follow or encounter the subject, the risk of reactivity is minimal. This can be very valuable in activities like hunting, where the observer's presence is highly likely to lead the hunters to modify their route, pace, and perhaps the game being sought. The method is also highly compatible with other ethnographic activities.

The real limitation of the method is the ambiguity of interpreting the results. Just what do the data indicate in levels of time and effort? Two individuals may be reported to spend the same number of person-days at work, but for one this may represent a few hours of labor whereas for another full days at work. This problem can be addressed by using participant observation or systematic behavior observation to detail daily patterns of activity among a subset of individuals that can then be used to interpret person-day records.

Recording Strategies

Descriptions and Codes

At the moment of recording observations, we have two approaches open to us: Describe the activities we observe or code them. At one end, behavioral descriptions are open-ended textual accounts of behavior; at the other end, codes are brief, usually symbolic representations with a selective, explicit, and preferably unambiguous meaning. This leaves us with three options: (1) avoid coding entirely by keeping textual descriptions and treating our data as a corpus of qualitative narratives; (2) collect textual descriptions to be coded later using categories developed once the research is complete; or (3) code activities at the moment of observation using categories developed prior to or during early phases of the research.

Text descriptions have the advantage of being like conventional ethnographic description and may be used as such during analysis. They can be as detailed and topically broad as the situation allows and as finely contextualized as necessary. They have a potential richness that can allow reanalysis at a later date or by different researchers. The recording style is free to adapt as the research progresses and the goals of the research change or become refined. On the other hand, use of text descriptions of behavior allows conceptual confusion to lay buried in ways that would be immediately exposed by requiring explicit rules of description. It allows for descriptions of similar events to vary greatly from one instance to the next, and places great demands on the observer.

Coding has its own advantages. It calls for a degree of selectivity: The goal of coding is not to capture reality in all its complexity but to highlight those aspects we consider significant in the context of the research. Codes are ideally explicitly defined and objective, typically in a detailed codebook that spells out how codes are to be applied so that different coders can achieve a high degree of interobserver reliability. With codes, it is ideally possible to have a complete set of codes to cover all activities, with discrete codes for discrete activities, minimizing overlap (mutually exclusive and exhaustive; Robson 1993). These strengths of coding are also, in some contexts, limitations: codes reduce the complexity and ambiguity of real behavior and to that degree represent a loss of information in exchange for order and clarity.

The Behavior Record

Each observation in a behavior record should have a unique identification code for record keeping. Each subject, too, will have a unique identification code. As part of a general ethical requirement to protect the anonymity of research subjects, these codes will not, as a rule, identify the subject to a casual outside observer. The subject should be on a census list that contains relevant information like age, gender, household, position in the family, and perhaps other information like occupation, ethnicity, and health status. Each observation should also pinpoint the time of observation on a 24-hour clock

Structural and Functional Descriptions

Researchers have distinguished two sorts of behavioral descriptions: structural descriptions of an actor's physical movements and functional descriptions of the presumed objectives or consequences of the behavior (Borgerhoff Mulder and Caro 1985; Hames 1992). Structural descriptions document the actor's posture (sitting, walking, climbing, etc.), manipulatory movements (carrying, handling, touching, etc.), and social interactions (speaking, striking, receiving an object, etc.). Structural descriptions may be conveniently recorded in grammatical data "sentences"— "individual X walks rapidly" (subject-verb-adverb) or "individual Y peels potato" (subject-verb-object). Since structural codes are straightforward descriptions of observable actions, they can be recorded reliably and objectively, with minimal inference on the part of observers.

However, the same physical act can have very different consequences depending on the context. For example, the action of repeatedly raising and lowering a hoe while standing may have different outcomes depending on whether it is performed while weeding a garden, clearing an irrigation ditch, or killing a snake that wandered into the yard. The goal of functional description is to characterize—at least in a general way—the purposes and likely outcomes of the actor's movements.

Thus, rather than recording in detail all the component movements of the actor's behavior, the observer describes the action using broader functional categories such as food production, child care, cooking, hygiene, and so forth. The specific functional activity classification scheme—which is best worked out in advance of making observations—depends on the nature of the research problem and the habitual activity patterns of the study population. A period of informal observation at the beginning of fieldwork can be invaluable for testing and refining activity classification schemes.

The field worker need not choose between structural and functional description: There are good reasons for collecting both simultaneously. Recording both physical actions and their presumed consequences increases confidence that measurement was not biased by preconceived notions of function, improves the richness of our descriptions of general (functional) activity categories such as "production" and "leisure," and preserves information on both what the observer saw and how she or he interpreted it (Borgerhoff Mulder and Caro 1985).

Coding

To facilitate cross-cultural comparisons of activity patterns, Gross (1984:542) calls on investigators to "standardize their coding of behavior into a set of broad descriptive categories of behavior. This would," he points out, "make the results of different investigators collected for different purposes usable for comparative purposes." With Gross (1984), we stress that any standardized coding system can be modified, with sub-categories added that are appropriate to particular cases. Table 3 shows a hierarchical coding scheme developed for use across cultures in small-scale and peasant societies (Johnson and Johnson 1988). Analogous coding schemes have been used by sociologists working in urban societies since the 1960s (Szalai 1972).

TABLE 3
Standardized Hierarchical Activity Codes Designed for
Cross-Cultural Comparisons of Time Use Patterns.

F   Food production
Includes foraging, agriculture, and husbandry producing food for household consumption, including travel to and from site of food production, cultivation of nonfoods or cash crops if these are undifferentiated from subsistence production, and soil preparation.
- FA   Agriculture
- FC   Collecting wild plant foods
- FF   Fishing
- FH   Hunting and fowling
- FL   Tending food and draft animals
- FX   Other food production
- FU   Food production, type unknown

C   Commercial activities
Activities oriented toward the production and exchange of money and trade goods.
- CA   Cash cropping, raising livestock for sale
- CC   Collecting wild/natural products for sale, including mining
- CM   Manufacturing articles for sale
- CS   Shopping, buying and selling, and bartering
- CW   Wage laboring, selling labor to others, service for money
- CX   Other commercial activity
- CU   Commercial activity, type unknown

M   Manufacture
Making and repairing the household, furnishings, implements, clothing (all for household use); nonpaid work on facilities such as roads, fences, irrigation channels, traps, etc.
- MA   Making or repairing portable artifacts
- MC   Making or repairing clothing
- MF   Building or repairing immobile facilities
- MM   Acquiring materials for manufactures
- MX   Other manufacture
- MU   Manufacture, type unknown

P   Food preparation
Processing, storing, and serving food.
- PC   Cooking food
- PG   Handling or processing food for storage
- PH   Handling or processing food for consumption in the near future
- PS   Serving or transporting food
- PX   Other food preparation
- PU   Food preparation, type unknown

H   Housework
Household tidying and cleaning chores, cleaning related to meals, managing household water and fuel, pet care, cleaning clothing.
- HH   Housekeeping, tidying, cleaning
- HM   Fetching and managing household water and fuel

    HX   Other housework
    HU   Housework, type unknown

E   Eating
    Eating and other meal-time activities.
    EE   Eating, drinking, and ingestion of nonfoods
    ES   Suckling
    EX   Other food consumption
    EU   Food consumption, type unknown

S   Social
    Includes a broad range of activities not better classified into the above categories, which are distinguished by social exchanges.
    SC   Child care, actively tending child
    SE   Acquiring or giving education, information, socialization in a face-to-face context
    SO   Care for another (nonchild), receiving care
    SP   Group ceremony, ritual, political activity (including both spectating and participating)
    SR   Group recreational activity or public entertainment (participating or spectating)
    SS   Socializing, chatting, visiting
    SX   Other social activity
    SU   Social activity, type unknown

I   Individual
    Self-involved activities that do not fit well into other categories.
    IE   Acquiring education or information, alone
    IG   Self-grooming, dressing, hygiene
    II   Idle due to illness
    IN   Idle "doing nothing"
    IP   Participating in individual religious observance
    IR   Participating in individual recreation or entertainment
    IS   Sleeping, napping
    IX   Other individual activity
    IU   Individual activity, type unknown

U   Away from community unobserved
    This category applies only to activities that take place outside of the specified geographical range of the behavior study (for example, on an extended trip visiting another community). Secondary codes refer to the primary activity best describing the purpose of the trip, giving priority to those activities earlier in the list. Note: this code is not to be used to distinguish unobserved activities ("time-outs") when the subject is temporarily out of sight.
    UF   Away to do food-producing activity
    UC   Away to do commercial activity
    UM   Away to do manufacturing activity
    UP   Away to do food preparation (possible, but probably unlikely)
    UH   Away to do housework activity (also unlikely)
    UE   Away to eat (unlikely)
    US   Away to do social activity
    UI   Away to do individual activity
    UX   Away to do activity classified as "Other"
    UU   Away for unknown purpose

X   Other
     Activity that does not fit into any of the above categories. No secondary codes suggested, although field workers using this activity list undoubtedly will want to subdivide and specify this residual category.

SOURCE: Based on Standard Activity Codes, UCLA Time Allocation Project (see Johnson and Johnson 1988).

Three problems that confront the researcher during coding are *simultaneity*, *reliability*, and *context*.

1. *The simultaneity problem.* What do we record when an actor is performing what could be coded as two different activities? A common example is a woman nursing a baby while tending a cooking pot: is her behavior "child care" or "food preparation"? A small but significant proportion of activities are not mutually exclusive in this sense; such doubling-up of activities is actually an interesting empirical question: For example, it is often argued that women's activities are constrained by their responsibility for child care, so that their other activities must be compatible.

Strategies for handling the simultaneity problem:

1. Use a structural coding system and describe physical acts, perhaps along with a functional activity code (Borgerhoff Mulder and Caro 1985), thus preserving information about simultaneity.
2. Code both activities as a full observation. This preserves information about simultaneity but raises the problem of double accounting (inflated n).
3. Code both activities, but treat each as a half-observation. This avoids the problem of inflated n but discounts activities performed simultaneously: nursing a baby while cooking only counts half as much as nursing a baby alone.
4. Establish priority rules, such as coding food preparation over child care: In this case, the woman would only be counted as cooking. This solves the problem of inflated n but loses information about simultaneity.
5. Code the different activities as separate dimensions of behavior. In this case, there might be an activity code (cooking) and a social code (child care).
6. Develop combination codes such as cooking/child care to cover the most common cases of simultaneity.

Each of these solutions has its strengths and shortcomings. Whichever is chosen must be consistently adhered to and made explicit in publishing the data.

2. *The reliability problem.* There are two questions that frame this problem: Does a single observer consistently record the same behavior in the same way (intracoder reliability)? Do two observers consistently code the same behavior in the same way (intercoder reliability)? The reliability problem must be addressed early in the research —even prior to it —so that a detailed codebook can be constructed. The codebook should do more than just list the complete set of codes. It should spell out how the codes will be applied. Codes must be applied in practice and evaluated for usefulness; coders must practice also and

learn how to increase their consistency. A steep learning curve means that a few weeks of practice may be needed in order to stabilize recording or coding and achieve a high degree of intercoder reliability (Robson 1993).

3. *The context problem.* We use context both to help us interpret behavior and to look for connections between environment and behavior. As noted above, this is only possible to the degree that our descriptions of behavior are separate from our descriptions of context. Some aspects of context are *constant*, in the sense that they change little or not at all during the research (for example, political institutions, roads, markets). A census, map, and a general ethnographic description often suffice to supply this information. Other aspects of context are *variable* and must be recorded on each observation. Common context variables include date and time, weather, location, social interaction, and technology used. It is possible, however, to go overboard with context descriptions: in our experience few anthropologists do much with the context data they collect—people tend to do agriculture in their fields, housework in their homes, etc. As with behavioral descriptions, effort put into context descriptions should be constrained by the question: What are the data for?

Understanding of context can also be enhanced by attention to: (1) *methodological details* needed to establish the reliability of the observation, such as whether the behavior was directly observed or established by hearsay; and (2) *provision for open-ended comments* on the circumstances of the observation, amplification of the data recorded, or general ethnographic observations.

Conclusion

In ethnography, what people *do* matters. Much of ethnographic description is intended to tell us how members of a group behave: how they make a living, raise children, resolve conflicts, worship, celebrate, mourn. The accuracy, fairness, completeness—in a word, verisimilitude—of ethnographic descriptions is of central importance to us, yet we as ethnographers are astonishingly cavalier about how we develop our descriptions of behavior. We do not take seriously enough the severe limitations that the cultural construction of long-term memory place on the ability of both research subjects and fieldworkers to develop accurate descriptions of ongoing behavior.

Accurate descriptions of behavior matter because, from the most theoretically abstract to the most immediately applied concerns, our understanding of the causes and consequences of human behavior depends on them. We would ordinarily have little respect for theories or policies based on data that had error rates ranging from 50%–80%. Yet participant observation typically produces descriptions of behavior with such error rates, unless the observations are carefully recorded immediately as the behavior occurs.

Once it is accepted that accurate descriptions of the behavior of members of a community matter, the methodological issues we have addressed in this chapter become paramount. What does it mean to describe an activity? Whom should we observe, when, and where? At what level of detail? How can we sample from the stream of behavior in a community to generate a fair representation of people of differing age, gender, and status, in all the relevant contexts of their lives?

These are issues that we should address as far as possible in the design phase of research. But, because research in real communities is always unpredictable to some degree, we must remain flexible and ready to change methods to meet contingencies. The best way to do this is to develop skills in a variety of methods of direct systematic observation and an understanding of the rationales behind them. Researchers who do so will be able to make the inevitable compromises fieldwork entails while achieving the most accurate and representative descriptions possible.

REFERENCES

Alexander, R. M. 1992. *The Human Machine.* New York: Columbia University Press.

Altmann, J. 1974. The Observational Study of Behavior. *Behavior 48*:1–41.

Bailey, R. C., and N. Peacock. 1988. *Time Allocation of Efe Pygmy Men and Women of the Ituri Forest, Zaire.* Vol. 3 in *Cross-Cultural Studies in Time Allocation.* New Haven: Human Relations Area Files.

Baksh, M. 1989–90. The Spot Observations Technique in Time Allocation Research. *Cultural Anthropology Methods 1*:3; 2:6–7; 3:4–5.

Baksh, M. 1990. *Time Allocation among the Machiguenga of Camana.* Vol. 7 in *Cross-Cultural Studies in Time Allocation.* New Haven: Human Relations Area Files.

Bernard, H. R., P. J. Pelto, O. Werner, J. Boster, A. K. Romney, A. Johnson, C. R. Ember, and A. Kasakoff. 1986. The Construction of Primary Data in Cultural Anthropology. *Current Anthropology 27*:382–396.

Bernard, H. R., and P. D. Killworth. 1993. Sampling in Time Allocation Research. *Ethnology 32*:207–215.

Bernard, H. R. 1994. *Research Methods in Anthropology: Qualitative and Quantitative Approaches,* 2d ed. Walnut Creek, CA: AltaMira Press.

Betzig, L. L., and P. Turke. 1985. Measuring Time Allocation: Observation and Intention. *Current Anthropology 26*:647–650.

Borgerhoff Mulder, M. B., and T. M. Caro. 1985. The Use of Quantitative Observation Techniques in Anthropology. *Current Anthropology 26*:323–336.

Bornstein M. H., and H. G. Bornstein. 1976. The Pace of Life. *Nature 259*:557–559.

Carlstein, T. 1982. *Time Resources, Society, and Ecology.* Vol. 1, *Preindustrial Societies.* London: George Allen and Unwin.

Chapple, E. D., and C. M. Arensberg. 1940. Measuring Human Relations: An Introduction to the Study of the Interaction of Individuals. *Genetic Psychology Monographs 22*:3–147.

D'Andrade, R. 1974. Memory and the Assessment of Behavior. In *Measurement in the Social Sciences*. H. Blalock, ed. Pp. 159–186. Chicago: Aldine.

D'Andrade, R. 1995. *The Development of Cognitive Anthropology*. Cambridge: Cambridge University Press.

Dufour, D. L. 1984. The Time and Energy Expenditure of Indigenous Women Horticulturalists in the Northwest Amazon. *American Journal of Physical Anthropology 65*:37–46.

Dunbar, R.I.M. 1976. Some Aspects of Research Design and Their Implications in the Observational Study of Behavior. *Behavior 58*:78–98.

Engle, P., and J. Lumpkin. 1991. How Accurate Are Time Use Estimates? Effects of Cognitive Enhancement and Cultural Differences on Recall Accuracy. *Applied Cognitive Psychology 6*:141–159.

Feldhutter, I., M. Schleidt, and I. Eibl-Eibesfeldt. 1990. Moving in the Beat of Seconds. *Ethology and Sociobiology 11*:511–520.

Flinn, M. 1988. Parent-Offspring Interactions in a Caribbean Village. In *Human Reproductive Behavior: A Darwinian Perspective*. L. L. Betzig, M. Borgerhoff Mulder, and P. Turke, eds. Pp. 189–200. Cambridge: Cambridge University Press.

Gross, D. R. 1984. Time Allocation: A Tool for the Study of Cultural Behavior. *Annual Reviews in Anthropology 13*:519–558.

Hames, R. 1979. A Comparison of the Efficiencies of the Shotgun and Bow in Neotropical Forest Hunting. *Human Ecology 7*:219–252.

Hames, R. 1992. Time Allocation. In *Evolutionary Ecology and Human Behavior*. E. A. Smith and B. Winterhalder, eds. Pp. 203–235. New York: Aldine.

Harris, M. 1964. *The Nature of Cultural Things*. New York: Random House.

Harris, M. 1990. Emics and Etics Revisited. In *Emics and Etics: The Insider/Outsider Debate*. T. M. Headland, K. L. Pike, and M. Harris, eds. Pp. 48–61. Thousand Oaks, CA: Sage Publications.

Hawkes, K., H. Kaplan, K. Hill, and A. M. Hurtado. 1987. A Problem of Bias in Scan Sampling. *Journal of Anthropological Research 43*:239–246.

Hill, K., H. Kaplan, K. Hawkes, and A. M. Hurtado. 1985. Men's Time Allocation to Subsistence Work among the Ache of Eastern Paraguay. *Human Ecology 13*(1):29–47.

Hurtado, A. M., and K. R. Hill. 1987. Early Dry Season Subsistence Ecology of Cuiva (Hiwi) Foragers of Venezuela. *Human Ecology 15*:163–187.

Johnson, A. 1975. Time Allocation in a Machiguenga Community. *Ethnology 14*: 301–310.

Johnson, A., and O. R. Johnson. 1988. *Time Allocation among the Machiguenga of Shimaa*. Vol. 1 in *Cross-Cultural Studies in Time Allocation*. New Haven: Human Relations Area Files.

Lee, R. B. 1979. *The !Kung San*. Cambridge: Cambridge University Press.

Levine, R. V. 1990. The Pace of Life. *American Scientist 78*:450–459.

Lhermillier, A., and N. Lhermillier. 1983. Vida economica y social de un nucleo familiar Yanomami. *Boletin Antropologico 3*:39–65.

Martin, P., and P. Bateson. 1993. *Measuring Behavior: An Introductory Guide*, 2d ed. Cambridge: Cambridge University Press.

Montoye, H. J., H.C.G. Kemper, W.H.M. Saris, and R. A. Washburn, 1996. *Measuring Physical Activity and Energy Expenditure*. Champaign, IL: Human Kinetics.

Niemi, I., S. Kiiski, and M. Liikkanen. 1981. *Use of Time in Finland, 1979.* Helsinki: Central Statistical Office of Finland.

Panter-Brick, C. 1989. Motherhood and Subsistence Work: The Tamang of Rural Nepal. *Human Ecology 17*:205–228.

Paolisso, M. J., and R. Sackett. 1988. *Time Allocation among the Yukpa of Venezuela.* Vol. 2 in *Cross-Cultural Studies in Time Allocation.* New Haven: Human Relations Area Files.

Robson, C. 1993. *Real World Research: A Resource for Social Scientists and Practitioner-Researchers.* Oxford: Blackwell.

Romney, A. K., S. Weller, and W. Batchelder. 1986. Culture as Consensus: A Theory of Culture and Informant Accuracy. *American Anthropologist 88*:313–338.

Sackett, R. 1996. Time, Energy, and the Indolent Savage: A Cross-Cultural Test of the Primitive Affluence Hypothesis. Ph.D. diss., Department of Anthropology. Los Angeles: University of California.

Scaglion, R. 1986. The Importance of Nighttime Observations in Time Allocation Studies. *American Ethnologist 13*:537–545.

Shweder, R. A. 1982. *Fact and Artifact in Trait Perception: The Systematic Distortion Hypothesis.* Vol. 11 in *Normal Personality Processes: Progress in Experimental Psychology Research.* B. A. Maher and W. B. Maher, eds. Pp. 65–100. New York: Academic Press.

Szalai, A., ed. 1972. *The Use of Time: Daily Activities of Urban and Suburban Populations in Twelve Countries.* The Hague and Paris: Mouton.

Whiting, B., and J.W.M. Whiting. 1973. Methods for Observing and Recording Behavior. In *A Handbook of Method in Cultural Anthropology.* R. Naroll and R. Cohen, eds. Pp. 282–315. New York: Columbia University Press.

Whiting, B., and J.W.M. Whiting. 1975. *Children of Six Cultures: A Psycho-Cultural Analysis.* Cambridge: Harvard University Press.

ROBERT I. LEVY
DOUGLAS W. HOLLAN

Ten

Person-Centered Interviewing and Observation

Introduction

A major problem for contemporary anthropology is to clarify theoretically and empirically the nature of the relations in various communities—and various *kinds* of communities—between individual members of the community and their historical and current sociocultural and material contexts. How are community members *constituted* by their contexts? To what degree and in what way are they at least partially autonomous individuals, engaged in a dynamic, sometimes coercive, sometimes enabling interplay with a context that is in some way *separate* from and alien to them? What, then, is the nature and location of such constructs as self, identity, agency, cognition in different kinds of communities? How are the phenomena relevant to these constructs differentially formed, stabilized, and located in the interplay between public and private spheres? What, in a particular place and in relation to a particular person, is to be thought of as a communal (sociocultural) form; what as an intrapersonal (psychological) form? When is this traditional dichotomy misleading, so that some synthesizing concept of behavioral locus and integration might be warranted? What do these various *locations* of local influences on thought, emotion, morality, and action have to do with social process and with the implications of history, stability, and change—and, indeed, with the idea of freedom?

In this chapter, we will be concerned with certain techniques for investigating these relations of individual and context. A number of preliminary cautions and

333

assertions are necessary. Our focus is on the relatively neglected anthropological study of individuals[1] (neglected in comparison with studies of "culture" and "society"). It is important to note that these methods are not attempts to study individuals primarily in or within themselves (for, say, the purposes of some comparative personality theory, or some issue in general psychology, or to humanize an ethnography by appending life stories to it). Rather, they are attempts to clarify the relations of "individuality," both as output and input, to its sociocultural contexts. The implication is that the study of individuals is an essential component of adequate social theory. We assume that the local forms of individuality and individual-social transactions have to be studied empirically in each particular setting and for each kind of problem (although we will also argue for a concept of "types" of settings for some purposes) and that we cannot thus use some a priori generic model of "anthropological man and woman."

The interviews we will be centrally concerned with are not just samples of *discourse*—not one kind of local discourse among others, not just narratives, not just life histories or autobiographies. They are in part such things, but they are conducted in an attempt to attenuate and disrupt ordinary and conventional patterns of social discourse. In so doing, we hope to elicit behavior that moves beyond role-determined surface scripts to suggest hidden or latent dimensions of the organization of persons and of the sociocultural matrix and their interactions.

We are not only concerned with the nature and interaction of what we may gloss as "relatively private" and "relatively public" forms in one or another *particular* community, although almost all studies have been ethnographic and local. We also are concerned with the probability that such local forms are, in some of their dimensions, results of *typological* features shared by other communities (for example, scale, density, complexity, isolation, nature of embeddedness in larger systems, colonial or postcolonial relations, and subsistence, market, exchange or cash economies), which, in some sense, partially determine private and public forms and their relations, and are, therefore, of systematic comparative interest.[2]

We are, of course, aware of the ideological and methodological disagreements that some anthropologists will have with the quasi-positivistic or "cookbook" way in which we have necessarily phrased this methodological manual. We believe that the distortions implicit in method—embodying differential power and status and Western ethnocentrism and self-interest—are aspects of the kinds of at least partially correctable interview distortions that we will discuss and which can be brought to consciousness and in part rectified.

Person-centered interviewing and observations are not made up of standard "reliable" techniques such as those used by "scientific" technicians to assure what they take to be valid and reliable (that is easily replicable) results. The interviewing and observing discussed here are rather performing arts, and this manual is something like a musical score. You have to know how to do it (or something very like it) in some important sense beforehand; you have to already be a "musician." You have to make use of social, psychological, and probably evolutionary skills of social knowing and interpersonal interaction that you bring to the "score," to the manual. This means that none of what follows is to be followed mechanically. It is rather to be taken as a series of examples, of guides for the mobilization and education of a preadapted understanding. These methodological prescriptions are no more mechanical and positivistic than is a musical score for skilled performers. And as not everyone can go from the score to a satisfactory performance, not everyone can grasp skillfully (or is interested in) person-centered aspects of social behavior.

This manual of technique has another problem. Particular practices will be sketched and related to topics of inquiry and categories of analysis. But those topics and categories are tentative and may have to be changed as a result of trying to use them. They are often crudely approximate and are rough starting places, which may well be criticized, altered, and undermined as a result of the successful inquiries that they generate. They are simply used to get started.

One final issue needs comment. The three communities where we have worked the most—a remote Tahitian village, a city in Nepal's Kathmandu Valley, and a community in Sulawesi in Indonesia—were at the time of the original study quite remote, considerably inwardly turned, and, in regard to the aspects of life we were principally concerned with at the time, conservative. Much of our discussion is directed at the problems and issues relevant to such kinds of communities. These were the sorts of places that generated traditional anthropological thought, achievements, and errors. There are still some of them about, but insofar as traditional communities have changed, and insofar as anthropologists are working in other kinds of places, the problems sketched here of studying and thinking about individual organization and person-context integrations become significantly transformed and even more complex. But one can begin, at least—as anthropology began—with considerations arising from smallish and inwardly turned places.

Our main concern here is with interviewing in person-centered anthropological studies and only tangentially with other types of person-centered study, but interviewing must be conducted in conjunction with traditional community studies that elucidate context, determine the issues to be covered in the interviews, and make the interview materials intelligible. Person-centered interviews must also be augmented by special studies dictated by the investigator's interests and developing sense of significant problems.

To the extent that person-centered interviews engage the interviewee as an "informant," that is as a knowledgeable person who can tell the anthropologist-interviewer about culture and behavior in a particular locale, these interviews are similar to other types discussed in the social science literature.[3] But person-centered interviews also engage the interviewee as a "respondent," as an object of systematic study and observation in him- or herself. The interviewer observes and studies the interviewee as he or she behaves in the interview setting, as he or she reacts or responds to various probes, questions, and topics.[4] It is the balanced combination of informant and respondent modes of interviewing that is characteristic of person-centered interviews and that distinguishes them from most other types of interviews.[5]

The Interviewee as Informant and as Respondent

There is a significant difference between asking a Tahitian interviewee something like "Please describe for me exactly how and why supercision (a penis-mutilating rite of passage) is done by Tahitians," and asking him "Can you tell me about *your* supercision?" "What happened leading up to it?" "What happened that day?" "Did it change your life in any way?" "How?" "What did you think and feel about it then?" "What do you think and feel about it now?"

The first question uses the interviewee as an informant, as an expert witness (albeit with a limited and special perspective) about some community procedure. The second set of questions treats the interviewee as a respondent, as an object of study in him- or herself; it explores what he or she makes of the procedure. The relation between the two sets of answers is directly informative (see Levy 1973: 117–122) and illuminates the force of supercision on males in a way that the informant-based cultural description does not, so that the two types of description complement each other, both for social and psychological interpretations.

Person-centered interviewing moves back and forth between the informant and the respondent modes. A remark of a young woman informant: "I felt very shy and embarrassed at that time" might be followed by a respondent-type probe: "Tell me more about how you felt" or by the informant-type questions: "What do girls usually feel under those circumstances?" "How do they usually act?" "If they don't feel or act like that, what do people think?"

These oscillations between respondent and informant modes illuminate the spaces, conflicts, coherences, and transformations, if any, between the woman-in-herself (either in her own conception, or in the interviewer's emerging one) and aspects of her perception and understanding of her external context. Notice that if we stay at the descriptive and phenomenal level, this unpacking of phenomena is not too difficult. Problems arise when we try to *theorize* these separations and relations—we cannot in any satisfactory way simply force private into something like "mental" or "personality," and public or external-to-the-individual into some contrary realm of "culture" or some related idea. The tensions and apparent polarities that person-centered interviewing reveal present a challenge in theorization to each worker.[6]

Person-centered interviewing *generates* a field of often new phenomena, of reports and behaviors, that are then subject to interpretation. We will consider the mechanics of the interview and note sources of distortion and misinterpretation before turning to aspects of interpretation and the theoretical issues to which they are related.

How to Conduct Person-Centered Interviews

Person-centered interviews are a mixture of informant and respondent questions and probes. A probe is an intervention to elicit more information, not necessarily in the form of a question. An encouraging grunt may be a probe, as is a verbal directive like: "Tell me more about that." Questions and probes may be relatively focused or "closed" ("Exactly what did he say that made you feel like that?") or relatively vague or "open ended" ("What was going on?").

Open-ended probes are purposely ambiguous. This leaves the respondent a relatively wide choice of responses, dictated less by the exact answer to a factual question than by, presumably, some private concern or orientation. The interviewer tries to widen the constraints of the question as much as is relevant to what he or she is interested in at the moment. "Tell me about your childhood" is more open than "Tell me about the people around you in your childhood family," which is more open than "Tell me about your parents," which is more open than "Tell me about your mother," which is more open than "Tell me about how your mother disciplined you." (We will return to open and closed interventions.)

The specific choices and emphases in the *contents* of responses as well as the *form* of the responses made by the respondent within the relatively wide constraints of the probe are important material for analysis.

When to Begin Person-Centered Interviewing

Several factors determine when in the course of the fieldwork the person-centered interviewing should begin:

Linguistic Competence

Person-centered interviewing depends, of course, on adequate linguistic competence. Many anthropologists don't achieve enough fluency in the local language to do person-centered interviewing. It is not only harder to shape questions for respondent probes than for informant probes (it is harder to be properly vague in a foreign language than properly precise), but the linguistic nuances in the respondent's discourse that convey personal information are often meaningful variations of the standard language. One has to know enough of the standard language to realize that the respondent is talking in a peculiar or significant way.

Some anthropologists don't work in the native language. When informants are bilingual, they may work in the areal lingua franca, the national language (pidgin, trade Malay, Nepali etc.), or the former colonial language. Where an informant is monolingual in some local language, the anthropologists may use bilingual assistants. Any of these shortcuts will systematically affect and distort the respondent's behavior in often obscure ways. Different aspects of identity, morality, self-presentation, and mind are organized around and evoked by the use of each of the two (or more) languages the respondent uses. The local language is almost certainly most closely related to people's private realms of experience and to their personal organization. It may be productive and theoretically interesting to work with informants in both languages for comparison, but it is deeply distorting not to work primarily in the respondent's core language.

Many of the language forms used during respondent interviewing are different from many aspects of the language that the anthropologist learns for public discourse and informant interviewing. So it's often necessary to work out the vocabulary and phrasing of questions and probes with the help of a patient informant. It is also very helpful to try some pilot interviews with people who will not be major respondents. This way if things go wrong it won't compromise essential studies. (It's sometimes a good idea to do these interviews and the linguistic preparation with someone who lives outside of the community; this minimizes community members' expectations about the interviews.) The most helpful way to improve interviewing skills is to study closely the errors and misunderstandings revealed by tape recordings of interviews.

Understanding the Culture

In the same way as the interviews will drift from public to private realms (below), so does the understanding of the anthropologist. It takes considerable general knowledge about a place and its people before we can begin to understand the presence and significance of private variants and transformations of local cultural and social forms. The field worker must, therefore, function as a general ethnologist before turning to person-centered studies, and, therefore, relatively long periods of fieldwork are required.

Trust and Repondents' Motivations

In the United States, people are often willing to discuss personal matters freely with experts who are strangers to them and to do so in many public arenas. In traditional societies, where face and reputation are essential, one doesn't discuss potentially reputation-threatening private worlds with someone unless one trusts him or her deeply. This is particularly true in relation to the anthropologist who will be living in the community and who will be in daily contact with many different local people, including the interviewee's superiors and enemies. Much close observation of and contact with the anthropologist (insofar as that observation and contact leads to trust) is necessary before local people will consent to being relatively frank respondents.

We must ask at this point why interviewees engage in interviews at all. It is easier to grasp—especially in small communities where anxieties about public reputation require much self-censorship and self-control or in communities where political positions may be full of danger—why people would *not* want to participate. But it has been our experience in several traditional communities that almost all people we asked (representing a cross-section of their communities) were willing to become and remain respondents.

Early in the anthropologist's stay, people (unless they have good reason to keep silent) are motivated to engage superficially, at least, with the anthropologist and his or her interviews through politeness, hospitality, compassion for the naive and confused field worker, and curiosity. In some kinds of communities, there is a sense that it is prestigious to be chosen as an expert.

In most premodern places, the respondent assumes that an exchange relation is being set up and that some sort of obligation on the part of the interviewer will result. Essentially, a long-lasting relationship of mutual obligation is being entered into, initiated by the respondent's generosity. Thus, overt quid-pro-quo offers of payments "settling" the interviewer's obligation are disturbing and, often, insulting to the respondent. In the kinds of communities we have worked in, it would have been a serious violation of the conventions of exchange to offer money at the start, that is to *hire* respondents. We gave substantial gifts or reciprocal services to respondents (sometimes, as in Nepal, gifts of money to poor respondents), usually at the end of the interview series. We also found that we had assumed some very long-term obligations to informants and their families.

Under modern conditions, informants and respondents do become professionalized, and in exchange for their time and expertise, one may hire them, as one does a Western expert. Such interviews may be problematic unless the respondent becomes engaged for the sorts of personal reasons we discuss below.

All interviews provide some kind of immediate psychological reward for interviewees. They perceive themselves to be taken seriously by someone they may perceive as having high status. They are selected over their peers and treated as an expert, a master. High-status interviewees, on the other hand, may consider helping the anthropologist to be part of the responsibility (and validation) of their status.

Such motivations may operate in the beginning phases of a respondent interview, but the interviewee soon realizes that something strange is going on. He or she is not being treated for the most part as a cultural expert, nor in his or her public role, but as an individual, and in a rather deep and comprehensive way.

In contrast to informant interviews, which may be successful no matter whether the reward is intrinsic or extrinsic, the respondent interviewee must develop additional motivations for the interview to proceed properly. It has been our experience in very diverse communities that insofar as respondent-centered interviews are being conducted properly (in ways we shall try to specify), they become, when people slowly grasp what is going on, deeply meaningful to interviewees. More often than not, they express regret at the conclusion of the interview series, no matter how lengthy it has seemed to the interviewer. Why should this be?

It seems that the opportunity to talk about, express, share, and construct aspects of one's private world in conditions where this proves safe—away from immediate external communal censorship, in an interaction with someone who is sympathetic, nonjudgmental, disinterested, and trustworthy—is of considerable value for many, perhaps most people. This is *particularly* true in small, traditional communities (or those under some sort of rigid social control) where it may be difficult to express, articulate, or explore private worlds even with friends or family. Obviously, these are the very communities in which self-exposure is most dangerous.

In these, and in all communities, it is essential to protect rigorously the reputation (and sometimes life and liberty) of individuals. Clearly, this provides profound responsibilities for the anthropologist, who must protect the respondent through guarding and disguising field materials (for example, through writing some things in a coded language) and must resist any temptation to gossip. There may be some topics that are so sensitive and dangerous that they should not even be asked about, and certainly not recorded in ways that could possibly implicate the interviewee. Political participation in many countries is one such matter, and so are behaviors defined as "crime," and any behavior the exposure of which would cause a significant threat to reputation. On other occasions, it may be safe to talk about some subject so long as no recordings are made and so long as written notes are coded or disguised in some other manner.

Location of Interviews

To maximize private responses, it is essential to interview the respondent as far as possible in isolation from his or her family, friends, and acquaintances. The presence of others automatically shifts behavior and discourse toward public behavior and socially proper responses. In many communities, the search for a private place for interviewing is a most difficult, sometimes impossible, matter. Often, isolated, private, and secret conversations (even among friends and/or spouses, the latter being the case in many traditional Indian families) are deeply suspect as an escape from communal or familial controls. The problem is deepened in cases of cross-sexual interviews. In some communities, a woman may be interviewed by a man if she brings a baby or young child with her. In others, such interviews are possible if the interlocutors have some sort of (and the proper kinds of) fictive kinship relation, a relationship that is often given to outsiders in traditional kin-organized societies to facilitate social relationships.

Interview Topics

The subject matter of an interview series consists of discussions of as wide a range as possible of the issues in the interviewee's life that seem important to him or her and/or the interviewer. Most of these will concern, on the one hand, the forms and encounters of local social, comparative, and historical importance (such as, for example, being an untouchable, or a wife in an arranged marriage, or about life lived in the narrow constraints of a tiny village), and, on the other hand, significant matters of more or less general human concern. These accounts of aspects of lives are approached first descriptively, then with an emphasis on the interviewee's personal experience and interpretations—that is to say sometimes in the informant mode, sometimes in the respondent mode.

Person-centered interviews consist, then, of *topics of inquiry* that are approached and dealt with in certain ways. We will consider the topics first and aspects of how to deal with them in later sections. Inquiries into specific topics generate stories. "This is the day-by-day life of us untouchables." Those stories are directly meaningful in themselves, but the *form* in which they are told also yields a good deal of general information about aspects of personal organization, local context, and person-context relations that cut across many different topics.

It is essential to note that our list is selected and biased in certain ways.[7] Other interviewers in other settings must develop their own lists, although it may be useful to cover most of the topics listed here for comparison with other studies and because they may prove to be valuable at a later time.

Our list emphasizes the personal pole of person-context interactions. In actual interviews, both poles have to be dealt with. There are several reasons for our present emphasis. Relevant social and cultural patterns vary in different kinds of communities. The problems addressed in a caste system are different from those of a small, relatively egalitarian village, for example. A generalized list cannot deal with such variables. The topics of the personal pole, at least at the level of abstraction we are using here ("identity," "feeling") are perhaps more general than social variables. But the main reason for our present emphasis is that general aspects of context—economic forms, kinship structures, religious forms, modernization, and so on—are the familiar subject matter of general anthropological method. The categories of the person-pole interacting with these public forms are relatively less familiar to anthropologists.

Although many of these person-centered categories may have intrapsychic implications (they were, in large part, developed historically for the purposes of some model or other of intrapsychic personality description), we understand them, as we have noted, as being open and interactional aspects of context-person relations. (Conversely, at the social level, we would similarly expect such categories as "production" or "exchange" to be so understood for our purposes).

Many topics are relevant to all respondents, but some categories of people (women in their defining contrasts to men, high status versus low status, young versus old, and people with specialized roles—mothers, local leaders, deviants, etc.) will obviously call for particular topics of inquiry.

We can only suggest briefly what we mean by any particular topic category. For further understanding, it may be helpful to the reader to see how the categories are used in the literature we have cited.

Locating Information

This cluster of issues locates individuals in the various significant components of their community's social structure, both in their current activities and in their earlier life. It guides the inquiry of the first stages of the interviews and covers such matters as social roles, patterns of association, friends and enemies, economic status and activities, marital status, children—and whatever else may be socially and culturally significant for placing respondents in the local social network. Of importance here are not only specific relationships but generalized ones, with classes of superiors and inferiors, with allies and opponents, with equals, with people of the same and opposite sex, with relatives and nonrelatives, with people in the local community, and with various kinds of outsiders.

Not only is the individual to be located in his or her current life, but also developmentally in relation to what is taken to be significant past experience, particularly those matters having to do with learning and with the developmental aspects of people's present orientations and behavior. Here we may include such things as patterns of life in the family of origin, parents' and other caretaking adults' roles and characteristics, sibling patterns, household caretaking and teaching practices, early economic activities, formal education, travel, and other putatively formative and socially differentiating matters. In those societies that have rites of passage, it is important to explore memories and interpretations of the rites, and their effects, if any, on the respondent.

In the early phases of the interview series, locating data are gathered principally in informant and conversational modes. One may ask the village headman what a headman does, how people achieve status, etc. It is only at some later point in the interview series that certain items in the locating data may be returned to in respondent mode ("How do you feel about being a headman?" "What about the work makes you anxious?" "What is difficult about the work?" "What is reward-ing?" "How do people judge and react to what you do?").[8]

Patterns of Identification and Identity Formation

The locating data and patterns of relationship are all related to the interviewee's position in a historical and social nexus. This position is reflected and becomes a behavior-directing force, in part, in his or her "identity," understood as the inter-section of (aspects of) an individual and (aspects of) his or her communally provided social roles and social definition.

Identity is reflected in the behavior-guiding orientation to the issue of "Who am I?" as it is formulated in different contexts.[9] Answers such as "I am an aristocrat,"

"I am myself," "I am a member of such and such a family," "I am a farmer," "It depends on whom I am with,"[10] etc., are all obviously of differential importance. These matters can be discussed directly with the respondent as well as inferred from other interview materials and from observations of the informant. In our experience, the direct question "What would you answer if I asked 'Who are you?'," addressed to someone who knows that you already know who he or she is in some sense, produces very informative discussions.

Ethnic, class, familial, gender, and other components of identity can be approached directly. Questions such as "What does it mean to be a Tahitian?" and "In what way are you like, or different from that?" directly probe aspects of categorization of self and, in defining contrast, others.

The processes of identity *formation* can be approached through questions like "Who (an individual or class of people) did you want to be like when you were a child?," "In what ways?," "Why?," "At what age?," and "Who did you wish *not* to be like?." One can trace the interviewee's sense of developing consciousness of identity, and of shifting, multiple, or unified identities by discussing these issues directly—as well as by inferences from other interview materials.

An important aspect of identity is, of course, locally constructed sexual identity. This entails definitions of the sexual other (as all identity categories define classes of others). It is also closely related to and in part distinct from ideas and behaviors about physical sexuality and general orientations about bodies. Direct probes at sexual identity include the repondent's definitions and evaluations of "men" and "women" and their lives, self-definition in relation to these general definitions, envy or disapproval of aspects of opposite sex roles and characteristics, and advantages and disadvantages of being male or female. What traits does the interviewee sense in him- or herself to be masculine or feminine? Does he or she wish sometimes in fantasy to change sex? All this overlaps with local and private forms, meanings and attitudes about "heterosexuality" in its defining contrast to "homosexuality."

Aspects of Self

Quite different from the idea of identity is the local (and individual's) conception about and the actual forms of "self," if self is taken to be that subsystem of a larger mind that is the locus of "I," of experientially autonomous action and, thus, of moral responsibility. An individual's thoughts and feelings and behaviors are variously sorted as belonging to self or to nonself. Nonself phenomena may be variously explained by respondents and/or their communities as emanating from some natural or supernatural source, alien to some essence of what it is to be a conscious and responsible individual.

The concept of self is related to the idea of "person" in that a community's ideas about which members are socially responsible ("persons") implies that they possess competent selves in one or another sense that must be locally investigated. Although the interviewer's understanding of local ideas about selves and actual local structures of self are, for the most part, based indirectly on a range of miscellaneous interview materials, it is possible, usually late in the interview series, to ask about the respondent's sense of which actions or thoughts are really his or hers, which just conventional actions, and which come from outside the self, and if from "the outside," then, from where.[11] Such conceptions are related to the moral issue (below) of which thoughts and behaviors one (and one's associates) are responsible for, and the somewhat different issue of which behaviors respondents believe they can or cannot control at some level of thought or action.

Probes can be used to investigate the relation of ideas about self—its separation, blending, congruence, or antagonism—to the body or to some spiritual entity or to other parts of mind; and one can investigate as well the stability or instability of the sense of self, the relation of self to different contexts, the relation of self to the local use of drugs and their effects (and to meditation and mystic experiences in some communities), the strength of the self in relation to internal and external pressures, the particular resources the self has to control itself, and so on. These latter issues are on the border of moral organization and conception.

Morality

Related to the conception of the self as the particular focus within the larger mind of moral responsibility is a large set of issues related to aspects of moral evaluation and, especially, to self-control and attempts to control others that can be approached directly—as well as being implied and illustrated in discussions of many topics. One can explore respondents' ideas about *what* constitutes good and bad behavior. *Why* is a particular behavior good or bad? What kinds of feelings and personal consequences are associated with doing good, doing bad? What kinds of things is the respondent aware of wanting to do, but refrains from doing? Why? Ideas (and relevant episodes) bearing on what we would gloss as shame, guilt, sin, embarrassment, repentance, rectification, justice, and the like can be explored directly. Tensions between public ideas about moral matters and those of the respondent, and the relation of those tensions to his or her actions are all important here.[12]

The Body

One of the principal foci of private experience is the ways that people in various communities live in and through their bodies, their sense and evaluations of the functions and form of their own bodies and the bodies of others, and the relation of bodies to action, to a person's value, to a person's nature and constitution, to self and identity. Various miscellaneous matters are relevant here—body-centered sociocultural topics such as eating, cleanliness, pollution, excretion, menstruation, procreation, and physical sexuality. All of these can be explored directly.

Stress, Illness, and Healing

Essential information about any systematically organized arena, particularly the personal and social forms we are concerned with here, is derived from how it breaks down, is defended from breakdown and is, if possible, ultimately restored. Various phenomena (locally interpreted in various ways) indicate problems (symptoms) in people's internal adjustment and external adaptations and local ways of attempting to prevent, deal with, and relieve the corresponding discomforts and socially troubling behaviors. These symptoms and healing and control techniques can be asked about directly and are important clues about local personal and social organization. Included here are such things as indications of the presence of and contexts for generating "psychophysiological stress" (for example, anxiety, headaches, insomnia, sweating palms, poor appetite), "mental disorders" (as defined in local judgment, and/or in what seem to be some transculturally recognized form), and other symptoms of anxiety or depression, drinking and drugs, suicide, violence—and, in response to such things, local healing and problem-preventing practices.

Death

Ideas, feelings, and responses about the respondent's own death as well as the deaths of others are rich sources of information about self and identity, about orientations to time, ideas of guilt and punishment, about defense mechanisms, meanings of intimate relationships, aspects of aggression, and so on. These areas of investigation often show clearly the interplay between public doctrines and private orientations.

Emotion

As many studies (for example, Levy 1984) have shown, it is possible to approach feeling and emotion directly, by exploring categories, terminology, experience, behavior, and evaluations of the respondent in relation to a range of what the interviewer considers (taking account of local definitions) to be the domain of emotions. Such an approach is supplemented by (and often clarifies) accounts of emotional responses in respondents' stories about other matters, and by direct observations of respondents' reactions during the interviews.

Religion and the Supernatural

In early psychological anthropology, certain areas of local culture were thought of as "projections." These were areas that because of a lack of material constraints (in contrast to the reality-constrained procedures of, say, farming or fishing), were thought to reveal "deep" psychological orientations. Foremost among these projective areas were religion and its associated symbols, rites, and rituals. The opposition between realistic and projective culture is problematic, but the exploration of the respondent's understandings and uses of the culturally constituted realm of the "supernatural" is another rich source of psychocultural information. These personal understandings, uses, and experiences of the supernatural reveal meanings and functions of community religion that may be obscure at the level of cultural description. (See, for example, Levy's [1990:323–335] discussion of blood sacrifice in Bhaktapur and Hollan's [1996] analysis of spirit possession in Toraja.)

Fantasy, Creative Art, Dreams

Our discussion about "projective culture" is also relevant to the relatively private creations of fantasy, plastic or literary art, and dreams—projective activities generated or, at least, arranged out of cultural pieces by the respondent him- or herself.

Children

The respondent's discussion of his or her own children is a rich source of information on education, learning, morality, ideas of the self, etc. Ideas about what children are like and how they should be dealt with illuminate a good deal of the respondent's central orientations as well as providing clues to what formative experiences respondents had during their own childhoods (Levy 1996a).

Conducting the Interviews

Topic areas suggest what issues the person-centered interviews might be directed toward, but not how to actually conduct them, nor how to think about them. As we have noted, it is not only the particular topic areas that make these person-centered or respondent-oriented anthropological interviews, but also *how* the interviews are conducted. We now discuss how the interviews should be carried out.

The General Stance of the Interviewer

Perhaps the most basic technical matter in conducting interviews is the general stance of the interviewer toward the respondent. It closely resembles a familiar one in ordinary social interactions, the first phases of talking with a friend who has something important to discuss. One listens sympathetically and nonjudgmentally, drawing the friend out and trying to help him or her say what is on his or her mind. One doesn't break off the friend's report by changing the subject, by talking about oneself, by prematurely advising or moralizing, or by showing one's cleverness. One's responsibility in this phase of listening is (1) to facilitate the friend's communication; and (2) to try to fully understand what he or she is trying to communicate. The conversation with the concerned friend then may move on to a second stage— that of trying to be helpful. If it moves on too quickly to the advice stage, one suspects the listener-friend of not doing the job rightly, of being too egoistic.

For our purposes of trying to understand the respondent, the anthropological interview maintains itself in this first phase. Being helpful is not our present concern (at least in our immediate role as ethnographers)—although we have argued that skillful listening and interviewing seems, in itself, to be helpful to the respondent. But just how does a friend listen properly and encourage his or her partner's talking, thinking, and feeling? What are the interventions he or she uses? Here a discussion of specific elements of technique will be relevant; but we must first consider the basic problem of interview distortion.

Interview Distortion

The Need for Self-Monitoring

The validity, the nonfactitiousness, of loosely structured interviews depends almost entirely on the quality of the anthropologist's interviewing, its constant correction through feedback from studying the interviews, and from self-monitoring during the interviews. We are not concerned here with straightforward unskilled errors in technique (which can be corrected relatively easily). Rather, we are talking about *systematic* distortions in understanding that can profoundly bias an otherwise excellent technique, errors that good technique and skillful theoretical rhetoric, in fact, obscure. We may roughly differentiate two overlapping sorts of distortion of understanding—cognitive and motivated. We will say most about the latter.

"Cognitive distortion" is a misunderstanding of what is going on, based on the interviewer's prior intellectual experience with other kinds of people (than the respondent) and with other kinds of contexts (than the respondent's). At least some of this cognitive distortion is correctable through ordinary learning based on what is often a pleasurable and rewarding perception of correctable error. This corrective learning is, in fact, the whole point of the field study.

But distortion may be *motivated* to serve some personal need (including guarding some deeply and centrally organizing cognitive orientations). There is a significant difference here from simple ignorance. In the motivated case, the uncongenial true state of affairs may well be somehow known or intuited, stirring up defensive maneuvers and self-protective distortions generated within the interviewer, blunting or closing off threatening new understandings. *These motivated processes tend to signal themselves*. That is, if interviewers are attentive to their own sensations and responses, they can become aware of signs of the *process* of distortion while it is going on, although they may well be uncertain as to what, exactly, is going on.

During an interview, the interviewer may be aware that something "psycho-logical" is going on about which he or she is unclear—the unclarity being the point of the defensive operation. What the interviewer senses are abrupt and often mysterious alterations in his or her feelings. The interviewer perceives an alteration of his or her state of concentration, alertness, or interest and may feel anxious, bored, cloudy-minded, inattentive, irritated, excited, or whatever. The interviewer must struggle to understand what happened (either during the interview—in which case, a brief note of the response and of what seemed to be going on in the interview should be made—or later while listening to the tape recording of the interview). What was going on just before the disturbance? Was there a pattern to such feelings and alterations? Did they happen with certain kinds of respondents, with certain kinds of materials under discussion, with certain developments in relations with respondents?

It is difficult to grasp what is going on while an interview is taking place. Tape recordings (below) are invaluable—for two main reasons. (1) Listening to the recordings will usually make evident what was occurring at the time of altered awareness. While listening to the tape, the reaction may be generated again. (2) But the tapes have another kind of essential information on self-motivated distortion. They show the *effects* of these alterations on the interview process. For if the interviewer's first response to uncongenial material is a matter of feeling, the next response is liable to be an action, distorting the interview and suppressing the disturbing material.

There are various ways the interviewer may, more or less unconsciously, deflect the disturbing interview phenomena. For example, one may simply not hear what the respondent was trying to talk about, one may intervene to change the subject or deflect it, or one may signal one's own anxiety, anger, or disapproval in some (often quite subtle) way.

However they are produced, the distortions of the interview, and thus the understanding of what is going on, are usually evident when the tapes and transcripts are studied closely. In our experience in our own interviewing and in teaching interviewing, the (always embarrassing and painful) awareness of these distorting responses and maneuvers leads to significant self-corrections and learning.[13]

Guarding Against Forcing a Wished-for Response

It is essential that interviewers be particularly careful to be nondirective as they approach material that they sense they wish to make come out in a certain way, something, for example, that will serve to strengthen an attractive developing hypothesis or bolster a cherished world view. A kind of preemptive blandness is called for at these points.

Exaggerating the Fragility of the Interviewee

In other sections we comment on the sensitivity of certain topics that have to be recorded with care and sometimes avoided. Inexperienced interviewers sometimes, however, avoid topics of importance that they *inappropriately* fear are too sensitive.

For many, this is a matter of an exaggerated fear of the fragility of the respondent in regard to emotionally loaded material that might stir up feelings of anxiety, anger, or sadness. Clearly, interviewers can be brutal, sadistic, and insensitive. More likely, though, they will be much too cautious, and in so being (and by avoiding certain topics and by signaling back their anxiety to the interviewee, covertly entreating him or her to change the subject) close off the discussion of critically informative feelings, evaluations, concerns, and experiences.

Beginning the Interview Series, Introductory Topics

The interview series must start with topics and in a manner that seems natural to the respondent. Thus, we begin with locating data—the usual ways of getting to know someone—and in an informant mode. Examples might be "Where were you born?," "Where do you live now?," "Describe your house to me," "What do you do for a living?," "How do you spend a day," and the like—developed subsequently in some systematic way. The anthropologist asks for locating information, or information about the informant's corner of public culture, treating the interviewee as an expert informant. Follow-up questions at this stage are to expand informant information, and questions about feelings and private interpretations are avoided.

It's necessary at first to begin to map out via the informant mode the public world in which the informant exists, which is the world that provides the context for respondent studies. In the early phases, premature respondent-type interviewing would probably be unnecessarily disturbing to the interviewee. Shifts to the respondent mode come gradually over the set of interviews as the interviewer approaches more personal target topics, asks questions probing personal feelings and ideas, and uses open-ended interviewing. The shift will begin when some mutual trust, sympathy, and understanding has been built up. The early phase allows the interviewee and interviewer time to get to know one another, at least in a preliminary way.

Interventions and Open and Closed Probes

Open-ended interviews can be used in the early stages of investigating any socio-cultural phenomena (for example, to understand the range of a domain and the relative saliency of items in it—"Tell me about how people fish"), but such probes quickly lead to more focused, fact-finding questions. In person-centered, open-ended interviewing, there is a continuous back-and-forth movement between the open-ended probes and more specific questions.

The interviewer's responses in the interview may be called "interventions." One purpose of interventions is simply to keep the interview going—grunts and nods signaling that the interviewer is listening and interested serve this purpose; without such signals most interviews quickly dry up. But interventions—probes, questions, grunts, "uh huh," "go on," and the like—not only indicate attention, but are so placed as to guide the direction of the interview or to encourage the continuation of some topic.

As the introduction to this section notes, the ideal purpose of an open intervention (open in that it gives the interviewee maximum options in his or her response) is to encourage the interviewee to form the response as far as possible in terms of his or her personal organization. Closed interventions narrow the options for response, and often, but not necessarily, shift the response in the direction of objective, that is public, information. The openness or closedness of interventions is relative, on a continuum. Within the investigative arena of "mother" (all other areas having been for the moment closed off), "Tell me about your mother" is quite open; the interviewee must choose how to respond out of a large permissible universe of responses. "What did she look like?" is narrower, but there are still significant respondent choices. "What color hair did she have?" is still narrower and a function of the interviewee's descriptive competence, the interviewee now acting presumably mostly as an informant.

Interviewees are often at least mildly uncomfortable with very open-ended questions that tend to violate the expectations of normal dialogue. Respondents, anxious about the unfamiliar mode of questioning or unsure of the intent or linguistic competence of the anthropologist, may ask something like "Just exactly what about my childhood do you want to know?" Usually just repeating the question or slightly rephrasing it will produce a response, especially where interviewees are just checking to make sure that anthropologist really meant to be so vague.

The interview is not a debate, nor, properly speaking, a dialogue. At first, the respondent will try to deal with the interview in the mode of two-person conversation familiar to him or her, and the interviewer must tactfully deflect this into interview form. Respondents often pose polite questions to the interviewer such as "What do *you* think about this?," or "How do you folks do this?" Such questions can be temporarily deflected by a response like "Let's talk about this after the interview." Insofar as the respondent's question was dictated by politeness rather than curiosity, he or she will not bring it up after the interview, and the interviewer may want not to bring it up him- or herself, at least until the interview series is over.

While the discussion of an area is going on, the interviewer listens and signals that he or she is listening. The ability to listen attentively and accurately is critical to the interviewing process. This attentive listening not only helps the interviewer determine proper interventions, it also communicates to the respondent that the interviewer is interested in what he or she has to say. And it enables the interviewer to encourage the respondent further to elaborate on a particular topic by referring back to something already stated. Shy or fearful respondents who worry that they have nothing more of interest to say (or fear the interviewer is not hearing them properly) can be encouraged to go on by the interviewer asking, "A while ago you mentioned X. Could you tell me more about what that was like, how it felt, etc.?"

One of the hardest things for an inexperienced interviewer is to tolerate silence, the interviewee's and his or her own. Open interviews are full of silences, as the respondent wonders whether it is all right to go on and continue to monopolize the discourse, pauses to choose where to go next, or struggles internally with what he or she is about to say. If the silence persists too long, the interviewer may say something like, "Yes?," or "What are you thinking?," or "Why are you hesitating?"

If the interviewee's discussion of some topic really seems at an end, the interviewer must move on. If the respondent has been describing an event, a situation, a social form, he or she may now be asked questions that move the discussion further into the personal realm—"How did you feel about that?," or "What is your own opinion about that?," or "Do you agree with what people say about it?" If the interviewer feels the topic is temporarily exhausted, he or she may move to related topics, or, if warranted, to some quite different area, excusing abruptness with a remark such as, "Let's now talk about something else."

Sensitive Topics

Sometimes a topic that the interviewer senses may be uncomfortable for the respondent (for example, matters related to the body and sexuality or to moral behavior) can be approached indirectly. One can, for example, ask first "What do other people really do in these circumstances?," "What do wives really feel about their mothers-in-law?," "Do young men go with prostitutes?" These discussions of others' behavior prepare the interviewer and interviewee for the possible next probe, "What about you?"

There is another way of approaching some of the potentially delicate topics related to body-centered states, sexuality, menstruation, and some aspects of stress and emotion. People in most places are accustomed to talking about illness. Discussing the history of illness and the physical symptoms of what are locally taken to be effects of illness can serve as a natural entrance into discussions of other areas where physical states and bodily sensations are important.

Ending the Interview Series

Ending the interview series requires as much tact as beginning it. The respondent must be prepared for closing in previous interviews with, perhaps, something like, "There will just be a few more things we need to talk about, and then we'll be finished with these interviews."

A busy anthropologist who has been closely involved with a particular respondent for weeks might be tempted to suddenly drop the previous respondent when beginning with a new one. This would violate local (and universal) understandings of relationship and exchange. The anthropologist has to find ways of keeping the relationship going.

Number and Length of Interviews

How many interviews are necessary in the study of a respondent? How long should each interview take?

The distinction between informant and respondent is relevant in approaching these questions. An informant is asked to give systematically a set of verbal descriptions of local phenomena. This can be accomplished *comparatively* quickly. A respondent, on the other hand, is asked, in a sense, to *react* to a set of questions and probes.

It is the shifting play of these reactions that provide the materials for a growing understanding of the respondent's private world. And although only the coherent discursive statements of an informant are useful, almost any verbal and bodily behavior of the respondent may prove informative. In contrast to an informant's responses, those of a respondent do not get used up so quickly; they only begin to become uninformatively redundant and undemanding of further contextualizing after a large number of responses have been observed. It thus takes a number of interviews to discern patterns in the respondent's responses. Finally, it will also take a certain number of interviews to cover the list of the target topics that the anthropologist has chosen to cover.

The length of the interview series is an important technical tool in itself. The respondent's personal world becomes more and more clarified as he or she comes to trust the interviewer and rapport deepens; as he or she gets some sense of what these peculiar interviews are about; as he or she returns with different perspectives to major private concerns; and as public role behavior begins to shift to private, more intimate modes of response. The depth, significance, and honesty of respondent responses tends to grow over the course of a series of interviews. Inexperienced interviewers fear that they will run out of questions, that the interviews will become sterile, that the respondent will become annoyed. This is not what happens in well-conducted interviews where understanding deepens, and where, as we have noted, the respondent usually regrets having the series discontinued.

There are so many variables determining the length of the interview series that it is not possible to give more than very rough numbers. In our experience, depending one one's goals, something between 6 (if goals or time are limited) and 20 or more interviews may be reasonable. For special purposes (to check, for example, the generality of some form among some class of respondents), 1 or 2 interviews may be sufficient.

The question of the length of individual interviews is simpler—it is a question of how long the participants can pay close attention to each other. This is particularly problematic for the anthropologist who needs to be at his or her most alert. In our experience, it is difficult to be properly alert in a interview of more than an hour or so, although respondents' limited availability often requires that the interviewer be prepared to conduct longer interviews.

Recording and Transcribing the Interviews

Note Taking During the Interview

It is best to keep note taking to a minimum. Writing may interfere with paying attention and it sends signals (often wrong ones) to the respondent that whatever he and she is doing at the moment of note taking is more interesting than non-noted behaviors. This can skew the interview. Most notes about interviews will come from recall immediately after the interview and from the study of tape recordings.

However, it may be necessary to note certain matters briefly for mnemonic purposes, notes which can then be expanded in writing after the interview. These notes may include: (1) important *visual* aspects of the respondent's behavior (which, of course, would not be picked up by the tape recorder); (2) significant events and shifts in the interviewer's internal experience; and (3) guesses about some potentially illuminating and organizing hypothesis. These matters should be noted along with their context—that is, what seems to be happening in the interview at the moment. They should be recorded as briefly as possible.

Note Taking After the Interview

As soon as possible after each interview, written notes should be made. These should include a list of the topics covered in the interview, a list of new topics and questions suggested by the interview for later follow-up, an impression of the significant behavior of the respondent, comments on the interactions between interviewer and respondent, comments on visual behaviors, and comments on the interviewer's reactions to various parts of the interview. The written notes should attend to all the matters that the interviewer thinks might be missed or obscured in the details of the tape recordings.

Tape Recording

The most frequently used recording device for respondent interviews is tape recording. Tape recordings of well-conducted interviews contain an enormous amount of the kinds of information that allow interpretation of respondent-interviewer interactions and of the respondent's personal world. Although audio recordings obviously cannot capture the visual data of video recordings, we believe that respondents generally may find them to be less distracting and obtrusive.[14]

Listening to and transcribing tapes, particularly in the early stages of doing interviews, are excellent ways to improve language competence and to become aware of linguistic and interviewing mistakes. Problems in pronunciation, vocabulary, grammar, and intervention phrasing can be spotted, and, if necessary, clarified in discussions with local people.

Beyond their help in improving linguistic and interviewing skills, tape recordings are essential for capturing the content and the form of interviews and are the only way (aside from video recordings) to catch the kinds of micropatternings that are (as we shall see) essential phenomena for trying to understand the personal organization of respondents and their relations to their public cultures. Further, they are essential sources of information about the anthropologist's conscious and unconscious biases and the linguistic and cultural blind spots that may critically distort interviews.

Most beginning interviewers fear that tape recording may disturb respondents. In our experience, if respondents agree to be interviewed, the tape recorder is not usually an additional disturbance. The respondent must be able to trust the interviewer that his or her privacy and interests will be rigorously protected. If trust has been established, the tape recorder does not usually make a difference, especially after the respondent has gotten used to the recorder in the first interview or two. It is evident that the physical presence of the recorded tape is even more potentially dangerous in its transcription of potentially compromising materials than are written notes. It is sometimes necessary to turn off the tape recorder and make written (and coded) notes in discussing certain kinds of material.

Transcribing the Tapes

Logging the Tape

It is difficult to find your way around in tape-recorded material, especially to relocate important material after the tape is first heard. As you listen to the tape, it is necessary to make a written log locating all potentially significant data by means of the number on the tape counter. This preliminary logging is still a fairly crude locating index of important materials—one does not know what may be important until one has done later interviews with the respondent and with other respondents.

Written Transcriptions

The ideal way of working with tapes is to have written or typed transcriptions. These may be limited to those sections of the tape that the anthropologist thinks are important or may include the entire interview—which is often of great value during later study of material.[15]

The anthropologist will almost certainly need help to make full written transcriptions of tapes, because this requires a great deal of time and work. If at all possible, adequate money for the preparation of written transcriptions should be written into the grant budget. Sometimes linguists studying in the area may welcome the chance to transcribe interviews as samples of local linguistic forms. In some places, there are people working as professional scribes who would find transcription related to their usual work. Sometimes, on returning from the field, you can find people from the language area who are studying or working abroad and who may be willing to do the transcriptions. In all these cases, obviously, the greatest care must be used not to compromise the respondents. All sensitive materials must be protected, and it is often better not to have tapes dealing with certain subjects transcribed in written form.

Written transcriptions prepared by others are really only first drafts that have to be corrected and augmented while the interviewer listens to the tape. The transcriber will not be able to capture much of the significant audible material on the tapes that the anthropologist will need. The transcriber will clean up the tape, neglecting errors, stutterings, abrupt changes, and hesitations in the flow of discursive speech, essential data for respondent analysis. The written transcription must be corrected against the aural recording, and the interviewer must indicate the presence of significant formal auditory features of the tapes, features that reveal aspects of the state of the speaker and also how a segment of discourse is intended by the speaker to be understood. These additions require the development of a simple code for indicating significant auditory forms (for some suggestions for coding certain features, see Pittenger et al. 1960).

Analysis of the Interviews

Types and Levels of Meaningful Phenomena

The person-centered interview with its special topics and rhythms of open and closed questions *generates* the phenomena that the anthropologist must attend to and find ways of thinking about. We can sort some of the meaningful phenomena of the interviews into types and levels.

Content as Meaningful Story

The interviews are full of stories recounted in the surface text. These are in part directly meaningful, but their meaning is modified significantly in the light of the formal aspects of the stories and their disruptions and in the qualities of the voice in which they are recounted.

Because of our saturation in written texts and our habits of ordinary listening when we are considering speech as a report on reality (or as a story), we are most conscious of that part of a complex verbal communicative act that can be expressed as a written set of words—written in a certain way, with the hesitations and errors often treated as "noise" and filtered out both in transcription and, to a large degree, even in our hearing of the oral statement. This is what we usually think of as the text of a communication, of an utterance, of a conversation.[16]

There is much significant material in the story so heard, the story-in-itself, for the relations of individuals to their culture. "I think ritual animal sacrifice is wonderful now, but when I was young I could feel the sacrificial knife against my own throat, and I thought, if adults could do that to animals, what would they do to me if they ever got angry at me" (see Levy 1990:332ff). This is directly meaningful as a story. Meanings conveyed in the *form* of the story itself, in the *disruptions* of the story text, and in *how* it is told in its concrete telling are attended to by the interviewer in a sort of intuitive and "calibrating" mode as he or she listens to the story—and are often registered as peripheral impressions. These features are often lost in conventional written transcriptions and in paraphrases of respondents' stories. Different people are differentially sensitive to formal qualities of discourse. Not everyone is equally intuitive or "psychologically minded." But it is possible to get intuition and its sources under considerable methodological and intellectual control.

Meanings in the Organization of the Surface Text

As we listen to a story, a statement, an account, we often come to know more about it than what it seems to say on the surface. That extra knowing is often treated as being different from what we know from the surface discourse. We sense that "There is something strange about this," or "Now I understand what he is trying to say," or "He doesn't really mean what he is saying."

Some of this intuited meaning is in the organization of the story. The way the story is told at the level of story (in contrast to interferences and paralinguistic phenomena that are not at the level of the story itself and which we deal with below) gives us much information. These formal characteristics of the story itself are facilitated by the freedom to proceed in story telling, encouraged by open-ended interviewing. (Of course, some of these story forms are culturally conventional, but others have to do—also or instead—with personal organization.)

At the "level of the story," we would look, among other things, at the following: What are the themes of the stories? Are any themes habitually introduced early in the discussions of a range of topics? Are there repeated or obsessive themes? What are *not* talked about, if the context would have made talking about them expectable in some sense? Thus, in response to the relatively open query, "Tell me about your childhood family," it would be perhaps significant if, say, the respondent said nothing about his father. How are the themes related in the discourse? How does the story flow from one thematic area to another? Is it possible that these flowings show some logic of relationship and implication of different themes?

Disturbances of the Surface Text

Personal meanings play beneath the surface of the story and put pressure on the story as shown in the organization of themes. Aspects of personal meaning also show themselves as disruptions of the ideal and culturally and linguistically correct surface form. These disruptions are of various kinds. They are often missed in ordinary listening, often going by too rapidly, and tape recordings are essential here.

One of the classic kinds of disruption is "slips of the tongue," where an error erupts into the surface. A Tahitian village informant calling the missionary-introduced Christian god "they" instead of "he" (which she subsequently denied and was then embarrassed about when she heard it on the tape), seemed to suggest a submerged personal protopolytheistic sense of deity, a residue of old ideas and persisting family structure.

Most disruptions are not slips of the tongue in which some unexpected meaningful content appears at the verbal or phonemic level. They are rather hesitations, stammerings, interruptions, incompletions, or abrupt switches to a new direction. These suggest tensions and dynamics of organization that produce pressures on ideal discourse, which are often clarified by their locations in the story context. These disturbances must be indicated by some convention on the written transcriptions of the tape.

Another kind of disruption of ideal communication may be noted here. This is the matter of what the respondent makes of the interviewer's probes and questions. (We assume for this purpose that the probes and questions are correct in terms of local rules for communication.) Those interventions that are ignored, mishcard, or misinterpreted in comparison with the respondent's usual responses can be treated as potentially meaningful disturbances of communication.

Paralinguistic Phenomena

There is another set of phenomena, which overlaps in part "disruptions of communication." This is the set that has been called "paralinguistic" phenomena, qualities of voice, breath, resonance, pitch, etc., which indicate "the relation of the speaker to his utterance" as well as the kind of utterance it is to be taken to be (Pittinger et al. 1960). These are ways that we convey (in alliance with contextual and visible clues) that a verbal statement, for example, "I went to town this morning" is (variously) a declaration, a question, full of some special importance, the introduction to a ghost story, uncertain, sincere, ironic, and much more—and also what kind of emotion is involved in the statement—rage, sadness, joy, fear, etc.

It is our experience that most of these paralinguistic markers are universals or else directly readable cross-culturally because they are *iconic* signs (in C. S. Peirce's sense) or direct (or simulated) *indexes* of body states. These paralinguistic comments on the story text are relatively easy to grasp, and it is often possible in listening to tapes to locate the form (a quivering voice, a strong emphasis, a slowing of tempo, a quality of breathing) that is conveying the information.

Visual Phenomena

Much information about the respondent's momentary or characteristic organizat-ion (tension, stress, animation, excitement, relaxation, depression), information about emotion, about the meaning of some segment of speech, about the relations of cultural forms and private worlds, is visual—facial expression, body posture, and movements. If video tape isn't being used, the interviewer must make brief notes during the interview on what he or she observes—and expand them as soon after the interview as possible, trying to discern what is being signalled by visual phenomena, and ideally, exactly which visual phenomena convey the impression.

Some Miscellaneous Aspects of Analysis

Categorization of Personal Forms

We need a language to talk about—and think about—aspects of individuals and of social processes. When, focusing on the person at the center of some world, we begin to tell our stories about their stories, we use our common sense and its largely unexamined terms or categories—this is how he or she feels, thinks, copes. But when it is necessary to theorize beyond the first tentative theoretical modeling of the respondent's story, more practice-specific theoretical terms are required, terms derived from our professional intellectual history. The considerable danger of the terms bearing on the personal pole of social experience is, as we have noted, that they have an intrapsychic, within-the-head, bias and much a priori and hidden theoretical baggage. Nevertheless, with due caution, many of the standard items of personality psychology and more general psychology have proved productive as first approximations—with the caution that the anthropological task is to discover which items have to be added to, opened up, altered or, perhaps, rejected for the purposes of accounts of the differential effects of history and community on individuals, and individuals' effects, in turn, on that history and community.

Useful person-centered foci of theorization include such categories as self, identity, person, thinking, feeling and emotion, moral controls, defense mechanisms (to deal with problematic internal matters), and coping mechanisms (how an individual tries to deal with problematic external problems), and conscious and unconscious aspects of mind, unconscious forms being deduced by the interviewer from various forms of the respondent's discourse and behavior. (The reader is referred to the reference citations and to the vast literature of person-description for implications and use of these foci). In relation to the problem of unconsciousness, it is useful to try to distinguish a "cognitive unconscious," the inability to know things that are not named or cognitively discriminated by the local culture from a "dynamic unconscious," the repression of painful knowledge that is disruptive or uncongenial to the self.[17] Some of these categories can be approached directly as interview topics, but all of them can be discerned in the examination of various kinds of content and forms in the course of the interviews.

The Extent and Locus of Personal Forms

Suppose we perceive the respondent is, say, anxious. It makes a significant difference if he or she is anxious because of the *interview situation* in general, because of some aspect of his or her shifting or sustained *relationship* to the interviewer, because of the *topic* being discussed, or because anxiety is a diffuse *characterological* aspect of the respondent. Of course, these aren't necessarily independent, the anxiety may be due to a combination of factors—discussing a particular subject with this particular interviewer. A common source of error is to observe accurately but misplace or overgeneralize the significance of a behavior.

Expression Versus Communication

It is useful to attempt to make a distinction between expressive interview phenomena that indicate directly and unintendedly something about the state of the respondent (such as tearing, blushing, flushing, trembling and other involuntary meaningful acts) from acts intended as communication, intended to influence the auditor. Many behaviors, of course, are mixed, and it is possible to simulate purposely some expressive behavior for an intended communicative end. But it is also clear that some behaviors are relatively more shaped by personal organization, some more by the motivated use of some convention for the purposes of communicating an impression. Being able to distinguish between the two is essential to the analyses we wish to make.

A Note on Observations Outside of the Interview

Interviewers obviously meet interviewees to various extents outside of the interview. In a large and stratified community, they may meet only rarely; in a small village community respondents may be met every day and in a wide range of settings and situations. We can't deal here with observation of individuals in public contexts. These public behaviors must be brought into relation to interview behaviors and are, wherever available, essential sources for observing the consonances, conflicts, and transformations of behavior and discourse in different local settings.

Concluding Note

The main concern of person-centered interviewing and observation is to find ways to explore the relations—spaces, condensations, unities, divisions, transformations, tensions, and coercions—that operate in the interplay of more public realms of experience, situated at different distances in space and time from individuals, and the more private ones constituting and impacting immediately on individuals. How do these realms affect and construct each other? To what degree are they relatively autonomous?

The major difficulty in talking about how to do and think about person-centered studies is our heritage of folk, social science, and psychological conceptions. In its mainstream at least, this makes us separate person and context too neatly into different realms—the person and the community—and makes "person" too stable. This separation and reification of individual and context is based on only one aspect of our experience of living and has traditionally served to support many compelling moral, religious, and ideological purposes.

Another, and more peripheral, mood and ideology (shared by mystics and "classical" structuralists and poststructuralists) is to make the individual and individual agency an illusion, a node in some field of history or context.[18] The actual relations of individuals and individuality and agency to context vary according to different kinds of communities, different positions in each community, different individual temperaments, and different situations. This complex and shifting interplay is, however, more than a formless and ungraspable kaleidoscope of shifting shapes. These various forms and relations have explanations and are affected by the kinds of historical, communal, and personal forms that we know a good deal about. Person-centered ethnography is work in progress toward the slow empirical and conceptual elucidation of the interplay of social and personal forces.

NOTES

1. See Hollan and Wellenkamp (1994:3–7) and Hollan (In preparation) for a summary and critical analysis of early research in "culture and personality studies" and "psychological anthropology."

2. For programmatic notes on typological contrasts, see Levy (1989, 1994).

3. There is a vast literature on interviewing methods and procedures in the social sciences, for example, Kluckhohn (1945); Payne (1951); Merton et al. (1956); Kahn and Cannell (1957); Whyte (1960); Whyte and Whyte (1984); Richardson et al. (1965); Gorden (1975, 1992); Hyman and Cobb (1975); Bradburn and Sudman (1979); Spradley (1979); Garrett and Zaki (1982); Douglas (1985); Briggs (1986); Werner et al. (1987); Bernard (1988, 1994); McCracken (1988); Fontana and Frey (1994); Holstein and Gubrium (1995); Rubin and Rubin (1995).

4. For discussions of the interviewee as respondent, see Rogers (1942), Sullivan (1954), Pittenger et. al. (1960), Devereux (1967), and Greenson (1967).

5. For contemporary examples of studies based on person-centered interviewing in anthropology, see Levy (1973, 1977, 1990), Kracke (1978), Obeyesekere (1981), Herdt and Stoller (1990), Csordas (1994), Hollan and Wellenkamp (1994, 1996), and Parish (1994, 1996).

6. A closely related problem is how one judges that the interviewee is giving "objectively valid" information as an informant. This determination, always tentative, starts with an interpersonal skill that we use in all conversation. It is based on the interviewer's sense of consistency, a knowledge of other people's reports, a sense of the informant's biases and peculiarities—biases and peculiarities that, paradoxically, sometimes make the informant a more valid reporter than is a more "normal" informant.

7. See Levy (1973:509–511) and Hollan and Wellenkamp (1994:227–229, 1996:205–206) for more complete lists of interview topics.

8. It must be emphasized in this case and in general, that these "private" responses to public roles, may be deeply informative about such centrally social matters as, in this case, the dynamics and problems of authority and governance in a particular community.

9. This conception of "identity" derives largely from the works of Erik Erikson (1950, 1959, 1968).

10. This example is from a respondent in a Nepalese Hindu city. See Levy (1990:31, n. 11).

11. Possession phenomena are centrally relevant to these issues (Levy 1996b).

12. Parish (1994) is relevant to these issues.

13. In the early days of psychological anthropology, psychoanalytically inclined anthropologists, following the claims of the earliest psychoanalytic anthropologists such as Geza Roheim, occasionally proposed that extended psychoanalysis was necessary to avoid motivated distortions. Our experience has been that short and intensive training (during one semester) in tape-recorded practice interviewing with interviewees chosen because they have some interesting or exotic public social role, and with interviews focused on the interrelations between that public role and the informant's private world also serves this purpose. It alerts graduate students to problems in interviewing techniques, and to their habitual motivated distortions, and, particularly, to the perception of the signs and symptoms of the personal needs that lead to distortion.

14. People who use video recordings have a special set of technical and methodological problems that we are unqualified to deal with. The present chapter is relevant to such recordings, but there are obviously extensive additional problems of administration and analysis.

15. Levy used completely transcribed written copies of all interviews in his work in Tahiti and Nepal.

16. Such texts were characteristic of life history accounts in anthropology and provide a limited kind of information.

17. This distinction is related to our discussion of the difference between cognitive distortion and motivated distortion.

18. For a discussion of individual agency versus sociocultural determinism, see Levy (In press).

REFERENCES

Bernard, H. Russell. 1988. *Research Methods in Cultural Anthropology*. Thousand Oaks, CA: Sage Publications.

Bernard, H. Russell. 1994. *Research Methods in Anthropology: Qualitative and Quantitative Approaches*, 2d ed. Walnut Creek, CA: AltaMira Press.

Bradburn, Norman M., and Seymour Sudman. 1979. *Improving Interview Method and Questionnaire Design*. San Francisco: Jossey-Bass.

Briggs, Charles L. 1986. *Learning How To Ask: A Sociolinguistic Appraisal of the Role of the Interview in Social Science Research*. New York: Cambridge University Press.

Csordas, Thomas J. 1994. *The Sacred Self: A Cultural Phenomenology of Charismatic Healing*. Berkeley: University of California Press.

Devereux, George. 1967. *From Anxiety to Method*. New York: Humanities Press.

Douglas, Jack D. 1985. *Creative Interviewing*. Beverly Hills, CA: Sage Publications.

Erikson, Erik. 1950. *Childhood and Society*. New York: W. W. Norton

Erikson, Erik. 1959. Identity and the Life Cycle. *Psychological Issues 1*(1). New York: International Universities Press.

Erikson, Erik. 1968. *Identity: Youth and Crisis*. New York: W. W. Norton.

Fontana, Andrea, and James H. Frey. 1994. Interviewing: The Art of Science. In *Handbook of Qualitative Research*. Norman K. Denzin, Yvonna S. Lincoln, eds. Pp. 361–376. Thousand Oaks, CA: Sage Publications.

Garrett, Annette Marie, and Elinor P. Zaki. 1982. *Interviewing, Its Principles and Methods*, 3d ed., rev. by Margaret M. Mangold and Elinor P. Zaki. New York: Family Service Association of America.

Gorden, Raymond L. 1975. *Interviewing: Strategy, Techniques, and Tactics*, rev. ed. Homewood, IL: Dorsey Press.

Gorden, Raymond L. 1992. *Basic Interviewing Skills*. Itasca, IL: F. E. Peacock Publishers.

Greenson, Ralph R. 1967. *The Technique and Practice of Psychoanalysis*. New York: International Universities Press.

Herdt, Gilbert, and Robert J. Stoller. 1990. *Intimate Communications: Erotics and the Study of Culture*. New York: Columbia University Press.

Hollan, Douglas W. 1996. Cultural and Experiential Aspects of Spirit Beliefs among the Toraja. In *Spirits in Culture, History, and Mind*. Jeanette Mageo and Alan Howard, eds. Pp. 213–235. London and New York: Routledge.

Hollan, Douglas W. In preparation. Developments in Person-Centered Ethnography. In *The Psychology of Cultural Experience*. H. Mathews and C. Moore, eds. New York: Cambridge University Press.

Hollan, Douglas W., and Jane C. Wellenkamp. 1994. *Contentment and Suffering: Culture and Experience in Toraja*. New York: Columbia University Press.

Hollan, Douglas W., and Jane C. Wellenkamp. 1996. *The Thread of Life: Toraja Reflections on the Life Cycle*. Honolulu: University of Hawaii Press.

Holstein, James A., and Jaber F. Gubrium. 1995. *The Active Interview*. Qualitative Research Methods Series, Vol. 37. Thousand Oaks, CA: Sage Publications.

Hyman, Herbert H., and William J. Cobb. 1975. *Interviewing in Social Research*. Chicago: University of Chicago Press.

Kahn, Robert L., and Charles F. Cannell. 1957. *The Dynamics of Interviewing*. New York: Wiley.

Kluckhohn, Clyde. 1945. The Personal Document in Anthropological Science. In *The Use of Personal Documents in History, Anthropology, and Sociology*. L. Gottschalk et al., eds. Pp. 79–173. New Science Research Council Bulletin 53.

Kracke, W. 1978. *Force and Persuasion: Leadership in an Amazonian Society*. Chicago: University of Chicago Press.

Levy, Robert I. 1973. *Tahitians: Mind and Experience in the Society Islands*. Chicago: University of Chicago Press.

Levy, Robert I. 1977. Tahitian Gentleness and Redundant Controls. In *The Socialization of Aggression*. Ashley Montagu, ed. Pp. 222–235. Oxford: Oxford University Press.

Levy, Robert I. 1984. Emotion, Knowing and Culture. In *Culture Theory: Essays on Mind, Self, and Emotion*. Richard A. Shweder and Robert A. LeVine, eds. Pp 214–237. Cambridge: Cambridge University Press.

Levy, Robert I. 1989. The Quest for Mind in Different Times and Different Places. In *Social History and Issues in Human Consciousness*. Andrew Barnes and Peter Stearns, eds. Pp. 3–40. New York: New York University Press.

Levy, Robert I. 1990. *Mesocosm: The Organization of a Hindu Newar City in Nepal*. Berkeley: University of California Press.

Levy, Robert I. 1994. Person-Centered Anthropology. In *Assessing Cultural Anthropology*. Robert Borowsky, ed. Pp. 180–187. New York: McGraw Hill.

Levy, Robert I. 1996a. Essential Contrasts; Differences in Parental Ideas about Learners and Teaching in Tahiti and Nepal. In *Parents' Cultural Belief Systems*. Sarah Harkness and Charles Super, eds. Pp. 123–142. New York: Guilford Publications.

Levy, Robert I. 1996b. Gods, Spirits and History: A Theoretical Perspective. In *Spirits in Culture and Mind*. Jeannette Mageo and Alan Howard, eds. Pp. 11–28. London and New York: Routledge.

Levy, Robert I. In press. Selves in Motion. In *Selves in Time and Place: Identities, Experience and History in Nepal*. Debra Skinner, Al Pach, and Dorothy Holland, eds. Lanham, MD: Rowman and Littlefield.

McCracken, Grant David. 1988. *The Long Interview*. Qualitative Research Methods Series, Vol. 13. Thousand Oaks, CA: Sage Publications.

Merton, Robert K., Marjorie Fiske, and Patricia L. Kendall. 1956. *The Focused Interview: A Manual of Problems and Procedures*. Glencoe, IL: Free Press.

Obeyesekere, Gananath. 1981. *Medusa's Hair: An Essay on Personal Symbols and Religious Experience*. Chicago: University of Chicago Press.

Parish, Steven M. 1994. *Moral Knowing in a Hindu Sacred City*. New York: Columbia University Press.

Parish, Steven M. 1996. *Hierarchy and Its Discontents*. Philadelphia: University of Pennsylvania Press.

Payne, Stanley L. 1951. *The Art of Asking Questions*. Princeton: Princeton University Press.

Pittinger, Robert E., C. F. Hockett, and J. J. Danehy. 1960. *The First Five Minutes: A Sample of Microscopic Interview Analysis*. Ithaca: Paul Martineau.

Richardson, Stanley A., Barbara S. Dohrenwend, and David Klein. 1965. *Interviewing: Its Forms and Functions*. New York: Basic Books.

Rubin, Herbert J., and Irene S. Rubin. 1995. *Qualitative Interviewing: The Art of Hearing Data*. Thousand Oaks, CA: Sage Publications.

Rogers, Carl. 1942. *Counseling and Psychotherapy*. New York: Houghton Mifflin.

Spradley, James P. 1979. *The Ethnographic Interview*. New York: Holt, Rinehart and Winston.

Sullivan, Harry S. 1954. *The Psychiatric Interview*. New York: W. W. Norton.

Werner, Oswald, G. Mark Schoepfle, and Julie Ahern. 1987. *Systematic Fieldwork*. Thousand Oaks, CA: Sage Publications.

Whyte, William Foote. 1960. Interviewing in Field Research. In *Human Organization Research*. Richard N. Adams and Jack J. Preiss, eds. Pp. 352–374. Homewood, IL: Dorsey Press.

Whyte, William Foote, and Katherine King Whyte. 1984. *Learning from the Field: A Guide from Experience*. Beverly Hills, CA: Sage Publications.

SUSAN C. WELLER

Eleven

Structured Interviewing and Questionnaire Construction

Introduction and Overview

Studies of humans can be based on different forms of information: observations, archival records, and interviews. I focus here on developing interview materials for studies that rely on direct informant-based information. The chapter is organized by interview *purpose*; I describe different approaches to interviewing and questionnaire construction within the context of the overall study goals. The best format for a question or series of questions depends on the type of information desired. In general, the less that is known about an area, the more appropriate are unstructured, open-ended methods. The same is true with interviewing.

The initial stage of any project should include a descriptive exploration of the topic under study. A variety of strategies are available for conducting semistructured individual or group interviews. Your goal is to develop a set of items relevant to the area of interest and to the people to be interviewed. This phase may elicit a set of relevant items for further inquiry or generate descriptive cultural models.

The second stage incorporates the results into structured interview materials for systematic examination. In anthropology, descriptive information may be used to design a detailed study of cultural models, assertions, or beliefs. In cross-cultural psychology, descriptive results may be used to modify existing materials (for example, standardized scales) or to check their validity. A combination of initial descriptive exploration and subsequent systematic interviewing produces a study superior to one based on either method alone, although it involves a greater commitment of time and energy.

Projects that rely solely on either responses to open-ended questions or to a series of agreement rating scales can be biased and thus inaccurate. Responses to open-ended questions are limited by memory bias: People can *recall* fewer items (reasons, cases, etc.) than they can *recognize* when presented with a complete list of relevant items. This means that spontaneous, unstructured requests for information, while retrieving important information, may not retrieve all of it. When a respondent doesn't mention a particular item, it may mean that the item is unimportant or that it's been forgotten. Also, some informants provide long, detailed answers while others give short ones. Using different probes or different amounts of probing across individuals effectively changes the questions and makes it difficult to compare responses across individuals.

Using a standardized list of items or set of statements helps you minimize or avoid the problem of obtaining inconsistent or noncomparable data across informants and helps you make systematic comparisons across individuals and groups. However, if the questions or items to be explored are generated by you and not preceded by descriptive interviewing, the interview may focus on items of interest to you and may misrepresent or entirely miss topics of importance to informants. A preferable approach is to combine both methods: Use open-ended questions to explore a topic and develop an understanding of relevant questions and responses, then collect further systematic data based on the responses.

In the second phase of a study, you develop structured interview materials to examine in detail knowledge, attitudes, beliefs, and reported practices. A variety of question formats are available. For example, most interview-based studies contain some *general information* questions covering sociodemographic characteristics of the respondent. These questions can be constructed in a variety of formats (close ended, multiple choice, or open ended) and are designed to collect specific information like gender, religious affiliation, racial/ethnic identity, age, years of education, number of children, etc. There may also be questions about behaviors ("In the last year, how many times did you visit a doctor?") or relationships ("Name the people with whom you have discussed important personal matters during the past six months.").

Another type of study where questions are used is in assessment of *knowledge*. Knowledge tests evaluate the degree to which an individual or group possesses knowledge about a particular topic. You may construct tests with multiple choice, true/false, or open-ended questions. A specific assumption of a knowledge test is that the correct answer to each question is known, so that respondents' answers may be scored as correct/incorrect.

A related type of study assesses *attitudes*. Attitudinal studies attempt to measure the degree to which individuals demonstrate a specific a priori defined concept that is usually psychological, such as authoritarianism, feminine role identity, accultura-tion, or aggressiveness. The most common format for such studies is to have a series of statements, with a rating scale for each; respondents are asked to express their relative agreement with each statement. Similar to knowledge tests, responses are "scored" according to the a priori defined standard or criterion.

A fourth type of study describes the categories or dimensions people use to discriminate among items in a set to describe their *classification* of items. Classification studies try to uncover respondents' dimensions of discrimination rather than assess their adherence to a priori defined dimensions. You ask informants to compare items in terms of their similarity without reference to any specific dimensions or criteria. Formats appropriate for collecting similarity data include: pile-sorting tasks (items are sorted into piles according to their similarity); paired-comparisons of items (similarity is rated on a rating scale); and triadic comparisons of items (respondents pick the most different item from a set of three). Classification procedures are often used to study relations or structure in a face-to-face or closed-group social network.

Finally, the purpose of a study may be to describe the *beliefs* of a group of respondents. Whereas classification studies examine respondents' beliefs (such as how they divide up the world into sets and subsets), beliefs may be examined in greater depth by administering a series of related questions on a single topic. For example, questions might refer to attributes relevant to a specific topic or to assertions contained in a cultural model. Question formats differ from those appropriate for classification studies and include: open-ended, multiple choice, ordered or ranked items, and interval or frequency estimate questions.

Classification and belief studies depart meaningfully from knowledge and attitudinal studies in how informants' responses are handled. In classification and belief studies, responses are not recoded or scored against a predetermined standard. Thus, while many formats are applicable across a variety of study purposes, not all formats lend themselves to every purpose.

Phase I: Exploratory Interviewing and Item Generation

The first phase of a project should be about gaining a broad understanding of the area of study. Without general background knowledge, it's impossible to know what questions are appropriate. So, depending on how familiar you are with the topic and informants, begin with unstructured and semistructured interviews and progress to more structured ones. Initial interviews may explore a topic in general to gain broad understanding of the topic and terminology. The first step in this phase of interviewing, however, focuses on learning whether your topic is relevant to the population and discovering the "right" questions to ask. Spradley's books (1970, 1979) are helpful in this phase. After eliciting the information, you may use it to develop new interview materials or to check the appropriateness of existing materials.

Results of the initial interviews may be used to modify existing materials or to develop new ones. Items should be elicited from informants in their own words. (Without such elicitation, items may reflect your ideas and not theirs.) The set of items is sometimes called a semantic or cultural "domain." A domain is a set of related words, concepts, or statements about a single theme. The set typically is defined as the items with the highest agreement across informants. Examples of domains include: color terms (Berlin and Kay 1969; Kay 1975), plants (Berlin et al. 1974), kinship terms (Romney and D'Andrade 1964), animals (Henley 1969; Rummelhart and Abramson 1973), illnesses (Frake 1961; D'Andrade et al. 1972; Lieberman and Dressler 1977; Young 1978; Weller 1983, 1984); types of pain (Moore et al. 1986); and emotions (Fillenbaum and Rapoport 1971; Romney et al. 1997).

Free-Recall Listing

Free-recall listing is a technique where an open-ended question is used to obtain a list or partial set of items from each informant. (What kinds of _____ s are there? Name all the _____ s you know.) The goal is to get a comprehensive sample of items. Some domains may be predefined with items belonging to a clear set, like months of the year or days of the week. Usually, however, the boundaries are unknown, and you use interview responses to define the set and its boundaries.

After deciding on a general subject, you have to find a meaningful question. Some areas or topics are so clearly defined that a single question can elicit domain items. Such a question is usually of the form, "Name all the Xs that you know of." For example, in a study comparing the perception of illnesses by urban Guatemalan and U.S. women, Weller (1984) began by eliciting a set of illness terms well known to the informants. To do this, Weller asked 20 women in each country to name all the illnesses that they knew (and to describe each). In the United States she said, "I would like you to name illnesses or expressions for being sick. Could you please tell me all the diseases or illnesses that you can think of?"

Table 1 shows the distribution of response frequencies for the U.S. sample for items mentioned by three or more respondents. Note the number of respondents mentioning each item: The first item was mentioned by three-fourths of the sample; 6 items were mentioned by about half (9/20) of the sample; and 30 items were mentioned by at least 15% (3/20) of the respondents. The 30 items formed the set of items for further interviews with U.S. women.

You may ask questions in a variety of formats. A series of related questions may elicit more exhaustive lists from informants. Some informants may perceive such a series as being all the same, but others respond differently to each question and provide detailed responses to some questions and not to others. In a study of women's preferences for different infant-feeding methods, Weller and Dungy (1986)

TABLE 1
American-English Illness Terms

Frequency	Disease Term	Frequency	Disease Term
15	Cancer	5	Scarlet Fever
13	Mumps	5	Venereal Disease
12	Measles	4	Arthritis
9	Chicken Pox	4	Migraine
9	Leukemia	4	Whooping Cough
9	Tuberculosis	3	Diphtheria
7	Diabetes	3	Headache
7	Multiple Sclerosis	3	Hepatitis
7	Pneumonia	3	Mental Illness
6	Cold	3	Mononucleosis
6	Flu	3	Rubella
6	Muscular Dystrophy	3	Smallpox
5	Emphysema	3	Strep Throat
5	Heart Disease	3	Stroke
5	Polio	3	Ulcers

used a series of questions to tap the set of reasons that might influence a woman to either breast- or bottlefeed. Weller and Dungy asked multiple questions of each informant, to capture positive and negative aspects of each feeding method. In all, each woman was asked 18 related questions.

> Please tell me the reasons why you want to breastfeed.
> Why do you think some people breastfeed?
> Why did you decide not to bottlefeed?
> What are the advantages of breastfeeding?
> What are the disadvantages of breastfeeding?
> What are all the things you like about breastfeeding?
> What are all the things you *dislike* about breastfeeding?
> When is breastfeeding appropriate?
> In what situations would you *not* want to breastfeed?
> (THEN, each question was repeated, substituting bottlefeeding for breastfeeding.)

A related format, when using multiple questions, is contrasting questions. Here, items may be compared (in pairs) and informants asked about their distinguishing features. Young (1980) used this format to study health care choices. To elicit reasons for choosing a particular health care source, he asked informants why they might go to a doctor and *not* a pharmacist, why/when they would consult a folk healer and *not* a doctor, etc. Such questions help get more details than "Why/when would you go to a doctor?" or "Why/when would you go to a folk healer?"

Informant-generated lists can be supplemented with items from other sources. In a study of possible cultural differences in the definition of punishment and child abuse, "punishment" items listed by Anglo and Hispanic adolescents were supplemented with examples of physical abuse (Weller et al. 1987). Because Hispanics appeared in the child-abuse registries at a rate exceeding that of Anglos, the study sought to discover if the difference was due to a greater use and possible acceptance of corporal punishment among Latinos or if there might be bias in reporting statistics. Interviews conducted with Anglo and Hispanic adolescents explored adolescent "misbehaviors" and "adult disciplinary responses." Verbatim responses of 29 Anglo and 27 Hispanic adolescents (with approximately equal numbers of males and females) were recorded. Each interview took one–two hours to complete and consisted of open-ended free-listing questions, descriptive answers, and probes by interviewers to seek further explanations. The following issues were explored:

1. "What things do you (or other teenagers) do that make your parents/mother/father/adults/etc., angry?"
2. (For each response to the previous question)
   "When you do _____, what do your parents, etc., do?"
3. "What other things might be likely to make adults upset or angry?"
4. (For each item mentioned) "And if _____ makes adults/etc., angry, what might they do in response?"

To elicit as exhaustive a list as possible for each question, Weller et al. (1987) changed the question slightly and asked it again as informants exhausted their list. These questions elicited two related lists: the set of things teenagers do and the set of things adults do in response. Weller et al. tabulated the responses across all 56 adolescents. Because extreme forms of punishment and abuse are infrequent enough so that they would not be expected to appear in such a small sample size, a list of the most frequently reported forms of physical abuse were incorporated into the list of items from the log of the university hospital emergency room.

Informants should be able to generate lists of about a dozen items. If lists are short, try probing more. Avoid asking questions that can be answered with "yes" or "no." Rather than asking, "Are there any more ___s?," say, "You said that ____ and ____ are kinds of ____s. What other kinds of ____s are there?" This reminds the informant what he or she was thinking and conveys the message that you're looking for a more complete listing. If such probes fail to generate richer lists, you might try a different format for the focus of the question, by using multiple or contrasting questions, or try an altogether different focus. It is possible that the "set" may exist in your mind, but not in those of the informants.

Record responses verbatim. Clarify all ambiguous phrases and thoughts. You want to elicit statements or themes that are clear so that only one meaning is conveyed (for example, if a statement is repeated to others, they will understand the *exact* meaning implied by the informant). In the infant-feeding study, some women said that they had chosen breastfeeding because it was "convenient." Others said they had chosen bottlefeeding because *that* was "convenient." Further probing revealed that the breastfeeders meant that they could feed their infant without having to prepare or clean bottles and the bottlefeeders meant that they could feed their baby anywhere without exposing their breasts. Thus, the latter statements more clearly expressed the reasons for choosing a particular feeding method. A goal in recording responses is to be sure that you have captured the essence or underlying meaning *in the informants' own words*, so that you may use specific statements, phrases, and idioms in subsequent interviews.

Responses should also be at the same level of contrast. Simply, there should not be any set-subset relationships among items in a list. Suppose an informant is asked to name fruits and the list contains the following: berries, strawberries, blueberries, oranges, lemons, and citrus fruits. Further questioning should clarify possible relationships among items on the list: "Is a berry a kind of strawberry? Is a strawberry a kind of blueberry? . . . Is a berry a kind of citrus fruit?" Responses should clarify the relationships and would eliminate berries and citrus fruits from the list. Alternatively, asking "What *kinds* of fruits are there?" may elicit classes or subtypes of fruit. The taxonomic relationships among items in a set may be elicited through detailed interviewing about what *kinds* of things there are in the world (see section below on Taxonomic Elicitation).

Unique, verbatim answers are tabulated across respondents. Tabulate answers *by informant*, not by question. This is especially important when using multiple questions to elicit items, so that when someone mentions something more than once, it is counted only once—for that informant. The final tabulation list, then, should reflect the number of people who mentioned each item.

The final statements should be in clear language with consistent syntax. Statements should convey the same meaning to each and every reader. In the infant-feeding study, Weller and Dungy (1986) chose the 18 most frequently mentioned themes from the English-speaking Anglo and the Spanish-speaking Hispanic lists for study. They used two separate statements to capture the notion of convenience. They changed all statements to a neutral form: "A way to feed your baby that . . ." The list was balanced, so that half of the items referred to breast- and half to bottlefeeding; half contained "positive" attributes and half "negative" ones. Although the list had a culled and modified set of the multitude of statements collected, the language and ideas were concordant with those in the original interviews.

The necessary sample size for open-ended interviews is a function of variability. This is true for both qualitative and quantitative research. The less variation there is (that is, the more homogeneous the responses), the fewer informants are necessary. With high agreement and repetitive responses across informants, a small sample size may suffice. For some domains, a sample size of 10 may be sufficient; for other domains, or for increased accuracy, sample sizes of 50 or more may be needed. Typically, about 20 informants is adequate. As the number of interviewed informants increases, say in increments of 5, a point will be reached where little new information is added. Thus, the sample size is adequate when the addition of new informants doesn't alter the frequency distribution of items.

By attempting to get a *list* of items from each informant, more information is obtained per informant and fewer informants are needed. With a meaningful question, each informant should be able to generate a list of approximately 10 items (6–14 items). Agreement on items, statements, or themes is estimated by counting the number of informants that mentioned each. The set or domain is defined for the group by the overlap across informants. The most frequently mentioned items are the most salient ones interviewed. Psychologists have shown that the most salient items will be named by more people and those will appear higher up in individual lists. While the set of items obtained with free-recall listing is not necessarily definitive or complete, it should nevertheless capture well-recognized items.

Group Interviews

Lists generated from group interviews do not necessarily reflect the thoughts of each person. Individual lists generated in a group setting are not independent because of interaction among informants. Thus, only one list is generated per group. An exception to this is the initial request for written free-recall lists from individuals and the collection of the lists, *before* any discussion begins. When lists are collected after discussion begins, sample size is the number of groups and not the total number of individuals in the groups.

Taxonomic Elicitation

Structured interviews may be used to elicit an entire taxonomy from a single (or multiple) informant(s). General questioning of the sort, "What kinds of ___s are there?" with comparative and contrastive questions like, "Is ___ a ___?" can be used to construct a taxonomy of domain items. This form of questioning and the resultant description or model of beliefs can be seen in the work of Meztger and Williams (1963a, 1963b, 1966), Frake (1961), and Conklin (1969). This type of interviewing is excellent for mapping-out terminology (especially in a new language) and gaining an understanding of the interrelations among items. Interviews may focus on collecting all terms related to a particular topic. For example, Frake elicited all illness terms in the Subanum language (the lexicon) and identified features that distinguished classes of illnesses. Berlin et al. (1974) detailed indigenous knowledge of plants, and Berlin and Kay (1969) described color terms. Kay (1977) described a taxonomy of kinds of illnesses for Mexican Americans, and Spradley (1970) described kinds of "drunks."

Narratives and Cultural Models

Another way to learn about a topic or domain is to collect narratives or individual accounts (case histories). Common themes can then be extracted from textual materials and studied. Quinn (1987) created a descriptive account or "model" of American beliefs about marriage based on informants' descriptions of it. Chavez et al. (1995) recorded descriptions of possible cancer etiologies and used the common or recurring themes across informants to compare beliefs across different informant groups. Kempton, Boster, and Hartley (1995) also began their study of U.S. environmental beliefs by collecting narratives and then systematically explored the salient themes.

Narrative analyses can only *suggest* possible interconnections and relationships among themes. Unstructured methods of interviewing are excellent for suggesting hypotheses, but you need systematic data to test the validity of observations and to make comparisons across groups. Personal narratives sometimes yield more detail on a single case, but typically require a larger sample size to cover the breadth of cases. For example, interviews with individuals about "all the illnesses they know" can uncover information on the diagnosis, symptoms, and treatments for a variety of illnesses. In contrast, a detailed case history of the last illness case that occurred in the household collects information on only one case of one illness. Furthermore, it's difficult to get case information on rare events. The appropriate sample size for collecting narrative materials—as with any technique—is determined by the degree of homogeneity in the sample. If a high degree of redundancy (say 50%–75% overlap in themes) is reached within a homogeneous category of informants (for example, gender and SES), then only a few interviews (say 10–20 informants) may be necessary. However, as with all interviewing, sample size minimums apply to each category (gender and/or SES groupings) of informants.

Phase II: Structured Interviewing Techniques and Questionnaire Construction

After you establish the items for study, you can pursue a more structured interview format. Open-ended, semistructured formats facilitate the collection of new information, providing the flexibility to explore different topics in-depth with different informants. Meaningful comparisons across people may not be possible, however; informants have been encouraged to discuss different items, so they haven't really been asked the "same" questions. Structured formats let you make comparisons across people and groups.

In this section, I describe a variety of question formats. The focus is on designing interview materials (questions, tests, and tasks) appropriate for the goal of the study. Thus, the section is organized by study purpose: general information questions, knowledge tests, attitude scales, classification studies, and assessment of cultural beliefs.

General Information Questions

Most studies collect general information. Questions in such studies may be straightforward requests for information: age, gender, ethnicity, household composition, length of residency, and reports of familial practices. Some questions provide information about respondents' sociodemographic characteristics. These questions most closely parallel those found in surveys.

The term "survey," however, is often used to refer to a combination of methodologies: the selection of respondents, method of interviewing, and questionnaire design (Fowler 1993). Sampling procedures in survey research usually focus on different procedures for selecting a *random* sample. There are many disadvantages to nonrandom or convenience samples (for example, they may not be representative and it's impossible to estimate the degree of bias that they contain). Nevertheless, convenience samples can sometimes be useful, especially when they're chosen from specific segments of the population (Johnson 1990).

The method of interviewing refers to whether interviews are conducted in person, on the phone, or by mail. In-person or face-to-face interviews may be administered by an interviewer or be self-administered and tend to have the highest participation rates. Phone interviews can only be administered by an interviewer, but may be computer assisted by having the questionnaire on a computer. With computer-assisted telephone interviews (known as CATI in the sociological literature), the interviewer enters responses directly into a computer. Mail interviews must be self-administered. More complex responses can be obtained in face-to-face interviews, with the use of visual aids, if necessary. Questions and responses must be simplified for oral/phone presentation. Self-administered open-ended questions usually do not produce useful information, due to the lack of probing for clarification.

Participation rates for the three different approaches parallel their costs. In general, face-to-face interviews have the highest participation rates and are the most expensive. Phone and mail methods tend to be less expensive, but also have lower rates of participation. As follow-up procedures (call backs and remailings) are intensified, phone and mail participation rates (and costs) increase. A minimal participation rate of 75% is required for surveys contracted by the U.S. government.

The biggest weakness in questionnaire design occurs when an investigator drafts a set of questions without sufficient background. The result is often a set of poorly worded questions with unclear response categories. Sociologists and psychologists have spent an enormous amount of time studying the effect of different wordings and orders of questions. The interactive context of an interview has long been recognized and studied by sociologists. It's a waste of research effort not to take advantage of their experience and knowledge. Recommendations on wording and ordering of items can be found in the sociology literature. See, for example, Sudman and Bradburn's (1982) book *Asking Questions?* or the Sage Series, *The Survey Kit* (Fink 1995). It's worth investing a weekend or a full week to review some of these materials.

Question formats include: open-ended, close-ended multiple choice, and rating scales. Open-ended questions should be simple and seek clear, short answers. For example, "What was your age at your last birthday?," "What is your birthdate?," or "How many times have you been to the hospital this year?" Social network information may be requested from informants who do not have overlapping networks and who are not necessarily describing the same people with questions that parallel those used in the General Social Survey (Burt [1984] appends the actual questions). Close-ended questions should be concise, with a complete listing of mutually exclusive response categories. Rating scales are usually appropriate only for literate informants with a moderate degree of education, although they may be simplified sufficiently to be handled in an oral interview (Weller and Romney 1988).

In general, questions should proceed from broad, general requests for information to those requesting specific or more detailed information. This is done so that questions requesting detailed information don't bias responses for more general information. Similarly, less personal questions should precede those perceived as more private or threatening. Questions requesting sociodemographic information may be asked initially, especially if they help establish whether the informant fits the study's inclusion criteria. Some sociodemographic questions may be asked at the very end of the interview, as is often done with questions in the United States regarding income.

Inclusion and exclusion criteria for interviewing informants should be part of the study design or protocol. If you want to study Latina women, then before interviewing anyone you should define who is and who is not a Latina woman. Thus, the initial questions may seek to establish the informant's gender, ethnicity (by self-report and possibly by birthplace and language preference), and age (in years or parental status). The advantage of having all inclusion and exclusion criteria-related questions first is that an interview may be terminated quickly for people who don't meet study criteria. Sometimes, though, it may be necessary to collect some information on the excluded individuals so that they are not offended by a short interview.

Only questions relevant to the study should be included in the interview (that is, factors implicated by theory, factors mentioned in the literature, and factors that might potentially affect results). Too often, extraneous questions are included without considering how responses will be handled. For example, a question on marital status ("Are you married, single, divorced, or widowed?") might be included, but if you're really interested in whether a woman is living with the father of her child, then a direct question about that would provide more useful information. Still, it's best to ask too many rather than too few questions: A question/answer can always be ignored after it's collected but it's usually difficult or impossible to go back and ask a question that was omitted inadvertently.

If you want to know how your sample compares with a larger population, use questions from large or national surveys. Not only can you compare responses with those in the larger survey, but you can take advantage of the time and effort that went into the development and wording of the questions. Also, you can compare different sets of questions purported to measure the same thing. For example, questions about ethnicity can come from multiple sources: the categories used in a national census and/or from questions you have developed that you believe are more appropriate indicators. Using the census categories allows you to discuss the results in terms of those categories and to compare findings with other reports. Using a new series of questions in conjunction with the census questions would allow direct comparison of the two ways to define ethnicity. When beginning to design a questionnaire, take advantage of previous scholarly work and look for published questions (and responses) and don't hesitate to use them if they're good.

Combining Responses to Create Scales and Indices

As the requested information becomes more abstract (that is, as questions move from simple ideas like gender and age to more complex ideas such as social class), more questions are needed to get a reliable estimate of the concept. For concepts that can't be measured simply or directly, use proxy questions to get information associated with or indicative of the underlying concept. Then, combine responses to obtain a more reliable and accurate estimate. For example, we believe that social class or socioeconomic status exists, even though there is no direct, single question or ruler by which we can assess or categorize an individual or household.

In developed countries, we often use combinations of educational level, income, and occupation as proxy measures for social class (see Haug 1977). In less-developed countries and among populations with little variability in occupation, education, and income, such variables may not be helpful in differentiating social strata. In lesser developed and rural areas, it's more helpful to ask a series of questions related to or indicative of socioeconomic status (for example, house construction, water source, type of stove, etc.) and to combine responses to differentiate households.

A summative score across variables creates an index or scale. The choice of questions whose content is related to the underlying concept ensures the *content validity* of such a scale. Thus, the choice of a set of reasonable questions or proxy variables and a combination of responses to those variables should also provide a reasonable estimate. Another kind of validity is *construct validity*, or whether the scale is correlated with other measures of the same concept. An additional check on construct validity is to ensure that items selected for combination in a scale are in fact *scalable* (that is, whether they are mathematically correlated). Questions measuring the same thing should have similar responses across respondents and should be correlated. Principal components analysis provides a solution of how to optimally combine variables that are in different units of measurement. A principal components analysis clusters items into groups according to their intercorrelations; items with the same pattern of responses across people (those that have the same pattern of high values and low values across people) are grouped together.

In developing a scale of financial resources in rural Guatemala, Weller et al. (1997) asked over two dozen questions about household composition, characteristics of head of household (gender, age, education, ability to read, ability to write), house construction, and assets (ownership of land, appliances, vehicles, and animals). Some questions requested yes/no responses: "Do you own your house?," "Do you have a bicycle?" Others requested the number of people or animals. Weller et al. created codes for questions with multiple responses (for example, household construction).

In seeking to develop a scale concordant with community perceptions (construct validity), Weller et al. (1997) asked three informants in six villages to rank ten families according to their economic resources and retained only those questionnaire items that correlated with the community judgments (10 of the original 28 questions). A principal components analysis of those questions showed that variables most indicative of financial resources (including monthly income) grouped together on the first factor, and variables representing other dimensions of socioeconomic status (educational level and household size) grouped on successive factors.

Weller et al. (1997) wanted a relatively simple scale that could be used in other studies in the region, so they used the principal components solution to identify which variables should be combined (those on the first factor), but not for a weighted combination of variables. To overcome the problem of different units of measure, variables were dichotomized (so they would be in the same units) and summed. Each household received a cumulative score (+1) for the presence of each indicator: monthly income greater than the median; ownership of any appliance; more than two rooms in the house; nondirt floor; more than three chickens; adobe, brick, or block walls (as opposed to bamboo, wood, or plastic); land ownership; and ownership of a bicycle. Summing across the eight variables created a nine-point (0–8) scale. The final scale was concordant with other scales previously constructed to assess socioeconomic status in rural Guatemala (Freeman et al. 1977; Johnston et al. 1987). Such scales are surprisingly similar across rural regions of the world and use indicators such as floor construction (dirt versus other), type of cooking fuel, and availability of animals for sale.

Guttman scaling is another way to combine household indicators of socioeconomic status. DeWalt (1979:106–115) created a nine-point "material style of life" scale by combining responses across the presence or absence of eight variables: iron, radio, bed, cooking facilities off the floor, sewing machine, wardrobe, stove, and television. Guttman scaling of households by these eight variables reveals the cumulative and sequential ordering of the variables: If a household has an item on the list, it tends to have objects that precede it. Similarly, if a household lacks an item, it tends to lack subsequent items. DeWalt checked the validity of the scale by comparing the final scale to informant ratings of wealth and found them highly correlated. Another example of Guttman scaling of consumer goods for Polynesian households appears in Kay (1964; and see Weller and Romney 1990:79–83).

Responses can be combined across related questions or variables to create a single scale or index. Such indices are more reliable and accurate than a single question, especially when the question requests more than simple information like someone's age, height, or weight. While the combination of simple questions about households may be combined to estimate the socioeconomic status of a household, a variety of other variables may be similarly combined to obtain better estimates of behaviors and experiences. Handwerker (1996) describes the combination of responses from questions regarding household activities and responses about experiences of violence and affection.

Challenges to Validity

Accuracy of responses can be compromised by questions that are interpreted differently by different respondents. Questions should be in complete, grammatically correct language to minimize the possibility of reading questions one way with some informants and another way with other informants. A technique psychologists use to understand how informants interpret a question is to ask individuals to think out loud, to describe their interpretation of the question and the process of answering, and to list possible answers.

Another source of inaccurate responses is the informants' own memory. Informants may report an event that actually happened 12 months ago as occurring 6 months ago. Marking a period with an important or widely recognized event (since ____ occurred . . .) reduces this telescoping effect (Loftus and Marburger 1983). Informants also may misremember an event, reporting instead what they think happened or what usually happens. Informants are much better at telling you what they typically do than what happened at a specific time. Freeman et al. (1987) asked a group of individuals about attendance at a group presentation the previous week. Errors consistently counted those who usually were in attendance, but were not there, as being there; and those who usually were absent, but were there, as absent.

In another study of systematic errors caused by memory (described in D'Andrade 1974), two groups of individuals observed interactions among members of a small group and rated the occurrence of specific behaviors. One group rated behaviors simultaneously while they were watching the film and the other group recorded the behaviors immediately after the film was over. The responses of the group that rated the behaviors after the film was over corresponded more to the similarity among the words or adjectives than to the ratings of the first group. In other words, if someone was remembered as having smiled, then they were more likely to be attributed with actions associated with smiling like having been facilitative, friendly, and so on whether they were or not. Again, reports may reflect broader patterns of occurrence rather than a specific instance. The series of studies by Bernard et al. (1980; see also Bernard et al. 1985) also reflect this: Although informants were asked about social interactions during a specific time period, the longer the observational period (a better sample of typical interactions), the higher the informants' accuracy.

Accuracy of responses may also be affected by the interview itself. Contextual effects have long been documented and studied by sociologists and, generally, better responses are obtained when the interviewer and the informant share characteristics such as gender and ethnicity. An informant's lack of experience with the interview process may decrease accuracy, and informants may offer socially desirable responses or may deliberately mislead you. It isn't necessarily true, however, that because information comes from a structured interview with a stranger that the information won't be accurate. Stone and Campbell (1984) found that when individuals were first interviewed with a survey administered by a stranger and then reinterviewed in an unstructured format by someone known to them, the second interview reflected greater family-planning awareness. Unfortunately, without a group of informants interviewed in an unstructured way followed by a survey, it's impossible to tell if the difference in reporting is due to a difference in interview format or if results reflect increased awareness due to the prior interview on the same topic.

Knowledge Tests

A knowledge test consists of a series of questions designed to test someone's ability or knowledge. The answers—the correct answers—to the questions are known, and responses are scored or *recoded* as correct/incorrect. First, a domain of questions is established that covers the subject matter or ability to be tested. Then, test questions are drafted. Question format may be multiple choice (with two or more choices) or open ended (requesting single-word or short-phrase answers). Performance of respondents is usually described as the percentage of correct responses (of the total number of questions) or as a percentile, comparing performance of respondents to one another from the distribution of scores across respondents. Just as sociologists have much expertise in writing general information questions, psychologists have extensive expertise in developing knowledge tests. Nunnally's (1978) book, *Psychometric Theory*, presents a thorough review of issues involved in developing a test.

Unfortunately, some tests are simply drafted, administered, scored, and reported without assessing the reliability of the test. An assessment of a test's reliability and modification of the test, can greatly improve a test's ability to discriminate between knowledgeable and less knowledgeable informants. Reliability is the degree to which a variable or test yields the same result when administered to the same people, under the same circumstances. A test with low reliability is analogous to a sloppy measuring device—it may be valid, but it has a lot of measurement error. For example, if you measured the height of a sample of college undergraduates with a weight-height measuring device typically found in a physician's office and again with a 6" pocket-ruler, you might find that the pocket-ruler estimates could contain measurement error large enough to mask the difference in height between men and women. The more accurate the measuring device, the greater the ability to detect smaller differences. The same is true for tests. If a test can be streamlined and *limited* to questions that best differentiate degree of knowledge of the subject matter (thus, increasing the reliability), it can be a shorter, more accurate, and hence a more powerful test.

Reliability

Reliability of a test can be assessed in a variety of ways. One way to assess reliability is to give the same test twice, after an interval of time, to the same individuals. Reliability is estimated by the correlation between the two sets of scores. Because the Pearson Correlation Coefficient is used, reliability ranges from zero to one. This type of reliability, *test-retest reliability*, is limited because scores may improve due to practice or learning effects. Two equivalent, but nonidentical tests can be administered, but it is difficult to develop "equivalent but nonidentical" tests and the individuals being assessed may change during the time interval. Another approach is to create "two" tests by arbitrarily dividing a test in half and calculating separate scores for odd-numbered and even-numbered items. This type of reliability, *split-half reliability*, is estimated by the correlation between the two sets of scores. The best overall estimate of reliability, because it subsumes the previous estimates, is provided by the *reliability coefficient*. The reliability coefficient, sometimes called coefficient alpha or Cronbach's alpha, is mathematically equivalent to calculating all possible split-half reliabilities, and, while it may sound complex, it is widely available as an easily accessible option in most statistical software packages.

For a test to have high reliability, all the questions must be on only a single topic and be at the same general level of difficulty. This means that items should be intercorrelated, and performance on individual items should be concordant with the overall score. A test question would not be a good estimate of ability if the "best" or high scorers got it wrong and those with lower total scores tended to get it right. Such questions reduce the accuracy of the total score. An *item analysis* helps identify items that do and do not parallel the total score. The *item-to-total* correlation for each question tells how well responses for each question parallel the total score. If the correlation is not positive, or if the correlation is weak (less than +.20 or +.30), the item should be dropped. Items considered for omission can be dropped or modified. Writing good multiple choice answers is very difficult! The overall reliability of a test, the reliability coefficient alpha, is a function of the intercorrelation among the questions (the degree to which they measure the same concept) and the number of items (the more items on a single topic the more accurate the estimate):

$$\text{Reliability} = k\,\bar{r} / (1 + (k - 1)\,\bar{r})$$

where k is the number of questions and $\bar{r}$ is the average Pearson Correlation Coefficient between questions. Thus, a reliable test can be created with a few, highly correlated items or with a lengthy test of weakly related items. When dichotomous responses are analyzed, this formula is called Kuder-Richardson 20 (KR-20). The overall reliability coefficient and the reliability of each item can be readily obtained with the Reliability Procedure in the Statistical Package for the Social Sciences (SPSS 1990) or other statistics programs.

Example

In a study on the Pacific South Coast of Guatemala, Ruebush et al. (1992) developed a test to assess local knowledge about the causes, symptoms, and treatment of malaria. Experience both with residents of the region and the National Malaria Service led to a draft questionnaire or test with 65 true/false items. Since the correct answers to the questions comprised the scientific or biomedical model of malaria transmission and treatment, an initial pilot of the test was a very simple test to see if National Malaria Service workers (those with more biomedical experience) scored higher than the rural residents. This involved a day's worth of interviewing, going household to household, interviewing a half a dozen respondents and National Malaria Service workers.

A quick tabulation of responses and scores, in the field, helped identify obvious problems with the test. A revised version with 65 true/false questions was administered to a larger sample of residents and National Malaria Service workers. Responses, where 0 = no/false and 1 = yes/true, were compared to the correct answers and recoded to 1 if answers matched and the answer was correct and to 0 if answers were incorrect. A reliability analysis, especially the item analysis, helped identify items that did not perform well because they did not contribute to the total score. The 65-item test had a reliability coefficient of .82. The reliability analysis indicated that reliability could be improved by *omitting* items with low item-to-total score correlations. The omission of 25 items created a 40-item test with a reliability coefficient of .91. Thus, the shorter version of the test had better discriminatory ability and comparisons between groups could be made with greater precision.

Scores from knowledge tests indicate how much someone knows the correct answers. In the above example, the correct answers constituted the scientific or the biomedical model of malaria, but the scores did not indicate whether wrong answers were due to a lack of knowledge or whether they were due to different beliefs. In the malaria study, Ruebush et al. (1992) also analyzed responses in their original form without coding them as correct/incorrect, and used the modal response for each question as an estimate for local *beliefs* regarding the answers. Cultural beliefs can then be compared to the scientific answer key used to score the knowledge test. Similarly, Trotter et al. (1997) compared Latino beliefs about AIDS to national survey results about AIDS knowledge. They found that although Latinos made more errors on knowledge tests (for example, they knew the biomedical or scientific model of AIDS less well than other groups [Anglos]), many of the items that the Latinos got wrong were *not* because Latino beliefs differed from the biomedical model. Rather, many items tapped areas about which there were no strong cultural beliefs (see section below on Exploration of Specific Beliefs).

Attitude Scales and Tests

Similar to knowledge tests, attitudinal scales or tests measure the degree to which individuals and groups possess specific constructs. (A construct is an a priori defined concept.) Development of attitudinal scales begins by defining the domain of items relevant to the particular attitude being studied. Statements are generated that describe the attitude. The statements are then administered to respondents, usually with a checklist or rating scales. Informants indicate whether the statements describe their feelings and thoughts. Responses are scored by reversing or *reflecting* some responses (for example, reversing scale values by subtracting them from the value of the largest anchor point), so that the meaning of the values is consistent and small (or large) scores all indicating the absence (or presence) of the attribute. Thus, scale responses to some questions are reversed (by subtraction or by multiplication with -1). This reflection of responses parallels the handling of responses with knowledge tests, in that responses are scored in accordance with a previously determined standard. Attitude scales have been developed for a variety of topics, like depression, acculturation, and quality of life. Question formats can be dichotomous or checklist questions, but are usually rating scales.

Adapting Existing Materials and Scales

There are considerable advantages to using existing interview materials. Most importantly, it allows you to take advantage of the large amount of work that goes into the development of an interview protocol and facilitates communication with a larger group of scholars. Even for the seemingly simplest things, like collecting sociodemographic information, use of *exact wording* from national surveys allows for the comparison of sample results with those for the total population. The main disadvantage in using existing materials, especially standardized attitudinal scales, is the questionable validity of the results. A scale designed for one population may not be transferable to another population and conclusions based on one population may be erroneously generalized to another. Also, applying existing materials in a new setting may miss concepts important to the new group. There may be ideas or elaborations of ideas that are relevant in the new population that were not tapped or fully articulated in the original scale.

Nevertheless, the advantages of adopting existing interview materials, when and where they exist, usually outweigh the disadvantages. One approach is to borrow and adapt materials as necessary. A thorough discussion of how to translate and modify materials (especially, tests) is presented by Brislin (1986) in the edited volume *Field Methods in Cross-Cultural Research*. Cross-cultural psychologists have extensive expertise in the development of tests and materials that are comparable across cultural boundaries.

The first step in adapting a test for another culture or another setting is to translate statements and rating scales. Materials should be translated from the source language to the target language by one person and then translated back into the source language by another person. Brislin recommends two full translation loops (four people). Taking statements through such loops allows the investigator to see which concepts translate. Statements that retain their meaning through translation and retranslation are easily and directly usable. Statements that change meaning or that cannot be captured across translations need to be modified.

The next step involves ensuring that test questions are appropriate. One way to validate the items of a test or the statements for an attitude scale is to generate the item pool *de novo*. When applying a test to a new group, even within the same language group, it's advisable to generate new items. Open-ended questions with a small sample can sometimes reveal quickly and directly the validity of the items in a test. If newly generated items match or overlap statements and concepts already on the test, the test probably needs little or no modification. If, on the other hand, descriptive interviews elicit many ideas and themes not well developed or measured on the test, then the test probably needs revision. One solution is to add new questions at the end of the set of standard questions. Adding new questions at the end allows you to score the scale in the traditional way and build on the body of literature relevant to the scales as well as to base an analysis on a new set of items.

In a study of preterm deliveries among inner-city African American women, a standardized measure of stress was modified for that population. Stress, defined as the fit between an individual and his or her environment, was measured with the Holmes and Rahe (1967) Social Readjustment Rating Scale. The scale is a checklist of 43 life events that may have occurred in the past year, such as death of spouse and change in residence, where a greater number of positive answers is assumed to be indicative of higher stress. Before using the scale in a larger study of inner-city women, the investigators conducted open-ended, descriptive interviews with pregnant African American women about the stress in their lives.

Interviews began with a discussion of stress itself, to discover how it was defined and understood. Then, discussions covered the kinds of things that caused them stress. The results showed that although the women shared a general definition of stress and had experienced similar stress-causing situations, their stressful life events didn't correspond completely with those in the Holmes and Rahe scale. For example, they experienced stressful events not captured in the scale, such as loss of heat or electricity, being beaten or hit by a husband or boyfriend, and being evicted from home (being homeless). To be able to communicate with a larger group of researchers who might use the same scale, the investigators added new items to the end of the scale, rather than modify the scale itself. This gave them the flexibility to analyze stress in terms of either the standardized approach or as a modified test.

A limitation with attitudinal scales is their questionable validity when used on populations different from that on which the scale was developed. In general, this does not indicate a problem with the test, but one with the application and conclusions. Validity, most generally, is the degree to which something does what it is supposed to do. A valid question, scale, or test measures what it is intended to measure. Content validity refers to the appropriateness of the items: Does the content of the test items seem relevant to the topic and people being assessed? If responses from open-ended interviews with members of the target population overlap with the items and ideas contained in the existing set of questions, the questionnaire is appropriate for the new application. When the two sets of items overlap on many ideas but not all, the existing materials can be modified or expanded. If there is little overlap in the ideas and themes captured by the two approaches, an alternative or new test is needed.

Creating a New Scale

Nunnally (1978:604–609) describes the process of creating an attitude scale. His discussion is summarized here as five steps.

1. An item pool is created by writing about 40 items on a single topic. Half of the items should be moderately positive and half should be moderately negative. Statements where all or most respondents tend to answer similarly do not help to differentiate people. Thus, neutral statements are not helpful nor are very strong statements.
2. Statements are composed into a draft questionnaire and administered to individuals similar to whom the scale will eventually be administered (the target population). Questions may have dichotomous or rating scale responses. The

number of respondents should be approximately ten times the number of items. (The sample size recommendation is because principal components analysis is used to ensure that statements are intercorrelated and cluster together as a single conceptual group.)

3. Responses are scored so that high scores all indicate the presence of the concept or trait and low scores indicate an absence of the trait. This means that some responses must be reflected prior to analysis. If items were rated on 7-point scales where 1 = agree and 7 = disagree for *positive* statements, then responses for *negative* items need to be subtracted from 8 so that 1 = disagree and 7 = agree. Similarly, when responses are dichotomous and 0 = no and 1 = yes, then coding for negative statements should be reversed prior to analysis to obtain consistency in the meaning of scores.

4. An individual's score is the sum of his or her responses across items (after appropriate reversal of some items). Reliability of the total score is calculated from the average correlation among items and the number of items (alpha or KR-20). Reliability of individual items is determined by each item's correlation to the total score (item-to-total correlation). All items should have a positive item-to-total correlation. (Items with a negative item-to-total correlation need to be reflected; see step 3).

5. The final items are selected with high item-to-total correlations, say 10 positive and 10 negative statements from the original 40. A 20-item summative scale should have a reliability coefficient greater than .80.

Development of reliable and valid attitudinal scales is usually an iterative process involving data collection from several samples of informants. For example, Lewis et al. (1984) were interested in measuring stress in preadolescent children. Previous studies of stress contained items relevant to adults or items *thought to be relevant* for children. The investigators began with individual and small group interviews with 50–60 fifth and sixth graders. They asked, "What happens that makes you feel bad, nervous, or worry?" From the responses to this question (three questions), the researchers compiled a list of 22 items *agreed on by the group*. These statements, responses, or themes then formed the set of items defined and generated by the people to be studied.

The degree to which the items were well captured and expressed in existing scales of stress for children provides evidence for the validity of those scales. The degree to which the items were mutually exclusive with existing scales, challenges the valid use of such scales with children. The researchers determined that the set of items was unique to this population, and thus, proceeded to create a new scale. Their next step was to pretest the 22 items as a questionnaire, rated on five-point scales as to "How bad each would make you feel" and "How often each occurs." The results of the pretest indicated that two items were almost always rated as "not bad," and so were eliminated. The final 20-item test was then administered to 2,400 fifth graders.

Classification Studies

In a departure from knowledge tests and attitudinal scales where answers are known, classification studies seek to understand and describe ways in which individuals classify items into categories. For a set of items, similarity data are collected from respondents without directing informants as to the criteria for making comparisons; judgments are made only in terms of the similarity or difference between items. Formats appropriate for similarity data collection are: pile sorting of items and paired or triadic comparisons of items. Similarity between items may also be estimated indirectly as a function of their shared attributes. Typically, responses are aggregated across informants and the similarity information is represented with a spatial plot or tree structure to summarize the relationships among items.

A classification study has at least three parts. First, the set of items for study must be defined. Second, similarity between each pair of items is estimated. Third, the similarity data are represented in a spatial or tree model. Similarity information can be collected *directly* with judged similarity or *indirectly* with a measure of similarity between pairs of items across a series of questions (their similarity in profiles). Direct, judged similarity may be collected with the names of items written on cards and sorted into piles according to their similarity (pile sort); with items arranged into sets of two and each pair is rated on the degree of similarity (paired comparisons); or items can be arranged in sets of three and the most different item is selected (triadic comparisons). For the collection of social network data, the question/task is modified slightly to emphasize the relationship being studied. Network studies often use an indirect estimate of similarity by calculating the similarity between informants' lists of group members' names. (For more detail on social network data collection, consult Wasserman and Faust [1994:45–55].)

Pile Sorting

After the set of items for study has been defined, the name of each can be written on a card or visual stimuli (pictures or objects) can be used. Informants are asked to read or review all of the items and to put them into piles, so that similar items are together in the same pile. Instructions are deliberately kept at a general level: Group the items according to their similarity without providing any specific criteria or examples. Individuals may make as many or as few piles as they wish. Pile sorting was originally described by Miller (1969) and is reviewed in Weller and Romney (1988). Some applications include the study of social networks (Miller and Johnson 1981; Johnson and Miller 1983; Freeman et al. 1988, 1989), recreational activites (Roberts and Chick 1979; Roberts and Nattrass 1980; Roberts et al. 1981; Miller and Hutchins 1989), concepts of success and failure (Romney et al. 1979; Freeman et al. 1981), and pilot error (Roberts et al. 1980).

For example, Kirk and Miller (1978) were interested in the perception of coca in South America and attempted to discover if it was considered a food product, a beverage, or a drug. They collected pile sort similarity data on 16 words, including foods, condiments, beverages, cigarettes, and drugs. They selected samples of 12 informants from each of 12 different sites: 2 cities in Colombia, 1 in Ecuador, and 6 locales in Peru (with 4 separate samples in Lima). Because Kirk and Miller used small, convenience samples, they used multiple samples to check the reliability of their results. Although some would argue for a single, large representative (random) sample to accurately represent the perceptions of a group, multiple, diverse, convenience samples can provide similar information—*if* the results are consistent across the diverse groups. If the results differ, then further work is necessary to discover what factors are associated with the difference. In this case, results were similar across samples, so they were combined.

The classification or grouping of items appears in Figure 1 as a treelike representation. Here, "meat" and "food" are the most similar pair and are linked together

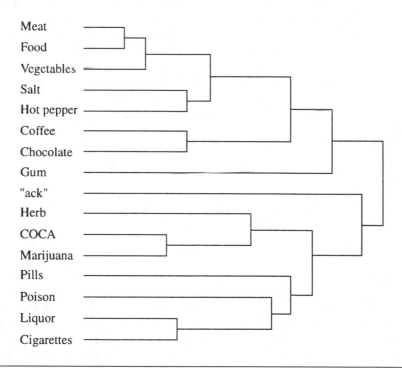

Figure 1: Perceived similarity among foods and drugs (adapted from Figure 2 in Kirk and Miller 1978:144; reprinted with permission).

at the lowest level of the tree, indicating the highest level of similarity. A cluster of edible things is then formed with other foods and condiments: meat, food, and vegetables join with salt and hot pepper. The beverages, coffee and chocolate also belong to this cluster. Another cluster contains the drugs: herb, COCA, and marijuana are in one subgroup; and liquor, cigarettes, poison, and pills are in another. Thus coca, although chewed often and drunk as tea, is perceived to be a drug, similar to marijuana.

The pile sort is a widely used and quick way to estimate similarity among items for a group of people. The task is easily understood and can facilitate conversation. After an individual has finished sorting items, she or he can describe the groupings. The data are best used to describe a group of individuals, rather than a single individual because the data are sparse. Information from each individual only indicates if an item is paired with another or not. Thus, only dichotomous (yes/no or one/zero) data are collected for each pair from each individual. Because of the sparsity of information at the individual level, the method is recommended for larger samples of people (at least 30 people) and for larger sets of items (two dozen or more items, where other methods of data collection such as triadic and paired-comparisons become prohibitive).

To collect pile sort data, write or type the names of items on cards (and number the backs of each card). Then, shuffle (and randomize) the cards and present them to an informant. Ask the informant to sort the cards according to their similarity. You can record responses immediately or later, by putting colored cards between the piles and putting a rubber band around the total set. Record responses by piles. For example, if someone sorts seven things into four piles:

1 = 1, 2, 3
2 = 4, 5
3 = 6
4 = 7

This can be recorded as above, indicating the item numbers in each pile or, the item numbers can be separated by slashes:

1 2 3 / 4 5 / 6 / 7

Here, seven items have been sorted into four piles: items 1, 2, and 3 are together; and items 4 and 5 are together. Items 6 and 7 were not put into piles with any other items. Similarity between *each pair* of the seven items is then recorded into a square, symmetric table or matrix. Since items 1, 2, and 3 are together, each pair in the group (1 and 2, 2 and 3, 1 and 3) are tabulated as similar. Items 4 and 5 also occur together and are tabulated as similar. All other pairs are not perceived to be similar and are coded with zeros (see below).

Responses are tabulated into a matrix for each individual and then summed together into an aggregate matrix for the entire sample of informants. The tabulation of responses can be done by hand or with the aid of computer software. The ANTHROPAC program (Borgatti 1992) accepts pile sort information (item numbers separated by slashes), and provides both the individual and group matrices. Here is the individual matrix for the example above:

	1	2	3	4	5	6	7
1							
2	1						
3	1	1					
4	0	0	0				
5	0	0	0	1			
6	0	0	0	0	0		
7	0	0	0	0	0	0	

Variations on pile sorting include: allowing informants to split items, so that an item may go into more than one pile; constraining the number of piles an informant may make; or collecting successive pile sorts from each individual. Steffire (1972) asked informants, when they were finished sorting items, if any items should go into more than one pile. Items or cards were then split and put into multiple piles.

In the unconstrained version of the pile sort, informants may make as many or as few piles as they wish. In the constrained version; informants are instructed to make a specific number of piles, say between seven and nine piles (Romney, Smith et al. 1979). The constrained version of the pile-sort attempts to control for individual differences in style; some individuals make finer discriminations between items (splitters) than others (lumpers). Burton (1975) proposed a method for assigning greater weight to the responses of splitters in an unconstrained sorting task. Because of the strong effect of such style differences, sorting tasks are usually not appropriate for comparisons between informants (Boorman and Arabie 1972; Arabie and Boorman 1973; Boorman and Olivier 1973). Comparisons between informants, rather than items, can be made only with an equal number of piles per informant or with successive pile sorts (Truex 1977; Boster 1986a; see Weller and Romney 1988 for more information on successive sorts).

Paired-Comparison and Triads Similarity Data

Since similarity data technically concern pairs of items, sets of items can be created and informants asked directly about each pair. The advantage of such a design is that much more information can be collected per informant. With m items there are $m(m-1)/2$ pairs or relationships to be estimated. Pile sort similarity data provide only dichotomous information (two values; co-occur = 1, do not co-occur = 0) on the $m(m-1)/2$ pairs for each informant. A direct rating of pairs, say on a nine-point rating scale, theoretically provides a nine-point range of information for each pair for each informant. A triad design offers a measurement range that is equal to the number of times each pair occurs in the design. Thus, a paired-comparison design or a triadic design collects the same type of information as the pile sort, but collects more detail from each informant. The tradeoff is that although more information is collected, the tasks may be somewhat less interesting to informants than doing a pile sort.

In triad designs, items are systematically arranged into sets of three (see Weller and Romney 1988). Usually informants are instructed to pick the most different item in each set, which, in turn, identifies the most similar pair (the two remaining items). Pairwise similarity is thus estimated from responses. Picking the most different item is simple and can be done orally. Because of that, it is the method preferred by anthropologists. Psychologists, working in more controlled conditions like classroom data collection, sometimes collect much more detailed information per informant. For example, because a triad of items actually contains three pairs, some have asked informants to identify the *most* similar pair in each triad and the *least* similar pair. In that way, all three pairs within each triad are ranked (1 = least, 2 and 3 = most similar). This latter method is much more intensive than the simple, "pick the most different one," and provides much more information per informant, but is not practical for most field applications.

Tasks collecting judged similarity through designs that use subsets of items can collect more detailed information per informant, but the task can be lengthy and cumbersome. With m items there are $m(m-1)/2$ pairs in any set of items and $m!/[3!(m-3)!]$ triads.

Thus, with 10 items there are 45 pairs and 120 triads; with 21 items there are 210 pairs and 1,330 triads. Because the subset designs quickly become cumbersome, there are special designs to limit the number of necessary subsets and still collect similarity judgments on all pairs of items. These are called *balanced-incomplete-block designs* and can be found in Burton and Nerlove (1976) or in Weller and Romney (1988). The designs are identified by the number of items to be compared (m), the size of the subsets (2 = pairs, 3 = triads, etc.), and the number of times each pair appears (lambda). A complete triads design with 7 items requires 35 triads, but designs may be created where each pair appears once (creating 7 triads), twice (14 triads), three times (21 triads), four times (28 triads), and five times (35 triads in the complete set). A complete triads design for 21 items contains 1,330 unique sets of 3 items, but only 70 triads are necessary if a design is created where each pair occurs only once. A lambda-one design for 21 items has a large enough number of items to provide interesting results and yet is simple enough to be administered orally in the field.

To create a triad design for a set of items, first enumerate all unique sets of three items. Because the number of triads increases quickly, triads are most useful with two dozen or fewer items. If a balanced-incomplete-block design is to be used to reduce the number of triads, first make sure a solution exists for the number of items that you have (check Weller and Romney 1988). Often an item may need to be added or deleted from the set, since designs exist for only certain size domains. After all triads have been listed, the order of the sets and the order of items within each set must be randomized (see Weller and Romney 1988:33–34). Failure to randomize items can lead to biased selections by informants and might confound results (Romney et al. 1979). Subset designs are created in a systematic way to insure that all pairs are included. The computer program ANTHROPAC (Borgatti 1992) has an option to develop and print the data collection forms for some of the triad designs. Clear instructions should be given and informants should be provided with a few practice sets. When examples are given, they should have obvious answers, they should come from a different domain, and the correct answer in each should be in a different position within the set (first, second, third item).

The triad selections for each individual can be typed into a computer file, and ANTHROPAC will tabulate them into a matrix. The similarity matrix containing the aggregate responses across all informants (whether from pile sorting, triads, or paired-comparisons) can be analyzed to determine the perception or categorizations for the group.

Responses are tabulated into a similarity matrix just as for the pile sort judgments. A square *m* by *m* table is created, and responses corresponding to each pair are tallied into each cell. With a triad task, where each informant is asked to pick the most different item, the two items that were not picked form the pair that is tallied as similar. Each triad (A, B, C) contains information on three pairs (AB, AC, and BC). For four items, say measles, chicken pox, cancer and AIDS, there are four unique triads:

1. MEASLES	CANCER	CHICKEN POX
2. AIDS	CHICKEN POX	MEASLES
3. CHICKEN POX	AIDS	CANCER
4. CANCER	MEASLES	AIDS

If CANCER is selected as the most different in the first triad, then MEASLES and CHICKEN POX receive a point of similarity. Similarity relations are symmetric, so the relation between A and B is the same as that between B and A. If AIDS is chosen in the second triad, then MEASLES and CHICKEN POX receive an additional point of similarity. If CHICKEN POX is chosen in the third triad, then AIDS and CANCER receive a point of similarity. If MEASLES is chosen in the last set, then CANCER and AIDS receive an additional point of similarity. Thus, the responses from this one individual can be tabulated into a matrix:

	M	CP	A	Ca
Measles				
Chicken Pox	2			
AIDS	0	0		
Cancer	0	0	2	

If pairs are rated, the first step is to list all possible pairs of items. Next, the ordering of the pairs and the order of items within each pair is randomized. A rating scale is then created, where the smallest number indicates the least similarity and the largest number indicates the highest similarity. Informants judge the similarity of items in each pair on the rating scales. The rating scale value selected for each pair is tallied into a matrix. An example with the four illness terms from above yields the following pairs:

	Minimum				Maximum	
1. CHICKEN POX—MEASLES	1	2	3	4	5	6
2. CANCER—CHICKEN POX	1	2	3	4	5	6
3. CANCER—MEASLES	1	2	3	4	5	6
4. AIDS—CHICKEN POX	1	2	3	4	5	6
5. CANCER—AIDS	1	2	3	4	5	6
6. AIDS—MEASLES	1	2	3	4	5	6

If someone responded to these six rating scales selecting 6 for the first pair and 2, 1, 2, 5, and 1 for subsequent pairs, the values would be tabulated into a similarity matrix as:

	M	CP	A	Ca
Measles				
Chicken Pox	6			
AIDS	1	2		
Cancer	1	2	5	

Applications using triads to collect similarity data include the study of kinship terms (Romney and D'Andrade 1964), animals (Henley 1969), occupations (Burton 1972; Burton and Romney 1975; Magaña et al. 1995), illness terms (Lieberman and Dressler 1977; Young and Garro 1982; Weller 1983), and personality descriptors (Kirk and Burton 1977; Burton and Kirk 1979). In a recent study, Romney et al. (1997) compared monolingual English- and monolingual and bilingual Japanese-speakers' judgments of 15 emotion terms. Figure 2 shows the similarity between terms and across the two monolingual samples in a spatial representation. Correspondence analysis was used to represent the similarity data in two dimensions. The figure may be interpreted as a "map," where closeness in the picture indicates similarity. Thus, "disgust," "anger," and "hate" are perceived as similar to one another and different from "sad" or "happy." Differences between the two samples are negligible for 4 terms, small for 8 terms (for example, "disgust/*mukatsuku*," "hate/*kirai*," and "anger/*haragatatsu*"), and large for 3 terms ("shame/*hazukashii*," "anxious/*fuan*," and "bored/*tsumaranai*"). Romney et al. conclude that there is a substantial amount of shared meaning in emotions between the English and Japanese samples.

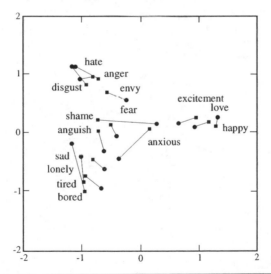

Figure 2. Correspondence analysis of similarity among Japanese and English emotion terms (adapted from Romney et al. 1997; reprinted with permission, copyright © 1997, National Academy of Sciences, U.S.A.).

In a study of societal problems, Wish and Carrol (presented in Kruskal and Wish 1990:36–41) asked 14 individuals to rate 22 societal problems in terms of their similarity. Rating scales were used to collect judged similarity on all 231 pairs.

Additional rating scales were used to rate the problems on various dimensions; for example, the degree to which the problem affects people. The similarity among the 22 items (aggregated across informants) was represented spatially in three dimensions using multidimensional scaling. Multidimensional scaling is another multivariate analysis appropriate for the analysis interitem similarity data. Similarity relations are translated into Euclidean distances creating a spatial representation like a map. Thus, closeness in the representation indicates similarity.

The three dimensions that best explained informants' perception of the societal problems were the degree to which the problem affected people, the degree to which the problem was the responsibility of local government, and the degree to which the problem was technological. Figure 3 shows the latter two dimensions. In the lower-left quadrant of the figure are problems ("Failures in welfare") thought to be the responsibility of local government; and in the upper-right quadrant are those that are not the responsibility of local government ("Inflation"). Technological problems are in the lower-right quadrant and nontechnological problems in the upper-left.

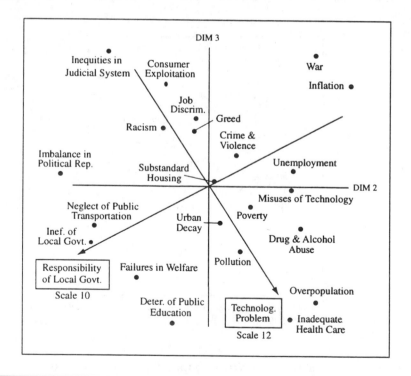

Figure 3. Multidimensional scaling of similarity among societal problems in the United States (from Kruskal and Wish 1990; reprinted with permission).

Sentence-Substitution or Profile Data

As discussed, similarity between items can be collected directly with judgments of similarity (pile sorting, triads, or paired-comparisons), or similarity can be estimated indirectly, between the "profiles" of pairs of items across a series of questions. For example, D'Andrade et al. (1972) asked about the attributes of 50 illness terms by repeating a set of 50 attribute questions for each illness (2,500 questions); then they estimated the similarity between the illnesses from their proportion of shared attributes. This interviewing procedure—the systematic comparison of a set of items with a set of attributes or features—is sometimes called sentence-substitution data collection because the items are systematically substituted into sentence-frames containing the attributes for the interview.

Sentence-substitution interviews begin with two related lists. The first list is the set of domain items and the second list is a set of statements about the domain items. The latter list may include descriptive statements, attributes, features, or uses (behaviors) relevant to the domain items. In the interview, each item is paired with every attribute, and informants are asked to judge the acceptability or veracity of the newly formed statement. The task is easy to understand and may be administered orally. For oral administration, a matrix can be used to indicate the intersection of the two lists (rows as attributes and columns as domain items). For written administration, all statements should be completely written out with correct syntax. Responses are usually dichotomous yes/true or no/false. Usually, informants' responses are summed into a single item-by-attribute table. Aggregated responses may then be dichotomized so that item-attribute pairs with majority affirmative responses are recoded to "X" (or 1) and others are recoded to blanks (or 0).

Similarity among *items* may be calculated from their shared attributes (or similarity among attributes can be calculated from their co-occurrence in items). From either, a square symmetric matrix of similarities is obtained. In D'Andrade et al.'s (1972) study of illnesses and illness attributes, the similarity between each pair of illnesses (across attributes) was calculated with a Pearson correlation coefficient. The item-by-item correlation matrix was represented with both multidimensional scaling and hierarchical clustering. Clustering results can be used to interpret the similarity between items and to reorder the rows (items) and columns (attributes) in the aggregate item-by-attribute response table so that the joint item-attribute clusters can be seen.

Stefflre (1972), D'Andrade et al. (1972), Young (1978), and Weller et al. (1987) used hierarchical clustering to reorder the rows and columns of item-by-attribute response tables to aid interpretation. D'Andrade (1976) and Young (1978) also tried to identify attributes that best differentiated illness categories. Weller et al. (1987) and Garro (1986) collected sentence-substitution data, but examined variation between informants. Sentence-substitutions provide rich and valuable information, but the interview can be lengthy. Interviews like Stefflre's (1972) and D'Andrade et al.'s (1972) comparison of 50 items and 50 attributes (2,500 questions) were carried out over a few days, and informants were reimbursed for their time.

A more general form of this type of interviewing is systematic collection of information on any two related lists of items to create a profile of information for one set of items based on the second set of items. For example, interviews with members of a small face-to-face social group may ask that each group member "Name the individuals with whom you interact the most," "Name the three people with whom you interact most," or "Rate each member in terms of how much you interacted with them in the last month." Although these three questions vary from unconstrained and constrained dichotomous responses (those named and those not named) to responses for all members (rating or ranking), the information refers to the set of all group members. The two related lists each contain the names of all members: The first list indicates the informant or member interviewed, and the second list indicates that informant's responses, choices, or names of members selected by that informant. Similarity is then calculated between informants, based on their profile of responses or choices. Similarity in their pattern of choices may be calculated with a Pearson correlation coefficient or other measure and represented spatially with multidimensional scaling, correspondence analysis, or graph theoretic techniques (Wasserman and Faust 1994).

Reliability and Validity of Similarity Data Representations

Data collection and analysis for the study of classifications include three steps: (1) collecting similarity data; (2) tabulating the data into a single table or matrix for each group; and (3) getting a descriptive model or representation of the similarity relationships. Similarity data may be collected directly with pile sorting, triads, or paired-comparisons or indirectly from the shared attributes across items. With direct judged similarity, a similarity matrix is created for each individual and then the matrices are summed together. Tabulation of similarity can be done by hand or by computer (Borgatti 1992). With indirect measures of similarity, a matrix of similarity coefficients (for example, Pearson correlation coefficients) is usually generated by a computer program. Finally, aggregate similarity information in the form of a square, symmetric matrix of similarities is represented with a descriptive multivariate technique.

Descriptive statistical analyses used for the representation of similarity data include hierarchical clustering (Mezzich and Solomon 1980), nonmetric multidimensional scaling (Mezzich and Solomon 1980; Kruskal and Wish 1990), and correspondence analysis (Weller and Romney 1990). These analyses are available in most major statistical packages. Hierarchical clustering represents the relationships between items in a treelike structure or dendrogram, like a taxonomy and is available in SAS (SAS Institute 1989) and BMDP (Dixon et al. 1990). Although there are about three dozen different clustering algorithms, some are better than others in accurately representing the structure in data. The most widely available and probably best method is the average-link method, sometimes called UPGMA (Sokal and Sneath 1963). D'Andrade's (1978; and see Buchholtz and Weller [1985] and Weller and Buchholtz [1986]). U-Statistic, or median-linking method, is also good.

Both nonmetric multidimensional scaling (MDS) and correspondence analysis spatially represent data so that similar items are closer together on a map or plot of items. Correspondence analysis is a sister of principal components, appropriate for scaling qualitative/categorical data. When using correspondence analysis on similarity data, a large or the largest number must appear down the main diagonal. (The largest possible similarity number plus one may be used.) Correspondence analysis is less sensitive to artifactual effects than MDS and allows for simultaneous scaling of two or more groups of informants. Multidimensional scaling is available in ALSCAL in SAS. Correspondence analysis is in BMDP (Moran et al. 1990), SPSS (SPSS, Inc. 1990), and SAS.

A variety of studies have tested the validity and reliability of using one of these multivariate models to represent similarity data. Simple exercises include submitting a set of interpoint distances (where similarity is the degree of propinquity) for analysis and checking to see if the same information can be retrieved. As mentioned, although there are many types of hierarchical clustering, the average-link method outperforms others in being able to retrieve known structures (Milligan 1980). Green and Carmone (1970) illustrate MDS's ability to translate such information into an accurate map with a configuration of points representing the letters "A" and "M"; Kruskal and Wish do so with a map of the United States. Weller and Romney repeat Kruskal and Wish's example and show that correspondence analysis also accurately maps the location of cities. Magaña et al. (1981) studied the perception of a college campus and compared estimates of distances, triad judgments, and distances from hand-drawn maps and found the MDS representations to accurately reflect true distances.

A more complicated form of validation concerns the degree to which such models accurately represent what people think. Friendly (1977) used hierarchical clustering and MDS models of free-recall listing and similarity data to successfully predict memory performance tasks. Similarly, Romney et al. (1993) used an MDS model of similarity data to predict list length in a free-recall listing task. Hutchinson and Lockhead (1977) found the MDS model of similarity data predicted reaction time judgments of the same stimuli. Rumelhart and Abrahamson (1973) used an MDS model to predict informants' responses on analogical reasoning tasks.

Most studies have found similarity judgments to be highly reliable. This means that there tends to be little intracultural variation in them. Romney, Smith et al. (1979), in a study of concepts of success and failure, compared results across several samples and found them to be highly concordant. A check on the internal concordance in similarity judgments is an important step in justifying an aggregate representation. Similarity between items from direct judged similarity or from shared attributes is usually concordant (compare D'Andrade et al. [1972] and Weller [1983]; and see Young and Garro [1982]). Tversky (1977) proposed that similarity between items is a function of their shared attributes.

Exploration of Specific Beliefs

A series of questions on a single topic may be used to evaluate knowledge, attitudes, or beliefs. In studies of beliefs, however, the purpose is discover the answers and not to measure deviance from a standard. Thus, only original responses are used; they are not transformed or recoded *in any way*. Studies focusing on beliefs are similar to classification studies, except that classification studies rely on similarity data generally without reference to specific criteria and studies of beliefs may explore specific criteria. Question formats include: open-ended questions requesting short answers or phrases; questions with predetermined multiple choice response categories (including dichotomous yes/no or true/false); requests to order or rank items on a specific topic; and open-ended questions requesting numeric answers (interval estimates, like frequencies, distances, or ages). Typically, responses are summarized by aggregating responses across informants.

Interviews are conducted with a series of statements or questions on the same topic, in the same format, and at the same level of difficulty. As with all interview materials, the items should be relevant to the informants and developed from open-ended interviewing. The actual format of questions is guided by the purpose of the study. If the purpose is to discover detailed beliefs, for example a cultural model of the causes, symptoms, and treatments for an illness, then an appropriate format may be a series of yes/no or true/false questions covering all of the potential attributes of the illness (Garro 1986, 1987; Weller et al. 1993).

Alternatively, a project might focus on a single question, "What causes breast cancer?" (Chavez et al. 1995) or "What are the reasons that influence a woman to choose breast or bottlefeeding?" (Weller and Dungy 1986). Here, the set of items would consist of all possible causes of breast cancer or all possible reasons influencing the choice of an infant feeding method. Data collection could include either yes/no judgments for each item or the items can be ordered from most to least likely. Or, a researcher may wish to study land ownership (Sankoff 1971) or names of plants (Boster 1985) by asking simple open-ended questions such as, "Who owns this land?" or "What do you call this?" Finally, if you are interested in numeric information, say cultural beliefs about infant development, you can ask informants the age at which certain behaviors typically occur (Pachter and Dworkin 1997).

Description of beliefs from the responses to a series of questions usually involves some summarization procedure across informants. Intuitively, the best estimate of an answer is provided by the majority response or an average across informants

(D'Andrade 1987). Such measures, called *central tendency* measures in statistics, provide the best single description of responses to a question. Thus, open-ended or categorical responses are best described by the majority or modal response, and ranked or interval data are best described by the median (midpoint) or mean (average) response.

Aggregate measures, however, are accurate only to the degree that there is little to moderate variability in responses. That is why basic statistical descriptions also report an indicator of the spread or range of values in a variable. If responses are truly heterogeneous, a description based on pooled or aggregate data would be misleading. For example, if 95% of informants say "yes" to a question and 5% say "no," there is a clear cultural preference for "yes." In contrast, if 51% say "yes" and 49% say "no," the majority response is "yes," but there is no strong cultural preference for that answer. When responses to a single question are analyzed, a binomial test (or chi-square test) can determine when responses exhibit a strong cultural preference and thus are significantly different from a 50:50 split. Since the description of cultural beliefs—modal beliefs—involves an aggregation of responses, the first question is whether there is sufficient agreement in responses to identify culturally preferred answers.

The notion of sufficient agreement in responses for a single question can be generalized to a set of questions. Agreement across informants' responses for a series of questions can be assessed with a concordance measure. Anthropologists have often noted that agreement is related to accuracy (Young and Young 1962), and this can be expressed as a general principle of aggregation. The accuracy of a set of aggregated responses is a function of the concordance among the informants and the number of informants (the Spearman-Brown Prophesy Formula described in Weller and Romney 1988). In other words, if the agreement between *each pair* of informants is measured with a Pearson correlation coefficient and averaged across all pairs of informants, the higher the agreement among informants the fewer informants are necessary to achieve an accurate estimate of the "true" answers. Thus, cultural beliefs can be estimated by pooling the responses of a group of informants to a set of questions (all on the same topic and all in the same format) if there is sufficient agreement among informants. A summarization of responses must include an assessment of the degree of intracultural variation and only when concordance is high can responses be summarized meaningfully.

Cultural Consensus Model

An analytical model that estimates the culturally appropriate answers and the degree to which each informant shares those beliefs is the cultural consensus model (Romney et al. 1986). The model assumes that the ethnographer does not know the answers to the questions, nor how much each informant knows about the domain under consideration. The analysis first determines *if* there are highly shared beliefs and, if so, provides an estimate of the answer for each question and an estimate of how much each informant knows the shared beliefs. Open-ended (single word or short phrase) responses, multiple choice, and full-rank/interval responses can each be accommodated. The model also includes a method for estimating the number of informants needed to provide given levels of confidence in the answers for different levels of shared cultural knowledge. With highly shared beliefs, accurate results can be obtained with few informants.

The analysis focuses on the degree of agreement among informants and begins by assessing the similarity between all pairs of respondents. The proportion of matching responses is calculated for responses that are categorical (open-ended or multiple-choice)(Romney et al. 1986). If responses are dichotomous (yes/no or true/false categories), similarity can be measured with the match coefficient or covariance (Batchelder and Romney 1988). The next step evaluates the degree of homogeneity or agreement in responses. The matrix of similarity between pairs of informants is factored to solve for individual knowledge or cultural competency levels. The analysis parallels a principal components of people (with missing values on the main diagonal). Whether or not the solution is a single factor solution is used to determine if there is a single pattern in responses. If the ratio of the first-to-second eigenvalues is greater than three and if the competency values are all between zero and one, inclusive, then the solution is said to fit the model and thus represent homogenous responses.

If responses are sufficiently homogeneous to meet these criteria and thus fit the cultural consensus model, then the cultural knowledge of each individual can be estimated and the estimates are used to weight the responses prior to aggregating. Thus, responses of more knowledgeable informants are weighted more heavily. For categorical response data this is done by adjusting the prior probabilities and calculating a Bayesian posterior probability (confidence level) for each answer.

Applications include the study of illness beliefs and plant naming. Garro (1987) studied Ojibwa beliefs about hypertension with a series of yes/no questions concerning various aspects of the condition. Similarly, she asked a series of questions about illnesses and their attributes and compared the beliefs of Tarascan Indian women with those of specialized healers (Garro 1986). Weller et al. (1993) studied the beliefs of Latinos in Connecticut, Texas, Mexico, and Guatemala regarding the folk illness *empacho*. Pachter et al. (1996) compared the beliefs of Puerto Rican and African American parents with those of health care providers. Open-ended responses of words or short phrases can also be used. Boster (1985, 1986b) walked Jivaro women through a garden and asked them to name specific plants.

The model also extends to rank-order data (Romney et al. 1987). For full-rank or interval-scaled response data, similarity between people is measured with a Pearson correlation coefficient, and the person-by-person correlation matrix is factored to obtain knowledge scores. If a single factor solution is obtained, the cultural knowledge scores for individuals appear as the first set of factor *loadings*. The weighting procedure that is used to find the answer key is the simple linear combination of standardized responses weighted by the individual knowledge scores. The solution or answer key is provided as the first set of factor *scores* and contains a numeric value for each item. Chavez et al. (1995) compared the beliefs of four different groups of Latinas and one group of physicians by having each group of informants rank order 30 potential causes of breast cancer. Magaña et al. (1995) compared U.S., Mexican, and Guatemalan perceptions of socioeconomic status and prestige by comparing informants' orderings of occupations. The full-rank/interval model also accommodates open-ended requests for numerical information.

With high agreement few informants are needed to get stable, accurate estimates of beliefs (Weller and Romney 1988). For dichotomous response data, low levels of cultural sharing (.50) with high accuracy (.99 of answers correct) and a high degree of confidence (.95 Bayesian posteriori probability) requires at least 29 informants. For the same accuracy and confidence, but with high cultural sharing (.70), only 10 informants are necessary. Similarly with ranked data, low levels of sharing (.25 average Pearson correlation coefficient between informants) and high accuracy (.95 correlation between the aggregate answers and the *true* answers) requires a sample size of 28. For the same level of accuracy and higher agreement among informants (.49), 10 informants are necessary. The square root of the average Pearson Correlation coefficient estimates the level of shared cultural knowledge (Weller 1987).

A limitation of the consensus model, as currently formulated, is that it is very simplistic and cannot handle complex conditions. For example, "I don't know" responses cannot be accommodated. It is assumed that informants will answer *every* question, and the match coefficient corrects for possible guessing. A more complex model is needed to estimate the individual thresholds for using the "I don't know" option. Also, the match coefficient assumes that there is no response bias in the data. Response bias can have many forms; with field data it may be the simple pattern of respondents to tend to say "yes" to all questions about which they have doubt or conversely to say "no." Thus, analyses based on the match method are sensitive to such bias and accurate only to the degree that they do not contain bias (Weller and Mann 1997).

The covariance method assumes that the investigator can estimate the proportion of positive answers (the proportion of answers that will be "yes"). While this can be estimated, especially since the investigator defines the set of items and creates the interview, the answers are truly unknown to the investigator (hence the purpose of the study) and a very skewed distribution (very few positive answers or very few negative answers) may affect the model's estimates. Thus, use of the covariance method is dependent on the accuracy of the estimate of the proportion of answers that are really yeses and a very skewed distribution (very few positive answers or very few negative answers) may affect the model's estimates.

Summary

This chapter briefly describes the variety of methods available for conducting interviews. Choice of an approach varies, depending on the amount of knowledge of the subject matter and the people to be interviewed. Taxonomic interviews are a good beginning point when there is little prior knowledge of the topic and little experience with appropriate language or terminology (lexicon). With increased understanding of the topic or domain, questions can be formulated that are relevant to the topic and the informants. Interviews with individuals or groups to further elaborate the domain may be conducted with listing tasks or case descriptions. Such descriptive interviewing techniques provide understanding of a topic and suggest ideas that can be explored further. Systematic interviewing with questionnaires or specific tasks (such as pile sorts) may then be used to explore ideas and test assertions.

This "bottom-up" approach describes the development of materials from the beginning of a study with unstructured methods followed by structured methods. A "top-down" approach is also valid. One might begin with survey results collected by someone else (a national survey, the census, etc.) and supplement their findings with more detailed open-ended work on the same topic. Kempton et al. (1995) gave the context and rationale for their study of U.S. environmental values by presenting results from national surveys (based on representative samples of the U.S. population) on environmental issues. Baer (1996) conducted in-depth interviews with Mexican migrant workers in Florida and explored informants' understandings of U.S. census questions about mental health. Survey results are good at providing a representative picture of what the population may be doing or thinking, but are limited in the depth with which they may explore a topic.

REFERENCES

Arabie, P., and S. A. Boorman. 1973. Multidimensional Scaling of Measures of Distances Between Partitions. *Journal of Mathematical Psychology 10*:148–203.

Baer, R. D. 1996. Health and Mental Health among Mexican American Migrants: Implications for Survey Research. *Human Organization 55*(1):58–66.

Batchelder, W. H., and A. K. Romney. 1988. Test Theory Without an Answer Key. *Psychometrika 53*:71–92.

Bernard, H. R., P. D. Killworth, and L. Sailer. 1980. Informant Accuracy in Social Network Data IV: A Comparison of Clique-Level Structure in Behavioral and Cognitive Network Data. *Social Networks 2*:191–218.

Bernard, H. R., P. D. Killworth, D. Kronenfeld, and L. Sailer. 1985. On the Validity of Retrospective Data: The Problem of Informant Accuracy. *Annual Review in Anthropology*:495–517. Stanford: Stanford University Press.

Berlin, B. O., D. Breedlove, and P. Raven. 1974. *Principles of Tzeltal Plant Classification*. New York: Academic Press.

Berlin, B. O., and P. D. Kay. 1969. *Basic Color Terms*. Berkeley: University of California Press.

Boorman, S. A., and P. Arabie. 1972. Structural Measures and the Method of Sorting. In *Multidimensional Scaling: Theory and Applications*, Vol. 1. R. Shepard et al., eds. Pp. 225–249. New York: Seminar Press.

Boorman, S. A., and D. C. Olivier. 1973. Metrics on Spaces of Finite Trees. *Journal of Mathematical Psychology 10*:26–59.

Borgatti, S. P. 1992. ANTHROPAC, Version 4.93. Columbia, SC: Analytic Technologies.

Boster, J. S. 1985. Requiem for the Omniscient Informant: There's Life in the Old Girl Yet. In *Directions in Cognitive Anthropology*. J. Dougherty, ed. Pp. 177–197. Urbana: University of Illinois Press.

Boster, J. S. 1986a. Can Individuals Recapitulate the Evolutionary Development of Color Lexicons? *Ethnology 25*(1):61–74.

Boster, J. S. 1986b. Exchange of Varieties and Information Between Aquaruna Manioc Cultivators. *American Anthropologist 88*:428–436.

Brislin, R. W. 1986. The Wording and Translation of Research Instruments. In *Field Methods in Cross-Cultural Research*. W. J. Lonner and J. W. Berry, eds. Pp. 137–164. Thousand Oaks, CA: Sage Publications.

Buchholtz, C., and S. C. Weller. 1985. 4M: A Pascal Program for Min, Max, Mean, and Median Hierarchical Clustering. Unpublished software. Philadelphia: University of Pennsylvania.

Burt, R. S. 1984. Network Items and the General Social Survey. *Social Networks 6*: 293–340.

Burton, M. L. 1972. Semantic Dimensions of Occupation Names. In *Multidimensional Scaling: Theory and Applications in the Behavioral Sciences*, Vol. 2. A. K. Romney et al., eds. Pp. 55–77. New York: Seminar Press.

Burton, M. L. 1975. Dissimilarity Measures for Unconstrained Sorting Data. *Multivariate Behavioral Research 10*:409–424.

Burton, M. L., and L. Kirk. 1979. Sex Differences in Maasai Cognition of Personality and Social Identity. *American Anthropologist 81*:841–873.

Burton, M. L., and S. B. Nerlove. 1976. Balanced Designs for Triads Tests: Two Examples from English. *Social Science Research 5*:247–267.

Burton, M. L., and A. K. Romney. 1975. A Multidimensional Representation of Role Terms. *American Ethnologist 2*(3):397–407.

Chavez, L. R., F. A. Hubbell, A., J. M. McMullin, R. G. Martinez, and S. I. Mishra. 1995. Structure and Meaning in Models of Breast and Cervical Cancer Risk Factors: A

Comparison of Perceptions among Latinas, Anglo Women, and Physicians. *Medical Anthropology Quarterly* 9(1):40–74.

Conklin, H. 1969. Lexicographical Treatment of Folk Taxonomics. In *Cognitive Anthropology*. Stephen Tyler, ed. Pp. 41–59. New York: Holt, Rinehart and Winston.

D'Andrade, R. G. 1974. Memory and the Assessment of Behavior. In *Measurement in the Social Sciences*. H. M. Blalock, ed. Pp. 139–186. Chicago: Aldine.

D'Andrade, R. G. 1976. A Propositional Analysis of U.S. American Beliefs about Illness. *American Ethnologist* 2(3):397–407.

D'Andrade, R. G. 1978. U-Statistic Clustering. *Psychometrika* 43(1):59–67.

D'Andrade, R. G. 1987. Modal Responses and Cultural Expertise. *American Behavioral Sciences 31*:194–202.

D'Andrade, R. G., N. Quinn, S. B. Nerlove, and A. K. Romney. 1972. Categories of Disease in American-English and Mexican-Spanish. In *Multidimensional Scaling: Theory and Applications in the Behavioral Sciences*, Vol. 2. A. K. Romney et al., eds. Pp. 9–54. New York: Seminar Press.

DeWalt, B. R. 1979. *Modernization in a Mexican* Ejido*: A Study in Economic Adaptation*. Cambridge: Cambridge University Press.

Dixon, W. J., M. B. Brown, L. Engelman, M. A. Hill, and R. I. Jennrich, eds. 1990. *BMDP, Statistical Software Manual*, Vols. 1 and 2. Los Angeles: University of California Press.

Fillenbaum, S., and A. Rapoport. 1971. *Structures in the Subjective Lexicon*. New York: Academic Press.

Fink, A. 1995. *How to Ask Survey Questions. The Survey Kit*, Vol. 2. Thousand Oaks, CA: Sage Publications.

Fowler, F. J. 1993. *Survey Research Methods*. Applied Social Research Methods Series, Vol. 1. Newbury Park, CA: Sage Publications.

Frake, C. O. 1961. The Diagnosis of Disease among the Subanun of Mindanao. *American Anthropologist 63*(1):113–132.

Freeman, H. E., R. E. Klein, J. Kagan, and C. Yarbrough. 1977. Relations Between Nutrition and Cognition in Rural Guatemala. *American Journal of Public Health 67*:233–239.

Freeman, H. E., A. K. Romney, J. Ferreira-Pinto, R. E. Klein, and T. Smith. 1981. Guatemalan and U.S. Concepts of Success and Failure. *Human Organization 40*(2):140–145.

Freeman, L. C., Freeman, S. C., and A. G. Michaelson. 1988. On Human Social Intelligence. *Journal of Social and Biological Structures 11*:415–425.

Freeman, L. C., S. C. Freeman, and A. G. Michaelson. 1989. How Humans See Social Groups: A Test of the Sailer-Gaulin Models. *Journal of Quantitative Anthropology 1*:229–238.

Freeman, L. C., A. K. Romney, and S. C. Freeman. 1987. Cognitive Structure and Informant Accuracy. *American Anthropologist 89*(2):310–325.

Friendly, M. L. 1977. In Search of the M-Gram: The Structure of Organization in Free-Recall. *Cognitive Psychology 9*:188–249.

Garro, L. C. 1986. Intracultural Variation in Folk Medical Knowledge: A Comparison Between Curers and Noncurers. *American Anthropologist 88*(2):351–370.

Garro, L. C. 1987. Explaining High Blood Pressure: Variation in Knowledge about Illness. *American Ethnologist 15*(1):98–119.

Green, P. E., and F. J. Carmone. 1970. *Multidimensional Scaling and Related Techniques in Marketing Analysis*. Boston: Allyn and Bacon.

Handwerker, W. P. 1996. Constructing Likert Scales: Testing the Validity and Reliability of Single Measures of Multidimensional Variables. *Cultural Anthropology Methods 8*(1):1–6.

Haug, M. R. 1977. Measurement in Social Stratification. *Annual Review in Sociology 3*:51–77.

Henley, N. M. 1969. A Psychological Study of the Semantics of Animal Terms. *Journal of Verbal Learning and Verbal Behavior 8*:176–184.

Holmes, T. H., and R. H. Rahe. 1967. The Social Readjustment Rating Scale. *Journal of Psychosomatic Research 11*:213–218.

Hutchinson, J. W., and G. R. Lockhead. 1977. Similarity as Distance: A Structural Principle for Semantic Memory. *Aluman Learning and Memory 6*:660–678.

Johnson, J. C. 1990. *Selecting Ethnographic Informants*. Qualitative Research Methods Series, Vol. 22, Thousand Oaks, CA: Sage Publications.

Johnson, J. C., and M. L. Miller. 1983. Deviant Social Positions in Small Groups: The Relations Between Role and Individual. *Social Networks 5*:51–69.

Johnston, F. E., S. M. Low, Y. deBessa, and R. B. MacVean. 1987. Interaction of Nutrition and Socioeconomic Status as Determinants of Cognitive Development in Disadvantaged Urban Guatemalan Children. *American Journal of Physical Anthropology 73*:501–506.

Kay, M. A. 1977. Health and Illness in a Mexican American Barrio. In *Ethnic Medicine in the Southwest*. E. H. Spicer, ed. Pp. 99–166. Tucson: University of Arizona Press.

Kay, P. 1964. A Guttman Scaling Model of Tahitian Consumer Behavior. *Southwestern Journal of Anthropology 20*:160–167.

Kay, P. 1975. Synchronic Variability and Diachronic Change in Basic Color Terms. *Language in Society 4*:257–270.

Kempton, W., J. S. Boster, and J. A. Hartley. 1995. *Environmental Values in American Culture*. Cambridge: M.I.T. Press.

Kirk, L. and M. Burton. 1977. Meaning and Context: A Study in Contextual Shifts in Meaning of Maasai Personality Descriptors. *American Ethnologist 4*(4):734–761.

Kirk, J., and M. L. Miller. 1978. Cognitions of Coca in Columbia, Ecuador, and Peru. In *A Multicultural View of Drug Abuse*. D. E. Smith, S. M. Anderson, M. Buxton,

N. Gottlieb, W. Harvey, and T. Chung, eds. Pp. 132–146. Cambridge: Schenkman Publishing.

Kruskal, J. B., and M. Wish. 1990. *Multidimensional Scaling*. Quantitative Applications in the Social Sciences Series, Vol. 11. Thousand Oaks, CA: Sage Publications.

Lewis, C. E., J. M. Siegel, and M. A. Lewis. 1984. Feeling Bad: Exploring Sources of Distress Among Pre-Adolescent Children. *American Journal of Public Health 74*: 117–122.

Lieberman, D., and W. M. Dressler. 1977. Bilingualism and Cognition of St. Lucian Disease Terms. *Medical Anthropology 1*:81–110.

Loftus, E., and W. Marburger. 1983. Since the Eruption of Mt. St. Helens Did Anyone Beat You Up? Improving the Accuracy of Retrospective Reports with Landmark Events. *Memory and Cognition 11*:114–120.

Magaña, J. R., M. Burton, and J. Ferreira-Pinto. 1995. Occupational Names in Three Nations. *Journal of Quantitative Anthropology 5*:1149–1168.

Magaña, J. R., G. W. Evans, and A. K. Romney. 1981. Scaling Techniques in the Analysis of Environmental Cognition Data. *Professional Geographer 33*: 294–310.

Meztger, D., and G. Williams. 1963a. Formal Ethnographic Analysis of Tenejapa Ladino Weddings. *American Anthropologist 65*:1076–1101.

Meztger, D., and G. Williams. 1963b. Tenejapa Medicine I: The Curer. *Southwestern Journal of Anthropology 19*:216–234.

Meztger, D., and G. Williams. 1966. Some Procedures and Results in the Study of Native Categories: Tzeltal Firewood. *American Anthropologist 68*:389–407.

Mezzich, J. E., and H. Solomon. 1980. *Taxonomy and Behavioral Science*. London: Academic Press.

Miller, G. A. 1969. A Psychological Method to Investigate Verbal Concepts. *Journal of Mathematical Psychology 6*:169–191.

Miller, M. L., and E. Hutchins. 1989. On the Acquisition of Boardsailing Skill. In *The Content of Culture: Constants and Variants, Studies in Honor of John M. Roberts*. R. Bolton, ed. Pp. 153–170. New Haven: HRAF Press.

Miller, M. L., and J. C. Johnson. 1981. Hard Work and Competition in an Alaskan Fishery. *Human Organization 40*(2):131–139.

Milligan, G. W. 1980. An Examination of the Effect of Six Types of Error Perturbation of Fifteen Clustering Algorithms. *Psychometrika 45*:325–342.

Moore, R., M. L. Miller, P. Weinstein, S. F. Dworkin, and H. Liou. 1986. Cultural Perceptions of Pain and Pain Coping among Patients and Dentists. *Community Dental Oral Epidemiology 14*:327–333.

Moran, A., L. Engelman, E. Stephen, and G. FitzGerald. 1990. Correspondence Analysis. In *BMDP, Statistical Software Manual*, Vols. 1 and 2. W. J. Dixon, M. B. Brown, L. Engelman, M. A. Hill, and R. I. Jennrich, eds. Los Angeles: University of California Press.

Nunnally, J. C. 1978. *Psychometric Theory*. New York: McGraw-Hill.

Pachter, L. M., and P. H. Dworkin. 1997. Maternal Expectations about Normal Child Development in Four Cultural Groups. *Archives of Pediatrics and Adolescent Medicine* *151*:1144–1150.

Pachter, L. M., S. Niego, and P. J. Pelto. 1996. Differences and Similarities Between Health Care Providers and Parents Regarding Symptom Lists for Childhood Respiratory Illnesses. *Ambulatory Child Health* *1*:196–204.

Quinn, N. 1987. Convergent Evidence for a Cultural Model of American Marriage. In *Cultural Models in Language and Thought*. D. Holland and N. Quinn, eds. Pp. 173–192. Cambridge: Cambridge University Press.

Roberts, J. M., and G. E. Chick. 1979. Butler County Eight Ball: A Behavioral Space Analysis. In *Sports, Games, and Play: Social and Psychological Viewpoints*. J. H. Goldstein, ed. Pp. 65–99. Hillsdale, NJ: Lawrence Erlbaum.

Roberts, J. M., G. E. Chick, M. Stephanson, and L. L. Hyde. 1981. Inferred Categories for Tennis Play: A Limited Semantic Analysis. In *Play as Context*. A. B. Cheska, ed. Pp. 181–195. West Point, NY: Leisure Press.

Roberts, J. M., T. V. Golder, and G. E. Chick. 1980. Judgment, Oversight and Skill: A Cultural Analysis of P-3 Pilot Error. *Human Organization* *39*(1):5–21.

Roberts, J. M., and S. H. Nattrass. 1980. Women and Trapshooting: Competence and Expression in a Game of Skill with Chance. In *Play and Culture*. H. B. Schwartzman, ed. Pp. 262–291. West Point, NY: Leisure Press.

Romney, A. K., W. H. Batchelder, and S. C. Weller. 1987. Recent Applications of Consensus Theory. *American Behavioral Scientist* *31*:163–177.

Romney, A. K., D. D. Brewer, and W. H. Batchelder. 1993. Predicting Clustering from Semantic Structure. *Psychological Science* *4*:28–34.

Romney, A. K., and R. G. D'Andrade. 1964. Cognitive Aspects of English Kin Terms. *American Anthropologist* *66*(3):146–170.

Romney, A. K., M. Keiffer, and R. E. Klein. 1979. A Normalization Procedure for Correcting Biased Response Data. *Social Science Research* *2*:307–320.

Romney, A. K., C. C. Moore, and C. D. Rusch. 1997. Cultural Universals: Measuring the Semantic Structure of Emotion Terms in English and Japanese. *Proceedings of the National Academy of Science USA, 94*:5489–5494.

Romney, A. K., T. Smith, H. E. Freeman, J. Kagan, and R. E. Klein. 1979. Concepts of Success and Failure. *Social Science Research* *8*:302–326.

Romney, A. K., S. C. Weller, and W. H. Batchelder. 1986. Culture as Consensus: A Theory of Cultural and Informant Accuracy. *American Anthropologist* *88*(2): 313–338.

Ruebush, II, T. K., S. C. Weller, and R. E. Klein. 1992. Knowledge and Beliefs about Malaria on the Pacific Coastal Plain of Guatemala. *American Journal of Tropical Medicine and Hygiene* *46*:451–459.

Rumelhart, D. E., and A. A. Abrahamson. 1973. A Model for Analogical Reasoning. *Cognitive Psychology* *5*:1–28.

Sankoff, G. 1971. Quantitative Analysis of Sharing and Variability in a Cognitive Model. *Ethnology 10*:389–408.

SAS Institute, Inc. 1989. *SAS/STAT User's Guide, Version 6*, 4th ed., Vol 1. Cary, NC: SAS Institute.

Sokal, R., and P. Sneath. 1963. *Principles of Numerical Taxonomy*. San Francisco: W. H. Freeman.

Spradley, J. P. 1970. *You Owe Yourself a Drunk*. Boston: Little Brown.

Spradley, J. P. 1979. *The Ethnographic Interview*. New York: Holt, Rinehart and Winston.

SPSS, Inc. 1990. *SPSS-PC*. Chicago: SPSS, Inc.

Stefflre, V. J. 1972. Some Applications of Multidimensional Scaling to Social Science Problems. In *Multidimensional Scaling: Theory and Applications in the Behavioral Sciences*, Vol. 2. A. K. Romney et al., eds. Pp. 211–243. New York: Academic Press.

Stone, L. and J. G. Cambell. 1984. The Use and Misuse of Surveys in International Development: An Experiment from Nepal. *Human Organization 43*:27–37.

Sudman, S., and N. M. Bradburn. 1982. *Asking Questions*. San Francisco: Jossey-Bass.

Trotter, II, R., S. C. Weller, R. D. Baer, L. M. Pachter, M. Glazer, J. E. García de Alba García. 1998. Consensus Theory Model of AIDS/SIDA Beliefs in Four Latino Populations. Manuscript under review.

Truex, G. F. 1977. Measurement of Intersubject Variations in Categorizations. *Journal of Cross-Cultural Psychology 8*(1):71–82.

Tversky, A. 1977. Features of Similarity. *Psychological Review 84*:327–352.

Wasserman, S. and K. Faust. 1994. *Social Network Analysis*. Cambridge: Cambridge University Press.

Weller, S. C. 1983. New Data on Intra-Cultural Variation: The Hot-Cold Concept. *Human Organization 42*:249–257.

Weller, S. C. 1984. Cross-Cultural Concepts of Illness: Variation and Validation. *American Anthropologist 86*:341–351.

Weller, S. C. 1987. Shared Knowledge, Intercultural Variation and Knowledge Aggregation. *American Behavioral Scientist 31*(2):178–193.

Weller, S. C., and C. H. Buchholtz. 1986. When Single Clustering Creates More than One Tree: A Reanalysis of the Salish Languages. *American Anthropologist 88*(3): 667–674.

Weller, S. C., and C. I. Dungy. 1986. Personal Preferences and Ethnic Variations among Anglo and Hispanic Breast and Bottle Feeders. *Social Science and Medicine 23*(6): 539–548.

Weller, S. C., and N. C. Mann. 1997. Assessing Rater Performance Without a "Gold Standard" Using Consensus Theory. *Medical Decision Making 17*:71–79.

Weller, S. C., L. M. Pachter, R. T. Trotter, II, and R. D. Baer. 1993. Empacho in Four Latino Groups: A Study of Intra- and Inter-Cultural Variation in Beliefs. *Medical Anthropology 15*:109–136.

Weller, S. C., and A. K. Romney. 1988. *Systematic Data Collection.* Qualitative Research Methods Series, Vol. 10. Thousand Oaks, CA: Sage Publications.

Weller, S. C., and A. K. Romney. 1990. *Metric Scaling: Correspondence Analysis.* Quantitative Applications in the Social Sciences Series, Vol. 75. Thousand Oaks, CA: Sage Publications.

Weller, S. C., A. K. Romney, and D. P. Orr. 1987. The Myth of a Sub-Culture of Corporal Punishment. *Human Organization 46*: 39–47.

Weller, S. C., T. R. Ruebush, II, and R. E. Klein. 1997. Predicting Treatment-Seeking Behavior in Guatemala: A Comparison of the Health Services Research and Decision-Theoretic Approaches. *Medical Anthropology Quarterly 11*:224–245.

Young, F. W. and R. C. Young. 1962. Key Informant Reliability in Rural Mexican Villages. *Human Organization 20*:141–148.

Young, J. C. 1978. Illness Categories and Action Strategies in a Tarascan Town. *American Ethnologist 5*:81–97.

Young, J. C. 1980. A Model of Illness Treatment Decisions in a Tarascan Town. *American Ethnologist 7*(1):106–131.

Young, J. C. and L. Y. Garro. 1982. Variation in the Choice of Treatment in Two Mexican Communities. *Social Science and Medicine 16*:1453–1465.

BRENDA FARNELL
LAURA R. GRAHAM

Twelve

Discourse-Centered Methods

Discourse analysis comprises methods used by researchers across the social sciences as well as in literary studies (see, for example, Josselson 1953 and Bernard and Ryan in this volume). It is also used in clinical fields (see, for example, Labov and Fanshel 1977; Cicourel 1981, 1982, 1992; West 1984). What unites this work is analytic attention to the use of *language in social contexts*.

The term "discourse centered" (Sherzer 1987; Urban 1991) is an expedient label with which to describe recent movements in linguistic anthropology. It does not, however, constitute a single theoretical "school."[1] Discourse-centered approaches draw on theoretical resources from several intellectual ancestries and build on earlier work in sociolinguistics, the ethnography of speaking/communication, and performance approaches to language.[2] These approaches distinguish themselves by focusing on the dialogical processes through which persons, social institutions, and cultural knowledge are socially constructed through spoken discourse and other signifying acts/forms of expressive performance.

In current anthropological practice, discourse-centered methods are used in participant observation, within the context of ethnographic fieldwork. Within this general orientation, researchers pay close attention to how language is used in and across social situations, focusing particularly on "naturally occurring discourse"— that is, utterances that occur in the context of social interaction, in contrast to utterances specifically elicited by a linguist or ethnographer.

We focus here on approaches in linguistic anthropology in which discursive practices are seen as constitutive of culture. That is, culture and self are viewed as actually *constituted by* speech and other signifying acts. Discourse-centered work emphasizes the heterogeneous, multifunctional, and dynamic character of language use and the central place it occupies in the social construction of reality. A central proposition of discourse-centered research is that "culture is localized in concrete publicly accessible signs, the most important of which are actually occurring instances of discourse" (Urban 1991:1). Edward Sapir (1949) prefigured discourse-centered approaches when he wrote: "The true locus of culture is in the interactions of specific individuals and, on the subjective side, in the world of meaning which each one of these individuals may unconsciously abstract for himself from his participation in these interactions" (p. 515).

According to a discourse-centered framework, culture is an emergent dialogic process, historically transmitted but continuously produced and revised through dialogues among its members. It is constantly open to new associations and interpretive moves. Such perspectives open up new discursive spaces within the discipline of anthropology that embody Saussure's original vision of a scientific study of "the functioning of signs within social life" (Saussure 1916:33; see also Mertz and Parmentier 1985; Thibault 1997).

New theoretical insights and questions lead to methodological challenges, and in this chapter we examine methods of research in light of the theoretical developments that gave rise to them. As Harré (1986c) said, "a theory determines where, in the multiplicity of natural phenomena, we should seek for its evidence" (p. 83). In our particular case, increasing theoretical attention to language in social contexts and an emerging understanding of discursive practices as constitutive of culture, have required, and are reinforced by, new ways of collecting and analyzing data.

For example, discourse-centered approaches contrast with the formalist logicism and mentalism that define the notion of grammar characteristic of Chomskian generative linguistics. In that paradigm, linguistic utterances are analyzed as if they are generated by an idealized, individual, speaker-hearer independent of sociocultural context. Linguistic anthropologists have long been critical of this view of language (see, for example, Hymes 1964, 1971, and, for a recent cogent critique, see Ellis 1994). When discourse is considered from the point of view of language use in social contexts, the assumption that there is a single underlying abstract grammar or that languages can be considered as discrete and monolithic codes becomes questionable. Linguistic anthropologists find multiple linguistic varieties and styles existing simultaneously within a culture and deem traditional notions of descriptive grammar and linguistic structure inadequate (see Hymes 1971; Silverstein 1976; Woodbury 1987; Urciuoli 1996).

Many researchers using discourse-centered approaches consider the rules of grammar to be imminent in conversational and other expressive practices not located in "mental structures" (Harré and Gillet 1994). A widely held position in discourse-centered research is succinctly captured in the statement, "People use rules to assess the correctness of their actions; rules do not use people as the vehicles of their causal efficacy to generate actions" (paraphrase of Wittgenstein in Mülhäusler and Harré 1990:7).

The theoretical presuppositions that inform discourse-centered methods are a shift away from approaches to ethnography that define "language" and "culture" as transcendent realms or abstract systems that interact with or determine social practices, or as preexistent patterns imperfectly expressed by each individual participant. Instead, discourse-centered perspectives present a view of language use *as social action* and cultural events as the scenes where culture emerges from interaction among participants (Mannheim and Tedlock 1995:2). For example, the dialectic between linguistic performances and wider sociocultural and political-economic contexts is being explored (Hill and Hill 1986; Handler 1988; Irvine 1989; Woolard 1989; Urciuoli 1996). Investigators are also interested in how individuals gain rights to particular modes of transforming discourse, or are denied such rights, and how the signifying acts of those with status and power achieve performativity (that is, are effective) while those of others fail. Investigating how these kinds of processes operate places language *in* culture in new ways. Positioning discursive practices as a central locus of cultural creativity opens up new possibilities for studying how processes of cultural continuity and cultural change take place. Discussions of "entextualization, decontextualization, and recontextualization" as processes that connect discourse with wider sociocultural concerns can be found in Bauman and Briggs (1990) and Silverstein and Urban (1996).

Discourse-centered approaches don't focus on language forms alone, but on forms and processes. "Meaning does not inhere to words or grammar alone, and language function—the social meaning of what people say—goes well beyond the semantic-referential function or dictionary sense of meaning" (Urciuoli 1996:5). In discourse-centered approaches, the referential (word and grammar meaning, independent of context) is but one aspect of linguistic function, such that attention to language as "code" (that is, English, Spanish, Kwakiutl, etc.) is not the primary or sole focus of analysis. The principle objectives are to discover the social meanings inhering in language forms and their relationship to social formations, identity, relations of power, beliefs, and ideologies.

This doesn't mean that discourse-centered methods eschew formalist concerns. On the contrary, formal investigation has helped us understand exactly how discourse structures a socialized world (Hill and Irvine 1993).

Quantitative approaches to linguistic variation in sociolinguistics have also proved inadequate to handle discursive data. For example, ethnographic research has shown that aspects of discourse such as accent and code switching play important roles in the interactive performance of identity and so cannot be understood adequately if reduced to quantifiable variable phonemes and variable rules (Urciuoli 1996:5).

Below, we provide a brief overview of some of the shared features of discourse-centered approaches in linguistic anthropology and point out their utility for addressing issues that concern anthropologists and social theorists. Later, we discuss methods and methodological issues related to discourse-centered work.

Why Study "Discourse"?

Discourse-centered approaches in linguistic anthropology seek to dissolve the long-standing dilemma in Western social theory of how to connect "social structure" and/or "culture" with individual human agency. The problem has been labeled variously as a tension between structure/event (Rosaldo 1980:109), individual action/ collective representations (Sahlins 1985:108), structure/practice (Bourdieu 1977a), and structure/agency (Giddens 1984). The enduring problem has been how to avoid the twin errors of individualism and the reification of internal unconscious mental structures, on the one hand (for example, Freud, Chomsky, Lévi-Strauss, and Searle), and collectivism and the reification of external social structures, on the other (for example, Durkheim and variations). These positions have been exposed as violating the logic of "causal powers" and, as a result, mislocating human agency (see Varela 1995; Varela and Harré 1996).

When such psychological and sociological determinisms are abandoned and persons are viewed instead as causally empowered embodied agents with unique powers and capacities for making meaning, discursive practices emerge as the means by which social action, cultural knowledge, and social institutions are achieved and enacted (Williams 1982; Farnell 1994, 1995b; Harré and Gillett 1994; Graham 1995; Urciuoli 1995; Silverstein and Urban 1996; Urban 1996b). Discourse-centered approaches thus offer social theorists a number of principles that should be central to their goal of achieving more dynamic views of culture and the relationships between the individual and society (for example, Sahlins 1976, 1985; Bourdieu 1977a, 1977b, 1991; Giddens 1979, 1984).

Earlier generations of ethnographers necessarily acquired much of their knowledge through the discursive practices of their informants. Yet many ethnographers tended to overlook the fact that the discursive forms in which this knowledge is packaged are themselves unique cultural forms. In traditional ethnography, Sherzer and Urban (1986a) note, "Discourse is invisible, a glass through which the ethnographer comes to perceive the reality of social relations, of ecological practice, and of belief. Little attention is given to the glass itself. We are rarely informed about the structure of the discourse through which knowledge is produced, conceived, transmitted and acquired by members of societies and by researchers" (pp. 1–2).

Many discourse-centered researchers also take the position that persons constitute themselves as a "self," an embodied moral unit in the world through discursive practices of reflexive talk. Basso (1979) offers a pioneering ethnographic example of ways in which discourse is central to the cultural construction of self (see also Rosaldo 1982; White and Kirkpatrick 1985; Harré 1986a; Lutz 1988; Mühlhäusler and Harré 1990; Abu-Lughod 1993; Harré and Gillett 1994). The works of Brenneis (1984, 1986), Du Bois (1993 [1987]), Duranti (1986), Keane (1991), and Graham (1993) show how the "I" of discourse (Urban 1989) can project different selves and the organization of talk can be linked to notions of the construction of "truth" and individual accountability.

This reorients theories of person, self, and agency away from an ethnocentric, individualistic psychologism toward sociocultural dimensions of communication, cross-cultural variability (Hill and Irvine 1993), and the enactment of indexical dynamics (Urciuoli 1996). The assigned locus of "meaning" shifts correspondingly from internal (private) mental structures (for example, the Freudian "unconscious" or Searle's "psychological states") and the individual speaker/signer, and toward the dialogic, interactional processes within which meanings are constructed.

Performativity and Indexicality

In addition to resources provided by sociolinguistics, the ethnography of speaking, and performance approaches to language, a second set of resources used in discourse-centered approaches draws on the "linguistic turn" in philosophy (see Taylor 1985; Rorty 1992 [1967]) and the development of Peircian and Jakobsonian ideas about indexical signs (see Jakobson 1971 [1957]; Silverstein 1976). Benveniste recognized an important connection between indexicality in personal pronouns (1971a [1956]) and performativity in certain verbs (1971b [1958]), thereby drawing attention to the construction of person through discourse.

The linguistic turn contributed Wittgenstein's post-Cartesian emphasis on the social construction of mind, language, and emotion to linguistic anthropology (see Rosaldo 1982; Harré 1986a; Lutz 1988; Lutz and Abu-Lughod 1990). Wittgenstein's insights have been complemented by the social constructionism of Vygotsky and G. H. Mead in a relocation of agency toward a discursive view of mind and person (see Harré 1984, 1986b, 1987; Harré and Gillett 1994). Austin's speech act theory (1962) introduced the notion of "performativity" into the study of language practices. Ethnographically grounded critical discussions of speech act theory stimulated important challenges to Western philosophical assumptions (see Rosaldo 1982; Bauman and Briggs 1990). The central insight that language is "performative" (that is, achieves social action) has remained important, however, and has been developed further through the Peircian notion of indexicality and Jakobson's discussion of "shifters"—words that "shift" their reference depending on the context in which they are used (for example, demonstratives such as this/that, here/there and pronouns) (Jakobson 1960, 1971; Silverstein 1977).

Silverstein argues that the preoccupation with the "semantico-referential" function of language (that is, where the meaning of words derives from their naming things, and their relationships to other words, as in dictionary definitions) provided the basis for a uniquely biased Western linguistic ideology. In this ideology, other functions of language, especially "nonreferential" indexical functions (ways in which linguistic utterances also carry social/pragmatic meanings through spatio-temporal contiguities to the social context) are accorded secondary importance. Prague School linguists and the Russian formalists advanced theories of the multifunctionality of language. Until Jakobson's work became influential in Western linguistic circles, however, these ideas were little known outside of the former Soviet Union (see Hymes 1975).

The defining properties of meaningful action are precisely those not visible in a grammatical-semantic model, the units and rules of which are essentially divorced from social and historical contexts. Urciuoli (1995) synthesizes insights from Jakobson, Hymes, and Silverstein to describe exactly how indexical language is constitutive of self and social action:

> The property that language shares with all sign systems is its indexical nature: its maintenance and creation of social connections, anchored in experience and the sense of the real. Linguistic indexes may be grammaticalized or lexicalized as "shifters"—devices that locate actions in time and space: personal pronouns, verb tenses, demonstratives, and time and space adverbs. These are deictic in that they point outward from the actor's location. The structure of action fans out from the center, the locus of I and you, to delineate where and when everything happens relative to the central actors: he and she versus I and You; there versus here; then versus now; present versus non-present (past or future). . . . The indexes that embody discourse extend beyond pronouns, adverbs and verbal categories both to the sounds and shapes of speech that identify the actor with a particular group and to the speech acts marking the actor's intent as others recognize it. In short indexes make the social person. (p. 190)

This interest has prompted ethnographic studies of spatial and temporal deixis as well as the social functions of pronouns. (For ethnographic studies of deixis, see Hanks 1990; Haviland 1993; Farnell 1995a.[3]) Fundamental connections between indexicality and performativity are at work because:

> Indexicality, a *sine qua non* of language, may be more or less creative: the more an index creates the who, what, when and where of the action, the more performative it is. The more an index maintains the *status quo* of action, the more presupposed (and less performative it is). Performativity may be thought of as a process that sometimes surfaces as an explicit formula (commands, promises etc.) but it is more often implicit. Any index can be performative, depending on the dynamics of the context. (Urciuoli 1995:190; see also Silverstein 1977)

Formal discourse features frequently carry indexical value. For example, speakers may use reported speech as a means to distance themselves from the content of their utterances, or it may be used to add the moral weight of other voices to the speaker's own (see, for example, Bakhtin 1986; Hill and Irvine 1993:6–7). Speakers can use evidential particles to index their orientation to a message (see papers in Hill and Irvine 1993; also Basso 1995). The analysis of person markers and other deictics has been particularly fruitful to the study of issues in the social construction and representation of identity and personhood. Formal pragmatic devices such as honorifics frequently convey significant information about social relationships between individuals (see Brown and Gillman 1960; Irvine 1992; Agah 1996; Pressman 1997). Ethnographic studies that use these resources have focused attention on such topics as political economies of language (see Irvine 1989), language ideologies (Silverstein 1976; Woolard 1989, 1992; also Kroskrity et al. 1992), conflict resolution (Murphy 1990; Watson-Gegeo and White 1990), and the discursive construction of asymetries of power (for example, Hill and Hill 1986; Handler 1988; Urciuoli 1996; see also Bauman and Briggs [1990] for further discussion).

A third important source of theoretical insights has been the symbolic interactionism of G. H. Mead, Goffman's microsociology (1972 [1967], 1974, 1981), and the sociological study of conversation (sociolinguistics, ethnomethodology), with its emphasis on the negotiated and emergent quality of meanings and the interactional construction of social structure and institutions. Researchers who specialize in conversational analysis, a tradition that developed largely within sociology with the work of Sacks and Schegloff, focus especially on cultural strategies that make conversations function effectively or not (see, for example, Schegloff 1972; Schegloff and Sacks 1973; Sacks et al. 1974; see also Fishman 1968, 1970; Garfinkel 1967, 1972; Goodwin 1981; Gumperz 1982; Tannen 1982, 1984, 1994; Goodwin and Heritage 1990; Grimshaw 1990, 1994).

These studies note strategies for turn-taking, conversational overlap, utterance length (holding the floor), patterns of interruption, and conversational "repair," for example. This line of inquiry has been fruitful in analyzing how gender roles are created and enacted through talk (see, for example, M. Goodwin 1990 and papers in Tannen 1994). Although a great deal of work in conversational analysis focuses on patterns of communication among English speakers, this approach has also been fruitful in cross-cultural contexts (for example, Moerman 1988; also Testa 1988).

Reflexive Dimensions

Recognizing that language ideologies are as much at work in our own disciplinary discourse as in the discursive practices of the peoples we study, many discourse-centered researchers explore reflexive dimensions of their research and seek to deconstruct and challenge dominant Western conceptions of language and social life. (For discussion of language ideologies, see Lucy [1990] and papers in Kroskrity et al. [1992].) Several ethnographic studies challenge Western "personalist" (individualist) notions of discourse (Holquist 1983), in which the individual is understood to be solely responsible for utterance production (for example, Searle 1969). These studies reveal language ideologies in which discourse is thought to be the product of multiple speakers (Rosaldo 1982; Brenneis 1984, 1986; Duranti 1986, 1993; Keane 1991; Chafe 1993; Du Bois 1993 [1987]; Graham 1993; Hill and Zepada 1993; Irvine 1996). Reflexive studies thus seek to expand traditional definitions of what counts as discourse, discourse production, and interpretive processes in ways that allow a better understanding of indigenous classifications.

Studies that include consideration of complementary vocal acts such as wailing, chanting, laughter, the use of sound symbolism, the blurring of boundaries between music and speech, and the coproduction of utterances expand the traditional boundary within the modality of socially produced and meaningful sound (List 1963; Brenneis 1986; Duranti 1986; Urban 1988; Feld 1990 [1982]; Nuckolls 1992; Graham 1993; Feld and Fox 1994). Ethnographic studies of sign languages and the coproduction of speech and gesture seek to make problematic the reductionism inherent in the conflation of discourse with speech. Including the modality of bodily action into what counts as discourse challenges the traditional Western division of communicative practices into "verbal" and "nonverbal" (Farnell 1995a) and reconceives discourse as the simultaneous production of vocal signs and action signs (Farnell 1995a; see also Heath 1986; Kendon 1989; McNeill 1985, 1992; and the section Embodiment of Discourse).

In this critically reflexive arena, meta-level discourses on language and social life provided by native speakers are no longer simply sources of data for the presentation of a problem-free "indigenous perspective." Speakers become intellectual collaborators who can make substantial theoretical contributions. Greater reflexive awareness of the very processes of recording and analysis have been called for and demonstrated (Briggs 1986; Ardener 1989 [1978]; Bauman and Briggs 1990; Farnell 1994; Haviland 1996; Urban 1996a).

Context

Expanding what counts as discourse beyond "naturally occurring speech" to "naturally occurring speech and bodily action" prompts reflection about what an adequate theory of context might look like. Clearly, a theory of context must take into account the copresence of other semiotic practices. Conceptions of context must also be elaborated to account for events taking place elsewhere in space or time that give meaning to novel events and actions. Emergent performances are necessarily situated in cultural histories and long-term patterns of action. Performances are situated within the context of histories of performance and cultural knowledge. (For further discussion of context in discourse-focused work, see Introduction and papers in Goodwin and Duranti [1992].)

Actors also bring individual perspectives to the situations in which they operate, and a context analysis must account for the strategies actors use "to constitute the culturally and historically organized social worlds that they inhabit" (Duranti and Goodwin 1992:5). This means defining context "from the inside" rather than, as in traditional approaches to folklore, considering context "from the outside in"; context is not some kind of "surround" that exerts influence on expressive forms and texts (Bauman 1992:142). It is agent-centered, emergent, and may vary across participants in a given event. Social actors position themselves in conversations according to their personal histories and goals and are simultaneously positioned by others according to factors such as class, ethnicity, and gender (Davies and Harré 1990).

Previous discourse is a further dimension of context because discourse itself is the source of much presupposed knowledge. Discourse is highly intertextual: Any present utterance, as Bahktin observed, is "replete with echoes, allusions, paraphrases, and outright quotations of prior discourse" (Mannheim and Tedlock 1995:7). Utterances and narratives typically reference other texts, and pieces of previous discourse are frequently inserted into newly created texts (see Bauman 1992). Often references to prior discourse take the form of direct or indirect quotations (see, for example, Bakhtin 1981; Briggs 1992; Lucy 1990; Silverstein 1985; Tannen 1995; Urban 1984). These "entextualized" pieces of discourse import meanings from other situations and contribute to the creation of emergent meanings in novel contexts (see Bauman and Briggs 1990; also Kuipers 1990; Urban 1996a; Silverstein and Urban 1996; Graham In press).

Methods: Text Collection and Elicitation

The ethnographic focus on socially situated discourse contrasts with earlier methods for language study in American anthropology, as well as those adhered to by contemporary descriptive linguists. Two traditional methods for studying language that became central to the Boasian tradition of the study of North American Indian languages are text collection and elicitation (see, for example, Boas 1940; Radin 1949).

Texts

In this tradition, linguists take written texts as the starting point for linguistic analyses (see Bernard and Ryan, this volume). These texts are typically elicited from native speakers by a field worker who analyzes grammatical structure based on the patterns that emerge in the texts. Before the use of tape recorders, this process necessarily involved a stop-start process of dictation, which destroyed the natural flow of a storytelling performance or other speech event, and texts were usually collected outside of normal cultural contexts of narration.[4]

Such limited technological means precluded any detailed attention to the role of naturally occurring discourse within social life. Analytical goals centered on grammatical structure, the mythological, and other ethnographic content of narratives. As Tedlock (1993:38–39) notes, only after new recording technologies emerged could linguistic anthropologists and folklorists turn their theoretical attention to features of oral performance that could not be captured through dictation or elicitation. Throughout the late 1970s and early '80s, the emphasis on narrative performance of verbal art directed attention away from the study of formal patterning and symbolic content of texts typical of the Boasian tradition and an earlier poetics. The focus instead was on the emergence of verbal art in social interaction and fine-grained analyses of speech events. This interest connects with a long tradition of thinking about language and society that emerges clearly in the writings of Vico, Herder, and von Humboldt, who argue that verbal art is a central dynamic force in shaping linguistic structure and study. Attention to poetics from Sapir, the Russian formalists, and members of the Prague school contributed to the development of performance and poetics in the 1970s and 1980s (Bauman and Briggs 1990:59).

Elicitation

In this second method, a linguist elicits words and sentences from a native speaker and transcribes the sounds into a written form. Usually, the linguist works with one or a small number of informants. Each utterance produced by the native speaker is seen as an instantiation, a token, of the abstract code or language. Through elicitation of words and sentences, the linguist tries to determine the structure of the grammar underlying the spoken utterances. In this way, it's possible to determine and describe such things as the sounds of a language (its phonetic inventory), the way these sounds combine (the phonology), and syntactical patterns (word order, grammatical particles). Descriptive linguists, who aim to describe language structure, use this methodology.

Although discourse-centered research incorporates both elicitation and text-focused methods of analysis, it differs from earlier approaches by taking contextually situated discourse as the starting point for analysis. Elicitation and text-focused analysis are often incorporated at later stages, as specific problems emerge.

Identifying, Collecting, and Recording Situated Discourse

There is no single best method of collecting information on language use within a community. The starting point, though, is to seek, or discover, through participant observation, those forms of discourse that will form the data for analysis. (For an excellent discussion of ethnographic methods and transcription see Duranti 1997: 84–161). Appropriate procedures will depend on the theoretical focus of the research, the relationship of the ethnographer to the community, and the specific situation.

One method advocated as a way to make "ethnographies of communication" (for example, Gumperz and Hymes 1964; Hymes 1967, 1974; Sherzer and Darnell 1972; Bauman and Sherzer 1989; Saville-Troike 1989) involves making an inventory of distinct spoken forms, both marked (not typical) and unmarked (typical), and the contexts in which they occur. Recording a broad range of spoken discourse provides data from which to compare and contrast distinct expressive forms and styles along formal and functional lines. A researcher may want to learn if speakers change how they talk when addressing certain individuals (such as elders, relatives, or those of certain social roles or genders) or in distinct social settings (for example, ceremonial contexts), or if there are special oratorical styles or styles of interacting when telling stories or myths. If special forms or styles of speech do exist, then the researcher would attempt to map their social distribution (that is, find out who has the capacity and authority to use these forms) and try to discover how the forms are learned and in what situations they can occur.

Depending on the researcher's theoretical focus, it might also be important to note whether some expressive modes of speaking stimulate other forms of expression (see Feld 1990 [1982]) and to determine the relationships between speech, gesture, facial expression, body position, and spatial orientation (for example, Goodwin 1984; Wiget 1987; Kendon 1989; Hanks 1990; Duranti 1992; Streeck 1993; Farnell 1995a, 1995c; Kaeppler 1995) and other sensory modalities.

The notion of a "soundscape" (Schafer 1997) has directed researchers' attempts to record and describe the full range of socially meaningful sounds used within a community (see Feld 1990 [1982]; Graham 1995). A soundscape describes the sounds that people make and use over a 24-hour period, together with explanations of their meanings. It includes talk, musical forms, silences (Basso 1972), and attention to groups that are silenced (Lederman 1984; Gal 1991). Description of a soundscape might include variations in the social use of sound that occur due to seasonal changes, in response to (or to provoke) natural events, and in conjunction with ceremonial cycles. The concept of soundscape draws attention to the fact that speech is just one modality within an entire arena of socially constructed and meaningful sound production. Distinct genres, such as lament, song, and oratory, may have important interconnections yet contrast in significant ways (see Graham 1984, 1986). Moreover, communities vary in the way that they divide the continuum between speech and song (see List 1963). In a soundscape, expressive forms that sound like speech (or song) to Western ears may be classified in ways that challenge ethnographers' assumptions (see Seeger 1986). The notion of soundscape has proven useful in calling researchers' attention to unmarked forms of speech, which tended to be overlooked in earlier ethnographies of communication.[5]

Everyday or unmarked forms of discourse constitute important data for analysis because they contain information about language ideology, socialization, and ways in which gender, age, ethnic identity, and power relationships are linguistically constructed and conceived. These unmarked forms provide a basis against which more salient forms (oratory, storytelling, poetry, etc.) can be compared and contrasted. Moreover, marked forms derive some of their meaning through their contrasts with everyday forms of expression (see, for example, Urban 1985).

If the research focus is more specifically defined at the outset, as in studies of language and gender (see papers in Philips et al. 1987; Hall and Bucholtz 1995) or language socialization, (for example, Schieffelin and Ochs 1986a 1986b; Ochs 1988; Schieffelin 1990), then the researcher would select those social contexts that facilitate observation of the linguistic features targeted for investigation. For example, in her study of language socialization among Kaluli children, Schieffelin (1990) used ethnographic observation to determine the activities and times of day when caregivers and children interact most intensively. She found that opportunities for lively interaction occurred in the early morning when families awaken and begin to prepare the first meal. Interactions during the late afternoon when mothers return from the garden and begin preparations for the evening meal and during trips to the stream for bathing were other opportunities for lively interaction and were particularly fruitful occasions for studying socialization practices (p. 25). Like time, space may be another dimension that permits access to distinct types of social interaction. Thus, once Ochs (1988) broke through the "honored guest" status in the Samoan household, she was able to enter the domestic space at the back of the house where previously inaccessble forms of interaction between caregivers and children take place. Garvey (1984) and Ochs (1979b) show how the study of children's talk is an area with its own methodological problems.

A crucial element of the research process is to make recordings of discourse as it unfolds in social settings. Typically, this involves using a high-quality portable audiotape recorder and microphones. (Internal microphones are generally of poor quality. For practical advice regarding recording techniques in natural settings, see Goodwin 1993; Ives 1995). In recent years, as video-recording equipment has become more affordable and portable, researchers have incorporated this technology into their fieldwork so that visual-kinesthetic aspects of discursive practices can be incorporated into analyses (see Kendon 1989; Streeck 1993; Farnell 1995a).

Carrying a recording device in the field as much as possible can provide a researcher with many samples and a variety of types of naturally occurring discourse for later analysis. Recording devices may present problems, however, and a researcher must take into account ethical concerns about privacy, access to restricted information, and rights to ownership, as well as the ways in which, like the presence of the ethnographer, the presence of recording devices may significantly alter the events themselves. In many communities, expressive forms such as songs are considered intellectual property (Seeger 1991, 1997), and intellectual property issues associated with field recordings are increasingly likely to confront researchers. (See Shuy [1986] and Murray and Ross Murray [1992] for discussion of the legality of surreptitious recording. For discussion of ethical dimensions of fieldwork, see Fluehr-Lobban, this volume.)

The advent of affordable recording technologies has in some cases enabled our research subjects to own and operate their own recording devices. Situations where outside researchers no longer have a monopoly over recording technologies challenge us to think of the power vested in our control of technologies. In some cases, new technologies have stimulated changes in the form or use of expressive genres (see Abu-Lughod 1989; Caton 1990; Manuel 1993; also Turner 1991. Spitulnik [1993] provides an excellent overview of anthropological studies of mass media). Local control of recording technologies may also open up new possibilities for collaboration (see Michaels 1994). Ways in which such ownership affects discourse-focused research is an area for further ethnographic investigation.

Participants may be self-conscious or conscious of addressing audiences beyond those immediately present when they know they are being recorded, and their language use can reflect this. Alternatively, people may forget that they are being recorded and after several minutes of self-conscious interaction, they may settle into familiar communicative patterns and activities will proceed as usual (Hymes 1981; Tedlock 1983:18, 302–311; Briggs 1986; Darnell 1989 [1974]; Graham 1995; Haviland 1996; Urban 1996a). Members of a community can become accustomed to the constant presence of electronic technology in much the same way that people often become accustomed to seeing ethnographers writing things in notebooks. Individuals have also been known to comment on the tape recorder or camera's absence when it's not present and wonder why an event is not being recorded.

In situations where participants are sensitive to intrusive technologies, a small tape recorder, which is less obtrusive than a camcorder, may be allowed. In some cases, however, participants may refuse to speak or perform when a recording device is present, or the ethnographer may be excluded from an event if carrying such devices. One option in such cases would be to explore the possibility of recording an elicited or "staged" performance at a later time. This will, of course, be different in many ways, but is not thereby rendered inauthentic nor is it without considerable analytic value. The presence of the ethnographer and recording devices will almost certainly affect people and their interactions, but reflexive consideration of these factors, rather than being denied, can be incorporated into analyses with interesting results. Labov (1972) recognized the problem of how to observe people's interaction without their being self-conscious as an "observer's paradox" in sociolinguistic research and developed various fieldwork techniques to attempt to transcend this dilemma.

Certainly, good field recordings of contextually situated interaction either audio or audiovisual, are essential to discourse-focused work. This doesn't negate the usefulness of field notes, however, which are often essential companions to recorded data. For example, field notes can be used to document important contextual observations that can later be incorporated into transcriptions. Alternately, comments can be spoken into the tape recorder/video camera itself. A useful technique is to correlate numbers on a tape/video recorder counter with notes written in a notebook (for example, Schieffelin 1990:30).

In and of themselves, however, field notes are insufficient as records because they are only fragments of discourse or descriptions of it at best; they don't provide records adequate to analyze the richness and nuances of discourse as performed. Tedlock (1983:38–39), for example, observed that the Zuni texts he recorded using a tape recorder, were nearly twice as long as those recorded by Benedict. Among the reasons for this is that narratives given for dictation tended to be condensations of what a performer would tell in a normal, spontaneous situation and because a responsive audience was lacking. At the time field recordings are made, a researcher may be unaware of components that subsequent analysis of audio/videotape reveal as significant carriers of social meaning (see discussion of the two tape recorder/two video method below).

Processes of Translation and Transcription

The extensive use of tape recorders and, more recently, video cameras, has neither replaced nor reduced the need for adequate methods of written transcription. On the contrary, innovations in electronic recording technologies have facilitated the development of written transcription systems more adequate to the analytic tasks at hand. The processes of transcription and translation are themselves interpretive analytic tasks; they are re-presentations of performance that are necessarily informed by explicit and implicit theoretical assumptions (see Ochs 1979a; Hymes 1981; Tedlock 1983; Woodbury 1985; Sherzer and Urban 1986a:11–12; Sherzer 1992; Swann 1992). As Ardener (1989) reminds us, particular events that are registered depend on our modes of registration and specification—that is, the means by which they are apperceived. He advises us to know as much as possible about these modes because "our definition of . . . the events depends upon the modes of registration available to us" (p. 87). The techniques we use to complete the tasks of transcription and translation influence the interpretation of texts and the ways in which meanings are understood to emerge from socially situated discourse. Similarly, the phonological patterns or grammatical categories of the translator's language may affect the transcription and translation of texts (see Whorf 1956; also Sherzer 1987).

MacMahon (1996:831–837) provides an excellent history of the interest in and development of phonetic transcription systems that can be traced back, in England and North America, to the late sixteenth century. Interest in Asian languages and cultures at the end of the eighteenth century first led scholars to question the adequacy of characters from the Roman alphabet to represent spoken pronunciation in foreign tongues. In other contexts, the need to incorporate information about pronunciation into dictionaries, interest in transcribing local dialects of European languages, and intensive Christian missionary activity in Africa and elsewhere also led to specific methods of transcribing speech (MacMahon 1996).

A group of modern language teachers in the International Phonetic Association incorporated many of these efforts into the International Phonetic Alphabet (IPA) in 1888. Although it has undergone subsequent changes and additions, the IPA remains the major phonetic alphabet in use today. It comprises an extensive set of symbols and diacritics derived from the Roman alphabet and has symbols for consonants, vowels, and some prosodic features such as stress and intonation.[6]

It is worth remembering that in the era of dictation (an era stretching back to the making of Homeric texts and lasting until well into the Boasian era) the *only* language-recording technology was writing. Before the invention of the tape recorder, important collections of spoken language and other vocal expressive forms were recorded on wax cylinders, glass acetate, and aluminum phonograph discs.[7] Materials recorded with these technologies are deposited in the Archives of Traditional Music at Indiana University and in the Smithsonian Institution. In addition to collections made by Boas and his students such as Radin and Fletcher, Haugen's study of Norwegian language change in the Midwest (1969) and Turner's collection of Sea Island Gullah (1969) included samples of situated discourse.[8]

As mentioned above, the advent of the tape recorder transformed the field worker's ability to record oral discourse (Tedlock 1983:38–39), and only subsequently did the examination of native poetic structure (ethnopoetics) and the adequate translation of verbal art emerge as central concerns.

At this point, analytical limitations of conventional transcriptions began to emerge. Ironically perhaps, the very success of phonetic notation systems had led investigators to limit their definitions of "language" to those segmentable components that could be represented with the Roman alphabet and its extensions. New technologies and innovative forms of transcription have exploded limiting theoretical assumptions about language and enabled anthropologically oriented linguists to expand notions of linguistic functionality.

With the explicit goal of exploring native poetic structures, Hymes (1981), Tedlock (1983), and others began to expand the notational repertoire to include conventional poetic and dramatic devices. Figure 1 illustrates how Tedlock (1983:84) used line breaks to indicate short pauses and dots to indicate longer pauses, thereby inviting the reader to listen more closely to the rhythms of speech and silence in performance. Upper-case letters mark louder speech and marginal parentheses guide the reader's attention to voice quality and volume. A vowel followed by a long dash indicates vowel lengthening; repeated letters indicate drawn-out sounds; letters spilling downward on the page indicate descending glissando; and split lines indicate tonal changes in chants.

Now there's a voice
and she hears it.
"Perhaps
you are
someone from the village who's lost the way
and you're calling out.
Well, I'll answer you, and
perhaps I could depend on you for the night."
That's how the poor girl felt.
She quickly put on her snow boots, then
she went out in the clearing to the edge of the firelight.
(*as if from a distance, and very high*)
hoooooooooooohaaaaaaaaaaaaaaaaaaaaaaaa
                                    a
                                  a
                               a
                             a
                            ay it said.
(*calling out*) "Come over here, I'm spending the night here," the girl
   said.

And then
there was another call then:
hooooooooooooooooooooohaaaaaaaaaaaaaaaaaaaaaaaaaaa
                                         a
                                      a
                                    a
                                  ay it said.
(*calling out*) "Come over here, I'm spending the night here," the girl
   said again.

The girl went inside and PUT MORE WOOD ON, the fire was really
   blazing, then it came CLOSER.
It came closer
calling
hooooooooooooooooooooooooooohaaaaaaaaaaaaaaaaaaa
                                           a
                                        a
                                     a
                                 ay it said.
The girl heard it very clearly now.
(*gasping*) "Eeee! this is why you
warned me.
Why did I answer?
So this is why you told me
that I shouldn't have a fire late at night.
Well, I asked for it," she said, and the girl

Figure 1. Transcription designed to convey features of oral performance such as volume, pause structure, utterance length, and pitch (from *The Spoken Word and the Work of Interpretation* by Dennis Tedlock. Copyright © 1983 University of Pennslyvania Press. Reprinted by permission of the publisher.).

Tedlock called for punctuating according to rising and falling contours of oratory, and shaped lines and stanzas according to the stops and starts of dramatic timing. His explicit aim was to create "open or performable texts" that "open the ear" to the sounds of vocal performance (1983:62). Students of "the ethnography of speaking" contributed to these developments, choosing from these transcription options according to their analytic purposes. Papers in Edwards and Lampert (1993) discuss a number of transcription and coding systems for discourse analysis from contrasting theoretical perspectives, highlighting the point that a transcription format should be related to the goals of analysis.

Of course, no transcription can ever be so detailed and precise as to provide for the full re-creation of the sound (or vision) of a tape: The hypothetical goal of total notation is a positivist's dream. In light of this, some researchers supplement their written publications with audiotapes (Bowen 1991a,1991b; Feld 1990 [1982]; Sherzer and Urban 1986b; Seeger 1987) and CD-ROMs (Farnell 1995c). Individuals and communities can also exert influence over transcription conventions. For example, Becker (1983) describes how his Burmese consultant objected to phonetic transcription and insisted on using the Burmese writing system because it related to Buddhist understanding of the language. Elizabeth Brandt (1981) describes an extreme case where members of a speech community entirely rejected the writing of their languages.

Computer-Assisted Analyses

Recently, scholars have experimented with computer programs, such as SoundEdit and Signalyze, to digitize sound for visual display.[9] Such programs provide graphic representations of wave forms that can be useful for analysis and representation of patterning in amplitude, pause structure, and pitch (using spectrographs). Digitized images can be especially productive in analysis because they enable researchers to capture microfeatures of performance and to perform analytic tasks involving looping, splicing, and juxtaposition of instances of speech or other sounds. For example, it is possible to create a "tape loop" of a recorded segment and replay it repeatedly in order to listen—and see—aspects of sound such as utterance or pause length and amplitude. Sound segments can also be juxtaposed to discern the existence of regularities or microvariations across instances.

Digitized sound samples enabled Roseman (1991:171) to recognize an acoustic iconicity between cicada buzzing, certain bird calls, and Temiar bamboo tube drumming, which were essential to efficacious performance. The digitized representations shown in Figure 2 illustrate the striking resemblance between the wave forms of sounds Temiar link with performance and associate with evocative power. Urban uses digitized samples to represent the regularity of utterance length and amplitude in an excerpt from the Shokleng origin myth to illustrate the syllable-by-syllable dialogic nature of the performance (1991:109; see also 1996b: 201). Digitized figures also illustrate the regularities of Warão lament performance in Briggs's analysis (1993). Sherzer uses digitized samples to display visually the parallelism of amplitude (from high to low) that characterizes certain genres of Kuna oral performance, as well as pitch and volume patterns (1992: 430, 435–438).

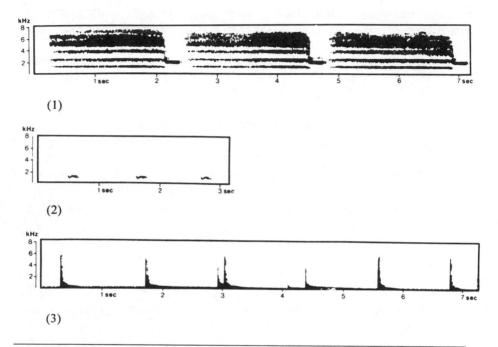

Figure 2. Digitized samples of (1) cicadas, (2) the golden-throated barbet (*Megalaima franklini*), and (3) the beat of bamboo tubes illustrate an iconicity that is essential to efficacious Temiar performance (from Roseman 1991:170. Reproduced by permission of the University of California Press from *Healing Sounds from the Malaysian Rainforest: Temiar Music and Medicine.* Copyright © 1991.).

Researchers also experiment with transcriptions that depict pitch variations and other features of speech, plus other musical or music-like vocal genres. Spectographs may be used or graphs may best represent the salient features that a scholar seeks to illustrate. Modified Western musical staffs can also be suitable for depicting features of vocal performance. Linguistic anthropologists, often working in collaboration with ethnomusicologists (for example, Sherzer and Wicks 1982; Graham 1984, 1994, 1995), or those with ethnomusicological training (for example, Seeger 1987; Feld 1990 [1982]), have developed innovative ways to represent melodic genres. Figure 3 (in two parts) shows a transcription of a Xavante musical performance in which the musical staff has been reduced from five to three lines to highlight the reduced pitch inventory of this musical genre. Notes with indistinct pitch appear as "x," and slanting lines before notes indicate a slide up or down to the indicated pitch (transcription by Scruggs in Graham 1994:734–735, 1995:120–121).

By contrasting four representational modes of the same stretch of Kuna chanting, Sherzer (1992:434–435) shows how a variety of transcription modes are suitable for

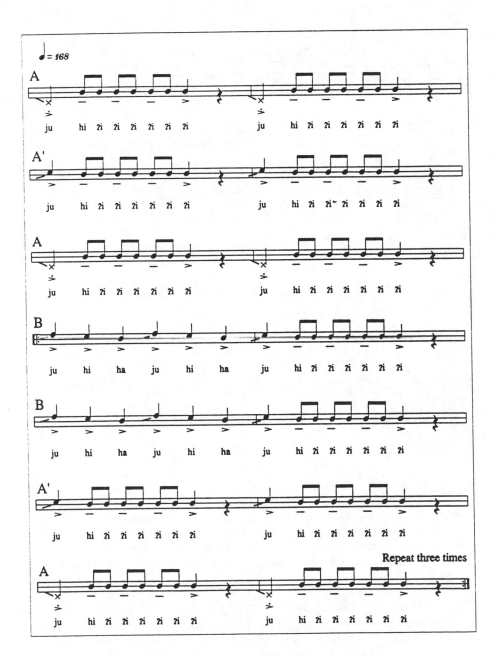

Part 1

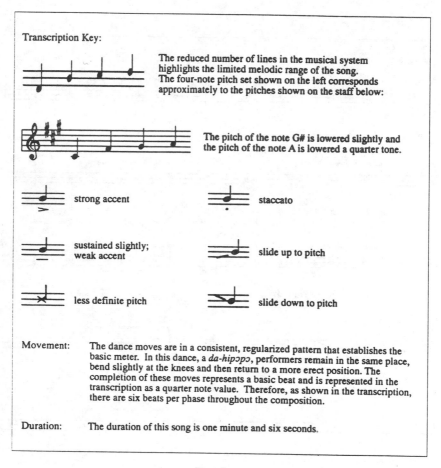

Transcription Key:

The reduced number of lines in the musical system highlights the limited melodic range of the song. The four-note pitch set shown on the left corresponds approximately to the pitches shown on the staff below:

The pitch of the note G# is lowered slightly and the pitch of the note A is lowered a quarter tone.

strong accent

staccato

sustained slightly; weak accent

slide up to pitch

less definite pitch

slide down to pitch

Movement: The dance moves are in a consistent, regularized pattern that establishes the basic meter. In this dance, a *da-hipɔpɔ*, performers remain in the same place, bend slightly at the knees and then return to a more erect position. The completion of these moves represents a basic beat and is represented in the transcription as a quarter note value. Therefore, as shown in the transcription, there are six beats per phase throughout the composition.

Duration: The duration of this song is one minute and six seconds.

Part 2

Figure 3. This musical transcription of Xavante *da-ño're* illustrates how modifications of the conventional Western musical notation system may highlight salient features of non-Western musics. Here, the Western musical staff is reduced to call attention to the pitch inventory and notation is designed to indicate sliding pitch and less definite pitch (transcription by T. M. Scruggs in Graham 1994:734–735, 1995:120–121. Reproduced by permission of the American Anthropological Association from *American Ethnologist*, 1994. Not for sale or further reproduction.).

distinct analytic ends (see Figure 4, in four parts). These alternative modes of representation and transcription can be used to highlight or downplay the importance of varied linguistic and stylistic features that serve various expressive and aesthetic ends (see also Hymes 1981; McClendon 1981; Tedlock 1983, 1987; Silverstein 1984; Woodbury 1985, 1987).

kurkin ipekantinaye.
Owners of kurkin.
olopillise pupawalakan akkuekwiciye.
Your roots reach to the level of gold.

kurkin ipekantinaye.
Owners of kurkin.
olopillise pe maliwaskakan upoekwiciye.
Your small roots are placed into the level of gold.

kurkin ipekantinaye.
Owners of kurkin.
olopillise pe maliwaskakana pioklekekwiciye.
Your small roots are nailed into the level of gold.

kurkin ipekantinaye.
Owners of kurkin.
olopillipiiye   apikaekwiciye kurkin ipekantinaye.
You are resisting within the very level of gold owners of kurkin.

olopilli aytikkimakkekwici kurkin ipekantinaye.
You weigh a great deal in the level of gold owners of kurkin.

olopilli kwamakkekwici kurkin ipekantinaye.
You are firmly placed in the level of gold owners of kurkin.

olopilli aytitimakkekwakwiciye kurkin ipekantinaye.
You are moving in the level of gold owners of kurkin.

Part 1

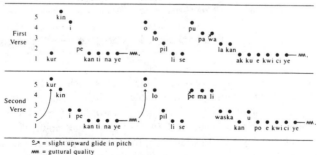

⌐↗ = slight upward glide in pitch
ᴡᴡ = guttural quality
· = breath intake

Part 2

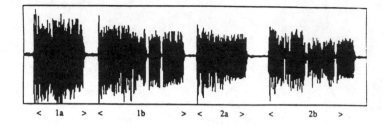

1a kurkin ipekantinaye.
    Owners of kurkin.
1b olopillise pupawalakan akkuekwiciye.
    Your roots reach to the level of gold.

2a kurkin ipekantinaye.
    Owners of kurkin.
2b olopillise pe maliwaskakan upoekwiciye.
    Your small roots are placed into the level of gold.

Part 3

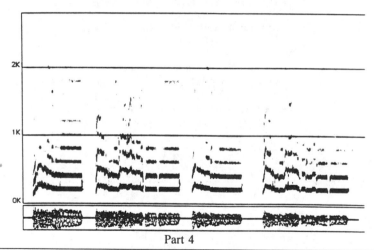

Part 4

Figure 4. Four representational modes of the same stretch of Kuna chanting illustrate a variety of transcription modes uniquely suitable for distinct analytic ends. Part 1 provides a segmental transcription of sounds, morphemes and words in which line and verse structure is based on musical and pause patterns; Part 2 is a graph that captures pitch and tempo; Part 3 is a SoundEdit display that illustrates amplitude and pause patterns; and Part 4 is pitch tracking (of formant structures) that shows the falling pitch and volume that is characteristic of this genre, as well as long pauses between lines. Parts 1, 3, and 4 from Sherzer 1992:434–436 reproduced by permission of the Smithsonian Institution Press; Part 2 reproduced by permission of Joel Sherzer and Sammie Wicks and *Latin American Music Review*, of the University of Texas Press. Copyright © 1982.).

The Embodiment of Discourse

The shift to performance and the inclusion of context in linguistic analyses also opened up theoretical space within which to add the embodiment of social actors to the notion of language-in-use (Farnell 1995a:9). Several investigators have recognized that the visual-kinesthetic components of discourse, such as gestures, postures, gazes, facial expressions, and spatial orientation, are meaningful components of linguistic utterances in social contexts (for example, Goffman 1961, 1974; Sherzer 1973; Kendon 1980, 1983; Goodwin 1981; Tedlock 1983; Wiget 1987; Hanks 1990; Duranti 1992; Haviland 1993; Keating 1998, In press). Until recently, however, a way of making the analysis of body movements in spatial contexts part of the normal ethnographer's tool kit had not been developed. In the 1970s, Birdwhistell's "kinesics" promised a solution, but failed because bodily movements were still seen as "behaviors" rather than signifying acts—that is, as agentic, semiotic practices that are shared expressive resources which require translation from one culture to another. Kinesic analyses and attempts to create an adequate transcription system dissolved under the weight of ever-increasing microscopic behavioral detail. Also absent from earlier conceptions was an adequate analytic framework for dealing with the multidimensional spaces within which humans move; spaces that are simultaneously physical, conceptual, moral, and ethical (Williams 1995:52).

Williams's "semasiological theory" of human action with its central concept of the "action sign," has provided investigators with new theoretical resources more adequate to this task (see Williams 1975, 1982, 1991, 1995, 1996). From a semasiological perspective, discourse is necessarily embodied because persons are conceived as subjects empowered to perform signifying acts with both vocal signs (speech) and action signs (bodily movements). In addition, a new emphasis on acquiring a literacy specific to the medium (that is, the ability to read and write body movement) has been achieved through a movement transcription system called "Labanotation" (Page 1990, 1996; Williams and Farnell 1990; Farnell 1994). The introductory essay in Farnell (1995b) offers an overview of recent theoretical developments in the anthropology of human movement systems. Ethnographic studies can be found in Farnell (1995b), Williams (1996) and in the *Journal for the Anthropological Study of Human Movement*.

An alphabetic script for writing body movement must solve the problem of how to represent all the parts and surfaces of the body with two-dimensional graphic signs (see Figure 5). It must also make finite in some way the space(s) in which the body moves. Figure 6 illustrates how the Laban script uses simple set theory to represent spatial directions viewed from the actor's perspective. Locating this imaginary three-dimensional "cross of axes" at each joint of the body achieves a remarkable economy of graphic signs: The same scheme specifies the direction of individual limbs and smaller body parts and provides a framework for indicating the direction of pathways for the whole body (as when a person moves from one location to another). These graphic signs for body parts and spatial directions are arbitrary but iconically motivated to assist reading fluency.

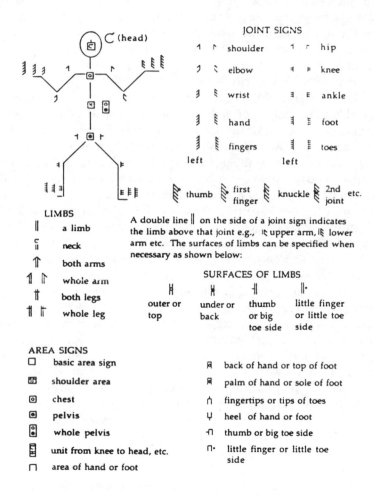

Figure 5. Labanotation: graphic signs for body parts and surfaces (from Farnell 1995a. Reproduced by permission of the University of Texas Press.).

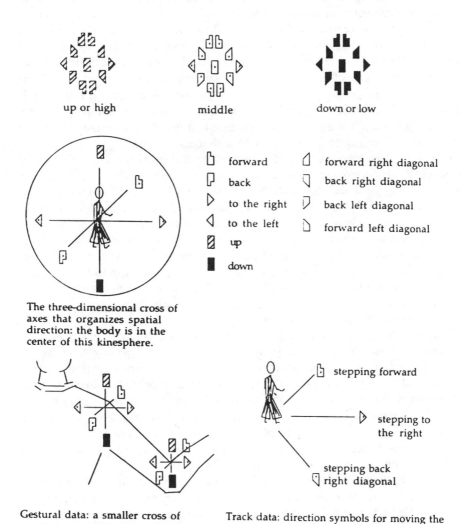

up or high middle down or low

⌐	forward	⌐	forward right diagonal
Ц	back	⌐	back right diagonal
▷	to the right	⌐	back left diagonal
◁	to the left	⌐	forward left diagonal
⌐	up		
■	down		

The three-dimensional cross of axes that organizes spatial direction: the body is in the center of this kinesphere.

stepping forward

stepping to the right

stepping back right diagonal

Gestural data: a smaller cross of axes is imagined at the center of each joint so that direction for each part of a limb can be specified.

Track data: direction symbols for moving the whole body from one place to another. These would be placed in the central support column on the staff.

Figure 6. Labanotation: graphic signs for specifying spatial direction (from Farnell 1995a. Reproduced by permission of the University of Texas Press.).

Movement necessarily takes place through time and the flow of action and direction of reading in texts written with the Laban script is upward. Placing symbols in different columns on a vertical staff organizes the flow of action; a central dividing line separates left and right sides of the body. The Laban script can be divided into bars like a musical score if metrical timing is required, or it can be used without if not—the length of spatial symbols indicating relative timing instead. Farnell's ethnography of the simultaneous production of spoken Nakota and Plains Sign Language in the storytelling practices of Assiniboine elders illustrates this approach (1995a, 1995c). Figure 7 is an example of a transcription of speech and gestural signs from a storytelling performance that was first videotaped and then transcribed and translated in collaboration with the storyteller.

Concepts of the body, systems of spatial orientation, and concepts of time differ considerably across languages and cultures, and the Laban script has proven flexible enough to take these into account (see Williams and Farnell 1990; Farnell 1994, 1996; Williams 1995; Page 1996). For example, Farnell (1995a:141–154) found that understanding Assiniboine conceptions of the cardinal directions was, among other things, central to understanding deictic utterances in speech and gesture. (This applied to unmarked forms of everyday discourse as well as storytelling performances.) Such a conception was incorporated into the transcription by placing a "spatial orientation key" at the start of the movement score; this tells the reader that this particular conception is in operation throughout, much like the key of C# minor might operate at the start of a musical score.

We know as much as we do about the speech components of discursive practices because we remove them from the flow of "real time" by writing them down. Alphabetic scripts are a clear mode of specification for components of spoken languages at a phonological level. A script designed to produce movement texts establishes similar conditions for the specification and registration of the bodily, spatial, and dynamic components of actions. This makes translation into words unnecessary for creating ethnographically appropriate descriptions of action. In addition, when actions and words integrate, as is most often the case in social interaction, both can be given equal analytical weight.

In addition, embodied aesthetic sensibilities such as voice quality and melody can underlie notions of propriety, correctness, appropriateness, and honorification in language use. Laderman (1987), for example, illustrates how only "beautiful voices" are efficacious in Malay ritual. Irvine (1992) demonstrates how Wolof speakers ideologically associate vocally embodied affectivity with honorification.

Collaboration with Native Speakers

Since meanings of utterances are embedded within the context in which they occur, it's important to note not only what explicit propositions are made but other

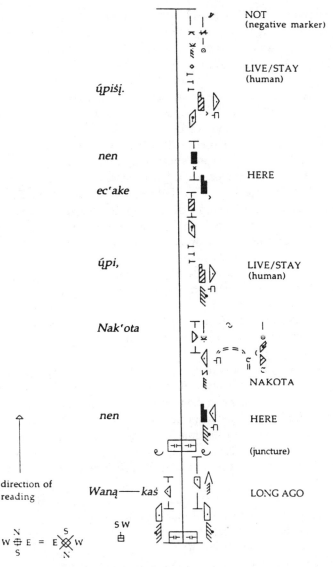

1. *Waną—kaś, nen, Nak'ota úpi,   ec'ake   nen   úpiśį.*
   Long ago   here Nakota they live/ be always   here they live not
   Lo—ng ago, the Indians that live here now, did not always live here.

Figure 7. Assiniboine storytelling with Plains Sign Talk and Nakota: p. 1 of the Labanotated score (from Farnell 1995a:83. Reproduced by permission of the University of Texas Press.).

features of the environment that might have some relationship to an utterance's meanings. Many studies show how meaning emerges from context; others show how the internal structure of stories reflects embeddness in larger interactive processes (M. Goodwin 1982a, 1982b; Heath 1983;Goodwin and Duranti 1992:11). Since consultants are always active participants, collaborating with them during transcription, translation, and interpretation is crucial to discovering presupposed knowledge, interpretive frames, and the relevance of prior discourse. Basso (1979, 1990), Briggs (1986, 1988), and Hymes (1981), among others, illustrate the advantages of long-term collaborations with consultants. Farnell (1995a), Graham (1995), and Valentine (1995) explicitly address how consultant and community concerns can influence the shape and scope of research. The methods used will depend on research goals as well as practical and political realities of the fieldwork situation.[10] Collaboration itself is a socially constructed relationship that develops throughout fieldwork.

To better understand native perspectives in instances of socially situated speech, recent discourse-focused research has attempted to directly involve native speakers in transcription and analysis. In transcribing and analyzing the speech of Kaluli children, for example, Schieffelin worked with the mothers of children she had recorded (1990:30–32). They helped with initial transcription by repeating back their own and others' speech as they listened to the tape-recorded samples. Schieffelin notes that this was especially helpful in glossing special forms children used, identifying speakers in multiparty talk, and specifying the history and ownership of objects involved in the interactions.

The women also provided important metalinguistic commentary that made explicit Kaluli notions about proper language use. Schieffelin took careful notes on the women's comments and incorporated them into the extensive contextual notes she had made while recording. This metacommentary became part of extensive text annotatations and Schieffelin used it to generate further questions about interactional patterns, classifications of speech acts and events, and notions of what constituted "good talk" (1990:30). She notes that for every hour of recorded speech, she spent an additional 20 hours preparing the annotated and translated transcript. Given the recognition that discourse is both saturated with and constitutive of social meaning, this is neither surprising nor atypical for discourse-centered work.

To obtain further insights into the recorded interactions, Schieffelin incorporated a "reliability check" into her work (1990:30–31). This involved relistening and reviewing the transcriptions with a young man who hadn't participated in the interactions. Schieffelin originally conceived of this exercise as a means to check her initial transcriptions, but she discovered that it was a way of "extending and enriching the contextualizing ethnographic and linguistic information" (p.31) that the mothers had provided. Work with the young man revealed that devices such as prosody, voice quality, and affect-marked affixes convey significant affective information and that pragmatic uses of word order can disambiguate utterances and clarify issues. To avoid influencing consultants' interpretations of video-recorded data, Erickson and Shultz (1982:59–63) developed a technique that allowed consultants to stop the tape wherever they found items worthy of attention and to comment on them in interactions they were watching. They found that consultants usually chose to stop at points where discourse topics or conversational routines had just been completed.

Graham (1995:15–16) worked with Xavante assistants in ways similar to Schieffelin but used two tape recorders as she was transcribing and translating field recordings with native speakers. While one tape recorder was used to play back recorded instances of contextually situated discourse, the other recorded the consultants' explanations and responses to questions Graham posed about the interactions and language use.

Using two tape recorders enables the investigator to return repeatedly to informants' responses to the original taped utterances. It also permits the researcher to discover discrepancies between forms that appear in an initial recording and what informants "repeat" for transcription (see Urban 1996a). Such discrepancies may be due to a straightforward difference between citation form (pronunciations given in elicitation or interview contexts) and those used in actual practice, but not necessarily. Factors such as a difference in age, class, or gender may be at work, and comparisons may reveal social and pragmatic meanings associated with such alternative forms. It was in using this technique, for example, that Graham discerned significant pragmatic phenomena such as features associated with the speech of elders and alternative patterns of person marking and verb morphology used in speech to, or about, certain kin and affines. These forms, Graham (1990) ascertained, are not typically given in elicitation situations.

In a similar manner, Farnell made important discoveries about Assiniboine conceptions of the integrated nature of speech and signing and the primacy of movement in indigenous classifications by videotaping her own interaction with informants during collaborative transcription and translation sessions as they watched and listened to their own previously recorded storytelling performances (Farnell 1995a:247). She had to change her methodological decision to transcribe first the speech and then the action because one of her informants consistently failed to repeat the words he had spoken on the videotape. It became apparent that he was adding spoken material in order to ensure that meanings contained in the gestural component of his utterances were also included. Only when both speech and action were discussed and transcribed simultaneously was he satisfied that what he had "said" was all there. As in most discourse centered research, consultants' comments on recorded texts provided rich contextualizing information and can be used to generate further questions and elicitations. Briggs (1986:99–100) also notes that participants commented extensively whem reviewing their videotaped interactions.

As these examples show, discourse-centered research incorporates elicitation as a fieldwork technique. However, such elicitation never substitutes for socially situated utterances: Elicitation and interviewing always follow and support the former. Elicitation is limited because, although it frequently enables researchers to determine basic grammatical patterns, when and why social actors use certain forms in specific situations for what kind of pragmatic ends remain to be investigated.

Interviews, too, can supplement direct observation by providing important information. (For an excellent discussion of problems in interview based research, see Briggs [1986] and Urban [1996b]). Communities and individuals within communities vary in the extent to which they are able to provide metalinguistic commentary (that is, talk about) any formal features of discourse or criteria for judging performance (see Hymes 1981; Silverstein 1981). In cultures that don't engage in elaborate metalinguistic glossing, native speakers may not identify distinctive styles or genres or may not be able to describe characteristics of speech or criteria for evaluating performance. Observing how participants in an event react to performances can shed light on such features. For example, noting aside commentary and what causes laughter, smiling, frowning, silence, changes in bodily postures, or responsive gestures can be very instructive. Such visible responses also require careful translation from one cultural context to another, however, and potential meanings associated with such "action signs" or "body languages" must also be ascertained ethnographically, rather than assumed.[11]

Transcription and translation themselves must be viewed as contextually situated, emergent dialogic acts which may generate novel meanings. Accordingly, these tasks have become the focus of productive and provocative analytic inquiry (see Tedlock 1983; Haviland 1996; Urban 1996a; also papers in Sammons and Sherzer In press). Recent studies of roles of native informants in language-focused work challenge researchers to reflect on the situated nature of producing transcriptions, translations, and analyses. Anthropologists have long recognized the significance individual informants and their social positions play in research endeavors. In discourse-focused work, native consultants play important and unique roles. Not only can their social position influence whether they will transcribe or translate the speech of certain individuals (see Graham 1995:13–16), but relationships between speakers and consultants may influence the meanings that are understood to be encoded in texts, and even how speech itself is transcribed.

Haviland (1996) examines how Tzotzil Mayas from the highlands of Chiapas, who have little experience with reading and writing, transform aspects of recorded conversation in producing native written texts of multiparty talk. He notes that natives change written texts in ways that "normalize" significant pragmatic features of conversational situations. This includes erasing context-specific elements of speech, such as quotative particles and evidentials that relate utterances to previous conversation. Natives also smooth "interactional edges," eliminate false starts, disfluencies, asides, and Spanish loan words from their transcriptions.

Urban (1996a) observes that there may be predictable regularities in how native transcriptions of recorded speech differ from original utterances. He proposes that when replication occurs in relatively deliberate contexts (as in transcription) the copy may include segmentable forms that do not occur in the original but that encode meanings that are only pragmatically inferable from the original. He also notes that native transcribers may delete metadiscursive instructions, especially indications of mistakes or deviations from an intended "text" (as in a myth), and may "correct" mistakes indicated by such remarks. Urban proposes that power relations between the speaker of the original text and the "copier" (or transcriber) may influence the production of a written text. He says that when the relationship between the originator and copier is more symmetrical and egalitarian, there will be a greater divergence between the copy and the original; the copier is also more likely to respond to the originator. In contrast, where there is greater power differential, transcribers attempt to render versions that are more faithful to the original text. These observations have important consequences because the ways in which a text is transcribed influences its subsequent translation and analysis.

Concluding Remarks

Discourse-centered approaches in linguistic anthropology position speech and other expressive acts as the principle means by which social actors create and recreate social life. They thus open up new ways to conceive of "culture." This perspective offers new resources for investigating some traditional problems in anthropology and related disciplines, and for discovering how processsses of cultural change and continuity take place.

The focus of analysis in discourse-centered methods is on data collected in actual social life. With a corpus of transcribed and translated texts in hand, researchers may examine formal discourse features and grammatical patterning to discover ways in which such devices are implicated in broader social and cultural phenomena. Scholars have examined such features as evidentials, deictics, reported speech, metadiscursive particles and phrases, semantic and grammatical patterning, as well as formal features of performance such as the organization of talk.

In addition to such microconstituents, formal analysis may focus on macro structures such as the formal organization of entire narrative texts (see Hymes 1981; Urban 1986; also Bernard and Ryan, this volume) or on relationships between entire genres (see Graham 1986; Seeger 1986). Work with native assistants in transcription and translation, including metacommentary and elicitation, will help tease out further significant features. Through detailed attention to such formal elements, as well as examination of the ways in which creative indexical reference conveys additional social meaning in communicative acts, researchers seek to discover how social phenomena, such as relations of power, kinship, identity, gender relations, aesthetics, ideologies and affect, are discursively constituted and negotiated.

Ways in which wider social phenomena will be encoded in discourse can rarely be anticipated before ethnographic fieldwork is well underway. They are usually discovered during fieldwork and necessarily vary according to such factors as interactions between the ethnographer and the individuals and community with whom she or he works, as well as formal elements of the texts themselves. Moreover, just as meanings and interpretations are co-produced among interactants in any ethnographic situation, anthropological understandings of discourse forms are intersubjectively achieved in field research. Outside of the context of fieldwork, interpretations continue to be intersubjectively achieved in dialogue with academic colleagues and the intellectual capital of linguistic anthropology.

Discourse-centered research also entails ongoing relationships between technologies, method, and theory. In an ever-evolving dynamic process, new theoretical questions and insights challenge researchers to devise new methods and adopt or devise new technologies which, in turn, stimulate more theoretical questions and so on. Since theory and method are closely intertwined and are part of the dialogical processes through which we, as social scientists construct ethnographic knowledge, we can expect that new methods of research will continue to arise.

NOTES

We thank Russ Bernard and Jane Hill for their helpful suggestions and the opportunity for collaboration. We also thank Andy Orta, Jon Pressman, Joel Sherzer, Bambi Schieffelin, Greg Urban, and Bonnie Urciuoli for their comments on an earlier version. We are grateful to Tony Seeger, Marilyn Graf, and Judith Gray for helping us find information about early recordings and technologies. We appreciate the help of Jon Wolseth and Jerry Wever in preparing the manuscript. Each author thanks the other for patience, good humor and intellectual companionship. Our contributions are shared; our names appear in alphabetical order.

1. We do not attempt an exhaustive survey of the literature on discourse analysis or linguistic anthropology generally. See Gumperz and Hymes (1986 [1972]) for a survey of work in sociolingistics and the ethnography of speaking up to that date. See Bauman and Briggs (1990) for later contributions.

2. See Hymes (1971) for a historical overview of the emergence of sociolinguistics and the ethnography of speaking as a contrast to the canon in mainstream linguistic theory of the 1960s and 1970s. For further background, see Hymes (1974), Bauman (1977), Bauman and Sherzer (1989), and Bauman and Briggs (1990).

3. See papers in Jarvella and Klein (1982) and Pick and Acredolo (1983) for further references on this topic. Agah (1996), Benveniste (1971 [1956]), Graham (1995:175–206), Mühlhäusler and Harré (1990), and Urban (1989) provide studies of pronoun systems and uses.

4. Urban (1991:16) notes that among Boasian anthropologists, Paul Radin's work stands out because he discusses the methods by which texts in the native language were collected prior to the invention of the tape recorder. These consist of standard informant elicitation and dictation, the writing down of myths in the Winnebago syllabury by the Winnebego themselves, and the use of the Edison phonograph to record elicited tales from which

transcriptions were made (Radin 1949). Radin's work strikes us as remarkably contemporary because he employed the discourse of native accounts in his "method of reconstruction from internal evidence" (1965 [1933]:183–252).

5. In calling for ethnographies of communication, Gumperz and Hymes (1964) did not intend to stimulate disproportionate attention to marked speech styles. This may have occurred because researchers sought to call attention to the richness of verbal life cross-culturally. The tendency parallels disproportionate attention to ritual activities and ceremonial life on the part of sociocultural anthropologists generally. Recent ethnography, both socio-cultural and linguistic, seeks to remedy this through increased attention to "everyday" life. See, for example, Abu-Lughod (1993), Schieffelin (1990), and Ochs (1988).

6. For a guide to IPA and other systems of phonetic representation, both linear and parametric, see MacMahon (1996). Articulatory phoneticians concerned with the dynamics of vocal production now use moving x-ray video images to study the production of "vocal gestures" (see Studdert-Kennedy and Goodall 1992).

7. For discussion of early recording technologies, see Gelatt (1977) and Welch and Burt (1994); see also Copeland (1991).

8. Turner recorded Sea Island Gullah dialects on 154 12-inch aluminum discs, recorded at 78 rpm. The technology he used to make these field recordings was very cumbersome.

9. SoundEdit 16 is available from MacroMedia. Signalyze is available from Network Technology Corporation, 91 Baldwin St, Charlestown, MA 02129. Other sound analysis programs include Capmedia and Kay CSL (computerized speech lab).

10. The political entailments of field research are widely acknowledged in anthropology (see Rabinow 1977; Fox 1991; Clifford and Marcus 1986). They have received less attention in linguistics (see Aissen 1992). Briggs (1986) discusses assymetries of power in linguistic anthropology with a focus on the interview.

11. Anthropologists of Human Movement use the term "body language" to mean systems of action signs with distinct spatial grammars and multiple functions that constitute one of the semiotic practices distinctive of human life. These are often closely integrated with spoken language conceptions, often having given rise to spoken propositional forms, and are certainly never independent of them. We do not intend to invoke popular misconceptions of the term "body language" that connote one-to-one correlations between a movement and "its" meaning. See Williams (1991) and Farnell (1995b) for further information on this subfield.

REFERENCES

Abu-Lughod, Lila. 1989. Bedouins, Cassettes, and Technologies of Public Culture. *Middle East Report 159*:7–11.

Abu-Lughod, Lila. 1993. *Writing Women's Worlds: Bedouin Stories*. Berkeley: University of California Press.

Agah, Asif. 1996. Honorifics. *Annual Review of Anthropology 22*(4):473–488.

Aissen, Judith. 1992. *Fieldwork and Linguistic Theory. International Encyclopedia of Linguistics*, Vol. 2. William Bright, ed. Pp. 9–10. New York: Oxford University Press.

Ardener, Edwin. 1989 [1978]. Some Outstanding Problems in the Analysis of Events. In *Edwin Ardener: The Voice of Prophecy and Other Essays*. M. Chapman, ed. Pp. 86–104. Oxford: Basil Blackwell.

Austin, John L. 1962. *How to Do Things with Words*, 2d ed. J. O. Urmson and M. Sbisa, eds. Cambridge: Harvard University Press.

Bakhtin, M. M. 1981. *The Dialogic Imagination*. C. Emerson and M. Holquist, trans. Austin: University of Texas Press.

Bakhtin, M. M. 1986. *Speech Genres and Other Late Essays*. V. W. McGee, trans. Austin: University of Texas Press.

Basso, Ellen. 1995. *The Last Cannibals: A South American Oral History*. Austin: University of Texas Press.

Basso, Keith. 1972. "To Give Up on Words": Silence in Western Apache Culture. In *Language and Social Context*. Pier Paolo Giglioli, ed. Pp. 67–86. Harmondsworth, England: Penguin Books.

Basso, Keith. 1979. *Portraits of the Whiteman: Linguistic Play and Cultural Symbols among the Western Apache*. New York: Cambridge University Press.

Basso, Keith. 1990. *Western Apache Language and Culture*. Tucson: University of Arizona Press.

Bauman, Richard. 1977. *Verbal Art as Performance*. Rowley, MA: Newbury House. Reprinted by Waveland Press, 1984.

Bauman, Richard. 1992. Contextualization, Tradition and the Dialogue of Genres: Icelandic Legends of the Kraftaskáld. In *Rethinking Context: Language as an Interactive Phenomenon*. C. Goodwin and A. Duranti, eds. Pp. 125–145. Cambridge: Cambridge University Press.

Bauman, Richard, and Charles Briggs. 1990. Poetics and Performance as Critical Perspectives on Language and Social Life. *Annual Review of Anthropology 19*:59–88.

Bauman, Richard, and Joel Sherzer, eds. 1989 [1974]. *Explorations in the Ethnography of Speaking*, 2d ed. Cambridge: Cambridge University Press.

Becker, A. L. 1983. Biography of a Sentence: A Burmese Proverb. In *Text, Play, and Story: The Construction and Reconstruction of Self and Society*. Edward M. Bruner, ed. Pp. 185–210. Proceedings of the American Ethnological Society, American Anthropological

Association. Reprinted in 1995 in *Beyond Translation: Essays Toward a Modern Philology*. Ann Arbor: University of Michigan Press.

Benveniste, Emile. 1971a [1956]. The Nature of Pronouns. In *Problems in General Linguistics*. M. E. Meek, trans. Pp. 217–222. Coral Gables: University of Miami Press. Originally published in 1956 in *For Roman Jakobson*. M. Halle, H. G. Lunt, H. McLean, and C. H. van Schooneveld, eds., pp. 34–37. The Hague and Paris: Mouton.

Benveniste, Emile. 1971b. Subjectivity in Language. In *Problems in General Linguistics*. M. E. Meek, trans. Pp. 223–230. Coral Gables: University of Miami Press.

Boas, Franz. 1940. *Race, Language and Culture*. New York: Macmillan.

Bourdieu, Pierre. 1977a. *Outline of a Theory of Practice*. R. Nice, trans. Cambridge: Cambridge University Press.

Bourdieu, Pierre. 1977b. The Economics of Linguistic Exchanges. *Social Science Information 16*:645–668.

Bourdieu, Pierre. 1991. *Language and Symbolic Power*. Cambridge: Harvard University Press.

Bowen, John. 1991a. *Gayo Speech and Song*. Audiotape. New Haven: Yale University Press.

Bowen, John. 1991b. *Sumatran Politics and Poetics: Gayo History, 1900–1989*. New Haven: Yale University Press.

Brandt, Elizabeth 1981 Native American Attitudes Toward Literacy and Recording in the Southwest. *The Journal of the Linguistic Association of the Southwest 4*(2):185–195.

Brenneis, Donald. 1984. Straight Talk and Sweet Talk: Political Discourse in an Occasionally Egalitarian Community. In *Dangerous Words: Language and Politics in the Pacific*. D. L. Brenneis and F. R. Myers, eds. Pp. 69–84. New York: New York University Press.

Brenneis, Donald. 1986. Shared Territory: Audience, Indirection, and Meaning. *Text 6*(3):339–347.

Briggs, Charles. 1986. *Learning How to Ask? A Sociolinguistic Appraisal of the Role of the Interview in Social Science Research*. Cambridge: Cambridge University Press.

Briggs, Charles. 1988. *Competence and Performance: The Creativity of Tradition in Mexicano Verbal Art*. Philadelphia: University of Pennsylvania Press.

Briggs, Charles. 1992. "Since I Am a Woman, I Will Chastize My Relatives": Gender, Reported Speech and the (Re)Production of Social Relations in Warao Ritual Wailing. *American Ethnologist 19*(2):336–361.

Briggs, Charles. 1993. Personal Sentiments and Polyphonic Voices in Warao Women's Ritual Wailing: Music and Poetics in a Critical and Collective Discourse. *American Anthropologist 95*(4):929–957.

Brown, Roger, and Albert Gillman. 1960. The Pronouns of Power and Solidarity. In *Style in Language*. T. Sebeok, ed. Pp. 253–276. Cambridge: M.I.T. Press.

Caton, Steve. 1990. *"Peaks of Yemen I Summon": Poetry as Cultural Practice in a North Yemeni Tribe*. Berkeley: University of California Press.

Chafe, Wallace. 1993. Seneca Speaking Styles and the Location of Authority. In *Responsibility and Evidence in Oral Discourse*. Jane Hill and Judith Irvine, eds. Pp. 72–87. Cambridge: Cambridge University Press.

Cicourel, A. V. 1981. Language and Medicine. In *Language in the USA*. C. A. Ferguson, and S. B. Heath, eds. Pp. 407–429. New York: Cambridge University Press.

Cicourel, A. V. 1982. Language and Belief in a Medical Setting. In *Contemporary Perceptions of Language: Interdisciplinary Dimensions*. Heidi Byrnes, ed. Pp. 48–78. Washington, DC: Georgetown University Press.

Cicourel, A. V. 1992. The Interpenetration of Communicative Contexts: Examples from Medical Encounters. In *Rethinking Context: Language as an Interactive Phenomenon*. C. Goodwin and A. Duranti, eds. Pp. 1–42. Cambridge: Cambridge University Press.

Clifford, James, and George E. Marcus. 1986. *Writing Culture: The Poetics and Politics of Ethnography*. Berkeley: University of California Press.

Copeland, Peter. 1991. *Sound Recordings*. London: The British Library.

Darnell, Regna. 1989 [1974]. Correlates of Cree Performance. In *Explorations in the Ethnography of Speaking*, 2d ed. Richard Bauman and Joel Sherzer, eds. Pp. 315–336. New York: Cambridge University Press.

Davies, Bronwyn, and Rom Harré. 1990. Positioning: The Discursive Production of Selves. *Journal for the Theory of Social Behavior 20*(1):43–63.

Du Bois, John. 1993 [1987]. Meaning Without Intention: Lessons from Divination. *Papers in Pragmatics 1*(2):80–122. Reprinted in *Responsibility and Evidence in Oral Discourse*. Jane Hill and Judith Irvine, eds. Pp. 48–71. Cambridge: Cambridge University Press.

Duranti, Alessandro. 1986. The Audience as Co-Author. *Text 6*(3):239–247.

Duranti, Alessandro. 1992. Language and Bodies in Social Space: Samoan Ceremonial Greetings. *American Anthropologist 94*(3):657–691.

Duranti, Alessandro. 1993. Intentions, Self, and Responsibility: An Essay in Samoan Ethnopragmatics. In *Responsibility and Evidence in Oral Discourse*. Jane Hill and Judith Irvine, eds. Pp. 24–47. Cambridge: Cambridge University Press.

Duranti, Alessandro. 1997. *Linguistic Anthropology*. Cambridge: Cambridge University Press.

Duranti, Alessandro, and Charles Goodwin, eds. 1992. *Rethinking Context: Language as an Interactive Phenomenon*. Cambridge: Cambridge University Press.

Edwards, Jane A., and Martin D. Lampert. 1993. *Talking Data: Transcription and Coding in Discourse Research*. Hillsdale, NJ: Lawrence Erlbaum.

Erickson, Frederick, and Jeffrey Shultz. 1982. *The Counselor as Gatekeeper: Social Interaction in Interviews*. New York: Academic Press.

Ellis, John. 1994. *Language, Thought, and Logic*. Evanston, IL: Northwestern University Press.

Farnell, Brenda. 1994. Ethno-Graphics and the Moving Body. *Man: Journal of the Royal Anthropological Institute 29*(4):929–974.

Farnell, Brenda. 1995a. *Do You See What I Mean?: Plain Indian Sign Talk and the Embodiment of Action.* Austin: University of Texas Press.

Farnell, Brenda. 1995b. Introduction. In *Human Action Signs in Cultural Context: The Visible and the Invisible in Movement and Dance.* B. Farnell, ed. Pp. 1–28. Metuchen, NJ: Scarecrow Press.

Farnell, Brenda. 1995c. *Wiyuta: Assiniboine Storytelling with Signs.* CD-ROM. Austin: University of Texas Press.

Feld, Steven. 1990 [1982]. *Sound and Sentiment: Birds, Weeping, Poetics, and Song in Kaluli Expression,* 2d ed. Philadelphia: University of Pennsylvania Press.

Feld, Steven, and Aaron A. Fox 1994. Music and Language. *Annual Review of Anthropology* 23:25–53.

Fishman, Joshua. 1968. *Readings in the Sociology of Language.* The Hague and Paris: Mouton.

Fishman, Joshua. 1970. *Sociolinguistics: A Brief Introduction.* Rowley, MA: Newbury House.

Fox, Richard. 1991. *Recapturing Anthropology: Working in the Present.* Santa Fe: School of American Research Press.

Gal, Susan. 1991. Between Speech and Silence: The Problematics of Research on Language and Gender. In *Gender at the Crossroads of Knowledge: Feminist Anthropology in the Postmodern Era.* Michaela Di Leonardo, ed. Pp. 175–203. Berkeley and Los Angeles: University of California Press.

Garfinkel, Harold. 1967. *Studies in Ethnomethodology.* Englewood Cliffs, NJ: Prentice Hall.

Garfinkel, Harold. 1972. Remarks on Ethnomethodology. In *Directions in Sociolinguistics.* J. Gumperz, ed. Pp. 301–324. New York: Holt, Rinehart and Winston.

Garvey, Catherine. 1984. *Children's Talk.* Cambridge: Harvard University Press.

Gelatt, Roland. 1977. *The Fabulous Phonograph 1877–1977,* 2d rev. ed. New York: Macmillan.

Giddens, Anthony. 1979. *Central Problems in Social Theory: Action, Structure and Contradiction in Social Analysis.* Berkeley: University of California Press.

Giddens, Anthony. 1984. *The Constitution of Society.* Berkeley: University of California Press.

Goddard, Ives. 1996. The Description of the Native Languages of North America Before Boas. In *Handbook of North American Indians.* Vol. 17, *Languages.* William C. Sturtevant, ed. Pp. 17–42. Washington DC: Smithsonian Institution Press.

Goffman, Erving. 1961. *Encounters: Two Studies in Social Interaction.* Indianapolis: Bobbs-Merrill.

Goffman, Erving. 1972 [1967]. *Interaction Ritual.* Harmondsworth, England: Penguin Books.

Goffman, Erving. 1974. *Frame Analysis.* New York: Harper and Row.

Goffman, Erving. 1981. *Forms of Talk.* Philadelphia: University of Pennsylvania Press.

Goodwin, Charles. 1981. *Conversational Organization: Interaction Between Speakers and Hearers.* New York: Academic Press.

Goodwin, Charles. 1984. Notes on Story Structure and the Organization of Participation. In *Structures of Social Action*. M. Atkinson and J. Heritage, eds. Pp. 225–246. Cambridge: Cambridge University Press.

Goodwin, Charles. 1993. Recording Human Interaction in Natural Settings. *Pragmatics* 3(2):181–209.

Goodwin, Charles and John Heritage. 1990. Conversational Analysis. *Annual Review of Anthropology 19*:283–307.

Goodwin, Charles, and Alessandro Duranti. 1992. Rethinking Context: An Introduction. In *Rethinking Context: Language as an Interactive Phenomenon*. C. Goodwin and A. Duranti, eds. Pp. 1–42. Cambridge: Cambridge University Press.

Goodwin, Majorie. 1982a. "Instigating": Storytelling as a Social Process. *American Ethnologist 9*:799–819.

Goodwin, Majorie. 1982b. Processes of Dispute Management among Urban Black Children. *American Ethnologist 9*:76–96.

Goodwin, Majorie. 1990. *He-Said-She-Said: Talk as Social Organization Among Black Children*. Bloomington: Indiana University Press.

Graham, Laura R. 1984. Semanticity and Melody: Parameters of Contrast in Shavante Vocal Expression. *Latin American Music Review 5*(2):161–185.

Graham, Laura R. 1986. Three Modes of Shavante Vocal Expression: Wailing, Collective Singing, and Political Oratory. In *Native South American Discourse*. J. Sherzer and G. Urban, eds. Pp. 83–118. Berlin: Mouton.

Graham, Laura R. 1990. The Always Living: Discourse and the Male Lifecycle of the Xavante Indians of Central Brazil. Ph.D. diss., Austin: University of Texas.

Graham, Laura R. 1993. A Public Sphere in Amazonia? The Depersonalized Collaborative Construction of Discourse in Xavante. *American Ethnologist 20*(4):717–741.

Graham, Laura R. 1994. Dialogic Dreams: Creative Selves Coming into Life in the Flow of Time. *American Ethnologist 21*(4):719–741.

Graham, Laura R. 1995. *Performing Dreams: Discourses of Immortality Among the Xavante of Central Brazil*. Austin: University of Texas Press.

Graham, Laura R. In press. The One With the Long Hair: Tellings, Meanings, and Inter-Textuality in the Translation of Xavante Narrative. In *Translating Native Latin American Verbal Art: Ethnopoetics and Ethnography*. K. Sammons and J. Sherzer, eds. Washington, DC: Smithsonian Institution Press.

Grimshaw, Allan D., ed. 1990. *Conflict Talk: Sociolinguistic Investigations of Arguments in Conversations*. Cambridge: Cambridge University Press.

Grimshaw, Allan D. 1994. *What's Going on Here? Complementary Studies of Professional Talk*. Norwood, NJ: Ablex Press.

Gumperz, John J. 1982. *Discourse Strategies*. Cambridge: Cambridge University Press.

Gumperz, John J., and Dell Hymes, eds. 1964. *The Ethnography of Communication*. *American Anthropologist*, Special Publication 66, Number 6, Part II.

Gumperz, John J., and Dell Hymes, eds. 1986 [1972]. *Directions in Sociolinguistics: The Ethnography of Communication*. Oxford and New York: Basil Blackwell.

Hall, Kira, and Mary Bucholtz. 1995. *Gender Articulated: Language and the Socially Constructed Self.* New York: Routledge.

Handler, Richard. 1988. *Nationalism and the Politics of Culture in Quebec*. Madison: University of Wisconsin Press.

Hanks, Willam. 1990. *Referential Practice: Language and Lived Space among the Maya*. Chicago: University of Chicago Press.

Harré, Rom, ed. 1984. *Personal Being*. Cambridge: Harvard University Press.

Harré, Rom. 1986a *The Social Construction of Emotions*. Oxford: Basil Blackwell.

Harré, Rom. 1986b. Mind as a Social Formation. In *Rationality, Relativism and the Human Sciences*. J. Margolis, M. Krausz, and R. M. Burien, eds. Pp. 91–106. Dortrecht, the Netherlands: Martinus Nijhoff.

Harré, Rom. 1986c. *Varieties of Realism*. Oxford: Basil Blackwell.

Harré, Rom. 1987. The Social Construction of Selves. In *Self and Identity: Psycho-social Perspectives*. K. Yardley and T. Honess, eds. Pp. 41–52. New York: John Wiley.

Harré, Rom, and Grant Gillett. 1994. *The Discursive Mind*. London: Sage Publications.

Haugen, Einar. 1969. *The Norwegian Language in America*. Bloomington: Indiana University Press.

Haviland, John. 1993. Anchoring, Iconicity and Orientation in Guugu Yimithirr Pointing Gestures. *Journal of Linguistic Anthropology* 3(1):3–45.

Haviland, John. 1996. Text from Talk in Tzotzil. In *Natural Histories of Discourse*. M. Silverstein and G. Urban, eds. Pp. 45–78. Chicago: University of Chicago Press.

Heath, Christian. 1986. *Body Movement and Speech in Medical Interaction*. Cambridge: Cambridge University Press.

Heath, Shirley Brice. 1983. *Ways with Words: Language, Life and Work in Communities and Classrooms*. Cambridge: Cambridge University Press.

Hill, Jane, and Kenneth Hill. 1986. *Speaking Mexicano: Dynamics of Syncretic Language in Central Mexico*. Tucson: University of Arizona Press.

Hill, Jane, and Judy Irvine. 1993. *Responsibility and Evidence in Discourse*. Cambridge: Cambridge University Press.

Hill, Jane, and Olivia Zepeda. 1993. Mrs. Patricio's Trouble: The Distribution of Responsibility in an Account of Personal Evidence. In *Responsibility and Evidence in Oral Discourse*. Jane Hill and Judith Irvine, eds. Pp. 197–225. Cambridge: Cambridge University Press.

Holquist, Michael. 1983. The Politics of Representation. *Quarterly Newsletter of the Laboratory of Comparative Human Cognition* 5(1):2–9.

Hymes, Dell. 1962. The Ethnography of Speaking. In *Anthropology and Human Behavior*. T. Gladwin and William C. Sturtevant, eds. Pp. 13–53. Washington, DC: Anthropological Society of Washington.

Hymes, Dell. 1964. Introduction: Toward Ethnographies of Communication. In *The Ethnography of Communication*. John J. Gumperz and Dell Hymes, eds. American Anthropological Association Special Publication 66, Number 6, Part II:1–34.

Hymes, Dell. 1967. Models of the Interaction of Language and Social Setting. *Journal of Social Issues 23*(2):8–28.

Hymes, Dell. 1971. Sociolinguistics and the Ethnography of Speaking. In *Social Anthropology and Language*. Edwin Ardener, ed. Pp. 47–94. London: Tavistock Press.

Hymes, Dell. 1974. *Foundations in Sociolinguistics: An Ethnographic Approach*. Philadelphia: University of Pennsylvania Press.

Hymes, Dell. 1975. The Pre-War Prague School and Post War American Anthropological Linguistics. In *Transformational Generative Paradigm and Modern Linguistic Theory*. E.K.F. Koerner, ed. Pp. 359–381. Amsterdam: John Benjamins.

Hymes, Dell. 1981. *"In Vain I Tried to Tell You": Essays in Native American Ethnopoetics*. Philadephia: University of Pennsylvania Press.

Irvine, Judith. 1989. When Talk Isn't Cheap: Language and Political Economy. *American Ethnologist 16*:248–267.

Irvine, Judith. 1992. Ideologies of Honorific Language. *Pragmatics 2*(3):251–262.

Irvine, Judith. 1996. Shadow Conversations: The Indeterminacy of Participant Roles. In *Natural Histories of Discourse*. G. Urban and M. Silverstein, eds. Pp. 131–159. Chicago: University of Chicago Press.

Ives, Edward D. 1995. *The Tape Recorded Interview: A Manual for Field Workers in Folklore and Oral History*, 2d ed. Knoxville: University of Tennessee Press.

Jakobson, Roman. 1960. Linguistics and Poetics. In *Style in Language*. Thomas Sebeok, ed. Pp. 350–377. Cambridge: M.I.T. Press.

Jakobson, Roman. 1971 [1957]. Shifters, Verbal Categories and the Russian Verb. In *Selected Writings of Roman Jakobson* 2:130–147. The Hague and Paris: Mouton.

Jarvella, Robert J. and Wolfgang Klein, eds. 1982. *Speech, Place and Action: Studies in Deixis and Related Topics*. New York: John Wiley.

Josselson, Harry Hirsh. 1953. *The Russian Word Count and Frequency Analysis of Grammatical Categories of Standard Literary Russian*. Detroit: Wayne State University Press.

Kaeppler, Adrienne. 1995. Visible and Invisible in Hawaiian Dance. In *Human Action Signs in Cultural Context: The Visible and Invisible in Movement and Dance*. B. Farnell, ed. Pp. 31–43. Metuchen, NJ: Scarecrow Press.

Keane, Web. 1991. Delegated Voice: Ritual Speech, Risk, and the Making of Marriage Alliances in Anakalang. *American Ethnologist 18*:311–330.

Keating, Elizabeth. 1998. A Woman's Role in Constructing Status Hierarchies: Using Honorific Language in Pohnpei, Micronesia. *International Journal of the Sociology of Language* 129:103–115.

Keating, Elizabeth. In press. *Power Sharing: Language, Rank, Gender and Social Space in Pohnpei, Micronesia*. Oxford: Oxford University Press.

Kendon, Adam. 1980. Gesticulation and Speech: Two Aspects of the Process of Utterance. In *The Relationship of Verbal and Non-Verbal Communication.* M. R. Key, ed. Pp. 207–227. The Hague and Paris: Mouton.

Kendon, Adam. 1983. Gesture and Speech: How They Interact. In *Nonverbal Interaction.* J. M. Wieman and R. P. Harrison, eds. Pp. 13–45. Sage Annual Reviews of Communication Research, Vol. 11. Beverly Hills, CA: Sage Publications.

Kendon, Adam. 1989. *Sign Languages of Aboriginal Australia.* Cambridge: Cambridge University Press.

Kroskrity, Paul, Bambi Schieffelin, and Kathryn Woolard, eds. 1992. Language Ideologies. Special issue of *Pragmatics* 2(3).

Kuipers, Joel. 1990. *Power in Performance: The Creation of Textual Authority in Weyewa Ritual Speech.* Philadelphia: University of Pennsylvania Press.

Labov, William. 1972. *Sociolinguistic Patterns.* Philadelphia: University of Pennsylvania Press.

Labov, William, and David Fanshel. 1977. *Therapeutic Discourse: Psychotherapy as Conversation.* New York: Academic Press.

Laderman, Carol. 1987. The Ambiguity of Symbols in the Structure of Healing. *Social Science and Medicine* 24(4):293–301.

Lederman, Rena. 1984. Who Speaks Here? In *Dangerous Words: Language and Politics in the Pacific.* D. L. Brenneis and F. R. Myers, eds. Pp. 85–107. New York: New York University Press.

List, George. 1963. The Boundaries of Speech and Song. *Ethnomusicology* 7:1–16.

Lucy, John, ed. 1990. *Reflexive Language: Reported Speech and Metapragmatics.* Cambridge: Cambridge University Press.

Lutz, Catherine. 1988. *Unnatural Emotions: Everyday Sentiments on a Micronesian Atoll and Their Challenge to Western Theory.* Chicago: University of Chicago Press.

Lutz, Catherine, and Lila Abu-Lughod, eds. 1990. *Language and the Politics of Emotion.* Cambridge: Cambridge University Press.

MacMahon, Michael K. C. 1996. Phonetic Notation. In *The World's Writing Systems.* Peter Daniels and William Bright, eds. Pp. 821–846. Oxford and New York: Oxford University Press.

Mannheim, Bruce, and Dennis Tedlock. 1995. Introduction. In *The Dialogic Emergence of Culture.* Bruce Mannheim and Dennis Tedlock, eds. Pp. 1–32. Urbana: University of Illinois Press.

Manuel, Peter. 1993. *Cassette Culture: Popular Music and Technology in North India.* Chicago: University of Chicago Press.

McClendon, Sally. 1981. Meaning, Rhetorical Structure, and Discourse Organization in Myth. In *Analyzing Discourse: Text and Talk.* Deborah Tannen, ed. Pp. 284–305. Georgetown University Roundtable on Language and Linguistics, Washington, DC: Georgetown University Press.

McNeill, David. 1985. So You Think Gestures Are Non-Verbal? *Psychological Review* *92*(3):350–371.

McNeill, David. 1992. *Hand and Mind: What Gestures Reveal about Thought*. Chicago: University of Chicago Press.

Mertz, Elizabeth, and Richard Parmentier. 1985. Introduction. In *Semiotic Mediation*. E. Mertz and R. Parmentier, eds. Pp. 1–19. New York: Academic Press.

Michaels, Eric. 1994. *Bad Aboriginal Art: Tradition, Media and Technological Horizons*. Minneapolis: University of Minnesota Press.

Mithun, Marianne. 1996. The Description of the Native Languages of North America: Boas and After. In *Handbook of North American Indians*. Vol. 17, *Languages*. William C. Sturtevant, ed. Pp. 43–63. Washington DC: Smithsonian Institution Press.

Moerman, Michael. 1988. *Talking Culture: Ethnography and Conversation Analysis*. Philadelphia: University of Pennsylvania Press.

Mühlhäusler, Peter, and Rom Harré. 1990. *Pronouns and People: The Linguistic Construction of Social and Personal Identity*. Oxford: Basil Blackwell.

Murphy, William. 1990. Creating the Appearance of Consensus in Mende Political Discourse. *American Anthropologist 92*:24–41.

Murray, Thomas E., and Carmin Ross Murray. 1992. *Legal and Ethical Issues in Surreptitious Recording*. Publication of the American Dialect Society 76. Tuscaloosa: University of Alabama Press.

Nuckolls, Janice. 1992. Sound Symbolic Involvement. *Journal of Linguistic Anthropology 2*(1):51–80.

Ochs, Elinor. 1979a. Transcription as Theory. In *Developmental Pragmatics*. Elinor Ochs and Bambi B. Schieffelin, eds. Pp. 43–72. New York: Academic Press.

Ochs, Elinor, 1979b. Introduction: What Child Language Can Contribute to Pragmatics. In *Developmental Pragmatics*. Elinor Ochs and Bambi B. Schieffelin, eds. Pp. 1–17. New York: Academic Press.

Ochs, Elinor. 1988. *Culture and Language Development: Language Acquisition and Language Socialization in a Samoan Village*. New York: Cambridge University Press.

Page, JoAnne. 1990. A Comparative Study of Two Movement Writing Systems: Laban and Benesh Notation. Master's Thesis, University of Sydney.

Page, JoAnne. 1996. Images for Understanding: Movement Notations and Visual Recordings. *Visual Anthropology 8*(2–4):171–196.

Philips, S., S. Steele, and C. Tanz, eds. 1987. *Language, Gender and Sex in Comparative Perspective*. Cambridge: Cambridge University Press.

Pick, H. L., and L. P. Acredolo, eds. 1983. *Spatial Orientation: Theory, Research and Application*. New York and London: Plenum Press.

Pratt, M. L. 1987. The Ideology of Speech Act Theory. *Centrum* N.S. *1*:5–18.

Pressman, Jon. 1997. Honorification and Projection on Saint Barthélemy. *Anthropological Linguistics 39*(1):111–150.

Rabinow, Paul. 1977. *Reflections on Fieldwork in Morocco*. Berkeley: University of California Press.

Radin, Paul. 1949. *The Culture of the Winnebago: As Described by Themselves*. Indiana University Publications in Anthropology and Linguistics, Memoir 2. Baltimore: Waverly Press.

Radin, Paul. 1965 [1933]. *The Method and Theory of Ethnology: An Essay in Criticism*. New York: Basic Books.

Rorty, Richard ed. 1992 [1967]. *The Linguistic Turn*. Chicago: University of Chicago Press.

Rosaldo, Michelle. 1982. The Things We Do with Words: Ilongot Speech Acts and Speech Act Theory in Philosophy. *Language in Society 11*:203–235.

Rosaldo, Renato. 1980. *Ilongot Headhunting 1883–1974: A Study in Society and History*. Stanford: Stanford University Press.

Roseman, Marina. 1991. *Healing Sounds from the Malaysian Rainforest: Temiar Music and Medicine*. Berkeley: University of California Press.

Sacks, Harvey, Emanuel A. Schegloff, and Gail Jefferson. 1974. A Simplest Systematics for the Organization of Turn-Taking Conversation. *Language 50*:696–735.

Sahlins, Marshall. 1976. *Culture and Practical Reason*. Chicago: University of Chicago Press.

Sahlins, Marshall. 1985. *Islands of History*. Chicago: University of Chicago Press.

Sammons, Kay, and Joel Sherzer. In press. *Translating Native American Verbal Art: Ethnopoetics and Ethnography of Speaking*. Washington, DC: Smithsonian Institution Press.

Sapir, Edward. 1949. *Selected Writings of Edward Sapir in Language Culture and Personality*. David Mandelbaum, ed. Berkeley: University of California Press.

Saussure, Ferdinand de. 1916. *Course de linguistique générale*. Charles Bally and Albert Sechehaye, eds. Paris: Payot.

Saville-Troike, Muriel. 1989. *The Ethnography of Communication: An Introduction*, 2d ed. New York: Basil Blackwell.

Schafer, Murray R. 1997. *The Tuning of the World*. New York: Knopf.

Schegloff, Emanuel A. 1972. Sequencing in Conversational Opening. In *Directions in Sociolinguistics*. J. Gumpertz, ed. Pp. 346–380. New York: Holt, Reinhart and Winston.

Schegloff, Emanuel A., and Harvey Sacks. 1973. Opening Up Closings. *Semiotica 7*:289–327.

Schieffelin, Bambi. 1990. *The Give and Take of Everyday Life: Language Socialization of Kaluli Children*. New York: Cambridge University Press.

Schieffelin, Bambi, and Elinor Ochs. 1986a. *Language Socialization Across Cultures*. New York: Cambridge University Press.

Schieffelin, Bambi, and Elinor Ochs. 1986b. Language Socialization. *Annual Review of Anthropology 15*:163–191.

Searle, John R. 1969. *Speech Acts: An Essay in the Philosophy of Language*. Cambridge: Cambridge University Press.

Seeger, Anthony. 1986. Oratory Is Spoken, Myth Is Told, and Song Is Sung, But They Are All Music to My Ears. In *Native South American Discourse*. Joel Sherzer and Greg Urban, eds. Pp. 59–82. Berlin: Mouton.

Seeger, Anthony. 1987. *Why Suyá Sing: A Musical Anthropology of an Amazonian People*. Cambridge: Cambridge University Press.

Seeger, Anthony. 1991. Singing Other Peoples' Songs. *Cultural Survival Quarterly 15*(3): 36–39.

Seeger, Anthony. 1997. Ethnomusicology and Music Law. In *Borrowed Power: Essays on Cultural Appropriation*. Bruce Ziff and Pratima V. Rao, eds. Pp. 52–67. New Brunswick, NJ: Rutgers University Press.

Sherzer, Joel. 1973. Verbal and Nonverbal Deixis: The Pointed Lip Gesture among the San Blas Kuna. *Language in Society* 2:117–131.

Sherzer, Joel. 1987. A Discourse-Centered Approach to Language and Culture. *American Ethnologist 89*:295–309.

Sherzer, Joel. 1992. Modes of Representation and Translation of Native American Discourse: Examples from the San Blas Kuna. In *On the Translation of Native American Literatures*. Brian Swann, ed. Pp. 426–440. Washington, DC: Smithsonian Institution Press.

Sherzer, Joel, and Regna Darnell. 1972. Outline Guide for the Ethnographic Study of Speech Use. In *Directions in Sociolinguistics: The Ethnography of Communication*. John J. Gumperz and Dell Hymes, eds. Pp. 548–554. New York: Holt.

Sherzer, Joel, and Greg Urban. 1986a. Introduction. In *Native South American Discourse*. Joel Sherzer and Greg Urban, eds. Pp. 1–14. Berlin: Mouton.

Sherzer, Joel, and Greg Urban, eds. 1986b. *Native South American Discourse*. Berlin: Mouton.

Sherzer, Joel, and Sammie Wicks. 1982. The Intersection of Language and Music in Kuna Discourse. *Latin American Music Review 3*:147–164.

Shuy, Roger. 1986. Ethical Issues in Analyzing FBI Surreptitious Tapes. *International Journal of the Sociology of Language 62*:119–128.

Silverstein, Michael. 1976. Shifters, Linguistic Categories, and Cultural Description. In *Meaning in Anthropology*. K. H. Basso and H. A. Selby, eds. Pp. 11–56. Albuquerque: University of New Mexico Press.

Silverstein, Michael. 1977. Cultural Prerequisites to Grammatical Analysis. In *Georgetown University Round Table on Languages and Linguistics: Linguistics and Anthropology*. M. Saville-Troike, ed. Pp. 139–151. Washington, DC: Georgetown University Press.

Silverstein, Michael. 1981. *The Limits of Awareness*. Austin: Southwest Educational Laboratories.

Silverstein, Michael. 1984. On the Pragmatic "Poetry" of Prose. In *Georgetown University Roundtable in Linguistics*, Vol. 18. D. Schiffrin, ed. Pp. 181–199. Washington, DC: Georgetown University Press.

Silverstein, Michael. 1985. The Culture of Language in Chinookan Narrative Texts; or On Saying That . . . in Chinook. In *Grammar Inside and Outside the Clause: Some Approaches to Theory from the Field*. J. Nichols and A. C. Woodbury, eds. Pp. 132–171. Cambridge: Cambridge University Press.

Silverstein, Michael, and Greg Urban. 1996. Introduction. In *Natural Histories of Discourse*. Greg Urban and Michael Silverstein, eds. Pp. 1–20. Chicago: University of Chicago Press.

Spitulnik, Debra. 1993. Anthropology and Mass Media. *Annual Review of Anthropology* 22:293–325.

Streeck, Jürgen. 1993. Gesture as Communication I: Its Coordination with Gaze and Speech. *Communication Monographs* 60:275–299.

Studdert-Kennedy, Michael, and Elizabeth Whitney Goodall. 1992. Gestures, Features and Segments in Early Child Speech. *Haskins Laboratory Status Report on Research*. SR 111/112. Pp. 89–102.

Swann, Brian, ed. 1992. *On the Translation of Native American Literatures*. Washington, DC: Smithsonian Institution Press.

Tannen, Deborah, ed. 1982. *Analyzing Discourse: Text and Talk*. Washington, DC: Georgetown University Press.

Tannen, Deborah. 1984. *Conversational Style: Analyzing Talk Among Friends*. Norwood, NJ: Ablex Press.

Tannen, Deborah. 1994. *Gender and Discourse*. New York: Oxford University Press.

Tannen, Deborah. 1995. Waiting for the Mouse: Constructed Dialogue in Conversation. In *The Dialogic Emergence of Culture*. Bruce Mannheim and Dennis Tedlock, eds. Pp. 198–218. Urbana: University of Illinois Press.

Taylor, Charles. 1985. *Human Agency and Language*. Cambridge: Cambridge University Press.

Tedlock, Dennis. 1983. *The Spoken Word and the Work of Interpretation*. Philadelphia: University of Pennsylvania Press.

Tedlock, Dennis. 1987. Hearing a Voice in an Ancient Text: Quiché Maya Poetics in Performance. In *Native American Discourse*. Joel Sherzer and Anthony Woodbury, eds. Pp. 140–175. Cambridge: Cambridge University Press.

Testa, Renata. 1988. Interruptive Strategies in English and Italian Conversation: Smooth Versus Contrastive Linguistic Preferences. *Multilingua* 7(3):285–312.

Thibault, Paul J. 1997. *Re-Reading Saussure: The Dynamics of Signs in Social Life*. London and New York: Routledge.

Turner, Lorenzo Dow. 1969. *Africanisms in the Gullah Dialect*. New York: Arno.

Turner, Terence. 1991. Representing, Resisting, Rethinking: Historical Transformations of Kayapo Culture and Anthropological Consciousness. In *Colonial Situations. History of Anthropology*. Vol. 7. George Stocking, ed. Pp. 285–313. Madison: University of Wisconsin Press.

Urban, Greg. 1984. Speech about Speech and Speech about Action. *Journal of American Folklore 97*:310–328.

Urban, Greg. 1985. Semiotics of Two Speech Styles in Shokleng. In *Semiotic Mediation*. E. Mertz and R. Parmentier, eds. Pp. 311–329. New York: Academic Press.

Urban, Greg. 1986. Semiotic Functions of Macro-Parallelism in the Shokleng Origin Myth. In *Native South American Discourse*. Joel Sherzer and Greg Urban, eds. Pp. 15–58. Berlin: Mouton.

Urban, Greg. 1988. Ritual Wailing in Amerindian Brazil. *American Anthropologist 90*(2): 385–400.

Urban, Greg. 1989. The "I" of Discourse. In *Semiotics, Self, and Society*. Greg Urban and Benjamin Lee, eds. Pp. 27–51. New York: Mouton.

Urban, Greg. 1991. *A Discourse-Centered Approach to Culture: Native South American Myths and Rituals*. Austin: University of Texas Press.

Urban, Greg. 1996a. Entextualization, Replication, and Power. In *Natural Histories of Discourse*. G. Urban and M. Silverstein, eds. Pp. 21–44. Chicago: University of Chicago Press.

Urban, Greg. 1996b. *Metaphysical Community: The Interplay of the Senses and the Intellect*. Austin: University of Texas Press.

Urciuoli, Bonnie. 1995. The Indexical Structure of Visibility. In *Human Action Signs in Cultural Context: The Visible and Invisible in Movement and Dance*. B. Farnell ed. Pp. 189–215. Metuchen NJ: Scarecrow Press.

Urciuoli, Bonnie. 1996. *Exposing Prejudice: Puerto Rican Experiences of Language, Race and Class*. Boulder: Westview Press.

Valentine, Lisa. 1995. *Making It Their Own: Severn Ojibwe Communicative Practices*. Toronto: University of Toronto Press.

Varela, Charles R. 1995. Ethogenic Theory and Psychoanalysis: The Unconscious as a Social Construction and a Failed Explanatory Construct. *Journal for the Theory of Social Behavior 25*(4):363–385.

Varela, Charles, and Rom Harré. 1996. Conflicting Varieties of Realism: Causal Powers and the Problems of Social Structure. *Journal for the Theory of Social Behavior 26*(3): 313–325.

Verschueren, J. 1985. *What People Say They Do with Words*. Norwood, NJ: Ablex.

Watson-Gegeo, Karen Ann, and Geoffrey White, eds. 1990. *Disentangling: Conflict Discourse in Pacific Societies*. Stanford: Stanford University Press.

Welch, Walter, and Leah Brodbeck Stenzel Burt. 1994. *From Tinfoil to Stereo: The Acoustic Years of the Recording Industry 1877–1929*. Gainesville: University Press of Florida.

West, Candace. 1984. *Routine Complications*. Bloomington: Indiana University Press.

White, Geoffrey M., and John Kirkpatrick, eds. 1985. *Person, Self and Experience: Exploring Pacific Ethnopsychologies*. Berkeley: University of California Press.

Whorf, Benjamin Lee. 1956. *Language Thought, and Reality*. Cambridge: M.I.T. Press.

Wiget, A. 1987. Telling the Tale: A Performance Analysis of a Hopi Coyote Story. In *Recovering the Word: Essays in Native American Literature*. B. Swann and A. Krupat, eds. Pp. 297–338. Berkeley: University of California Press.

Williams, Drid. 1975. The Role of Movement in Selected Symbolic Systems. D. Phil., Oxford University.

Williams, Drid. 1982. Semasiology. In *Semantic Anthropology*, ASA Vol. 22. D. Parkin, ed. Pp. 161–181. London: Academic Press.

Williams, Drid. 1991. *Ten Lectures on Theories of the Dance*. Metuchen, NJ: Scarecrow Press.

Williams, Drid. 1995. Space, Intersubjectivity and the Conceptual Imperative: Three Ethnographic Cases. In *Human Action Signs in Cultural Context: The Visible and the Invisible in Movement and Dance*. B. Farnell, ed. Pp. 44–81. Metuchen, NJ: Scarecrow Press.

Williams, Drid, ed. 1996. Special Issue: Human Action Signs. *Visual Anthropology 8*(3/4).

Williams, Drid, and Brenda Farnell. 1990. *A Beginning Text on Movement Writing for Non-Dancers*. Canberra: Australian Institute for Aboriginal Studies.

Woodbury, Anthony. 1985. The Functions of Rhetorical Structure: A Study of Central Alaskan Yupik Eskimo Discourse. *Language in Society 14*:153–190.

Woodbury, Anthony. 1987. Rhetorical Structure in a Central Alaskan Yupik Eskimo Traditional Narrative. In *Native American Discourse*. J. Sherzer and A. Woodbury, eds. Pp. 176–239. Cambridge: Cambridge University Press.

Woolard, Katherine. 1989. *Double Talk: Bilingualism and the Politics of Ethnicity in Catalonia*. Stanford: Stanford University Press.

Woolard, Katherine. 1992. Language Ideologies: Issues and Approaches. *Pragmatics 2*(3):235–249.

Thirteen

From Pictorializing to Visual Anthropology[1]

Introduction

Visual anthropology traces its roots to the advent of modern photographic (and sound) technology invented in Europe and the United States; its founders were Alfred Cort Haddon, Baldwin Spencer, Franz Boas, Marcel Griaule, Gregory Bateson, and Margaret Mead, among others. The term "visual anthropology," however, was coined only after Word War II and became associated with the idea of using cameras to make records about culture (Worth 1980:7). In Europe, visual anthropologists have focused almost exclusively on ethnographic film. In the United States, all visual formats and media developed for teaching, recording, research, and analysis are considered part of visual anthropology.

This is an issue-, method-, and theory-oriented chapter. What has come to be known as the humanistic orientation is not posed here in a polarity of humanistic/scientific contrasts. Instead, an overview of the various methods in visual anthropology and a critique of the diverse anthropological approaches to the visual medium includes humanistic and other orientations. Also addressed here is the non-Western critique of the Western tradition of visual anthropology, which brings out pertinent issues of cross-cultural representationality.

Visual anthropology embraces many interests, methods, and specializations, including communication kinesics (Birdwhistell 1952, 1970), proxemics (Hall 1959, 1966), semiotics (Worth 1969, 1972, 1980, 1981a, 1981b), the study of gestures (Kendon and Ferber 1973), and choreometrics (Lomax 1975, 1978 [film]; Lomax et al. 1969). Synchronous sound was developed in the 1960s, but even before that, archaeologists, primatologists, and ethnologists used photographic (still and moving) technologies for gathering data, for cross-checking facts, and for building records (see Blackman 1986, 1992; Caldarola 1987; Edwards 1992; Faris 1992; Scherer 1992). Video technology has made filming easy and accessible, leading to further innovations. Today, multimedia technology simultaneously and interactively combine various media and formats, allowing for maximum flexibility in application and for methodological and analytic rigor.

In 1964 a conference was held on filmmaking in anthropology. Other than that, there were vitually no programs, publications, or regular meetings on ethnographic film or visual anthropology. In subsequent years, the Program in Ethnographic Film (PIEF) was established, and by 1973 it had become the Society for the Anthropology of Visual Communication (SAVICOM). This society functioned under the wing of the American Anthropological Association. The founding group behind this effort, namely Jay Ruby along with a number of anthropologists and researchers, also set up the National Anthropological Film Center (directed by E. Richard Sorenson) at the Smithsonian Institution. The *PIEF Newsletter*, begun by Jay Ruby and Carroll Williams in 1969, continued as the *Society for the Anthropology of Visual Communication (SAVICOM) Newsletter*. This was later incorporated into the *Anthropology Newsletter* of the AAA. In 1974, SAVICOM began a more formal publication series, edited by Sol Worth.

Ethnographic films have been reviewed in the *American Anthropologist* since 1965. Since 1966, ethnographic film sessions have been a regular feature of the AAA annual meetings. In 1969, Jay Ruby began the annual Conference on Visual Anthropology at Temple University in Philadelphia.

In 1984, the Society for Visual Anthropology (SVA) was formed as a constituent section of the American Anthropological Association. The SVA produced a regular newsletter—now *Visual Anthropology Review*—out of which a select group of articles were recently published (Taylor 1994). SVA's scope is as follows:

> [T]he use of images for the description, analysis, communication and interpretation of human (and sometimes nonhuman) behavior—kinesics, proxemics and related forms of body motion communication (e.g., gesture, emotion, dance, sign language) as well as visual aspects of culture, including architecture and material artifacts. It also includes the use of image and auditory media, including still photography, film, video and noncamera generated images, in the recording of ethnographic, archeological and other anthropological genres—how aspects of culture can be pictorially a source of ethnographic data, expanding our horizons beyond the reach of memory culture. It is the study of how indigenous, professional, and amateur forms of pictorial/auditory materials are grounded in personal, social, cultural, and ideological contexts.

On the tenth anniversary of the annual SVA Film/Video Festival (El Guindi and Williams 1995:xv–xvi), the SVA published a list of all the films and videos given awards during the preceding years, along with a detailed scholarly commendation (Blakely and Williams 1995; Williams et al. 1995). That year, the AAA published another listing of films (Heider and Hermer 1995).

In the first—and still classic—collection of articles on visual anthropology, Hockings (1975) lamented that "of the various English handbooks now available on research methodology, only one devotes as much space as two pages (out of a thousand) to some applications of cinematography in anthropology" (p. 477).

That was then. In the rest of this chapter, I present an extended historical/ methodological overview of visual anthropology. It's worth restating the earlier call: "It is not sufficient to give lectures at the universities and use films to illustrate those lectures. We have much to teach mankind about itself; let us do so through all the visual media available to us" (Hockings 1975:480).

Film: Technology and Ethnography

Motion film technology was invented in Europe and America shortly before the turn of the century, decades after the invention of still photography. At first, the new technology was crude, bulky, and awkward. It was dangerous to work with and cumbersome to transport. As Rouch (1975) put it:

> One almost needed to be crazy to try using (as did some ethnographers) a tool as forbidding as the camera. When we see today the first clumsy attempts to use it correctly in Marcel Griaule's *Au pays des Dogons* (In the Land of the Dogon) (Griaule 1935 [film]) and *Sous le masque noir* (Beneath the black mask) (Griaule 1938 [film]), we can understand their discouragement with the results of their efforts. Their admirable documentation was put through the filmmaking machine. There was wild, insensitive editing, oriental music, commentary in the style of a sportscast. . . . It is this sort of travesty that Margaret Mead and Gregory Bateson were able to avoid when they produced their series *Character Formation in Different Cultures* (Mead and Bateson 1930s–1950s [film]) at about the same time (1936–1938). [The films in the series include: *Bathing Babies* (Mead and Bateson 1954 [filmed 1930s]); *Childhood Rivalry in Bali and New Guinea* (Mead and Bateson 1952); and *First Days in the Life of a New Guinea Baby* (Mead 1952, approx.)] They were successful because they had the financial aid of American universities which understood before others did that it is absurd to try to mix research and business. (p. 88)

Cameras were fixed on tripods, and film was suitable only for shooting in broad daylight or with artificial light. Yet, like our human ancestors who pictorialized incessantly despite the awkwardness and difficulties, some anthropologists immediately saw the innovative potential of the new technology.

Félix-Louis Regnault, a physician specializing in pathological anatomy, became interested in anthropology around 1888—the year Jules-Etienne Marey, the inventor of "chronophotography" demonstrated his new camera to the French Académie des

Sciences using celluloid roll film. Some consider Marey the first to make an ethnographic film.

Six months before the Lumière brothers made their first public projection of cinématograph films (Lumière 1895), Regnault filmed a Wolof woman making pots at the Exposition Ethnographique de l'Afrique Occidentale. "The film showed the Wolof method of making pottery, using a shallow base which is turned with one hand while the clay is shaped with the other" (de Brigard 1975:15).

Regnault claimed that he was the first to observe this method which, he said, illustrated the transition from pottery made without any wheel to pottery made on the horizontal wheel, as in ancient Egypt, India, and Greece. The movie camera was used as if someone were producing multiple still images rather than a single moving sequence. Tuareg (1983:68) describes the images as "actually closer to serial photography than to film, taken with the method of 'chronophotography,' which had been developed by J. E. Marey around 1888."

Regnault carried out a cross-cultural, comparative study of body movement some 40 years before Marcel Mauss wrote his famous essay on *Techniques du corps* (Rouch 1975:85). Using time-sequence photography, Regnault filmed the "ways of walking, squatting, climbing" (1896a, 1896b, 1897). In addition to sequences of a Wolof woman from Senegal making a claypot, he shot a Wolof woman thrashing millet, three Muslims performing a salaam, and four Madagascans passing the camera while carrying the photographer on a palanquin (Marks 1995:339; and see de Brigard 1971). In 1900, Regnault and his colleague, anthropologist Azoulay, were the first to use Edison sound-record cylinders to record sound (see Azoulay 1900a, 1900b). Regnault (1923:681) described his records as "physiologie ethnique comparée" (comparative ethnic physiology). He wrote about and published his experiment, including line drawings taken from the film (Lajard and Regnault 1895). This was the earliest known attempt to use film for controlled comparison of human behavior and movement.

Sol Worth found that motion pictures antedated Regnault. "The first set of photographs called motion pictures was made by Eadweard Muybridge in 1877, as scientific evidence of a very serious kind. He invented a process of showing things in motion in order to settle a bet for Governor Leland Stanford of California about whether horses had all four feet off the ground when they ran at a gallop" (Worth 1980:3; see also Muybridge 1887).[2]

In 1898, the Cambridge Anthropological Expedition to the Torres Straits, led by former zoologist Alfred Cort Haddon, set out to do salvage ethnography on Torres Straits culture, studying physical anthropology, psychology, material culture, social organization, and religion (see Banks 1996). The team was equipped with a variety of recording tools, from W.H.R. Rivers' genealogical method, to photography, to wax-cylinder sound recording, to the Lumière motion camera. Haddon collected over 7,000 feet of film (chiefly of ceremonies) and made a number of wax cylinders. The ethnographic footage that resulted is the earliest known to have been made in the field.[3]

Franz Boas used still photography in the field beginning in 1894. In 1930, when he was 70, he took a motion picture camera and wax cylinder sound-recording machine to the Northwest Coast. It was his last field trip to the Kwakiutl, whom he had studied for more than 40 years. He was accompanied by Yulia Averkieva, a Russian anthropologist. Ruby (1983:27) notes that Boas "wrote nothing about film as a scientific tool or even about his views of the role of the cinema in our society, [yet he] undoubtedly knew that some anthropologists such as Regnault or Haddon in the 1897 Torres Straits expedition had taken movie cameras into the field." Ruby (p. 27) wondered why "Boas never reacted formally to Robert Flaherty's film, *Nanook of the North*—a popular film about people he had studied [and which] must have been a topic of conversation [in Boas's circle]."

During that trip, Boas shot 16-mm film of dances, games, manufacturing, songs, music, and other aspects of life. The task was completed in 1973 when Bill Holm edited the sequences into a two-reel film with the assistance of several Kwakiutl informants (Boas 1973 [filmed 1930]). Morris (1994:56–66) analyzes the "film" in detail, referring to it as "extraordinary collage," "a fragmented totality," "a rough-hewn montage." She concludes that "taken as a whole, the footage provides a powerful demonstration of the degree to which photographic and filmic imagery arrests social process, stripping objects from their systems of meaning in the moment of their inscription" (p. 60). To Ruby, it was evident that the footage was shot primarily for research, not for an edited production, and that Boas's theory of culture (see Stocking 1974) generated his approach to imaging—events and bits of behavior out of normal contexts for purposes of recording and analysis. Though Boas neither completed the analysis of the visual data nor published the results, Ruby (1983:27, 29) suggests that Boas be regarded as a father figure in visual anthropology for making picture-taking a normal part of the anthropologist's field experience.

MacDougall (1975) observes that perhaps "the very invention of the cinema was in part a response to the desire to observe the physical behavior of men and animals." He remarks that Regnault and Baldwin Spencer quickly went beyond the popular, commercial interests of Lumière, making essentially observational film records of technology and ritual in traditional societies. MacDougall proposed that "the notion of the synchronous-sound ethnographic film was born at the moment Baldwin Spencer decided to take both an Edison cylinder recorder and a Warwick camera to Central Australia in 1901" (p. 111).

Yet, when highly portable synchronous-sound cameras were finally developed around 1960, few ethnographic filmmakers jumped to use them. (Two exceptions were Jean Rouch in France and John Marshall in the United States.) In contrast, Loizos (1993) points out that still cameras and tape recorders were accepted rapidly and virtually without question by most anthropologists. Toward the end of his life, Regnault felt that his urgings to use film for ethnography had not been effective (de Brigard 1975:16).

In France, Jean Rouch,[4] an ethnographic and avant-garde filmmaker and ethnologist with an international reputation, received his initial training in engineering. Rouch crossed freely between shooting styles with the camera, which he himself held, and between the conventions of cinema and anthropology (see also Stoller 1992).[5] In 1960, Rouch and Edgar Morin (sociologist-cinéast) made a path-breaking documentary, *Chronique d'un été* (1961 [film]), that questioned the line drawn between documentary and fiction film.

Changes in camera and sound-recorder technology from 1960 on enabled simultaneous recording of image and speech. Also, 16-mm color film became accessible and faster film enabled filming in poor light (inside houses, huts, evening rituals, etc.). These changes made possible more intimacy, more flexibility, more spontaneity, and more shooting-style innovations. Rouch demonstrated the profound impact of the changes in both his participatory camera and catalytic shooting style. De Brigard (1975) states that Rouch was one of a few who pioneered a change in technology and shooting—synchronous sound filming combined with the hand-held camera—in the 1960s. Loizos (1993) observes that "Rouch in interviews sometimes makes it sound as if he discovered the use of the hand-held camera [but that] combat cameramen in World War II had been hand-holding their 16-mm cameras" (p. 65).

Loizos identifies four qualities that describe Rouch's contributions: documentation, collaboration, interrogation, and improvisation and fantasy. For Rouch, the "camera is not confined to the role of a passive recording instrument," as in observational cinema, but becomes "rather an active agent of investigation and the camera user can become an interrogator of the world" (1993:46).

Loizos entered academic anthropology after a career in documentary filmmaking for television. He was involved in producing 15 films on topics that included nursing and dying, mental disabilities, perceptual psychology, physics, and technological innovation. Loizos (1993:1) also worked on "two political propaganda films" and "three ethnographic documentaries." In ethnography, Loizos worked in a locale chosen for personal reasons: It was his father's village—a developing, postpeasant society in rural Cyprus. He rejects any formalizing in ethnography and film, referring to Rouch's films as the earliest challenge to the "innocence of early documentation filming and its claims to objectivity and truth" (p. 2). Recently, Loizos presented what is primarily his film-by-film reading of segments from his choice of some ethnographic films that appeared over three decades, ending in 1985.

Heider appreciates the methodological dimension in Rouch's editing. In *Les maîtres fous* (Rouch 1954 [film]), Heider (1983) says that Rouch used montage to show the referent of a symbol:

[W]hen the egg is smashed on the head of the possessed man playing the governor-general, Rouch cuts, interrupting the possession ceremony of the Hauka, to a shot of the real governor-general of the colony in full regalia to show us the white ostrich plume streaming down his hat and tells us, visually as well as verbally, that the egg is meant to symbolize the feather (this cross-cutting has a parallel in a written analysis of a myth). (p. 5)

Heider notes that Rouch used flashbacks in the final sequence to juxtapose the men as they appear in their everyday contexts with their exalted forms in their possession states. In other words, his film was an analyzed ethnographic presentation and had value for its development of the visual medium as ethnography, not only as data.

In Germany, the Institut für den Wissenschaftlichen Film was reorganized after World War II. German anthropologists resumed filming in Melanesia, Africa, and Europe, emphasizing scientific purity (Husmann 1983; Koloss 1983). Their program produced "Rules for Film Documentation in Ethnology and Folklore" in 1959. The rules said that filmmaking must be done by persons with sound anthropological training or supervision. Further, an exact log must be kept, recording authentic events. Finally, the filming must be done without using dramatic camera angles or movement and must be edited for representativeness.

In 1952, the first systematic anthropological film archive, a scientific encyclopedia in film form, was established at Göttingen, Germany (Wolf 1972 [film]). Konrad Lorenz and others assembled and arranged several thousand films on anthropological and biological subjects. Each film consisted of a single "thematic unit," such as dance, work, or ritual, grouped according to different cultures (see Wolf 1967; Tuareg 1983) and arranged to facilitate comparisons of behavior across cultures (Wolf 1972). The majority are silent. Most also have a printed document with background and technical information. The document is in the language of its author (German, French, or English—the official languages of the *Encyclopedia*).

Work on an ethnohistorical atlas of the Soviet Union began in the 1960s. By mid-1970, the classical methods of collecting ethnographic materials had been complemented with ethnographic filming. A number of Soviet research institutions have used ethnographic filming. Filming began to be used for scientific purposes at the State Ethnographical Museum of the Estonian Soviet Socialist Republic in 1961 (Peterson 1975:185).

In 1970, a Japanese archive was established at Tokyo. In 1972, Japanese anthropologists, TV journalists, and artists formed the Japanese Committee of Film on Man, in collaboration with Jean Rouch. Its aim was to support the production of ethnographic films in collaboration with the National Institute of Ethnological Studies (see Ushiyama 1975; Hockings and Omori 1988; Ushijima 1988).

In 1974, the National Anthropological Film Center was started at the Smithsonian (see Sorenson 1975:463–476). This led to the Human Studies Film Archives, which houses a large collection of film and visual material (see Wintle and Homiak 1995).

The situation was different in non-Western countries. Egypt (see al-Bindari 1981; Abdullah 1984) and India (see Sahay 1983) had a strong, early cinematic tradition of realistic fiction and social documentary, but no tradition of ethnographic films that were viewed as products of racist powers. In their view, colonial filmers were filming the colonized, the East is orientalized by the West (Said 1978; Amin 1989), and anthropology's colonial roots were being revisited through visual anthropology.

Adolfo Colombres situates the ethnographic film genre, like anthropology itself, within colonial encounters and dominating relationships. To him, Malinowski and Flaherty were romantics who, in the 1920s, escaped civilization by going to remote lands and introduced methods of recording, thus sidestepping the political context of a colonial situation. Colombres points out that Flaherty admitted that he wasn't interested in the demise of the people he was filming—a demise brought about by white domination. Rather, Flaherty's goal was to demonstrate "their originality and majesty before whites annihilated not only their identity, but the people themselves" (Colombres 1985a:12, 1985b). In other words, Flaherty's sentimental nostalgic view of culture would freeze a reconstructed pre-Contact "noble savagery."

Marks's analysis of the 1895 footage by Regnault supports the claim of the colonial orientation of anthropological film. First, the film depicted tribal peoples, hence fixing its subject matter. Second, the last of four sequences, in which the Madagascans carry the photographer on the palanquin, evokes the image of servile native bearers carrying the dominant European photographer (Marks 1995:339).

In 1946, Jean Rouch, inspired by Robert Flaherty, Dgiza Vertov, and Jean Vigo and a second-hand camera, set out to film reality. Colombres observes that when Rouch filmed that year in Niger, he was a member of the French colonial society, launching a spiritual adventure inside colonially dominated French West Africa. Rouch avoided politics, however, and the political context. In *Moi, un noir* (1957 [film]), about immigrants from Niger to the Ivory Coast, Rouch gives voice, for the first time, to the colonized so that they could express their view of the world. But Colombres asks (1985a:17) to whom Rouch designated the responsibility of the African consciousness? Was it to an immigrant Nigerian from British West Africa who danced well, as was expected of an African black? The film confirms the racist stereotypes of the colonizer and is a cinema of the exotic, an important component of colonialism.

Others echo this perspective. In India,[6] Singh (1992b) criticizes the anthropology about India. He said it overstresses divisions and tribalism, particularly during the colonial period, when ethnography was concerned primarily with tribes. This legacy continued. Colonial ethnography, Singh writes (1992a:9), "created the categories of caste and tribe—simplifying a very complex structure (of) India as a feeling, as a vision, as a dream shared by all of us." Singh proposes research and filming that would show an understanding of the nature of Indian pluralism as a "melting pot, a mosaic, a fishing net into which have been drawn peoples and races . . .

(reflecting) the unity of the people, shaped by geography and environment, by history and culture, that developed as communities and regions have interacted over time. This process is called unity in diversity, some call it diversity in unity" (pp. 8–10).

Singh's alternative approach to the study of India consists of a comprehensive study in which "community," as identified and defined by the people themselves, is the unit of study. The project would include visual documentation by films (1992a:11, 12). Roy and Jhala (1992:28) see a role for visual anthropology in India in that it "could initiate discourse across the illiteracy barrier and provide a platform from which the cultures of India could gain both 'voice' and 'representation.'" They regard "technological feasibility, political desirability, international example, and the promise of international cooperation as incentives for undertaking visual anthropology in India" (p. 21). Singh (1992a:14) supports development of a visual anthropology that respects premises of cultural integrity and finds great value in scientific visual documentation for influencing consciousness and intervention strategies during crises in a way that fiction film can't.

This critical ideological perspective from Latin America, Egypt, India, and elsewhere hasn't led to a methodological framework for ethnographic film that deals with the premises underlying the critique. Filmmakers there concentrated on fiction and, in a somewhat limited way, adopted the documentary form in three genres—journalistic, propaganda, and folkloric (the latter presented as ethnographic).

Reverse visual anthropology is, perhaps, one attempt to subvert domination. Three decades after Rouch began filming in Africa, Manthia Diawara, head of the African Studies Program at New York University and commentator on West African film, experimented with the idea of "visual anthropology in reverse." Diawara filmed Rouch in Paris to see if "shared anthropology," a phrase coined by Rouch, could shed light on cross-cultural relations between the powerful and the disempowered (see Diawara 1989). In a review of Diawara's (1995) film, Michael Fischer observes that Rouch had proposed a journey through the sculptures of Paris as his way of presenting the "public Rouch." Diawara came to realize that "He was taking me on a tour of my own French education and showing me how much of it I still carry." And Diawara was made to recite in front of one sculpture the childhood verse La Fontaine's fable of *Monsieur Fox and Monsieur Crow*. Fischer asks (1997: 142): "Is this an unsuccessful effort by the filmmaker, a political blockage in Rouch, or an example of the wily Rouch's upstaging, inverting the power relation between filmmaker and film subject, the very thing that Diawara has been warned about and warns us about both early and late in the film?"[7]

Early in the 1950s, John Marshall became involved with *Ju/hoasi* (*!Kung Bushmen or San*) in the Kalahari desert. He recorded aspects of their lives on mute, 16-mm film, which, after several expeditions, resulted in more than 250 hours of footage. This material was subsequently logged, partially annotated, and edited to produce complex ethnographic works such as *The Hunters* (Marshall 1957 [film]), *Bitter Melons* (Marshall 1971 [film]), *N/umTchai: The Ceremonial Dance of the !Kung Bushmen* (Marshall 1966 [film]), and a number of short films such as *A Curing Ceremony* (Marshall 1969a [film]), which focused on a specific event, type of relationship, or activity.

These films used informative commentaries, indigenous music, sound effects, and renderings of the subjects' speech in English. The early ones had not been shot with synchronous sound and have been carefully edited and "postsynchronized." Others, such as *A Joking Relationship* (Marshall 1962 [film]), *The Meat Fight* (Marshall 1974 [film]) and *An Argument about a Marriage* (Marshall 1969b [film]), were shot in 1957 and 1958 with synchronous sound. They concentrate on intimate interpersonal interaction. Loizos describes these films as "unrivaled in the intimacy and vividness with which [they] conveyed hunter-gatherer lives, including quarrels, and the dramatic intensity of the rituals needed to effect curing. The ability of Marshall and his co-workers to give his subjects, who were also by this time either friends or people he knew very well, vividness and authenticity as skilled, three-dimensional individuals was at the time unrivaled" (1993:21–22; see Ruby 1993). These film episodes were shown in an introductory anthropology course at Harvard to illustrate concepts such as avoidance and reciprocity.

In the early 1960s, Timothy Asch, a young photographer with anthropological training, helped Marshall edit some of the *Ju/hoasi* films. Several innovations came out of this teamwork. One innovation was the emphasis on "sequence filming." Sequence, Loizos explains, is where Marshall and Asch broke down the "story" into something more like a bare, descriptive case-history, as in *The Meat Fight* (Marshall 1974), or where the on-screen event was a single continuous one, with minor excisions, but no transcending synthesis (Loizos 1993:23). Asch describes his technique as "continuous filming of an interaction" (Asch and Asch 1988:171). Marshall and de Brigard write that a sequence can be thought of as the verifiable film record of a small event. Sequence filming replaces the ordinary process of shooting and editing a thematic film, or overview, with an attempt to report the events themselves in as much detail and for as long as possible. "Film can follow small events closely, letting them take their own time and produce their own content. The result is a sequence notable for the lack of conceptual and contextual framework which other forms of film attempt to supply. Most filmmakers would be unwilling to call a sequence a film" (Marshall and de Brigard 1975:133, 134).

Asch was also instrumental in putting subtitles on some of Marshall's *Ju/hoasi* sequence films. A number of these very short films were released. They had qualities of simplicity and self-containment—no background or introduction—but were, in many cases, supported by detailed study guides.

Asch then sought to enter into a collaborative relationship with an anthropologist,[8] aiming for a major filming project. He wanted to follow up Marshall's sequences idea, but instead of breaking footage into sequences at the editing table, he wanted to shoot sequences in the field, with synchronous sound to capture social interactions at length and without significant breaks.

Asch was contacted by anthropologist Napoleon Chagnon, who had studied the Yanomamo of Venezuela and had done some filming himself. In 1968 and 1971, Asch and Chagnon went on major ethnographic and filming expeditions to the Yanomamo and made some 37 ethnographic films. In these films, Asch applied several techniques that he and Marshall had developed together. For example, Asch and Chagnon used stills as an orientation device to get the audience familiar with the persons, relationships, and events that would be seen later as live action—a technique developed on some of the *Ju/hoasi* films.

One of the more powerful films was *Magical Death* (Chagnon 1970 [film]), in which some shamans brought their powers to bear in a psychic attack on an enemy village. Another, *A Father Washes His Children* (Asch and Chagnon 1974 [film]), shows the same man as *Magical Death*. In *Magical Death*, the man was a shaman conducting a campaign of roaring aggression against an enemy village; in the later film, he was as a gentle man handling children peacefully in the stream. Asch offered this as a beginning of "his own view" of the culture, the "other side" he called it. Loizos considers this film a valuable complement to the image of a battle-ready Yanomamo warrior. Collier (1988) sees all the Yanomamo films as humanizing the Yanomamo people, a quality not revealed in the written ethnography.

The Ax Fight (Asch and Chagnon 1971 [film]) is a good example of "shooting a sequence in the field." It's an innovative film showing a "live" field situation—a spontaneous fight that broke out in the Yanomamo village and the spontaneous reaction of the ethnographer. In the film, both the ethnographer and the filmmaker try to understand and explain as they observe the fight and film it. The film's value lies in the editorial decision to include footage and sound usually inaccessible and to replay this footage to reveal the ethnographer's understanding to the viewer. In written ethnography and most films, we're rarely, if ever, given a record of an ethnographer's struggle to make sense of ambiguous events. *The Ax Fight* is both ethnographic and about the ethnographic process. Ruby (1975:109) articulated the significance of such revelations: "A filmic ethnographic work must include a scientific justification for the multitude of decisions that one makes in the process of producing a film." The scientific justification for *The Ax Fight*'s specific construction is evident. What's lacking is a methodological paradigm that provides a sound ethnographic basis for determining and selecting sequences.[9]

The effort to provide information alongside the visual for research and teaching purposes motivated early innovations. Sorenson (1967:448) had proposed editing sequences in chronological order in the original or in a copy, then printing from a copy or from a duplicate of the chronological edit. This last copy, marked with titles and subtitles, immediately receives the magnetic track in the margin for recording information useful for scientific reasons. All these operations are done on regular film.

In the past few years, there have been dramatic, technological changes combining media, formats, and bodies of data for enhancing information. The video format has presented new areas of application and facilitated filming with sound. And with digitization, nonlinear editing, hypermedia, multimedia, web sites, CD-ROM, technology, and other innovative technology, new directions have become a reality (Seaman and Williams 1992, 1993).

Computer-based technology has also made it feasible to make visual imagery central to formal analysis, not as illustration, but as the medium for developing formal models with interactive, computer-generated, graphic modeling of, for example, kinship terminology structure (Read and Behrens 1990). Gary Seaman and Peter Biella have been working with Chagnon on the Yanomamo materials (Biella et al. 1997), combining different kinds of data in one format using hypermedia techniques and CD-ROM technology (Biella 1993a, 1993b). Biella (1996) says: "Since the invention of interactive media technology 20 years ago, students of ethnographic film have awaited fulfillment of its promise for education and scholarship. Laser discs' nonlinear access to films, along with keyboard and computer control over that access, permits dramatic, new intellectual possibilities for film and video in anthropology" (p. 595).

Research Film and Photography

General anthropologists are familiar with ethnography on film because they're using it increasingly in teaching, particularly in its more accessible video format. Less is known of using film and photography as data in research, referred to as research film. This usage is ambiguous—confounding purpose, technique, format, and a phase in the research cycle. But it does stress the scientific quality: visual tools are used to gather, discover, or elicit data for analysis. A research film is one in which cinematography is applied to the systematic search for new scientific knowledge (Michaelis 1955:1; and see Wolf 1961:16–20). It's different in format and use from films that are constructed to reveal an anthropologist's understanding of a culture, commonly referred to as ethnographic film. Research film, which Sorenson also calls "record footage," is meant to provide a credible source of information for continued analysis and rework (1976:248). From this perspective, the visual medium is considered a relatively exact tool that ensures data accuracy and enhances analysis objectivity.

Sorenson made still and moving records of events in day-to-day life in New Guinea. In this photographic ethnography on Fore childhood, Sorenson developed the concept of the research film as a method that turns exposed footage into research documents after filming. He systematized the use of film and created a "research film theory and methodology." The method deals primarily with assembling and annotating film footage taken by anyone for any purpose in order to maximize its scientific potential. Sorenson used still cameras to capture data on items, locations, positions, and context, and he used motion pictures to gather information on patterns and subtleties of process and development in behavior and social interaction (1976:147). For Sorenson, visual records facilitated original and validative inquiry in several ways: discovery, preservation for restudy, the level of detail, and as primary data. He likened the visual record to a fossil—it preserves primary data, permits reexamination from new points of view and perspectives, and facilitates discovery beyond earlier knowledge (p. 146). It's a permanent scientific resource (Sorenson and Jablonko 1975:151).

Archaeologists began to use film around 1900. They found the camera quicker than making drawings of the artifacts they uncovered and more accurate as a record of life and artifact. Worth suggests that it was from the use to which archaeologists put photographs that cultural anthropology developed its first, and still important, conceptual paradigm about using pictures as records of such cultural artifacts as arrowheads, potsherds, houses, persons, dances, ceremonies, or any performed behaviors. (See Struever [1975] for a discussion on the role of film in archaeology.) Collier (1975) notes that in digs, the still camera provides archaeologists with a record of an invaluable mapping process that corresponds with phases in their exploration. He says that John Paddock of the University of the Americas in Mexico City regularly surveyed ongoing excavations so that the exact relationships of structure and stratification could be carefully recorded each day before descending to lower levels.

According to Collier and Collier (1986), aerial photography for mapping surveying is one of the most accepted uses of the camera. Interpretation of aerial photographs has been pushed further than any other application because mappers seized photography as a useful device (1986:29–44). Vogt and Collier used photographic aerial reconnaissance to collect sociocultural data in the Harvard University Chiapas Project, a major community study (Vogt 1974).

Regnault was the first to film cultural practice with scientific intent. In 1931, he surveyed the status of film in anthropology, formulated a typology of film according to its use (entertainment, education, or research), and asserted that the importance of film in scientific research had been forgotten (Regnault 1931:306, cited in de Brigard 1975:20).[10] By the 1920s, however, there was reasonable use of photography and film. Some films focused on a single cultural activity, a few dealt with cross-cultural comparison. Museums and universities began to foster the use of film in anthropological teaching and for public education.[11] By the mid-1920s, anthropological film was accessible as a teaching tool. By the mid-1930s, a minor shift had occurred in anthropology toward accepting the visual. Although not fully integral to research and anthropological methodology, anthropologists like Melville Herskovits and Marcel Griaule used film to illustrate ethnography.

Films were not yet being cited in publications or referenced as films for discussion in scholarly works,[12] but this would soon change, as film became an instrument for the systematic microanalysis of human behavior, an instrument for recording and discovery (Marshall and de Brigard 1975:133). Margaret Mead and Gregory Bateson pioneered systematic film use over an extended period of research and across cultures. In Bali and New Guinea from 1936–1938, they shot 22,000 feet of 16-mm film and 25,000 stills. Their goal was to describe the "ethos" of a people using visual data. Technical advances and the 16-mm format, which Eastman Kodak had developed in 1923 expressly for the school market, facilitated using film technology in the field.

Bateson, an experienced photographer, took pictures, while Mead took copious field notes of events. "Mead had developed a technique of writing in a notebook while hardly looking at what she was doing, so that she could at the same time focus on what was going on in the field in order to select and direct Bateson's next shot" (Chaplin 1994). They had no sound-recording equipment. Pictures were valuable because, as Mead (1963:174) put it, there was neither vocabulary nor conceptualized methods of observation for recording certain types of nonverbal behavior. Observation had to precede codification. Pictures and notes were carefully cross-referenced. After building a large corpus of photographed data, Bateson and Mead used photos in systematic comparison—those taken before a specific hypothesis was formulated with those made afterward. After 1938, they spent another six months in New Guinea, collecting comparative data among the Iatmul.

Bateson and Mead viewed 25,000 stills in original sequence and selected and arranged 759 of them in 100 plates, thematically juxtaposing related details without "violating the context and integrity of any one event" (Mead 1972:235). They had made the "first saturated photographic research in another culture" (Collier and Collier 1986:12; see also Jacknis 1988a) and published their results (Bateson and Mead 1942). Both continued to use photography in their joint and complementary research. Mead's research focused on child development (Mead and MacGregor 1951) using photographs taken by Bateson and analyzed according to Gesell categories (Gesell 1945). Bateson's research focus was nonverbal communication (Bateson 1963).

The footage they shot was edited either chronologically (Mead and Bateson 1991 [ca. 1952] [film]) or according to contrasting behaviors (Mead and Bateson 1952 [film]). Several films, released after World War II, resulted from this field project (Mead and Bateson 1930s–1950s [film]).

Margaret Mead was critical of anthropology's passivity and resistance to using pictures in field research. She (1975) criticized ethnographic inquiry that came to "depend on words, and words and words," anthropology for "becoming a science of words," and anthropologists who relied on words and "have been very unwilling to let their pupils use the new tools" (p. 5).

Collier (1988:74), too, recognized that photography's potential contribution to anthropology had not been exploited. He found it ironic that anthropologists doubted the photographic fact (for its scientific value), whereas photography had already been widely used in the hard sciences (where data control is more of an issue). Collier and Collier (1986:10) note that "early ethnographers were enthusiastic photographers, for the camera gathered the descriptive details sought for in the material inventory phase of anthropology . . . [whereas] modern anthropologists generally use photographs strictly as *illustrations"* (emphasis in the original). Physical anthropologists and archeologists seem to have trusted the camera to record scientific observations. Yet, with still photography, chronophotography, moving pictures, and later video, visual documentation of cultural differences has long been part of the anthropological research process from Muybridge to Regnault, from Haddon to Spencer to Mooney (see Jacknis 1990) to Boas (see Jacknis 1984, 1988b, 1992), developing alongside anthropology as a discipline.

Ruby (1983:27, 29) sheds light on Boas's unused footage—the film he shot in 1930 among the Kwakiutl. Boas's interest in body movements and dance brought together several lifelong themes in his work—the relationship between race and culture to behavior and the study of expressive and aesthetic forms of culture. He espoused a theory of rhythm that encompassed dance, music, song, and many other aspects of culture, and it's possible that he made the footage and sound recordings to study rhythm. Benedict confirms this in a letter to Mead (Mead 1959:495–496; and see Mead 1977). Boas may have assumed that he could synchronously record sound and image, but he didn't have sufficient technical knowledge to realize that it was impossible to do synchronous sound filming in the field in 1930.

Visual representation is increasingly important in cross-cultural studies of human communication, which is as much visual as oral (see Goodwin 1994). Semiotic analysis and evocative techniques have joined the long-established use of film by anthropologists for both purposes: as a note-taking tool for events that are too complex, too rapid, or too small to be grasped with the naked eye or recorded in writing, and for gathering data for synchronic and diachronic comparison.

Ray Birdwhistell, who adapted methods of descriptive linguistics to the study of culture, used film to map the kinesics of American English using a written notation system (1952). His discovery of subtle, visible components in communication from film records showed that film was indispensable in detailed analyses of human interaction (1964 [film]). This was further supported by Hall's demonstration of cultural differences in nonverbal human interaction.

Alan Lomax has been directing a cross-cultural study of expressive style, including song, dance, and speech, since 1961. The Choreometrics Project (Lomax et al. 1969) is concerned with movement style, and Lomax has collected film of work and dance from nearly two hundred cultures. His study of patterns of human movement in work and dance, and their relation to social and economic evolution, would not have been possible without a growing body of anthropological films containing retrievable data that were not necessarily sought or recognized by the makers of the films. Most footage was filmed by others, but Lomax and his team selected and coded them using a descriptive system based on the Laban Effort-Shape theory (Laban 1926). Ratings were computerized for multifactor analysis. The aim of the project has been to develop an evolutionary taxonomy of culture (Lomax 1968, 1973).

With recent advances in videotape techniques, anthropologists are increasingly able to provide sophisticated analyses of expressive aspects of verbal communication. For example, they have used videotapes to examine silent cultural cues in social interactions, including distance between interactants, body posture, facial expressions, hums and murmurs, head movements, eye movements, hand gestures, etc., to determine messages being communicated in the interaction. These are so different from one culture to another that without videotape, a verbally fluent but culturally naive speaker could conclude that the audience is agreeing with the points being made, when, in fact, it is politely disagreeing or remaining neutral.

I accidentally discovered the significance of nonverbal behavior and its value as a cultural cue for synching 16-mm sound and picture. During the synching session and rough assembly of a film now in progress, I was unable to locate the synch sound to match a visual segment. After repeatedly running the film and sound back and forth and just before giving up, I noted a subtle, face-hand gesture by the woman in the image. I knew that this gesture only occurs when accompanied by specific words. Using this verbal/nonverbal linkage as a cue, I recalled hearing those words earlier on the tape, so I rolled the tape again. After locating the cue words, I synched words with cue gesture (rather than lip movement), and successfully completed the segment.

Crawford (1992:66–82; Crawford and Turton 1992) sees no need to analyze raw film. He argues that unedited film footage is already so coded that an audience can decode the images *as is* and derive meaning. What kind of meaning will be derived when raw footage is viewed without analysis? What interpretation will be assigned to "mute" facts that aren't contextualized by ethnographic background and knowledge? In his criticism of the antiexegetic stance of observational filming, Loizos (1993) supports this position when he says that unfamiliar ritual in an unfamiliar culture cannot possibly yield its meaning—culture translating itself, as it were. Sorenson (1976:247) stresses the importance of method: "Method is crucial—in order for visual records of changing ways of life to be a valid scholarly resource, they need to be shaped by scientific methodological considerations that govern the investigation of nonrecurring phenomena. Interpretability and verifiability must be stressed. Credibility is key."

Native Knowledge Through Visual Methods

The relationship with, and the role of, the people of observed cultures is a fundamental dimension in the perspective and method of anthropology. As informants, native culture-bearers, collaborators, native ethnographers, filmers, or filmed, their views of culture are essential aspects of what anthropologists seek. Collier (1967:49) wrote: "[M]ethodologically, the only way we can use the full record of the camera is through the projective interpretation by the native."

Elicitation Techniques

Margaret Mead (1956) described how anthropologists were always looking for better recording methods. Still photography was the first technical aid given full use, "partly because of cost" and simplicity and "partly because our methods of analysis were still so rudimentary." Photographs were intended for recording, while preserving "the complexity of the original material" and "simultaneity in which the memory of the investigator is at a minimum during the analysis" (pp. 79–80).

Much information is gained by analyzing photographs directly. But John Collier (1967), photographing since the 1930s, noted that pictures can be used to gain other knowledge beyond that gained from direct analysis—an understanding of culture informed by indigenous interpretations. And Prost (1975:302) saw "nothing new in using film to elicit responses from informants: Darwin did it more than a century ago." The combination of advancing visual technology and the basic anthropological premise of seeking the local view of reality process led to experimentation with methodological techniques and innovative approaches to data gathering. One important technique is the photo/film elicitation technique.

Visual elicitation as technique can be traced to psychological research going back to 1909 and became common in psychiatry during World War II (see Prados 1951; de brigard 1975). In 1925, Mead introduced photo elicitation in anthropology—using still photos to elicit responses from Samoan children. The manifold applications of photography in anthropology steadily increased.

Drawing on linguistics and ethnoscience, the elicitation technique sought to discover how members of a society experience, label, and structure the world in which they live (see Sturtevant 1964). In early studies using still photography, researchers used photographs to discover or illustrate analytical concepts. Collier (1975:213) distinguished between projective and elicitive uses. He wrote that "There really are no other ways to use photographic records scientifically, except to use photographs as stimuli in interviewing. The projective use offers a rich recovery of data, but so do old maps and ink blots. In terms of direct research, projective use of photographs is a secondary research potential."

Although Collier (1967) and Bateson and Mead (1942) did their own photography, they suggested that detailed visual studies can be applied to substantive areas (see also Mead and MacGregor 1951). Both studies were concerned with capturing events and behaviors in natural settings and explaining the attitudes and behaviors of their subjects—by elicitation in Collier's case and by research analysis for Mead and Bateson. Collier thought that elicitation could uncover informants' conceptions of the entire community and its social organization.

In my Zapotec work, I used still photography (El Guindi 1986b) for data cross-checking and elicitation "to stimulate a number of lines of enquiry that have hitherto been unexplored" (Olien 1968:837). Following a regular, in-depth interview with Martín Hernández, an informant I relied on in the area of myth, I showed him slides I had taken of ritual events and recorded his comments and reactions to them. I had no fixed notion as to what to expect nor what specific questions to ask him. Most comments involved recognition and identification of persons and places, some of which led to discussions of kinship and social networks. Only some data were useful and they were more confirmatory than informative. There were exceptions—two noteworthy observations made toward the latter part of the slide show.

In one instance, as I was showing a slide of the cemetery with a focus on the cemetery shrine, the informant pointed to two stones placed on the shrine and volunteered valuable information about the "sacredness" of the two stones (which, as I had observed frequently, were regularly used by the village caretakers to pound dirt on the grave after burial). The other instance concerned a slide of the church altar decorated elaborately for the Christmas ceremonies. In an enthusiastic burst, Martín pointed to the altar saying: "Ha, there is the little house already raised." This comment led to an extended discussion revealing rich data on various aspects of Christmas- and Easter-related rituals and myth.

Most elicited data were in the hidden, ideational realm, but made observable through the slide-elicitation technique. My use of still photography was important because it showed that: (1) It can be productive in cross-checking with the people about their culture; and (2) It was an additional means of eliciting data by combining visual aids with interviews (El Guindi 1986b:21, 43).

The elicitation technique has developed in formal terms and out of what was in the 1960s known as the "new ethnography." The interview with photo/film procedure was adapted from field linguistics (Krebs 1975:285). Advances in visual documentation brought linguistics closer to visual anthropology. To build a corpus of conceptual categories, the film elicitation technique used such interview procedures as "nontranslational linguistics" (tell me about); "interactive elicitation" (what is this? who made it? what is this part called?); and the "word-to-text technique" (to elicit labels and concepts within informant's competence, and then to use these to talk about the subject) (Samarin 1967:83). *Ghurbal* (El

Guindi 1995c [film]) is one of the few films consisting entirely of an anthropologist's spontaneous interviews seeking and eliciting original information on camera in the field.

Film Elicitation Followed Photo Elicitation

Important research was done using film in studies based on careful observation, as in kinesics and choreometrics, sometimes using film projected frame-by-frame (Lomax 1968; Birdwhistell 1970). Krebs (1975) used both photo and film for elicitation during her fieldwork in Bangkok on the ancient form of Thai dance-drama called *Khon* (1970–73). But her focus was more on film elicitation, using it with native informants "to elicit conceptual categories of culture from members of the filmed society . . . [and to] . . . discover how they conceptualize and categorize the phenomena of the world in which they live" (Krebs 1975:283). Krebs showed an informant a carefully shot and edited film of some event or happening within the culture, and, through questioning, learned how he or she structured that "slice of reality" shown on the screen. Krebs used a composite workprint of a complete Khon dance-drama outdoor performance with an optical sound track along the edge and frame-by-frame numbering to facilitate recording informants' responses as the basis for film elicitation interviews. Drawing on experimentation and categorization from the Choreometrics Project of Columbia University (Lomax 1978 [film]), Krebs empirically established the existence of gestures and the multivocality of the same gestures in different contexts.

Prost (1975:302) summarizes the uses of film in Krebs's project: (1) a memory device—informants recalled their intentions as they observed something they did; (2) a standardization tool—people commented on the same filmed slice of reality; and (3) a vehicle for experimental control—informants responded to a film where one or another variable has been controlled, either a doctored film or a simulated portrayal. With this technique, researchers can explore the full variety of meanings among their informants.

Feedback as Method

Rouch wants to know: "For whom have you produced this film, and why?" (1975:95). He said, "[M]y prime audience is the other person, the one I am filming" (p. 99). It's an indispensable step to present "the first rushes from beginning to end to the people who were filmed whose participation is essential" (p. 98). Rouch's notion of participation refers to the camera's role: "The anthropologist has at his disposal the only tool—the participant camera—which can provide him with the extraordinary opportunity to communicate with the group under study," what some of us call "shared anthropology" (p. 98).

Feedback, to Rouch, is an "extraordinary technique [which] turned those filmed into participants with the film acting as a *stimulant for mutual understanding and dignity*" (1975:100, emphasis added). In the early 1960s, Rouch and Morin filmed their actors' comments and exclamations as those actors saw themselves on screen in *Jaguar*. Rouch went further by using the presence of cameras and cameramen to provoke psychodramas (de Brigard 1975:31). In most cases, feedback was used to meet the filmers' obligation to the people filmed. Rouch calls this "sharing" anthropology.

Timothy Asch introduced something different in 1978, when he embarked on a project with Patsy Asch and in collaboration with Linda Connor, who had worked closely with Balinese healers and mediums. The project resulted in four films and a monograph, which "represent collaborative ethnographic documentation [with] Jero Tapakan (the Balinese medium) as the most important person in this collaboration" (Connor et al. 1986:xi). The monograph fulfilled Asch's objective of integrating written teaching materials with film so they were available in one package.

A Balinese Trance Seance (Asch et al. 1980 [film]) was the first in the series; it was filmed in 1978 in straightforward documentation style, but in collaboration with Connor. Loizos (1993:40) describes it this way: We see Jero as therapeutic specialist being consulted by several different clients, who are recently bereaved and troubled by anxieties and need to understand what their dead need from them. Jero questions them, goes into possession, and her words become the words of various deities or of the recently dead. Through her, the bereaved receive communication and, subsequently, advice. To explore the value of showing people a film of themselves, Asch et al. made a second film, *Jero on Jero* (1981 [film]), in which they show Jero's reactions viewing the first film.

Loizos raises questions prompted by this experiment. Should this second film be given the same status as the first film, which merely shows Jero at work? Or, do we now need a typology of documents, primary, secondary, tertiary, in which this becomes a metadocument? In the second film, Loizos (1993) sees Jero's strong ego in a nontraditional context, encountering an objectified representation of her as a person, and as a healer, on film. He proposes that this film be considered a metadocument to be treated with care. He finds the most important aspect resulting from this experiment is how this whole process has affected Jero's character (p. 41). This project—films and monograph—is a package intended to aid in teaching.

Native Film as Experiment

Informant-made films can show overall views of selected activities in the community, particularly when the film is used to record naturally occurring activities. In 1966, Worth and Adair began experimenting with such films. They undertook to teach a group of Navajo men and women how to make their own motion pictures, on any subject they wanted, to elicit a "visual flow" that could be analyzed "in terms of the structure of images and the cognitive processes of rules used in making those images" (Worth and Adair 1972:27–28). Worth and Adair hypothesized that motion picture film—conceived, photographed, and sequentially arranged by a people, in this case, the Navajo—would reveal aspects of coding, cognition, and values that may be inhibited, not observable, or not analyzable when the investigation is totally dependent on verbal exchange—especially when such research must be done in the language of the investigator.

Within two months, the Navajo produced short exercises and seven silent films. The films were analyzed and shown to the Navajo community. They were eventually distributed and gained popularity in experimental film circles (The Navajo People 1966 [film]). "Our own study of Navajo films shows clearly that what the Navajos show us about themselves in their films is very different from what an anthropologist shows in his. Even in a film about weaving, the Navajo concentrates the bulk of his film on things that are never seen in an anthropologist's film on the same subject" (Worth and Adair 1972).

A little over a decade later, Bellman and Jules-Rosette (1977:v) carried out a controlled and comparative study on the introduction of media to two African communities—a traditional rural village on the Liberian-Guinea border and a shanty town compound on the outskirts of Lusaka, Zaire. Both anthropologists carried out extended fieldwork and both asked informants to videotape or film different kinds of social interactions, palavers, and rituals. Their materials do contain a particular kind of editing process. The informant camera persons edited in-camera by using the techniques of turning the camera on and off, zoom (in and out), dolly (toward and away from the action), pan (horizontal and vertical), tilt, follow shots, narration, and various combinations of the above (pp. 4, 5).

Bellman and Jules-Rosette extended in-camera editing to include not only the filmer's selection of shots but also the techniques used to produce them. They knew that there was a limited time on the battery (no electricity) and amount of tape or film in the camera. Consequently, they carefully chose which occurrences were significant. For example, in one of the Kpelle research tapes, a high-ranking member of the Poro (men's secret society) priesthood recorded an important ritual of the Sande (women's secret society) and its Zo (priestess-leadership). The tape, approximately 25 minutes long, has 18 recognizable segments. Each, in turn, is segmented by different camera techniques that serve as markers to show particular actors, follow central action, study interesting movements, display instruments, etc.

Borrowing the concept of cademe from Worth and Adair (1972), these meaningful units are tape-film components or cademic markers. In the Navajo experiment, 16-mm films were made by Navajo living on an Arizona reservation. Worth and Adair defined a cademe as "that unit obtained by pushing the start button of the camera and releasing it, producing one continuous image event" (p. 89).

Bellman and Jules-Rosette (1977:4-5) extended the definition to include in-camera editing techniques. "Our concept of cademic marker refers to the location of meaningful camera techniques in the analysis."

Years later, cameras were given to indigenous populations for advocacy, political purposes, and as devices for cultural and political self-representation to resist encroachment on their territories and exploitation of their resources (Turner 1991, 1995). Video technology with automatic synchronous sound further facilitated this genre and became an additional resource available to informants in their productions.

Culture Reconstruction

In anthropology, deconstruction and reconstruction of ancient or traditional culture or culture artifacts are used experimentally to shed light or test scientific hypotheses on the past. In archaeology, James Hill (1977; Hill and Gunn 1977) devised a method to discover and identify which artifacts in prehistoric contexts were made or used by specific prehistoric individuals. First, a collection of ceramic vessels was painted in Tijuana, Mexico, by local artisans. When the painting was completed, the pots were photographed and then broken into sherds to resemble the pottery remnants dug up by archaeologists. The sherds were analyzed and grouped. The archaeologists matched the sherds with the recorded information (photo and labeling) on the original pots groups, showing correspondence to individual artisans (see Hill and Gunn [1977:55–108] for the published results). Photography is regularly used in scientific archaeology as integral to the data-recording methodology and for replication. In this case, it was used to reconstruct culture.

Asen Balikci is the visual anthropologist best associated with reconstructing culture on film. His aim is to partially reconstruct sequences of traditional behavior, especially where there is loss of indigenous cultures, without portraying the extraordinary or the unique. Balikci (1975) views this as a way to "in a sense reverse the acculturative process and salvage elements of traditional behavior for posterity" (p. 191). Working among the Netsilik Inuit, he tried to reconstruct the "old pattern"— vividly remembered by middle-aged Inuit—to provide instructional materials for classroom use about the Netsilik traditional past.

Boas filmed the Kwakiutl in 1930 because of an urgent need to salvage and, if necessary, reconstruct as much of their traditional culture as possible. Boas assumed a theory of culture that allowed him to remove bits of behavior from their normal context for recording and analysis (see Ruby 1983). He filmed two Kwakiutl chiefs boasting (that is, making speeches). Normally, these speeches would have occurred inside, at night within the context of a particular ceremony, and in front of an audience. In the film, the two men are outside, in daylight, without ceremony or audience.

Morris (1994:64) sees in the footage "the props of reconstruction: the make-shift stage, the self-conscious performance, even the recording equipment in one corner of the frame"—a reconstruction, she argues, "that effaces the supposed impurities of cultural change, and thereby elides the reality of cultural contact, colonization, and historical process." Morris considers this methodological tool as perpetuating "a vision of the Native as Adamic, as originary . . . the image of the savage as custodian of the paradisiacal garden . . . abundance assumed to have been the basis of pre-contact cultures on the Northwest Coast" (p. 63). However, in line with the argument by Colombres (1985b:12, 13) about Flaherty, Morris points out that when Boas made *The Kwakiutl of British Columbia,* the population was reduced by disease, the ceremonial life was virtually strangled by federal (Canadian) legislation banning the potlatch, there was limited access to the resources that had been the staple of their life, and they suffered from widespread poverty and cultural dislocation. "Boas was not simply recording the processes of the present, but reconstructing a culture—an imaginary culture—still pristine and innocent of Euro-Canadian ways" (Morris 1994:63–64). Ruby (1983:29) considers Boas's methodology of reconstruction as valid in the context of his general theory of culture, in which case the staged boasting performance still retained those elements Boas wished to study.

The well-known works of Robert Flaherty, an explorer/artist with no claims to training in anthropology, exemplify a nonscientific approach to reconstruction. When he "directed a South Seas love story for Hollywood" (de Brigard 1975:22), his perspective was that film is a purely personal interpretation of the local culture. He observed closely, and for extended periods, the way of life of the indigenous people he was to film and then selected an "actor(s)" from among the local population to become the local interpreter(s) of culture on camera.

Flaherty's most talked-about film is *Nanook of the North* (1922 [film]). The other two are *Moana* (1926 [film]) and *Man of Aran* (1934 [film]). A spokesman for the Asia Society described *Nanook* as "drama, education, and inspiration combined." And John Grierson (cited in de Brigard 1975), wrote: "*Moana*, being a visual account of events in the life of a Polynesian youth, has documentary value" (de Brigard 1975:23).

Flaherty's favorite theme was the continuously heroic struggle of total, primordial man against infinitely powerful and hostile elements. Messenger (1966) wrote that Flaherty was so deeply influenced by primitivism and his philosophy of aesthetics that he created new customs, such as shark fishing—a central theme of his work—and seriously distorted numerous indigenous customs to make the "man of Aran" fit his preconceptions. "As to the soil building and associated seaweed collecting technique it is faulty to the point of being ridiculous. And for the most dramatic scene depicting the wrecking of the craft on shore while landing, local informants agreed that weather conditions were not as severe nor the situation as perilous as illustrated on the film" (p. 21). According to Balikci (1975:195), *Man of Aran* wouldn't qualify as "ethnographically valid reconstruction of the local culture." Heider (1976:23) criticized the claim of native feedback, although he says that "the Flaherty legend relates how Flaherty developed his footage each evening and screened it for his subjects, getting their reactions and advice and thus making them real collaborators in the filmmaking process." Heider found no evidence that this was a serious attempt at reaching the natives' insight into their own culture. For more details on the making of *Man of Aran* and *Desert People*, see Balikci's account (1975:191–199).

Another film of culture reconstruction is *Desert People*, by Ian Dunlop and Robert Tonkinson (1969 [film]). At a mission station, Dunlop and Tonkinson found a family of Aborigines who, until a short time before, had been living off the land. They asked the family to return to its traditional grounds for a period of time to be filmed. The family accepted and left for the bush, armed only with traditional tools, leaving behind imported goods they owned at the mission station. The director concentrated on various daily routines. The reconstruction of the traditional family life was so successful that even the critical ethnographer remains oblivious to the powerful, intrusive society encircling this Aboriginal group (for more on ethnographic filmmaking in Australia, see Dunlop 1983).

Reconstructing the traditional life of the Netsilik Inuit was different. From 1959–1960, Asen Balikci did ethnographic fieldwork among the eastern Netsilik Inuit living around Pelly Bay. At that time, the band numbered about a hundred individuals and had gone through several acculturative stages. The introduction of the rifle had caused profound changes in settlement pattern, subsistence techniques, and economic organization. In traditional times, a group hunt for seals was a complex system of meat sharing at the community level. In the 1950s, the Pelly Bay band still lived in igloos, drove dog teams, preferred caribou leather for clothing, and relied exclusively on local food. But by that time, hunters preferred to shoot seals at the ice edge and didn't share—seals that were shot belonged to the hunter. Caribou hunting from kayaks had been completely abandoned. With a rifle, a Netsilik could search for herds in the vast tundra and make a kill in any season. The middle aged and elderly vividly remembered the old ways (Balikci and Mary-Rousselière 1967–68 [film]).

"In 1962," Balikci (1975) writes, "I received an assignment to reconstruct on film the traditional migration pattern of the Pelly Bay band with the aim of preparing instructional material for social science courses at the elementary level" (pp. 196–197). In the Flaherty tradition, Balikci selected a principal "actor"— Itimanguerk, 50 years old. Itimanguerk was a camp headman, thus free to select his camp fellows and instruct them in the old ways without intervention or instruction by the anthropologist. Gradually, Balikci became more and more involved with the recording procedures and selecting what to film and what to leave out. This process highly depends on the anthropologist's ethnographic knowledge and understanding of Inuit traditional life.

How does an anthropologist determine the domain to be filmed without leaving it entirely to spontaneity and chance during shooting? In what way was Balikci's reconstruction that of a "whole" culture as he claims? Below, in the section on Visual Ethnography, I discuss establishing field and analytic methodology to address these questions.

Spurious Arguments, Reifying Terms, Confounding Players

"To appreciate *this,* one need only contrast Bateson and Mead's *Childhood Rivalry* in 1940 and the work of the MacDougalls in East Africa in the 1970s." By *this,* Crawford (1992:72) was referring to the new technologies of cinema and, presumably, their influence on the quality of productions. But other than quality of production and aesthetics, these two are very different projects. Bateson and Mead are anthropologists who, as a team, used film for research purposes, and their project is a systematic and comparative ethnographic study. Mead made their project's priority explicit. She stated that they weren't filming "for the purpose of making documentary films and photographs for which *one decides a priori upon the norms and then gets the Balinese to go through these behaviors in suitable lighting"* (Bateson and Mead 1942:49, emphasis added). The reference here is to the relative staging of behaviors and events to accommodate the limitations of technology (light conditions).

The MacDougalls' filmmaking project is about culture, any culture. The project calls for no prerequisite culture or language training. I see a problem in that. In a recent discussion with David MacDougall (El Guindi 1995a), I noted an emergent homogenization of people he filmed—that is, despite the cultural diversity of the people he films (Africans, Indians, Australians, or Sardinians), they either don't talk or they talk in a paced, slow, measured way. In contrast, all the people in my fieldwork talk a lot, on and off camera. Such rich verbal behavior often contains subtle cultural nuances that I feel shows their cultural identity and shouldn't be selected out on technical or artistic grounds.

From my perspective, a people are humanized when their representation is grounded in culture identity. Despite a sensitive empathy with the people, a dehumanizing homogenization may result from filmic conventions. The challenge then becomes, as in my own films, how to present rich verbal information within the film document. In the last film I completed, *Ghurbal* (El Guindi 1995c), I faced a formidable problem with selection in subtitling because of the rich verbosity that I knew was culturally characteristic and relevant and that I wished to include.

Crawford (1992:72) sees the problem as being that "Ethnographic film-making has always run the risk of falling between the two stools of anthropology and cinematography." But Margaret Mead was certain about the place of film. To Margaret Mead (1962:138), visual tools were used for research data and discovery: "Film materials . . . have made it possible to explore ways of tapping the theoretical insights of other disciplines through the use of visual materials and of providing a continuing resource for the exploration of new hypotheses as the behavior, recorded on film, can be viewed repeatedly in the light of other new materials." "[Mead and Bateson] studied child development with the camera" (Collier 1988:74). As such, Mead didn't distinguish between moving and still photography (1963).

But MacDougall (1978:405) places ethnographic film in cinema and calls for film to be considered a cultural artifact serving "as a source of data for social science in the manner of myths, rock paintings, and government papers." Loizos (1993) concurs, suggesting that we look at ethnographic film from the cinematic point of view, as a kind of documentary cinema, lest it become "narrowly concerned with ghetto-culture called 'ethnographic films'" (1993:1). He calls on anthropologists to "unlearn the idea that formal conceptual analysis rules the academy—and rules alone" (1993:64). In this tradition, the stress is on multiple subjectivities and plural learning systems rather than on systematic characteristics of human behavior and patterned culture. The concern is not with film for research, elicitation, discovery, recording, or archiving. It situates film in cinema, rather than in the social science tradition of anthropology, and draws inspiration from literary theory, which challenges objectivity and facts.

In my view, the need to listen to indigenous voices has always been a core part of anthropology's perspective and a central premise underlying its formal conceptual thinking. Poetry, painting, novels, and songs have always been included, along with sex, food, child rearing practices, etc., in the cultural repertoire of traditional ethnographies. Even cinema is included as a cultural element for analysis (see Heider's 1991 analysis of Indonesian cinema as a window on national culture). Loizos (1993:80) said that in the 1980s more anthropologists came to see their informants "as more rounded than they had been as producers of kinship systems, economic data, myths and cosmologies." My question is: Other than for reasons of a researcher's personal preference, why are people more rounded when they recite a poem than when they exchange necklaces?

Mead's observation (1963) about forgetting that other things are happening when the camera is pointing in one direction, or that other things are happening outside the frame, was misused to raise spurious arguments about objectivity, selectivity, and representationality. Sorenson (1975:466) notes that "A peculiar myth that has developed in recent years is that anthropological films cannot be scientific because their content is always governed by selective interests. This absurd notion ignores the degree to which selectivity and special interest underlie all scientific inquiry. Method is crucial. In order for visual records to be a valid scientific resource, they need to be shaped by the scientific methodological considerations that govern the investigation of nonrecurring phenomena."

Rather, the point to be made from Mead's remark is about the importance of visual research data and their use for discovery. Heider (1983) discusses research footage (not intended for inclusion in a finished film) used by an ethnographer to capture an image of behavior for careful frame-by-frame analysis. "Research with film and videotape allowed people like Bateson, Birdwhistell, Lomax, and Kendon to demonstrate how much important information is continually being expressed and communicated in whole bodies and in both sides of the conversation. Their research has had a direct impact on thinking about ethnographic film" (pp. 2–10). Adam Kendon shot his footage of greeting behavior in wide angle to pick up unexpectedly early stages of a greeting sequence (Kendon and Ferber 1973).

Heider observes that random focusing on some behavior of interest might sacrifice other, potentially important data. This is well demonstrated by the case where John Collier worked with Bernard Siegel on an ethnography of Picuris Pueblo—a dwindling pueblo of the Tiwa language group. Collier's contribution was to make photographs for Siegel to use in photo interviewing. Both presumed that ceremonial dances were the heart of Pueblo religious life. San Lorenzo Day, a summer fiesta, took place during the research, and Collier photographed the theatrically exquisite Deer Dance. During photo interviewing, however, Collier and Siegel learned that the dance held a relatively low place in the day's ceremony. As one collaborator said, "We do this to please the white people" (Collier 1988:90).

MacDougall (1978:405) first dismisses ethnographic film totally, saying that it "cannot be said to constitute a genre, nor is ethnographic film-making a discipline with unified origins and an established methodology." In fact, as the overview in this chapter shows, there is unified origin and a sustained interest in establishing methodology. Griaule sustained Regnault's concept of ethnographic filming as a scientific activity concerned with traditional ethnographic subjects. He distinguished three film types: archive footage for research, training films for anthropology courses, and public education films, occasionally including "works of art" (Griaule 1957). André Leroi-Gourhan applied the term ethnological (to film) and introduced another tripartite classification: the research film, the "exotic" travel film (to be abhorred as superficial and exploitative), and the "film of environment," produced with no scientific aim but deriving an ethnological value from its exportation (1948). Chanock and Sorenson (1975:432) refer to the research film method, which provides identified and annotated visual records, unedited, not designed to impose preconceived ideas, and focused on films based on ethnographic understandings of a culture.

Loizos (1993) avoids classification and remarks instead on films from specific periods as examples of innovations and modalities. The innovations he identifies are (1) production technology; (2) diverse subject matter; (3) widened range of strategies of argument used by filmmakers—that is, films that combine several modes of representation; and (4) enhanced ethnographic contextualizing devices. He proposes the following modalities: documentation, explanatory, explanation rejected (film modality that rejects conceptual explanation root and branch), and context enrichment.

MacDougall (1978:405) finds one distinction useful: ethnographic footage (raw material that comes out of a camera, like field notes, used for a variety of purposes including the making of films) and ethnographic films (structured works made for presentation to an audience). Then he further divides ethnographic footage into two major forms: research footage to serve specific scientific inquiries, and record footage made to provide more general documents for archiving and future research—footage for research purposes.

To Heider (1983:5), "ethnographic films must themselves be ethnographically accountable" and "the better the ethnographicness, the better the cinema." Omori (1988) focused his discussion on footage film and ethnographic film. He draws the analogy from print ethnography and sees a correspondence between footage film and field notes, on the one hand, and ethnographic film and monograph, on the other. He states that within visual anthropology there are two main forms that films take. First, there are simple footage films taken as field notes. Second, there is the ethnographic film (like a monograph) that is shot in a comprehensive way and organized around a theme related to the entire culture being studied (p. 192). Footage films are short films recording a technical process or scenes of human behavior within a group. The monograph film tends to be longer and it has a story that is constructed on a specific theme. Omori characterized the difference as part/whole, analytic/interpretive, scientific/ethnographic, or differential length (pp. 192, 194, 196). Wolf believed that there were three kinds of scientific film: the research film, the scientific documentation film, and the university instructional film (1961:16–20). Increasingly, there are visual studies that focus on popular media, home photography, and public culture (Chalfen 1975, 1987, 1992; Ruby 1981; Ginsburg 1995; El Guindi 1996b).

These progressive developments placed filming squarely within anthropology rather than documentary cinema—a position expressed by many anthropologists to this day. Sol Worth (1969, 1972; also see Gross and Worth 1997) referred to ethnographic film as a set of signs to study the behavior of a people, used either as a recording of data about culture or as data of culture. Jay Ruby (1975) proposed four criteria for ethnographic films. They should be (1) films about whole cultures, or definable portions of cultures; (2) informed by explicit or implicit theories of culture; (3) explicit about the research and filming methods they had used; and (4) use a distinctively anthropological lexicon. In a now-classic monograph, Karl Heider said (1976:75) that satisfactory ethnographic films are those revealing "whole bodies, and whole people, in whole acts." He sketched a system for discussing different attributes that contribute to the ethnographicness of a film.

Balikci (1988) discussed degrees of ethnographicness on the basis of six premises used "to define what is ethnographic in a film" (pp. 33–34).

Rollwagen (1988a, 1988b) stressed the disciplinary framework within which ethnographic film is situated, ethnography being a scientific description conducted within a theoretical framework. This puts film/photography within anthropology, not cinema, and entails the premise that the visual medium is integral to research or, in the case of ethnographic film, is based on a significant amount of research prior to filming (see Ruby 1983 on the role of photography in research by Boas). Clearly, ethnographic film isn't merely involvement in other cultures.

I propose grouping film in a way that is both inclusive of all the relevant visual forms and sufficiently differentiating in form, purpose, and character to have anthropological value. All require culture knowledge and are suitable, even recommended, for classroom teaching and public lecturing. They are (1) the visual medium as a recording tool of data for analysis and/or archival purpose; (2) the visual medium for elicitation and discovery; (3) the visual medium used for experimental culture reconstructions; and (4) the visual medium as ethnography—visual ethnography.

Visual Ethnography

In 1972, 13 years before my formal involvement with visual anthropology and before making my first visual ethnography (El Guindi 1986c [film]), Sol Worth (1972:8–12) called for the development of new methods of analysis (for the visual mode) tied to anthropological problems and theories. It is crucial, he stressed, to integrate the study of ethnographic film into anthropology.

I earned my Ph.D. in anthropology that year, after doing more than 32 months of fieldwork in rural Oaxaca, Mexico, among the valley Zapotec. In my research (El Guindi 1986b), I had established a methodological base for formal collaboration with indigenous informants in formulating an ethnography on Zapotec ritual. I called this collaborative method "native ethnography."[13]

While building an analytic framework, I also developed a notion of adequacy, linking data gathering, data analysis (grounded in anthropological insights), and ethnography construction into an interdependent process. This was the anthropological framework for my film *El Sebou*[14] (El Guindi 1986c; also see *Film Study Guide* [El Guindi 1996a]). The film was about the Egyptian birth ceremony that I had been studying between 1983 and 1985.[15] It was to be a visual ethnography.

Triadic Relations in Film

Two notions attributed to Jean Rouch—*participant camera* and *cinema direct*—are useful for defining the quality of, and distance between, filmer and filmed.

Participant camera links camera and people, turning filmmaking into a stimulant for mutual understanding and dignity. It is a visual field technique of both humanistic and methodological value for enhancing the quality of field filming. Cinema direct refers to direct filming of actions and direct contact between filmers and filmed. The intent is to maximize dignity and respect for the people as the quality of recorded data is simultaneously enhanced.

The quality of the relationship between filmmaker and people filmed is crucial but sometimes overromanticized, as rapport often is in general anthropology (El Guindi 1986b:7–43). The phrase, "style of interacting with people" (Asch and Asch 1988:172–173), becomes meaningful when placed in the process of building an analytic framework and when film construction is subjected to rigor as field technique. Establishing rapport and having a good relationship with the indigenous population doesn't magically translate into quality anthropological data gathering, visual or nonvisual.

Obviously, in print ethnography there's a third partner to the team of ethnographer/people—those who read the completed ethnography and interpret/misinterpret what the ethnographer wrote. Crawford (1992) turns this upside down when he asserts that "unedited film footage may be shown to an audience able to decode the images whereas the data providing the raw material for ethnographic writing needs to go through some degree of codification in order to make any sense to other than the producer" (p. 73). In my view, neither raw film nor raw field notes can be decoded without context, unless, of course, the image or the text is taken as pure art—uncontextualized in culture.

Templin (1982:138) finds that for images "there are two contexts that yield meanings"—the context in which they are made and the context in which they are viewed. Crawford and Simonsen (1992:3) see three dyadic relations, namely filmer/filmed, filmer/audience, and filmed/audience. Rollwagen (1988b:xv) observes at least three interpretations in any communication: that of the individual participant in a cultural system being studied, that of the anthropologist, and that of the reader of the written work or the viewer of the anthropological film.

Some studies went further by exploring the kind of interpretation attributed to ethnographic film images. Omori (1988:184) uses the notion of reflexivity to refer to the experience of viewing film as taking on "the thoughts and consciousness of a participating member from a different culture. . . . The emotionally involved viewer seems to enter the screen, and then experiences an identification with the people who appear in the scene, a temporary emotional tie between the viewer and the image called *participation affective* by Edgar Morin . . . a mental process of becoming one with the image on the screen." Wilton Martinez (1990, 1992) found that American students in anthropology classes interpret ethnographic films in ways that reinforce ethnocentric stereotypes of non-Western cultures. Evidence of such reactions has become the subject of much recent debate in visual anthropology.

Parameters for Visual Ethnography

This section describes the methodological framework I developed while making *El Sebou'*: *Egyptian Birth Ritual* (El Guindi 1986c [film]), the film about a traditional ceremony of the same name. The ceremony is held in many parts of rural and urban Egypt (and elsewhere in the Arabic-speaking region), by Muslims and Copts. It celebrates a child's "coming out" (the *sebou'* in the film is that of boy-girl twins). It also provides a ritualized cultural context to establish a child's identification with his or her own gender group and with the family.

During the filming process, I made spontaneous innovations, selected specific modes, and defined premises. Altogether, these constitute the methodological base for the film project and for a theory of visual ethnography. I will discuss these innovations, modes, and premises in terms of perspective, technique, and conceptual parameters.

Perspective refers to the source of premises that influence the orientation I adopted in filming. The orientations were anthropology and its core principles of holism, a comparative base for analysis, fieldwork, cultural knowledge, mastery of field language, and rapport with and respect for the people. Another dimension to perspective is self-sufficiency of the ethnographic filmic account on the subject matter. What if the film is the only source of information for the viewer? Deciding on self-sufficiency is not trivial since it relates to the use of a number of filmic techniques to provide the background and support information that is not evident in images alone.

Perspective is also about the target audience. Is the film for local or Euro American viewing? Is it for television? For public audiences? For classroom teaching? For discussion in anthropology classes or in classes on Middle East Studies? The most constraining, yet financially rewarding target, is television. But for television, ethnographic standards might have to be overlooked and television filming needs to be well financed. Finally, there is the dual context-triadic participation mentioned earlier. I was alert to the prejudicial portrayals and attitudes against things Arabic and Islamic and knew that this realization would guide my decisions. For me, the primary audience context is education and communication through direct classroom teaching and public viewing.

The second aspect is technique in shooting and editing. Whose eye will be behind the camera? How will the perspective described above translate into a coherent visual document? How will field-gathered data inform filming? How can we convey most of the information without much accompanying textual material? How will the filmic medium translate culture and cultural knowledge?

I devised three specific methods/techniques during the shooting and editing to deal with some of the questions raised above. They are: layering,[16] charting content, and freezing structure. Layering refers to using multiple techniques for culture translation and communication, all layered within the film itself. This was the technique of choice for *El Sebou'* and for *El Moulid* (El Guindi 1990 [film]). The multiple modes are: bottom-of-screen English subtitling of Arabic statements made by the people in the film, segment-by-segment English titling of Arabic songs, subjective voice (English rendition of voices faithful in diction and mannerism), and objective voice (analytic narrative). This mode has never been in vogue cinematically. The two other techniques are discussed below.

The third and final aspect is conceptual parameters. These include internal contextualizing, determining and visualizing the rite-of-passage form, and defining the cultural domain of ritual. Contextualizing[17] refers to the inclusion of images that are culturally and structurally relevant. Ethnographic analysis determines all three—the relevance of contextual images, the ceremony as a rite-of-passage, and the domain of the ritual.

Charting Content

After shooting some contextual material, I realized that I had to inform the entire team of my analysis to ensure smooth coordination, particularly during the focal ceremony. The team included an Egyptian cameraman and soundman, whose background was in both news photography and nonsync sound documentary tradition. Directing camera moves and framing during the shoot, a mode French anthropologist/filmmaker Colette Piault used when she filmed daily life in a Greek village (1988), wouldn't be suitable for a ritual event where the pace is fast and involves spontaneity and on-the-spot choices.

Sharing the analysis was also meant to ensure comprehensive coverage of concrete, events, and movements, and abstract aspects of the cultural activity, such as family warmth and gender intimacy. The *Sebou'* took two days. First, there are related ceremonies and events that occur on the eve of the *Sebou'* in the same home as the *Sebou'*. The second day is the *Sebou'* itself. Other components of the event included purchasing special foods and specific beverages, crafting ceremonial candles, and the like. These took another two days, so the ceremony was to be covered in four days of shooting.

In the field and in preparation for the spontaneous "team seminar" held before shooting, I had made a chart describing all aspects of the ceremony and divided these elements into three groups—Aspects, Actions, and Objects (see Figures 1 and 2). *Aspects* refers to abstract observations, which can be indirectly shown through concrete illustrations. *Actions* refers to concrete movements (lighting candles, the ritual meal, and symbolically winnowing the babies in a sieve). *Objects* covers ceremonial crafts and physical objects such as the ceremonial pots, the sieve, the candles, the candy sacks, etc.—all part of the ceremony.

Discussion with the filming team was useful in many ways.[18] Only one 16-mm camera would be used because it would be less intrusive, and this is an intimate family ceremony taking place in a small physical space. The cameraman said that he was already familiar with the *Sebou'* and knew exactly what to shoot and how to frame. In the discussion, it became evident that his knowledge was based on his personal, concrete experience and wasn't generalizable. Also, there were aspects that he simply "didn't see" or "consider marked." And he expected certain occurrences to occur exactly the way he had experienced them.

There are two central rites in the ritual: (1) winnowing of the baby and (2) carrying the baby down the stairs in a candle procession. Either (1) or (2) will occur first. Based on ethnographic knowledge, I shared the observation about limited possibilities. The cameraman preferred one possibility. For nonintervention with the natural flow of events, I insisted we prepare for either. In our filmed event, the ritual leaders led the procession down the stairs first, then winnowed the twin babies. The film team rushed to catch both sequences on film. We succeeded.

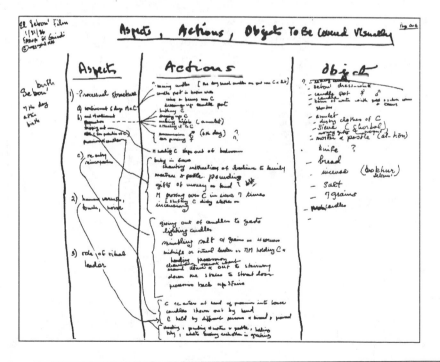

Figure 1. Original chart (Part 1) hand drawn spontaneously in the field in January 1986 by the anthropologist. It was used to guide film team preshooting discussion.

ASPECTS, ACTIONS, OBJECTS
To Be Covered Visually

ASPECTS	ACTIONS	OBJECTS
1) Processual Structure		
	? naming candles/ 7 candle lit by head of NB	naming candles
a) confinement of newborn 6 days	Eve of Sebou' (6th day)	incense candlepot

	candle pot in water basin w/ coins & beans
	   near child
	"dressing up" candle pot
	filling gift sacks w/ candy & peanuts/chickpeas
	serving "mughat"
		pot candle
		basin w/ water
		  & beans
		bowl w/ 7 grains
		gift sacks, candy,
		peanuts

b) end of confinement
      7th day
  1- preparation
	bathing child
	dressing up child
	making "hijab" (amulet)
	attaching it to child
		white sebou' dress
		dirty diaper
		amulet
		scissors

2- stepping out
    threshold crossing
	MM carries NB out of bedroom
	   Candlepot also brought out	

3- candle procession	Candles given out to everyone and lit
	RL holds dish with 7 grains & salt
	MW/RL/MM holds NB & heads procession down
	   building
	Chanting sebou' chants
	Sprinkling of grains in 4 directions
	Procession down stairs, to street gate and back
	   into flat
		procession candles
		dish of 7 grains
		incense

4- initiation rite	NB in sieve pounding brass mortar & pestle chanting obedience instructions to NB M stepping over NB 7 times incensing dirty diaper & knife shifting winnowing NB noqut/gifts of money over NB	

	-- 	
	      missing from field chart
	      (rolling sieve across room)
	-- 		

c) re-entry/ reincorporation	NB held by different persons, touched, kissed Giving out candy sacks to children Dancing Ceremonial meal/fatta-	
2) proxemics - human warmth, touch, noise		
3) role of ritual leader		

4) bonding
  M/Ch
  Women
  Family		

Figure 2. Chart retyped for clarity from original after return from the field (Fadwa El Guindi ©1986).

In the discussion I inadvertently omitted the action of sieve rolling, the one element later missed during shooting although it occurred in front of the cameraman. The chart was valuable for accuracy in coverage and economy in footage. Envisioning the contextual scenes as integral to the ceremony—a nonlinear approach—turned out to be a major strength of the film (see Lobban [1988] for a review of this film).

Freezing Structure

Three qualities underlie structuring *El Sebou'* as a visual ethnography—linearity, duality, and breaking linearity. Linearity is achieved through rites of passage. *El Sebou'* follows the form identified by van Gennep 1960 (1909) as universal for rites of passage in which participants pass from a marked state of separation to one of incorporation, with a transitional period of liminality in between. *El Sebou'* marks the end of the phase of liminality for the babies.

Duality arises in analysis of Egyptian ritual in general. A cursory examination of major Egyptian life cycle rituals shows the duality of 7 and 40. For example, the duration of mourning for a deceased person is 40 days, while celebrating the birth of a 12th-century holy man lasts 7 days (El Guindi 1995b). *Sebou'* is an Arabic word from the root *sab'a*, meaning 7. The ceremony occurs on the 7th day after birth. Seven recurs as a theme throughout the ceremony—7 grains sprinkled around the house, the mother crosses 7 times over the newborn—among others.

It was necessary to determine where in the ceremony the duality could be seen visually. I determined that 7 is best expressed when the newborn twins are carried out of the bedroom past the threshold dividing private from public sections of the home. This also marks the end of the phase of liminality when the babies are ceremonially incorporated into the cultural world of their parents. The mother remains secluded for 40 days after giving birth. So 40 is best represented by showing her standing on the side at the top of the stairs of the building, clearly not joining the procession of men, women, and children in the family.

Once I determined both qualities of the duality, I explored filmic techniques to represent it. I decided to use the freeze frame to mark the duality of the ritual structure. Seven and 40 corresponded to child and mother since the child comes out of the separation period on the 7th day while the mother comes out of the separation period on the 40th day after giving birth. A frame was stopped at each of the two points, marking the complementary opposition of child/mother and 7/40. By freezing the frame, one is freezing properties of the structure, as it were.

The third quality—breaking linearity—was the mode adopted for contextualizing the temporal ceremony by cutting to contextualizing sequences and events. Three kinds of events provided the visual material for this purpose: interviews with the ritual leaders (three women relatives), the making of ceremonial crafts, and the purchasing of foods and items needed for the ceremony in preparation for the ritual.

The film opens with a scene of a *Sebou'* shop in the bazaar and a woman, called Umm Sayyid, at the counter facing the salesman in a *Sebou'* shop. Another scene shows a man carrying decorated candles coming out of a candle-decorating shop into the winding alleys of Khan El-Khalili bazaar in Cairo. These sequences establish the context of ceremony in the film. This is ritually relevant context. Then the camera brings us into the intimacy of a family home, usually inaccessible to "outsiders." We see two babies, almost completely covered (with a part of their heads showing from under the blanket) sleeping in a large bed, in a bedroom, surrounded by family members, one of whom is blowing incense around the room by swinging a long-chained brass incensor, with smoke blowing from the burning incense. On each side of the bed is a clay pot, concealed by commercial decorations and battery operated lights. The clay pot is a key ritual object. The shape of the pots reflects gender difference (see Figure 3). Then, gender is further reinforced during the ceremony when the pots are "dressed up," the male-representing pot by the father and the female-representing pot by the mother.

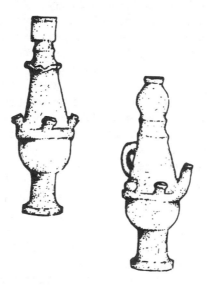

Figure 3. Gendered claypots: *ollah* (female) and *abri'* (male).

The objects used to "dress up" the clay pots are also consistent. The boy's pot is dressed with the father's prayer beads and the girl's pot is dressed with the mother's gold jewelry. This reinforces the identification of the child with two aspects of the cultural system that are most relevant to his or her identity—the family and gender. In essence, the clay pot becomes the symbol of creation—clay being associated with birth and creation in the cosmological imagery of Egypt's past. In ancient Egyptian mythology, the creator Khnum "creates" humankind by fashioning the child and "the other" out of clay. The shape of the pot is revealing and since the modern-day pots are covered with decorative elements hiding their original shape, a sequence of clay-pot crafting was used after the clay-pot dressing-up sequence. Linear time is broken by images of clay pot crafting filmed in the pottery village in Old Cairo where these pots are made.

But by the end of the eve of the *Sebou'* (before the segment on the main day itself) the film has already shown key ceremonial objects: clay pots, incense, seven grains, beans soaking in water, and candles and several key activities and rites: buying ceremony related objects and foods, lighting the candle in the clay pot, measures to protect the newborns from harm, "dressing up" the gendered pots, drinking the ceremonial drink *mughat*, and packing candy and peanuts in *Sebou'* special sacks. And on the actual day of the *Sebou'* in the film, sequences show candle making, general purchasing scenes, and segments of interviews. Folk songs spontaneously sung during the ceremonies are subtitled in verse-by-verse form (rather than phrase by phrase) to preserve the viewers' reading continuity.

Ritual Space Within Culture Space

Ritual space is structured by the processual linear universal form characterizing rites-of-passage and by the thematic duality characterizing Egyptian life-cycle ritual as a whole. That is, the two modes—the linear mode and the duality mode—together constitute the abstract parameters that demarcate *Sebou'* ritual space. Throughout the *Sebou'*, the ceremony takes place in the privacy of the home and the family. It would have been possible to limit the film by the boundary of ritual space and still have an interesting film. It would also have been possible to open the film in the more commonly used way, by situating the ceremony and the ceremony home geographically or using general scenery. However, according to the criteria established for visual ethnography discussed above, contextualizing images are ritually relevant images that establish culture identity by embedding the ceremony in the large culture space and by intermittently using indigenous voices. The indigenous voice mode is done by using interview segments from three key women in the family, the ritual leaders, interpreting events and customs. This contextualizing mode led to the layering technique described above in which several modes of presentation were used for complementary purposes.

By intermittently suspending ritual time and space by means of key ritual personnel and contextualising segments, we move out of the linear mode, breaking the ritual chronology as it were, to see ritual-relevant activities interpreted by indigenous voices: clay pot crafting, candle crafting, herbs, incense, spices, candy purchasing, etc. This technique links ceremonial events taking place within ritual time and space to the wider cultural space without losing the consistency or the momentum of the main event that is the focal subject of the visual ethnography. This linkage between ritual space and its wider cultural space is diagrammatically represented in Figure 4.

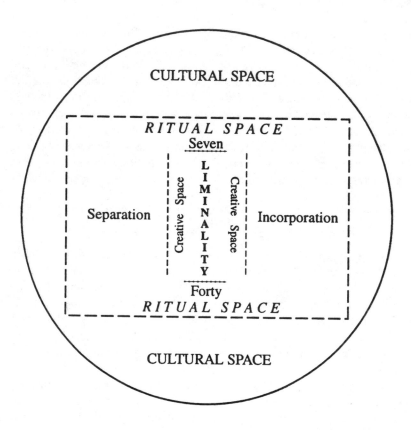

Figure 4. Diagram representing the film theory. It informs all phases of visual ethnography of *El Sebou'*. This shows the relation between universal ritual form, Egyptian ritual structure, ritual space, and culture space.

Conclusion

In this chapter I gave an overview of the methodological history of visual anthropology and discussed various uses of film in research and ethnography.

Critique grew around ethnographic film both within visual anthropology and from anthropology at large. For Heider (1976:8), "Ethnographic film is film which reflects ethnographic understanding . . . it is more than the simple sum of ethnography plus film." This observation is nontrivial in light of the course along which ethnographic film has developed—distanced from the anthropological process.

One reaction proposes to leave the label "ethnographic film" out of anthropology for films essentially not ethnographic, and to adopt an alternative term, such as "anthropological filmmaking" to reflect a film based on anthropological theory (Rollwagen 1988b:287). Another reaction is exemplified by Ruby. He calls for removing ethnographic film altogether from visual anthropology (which should focus on research film and photography in studies of communication), unless ethnograpic film "become(s) more scientific, describing culture from clearly defined anthropological perspectives" (cited in MacDougall 1978:421).

Anthropologists today accept using visual media—photographic, filmic, interactive, etc.—in the anthropological process. The challenge is how to use any visual medium, particularly film, while positioning it within the "disciplinary framework," as Rollwagen put it (1988b:288), that approaches ethnography as scientific description grounded in anthropological theory. Anthropologists haven't persuasively communicated the anthropological perspective to a public that has become more globally and visually communicative. Film can be a vital tool in this effort. It is in anthropology's interest to build that tool so that it is adequate to the task of reflecting, as well as producing, knowledge about the range of cultures and about culture itself.

The last section of this chapter proposes a theory of film that's grounded in systematic knowledge aimed at "preserving the integrity of persons, objects, and events in relation to their context and their culture" (Heider 1976:24). The process shifts to formulating a visual ethnography embedded in an empirically based, analytic framework. It builds on and feeds into systematic observation, in a research cycle that begins with data gathering and leads to visual ethnography construction that is anthropological in method, process, and product.

NOTES

1. An early version of my analysis of the methodological basis of film was presented in "The Making of *El Sebou*': Methodological Considerations for Ethnographic Film" on the panel Visual Research Strategies—Visual Anthropology in the '80s, at the 12th International Congress of Anthropological and Ethnological Sciences (IUAES), Zagreb, Yugoslavia, July 28, 1988. I presented a revised version at the Film as Ethnography conference at the 2d Royal Anthropological Institute Film Festival, Manchester, England, September 24–28, 1990, published in Rollwagen (1993; and see El Guindi 1993). This chapter is original and my analysis of film methodology describes my current position. Michael Hickey, a graduate

student of anthropology at the University of Southern California, provided research assistance, particularly in compiling bibliographic references.

2. Edison in the United States and Lumière in Europe invented more sophisticated machines for taking motion pictures. The first films made with those primitive motion picture cameras between 1895 and 1900 had much of the spirit of "ethnographic filmmaking." Lumière's first film showed French workers in the Peugeot auto factory outside Paris lining up to punch a time clock. Edison's first film showed his assistant sneezing. Other films depicted scenes of people walking in the street, bathing at the beach, eating, embarking on a train, and so on (see Worth 1980).

3. What remains is seven minutes long and shows three men's dances and an attempt at firemaking. See de Brigard (1975) for more details.

4. De Brigard (1975:28) describes Rouch as "a leader of the ethnographic film wave in Europe and an indefatigable producer and popularizer." Rouch decided to study anthropology during World War II, which he spent in French West Africa supervising the construction of roads and bridges. When Rouch wasn't selected to join the Ogooua-Congo Expedition of explorers-filmmakers, he "floated down the Niger with two friends, making films by trial and error with a 16-mm Bell and Howell from the flea market." When the tripod fell overboard, "necessity nudged Rouch toward an original shooting style" (Rouch 1955, cited in de Brigard 1975:28).

5. The Rouchian forum at the Musée de l'Homme in Paris, the Bilan du Film Ethnographique, engages anthropologists and the public in a way unlike anything I have seen in ethnographic film. The first conference on ethnographic film was held there 30 years ago.

6. The first International Seminar on Visual Anthropology in India was held in Jodhpur, December 1987. It was organized jointly by the Anthropological Survey of India and the Indian National Trust for Art and Culture. The issues addressed included cultural pluralism and visual anthropology, the ethics of ethnographic filmmaking, and the potential role of visual anthropology in the Indian context (see Singh 1992a).

7. Tension will persist as long as imbalance favors Euro American anthropological cinema. Euro American white dominance is reflected in the composition of juries, selection committees, and evaluative boards of ethnographic film conferences and festivals and in most writing about film and visual anthropology. The unrecognized sense of domination by visual anthropologists vis-à-vis the non-Western world is best exemplified, in my opinion, in international film conferences/festivals such as Eyes Across the Water II held in Amsterdam in 1992. There, films on Asia by Asians and on Africa by Africans were discussed, but there was no section on films about Europe by Europeans—as if this weren't a subject that could or should be scrunitized.

8. Asch subsequently adopted the idea of a collaborative filming team consisting of one ethnographer and one camera/sound person. He tried to establish this as a model in the film-training program of the Center for Visual Anthropology at the University of Southern California. The experiment failed to produce any working teams or significant films. In his later years, and in personal communication, Asch mentioned that he would not collaborate with senior anthropologists again; it was easier to work with junior anthropologists or graduating students doing ethnography.

9. In his last film, A *Celebration of Origins* (1992), Asch abandoned his signature sequence film genre. The film was edited in thematic film style, festival-qualifying mode. The awarding structure developed by film festivals may have influenced that change, since sequence or research films remain outside the festival award system.

10. This wasn't quite true, since film had by then become established in the laboratory.

11. Museums were well suited to produce films on anthropological subjects, since they could send cameramen on their expeditions and attract steady audiences to their programs. In 1923, F. W. Hodge, ethnologist, and Owen Cattell, cameraman, made an excellent series about the Zuni for the Heye Foundation-Museum of the American Indian. An overview film, *Land of the* Zuñi *and Community Work*, shows planting, threshing, water carrying, children at play, and gambling, by men, women, and children who appear to be going about their daily occupations (de Brigard 1975:20–21). Three films of ceremonials show dancing and the planting of sacred wands. The rest of the series covers hairdressing, house building, bread baking, and the tanning and wrapping of deerskin leggings.

12. Quality, in this kind of filming, still meant 35mm films and, if possible, a trained cameraman. But Norman Tindale, in Australia, and Franz Boas, in British Columbia, took their own 16-mm films (de Brigard 1975).

13. See El Guindi (1986b:7–43) for a full discussion on this notion and the methodology that produced it. See also the publication by Bernard (1989) using the same methodological concept

14. *El Sebou'* (El Guindi 1986c) is my first film. An analytic *Film Study Guide* (El Guindi 1996a) is companion material for teaching purposes.

15. This emerged during my research on the Islamic movement, which I began in 1976 (see El Guindi 1981, 1982, 1983, 1986a, 1987). I raised the question about "growing up" Muslim, because the movement began in the early 1970s overwhelmingly by youth and college students of both sexes. This query led to the study of birth and the *Sebou'*—a ceremony that occurs on the seventh day of life of both sexes.

16. I believe it was Marcus Banks at a film showing of *El Moulid* at Oxford University, which he and Howard Murphy kindly arranged, who first used this term in the context of the multiple modes of presentation used in my film.

17. Loizos (1993) uses contextualization to mean print ethnographic material as textual support to observational film. He mentions three attempts of contextualizing—some deliberately convergent, like the Marshall/Asch texts for the San (Bushmen) films, and the Asch/Connors/Asch material on Jero; others are parallel, such as Chagnon/Asch examples, and others fairly independent and divergent, such as Dunlop's Baruya films and Godelier's writings.

18. The highly structured preshooting session worked well in sorting out roles and jobs for different team members, enhancing coordination. In the field, I established my position as director of the project vis-à-vis the cameraman and crew. This was further reinforced by having everyone address me as "*doctora*." The title provided the Egyptian male team members with a familiar authority structure, which allowed them to transcend gender in the hierarchy, particularly in light of my then evident ignorance of the technical aspects of filming.

REFERENCES

Abdullah, Mohammad. 1984. *Tagarub Fi al-Cinema al-Tasgiliyya (Experiments in Documentary Cinema)* (Arabic). Cairo: Al-Hay'a Al-Misriyya Al-'Amma Lil Kitab.

al-Bindari, Mona. 1981. *Al-Cinema Al-Tasgiliyya Fi Misr Hatta Akhir Sanat 1980 (Documentary Cinema in Egypt Through 1980)* (Arabic). Cairo: Dar al-Sha'b Publishers.

Amin, Samir. 1989. *L'Eurocentrisme*. Russell Moore, trans. New York: Monthly Review Press.

Asch, T., and P. Asch. 1988. Collaboration in Ethnographic Filmmaking: A Personal View. In *Anthropological Filmmaking: Anthropological Perspectives on the Production of Film and Video for General Public Audiences*. J. R. Rollwagen, ed. Pp. 1–30. New York: Harwood.

Azoulay, L. 1900a. L'ere nouvelle des sons et des bruits. *Bulletins et Memoires de la Société d'Anthropologie de Paris 1*:172–178.

Azoulay, L. 1900b. Sur la constitution d'un musée photographique. *Bulletins et Memoires de la Société d'Anthropologie de Paris 1*:222–226.

Balikci, Asen. 1975. Reconstructing Cultures on Film. In *Principles of Visual Anthropology*. Paul Hockings, ed. Pp. 191–200. The Hague and Paris: Mouton.

Balikci, Asen. 1988. Anthropologists and Ethnographic Filmmaking. In *Anthropological Filmmaking*. J. R. Rollwagen, ed. Pp. 31–46. New York: Harwood.

Bateson, Gregory. 1963. Exchange of Information about Patterns of Human Behavior. In *Information Storage and Neural Control*. W. Abbott and W. Fields, ed. Pp. 173–186. Springfield, IL: Charles C. Thomas.

Bateson, Gregory, and Margaret Mead. 1942. *Balinese Character: A Photographic Analysis*. New York: New York Academy of Sciences.

Bellman, Beryl L., and Bennetta Jules-Rosette. 1977. *A Paradigm for Looking: Cross-Cultural Research with Visual Media*. Norwood, NJ: Ablex.

Bernard, H. Russell. 1989. *Native Ethnography: A Mexican Indian Describes His Culture*. Thousand Oaks, CA: Sage Publications.

Biella, Peter. 1993a. Beyond Ethnographic Film: Hypermedia and Scholarship. In *Anthropological Film and Video in the 1990s*. J. R. Rollwagen, ed. Pp. 131–176. Brockport, NY: The Institute, Inc.

Biella, Peter. 1993b. The Design of Ethnographic Hypermedia. In *Anthropological Film and Video in the 1990s*. J. R. Rollwagen, ed. Pp. 381–416. Brockport, NY: The Institute, Inc.

Biella, Peter. 1996. Interactive Media in Anthropology: Seed and Earth—Promise of Rain. *American Anthropologist 98*(3):595–616.

Biella, Peter, Gary Seaman, and Napoleon Chagnon. 1997. Yanomamo Interactive. CD-ROM Analysis of the Film *The Ax Fight*. (Packaged with Napoleon Chagnon, *The Yanomamo*, 5th ed.) Fort Worth: Harcourt Brace.

Birdwhistell, Raymond L. 1952. *Introduction to Kinesics*. Louisville: University of Louisville Press.

Birdwhistell, Raymond L. 1970. *Kinesics and Context*. Philadelphia: University of Pennsylvania Press.

Blackman, Margaret B. 1986. Visual Ethnohistory: Photographs in the Study of Culture History. In *Studies in Third World Societies Publication 35*. Dennis Weidman, Gerry Williams and Mario Zamora, eds. Pp. 137–166. Williamsburg: College of William and Mary.

Blackman, Margaret B. 1992. Of "Peculiar Carvings and Architectural Devices": Photographic Ethnohistory and the Haida Indians. In *Anthropology and Photography 1860–1920*. Elizabeth Edwards, ed. Pp. 137–142. New Haven and London: Yale University Press in association with The Royal Anthropological Institute.

Blakely, Thomas D., and Joan S. Williams. 1995. *Anthropological Excellence in Film: Ten Years of Award Winners in the SVA/AAA Film and Video Festival*. Society for Visual Anthropology Publications. Arlington: Society for Visual Anthropology, a section of the American Anthropological Association.

Caldarola, V. 1987. The Generation of Primary Photographic Data in Ethnographic Fieldwork and the Problem of Objectivity. In *Visual Explorations of the World*. M. Taureg and J. Ruby, eds. Pp. 217–227. Aachen, Germany: Edition Heredot.

Chalfen, Richard. 1975. Cinema Naiveté: A Study of Home Moviemaking as Visual Communication. *Studies in the Anthropology of Visual Communication* 2(2):87–103.

Chalfen, Richard. 1987. *Snapshot Versions of Life*. Bowling Green, OH: Bowling Green State University Popular Press.

Chalfen, Richard. 1992. Picturing Culture Through Indigenous Imagery: A Telling Story. In *Film as Ethnography*. Peter Ian Crawford and David Turton, eds. Pp. 222–241. Manchester and New York: Manchester University Press.

Chanock, Foster O., and E. Richard Sorenson. 1975. Research Films and the Communications Revolution. In *Principles of Visual Anthropology*. Paul Hockings, ed. Pp. 431–438. The Hague and Paris: Mouton.

Chaplin, E. 1994. *Sociology and Visual Representation*. London and New York: Routledge.

Collier, John, Jr. 1967. *Visual Anthropology: Photography as a Research Method*. New York: Holt, Rinehart and Winston.

Collier, John, Jr. 1975. Photography and Visual Anthropology. In *Principles of Visual Anthropology*. Paul Hockings, ed. Pp. 211–230. The Hague and Paris: Mouton.

Collier, John, Jr. 1988. Visual Anthropology and the Future of Ethnographic Film. In *Anthropological Filmmaking*. J. R. Rollwagen, ed. Pp. 73–96. New York: Harwood.

Collier, John, Jr., and Malcolm Collier. 1986. *Visual Anthropology: Photography as a Research Method*, rev. and exp. ed. Albuquerque: University of New Mexico Press.

Colombres, Adolfo. 1985a. *Ciné, antropologìa y colonialismo*. Buenos Aires: Ediciones del Sol: CLACSO.

Colombres, Adolfo. 1985b. Prologo. In *Ciné, antropología y colonialismo*. Adolfo Colombres, ed. Pp. 11–54. Buenos Aires: Ediciones del Sol: CLACSO.

Connor, L., P. Asch, and T. Asch. 1986. *Jero Tapakan: Balinese Healer: An Ethnographic Film Monograph*. Cambridge: Cambridge University Press.

Crawford, Peter Ian. 1992. Film as Discourse—The Invention of Anthropological Realities. In *Film as Ethnography*. P. I. Crawford and D. Turton, eds. Pp. 66–82. Manchester: Manchester University Press.

Crawford, Peter Ian, and Jan Ketil Simonsen. 1992. Introduction. In *Ethnographic Film Aesthetics and Narrative Traditions, Proceedings from NAFA II*. Pp. 1–13. Aarhus, Denmark: Intervention Press.

Crawford, Peter Ian, and David Turton, eds. 1992. *Film as Ethnography*. Manchester: Manchester University Press.

de Brigard, Emilie Rahman. 1971. History of Ethnographic Film. Unpublished Master's Thesis, Department of Theater Arts. Los Angeles: University of California.

de Brigard, Emilie. 1975. The History of Ethnographic Film. In *Principles of Visual Anthropology*. Paul Hockings, ed. Pp. 13–45. The Hague and Paris: Mouton.

Diawara, Manthia. 1989. Oral Literature and African Film: Narratology in Wend Kuuni. In *Questions of Third Cinema*. Jim Pines and Paul Willemen, eds. Pp. 199–121. London: British Film Institute.

Dunlop, Ian. 1983. Ethnographic Filmmaking in Australia: The First Seventy Years (1898–1968). *Studies in Visual Communication* 9(1):11–18.

Edwards, Elizabeth. 1992. Science Visualized: E. H. Man in the Andaman Islands. In *Anthropology and Photography 1860–1920*. Elizabeth Edwards, ed. Pp. 108–121. New Haven and London: Yale University Press in association with The Royal Anthropological Institute.

El Guindi, Fadwa. 1981. Veiling Infitah with Muslim Ethic: Egypt's Contemporary Islamic Movement. *Social Problems 28*(4):465–485.

El Guindi, Fadwa. 1982. The Emerging Islamic Order: The Case of Egypt's Contemporary Islamic Movement. *Journal of Arab Affairs 1*(2):245–262.

El Guindi, Fadwa. 1983. Veiled Activism: Egyptian Women in the Islamic Movement. *Peuples Mediterranéans* (Special issue: *Femmes de la Mediterranée) 22–23*:79–89.

El Guindi, Fadwa. 1986a. The Egyptian Woman: Trends Today, Alternatives Tomorrow. In *Women in the World: 1975–1985, The Women's Decade*. L. Iglitzin and R. Ross, eds. Pp. 225–242. Santa Barbara: Clio Press.

El Guindi, Fadwa. 1986b. *The Myth of Ritual: A Native's Ethnography of Zapotec Life-Crisis Rituals*. Tucson: The University of Arizona Press.

El Guindi, Fadwa. 1987. Das Islamische Kleid "al-Hidschab." In *Pracht und Geheimnis: Kleidung und Schmuck aus Palastina und Jordanie*. G. von Volger, K. v. Welck, and K. Hackstein, eds. Pp. 164–167. Cologne: Rautenstrauch-der Stadt Köln.

El Guindi, Fadwa. 1993. Charting Content, Freezing Structure: A Methodological Base for Visual Ethnography. In *Anthropological Film and Video in the 1990s*. J. R. Rollwagen, ed. Pp. 11–36. Brockport, NY: The Institute, Inc.

El Guindi, Fadwa. 1995a. Fikra. *Anthropology Newsletter* April, 29–30.

El Guindi, Fadwa. 1995b. Voice of Islam, Experience of Muslims—The Television Series, Review of Living Islam. *Anthropology Today 11*(1):24–26.

El Guindi, Fadwa. 1996a. *Film Study Guide: Egyptian Celebration of Life Series—El Sebou'*. Los Angeles: El Nil Research.

El Guindi, Fadwa. 1996b. Shades of Los Angeles: From Albums to Archives—The Middle Eastern Project. *The Washington Report on Middle East Affairs* CVI (1):61, 104.

El Guindi, Fadwa, and Joan Williams. 1995. The Society for Visual Anthropology Film/Video Festival: A Short History. *Program*. Pp. xv–xvi. American Anthropological Association, 94th Annual Meeting, Washington, DC, November 15–19.

Faris, James C. 1992. Anthropological Transparency: Film, Representation and Politics. In *Film as Ethnography*. Peter Ian Crawford and David Turton, eds. Pp. 171–182. Manchester: Manchester University Press.

Fischer, Michael M. J. 1997. Raising Questions about Rouch. *American Anthropologist 99*(1):140–143.

Gesell, Arnold. 1945. Cinemanalysis: A Method of Behavior Study. *Journal of General Psychology 47*:3.

Ginsburg, Faye. 1995. The Parallax Effect: The Impact of Aboriginal Media on Ethnographic Film. *Visual Anthropology Review 11*(2):64–76.

Goodwin, Charles. 1994. Professional Vision. *American Anthropologist 96*(3):606–633.

Griaule, Marcel. 1957. *Methode de l'ethnographie*. Oarus: Presses Universitaires de France.

Hall, Edward T. 1959. *The Silent Language*. Garden City: Doubleday.

Hall, Edward T. 1966. *The Hidden Dimension*. Garden City: Doubleday.

Heider, Karl G. 1976. *Ethnographic Film*. Austin: University of Texas Press.

Heider, Karl G. 1983. Fieldwork with a Cinema. *Studies in Visual Communication 6*(9):2–10.

Heider, Karl G. 1991. *Indonesian Cinema: National Culture on Screen*. Honolulu: University of Hawaii Press.

Heider, Karl G., and Carol Hermer. 1995. *Films for Anthropological Teaching*. Special Publication of the American Anthropological Association: Professional Series. Arlington: American Anthropological Association.

Hill, James N. 1977. Individual Variability in Ceramics and the Study of Prehistoric Social Organization. In *The Individual in Prehistory: Studies of Variability in Style in Prehistoric Technologies*. J. N. Hill and Joel Gunn, eds. Pp. 55–108. New York: Academic Press.

Hill, James N., and Joel Gunn, eds. 1977. *The Individual in Prehistory: Studies of Variability in Style in Prehistoric Technologies*. Studies in Archeology. New York: Academic Press.

Hockings, Paul, ed. 1975. *Principles of Visual Anthropology*. The Hague and Paris: Mouton.

Hockings, Paul, and Yasuhiro Omori. 1988. *Cinematographic Theory and New Dimensions in Ethnographic Film*. Osaka: National Museum of Ethnology.

Husmann, Rolf. 1983. Film and Fieldwork: Some Problems Reconsidered. In *Methodology in Anthropological Filmmaking: Papers of the IUAES Intercongress, Amsterdam, 1981*. Nico C. R. Bogaart and Henk W.E.R. Ketelaar, eds. Pp. 93–112. Göttingen, Germany: Edition Herodot.

Jacknis, Ira. 1984. Franz Boas and Photography. *Studies in Visual Communication 10*(1): 2–60.

Jacknis, Ira. 1988a. Margaret Mead and Gregory Bateson in Bali: Their Use of Photography and Film. *Cultural Anthropology 3*(2):160–177.

Jacknis, Ira. 1988b. The Picturesque and the Scientific: Franz Boas's Plan for Anthropological Filmmaking. *Visual Anthropology 1*(1):59–64.

Jacknis, Ira. 1990. James Mooney as an Ethnographic Photographer. *Visual Anthropology 3*(2–3).

Jacknis, Ira. 1992. George Hunt, Kwakiutl Photographer. In *Anthropology and Photography 1860–1920*. Elizabeth Edwards, ed. Pp. 143–151. New Haven and London: Yale University Press in association with The Royal Anthropological Institute.

Kendon, Adam, and Andrew Ferber. 1973. A Description of Some Human Greetings. In *Comparative Ecology and Behavior of Primates*. R. P. Crook and J. H. Michael, eds. Pp. 591–668. London: Academic Press.

Koloss, Hans-Joachim. 1983. The Ethnological Film as a Medium of Documentation and as a Method of Research. In *Methodology in Anthropological Filmmaking: Papers of the IUAES Intercongress, Amsterdam, 1981*. Nico C. R. Bogaart and Henk W.E.R. Ketelaar, eds. Pp. 87–92. Göttingen, Germany: Edition Herodot.

Krebs, Stephanie. 1975. The Film Elicitation Technique. In *Principles of Visual Anthropology*. Paul Hockings, ed. Pp. 283–302. The Hague and Paris: Mouton.

Laban, R. 1926. *Choreographie*. Jena, Germany: Eugen Diederichs.

Lajard, J., and Félix-Louis Regnault. 1895. Poterie crue et origine du tour. *Bulletin de la Société d'Anthropologie de Paris 6*:734–739.

Leroi-Gourhan, André. 1948. Cinema et sciences humaines—Le film ethnologique exist-t-il? *Revue de Geographie Humaine et d'Ethnologies 3*:42–51.

Lobban, Jr., Richard A. 1988. Review of *El Sebou': Egyptian Birth Ritual*, by Fadwa El Guindi. *American Anthropologist 90*(1):242–243.

Loizos, Peter. 1993. *Innovation in Ethnographic Film: From Innocence to Self-Consciousness, 1955–85*. Chicago: University of Chicago Press.

Lomax, Alan. 1968. *Folk Song Style and Culture: A Staff Report on Cantometrics*. Publication 88. Washington DC: American Association for the Advancement of Science.

Lomax, Alan. 1973. Cinema, Science, and Culture Renewal. *Current Anthropology 14*: 474–480.

Lomax, Alan. 1975. Audiovisual Tools for the Analysis of Culture Style. In *Principles of Visual Anthropology*. Paul Hockings, ed. Pp. 303–324. The Hague and Paris: Mouton.

Lomax, Alan, Irmgard Bartenieff, and Forrestine Paulay. 1969. Choreometrics: A Method for the Study of Cross-Cultural Pattern in Film. *Research Film/Le Film de Recherche/ Forschungsfilm* 6:505–517.

MacDougall, David. 1975. Beyond Observational Cinema. In *Principles of Visual Anthropology*. Paul Hockings, ed. Pp. 109–124. The Hague and Paris: Mouton.

MacDougall, David. 1978. Ethnographic Film: Failure and Promise. *Annual Review of Anthropology* 7:405–425.

Marks, Dan. 1995. Ethnography and Ethnographic Film: From Flaherty to Asch and After. *American Anthropologist* 97(2):339–347.

Marshall, John, and Emilie de Brigard. 1975. Idea and Event in Urban Film. In *Principles of Visual Anthropology*. Paul Hockings, ed. Pp. 133–145. The Hague and Paris: Mouton.

Martínez, Wilton. 1990. Critical Studies in Visual Anthropology: Aberrant Versus Anticipated Readings of Ethnographic Film. *Commission on Visual Anthropology Revue* (Spring): 34–47.

Martínez, Wilton. 1992. Who Constructs Anthropological Knowledge? Toward a Theory of Ethnographic Film Spectatorship. In *Film as Ethnography*. Peter Ian Crawford and David Turton, eds. Pp. 131–164. Manchester: Manchester University Press.

Mead, Margaret. 1956. Some Uses of Still Photography in Culture and Personality Studies. In *Personal Character and Cultural Milieu*. D. G. Haring, ed. Pp. 79–105. Syracuse: Syracuse University Press.

Mead, Margaret. 1959. *An Anthropologist at Work: Writings of Ruth Benedict*. Boston: Houghton Mifflin.

Mead, Margaret. 1962. *Retrospects and Prospects. Anthropology and Human Behavior*. Washington, DC: The Anthropological Society of Washington.

Mead, Margaret. 1963. Anthropology and the Camera. In *The Encyclopedia of Photography*, Vol. 7. Willard D. Morgan, ed. Pp. 166–184. New York: Greystone Press.

Mead, Margaret. 1972. *Blackberry Winter: My Earlier Years*. New York: Morrow.

Mead, Margaret. 1975. Visual Anthropology in a Discipline of Words. In *Principles of Visual Anthropology*. Paul Hockings, ed. Pp. 3–12. The Hague and Paris: Mouton.

Mead, Margaret. 1977. *Letters from the Field 1925–1975*. New York: Harper and Row.

Mead, Margaret, and F. C. MacGregor. 1951. *Growth and Culture: A Photographic Study of Balinese Childhood*. New York: Putnam.

Messenger, John C. 1966. *Man of Aran* Revisited: An Anthropological Critique. *University Review* (Dublin) 3(9):21.

Michaelis, Anthony R. 1955. *Research Film in Biology, Anthropology, Psychology and Medicine*. New York: Academic Press.

Morris, Rosalind C. 1994. *New Worlds From Fragments: Film, Ethnography, and the Representation of Northwest Coast Cultures. Studies in Ethnographic Imagination*. Boulder: Westview Press.

Muybridge, Eadweard. 1887. *Animal Locomotion: An Electro-Photographic Investigation of Consecutive Phases of Animal Movements* (16 vols.). Philadelphia: Lippincott.

Olien, M. D. 1968. Review of *Visual Anthropology: Photography as a Research Method*, J. Collier, Jr., ed. *American Anthropologist 70*(4):837.

Omori, Yasuhiro. 1988. Basic Problems in Developing Film Ethnography. In *Cinematographic Theory and New Dimensions in Ethnographic Film*. Paul Hockings and Yasuhiro Omori, eds. Pp. 191–201. Osaka: National Museum of Ethnology.

Peterson, Alexei Y. 1975. Some Methods of Ethnographic Filming. In *Principles of Visual Anthropology*. Paul Hockings, ed. Pp. 185–190. The Hague and Paris: Mouton.

Piault, Colette. 1988. European Visual Anthropology: Filming in a Greek Village. In *Anthropological Filmmaking: Anthropological Perspectives on the Production of Film and Video for General Public Audiences*. Jack Rollwagen, ed. Pp. 273–286. Chur, Switzerland: Harwood.

Prados, Miguel. 1951. The Use of Film in Psychotherapy. *American Journal of Orthopsychiatry 21*:36–46.

Prost, J. H. 1975. Comment on "The Film Elicitation Technique" by Stephanie Krebs. In *Principles of Visual Anthropology*. Paul Hockings, ed. P. 302. The Hague and Paris: Mouton.

Read, D., and C. Behrens. 1990. KAES: An Expert System for the Algebraic Analysis of Kinship Terminologies. *Journal of Quantitative Anthropology 2*:353–393.

Regnault, Félix-Louis. 1896a. Les attitudes du repos dans les races humaines. *Revue Encyclopédique 1896*:9–12.

Regnault, Félix-Louis. 1896b. La locomotion chez l'homme. *Cahiers de Recherche de l'Académie 122*:401.

Regnault, Félix-Louis. 1897. Le grimper. *Revue Encyclopédique 1897*:904–905.

Regnault, Félix-Louis. 1923. Films et musées d'ethnographie. 11. *Compte-Rendu de la Session de l'Association Française pour l'Avancement des Sciences 11*:680–681.

Regnault, Félix-Louis. 1931. Le role du cinéma en ethnographie. *La Nature 59*:304–306.

Rollwagen, Jack R., ed. 1988a. *Anthropological Filmmaking: Anthropological Perspectives on the Production of Film and Video for General Public Audiences*. New York: Harwood.

Rollwagen, Jack R. 1988b. The Role of Anthropological Theory in "Ethnographic Film-Making." In *Anthropological Filmmaking: Anthropological Perspectives on the Production of Film and Video for General Public Audiences*. Pp. 287–315. New York: Harwood.

Rollwagen, Jack R., ed. 1993. *Anthropological Film and Video in the 1990s. Case Studies in Documentary Filmmaking and Videomaking*, Vol. 1. Brockport, NY: The Institute, Inc.

Rouch, Jean 1955. Renaissance du film ethnographique. *Connaissance du Monde 1*:69–78.

Rouch, Jean. 1975. The Camera and Man. In *Principles of Visual Anthropology*. Paul Hockings, ed. Pp. 83–102. The Hague and Paris: Mouton.

Roy, Rakhi, and Jayasinhji Jhala. 1992. An Examination of the Need and Potential for Visual Anthropology in the Indian Social Context. In *Visual Anthropology and India: Proceedings of a Seminar*. K. S. Singh, ed. Pp. 16–30. Calcutta: Anthropological Survey of India.

Ruby, Jay. 1975. Is an Ethnographic Film a Filmic Ethnography? *Studies in Visual Communication* 6(2):104–111.

Ruby, Jay. 1981. Seeing Through Pictures: The Anthropology of Photography. *Camera-Lucida: The Journal of Photographic Criticism* (Spring):19–32.

Ruby, Jay. 1983. An Early Attempt at Studying Human Behavior with a Camera: Franz Boas and the Kwakiutl—1930. In *Methodology in Anthropological Filmmaking: Papers of the IUAES Intercongress, Amsterdam, 1981*. Nico C. R. Bogaart and Henk W.E.R. Ketelaar, eds. Pp. 25–38. Göttingen, Germany: Editions Herodot.

Ruby, Jay, ed. 1993. *The Cinema of John Marshall*. Philadelphia: Harwood.

Sahay, K. N. 1983. Ethnographic Films in India: Prospect, Priorities and Proposals. In *Methodology in Anthropological Filmmaking: Papers of the IUAES Intercongress, Amsterdam, 1981*. Nico C. R. Bogaart and Henk W.E.R. Ketelaar, eds. Pp. 49–60. Göttingen, Germany: Edition Herodot.

Said, Edward W. 1978. *Orientalism*. New York: Pantheon Books.

Samarin, William J. 1967. *Field Linguistics*. New York: Holt, Rinehart and Winston.

Scherer, Joanna C. 1992. The Photographic Document: Photographs as Primary Data in Anthropological Enquiry. In *Anthropology and Photography 1860–1920*. Elizabeth Edwards, ed. Pp. 32–41. New Haven and London: Yale University Press in association with The Royal Anthropological Institute.

Seaman, Gary, and Homer Williams. 1992. Hypermedia in Ethnography. In *Film as Ethnography*. P. I. Crawford and D. Turton, eds. Pp. 300–311. Manchester: Manchester University Press.

Seaman, Gary, and Homer Williams. 1993. Processing Visual Data in Ethnography: Fieldwork, Filework, and Fieldinfo. In *Eyes Across the Water*. Robert M. Boonzaher and Douglas Harper Blaes, eds. Pp. 143–158. Amsterdam: Het Spinhuis Publishers.

Singh, K. S. 1992a. Cultural Policy, Cultural Pluralism and Visual Anthropology: An Indian Perspective. In *Visual Anthropology and India: Proceedings of a Seminar*. K. S. Singh, ed. Pp. 7–15. Calcutta: Anthropological Survey of India.

Singh, K. S., ed. 1992b. *Visual Anthropology and India: Proceedings of a Seminar*. K. S. Singh, ed. Calcutta: Anthropological Survey of India.

Sorenson, E. Richard. 1967. A Research Film Program in the Study of Changing Man: Research Filmed Material as a Foundation for Continued Study of Non-Recurring Human Events. *Current Anthropology* 8:443–469.

Sorenson, E. Richard. 1975. Visual Records, Human Knowledge, and the Future. In *Principles of Visual Anthropology*. Paul Hockings, ed. Pp. 463–476. The Hague and Paris: Mouton.

Sorenson, E. Richard. 1976. *The Edge of the Forest*. Washington, DC: Smithsonian Institution Press.

Sorenson, E. Richard, and Allison Jablonko. 1975. Research Filming of Naturally Occurring Phenomena: Basic Strategies. In *Principles of Visual Anthropology*. Paul Hockings, ed. Pp. 151–166. The Hague and Paris: Mouton.

Stocking, George. 1974. *The Shaping of American Anthropology, 1883–1911—A Franz Boas Reader*. New York: Basic Books.

Stoller, Paul. 1992. *The Cinematic Griot: The Ethnography of Jean Rouch*. Chicago and London: The University of Chicago Press.

Struever, Stuart. 1975. The Role of Film in Archeology. In *Principles of Visual Anthropology*. Paul Hockings, ed. Pp. 201–207. The Hague and Paris: Mouton.

Sturtevant, William C. 1964. Studies in Ethnoscience. *American Anthropologist 66*:99–131.

Taylor, Lucien. 1994. Foreword. In *Visualizing Theory: Selected Essays from V.A.R. 1990–1994*. Lucien Taylor, ed. Pp. xi–xviii. New York and London: Routledge.

Templin, Patricia. 1982. Still Photography in Evaluation. In *Communication Strategies in Evaluation*. Nick Smith, ed. Pp. 121–175. Beverly Hills, CA: Sage Publications.

Tuareg, Martin. 1983. The Development of Standards for Scientific Films in German Ethnography. In *Methodology in Anthropological Filmmaking: Papers of the IUAES-Intercongress, Amsterdam 1981*. Nico C. R. Bogaart and Henk W.E.R. Ketelaar, eds. Pp. 61–86. Göttingen, Germany: Edition Herodot.

Turner, Terence. 1991. The Social Dynamics of Video Media in an Indigenous Society. *Visual Anthropology Review 7*(2):68–76.

Turner, Terence. 1995. Representation, Collaboration, and Mediation in Contemporary Ethnographic and Indigenous Media. *Visual Anthropology Review 11*(2):102–106.

Ushijima, Iwao. 1988. The Situation of Visual Anthropology in Japanese Universities. In *Cinematographic Theory and New Dimensions in Ethnographic Film*. Paul Hockings and Yasuhiro Omori, eds. Pp. 135–150. Osaka: National Museum of Ethnology.

Ushiyama, Junichi. 1975. Anthropological Programming in Japanese Television. In *Principles of Visual Anthropology*. Paul Hockings, ed. Pp. 445–447. The Hague and Paris: Mouton.

van Gennep, Arnold. 1960 (French 1909). *Rites of Passage*. Chicago: University of Chicago Press.

Vogt, Evon Z., ed. 1974. *Aerial Photography in Anthropological Research*. Cambridge: Harvard University Press.

Williams, Joan S., Allison Jablonko, Thomas D. Blakely, Fadwa El Guindi, and P.A.R. Blakely. 1995. SVA/AAA Film and Video Festival: A Short History Revisited. In *Anthropological Excellence in Film: Ten Years of Award Winners in the SVA/AAA Film and Video Festival*. Thomas D. Blakely and Joan S. Williams, eds. Pp. vii–viii. Arlington: Society for Visual Anthropology, a section of the American Anthropological Association.

Wintle, Pamela, and John P. Homiak. 1995. *Guide to the Collections of the Human Studies Film Archives*. Washington, DC: National Museum of Natural History, Smithsonian Institution.

Wolf, Götthard. 1961. Der Systematischen Filmischen Bewegungsdokumentation. In *Der Film in Dienste der Wissenschaft: Festschrift zur Einweihung des Neubaues für das IWF.* Götthard Wolf, ed. Pp. 16–20. Göttingen, Germany: IWF.

Wolf, Götthard. 1967. *Der Wissenschaftliche Dokumentationsfilm und die Encyclopaedia Cinematographica.* Munich: J. A. Barth.

Worth, Sol. 1969. The Development of a Semiotic Film. *Semiotica 1*:282–221.

Worth, Sol. 1972. A Semiotic of Ethnographic Film. *Program in Ethnographic Film (PIEF) Newsletter 3*:8–12.

Worth, Sol. 1980. Margaret Mead and the Shift from "Visual Anthropology" to the "Anthropology of Visual Communication." *Studies in Visual Communication 6*(1):15–22.

Worth, Sol. 1981a. Pictures Can't Say Ain't. In *Studying Visual Communication.* Larry Gross, ed. Pp. 162–184. Philadelphia: University of Pennsylvania Press.

Worth, Sol. 1981b. *Studying Visual Communication.* L. Gross and S. Worth, eds. Conduct and Communication Series, Virtual Edition GAVA, Temple University. Philadelphia: University of Pennsylvania Press.

Worth, S, and J. Adair. 1972. *Through Navajo Eyes: An Exploration in Film Communication and Anthropology.* Bloomington: Indiana University Press.

FILMS

Asch, T. 1992. *A Celebration of Origins.* DER. 45'; color.

Asch, T, and N. A. Chagnon. 1971. *The Ax Fight.* DER. 30'; color.

Asch, T., and N. A. Chagnon. 1974. *A Father Washes His Children.* DER. 13'; color.

Asch, T., P. Asch, and L. Connor. 1980. *A Balinese Trance Seance.* DER. 30'; color.

Asch, T., P. Asch, and L. Connor. 1981. *Jero on Jero: A Balinese Trance Seance.* DER. 17'; color.

Balikci, A., and G. Mary-Rousseliere. 1967–68. *The Netsilik Eskimo Series.* Canada. 9 films, 21 ½ hr segments; color.

Birdwhistell, Raymond L. 1964. *Kinesics.* PSU. 73'; b&w.

Boas, Franz. 1973 (filmed 1930). *The Kwakiutl of British Columbia.* (Edited by Bill Holm.) University of Washington Burke Museum; b&w.

Chagnon, Napoleon. 1970. *Magical Death.* DER. 29'; color.

Diawara, Manthia. 1995. *Rouch in Reverse.* Parminder Vir. California Newsreel. 51'; color.

Dunlop, Ian, and Robert Tonkinson. 1969. *Desert People.* CMH. 51'; b&w.

El Guindi, Fadwa. 1986c. *El Sebou': Egyptian Birth Ritual.* El Nil Research. 27'; 16-mm; color.

El Guindi, Fadwa. 1990. *El Moulid: Egyptian Religious Festival.* El Nil Research. 38'; 16-mm; color.

El Guindi, Fadwa. 1995c. *Ghurbal*. El Nil Research. 30'; 16-mm; color.

Flaherty, Robert. 1922. *Nanook of the North*. CMH. 55'; b&w (original silent version available from MOMA).

Flaherty, Robert. 1926. *Moana, A Romance of the Golden Age*. MOMA. 85'; b&w; silent.

Flaherty, Robert. 1934. *Man of Aran*. CMH. 77'; b&w.

Griaule, Marcel. 1935. *Au pays des Dogons*. Comité du Film Ethnographique (Paris). 15'; 16 mm; b&w.

Griaule, Marcel. 1938. *Sous le masque noir*. NSFL. 50'; color.

Lomax, Alan. 1978. *Choreometrics Project (Step Style; Palm Play)*. Columbia University. 29' each; 16mm; color.

Lumière, Louis. 1895. *La sortie des usines (Leaving the Factories)*. Not available. 20'; b&w.

Marshall, John. 1957. *The Hunters*. DER. 74'; color.

Marshall, John. 1962. *A Joking Relationship*. DER. 13'; b&w.

Marshall, John. 1966. *N/Um Tchai: The Ceremonial Dance of the !Kung Bushmen*. DER. 25'; color.

Marshall, John. 1969a. *A Curing Ceremony*. DER. 8'; b&w.

Marshall, John. 1969b. *An Argument about a Marriage*. DER. 18'; color.

Marshall, John. 1971. *Bitter Melons*. DER. 30'; color.

Marshall, John. 1974. *The Meat Fight*. DER. 14'; color.

Mead, Margaret, and Gregory Bateson. 1930s–1950s. *Character Formation in Different Cultures Series*. NYU., a series of six films; b&w.

Mead, Margaret, and Gregory Bateson. 1952 (approx.). *First Days in the Life of a New Guinea Baby*. NYU. 19'; b&w.

Mead, Margaret, and Gregory Bateson. 1952. *Childhood Rivalry in Bali and New Guinea*. NYU. 17'; b&w.

Mead, Margaret, and Gregory Bateson. 1954 (filmed 1930s). *Bathing Babies Three Cultures*. PSU. 9'; b&w.

Mead, Margaret, and Gregory Bateson. 1991 (ca. 1952). *Trance and Dance in Bali*. NYU. 22'; b&w.

Rouch, Jean. 1954. *Les maîtres fous*. Films de la Pleiade. 35'; color.

Rouch, Jean. 1957. *Moi, un noir*. Films de la Pleiade. 80'; color.

Rouch, Jean, and Edgar Morin. 1961. *Chronique d'un été*. Argos Films, Paris. 90'; b&w.

The Navajo People. 1966. *Navajos Film Themselves Series*. NYU. 7 films. 55'; b&w.

Wolf, Götthard. 1972. *Encyclopaedia Cinematographica 1972*. Institut für den Wissenschaftlichen Film; information not available as to color or b&w.

WEBSITES

Banks, Marcus. 1996. Haddon: The Online Catalogue of Archival Ethnographic Film Footage 1895–1945. University of Oxford.
http://www.rsl.ox.ac.uk/isca/haddon/HADD_home.html

Gross, L., and Tobia Worth. 1997. Sol Worth's Homepage. Temple University.
http://www.temple.edu/anthro/worth/worth.html

CAROLINE B. BRETTELL

Fourteen

Fieldwork in the Archives
Methods and Sources in
Historical Anthropology

Introduction

In 1899 Frederick Maitland penned his frequently quoted declaration "By and by anthropology will have to make the choice between being history and being nothing" ([1975]:295). Although disagreed with, Maitland's categorical statement offered an alternative approach to nineteenth-century evolutionists who had formulated a generalized history of broad and supposedly cross-culturally uniform stages of structural change. Maitland began a debate among anthropologists that continues to the present, and it assumes new form with each paradigm shift within the discipline. Early twentieth-century Boasian historical particularism, which emphasized that societies are created by their own historical circumstances, was, in some sense, a direct response to the gauntlet tossed out by Maitland.

By contrast, the functionalist paradigm that predominated in the 1940s and 1950s was ahistorical. Radcliffe-Brown, for example, argued that in the societies "without written history" that are generally the subject of anthropological investigation, historical study could be nothing more than conjectural and hence suspect.[1] The implications of the functionalist position are clear. As Burke (1992:13) stated it, "It is hard to say whether it was the spread of fieldwork which led to the rise of functionalism or vice versa. Slipping into the idiom of the functionalists themselves, one might say that the new explanation and the new method of research 'fitted' each other. Unfortunately, they reinforced the tendency of social theorists to lose interest in the past." The result was a kind of essentialism that often set the "people without history" into a fixed and static framework of analysis.

It was to the ahistoricism of structural-functionalism that E. E. Evans-Pritchard addressed himself in a commentary on anthropology and history that is by now perhaps as well known as Maitland's dictum. Anthropology, Evans-Pritchard argued, is "a special kind of historiography" and only as such could it be "empirical, and, in the true sense of the word, scientific" (1962:26). He questioned the isolation of the small-scale societies that anthropologists were used to studying: "If still fairly simple in structure [these communities are] enclosed in, and form part of, great historical societies. . . . [Anthropologists] can no longer ignore history . . . but must explicitly reject it or admit its relevance" (p. 21).

Although some British social anthropologists were producing historically framed ethnographies (Schapera 1962; Lewis 1968), it took time for the discipline as a whole to liberate itself from the functionalist paradigm. Even those anthropologists who began working in parts of the world with rich written records of the past tended to treat the records superficially, or not at all. William Douglass (1984:xiii) describes the trepidation with which he approached the municipal archives of Echalar, in the province of Navarra in Spain. "The wall of the council chambers was lined with a chaotic mass of parchment and paper, some dating back to the fifteenth and sixteenth centuries. I made the rather arbitrary decision to use the earliest available (mid-nineteenth century) household census as a base line so that I could ignore all earlier documentation." When historical materials were considered by anthropologists, they were primarily "background to the ethnographic present rather than . . . an integral part of anthropological analysis" (Silverman 1979:413).[2]

The exceptions, of course, were anthropologists who called themselves ethnohistorians and who worked primarily on the past of Native American populations. To many, ethnohistory involves reconstruction of the past of a region and a people who have no written history. To others, it involves a history from the insider's point of view (Gewertz and Schieffelin 1985).[3] More recently, some have defined ethnohistory as the study of historical consciousness (Dening 1991). Still others emphasize the application of anthropological theory and method to history, thereby bringing ethnohistory closer to historical anthropology.

No doubt the prolific work of ethnohistorians provided the foundation for the shift toward diachronic and processual modes of analysis described by Ortner (1984) in "Theory in Anthropology Since the 1960s." Among the major works of anthropology that substantiate this shift are *Europe and the People Without History* (Wolf 1982), *Islands of History* (Sahlins 1985), *Sweetness and Power* (Mintz 1985), *Sepik River Societies: A Historical Ethnography of the Chambri and their Neighbors* (Gewertz 1983), *High Religion: A Cultural and Political History of Sherpa Buddhism* (Ortner 1989), *Culture and Political Economy in Western Sicily* (Schneider and Schneider 1976), *Emigration in a South Italian Town: An Anthropological History* (Douglass 1984), and *Body of Power, Spirit of Resistance: The Culture and History of a South African People* (Comaroff 1985). Fifty years ago we could not claim what we can claim now—that history has found a new, serious, and most likely permanent place in the ethnographic perspective and therefore in anthropological method.

What has motivated this rapprochement with history in the form of historical anthropology?[4] For Ohnuki-Tierney (1990a:1), there are two reasons: (1) the realization that "there has never been a culture without history"; and (2) an increasing number of anthropologists are engaged in the study of so-called more complex societies with long historical traditions. Chance (1996:392) focuses on avoiding the attribution of "greater antiquity to certain practices and beliefs than they in fact possess," a perspective that locates change rather than continuity at the center of our analyses. To these, we should add recent challenges to the boundedness of the concept of culture, challenges that ask us to explore and understand how the lives of individuals, families, and communities are historically produced and altered not only by local, but also by global forces.

Some suggest that history offers anthropologists the opportunity to extend the comparative method by increasing—in time rather than in space—the number of cases that we study.[5] Silverman (1986:125) notes that the anthropologist working alongside the historian in a dusty provincial Italian archive may be studying the same documents but the goals and problems that he or she is addressing are shared with "the ethnographer of New Guinea, the archeologist of the pre-Conquest Maya, the primatologist observing the social behavior of our chimpanzee relatives, and the urban anthropologist studying Korean greengrocers in contemporary Manhattan." Historical anthropologists tend to address big problems in local places and to frame their questions in terms of cross-cultural comparison. Thus, Jane and Peter Schneider (1996:3) open their study of fertility decline and the ideology of class in Sicily with the following statement: "The drama, and the trauma, of world population history since the mid-eighteenth century, and the ways people interpret it, are the broadest concerns of this study. The expansion and contraction of the population of one Sicilian community between, roughly, 1860 and 1980, are its narrowest concerns."

Although much has been written about the rapprochement between anthropology and history (Cohn 1962, 1980, 1981; Davis 1981; Adams 1982; Sahlins 1983; Kertzer et al. 1986; Medick 1987; Biersack 1989, 1991; Roseberry 1989; Kellogg 1991; Comaroff and Comaroff 1992; Silverman and Gulliver 1992; Dirks 1996), methods in historical anthropology are rarely discussed.[6] The implicit assumption, of course, is that historical anthropology is a reconstruction of the past of a society through the use of documents. But what are these documents? How are they to be assessed and used? And are those who call themselves historical anthropologists doing something different from historians or, for that matter, from those who continue to call themselves ethnohistorians? How does one *do* fieldwork in the archives?

Certainly, the historical field methods used will be shaped by the particular questions asked.[7] Renato Rosaldo (1980) relied primarily on oral history to explore the cultural construction of warfare among the Ilongot headhunters of Northern Luzon in the Philippines. Brettell (1986) and Netting (1981) used nominal record linkage to examine changes in demographic patterns and relations of kinship over two or three centuries in a Portuguese village and a Swiss mountain community respectively. Kertzer (1984) used similar methods to focus on household and family structure in central Italy in a 30-year period of time set completely in the past. Sahlins (1981, 1985) has juxtaposed an analysis of myth with an analysis of historical documents to explore differences in the emic and etic interpretations of Captain Cook's death at the hands of Hawaiians in 1779.[8] Bernard Cohn (1987, 1996), during a lifetime of fieldwork in the archives, has approached a range of documentary sources (legal codes, statistical enumerations, official surveys and other published reports, travel accounts, gazetteers, administrative histories, and museum exhibition catalogues) as texts that can be deconstructed to reveal the nature of colonial society in India. Finally, Marla Powers (1986) has used a biographical method and life histories to document change over time in the lives of Oglala Sioux women.

In the remainder of this chapter, I will develop my discussion of these varying historical methods further. I begin with documentary sources and how anthropologists have used them to study family history, demographic history, and political-economic history. I focus, in particular, on the application of quantitative and qualitative methods and on the differences between micro- and macrohistorical approaches. Next, I discuss life history and oral history. I then address briefly other sources and methods that can be used in historical anthropology, specifically material culture and visual images. I end by considering the relationship between ethnographic fieldwork and archival research—that is, the efforts to link the past to the present. Two things will be evident in this discussion: (1) sources, methods, modes of analysis, and theory are ultimately inseparable; and (2) research strategies and methods of historical anthropologists are best studied by examining the products of their work. What Charles Tilly (1981) and Theda Skocpol (1984:361) have claimed for historical sociology is equally true for historical anthropology: There are no mechanical recipes for proper methods.

Documentary Evidence: Evaluating Sources

In the early days of ethnohistorical research, anthropologists such as Bruce Trigger were extremely critical of the lack of rigor in the use of documentary evidence. "Statements are considered without reference to their immediate context, and no effort is made to assess the biases or abilities of the recorder. The result is a mixture of arrogance and naiveté in the use of material which frequently repels the professional historian" (1976:12).[9]

How, then, does one begin to acquire the skills necessary to evaluate critically documentary sources? An old but still useful introduction to the documentary record can be found in Pitt's concise *Using Historical Sources in Anthropology and Sociology* (1972). He covers the diverse range of archives—public and official, religious, institutional, business and company sources, private papers, and data banks—as well as methods of critical analysis. When anthropologists venture into archives, they must learn about and apply the same evaluative criteria used by historians to determine the reliability of documentary evidence.[10] Such criteria include an assessment of the social position, intelligence, and linguistic abilities of the observer; of the attitudes that may have influenced the observations; of what is included and what is omitted; of intended audience and the motivation for creating the document; and of narrative style.

However, historical anthropologists bring additional questions to their use of documents. These questions are often based on their knowledge of contemporary ethnography, of ethnocentrism, of power politics in the context of colonial encounter, and of the difficulty for any outsider of understanding another culture. Most historical anthropologists have conducted fieldwork among the people whose history they are writing and can draw on the perspective gained from this ethnographic knowledge to assess the kind of cultural understanding that the observer who left the written record possessed. Sturtevant (1968:458) offers a good example. A historian, writing in 1944 about the 1837 escape of the Seminole leader Coacoochee (Wildcat) from Fort Augustine through a small cell window, doubted the report that Wildcat used "medicinal roots" to reduce his weight to squeeze through the opening. Sturtevant suggests that knowledge of the magical practices and beliefs of the modern Seminole allowed the anthropologist "to accept this detail as a reliable report." The issue here is not about medicinal roots having the effect described, but about a particular emic explanation that is valid to the Seminole and therefore a distinct kind of historical fact subject to a different set of scholarly judgments.

Ethnographic knowledge can also be brought to bear on the evaluation of enumerative sources. Shoemaker (1992) addresses the methodological problems that face family historians who use census data to analyze Native American household structure. Specifically, she identifies the attempts to fit Native Americans into a Euro American mold and to use enumerative data to test the success of particular government policies of resettlement and reorganization. Translation problems are significant, particularly as applied to relationship terms. Census data for the Cherokee, she argues, are probably of higher quality than that for the Navajo because of their greater command of English and hence familiarity with Euro American culture.

A broad understanding of cultural models can also be brought to bear on the evaluation of sources. Thus, a missionary description of a high chief of the Calusa

Indians of South Florida marrying his full sister is reasonable, given the exceptions to incest taboos in other stratified societies around the world (Sturtevant 1968:458). Similarly, the richer ethnohistoric information about one Native American group, the Iroquois for example, can, with caution, be used to help piece together the scantier data on another group such as the Huron (Trigger 1976).

Finally, a sophisticated understanding of the impact of culture contact, conquest, and colonialism as historical processes can deter misinterpretation. Obeyesekere (1992:9) illustrates this by contrasting the treatment of a British civil servant named Woolf in Kandy, Sri Lanka, in 1907 (well after the British took over the role of local chiefs) with that of Robert Andrews, British ambassador to the court of the independent Kandyan Kingdom in 1796. In the first case, the Sri Lankans prostrated themselves before Woolf; in the second, Andrews was required to kneel and those in his entourage had to prostrate themselves before the sovereign. The difference reflects a change in historical conditions and power relationships that affected both ceremonial life and the treatment of outsiders.

Obeyesekere moves from this issue to an analysis of what he argues is an uncritical reading of texts related to the death of Captain James Cook in Hawaii in 1779 and, by extension, a misrepresentation of native thought. He cites several specific examples from Marshall Sahlins's book *Historical Metaphors*. Sahlins (1995) offers a convincing and rigorous rejoinder. In several appendices to his book *How Natives Think*, he addresses quite specifically the particular sources that he has been accused of overlooking or misreading. He thereby raises intriguing methodological issues about the use of historical evidence that make the book, in one reviewer's opinion, "an excellent choice for any advanced course in historical anthropological method" (Friedman 1997:262; see also Borofsky 1997). Despite their differences, there are two points about which Sahlins and Obeyesekere would, I think, agree in general if not in the specifics. (1) Historical documents should be read with a sensitivity to the social, political, and cultural context within which they were produced. (2) We must work not only to identify the ethnocentrism of the writer of a document but our own ethnocentrism as evaluators of that document.

Methods in Family History and Historical Demography

A range of quantitative methods of data collection and analysis has been developed in the fields of family history and historical demography. Many of these have been used successfully by anthropologists, particularly those working in Europe, and by those conducting research in some of the more traditional regions of anthropological fieldwork such as Africa (Howell 1979; Cordell et al. 1996) and East Asia (Skinner 1957; Wolf and Huang 1980; Hanley and Wolf 1985; Davis and Harrell 1993; Harrell 1995). Among the general works that review the application of quantitative methods to historical data are Haskins and Jeffrey (1990) and Jarausch and Hardy (1991). Equally useful is the bibliography prepared by Grossbart (1992). However, the best general discussion of sources and methods in historical demography is that of Willigan and Lynch (1982), who not only review the types of sources—parish and civil registration records, enumerations and censuses, genealogies and population registers, organizational and institutional records—but also engage in a detailed discussion of specific methods of population reconstruction and analysis, including nominal record linkage and family reconstitution, computer simulation, regression, time series, and log-linear modeling, and factor analysis.[11]

Nominal record linkage involves finding the same individual in a variety of documents that come from a range of sources. Family reconstitution is then a procedure whereby these individuals are grouped into family units. Although problems of incomplete sources, accurate identification, changes of name, and a mobile and fluid population are inherent to these methods, together they have provided one of the most productive avenues to reconstruct the daily lives of the "ordinary" people of the past.[12]

Winchester (1992) offers an excellent survey of 20 years of the development and applications of these methods, including their adaptation to the world of micro-computers. Among the examples of anthropological work using record linkage and/or family reconstitution are Kertzer (1984) and Kertzer and Hogan's (1989) research on the population of Casellechio in central Italy in the late nineteenth century; Brettell's (1986) study of migration, marriage, fertility, and illegitimacy in northern Portugal between 1700 and the present; Birdwell-Pheasant's (1993) reconsideration of the nineteenth- and early twentieth-century Irish stem family; Schneider and Schneider's (1996) study of fertility decline in Sicily between 1860 and 1980; Wolf and Huang's (1980) study of marriage and adoption in Taiwan between 1845 and 1945; and Netting's (1981) study of ecological change and continuity in a Swiss mountain community from 1700 to 1980.

In Netting's case, the method worked particularly well because he was dealing with a closed-corporate community with relatively little mobility for much of its history. Well over 90% of resident families could be fully or partially reconstituted and supplementary data available in published genealogies, census manuscripts, and tax listings made rigorous cross-checking possible. Kertzer's focus was less on demographic rates than on household composition and patterns of coresidence. Drawing on Italian population registers, a range of other historical sources, and the household typology developed by Eugene Hammel (Hammel and Laslett 1974), Kertzer and his colleague Dennis Hogan were able to reconstruct family life in complex sharecropping households in central Italy in the latter nineteenth and early twentieth centuries.[13]

What is most innovative about the work of Kertzer and Hogan is the application of the life course method. This method, also adopted by historian Tamara Hareven (1982), in her study of industrial workers in New England, and by historian George

Alter (1988) in his study of women in Verviers, Belgium, in the mid-nineteenth century, makes individuals the center of analysis and focuses on how their lives are affected by changing historical circumstances. The method offers an alternative model to the more normative and fixed family or developmental cycle model. It is thoroughly delineated in many of the writings of the sociologist Glen Elder (1975, 1977, 1987; see also Hareven 1978; Kertzer and Schiaffino 1983).

Somewhat different is the method of cohort analysis used by Rosaldo (1980) in his historical study of the Ilongot. Rosaldo suggests that "cohort analysis directs inquiry toward the various developmental processes, through which groups reproduce themselves, perpetuating, modifying or abruptly changing their social structure" (p. 112). Like the life course method, cohort analysis is drawn from sociology (Ryder 1965) but has been used in historical research aimed at a longitudinal analysis of the collective destinies of groups of individuals (Mason et al. 1973; Willigan and Lynch 1982).[14]

Within anthropology, the genealogical method is a well-accepted technique for historical reconstruction and has a long tradition among British social anthropologists working in Africa (Bohannan 1952; Lewis 1962). One of the most complete discussions of the methods of genealogical analysis for demographic history is Bennett Dyke and Warren Morrill's edited volume *Genealogical Demography* (1980). In their introduction, the editors evaluate the ethnographic and documentary approaches to genealogy to show how much can be missed in an "informants" list when it is checked against a "records" list. Of equal value is Willigan and Lynch's (1982) coverage of types of genealogies, of the problems with genealogical sources, and of some of the methods used to extract marriage and fertility rates from genealogical data.

A good example of the application of this method can be found in Freeman's (1979) study of the Pasiegos of northern Spain. Through informant interviews, Freeman constructed Pasiego genealogies and then linked this information to census manuscript data. In an unpublished paper explicating the method, Freeman (1981) notes that a range of other data is transmitted in the process of collecting a genealogy—the politics of marriage, issues of property transmission, the dynamics of household formation, migration, interpersonal and intracommunal relations, and snippets of gossip and scandal. She argues that these genealogies can then serve as a backdrop for the interpretation of written sources such as church and civil archives, tax records, and land cadastres (1981:6). In particular, they may help to reveal certain recording conventions that obscure specific behavioral practices such as fosterage. Written records themselves can be used to extend genealogies backward and to evaluate ethnographic statements. Thus, a shorter time depth for some family lines can be set against the statement "We have always been here" and lead the anthropologist to a more considered evaluation of the real and symbolic significance of the statement itself (1981:10).

Other anthropologists and historians, especially those conducting research on European, Asian, and American family history, have turned to published genealogies rather than to construct them by means of interviews (Meskill 1970; Sabean 1970; Ahern 1976; Adams and Kasakoff 1980; Netting 1981; Hanley and Wolf 1985; Knodel 1988; Ortner 1989). These genealogies are often subjected to methods of quantitative analysis similar to those applied to families reconstituted from vital registers.

From Family History to Local Social, Economic, and Political History

Historical anthropologists often move beyond the reconstruction of family and demographic history based on the data available in vital records, census enumerations, population registers, and oral or written genealogies to explore a range of other qualitative historical sources that shed light on social and economic life in the past as well as on the significance of particular events in the lives of local populations.

Galt (1986, 1991) links household census data to tax registers, data drawn from notarial transactions, and police and judicial records in order to reconstruct settlement patterns and aspects of social class in an Apulian town in southern Italy from the eighteenth to the twentieth centuries. By analyzing both the remembered and the documented past, he is able to show the historical depth of specific elements of the present-day economic and social landscape. In his discussion of kinds of evidence, Galt notes that many anthropologists begin their foray into history in places where they have previously worked as ethnographers and hence must cope with limitations in the historical documents available (1991:67).

In a more narrative format, Rosenberg (1988) uses numerous historical sources to trace changes in a Swiss Alpine community as it gradually came under the influence of the state and was affected by the spread of capitalism. Using a model of negotiation, and centering her analysis on subsistence patterns, market conditions, and class formation, Rosenberg looks at how village people coped with the changing demands on their community that were introduced from outside. Among her primary sources are property and tax records and wills—both of which offer invaluable information on property relations—land transactions, and long-term trends in class formation and inequality.[15] A number of other anthropologists and ethnohistorians have used wills, notarial records, and other legal documents to reconstruct residence patterns, family relations and values, as well as changing attitudes toward death and religion (Obeyesekere 1967; Davis 1973; Goody et al. 1976; Aries 1981; Behar 1986; Cline 1986; Brettell 1991), and a broad range of court records have been analyzed to shed light on the structure and meaning of colonialism in places such as India and Africa (Mann and Roberts 1991; Cohn 1996).

Maddox's (1993) history of the dynamics of local sociopolitical relations in a southern Spanish town from the seventeenth to the twentieth centuries is painted in much broader brushstrokes than the local histories produced by Galt and Rosenberg. It's divided into three phases. Maddox addresses the themes of religion, honor, and patronage and how they shaped a local ethos during the traditional phase of the *Ancien Régime*. Local history is tied into the national history of formal charters, exacted tribute, and external authority. This phase of tradition and domination is displaced in the nineteenth and early twentieth centuries by the forces of agrarian capitalism and a crisis among the rural aristocracy and within ecclesiastical institutions. The final phase covers the period of "tradition liberalized," when class society was reformed after the Spanish Civil War. Of methodological distinction in Maddox's approach is his frequent use of key historical, literary, or religious texts to ballast his discussion of the relationship between forms of discourse and forms of life at different periods in the history of the town of Aracena.

Perhaps the most remarkable recent example of a localized study in historical anthropology over the *longue durée* is Gulliver and Silverman's (1995) analysis of shopkeepers and merchants in the southeast Irish market town of Thomastown from the mid-seventeenth century to the present. The time frame they tackle requires them to deal with varying qualities of data and to make creative linkages between one period and the next. They offer a historical study "which increases in ethnographic detail and analytical depth as we come closer to the present, as archival materials improve, and as field data intersect with archival data" (p. 9). Tax records, land surveys, and a census offer insight into the local experience of the Cromwellian conquest and how the population became divided along ethnic and status lines. Parish registers provide information on the rise and fall of population, and data from deeds help to develop a picture of changing economic conditions as well as the history of local enterprises.

Once Gulliver and Silverman's narrative is situated in the nineteenth century, commercial directories, town plans, shop book accounts, minute books of the Board of Guardians and Rural District Councils, and county newspapers are brought into play to describe a flourishing local economy built on retailing. The discussion culminates in a chapter on the political-economy of Thomastown from 1840–1991 that addresses and challenges analytical models such as core-periphery and the geography of domination. This is followed by treatment of family entrepreneurship and other aspects of kinship and heirship. Case histories of three family enterprises based on a method of record linkage and reconstruction from a variety of archival sources, from family oral histories, and from informants' accounts, offer depth to the more general statistical analysis. Gulliver and Silverman conclude that Thomastown, while located spatially at the margins of Europe, nevertheless occupies a central place "at a particular level in an evolving hierarchy of domination" (1995:339). Thomastown, in their view, is neither typical nor unique. Its history is more than another ethnographic case. It contributes to theory building: "We have a particular view of how meaningful understandings are reached—not by macro studies, quantitative analysis and modelling, but by careful and controlled comparison in the context of a cross-cultural method which uses empirical case studies of agents, networks, resources, and interests" (p. 341).[16]

Big Problems in Small Places: The Global Perspective in Political Economic History

The local histories discussed in the previous section illustrate one of the major differences between history and anthropological history noted by Cohn (1980:220). "The units of study in anthropological history should be cultural and culturally derived: power, authority, exchange, reciprocity, codes of conduct, systems of social classification, the construction of time and space, rituals. One studies these in a particular place and over time, but the study is about the construction of cultural categories and the process of that construction, not about place and time." Although some may quibble with Cohn's statement, it is perhaps best illustrated by those studies that adopt a macro and global historical perspective.

Any number of historical anthropologists work with this perspective. Thus, Friedrich's (1977:ix) study of the community of Naranja in Mexico is really about "the origin and growth of agrarian reform and agrarian politics, the formation of an agrarian ideology, and of the techniques of agrarian revolt." To engage in this study, he reconstructs the past of the late nineteenth century through both ethnological methods (interviews with older natives, internal analysis of present-day life of the community, and comparisons with other Tarascan pueblos) and research in government and agrarian archives. A significant portion of the book focuses on a biographical history of the revolutionary leader Primo Tapia. In a subsequent volume, Friedrich (1986) outlines his "anthrohistorical methods" more fully. This is one of the most intriguing statements on linking local, regional and national historical discourse, as well as on the interpretation of "shattered bits" of ethnography in general.

By far the majority of those historical anthropologists who address the big problem in small places are looking at the impact of culture contact, colonialism, and capitalist and state penetration (Wallace 1972, 1981; Schneider and Schneider 1976, 1996; Comaroff 1985; Dirks 1987; Gailey 1987; Silverblatt 1987; Hansen 1989; Linnekin 1991; Kahn 1993). One of the best examples of such work is Roseberry's (1983) Marxist analysis of the formation and transformation, over four centuries, of a property-owning, commodity-producing Venezuelan peasantry. He is interested in elevating local facts to the level of world-historical facts, and thus writes a history that deepens our understanding of the capitalist mode of production and uneven capitalist development (p. 202). Roseberry draws on local documents dealing with land use and land rights, the files of a local coffee cooperative, local newspapers, municipal tax records, census data for the twentieth century, and a host of secondary sources to write this sweeping history of transformation. Secondary sources, in his view, are essential to the historical anthropologist who must wrestle with the tension between a national and a local history. Roseberry describes his method as follows: "It is the application of a theoretical framework to a particular situation, the modification of that framework as the data I was gathering presented surprises, and the search for new data as the theoretical revisions suggested new questions" (p. 212).

Richard Fox (1985) adopts a somewhat different approach in his analysis of how beliefs about the racial division of humankind shaped British attitudes toward the Sikhs in early twentieth-century Punjab, licensed the treatment of Singhs (Lions) as a separate species, rationalized and constructed colonial oppression, and caused the Singh Sabha protest movement. Relying largely on secondary sources, Fox analyzes "the peculiar historical conjunction of material conditions and cultural meanings that constituted the political economy of the Punjab in the first decades of the twentieth century" (1985:10). Ultimately, however, he writes a history about the construction of identity in situations of culture contact where a particular region is progressively integrated into the world economy. Fox argues that members of the dominated class appropriate the hegemonic model of the dominant class and alter and use it in their resistance. This leads him to a conceptual "re-situation" of the concept of culture itself as always in a state of becoming. This is his affirmation of "a history that engages the particulars of systems of domination and their relevant cultural codes," a history whose objective is "to explain real social processes and practices, carried on and developed over time in social actions" (p. 206).

Ortner (1989) also weaves the perspectives of political economy and culture together in what she calls an ethnographic history that outlines not only the impact of the state, colonialism or capitalism but also how this impact is interpreted at the receiving end.[17] Anthropologists, she argues, "must use the cultural frames and structural contradictions of the local society as a kind of lens through which to view the practices and politics of the larger system because it is these cultural frames and structural contradictions that mediate both the meaning and the impact of the larger political and economic forces in question" (p. 83).

Historical Applications of Ethnographic Methods of Analysis

Some anthropologists have engaged history by adapting the method of event-centered analysis (Pelto and Pelto 1978:200–208; Fogelson 1989). The focus of their research is on a single event and its lasting impact on a local community or population. Depending on the historical depth of the event the sources are oral, documentary, or a combination of both. Marshall Sahlins's (1981) exploration of the death of Captain Cook is a good example of this method, as is his more recent analysis of the Fijian War of 1843–1855 (Sahlins 1991), but there are others. Vincent (1992) relies on documentary sources—published and unpublished reports of local and national commissions, reconstructed genealogies and family histories, as well as on an examination of material culture—to explore the impact of a single incident involving a board meeting of the guardians of the Enniskillen Poor Law Union that shaped the response to the famine in one Irish county. Collier (1987) draws extensively on oral history (supplemented with archival sources) to document the effects of a series of political assassinations on the construction of socialism in the southern Spanish community of Los Olivos.

Certainly, Victor Turner's (1957, 1974) concept of social drama and his extended case-study method have much in common with the method of event-centered analysis. Taylor (1983) draws on Turner's method to develop his ethnohistorical analysis of a Dutch immigrant community in New England. He focuses this ethnohistory on two prolonged disputes, each with its moments of dramatic confrontation, each with its leading actors, extras, and cameo-roles. In his discussion of the advantages of this method as applied to history, Taylor notes the "opportunities for exploring (1) the underlying normative conflicts that may be generating such observable confrontations; (2) the manner in which individuals manipulate norms in pursuance of self-interest, and (3) the collective, symbolic assertion of a moral order as over against the disorder of life" (1983:185).[18]

Turner is also a key figure in the development of symbolic anthropology, and his method of symbolic analysis, broadly conceived, has been successfully applied to history by some anthropologists. The best example is Ohnuki-Tierney's (1987, 1990b) exploration of the changing meaning of the monkey as a metaphor for the self in Japanese culture from the eighth century to the present. Documentary sources, including ancient texts and folktales, reveal, for example, that the dominant meaning of monkey as mediator in the medieval period was transformed into the monkey as scapegoat by the early modern period. By the modern period, another meaning, the monkey as clown, had emerged. These transformations, Ohnuki-Tierney argues, coincided with major transitions in Japanese history.

Mid-thirteenth- and fourteenth-century Japan was characterized by political chaos, and unprecedented mobility, flexibility, and openness to foreigners. By the early modern period, however, a consolidation process resulted in a highly stratified and less dynamic society that was closed to outsiders. It was only in the late nineteenth century that Japan again opened itself up to the outside world, heralding another period of change.[19]

Horwitz draws on an ethnoscientific methodology to discover "the cultural context of social relations in a nineteenth century community" (1978:27). His approach is based on semantic analysis and proceeds from an examination of primary sources to record terms of reference or address, and the contexts within which they are used. He then develops a set of domains or a taxonomy of the types of statements that, through an analysis of components, lead to general principles of social organization.

In a somewhat different vein, discourse is also the focus of the historical work of Taylor (1992) and Comaroff and Comaroff (1992). The Comaroffs analyze the chronicles of Non-Conformist missions in South Africa and expand their analysis to other written sources, including newspapers and official publications, novels, popular songs, drawings, and children's games. Through discourse analysis, they can trace the transformation of a text such that a single, consistent, and coherent ideology emerges from disparate voices and modes of expression. Taylor applies the method to an analysis of religious narratives (a folk story, a magazine piece, and a Redemptorist sermon) in nineteenth-century Donegal to arrive at a more complete understanding of competing cultural and social realities and regimes.

Finally, mention should be made of the comparative method used successfully by ethnohistorians who draw comparisons across time based on certain assumptions about cultural and social regularities under similar conditions (Chance 1996). Among historical anthropologists, this method has been used by Eric Wolf throughout his career for both micro- (1957; Cole and Wolf 1974) and macrolevel studies (1982) and by Goody (1983) in his sweeping study of the development of marriage and the family in Europe. However, Clark (1992) has called for its wider application, and Hansen (1989) suggests, rather than rigorously pursues, the idea that her study of domestic service in Zambia can cast a critical light on similar issues in the United States and ultimately contribute to our understanding of the place of paid household work under the economic conditions of advanced capitalism.

Life History

Any discussion of historical methods in anthropology must address the life history. Although a form of oral historical data, a life history is distinct in being an extensive record "of a person's life told to and recorded by another, who then edits and writes the life as though it were autobiography" (Langness 1965:4–5).

Emerging from research to recapture the past of Native American populations, the life history method flourished during the 1920s, 1930s, and 1940s and culminated in a Social Science Research Council seminar focusing on the use of personal documents in the social sciences (Gottschalk et al. 1947). As a method of research, life history has been controversial, largely because of questions of reliability, validity, and representativeness. These questions led to its dwindling use in the postwar years.[20] However, in recent years life histories have reemerged, to a large extent in connection with reflexive and feminist anthropologies. Although the method can be studied indirectly by looking at specific ethnographic applications (Crapanzano 1980; Shostak 1981; Blackman 1982; Friedrich 1986; Kendall 1988;

Gmelch 1991; Behar 1993; Brettell 1995), there are also some publications that deal with it more directly (Langness 1965; Bertaux 1981; Bertaux and Kohli 1984; Crapanzano 1984; Watson and Watson-Franke 1985; Behar 1990; Rosenwald and Ochberg 1992; Linde 1993). Langness and Frank (1981), in particular, offer numerous suggestions for how to handle the problem of reliability and how to supplement life history data with other kinds of data in order to arrive at a more complete understanding. Certainly, many of the concerns that pertain to participant observation more generally—rapport, language facility, interviewing techniques, and ethics—are equally pertinent to the collection of life histories.

Although life histories have been used to study personality, to examine the relationship of an individual to his or her society or culture, or to explore the "phenomenology of subjective experience" (Watson and Watson-Franke 1985), in the context of this essay we need to ask about the nature of the life history as a historical method. Here, the conceptual distinctions outlined by Peacock and Holland (1993) are useful. They contrast a life-focused approach with a story-focused approach. One treats the narrated life as a window on objective facts of historical and ethnographic events, and the other focuses on the subjective experiences of narrator. Issues of validity come into play in the first case, but the emphasis is largely on the way that change can be documented through its impact on individual lives. However, the second perspective is equally relevant to historical analysis. Indeed, historians have borrowed the life history method to gain access to an inside view of slavery among women in East, West, and Central Africa (Alpers 1983; Strobel 1983; Wright 1993), colonialism in East Africa (LeVine 1979), caste and ethnicity in Central Africa (Codere 1973), labor among Chinese women (Sheridan and Salaff 1987), or migration between the wars in Europe (Bertaux-Wiame 1982).[21]

Generated by the anthropologist in interaction and dialogue with an informant in the field, life histories are similar to a range of other personal or subjective documents—letters, diaries, autobiographies, oral narratives—used by historians to reveal the participant's view of the experiences in which he or she has been involved (Yans McLaughlin 1990; Maynes 1992; West 1992). Recently, Graff (1994) has assembled a useful bibliography of works using such sources. Some of these works may provide useful guidelines for the anthropologist who wants to juxtapose life history material with documented life stories.

Oral History

The life history provides one form of oral historical data, but oral history itself has much broader applications. The pioneer in using oral history among "people without history" was Jan Vansina. Working in Africa, Vansina argued that oral traditions are as solid an historical source as any other, especially when they can be evaluated through comparisons with written records, archaeological evidence, and linguistic patterns (1970, 1985). Vansina outlined a range of oral traditions: slogans and formulas; place names; official and private poetry; stories; and legal and other commentaries.

In the post-Vansina era, a number of historians have produced volumes dealing with the methods of oral history (Grele 1975; Hoopes 1979; Henige 1982; Thompson 1988; Dunaway and Baum 1996). These works tackle such issues as the relationship between history and oral history, the authority of the story teller, the interview process, balancing subjectivity and objectivity, and problems of editing and bias. The oral history method has been applied to economic history, labor history, the history of science, social history, family history, and women's history. Historians generally elicit oral histories using a rather formal method of interviewing. Many anthropologists do the same, but some weave together oral history from nonnarrative oral traditions—informal discussions, passing comments, and daily verbal interactions (Taylor 1983; Besteman 1993).[22]

An examination of works in historical ethnography that draw on oral history reveals a common thread in the emphasis on a dialogue between data gathered through oral history and that collected in the archives so that "The meaning of each set of data [is] satisfactorily elucidated only with reference to the other" (Rogers 1992:25). Thus, one aim of the dialogic approach is to arrive at a more complete record of an event or historical structure. Stockard (1989) elicited oral histories (or what she calls retrospective interviews) with 150 elderly women to document an unorthodox marriage pattern (delayed transfer marriage) that was characteristic of the population of the Canton Delta in traditional times and that was produced in association with silk cultivation. In fact, a project that was initially intended to focus on the present turned to a focus on the past because of a casual comment made by an informant. To verify the accounts that were coming from oral history, Stockard began to examine other written records—gazetteers, missionary accounts, histories, travel literature—in search of a "confirmation" of the oral accounts.

Another aim of this dialogic juxtaposition of oral history and the written record is to access different voices and different interpretations of the same historical experience. There are numerous examples of the application of this method (Stolcke 1988; Poyer 1994). For example, Hoehler-Fatton (1996) uses (or, as she says, "privileges") oral tradition to access the contributions of women to the rise of charismatic Christian movements among the Luo of western Kenya during the colonial era. "Although colonial and missionary reports may be more reliable as far as basic chronology is concerned, they highlight the activities of male leaders exclusively. When women are mentioned in these written texts, it is usually in collective (and dismissive) terms. As we will see, women have always been the backbone of this popular religion. A history that is silent with respect to their activities would be seriously skewed" (Hoehler-Fatton 1996:8).

Different class-based historical narratives are the focus of Jerome Mintz's (1982) study of the anarchist rebellion in Casas Viejas, Spain in the early twentieth century.

Mintz compares oral tradition with the documentation in anarchist and local newspapers, parliamentary debates and reports, letters and journals, and church and court records. The written record contains the narratives of the well-born, while oral accounts and traditions belong to the campesino. The first narrative portrays the monks of the Carmelite monastery in Casas Viejas as spiritual nourishers; the other as oppressors. Similarly, one account attributes the decline of the local monastery in the early nineteenth century to the French invasion; the other suggests that the decline was the result of the lust and rivalry of the monks themselves (p. 77).

In a study of narratives of the Klondike goldrush, Cruikshank (1992) contrasts the western story of expansion, individualism, and hegemony with the native narrative of resilience and assertion of autonomy.[23] In commenting on the value of the oral account as opposed to the written record, she suggests that "the exercise . . . is less one of straightening out facts than of identifying how such cognitive models may generate different kinds of social analysis, leading to different interpretations of a given event, one of which is included in official history while the other is relegated to collective memory" (p. 22).

Ortner (1989), in her ethnohistory of high religion among the Sherpas of Nepal, describes a somewhat different experience with the multivocality of history as it derives from the juxtaposition of oral tradition and the written record. She collected stories and personal memories from individuals who could talk about the foundation of the monasteries and temples that were part of their history. In the process, she unearthed an emic view of authoritative knowledge—although she wanted a variety of views, she was consistently referred to the lamas who "really knew." This historical work made much more sense to her informants than did her earlier ethnographic work and information was therefore easier to obtain. What was more challenging was the construction of narrative history from the shreds of evidence.

Perhaps the most masterful works in this dialogic genre are Richard Price's monumental volumes *First-Time* and *Alabi's World*. First-Time, for the Saramaka of Surinam, is the sacred history of their formative years. It was not a subject open to Price during his initial fieldwork. Only after several years in the field was he able to broach the subject with the elders to whom he offered his own sense of history gleaned from archives in the Netherlands. He elicited this oral history of First-Time from a number of elders under conditions that made them feel comfortable talking about something they did not like to share with outsiders.

Price's method (1983) is to focus on the event. "Taking fragments (often a mere phrase) from many different men, comparing them, discussing them with others, challenging them against rival accounts, and eventually holding them up against contemporary written evidence, I try to begin to develop a picture of what the most knowledgeable Saramakas collectively know, and why they know and preserve it" (p. 25). He applies the same method to the incomplete written record, carefully considering "a complicated bundle of evidence, often including apparently contrary facts . . . which I am ultimately able to dismiss by critical consideration of the sources" (p. 40).

In the comparisons that he made with written evidence, he was consistently aware of the risk of establishing a canonical or authorized version of Saramaka history. His solution was to publish his book with varying typefaces so that the two histories—both equally fragmented—could be kept distinct. His second book, *Alabi's World*, focuses on the period from 1762 forward and draws on a range of new written sources that are unavailable for the earlier period. In it, he continues the method of juxtaposing voices—that of the Saramakas, that of Moravian missionaries, that of Dutch colonial officials, and that of the ethnographic historian —and hence histories. For the ethnographic historian, Price suggests, the goal should be "to penetrate existential worlds different from his own and to evoke their texture, by bridging, but never losing sight of, the cultural and semantic gulf that separates the anthropologist from the historical actors and from the historical observers (those who create the sources) which themselves possess and represent complex prior histories" (Price 1990:xix).

Material Culture and Visual Images

Perhaps inspired by the archaeological branch of their discipline, some historical anthropologists have looked to material culture as a valuable source for the writing of history. An equally important stimulus to this approach is the work of the French social historian Marc Bloch, whose book *Caractères originaux de l'histoire rurale française* was originally published in Paris in 1931 and eventually translated into English under the title *French Rural History* (Bloch 1966). Bloch drew on everything from serial maps to plows to write the history of rural France. One of the earliest anthropological examples of the use of material culture to write history is Kroeber and Richardson's (1940) careful examination of cycles of change in the style of women's clothing in Europe across a 300-year period. They link these changes to periods of stress and crisis.

More recently, Cohn (1996) has explored the relationship between cloth, clothes, and colonialism in nineteenth-century India.[24] Mintz (1985) has used cookbooks as a window on the tastes of the nineteenth-century English working class, and Frykman and Lofgren (1987) draw, among other things, on an analysis of domestic space to access the culture of the Swedish bourgeoisie between 1880 and 1910. Fernandez (1990) and Behar (1986) also "read" domestic spaces for what they tell us about the past. McDonogh (1986) carefully analyzes the opera house and cemeteries to study the urban elite of nineteenth-century Barcelona. On a more global scale, Goody (1993) also makes extensive use of cemeteries, as well as other ancient monuments and works of art, to produce his massive study of the symbolic and transactional use of flowers across time and space. Even Ohnuki-Tierney (1990b) finds some of her representations of monkey symbolism on lacquerware boxes. Schneider and Schneider (1996:94) actually mention a material culture survey. "We asked elderly people of different class backgrounds to tell us how their parents and grandparents lived, illustrating their accounts wherever possible with artifacts of past households, wardrobes, and occupations."

Visual images (paintings, photographs, sculpture) are also part of material culture and hence a valuable source for writing history (Szabo 1994). Perlmutter (1994) suggests that the visual historian can ask about the social and historical forces that influenced the origin, production, dissemination, function, ideology and survival of visual images and how the images themselves may have influenced and shaped thinking and events. He outlines a series of meanings that can be explored in the analysis of images, including production, content identification, functional, expressional, figurative, rhetorical moral, societal or period, and comparative.

While historians have been using such visual images for some time, only a handful of historical ethnographers have moved beyond written sources. John and Jean Comaroff found this a necessary avenue to the unheard voices. Methodologically, the dominant narrative commanded them "to peruse the colonizing gesture beyond audible ideologies and visible institutions into the realm of such unspoken forms as bodies, buildings, magic, and merchandise. And this, in turn, took us back to our archives—to letters, lists, illustrations, and photographs—albeit now less for what they declared than for what they disclosed as maps of the mundane" (Comaroff and Comaroff 1992:36). The Comaroffs call for historical ethnographers to construct their own archive. "As anthropologists, . . . we must work both in and outside the official record, both with and beyond the guardians of memory in the societies we study" (p. 34).

Conclusion: Linking the Past to the Present and History to Ethnography

In the preface to her study of domestic workers in Zambia, Karen Hansen (1989:xiii) describes the calculated leaps that she took from the documents of the past to observations in the present and from Zambia's capital to the metropolitan United States. She suggests that these leaps, and the sacrifice of detail to theoretical insights, might make the historian wince. However, they are the leaps often made by anthropologists who enter the archives through the back door of ethnography. One of the ways in which historical anthropology is different from history is precisely in the effort to link the past to the present.

In an earlier article (Brettell 1992), I explored a number of important issues that arise from this linkage. I noted that the method of participant-observation can generate relevant questions for historical research and that patterns of social relations that the anthropologist sees on the ground can be suggestive in formulating hypotheses about social interaction in the past. I also noted that historical research can bring us to a clearer understanding of the relationship between the ideal and the actual, as well as of the idealization of the past.[25] To these Gulliver (1989:332) adds the use of informants to "flesh out the facts of a government report, a deed or a newspaper article" or the use of an historical document to jog the memory of informants or provide the basis for an interview or a discussion. Schneider and Schneider (1996) used a similar method to help them interpret vital registers and household files and understand fully the practice of coitus interruptus in the past.

As ethnographers, we bring a broad range of methods into the field. Similar methods can be applied to our fieldwork in the archives. Indeed, it has been suggested that the objective of historical work should be good ethnography. "This means finding ways of seeing regularities in the evidence of specific events and ways of bringing together documents of individual lives and the societal processes in which they are embedded" (Silverman 1986:125).

In summary, it seems that work in historical anthropology follows one of two directions, each of which calls for distinct kinds of methods of research and neither of which is, necessarily, mutually exclusive of the other. For some, to be a historical ethnographer means to interpret historical events through the eyes of others. The ethnohistorical method, DeMaillie argues, is aimed at "understanding the past in its own terms, of reading the record of the past in a manner that as fully and ver-isimilarly as possible represents events as they were perceived by the actors, and then uses this knowledge to write culturally grounded histories and historical ethnographies" (1993:553). For others, the major focus of historical anthropology is cross-cultural and comparative understanding of the social, political, economic, and cultural processes that characterize human behavior in the past as well as in the present.

NOTES

I thank Dennis Cordell, Bonnie Wheeler, Jeremy Adams, Russ Bernard, and David Kertzer for their careful reading of the first draft of this chapter.

1. Early historians looked at the non-Western world in a similar way. Krech points to Trevor Roper's claim that only the history of Europeans in Africa was worthwhile because the rest was largely darkness. "We should not amuse ourselves with unrewarding gyrations of barbarous tribes in picturesque but irrelevant corners of the globe" (Trevor Roper 1965; quoted in Krech 1991:345).

2. According to Chance (1996), anthropologists working in Mesoamerica in the 1950s and 1960s were also slow to exploit the rich historical documents available to them.

3. For a recent review of the state of ethnohistory, see Krech (1991).

4. Simultaneously, there was a turn toward anthropology among some historians. Exemplary works include Andaya (1993), Bynum (1992), Darnton (1984), Davis (1975), and Isaac (1982). Davis (1981:267) notes four aspects that make anthropology useful to historians: close observations of living processes of social interaction; interesting ways of interpreting symbolic behavior; suggestions about how the parts of a social system fit together; and a comparative framework. Recently, several historians of Africa have discussed their own methods of fieldwork (Adenaike and Vansina 1996). On this latter topic, also see the pages of the journal *History in Africa*.

5. Silverman and Gulliver (1992:55) refer to a place "called Thepast, that has been added to the list of exotic places in which anthropologists may do fieldwork."

6. Blok (1992:123) argues that "the ambiguity of the term 'history' still hovers over the heads of anthropologists, for whom 'history' primarily signifies the past (and representations of the past) but leaves little room for historiography." For an interesting discussion by a historian of the application of a meaning-centered ethnographic method to history, see Isaac (1982). For one of the few thorough discussions of methods by a historical anthropologist see Gulliver (1989). Bernard (1994:1) outlines three different meanings of the word "method": (1) an epistemology—how we know things; (2) a set of strategic choices—whether to do participant observation fieldwork, library research, experimental research; (3) and a set of research techniques—how and what kind of sample to select, whether to do face-to-face or telephone interviews, etc. These three meanings are interconnected, hence all are part of my use of the word "methods" in this chapter.

7. Roseberry (1989.5) notes that there are a "variety of anthropologists appropriating a variety of histories." The political-economy approach of Eric Wolf—one that explores the construction of economic and political inequality within a global system—is quite different from the cultural approach of Clifford Geertz or the structuralist approach of Marshall Sahlins. Ortner (1989) describes a bifurcation of historical anthropology into political economy, on the one hand, and structural or ethnographic history, on the other.

8. A heated debate has emerged about whether the apotheosis of Captain Cook was linked to a Hawaiian myth or to European assumptions about native modes of thought, and hence to European mythmaking (Obeyesekere 1992; Sahlins 1995; Borofsky 1997). This debate has raised intriguing questions about native voice and agency and about the nature of historical anthropological research and explanation itself. I return to this debate in the next section of the paper. For further discussion of the relationships between myth and history, see Hill (1988).

9. Trigger also offers an excellent discussion of how ethnohistory differs from conventional history, including its reliance on the auxiliary fields of archaeology, physical anthropology, and linguistics. For another discussion of the interaction between archaeology and historical ethnography, see Kirch and Sahlins (1992).

10. In fact, anthropologists would be wise to begin their historical work by consulting several general books about history and the historian's craft, among them E. H. Carr's (1961) classic *What Is History*, Mark Bloch's (1984; orig. 1954) *The Historian's Craft*, and, more recently, the co-authored volume by Appleby, Hunt, and Jacob (1994). The latter volume tackles the diverse voices of history in the age of multiculturalism and the nature of historical truth and historical objectivity. The authors also deal with the textuality of historical texts and

with problems of linguistic translation. Of equal importance is an exploration of the work of ethnohistorians who have occasionally written about the topic of source evaluation. See, for example, Meister (1980), Moore and Campbell (1989), and Trigger (1976).

11. Many of these methods, and others, are discussed in the pages of the journal *Historical Methods*. This journal is an invaluable source for those anthropologists interested in exploring modes of analysis that can be applied to historical data. See, for example, Ruggles (1993) for a more recent discussion of simulation models in demographic and family history. And see Cordell et al. (1996) for a discussion of how various sources, including retrospective migration surveys, were used to develop a social history of a migration system in West Africa.

12. Those who want to explore the original discussion of the methods of nominal record linkage and family reconstitution should consult the works of Louis Henry (1956, 1967). Schneider and Schneider (1996:90ff) offer some useful comments on the problems of dealing with out-migration.

13. Kertzer (1984) provides a well-reasoned assessment of the positive and negative aspects of the comparative household typology developed by Hammel and Laslett. He and other anthropologists (Brettell 1986) have modified the typology to suit local variations in household composition and patterns of coresidence. The Appendix in Kertzer and Hogan (1989) offers a rare explication of the range of sources used and the methods of record linkage applied to the construction of an individual-level database; it is well worth reading.

14. See, however, Wells (1978) for a cautionary note on constructing cohorts in historical demographic research.

15. See Steckel (1994) for further discussion on the use of tax lists.

16. A complete and extremely interesting discussion of the sources and methods used by Gulliver and Silverman, as well as a justification for close, local-level investigation can be found in Gulliver (1989).

17. Additional examples of a historical anthropology method that approaches political economy from a culturalist position are Linnekin (1991) and Collier (1987).

18. Taylor (1985) applies a similar method in a study of estate agents and priests in late nineteenth-century Ireland. For a critique of Turner's ideas, as applied to historical material, see Bynum (1984; reprinted in Bynum 1992).

19. For other examples of the application of symbolic analysis, see Fernandez (1990) and Hawkins (1984).

20. One major exception was the work of Oscar Lewis, specifically *The Children of Sanchez* (1959) and *Five Families* (1961).

21. For an interesting methodological statement, see Townsend (1990).

22. See the introduction in Pitkin (1985) for a useful discussion of the methods of oral history applied to family history. Of interest also is Elizabeth Tonkin's (1992) book on the social construction of oral history.

23. The historian Luise White (1995) uses similar methods of juxtaposition, comparing oral accounts of African rumors that white people captured Africans and took their blood to medical missionary writings about the triumph of Western biomedicine.

24. See Weiner and Schneider (1989) for other explorations of cloth and culture.

25. Birdwell-Pheasant (1992) also focuses on the difference between ideal and actual in her reconsideration of the Irish stem family. For discussions by historians of their own attempts to link the present to the past, see the essays in Adenaike and Vansina (1996).

REFERENCES

Adams, John W. 1982. Anthropology and History in the 1980s: Consensus, Community, and Exoticism. In *The New History: The 1980s and Beyond*. Theodore K. Rabb and Robert I. Rotberg, eds. Pp. 253–265. Princeton: Princeton University Press.

Adams, John W., and Alice B. Kasakoff. 1980. Migration at Marriage in Colonial New England: A Comparison of Rates Derived from Genealogies with Rates from Vital Records. In *Genealogical Demography*. Bennett Dyke and Warren T. Morrill, eds. Pp. 115–138. New York: Academic Press.

Adenaike, Carolyn Keyes, and Jan Vansina, eds. 1996. *In Pursuit of History: Fieldwork in Africa*. Portsmouth, NH: Heinemann.

Ahern, Emily. 1976. Segmentation in Chinese Lineages: A View Through Written Genealogies. *American Ethnologist* 3:1–15.

Alpers, Edward. 1983. The Story of Swema: A Note on Female Vulnerability in Nineteenth-Century East Africa. In *Women and Slavery in Africa*. Claire C. Robertson and Martin A. Klein, eds. Pp. 185–219. Madison: University of Wisconsin Press.

Alter, George. 1988. *Family and the Female Life Course: The Women of Verviers, Belgium, 1849–1880*. Madison: University of Wisconsin Press.

Andaya, Leonard. 1993. *The World of Maluku: Eastern Indonesia in the Early Modern Period*. Honolulu: University of Hawaii Press.

Appleby, Joyce, Lynn Hunt, and Margaret Jacob. 1994. *Telling the Truth About History*. New York: W. W. Norton.

Aries, Philippe. 1981. *The Hour of Our Death*. New York: Knopf.

Behar, Ruth. 1986. *Santa Maria del Monte: The Presence of the Past in a Spanish Village*. Princeton: Princeton University Press.

Behar, Ruth. 1990. Rage and Redemption: Reading the Life Story of a Mexican Marketing Woman. *Feminist Studies 16*: 223–258.

Behar, Ruth. 1993. *Translated Woman: Crossing the Border with Esperanza's Story*. Boston: Beacon Press.

Bernard, H. Russell. 1994. *Research Methods in Anthropology: Qualitative and Quantitative Approaches*, 2d ed. Walnut Creek, CA: AltaMira Press.

Bertaux, Daniel, ed. 1981. *Biography and Society: The Life History Approach in the Social Sciences*. Beverly Hills, CA: Sage Publications.

Bertaux, Daniel, and Martin Kohli. 1984. The Life Story Approach: A Continental View. *Annual Review of Sociology 10*:215–237.

Bertaux-Wiame, Isabelle. 1982. The Life History Approach to the Study of Internal Migration: How Women and Men Came to Paris Between the Wars. In *Our Common History: The Transformation of Europe*. Paul Thompson and Natasha Burchardt, eds. Pp. 186–199. Atlantic Highlands, NJ: Humanities Press.

Besteman, Catherine. 1993. Public History and Private Knowledge: On Disputed History in Southern Somalia. *Ethnohistory* 40:563–586.

Biersack, Aletta. 1989. Local Knowledge, Local History: Geertz and Beyond. In *The New Cultural History*. Lynn Hunt, ed. Pp. 72–96. Berkeley: University of California Press.

Biersack, Aletta, ed. 1991. *Clio in Oceania: Toward a Historical Anthropology*. Washington, DC: Smithsonian Institution Press.

Birdwell-Pheasant, Donna. 1992. The Early Twentieth-Century Irish Stem Family: A Case Study from County Kerry. In *Approaching the Past: Historical Anthropology Through Irish Case Studies*. Marilyn Silverman and P. H. Gulliver, eds. Pp. 205–235. New York: Columbia University Press.

Birdwell-Pheasant, Donna. 1993. Irish Households in the Early Twentieth Century: Culture, Class and Historical Contingency. *Journal of Family History* 18:19–38.

Blackman, Margaret. 1982. *During My Time: Florence Edenshaw Davidson, A Haida Woman*. Seattle: University of Washington Press.

Bloch, Marc. 1966 (orig. pub. 1931 as *Caractères originaux de l'histoire rurale française*). *French Rural History*. Berkeley: University of California Press.

Bloch, Marc. 1984 (orig. pub. 1954). *The Historian's Craft*. Manchester, England: Manchester University Press.

Blok, Anton. 1992. Reflections on Making History. In *Other Histories*. Kirsten Hastrup, ed. Pp. 121–127. London: Routledge.

Bohannan, Laura. 1952. A Genealogical Charter. *Africa* 22:301–315.

Borofsky, Robert. 1997. Cook, Lono, Obeyesekere, and Sahlins. *Current Anthropology* 38: 255–281.

Brettell, Caroline B. 1986. *Men Who Migrate, Women Who Wait: Population and History in a Portuguese Parish*. Princeton: Princeton University Press.

Brettell, Caroline B. 1991. Kinship and Contract: Property Transmission and Family Relations in Northwestern Portugal. *Comparative Studies in Society and History* 33:443–465.

Brettell, Caroline B. 1992. Archives and Informants: Reflections on Juxtaposing the Methods of Anthropology and History. *Historical Methods* 25:28–36.

Brettell, Caroline B. 1995. *We Have Already Cried Many Tears: The Stories of Three Portuguese Migrant Women*. Prospect Heights, IL: Waveland Press.

Burke, Peter. 1992. *History and Social Theory*. Ithaca: Cornell University Press.

Bynum, Caroline Walker. 1984. Women's Stories, Women's Symbols: A Critique of Victor Turner's Theory of Liminality. In *Anthropology and the Study of Religion*. Frank Reynolds and Robert Moore, eds. Pp. 105–125. Chicago: Center for the Scientific Study of Religion.

Bynum, Caroline Walker. 1992. *Fragmentation and Redemption: Essays on Gender and the Human Body in Medieval Religion*. New York: Zone Books.

Carr, Edward Hallett. 1961. *What Is History?* New York: Vintage Books.

Chance, John K. 1996. Mesoamerica's Ethnographic Past. *Ethnohistory 43*:379–403.

Clark, Samuel. 1992. Historical Anthropology, Historical Sociology, and the Making of Modern Europe. In *Approaching the Past: Historical Anthropology Through Irish Case Studies*. Marilyn Silverman and P. H. Gulliver, eds. Pp. 324–351. New York: Columbia University Press.

Cline, S. L. 1986. *Colonial Culhuacan, 1580–1600. A Social History of an Aztec Town*. Albuquerque: University of New Mexico Press.

Codere, Helen. 1973. *The Biography of an African Society, Rwanda, 1900–1960*. Tervuern, Belgium: Musée Royale de l'Afrique Centrale.

Cohn, Bernard. 1962. An Anthropologist among the Historians: A Field Study. *The South Atlantic Quarterly 61*:13–29.

Cohn, Bernard. 1980. History and Anthropology: The State of Play. *Comparative Studies in Society and History 22*:198–221.

Cohn, Bernard. 1981. Anthropology and History in the 1980s: Toward a Rapprochement. *Journal of Interdisciplinary History 12*:227–252.

Cohn, Bernard. 1987. *An Anthropologist Among the Historians and Other Essays*. Delhi: Oxford University Press.

Cohn, Bernard. 1996. *Colonialism and Its Forms of Knowledge: The British in India*. Princeton: Princeton University Press.

Cole, John W., and Eric R. Wolf. 1974. *The Hidden Frontier: Ecology and Ethnicity in an Alpine Valley*. New York: Academic Press.

Collier, George H. 1987. *Socialists of Rural Andalusia*. Stanford: Stanford University Press.

Comaroff, Jean. 1985. *Body of Power, Spirit of Resistance: The Culture and History of a South African People*. Chicago: University of Chicago Press.

Comaroff, John, and Jean Comaroff. 1992. *Ethnography and the Historical Imagination*. Boulder: Westview Press.

Cordell, Dennis D., Joel W. Gregory, and Victor Piché. 1996. *Hoe and Wage: A Social History of a Circular Migration System in West Africa*. Boulder: Westview Press.

Crapanzano, Vincent. 1980. *Tuhami: Portrait of a Moroccan*. Chicago: University of Chicago Press.

Crapanzano, Vincent. 1984. Life Histories. *American Anthropologist 86*:953–959.

Cruikshank, Julie. 1992. Images of Klondike Gold Rush Narratives: Skookum Jim and the Discovery of Gold. *Ethnohistory 39*:20–41.

Darnton, Robert. 1984. *The Great Cat Massacre and Other Episodes in French Cultural History*. New York: Basic Books.

Davis, Deborah, and Stevan Harrell, eds. 1993. *Chinese Families in the Post-Mao Era*. Berkeley: University of California Press.

Davis, John. 1973. *Land and Family in Pisticci*. London: Athlone Press.

Davis, Natalie Z. 1975. *Society and Culture in Early Modern France*. Stanford: Stanford University Press.

Davis, Natalie Z. 1981. Anthropology and History in the 1980s: The Possibilities of the Past. *Journal of Interdisciplinary History 12*:267–275.

DeMaillie, Raymond J. 1993. 'These Have No Ears': Narrative and the Ethnohistorical Method. *Ethnohistory 40*:515–538.

Dening, Greg. 1991. A Poetic for Histories: Transformations that Present the Past. In *Clio in Oceania*. Aletta Biersack, ed. Pp. 347–380. Washington, DC: Smithsonian Institution Press.

Dirks, Nicholas B. 1987. *The Hollow Crown: Ethnohistory of an Indian Kingdom*. Cambridge: Cambridge University Press.

Dirks, Nicholas B. 1996. Is Vice Versa? Historical Anthropologies and Anthropological Histories. In *The Historic Turn in the Human Sciences*. Terrence J. McDonald, ed. Pp. 17–52. Ann Arbor: University of Michigan Press.

Douglass, William A. 1984. *Emigration in a South Italian Town: An Anthropological History*. New Brunswick, NJ: Rutgers University Press.

Dunaway, David K., and Will K. Baum. 1996. *Oral History: An Interdisciplinary Anthology*, 2d ed. Walnut Creek, CA: AltaMira Press.

Dyke, Bennett, and Warren T. Morrill, eds. 1980. *Genealogical Demography*. New York: Academic Press.

Elder, Glen H., Jr. 1975. Age Differentiation and the Life Course. *Annual Review of Sociology 1*:165–190.

Elder, Glen H., Jr. 1977. Family History and the Life Course. *Journal of Family History 2*:279–304.

Elder, Glen H., Jr. 1987. Families and Lives: Some Developments in Life-Course Studies. *Journal of Family History 12*:179–199.

Evans-Pritchard, E. E. 1962. Social Anthropology: Past and Present—The 1950 Marett Lecture. In *Essays in Social Anthropology*. Pp. 139–154. London: Faber and Faber.

Fernandez, James. 1990. Enclosure: Boundary Maintenance and Its Representations over Time in Asturian Mountain Villages (Spain). In *Culture Through Time: Anthropological Approaches*. Emkio Ohnuki-Tierney, ed. Pp. 94–127. Stanford: Stanford University Press.

Fogelson, Raymond. 1989. The Ethnohistory of Events and Non-Events. *Ethnohistory 36*:133–147.

Fox, Richard G. 1985. *Lions of the Punjab: Culture in the Making*. Berkeley: University of California Press.

Freeman, Susan Tax. 1979. *The Pasiegos: Spaniards in No Man's Land*. Chicago: University of Chicago Press.

Freeman, Susan Tax. 1981. From Present to Past: The Genealogical Approach to Local History. Unpublished paper, delivered at the meetings of the Society for Spanish and Portuguese Historical Studies, Toronto.

Friedman, Jonathan. 1997. Review of *How Natives Think: About Captain Cook For Example* by Marshall Sahlins. *American Ethnologist 24*:261–262.

Friedrich, Paul. 1977. *Agrarian Revolt in a Mexican Village*. Chicago: University of Chicago Press.

Friedrich, Paul. 1986. *The Princes of Naranja*. Austin: University of Texas Press.

Frykman, Jonas, and Orvar Lofgren. 1987. *Culture Builders: A Historical Anthropology of Middle-Class Life*. New Brunswick, NJ: Rutgers University Press.

Gailey, Christine Ward. 1987. *Kinship to Kingship: Gender Hierarchy and State Formation in the Tongan Islands*. Austin: University of Texas Press.

Galt, Anthony. 1986. Social Class in a Mid-Eighteenth Century Apulian Town: Indications from the Catasto Onciario. *Ethnohistory 33*:419–447.

Galt, Anthony H. 1991. *Far from the Church Bells: Settlement and Society in an Apulian Town*. Cambridge: Cambridge University Press.

Gewertz, Deborah. 1983. *Sepik River Societies: A Historical Ethnography of the Chambri and Their Neighbors*. New Haven: Yale University Press.

Gewertz, Deborah, and Edward Schieffelin, eds. 1985. *History and Ethnohistory in Papua New Guinea*. Sydney: University of Sydney, Oceania Monographs #28.

Gmelch, Sharon. 1991. *Nan: The Life of an Irish Travelling Woman*. Prospect Heights, IL: Waveland Press.

Goody, Jack. 1983. *The Development of the Family and Marriage in Europe*. Cambridge: Cambridge University Press.

Goody, Jack. 1993. *The Culture of Flowers*. Cambridge: Cambridge University Press.

Goody, Jack, Joan Thirsk, and E. P. Thompson, eds. 1976. *Family and Inheritance*. Cambridge: Cambridge University Press.

Gottschalk, Louis, Clyde Kluckhohn, and Robert Angell. 1947. *The Use of Personal Documents in History, Anthropology, and Sociology*. New York: Social Science Research Council.

Graff, Harvey J. 1994. Using First-Person Sources in Social and Cultural History: A Working Bibliography. *Historical Methods 27*:87–93

Grele. Ronald K., ed. 1975. *Envelopes of Sound*. Chicago: Precedent Publishing.

Grossbart, Stephen R. 1992. Quantitative and Social Science Methods for Historians: An Annotated Bibliography of Selected Books and Articles. *Historical Methods 25*: 100–120.

Gulliver, P. H. 1989. Doing Anthropological Research in Rural Ireland: Methods and Sources for Linking the Past and the Present. In *Ireland from Below: Social Change and Local Communities*. Chris Curtin and Thomas M. Wilson, eds. Pp. 320–338. Galway, Ireland: Galway University Press.

Gulliver, P. H., and Marilyn Silverman. 1995. *Merchants and Shopkeepers: A Historical Anthropology of an Irish Market Town, 1200–1991*. Toronto: University of Toronto Press.

Hammel, Eugene A., and Peter Laslett. 1974. Comparing Household Structure over Time and Between Cultures. *Comparative Studies in Society and History* 16:73–109.

Hanley, Susan B., and Arthur P. Wolf, eds. 1985. *Family and Population in East Asian History*. Stanford: Stanford University Press.

Hansen, Karen Tranberg. 1989. *Distant Companions: Servants and Employers in Zambia, 1900–1985*. Ithaca: Cornell University Press.

Hareven, Tamara K. 1978. Cycles, Courses and Cohorts: Reflections on Theoretical and Methodological Approaches to the Historical Study of the Family. *Journal of Social History* 2:97–109.

Hareven, Tamara K. 1982. *Family Time and Industrial Time*. Cambridge: Cambridge University Press.

Harrell, Stevan, ed. 1995. *Chinese Historical Microdemography*. Berkeley: University of California Press.

Haskins, Loren, and Kirk Jeffrey. 1990. *Understanding Quantitative History*. Cambridge: MIT Press.

Hawkins, Jack. 1984. *Inverse Images: The Meaning of Culture, Ethnicity and Family in Post-Colonial Guatemala*. Albuquerque: University of New Mexico Press.

Henige, David. 1982. *Oral Historiography*. New York: Longmans.

Henry, Louis. 1956. *Anciennes familles genevoises: Etude démographique, XVIe–XXe siècle*. Paris: Presses Universitaires de France.

Henry, Louis. 1967. *Manuel de démographie historique*. Paris: Librarie Droz.

Hill, Jonathan D., ed. 1988. *Rethinking History and Myth: Indigenous South American Perspectives on the Past*. Urbana: University of Illinois Press.

Hoehler-Fatton, Cynthia. 1996. *Women of Fire and Spirit: History, Faith and Gender in Roho Religion in Western Kenya*. Oxford: Oxford University Press.

Hoopes, James. 1979. *Oral History*. Chapel Hill: University of North Carolina Press.

Horwitz, Richard P. 1978. *Anthropology Toward History: Culture and Work in a 19th-Century Maine Town*. Middletown: Wesleyan University Press.

Howell, Nancy. 1979. *The Demography of the Dobe !Kung*. New York: Academic Press.

Isaac, Rhys. 1982. *The Transformation of Virginia, 1740–1790*. Chapel Hill: University of North Carolina Press.

Jaraush, Konrad, and Kenneth Hardy. 1991. *Quantitative Methods for Historians: A Guide to Research, Data, and Statistics*. Chapel Hill: University of North Carolina Press.

Kahn, Joel S. 1993. *Constituting the Minangkabau: Peasants, Culture, and Modernity in Colonial Indonesia*. Providence: Berg Publishers.

Kellogg, Susan. 1991. Histories for Anthropology: Ten Years of Historical Research and Writing by Anthropologists, 1980–1990. *Social Science History* 15:417–455.

Kendall, Laurel. 1988. *The Life and Hard Times of a Korean Shaman: Of Tales and the Telling of Tales*. Honolulu: University of Hawaii Press.

Kertzer, David I. 1984. *Family Life in Central Italy, 1880–1910: Sharecropping, Wage Labor, and Coresidence*. New Brunswick, NJ: Rutgers University Press.

Kertzer, David I., and Dennis P. Hogan. 1989. *Family, Political Economy, and Demographic Change: The Transformation of Life in Casalecchio, Italy 1861–1921*. Madison: University of Wisconsin Press.

Kertzer, David I., and Andrea Schiaffino. 1983. Industrialization and Coresidence: A Life Course Approach. In *Life Span Development and Behavior*. Paul B. Baltes and Orville G. Brim, Jr., eds. Pp. 359–391. New York: Academic Press.

Kertzer, David I., Sydel Silverman, Darrett B. Rutman, and Andrejs Plakans. 1986. History and Anthropology: A Dialogue. *Historical Methods 19*:119–128.

Kirch, Patrick V., and Marshall Sahlins. 1992. *Anahulu: The Anthropology of History in the Kingdom of Hawaii*. Chicago: University of Chicago Press.

Knodel, John. 1988. *Demographic Behavior in the Past: A Study of Fourteen German Village Populations in the Eighteenth and Nineteenth Centuries*. Cambridge: Cambridge University Press.

Krech, Shepard, III. 1991. The State of Ethnohistory. *Annual Review of Anthropology 20*:345–375.

Kroeber, Alfred L., and Jane Richardson. 1940. Three Centuries of Women's Dress Fashions. *Anthropological Records 5*:111–153.

Langness, L. L. 1965. *The Life History in Anthropological Science*. New York: Holt, Rinehart and Winston.

Langness, L. L., and Gelya Frank. 1981. *Lives: An Anthropological Approach to Biography*. Novato, CA: Chandler & Sharp.

LeVine, Sara. 1979. *Mothers and Wives: Gusii Women of East Africa*. Chicago: University of Chicago Press.

Lewis, I. M. 1962. Historical Aspects of Genealogies in Northern Somali Social Structure. *Journal of African History 3*:35–48.

Lewis, I. M. 1968. *History and Social Anthropology*. London: Tavistock Publications.

Lewis, Oscar. 1959. *Five Families*. New York: Basic Books.

Lewis, Oscar. 1961. *The Children of Sanchez*. New York: Random House.

Linde, Charlotte. 1993. *Life Stories: The Creation of Coherence*. New York: Oxford University Press.

Linnekin, Jocelyn. 1991. Inside, Outside: A Hawaiian Community in the World System. In *Clio in Oceania*. Aletta Biersack, ed. Pp. 165–203. Washington, DC: Smithsonian Institution Press.

Maddox, Richard. 1993. *El Castillo: The Politics of Tradition in an Andalusian Town*. Urbana: University of Illinois Press.

Maitland, Frederick W. 1899 [1975]. The Body Politic. In *Selected Essays*. Frederick W. Maitland, ed. Pp. 285–303. Cambridge: Cambridge University Press.

Mann, Kristin, and Richard Roberts. 1991. *Law in Colonial Africa*. Portsmouth, NH: Heinemann.

Mason, Karen Oppenheim, William M. Mason, H. H. Winsborough, and W. Kenneth Poole. 1973. Some Methodological Issues in the Cohort Analysis of Archival Data. *American Sociological Review 38*:242–258.

Maynes, Mary Jo. 1992. Autobiography and Class Formation in Nineteenth-Century Europe: Some Methodological Considerations. *Social Science History 16*:517–537.

McDonogh, Gary Wray. 1986. *Good Families of Barcelona: A Social History of Power in the Industrial Era*. Princeton: Princeton University Press.

Medick, Hans. 1987. 'Missionaries in the Row Boat'? Ethnological Ways of Knowing as a Challenge to Social History. *Comparative Studies in Society and History 29*:76–98.

Meister, Cary W. 1980. Methods for Evaluating the Accuracy of Ethnohistorical Demographic Data on North American Indians: A Brief Assessment. *Ethnohistory 27*: 153–168.

Meskill, Johanna M. 1970. The Chinese Genealogy as a Research Source. In *Family and Kinship in Chinese Society*. Maurice Freedman, ed. Pp. 139–161. Stanford: Stanford University Press.

Mintz, Jerome R. 1982. *The Anarchists of Casas Viejas*. Chicago: University of Chicago Press.

Mintz, Sidney W. 1985. *Sweetness and Power: The Place of Sugar in Modern History*. New York: Viking Penguin.

Moore, John H., and Gregory Campbell. 1989. An Ethnohistorical Perspective on Cheyenne Demography. *Journal of Family History 14*:17–42.

Netting, Robert McCormick. 1981. *Balancing on an Alp: Ecological Change and Continuity in a Swiss Mountain Community*. Cambridge: Cambridge University Press.

Obeyesekere, Gananath. 1967. *Land Tenure in Village Ceylon: A Sociological and Historical Study*. Cambridge: Cambridge University Press.

Obeyesekere, Gananath. 1992. *The Apotheosis of Captain Cook: European Mythmaking in the Pacific*. Princeton: Princeton University Press.

Ohnuki-Tierney, Emiko. 1987. *The Monkey as Mirror: Symbolic Transformation in Japanese History and Ritual*. Princeton: Princeton University Press.

Ohnuki-Tierney, Emiko. 1990a. *Culture Through Time: Anthropological Approaches*. Stanford: Stanford University Press.

Ohnuki-Tierney, Emiko. 1990b. The Monkey as Self in Japanese Culture. In *Culture Through Time: Anthropological Approaches*. Emiko Ohnuki-Tierney, ed. Pp. 128–153. Stanford: Stanford University Press.

Ortner, Sherry. 1984. Theory in Anthropology Since the Sixties. *Comparative Studies in Society and History 26*:126–166.

Ortner, Sherry. 1989. *High Religion: A Cultural and Political History of Sherpa Buddhism.* Princeton: Princeton University Press.

Peacock, James L., and Dorothy C. Holland. 1993. The Narrated Self: Life Stories in Process. *Ethos 21*(4):367–383.

Pelto, Pertti J., and Gretel H. Pelto. 1978. *Anthropological Research: The Structure of Inquiry.* Cambridge: Cambridge University Press.

Perlmutter, David D. 1994. Visual Historical Methods: Problems, Prospects, Applications. *Historical Methods 27*:167–184.

Pitkin, Donald S. 1985. *The House that Giacomo Built: History of an Italian Family, 1898–1978.* Cambridge: Cambridge University Press.

Pitt, David C. 1972. *Using Historical Sources in Anthropology and Sociology.* New York: Holt, Rinehart and Winston.

Powers, Marla N. 1986. *Oglala Women: Myth, Ritual, and Reality.* Chicago: University of Chicago Press.

Poyer, Lin. 1994. *The Ngatik Massacre: History and Identity on a Micronesian Atoll.* Washington, DC: Smithsonian Institution Press.

Price, Richard. 1983. *First-Time: The Historical Vision of an Afro-American People.* Baltimore: The Johns Hopkins Press.

Price, Richard. 1990. *Alabi's World.* Baltimore: The Johns Hopkins Press.

Rogers, Susan Carol. 1992. When the Shoe Fits: Census Data, Oral History, and Stem Families in Southwest France. *Historical Methods 25*:20–27.

Rosaldo, Renato. 1980. *Ilongot Headhunting, 1883–1974: A Study in Society and History.* Stanford: Stanford University Press.

Roseberry, William. 1983. *Coffee and Capitalism in the Venezuelan Andes.* Austin: University of Texas Press.

Roseberry, William. 1989. *Anthropologies and Histories.* New Brunswick, NJ: Rutgers University Press.

Rosenberg, Harriet G. 1988. *A Negotiated World: Three Centuries of Change in a French Alpine Community.* Toronto: University of Toronto Press.

Rosenwald, George C., and Richard L. Ochberg. 1992. *Storied Lives: The Cultural Politics of Self-Understanding.* New Haven: Yale University Press.

Ruggles, Steven. 1993. Concessions of a Microsimulator: Problems in Modeling the Demography of Kinship. *Historical Methods 26*:161–169.

Ryder, Norman. 1965. The Cohort as a Concept in the Study of Social Change. *American Sociological Review 30*:843–861.

Sabean, David. 1970. Household Formation and Geographical Mobility: A Family Register Study for Wurttemberg Village, 1760–1900. *Annales de Démographie Historique*, pp. 75–294.

Sahlins, Marshall. 1981. *Historical Metaphors and Mythical Realities: Structure in the Early History of the Sandwich Islands Kingdom.* Ann Arbor: University of Michigan Press.

Sahlins, Marshall. 1983. Other Times, Other Customs: The Anthropology of History. *American Anthropologist 85*:517–544.

Sahlins, Marshall. 1985. *Islands of History*. Chicago: University of Chicago Press.

Sahlins, Marshall. 1991. The Return of the Event, Again: With Reflections on the Beginnings of the Great Fijian War of 1843 to 1855 Between the Kingdoms of Bau and Rewa. In *Clio in Oceania*. Aletta Biersack, ed. Pp. 37–99. Washington, DC: Smithsonian Institution Press.

Sahlins, Marshall. 1995. *How Natives Think: About Captain Cook For Example*. Chicago: University of Chicago Press.

Schapera, I. 1962. Should Anthropologists Be Historians? *Journal of the Royal Anthropological Institute 92*:143–156.

Schneider, Jane C., and Peter T. Schneider. 1976. *Culture and Political Economy in Western Sicily*. New York: Academic Press.

Schneider, Jane C., and Peter T. Schneider. 1996. *Festival of the Poor: Fertility Decline and the Ideology of Class in Sicily, 1860–1980*. Tucson: University of Arizona Press.

Sheridan, Mary, and Jane Salaff, eds. 1987. *Chinese Working Women*. Bloomington: Indiana University Press.

Shoemaker, Nancy. 1992. The Census as Civilizer. *Historical Methods 25*:4–11.

Shostak, Marjorie. 1981. *Nisa: The Life and Words of a !Kung Woman*. Cambridge: Harvard University Press.

Sider, Gerald M. 1986. *Culture and Class in Anthropology and History: A Newfoundland Illustration*. Cambridge: Cambridge University Press.

Silverblatt, Irene. 1987. *Moon, Sun, and Witches: Gender Ideologies and Class in Inca and Colonial Peru*. Princeton: Princeton University Press.

Silverman, Marilyn, and P. H. Gulliver. 1992. *Approaching the Past: Historical Anthropology Through Irish Case Studies*. New York: Columbia University Press.

Silverman, Sydel. 1979. On the Uses of History in Anthropology: The Palio of Siena. *American Ethnologist 6*:413–436.

Silverman, Sydel. 1986. Anthropology and History: Understanding the Boundaries. *Historical Methods 19*:123–126.

Skinner, G. William. 1957. *Chinese Society in Thailand: An Analytical History*. Ithaca: Cornell University Press.

Skocpol, Theda. 1984. Emerging Agendas and Recurrent Strategies in Historical Sociology. In *Vision and Method in Historical Sociology*. Theda Skocpol, ed. Pp. 356–391. Cambridge: Cambridge University Press.

Steckel, Richard H. 1994. Census Manuscript Schedules Matched with Property Tax Lists: A Source of Information on Long-Term Trends in Wealth Inequality. *Historical Methods 27*:71–85.

Stockard, Janice E. 1989. *Daughters of the Canton Delta: Marriage Patterns and Economic Strategies in South China, 1860–1930*. Stanford: Stanford University Press.

Stolcke, Verena. 1988. *Coffee Planters, Workers and Wives: Class Conflict and Gender Relations on São Paulo Plantations, 1850–1980.* New York: St. Martins Press.

Strobel, Margaret. 1983. Slavery and Reproductive Labor in Mombasa. In *Women and Slavery in Africa.* Claire C. Robertson and Martin A. Klein, eds. Pp. 111–129. Madison: University of Wisconsin Press.

Sturtevant, William C. 1968. Anthropology, History and Ethnohistory. In *Introduction to Cultural Anthropology: Essays in the Scope and Methods of the Science of Man.* James Clifton, ed. Pp. 451–475. Boston: Houghton Mifflin.

Szabo, Joyce M. 1994. Shields and Lodges, Warriors and Chiefs: Kiowa Drawings as Historical Records. *Ethnohistory 41*:1–24.

Taylor, Lawrence. 1983. *Dutchmen on the Bay: The Ethnohistory of a Contractual Community.* Philadelphia: University of Pennsylvania Press.

Taylor, Lawrence. 1985. The Priest and the Agent: Social Drama and Class Consciousnness in the West of Ireland. *Comparative Studies in Society and History 27*:696–712.

Taylor, Lawrence. 1992. The Languages of Belief: Nineteenth-Century Religious Discourse in Southwest Donegal. In *Approaching the Past: Historical Anthropology Through Irish Case Studies.* Marilyn Silverman and P. H. Gulliver, eds. Pp. 142–175. New York: Columbia University Press.

Thompson, Paul. 1988. *The Voice of the Past: Oral History,* 2d ed. Oxford: Oxford University Press.

Tilly, Charles. 1981. *As Sociology Meets History.* New York: Academic Press.

Tonkin, Elizabeth. 1992. *Narrating Our Pasts: The Social Construction of Oral History.* Cambridge: Cambridge University Press.

Townsend, Leslie H. 1990. Out of Silence: Writing Interactive Women's Life Histories in Africa. *History in Africa 17*:351–358.

Trevor-Roper, H. H. 1965. *The Rise of Christian Europe.* New York: Harcourt, Brace and World.

Trigger, Bruce. 1976. *The Children of Aataentsic: A History of the Huron People to 1660.* Montreal: McGill-Queen's University Press.

Turner, Victor. 1957. *Schism and Continuity in an African Society.* Manchester, England: Manchester University Press.

Turner, Victor. 1974. Hidalgo: History as Social Drama. In *Dramas, Fields and Metaphors.* Pp. 98–155. Ithaca: Cornell University Press.

Vansina, Jan. 1970. Culture Through Time. In *A Handbook of Method in Cultural Anthropology.* Raoul Naroll and Ronald Cohen, eds. Pp. 165–179. New York: The Natural History Press.

Vansina, Jan. 1985. *Oral Tradition as History.* Madison: University of Wisconsin Press.

Vincent, Joan. 1992. A Political Orchestration of the Irish Famine: County Fermanagh, May 1847. In *Approaching the Past: Historical Anthropology Through Irish Case Studies.*

Marilyn Silverman and P. H. Gulliver, eds. Pp. 75–98. New York: Columbia University Press.

Wallace, Anthony F. C. 1972. *Rockdale: The Growth of an American Village in the Early Industrial Revolution*. New York: W. W. Norton.

Wallace, Anthony F. C. 1981. *St. Clair: A Nineteenth-Century Coal Town's Experience with a Disaster-Prone Industry*. Ithaca: Cornell University Press.

Watson, Lawrence C., and Maria Barbara Watson-Franke. 1985. *Interpreting Life Histories: An Anthropological Inquiry*. New Brunswick, NJ: Rutgers University Press.

Weiner, Annette B., and Jane Schneider. 1989. *Cloth and Human Experience*. Washington, DC: Smithsonian Press.

Wells, Robert V. 1978. On the Dangers of Constructing Artificial Cohorts in Times of Rapid Social Change. *Journal of Interdisciplinary History 9*:103–110.

West, Barbara A. 1992. Women's Diaries as Ethnographic Resources. *Journal of Narrative and Life History 2*:333–354.

White, Luise. 1995. "They Could Make Their Victims Dull": Genders and Genres, Fantasies and Cures in Colonial Southern Uganda. *American Historical Review 100*:1379–1402.

Willigan, J. Dennis, and Katherine Lynch. 1982. *Sources and Methods of Historical Demography*. New York: Academic Press.

Winchester, Ian. 1992. What Every Historian Needs to Know About Record Linkage for the Microcomputer Era. *Historical Methods 25*:149–179.

Wolf, Arthur P., and Chieh-shan Huang 1980. *Marriage and Adoption in China, 1845–1945*. Stanford: Stanford University Press.

Wolf, Eric R. 1957. Closed Corporate Peasant Communities in Mesoamerica and Central Java. *Southwestern Journal of Anthropology 13*:1–13.

Wolf, Eric R. 1982. *Europe and the People Without History*. Berkeley: University of California Press.

Wright, Marcia. 1993. *Strategies of Slaves and Women: Life Stories from East/Central Africa*. New York: Lillian Barber Press.

Yans McLaughlin, Virginia. 1990. Metaphors of Self in History: Subjectivity, Oral Narrative, and Immigration Studies. In *Immigration Reconsidered: History, Sociology, and Politics*. Virginia Yans-McLaughlin, ed. Pp. 254–290. New York: Oxford University Press.

PART III
INTERPRETING INFORMATION

W. PENN HANDWERKER
STEPHEN P. BORGATTI

Fifteen

Reasoning with Numbers

This chapter explains the reasoning behind numerical methods and illustrates their application to questions we ask when we carry out ordinary ethnographic research. *Numerical methods* encompass a wide variety of interlinked techniques that range from basic mathematical tools (for example, matrix algebra) and simple descriptive statistics (modes, medians, means, percentages, ratios), to visualization and data-reduction techniques (for example, multidimensional scaling and factor analysis), to classical statistical tools (for example, t-tests and regression). *Numerical reasoning* consists of answering important research questions with appropriate numerical methods.[1]

Most of the techniques we illustrate go well beyond the content of introductory statistics courses. Nonetheless, we hope to show that even simple forms of numerical reasoning add important components to ethnographic research, that more sophisticated methods answer questions that may prove crucial in your research, and that explicit reasoning with numbers reveals things you'd otherwise miss. Since this chapter can't substitute for formal study, we direct you to literature that can help you master techniques you find intriguing.

Answering Questions We Ask in the Field

All ethnographic research begins by collecting data from one person. When we go to the next person, we always find something different, as well as something much is much the same. And so it goes. We keep track of similarities, note variability, and keep at it until we no longer find significant cultural or behavioral variability. Then, we construct a story from the inferential generalizations we arrived at about the people we worked with: about their lives and the circumstances in which they have lived; about what those people now think, feel, and do; about who agreed with whom about what and to what extent; and about who is similar to whom and to what extent, and how they differ from others and to what extent.

This considerably simplified account highlights eight activities entailed by ordinary ethnographic fieldwork:

1. We *measure*. Measurement transforms sensory information into intelligible mental constructions. Measurement thus refers to what we do when we make and record observations about what we experience in the field. Much ethnography entails altering the constructions we took into the field in ways that improve their correspondence with those used by the people in our field setting. We also may create new ways of thinking about the world to help us better understand what we experience in the field. In either event, we aspire to an understanding of what we see during fieldwork that corresponds with what our informants tried to teach us and take that understanding a step further. This corresponds with the research design issue of *internal validity* (see Campbell and Stanley 1966).

   - We measure two fundamentally different kinds of data: *cultural* data and *life experience* data. *Cultural* data, as we use the term, are measurements of the systems of mental constructions people use to interpret themselves and the world around them and of the behavior isomorphic with those systems of meaning. *Life experience* data, as we use the term, are measurements of individual characteristics (like age, gender, height, or weight) and events or processes that mark the life experience of particular people (like how many years a person spent in school, whether they grow cash crops, if they grew up in poor or wealthy households, how often they use condoms when having sex, or the degree to which they experienced one or another form of violence as a child). We highlight the operationally important differences between these two kinds of data in later sections of this paper.

   - *Measurement error* constitutes a principal source of invalid research findings. Intensive and prolonged interaction predicated on personal relationships with informants is one check on this source of error. *Triangulation* using a variety of data collection and analysis tools to address any one question or issue helps even more (McNabb 1990).

2. We pay attention to *variables*. Variables consist of phenomena that may vary from one observation to another. Variation in a phenomenon may exhibit qualitatively different assignments of meaning. The variable *kin* may be brother, sister, husband, or wife, for example. *Gender* may be woman, man, girl, or boy.

Variation may exhibit quantity. *Family size* may be small, medium, or large (an *ordinal* form of measurement, which only entails relative rank); or 5, 10, and 20 (a *ratio* form of measurement characterized by a true zero, which allows any two values to be expressed as a meaningful ratio of the other).[2]

3. We aim to identify *what is typical* in one sense or another. For one purpose or another, we may want to know

   • How *most* people conceptualize specific people, events, and processes (measured explicitly by a statistic called the *mode*).

   • The age at which, on average (measured explictly by a statistic called the *mean*), as well as how, children become adults, and people first have sex, marry, give birth, and become grandparents.

   • Important and unimportant people, events, and processes; or people who move into adulthood, first have sex, marry, give birth, and become grandparents early or late. The warrant for judgments about relative placement consists of a middle point (measured explicitly by a statistic called the *median*) that distinguishes important from unimportant, or early from late.

   • The *median* is one of a set of statistics called *quantiles*, which measure relative placement in a distribution. The median, for example, is the 50th percentile. Other quantiles include the 10th percentile (which identifies the location below which lies the earliest or lowest set of cases), the 25th and the 75th percentiles (between which the middle 50% of the cases lie), and the 90th percentile (which identifies the location above which lies the latest or highest set of cases).

4. We evaluate *variation from what is typical*. For one purpose or another, we may want to know

   • How commonly we find a particular way of conceptualizing specific people, events, and processes. We can explicitly measure how commonly something occurs as a simple count (*frequency*) of the number of people who take one point of view or another. The *modal frequency* is the point of view with the highest count. More usefully, we can express this number as a *proportion* (the modal frequency/the total count), a *percentage* (100*a proportion), or a *ratio* (for example, the number of people who express the most common point of view/the number of people who express any other point of view). We might be inclined to generalize a consensus if 80% of the people we talk with express the most common (*modal*) point of view, for example. We probably would infer much cultural diversity if we find many ways of thinking about an issue and only 20% express the most common (*modal*) view. In the former case, the modal view occurs (80%/20%), four times (400%) more often than any alternative; in the latter, it occurs (20%/80%), 25% less often than the alternatives. Great variation suggests the operation of many contingencies that influence how people conceptualize themselves and the world around them. Little variation suggests the operation of significant constraints.

- How much variation, on average, exists in the age at which children become adults and people first have sex, marry, give birth, and become grandparents (measured explicitly by a statistic called the *standard deviation*). Great variation suggests the operation of many contingencies that influence when and, perhaps, how life course events occur. Little variation suggests the operation of significant constraints bearing on life course events.

- The earliest point at which an event occurs in people's lives (the *minimum*), the latest point that event occurs (the *maximum*), the distance between these points (the *range*), and the relative frequency with which an event occurs between these points (a variable's *frequency distribution*). The distribution of events may be *skewed* over a given range of occurrence—most people marry first at relatively young ages, but some marry first late in life, for example. A distribution may be *symmetrical*, or approximately so, as might be the case for the age at which children undergo one or another puberty rite.

- Events that occur unusually early or late (*outliers*) relative to others.

  Pictures of the distribution of a variable—*stem-and-leaf plots, box plots,* or *quantile plots,* for example—make it easy to evaluate these salient characteristics of a variable's distribution.

5. We try to identify the people, events, and processes that go together and those that don't. *Similarity* coefficients, each in different ways, explicitly measure the extent to which two phenomena go together or not. *Dissimilarity* coefficients, each in different ways, explicitly measure the extent to which two phenomena don't go together. Explicit measurements of relationships among even a few people, events, and processes produce hundreds if not thousands of details, which human minds appear particularly unsuited for comprehending. Tools like *factor analysis, cluster analysis, multidimensional scaling, and correspondence analysis,* reduce this complexity and transform these details into pictures, which human minds appear particularly well suited for comprehending.

6. We try to identify who agrees with whom about what and to what extent, which we can measure explicitly with *similarity* coefficients. A set of techniques called *consensus analysis,* which uses a specific form of *factor analysis,* tests for the existence of cultural consensus.

7. We aspire to an understanding of what we see during fieldwork that goes beyond the few people we had a chance to learn from. This aim corresponds with the issue of *external validity* (to whom, if anyone, can we generalize?) and recognizes that, having studied with only a handful of teachers, we generalize to a community of hundreds, perhaps hundreds of thousands of people we never met. This goal signals the difference between using statistics to *describe*

characteristics of the people we spoke with (*descriptive* statistics) to using the same statistics to *infer* something about a larger population (*inferential* statistics). Research design and sampling procedures address these questions (see Kish [1965] for sampling of life experience data and Handwerker [1998] for sampling of cultural phenomena).

- All data collection entails sampling—gathering information from only *some* of an indefinitely large number of people, places, and times. Gathering information from other people, or the same people at different times (the next day) and places (next door), almost always yields different findings even when population characteristics (*parameters*) don't change. We can't tell from looking at differences—whether they appear in our fieldnotes or in survey results—whether they represent something real (people changed, people living in different neighborhoods think and act differently) or not (people haven't changed, and people living in different neighborhoods think and act pretty much the same). *Statistical tests* yield *probabilities* that tell us how often specific differences could occur merely by chance.

- *Inferential* data analysis consists of *measuring* characteristics of an unbiased ("random") sample of independent cases, computing *statistics*, and *estimating* population parameters. So long as you draw an unbiased ("random") sample of independent cases, any statistic (identified by Latin letters, like b or mean) can be taken as a *point estimate* of a population parameter (identified by Greek letters, like β or μ). The statistic (which you compute) constitutes your single best guess at the parameter (which you can't compute). You can also compute *confidence intervals* for a statistic. Ninety-five percent confidence intervals computed for 100 different samples of the same size from the same population will contain the population parameter 95 times, for example. Classical statistical tests (*chi-squared, t-tests, F-ratios*) yield valid probabilities that tell you how often to expect a specific finding just by random sampling fluctuations—so long as you test an explicit hypothesis.[3]

- The socially constructed nature of cultural phenomena, however, means that any one person who knows about a particular cultural phenomenon participates with other experts in its construction. This means that a random sample of people does not constitute a random sample of the cultural phenomenon you want to study, since talking with any one person yields data very much like that provided any other (see Handwerker and Wozniak 1997; Handwerker et al. 1997). Although case-dependence like this means that standard kinds of statistical tests won't give us the information we need for valid analysis of cultural data, Weller (1987) has shown that the Spearman-Brown Prophesy Formula can be applied to informants rather than items, which allows us to measure the reliability and validity of the cultural data we report. Ethnographic findings based on information from small numbers of informants (3–36, depending on the average level of agreement), exhibit exceptional reliability (.90–.99) and validity (.95–~1).

- *Bootstrap* (Efrom and Tibshirani 1991; Mooney and Duval 1993) and *jacknife* (Tukey 1958) procedures create sampling distributions for statistics from the data at hand, and yield valid parameter estimates for life experience data for situations in which the theoretical sampling distribution of a statistic, on which classical statistical tests rely, remains unknown (for example, Handwerker 1988). *Permutation tests* give valid probabilities (Fisher 1935; Edginton 1980) for any set of data. Permutation tests yield exact probabilities by expressing the observed findings (and all more extreme findings) as a ratio of all possible events. ANTHROPAC (Borgatti 1992) offers permutation tests; SYSTAT 7.0 (Wilkinson 1997) has integrated bootstrap and jacknife options into its regression module, and others where appropriate.

8. We may go further than mere description to try to determine why and how the patterns and variability we found might have come into being, why and how they persist over time, and why and under what circumstances they may change. We aim to explain variability in culture and behavior as a function of variability in experience, and search for concrete events and circumstances that shape those experiences. We also understand that what people think and do must reflect not only their individual life history, but broader regional and global histories of people, events, and social interaction into which they were born and in which they grew up. So we try to identify events, circumstances, and processes that provide one set of choices to some people and a different set of choices to others. We ask individuals to identify life experiences that were significant to them, and to help us understand why those experiences were significant.

- Similarity coefficients and statistical tests applied to data like these can tell us what goes with what and how strongly, and thus provide a warrant for believing that a given relationship is *real*, not merely a figment of our imagination (McEwan 1963). Handwerker and Crosbie (1982) showed that the relationship between gender and social dominance (men tend to be dominant over women) is real, for example. Unfortunately, analysis of the relationship between only two variables (*zero-order analysis*) tells us next to nothing in which we can have confidence. Adding another variable to the analysis may produce dramatic changes—a zero-order similarity coefficient may disappear, grow stronger, or change from positive to negative.

• Research that goes beyond cultural description thus raises *internal validity* issues that go beyond the simple problem of *measurement error* mentioned earlier. Warrant for inferring that a relationship is *determinant* as well as *real* (McEwan 1963) requires us to isolate a suspected relationship so we can tell whether or not it exists, and its strength, when we rule out the other internal validity possibilities. *Experimental research designs* (for example, Campbell and Stanley 1966; Cook and Campbell 1979) were created to do just that. Although ethnographic research rarely allows for the use of experimental designs, experimental design principles apply to all research. *Multiple regression* techniques approximate the goals of experimental designs and have many uses in ethnographic research. Handwerker and Crosbie (1982) used a form of multiple regression called *path analysis* to show that, although the relationship between gender and dominance was real, it wasn't determinant: social dominance followed from control over access to resources and, independently, from relative size. Larger people tended to dominate smaller people. Men tend to dominate women only because, generally, men are larger than women. But just as larger women tend to dominate smaller women and larger men tend to dominate smaller men, larger women tend to dominate smaller men.

What Numerical Analysis Does

Numerical methods thus constitute nothing more than explicit tools of data collection and analysis that address core research questions: "Did we get it right?" and "To whom, if anyone, can we validly generalize?" The operationally important difference between one or another numerical method is the question it answers. Each technique answers a different question. Table 1 shows the correspondence between specific numerical methods and specific questions we ask in the course of conducting ordinary ethnographic research. *Numerical reasoning* consists of answering important ethnographic questions with the appropriate numerical method.

Research consists of a search for ways to distinguish mental constructions that consist largely of error from constructions that consist of less. *Validity* consists of a relationship between the definitions of specific mental constructions and specific observations. It follows that we assess data and finding validity with reference to whether or not, or the degree to which, specific mental constructions correspond with specific observations. Being explicit helps immensely when you and others try to find errors in judgment that, once identified, prod you to think about the world in new, more interesting, and, perhaps, more useful ways. Judgment errors come in three main ways. First, you may construct your study phenomena from the wrong components. Second, you may construct arguments with questionable assumptions

TABLE 1

*Correspondence Between Selected Numerical Analysis Tools
and Questions Anthropologists Try to Answer*

NUMERICAL ANALYSIS TOOLS	RESEARCH QUESTIONS					
	Who agrees with whom about what and to what agree?	What's the agreement about?	What's there to be explained?	Who (what) acts (looks) like whom (what) and to what degree?	What goes with what and to what degree?	Can we see a suspected relationship even after we control for everything else we can think of?
Consensus Analysis	▓		▓			
Multidimensional Scaling (MDS)	▓	▓			▓	
Quadratic Assignment (QAP)	▓			▓	▓	
Similarity and dissimilarity coefficients	▓	▓		▓		
Cluster Analysis	▓	▓		▓	▓	
Correspondence Analysis	▓	▓		▓	▓	
Perceptual Mapping/PROFIT Analysis	▓			▓	▓	
Factor Analysis	▓	▓			▓	
Simple Summary Statistics	▓		▓			
Numerical Transformations						▓
Graphical Analysis Tools for Single Variables			▓			▓
Graphical Analysis Tools for 2 or More Variables			▓		▓	▓
Survival Analysis			▓			▓
Ordinary Least Squares (OLS) Multiple Regression			▓			▓
Logistic Multiple Regression			▓			▓
Probabilities	▓	▓	▓	▓	▓	▓

or make logical errors. Third, you may mistake what you would like to be with what is. The first source of judgment errors constitutes the focus of debates and arguments over theory. Explicit identification of the assumptions used to construct different theories helps clarify what arguments are all about and uncover logical errors and thus minimize the second source of error. But arguments over logically sound theory are resolvable—albeit only temporarily—only by reference to assessments of the fit between specific constructs and specific observations. Explicit numerical reasoning helps minimize this third source of judgment error and allows us to see things we'd otherwise miss.

Cultural Data: A Look at Families and Kin Relations

Danielle Wozniak's recent research among foster mothers in the United States (Wozniak 1997) addresses a question at the core of cultural anthropology since its inception: What is a "family?" We shall use her data as a running example to illustrate the numerical methods most suited for the analysis of cultural data.

Like most ethnographic research, Wozniak relied on extensive participant-observation over a three-year period, involving day-long periods of observation, two–three hours of taped interviews, and active involvement in the lives of foster mothers. One of the most important themes that emerged in the texts of daily conversations and transcribed interviews involved criteria her informants used to talk about themselves and other women as "mothers" and how other people—husbands, children, social workers, friends, and relatives—used or didn't use these criteria in equivalent ways. She felt these women telling her that how they assessed the relative importance of motherhood criteria was at least as important—probably more important—than knowing which criteria they used to make sense of themselves and their activities as mothers.

Wozniak asked women to evaluate the importance of nine criteria her informants had identified as ones used, not used, or used differently, when they thought about themselves and other women as mothers, carrying out mothering activities. These criteria included that a child: (1) be born to a woman; (2) be born to a family member; (3) contribute work or income; (4) be loved by a woman; (5) be taken care of by a woman; (6) live with a woman for a long time; (7) be adopted; (8) be thought of by the woman as being the child's mother; and (9) that the child think of the woman as her or his mother. These questions thus asked about conventionally recognized legal, biological, and instrumental criteria as well as self-defined affective criteria that foster mothers had mentioned. To avoid having the order of presentation influence women's responses, Wozniak randomized the order in which women were asked these questions.

Sixty-nine foster mothers—Black, white, rich, poor, old, and young—rated each criterion on a four-point scale from "not at all important" to "very important."

Scales like this can be treated either as an ordinal sequence of quantities or qualitatively different assignments of meaning. In most subsequent analyses, we treat the points on these scales as qualitatively different assignments of meaning.

Matrices and Matrix Operations

All numerical analysis begins with the construction of a data matrix. Typically, matrix rows correspond to individual informants (*cases*) and the columns express what they tell us or what we see (*variables* and their *attributes* or *values*). Each column consists of a vector of numbers or characters, and a matrix consists of a collection of vectors. The following matrix, for example, shows a portion of Wozniak's data on the race of her foster mother informants and their rating of various affective motherhood criteria. Wozniak's data comprise a *cross-sectional profile matrix*. Her data are cross-sectional in that they were collected for a specific point in time. The data also include specific information for each individual informant and thus give us a profile of each. If Wozniak had collected data on the same variables for two or three sequential periods in time (for example, Day 1, Day 10; or 1985, 1995), her matrix would consist of *panel* data (for example, see Markus 1979). If Wozniak collected data on the same variables for an increasing number of sequential time periods (for example, Day 1, Day 2, Day 3 . . . Day k; or 1950, 1955, 1960 . . . 1995), her matrix would consist of *time-series* data.

RACE$	AFFEC1	AFFEC2	AFFEC3	AFFEC4
W	4	4	4	4
B	4	4	4	4
B	4	4	4	4
W	4	4	3	3
W	4	4	4	2
B	4	4	4	3
B	4	4	4	4
B	4	4	4	2
W	4	4	4	4
W	3	4	4	3

Numerical analysis consists of operations carried out on matrix rows or columns (*vectors*) or both (for example, Namboodiri 1984). For example, summing each column of numbers and dividing by the number of cases provides a convenient summary (the average, or *mean*) of the importance of each motherhood criterion. Counting the number of Ws and Bs tells us the number of Euro and African American women in the sample. Dividing one of these sums by the total number of cases tells us the proportion of Euro and African American women Wozniak interviewed; multiplying that number by 100 converts them to percentages (47.8%

of her informants identified themselves as African American). We might want to recode the affective criteria to create *binary* (sometimes called *dummy*) variables with only two values, "1" and "0." If we assign a "1" to any value greater than 2 and "0" for all other values, the sum for each row would tell us the number of criteria that each woman felt important. The average of 1s and 0s for any one motherhood criterion would tell us the proportion of women who felt it important.

When we apply other descriptive statistics mentioned earlier to Wozniak's data, we learn, among other things, that one person was a newly licensed foster mother who had not yet fostered a child (the minimum) and another had fostered around 250 children (the maximum); and that the women who answered her questions ranged in age from 28–78 and averaged 44 years of age, give or take (the standard deviation) about 9 years. Answers to questions like these help us evaluate the extent to which Wozniak's sample differs from all currently licensed foster mothers, but they don't tell us anything interesting about the central question: What criteria do you apply to determine whether or not, or the extent to which, you are a mother? We need to apply other matrix operations.

Figure 1, for example, juxtaposes stem-and-leaf and box-and-whisker plots of four variables, one representing biological criteria of motherhood (gave birth to the child), one representing instrumental criteria (a child's contribution of work or income), one representing legal criteria (adoption), and one representing affective criteria (giving care to the child) (see, for example, Tukey 1977; Cleveland and McGill 1985; and SYSTAT's graphics module documentation). Stem-and-leaf plots identify the minimum and maximum scores (1 and 4), the median, and the upper and lower hinges (the 25th and 75th percentiles). The plot stem identifies the values (1, 2, 3, 4); one leaf appears next to each value for each informant who reported that assessment. Box plots tell us the location of the middle 50% of cases with a box. These boxes are notched to show an interval that contains the value of the middle case (median) for the entire population 95% of the time (a *confidence interval*). Whiskers extend to the lowest and the highest 25% of cases. Unusually high or low cases (*outliers*), as on the last plot, appear as dots. Examination of these plots reveals, rather dramatically, that Wozniak's informants expressed much variation in their assessments of the importance of biological, instrumental, and legal criteria of motherhood, and little about the importance of an affective criterion. Indeed, so many women rated the affective motherhood criteria as "very important" that the median and both hinge cases are buried at a single point, and the box-plot shows no box. All other ratings (3, 2, or 1) constitute outliers.

Assessing Similarities and Differences

This finding raises two questions: (1) Do these women see these criteria as the same kinds of things, or differently?; and (2) Which women agree with which others

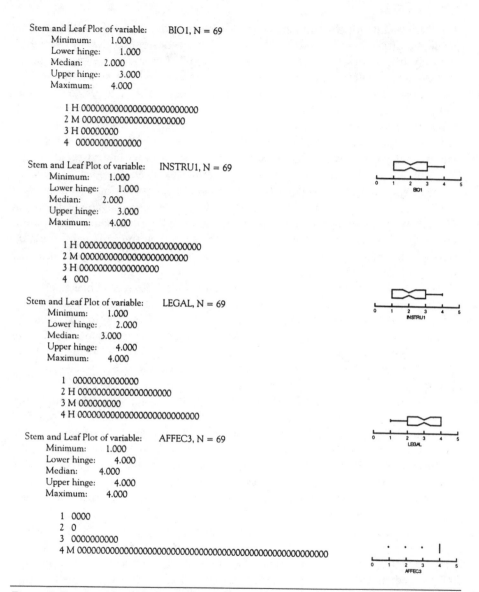

Stem and Leaf Plot of variable: BIO1, N = 69
    Minimum: 1.000
    Lower hinge: 1.000
    Median: 2.000
    Upper hinge: 3.000
    Maximum: 4.000

        1 H 000000000000000000000000000
        2 M 000000000000000000000000
        3 H 00000000
        4 00000000000000

Stem and Leaf Plot of variable: INSTRU1, N = 69
    Minimum: 1.000
    Lower hinge: 1.000
    Median: 2.000
    Upper hinge: 3.000
    Maximum: 4.000

        1 H 0000000000000000000000000000
        2 M 00000000000000000000000
        3 H 0000000000000000
        4 000

Stem and Leaf Plot of variable: LEGAL, N = 69
    Minimum: 1.000
    Lower hinge: 2.000
    Median: 3.000
    Upper hinge: 4.000
    Maximum: 4.000

        1 00000000000000
        2 H 00000000000000000000000
        3 M 000000000
        4 H 00000000000000000000000000000

Stem and Leaf Plot of variable: AFFEC3, N = 69
    Minimum: 1.000
    Lower hinge: 4.000
    Median: 4.000
    Upper hinge: 4.000
    Maximum: 4.000

        1 0000
        2 0
        3 0000000000
        4 M 00000000000000000000000000000000000000000000000000000000000

Figure 1. Stem-and-leaf and box plots of foster mother's assessments of the importance of different mothering criteria.

about the nature and relative importance of these criteria? Matrix operations that tell us how much any two cases or variables exhibit similarity or difference yield a wide variety of similarity and dissimilarity coefficients (for example, Sneath and Sokal

1973). Common *similarity coefficients* include Pearson's r (*the* correlation coefficient), r^2, and, for binary data, Driver's G, the positive matching coefficient, the simple matching coefficient, and Jaccard's coefficient. Common *dissimilarity coefficients* include Euclidean distances, city-block distances, positive nonmatching coefficients, and simple nonmatching coefficients.

For ratio data,[4] Pearson's r, which tells us the extent to which variation in one phenomenon accompanies variation in another, varies between ± 1.00. Positive coefficients tell you that one variable goes up when the other goes up; negative coefficients tell you that one variable goes up when the other goes down; values close to ± 0.00 tell you that what one variable does has nothing to do with what the other variable does. The coefficient of determination, r^2, tells the proportion of variation shared by two phenomena. Euclidean distance coefficients express the square root of the summed squared distances. The Euclidean distance is zero when the variables are identical and gets larger as the values of the two variables get more and more different. City-block distance coefficients just constitute the sum of the absolute distances (like the number of miles between cities, or the length of different city blocks).

Similarity and dissimilarity coefficients for binary data (present-absent) come from cross-tabulation tables like the following:

		X		
		1	0	
Y	1	a	b	a+b
	0	c	d	c+d
		a+c	b+d	N

Y and X represent variables, like whether or not a person assesses "giving birth" or "adoption" as important criteria for "motherhood." The letters *a,b,c,* and *d* represent the number of informants who fall into particular cells of the table. For example, the value of *a* would tell us the number of foster mothers who thought that both "giving birth" and "adoption" constituted important motherhood criteria. The value of *d* would tell us the number of foster mothers who thought that neither "giving birth" nor "adoption" constituted important motherhood criteria. Sums across rows (*a+b, c+d*) and down columns (*a+c,b+d*) yield marginal frequencies, which sum to N, the total number of cases.

Positive matching coefficients tell you the number of times that X and Y share the presence of something (*a*) as a proportion of the total (N). Simple matching coefficients tell you the number of times that X and Y share both the presence and absence of something (*a+d*) as a proportion of the total (N). The dissimilarity positive and simple nonmatching coefficients constitute mirror images of their similarity cousins. By contrast, Driver's G and Jaccard's coefficients ignore phenomena X and Y do not share (the frequency of cell *d*). Matching coefficients, under some circumstances, make some people, households, societies, and organisms look similar largely because they share so little. To avoid this problem, Jaccard's coefficient tells you the number of times that X and Y share the presence of something (*a*) as a proportion of all of the times X and Y share something (*a+b+c*). Driver modified Pearson's correlation coefficient for binary data by eliminating the value of *d*:

$$\text{Driver's G} = a/ (\text{sqr}(a+b)*\text{sqr}(a+c))$$

Analysis of similarities or dissimilarities among sets of variables begins with the construction of matrices made up of similarity or dissimilarity coefficients, like the following Pearson correlation matrix for the motherhood criteria Wozniak studied.

The unities (1.000) across the diagonal just tell us the obvious—variables covary perfectly with themselves. The interesting coefficients tell us the degree to which women assessed the different motherhood criteria in identical ways. The correlation coefficient of .585 tells us that Wozniak's informants assessed giving birth (BIO1) and children contributing work and money (INSTRU1) in reasonably similar ways. They assessed children contributing work and money (INSTRU1) and giving care to children (AFFEC3) in essentially unrelated ways (the correlation of .041 is very close to zero).

	BIO1	INSTRU1	LEGAL	AFFEC3
BIO1	1.000			
INSTRU1	0.585	1.000		
LEGAL	0.445	0.361	1.000	
AFFEC3	0.246	0.041	0.308	1.000

Number of observations: 69

It's hard to say much more with confidence about the relationships among all variables. Eye-balling the coefficients suggests that women tended to assess the importance of biological, instrumental, and legal criteria in similar ways, in ways related little if at all to their assessment of affective criteria. But the correlation of .308 between the legal criterion and the affective criterion clouds this judgment. To make clearer evaluations of how women made their assessments, we need to analyze a matrix showing the interrelationships of all nine variables simultaneously. Trying to make judgments about 36 similarity coefficients at once just intensifies the information overload we've stumbled into (Miller 1956). Moreover, sets of similarity coefficients may exhibit relationships due solely to chance (for example, see Handwerker 1991).

Data-reduction techniques that make this information load manageable include factor analysis (see Rummel 1970; Harman 1976; see also Driver and Schuessler

1957), cluster analysis (see Sokal and Sneath 1963; Sneath and Sokal 1973; Aldenderfer and Blashfield 1984), and multidimensional scaling (see Kruskal and Wish 1978). These techniques also help us distinguish matrices with *structure* (relationships among variables that don't exist solely by chance) from matrices with none (relationships that exist solely by chance).

Factor Analysis

Let's turn to the question of whether women assessed the importance of biological, instrumental, and affective criteria in similar ways, in ways related little if at all to their assessment of affective criteria. If they did, that suggests that women experience and respond to biological, instrumental, and legal criteria in ways fundamentally different from the way in which women experience and respond to affective dimensions of motherhood. Indeed, distinctions like this may exist only on the edge of consciousness. Women might not have the words to describe such differences, which nonetheless may significantly influence how they experience and respond to the world, and shape their family relationships in fundamental ways.

Factor analysis constructs a small set of variables (*factors* or *principal components*) from additive combinations of existing similarities among variables or cases.[5] Each factor infers the existence of one or more underlying, unmeasured variables that might explain the observed pattern of similarities. Handwerker (1997), for instance, used factor analysis to show that people who live dramatically different lives—descendants of former plantation slaves who make a living in tourist economies in the West Indies and people who continue to hunt, gather, and herd in the Alaskan and Siberian Arctic—agree about components that comprise unitary phenomena legitimately called "violence" and "affection." In a factor analysis, the first principal component extracted accounts for the maximum amount of variance in a matrix. The second factor or principal component accounts for the maximum amount of the remaining variance. The subsequent principal components account for the maximum amount of the variance left by previously extracted factors.

Factor analysis output includes correlations between each factor and either your cases or variables, called *loadings*. The square of a loading tells you how much variability a case or variable shares with the unobserved variable represented by each factor. The sum of squared loadings for a factor (its *eigenvalue* or *latent root*) tells you how much variation *all* your cases or variables share with a factor. A factor's eigenvalue divided by the sum of eigenvalues for all factors expresses the factor's explanatory power as a proportion.

Look at the eigenvalues from a principal components analysis of the similarity matrix for all motherhood criteria (SYSTAT output):

1	2	3	4	5	6	7	8	9
3.908	1.714	0.936	0.764	0.567	0.425	0.292	0.256	0.138

Note that the eigenvalues drop precipitously after the first and level off after the second, where they fall below 1. Judgments about how many real factors a matrix may contain should reflect close analysis of the eigenvalues. Matrices that contain real underlying structure exhibit a very sharp drop in the size of eigenvalues and a clearly identifiable point at which eigenvalues level off (shown in *scree plots* [after the debris, called scree, that accumulates at the base of cliffs; see Figure 2]). Contrast the first scree plot with the second, which comes from eigenvalues generated by an identical principal components analysis of similarities among variables related only by chance.

The kinship data yielded only two of nine eigenvalues over 1.0 whereas the second set of data yielded five eigenvalues over 1.00, five under 1.00, and no perceptible scree. The differences between the two distinguish matrices containing real factors (like Wozniak's data on mothering) from matrices with no underlying structure (random relationships). Just by chance, sample items may show great similarity. Factor analysis of matrices like this will find some eigenvalues over 1.0 and some high loadings just by chance. But matrices that contain no real factors will generate random distributions of eigenvalues and loadings.

Latent Roots (Eigenvalues)

1	2	3	4	5	6	7	8	9	10
1.633	1.299	1.204	1.144	1.088	0.986	0.891	0.634	0.618	0.503

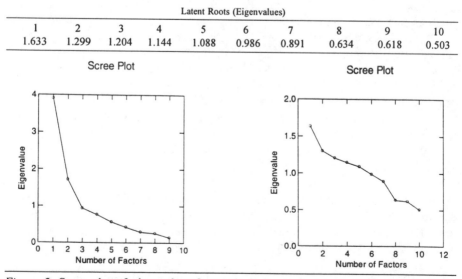

Figure 2. Scree plot of eigenvalues from principal components analysis of (left) foster mothers' assessments of the similarity among mothering criteria and (right) similarities among variables related only by chance.

Further analysis of Wozniak's kinship data focused on the first two factors identified in the scree plot in Figure 2. An operation called *rotation* clarifies the differences between factors. Rotation using the Varimax criterion maximizes the differences between the factors. The rotation process redistributes the proportion of variation each factor explains, but the total remains the same. Two factors account for just over 62% of the variability in these women's assessments of the relative importance of nine criteria bearing on mothering and mothering activities:

Rotated Loading Matrix (VARIMAX)

	1	2
BIO1	0.863	0.066
BIO2	0.851	0.125
LEGAL	0.709	0.332
INSTRU1	0.708	0.033
INSTRU2	0.544	0.436
AFFEC2	0.093	0.835
AFFEC1	0.018	0.798
AFFEC3	0.156	0.765
AFFEC4	0.321	0.690

Variance Explained by Components before Rotation

1	2
3.908	1.714

Percent of Total Variance Explained

1	2
43.425	19.048

"Variance" Explained by Rotated Components

1	2
2.907	2.716

Percent of Total Variance Explained

1	2
32.295	30.177

Note that this output also sorted the variables by loading size, for loadings equal to or larger than .5 (loadings of .5 or larger mean that a factor and a variable share at least 25% of the observed variance). BIO1, BIO2, LEGAL, INSTRU1, and INSTRU2 load highly on one factor; all AFFEC variables load highly on the other. These findings suggest that Wozniak's informants responded to formal biological, legal, and instrumental motherhood criteria in one way and responded to personal affective criteria in another. Cluster analysis gives similar results.

Cluster Analysis

Cluster analysis assigns cases or variables to groups based on relative similarity or dissimilarity. There are a large variety of clustering methods, based on different algorithms and different criteria for constructing groups.

In a study of the class structure of Mexican villages, for example, Allison Bingham (1995) used a *k-means cluster analysis* to show that the historical *ejidatario-avecendados*/landed-landless class structure had been completely reconfigured. K-means cluster methods split cases (households, in this instance) into hypothesized numbers of groups maximizing the differences between groups and minimizing the differences within groups. The *ejidatario-avecendados* (two-class) distinction held when she looked only at legal land ownership, but fell apart as she added other pertinent variables. What began historically as a two-class structure had acquired multiple levels. The wealthiest community members owned stores and/or drew on income from migrant family members, and turned liquidity into de facto land ownership, acquiring land from *ejidatarios* who had no other sources of credit for farm operations.

Probably the most commonly used clustering methods, however, use Johnson's hierarchical clustering technique, which itself contains several variations. The basic variants apply *single-link* or *complete-link* criteria to matrices of similarity or dissimilarity coefficients. Both variants begin by assigning each item being clustered (cases or variables) into a cluster by itself, yielding N clusters (where N is the number of items). Then it determines which pair of clusters is the most similar (or the least dissimilar) and combines the two, resulting in N−1 clusters.

This process continues until only one cluster remains, which contains all the items. The difference between single-link and complete-link methods consists of the criteria applied to determine similarity between existing pairs of clusters. Single linkage procedures match up cases or variables based on the similarity between a candidate member and any *one* existing member.

Complete linkage procedures match up cases or variables based on the similarity between a candidate member and *all* existing members. Figure 3 shows a complete linkage cluster analysis of women's assessment of motherhood criteria. The results tell us that women assessed affective criteria one way and biological, instrumental, and legal criteria in another. Contrast the complete linkage clusters of motherhood criteria with complete link clusters of random relationships.

Multidimensional Scaling (MDS)

Multidimensional scaling (MDS) transforms a matrix of similarities or differences into a map. MDS transforms a matrix of distances among cities in the United States (city-block dissimilarities) into map coordinates of the United

States, for example. MDS coordinates thus express strong similarities (small dissimilarities) as spatial closeness and weak similarities (great dissimilarities) as spatial distance.

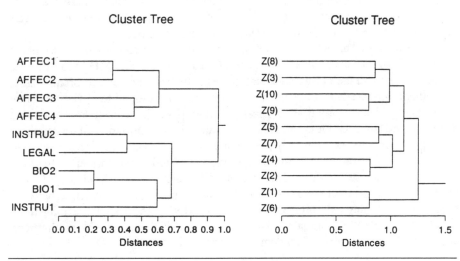

Figure 3. Cluster trees of foster mothers' assessments (left) of similaries among mothering criteria and similarities (right) among variables related only by chance.

MDS transforms similarity and dissimilarity coefficients into coordinates for two, or for several dimensions. In a study of dance among Northern Ute and the predominantly Mormon Anglos living in adjacent communities, for example, Stephanie Reynolds (1990) used a three-dimensional MDS analysis to show that, whereas Anglos differentiated the meanings of dance, the meaningfulness of dance, its purpose and function, and clearly separate it from their history and way of life, Utes equated the meanings of dance, the meaningfulness of dance, its purpose and function, with each other and with Ute history and way of life. In a study of Alaskans affected by the Exxon Valdez oil spill, Joseph Jorgensen (1995) used three-dimensional MDS to show that natives configured their subsistence economy in ways qualitatively different from nonnatives, despite undertaking many of the same activities, living in the same communities. Where natives experienced spiritual dimensions to the environmental damage and responded communally, non-natives, sensitive to commoditized properties of the environment, responded as individuals.

Like the Cartesian coordinates that mapmakers use, the axes of an MDS picture are arbitrary and uninterpretable. The only thing that matters is the relative placement of cases or variables on the MDS map. Two-dimensional coordinates map a plane; three-dimensional coordinates map volume; larger numbers of dimensions probably can't be interpreted. A value called *stress* measures the extent to which mapping distorts the distance between pairs (of cases or variables). Stress varies between 0 and 1. A stress value of 0.0 means that no distortion took place. Stress values below .10 constitute evidence of an excellent fit between the matrix and the mapped coordinates; stress values up to around .15 exhibit at least reasonable levels of fit; stress values over .20 call for additional dimensions.

Figure 4 shows an MDS plot of the similarity coefficients among women's assessments of various motherhood criteria (stress = .075). The MDS plot, like the factor analysis and the cluster analysis, suggests the existence of two broad classes of motherhood criteria that women may experience and respond to in very different ways: personal and formal. It suggests, further (like the cluster analysis), that different kinds of affective criteria may exist that reflect important differences about how foster mothers experience being mothers and carry out mothering activities. Text (from conversations and formal interviews) hinted at the former distinction, which these analyses confirm. The possible difference between kinds of affective motherhood criteria remained hidden. So did a possible equivalence between adoption, the biological child of a relative, and living together for a long time, which only the MDS map suggests. Contrast the MDS map of the motherhood criteria with the mapping of randomly generated variables.

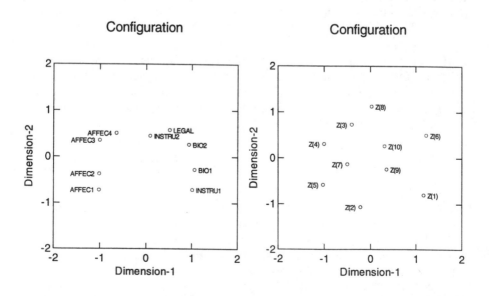

Figure 4. MDS maps of (left) foster mothers' assessments of similaries among mothering criteria and (right) similarities among variables related only by chance.

Consensus Analysis

Consensus analysis (for example, Romney et al. 1986; Weller and Romney 1988; see Boster 1981, 1987, 1988) answers what may be the single most important question of ethnography: Who agrees with whom about what and to what degree? Consensus analysis thus answers the second question raised by examination of the stem-and-leaf and box plots of Wozniak's data: Which foster mothers agree with whom about which motherhood criteria and to what degree?

Consensus analysis is a singularly valuable analytical tool that contributes directly to the ongoing reorientation of theory and research in ways that transform ethnography into ethnology by a focus on cultural variability between individuals rather than between reified and essentialized groups (see Bidney 1944; Barnett 1953; Wallace 1961; Murdock 1971; Pelto and Pelto 1975; Wolf 1982; Keesing 1994). For a given domain of meaning and behavior, variation in the data we collect in the field may reflect three conditions:

1. random variation around a single consensus about the domain or some aspect of it, which may be weak or strong;
2. subpopulation differences in the strength of agreement with the single consensus, or two or more systematically different sets of meanings and behavior, which may differ little or be polar opposites; or
3. no consensus about the domain or some aspect of it.

The first condition identifies the absence of *cultural boundaries* (after Keesing 1994) within a given population and, thus, the absence of significant cultural variability. The second condition identifies the existence of cultural boundaries within a given population and, thus, the presence of significant subpopulation variability. The third condition signals the presence of such widespread disagreement within a population that the data can't be distinguished from random data.

Historically, we have used assumptions, not evidence, to equate cultural boundaries with social identities like Nuer, Navaho, and African American, and have dismissed, overlooked or downplayed both cultural variation among people who use the same social identity and cultural consensus among people who use different social identities. Consensus analysis procedures and diagnostics allow us to test explicitly for the presence or absence of cultural boundaries and to identify disagreements bearing on specific domains of meaning and behavior.

Consensus analysis thus promotes an important new rigor in cultural description and explanation. In a study of American culture, for example, Kempton et al. (1995) found consensus about environmental values that was integrated with other core American values, including religion and parental responsibility, and which was shared by people as diverse as members of Earth First! and laid-off sawmill workers. They found little antienvironmental sentiment and no coherent set of values that contrasted with or was an alternative to the coherent and widely shared proenvironmental values.

William Dressler used consensus analysis to construct regionally and historically specific measures of poverty (see Dressler 1996, 1997; Dressler et al. 1996) based not on the conventional and narrow biological conception of need, but on one more germane to understanding meaning and behavior—relative deprivation in lived experiences (for example, Aberle 1966). The resulting measure of *cultural consonance* encompasses the lived experience of poverty with its multiple dimensions—income, education, age, marital status, occupation, and social support and integration—and thus offers a new, explicit tool for understanding the sources, patterning, and implications of disadvantage in human communities.

Dressler's work documents clear health implications. Similarly, efficient sampling strategies for cultural data focus on the selection of knowledgeable informants whose lives encompass experiential variability that may influence the phenomena studied, track levels of agreement, and expand sample sizes and sampling criteria consistent with levels of agreement and identified cultural boundaries (Handwerker and Wozniak 1997). Consensus analysis combined with explicit sampling frames addresses the problems of internal and external validity and yields findings generalizable to a population defined by an explicitly identified set of life experiences (Handwerker 1998).

Consensus analysis procedures came from a theory that defines culture as knowledge and that distinguishes variation due to the use of different configurations of knowledge (usually called subcultural variation) from variation due to differences in how much individuals know about a given cultural domain. For example, Boster (1981) noticed that the Aguaruna women who agreed most often with others on questions about a set of manioc plants were also the ones who knew the most about it. Similarly, on a multiple-choice examination in which the teacher defines the culturally correct answer key, students who know most of the answers tend to agree a lot with each other because they agree closely with the common answer key. At the same time, students who know very little of the material give answers that agree little with anyone.

Romney et al. (1986) showed that one can use patterns of agreement to reliably infer how much informants know about a domain when three conditions hold: (1) There is a single right answer to every question; (2) Conditional on the answer key, people's answers to questions are independent of each other (that is, students are not cheating and answering one question does not affect one's answer to another); and (3) Questions are drawn at random from one domain of knowledge (for example, the test doesn't mix questions about tennis with questions about anthropology). Given these conditions, we don't need the answer key to work out how much of the material each student knows. A factor analysis of a chance-adjusted person-by-person agreement matrix estimates a person's knowledge score based on the correlation between their responses and everyone else's. Once we estimate how much each person knows, we can infer the right answers by the application of *Bayesian* statistical methods.

Consensus analysis procedures thus lend themselves particularly well to the analysis of cultural domains for which there exist unique culturally correct answers and variation in knowledge about the domain. Examples include the correct way to give birth, hold girls' or boys' puberty rites, or marry—or any form of *evaluation research*. Evaluation research tests the efficacy of interventions designed to induce specific forms of cultural change. Example interventions include bicycle safety programs designed to increase the chances that a child will use a helmet while riding, training of health care providers designed to improve their ability to carry out accurate physical examinations, and lesson-delivery that requires fifth-grade students to participate in the construction of mathematics problems designed to improve mathematics problem-solving skills.

Interventions assume the existence of, and teach, "correct" answers—riding with, not without helmets; the correct way to conduct physical examinations; the skills to achieve correct solutions to specific mathematics problems. Evaluation research assesses the degree to which trainees exhibit "correct" answers. People subject to intervention activities constitute "cases;" people not subject to intervention activities constitute "controls." One way to state the evaluation research hypothesis is that cases exhibit greater cultural similarities with the "correct" answers than do controls. Thus, a direct test of the evaluation research hypothesis comes from a consensus analysis carried out on a matrix that includes the intervention-defined answers coded as 1 (correct), the answers given by cases coded as 1 (if correct) or 0 (if not), and the answers given by controls coded as 1 (if correct) or 0 (if not).

The consensus procedure in ANTHROPAC generates four key sets of output data: (1) eigenvalues of each factor, the percentage of variability in informant responses that each factor accounts for, and the ratio of the largest eigenvalue to the next largest; (2) factor loadings (ANTHROPAC's KNOWLEDGE scores), which identify the correlation between the responses of individual informants and the first factor, and the average level of agreement among all informants; (3) the similarities among the responses of your informants (ANTHROPAC's AGREE data file), on which the factor analysis was performed; and (4) an answer key. The first set provides provisional information with which to judge whether or not your informants express a consensus about the issue you're studying. A large proportion of the variance among individuals explained by a single factor the eigenvalue of which is three or more times larger than the next largest—a dramatic scree fall—constitutes evidence (subject to diagnostic analysis) of the existence of a single answer key around which all variation in responses is draped. The last three sets provide critical diagnostic information. Negative factor loadings (KNOWLEDGE scores), for example, signal the possible presence of two or more systematically different sets of meanings within the population. A run of particularly low factor loadings (KNOWLEDGE scores) warns you of significant subpopulation cultural differences.

In the evaluation research example, for example, evidence that the intervention worked and that cases acquired higher levels of competence (wearing helmets, physical exam procedures, mathematics) than did controls consists of a factor loading (KNOWLEDGE score) for the intervention-defined answers approximating 1.00, high factor loadings (KNOWLEDGE scores over .5) for cases, and low factor loadings (KNOWLEDGE scores under .5) for controls. We could count the number of intervention-defined correct answers provided by cases and controls and use a permutation test to find out how often we could find those differences just by chance. However, consensus analysis procedures allow us to look for intervention-induced alternatives or opposing sets of agreements, as well as subpopulation differences in the degree of agreement with intervention-defined correct answers. Consensus analysis thus adds a rich complement to the more straightforward technique.

In the general case, a large number of negative or low factor loadings tell you to disaggregate your data (for example, see Boster and Johnson 1989) and possibly return to your informants to search out the sources of difference. Is this a domain for which there exist acknowledged cultural experts and the low or negative knowledge scores reflect the ignorance of particular informants? Do there exist two or more systematically different sets of meanings and behavior? Are there domain items about which people show no agreement?

Although the theory that led to consensus analysis conceptualized culture as a mental phenomenon, consensus analysis procedures apply equally well to the behavior isomorphic with a given body of knowledge (observational data on how women give birth, how puberty rites are carried out, how people marry—and whether people act differently after an intervention). Data appropriate for consensus analysis might come from text collected by various forms of informal or semi-structured interviews (so long as all informants responded to the same questions), from structured observations, or from structured interview formats like sentence frames, pile sorts, triads tests, or rating scales.

Moreover, since the factor analysis infers the existence of a coherent (albeit otherwise unobserved) agreement about a domain or some aspect of it, consensus analysis procedures also lend themselves to the analysis of cultural domains where the metaphor of an answer key fits awkwardly. In many if not most cultural domains, everyone is a cultural expert. All women are experts about being women; all men are experts about being men. Everyone living in the United States is an expert on life in the United States, and all Americans are experts on American environmental values, for example. Lack of agreement doesn't imply that one person knows more than another. In these circumstances, consensus analysis procedures allow us to infer a coherent, shared agreement about meanings or behavior.

A first eigenvalue massively larger than the second signals a clear consensus and ANTHROPAC's answer key tells us what the agreement is all about. But factor loadings tell us the strength of agreements, not how much someone knows about the domain. Low or negative factor loadings signal cultural differences arising from life experiences that differ in significant ways. Diagnostic analysis can tell us whether low or negative factor loadings mean a weak consensus with generally low levels of agreement, subpopulation differences in the level of agreement, or the existence of alternative or opposed subpopulation agreements about the domain or some domain items.

Consensus analyses of Wozniak's data, treated as qualitative assignments of meaning (multiple choice data), yielded the following:

		Eigenvalues		
Factor	Value	%	Cum %	Ratio
1:	25.451	61.3	61.3	2.830
2:	8.994	21.6	82.9	1.266
3:	7.103	17.1	100.0	

Note: It would be better if the first factor accounted for more than three times the variance of the second.

Although the first factor accounts for 61.3% of the variability in informant responses, the second accounts for 21.6%. A consensus may exist among some women about some criteria, but these findings suggest the possibility of subpopulation cultural differences. Subpopulations might differ in the degree to which they concur with the overall consensus. There may be two or more coherent sets of agreements. A subpopulation might strongly agree among themselves and sharply disagree with the majority. A subpopulation might agree with some of the overall consensus and strongly agree among themselves about an alternative set of answers to some domain items. To know, we need to disaggregate the data. Maybe Black foster mothers thought about what it takes to be a mother differently than did white foster mothers. Maybe cultural differences reflected how long a woman had fostered, her age, whether her biological children were grown, or whether she was poor.

Subsequent diagnostic analysis, guided by informant interview texts, revealed that none of these speculations bore out. Indeed, they revealed another dimension to the distinction between personal and formal criteria of motherhood examined earlier. *All* women—Black or white, rich or poor, old or young—agreed on the importance of the self-defined affective criteria of motherhood. Consensus analysis of respondent evaluations of the importance of affective criteria yielded a first eigenvalue 7.4 times larger than the second, which accounted for 83.5% of the variability in informant evaluations; the average level of agreement among informants was .76. By contrast, there existed no agreement about the conventional biological, legal, and instrumental criteria of "motherhood." For these latter criteria, the ratio of the first to the next largest eigenvalue was only 1.3, the first factor accounted for only 42.9% of variability in informant evaluations, and the average level of agreement among informants was only .01.

The similarity matrices among informant cases analyzed by consensus procedures may exhibit one of at least four different patterns. First, a very high degree of consensus among informants would appear as a tight centralized cluster of cases with increasing degrees of random scatter as one moved away from the answers that constituted the common agreement (although you might not see the fried-egg pattern if high average levels of agreement place everyone in the core). Second, a weaker consensus might appear as a more uniformly distributed, but still clearly clustered, scatter of cases. Third, the absence of consensus would appear as a random scatter of cases. Finally, the existence of two or more distinct consensuses—as would exist, for example, if Black and white foster mothers responded to the affective dimensions of mothering in different ways—might appear as two or more foci in the MDS map. Figure 5 shows the MDS map of agreements concerning the importance of affective criteria for judging oneself a "mother" (stress = .0517) with the MDS map of agreements concerning the importance of biological, legal, and instrumental criteria (stress = .1237). The first exhibits the very strong consensus identified by the factor analysis (the plot points contain a small amount of random variation—jittering—otherwise the cluster in the center would have appeared as a single point, it was packed so densely). The second exhibits random scatter.

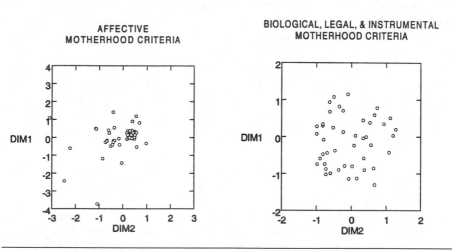

Figure 5. MDS maps of informant agreement about mothering criteria.

In short, through their responses to structured questions about the relative importance of different mothering criteria, Wozniak's informants told her that personal, affective dimensions of mothering guided and rationalized their mothering activities in important ways. Black or white, rich or poor, old or young, foster mothers experienced formal dimensions of mothering that receive wide social recognition—giving birth to a child, receiving help from a child, adopting a child—as very different from, albeit in almost idiosyncratic ways, the core affective dimensions of mothering and family relationships.

Triangulation

Numerical analysis integrated into the actual fieldwork process builds method triangulation to assess data validity and reliability (see McNabb 1990). By helping you see things you'd otherwise miss, it also identifies questions that lead to a greater depth of understanding. MDS maps and other plots are particularly handy output to take to informants, individually or in focus groups. For example, findings from consensus analysis of Wozniak's informants' assessments of family members and their permanency revealed a highly puzzling finding: Foster mothers thought of foster sons as "very" permanent family members but thought of foster daughters as only "somewhat" permanent family members. She presented this and other findings to focus groups of foster mothers and asked if they thought the findings were true and, if so, why. Group discussions revealed that foster mothers experienced a family dynamic common to biological mothers: Once foster daughters reached their teens, foster mothers and daughters often began to experience conflicts over the daughter's sexual and reproductive behavior. Characteristically, these conflicts escalated and culminated with the pregnant daughter leaving or being told she must leave.

Foster mothers and daughters subsequently had little if any contact for several years. Once daughters established their own families, however, they usually reestablished relationships with their foster mothers. One woman's foster son might well be the father of another woman's foster daughter's child. But foster sons were "very" permanent family members: sons brought home the baby and the girlfriend and foster mothers incorporated both into their families.

Life Experience Data: Modeling Relationships
Among Lives, History, and Region

Numerical reasoning thus provides explicit validation for the inferential generalizations about cultural phenomena that we arrive at during the course of ordinary ethnographic research. Ordinary Least Squares (OLS) regression (for example, Schroeder et al. 1986; Gujarati 1995) provides explicit tests for speculations about why and how the patterns and variability we found might have come into being, why and how they persist over time, and why and under what circumstances they may change.

Conceptualizing human beings in ways that coherently incorporate the implications of being born at a specific time and place, the effects of maturation, and the experience of specific historical events and processes at specific ages, constitutes a major theoretical challenge. Historical and regional explanation appears essential. However, historical and regional explanations usually create linkages between temporal sequences of events and processes with ad hoc or post hoc claims that people act for specific intentions, out of specific dispositions, or for specific reasons.

Long experience with (and analysis of) reasons, intentions or motivations found in text provided by informants living or long dead tells us that this information *cannot* decide these issues (see Brown 1963; Hammel 1990). Indeed, this information may mislead us far more than they provide us insight. People lie. People forget. People rationalize what they do. People do things for many reasons. People aren't aware of all or even most of the influences on what they do. People may be completely *unaware* of the most important influences on what they do, particularly when those influences are historical, macrolevel phenomena that can't be perceived clearly in the minutiae of day-to-day living. People misjudge the relative importance of their reasons, intentions, or motivations. Shweder (1977) and many others have documented how easy people find it to tell what is *like* what and how hard people find it to tell what *goes* with what.

Moreover, attempts to explain specific behavior from specific reasons, intentions, or motivations necessarily produce covert tautologies because, if we "explain" a specific behavior by reference to a *different* reason, intention, or motivation, we'd contradict ourselves. Reasons, intentions, motivations, and other internal mental states consitute part of our *descriptions* of cultural phenomena—which call for explanation.

One way to avoid this dilemma is to link theoretical or empirical generalizations to initial conditions established by specific (albeit ungeneralizable) temporal sequences of events and processes. Historical events and processes in specific regions establish initial sets of conditions that people may experience and to which they may respond in predictable ways.

For example, explanations for childbearing during adolescence range from speculations about the influence of (1) the operation of evolved neural architectures designed to optimize reproductive success (for example, see Tooby and Cosmides 1992), to (2) social circumstances, to (3) gender and intergenerational inequalities bearing on means by which women gain access to resources. An important formulation for the first appeals to girls' early sensitive learning-period responses to father-absent rearing, or to maternal messages about father-absent rearing (Draper and Harpending 1982, 1988). The most popular example of the second appeals to the frustrations, stresses, and strains of poverty. Childbearing, however, might reflect social relations.

On the principle that one must eat before one can reproduce effectively, our central nervous system should have an evolved neural architecture designed to optimize access to resources, and humans gain access to resources through social relations. If childbearing yields the best resource access, as it did in the West Indies when women were dependent on men for income and women used childbearing to legitimize claims of support from men during their youth and to equalize gender inequalities by middle age, women should bear lots of children. If good jobs requiring high levels of educational attainment yield the best resource access, as occurred recently in the West Indies with structural change in regional economies that equalized gender inequalities, women should go far in school and have few if any children. Early sensitive period learning may bear on optimizing resource access, as well as reproductive success. Women who experience exploitative violence (sexual abuse) as children may act in ways that correspond more closely with optimum resource access than their unexploited peers (for example, see Liem et al. 1992). Sexually abused girls thus might have more children than their peers, when childbearing yields the best resource access, and more education than their peers, when education yields the best resource access.

Multiple Regression Models

We indicated earlier that multiple regression methods approximate the goals of experimental designs and help us isolate relationships so we can tell whether or not they exist, and their strength, even after we control for other variables. Answers to "why" questions consist of a claim that one phenomenon is linked to another. Multiple regression is a way of thinking about these claims as general functions. General functions of the form $Y = f(X_k)$ constitute claims about the existence of a set of rules that allow us to translate values of *independent* variables (X_k)—explanatory variables like father-absent rearing, poverty, and inequalities—into values of one or more *dependent* variables (Y)—like adolescent childbearing. A simple additive (*linear*) model to test the possibilities outlined earlier looks like the following:

$$Y = \beta_0 + \beta_1 X_1 + \beta_2 X_2 + \beta_3 X_3 + \epsilon$$

where each X represents one of the three explanatory variables and the Greek epsilon (ϵ) constitutes explicit recognition that we will make the best predictions possible, but we anticipate prediction error. Alternatively, we could write the model as: adolescent childbearing = f(father-absent rearing, poverty, and inequalities), and write the equation with variable names:

ADOLESCENT CHILDBEARING $= \beta_0 + \beta_1$FATHER-ABSENT REARING $+ \beta_2$POVERTY $+ \beta_3$INEQUALITIES $+ \epsilon$

The Greek betas (β) represent the relationships that may exist between Y and each explanatory variable. Assume that we've measured the independent variables as simply present (1) or absent (0).

If there exist no father-absent rearing, no poverty, and no inequalities (all Xs equal 0), β_0 (the *constant*) shows the predicted number of children born during adolescence (ADOLESCENT CHILDBEARING = $\beta_0 + \beta_1*0 + \beta_2*0 + \beta_3*0 = \beta_0$).

If father-absent rearing exists but there exist neither poverty nor inequalities, $\beta_0+\beta_1$ shows the predicted number of children born during adolescence (ADOLESCENT CHILDBEARING = $\beta_0 + \beta_1*1 + \beta_2*0 +\beta_3*0 = \beta_0+\beta_1$).

If father-absent rearing, poverty, and inequalities all exist, $\beta_0+\beta_1+\beta_2+\beta_3$ shows the predicted number of children born during adolescence (ADOLESCENT CHILD-BEARING = $\beta_0 + \beta_1*1 + \beta_2*1 +\beta_3*1 = \beta_0+\beta_1+\beta_2+\beta_3$).

The *regression coefficients* (β_1, β_2, β_3) thus tell you how much adolescent childbearing changes with any change in the independent variables; regression coefficients may be negative or positive numbers, so they also tell you whether the number of children born goes up or down.

Introducing Complexities from the Intersection of Lives, History, and Region

Simple linear models fit an amazing number of real world situations. Simple modifications transform them in ways suitable to many real world non-linearities and situational, historical, and regional contingencies. For example, in poor homes adolescent childbearing may rise proportionally (may double, for example), not by fixed amounts (by one child, for example). The following model, which transforms the dependent variable units into logarithms, tests that possibility.

Ln(ADOLESCENT CHILDBEARING) = $\beta_0+\beta_1$FATHER-ABSENT REARING+β_2POVERTY +β_3INEQUALITIES+ϵ

Similarly, father-absent rearing, poverty, and inequalities may have nothing to do with adolescent childbearing—unless they all occur together (an *interaction* effect). The following equation tests this possibility:

ADOLESCENT CHILDBEARING = $\beta_0+\beta_1$FATHER-ABSENT REARING+β_2POVERTY +β_3INEQUALITIES+β_4(FATHER-ABSENT REARING*POVERTY *INEQUALITIES)+ϵ

If father-absent rearing, poverty, and inequalities (for *direct* effects of the variables) exert no influence on the number of children girls bear before they turn

20 unless they occur together, you couldn't distinguish the size of the first three regression coefficients from 0.00, and the final model would appear like:

ADOLESCENT CHILDBEARING = $\beta_0 + \beta_4$(FATHER-ABSENT REARING * POVERTY * INEQUALITIES) + ϵ

Regression also facilitates thinking of what people experience with *systems* of equations and, thus, modeling *pertinent* intersections of lives, history, and region. The regional and historical contingencies summarized earlier suggest the following (truncated and simplified) system of equations bearing on adolescent childbearing (see Handwerker 1989, 1993a, 1993b):

Childbearing leveled gender inequalities by a woman's middle age, for women subject to gender inequalities early in life. So, the extent to which women conceptualized childbearing as an investment activity rather than a consumption activity (their moral economy of childbearing) = f(job opportunities for women).

Women found education useful only to the extent that it gave them access to good jobs. So, educational attainment (by age 20) = f(moral economy of childbearing in the absence of job opportunities for women).

Given that childbearing levels gender inequalities by middle age, for women subjected to gender inequalities early in life: Childbearing during adolescence (to age 20) = f(moral economy of childbearing*length of time spent in one or another sexual union, for women with no biological constraints on fecundity, educational attainment, and the absence of job opportunities for women who experienced childhood sexual abuse).

This system of equations implies that adolescent birthrates will decrease and educational attainment will increase as job opportunities for women grow, and that women who experience adolescent childbearing will invest heavily in childbearing early in life, but only in the absence of job opportunities. In the presence of good job opportunities, these women will invest heavily in education.

We can evaluate systems of equations like this with *path analysis,* which uses *standardized* regression coefficients. Standardized regression coefficients allow ready comparison between different sets of data. For specific sets of data, however, unstandardized regression coefficients yield far more interesting findings because they provide a concrete picture of what happens in people's lives.

OLS Regression

Ordinary Least Squares (OLS) regression operations try to account for variability in a set of observations (some girls bear more children during adolescence than others). For any one equation, multiple regression operations estimate parameters (β_k) with statistics (b_k). OLS regression makes these estimates using the same criteria applied to the calculation of means. The result is a set of *regression coefficients* (b_k) which estimate values of the dependent variable (Y) in ways which guarantee that the sum of prediction errors (the absolute differences between the value of each case and the model estimate for the case, called *residuals*) equals 0.0. Each coefficient tells you the average change in Y for each change in one independent variable (X), after controlling for the effects of other independent variables.

The following SYSTAT output shows a test of the third equation listed earlier using data collected in Antigua:

DEP VAR: Number of Live Births by Age 20
N: 97
ADJUSTED SQUARED MULTIPLE R: .828
STANDARD ERROR OF ESTIMATE: 0.249

VARIABLE	COEFFICIENT	T	P2 TAIL
CONSTANT	0.752	3.317	0.001
Trajectory set by moral economy*Years in legal unions	0.688	7.634	0.000
Trajectory set by moral economy*Years in commonlaw unions	0.117	6.641	0.000
Trajectory set by moral economy*Years in visiting unions	0.051	6.070	0.000
Educational attainment by age 20	−0.064	−3.482	0.001
No job opportunities for girls sexually abused <16	0.602	3.103	0.003

The regression coefficients (the column of numbers labeled COEFFICIENT) tell us rates of childbearing during adolescence. The model's CONSTANT tells us that these Antiguan girls bore an average of about one (.752) child before age 20, irrespective of effects from independent variables. The remaining coefficients describe the effects of each independent variable. The coefficient of .688, for example, describes the birth trajectory for the interaction between the degree to which a girl looked on childbearing as a consumption or an investment activity (their moral economy score, which ranges from 0 to 4) and how long they spent in a legal marriage. For each year these Antiguan girls were legally married, for example, they bore an average of .688 children for each increase in the degree to which they thought of childbearing as a consumption or an investment activity. Childbearing rates fall off in commonlaw unions (.117) and visiting unions (.051). In concrete terms, this means that Antiguan girls who thought of childbearing only as a consumption activity (moral economy score of 0) bore an average of (.117*0), or 0 children, each year they spent in a commonlaw union. Antiguan girls who thought of childbearing as an extremely important investment activity (moral economy score of 4) bore (.117*4), or .468 children each year they spent in a commonlaw union—one child every two years, on average. Model estimates of the number of children born to any one girl before age 20 would include the constant (.752) and the effects of other independent variables.

For example, the coefficient for educational attainment by age 20 tells us that, for each year of schooling, the estimated number of children born by age 20 fell by .064 children. Thus, the model estimates that an Antiguan girl in a commonlaw union for five years who thought of childbearing as an extreme investment activity (moral economy score of 4) who had only 10 years of schooling (incompleted secondary education) bore (.752) + (.117*5*4 = 2.34) − (.064*10 = .64), or two (2.452)—maybe three—children by age 20. By contrast, if the girl thought of childbearing as a consumption activity (moral economy score of 1) and had completed 15 years of schooling, the model estimates that she would bear no children by age 20: (.752) + (.117*5*1 = .585) − (.064*15 = .96) = .377.

Sexually abused girls who grew up when the Antiguan economy offered women few good job opportunities, however, bore an additional .602 children before they were 20. Thus, for girls

- in a commonlaw union for five years,
- with only ten years of schooling,
- who thought of childbearing as an extremely important investment activity, and who *also*
- experienced childhood sexual abuse *and* grew up when few good job opportunities existed for women,

the model estimates (2.452 + .602 = 3.054), or about three children born during adolescence.

How can you tell if the model really works? Regression analysis divides the variation in the dependent variable (childbearing during adolescence), measured as the sum-of-squares of the dependent variable, into two components: (1) the residual sum-of-squares (5.641), unaccounted for by the equation; and (2) the regression sum-of-squares (29.018), which tells how much variability the model explains. These quantities appear in the ANALYSIS OF VARIANCE portion of the regression output, which follows this paragraph. A regression sum-of-squares that is large relative to the residual sum-of-squares suggests that something in the model works very well in predicting the dependent variable.

Expressing the regression sum-of-squares as a proportion of the total (regression + residual) gives R^2, which will grow each time you add an independent variable even if the variable doesn't have much effect. The adjusted R^2 of .828 tells you that the model accounts for about 83% of the variation in adolescent childbearing among these Antiguan women, even after controlling for the number of variables in the model. Removing the squaring from the residual sum-of-squares, once you divide it by the number of cases (minus the number of variables in the model), gives you a coefficient equivalent to a standard deviation, called the *standard error of the estimate*. The standard error of the estimate (.249) tells you how much error you make, on average, each time you estimate the dependent variable. This model's average error rate is about one quarter of a child. These numbers are remarkable for data collected from individuals, where R^2s of .25 or lower may signal important findings.

ANALYSIS OF VARIANCE

SOURCE	SUM-OF-SQUARES	DF	MEAN-SQUARE	F-RATIO	P
REGRESSION	29.018	5	5.804	93.617	0.000
RESIDUAL	5.641	91	0.062		

What appear as extremely strong relationships can find their way into our data merely by random sampling fluctuations (chance), however. The R^2 of .828 estimates a parameter ρ^2 (rho-squared). The F-ratio output (93.617) gives a probability, which tells you how often to expect the observed R^2 or any larger just by chance. The listed probability for the model as a whole (.000) tells you that we could get an R^2 of .828 or larger less than once in a thousand just by chance. This warrants the inference that something about the model works better than chance in estimating variation in adolescent childbearing among these Antiguan girls. T-tests tell you how often to expect the observed regression coefficients just by chance. The high t-test statistics correspond with low t-test probabilities, which tell you that each independent variable predicts adolescent childbearing in ways most unlikely to occur merely by chance.

OLS Regression Diagnostics

Inferences such as these depend on random sampling and an ideal world of data collection, in which you:

- include all pertinent and no irrelevant or extraneous variables,
- correctly specify the functional form of all supposed relationships between dependent and independent variables,
- measure all variables perfectly,
- predict dependent variables in such a way that the errors we make exhibit a normal distribution,
- select cases in such a way that independent variables exhibit no correlation, and
- findings of the model solution generate no correlated residuals.

Of course, the real world and the ideal world don't often correspond very closely. Sometimes, they match badly. Much data collection and analysis involves trying to determine which of these conditions are met acceptably and which are not, and correcting particularly bad matches between the ideal world and the real one. For example, the first assumption tells you to make your final evaluation of model variables by including only those variables for which you find evidence (low probabilities) that they belong. If you believe that you've met the other assumptions, do an appropriate post hoc test with all variables that otherwise appear extraneous to test for otherwise hidden additional effects. The following SYSTAT output comes from a post hoc test for significant additional effects on adolescent childbearing of growing up (1) in poverty; (2) with a stepfather; (3) in a stable nuclear family household; or (4) only with a mother; (5 and 6) the experience of father-absent rearing (measured directly by the presence or absence of the biological father during an hypothesized early sensitive learning period, and as father-absent rearing messages received from the mother; and (7) age (as a control for historical change). The high probability (.557) tells us that the effects of these variables could be found by chance nearly 60 times in 100. This finding warrants the inference that these variables either have no effect on adolescent childbearing, or effects so small we can't detect them.

TEST OF HYPOTHESIS

SOURCE	SS	DF	MS	F	P
HYPOTHESIS	0.369	7	0.053	0.841	0.557
ERROR	5.272	84	0.063		

The second assumption (correct functional form) tells you to assess possible nonlinearities. If relationships between variables exhibit proportional changes rather than fixed unit changes, logarithm transformations will produce a model that fits the data better. The third assumption (perfect measurement) cannot be fulfilled in the real world. But this assumption bears more on the precision of model estimates than on their accuracy. Random measurement error makes it harder to see real-world relationships, and measurement imperfections in the dependent variable exhibit minor effects compared with measurement imperfections for independent variables.

Violations of the fourth assumption (normally distributed residuals) rarely invalidate findings. However, violations of the fifth assumption (no correlation among independent variables) pose major dilemmas, and violations of the sixth (no correlation among model estimates) are deadly. These conditions mean that the F-ratio and t-tests don't yield valid probabilities. Sophisticated diagnostic techniques now allow us to evaluate whether or not our data violate these assumptions, and equally sophisticated techniques give us means to avoid the analytical confusion such violations create (for example, Gujarati 1995).

Explicit randomization in true experimental designs meets the fifth assumption, since it guarantees that relationships among independent variables exist only by chance. All other data violate the assumption that there are no relationships among independent variables. For all practical purposes, all data sets contain *multicollinearity*. Nonetheless, multicollinearity doesn't always invalidate probabilities. The following conditions signal the presence of enough multicollinearity to distort model estimates:

- *Condition indices* greater than 30 (see Belsley et al. 1980).
- Including a new variable increases rather than decreases the standard error of the estimate.
- A new variable exhibits a high probability and *also* raises the probability of a variable already in the model.
- The model exhibits a low F-ratio probability but exhibits no low t-statistic probabilities.
- Your software tells you that it can't solve for the coefficients.

Factor analysis offers one solution to multicollinearity problems. If the troublesome collinear variables load highly on a single factor, you can measure all simultaneously with *factor scores*. Factor scores measure the contribution of each variable to the underlying factor and thus integrate all variables into a single score. If you suspect that significant multicollinearity still gives you invalid probabilities, identify a promising model, enter additional (control) variables one-by-one, and report the t-tests.

Violations of the sixth assumption, that prediction errors associated with any one case remain uncorrelated with errors made for other cases, appear as patterned relationships among residuals called *heteroskedasticity*. For example, errors in estimation (*residuals*) may be small when you estimate low values of the dependent variable, and grow increasingly larger as you estimate increasingly high values of the dependent variable. Estimation errors may exhibit high similarity for people who live close to each other and decreasing similarity for people who live increasingly far away, a pattern now called *spatial autocorrelation*. Similarly, estimation errors may exhibit high similarity for cases that occur close to each other in time and decreasing similarity for cases increasingly far away, a pattern now called *temporal autocorrelation*. Models that make the dependent variable in one equation an independent variable in the other frequently produce OLS solutions in which the errors for dependent variable estimates correlate with the same variable used as an independent variable.

Finally, all cultural data necessarily entail a combination of both spatial and temporal autocorrelation. This observation dates from the first time an anthropologist used numerical methods—Edward B. Tylor's (1889) attempt to explain the origins and distribution of kin avoidances with a hodgepodge of psychological, functional, and evolutionary hypotheses. One of the originators of the numerical tools that we use today, Sir Francis Galton, asked Tylor how he knew his cases were independent, since the similarities he tried to explain by reference to individual needs and social functions might merely reflect social interaction mediated either by a common history or geographical propinquity. Tylor had no answer.

The second time an anthropologist used numerical methods, Franz Boas (1894) addressed this problem with a cluster analysis of regional and historical social relationships bearing on the distribution of myths and stories found among tribes of the Northwest Coast of North America, the adjacent plateau, and three widely scattered communities. Boas found that neighboring communities shared more than distant communities (for example, Northwest Coast tribes were more similar to each other than to tribes on the plateau, but Northwest Coast and plateau tribes shared more than either did with the interior Athapaskan, Ponca, and Micmac) and that people who may share a common ancestral community (who spoke languages from the same language family) shared more than people who spoke languages from different language families. Boas thus demonstrated case dependence in cultural data collected in and taken to characterize different communities.

Methods for diagnosing and correcting spatial and temporal autocorrelation may be fruitfully applied when the unit of analysis corresponds to an explicitly identifiable regional or historical unit. *Measurement unit transforms* (for example, logarithm transformations), *weighted least squares*, and *differencing* procedures may eliminate the correlated errors associated with cross-sectional heteroskedasticity and many forms of temporal and spatial autocorrelation (see Odland 1988). *Two-Stage Least Squares* (2SLS) procedures eliminate the correlated errors produced by sets of equations in which independent variables in one equation appear as dependent variables in the other. More recent research, which extends Boas's findings to cultural data collected from and taken to characterize different individuals (Handwerker and Wozniak 1997),[6] suggests that the complexity of spatial and temporal autocorrelation among individuals defeats corrective techniques like these. Cultural data require the application of the Spearman-Brown Prophesy formula to assess reliability and validity or bootstrap, jacknife, or permutation test probabilities, depending on the question you need answered.

Findings that survive exhaustive diagnostic tests warrant substantive interpretation. For example, the system of three equations listed earlier belongs to a more extensive set which tests hypotheses bearing on sexual precocity (when adolescent girls first have sex), sexual mobility (how many sexual partners they have during adolescence), their moral economy score, their educational attainment, and their adolescent childbearing. Solutions for each subsequent equation yield estimates for variables in later equations. Simulations based on these estimates help clarify the implications of the findings. If we assume that all models hold up under rigorous diagnostic scrutiny and we create simulations which fall into the range of values observed for all variables, we find that sexually abused girls invested in childbearing more than their peers if they grew up when the Antiguan economy offered few good job opportunities for women: Sexually abused girls (who averaged only 10 years of schooling, and 6 if they grew up in poverty) bore an average of two children and girls who weren't (who averaged 12 years of schooling, and 11 if they grew up in poverty) bore an average of one. We also find that sexually abused girls invested in education more than their peers, if they grew up after the Antiguan economy offered good job opportunities for women: Sexually abused girls who averaged zero children by age 20 attained an average of 15 years of schooling and girls who weren't who also averaged zero children by age 20 attained an average of 13 (12 if they grew up in poverty).

Conclusion

Our numerical analysis tool kit has grown prodigiously over the last decade or so, as a quick look through the contents of good software programs like SYSTAT and ANTHROPAC shows. At the beginning of this chapter, Table 1 summarized the correspondence between selected numerical methods and the principal questions we ask in the course of ordinary ethnographic research. But many more tools exist. *Andrew's Fourier Plots* and *Icon Analyses* provide graphical alternatives for diagnosing cultural consensus, cultural differences, and disagreements, for example. *Correspondence analysis* provides a graphical means to look at which informants tell us what (Greenacre 1984). *Property-Fitting (PROFIT)* analysis (in ANTHROPAC) and *Perceptual Mapping Analysis* (in SYSTAT) provide ways to assess the meanings that guide informant judgments about similarities or dissimilarities (for example, Carroll 1972). Decisions bearing on whether a test designed for one population (for example, a test for disability among middle-class Euro American children) can be validly applied to another (for example, children living in Puerto Rico) require a distinctive set of *test item analytical procedures* (for example, Gannotti 1998).

Evolutionary and developmental change—in which phenomenal properties at one point in time (t_1) are contingent on phenomenal properties at an earlier point in time (t_0)—can best be evaluated with *Guttman scaling* analyis (for example, Goodenough 1944, 1963; Carneiro 1962). *Linear programming* operations (for example, Chvatal 1983, Feiring 1986) provide tests for optimization hypotheses. When we change the analytical question from *How many* children does a girl bear on average before she turns 20? to What's *the likelihood* that a girl will bear a child before she turns 20? OLS regression yields impossible estimates (under 0 and over 1) and correlated residuals. When we analyze binary or qualitative dependent variables, *logistic regression* (Hosmer and Lemeshow 1989) substitutes for OLS regression to provide us modeling capabilities sensitive to situational, historical, and regional contingencies. *Time series* (see, for example, Gujarati 1995 or any good econometrics text) and *event-history* analyses (for example, Yamaguchi 1991) require specialized numerical methods. We need a distinctive set of numerical methods even to *conceptualize* the population processes and demographic characteristics so central to an understanding of human-environmental relationships and much cultural evolution and social change (for example, Handwerker 1990). In short, numerical methods apply to an indefinitely large number of questions.

Numerical reasoning often constitutes the only available means of answering important questions. For example, *Quadradic Assignment Procedures* (ANTHROPAC's *QAP*; see Hubert and Schultz 1976) give us the capability to test for relationships between multidimensional phenomena measured with a large number of variables on two populations or subpopulations. Allison Bingham (1998) measured activity patterns with more than 20 movement variables (for example, washing clothes, taking care of children, sitting out in the evening) and used QAP to test for differences in movement patterns between people with malaria and those without. James Boster (for example, see Boster and Johnson 1989, Kempton et al. 1995) has used QAP analyses to test for subpopulation differences in consensus agreement patterns.

Similarly, time-series graphics allow us to set cultural and life experience phenomena in context with historically and regionally specific processes. Handwerker used a *Fourier blob icon analysis* of a macroeconomic time-series for Antigua, W.I. to pinpoint the dates of structural change in the national economy. This made it possible to identify precisely which informants could provide first-hand accounts of the early years, how their world changed, and how they experienced those changes; which informants could provide first-hand accounts of the transition years, the conflicts that arose and how they came to be resolved (if they were); and which informants could provide first-hand accounts of life once the structural changes clarified themselves and how they see themselves differ from people in the older cohorts. By pinpointing the dates of change, moreover, this analysis also provided a foundation for construction of a microlevel measure of "employment opportunities for women" from the aggregated data on macrolevel changes in the Antiguan economy (Handwerker 1993b). This variable effectively identified powerful influences on women's view of childbearing and their reproductive behavior.

Unaided, our senses tell us about surface phenomena—the net effects of chance and complexly textured multidimensional influences on what we think, feel, and do that operate all the time. Numerical methods help us identify chance fluctuations in what we see, detect the subtle configurations of meaning that remain unspoken and, perhaps, unrealized, by our informants, and both identify and assess the relative importance of the multidimensional historical, regional, situational, and individual influences on meaning and behavior. Explicit reasoning with numbers thus lets us see things in and about people's lives we'd otherwise miss and answer questions in ways that help us pinpoint those errors in judgment that make us quintessentially human.

NOTES

We thank Robert Bee and several anonymous referees for helping us avoid unnecessary embarrassment by pointing out important ambiguities, errors, and other lapses in good judgment in earlier drafts. We take sole responsibility for what you see now.

1. As a first-year graduate student at Berkeley studying under A. L. Kroeber (Driver and Kroeber 1932), Harold Driver created a very effective similarity coefficient (Driver's G, which Ellegard [1959] worked out independently, along with its sampling distribution, 30 years later). Driver carried out the first explicit reliability assessment of cultural data (1938) and has written excellent reviews of the development and use of numerical methods in anthropology up to the last quarter of the twentieth century (1962, 1965, 1970). Jorgensen edited a volume (1974) that assesses Driver's own considerable accomplishments.

2. You will find ratio scales called interval scales. However, you will rarely come across true interval scales like the Farenheit and Celsius temperature scales. Interval scales like these do not contain a true zero, since 0 measures a degree of temperature (molecular movement), not the absence of temperature (as does 0 in the Kelvin temperature scale).

3. Computing a set of statistical tests to look for low probabilities produces invalid probabilities. Just by chance, you'll find low probabilities—5% of the time, you'll find probabilities equal or less than .05. You'll find it useful to see this yourself. Follow the procedures outlined in Handwerker (1991).

It's also a mistake to look just at probabilities. A large enough sample will show you that almost everything exhibits a nonchance relationship with everything else. Similarity coefficients for that sample will also show you that nearly all of these relationships are very, very weak and, so, inconsequential. Although anthropologists rarely use samples greater than 100 cases and almost never use samples greater than 500, you still need to focus on the *strength* of relationships, for relationships that don't appear due to sampling fluctuations.

4. Pearson's r computed for ordinal data usually is called Spearman's Rho; Pearson's r computed for binary data usually is called Phi.

5. We describe a *principal components* analysis. Classical forms of factor analysis, to which purists restrict the factor analysis name, reverse this procedure by looking for additive factors that account for observed similarities.

6. Indeed, Handwerker's appreciation of numerical methods owes much to both history and geographical propinquity. He received his degree from the University of Oregon, where he was heavily influenced by two lines of descent from Franz Boas, the first American anthropologist to publish a numerical analysis of cultural data. One line of descent runs through Alfred Kroeber and Harold Driver to his teacher, Joseph G. Jorgensen. The other runs through Melville Herskovits to his teacher, Vernon R. Dorjahn. The seeds of his understanding of cultural phenomena come from another, which runs through Alfred Kroeber to his teacher, Homer Barnett. We might learn much about cultural phenomena from a study of the social interaction influenced by descent and geography within our own discipline.

REFERENCES

Aberle, David F. 1966. *The Peyote Religion among the Navaho*. Chicago: Aldine.

Aldenderfer, M. S., and R. K. Blashfield. 1984. *Cluster Analysis*. Quantitative Applications in the Social Sciences, Vol. 44. Beverly Hills, CA: Sage Publications.

Barnett, Homer G. 1953. *Innovation*. New York: McGraw-Hill.

Belsley, D. A., E. Kuh, and R. E. Welsch. 1980. *Regression Diagnostics*. New York: John Wiley.

Bidney, David. 1944. The Concept of Culture and Some Cultural Fallacies. *American Anthropologist 46*:30–44.

Bingham, Allison. 1995. Household Economic Differentiation among Small Coffee Producers: A Case-Study from Soconusco Region, Chiapas, Mexico. Paper delivered at the 1995 meeting of the American Anthropological Association, Atlanta.

Bingham, Allison. 1998. The Malaria Ecosystem in Southern Mexico. Ph.D. diss., Storrs: University of Connecticut.

Boas, Franz. 1894. *Indianische Sagen von der Nord-Pacifischen Kuste Amerikas*. Berlin: Asher.

Borgatti, S. P. 1992. ANTHROPAC 4.0. Columbia, SC: Analytic Technologies.

Boster, James S. 1981. How the Exceptions Prove the Rule. Ph.D. diss., Berkeley: University of California.

Boster, James S. 1987. Introduction. *American Behavioral Scientist 31*:150–162.

Boster, James S. 1988. "Requiem for the Omniscient Informant": There's Life in the Old Girl Yet. In *Directions in Cognitive Anthropology*. Janet Dougherty, ed. Pp. 177–197. Urbana: University of Illinois Press.

Boster, James S., and Jeffrey C. Johnson. 1989. Form or Function: A Comparison of Expert and Novice Judgments of Similarity among Fish. *American Anthropologist 91*:866–889.

Brown, Robert. 1963. *Explanation in Social Science*. Chicago: Aldine.

Campbell, D. T., and J. C. Stanley. 1966. *Experimental and Quasi-Experimental Designs for Research*. Chicago: Rand McNally.

Carneiro, R. L. 1962. Scale Analysis as an Instrument for the Study of Cultural Evolution. *Southwestern Journal of Anthropology 18*:149–169.

Carroll, J. D. 1972. Individual Differences in Multidimensional Scaling. In *Multidimensional Scaling: Theory and Applications in the Behavioral Sciences*, Vol. 1. R. N. Shepard, A. K. Romney, and S. B. Nerlove, eds. Pp. 105–155. New York: Seminar Press.

Chvatal, Vasek. 1983. *Linear Programming*. San Francisco: W. H. Freeman.

Cleveland, William S., and Robert McGill. 1985. Graphical Perception and Graphical Methods for Analyzing Scientific Data. *Science 229*:828–833.

Cook, T. D., and D. T. Campbell. 1979. *Quasi-Experimentation: Design & Analysis Issues for Field Settings*. Boston: Houghton Mifflin.

Draper P., and H. Harpending. 1982. Father Absence and Reproductive Strategy: An Evolutionary Perspective. *Journal of Anthropological Research 38*:255–273.

Draper P., and H. Harpending. 1988. A Sociobiologial Perspective on the Development of Human Reproductive Strategies. In *Sociobiological Perspectives on Human Development.* K. B. MacDonald, ed. Pp. 340–372. New York: Springer-Verlag.

Dressler, William W. 1996. Culture and Blood Pressure: Using Consensus Analysis to Create a Measurement. *Cultural Anthropology Methods 8*(3):6–8.

Dressler, William W. 1997. Culture and Patterns of Poverty. Paper delivered at the 1997 meeting of the Society for Applied Anthropology, Seattle.

Dressler, William W., Jose Ernesto dos Santos, and Mauro Campos Balierio. 1996. Studying Diversity and Sharing in Culture: An Example of Lifestyle in Brazil. *Journal of Anthropological Research 52*:331–353.

Driver, Harold E. 1938. The Reliability of Culture Element Data. Culture Elements Distributions: VIII *Anthropological Records 1*:4, Berkeley: University of California Press.

Driver, Harold E. 1962. The Contribution of A. L. Kroeber to Culture Area Theory and Practice. *International Journal of American Linguistics 28*(2), Memoir 18.

Driver, Harold E. 1965. Survey of Numerical Classification in Anthropology. In *The Use of Computers in Anthropology.* Dell Hymes, ed. Pp. 301–344. The Hague and Paris: Mouton.

Driver, Harold E. 1970. Statistical Studies of Continuous Geographical Distributions. In *Handbook on Methods in Anthropology.* Raoull Naroll and Ronald Cohen, eds. Pp. 620–639. Garden City, NY: Natural History Press.

Driver, Harold E., and A. L. Kroeber. 1932. Quantitative Expression of Cultural Relationships. *University of California Publications in American Archaeology and Ethnology 31*:211–256.

Driver, Harold E., and Karl F. Schuessler. 1957. Factor Analysis of Ethnographic Data. *American Anthropologist 59*:655–663.

Edginton, E. S. 1980. *Randomization Tests.* New York: Marcel Dekker.

Efrom, Bradley, and Robert Tibshirani. 1991. Statistical Data Analysis in the Computer Age. *Science 253*:390–395.

Ellegard, A. L. 1959. Statistical Measurement of Linguistic Relationships. *Language 35*:131–156.

Feiring, B. R. 1986. *Linear Programming. An Introduction.* Quantitative Applications in the Social Sciences, Vol. 60. Thousand Oaks, CA: Sage Publications.

Fisher, R. A. 1935. *The Design of Experiments.* London: Oliver & Boyd.

Gannotti, Mary E. 1998. The Reliability and Validity of the Pediatric Evaluation of Disability Inventory for Children Living in Puerto Rico. Ph.D. diss., Storrs: University of Connecticut.

Goodenough, Ward H. 1944. A Technique for Scale Analysis. *Educational and Psychological Measurement 4*:179–190.

Goodenough, Ward H. 1963. Some Applications of Guttman Scale Analysis to Ethnography and Culture Theory. *Southwestern Journal of Anthropology 19*:235–250.

Greenacre, M. J. 1984. *Theory and Applications of Correspondence Analysis.* New York: Academic Press.

Gujarati, D. N. 1995. *Basic Econometrics.* New York: McGraw-Hill.

Hammel, E. A. 1990. A Theory of Culture for Demography. *Population and Development Review 16*:455–485.

Handwerker, W. Penn. 1988. Sampling Variability in Microdemographic Estimation of Fertility Parameters. *Human Biology 60*:305–318.

Handwerker, W. Penn. 1989. *Women's Power and Social Revolution.* Thousand Oaks, CA: Sage Publications.

Handwerker, W. Penn. 1990. Demography. In *Medical Anthropology.* Thomas M. Johnson and Carolyn F. Sargent, eds. Pp. 319–347. New York: Praeger.

Handwerker, W. Penn. 1991. Sampling Experiments as Teaching Tools: Part II, Fishing Expeditions Usually Catch Suckers. *Cultural Anthropology Methods 3*(1):8–9.

Handwerker, W. Penn. 1993a. Gender Power Differences Between Parents and High Risk Sexual Behavior by Their Children: AIDS/STD Risk Factors Extend to a Prior Generation. *Journal of Women's Health 2*:301–316.

Handwerker, W. Penn. 1993b. Empowerment and Fertility Transition on Antigua, WI: Education, Employment, and the Moral Economy of Childbearing. *Human Organization 52*(1):41–52.

Handwerker, W. Penn. 1997. Universal Human Rights and the Problem of Unbounded Cultural Meanings. *American Anthropologist 99*:799–809.

Handwerker, W. Penn. 1998. Consensus Analysis: Sampling Frames for Valid, Generalizable Research Findings. In *Using Methods in the Field: A Practical Introduction and Casebook.* V. De Munck and E. J. Sobo, eds. Pp. 165–178. Walnut Creek, CA: AltaMira Press.

Handwerker, W. Penn, and Paul V. Crosbie. 1982. Sex and Dominance. *American Anthropologist 84*:97–104.

Handwerker, W. Penn, Julie Harris, and Jeanne Hatcherson. 1997. Sampling Guidelines for Cultural Data. *Cultural Anthropology Methods 8*:7–9.

Handwerker, W. Penn, and Danielle F. Wozniak. 1997. Sampling Strategies for the Collection of Cultural Data. *Current Anthropology 38*:869–875.

Harman, H. H. 1976. *Modern Factor Analysis*, 3rd ed. Chicago: University of Chicago Press.

Hosmer, D., and S. Lemeshow. 1989. *Applied Logistic Regression.* New York: John Wiley.

Hubert, L. and J. Schultz. 1976. Quadratic Assignment as a General Data Analysis Strategy. *British Journal of Mathematical and Statistical Psychology 29*:190–241.

Jorgensen, Joseph G., ed. 1974. *Comparative Studies by Harold E. Driver and Essays in His Honor.* New Haven: HRAF Press.

Jorgensen, Joseph G. 1995. Ethnicity, Not Culture? Obfuscating Social Science in the *Exxon Valdez* Oil Spill Case. *American Indian Culture and Research Journal 19*:1–124.

Keesing, Roger. 1994. Theories of Culture Revisited. In *Assessing Cultural Anthropology*. Robert Borofsky, ed. Pp. 301–312. New York: McGraw-Hill.

Kempton, W., J. S. Boster, and J. A. Hartley. 1995. *Environmental Values in American Culture*. Cambridge: M.I.T. Press.

Kish, Leslie. 1965. *Survey Sampling*. New York: John Wiley.

Kruskal, J. B. and M. Wish. 1978. *Multidimensional Scaling*. Quantitative Applications in the Social Sciences, Vol. 11. Beverly Hills, CA: Sage Publications.

Liem, J. H., J. G. O'Toole, and J. B. James. 1992. The Need for Power in Women Who Were Sexually Abused as Children. *Psychology of Women Quarterly 16*:467–480.

Markus, G. B. 1979. *Analyzing Panel Data*. Beverly Hills, CA: Sage Publications.

McEwan, Peter J. M. 1963. Forms and Problems of Validation in Anthropological Research. *Current Anthropology 4*:155–183.

McNabb, S. 1990. The Uses of "Inaccurate" Data. *American Anthropologist 92*:116–129.

Miller, G. A. 1956. The Magical Number Seven, Plus Or Minus Two: Some Limits on Our Capacity for Processing Information. *Psychological Review 63*:81–97.

Mooney, Christopher Z., and Robert D. Duval. 1993. *Bootstrapping*. Quantitative Applications in the Social Sciences, Vol. 95. Thousand Oaks, CA: Sage Publications.

Murdock, George Peter. 1971. *Anthropology's Mythology. The Huxley Memorial Lecture*. Proceedings of the Royal Anthropological Institute.

Namboodiri, Krishnan. 1984. *Matrix Algebra*. Quantitative Applications in the Social Sciences, Vol. 38. Beverly Hills, CA: Sage Publications.

Odland, John. 1988. *Spatial Autocorrelation*. Scientific Geography Series, Vol. 9. Thousand Oaks, CA: Sage Publications.

Pelto, P., and G. Pelto. 1975. Intracultural Diversity: Some Theoretical Issues. *American Ethnologist 2*:1–18.

Reynolds, Mary Stephanie. 1990. Dance Brings About Everything: Dance Power in the Ideologies of Northern Utes of the Uintah and Ouray Reservation and Predominantly Mormon Anglos of an Adjacent Uintah Basin Community. Ph.D. diss., Irvine: University of California.

Romney, A. K., S. C. Weller, and W. H. Batchelder. 1986. Culture as Consensus. *American Anthropologist 88*:313–338.

Rummel, R. J. 1970. *Applied Factor Analysis*. Evanston: Northwestern University Press.

Schroeder, Larry D., Savid L. Sjoquist, and Paula E. Stephan. 1986. *Understanding Regression Analysis*. Quantitative Applications in the Social Sciences, Vol. 57. Thousand Oaks, CA: Sage Publications.

Shweder, Richard A. 1977. Likeness and Likelihood in Everyday Thought. *Current Anthropology 18*:637–658.

Sneath, P.H.A., and R. R. Sokal. 1973. *Numerical Taxonomy*. San Francisco: W. H. Freeman.

Sokal, R. R., and P.H.A. Sneath. 1963. *Principles of Numerical Taxonomy*. San Francisco: W. H. Freeman.

Tooby, John, and Leda Cosmides. 1992. The Psychological Foundations of Culture. In *The Adapted Mind*. J. H. Barkow, L. Cosmides, and J. Toomy, eds. Pp. 19–136. New York: Oxford University Press.

Tukey, J. W. 1958. Bias and Confidence in Not Quite Large Samples. *Annals of Mathematical Statistics 29*:614.

Tukey, J. W. 1977. *Exploratory Data Analysis*. Reading, MA: Addison-Wesley.

Tylor, Edward B. 1889. On a Method of Investigating the Development of Institutions; Applied to Laws of Marriage and Descent. *Journal of the Royal Anthropological Institution of Great Britain and Ireland 18*:245–272.

Wallace, A.F.C. 1961. *Culture and Personality*. New York: Random House.

Weller, S. C. 1987. Shared Knowledge, Intracultural Variation, and Knowledge Aggregation. *American Behavioral Scientist 31*:178–193.

Weller, S. C., and A. K. Romney. 1988. *Systematic Data Collection*. Qualitative Research Methods Series, Vol. 10. Thousand Oaks, CA: Sage Publications.

Wilkinson, Leland. 1997. *SYSTAT: The System for Statistics*. Chicago: SPSS, Inc.

Wolf, Eric R.. 1982. *Europe and the People Without History*. Berkeley: University of California Press.

Wozniak, Danielle F. 1997. Twentieth-Century Ideals: The Social Construction of U.S. Foster Motherhood. Ph.D. diss., Storrs: University of Connecticut.

Yamaguchi, Kazuo. 1991. *Event History Analysis*. Applied Social Research Methods Series, Vol. 28. Thousand Oaks, CA: Sage Publications.

H. RUSSELL BERNARD
GERY W. RYAN

Sixteen

Text Analysis
Qualitative and Quantitative Methods

Introduction

There is growing interest across the social sciences in the systematic analysis of "text."[1] Little wonder: Most of the recoverable data about human thought and human behavior is text of one kind or another. In this chapter, we survey methods of text analysis in the social sciences and particularly how anthropologists have used those methods to look for meaning and pattern in written text.[2]

We cover two broad types of text analysis: the *linguistic tradition*, which treats text as an object of analysis itself, and the *sociological tradition,* which treats text as a window into human experience. For the linguistic tradition, we review how anthropologists have collected and produced texts, analyzed indigenous literatures, discovered patterns and structures in performance styles, and compared the production of narratives within and across cultures. For the sociological tradition, we review the methods of schema analysis, grounded theory, classical content analysis, semantic network analysis, cognitive mapping, and Boolean analysis.

Throughout, we focus on methods for collecting and analyzing written texts such as political speeches, song lyrics, personal diaries, transcriptions of interviews, newspaper editorials, and so on. Many of these methods serve just as well in dealing with images, such as photographs, home movies, video tape, commercial movies, kinescopes of old television shows, etc.

In the study of text, some scholars use methods identified with the humanist tradition while others use methods identified with the positivist tradition. The former involves interpretation and the search for meaning. The latter involves the reduction of texts to codes that represent themes or concepts and the application of quantitative methods to find patterns in the relations among the codes. Nowhere is Eric Wolf's aphorism that "anthropology is the most humanistic of the sciences and the most scientific of the humanities" (1964:88) better demonstrated than in the practice of text analysis.

Anthropology: A Passion for Collecting Texts

Debates about the value of structuralism, functionalism, historical particularism, materialism, and postmodernism come and go, but the value of faithfully produced texts is undisputed. Among Franz Boas's lasting contributions is the corpus of texts he collected, translated. and published (or deposited in archives) from speakers of Bella Bella (1928b), Sahaptin and Salishan (1917), Keresan (1928a) and, with George Hunt, Kwakiutl (Boas and Hunt 1902–1905, 1906; Boas 1910, 1935–1943). In 1893, Boas taught Hunt to write Kwakiutl, Hunt's native language. By the time Hunt died in 1933, he had produced 5,650 pages of text—a corpus from which Boas produced most of his reports about Kwakiutl life (Rohner 1966).

To the extent possible before the invention of voice-recording devices, Boas trained his students and collaborators to collect verbatim texts.[3] Following Boas's example with Hunt, Paul Radin worked with Sam Blowsnake, a Winnebago. Blowsnake wrote the original manuscript (in Winnebago) that became (in translation) *Crashing Thunder: An Autobiography of a Winnebago Indian* (Blowsnake and Radin 1983 [1920, 1926]). Among Boas's other students, Swanton (1909), Goddard (1911), Kroeber (1907), Lowie (1930), and Sapir (Sapir and Dixon 1910; Sapir and Curtain 1974; Sapir and Swadesh 1978) collected and analyzed indigenous language text, and Margaret Mead produced hours and hours of cinema verité about Bali dance—a rich, textual record that can be turned to again and again as new insights and new methods of analysis become available.

The concern for the collection and archiving of text remains undiminished in anthropology. In the 1970s, Eric Hamp edited the Native American Texts Series of the *International Journal of American Linguistics* (see, for example, Furbee-Losee 1976; Bernard and Salinas Pedraza 1976). As the literary language of a pre–Colonial Era civilization, Maya has attracted particular attention. Munro Edmonson's translations of the books of *Chilam Balam* (1982, 1986) and Dennis Tedlock's translation of the *Popol Vuh* (1985) are outstanding examples.

Following the example of Boas with Hunt and Radin with Blowsnake, Bernard (Salinas Pedraza and Bernard 1978; Bernard and Salinas Pedraza 1989), El Guindi and Hernández Jiménez (1986), Lurie (1961), and Sexton (Bizarro and Sexton 1981, 1985), among others, have helped indigenous people create narratives themselves in indigenous languages. Bernard (1997) has provided indigenous people with the computer technology and training to produce their own books in their own languages. Here again, the emphasis is on the production of texts, not on their analysis. (See Salinas Pedraza [1997] and González Ventura [1997] for indigenous perspectives on the production of indigenous-language text by computer.)

Analysis of Indigenous Literature

There are about 240 languages in the world spoken by more than a million people. Some of those languages have very long literary histories, and while smaller languages are disappearing, other indigenous ones are developing new literary traditions. Postel-Coster (1977) studies an indigenous tradition of novels in Indonesia that goes back to around 1920 when a thriving production of new literature appeared in Malay by western Sumatran, or Minangkabau, writers.

Postel-Coster does not see such novels as a source of factual information, but as the modern continuation of the myth in nonliterary societies. Although novels can not be taken as documentaries, he says, important elements of social reality can be exposed in novels without allusion to actual events. In novels about young couples who must struggle against social rules and disapproval to marry, Postel-Coster finds that "many problems of Minangkabau culture are explicitly dealt with: matrilineal succession, polygynous marriage, the enormous impact of the extended family on an individual's life, and the question of *merantau*—the traditional emigration of young people, mostly men, to other areas" (1977:137).

Besnier (1995) has studied an indigenous literacy tradition on the Polynesian atoll of Nukulaelae. The texts produced by the people of Nukulaelae include letters, sermons, and announcements of events. Besnier analyzes correspondence by identifying and presenting exemplars of structural regularities. For example, the main body of letters on Nukulaelae "usually begins with a greeting identical to the greeting used in face-to-face interactions (*taalofa* "hello," a Samoan borrowing). This is followed by references to the health of everyone at the writer's and recipient's ends, and sometimes a very long series of invocations to God's grace and kindness" (Besnier 1995:86). Besnier follows this with a series of exemplars.

Besnier noticed that letter writers "always adhere to a religious reference scheme in opening themes, Christian for the majority, or Baha'i, etc., for the handful of religious converts. In letters written by younger people, the introduction is usually much shorter and more predictable in content than that of letters written by older individuals. These introductions bear many similarities to the beginning of formal speeches" (1995:87).

Using literary methods of analysis, then, Besnier identifies covariation between certain elements of style in text and independent variables like religious affiliation and age.

Patterns in Performance

The discovery of regularities in narrative performance is achieved mostly through the analysis of written text (for a review, see Hanks 1989). The work of Dell Hymes is of singular importance. In 1977, Hymes reported that "the narratives of the Chinookan peoples of Oregon and Washington can be shown to be organized in terms of lines, verses, stanzas, scenes, and what many call acts." Hymes felt that this discovery might be relevant to many indigenous languages of the Americas (1977:431).

Hymes looked at texts in Shoalwater Chinook and Kathlamet Chinook. The texts had been collected by Boas between 1890–1894 from one informant who happened to speak both mutually unintelligible languages. Hymes also examined texts from Clackamas Chinook (collected in 1930 and 1931 by Melville Jacobs) and in Wasco (Wishram) Chinook (collected by Sapir in 1905, by Hymes in the 1950s. and by Michael Silverstein in the 1960s and '70s). Hymes found that features of Chinook that might have seemed idiosyncratic to the speakers of Shoalwater, Kathlamet, and Clackamas Chinook "are in fact part of a common fabric of performance style" so that the three languages "share a common form of poetic organization" (Hymes 1977:431).

This was a truly important discovery, for it made clear that Native North American texts have something to contribute to a general theory of poetics and literature. Hymes discovered verses, not by counting lines of text "but by recognizing repetition within a frame. . . . Covariation between form and meaning, between units with a recurrent Chinookan pattern of narrative organization, is the key" (Hymes 1977:438).

In some texts, Hymes found recurrent linguistic elements that made the task easy. Linguists who have worked with precisely recorded texts in Native American languages have noticed the recurrence of elements like "Now," "Then," "Now then," and "Now again." These often signal the separation of verses and "once such patterning has been discovered in cases with such markers, it can be discerned in cases without them" (1977:439). The method is to look for "abstract features that co-occur with the use of initial particle pairs in the narratives" of other speakers who use initial particle pairs. The method, then, is a form of controlled comparison.

In a series of articles and books (1976, 1977, 1980a, 1980b, 1981) Hymes showed that most Native American texts of narrative performance (going back to the early texts collected by Boas and his students and continuing in today's narrative performance as well) are organized into verses and stanzas that are aggregated into groups of either fives and threes or fours and twos. Boas and his students organized the narratives of American Indians into lines. This hid from view "a vast world of poetry waiting to be released by those of us with some knowledge of the languages" (Virginia Hymes 1987:65).

According to Virginia Hymes (1987:67–68), Dell Hymes's method involves "working back and forth between content and form, between organization at the level of the whole narrative and at the level of the details of lines within a single verse or even words within a line." Gradually, an analysis emerges that reflects the analyst's understanding of the narrative tradition and of the particular narrator. Virginia Hymes emphasizes that it is "only through work with many narratives by many narrators that the analyst builds up a knowledge of the range of narrative devices used in the language and the variety of uses to which they may be put" (1987:67–68).

In his study of Zuni narratives, Tedlock (1972:221) found that such paralinguistic features as voice quality, loudness, and pausing are key indicators of performance (and see Woodbury [1987] for an examination of prosodic features in Yup'ik Eskimo narrative). Hymes points out that the texts recorded by people like Sapir and Jacobs often had paralinguistic features such as nonphonemic vowel length and non-phonemic stress (for emphasis) marked. Some linguists of the time emphasized phonemic transcription under "the unquestioned assumption that linguistic structure should be built up on the basis of referential function alone, to the exclusion of features serving stylistic function" (Hymes 1977:452–453). This wasn't, of course, how Boas and his students did things. They used all manner of conventions for indicating expressive as well as strictly phonemic features of narratives that they recorded.

Thus, says Hymes, the view of the Boasians that "one should regard and present conventional phonetic habits, expressive as well as referential, comes to seem in the context of ethnopoetics, not old hat, but a cause for gratitude" (1977:453).

Tedlock (1987) showed the exegetical power that linguistic methods can bring to text analysis. He had translated the *Popol Vuh*, a sixteenth-century Quiché Maya manuscript that had been written out by Francisco Ximénez, a missionary of the time. Suppose, Tedlock asked, we have an ancient text, one that was meant to have been narrated. Can we narrate it today as performers would have done in ancient times? In achieving his translation of the *Popol Vuh*, Tedlock had relied on Andrés Xiloj, a modern speaker of Quiché. Xiloj had not been trained to read Maya, but he was literate in Spanish and made the transition very quickly. "When given his first chance to look at the Popol Vuh text, he produced a pair of spectacles and began reading aloud, word by word" (Tedlock 1987:145).

As was true of many medieval manuscripts in Europe, Ximénez's rendition of the *Popol Vuh* was more or less an undifferentiated mass of text with almost no punctuation—that is, no clues on how a performer might have "emphasized or elided the boundaries of . . . segments of discourse through the use of intonational contours, or how he might have varied his timing through the placement of pauses" (Tedlock 1987:147).

The solution to this problem was to capture oral narratives (not just casual speech) from modern speakers of the language—speeches, prayers, songs, stories—and to look for "patterns in the wording that have analogs in the ancient text" and how these patterns are enunciated (Tedlock 1987:147). Tedlock devises conventions for marking pauses, accelerations, verse endings, and so on. It is in the very use of such written marks that we see Tedlock's analysis—that is, his understanding of how a performance went. He can apply the written conventions to ancient texts once the analysis of performance is done. Then, by using techniques from linguistics (such as systematic comparison to look for recurrent sound patterns that signify variations in meaning), Tedlock found that Quiché verse has the same structure as ancient Middle Eastern texts—texts that predate Homer. Indeed, he concluded it is the same structure found in all living oral traditions that have not yet been influenced by writing. This is a contribution to a general theory of poetics and literature of the sort that Hymes had envisioned a decade earlier for the methods of ethnopoetics.

Sherzer (1994) presents a detailed analysis of a two-hour performance by Chief Olopinikwa of a traditional San Blas Kuna chant. The chant was recorded in 1970. Like many linguistic anthropologists, Sherzer had taught an assistant, Alberto Campos, to use a phonetic transcription system. After the chant, Sherzer asked Campos, to transcribe and translate the tape. Campos put Kuna and Spanish on left- and right-facing pages (1994:907).

By studying Campos's translation against the original Kuna, Sherzer was able to pick out certain recurrent features. Campos left out the chanted utterances of the responding chief (usually something like "so it is"), which turned out to be markers for verse endings in the chant. Campos also left out so-called framing words and phrases (like "Thus" at the beginning of a verse and "it is said, so I pronounce" at the end of a verse). These contribute to the line and verse structure of the chant. Finally, "instead of transposing metaphors and other figurative and allusive language into Spanish" Campos "explains them in his translation" (Sherzer 1994:908).

A key method of text analysis in ethnopoetics is text presentation. It turns out that verse breaks are determined by the regular turn-taking between Chief Olopinikwa and the responding chief and that verses and lines have a regular melodic shape. In his presentation of Chief Olopinikwa's performance, Sherzer breaks the work into lines and verses, using the convention of beginning verses and lines flush on the left of each page and indenting the lines of the responding chief. Earlier, in his presentation of *The Hot Pepper Story*, Sherzer (1990:178) used a highly literal translation. The text repeats a small number of words and themes, and Sherzer felt that a more liberal translation would fail to capture the poetics of performance. So, Sherzer describes the thematic elements he sees in the text but uses the device of literalness in the translation to draw the reader's attention to those elements.

Text analysis produces new text, which in turn can be analyzed. Hanks (1988) reviewed Edmunson's (1982) translation of *The Book of Chilam Balam of Tizimin*.

Edmunson had translated and annotated the original Mayan corpus into 5,514 lines of text, changing the format of presentation in the process. In the original, the lines had run clear across the page, but Edmonson presented the text in short lines to emphasize what he considered to be the verse structure. Hanks analyzes not only the Mayan text, but the literary style that Edmonston used in his presentation.

In translating Ñähñu (Otomí) parables, folk tales, and jokes, Bernard and Salinas (1976) presented a fully literal translation and a fully liberal translation, in addition to a transcription of the Ñähñu. At the time, Bernard felt that there was no way to mediate between the characteristics of the original, free Ñähñu and a free English translation. Later, in translating Salinas's four-volume ethnography of the Ñähñu, Bernard tried a middle course—one in which the English is grammatical but also one which makes clear from the style that it is a translation (see Bernard and Salinas 1989).

Anthropologists are still experimenting with methods for presenting text of indigenous performance that capture the subtleties of performance. How can one know if a particular presentation does, in fact, capture regular features of narrative? Tedlock's work with Andrés Xiloj, Sherzer's with Alberto Campos, and Bernard's with Jesús Salinas are, we think, experiments in method.

Sherzer and Woodbury (1987) observed that highly artistic, creative performance may be based on an underlying cognitive representation. These representations are knowable, they said, by systematically comparing texts across performances. Thus, they pose the possibility that there are schemas for performance—schemas that go beyond the lexical and syntactic levels of grammar. We will return to the methods of schema analysis.

Inter- and Intracultural Comparisons of Narratives

Comparing how people produce narratives in different cultures has long been of interest to many social scientists. In 1975, Wallace Chafe and five colleagues received a grant from the National Institutes for Mental Health to conduct research on how people store knowledge in the mind. In the spirit of the pioneering work by F. C. Bartlett (1967 [1932]) on how people remembered and retold folk tales, Chafe and his colleagues hired a professional filmmaker and produced the *Pear Story* film.[4] They showed it to more than 50 speakers of English in California, and to 20 or more speakers of Chinese, Japanese, Malay, Greek, Thai, German, Haitian Creole, Persian, and Sapultec (a Mayan language in Guatemala). They asked their informants for narratives about the film within half an hour of viewing and transcribed the tapes verbatim (with lots of attention to pauses, pause filters, stutterings, and such).

Examining the *Pear Stories*, Chafe (1980) identified the existence of *idea units* (about six seconds long and containing about six words) commonly marked by an intonation contour that involves a rise in pitch or a fall. Chafe suggests "that these idea units, these spurts of language, are linguistic expressions of focuses of consciousness" (1980:15) that are packaged into sentences. Children often package entire narratives into a single unit, but so do adults sometimes.

Downing (1980) compared the 20 English and 20 Japanese *Pear* story narratives, marking all nominal references to concrete entities (1,363 in the English narratives; 786 in the Japanese). She found that speakers of both languages make extensive use of a similar body of "basic" lexemes, but that cognitive, stylistic, and textual constraints may cause individual speakers to substitute other words and phrases for the basic terms at a given point in the narrative.

Herzfeld (1977) analyzed multiple renditions of the *khelidonisma*, or swallow song, sung in modern Greece as part of the welcoming of spring. He collected texts of the song from ancient, medieval, and modern historical sources and recorded texts of current-day renditions in several locations across Greece. His purpose was to show that inconsistencies in the texts come not from "some putative irrationality in the processes of oral tradition" but are, in fact, reflections of structural principles that underlie the *rite de passage* for welcoming spring in rural Greece. To make his point, Herzfeld looks for anomalies across renditions—like "March, my good March" in one song compared to "March, terrible March" in another. Herzfeld claims that the word "good" is used ironically in Greek where the referent is a source of anxiety.

Is March a subject of symbolic anxiety for Greek villagers? Yes, says, Herzfeld, it is, as evidenced by widely observed practices such as avoidance of certain activities during the *drimata* (the first three days of March). Herzfeld supports his analysis by referring to the *drimes*, a word that denotes the first three days of August, which are associated with malevolent spirits. Since March is the transition from winter to summer and August is the transition from summer to winter, Herzfeld concludes that there is symbolic danger associated with these mediating months. He finds support for this analysis in the fact that February is never referred to with an unequivocally good epithet.

This is symbolic analysis—the search for symbols and their interconnection in the expression of culture. The method for doing this kind of analysis requires deep involvement with the culture, including an intimate familiarity with the langauge, so that the symbolic referents emerge during the study of those expressions—as in the study of texts here. You can't see the connections among symbols if you don't know what the symbols are and what they are supposed to mean.

Furbee (1996) is doing an ongoing study of a new cult in and around Lomantán, a Tojolabal Maya village in the state of Chiapas, Mexico. According the the local story, Dominga Hernández was cutting wood on April 30, 1994, when God appeared and gave her images to care for. The images included the Christ Child, the Virgin Mary, Saint Joseph, and animals of the crèche. Hernández was to keep the images in her house and have a church built in Lomantán. Then she could turn over care of the the images to the community. Within 43 days, Hernández had mobilized support for purchase of materials and for the donated labor that went into building the church that now houses the images.

In 1996, Furbee and Jill Brody collected 26 versions of the Lomantán miracle. The tellers of these stories come from eighteen different villages across the region, including ten that are loyal to the PDR (an opposition party) and eight that are loyal to the PRI (the ruling political party).

Spanish loan words in the texts run from 1.9%–12.5% (the high end is the tale told by Hernández herself), but the number of Spanish loan words in the texts from the PRI-affiliated villages is 22% greater than the number of loan words in the texts from the PDR-affiliated villages (the difference is statistically significant). In other words "the greater Spanish loan usage is where one would expect to find it, with people from villages sympathetic to prevailing power." The PDR-affiliated villages are more sympathetic to the Zapatista cause and the speech of those villages contains fewer Spanish loan words—"just what one might predict from those who oppose the prevailing hegemony and who are engaged in a revitalization movement" (Furbee 1996:13).

La Llorona (the weeping woman) is a morality tale told across Mexico. Mathews (1992) collected 60 tellings of it. Here is one telling, which Mathews says is typical:

> La Llorona was a bad woman who married a good man. They had children and all was well. Then one day she went crazy and began to walk the streets. Everyone knew but her husband. When he found out he beat her. She had much shame. The next day she walked into the river and drowned herself. And now she knows no rest and must forever wander the streets wailing in the night. And that is why women must never leave their families to walk the streets looking for men. If they are not careful they will end up like La Llorona. (1992:128)

In another telling, La Llorona kills herself because her husband becomes a drunk and loses all their money. In yet another, she kills herself because her husband is seen going with other women and La Llorona, in disbelief, finally catches him paying off a woman in the streets.

Borrowing from Mandler's (1984) notion that stories are composed of an ordered series of constituent units, Mathews builds a grammar of the La Llorona stories. It is this grammar, says Mathews, this schema, that accounts for the success of the tale's motivational force. The morality tale succeeds in shaping people's behavior because "the motives of the main characters draw upon culturally shared schemas about gendered human nature" (1992:129). Men, according to Mathews's understanding of the cultural model in rural mestizo Oaxaca, view women as sexually uncontrolled. Unless they are controlled, or control themselves, their true nature will emerge and they will begin (as the story says) to "walk the streets" in search of sexual gratification. Men, for their part, are viewed by women as sexually insatiable.

Men are driven, like animals, to satisfy their desires, even at the expense of family obligations. In her grammar of La Llorona tales, Mathews shows that women have no recourse but to kill themselves when they cannot make their marriages work.

Mathews, however, goes beyond simply identifying the schema; she offers an explanation of where key parts of the schema come from. Most marriages in the village where Mathews did her research are arranged by parents and involve some exchange of resources between the families. Consequently, "natal families are usually unwilling to take back a daughter permanently and thereby contribute to the break-up of a marriage. So the only option perceived to be open to a woman who wants to terminate her marriage is suicide" (1992:150). Thus, Mathews offers a materialist explanation of how structural features in the society effect superstructural outcomes (perceptions) and consequent behavior—the inclusion of suicide by the woman in virtually all tellings of the La Llorona morality tale, despite significant variations in the tellings by men and women.

We now turn to the sociological analysis of text, beginning with the search for schemas.

Schemas, Models, and Metaphors

Schema analysis combines elements of the linguistic and sociological traditions. It pays particular attention to linguistic and paralinguistic features such as metaphors, proverbs, repetitions, pauses, speaker transitions, turn taking, and interruptions in the search for mental models that motivate action (D'Andrade 1984, 1987, 1995). (For a review of the concept of mental models, see Johnson-Laird [1983, 1989].)

Schema analysis is based on the idea that there is too much information about reality for people to deal with and that people must carry around some simplifications that help make sense of the welter of information to which they are exposed (Casson 1983:430). Early work by Bartlett (1967 [1932]) on how people remember things suggested the existence of such simplifications or "building blocks of cognition" (Rumelhart 1980).

In an influential book, Schank and Abelson (1977) postulated that schemas—or scripts, as they called them—enable culturally skilled people to fill in details of a story. We often say things like "Fred lost his data because he forgot to save his work." We know that Fred's forgetting to save his work did not actually *cause* him to lose his data. A whole set of links are left out, but they are easily filled in by any listeners who have the background to do so. It is, says Wodak (1992:525), our schemas that lead us to interpret Mona Lisa's smile as evidence of her perplexity or of her desperation.

Some schemas may be universal. Piaget (1970) studied cognitive schemas in children that he thought were universal in human development. Some are surely idiosyncratic (each person speaks a language that is, in some ways, like no other).

Somewhere between universal and idiosyncratic schemas are *cultural schemas*: They are developed through experience but are held by a population (Rice 1980:154; D'Andrade 1995:130).

Rice (1980) developed what she called the American schema for telling a story, which she contrasted with the Eskimo schema for doing the same thing. Using an experimental design, she took two Eskimo stories, adjusted them to about 20 phrases each, and presented one of five, systematically distorted versions to 12 Americans. She also presented the complete, original Eskimo story (in English) or an Americanized version of the story to 12 people. Then she asked informants to recall and write down, in their own words, certain passages from the stories.

When the passages fit the American story schema (as they did in the Americanized versions of the stories), subjects agreed about which events they remembered. Furthermore, subjects recalled vastly more exactly worded phrases from the Americanized versions of the stories than from the Eskimo ones. Thus, people distort stories in recall to fit their cultural expectations (their schemas) about what stories ought to be like.

Cognitive scientists, including anthropologists like Rice, often study schemas by setting up experiments so that they can observe the act of reasoning under uncomplicated conditions. Hutchins takes a naturalist's perspective. "If what we want to know about is how people reason in the real world," he says, "let's look at them doing that" (1980:123). Hutchins (1980) recorded and transcribed a formal dispute in the Trobriands. Two men claim the right to cultivate a particular garden plot. The antagonists have different views of the facts but, as Hutchins shows, they share an underlying logic—a schema—for how land claims are to be understood (1980:128).

Of course, it is not always possible to record people who are reasoning about important issues in their lives. The intermediate step, between experiments on reasoning and recording natural discourse on reasoning, is to collect texts. In 1979, Naomi Quinn and her students collected and transcribed interviews about marriage from 11 North American couples. Some of the couples were recently married; others had been married a long time. The couples came from different parts of the country and represented various occupations, educational levels, and ethnic and religious groups. Each of the 22 people were interviewed separately for 15–16 hours, and the interviews were transcribed.

In a series of articles, Quinn (1982, 1987, 1992, 1996, 1997) has analyzed this body of text to discover and document the concepts underlying American marriage and to show how these concepts are tied together—how they form a cultural model shared by people from different backgrounds about what constitutes success and failure in marriage.

Quinn's method is to "exploit clues in ordinary discourse for what they tell us about shared cognition—to glean what people must have in mind in order to say the things they do" (1997:140). She begins by looking at patterns of speech and the repetition of key words and phrases, paying particular attention to informants' use of metaphors and the commonalities in their reasoning about marriage. For example, Nan, one of her informants, uses a popular metaphor, that "marriage is a manufactured product"—something that has properties, like strength and staying power, and that requires work to produce. Some marriages are "put together well," while others "fall apart" like so many cars or toys or washing machines (Quinn 1987:174).

Quinn's emphasis on metaphor owes much to the pioneering work by Lakoff and Johnson (1980). The object is to look for metaphors in rhetoric and deduce the schemas, or underlying principles, that might produce patterns in those metaphors. For instance, Quinn found that people talk about their surprise at the breakup of a marriage by saying that they thought the couple's marriage was "like the Rock of Gibraltar" or that they thought the marriage had been "nailed in cement." People use these metaphors because they assume that their listeners know that cement and the Rock of Gibraltar are things that last forever.

But Quinn reasons that if schemas or scripts are what make it possible for people to fill in around the bare bones of a metaphor, then the metaphors must be surface phenomena and cannot themselves be the basis for shared understanding. Quinn found that the hundreds of metaphors in her corpus of texts fit into just eight linked classes that she calls: lastingness, sharedness, compatibility, mutual benefit, difficulty, effort, success (or failure), and risk of failure. For example, Quinn's informants often compared marriages (their own and those of others) to manufactured and durable products ("it was put together pretty good") and to journeys ("we made it up as we went along; it was a sort of do-it-yourself project"). Quinn sees these metaphors, as well as references to marriage as "a lifetime proposition," as exemplars of the overall expectation of lastingness in marriage.

The classes of metaphors, the underlying concepts, are linked together in a schema that guides the discourse of ordinary Americans about marriage:

> Marriages are ideally lasting, shared and mutually beneficial. Marriages that are not shared will not be mutually beneficial and those not mutually beneficial will not last. Benefit is a matter of fulfillment. Spouses must be compatible in order to be able to fill each other's [emotional] needs so that their marriages will be fulfilling and hence beneficial. Fulfillment and, more specifically, the compatibility it requires, are difficult to realize but this difficulty can be overcome, and compatibility and fulfillment achieved, with effort. Lasting marriages in which difficulty has been overcome by effort are regarded as successful ones. Incompatibility, lack of benefit, and the resulting marital difficulty, if not overcome, put a marriage at risk of failure. (Quinn 1997:164)

Quinn presents extended excerpts from eight informants to illustrate the relationship between lastingness and success. She hopes that the examples she gives will familiarize readers with her mode of analysis and "convince them of the pattern exemplified" in the cases she presents. "Finding this structure," Quinn says, "was a methodological challenge" (1997:167).

Other examples of the search for cultural schemas in texts include Holland's (1985) study of the reasoning that Americans apply to interpersonal problems, Kempton's (1987) study of ordinary Americans' theories of home heat control, and Claudia Strauss's (1997) study of what chemical plant workers and their neighbors think about the free enterprise system.

Examining metaphors and proverbs are not the only linguistic features used to infer meaning from text. D'Andrade notes that "perhaps the simplest and most direct indication of schematic organization in naturalistic discourse is the repetition of associative linkages" (1991:294). He observes that "indeed, anyone who has listened to long stretches of talk—whether generated by a friend, spouse, workmate, informant, or patient—knows how frequently people circle through the same network of ideas" (1991:287).

In a study of blue-collar workers in Rhode Island, Claudia Strauss (1992) refers to these ideas as "personal semantic networks." She describes such a network from one of her informants. On rereading her intensive interviews with one of the workers, Strauss found that her informant repeatedly referred to ideas associated with greed, money, businessmen, siblings, and "being different." She displays the relationships among these ideas by writing the concepts on a page of paper and interconnected with lines and explanations.

Price (1987) observes that when people tell stories, they assume that their listeners share many assumptions about how the world works and so they leave out information that "everyone knows." Thus, in her study of 14 narratives of illness and misfortune in a Mestizo community in Ecuador, Price looks for what is *not* said in order to identify underlying cultural assumptions (1987:314).

If underlying schemas exist, then, with a native speaker's command of the language and a deep understanding of one another's metaphors (about marriage and so many other things), we can recognize the surface representations of those schemas. Understanding the complete lexicon of a language, then, makes it possible to do text analysis. Language competence is nine-tenths of method.

We turn next to the two methods most widely used across the social sciences for analyzing text: grounded theory and classical content analysis. Grounded theory emphasizes the discovery and labeling of concepts (variables) and the building of models based on a close reading of the text. Classic content analysis emphasizes the formal description of concepts and the testing of models and hypotheses.

Grounded Theory

Grounded theory is a set of techniques that: (1) brings the researcher close to informants' experiences; (2) provides a rigorous and detailed method for identifying categories and concepts that emerge from text; and (3) helps the researcher link the concepts into substantive and formal theories (Glaser and Strauss 1967; Lincoln and Guba 1985; Strauss 1987; Lonkila 1995; Charmaz 1990; Strauss and Corbin 1990; Wilson and Hutchinson 1996). Miles and Huberman (1994) refer to their own brand of text analysis as "soft-nosed positivism"—a good characterization of most work in grounded theory as well, in our view.

Grounded theory has been used to examine topics in public health (Hitchcock and Wilson 1992; Sohier 1993; Kearney et al. 1994, 1995; Irurita 1996; Wright 1997), social welfare (Silverberg et al. 1996), and business (Hunt and Ropo 1995; Locke 1996). It also has a long history in ethnographic case studies (Becker et al. 1961; Agar 1979, 1980, 1983). Journals such as *Nursing Research, Qualitative Health Research,* and *Qualitative Sociology* have been outlets for this type of research.

The mechanics of grounded theory are deceptively simple: produce verbatim transcripts of interviews and read through a small sample of text (usually line by line). Identify potential themes that arise. As analytic categories emerge, pull all the data (that is, exemplars) from those categories together and compare them, considering not only what text belongs in each emerging category but also how the categories are linked together. Use the relationships among categories to build theoretical models, constantly checking the models against the data—particularly against negative cases. Throughout the process, keep running notes about the coding and about potential hypotheses and new directions for the research. This is called "memoing" in the vocabulary of grounded theory. Grounded theory is an iterative process by which the analyst becomes more and more "grounded" in the data and develops increasingly richer concepts and models of how the phenomenon being studied really works.

Identifying Themes

Many researchers offer specific advice and schemes for inductive or "open" coding of text (Taylor and Bogdan 1984; Lincoln and Guba 1985; Strauss and Corbin 1990; Bogdan and Biklen 1992; Bernard 1994; Lofland and Lofland 1995; Agar 1996). Sandelowski (1995a:373) observes that analysis of texts begins with proofreading the material and simply underlining key phrases "because they make some as yet inchoate sense." Identifying the categories and terms used by informants themselves is called "*in vivo* coding" (Strauss and Corbin 1990). Spradley (1979:199–201) advised searching texts for evidence of social conflict, cultural contradictions, informal techniques of social control, methods that people use in managing impersonal social relationships, the methods by which people acquire and maintain achieved and ascribed status, and information about how people solve problems. Each of these arenas, he said, is likely to yield major themes in cultures.

Others suggest that coders start with some general themes derived from reading the literature and add more themes and subthemes as they go (Willms et al. 1990; Miles and Huberman 1994). Regardless of which strategy is used, by the time one identifies the themes and refines them to the point where they can be applied to the whole text, a lot of the interpretive analysis has been done. Miles and Huberman say simply: "Coding is analysis" (1994:56).

Building Models

The next step is to identify how themes are linked to each other in a theoretical model. Memoing is one of the principal techniques for recording relationships among themes. When reviewing the text, you continually write down your thoughts about what you're reading. These thoughts become a set of information on which to develop theory. We think of memoing as taking field notes on observations about texts.

Strauss and Corbin discuss three kinds of memos: code notes, theory notes, and operational notes (1990:18, 73–74, 109–129, 197–219). Code notes describe the concepts that are being discovered in "the discovery of grounded theory." In theory notes, the researcher tries to summarize his or her ideas about what's going on in the text. Operational notes are about practical matters.

Once a model starts to take shape, researchers specifically look for negative examples that do not fit the pattern. Negative case analysis is discussed in detail by Becker et al. (1961:37–45), Strauss and Corbin (1990:108–109), Lincoln and Guba (1985:309–313), Dey (1993:226–233), and Miles and Huberman (1994:271). Negative cases either disconfirm parts of the model or suggest new connections that need to be made. In either case, these negative examples need to be accommodated when results are presented.

When the steps of the grounded theory approach are followed, models or "theories" are produced that are, indeed, "grounded" in the text. These models, however, are not the final product of the grounded theory approach. In their original formulation, Glaser and Strauss (1967) emphasized that the building of grounded theory models is a step in the research process. The next, of course, is to confirm the validity of a model by testing it on an independent sample of data.

The grounded theory approach, including iterative coding and analysis by constant memoing, has been the inspiration for several of the most widely used software packages in text analysis, including Atlas/ti (Muhr 1991), NUD*IST (Richards and Richards 1991), and Kwalitan (Peters and West 1990). In fact, 17 of the 24 text analysis packages reviewed by Weitzman and Miles (1995:316–325) have some provision for writing memos on the fly and retrieving them during analysis.[5]

Displaying Concepts and Models

Much of grounded theory involves presenting segments of text—verbatim quotes from informants—as exemplars of concepts and theories. These illustrations may be prototypical examples of central tendency or they may represent exceptions to the norm. Grounded theory researchers may display their theoretical results in maps of the major categories and the relationships among them (Miles and Huberman 1994:134–137, Kearney et al. 1995). These "concept maps" are similar to the personal semantic networks described by C. Strauss (1992) and D'Andrade (1991) (see below).

An Example of Grounded Theory

Kearney et al. (1995) interviewed 60 women who reported using crack cocaine an average of at least once weekly during pregnancy. The semistructured interviews lasted from one–three hours and covered childhood, relationships, life context, previous pregnancies, and actions during the current pregnancy related to drug use, prenatal care, and self-care. Transcripts were coded and analyzed as soon as they became available so that data collection and data analysis were intricately linked. As new topics emerged, investigators asked about the topics in subsequent interviews.

Kearney et al. coded the data first for the general topics they used to guide the interviews. Later, they would use these codes to search for and retrieve examples of text related to various interview topics. Next, team members reread each transcript searching for examples of social psychological themes in the women's narratives. Each time they found an example, they considered "What is this an example of?". The answers suggested substantive categories that were refined with each new transcript.

Kearney et al. (1995) looked at how substantive categories were related. They recorded their ideas about these interactions in the forms of memos and developed a preliminary model. With each subsequent transcript, they looked for negative cases and pieces of data that challenged their emerging model. They adjusted the model to include the full range of variation that emerged in the transcripts.

To begin with, Kearney et al. identified five major categories, which they called: VALUE, HOPE, RISK, HARM REDUCTION, and STIGMA MAN-AGEMENT. (Capital letters are often for code names in grounded theory research, just as in statistical research.) Women valued their pregnancy and the baby-to-be in relation to their own life priorities (VALUE); women expressed varying degrees of hope that their pregnancies would end well and that they could be good mothers (HOPE) and they were aware that cocaine use posed risks to their fetus but they perceived that risk differently (RISK). Women tried in various ways to minimize the risk to the fetus (HARM REDUCTION) and they used various stratagems to reduce social rejection and derision (STIGMA MANAGEMENT).

By the time they had coded 20 interviews, Kearney et al. realized that the categories HARM REDUCTION and STIGMA MANAGEMENT were components of a more fundamental category that they labeled EVADING HARM. After about 30 interviews had been coded, they identified and labeled an overarching psychological process they called SALVAGING SELF that incorporated all five of the major categories. "Theoretical saturation" was reached at approximately 40 interviews and Kearney et al. conducted another 20 without discovering any new categories or relationships.

Kearney et al. (1995) present their model graphically with ties to supporting textual evidence. They describe in rich detail each of the major categories that they discovered. Finally, they checked the validity of their model by presenting it to knowledgeable informants (pregnant drug users), members of the project staff, and health and social service professionals who were familiar with the population under study.

Classical Content Analysis

While grounded theory is concerned with the discovery of data-induced hypotheses, content analysis comprises techniques for (1) reducing the symbol-laden artifacts produced by human behavior (including, but not limited to texts) to a unit-by-variable matrix and (2) analyzing that matrix quantitatively in order to test hypotheses. The matrix is produced by applying a set of codes to artifacts and checking the reliability of human coders against one another. When the artifacts are texts, the coding may be done by a computer, using a content analysis dictionary. In addition to written text, the symbol-laden artifacts of human effort include television sitcoms, political cartoons, advertisements, song lyrics, and clay pots. The object is to test hypotheses about the producers of the symbolic artifacts, the consumers, or both.[6]

Cowan and O'Brien (1990), for example, tested whether males or females were more likely to be survivors in slasher films. The corpus of "text" in this case was 56 slasher films. The films contained a total of 474 victims, who were coded for gender and survival. Conventional wisdom about slasher films holds that victims are mostly women and slashers are mostly men. While slashers in these films were, in fact, mostly men, it turned out that victims were equally likely to be male or female. Surviving as a female slasher victim, however, was strongly associated with the absence of sexual behavior and with being less physically attractive than nonsurviving females. The male nonsurvivors were cynical, egotistical, and dictatorial. Cowan and O'Brien conclude that, in slasher films, sexually pure women survive and that "unmitigated masculinity" ends in death (1990:195).

The methodological issues associated with content analysis are all evident here. Does the sample of 56 films used by Cowan and O'Brien justify generalizing to slasher films in general? Did the coders who worked on the project make correct judgments in deciding things like the physical attractiveness of female victims or the personality and behavioral characteristics of the male victims? These two issues in particular, sampling and coding, are at the heart of content analysis.

Sampling

There are two components to sampling. The first is the identification of the *corpus* of texts; the second is the identification of the units of analysis *within* the texts. If one collects 40 or 50 life histories, then the entire set of texts is analyzed. When the units of data run into the hundreds or even thousands (i.e., all television commercials that ran during prime time in August 1997, all front-page stories of *The New York Times* from 1887–1996, all campaign speeches by Bill Clinton and George Bush during the 1996 presidential campaign), then a representative sample of records must be made.

Gilly (1988) did a cross-cultural study of gender roles in advertising. She videotaped a sample of 12 hours of programming in Los Angeles (U.S.), Monterrey (Mexico), and Brisbane (Australia), from 8 a.m. to 4 p.m. on Tuesday and 7 p.m. to 11 p.m. on Wednesday. To control for seasonal variation between the hemispheres, the U.S. and Mexico samples were taken in September 1984, while the Australia sample was taken in February 1985. There were 617 commercials: 275 from the U.S., 204 from Mexico, and 138 from Australia. Because of her research question, Gilly used only adult men and women who were on camera for at least three seconds or who had at least one line of dialogue. There were 169 women and 132 men in the U.S. ads; 120 women and 102 men in the Mexican ads; and 52 women and 49 men in the Australian ads.

Cohen (1990) wanted to know whether the unpredictability of the environment (floods, drought, etc.) would be reflected in a society's folktales. He selected a sample of 19 societies using two criteria: (1) two independent coders had to agree on the presence of three variables about resources in a cross-cultural study of warfare done by Ember and Ember (1992); and (2) there had to be at least 9 folktales for each society in the Human Relations Area Files (as of 1988). Cohen then selected up to 10 folktales from each society. If there were more than that, he numbered them and selected them randomly. In all, Cohen had 187 different folktales to code and analyze.

Waitzkin and Britt (1993:1121) did an interpretive analysis of 50 encounters between patients and doctors by randomly selecting texts from 336 audiotaped encounters. Nonquantitative text analysis is often based on purposive sampling. Trost (1986) thought the relationship between teenagers and their families might be affected by five different dichotomous variables. To test this idea, he intentionally selected five cases from each of the 32 possible combinations of the five variables and conducted 160 interviews.

Nonquantitative studies in content analysis may also be based on extreme or deviant cases, cases that illustrate maximum variety on variables, cases that are somehow typical of a phenomenon, or cases that confirm or disconfirm a hypothesis. A single case may be sufficient to display something of substantive importance, but Morse (1994) suggests using at least six participants in studies in which one is trying to understand the essence of experience. Morse also suggests 30–50 interviews for ethnographies and grounded theory studies. Patton (1990: 169–186) and Sandelowski (1995b) provide useful reviews of the nonrandom strategies for sampling texts. Finding themes and building theory may require fewer cases than comparing across groups and testing hypotheses or models.

Once a sample of texts is established, the next step (called "unitizing" [Krippendorf 1980] or "segmenting" [Tesch 1990]) is to identify the basic, nonoverlapping units of analysis. The units may be the entire texts (books, interviews, responses to an open-ended question on a survey) or segments (words, word-senses, sentences, themes, paragraphs). Where the object is to compare across texts—to see *whether or not* certain themes occur—the whole text (representing an informant or an organization) is the appropriate unit of analysis. When the object is to compare the *number of times a theme occurs* across a set of texts, then what Kortendick (1996) calls a *context unit*—a chunk of text that reflects a theme—is likely to be the appropriate unit of analysis.

With a set of texts in hand, the next steps are to develop a codebook and mark (actually code) the text. This is the heart and soul of sociological text analysis, whether it is schema analysis, grounded theory, or classic content analysis. How to develop a codebook is covered in detail by Dey (1993:95–151), Crabtree and Miller (1992), Miles and Huberman (1994:55–72). Richards and Richards (1991) discuss the theoretical principles related to hierarchical coding structures that emerge out of the data. Araujo (1995) uses an example from his own research on the traditional British manufacturing industry to describe the process of designing and refining hierarchical codes. The development and refinement of coding categories has long been a central task in classical content analysis (for example, Bereleson 1952: 147–168; Holsti 1969:95–126) and is particularly important in the construction of concept dictionaries (Stone et al. 1966:134–168; Deese 1969). Krippendorff (1980: 71–84) and Carey et al. (1996) note that much of codebook refinement comes during the training of coders to mark the text and in the act of checking for intercoder agreement.

The word "code" has two quite different meanings. Codes are sometimes simply tags that mark off sections of text in a corpus and sometimes are values of a variable. When codes are used as tags, they are reference markers, like an index in the back of a book. When they are used as values of a variable, they identify nominal, ordinal, or even ratio characteristics of episodes, cases or persons (Bernard 1991, 1994:193–194; Seidel and Kelle 1995). Below we look more closely at these distinctions.

Inductive Coding

In hypothesis-testing content analysis, codes are typically formulated first and the codebook is then tested for reliability, using multiple coders and modified if necessary. In exploratory content analysis, inductive coding (*open coding* in grounded theory terms) is appropriate. Kortendick (1996), for example, interviewed 43 members of a three-generation extended family in Holland, all of whom were related to three sisters (the first generation) who had immigrated from Indonesia. Some of the interviews were done with individuals, others with groups of several people. After reading eight interviews carefully, Kortendick found that he was no longer identifying any new themes and he constructed a codebook.

Kortendick used a numerical coding scheme. (Miles and Huberman [1994:65] warn against this, but it's really a matter of taste—whatever works for individual researchers.) Kortendick applied his coding scheme to all the interview texts, tagging each text for things like the level of competence in Dutch versus Indonesian that people evinced, whether they mentioned any of 21 family myths that he had identified, and whether each person felt fully Dutch, fully Indonesian, or ambivalent about their identity. Kortendick built a matrix of informants-by-themes so he could count and compare references to these myths across all 43 informants.

Ryan and Weisner (1996) asked fathers and mothers to describe their adolescent children. Ryan and Weisner generated a list of the unique words in the corpus and the number of times each word was used. They used the list to look for differences between fathers and mothers and to look for themes that might be coded in a content analysis. Mothers, for example, were more likely to use words like *friends*, *creative, time*, and *honest;* fathers were more likely to use words like *school*, *good*, *lack, student, enjoys, independent*, and *extremely*.

Deductive Coding

Deductive coding is appropriate in confirmatory research. From her reading of literature on the theory of resources, Hirschman (1987) thought that she would find ten kinds of resources in personal ads: love, physical characteristics, educational status, intellectual status, occupational status, entertainment services (nonsexual), money status, demographic information (age, marital status, residence), ethnic characteristics, and personality info (not including sexual or emotional characteristics).

Hirschman formulated and tested hypotheses about which resources men and women would offer and seek in personal ads.

She selected 20 test ads at random from the *New York Magazine* and *The Washingtonian* and checked that the ten kinds of resources were, in fact, observable in the ads. Sexual traits and services were less than 1% of all resources coded. This was 1983–84, but even then, ads with explicit references to sexual traits and services were more common in other periodicals than in *The Washingtonian* and *New York Magazine*.

Hirschman next gave 10 men and 11 women the list of resource categories and a list of 100 actual resources ("young," "attractive," "fun loving," "divorced," "32-year-old," etc.) gleaned from the 20 test ads. The respondents were asked to match the 100 resources with the resource category that seemed most appropriate. This exercise demonstrated that the resource items were mutually exclusive and exhaustive: No resource items were left over and all could be categorized into just one of the ten resource categories.

When she was confident her codebook worked, Hirschman tested her hypotheses. She sampled approximately 100 female-placed ads and 100 male-placed ads from each magazine. A male and a female coder, working independently (and unaware of the hypotheses of the study) coded 3,782 resource items taken from the 400 ads as belonging to one of the ten resource categories. The coding took three weeks. This is not easy work.

A third coder was given the data and identified discrepancies between the first two coders. Of 3,782 resource items coded, there were theme contrasts on 636 (16.8%) and one of the coders failed to code 480 items (12.7%). The theme contrasts were resolved by Hirschman. The omissions were checked against the ads to see if, in fact, the one coder who had made an assignment had done so because the resource was in the ad. This was always the case, so the 480 resource items omitted by one coder were counted as if they had been assigned to the ad by both coders.

Hirschman found that men were more likely than women to offer monetary resources, whereas women were more likely than men to seek monetary resources. Women were more likely than men to offer physical attractiveness. It would be very interesting to repeat this study today with the same magazines. After all, Washington, DC and New York City are supposed to be hip places. Are the stereotypes of how men and women market themselves to one another today very different from what they were in 1983–84?

Confirmatory hypothesis testing and deductive coding are also used by anthropologists and other scholars who examine the Human Relations Area Files. The "codes" in the *Outline of Cultural Materials* are tags, however, not measurements. "Tagging" a paragraph in a text on the Yanomamo with "warfare" indicates textual material on the topic. It says nothing about how much the Yanomamo engage in warfare, or how intense their battles are, or whether Yanomamo men are at high or low risk of dying in battle. These kinds of measurements require a close reading of the segments of text that deal with warfare. Absent any prior knowledge about the Yanomamo, the tag "warfare" could just as well indicate that the Yanomamo are a peaceful people who despise and preach actively against violence. [Methodological issues associated with cross-cultural research are dealt with at length in Chapter 17 of this volume. *Ed.*]

Intercoder Agreement

The marking of text often involves multiple coders. The idea is to see whether the constructs being investigated are shared and whether multiple coders see the same constructs as applying to the same chunks of text. Carey et al. (1996) asked 51 newly arrived Vietnamese refugees in New York State 32 open-ended questions about tuberculosis. Topics included knowledge and beliefs about TB symptoms and causes, as well as beliefs about susceptibility to the disease, prognosis for those who contract the disease, skin testing procedures, and prevention and treatment methods. The investigators read the responses and created a code list based simply on their judgment. The initial code book contained 171 codes.

Next, the researchers broke the text into 1,632 segments (each segment representing a single informant's response to each of the 32 questions) and two coders independently coded 320 segments. Text segments could be marked with multiple codes. Segments were counted as reliably coded if both coders used the same codes on it. If one coder left off a code or assigned an additional code, then this was considered a coding disagreement. On their first try, only 144 (45%) out of 320 responses were coded the same by both coders. The coders discussed their disagreements and found that some of the 171 codes were redundant, some were vaguely defined, and some were not mutually exclusive. In some cases, coders simply had different understandings of what a code meant. When these problems were resolved, a new, streamlined codebook was issued and the coders marked up the data again. This time they were in agreement 88.1% of the time.

This seems like high reliability, but analysts typically apply a correction formula to take account of the fact that some fraction of agreement will always occur by chance. Cohen's *Kappa*, or K is a popular measure for taking these chances into account (Jacob Cohen 1960). When K is zero, agreement is what might be expected by chance.[7] When K is negative, the observed level of agreement is less than one expects by chance. Of the 152 codes in the new code list that had been applied to the 320 sample segments, the coders agreed perfectly (*kappa* = 1.0) for 82.9% of the codes. Only 17 (11.2%) of the codes had final K values ≤ 0.89. As senior investigator, Carey resolved any remaining intercoder discrepancies himself (Carey et al. 1996).

How much intercoder agreement is enough? The standards are still evolving, but Krippendorf (1980:147–148) advocates agreement of at least .70 and notes that some scholars (Brouwer et al. [1969] use a cutoff of .80. In developing software to create psychological scales from texts, Gottschalk and Bechtel (1993) ensured that the reliability of the computer scores were greater than .80 when compared to human coders. Including several measures of intercoder agreement in popular text analysis packages would encourage much needed research on this issue.[8]

Dictionaries

Computer-based, general-purpose content analysis dictionaries are a kind of automated codebook. To build such dictionaries, words are assigned, by hand, to one or more categories (there are typically 60–50 categories in computerized content analysis dictionaries), according to a set of rules. The rules are part of a computer program that parses new texts, assigning words to categories.

Work began in the 1960s on the best-known system, the *General Inquirer* and continues to this day (Stone et al. 1966; Kelly and Stone 1975; Zuell et al. 1989). The system comprises a computer program (the *General Inquirer*), which uses a dictionary (the *Harvard Psychosocial Dictionary*) in parsing text and categorizing text. An early version of the system was tested on 66 suicide notes—33 written by men who had actually taken their own lives, and 33 written by men who were asked to produce simulated suicide notes. The control group men were matched with the men who had written actual suicide notes on age, occupation, religion, and ethnicity. The *General Inquirer* program parsed the texts and picked the actual suicide notes 91% of the time (Ogilvie et al. 1966).

The 1975 update of the *Harvard Psychosocial Dictionary*, called *Harvard IV,* initially contained about 4,000 entries (Kelly and Stone 1975:47), and the Dartmouth adaptation of *Harvard IV* now contains about 8,500 (Rosenberg et al. 1990). The next version will contain around 10,000 (Philip Stone, personal communication).[9] Unlike its predecessors, the *Harvard IV* dictionaries can distinguish among multiple meanings of many words. If the program runs into the word "broke," for example, it looks at the context and determines whether the meaning is "fractured," or "destitute," or "stopped functioning," or (when the word is paired with "out") "escaped" (Rosenberg et al. 1990:303). Of course, dictionaries do not include all the words in a text, so investigators must still look at words that are not tagged and decide how to tag them independently.[10]

Content dictionaries do not need to be very big to be useful. In his study of Navaho and Zuni responses to thematic apperception tests, Colby's (1966) initial impression was that the Navajo regarded their homes as havens and places of relaxation, whereas the Zuni depicted their homes as places of discord and tension. To test this idea, Colby created a special-purpose dictionary that contained two word groups that he and his colleagues had developed before looking at the data.

One word group, the "relaxation" group, comprised the words *assist, comfort, easy, affection, happy,* and *play.* The other, the "tension" group, comprised the words *destruction, discomfort, difficult, dislike, sad, battle* and *anger.* Colby examined the 35 sentences that contained the word "home" *and* one of the words in either of the two word groups. The Navajos were more than twice as likely to use words from the relaxation group when they were talking about home as they were to use words from the tension group. The Zuni were almost twice as likely to use tension words as they were to use relaxation words.

Colby (1966) also found that the Navajo were more likely to use words associated with exposure such as storm, cold, freezing, hot, heat, and windy. Colby was not surprised at the results; he noted that the Navajo were sheep herders and were concerned about protecting their sheep from the elements, whereas the Zuni were crop growers and were concerned about the water they need to grow their corn. What *was* surprising was that the texts were generated from pictures that had nothing to do with sheep or crops. (See Jehn and Werner [1993] and Furbee [1996] for other examples of the application of a special-purpose content dictionary.)[11]

Content dictionaries are attractive because they are entirely reliable but, as Shapiro (1997) argues, this may be offset by a decrease in validity. In many cases, only humans can parse the subtleties of meaning reflected in context (Viney 1983), but dictionary-based markup of text is producing better and better results as time goes on, particularly in well-defined domains. For example, texts are now scored by computer for the Gottschalk-Gleser psychological scales (measuring various forms of anxiety and hostility) with greater than .80 reliability (Gottschalk and Bechtel 1993).[12] We expect to see increasing use of computer-based dictionaries in text analysis.

For additional examples of special-purpose dictionaries in content analysis, see Fan and Shaffer (1990), Holsti (1966), Laffal (1990, 1995), McTavish and Pirro (1990), and Schnurr et al. (1986).

Combining Grounded Theory and Content Analysis Approaches

Techniques from grounded theory and content analysis can be fruitfully combined. Jehn and Doucet (1996, 1997) asked 76 U.S. managers who had worked in Sino-American joint ventures to describe recent interpersonal conflicts with business partners. Each person described a situation with a same-culture manager and a different-culture manger. They made sure that the manager included the relationship to the person, who was involved, what the conflict was about, what caused the conflict, and how the conflict was resolved.

Jehn and Doucet used three quite different methods to identify themes in these data: (1) word counts combined with consensual coding by expert judges; (2) factor analysis of a traditional content-analysis (text unit-by-variable) matrix; and (3) multidimensional scaling of similarity judgments by experts of the scenarios.

1. *Word counts and consensual coding.* There were 7,479 unique words in the corpus on *inter*cultural conflicts compared to 2,747 in the corpus on the *intra*cultural conflicts. Jehn and Doucet wanted to identify words that were related to conflict, but did not want to impose their own definitions. They asked three expatriate managers who had experiences similar to those of their 76 informants and who were blind to the conditions of the study to go through both word lists and select the words that seemed related to conflict. The three judges went over the lists together and settled on a list of 542 conflict words from the intercultural list and 242 words from the intracultural list. Two out of three judges had to agree before a word was put on the final lists.

    In an open discussion to reach consensus, the judges assigned each conflict word to a category. The judges developed 15 subcategories for the intercultural data—things like *conflict, expectations, rules, power,* and *volatile*—and 15 categories for the intracultural data—things like *conflict, needs, standards, power, contentious,* and *lose.* Taking into consideration the total number of words in each corpus, conflict words were used more in intracultural interviews and resolution terms were more likely to be used in intercultural interviews.

2. *Traditional content analysis.* Next, two coders read the 152 conflict scenarios (76 intracultural and 76 intercultural) and evaluated (on a 5-point scale) each on 27 different themes. This produced two 76x27 scenario-by-theme profile matrices—one for the intracultural conflicts and one for the intercultural conflicts. The first three factors from the intercultural matrix reflect: (1) interpersonal animosity and hostility; (2) aggravation; and (3) the volatile nature of the conflict. The first two factors from the intracultural matrix reflect: (1) hatred and animosity with a volatile nature and (2) conflicts conducted calmly with little verbal intensity.

3. *Scenario comparisons.* Finally, Jehn and Doucet identified the 30 intracultural and the 30 intercultural scenarios that they felt were the most clear and pithy. Fifty *more* expatriate managers assessed the similarities (on a 5-point scale) of 60–120 randomly selected pairs of scenarios (each pair of scenarios was seen and judged by eight respondents) and described the basis for their judgments. When combined across informants, this produced two aggregate, scenario-by-scenario, similarity matrices—one for the intracultural conflicts and one for the intercultural conflicts. Multidimensional scaling of the intercultural similarity data identified four dimensions: (1) open versus resistant to change, (2) situational causes versus individual traits, (3) high- versus low-resolution potential based on trust, and (4) high- versus low-resolution potential based on patience. Scaling of the intracultural similarity data identified four different dimensions: (1) high versus low cooperation, (2) high versus low confrontation, (3) problem-solving versus accepting, and (4) resolved versus ongoing.

The research by Jehn and Doucet illustrates the rich combination of qualitative and quantitative methods now available for text analysis. Jehn and Doucet collected narratives from their informants and asked their informants to help identify the emic themes in the narratives. Informants sorted key words, coded each scenario for potential themes, and compared scenarios to each other. The analysis of the data from these tasks produced different sets of themes. All three emically induced theme sets have some intuitive appeal and all three yield analytic results that are useful.

In a series of articles on young adult "occasional" drug users, Agar (1979, 1980, 1983) described his grounded methods for content analysis. Agar conducted and transcribed three interviews with each of his three informants. In the 1979 article, Agar describes his initial, intuitive analysis. He pulled all the statements that pertained to informants' interactions or assessments of other people. He then looked at the statements and sorted them into piles based on their content. He named each pile as a theme and assessed how the themes interacted. Agar found that he had three piles. The first contained statements where the informant was expressing negative feelings for a person in a dominant social position. The second pile emphasized the other's knowledge or awareness. The third small cluster emphasized the importance of change or an openness to new experiences.

From this intuitive analysis, Agar felt that his informants were telling him that those in authority were only interested in displaying their authority unless they had knowledge or awareness; knowledge or awareness comes through openness to new experience; most in authority are close to new experience or change.

In his second article (1983), Agar systematically tested his intuitive understanding of the data. He used all the statements from a single informant and coded the statements for their role type (kin, friend/acquaintance, educational, occupational, or other), power (dominant, symmetrical, subordinate, or undetermined), and affect (positive, negative, ambivalent, or absent). Agar realized that he could analyze the covariations among role type, power, and affect, or he could examine the distribution of the themes as they occur throughout the text, or he could simply count the number of statements in the different categories.

Agar restricted his analysis to check his earlier primary finding: that for a given informant, a particular negative sentiment is expressed toward those in dominant social roles. He found that out of 40 statements coded as dominant, 32 were coded negative and 8 were coded positive. For the 36 statements coded as symmetrical, 20 were coded positive and 16 negative, lending support to his original theory.

Next, Agar looked closely at the deviant cases—the eight statements where the informant expressed positive affect toward a person in a dominant role. These counterexamples suggested that the positive affect was expressed toward a dominant social other when the social other possessed, or was communicating to the informant, knowledge that the informant valued.

Finally, Agar (1980) developed a more systematic questionnaire to further test his hypothesis with an independent set of data for one of his informants. He selected 12 statements, four from each of the control, knowledge, and change themes identified earlier. Some statements came directly from the informant. Others he made up. Then he selected eight roles from the informant's transcript (father, mother, employer, teacher, friend, wife, co-worker, and teammate). Each role term was matched with each statement and the informant was asked if the resulting statement was true, false, or irrelevant. (In no case, did the informant report "irrelevant.") Agar then took the responses and compared them to what his hypotheses suggested. The results both met and did not meet his expectations. On balance, there seemed to be general support for his hypothesis, but discrepancies between Agar's expectations and his results suggested areas for further research.

Increasingly, text analysis is about extracting models or schemas from transcriptions of human discourse. In the next section, we review some of the main currents: semantic network analysis, cognitive mapping analysis, Boolean analysis, and schema analysis.

Structural Analysis and Semantic Networks

The fundamental point of structuralism is that abstractions, called "structures," are in some important way responsible for, or govern, human action. Modern network analysis is based on this principle. Traditional sociological analysis involves a profile matrix—a matrix of things (rows) characterized by values on variables (columns) that characterize the things. Structural analysis, or network analysis, examines the properties that emerge from relations among a set of things. Here the matrix is one of similarities, where rows and columns represent the same things.

The relations among even a small a set of things (the relations among, say, the 30 households in a village, for example, or the 15 countries of the European Union) can be wildly complex. Seeing patterns, if they exist, in such complexity is made possible by applying graph-theoretic methods that enable the visualization of structure through the messiness of surface reality. Hage and Harary (1983) provide other examples of structuralist analysis in anthropology.

The application of graph-theoretic principles and methods to the study of meaning in text is sometimes called *semantic network analysis*. As early as 1959, Charles Osgood (1959) created word co-occurrence matrices and applied factor analysis and dimensional plotting to describe the relation of major factors to one another. The development of computers has made the construction and analysis of co-occurrence matrices much easier and has stimulated the development of this field (Danowski 1982, 1993; Barnett and Danowski 1992).

Jang and Barnett (1994) examined whether there was a national culture—U.S. or Japanese—discernible in the annual letters to stockholders of CEOs in U.S. and Japanese corporations. Jang and Barnett selected 35 Fortune 500 companies, including 18 U.S. and 17 Japanese firms, matched by their type of business. For example, Ford was matched with Honda, Xerox with Canon, and so on.

All of these firms are traded on the New York Stock Exchange, and each year stockholders receive an annual message from the CEO or president of these companies. (Japanese firms that trade on the New York Exchange send the annual letters in English to their U.S. stockholders.) Jang and Barnett read through the 1992 annual letters to shareholders and (ignoring a list of common words like "the," "because," "if," and so on) isolated 94 words that occurred at least eight times across the corpus of 35 letters. This produced a 94(word)-by-35(company) matrix, where the cells contained a number from 0–25, 25 being the largest number of times any word ever occurred in *one* of the letters.

Next, Jang and Barnett created a 35(company)-by-35(company) similarity matrix of companies, based on the co-occurrence of words in their letters. They analyzed the matrix by multidimensional scaling. Figure 1 shows the result—a two-dimensional plot of similarities between companies.

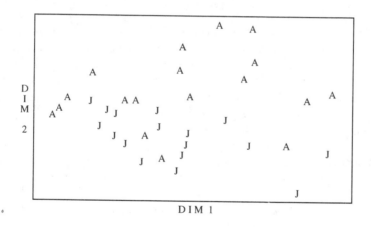

Figure 1. Multidimensional scaling, in two dimensions, of Jang's word co-occurrence matrix for 35 Japanese and American companies. J=Japanese company. A=American company. (Adapted from Jang and Barnett [1994:48]. Reprinted with permission of *Bulletin de Méthodologie Sociologique.*)

It's clear that there are two styles of corporate reporting to stockholders, one American and one Japanese. From a close reading of the texts, Jang concludes that U.S. executives discuss financial information and the structure of their organizations in their letters and Japanese executives focus more on organizational operations.

What is so appealing about word-by-word co-occurrence matrices is that they are produced by computer programs and there is no coder bias introduced other than to determine which words are examined. (See Borgatti [1992] and Doerfel and Barnett [1996] for computer programs that produce word-by-word co-occurrence matrices. See Schnegg and Bernard [1996] for another example of their use.) There is, however, no guarantee that the output of any word co-occurrence matrix will be meaningful, and it is notoriously easy to read pattern (and, thus, meaning) into any set of items.

Cognitive Maps

Cognitive map analysis combines the intuition of human coders with the quantitative methods of network analysis. Carley's work is instructive. If mental models, or schemas, are in there, she says, they are expressed in the texts of people's speech and can be represented as networks of concepts (Carley and Palmquist 1992:602), an approach also suggested by D'Andrade (1991). To the extent that mental models are widely shared, she asserts, even a very small set of texts will contain the information required for describing the models, especially for narrowly defined arenas of life.

In one study, Carley (1993) asked students some questions about the work of scientists. Here are two brief texts that address questions about the motivation of scientists and their collaboration with colleagues:

Student A: I found that scientists engage in research in order to make discoveries and generate new ideas. Such research by scientists is hard work and often involves collaboration with other scientists which leads to discoveries which make the scientists famous. Such collaboration may be informal, such as when they share new ideas over lunch, or formal, such as when they are coauthors of a paper.

Student B: It was hard work to research famous scientists engaged in collaboration and I made many informal discoveries. My research showed that scientists engaged in collaboration with other scientists are coauthors of at least one paper containing their new ideas. Some scientists make formal discoveries and have new ideas. (Carley 1993:89)

Carley compares these texts (one 64 words long, the other 48 words) by counting 11 concepts: I, scientists, research, hard work, collaboration, discoveries, new ideas, formal, informal, coauthors, paper. Each concept occurs exactly the same number of times in both texts, yet the texts clearly have different meanings. To analyze the differences in meaning, Carley produces maps of the relation between and among concepts. Concepts are coded for their strength, sign (positive or negative), and direction (whether one concept is logically prior to others), not just for their existence. Figure 2 shows Carley's maps of the two texts.

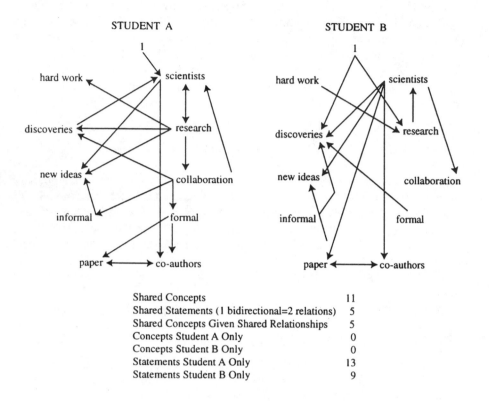

Figure 2. Coded maps of two student's texts (from Carley [1993:104]. Reprinted with the permission of the American Sociological Association).

This approach to text analysis holds a lot of promise, combining, as it does, the sensitivity of human intuition and interpretation with the labor-saving characteristics of automation. As Carley recognizes, though, a lot depends on who does the coding—just as in classical content analysis. Different coders (with more or less knowledge of the implicit culture lurking in a text) will produce different maps by making different coding choices. In the end, as with the search for schemas, competency in the native language is one of the fundamental methodological requirements for analysis (see also Carley and Palmquist 1992; Carley 1993, 1997; Carley and Kaufer 1993; Palmquist and Carley 1997).

Analytic Induction and Boolean Tests

Analytic induction is a formal, nonquantitative method for building up causal explanations of phenomena from a close examination of cases. It was proposed as an alternative to statistical analysis by Znaniecki (1934:249–331), and is discussed by Denzin (1978) and Manning (1982), among others. The method involves the following steps: First, define a phenomenon that requires explanation and propose an explanation. Examine a case to see if the explanation fits. If it does, then examine another case. An explanation is accepted until a new case falsifies it.

When a case is found that doesn't fit, then, under the rules of analytic induction, the alternatives are to change the explanation to include the new case or redefine the phenomenon to exclude the nuisance case. Ideally, the process continues until a universal explanation for all known cases of a phenomenon is attained. Explaining cases by declaring them all unique is not an option of the method. Classic examples of analytic induction include Lindesmith's (1947) study of drug addicts, Cressey's (1953) study of embezzlers, and McCleary's (1978) study of how parole officers decide when one of their charges is in violation of parole.

Ragin (1987, 1994) formalized the logic of analytic induction, offering a Boolean approach, and Romme (1995) applies the approach to textual data. Boolean algebra involves two states, true and false (present and absent). With just three dichotomous causal conditions (A and not A, B and not B, and C and not C) and one dependent variable (D and not D), there are 16 possible outcomes (A, B, C, D; A, not B, C, D; A, B, not C, D; and so on).

Schweizer (1991, 1996) applied Boolean logic in his analysis of conflict and social status in Chen Village, China. In the 1950s, the village began to prosper with the application of technology to agriculture. The Great Leap Forward and the Cultural Revolution of the 1960s, however, reversed the village's fortunes. Chan et al. (1984) reconstructed the recent history of Chen Village, focusing on the political fortunes of key actors there.

Schweizer coded the Chan et al. text for whether each of 13 actors experienced an increase or a decrease in status after each of 14 events (such as the Great Leap Forward, land reform and collectivization, the collapse of Brigade leadership, and an event known locally as "the great betrothal dispute"). Thus, he has a 13-actor-by-14-event matrix, where a 1 means that an actor had success in a particular event and a 0 means failure (loss of status). When Schweizer looked at the actor-by-event matrix he found that, over time, 9 of the actors consistently won or lost, but 4 of the actors lost sometimes and won other times. This produces 17 unique combinations of actors and outcomes.

Schweizer then partitioned the 17 unique cases according to three binary independent variables (urban versus rural origin, proletarian versus nonproletarian background, presence versus absence of external ties) and one dependent variable (whether the actor was a success overall). Table 1 shows the 16 possible outcomes, given four binary variables.

By setting up the logical possibilities, Schweizer was able to discern and test several hypotheses about success and failure in Chen Village. People from an urban background have an advantage, but inspection of Table 1 shows that it's not enough. To ensure success, you should come from a proletarian family or have good external ties and access to information and power at the regional level. Failure is predicted even better: If an actor has failed in the Chen Village disputes, then he or she is of rural origin (comes from the village) OR comes from a nonproletarian family AND has no ties to authorities beyond the village. The Boolean formula for this statement is: *Lack of success → nonurban v (nonproletarian & lack of ties).*[13] The substantive conclusions from this analysis are intuitively appealing: In a communist revolutionary environment, it pays over the years to have friends in high places; people from urban areas are more likely to have those ties; and it helps to have been born into a politically correct (that is, proletarian) family.

TABLE 1

The Outcome of 17 Cases from Schweizer's (1996) Text Analysis

Success Ties	External Background	Proletarian Origin	Urban	No. of Cases
0	0	0	0	2
0	0	0	1	2
0	0	1	0	1
0	0	1	1	0
0	1	0	0	0
0	1	0	1	0
0	1	1	0	2
0	1	1	1	0
1	0	0	0	1
1	0	0	1	3
1	0	1	0	0
1	0	1	1	0
1	1	0	0	0
1	1	0	1	1
1	1	1	0	4
1	1	1	1	1

Analytic induction helps identify the simplest model that logically explains the data. Like classic content analysis and cognitive mapping, it requires that human coders read and code the text into an event-by-variable matrix. The object of the analysis, however, is not to show the relationships between all codes, but to find the minimal set of logical relationships among the concepts that accounts for a single dependent variable. With three binary independent variables, as in Schweizer's data, two logical operators (OR and AND), and three implications ("if A then B," "if B then A," and "if A, then and only then, B"), there are 30 multivariate hypotheses: 18 when all three independent variables are used, plus 12 when two variables are used. With more variables, the analysis becomes much more difficult. Computer programs like QCA (Drass 1980) and ANTHROPAC (Borgatti 1992) test all possible multivariate hypotheses and find the optimal solution. (QCA is reviewed in Weitzman and Miles 1995.)

Computer-Assisted Text Analysis

One problem with text as data, as all field workers know, is that it piles up quickly. The sheer volume and the problems of handling and sorting through so much information has made text analysis less popular in the past than it is now. What has changed is the presence of computers and of programs that help researchers code and analyze text.

A useful review of the features of currently popular programs is given by Weitzman and Miles (1995). Each of the most popular programs has a devoted group of users who communicate regularly with one another (and with the authors of the programs) on Internet lists. Academic centers specializing in text analysis have also emerged, though mostly outside the United States. Centers at universities in Surrey (Centre for Computer Assisted Qualitative Data Analysis Software) and Kent, England (Centre for Social Anthropology and Computers), as well as Mannheim, Germany (Zentrum für Umfragen Methoden und Analysen) and La Trobe, Australia (Qualitative Solutions and Research) have helped to promote the use of qualitative data across the social sciences.

The panorama with regard to text-processing software is changing quickly. Like early word processors and database managers, the first generation of text processors was designed to help us do what we already did. Today's word processors let us do things that printing presses could not do before computers, and today's database managers, with built-in statistical analysis capabilities, let us do things at our desks that could only be done on a mainframe 15 years ago (and could not be done by anyone 60 years ago).

The first generation of text analysis programs made light work of chores like coding and finding the right quotes with which to illuminate a point in an article. Text processors today still focus on coding and retrieving, but more and more we find features that help with building conceptual models, linking concepts into networks, and producing numerical text-by-variable matrices. Eventually, we expect text processors to contain modules for doing word counts, concordances, KWIC (key-word-in-context) studies, Boolean analysis, map analysis, and semantic network analysis.

Some General Observations

Text analysis as a research strategy permeates the social sciences, and the range of methods for conducting text analysis is breathtaking. Investigators examine words, sentences, paragraphs, pages, documents, ideas, meanings, paralinguistic features, and even what is missing from the text. They interpret, mark, retrieve, and count. By turns, they apply interpretive analysis and numerical analysis. They use text analysis for exploratory and confirmatory purposes. Researchers identify themes, describe them, compare them across cases and groups, and try to explain them. Text analysis is used by avowed positivists and interpretivists alike.

Text analysts who are linguistically oriented rarely cite the work of their sociologically and anthropologically oriented colleagues, and vice versa. Even within the sociological tradition, the literatures on schema analysis, grounded theory, and content analysis are essentially distinct, though they all involve identifying and refining concepts (for example, categories, codes, themes), coding/marking concepts in text, and linking concepts into theoretical models. One of our goals in this chapter has been to make clear the importance of text analysis for all the social sciences.

We close this review by noting that some questions that might guide research on methods of text analysis include the following:

1. What effect does the selection of textual units (thematic segments, sentences, or words) have on the number, kind, and organization of themes that coders identify?
2. To what extent does increasing or decreasing the number of coders affect the size and composition of these themes?
3. Do different measures of intercoder agreement affect the content of themes?
4. How do different techniques for coding data (into thematic segments, sentences, or words) affect descriptions of the range, central tendency, and distribution of specific themes across informants?
5. Can different coding techniques produce contradictory findings? For example, does an analysis of text segments make groups appear more or less similar than does an analysis of words? Does an analysis of words suggest dimensions of similarity or dissimilarity that are not captured by thematic or sentence segments?
6. Do different methods for systematically treating text identify different sets of prototypical quotes for illustrating major and minor themes?
7. How can we use qualitative and quantitative instruments to produce complementary results? For example, can we identify informants who score high and low on particular survey scale variables based only on their textual data?

Answers to these questions will help us understand better how to make the outcomes and interpretations of qualitative data replicable.

NOTES

1. Holsti (1969) counted 2.5 content analysis studies per year, on average during the first two decades of this century. By the 1920s, the number had risen to 13.3 per year; in the 1930s it was 22.8, and in the 1940s it was 43.3. By the end of the 1950s, there were over 100 studies a year using content analysis. We did a keyword survey in mid-1997 and retrieved more than 500 book titles, including more than 200 books written since 1990, on "qualitative data analysis" or "text analysis." The number of journal articles runs into the thousands, with entire journals dedicated specifically to the analysis of qualitative data. These include: *Qualitative Sociology, Qualitative Inquiry, Journal of Contemporary Ethnography, Symbolic Interaction, Qualitative Health Research, Quality and Quantity, Studies in Qualitative Methodology*, and *International Journal of Qualitative Studies in Education*. In anthropology, *Cultural Anthropology Methods Journal* covers text analysis and other methods.

2. We do not review the fields of literary text analysis, biblical text analysis, authorship studies, or hermeneutics. Text analysis in the social sciences owes much to these fields. On hermeneutics, see Bleicher (1982), Bruns (1992), and Dilthey (1996). For a review of methods in literary text analysis, see Segre and Kemeny (1988). For an introduction to biblical hermeneutics, see Hayes and Holladay (1987). An important method, shared by all text analysts, is the production of concordances and KWIC (key-words-in-context) lists. Concordances are annotated lists, by page and/or line number, of the occurrence of every word, phrase, or theme in a text or set of texts. KWIC lists are created by finding all the places in a text where a particular word or phrase appears and printing it out in the context of some number of words (say, 30) before and after it. For examples of major concordances, see Young (1982), Kassis (1983), Spevack (1973), Prendergast (1971). See McKinnon (1993) and Burton (1981a, 1981b, 1982) on the use of concordances in modern literary studies. In authorship studies, differences in the use of words common to the writings of James Madison and Alexander Hamilton led Mosteller and Wallace (1964) to conclude that Madison and not Hamilton had written twelve of the *Federalist Papers*. See Yule (1944) and Martindale and McKenzie (1995) for other examples of authorship studies.

3. Not all of Boas's students agreed that faithful reproduction of narrative was important. Between 1903–1907, Clark Wissler collected 94 Blackfoot tales, all in English. His indigenous collaborator, D. C. Duvall, provided the English translations, which Wissler edited and revised for publication (Wissler and Duvall 1908). As it turned out, only a few of the tales were translated from actual texts. Wissler explained:

> In narration the Blackfoot often repeat sentences at irregular intervals, as if they wished to prevent the listener from forgetting their import. Naturally such repetitions were eliminated in the translations. A few narratives were recorded as texts. While texts will be indispensable for linguistic research, the present condition of Blackfoot mythology is such that its comparative study would not be materially facilitated by such records. Each narrator has his own version, in the telling of which he is usually consistent; and while the main features of the myths are the same for all, the minor differences are so great that extreme accuracy of detail with one individual would avail little. (p. 5)

We are sure that many Blackfoot today (not to mention linguists) would rather that Wissler had followed Boas's instructions to gather the texts in the original language and to record the texts as faithfully as possible. See Werner (1995) for a recent argument in favor of verbatim transcription of text.

4. The *Pear Story* chronicles what happens to a bushel of pears after they have been picked from a tree. The film is a series of scenes: A man picks the pears from a tree; another man and a goat pass by; a boy on a bicycle stops and rides off with a basket of pears; when the boy turns to look at a passing girl, his hat falls off, he runs into a rock and tips over; three other boys help him up; on walking off, one of the three boys finds the hat; a whistle is heard; and the hat is exchanged for three pears; the film returns to the picker who looks down at the baskets and scratches his head. The three boys appear eating their pears, and the picker watches them walk off into the distance.

5. For reviews of popular software for text analysis, see Weitzman and Miles (1995). This volume is the current best source of information on the features available in the array of software available for text analysis. For an early, but still useful discussion of software issues in text analysis, see Tesch (1990). For discussions of epistemological issues involved in using computers for the qualitative analysis of texts, see Kelle (1995, 1997), and Lee and Fielding (1995, 1996). Review articles are also found in the *Cultural Anthropology Methods Journal, Qualitative Sociology,* and *Computers and the Humanities.*

6. Content analysis has a long history in the social sciences. Good reviews are available in Krippendorf (1980) and Weber (1990). Monitoring newspapers by counting the space given to various themes was already in vogue in the late nineteenth century and early twentieth. By 1910, at the first meeting of the German Sociological Society, Max Weber proposed a major effort at content analysis of the German press (Krippendorf 1980:13). Weber's proposal was not implemented, but content analysis became, and remains, an important method for tracking the impact of news events across time and across print venues (see Danielson and Lasorsa [1997] and Kleinnijenhuis et al. [1997]—and many recent issues of *Journalism Quarterly*—for current examples).

Methods for content analysis were developed vigorously during World War II in studying speeches by Germany's leaders for clues about their intentions in the conduct of the war. In 1955, the Social Science Research Council's Committee on Linguistics and Psychology sponsored a conference on content analysis, bringing together experts from across the social sciences. Their contributions appear in a landmark volume, edited by de Sola Pool (1959). Since then, extensive reviews have appeared every decade or so: Gerbner et al. (1969), Holsti (1969), Krippendorf (1980), Weber (1990), and Roberts (1997).

Today, classical content analysis continues to be used across the social sciences in the study of media (Brouwer et al. 1969; Spiggle 1986; Hirschman 1987; Gilly 1988; Craig 1992; Cameron and Blount 1996; Fink and Gantz 1996; Kolbe and Albanese 1996), political rhetoric (Kaid, Tedesco, and McKinnon 1996; Franzosi 1997), business (Spears et al. 1996), medicine (Cardador et al. 1995; Potts et al. 1996; Sleath et al. 1997), psychiatry, clinical psychology, and counseling (Rosenberg 1990; Smith et al. 1992; Gottschalk 1994, 1997; Handron and Legget-Frazier 1994), and law (Imrich et al. 1995). Content analysis is represented in anthropology in cross-cultural hypothesis testing (White and Burton 1988; Bradley et al. 1990; Ember et al. 1992) and in quantitative, comparative studies of folklore (Colby et al. 1991; Johnson and Price-Williams 1997).

7. The amount of that fraction depends on the number of coders and the precision of measurement for each code. If two people code a theme present or absent, they could agree, *ceteris paribus,* on any answer 25% of the time by chance. If a theme, like wealth, is measured ordinally (low, medium, high); then the likelihood of chance agreement changes accordingly. Fleiss (1971) and Light (1971) expand Kappa to handle multiple coders. Another measure of intercoder agreement for two coders is Scott's pi (Scott 1955), which was generalized by Krippendorf (1980:147–154) for multiple coders, metric data, and any sample size. Craig (1981) generalized Scott's pi for subsets of coders. Craig's measure is particularly useful when one wants to use majority rule in making coding decisions like two out of three coders. See Holsti (1969) for several other measures.

8. Monte Carlo studies might prove helpful. Various types of error could be introduced to see how well a model performs under conditions of uncertainty. Ultimately, however, there may be no single solution but one that is derived within the context of each research problem (Holsti 1969:143).

9. The *General Inquirer* also uses the *Lasswell Value Dictionary* (Namenwirth and Weber 1987; Zuell et al. 1989). More dictionaries are being built for the system.

10. Developing rules for sorting words into dictionary categories requires an understanding of the multiple meanings of words. Concordances (see Note 2) and KWIC (pronounced "quick"), or key-word-in-context lists are used as aids in this process. KWIC lists are created by finding all the places in a text where a particular word or phrase appears and printing it out in the context of some number of words (say, 30) before and after it. Stone et al. (1966:158) created KWIC lists on a corpus of text that had more than a half million words to help revise the *Harvard III Psychological Dictionary*.

11. See Namenwirth and Weber (1987) and Zuell et al. (1989) for information on other dictionaries. Laffal (1990, 1995) created a 43,000-word dictionary that categorized each word into 1–5 of 168 potential concept categories to distinguish themes in different literary works.

12. Rosenberg et al. (1990) transcribed 71 speech samples from people who had been diagnosed with psychological disorders (depression, paranoia, somatisization) or cancer. The transcripts were hand scored by an expert and analyzed using various editions of the *Harvard Psychosociological Dictionary* (Schnurr et al. 1986). The human coder did better than the computer in diagnosing patients who had cancer, but the computer beat the human coder in identifying the transcripts of people who had been diagnosed with the various psychological disorders.

13. Here are the details of the logic of Schweizer's analysis. Three possible hypotheses can be derived from two binary variables: "if A then B," "if B then A," and "if A, then and only then, B." In the first hypothesis, A is a sufficient condition to B and B is necessary to A. This hypothesis is falsified by all cases having A and not B. In the second hypothesis, B is a sufficient condition to A and A is necessary to B. The second hypothesis is falsified by all cases of B and not A. These two hypotheses are *implications* or *conditional statements*. The third hypothesis (an *equivalence* or *biconditional statement*) is the strongest: whenever you see A, you also see B and vice versa; the absence of A implies the absence of B and vice versa. This hypothesis is falsified by all cases of A and not B, and all cases of B and not A.

Applied to the data from Chen Village, the strong hypothesis is falsified by many cases, but the sufficient condition hypotheses (urban origin implies success; proletarian background implies success; having external ties implies success) are true in 86% of the cases (this is an average of the three sufficient condition hypotheses). The necessary condition hypotheses (success implies urban origin; success implies proletarian background; success implies external ties) is true in just 73% of cases (again, an average). (There are 7 disconfirming cases in 51 possible outcomes of the 12 *sufficient condition* possibilities—4 possible outcomes for each of 3 independent variables and one dependent variable. There are 14 disconfirming cases in 51 possible outcomes of the 12 *necessary condition* possibilities.) To improve on this, Schweizer tested multivariate hypotheses, using the logical operators OR and AND.

REFERENCES

Agar, Michael. 1979. Themes Revisited: Some Problems in Cognitive Anthropology. *Discourse Processes 2*:11–31.

Agar, Michael. 1980. Getting Better Quality Stuff: Methodological Competition in an Interdisciplinary Niche. *Urban Life 9*:34–50.

Agar, Michael. 1983. Microcomputers as Field Tools. *Computers and the Humanities 17*:19–26.

Agar, Michael. 1986. *Speaking of Ethnography*. Qualitative Research Methods Series, Vol. 2. Thousand Oaks, CA: Sage Publications.

Agar, Michael. 1996. *The Professional Stranger*, 2d ed. San Diego: Academic Press.

Araujo, Luis. 1995. Designing and Refining Hierarchical Coding Frames. In *Computer-Aided Qualitative Data Analysis: Theory, Methods and Practice*. Udo Kelle, ed. Pp. 96–104. London: Sage Publications.

Barnett, George, and James Danowski. 1992. The Structure of Communication: A Network Analysis of the International Communication Association. *Human Communication Resources 19*:164–285.

Bartlett, F. C. 1967 [1932]. *Remembering: A Study in Experimental and Social Psychology*. Cambridge: Cambridge University Press.

Becker, Howard, B. Geer, E. C. Hughes, and A. L. Strauss. 1961. *Boys in White: Student Culture in Medical School*. Chicago: University of Chicago Press.

Berelson, Bernard. 1952. *Content Analysis in Communication Research*. Glencoe, IL: Free Press.

Bernard, H. Russell. 1991. About Text Management and Computers. *CAM Newsletter 3*(1):1–4, 7, 12.

Bernard, H. Russell. 1994. *Research Methods in Anthropology: Qualitative and Quantitative Approaches*, 2d ed. Walnut Creek, CA: AltaMira Press.

Bernard, H. Russell. 1997. Language Preservation and Publishing. In *Indigenous Literacy in the Americas*. Nancy H. Hornberger, ed. Pp. 139–156. Berlin: Mouton de Gruyter.

Bernard, H. Russell, and Jesús Salinas Pedraza. 1976. Otomí Parables, Folktales, and Jokes. *International Journal of American Linguistics*, Native American Texts Series *1*(2). Chicago: University of Chicago Press.

Bernard, H. Russell, and Jesús Salinas Pedraza. 1989. *Native Ethnography. A Mexican Indian Describes His Culture*. Thousand Oaks, CA: Sage Publications.

Besnier, Niko 1995. *Literacy, Emotion, and Authority. Reading and Writing on a Polynesian Atoll*. Cambridge: Cambridge University Press.

Bizarro Ujpan, Ignacio, and James Sexton. 1981. *Son of Tecun Uman: A Maya Indian Tells His Life Story*. Tucson: University of Arizona Press.

Bizarro Ujpan, Ignacio, and James Sexton. 1985. *Campesino: The Diary of a Guatemalan Indian*. Tucson: University of Arizona Press.

Bleicher, J. 1982. *The Hermeneutic Imagination: Outline of a Positive Critique of Scientism and Sociology*. London: Routledge and Kegan Paul.

Blowsnake, Sam, and Paul Radin (ed. and tr.). 1983. *Crashing Thunder: Autobiography of a Winnebago Indian*. Lincoln: University of Nebraska Press. Orig. pub. 1920 by the University of California Press and again in 1926 by Appleton.

Boas, Franz. 1910. *Kwakiutl Tales*. New York: Columbia University Press.

Boas, Franz. 1917. *Folk-Tales of Salishan and Sahaptin Tribes*. Lancaster, PA: American Folk-Lore Society.

Boas, Franz. 1928a. *Kerasan Texts*. New York: The American Ethnological Society.

Boas, Franz. 1928b. *Bella Bella Texts*. New York: Columbia University Press.

Boas, Franz. 1935–43. *Kwakiutl Tales, New Series*. New York: Columbia University Press.

Boas, Franz, and George Hunt. 1902–1905. *Kwakiutl Texts*. Leiden: E. J. Brill.

Boas, Franz, and George Hunt. 1906. Kwakiutl Texts, Second Series. *Memoirs of the American Museum of Natural History, 14*. New York: G. E. Stechert.

Bogdan, Robert, and Sari Knopp Biklen. 1992. *Qualitative Research for Education: An Introduction to Theory and Methods*, 2d ed. Boston: Allyn and Bacon.

Borgatti, Steven. 1992. ANTHROPAC 4.0. Columbia, SC: Analytic Technologies (www.analytictech.com).

Bradley, Candice, C. C. Moore, M. L. Burton, and D. R. White. 1990. A Cross-Cultural Historical Analysis of Subsistence Change. *American Anthropologist 92*:447–457.

Brouwer, M., C. C. Clark, G. Gerbner, and K. Krippendorff. 1969. The Television World of Violence. In *Mass Media and Violence: A Report to the National Commission on the Causes and Prevention of Violence*. R. K. Baker and S. J. Ball, eds. Pp. 311–339, 519–591. Washington, DC: Government Printing Office.

Bruns, Gerald. 1992. *Hermeneutics Ancient and Modern*. New Haven: Yale University Press.

Burton, Dolores M. 1981a. Automated Concordances and Word Indexes: The Early Sixties and the Early Centers. *Computers and the Humanities 15*:83–100.

Burton, Dolores M. 1981b. Automated Concordances and Word Indexes: The Process, the Programs, and the Products. *Computers and the Humanities 15*:139–154.

Burton, Dolores M. 1982. Automated Concordances and Word-Indexes: Machine Decisions and Editorial Revisions. *Computers and the Humanities 16*:195–218.

Cameron, G. T., and D. Blount. 1996. VNRs and Air Checks: A Content Analysis of the Use of Video News Releases in Television Newscasts. *Journalism and Mass Communication Quarterly 73*(4):890–904.

Cardador, M. T., A. R. Hazan, and S. A. Glantz. 1995. Tobacco Industry Smokers' Rights Publications—A Content Analysis. *American Journal of Public Health 85*(9): 1212–1217.

Carey, James W., Mark Morgan, and Margaret J. Oxtoby. 1996. Intercoder Agreement in Analysis of Responses to Open-Ended Interview Questions: Examples from Tuberculosis Research. *Cultural Anthropology Methods Journal 8*(3):1–5.

Carley, Kathleen. 1993. Coding Choices for Textual Analysis: A Comparison of Content Analysis and Map Analysis. In *Sociological Methodology*. P. Marsden, ed. Pp. 75–126. Oxford: Blackwell.

Carley, Kathleen. 1997. Network Text Analysis: The Network Position of Concepts. In *Text Analysis for the Social Sciences: Methods for Drawing Statistical Inferences from Texts and Transcripts.* Carl W. Roberts, ed. Pp. 79–100. Mahwah, NJ: Lawrence Erlbaum.

Carley, Kathleen, and D. S. Kaufer. 1993. Semantic Connectivity: An Approach for Analyzing Semantic Networks. *Communication Theory 3*:182–213.

Carley, Kathleen, and Michael Palmquist. 1992. Extracting, Representing, and Analyzing Mental Models. *Social Forces 70*:601–636.

Casson, Ronald. 1983. Schemata in Cultural Anthropology. *Annual Review of Anthropology 12*:429–462.

Chafe, W. 1980. The Deployment of Consciousness in the Production of Narrative. In *The Pear Stories. Cognitive, Cultural, and Linguistic Aspects of Narrative Production.* W. Chafe, ed. Pp. 9–50. Norwood, NJ: Ablex.

Chan, Anita, R. Madsen, and J. Unger. 1984. *Chen Village. The Recent History of a Peasant Community in Mao's China.* Berkeley: University of California Press.

Charmaz, Kathy. 1990. "Discovering" Chronic Illness: Using Grounded Theory. *Social Science and Medicine 30*:1161–1172.

Cohen, Alex. 1990. A Cross-Cultural Study of the Effects of Environmental Unpredictability on Aggression in Folktales. *American Anthropologist 92*:474–481.

Cohen, Jacob. 1960. A Coefficient of Agreement for Nominal Scales. *Educational and Psychological Measurement 20*:37–48.

Colby, B. N. 1966. The Analysis of Culture Content and the Patterning of Narrative Concern in Texts. *American Anthropologist 68*:374–388.

Colby, B. N., S. Kennedy, and L. Milanesi. 1991. Content Analysis, Cultural Grammars, and Computers. *Qualitative Sociology 14*:373–384.

Cowan, G., and M. O'Brien. 1990. Gender and Survival Versus Death in Slasher Films—A Content Analysis. *Sex Roles 23*(3/4):187–196.

Crabtree, Benjamin F., and William L. Miller. 1992. A Template Approach to Text Analysis: Developing and Using Codebooks. In *Doing Qualitative Research*. William L. Miller and Benjamin F. Crabtree, eds. Pp. 93–109. Thousand Oaks, CA: Sage Publications.

Craig, Robert T. 1981. Generalization of Scott's Index of Intercoder Agreement. *Public Opinion Quarterly 45*:260–264.

Craig, R. Stephen. 1992. The Effect of Television Day Part on Gender Portrayals in Television Commercials: A Content Analysis. *Sex Roles 26*(5/6):197–211.

Cressey, Donald R. 1973 (orig 1953). *Other People's Money: A Study in the Social Psychology of Embezzlement*. Montclair, NJ: Patterson Smith.

D'Andrade, Roy. 1984. Cultural Meaning Systems. In *Culture Theory: Essays on Mind, Self, and Emotion*. R. A. Shweder and R. A. Levine, eds. Pp. 88–119. Cambridge: Cambridge University Press.

D'Andrade, Roy. 1987. A Folk Model of the Mind. In *Cultural Models in Language and Thought*. N. Quinn and D. Holland, eds. Pp. 112–148. Cambridge: Cambridge University Press.

D'Andrade, Roy. 1991. The Identification of Schemas in Naturalistic Data. In *Person Schemas and Maladaptive Interpersonal Patterns*. Mardi J. Horowitz, ed. Pp. 279–301. Chicago: University of Chicago Press.

D'Andrade, Roy. 1995. *The Development of Cognitive Anthropology*. Cambridge: Cambridge University Press.

Danielson, Wayne A., and D. L. Lasorsa. 1997. Perceptions of Social Change: 100 Years of Front-Page Content in *The New York Times* and *The Los Angeles Times*. In *Text Analysis for the Social Sciences: Methods for Drawing Statistical Inferences from Texts and Transcripts*. Carl W. Roberts, ed. Pp. 103–116. Mahwah, NJ: Lawrence Erlbaum.

Danowski, James. 1982. A Network-Based Content Analysis Methodology for Computer-Mediated Communication: An Illustration with a Computer Bulletin Board. In *Communication Yearbook*. R. Bostrom, ed. Pp. 904–925. New Brunswick, NJ: Transaction Books.

Danowski, James. 1993. Network Analysis of Message Content. In *Progress in Communication Science, XII*. W. D. Richards and G. A. Barnett, eds. Pp. 197–221. Norwood, NJ: Ablex Publishing.

de Sola Pool, Ithiel, ed. 1959. *Trends in Content Analysis*. Urbana: University of Illinois Press.

Deese, James. 1969. Conceptual Categories in the Study of Content. In *The Analysis of Communication Content: Development in Scientific Theories and Computer Techniques*. George Gerbner, Ole R. Holsti, Klaus Krippendorff, William J. Paisley, and Philip J. Stone, eds. Pp. 39–56. New York: Wiley.

Denzin, N. K. 1978. *The Research Act. A Theoretical Introduction to Sociological Methods*, 2d ed. New York: McGraw-Hill.

Dey, I. 1993. *Qualitative Data Analysis: A User-Friendly Guide for Social Scientists*. London: Routledge and Kegan Paul.

Dilthey, Wilhelm. 1996. *Hermeneutics and the Study of History*. Princeton: Princeton University Press.

Doerfel, Marya L., and George A. Barnett. 1996. The Use of Catpac for Text Analysis. *Cultural Anthropology Methods Journal* 8(2):4–7.

Downing, Pamela. 1980. Factors Influencing Lexical Choice in Narrative. In *The Pear Stories. Cognitive, Cultural, and Linguistic Aspects of Narrative Production*. W. Chafe, ed. Pp. 89–126. Norwood, NJ: Ablex Publishing.

Drass, K. 1980. The Analysis of Qualitative Data: A Computer Program. *Urban Life* 9:332–353.

Edmonson, Munro S. 1982. *The Ancient Future of the Itza: The Book of Chilam Balam of Tizimin*. Austin: University of Texas Press.

Edmonson, Munro S., tr. and ed. 1986. *Heaven Born Mérida and Its Destiny: The Book of Chilam Balam of Chumayel*. Austin: University of Texas Press.

El Guindi, Fadwa, and Abel Hernández Jiménez. 1986. *The Myth of Ritual. A Native's Ethnography of Zapotec Life-Crisis Rituals*. Tucson: University of Arizona Press.

Ember, Carol R., and Melvin Ember. 1992. Resource Unpredictability, Mistrust, and War: A Cross-Cultural Study. *Journal of Conflict Resolution* 36:242–262.

Ember, Carol R., Melvin Ember, and B. M. Russett. 1992. Peace Between Participatory Polities: A Cross-Cultural Test of the 'Democracies Rarely Fight Each Other' Hypothesis. *World Politics* 44:573–599.

Fan, David P., and Carol L. Shaffer. 1990. Use of Open-Ended Essays and Computer Content Analysis to Survey College Students' Knowledge of AIDS. *College Health 38* (March): 221–229.

Fielding, Nigel G., and Raymond M. Lee. 1992. *Using Computers in Qualitative Research*, rev. ed. London: Sage Publications.

Fink, E. J., and W. Gantz. 1996. A Content Analysis of Three Mass Communication Research Traditions—Social Science, Interpretive Studies, and Critical Analysis. *Journalism and Mass Communication Quarterly* 73:114–134.

Fleiss, Joseph L. 1971. Measuring Nominal Scale Agreement among Many Raters. *Psychological Bulletin* 76:378–382.

Franzosi, Roberto. 1997. Labor Unrest in the Italian Service Sector: An Application of Semantic Grammars. In *Text Analysis for the Social Sciences: Methods for Drawing Statistical Inferences from Texts and Transcripts*. Carl W. Roberts, ed. Pp. 131–146. Mahwah, NJ: Lawrence Erlbaum.

Furbee, Louanna 1996. The Religion of Politics in Chiapas: Founding a Cult of Communicating Saints. Presented at the 96th Meeting of the American Anthropological Association, San Francisco.

Furbee-Losee, Louanna, ed. 1976. Mayan Texts I. *International Journal of American Linguistics*. Native American Texts Series, *1*(1). Chicago: University of Chicago Press.

Gerbner, G., O. R. Holsti, K. Krippendorf, W. J. Paisey, and P. J. Stone, eds. 1969. *The Analysis of Communication Content: Developments in Scientific Theories and Computer Techniques*. New York: Wiley.

Gilly, Mary C. 1988. Sex Roles in Advertising: A Comparison of Television Advertisements in Australia, Mexico, and the United States. *Journal of Marketing 52*(April):75–85.

Glaser, Barney G., and Anselm Strauss. 1967. *The Discovery of Grounded Theory: Strategies for Qualitative Research.* New York: Aldine.

Goddard, Pliny E. 1911. Jicarilla Apache Texts. *Anthropological Papers of the American Museum of Natural History 8.* New York: The Trustees.

González Ventura, Josefa. 1997. Experiences in the Development of a Writing System for Ñuu Savi. In *Indigenous Literacy in the Americas.* Nancy H. Hornberger, ed. Pp. 157–171. Berlin: Mouton de Gruyter.

Gottschalk, Louis A. 1994. The Development, Validation, and Applications of a Computerized Measurement of Cognitive Impairment from the Content Analysis of Verbal Behavior. *Journal of Clinical Psychology 50*(3):349–361.

Gottschalk, Louis A. 1997. The Unobtrusive Measurement of Psychological States and Traits. In *Text Analysis for the Social Sciences: Methods for Drawing Statistical Inferences from Texts and Transcripts.* Carl W. Roberts. ed. Pp. 117–129. Mahway, NJ: Lawrence Erlbaum Associates.

Gottschalk, Louis A., and R. J. Bechtel. 1993. *Psychologic and Neuropsychiatric Assessment Applying the Gottschalk-Gleser Content Analysis Method to Verbal Sample Analysis Using the Gottschalk-Bechtel Computer Scoring System.* Palo Alto, CA: Mind Garden.

Hage, Per, and Frank Harary 1983. *Structural Models in Anthropology.* New York: Cambridge University Press.

Handron, D.S., and N. K. Leggett-Frazier. 1994. Utilizing Content Analysis of Counseling Sessions to Identify Psychosocial Stressors among Patients with Type II Diabetes. *The Diabetes Educator 20*(6):515–520.

Hanks, William F. 1988. Grammar, Style, and Meaning in a Maya Manuscript. Review of *Heaven Born Mérida and Its Destiny: The Book of Chilam Balam of Chumayel. International Journal of American Linguistics 54*:331–369.

Hanks, William F. 1989. Texts and Textuality. *Annual Review of Anthropology 18*: 95–127.

Hayes, John, and Carl Holladay. 1987. *Biblical Exegesis*, rev. ed. Atlanta: John Knox Press.

Herzfeld, Michael. 1977. Ritual and Textual Structures: The Advent of Spring in Rural Greece. In *Text and Context.* Ravindra K. Jain, ed. Pp. 29–45. Philadelphia: Institute for the Study of Human Issues.

Hirschman, E. C. 1987. People as Products: Analysis of a Complex Marketing Exchange. *Journal of Marketing 51*:98–108.

Hitchcock, J., and H. S. Wilson. 1992. Personal Risking: Lesbian Self-Disclosure to Health Professionals. *Nursing Research 41*:178–183.

Holland, Dorothy. 1985. From Situation to Impression: How Americans Get to Know Themselves and One Another. In *Directions in Cognitive Anthropology.* J.W.D. Dougherty, ed. Pp. 389–412. Urbana: University of Illinois Press.

Holsti, Ole R. 1966. External Conflict and Internal Consensus: The Sino-Soviet Case. In *The General Inquirer: A Computer Approach to Content Analysis*. P. J. Stone, D. C. Dunphy, M. S. Smith, and D. M. Ogilvie, eds. Pp. 343–358. Cambridge: M.I.T. Press.

Holsti, Ole R. 1969. *Content Analysis for the Social Sciences and Humanities*. Reading, MA: Addison-Wesley.

Hunt, J. G., and A. Ropo. 1995. Multi-Level Leadership—Grounded Theory and Mainstream Theory Applied to the Case of General Motors. *Leadership Quarterly 6*:379-412.

Hutchins, Edwin. 1980. *Culture and Inference*. Cambridge: Harvard University Press.

Hymes, Dell. 1976. Louis Simpson's 'The Deserted Boy.' *Poetics 5*:119–155.

Hymes, Dell. 1977. Discovering Oral Performance and Measured Verse in American Indian Narrative. *New Literary History 8*:431–457.

Hymes, Dell. 1980a. Verse Analysis of a Wasco Text: Hiram Smith's "At'unaqa." *International Journal of American Linguistics 46*:65–77.

Hymes, Dell 1980b. Particle, Pause, and Pattern in American Indian Narrative Verse. *American Indian Culture and Research Journal 4*(4):7–51).

Hymes, Dell. 1981. *In Vain I Tried to Tell You: Essays in Native American Ethnopoetics*. Philadelphia: University of Pennsylvania Press.

Hymes, Virginia. 1987. Warm Springs Sahaptin Narrative Analysis. In *Native American Discourse: Poetics and Rhetoric*. Joel Sherzer and Anthony Woodbury, eds. Pp. 62–102. Cambridge: Cambridge University Press.

Imrich, D. J., C. Mullin, and D. Linz. 1995. Measuring the Extent of Prejudicial Pretrial Publicity in Major American Newspapers—A Content Analysis. *Journal of Communication 45*(3):94–117.

Irurita, V. F. 1996. Hidden Dimensions Revealed—Progressive Grounded Theory Study of Quality Care in the Hospital. *Qualitative Health Research 6*:331–349.

Jang, H-Y., and G. Barnett. 1994. Cultural Differences in Organizational Communication: A Semantic Network Analysis. *Bulletin de Méthodologie Sociologique 44* (September):31–59.

Jehn, Karen A., and Lorna Doucet. 1996. Developing Categories from Interview Data: Text Analysis and Multidimensional Scaling. Part 1. *Cultural Anthropology Methods Journal 8*(2):15–16.

Jehn, Karen A., and Lorna Doucet. 1997. Developing Categories for Interview Data: Consequences of Different Coding and Analysis Strategies in Understanding Text. Part 2. *Cultural Anthropology Methods Journal 9*(1):1–7.

Jehn, Karen A., and O. Werner. 1993. Hapax Legomenon II: Theory, A Thesaurus, and Word Frequency. *Cultural Anthropology Methods Journal 5*(1):8–10.

Johnson, Allen, and Douglass Price-Williams. 1997. *Oedipus Ubiquitous: The Family Complex in World Folk Literature*. Stanford: Stanford University Press.

Johnson-Laird, P. N. 1983. *Mental Models: Towards a Cognitive Science of Language, Inference, and Consciousness*. Cambridge: Harvard University Press.

Johnson-Laird, P. N. 1989. Mental Models. In *Foundations of Cognitive Science*. Michael I. Posner, ed. Pp. 469–500. Cambridge: M.I.T. Press.

Kaid, Lynda Lee, John C. Tedesco, and Lori Melton McKinnon. 1996. Presidential Ads as Nightly News: A Content Analysis of 1988 and 1992 Televised Adwatches. *Journal of Broadcasting Electronic Media 40*:297–308.

Kassis, Hanna. 1983. *A Concordance of the Qur'an*. Berkeley: University of California Press.

Kearney M. H., S. Murphy, and M. Rosenbaum. 1994. Mothering on Crack Cocaine—A Grounded Theory Analysis. *Social Science and Medicine 38*:351–361.

Kearney, M. H., S. Murphy, K. Irwin, and M. Rosenbaum. 1995. Salvaging Self—A Grounded Theory of Pregnancy on Crack Cocaine. *Nursing Research 44*(4):208–213.

Kelle, Udo. 1995. An Overview of Computer-Aided Methods in Qualitative Research. In *Computer-Aided Qualitative Data Analysis: Theory, Methods and Practice*. Udo Kelle, ed. Pp. 1–18. London: Sage Publications.

Kelle, Udo. 1997. Theory Building in Qualitative Research and Computer Programs for the Management of Textual Data. *Sociological Research Online 2*(2): http://www.socresonline.org.uk/socresonline/2/1/1.html.

Kelly, E. F., and P. J. Stone. 1975. *Computer Recognition of English Word Senses*. Amsterdam: North-Holland.

Kempton, Willett. 1987. Two Theories of Home Heat Control. In *Cultural Models in Language and Thought*. D. Holland and N. Quinn, eds. Pp. 222–242. Cambridge: Cambridge University Press.

Kleinnijenhuis, Jan, J. A. de Ridder, and E. M. Rietberg. 1997. Reasoning in Economic Discourse: An Application of the Network Approach to the Dutch Press. In *Text Analysis for the Social Sciences: Methods for Drawing Statistical Inferences from Texts and Transcripts*. Carl W. Roberts, ed. Pp. 191–208. Mahwah, NJ: Lawrence Erlbaum.

Kolbe, R. H., and J. P. Albanese. 1996. Man to Man: A Content Analysis of Sole-Male Images in Male-Audience Magazines. *Journal of Advertising 25*(4):1–20.

Kortendick, Oliver. 1996. *Drei Schwestern un ihre Kinder. Rekonstruktion von Familiengeschichte und Identitätstransmission bei Indischen Nederlanders mit Hilfe computerunterstützer Inhaltsanlyze*. Canterbury, England: University of Kent, Center for Anthropology and Computing.

Krippendorf, Klaus. 1980. *Content Analysis: An Introduction to Its Methodology*. Beverly Hills, CA: Sage Publications.

Kroeber, Alfred. 1907. Gros Ventre Myths and Tales. *Anthropological Papers of the American Museum of Natural History 1*(Part 3). New York: The Trustees.

Laffal, Julius. 1990. *A Concept Dictionary of English, with Computer Programs for Content Analysis*. Essex, CT: Gallery Press.

Laffal, Julius. 1995. A Concept Analysis of Jonathan Swift's *A Tale of a Tub* and *Gulliver's Travels*. *Computers and the Humanities 29*:339–361.

Lakoff, George, and Mark Johnson. 1980. *Metaphors We Live By*. Chicago: University of Chicago Press.

Lee, Raymond M., and Nigel G. Fielding. 1995. User's Experiences of Qualitative Data Analysis Software. In *Computer-Aided Qualitative Data Analysis: Theory, Methods and Practice*. Udo Kelle, ed. Pp. 29–40. London: Sage Publications.

Lee, Raymond M., and Nigel G. Fielding. 1996. Qualitative Data Analysis: Representations of a Technology—A Comment on Coffey, Holbrook and Atkinson. *Sociological Research Online 1*(4): <http://www.socresonline.org.uk/socresonline/1/4/lf.html>.

Light, Richard J. 1971. Measures of Response Agreement for Qualitative Data: Some Generalizations and Alternatives. *Psychological Bulletin 76*(5):365–377.

Lincoln, Yvonna S., and Egon G. Guba. 1985. *Naturalistic Inquiry*. Beverly Hills, CA: Sage Publications.

Lindesmith, A. R. 1968 [1947]. *Addiction and Opiates*. Chicago: Aldine.

Locke, K. 1996. Rewriting the Discovery of Grounded Theory—After 25 Years. *Journal of Management Inquiry 5*(3):239–245.

Lofland, John, and Lyn H. Lofland. 1995. *Analyzing Social Settings*, 3rd ed. Belmont, CA: Wadsworth.

Lonkila, Markku. 1995. Grounded Theory as an Emerging Paradigm for Computer-Assisted Qualitative Data Analysis. In *Computer-Aided Qualitative Data Analysis*. Udo Kelle, ed. Pp. 41–51. Thousand Oaks, CA: Sage Publications.

Lowie, Robert H. 1930. *A Crow Text, with Grammatical Notes*. Berkeley: University of California Press.

Lurie, Nancy. 1961. *Mountain Lone Wolf Woman, Sister of Crashing Thunder: The Autobiography of a Winnebago Woman*. Ann Arbor: University of Michigan Press.

Mandler, Jean. 1984. *Stories, Scripts, and Scenes: Aspects of Schema Theory*. Hillsdale, NJ: Lawrence Erlbaum.

Manning, Peter K. 1982. Analytic Induction. In *Handbook of Social Science Methods*, Vol. 2, *Qualitative Methods*. R. Smith and P. K. Manning, eds. Pp. 273–302. New York: Harper.

Martindale, Colin, and Dean McKenzie. 1995. On the Utility of Content Analysis in Author Attribution: The Federalist. *Computers and the Humanities 29*:259–270.

Mathews, Holly. 1992. The Directive Force of Morality Tales in a Mexican Community. In *Human Motives and Cultural Models*. Roy D'Andrade and Claudia Stauss, eds. Pp. 127–162. New York: Cambridge University Press.

McCleary, R. 1978. *Dangerous Men: The Sociology of Parole*. Beverly Hills, CA: Sage Publications.

McKinnon, Alastair. 1993. The Multi-Dimensional Concordance: A New Tool for Literary Research. *Computers and the Humanities 27*:165–183.

McTavish, Donald G., and E. B. Pirro. 1990. Contextual Content Analysis. *Quality and Quantity 24*:44–63.

Miles, Matthew, and A. Michael Huberman. 1994. *Qualitative Data Analysis*, 2d ed. Thousand Oaks, CA: Sage Publications.

Morse, J. M. 1994. Designing Funded Qualitative Research. In *Handbook of Qualitative Research*. Norman K. Denzin and Y. S. Lincoln, eds. Pp. 220–235. Thousand Oaks, CA: Sage Publications.

Mosteller, F., and D. L. Wallace. 1964. *Inference and Disputed Authorship: The Federalist Papers*. Reading, MA: Addison-Wesley.

Muhr, Thomas. 1991. Atlas/ti—A Protoype for the Support of Text Interpretation. *Qualitative Sociology 14*(4):349–371.

Namenwirth, J., and R. Weber. 1987. *Dynamics of Culture*. Winchester, MA: Allen and Unwin.

Ogilvie, D. M., P. J. Stone, and E. S. Schneidman. 1966. Some Characteristics of Genuine Versus Simulated Suicide Notes. In *The General Inquirer: A Computer Approach to Content Analysis*. P. J. Stone, D. C. Dunphy, M. S. Smith, and D. M. Ogilvie, eds. Pp. 527–535. Cambridge: M.I.T. Press.

Osgood, Charles. 1959. The Representational Model and Relevant Research Methods. In *Trends in Content Analysis*. Ithiels de Sola Pool, ed. Pp. 33–88. Urbana: University of Illinois Press.

Palmquist, Michael, Kathleen M. Carley, and Thomas Dale. 1997. Two Applications of Automated Text Analysis: Analyzing Literary and Non-Literary Texts. In *A Theoretical Map for Selecting among Text Analysis Methods*. C. W. Roberts, ed. Chap. 10. Mahwah, NJ: Lawrence Erlbaum.

Patton, Michael Q. 1990. *Qualitative Evaluation and Research Methods*, 2d ed. Thousand Oaks, CA: Sage Publications.

Peters, Vincent, and F. West. 1990. *Qualitative Analysis in Practice*. Nijmegen, Netherlands: University of Nijmegen.

Piaget, Jean. 1970. Piaget's Theory. In *Carmichael's Manual of Child Psychology*, 3rd ed., Vol. 1. P. Mussen, ed. Pp. 703–732. New York: Wiley.

Postel-Coster, Els. 1977. The Indonesian Novel as a Source of Anthropological Data. In *Text and Context*. Ravindra K. Jain, ed. Pp. 135–150. Philadelphia: Institute for the Study of Human Issues.

Potts R., D. Runyan, A. Zerger, and K. Marchetti. 1996. A Content Analysis of Safety Behaviors of Television Characters—Implications for Children's Safety and Injury. *Journal of Pediatric Psychology 21*(4):517–528.

Prendergast, Guy L. 1971. *A Complete Concordance to the Illiad of Homer*. Hildesheim, Germany: G. Olms.

Price, Laurie. 1987. Ecuadorian Illness Stories. In *Cultural Models in Language and Thought*. D. Holland and N. Quinn, eds. Pp. 313–342. Cambridge: Cambridge University Press.

Quinn, Naomi. 1982. 'Commitment' in American Marriage: A Cultural Analysis. *American Ethnologist 9*:755–798.

Quinn, Naomi. 1987. Convergent Evidence for a Cultural Model of American Marriage. In *Cultural Models in Language and Thought*. N. Quinn and D. Holland, eds. Pp. 173–192. Cambridge: Cambridge University Press.

Quinn, Naomi. 1992. The Motivational Force of Self-Understanding: Evidence from Wives' Inner Conflicts. In *Human Motives and Cultural Models*. Roy D'Andrade and Claudia Stauss, eds. Pp. 90–126. New York: Cambridge University Press.

Quinn, Naomi. 1996. Culture and Contradiction: The Case of Americans Reasoning about Marriage. *Ethos 24*:391–425.

Quinn, Naomi. 1997. Research on the Psychodynamics of Shared Task Solutions. In *A Cognitive Theory of Cultural Meaning*. Claudia Strauss and Naomi Quinn, eds. Pp. 189–209. Cambridge: Cambridge University Press.

Ragin, Charles C. 1987. *The Comparative Method: Moving Beyond Qualitative and Quantitative Strategies*. Berkeley: University of California Press.

Ragin, Charles C. 1994. Introduction to Qualitative Comparative Analysis. In *The Comparative Political Economy of the Welfare State*. T. Janowski and A. M. Hicks, eds. Pp. 299–317. Cambridge: Cambridge University Press.

Richards, Tom, and Lyn Richards. 1991. The NUDIST Qualitative Data Analysis System. *Qualitative Sociology 14*:307–325.

Rice, G. Elizabeth. 1980. On Cultural Schemata. *American Ethnologist 7*:152–171.

Richards, Thomas J. Using Computers in Qualitative Research. In *Handbook of Qualitative Research*. Norman K. Denzin and Yvonna S. Lincoln, eds. Pp. 445–462. Thousand Oaks, CA: Sage Publications.

Roberts, Carl W. 1997. A Theoretical Map for Selecting among Text Analysis Methods. In *Text Analysis for the Social Sciences: Methods for Drawing Statistical Inferences from Texts and Transcripts*. Carl W. Roberts, ed. Pp. 275–283. Mahwah, NJ: Lawrence Erlbaum.

Rohner, Ronald. 1966. Franz Boas, Ethnographer of the Northwest Coast. In *Pioneers of American Anthropology*. June Helm, ed. Pp. 149–212. Seattle: University of Washington Press.

Romme, A.G.L. 1995. Boolean Comparative Analysis of Qualitative Data: A Methodological Note. *Quality & Quantity 29*(3):317–329.

Rosenberg, Stanley D., P. P. Schnurr, and T. E. Oxman 1990. Content Analysis: A Comparison of Manual and Computerized Systems. *Journal of Personality Assessment 54*(1 and 2):298–310.

Rumelhart, David E. 1980. Schemata: The Building Blocks of Cognition. In *Theoretical Issues in Reading Comprehension: Perspectives from Cognitive Psychology, Linguistics, Artificial Intelligence, and Education*. R. J. Spiro, B. C. Bruce, and W. B. Brewer, eds. Pp. 33–58. Hillsdale, NJ: Lawrence Erlbaum.

Ryan, Gery, and Thomas Weisner. 1996. Analyzing Words in Brief Descriptions: Fathers and Mothers Describe Their Children. *Cultural Anthropology Methods Journal 8*(3): 13–16.

Salinas Pedraza, Jesús, and H. Russell Bernard. 1978. *Rc Hnychnyu. The Otomí*. Albuquerque: University of New Mexico Press.

Salinas Pedraza, Jesús. 1997. Saving and Strengthening Indigenous Mexican Languages: The CELIAC Experience. In *Indigenous Literacy in the Americas*. Nancy H. Hornberger, ed. Pp. 171–188. Berlin: Mouton de Gruyter.

Sandelowski, Margarete. 1995a. Qualitative Analysis: What It Is and How to Begin. *Research in Nursing and Health 18*:371–375.

Sandelowski, Margarete 1995b. Sample Size in Qualitative Research. *Research in Nursing and Health 18*:179–183.

Sapir, Edward, and Jeremiah Curtain. 1974 [1909]. *Wishram Texts*. New York: AMS Press.

Sapir, Edward, and Roland B. Dixon. 1910. Yana Texts. *University of California Publications in American Archeology and Ethnology 9*(1). Berkeley: University of California Press.

Sapir, Edward, and Morris Swadesh. 1978 [1939]. *Nootka Texts: Tales and Ethnological Narratives*. New York: AMS Press.

Schank, Robert C., and Robert P. Abelson, 1977. *Scripts, Plans, Goals, and Understanding: An Enquiry into Human Knowledge Structures*. Hillsdale, NJ: Lawrence Erlbaum.

Schnegg, Michael, and H. Russell Bernard. 1996. Words as Actors: A Method for Doing Semantic Network Analysis. *Cultural Anthropology Methods Journal 8*(2):7–10.

Schnurr, P. P., S. D. Rosenberg, T. E. Oxman, and G. Tucker. 1986. A Methodological Note on Content Analysis: Estimates of Reliability. *Journal of Personality Assessment 50*: 601–609.

Schweizer, Thomas. 1991. The Power Struggle in a Chinese Community, 1950–1980: A Social Network Analysis of the Duality of Actors and Events. *Journal of Quantitative Anthropology 3*:19–44.

Schweizer, Thomas. 1996. Actor and Event Orderings Across Time: Lattice Representation and Boolean Analysis of the Political Disputes in Chen Village, China. *Social Networks 18*:247–266.

Scott, William A. 1955. Reliability of Content Analysis. The Case of Nomimal Scale Coding. *Public Opinion Quarterly 19*:321–325.

Segre, Cesare, and T. Kemeny. 1988. *Introduction to the Analysis of the Literary Text*. John Meddemmen, tr. Bloomington: Indiana University Press.

Seidel, John, and Udo Kelle. 1995. Different Functions of Coding in the Analysis of Textual Data. In *Computer-Aided Qualitative Data Analysis: Theory, Methods and Practice*. Udo Kelle, ed. Pp. 52–61. London: Sage Publications.

Shapiro, Gilbert. 1997. The Future of Coders: Human Judgments in a World of Sophisticated Software. In *Text Analysis for the Social Sciences: Methods for Drawing Statistical Inferences from Texts and Transcripts*. Carl W. Roberts, ed. Pp. 225–238. Mahwah, NJ: Lawrence Erlbaum.

Sherzer, Joel. 1990. *Verbal Art in San Blas*. Cambridge: Cambridge University Press.

Sherzer, Joel. 1994. The Kuna and Columbus: Encounters and Confrontations of Discourse. *American Anthropologist 96*:902–925.

Sherzer, Joel, and Anthony Woodbury. 1987. Introduction. In *Native American Discourse: Poetics and Rhetoric*. Joel Sherzer and Anthony Woodbury, eds. Pp. 1–16. Cambridge: Cambridge University Press.

Silverberg, S. B., S. C. Betts, A. J. Huebner, and S. Cotarobles. 1996. Implicit Beliefs about Change: A Theory-Grounded Measure Applied to Community Organizations Serving Children, Youth, and Families. *Journal of Sociology and Social Welfare 23*(4):57–76.

Sleath, B., B. Svarstad, and D. Roter. 1997. Physician Versus Patient Initiation of Psychotropic Prescribing in Primary Care Settings: A Content Analysis of Audiotapes. *Social Science and Medicine 44*(4):541–548.

Smith, Charles P., S. C. Feld, and C. E. Franz. 1992. Methodological Considerations: Steps in Research Employing Content Analysis Systems. In *Motivation and Personality: Handbook of Thematic Content Analysis*. C. Smith, J. N. Atkinson, D. C. McClelland, and J. Veroff, eds. Pp. 515–536. Cambridge: Cambridge University Press.

Sohier, R. 1993. Filial Reconstruction: A Theory on Development Through Adversity. *Qualitative Health Research 3*(4):465–492.

Spears N. E, J. C. Mowen, and G. Chakraborty. 1996. Symbolic Role of Animals in Print Advertising—Content Analysis and Conceptual Development. *Journal of Business Research 37*(2):87–95.

Spevack, Marvin. 1973. *The Harvard Concordance to Shakespeare*. Cambridge: Belknap Press.

Spiggle, S. 1986. Measuring Social Values: A Content Analysis of Sunday Comics and Underground Comix. *Journal of Consumer Research 13*:100–113.

Spradley, James. 1979. *The Ethnographic Interview*. New York: Holt, Rinehart and Winston.

Stone, P. J., D. C. Dunphy, M. S. Smith, and D. M. Ogilvie, eds. 1966. *The General Inquirer: A Computer Approach to Content Analysis*. Cambridge: M.I.T. Press.

Strauss, Anselm. 1987. *Qualitative Analysis for Social Scientists*. Cambridge: Cambridge University Press.

Strauss, Anselm, and J. Corbin. 1990. *Basics of Qualitative Research. Grounded Theory Procedures and Techniques*. Thousand Oaks, CA: Sage Publications.

Strauss, Claudia. 1992. What Makes Tony Run? Schemas as Motive Reconsidered. In *Human Motives and Cultural Models*. Roy D'Andrade and Claudia Strauss, eds. Pp. 191–224. Cambridge: Cambridge University Press.

Strauss, Claudia. 1997. Research on Cultural Discontinuities. In *A Cognitive Theory of Cultural Meaning*. Claudia Strauss and Naomi Quinn, eds. Pp. 210–251. Cambridge: Cambridge University Press.

Swanton, John Reed. 1909. *Tlingit Myths and Texts*. Washington, DC: Government Printing Office.

Taylor, Steven J., and Robert Bogdan. 1984. *Introduction to Qualitative Research Methods*, 2d ed. New York: Wiley.

Tedlock, Dennis. 1972. *Finding the Center: Narrative Poetry of the Zuni Indians*. New York: Dial.

Tedlock, Dennis. 1985. *Popol Vuh: The Mayan Book of the Dawn of Life and the Glories of Gods and Kings*. New York: Simon and Schuster.

Tedlock, Dennis. 1987. Hearing a Voice in an Ancient Text: Quiché Maya Poetics in Performance. In *Native American Discourse: Poetics and Rhetoric*. Joel Sherzer and Anthony Woodbury, eds. Pp. 140–175. Cambridge: Cambridge University Press.

Tesch, R. 1990. *Qualitative Research: Analysis Types and Software Tools*. New York: Falmer Press.

Trost, J. E. 1986. Statistically Nonrepresentative Stratified Sampling: A Sampling Technique for Qualitative Studies. *Qualitative Sociology 9*:54–57.

Viney, L. L. 1983. The Assessment of Psychological States Through Content Analysis of Verbal Communications. *Psychological Bulletin 94*:542–563.

Waitzkin, Howard, and Theron Britt. 1993. Processing Narratives of Self-Destructive Behavior in Routine Medical Encounters: Health Promotion, Disease Prevention, and the Discourse of Health Care. *Social Science and Medicine 36*(9):1121–1136.

Weber, Robert. 1990. *Basic Content Analysis*, 2d ed. Quantitative Applications in the Social Sciences, Vol. 48. Thousand Oaks, CA: Sage Publications.

Weitzman, E., and M. Miles. 1995. *Computer Programs for Qualitative Data Analysis*. Thousand Oaks, CA: Sage Publications.

Werner, Oswald. 1995. The Case for Verbatim Cases. *Cultural Anthropology Methods Journal 7*(1):6–8.

White, Douglas R., and M. L. Burton. 1988. Causes of Polygyny: Ecology, Economy, Kinship, and Warfare. *American Anthropologist 90*:871–887.

Willms, D. G., J. A. Best, D. W. Taylor, J. R. Gilbert, D.M.C. Wilson, E. A. Lindsay, and J. Singer. 1990. A Systematic Approach for Using Qualitative Methods in Primary Prevention Research. *Medical Anthropology Quarterly 4*:391–409.

Wilson, Holly Skodol, and Sally Ambler Hutchinson. 1996. Methodologic Mistakes in Grounded Theory. *Nursing Research 45*(2):122–124.

Wissler, C., and D. C. Duvall. 1908. Mythology of the Blackfoot Indians. *Anthropological Papers of the American Museum of Natural History 2*(Pt. 1). New York: Trustees, AMNH.

Wodak, Ruth. 1992. Strategies in Text Production and Text Comprehension: A New Perspective. In *Cooperating with Written Texts*. Dieter Stein, ed. Pp. 493–528. New York: Mouton de Gruyter.

Wolf, Eric. 1964. *Anthropology*. Englewood Cliffs, NJ: Prentice-Hall.

Woodbury, Anthony C. 1987. Rhetorical Structure in a Central Alaskan Yupik Eskimo Traditional Narrative. In *Native American Discourse: Poetics and Rhetoric*. Joel Sherzer and Anthony Woodbury, eds. Pp. 176–239. Cambridge: Cambridge University Press.

Wright, K. B. 1997. Shared Ideology in Alcoholics Anonymous: A Grounded Theory Approach. *Journal of Health Communication* 2(2):83–99.

Young, Robert 1982. *Analytical Concordance to the Bible*. Nashville: T. Nelson.

Yule, G. U. 1968 [1944]. *The Statistical Study of Literary Vocabulary*. Hamden, CT: Archon Books.

Znaniecki, Florian. 1934. Analytic Induction in Sociology. In *The Method of Sociology*. New York: Farrar and Rinehart.

Zuell, C., R. P. Weber, and P. Mohler, eds. 1989. *Computer-Assisted Text Analysis for the Social Sciences: The General Inquirer III*. Mannheim, Germany: Center for Surveys, Methods, and Analysis (ZUMA).

CAROL R. EMBER
MELVIN EMBER

Seventeen

Cross-Cultural Research

Introduction

Cultural anthropology, among other things, is a comparative discipline. We who call ourselves cultural anthropologists like to emphasize how customs vary from place to place and how they may change over time. Indeed, we delight in the diversity of human cultures. Yet many cultural anthropologists are uncomfortable with the idea of explicit, systematic cross-cultural research—the subject of this chapter. One reason for the discomfort may be our emphasis on fieldwork. We train several years for our fieldwork and we spend a lot of time in the field. Fieldwork is central to our professional lives as well as to the discipline. The usual objective of fieldwork is to discover the details and particulars of a single community or culture. Those details remind us that each culture is unique, its combination of patterns of behavior and belief like no other.

To compare cultures is not to deny their uniqueness. Ethnography tells us what is distinctive about a particular culture; cross-cultural comparison tells us about what is generally true for some, or many, or even all cultures. To generalize across cultures, we build on the particulars of ethnographies to formulate statements about the similarities and differences of cultures, and what they may be related to. The serious epistemological issue is whether it is possible to formulate such general statements in the first place. Cross-culturalists argue that it is.

We focus in this chapter on methods for systematic comparisons across cultures—comparisons that, we expect, will answer questions about the incidence, distribution, and causes of cultural variation. The methods are familiar—unbiased sampling, repeatable measurements, statistical evaluation of results, etc. The relationship between cross-cultural research and ethnography is analogous to that between epidemiology and clinical practice in medicine. In ethnographic research and in clinical practice, the focus is on the individual case, while in cross-cultural research, as in epidemiology, the focus is on populations. Epidemiologists look at the incidence and distribution of diseases across populations and try to understand the causes of those diseases, primarily through correlational analyses of presumed causes and effects. Similarly, cross-cultural researchers are interested in causes and effects of cultural variation across the world or across regions of the world.

Uniqueness and Comparability

To illustrate how things can be unique and comparable at the same time, consider the following ethnographic statements (from C. R. and M. Ember, 1998) about sexuality in three different cultures:

1. The Mae Enga in the Western Highlands of Papua New Guinea believe that "copulation is in itself detrimental to male well-being. Men believe that the vital fluid residing in a man's skin makes it sound and handsome, a condition that determines and reflects his mental vigor and self-confidence. This fluid also manifests itself as his semen. Hence, every ejaculation depletes his vitality, and over-indulgence must dull his mind and leave his body permanently exhausted and withered." (Meggitt 1964:210)
2. "The Nupe men [of Nigeria], certainly, make much of the physically weakening effects of sexual intercourse, and teach the younger generation to husband their strength. . . ." (Nadel 1954:179)
3. "[T]he milk avoidances of the Nilotes [Shilluk of the Sudan] are dependent on fear of contamination associated with the sexual act. . . . Only small boys herd the cattle and milk them, for once a boy has reached maturity there is the danger that he may have had sexual contact, when if he milked, or handled manure, or even walked among the cattle in their pens, he would cause them to become sterile...If a man has had sexual relations with his wife or another he is considered unclean and does not drink milk until the sun has set the following day." (Seligman and Seligman 1932:73)

Each statement about male sexuality is unique, but there are also similarities in these statements that suggest a continuum—variation in the degree to which men in a society believe that heterosexual sex is harmful. Enga and Nupe men apparently think that heterosexual sex is harmful to them. If we ask "Do people believe that male heterosexuality (even with legitimate partners) brings some harm or danger?," we would have to say that all three of the cultures mentioned have such a belief.

Consider now the following ethnographic statements:

4. For the Cuna of Panama, "the sexual impulse is regarded as needing relief, particularly for males, and as an expression of one's *niga*, a supernatural attribute manifested in potency and strength. On the other hand, it is considered debilitating to have sexual relations too often, for this will weaken one's *niga*." (Stout 1947:39)

5. And in regard to the Bedouin of Kuwait: "It [sexual intercourse] is the one great pleasure common to rich and poor alike, and the one moment of forgetfulness in his daily round of troubles and hardships that Badawin [Bedouin] or townsmen can enjoy. Men and women equally love the act, which is said to keep a man young, 'just like riding a mare.'" (Dickson 1951:162)

The Bedouin beliefs contrast most sharply with the beliefs in the first three cultures: heterosexual intercourse appears to be viewed by them as purely pleasurable, with no negative associations. The Cuna seem somewhere in the middle. While they view sex as important, they appear to believe that too much is not good. The variable "degree of men's fear of sex with women" can be conceptualized as a continuum with gradations.

In a cross-cultural study of this variable, the first author identified four scale points: Societies with only negative statements (in the ethnography) about heterosexuality were considered high on men's fear of sex with women; societies with more or less an equal number of negative and positive statements were considered ambivalent; those with *mostly* positive statements were considered relatively low on men's fear of sex with women; and those with *only* positive statements were considered as lacking men's fear of sex with women. While the variable as operationally defined does not capture everything in a culture's beliefs about heterosexuality, it does capture some distinguishable similarities and differences across cultures (C. R. Ember 1978).

These examples show that if we focus on a specific aspect or dimension of variation, similarities and differences become apparent. Framing meaningful and answerable questions, and identifying useful dimensions to do so, is an art. To be meaningful, a question should have some theoretical (generally explanatory) importance. To be answerable, the question should be phrased in a way that allows us to get to an answer on the basis of research. In cross-cultural research, as in most social science research, framing the question (often in a single sentence) is half the battle. Once we frame a question in answerable terms, it is not hard to decide how to go about seeking an answer. And we do not have to limit ourselves to one possible answer; often cross-cultural research involves testing several, not necessarily alternative, answers to the question at issue.

Framing the Research Question:
The Kinds of Questions Asked

There are at least four kinds of questions we can ask in cross-cultural research:

1. Descriptive/statistical questions. These deal with the prevalence or frequency of a trait: How common is the belief that sex is dangerous to one's health? What proportion of societies have it?
2. Questions about causes of a trait or custom. Examples are: Why do some societies have the belief that heterosexual sex is harmful? Why do some societies insist on monogamous marriage, whereas most allow polygyny (multiple wives)? Why is war very frequent in some societies and less frequent in others?
3. Questions about the consequences or effects of a particular trait or custom. This kind of question may be phrased broadly: What are the effects of growing up in a society with a great deal of war? Or a consequence question may be phrased much more specifically: What is the effect of polygyny on fertility?
4. Questions that are nondirective and relational. Rather than theorizing about causes or consequences, a researcher may simply ask if a particular aspect of culture is associated with some other aspects. Is there a relationship between type of marriage and level of fertility? Is more war associated with more socialization for aggression in children? No causal direction is specified beforehand with a nondirective relational question.

Of the four types of questions, the descriptive/statistical type is the easiest to address because it tells the researcher what to count in a representative sample of societies. To estimate the frequency of monogamy versus polygyny, we need to establish what each society allows and make a count of each kind of society. The consequence and relational questions usually specify a set of concrete things to look at. If you want to know whether type of marriage has an effect on or is related to fertility, you know you need to measure both variables (type of marriage and fertility). Open-ended causal (and consequence) questions are the most challenging. The only thing specified in the open-ended causal question is the dependent variable (the variable to be explained); the only thing specified in the open-ended consequence question is the independent variable (the variable that may have effects). Exactly which variables may be causes or effects is something the investigator has to decide, often as suggested by some theory.

The basic assumption of cross-cultural research is that comparison is possible because repeated patterns can be identified. Cross-culturalists believe that all generalizations about culture require testing, no matter how plausible we may think they are. This applies to descriptive generalizations presumed to be true (for example, the presumption that hunter-gatherers are typically peaceful) as well as to presumed associations (for example, that hunting is more likely to be associated with patrilocality). As it turns out, *neither* presumption is generally true of hunter-gatherers (C. R. Ember 1975, 1978).

Before we discuss the advantages and disadvantages of the various kinds of comparative and cross-cultural research, here is a little historical background.

History of Cross-Cultural Research

The first cross-cultural study was published in 1889 by Edward B. Tylor. In that study, Tylor attempted to relate marital residence and the reckoning of kinship to other customs, such as joking and avoidance relationships. But, perhaps because of Francis Galton's objection to Tylor's presentation—see the Discussion section at the end of Tylor's paper—there was little cross-cultural research for the next 40 years. (We'll discuss what has come to be called "Galton's Problem" later.)

Cross-cultural research became more popular in the 1930s and 1940s, at the Institute of Human Relations at Yale. The person who led this rebirth was anthropologist George Peter Murdock (1897–1985). Murdock had obtained his Ph.D. at Yale in a combined sociology/anthropology department that called itself the "Science of Society" (its comparative perspective was established by its founder, William Graham Sumner).

Perhaps the major boost to cross-cultural studies was the Yale group's development of an organized collection of ethnographic information (first called the "Cross-Cultural Survey," the precursor of the "Human Relations Area Files") that scholars could use to compare the cultures of the world. In the early part of the twentieth century, Sumner had compiled voluminous materials on peoples throughout the world, but his compilation was limited to subjects in which he was personally interested. Later, at the Institute of Human Relations, the group of social and behavioral scientists led by Murdock (including psychologists, physiologists, sociologists, and anthropologists) set out to improve on Sumner's work by developing the Cross-Cultural Survey. The aim was to foster comparative research on humans in all their variety so that explanations of human behavior wouldn't be culture bound.

The first step was to develop a classification system that would organize the descriptive information on different cultures. This category system became the *Outline of Cultural Materials* (the most recent edition of which is Murdock et al. [1987]). The next step was to select well-described cases and to index the ethnography on them, paragraph by paragraph, sometimes sentence by sentence, for the subject matters covered on a page. As the aim was to file information by subject category to facilitate comparison, and since a page usually contained more than one type of information, the extracts of ethnographic information were typed using carbon paper to make the number of copies needed, which corresponded to the number of topics covered (carbon paper was used because the Cross-Cultural Survey antedated photocopying).

In 1946, the Cross-Cultural Survey directorship was turned over to Clellan S. Ford, who undertook to transform it into a consortium of universities. In 1949, first five, then eight universities joined to sponsor a not-for-profit consortium called the Human Relations Area Files, Incorporated (HRAF), with headquarters in New Haven. Over the years, HRAF added member institutions, and more and more cultures were added to its collection. In the early days, member institutions received the annual installments of information on xeroxed sheets of paper. Later, the preferred media became microfiche. Since 1994, the only media are electronic, first CD-ROM and now also the Internet. Technological changes have allowed the full-text HRAF Collection of Ethnography to become more and more accessible and more and more efficiently searchable. New cases are added each year. Today, when old cases are added to the electronic HRAF, they are almost always extensively updated. An updated case, if recent fieldwork has been done on it, may now have nearly 50% new material. (For more information on the evolution of HRAF, see M. Ember 1997.)

The accessibility that HRAF provides to indexed full-text ethnographic information has undoubtedly increased the number of cross-cultural studies. Considering just worldwide comparisons (the most common type of cross-cultural study), between 1889 and 1947 there were only ten worldwide cross-cultural studies. In the next 20 years, there were 127; and in the next 20 (ending in 1987), there were 440 (C. R. Ember and Levinson 1991:138). At present, there may be nearly 1,000 worldwide cross-cultural studies in the published literature. This trend is likely to continue for various reasons (see M. Ember 1997).

Types of Cross-Cultural Comparison

Cross-cultural comparisons vary along four dimensions: (1) geographical scope of the comparison—whether the sample is worldwide or is limited to a geographic area (for example, a region such as North America); (2) size of the sample—two-case comparisons, small-scale comparisons (fewer than ten cases), and larger comparisons; (3) whether the data used are primary (collected by the investigator in various field sites explicitly for the comparison) or secondary (collected by others and found by the investigator in ethnographies, censuses, and histories); and (4) whether the data on a given case pertain to (or date from) just one time period (a *synchronic comparison* of cases) or two or more time periods (a *diachronic comparison*). Although all combinations of the four dimensions are technically possible, some combinations are quite rare. Worldwide cross-cultural comparisons using secondary synchronic data (one "ethnographic present" for each case) are the most common in anthropology.

Comparative research is not only done in anthropology. Worldwide studies using ethnographic data are increasingly carried out by evolutionary biologists, sociologists, political scientists, and others. Cross-cultural psychologists often compare people in different cultures. And various kinds of social scientists compare across nations. The cross-national comparison is narrower than the worldwide cross-cultural one because the results of a cross-national comparison are generalizable only to a limited range of cross-cultural variation—that which encompasses only the complex societies (usually multicultural nation-states) of recent times. The results of a cross-cultural study are generalizable to all types of societies, from hunter-gatherers—with populations in the hundreds or a few thousand, to agrarian state societies—with populations in the millions, to modern nation-states—with populations in the hundreds of millions.

Cross-national research differs from cross-cultural research in ways other than generalizability. Economists, sociologists, and political scientists usually use secondary data when they study samples of nations, but the data are not generally ethnographic. That is, the measures used are not based on cultural information collected by anthropologists or other investigators in the field. Rather, the data used in cross-national comparisons are generally based on censuses and other nationally collected statistics (crime rates, gross national product, etc.), often documented over time. Cross-cultural psychologists are most likely to collect their own (primary) data, but their comparisons tend to be the most limited; usually only two cultures are compared.

Cross-historical studies are still comparatively rare in anthropology (but see Naroll et al. 1974). Few worldwide or even within-region cross-cultural studies have used data on a given case for more than one time period. But, as noted, some cross-national studies have been cross-historical studies as well. Such studies can be done by sociologists, political scientists, and economists because there are accessible historical data bases on nations. Since primary data are so hard and expensive to collect, it is not surprising that primary comparisons are likely to be small in scale. Large-scale comparisons, which almost always rely on secondary data (collected or assembled previously by others), are generally much less expensive.

Let us turn now to the advantages and disadvantages of the different types of cross-cultural comparison. Our discussion compares the different types with particular regard to theory formulation and theory testing. (Cross-cultural research may also be done to establish the incidence or relative frequency of something.)

Advantages and Disadvantages of the Different Types of Comparison

Worldwide cross-cultural comparisons have two major advantages, compared with other types of comparative research (M. Ember 1991). The major one, as noted, is that the statistical conclusions drawn from such comparisons are probably applicable to the entire ethnographic record, assuming that the sample is more or less free of bias. (See the section on Sampling, below.) This contrasts with results of a within-region comparison, which may or may not be applicable to other regions. And it contrasts with results of a cross-national comparison, which may or may not be applicable to the ethnographic record. The worldwide type of cross-cultural comparison, then, has a better chance than other types of coming close to the goal of knowing that a finding or observed relationship has nearly universal validity, consistent with the general scientific goal of more and more comprehensive explanations. (Most cross-cultural studies undersample modern industrial societies, but this deficiency will decrease as the ethnographic record increasingly includes results of ethnographic field studies in industrial countries.)

The other advantage of worldwide cross-cultural comparison is that it maximizes the amount or range of variation in the variables investigated. This may make the difference between a useful and a useless study. Without variation, it's impossible to see a relationship between variables. Even if there's some variation, it may be at just one end of the spectrum. We may think the relationship is positive or negative, because that's all we can observe in one region or in one society, but it may be curvilinear in the world, as John Whiting (1954:524–525) noted. This is what occurs when we plot socioeconomic inequality against level of economic development; there is little socioeconomic inequality in hunter-gatherer societies, there is a lot of inequality in premodern agrarian societies, and inequality is lower again—but hardly absent—in modern industrial societies (M. Ember et al. 1997).

If we only looked at industrial societies, it would appear that more equality goes with higher levels of economic development. But if we only looked at preindustrial societies, it would appear that more equality goes with *lower* levels of economic development. Thus, to be sure about the nature or shape of a relationship, we have to conduct a worldwide cross-cultural comparison because that shows the maximum range of variation and is the most reliable way to discover the existence and nature of relationships between or among variables pertaining to humans.

When a researcher compares many societies from different parts of the world, she or he is unlikely to know much about each one. If a tested explanation turns out to be supported, the lack of detailed knowledge about the sample cases isn't much of a problem. However, if the cross-cultural test is disconfirming, it may be difficult to come up with an alternative explanation without knowing more about the particular cases. More familiarity with the cases may help in formulating a revised or new theory that could be tested and supported (Johnson 1991).

Narrowing the scope of a comparative study to a single region may mean that you can know more about the cases and therefore may be more likely to come up with a revised theory if your first tests are unsuccessful. Restricting the study to a region doesn't allow you to discover that the results of the comparison apply to the whole world (see Burton and White 1991). Of course, even a regional comparativist may not know all the cases in the region. If the region is as large as North America, the comparativist is likely to know less about the cases than if the region studied is the American Southwest. And if you need to look at a sample of the rest of the world to discover how generalizable your results are, you might as well do a worldwide study in the first place!

The objective of large-scale within-region comparisons (using data on all or most of the societies in the region) is usually different from that of a worldwide cross-cultural study (Burton and White 1991). Using large numbers of cross-cultural traits, within-region comparativists generally try to arrive at classifications of cultures to make inferences about processes of diffusion and historical ancestry. Instead of trying to see how culture traits may be causally related to each other, within-region comparativists are usually more interested in how the cultures in the region are related to each another. But some regional comparativists are interested in pursuing both objectives at the same time (Jorgensen 1974). The importance of looking at worldwide as well as regional samples, especially if you're interested in relationships between or among variables, is indicated by the following discussion.

Consider the discrepancy between the findings of Driver and Massey (1957) and those of M. Ember and C. R. Ember (1971) and Divale (1974) concerning the relationship between division of labor by gender and where couples live after they get married. Driver and Massey found support in aboriginal North America for Murdock's (1949:203ff.) idea that division of labor by gender determined matrilocal versus patrilocal residence, but the Embers (and Divale) found no support for this idea in worldwide samples. The Embers found that the relationship varies from region to region. In North America there is a significant relationship, but in other regions the relationship is not significant. And in Oceania, there is a trend in the opposite direction—matrilocal societies there are more likely to have men doing more in primary subsistence activities. What might be the reason for the difference in the direction of the relationship in different regions? C. Ember (1975) found that the relationship between a male-dominated division of labor and patrilocal residence did hold for hunter-gatherers. She suggested that the frequent occurrence of hunter-gatherers in North America (see Witkowski n.d.) may account for the statistically significant relationship between division of labor and residence in North America.

Fred Eggan (1954) advocated small-scale regional comparisons, which he called "controlled comparisons," because he thought they would make it easier to control similarity in history, geography, and language. He presumed that the researcher could readily discern what accounts for an aspect of cultural variation within the region if history, geography, and language were held constant. However, the similarity of cases within a region may be a major drawback.

A single region may not show sufficient variability in the aspect (or presumed causes) the researcher is investigating. Unless a substantial number of cases lack what you're trying to explain, it would be difficult or impossible to discern what the phenomenon may be related to. For example, suppose almost all cases in a region share beliefs about sexuality being somewhat harmful. It would be difficult or nearly impossible to figure out what this belief is related to, because you couldn't tell which of the other regularly occurring regional practices or beliefs might explain the sexual beliefs. Only if some cases lack what you're trying to explain might you see that the hypothetical causes are also generally absent when the presumed effect is absent. So, unless there is sufficient variation in all possibly relevant variables, the controlled comparison strategy is a poor choice for testing theory.

Obviously, the controlled comparison is also a poor choice for describing the worldwide incidence of something (unless the region focused on is the only one of interest). While the strategy of controlled comparison may seem analogous to controls in psychology and sociology (which hold some possible causes, and their effects, constant), the resemblance is only superficial. Psychologists and sociologists typically eliminate certain kinds of variation (for example, in race, religion, ethnicity, or gender) only when they have prior empirical reasons to think that these factors partially predict the variable they are trying to explain. In contrast, those who do controlled comparisons in the anthropological sense usually only *presume* that common history, language, or geography have made a difference. If researchers aren't really controlling on predictors when they do a controlled comparison, they aren't necessarily getting any closer to the causal reality by restricting their study to a particular region.

The researcher must collect primary data in the field if he or she is interested in topics that are rarely (if ever) covered adequately by ethnographers. This was the major reason why John and Beatrice Whiting (see, for example, B. B. Whiting 1963), who were interested in children's behavior and what it was related to, decided that they had to collect new data in the field for the comparative study that came to be known as the Six Cultures project. Many aspects of socialization (such as particular practices of the mother) weren't typically described in ethnographies. Similarly, researchers interested in internal psychological states (such as sex-identity, self-esteem, and happiness) couldn't find out about them from ethnographies and would need to collect the data themselves, in the field. How time is allocated to various activities is a nonpsychological example of information that is also not generally covered in ethnographies, or not in sufficient detail.

Although it may always seem preferable to collect primary as opposed to secondary data, the logistics of cross-cultural comparisons using primary data are formidable in time and expense. And the task of maintaining comparability of measures across sites is difficult (R. L. Munroe and R. H. Munroe 1991a). So, if a researcher thinks that something like the needed information is already available in ethnographies, a comparison using secondary data is more economical than comparative fieldwork in two or more places. But comparative fieldwork may be the only viable choice when the information needed is not otherwise available.

Similarly, although it may seem preferable to use diachronic data (history) to test the temporal ordering implied in causal theories, such data are not often readily available. Because most societies that cultural anthropologists studied lacked native writing, there are usually no historical documents with which to measure variables for an earlier time. The alternative is to reconstruct the situation in a prior time period on the basis of oral history and occasional documents left by travelers, traders, and other visitors. Such reconstructions are notoriously subject to bias (because of wishful thinking by the researcher). It is also difficult to find diachronic data because different ethnographers have different substantive interests, so different ethnographers who may have worked in the same place at different times may not have collected information on the same variables.

For these reasons, most cross-culturalists think it's more efficient to test causal theories with synchronic data first. If a theory has merit, the presumed causes and effects should generally be associated synchronically. If they are, then we might try to make a diachronic or cross-historical test. It doesn't make sense to try to see if the presumed causes antedated the presumed effects unless we see first that the synchronic results show correlation. (Diachronic data should become increasingly available as the ethnographic record expands with updating, so we should see more cross-historical studies in the future.)

Sampling

Whatever questions cross cultural researchers want to answer, they always have to decide what cases to compare. How many cases should be selected for comparison and how should they be selected? If we want to answer a question about incidence or frequency throughout the world or in a region, then it is critical that all the cases (countries or cultures) be listed in the sampling frame (the list to be sampled from, sometimes also called the "universe" or "population"). And all must have an equal chance to be chosen (the major reason sample results can be generalized to the larger universe of cases). Otherwise, it's hard to argue that sample results are generalizable to anything!

It's rarely necessary to investigate all cases or even to sample a high proportion of cases from the sampling frame. In fact, except when relationships between contiguous cases are of interest, investigating all cases would be a colossal waste of time and resources. Political opinion polling is a case in point. The number of voters in the United States is a very large number. Yet, very accurate results can usually be obtained by randomly sampling a few hundred to a few thousand individuals. The size of the sample is not as important as selecting the cases in some random way from a more or less complete list of voters. If you're looking for a large difference between one kind of voter and another, or if the relationship you're examining is strong, you don't have to have a very large sample to obtain statistically significant results. The most important consideration is to sample in an unbiased way, preferably using some kind of random sampling procedure (M. Ember and Otterbein 1991).

Sampling in Comparisons Using Primary Data

There have been relatively few comparisons using primary data (collected by the researcher in two or more field sites) in anthropology. There have been a considerable number of two-case comparisons in cross-cultural psychology, usually comparing subjects in the United States with subjects in some other place. Generally, sampling in comparisons using primary data has been purposive rather than random. That is, the cases compared have not been randomly selected from some sampling frame. This is understandable, given the political realities of gaining permission to do fieldwork in certain countries. In terms of the cost of fieldwork, it's not surprising that two-case comparisons are more common than any other kind of comparison using primary data. Unfortunately, the scientific value of two-case comparisons is dubious. Years ago, Donald Campbell (1961:344) pointed out that a difference between two cases could be explained by *any* other difference(s) between the cases. Let's consider a hypothetical example.

Assume we are comparing two societies with different levels of fertility. We may think that the difference is due to a need for child labor, because much agricultural and household work has to be done. As plausible as this may sound, we should be skeptical about it because many other differences could be responsible for the difference in fertility. The high-fertility society may also have earlier weaning, a shorter postpartum sex taboo, better medical care, etc. There is no way, using aggregate or cultural data on the two societies, to rule out the possibility that any of the other differences (and still others not considered here) may be responsible for the difference in fertility. However, if you have data on a sample of mothers for each society, and measures of fertility and the possible causes for each mother, you could do statistical analyses that narrow down the causal possibilities in these two societies. Suggestive as these results might be, we can't be sure about what accounts for the difference at issue because we still have only two sample societies.

What is the minimum number of societies for a comparative test using primary data? If two variables are related, the minimum number of cases that might provide a statistically significant result—assuming unbiased sampling, errorless measurement, and a hypothesis that is true—is four (see R. L. Munroe and R. H. Munroe 1991b). Examples of four-case comparisons using primary data, which used theoretical criteria for case selection, are the project on culture and ecology in East Africa, directed by Walter Goldschmidt (1965), and the Munroes' project on socialization (R. H. Munroe et al. 1984; R. L. Munroe and R. H. Munroe 1992). In the East Africa project, which was concerned with the effect of ecology/economy on personality and social life, two communities (one pastoral and one agricultural) in each of four cultures (two Kalenjin speaking and two Bantu speaking) were selected. The Munroes selected four cultures from around the world to examine the effects of variation in degree of father-absence and in degree of male-centered social structure.

Sampling in Comparisons Using Secondary Data

You have to decide what your sampling frame is, what list of cases you want to generalize the sample results to. Will it be worldwide (all countries or all societies)? Will it be regional (a broad region like North America, or a narrower one like the cultures of the American Southwest)? When you specify your sampling frame, you're also specifying your unit of analysis.

A country isn't necessarily equivalent to a society or culture in the anthropological sense. A country (or nation-state) is a politically unified population; it may, and often does, contain more than one culture or society. Conventionally, a culture is the set of customary beliefs and practices characteristic of a society, which, in turn, is a population that occupies a particular territory and speaks a common language not generally understood by neighboring populations. Once you know what you want to generalize the sample results to, you should sample from a list containing all the eligible cases. Cross-national researchers have no problem constructing a list of countries. Cross-cultural researchers don't yet have a complete list of the world's described cultures, although such a list is currently under construction at HRAF. But there are large lists of cultures to sample from.

Several published lists of societies have served as sampling frames for most cross-cultural studies. A few claim to accurately represent the world's cultures, but we argue below that these claims are problematic and that cross-cultural researchers can't yet generalize sample results to all cultures. Any claim about a relationship or about the proportion of societies that have a particular trait should be tempered by recognizing that the generalization is only applicable to the list sampled from, and only if the particular cases investigated constitute an unbiased sample of the larger list.

Currently available cross-cultural samples include the following (from largest to smallest): (1) the "Ethnographic Atlas" (1962ff., beginning in *Ethnology 1* [1962]: 113ff. and continuing intermittently over succeeding years and issues of the journal), with a total of 1,264 cases; (2) the "Summary" version of the "Ethnographic Atlas" (Murdock 1967), with a total of 862 cases; (3) the "World Ethnographic Sample" (Murdock 1957), with 565 cases; (4) the *Atlas of World Cultures* (Murdock 1981), with 563 cases; (5) the annually growing HRAF Collection of Ethnography, which covered more than 360 cultures as of 1998 (the HRAF sample is a collection of full texts grouped by culture and indexed by topic for quick information retrieval; no precoded data are provided for the sample cases, in contrast to all the other samples except the next); (6) the "Standard Ethnographic Sample, 2d ed." (Naroll and Sipes 1973 and addenda in Naroll and Zucker 1974), with 273 cases; (7) the "Standard Cross-Cultural Sample" (Murdock and White 1969), with 186 cases; and (8) the "HRAF Probability Sample" (also called the "HRAF Quality Control Sample," for which some precoded data are available) (Naroll 1967; HRAF 1967; Lagacé 1979), with 60 cases. Before examining some claims made about these various samples, we first need to realize why it's necessary to use random sampling procedures.

According to sampling theory, only random sampling provides an unbiased or representative sample of some larger population or sampling frame (Cochran 1977:8–11; see also Kish 1987:16). For example, simple random sampling (using a table of random numbers or a "lottery" type of selection procedure) guarantees that every case in the sampling frame has had an equal chance to be chosen. (Equiprobability of selection is assumed in most tests that estimate the statistical significance, or likely truth-value, of sample results.) To sample in a simple random fashion, make sure that all cases in the sampling frame are numbered uniquely (no repeats, no cases omitted). Researchers may sometimes choose other kinds of random sampling, such as systematic sampling (every nth case is chosen after a random start) or stratified random sampling (first dividing the sample into subgroups or strata and then randomly sampling from each).

There are two kinds of stratified random sampling. In proportionate stratified random sampling, each subgroup is represented in proportion to its occurrence in the total population; in disproportionate stratified random sampling, some subgroups are overrepresented and others are underrepresented. Disproportionate stratified random sampling is used in cross-cultural research when the investigator needs to overrepresent a rare type of case to have enough such cases to study (as in a comparison of relatively rare hunter-gatherers with more common agriculturalists) or when he or she wants to derive an accurate estimate of some parameter (for example, mean, variance, or strength of an association) for a rare subgroup. Disproportionate stratified sampling usually requires larger sample sizes than simple random sampling. Proportionate random sampling may reduce the sample size needed when there are marked differences between subgroups. However, stratified random sampling may not improve much on the accuracy obtainable with a simple random sample (Kish 1987:33).

Comparing the Available Samples

Three of the existing cross-cultural samples were considered relatively complete lists when they were published. The largest is the complete "Ethnographic Atlas" (with 1,264 cases, published from 1962 on in *Ethnology*). But, as its compiler (Murdock 1967:109) noted, not even the Atlas is an exhaustive list of what he called the "adequately described" cultures; he acknowledged that East Eurasia, the Insular Pacific, and Europe were not well represented. For the smaller "summary" version of the Atlas (Murdock 1967), he dropped all the cases he considered poorly described. So, if you want your sampling frame to include only well-described cases (in Murdock's opinion), then the 1967 Atlas Summary (with 862 cases) is a reasonable list to sample from.

Raoul Naroll set out to construct a list of societies that met his stringent criteria for eligibility. Some of his criteria were: The culture had to lack a native written language; it had to have an ethnographer who lived for at least a year in the field; and the ethnographer had to know the native language. The resultant sample, which he called the "Standard Ethnographic Sample" (Naroll and Sipes 1973; see also Naroll and Zucker 1974), contains 285 societies. Naroll and Sipes claimed that this list was about 80–90% complete for the cultures that qualified at the time (eastern Europe and the Far East were admittedly underrepresented).

None of these lists has been updated. A more complete list of the world's described cultures is being developed at the Human Relations Area Files under the direction of Carol Ember and with the advice of the profession. This new list will be the sampling frame that HRAF uses, beginning in 1999, to add cases by simple random sampling to the HRAF Collection of Ethnography.

Three of the existing samples (from largest to smallest: the Atlas of World Cultures, the Standard Cross-Cultural Sample, and the HRAF Probability Sample Files) were developed to give equal weight to each of a number of culture areas (areas of similar cultures) in the world. Technically, the samples mentioned in this paragraph are all disproportionate stratified samples (only the HRAF Probability Sample Files uses random sampling to select cases for each culture area identified). The presumption behind all of these stratified samples is that the cultures in a given area are bound to be very similar by reason of common ancestry or extensive diffusion. The designers of these samples wanted to minimize Galton's Problem. In the next to last section of this chapter, we discuss whether Galton's Problem really is a problem, as well as nonsampling solutions to the presumed problem.

There are difficulties with these disproportionate stratified samples. First, exactly how we should define and separate culture areas requires empirical testing; Burton et al. (1996) have shown that social structural variables do not cluster consistently with Murdock's major cultural regions. Second, disproportionate stratified sampling is a less efficient way to sample (requires more cases) than is simple random sampling. Third, even if the disproportionate sample uses random sampling from each stratum, every case selected will not have had an equal chance to be chosen. This makes it difficult or impossible to estimate the commonness or uniqueness of a particular trait in the world. If we don't know how common a trait is in each culture area, we can't correct our counts by relative weighting, which we would need to do to make an accurate estimate of the frequency of the trait in the world.

Many have used all or some of the cases in the Standard Cross-Cultural Sample (Murdock and White 1969) for cross-cultural studies, at least partly because the published literature contains a large number of codes (ratings of variables) on those cases; many of these codes were reprinted in Barry and Schlegel (1980). This sample is claimed to be representative of the world's known and well-described cultures (as of 1969), but that's dubious for two reasons. First, disproportionate sampling doesn't give an equal chance for each culture to be chosen. Second, the single sample case from each cluster was chosen judgmentally, not randomly. (Judgmental criteria were also used to choose the five cases per culture area for the Atlas of World Cultures [Murdock 1981].)

Of the three samples discussed here, the HRAF Probability Sample is the only one using *random* sampling within strata (the 60-culture sample includes a random selection from each identified culture area). However, the other criteria for selection were so stringent (for example, at least 1,200 pages of cultural data focused on a community or other delimited unit; substantial contributions from at least two different authors), that only 206 societies in the world were eligible for inclusion when the sample was constructed (in the late 1960s).

Two other samples should be discussed briefly, because researchers have used them as sampling frames in cross-cultural studies. One is the World Ethnographic Sample (Murdock 1957). In addition to being based on judgmental sampling of cases within culture areas, it has one other major drawback. A time and place focus is not specified for the cases, as in the two Ethnographic Atlas samples (full and summary), the Standard Cross-Cultural Sample, and the Standard Ethnographic Sample. If researchers want to use some of the precoded data for the World Ethnographic Sample, they would have no idea what the "ethnographic present" is for a case. As we discuss later, focusing on the same time and place for all the measures on a case is usually called for in testing for an association; you may be introducing error if you don't make sure that the measures used pertain to the same time and place for the case.

Finally, let's turn to the entire HRAF Collection of Ethnography. Like most of the other samples, it, too, was based on judgmental selection. But because it covers many cultures all over the world and provides full-text ethnographic materials that are complexly indexed for rapid information retrieval, the collection has often been used as a sampling frame for cross-cultural studies. (As of 1998, the HRAF Collection covered more than 360 cultures, at least 40% of the world's well-described cultures if you go by Murdock's [1967] total of 862 in the summary version of the Ethnographic Atlas.)

The major advantage of the HRAF Collection is that only HRAF provides ethnographic texts on the cases. The other samples provide only coded data (usually) and only limited bibliography (usually). If the codes constructed by others don't directly measure what you're interested in, but you use them anyway, you may be reducing your chances of finding relationships and differences that truly exist. Hence, if you need to code new variables or you need to code something in a more direct way, you're likely to do better if you yourself code from the original ethnography (C. R. Ember et al. 1991). Library research to do so would be very time consuming, which is why HRAF was invented in the first place.

If you use the HRAF files, you don't have to devote weeks to constructing bibliographies for each sample case; you don't have to chase down the books and other materials you need to look at, which might otherwise have to be obtained by interlibrary loan; and you don't have to search through every page of a source (that often lacks an index) to find all the locations of the information you seek. The HRAF files give you the information you want on a particular topic, from all of the sources processed for the culture, in a single place. That place, with the electronic HRAF, is now your computer screen. If you want to examine the original ethnography on a case (with all the context), and particularly if you want to construct your own measures, there's no substitute for the HRAF Collection.

So, if you are starting out to do your first cross-cultural study, how should you sample? If you want to use some of the data already coded for one of the available samples, by all means use that sample *as your sampling frame*, particularly if it is one of the larger lists (such as the summary version of the Ethnographic Atlas [Murdock 1967]). The sampling frame becomes the list you are claiming to generalize to. (A larger claim that you are generalizing to the world is inappropriate.)

If you want to code all of your variables yourself, you can do so most economically by sampling from the HRAF Collection. If a sample size of sixty is large enough, the HRAF Probability Sample gives you a randomly selected case from each of sixty culture areas. If you want to code some variables yourself and use some precoded variables, you can sample from the intersection between HRAF and the sample with the precoded variables. Whatever sampling frame you use, you should select your cases in some standard random fashion, because only random sampling entitles you to infer that your statistically significant sample results are probably true for the larger universe. If for some reason you cannot sample randomly from some list, be sure to avoid selecting the cases yourself. The next best thing after a random sample is a sample constructed by others (who could not know the hypotheses you want to test). The wonderful thing about a random sample is that wherever your research stops, after 20 or 40 or 200 randomly selected cases, you will always be entitled to conclude that a statistically significant result in your sample is probably true for the larger universe.

Measurement

How you choose to measure some variable of interest to you depends at least partly on your implicit or explicit theory. After all, why are you interested in variable X in the first place? Your implicit or explicit theory specifies which variables are of interest and provides a model of how they may be related. Theories are generally evaluated by testing hypotheses derived from them. (What does the theory imply in the way of relationships?) The variables in a test can be fairly specific—such as whether a culture has a ceremony for naming a newborn child—or quite abstract— such as whether the community is harmonious.

Whether the concept is fairly specific or not, no variable is ever measured directly. This is true in the physical as well as social sciences. We are so used to a thermometer measuring heat that we forget that heat is an abstract concept that refers to the energy generated when molecules are moving. A thermometer reflects the principle that as molecules move more, a substance in a confined space (alcohol, mercury) will expand. We don't see heat; we see only the movement of the substance in the confined space. So all measurement is indirect. But some measures are better (more direct, more predictive, less errorful) than others.

The three most important principles in designing a measure are: (1) Try to be as specific as possible in deciding how to measure the theoretical variable you have in mind; (2) Try to measure the variable as directly as possible; and (3) Try to measure the variable in a number of different ways.

The first principle recognizes that science depends on replication; if we are to be confident about our findings, other researchers must be able to repeat them. To facilitate replication, the original researchers must be quite explicit about what they intended to measure and how they measured it.

The second principle recognizes that although all measurement is indirect, some measures are more direct than others. To learn how "rainy" an area is, you could count how many days it rains while you are there for a week's vacation and multiply by 52. But it would be better to count the number of rainy days, on average, over a number of years, and it would be best to measure the *total number of inches* of rain per year, on average, over a number of years.

The third principle recognizes that few measures measure exactly what they are supposed to, so it's better to use more than one way to measure the theoretical variable of interest. However, cross-cultural research is limited by what's available in ethnographies. So the availability of relevant information is the major constraint on the number of supposedly equivalent measures one might construct.

Measures have to be specified for each variable in the hypothesis. Devising a measure involves at least four steps: (1) theoretically defining the variable of interest (in words or mathematically); (2) operationally defining the variable, which means spelling out the empirical information needed to make a decision about where the case falls on the "scale" devised for measuring it; (3) pretesting the measure to see if it can be applied generally (to many if not most cases): designing a measure requires some trial and error, and if the scale is too confusing or too hard to apply (because the required information is too often lacking), the measure needs to be rethought; and (4) performing reliability and validity checks (reliability involves the consistency, replicability, and stability of a measure; validity involves the degree to which the measure reflects what it is supposed to reflect; for more discussion of these issues, see C. R. Ember et al. 1991). Because most attention has been paid to measurement issues in secondary comparisons, we focus mainly on them in what follows.

To illustrate processes involved in measurement, let's consider that a researcher has an idea about why many societies typically have extended families. Although the concept of extended families may appear straightforward, it needs to be defined explicitly. The researcher must decide whether to focus on extended family households or to include extended families that are not coresidential. The choice should depend on the theory. If the theory discusses labor requirements that would favor an extended family staying together (see Pasternak et al. 1997:237–239), then extended family households should be measured.

When this is decided, the researcher still needs to state what an "extended family" means and what a "household" means. And he or she has to decide on the degree (relative frequency) to which a sample society has extended family households. The researcher may choose to define a family as a social and economic unit consisting minimally of at least one or more parents and children; an extended family might then be defined as consisting of two or more constituent families united by a blood tie; and an extended family household might be defined as an extended family living coresidentially—in one house, neighboring apartments, or in a separate compound. Having defined the concepts, the researcher must then specify the counting procedure—how to measure the degree to which a society has extended family households. All these steps are involved in operationalizing the variable of interest.

Definitions are not so hard to arrive at. What requires work is evaluating whether an operational definition is useful or easily applied. For example, suppose by "degree" (of extended "family-ness") we operationally mean the percentage of households in the community that are extended families. The range of possible scale scores is from 0–100%. Suppose further that we instruct our coders to rate a case only if the ethnographer specifies a percentage or we can calculate one from a census of the households. If we did a pretest, we would find out that very few ethnographers tell us the percentage of extended family households or the results of censuses. Rather, they usually say things like "extended family households are the norm." Or, "extended families are typical, but younger people are beginning to live in independent households." So, our operational definition of percentage of extended family households, although perfectly worthy, may not be that useful if we can't find enough societies with reports based on household censuses.

What can we do? We can stick to our insistence on the best measure and study only societies for which a percentage is given (or can be calculated); we may have to expand our search (enlarge our sample) to find enough cases that have such precise information. Or, we can redesign our measure to incorporate descriptions in words that aren't based on census materials. Or, we can choose not to do the study because we can't measure the concept exactly how we want to.

Faced with these choices, most cross-cultural researchers would opt to redesign the measure to incorporate word descriptions. Word descriptions do convey information about degree, even though not so precisely. If an ethnographer says "extended family households are typical," we don't know if that means 50 percent or 100%, but we can be very confident it doesn't mean 0–40%. And we can be fairly sure it doesn't mean 40–49%. If the relative frequency of extended families (measured on the basis of words) is related to something else, we should be able to see the relationship even though we can't use a percentage measure based on numerical information. A measure going by words might read something like what follows.

Code extended family households as:

4. *Very high* in frequency if the ethnographer describes this type of household as the norm or typical in the absence of any indication of another common type of household. Phrases like "almost all households are extended" are clear indicators. Do not use discussions of the "ideal" household to measure relative frequency, unless there are indications that the ideal is also practiced. If there is a developmental cycle, such as the household splitting up when the third generation reaches a certain age, do not use this category. Rather, you should use scale score 3 if the extended family household remains together for a substantial portion of the life cycle or scale score 2 if the household remains together only briefly.

3. *Moderately high* in frequency if the ethnographer describes another fairly frequent household pattern but indicates that extended family households are still the most common.

2. *Moderately* low in frequency if the ethnographer describes extended family households as alternative or a second choice (another form of household is said to be typical).

1. *Infrequent or rare* if another form of household is the only form of household mentioned and if the extended family form is mentioned as absent or an unusual situation. Do not infer the absence of extended families merely from the absence of discussion of family and household type.

Don't know if there is no information on form of household, or there is contradictory information.

The next step is to pretest this measure, preferably with coders who haven't had anything to do with creating the scale. Four distinctions may be too difficult to apply to the word descriptions usually found in ethnographies, so a researcher might want to collapse the scale a little. Or, two coders may not agree with each other frequently. If so, the investigator may have to spell out the rules a little more. And if we decide to use the scale described above, what do we do when the ethnography actually gives us numbers or percentages for a case?

It's usually easy to fit numbers into the word scale (or to average two adjacent scale scores). So, for instance, if 70% of the households have extended families, and 30% are independent, we would choose scale score 3. But we might decide to use two scales: a precise one based on numerical measurement (percentages) for those cases with numbers or percentages, the other scale relying on words (when the ethnography provides only words). C. R. Ember et al. (1991) recommend using both types of scale when possible.

The advantage of using two scales of varying precision is that the more precise one (the quantitative scale) should be more strongly related to other variables than the less precise one. (The less precise scale should be less accurate than the more precise one, assuming that the former has to rely sometimes on ambiguous words.) Stronger results with the more precise scale would increase our confidence that the relationship observed even with the less precise one is true. We discuss the issue of validity in the next section and the issue of reliability in the section titled Minimizing Coder Error.

How to Minimize Error in the Design of Measures

Two kinds of measurement errors are usually distinguished: systematic and random errors. They have different effects on data analysis and each type is handled differently (Zeller and Carmines 1980:12).

Systematic error or bias exists if there is a consistent, predictable departure from the "true" score. Examples would be a scale that inflates everyone's weight by half a pound or a tendency by observers to ignore certain types of aggression in behavior observations. In cross-cultural research, systematic error can come from ethnographers, informants, design errors in measurement, or coders. Ethnographers may not mention or underreport something (for example, not mention the number of Western objects in the village). Or they may overreport (for example, overemphasize the unilineality of the descent system to fit reality into an ideal type). Informants may over- or underreport (for example, not mention an illegal or disapproved activity). Coders may interpret ethnography from the point of view of their own culture, their gender, or their personality. As discussed below, we may be able to detect possible bias by hypothesizing and testing for it. However, one major type of systematic error can't be detected so easily—the error that's introduced because the measure consistently under- or overestimates the theoretical variable (Blalock 1968; Cook and Campbell 1979:64; Zeller and Carmines 1980:11).

Random error, which is error in any direction, weakens correlations (Blalock 1972:414). Naroll (1962) called random errors "benign" perhaps because he and other social scientists commonly worry more about accepting a relationship as true that is false (Type I error) than about failing to accept a true relationship (Type II error). As Naroll (1962) pointed out, systematic error in two variables in the same direction could conceivably create a result when none is really there.[1] Thus, if our purpose is to find relationships when they are really there, we should take steps to minimize random error. But let's turn first to the problem of systematic error that's due to the lack of fit between the theoretical construct and the measure that presumes to tap that construct.

Even though all measurement is indirect so validity can't ever be established beyond a doubt (Campbell 1988), some measures are more direct and therefore more likely to be valid than others. More direct measures involve little question that they are measuring what they are supposed to measure. Other things being equal, we suggest that cross-culturalists try to use measures that are as direct as possible, because less inference and less guesswork generally yields more accuracy and hence stronger results (assuming that you are dealing with a true relationship). For example, when a cross-culturalist wants to measure whether a husband and wife work together, it's more direct to use a measure that's based on explicit ethnographers' reports of work patterns rather than to infer the work pattern from general statements about how husbands and wives get along.[2]

Some measures pose few validity problems. Where the operationalization is very close to the theoretical variable, for example, sex of a person (Blalock 1968:20), the measure requires so little inference that there is little question about its validity. Other measures seem to have "face validity," too—few researchers would question their validity. For example, if the theoretical variable is the rule of residence in a society, we usually think that the ethnographer's identification of the rule of residence is an operational measure with high face validity, despite the apparent lack of agreement between ethnographers Ward Goodenough (1956) and John Fischer (1958). The disagreement between them over Truk appears to have been interpreted by some anthropologists as an indication that a field worker's conclusions are bound to be subjective and therefore unreliable.

We think that there are two reasons why this interpretation is incorrect. First, the two investigators were in the field at different times, and practices can vary even over just a few years. Second, both Goodenough and Fischer found the Trukese to be predominantly matrilocal (Goodenough 71%, Fischer 58%). Indeed, they differed only with respect to 13% of the cases, which Goodenough classified as avunculocal and Fischer as patrilocal. (In some people's eyes, avunculocal residence is patrilocal because living with husband's mother's brother is living with *husband's* relatives.) So, with respect to the major or predominant residence pattern, the cross-culturalist would not misclassify the Trukese using Fischer's *or* Goodenough's data, even though they apparently disagreed on some details.

Unlike experimental psychologists, cross-cultural researchers are not able to use a great variety of validation techniques. There is rarely a standard measure to evaluate a new measure against. (If there were, we would always use the standard as the measure.) If there is little information in ethnographies on particular topics, it is sometimes difficult to think of multiple measures of the same theoretical variable. Cross-culturalists, unlike psychologists, can't collect new information—they must make do with what the ethnographic record gives them. Given this, it is best to use measures that are the most direct and therefore have the highest face validity.

However, many concepts of interest to cross-cultural researchers aren't easily measured directly. Two situations in which indirect measures might justifiably be used are when the theoretical variable can only be measured "projectively" (for example, unconscious fear of something as measured by how often proportionately folk tales mention it) or when very few ethnographies give information allowing a more direct measure.

Unconscious variables particularly do not lend themselves to direct measurement. Psychologists (and others) use projective testing and disguised measures when subjects cannot or will not give honest answers to certain questions. A field investigator can't simply ask a boy "Do you wish to be a woman?" and expect to get an answer that will reflect the boy's degree of feminine identification, any more than a survey researcher can ask "Are you prejudiced against Blacks?" and get an accurate response most of the time. Cross-cultural researchers may conclude, therefore, that culturally shared personality dispositions might be more accurately coded from folktales than from presumptions by ethnographers about unconscious feelings. And a researcher may choose indirect measures because a more direct one may be usable only for a small proportion of cases. Whatever the reason, the decision to use an indirect or proxy measure should be made only if the investigator can justify its use by showing why we should accept its validity. More on this below.

When the cross-culturalist decides to use a more indirect measure, we recommend strongly that he or she develop direct measures for some proportion of the cases (even if only a minority) to evaluate the validity of the more indirect measure. If it's not possible to correlate the two measures to validate the more indirect or proxy measure (because both kinds of information are hardly ever available for a particular case), the researcher could still see if the more indirectly measured cases show weaker correlations than the more directly measured ones. As noted above, if the more direct measure produces higher coefficients of association than the more indirect one, and the directions of the results are similar with both measures, we can be more confident that the indirect measure is probably tapping the same variable as the more direct one.

Researchers sometimes choose proxy measures over more direct measures because the proxy measures are readily available in precoded databases. But, unless it is shown that they correlate with more direct measures (which requires going back to the original ethnographies), we're skeptical about the validity of opportunistic proxy measures. We acknowledge that there's enormous value in having databases with codes provided by previous researchers. It isn't always necessary to code things anew, and using available codes when they fit your interests can allow time to code additional variables. But using precoded variables as proxies, without any attempts to validate them, deserves our suspicion. (Of course, the investigators originally responsible for the available codes are not to be blamed for how others use them.)

The designer of a measure also needs to consider the degree to which the information required is available in ethnographies. No matter how direct a measure may seem conceptually, it may require a high degree of inference by the coder if there's little relevant information in ethnographies. The terms "high-inference" and "low-inference" variables, first introduced by J.W.M. Whiting (1981), are useful for discussing this aspect of measurement design. Variables that require low inference on the part of the coder tend to deal with visible traits or customs, usually reported by ethnographers and easily located in ethnographies (Bradley 1987, 1989; Burton and White 1987; J.W.M. Whiting 1981; cf. White 1990).

High-inference variables often require complex coding judgments and are therefore difficult to code reliably. The codings of low-inference variables are less likely to contain error, and independent coders are therefore more likely to agree on codings. For example, Bradley (1987) compared her codings of presence versus absence of the plow with Pryor's (1985) codings for 23 societies; there was 96% agreement between the two data sets. The only disagreement was about a case that Pryor himself expressed uncertainty about. Thus, presence or absence of the plow, which ethnographers can observe and record without interpretation, is a low-inference variable. Others include the type of carrying device for infants, shapes of houses, domestic animals and major crops, and many elements of material culture (Bradley 1987; Burton and White 1987; Whiting 1981). Note that the dimension of low versus high inference may be uncorrelated with the dimension of more versus less direct measurement. Presence or absence of the plow may be measurable with low inference but if you consider it to be a proxy measure for the judgment that men do most of the agricultural work, then your measure would be low inference but indirect.

Because the measurement of some variables requires moderate levels of inference, such measures are more subject to random error. Relevant information is also missing more often, so you're likely to be able to code only a small proportion of the sample. In addition, when variables require moderate levels of inference, coders usually agree with each other less. Bradley (1989) presents evidence that coding the gender division of labor in agriculture requires moderate inference. Other examples of variables that require a moderate degree of inference are the proportion of day an infant is carried (J. W. M. Whiting 1981) and warfare frequency (Ross 1983; C. R. Ember and M. Ember 1992a). For moderate-inference variables, coders usually have to read through a considerable amount of ethnographic material that isn't explicitly quantitative in order to rate a case. Because of the imprecision, the coding decision is more likely to contain some error.

The highest degree of inference is required when researchers are interested in assessing general attitudes or global concepts such as "evaluation of children" (Barry et al. 1977). Such global concepts don't have obvious empirical referents to guide coders, and it's easy to see how coders focusing on different domains might justifiably code the same society differently. The most appropriate solution here, we believe, is to develop a series of more specific measures with clear empirical referents, as Whyte (1978) did for the various meanings of women's status and as

Ross (1983) did for the various dimensions of political decision making and conflict.

Random errors may be more likely if the investigator doesn't specify time and place precisely for all variables. Divale (1975), acting on the Embers' suggestion, has shown with a few examples how lack of time and place focus, which presumably increases random error, tends to lower correlations. The same time and place for a sample case should be attended to whether previous codes are used or new codes are developed. For example, M. Ember (1974, 1984/85) has presented evidence that polygyny is favored by a shortage of men because of high male mortality in war. If polygyny were present in a particular society as of 1900, but you measured the sex ratio in a later ethnography (after warfare ceased), you would be likely to find a more or less balanced sex ratio at the later time.

Would this case be exceptional to the theory that high male mortality (and an excess of women) favors polygyny? The answer of course is yes, but it wouldn't be appropriate to measure the two variables in this way. The two variables should be measured synchronically (for more or less the same time), or you could measure male mortality in war or the sex ratio for a slightly earlier time than you measure form of marriage. Otherwise, you may be introducing so much measurement error that the relationship between excess women and polygyny could be masked. (C. R. Ember's [1992?] concordance between cross-cultural samples can help you match time and place foci across samples.) Requiring that your measurements on each case pertain to the same time and place (or the appropriate relative times for a diachronic [over time] test) can only maximize your chances of seeing a relationship that truly exists.

Minimizing the Effect of Ethnographer (or Informant) Error

Measurement error caused by ethnographer or informant error is not often considered something we can deal with in the measurement process. But that's not necessarily true. Naroll (1962) proposed methods to deal with such errors and others have developed additional methods.

The supposedly poor or uneven quality of the ethnographic record is often cited as invalidating cross-cultural research. This is puzzling, given the usual high regard ethnographers have for their own work. If most anthropologists have high regard for their own work, how could the bulk of ethnography be poor unless most anthropologists were deluding themselves (C. R. Ember 1986:2)? Certainly there are errors in the ethnographic record and we must try to minimize their effects, but the critics' worry may derive from their ignorance about the effect of error on results.

Space here doesn't allow it, but we could show statistically that even a great deal of random error hardly ever produces a statistically significant finding. And even systematic error wouldn't normally produce a statistically significant finding that was, in fact, false. (Of course, there's always the possibility of deliberate cheating; but this probably doesn't happen often, and other investigators' attempts to replicate a result will eventually reveal cheating.) Statistically speaking, random error generally reduces the magnitude of obtained correlations. This means that more error lessens the likelihood of finding patterns that are there. And if error makes us *less* likely to infer statistical significance, it should not be assumed that significant cross-cultural results are generally invalid. It may seem paradoxical, but the more random error there is, the more likely the "true" results are better than the observed results!

Naroll (1962) proposed an indirect method—"data quality control"—to deal with systematic informant and ethnographer errors. His basic procedure involved identifying factors that might produce biases in the reporting of certain variables (for example, a short stay in the field would presumably make for underreporting of "secret" practices such as witchcraft). Indeed, Naroll found that short-staying ethnographers were significantly less likely to report witchcraft than were long-staying ethnographers. This suggests the possibility of systematic error due to length of stay. However, as Naroll himself was aware, there are other possible interpretations of the correlation. One is that short stays may be more likely in more complex cultures. If more complex cultures are less likely to have witchcraft beliefs than less complex ones, the correlation between length of stay and the presence of witchcraft would be spurious, not due to systematic underreporting by short-staying ethnographers.

Still, data quality factors could account for some results. For example, to exclude the possibility that a data quality factor may account for a correlation because that factor is correlated with both variables in the correlation, Naroll advised the researcher to control statistically for the data quality factor. Naroll's concern with the possible influence of data quality has persuaded researchers to test for systematic biases of various kinds (gender of ethnographer, type of training, knowing the native language, etc.) in evaluating their results. Naroll believed that the coding of information on qualities of the ethnographer and on conditions of the fieldwork should be a regular part of the coding process.

But C. R. Ember et al. (1991) don't agree, for two reasons. First, as Naroll (1977) also noted, it's very expensive to code for a large number of features that could, but probably do not, produce false correlations. Second, of the large number of studies done by Naroll, his students, and others (see Levinson 1978 for substantive studies using data quality controls), few have found that a data quality feature accounts for a correlation (but see Rohner et al. 1973; Divale 1976). Therefore, Ember et al. (1991) recommend that before investigating relationships between data quality variables and substantive variables, researchers should have plausible theoretical reasons for thinking they may be related. If we can't imagine how a data quality variable could explain a correlation, it isn't necessary to spend time and money coding for it. Only plausible alternative predictors should be built into a research design. However, Ember et al. (1991) recommend that researchers develop a specific data quality code for each substantive variable (for each case), to provide a direct assessment of the quality of the data in regard to that variable.

To illustrate the suggested procedure, compare the information in the following three statements, which a coder might use to measure the frequency of polygyny among married men: "Polygyny is the form of marriage that men aspire to," "Only the senior men have more than one wife," and "The household survey indicates that 15% of married men are married polygynously." Although none of these statements may contain error, and we can't assume that the one based on quantitative information is the most accurate, a coder trying to rate frequency of polygyny according to an ordinal scale would have the most trouble coding the first statement, because it tells us only that polygyny is present and preferred (at least by men).

The researcher could try to minimize error by instructing the coders not to make frequency judgments based on statements about what people prefer ("ideal culture"). But the researcher could also develop a data quality code for the measure of frequency of polygyny. The highest-quality score would be given to a code based on a census. The lowest-quality score would be given to information pertaining to ideal culture (such as the first statement listed above) or to a judgment based on inference (for example, polygyny is inferred to be not so common because only "senior" men are said to have more than one wife). A middle-quality score might be given to information such as: "The typical married man has only one wife."

With a data quality code by case for each variable in a correlational test, we could analyze the results with *and* without the "poorer" quality data. The omission of cases with scores based on poor-quality data (for example, vague ethnographic statements) should yield stronger results than in the data set that includes poor-quality data. (For how cases with poorer data quality can be omitted, see our discussion toward the end of the next section, on minimizing coder error.) And because the standard errors will be higher with more random error, our chances of finding a statistically significant relationship are greater with higher-quality data. We think the data quality control procedure suggested here offers two important advantages. First, it taps the quality of the ethnographic information more directly than Naroll's suggested strategy, which may not make any difference at all in regard to a particular correlation. Second, it can be done quite efficiently, at the same time substantive variables are coded, because reading more material is not required.

Another problem the ethnographic record poses to cross-cultural researchers is that in addition to errors in what is reported, there may also be problems about what is not reported. Ethnographers may not have gone to the field with a comprehensive guide to what kinds of information could be collected, as is provided by the *Outline of Cultural Materials* (Murdock et al. 1987). For this and other reasons, ethnographers often pay little or no attention to a question of interest later to the cross-cultural researcher. What should a cross-culturalist do?

We don't recommend inferring that something is absent if it's not reported, unless the cross-cultural researcher can be quite sure that it would have been reported if it had been present. For example, if an ethnographer didn't mention puberty rites but thoroughly discussed childhood and adolescence, absence of puberty rites could reasonably be inferred. If, however, the ethnographer didn't collect any information on adolescence, the fact that no puberty rites are mentioned shouldn't be taken to mean that they were absent. Researchers need to specify coding rules for inferring absence (see the measure of extended family households described above) or they need to instruct their coders not to make inferences.

A further strategy to deal with missing data is to interview the original ethnographers themselves (or others who have worked for extended periods in the society) to supplement the information not present in the published sources (Pryor 1977; Ross 1983; Levinson 1989). The cross-cultural researcher has to be careful to keep to the same time and place foci of the published data; if you call a recent ethnographer about a case, you should ask only about the time and place focus of the published information.

Finally, if data on some of the sample societies are missing, the cross-cultural researcher may decide to impute missing values. Burton (1996) has described and evaluated a number of procedures for doing so. The cross-cultural researcher needs to remember that any method of imputation is likely to increase measurement error. Therefore, the advantage of imputation (to increase sample size) has to be weighed carefully against the possible increase of error. Researchers who impute some data should consider doing analyses with and without this data to see if the imputing has misleadingly improved the results, just as we can compare data sets with and without dubious codings to see if including them has transformed a borderline or nonsignificant result into a significant one.

Minimizing Coder Error

The coding process itself can produce measurement error. If the investigator is also the coder, there is a possibility of systematic bias in favor of the theory being tested (Rosenthal 1966; Rosenthal and Jacobson 1968). For that reason alone, many researchers prefer to use "naive" or theory-blind coders. However, naive coders may not be as likely as experienced coders to make accurate judgments. Experienced researchers have skills that should make for more accurate coding, because they are more likely to be aware that an ethnographer's words should not always be taken at face value. For example, an experienced researcher is more likely to know that avunculocal residence might be called patrilocal residence, and that hunter-gatherers may get plenty of food (even if they have to move their camps frequently, that doesn't necessarily mean their food supply is precarious). Furthermore, experienced coders are more likely to pay attention to time and place foci—to know that when one ethnographer describes what Samoans do, he or she may not be talking about the particular time period or particular group of Samoans a previous ethnographer has studied and described (M. Ember 1985).

Bradley (1987) argues that naive coders can make systematic errors when coding instructions are insufficiently precise, especially when coding high-inference variables. For example, differences between her codes for the division of labor in agriculture and those of the coders for Murdock and Provost (1973) could be explained by the possibility that the Murdock and Provost coders were not instructed to consider differences between crop types or which phase of the agricultural sequence was to be coded. Naive coders might also be more likely to make judgments that are systematically biased toward their own cultural assumptions, as suggested by the experimental findings presented by D'Andrade (1974).

Researchers can try to minimize the error of inexperienced coders by being as explicit as possible in their coding instructions and by making sure that the codes don't surpass the information that's generally available in the ethnographic literature (Tatje 1970). Coding should have to make as few inferential leaps as possible. Trying to spell out all the possible obstacles to coding is an important part of the research design. Having at least one relatively inexperienced coder might be an advantage it might force the researcher to be as clear as possible in the operationalization of theoretical concepts.

Researchers may worry that coders will introduce systematic errors because of their gender, political ideology, personality, or faulty assumptions about different types of societies. But such contamination may not be so likely. Whyte (1978) did not find more significant relationships between gender of coder and his many indicators of women's status than would be expected by chance. His study suggests that systematic coding bias is most likely to occur when codes are very general (requiring a high degree of inference), which may allow the coder's personal background to exert an influence on the coding process. Whyte suggests that personal/cultural biases can be avoided if coders are asked to rate concrete or specific customs and behaviors.

Designing studies to test systematically for coder biases is normally quite expensive, because doing it properly requires more than one coder for each "bias-type." Thus, it's more cost effective for the investigator and a naive coder to rate the cases. Not only could we then compare the two sets of ratings for reliability, we could also see if both sets give similar results. If they don't, that would be something to worry about. It might only be that the naive coder's ratings contained more error; the results using only that coder's ratings should be weaker than the results using only the investigator's ratings. Maybe the best strategy is to test hypotheses using only cases that both raters agreed on. That way, you would probably be omitting the cases with more random error.

This brings us to the concept of interrater reliability—the extent to which different persons using the same measure achieve the same score or the same relative ranking for each case rated (Nunnally 1967:172; Zeller and Carmines 1980:6). Researchers who assess interrater reliability usually show a correlation coefficient between the two raters' judgements for at least a sample of the rated cases. Or, they may show the percentage of agreement. Both measures have advantages and disadvantages.

The percentage of agreement may detect systematic error, whereas a correlation coefficient may not. Suppose one coder always gives a score that's 1 point higher than the other. The correlation coefficient will be perfect (1.00); the percentage of agreement will be zero. On the other hand, the percentage of agreement measure can't distinguish between substantial disagreements and small disagreements. On a 10-point scale, a disagreement of one point counts the same as a disagreement of 10 points (R. P. Rohner and Katz 1970:1068). But percentage of agreement will detect differences between coders due to systematic inflation or deflation by one of the coders, whereas this kind of systematic bias will not affect a reliability correlation. Hence, it is useful to compute both kinds of measures of interrater reliability.

There is no clear decision point as to what is an acceptably high coefficient or percentage of agreement. Coefficients and percentages of agreement over .80 appear to be considered good and are usually reported without comment; more than .70 appears to be considered minimally acceptable; less than .70 leaves a feeling of unease. Neither method of measuring interrater reliability is a good way to deal with the situation where one rater does not make a rating (assign a number) and the other rater does. Correlation coefficients are easily computed; if some form of Pearson's r is used, it's easy to interpret—the square of the coefficient equals the proportion of variance explained. We expect that there will always be some interrater inconsistency (a study without any at all would probably be suspect). How do researchers deal with disagreements?

If a researcher does a reliability check on a small portion of the cases and the reliability coefficient is reasonably high, he or she usually uses the scores of the coder who rated all of the cases. If a researcher has two or more coders for each case, then a variety of strategies may be followed. Scores may be summed or averaged, or disagreements may be resolved by discussion. An advantage of the summing or averaging method is that both coders are given equal voice; personality differences between the coders can't influence resolutions. A second advantage is that the "effective reliability" is increased. Rosenthal and Rosnow (1984:163–165) indicate that if the correlation coefficient between two judges is .75, the reliability of the mean of the two judges' ratings is actually higher (.86). This is a better estimate of the reliability of the measure; it is an example of the Spearman-Brown prophecy formula, also known as Cronbach's alpha (Nunnally 1978:211–216; Romney 1989).

A disadvantage of the summing or averaging procedure is that one coder may be a better coder (more careful, more knowledgeable about the material), and the rating by that person might objectively deserve more weight. If coders are asked to discuss their disagreements and come to a resolution, the more knowledgeable coder might point to information that the other coder missed. This strategy might be particularly useful when each coder has read a large amount of ethnographic material.

There are also some disadvantages in the resolution method. First, as mentioned, one coder may have undue influence over the other. Certainly, if one coder was the investigator and the other a paid assistant, the resolution method might not be unbiased. But even if they were roughly equal in status, one personality may dominate the other. R. P. Rohner and E. C. Rohner (1981) discuss a procedure for testing for the influence of one coder over another. However, a major problem with their method is that it can't distinguish between influence because of power and influence because of more information. Another disadvantage is that it may add measurement error if the coders feel obliged to come to some resolution even when the data are too ambiguous to justify resolution.

We have found that results get stronger when we use only cases with the most reliable initial scores. This shouldn't be surprising. The most reliable scores are presumably those that independent coders will agree on initially, before any attempts to resolve disagreements. When we eliminate cases with disagreement, our results should get stronger because we're probably eliminating the more ambiguous cases, which are probably the ones more likely to be coded inaccurately. An interrater reliability coefficient may be acceptable, but you could still have a lot of cases that have been measured inaccurately. Even though the size of the sample is reduced when we eliminate the least reliable scores in some way, our chances of finding a true relationship are improved.

We think the best way to maximize the reliability of ratings and results is to use only those ratings (and cases) that the independent coders initially rated in exactly the same way (or very similarly), before any attempts at resolution. The researcher could provide a code that tells the reader how closely the raters agreed initially on the variable for a particular case (see C. R. Ember and M. Ember 1992b). This kind of reliability code (by variable, by case) would allow subsequent users of the data code to choose their own degree of reliability. Just as it's likely that results are more robust when we omit cases that didn't have higher quality data, so they should be more robust when we omit cases that weren't rated in much the same way initially. Chances are that more ambiguous ethnographic information will generally be coded with more error, and it does us no good to cloud the situation by including them in our analyses.

Minimizing Error Due to Sampling: Galton's Problem

Another major reason some question cross-cultural findings is referred to as "Galton's Problem." In 1889, Francis Galton heard Edward Tylor's presentation of what is generally considered the first cross-cultural study. Galton (see the end of Tylor 1889) suggested that many of Tylor's cases were duplicates of one another because they had similar histories; therefore Tylor's conclusions were suspect because the sample size was unjustifiably inflated. More recently, Raoul Naroll and others have considered Galton's Problem a serious threat to cross-cultural research. They have devised several methods to test for the possible effects of diffusion and historical relatedness (Naroll 1970). The concern behind these methods is that statistical associations couldn't be causal if they could be attributed mostly to diffusion (cultural borrowing) or common ancestry. Some cross-culturalists who were worried about Galton's Problem tried to solve it by making sure that their samples contained only one culture from a particular culture area (an area of related languages and cultures). For example, the Standard Cross-Cultural Sample (Murdock and White 1969) and the HRAF Probability Sample both contain only one culture per identified culture area.

How serious is Galton's Problem? Cross-culturalists disagree (see M. Ember and Otterbein 1991 for references; see also C. R. Ember 1990). Most but not all cross-culturalists think it's a serious one (Naroll, Schaefer, Loftin, Murdock and White, Dow—for references, see C. R. Ember 1990). We and others (Strauss and Orans, Otterbein—for references, see C. R. Ember 1990) think not, because we believe that random sampling of cases is the best way to prevent sampling bias. Also, the sample societies in most cross-cultural studies usually speak mutually unintelligible languages, which means that the speech communities involved have been separated for at least 1,000 years. If two related languages began to diverge 1,000 or more years ago, many other aspects of the cultures will also have diverged. So, such cases could hardly be duplicates of each other. If you push Galton's Problem to the limit and avoid any two cases that share a common history and language, then psychological studies with more than one individual per culture would be suspect!

We suggest that those who worry about Galton's Problem misunderstand two requirements of statistical inference—that sample cases be independent and that the measures on them should be independent (Kish 1965, 1987; Blalock 1972). Independence of cases means only that the choice of one case is not influenced by the choice of any other case (which random sampling guarantees). And the requirement of independent measurement means only that each case's score on a variable should be separately arrived at (the scores on two variables might be correlated, but that by itself doesn't violate the requirement that the measurements be made independently). An egregious example of nonindependent measurement would be to assign the same score on a variable to several cases just because they had the same score on another variable. (For further discussion of what independence means statistically, see M. Ember and Otterbein 1991.)

Until recently, whether or not you worried about Galton's Problem made a big difference in how you would do a study. Naroll's tests for the possibility of diffusion were quite time consuming to carry out. This was probably why most cross-culturalists altered their sampling strategy so as to eliminate multiple cases from the same culture area. Recently, however, mathematical anthropologists have developed statistical solutions and computer programs that treat the proximity of societies (in distance or language) as a variable whose influence can be tested in a multiple regression analysis. (This is called testing for spatial autocorrelation.[3]) Whether or not a researcher agrees that Galton's Problem is a problem, recent mathematical and computer solutions don't require a special sampling strategy, nor do they require expensive, time-consuming controls.

If you worry about Galton's Problem, all you have to do is test statistically for the possibility that proximity or common ancestry accounts for a result (Dow et al. 1984; Burton et al. 1996). Even without a statistical control for autocorrelation, cross-culturalists who randomly sample from a larger sampling frame can redo their analyses by randomly omitting more than a single case from the same culture area. If the results don't change substantially after multiple cases from an area are omitted, the original result can't be due to duplication of cases. Indeed, duplication may weaken results, because a set of historically related cases may be exceptional to a cross-cultural generalization rather than consistent with it. (For some evidence on this possibility, see M. Ember 1971.)

Maximizing the Information Value of Statistical Analysis

Most cross-cultural studies aim to test hypotheses, so some kind of inferential statistic is generally used to make a decision about whether the tested hypothesis should be accepted or rejected. This is where statistical researchers resort to the concept of level of significance. Cross-culturalists generally conform to the social science convention of accepting a hypothesis (at least provisionally) if there were 5 or fewer chances out of 100 ($p < .05$) of getting the result just by chance. That is, if 100 different random samples were examined, only 5 or fewer would show the same result or a stronger one.

Early cross-cultural studies usually relied on contingency tables and chi-square as a test of significance for those tables. But with the advent of statistical software packages for personal computers, increasing numbers of cross-culturalists realized that they could achieve more powerful and more informative statistical results in testing hypotheses if they measure ordinally (or intervally) rather than nominally.

Nominal measurement is putting a case into an appropriate set without implying that one set is higher or lower than another on some scale (for example, female versus male; extended family households versus independent family households). Often, nominal variables can be appropriately transformed to ordinal variables. Rather than classify societies as just having independent family households versus extended family households, our discussion earlier showed how to measure the degree to which a society has extended family households in terms of a four-point ordinal scale. In ordinal-scale measurement a higher (or lower) number implies more (or less) of the variable measured.

Cross-cultural researchers can rarely measure variables in terms of interval or ratio scales, where the distance between two adjacent numbers is equal to the distance between any other two adjacent numbers (the ratio-scale has a meaningful zero-point). But there are plenty of possible interval or ratio scales: number of people in the community, population density, average rainfall, average mean temperature (the Fahrenheit or Celsius scale is an interval scale because zero doesn't mean absence of temperature), altitude, etc. Labovitz (1967, 1970) has suggested that statistical tests originally designed for interval-level data may be used with ordinal data when the number of ordered scale scores isn't very small. For example, C. R. Ember and M. Ember (1992a, 1994) used multiple regression analysis when the dependent variables had five or more ordinal scale scores. Indeed, cross-cultural researchers are now more likely to use multivariate techniques to discover the relative effects of two or more predictors. These techniques are especially important for evaluating alternative theories that seem to be equally supported by the bivariate results.

Most cross-culturalists don't use mathematical formulas to decide on sample size in advance of their research. This is a pity, for a researcher often spends a good deal of effort trying to code a large number of cases in the belief that a large sample size is necessary. Generally speaking, you do not need a large sample to obtain a significant result. A small one can give you a trustworthy or significant result if it's strong. A large sample is necessary only if you want to detect a weak association or effect. Nominal-level tests (like chi-square) require the largest sample sizes; ordinal and interval-level tests require smaller sample sizes.

Kraemer and Tiemman (1987) have provided a master table to calculate approximately what sample size you will need, if you can specify how big an effect or correlation you are looking for, and how much possibility of error you can tolerate. (They also provide specific formulas for particular measures and tests of significance.) Suppose a researcher is looking for a correlation of .50 or better and wants to be 90% confident that he or she has found a true result, and one that has only a .05 chance of being false. The approximate number of cases required would be 30. If the researcher insists on a p value of .01, 45 cases would be required. To detect a weak correlation of only .24, a p value of .05 requires 144 cases; a p value of .01 requires 219 cases (Kraemer and Thiemann 1987).

Statistical techniques (factor analysis, multidimensional scaling, correspondence analysis) can evaluate whether there are one or more dimensions in a set of related measures. These techniques are especially useful for constructing complex scales from multiple indicators (for example, indicators of social complexity, status of women) and for exploring patterns in the data. Most of these techniques are not used for hypothesis testing.

While cross-culturalists aim to reject causal theories when the hypotheses derived from them are not supported by correlational tests, they generally can't differentiate between causes and effects even when hypotheses are supported. However, much more can be done than usually is. First, partial correlation and path analysis are designed to help evaluate alternative causal models. Only a few cross-cultural studies have used such techniques (Kitahara 1981; C. R. Ember and M. Ember 1992a, 1994). Second, more cultures than you might think have been studied for more than one time period. Cross-culturalists can use this diachronic information to study whether changes occur in time as predicted by our causal theories, but there's been little research of this kind as yet. (More will probably be done as the HRAF Collection of Ethnography increasingly includes information on more than one time period in the history of a case.) In the future, cross-archaeological studies will also be used to test theories diachronically (M. Ember and C. R. Ember 1995); such studies will become increasingly feasible as the new HRAF Collection of Archaeology (in electronic format) grows and becomes widely accessible.

Conclusion

Cross-cultural researchers don't deny the uniqueness of particular cultures, but they look at cultures in a different way—focusing on qualities or quantities that vary along some specified dimension. These variables don't capture everything about cultural attitudes, beliefs, values, or behaviors, but they do exhibit some distinguishable similarities and differences. A large part of the art of cross-cultural research is learning how to focus on dimensions of variation; so is learning how to frame a meaningful and answerable question. Questions range from being descriptive—dealing with the prevalence or frequency of a trait—to being about causes, consequences, or relationships without specified causal direction.

In addition to believing that comparison is possible, cross-culturalists generally assume that all generalizations require testing on some unbiased sample of cases. There are many types of cross-cultural comparison, from regional to worldwide, small or large, using primary or secondary data, synchronic or diachronic. They all have advantages and disadvantages. Large samples aren't necessarily better than small ones—what is most important is that the studied cases should fairly represent the universe of cases to which the results are generalizable; some kind of random sampling is the best way to ensure representativeness. Because theoretical variables are never measured directly, we have devoted a lot of space to various issues of measurement, including how to minimize error in designing measures and how to minimize the effects of ethnographer and coder error in cross-cultural tests using ethnographic data. We advocate the design of the most direct measures possible, those that require the least coder inference, and data quality scores for each variable for each culture.

Cross-cultural researchers don't agree unanimously about everything they do. They disagree about the seriousness of Galton's Problem, and how to deal with it, for instance. And of course they often disagree about causal interpretations. But with all their disagreement, they agree that it's necessary to do cross-cultural research (preferably a variety of cross-cultural studies—worldwide, regional, primary, secondary, synchronic, diachronic) to arrive at trustworthy and comprehensive explanations of human behavior that are probably true because they apply to the vast majority of cultures. We need to test our explanations in other ways, too—within cultures, ethnohistorically, cross-historically, experimentally, by computer simulations. But cross-cultural research is a necessary part of the social scientific enterprise because only a cross-cultural test gives us a relatively low-cost opportunity to discover whether a theory or explanation doesn't fit the real world of cultural variation and therefore should be rejected, at least for now.

NOTES

1. C. R. Ember has unpublished results that show that systematic error has to be enormous to produce a significant result when there really is none.

2. This paragraph and the next five are adapted from C. R. Ember et al. (1991:193–195).

3. For the newer treatments of Galton's Problem, see Burton and White (1991) for references; see also Dow (1991).

REFERENCES

Barry, Herbert, III, Lili Josephson, Edith Lauer, and Catherine Marshall. 1977. Agents and Techniques for Child Training; Cross-Cultural Codes 6. *Ethnology 16*:191–230.

Barry, Herbert, III, and Alice Schlegel, eds. 1980. *Cross-Cultural Samples and Codes*. Pittsburgh: University of Pittsburgh.

Blalock, Hubert M., Jr. 1968. Measurement Problem: A Gap Between the Languages of Theory and Research. In *Methodology in Social Research*. Hubert M. Blalock and Ann B. Blalock, eds. Pp. 5–27. New York: McGraw Hill.

Blalock, Hubert M., Jr. 1972. *Social Statistics*, 2d ed. New York: McGraw-Hill.

Bradley, Candice. 1987. Women, Children and Work. Ph.D. diss., Irvine: University of California.

Bradley, Candice. 1989. Reliability and Inference in the Cross-Cultural Coding Process. *Journal of Quantitative Anthropology 1*:353–371.

Burton, Michael L. 1996. Constructing a Scale of Female Contributions to Agriculture: Methods for Imputing Missing Data. *Cross-Cultural Research 30*:3–23.

Burton, Michael, and Douglas R. White. 1987. Cross-Cultural Surveys Today. *Annual Reviews of Anthropology 16*:143–160.

Burton, Michael, and Douglas R. White. 1991. Regional Comparisons, Replications, and Historical Network Analysis. (Special issue: *Cross-Cultural and Comparative Research: Theory and Method*) *Behavior Science Research 25*:55–78.

Burton, Michael L., Carmella C. Moore, John W. M. Whiting, and A. Kimball Romney. 1996. Regions Based on Social Structure. *Current Anthropology 37*:87–123.

Campbell, Donald T. 1961. The Mutual Methodological Relevance of Anthropology and Psychology. In *Psychological Anthropology: Approaches to Culture and Personality.* Francis L. K. Hsu, ed. Pp. 333–352. Homewood, IL: Dorsey Press.

Campbell, Donald T. 1988. *Methodology and Epistemology for the Social Sciences: Selected Papers.* E. Samuel Overton, ed. Chicago: University of Chicago Press.

Cochran, William G. 1977. *Sampling Techniques,* 3rd ed. New York: John Wiley.

Cook, Thomas D., and Donald T. Campbell. 1979. *Quasi-Experimentation: Design and Analysis Issues for Field Settings.* Chicago: Rand McNally.

D'Andrade, Roy. 1974. Memory and the Assessment of Behavior. In *Measurement in the Social Sciences.* H. M. Blalock, ed. Pp. 149–186. Chicago: Aldine-Atherton.

Divale, William T. 1974. Migration, External Warfare, and Matrilocal Residence. *Behavior Science Research 9*:75–133.

Divale, William T. 1975. Temporal Focus and Random Error in Cross-Cultural Hypothesis Tests. *Behavior Science Research 10*:19–36.

Divale, William T. 1976. Female Status and Cultural Evolution: A Study in Ethnographer Bias. *Behavior Science Research 11*:169–211.

Dow, Malcolm. 1991. Statistical Inference in Comparative Research: New Directions. (Special issue: *Cross-Cultural and Comparative Research: Theory and Method*) *Behavior Science Research 25*:235–257.

Dow, Malcolm M., Michael Burton, Douglas White, and Karl Reitz. 1984. Galton's Problem as Network Autocorrelation. *American Ethnologist 11*:754–770.

Driver, Harold, and William C. Massey. 1957. Comparative Studies of North American Indians. *Transactions of the American Philosophical Society 47*:165–456.

Eggan, Fred. 1954. Social Anthropology and the Method of Controlled Comparison. *American Anthropologist 56*:655–663.

Ember, Carol R. 1975. Residential Variation among Hunter-Gatherers. *Behavior Science Research 10*:199–227.

Ember, Carol R. 1978. Myths about Hunter-Gatherers. *Ethnology 17*:439–448.

Ember, Carol R. 1986. The Quality and Quantity of Data for Cross-Cultural Studies. *Behavior Science Research 20*:1–16.

Ember, Carol R. 1990. Bibliography of Cross-Cultural Methods. *Behavior Science Research 24*:141–154.

Ember, Carol R., and Melvin Ember. 1992a. Resource Unpredictability, Mistrust, and War: A Cross-Cultural Study. *Journal of Conflict Resolution 36*:242–262.

Ember, Carol R., and Melvin Ember. 1992b. Warfare, Aggression, and Resource Problems: Cross-Cultural Codes. *Behavior Science Research 26*:169–226.

Ember, Carol R., and Melvin Ember. 1994. War, Socialization, and Interpersonal Violence: A Cross-Cultural Study. *Journal of Conflict Resolution 38*:620–646.

Ember, Carol R., and Melvin Ember. 1998. On Cross-Cultural Research. In *Cross-Cultural Research for Social Science*. Carol R. Ember and Melvin Ember, eds. Pp. 107–126. Upper Saddle River, NJ: Prentice Hall/Simon & Schuster Custom Publishing.

Ember, Carol R., and David Levinson. 1991. The Substantive Contributions of Worldwide Cross-Cultural Studies Using Secondary Data. (Special issue: *Cross-Cultural and Comparative Research: Theory and Method*) *Behavior Science Research 25*:79–140.

Ember, Carol R., with the assistance of Hugh Page, Jr., Timothy O'Leary, and M. Marlene Martin. 1992. *Computerized Concordance of Cross-Cultural Samples*. New Haven: Human Relations Area Files.

Ember, Carol R., Marc H. Ross, Michael Burton, and Candice Bradley. 1991. Problems of Measurement in Cross-Cultural Research Using Secondary Data. (Special issue: *Cross-Cultural and Comparative Research: Theory and Method*) *Behavior Science Research 25*:187–216.

Ember, Melvin. 1971. An Empirical Test of Galton's Problem. *Ethnology 10*:98–106.

Ember, Melvin. 1974. Warfare, Sex Ratio, and Polygyny. *Ethnology 13*:197–206.

Ember, Melvin. 1984/85. Alternative Predictors of Polygyny. *Behavior Science Research 19*:1–23.

Ember, Melvin. 1985. Evidence and Science in Ethnography: Reflections on the Freeman-Mead Controversy. *American Anthropologist 87*:906–910.

Ember, Melvin. 1991. The Logic of Comparative Research. (Special issue: *Cross-Cultural and Comparative Research: Theory and Method*) *Behavior Science Research 25*:143–153.

Ember, Melvin. 1997. Evolution of the Human Relations Area Files. *Cross-Cultural Research 31*:3–15.

Ember, Melvin, and Carol R. Ember. 1971. The Conditions Favoring Matrilocal Residence Versus Patrilocal Residence. *American Anthropologist 73*:571–594.

Ember, Melvin, and Carol R. Ember. 1995. Worldwide Cross-Cultural Studies and Their Relevance for Archaeology. *Journal of Archaeological Research 3*:87–111.

Ember, Melvin, Carol R. Ember, and Bruce Russett. 1997. Inequality and Democracy in the Anthropological Record. In *Inequality, Democracy, and Economic Development*. Manus I. Midlarsky, ed. Pp. 110–130. Cambridge: Cambridge University Press.

Ember, Melvin, and Keith F. Otterbein. 1991. Sampling in Cross-Cultural Research. (Special issue: *Cross-Cultural and Comparative Research: Theory and Method*) *Behavior Science Research 25*:217–235.

Ethnographic Atlas. 1962–. *Ethnology 1*:113ff. and intermittently thereafter.

Fischer, John L. 1958. The Classification of Residence in Censuses. *American Anthropologist 60*:508–517.

Galton, Francis. 1889. Comment. In On a Method of Investigating the Development of Institutions Applied to the Laws of Marriage and Descent. Edward B. Tylor. *Journal of the Royal Anthropological Institute of Great Britain and Ireland 18*:245–272.

Goldschmidt, Walter. 1965. Theory and Strategy in the Study of Cultural Adaptability. *American Anthropologist 67*:402–408.

Goodenough, Ward. 1956. Residence Rules. *Southwestern Journal of Anthropology 12*:22–37.

HRAF. 1967. The HRAF Quality Control Sample Universe. *Behavior Science Notes 2*:63–69.

Johnson, Allen. 1991. Regional Comparative Field Research. (Special issue: *Cross-Cultural and Comparative Research: Theory and Method*) *Behavior Science Research 25*:3–22.

Jorgensen, Joseph G. 1974. On Continuous Area and Worldwide Sample Cross-Cultural Studies. In *Comparative Studies by Harold E. Driver and Essays in His Honor*. Joseph G. Jorgensen, ed. Pp. 195–203. New Haven: HRAF Press.

Kish, Leslie. 1965. *Survey Sampling*. New York: John Wiley.

Kish, Leslie. 1987. *Statistical Design for Research*. New York: John Wiley.

Kitahara, Michio. 1981. Men's Heterosexual Fear Due to Reciprocal Inhibition. *Ethos 9*:37–50.

Kraemer, Helena Chmura, and Sue Theimann. 1987. *How Many Subjects? Statistical Power Analysis in Research*.Thousand Oaks, CA: Sage Publications.

Labovitz, Sanford. 1967. Some Observations on Measurement and Statistics. *Social Forces 46*:151–160.

Labovitz, Sanford. 1970. The Assignment of Numbers to Rank Order Categories. *American Sociological Review 35*:515–524.

Lagacé, Robert O. 1979. The HRAF Probability Sample: Retrospect and Prospect. *Behavior Science Research 14*:211–229.

Levinson, David. 1978. Holocultural Studies Based on the Human Relations Area Files. *Behavior Science Research 13*:295–302.

Levinson, David. 1989. *Family Violence in Cross-Cultural Perspective*. Thousand Oaks, CA: Sage Publications.

Munroe, Robert L., and Ruth H. Munroe. 1991a. Comparative Field Studies: Methodological Issues and Future Possibilities. (Special issue: *Cross-Cultural and Comparative Research: Theory and Method*) *Behavior Science Research 25*:155–185.

Munroe, Robert L., and Ruth H. Munroe. 1991b. Results of Comparative Field Studies. (Special issue: *Cross-Cultural and Comparative Research: Theory and Method*) *Behavior Science Research 25*:23–54.

Munroe, Robert L., and Ruth H. Munroe. 1992. Fathers in Children's Environments: A Four Culture Study. In *Father-Child Relations*. Barry S. Hewlett, ed. Pp. 213–229. New York: Aldine de Gruyter.

Munroe, Ruth H., Harold S. Shimmin, and Robert L. Munroe. 1984. Gender Understanding and Sex Role Preference in Four Cultures. *Developmental Psychology 20*:673–682.

Murdock, George P. 1949. *Social Structure*. New York: Macmillan.

Murdock, George P. 1957. World Ethnographic Sample. *American Anthropologist 59*: 664–687.

Murdock, George P. 1967. Ethnographic Atlas: A Summary. *Ethnology 6*:109–236.

Murdock, George P. 1981. *Atlas of World Cultures*. Pittsburgh: University of Pittsburgh Press.

Murdock, George P., and Catarina Provost. 1973. Factors in the Division of Labor by Sex: A Cross-Cultural Analysis. *Ethnology 12*:203–225.

Murdock, George P., and Douglas R. White. 1969. Standard Cross-Cultural Sample. *Ethnology 8*:329–369.

Murdock, George P., Clellan S. Ford, Alfred E. Hudson, Raymond Kennedy, Leo W. Simmons, and John W. Whiting. 1987. *Outline of Cultural Materials*, 5th rev. ed. with modifications. New Haven: Human Relations Area Files.

Naroll, Raoul. 1962. *Data Quality Control—A New Research Technique: Prolegomena to a Cross-Cultural Study of Culture Stress*. New York: Free Press.

Naroll, Raoul. 1967. The Proposed HRAF Probability Sample. *Behavior Science Notes 2*:70–80.

Naroll, Raoul. 1970. Galton's Problem. In *A Handbook of Method in Cultural Anthropology*. Raoul Naroll and Ronald Cohen, eds. Pp. 974–989. Garden City, NY: Natural History Press.

Naroll, Raoul. 1977. Cost-Effective Research Versus Safer Research. *Behavior Science Research 11*:123–148.

Naroll, Raoul, Vern L. Bullough, and Frada Naroll. 1974. *Military Deterrence in History: A Pilot Cross-Historical Pilot Survey*. Albany: State University of New York Press.

Naroll, Raoul, and Richard G. Sipes. 1973. Standard Ethnographic Sample, 2d ed. *Current Anthropology 14*:111–140.

Naroll, Raoul, and Harold Zucker. 1974. Reply. *Current Anthropology 15*:316–317.

Nunnally, Jum C. 1967. *Psychometric Theory*. New York: McGraw-Hill.

Nunnally, Jum C. 1978. *Psychometric Theory*, 2d ed. New York: McGraw-Hill.

Pasternak, Burton, Carol R. Ember, and Melvin Ember. 1997. *Sex, Gender, and Kinship: A Cross-Cultural Perspective*. Upper Saddle River, NJ: Prentice Hall.

Pryor, Frederic L. 1977. *The Origins of the Economy: A Comparative Study of Distribution in Primitive and Peasant Economies*. New York: Academic Press.

Pryor, Frederic L. 1985. The Invention of the Plow. *Comparative Studies in Society and History 27*:727–743.

Rohner, Ronald P., and Leonard Katz. 1970. Testing for Validity and Reliability in Cross-Cultural Research. *American Anthropologist 72*:1068–1073.

Rohner, Ronald P., and Evelyn C. Rohner. 1981. Assessing Interrater Influence in Cross-Cultural Research: A Methodological Note. *Behavior Science Research 16*:341–351.

Rohner, Ronald P., Billie R. DeWalt, and Robert C. Ness. 1973. Ethnographer Bias in Cross-Cultural Research: An Empirical Study. *Behavior Science Notes 8*:275–317.

Romney, A. Kimball. 1989. Quantitative Models, Science and Cumulative Knowledge. *Journal of Quantitative Anthropology 1*:153–223.

Rosenthal, Robert. 1966. *Experimenter Effects in Behavioral Research*, enl. ed. New York: Irvington.

Rosenthal, Robert, and Ralph L. Rosnow. 1984. *Essentials of Behavioral Research: Methods and Data Analysis.* New York: McGraw-Hill.

Rosenthal, Robert, and L. Jacobson. 1968. *Pygmalion in the Classroom.* New York: Holt, Rinehart and Winston.

Ross, Marc Howard. 1983. Political Decision Making and Conflict: Additional Cross-Cultural Codes and Scales. *Ethnology 22*:169–192.

Seligman, C. G., and Brenda Z. Seligman. 1932. *Pagan Tribes of the Nilotic Sudan.* London: George Routledge & Sons.

Stout, David B. 1947. *San Blas Cuna Acculturation: An Introduction.* New York: Viking Fund Publications in Anthropology.

Tatje, Terrence A. 1970. Problems of Concept Definition for Comparative Studies. In *A Handbook of Method in Cultural Anthropology.* Raoul Naroll and Ronald Cohen, eds. Pp. 689–696. Garden City, NY: Natural History Press.

Tylor, Edward B. 1889. On a Method of Investigating the Development of Institutions Applied to the Laws of Marriage and Descent. *Journal of the Royal Anthropological Institute of Great Britain and Ireland 18*:245–272.

White, Douglas R. 1990. Reliability in Comparative and Ethnographic Observations: The Example of High Inference Father-Child Interaction Measures. *Journal of Quantitative Anthropology 2*:109–150.

Whiting, Beatrice B., ed. 1963. *Six Cultures: Studies of Child Rearing.* New York: Wiley.

Whiting, John W. M. 1954. Methods and Problems in Cross-Cultural Research. In *Handbook of Social Psychology*, Vol. 1. Gardner Lindzey, ed. Pp. 523–531. Cambridge: Addison-Wesley.

Whiting, John W. M. 1981. Environmental Constraints on Infant Care Practices. In *Handbook of Cross-Cultural Human Development.* Ruth H. Munroe, Robert L. Munroe, and Beatrice B. Whiting, eds. Pp. 155–179. New York: Garland.

Whyte, Martin K. 1978. Cross-Cultural Studies of Women and the Male Bias Problem. *Behavior Science Research 13*:65–80.

Witkowski, Stanley R. n.d. Environmental Familiarity and Models of Band Organization. Unpublished manuscript. New Haven: Human Relations Area Files.

Zeller, Richard A., and Edward G. Carmines. 1980. *Measurement in the Social Sciences: The Link Between Theory and Data.* New York: Cambridge University Press.

PART IV
APPLYING AND PRESENTING
ANTHROPOLOGY

ROBERT T. TROTTER, II
JEAN J. SCHENSUL

Eighteen

Methods in Applied Anthropology

Introduction to Applied Anthropology

Applied anthropologists conduct research so that the implications of their research can be used for direct interventions or to lead to recommendations for policy change. Applied anthropology publications underscore the globalization of applied anthropology and the appearance of applied anthropology networks in Africa, Southeast and South Asia, Latin America, Europe, the new Asian republics, and Australia (Baba and Hill 1996).

Two major factors have contributed to the growing recognition of applied anthropology as a resource for global problem solving. First, most critical U.S. social problems (health, consequences of poverty, violence, drug abuse, etc.) have a strong international component and cannot be solved in the United States alone. Second, the growth of cultural and ethnic consciousness, accompanied by widespread recognition of culture as a critical element to be considered in local and national problem solving, extends beyond single nation boundaries.

Applied anthropologists study conditions ranging from health and disease prevention to educational innovation and instructional improvement, community economic development, and environmental protection. Most of their work is based in or concerned with culturally diverse communities and populations. Increasingly, the research and interventions are conducted by partnerships that include anthropologists and representatives of the communities or countries in which the problem is to be addressed. This combination of complex and diverse subjects with plural cultural and political systems requires a very robust, and diverse tool kit, including methods that can be applied under less than ideal research conditions.

All research must be conducted with integrity, but two features of applied research place greater-than-usual responsibility on the shoulders of the researcher. First, the human, social, and ecological consequences of applied research are immediate, potentially significant, and sometimes critical to the life and survival of communities. Second, because the results are change oriented, they may be disruptive or threatening. Some researchers (for example, Campbell and Stanley 1963; S. Schensul 1985) have said applied social science research can and should be the most creative and rigorous of all social science research.

Types of Applied Situations

Applied anthropologists and other social scientists have delineated five types of applied research (see Schensul and Schensul 1978; Morgan 1983; Chambers 1987; Reason 1988; Van Willigen 1993):

1. **Policy Research**—research intended to assess the effects of a policy to adapt or change it or to generate new policies. Policy research in anthropology usually involves conducting ethnographic research and making suggestions for policy change through single events (press conferences or workshops). Less frequently, it involves describing the effects of implementing a set of policies on a target population and demonstrating the process of change as well as the need for policy change. In both approaches, the researcher speaks to the policymakers, but is generally not actively involved either in the process of policy-making or in penetrating the locations, networks, or policy clusters within which policy is made (J. Schensul 1985). The recognition that those who produce scientific knowledge for policymakers must be involved in significant ways in the policy-making process has been at the forefront of thinking in anthropology for the past decade. It is only recently, however, that anthropologists have provided written examples of their direct involvement with policy makers at governmental and other levels.

2. **Evaluation Research**—research intended to improve or evaluate the efficacy or outcome of a program (Trotter 1996). Generally, the evaluation identifies cultural patterns, networks, or other factors likely to help a program or be important in determining consistency of implementation and outcome. In many instances, the anthropologist isn't directly involved in developing or implementing the program and doesn't have the responsibility for translating research into program models or activities. At times, however, especially in participatory empowerment (Fetterman et al. 1993) or action research evaluation models, the evaluation researcher plays a role in implementation and thus should have some experience in managing the class of programs targeted by the evaluation.

3. **Cultural Intervention Research**—unlike evaluation research, this involves the applied anthropologist directly in the development, conduct, and evaluation of

a culturally based, theory-driven intervention. Here, the researcher conducts research that identifies cultural factors important in guiding interventions and uses the findings to generate or identify appropriate intervention theories (Trotter et al. 1995; Trotter et al. 1996). The creation and conduct of the intervention, based on cultural knowledge and theory development, also falls to the anthropologist, who, like the participatory evaluator, must know a great deal about methods of program implementation. Teamwork is advisable in cultural intervention research.

4. **Advocacy or Action Research**—specifically directed toward identifying, critiquing, and addressing imbalances in allocation of power, economic resources, social status, material goods, and other desired social or economic elements in a community, society, or globally. Advocacy research may include evaluation, policy research, and research and development. The end result is to increase, organize, and activate resistence in community groups, with unions, with groups representing underrepresented or excluded populations, and with those with limited (or perceived as limited) power to change their own conditions. Anthropologists engaged in advocacy research tend to do so from a "liberal" or "critical" perspective; thus, culturally based theories guiding advocacy research must recognize structural barriers to promote equity and consider such general factors contributing to social inequities as class and caste, power, gender, age, sexual preference, linguistic usage, and social race as well as those specific to local/national settings. Advocacy research in anthropology stems from the concept of action research first suggested by Sol Tax (1960), and reiterated in the work of Stephen and Jean Schensul (1978). It appears in the more recent work of such anthropologists as Alexander Ervin (1996) and Singer and Baer (1995). In this chapter, we use the term "advocacy research." "Action research" is a term now ubiquitous in social science literature; it refers to iterative research leading to any "action," rather than action guided by critical thinking (see Stringer 1996). Finally, advocacy research may or may not be participatory.

5. **Participatory Action Research**—research that involves several critical elements including: a long-term partnership with those who are going to take action (for example, to improve their program, to create and use a curriculum, to develop a new way of harvesting millet, etc.); continuous interaction of research with the action through joint researcher/actor data collection, analysis, reflection; and use. In the other forms of research outlined above, the means (research) leads to the end (an evaluation, a program, a policy change, etc). In participatory action research (PAR), the means is the end, and the conduct of research is embedded in the process of introducing or generating change. PAR is, first and foremost, locally specific and is intended to further local goals with local partners (see Stringer 1996). Since action depends on good information, the quality of the information obtained through PAR should ideally be outstanding. Early work, such as that of Holmberg and colleagues in their classic intervention in the Cornell-Vicos experiment, merged scientific research with ongoing contributions to improving agriculture, education, housing, and other social domains (Holmberg 1954, 1958, 1966).

More than any other form of research, PAR is subject to the constraints of time, local politics, and other contextual factors (Whyte 1991). Thus, participatory action researchers must be excellent group facilitators as well as researchers and should be familiar with techniques for conducting research with groups and individuals (for example, group pile sorts, group interviews, group elicitation techniques, etc.) in order to maximize the rigor of the research. Another consideration is that the research may or may not contribute to the development of scientific (that is, generalizable) knowledge on any given topic because the research, while meeting the rigors of application, may not meet the criteria for publication in scientific journals, or the researchers may not hold publication as a priority. Morgan (1983) and Reason (1988) discuss these issues with reference to qualitative techniques including group interviews and cooperative inquiry, narratives, and story-telling.

Applied anthropologists selecting one or another of these positions must consider with whom they wish to work, whether they have the skills or experience to conduct research *and* engage in practice, what their personal and professional values are, to what degree these values are rooted in particular theoretical frameworks, what position they occupy in the structure of the research setting, and where they wish to place themselves on the continuum from critical outsider to activist insider.

Applied researchers may conduct any or all of these forms of research, separately or even in the same field setting. In long-term relationships, it is easy to become confused about which role to play when. Confusion also arises when these approaches serve contradictory purposes (for example, are advocacy research and evaluation mutually exclusive?). It's important to identify which approach is being used (and why) so as to avoid or resolve possible challenges to researcher identity and to ensure proper presentation of self in the research site.

Building the Applied Setting

Applied research is embedded in a setting in which a problem has been identified and a group is present to address it. If these two conditions are not met, the research may be useful but it will rarely be used. An important component of "method" in applied anthropology involves close attention to the structures and relationships that affect the success or failure of the research mission.

The use of ethnography generally distinguishes anthropologists from other social scientists. In traditional ethnography, the anthropologist is a student of the culture and the indigenous expert is the teacher. Applied anthropology calls for reciprocal learning and sharing of expertise in identifying a problem, defining a researchable question, conducting research, and using results (what Stull and Schensul [1987] call collaborative research). The applied researcher is involved in shaping theory, design, and data collection to fit the requirements of the field situation and those of the field partners.

Common approaches to collaborative field research include consultations with bureaucracies, contract research or evaluations with governments or nonprofit organizations, and researcher-initiated collaborations with clinics, schools, community groups, or networks of nonprofit organizations (Chambers 1985; J. Schensul et al. 1987; Schensul and Schensul 1992). These partnerships are necessary for evaluating the implications of policy decisions or for developing and testing programmatic interventions. In these relationships, the applied anthropologist can be called "consultant," "evaluator," "administrator," or "principal investigator," titles also used in other fields.

In addition to understanding traditional anthropological theory and methods, applications research demands skills that are taught in only a small number of anthropology training programs, due to lack of time or to faculty inexperience. For example, to initiate a change-oriented program, it's critical to identify key actors who are influential leaders and who can engage in institutional change, program development, or policy advocacy. These individuals may or may not be key informants. They are people linked to service or policy systems—systems that also must be understood in order to introduce change efforts appropriately. Understanding the concept of program or intervention; being able to cross disciplinary boundaries in conceptualizing and writing intervention grants; designing and managing budgets; administering research, cultural interventions and interdisciplinary teams—all these are important skills. Finally, team building and group facilitation skills are central to endeavors in complex community or institutional settings. If researchers can't quickly grasp the "politics" of the setting and negotiate relationships to promote and achieve common goals across sectors, partnerships can fall apart.

Increasingly, anthropologists do research and act to improve conditions for their own ethnic/social/racial groups. These anthropologists speak as experienced social scientists as well as informed insiders and must contend with issues faced by any researcher conducting research in his or her own community. These issues are different from those encountered by researchers from the outside. Insiders are already "tracked" in their communities, by gender, class, family reputation, affiliation, education level, and so on. They must anticipate and confront expectations that they may or may not be able to meet. If they are faculty members in local colleges and universities, they are expected to recruit students from their communities of reference and nurture them through school. If they bring in outside grant resources, they must take special care to anticipate and avoid exacerbating divisions that may already exist in their communities.

For these "insider" anthropologists, the ability to remain in the community and to continue to conduct research with students and community members depends on the degree to which their research is successful in improving the quality of community life, meets the needs of residents, and minimizes negative effects or perceptions. They must juggle the demands of the outside world of funders, researchers, and policymakers with the demands of family friends and community politics. On the other hand, they are privy to insiders' information, understand local language and references, are more likely to recognize the utility of local social structures and networks and cultural beliefs in the development of interventions. As a result, they can more readily develop, test, and disseminate culturally appropriate research tools.

Building Testable Ethnographic Theory

Building and using strong, testable theory is the most crucial element for creating or selecting research methods in applied anthropology. Theory and methods are always bound together. The way theories are constructed and presented should suggest ways to test them. Theories imply directions in intervention or policy to be acted on once the research is done or while it is being conducted. Testing theory in the field, through research and intervention, improves understanding of the field situation, the cultural conditions to be modified or influenced, and human responses to both.

"Midrange" theory is what is tested most in applied anthropology. This term has several meanings. Pelto and Pelto (1978) refer to it as predictive generalizations arising from the time and space immediacy of field data and linked to broader theoretical approaches or paradigms such as structuralism; postmodernism; ecological, or systems theories; and Marxist/materialist or evolutionary theories. We agree with this definition but refine it in the following section by referring to "the next step down" in the Pelto and Pelto sequence—that is, to those midrange theories or approaches that have evolved from research in anthropology that precede and guide research in local settings, where that research has direct applications.

Midrange cultural theories are attempts to identify the important patterns of thought or behavior in specific domains of a culture—patterns representative of an identified group of people in a designated context (Trotter 1997). In other words, midrange theories are locally situated. Examples include constructing a cultural model of drug use and abuse in a specific urban setting, identifying the decision-making processes farmers use to decide whether to plant subsistence or cash crops, or producing a predictive model of factors accounting for contraceptive choice. These theoretical models describe, explain, and/or predict what is going on in one or more cultural domains in a specific local environment. Such models are generated from prior knowledge and field experience, are tested in the field, and are continually refined (Glaser and Strauss 1967; S. Schensul 1985; Trotter 1995, 1997). The cultural "frame" (that is, the lens through which culture is viewed and defined) may be cognitive, behavioral, structural, or critical. The choice of cultural frame influences (or is influenced by) the selection of a problem and theory. It also influences the selection of methods of sampling, data collection and data analysis. And it plays an important role in interpretation and utilization of the results of the research.

Some applied researchers use a combination of theoretical approaches. Midrange, descriptive cultural theories may predict cultural *choice* and point to general *intervention theories or actions* to be taken, but they don't always specify *how*, in detail, the intervention will be structured. For example, network theories (see below), suggest several directions for intervention: diffusion of information using opinion leaders, working with bounded networks to influence "peer norms," or mobilizing "social supports" for individuals through their ego-centered networks (Trotter et al. 1995b, 1995c, 1996). But those theories may not specify exactly how to work with opinion leaders. They may not specify all the approaches that are useful in diffusing information (regardless of the diffusion agent), or exactly what to do with social support networks to strengthen, modify, or eliminate selected behaviors. So, to bring about changes in individuals, systems, and policies, applied anthropologists often consider intervention theories in addition to those suggested by cultural research.

Midrange Theory Development in Applied Anthropology

Anthropological research typically uses a variety of data collection techniques, including observations, interviews, focused life stories, discussion groups, the analysis of social networks, decision modeling, projective techniques, and household surveys, to gain detailed knowledge about cultural contexts, patterns of social behaviors, sequences of events, and cultural norms or beliefs (Bernard 1994). When conducting research, anthropologists generally focus on cultural theories—that is, on theories that predict patterns of groups rather than theories that predict individual behavior. Efforts to bring about changes through the application of ethnographic research have mostly concentrated on group effects, and the changes promoted have generally been at the structural, policy, institutional, community, or group level. Here, we discuss cultural theories that have proven to have positive implications for change.

Sociocognitive Theories

Midrange theories on cultural beliefs and thought processes have been derived from the interface of cognitive psychology and psychological anthropology and investigate the mental aspects of cultural dynamics. A subset of these theories is concerned with links between cognition and behavior. The underlying assumption in these approaches is that culture is a mental phenomenon, consisting of identifiable conceptual domains that are shared and that can be identified and analyzed. In an applied context, this approach assumes that group change in behavior occurs through changes in cultural beliefs, attitudes, perceived norms, and concepts. These theories lend themselves to social marketing, to communications approaches to change, and to approaching change through individual learning and changes in beliefs or knowledge.

The midrange cognitive behavioral theories used most commonly in anthropology include cultural models approaches and cultural beliefs systematics. There is also renewed interest in Bateson's (1979) theory of epistemological shifts, in the practical application of new theories on cultural decision modeling (Gladwin 1989), and in the social construction of cultural norms (Nastasi et al. 1998; Schensul 1998c).

Cultural Models and Culture Congruency Theories

These include descriptive models of health beliefs, behaviors, and emic models of contagion or trauma (Kleinman 1980; Quinn and Holland 1987). Cultural congruency models (Trotter 1991; Trotter and Potter 1993; Schensul et al. 1993) are based on establishing similarities and differences between lay and professional models of health and healing. The cultural models theory can be applied to both groups and individuals. It can be used by change agents who wish to remove general or patient-specific barriers to access to professional health care by reducing cognitive incongruity between both parties, improving opportunities for shared meaning, and, at the same time, putting into place structures that improve access to care and care continuity (such as translators or transportation systems). The theory also allows the change agent to construct a common vocabulary or pattern of behavior for both groups. One key assumption is that there is a close relationship between belief and behavior such that change occurs in both simultaneously and probably interactively, or such that change in one condition creates a change in the other in a short time.

Consensus Theories

Consensus theory provides a method that allows ethnographers to explore a consensual description of a cultural domain while simultaneously assessing individual informants' expertise in that domain (Romney et al. 1987; Weller and Romney 1988). This allows for consensus validation and the simultaneous identification of important intragroup variation. Consensus theory models of culture are developed through a formalized set of questions about similarities and differences in shared experience and knowledge by informants. The method for testing the theory melds ethnographic survey questions with a formal mathematical model based on approaches used by psychometricians in test construction, and is influenced by signal detection theory and latent structural analysis procedures (Romney et al. 1986).

Some anthropologists involved in work on AIDS are attempting to use consensus theory to identify core versus peripheral values or norms (see Nastasi et al. 1998). Core values are those that most people agree on; peripheral values are those in which there is less agreement. Core elements of culture may be more difficult to change than peripheral areas or, alternatively, bringing about changes in core versus peripheral areas may have to be addressed in different ways, for example through social marketing versus targeted cognitive-behavioral interventions.

Social Construction Theories

These take the position that cultural knowledge, norms, skills, and behaviors are co-constructed through a negotiated group process in specific cultural contexts. According to this perspective, interpersonal exchange is essential to the development of individual cognitions and behavior and to the evolution and transmission of culture (see, for example, Berger and Luckman 1966; Vygotsky 1978; Bearison 1982; Damon 1983; Rogoff 1990; Wertsch, 1991). This approach suggests that new ways of thinking and behavior develop initially during social interactions in which more experienced or knowledgeable individuals mediate the person-environment interaction. With repeated exchanges in similar contexts, new ideas and behavior become internalized. Interpersonal relationships provide the context for reinforcing shared beliefs and behaviors, enhancing perceptions of competence and encouraging persistence of group norms. This theoretical framework lends itself to the use of group elicitation techniques for negotiating as well as documenting existing and changing group norms, and audiovisual recording methods for recording and understanding group processes. The approach can be used in group interventions and is linked to network theory and research since networks are natural groupings within which group interventions can be conducted.

Scripting Theories

These theories assume that patterns of conduct are locally situated and socially rooted. These behaviors are learned and change over time. Scripts are selectively used, modified, and adapted as people make choices in their lives. According to this theory, the scripts that people develop include a meshing of what both the cultural setting and the individual define as the cultural domain. The theory promotes the notion that both individuals and public institutions can be innovative while they are engaged in maintaining the way in which a cultural domain is represented. For example, middle-class suburban children's birthday parties are scripted in a particular way—including features such as balloons, paid entertainment, acceptable gift categories, appropriate clothes, acceptable foods, etc. Sufficient innovation—such as a decision to avoid giving gifts or to favor family parties—can change the cultural scripts in a society (see Brady and Levitt 1965; Castillo and Geer 1993; Gagnon and Simon 1987).

Different "master statuses" (that is, the important characteristics in a social setting that situate individuals structurally and determine who they can influence) are usually associated with different scripts and influence both the direction and probability of acceptance of innovation. Script theory is closely related to network theory since scripts as event sequences are socially negotiated through networks or groups (Parker and Gagnon 1995). Thus, a combination of social marketing (societal level), diffusion theory and influence or power (network level), and cognitive behavioral interventions (individual or dyad level) are necessary to bring about desired changes in cultural scripting.

Cultural Contexts Research

Anthropological midrange theories have helped establish the importance of cultural contexts and the organization and structure of human systems. We term this area cultural contexts research. This research addresses the cultural environment or conditions that have an impact on daily living (for example, environmental, political, economic, and social contexts of group beliefs, norms, and behaviors). Research derives from theories of kinship and social network analysis and the impact of cultural structures on human behavior. Theoretical models include diffusion theory approaches to cultural change and innovation; theories of organizational control and behavior; and theories on dynamics of social networks and the small-world phenomenon. Other context-specific theoretical models come from community participation research; gender, race, and power analysis; research on cultural diffusion, cultural resistance, and cross-cultural conflict. In this section we address only social network theories and the implications of ecological and critical theory for guiding midrange theory.

Social Network Theories

Network theories have evolved over the past 40 years within a number of research contexts germane to applied research (Galaskiewicz and Wasserman 1993; Wasserman and Faust 1993; Johnson 1994). Some of the broader midrange theories associated with these approaches are personal networks theory, social network structural theory, social support theory, and viewpoint theory. Network theory has been used in studies of family systems and adaptation (Bott 1957; Cross 1990); in diffusion studies concerned with the flow of innovation, information, or infection in populations (Trotter et al. 1995c); and in studies testing the efficacy of group interventions in contrived groups or networks (Trotter et al. 1996; Schensul and Berg 1997; Schensul et al. 1997; Nastasi et al. In press). Several primary methods (or methodological sets) have been used in conducting these studies, including ethnographic network mapping (Trotter et al. 1995b; Trotter et al. 1996), ego-centered network surveys (Trotter et al. 1995a), and full relational network analysis (Trotter et al. 1994; McGrady et al. 1995; Needle et al. 1995).

Cultural Ecological Theories

These relate cultural conditions to the context of humans within an ecological or political framework and are a third area of development and exploration for applied anthropology. The models derived from ecological theory are multifactoral and may include interaction with physical or bioenvironmental characteristics. In addition to consideration of multiple "independent variable domains" (that is, selected elements of larger systems) influencing individual or group behavior, two additional factors are important in ecologically driven investigation: the local nature of the investigation and the notion of "adaptation," which assumes that individuals and groups engage in continuous "adjustment" to environmental circumstances. Most prevention research now uses an ecological framework, identifying and attempting to address or rectify barriers to change at any level (for example, the family) in interaction with other levels (for example, health care system, individual constraints, school problems, etc.; see Bronfenbrenner 1977; Dryfoos 1990).

The midrange theories currently being tested include barriers to change research (referring to environmental factors impeding change or access to needed resources), cultural congruency models (which attribute results to differences in beliefs and practices between those seeking and those delivering services), human-biological interactions research, and comparative cultural models research. One example of midrange theory combined with observational methods in a cultural ecological context is a series of studies, supported by the National Institute on Drug Abuse, of needle sharing and needle hygiene practices. Part of HIV risk-reduction efforts, these studies focus on context-specific uses of injection equipment among drug users in the United States. Early descriptions (for example, Singer et al. 1991; Clatts 1994; Koester 1994) explore the meaning and the processes of injection drug use and needle sharing and the public health consequences of drug paraphernalia laws that restrict the possession of syringes that might be used for drug abuse. Later studies (Bourgois 1995a, 1995b; Needle et al. 1995) explore the consequences of needle hygiene and needle sharing at the microenvironmental level.

Critical Theory

Like ecological theory, in anthropology this theory uses a systems approach but its "value frame" substitutes resistence for adaptation (Giroux 1981a:113–126, 1981b; Freire 1995). It calls for examining cultural behaviors at the local level, in the context of the political economy of national systems in a global system dominated by nationalistic, capitalist, or other forms of hegemonic control over information and economic and human resources. Singer and Baer (1995), Hill (1991), Scheper-Hughes (1989), and others summarize and integrate cognitive/ cultural and behavioral domains into their critical theoretical framework. They have identified the importance of gender, race, ethnicity, and identity in the context of anthropological theory. Other anthropologists and cultural theorists, however, address these areas in greater detail (for example, Morgen 1993, Heath and McLaughlin 1993; Jordan and Weedon 1995; DeVos and Romanucci-Ross 1995), using a combination of postmodern and critical or Marxist theory. These authors generally view race and ethnicity as socially constructed, with localized meanings influenced by definitions of power and authority that are local manifestations of national or international systems. They argue against static definitions of racial, ethnic, or gender identity, suggesting that these are contested territories and, as such, don't lend themselves to acculturation, gender, or ethnic affiliation scaling techniques unless the tools of measurement are locally situated, constructed, and validated. While some of these theories have been transformed into applied midrange theory, others await testing both as models for applied interventions and for analysis as applicable theoretical models.

The next section describes successful models for selecting cultural experts in applied research settings; this is followed by descriptions of the methods that provide the research data in such settings.

Advances in Sampling Design Compatible with Ethnographic Theory and Methods

Applied research can only be conducted when there is an appropriate group of cultural experts who are willing to share their knowledge with the researcher. Midrange theories can only be tested where they are linked to systematic techniques that identify an appropriate representative selection of cultural experts (sampling techniques and key informant selection processes). This is a methodological condition that has been too long ignored in applied anthropological work.

Applied projects must be designed to create the highest level of confidence in the research results. To provide this confidence, quantitative social sciences have most commonly favored probabilistic (random) sampling techniques that allow for statistical analysis of the data collected. These techniques work well when the universe from which the sample is to be drawn can be identified and where everyone in a population (a school, a town, a country) has an equal chance of being chosen to express their viewpoint. It does not work for qualitative approaches, where other conditions apply.

For ethnographic purposes, it is generally inappropriate to draw simple random samples or to use random sampling procedures without using other techniques that are guaranteed to produce a qualitatively representative sample of information about the culture, not just a sample of people representing the group. For example, random sampling in multiethnic neighborhoods, when the target of study is a specific ethnic group, may fail produce a representative sample of members of that group. Instead, cultural representatives must be identified through ethnographic informant selection procedures (Johnson 1990) or cluster or stratified random sampling techniques.

Quantitative sampling techniques should be used as appropriate. Often, however, conditions for randomized or systematic sampling and quantitative surveying cannot be met or do not need to be met in an ethnographic context. Time and resource constraints may preclude survey research. Or research questions may call for the discovery of cultural patterns or range of variation at the cultural (group) but not at the individual level. Alternative approaches to sampling must often be used because the target population is hidden, rare, or difficult to find. The following sections provide options to probabilistic sampling in applied ethnographic research contexts.

Systematic Sampling Procedures

Ethnographic sampling processes focus on identifying individuals in the community who have extensive expertise in an important cultural domain. It is important to talk to individuals who are carefully selected for their expertise, in order to explore cultural domains and variations in cultural patterning, rather than randomly selecting someone from the general population who may not have the information needed to complete the study. Saturation sampling is often the preferable approach for exploring cultural domains or cultural consensus studies. This is the process of interviewing a succession of individuals to the point where no new information is obtained from a subsequent set of interviews. Saturation sampling depends on having sufficient information about the social setting to be able to identify key informants who represent the widest possible or anticipated range of views on the topic under investigation. For example, if the topic is microeconomic enterprises for women, key informants should include women involved in such enterprises—trainers, policymakers, representatives of lending agencies, design experts, educators, and community opinion leaders.

One form of saturation sampling is called universal interviewing—interviewing everyone, not just a sample. This approach has been the norm in small community research projects involving prolonged stays and repeated exposures to most individuals in that context. It is also used when the setting in which the research is being conducted can be bounded (for example, a classroom or alternative school) and the number of people involved is small enough so that each individual can be interviewed/observed at least once. Interviewing the whole population on a particular topic is an alternative for ensuring a representative sample and eliminates the need for complicated random or selective sampling designs.

A second form of saturation sampling is interviewing to "sufficient redundancy." This involves reviewing the accumulated knowledge from a set of interviews, as the interviews are conducted, and deciding that all the key information has begun to repeat. If research topics have very little intracultural variation, very few interviews may be needed; very complex issues with wide divergence of viewpoints need far more (up to and including the need to do appropriate probabilistic sampling for information that needs to be generalized to the entire population in question). Identification of respondents occurs in a known context in which sociodemographic and other forms of complexity are known. We would not assume that the full scope of responses has been covered in a multiethnic or multigenerational community, for example, unless we were sure that our sampling procedure covered all known or suspected sources of significant variation on the topic.

One consistent rule for qualitative or ethnographic interviewing is to identify the people who are experts in a particular cultural domain and to interview all of them, if they are all accessible. This approach is based on the assumption that they will provide the most accurate information about the details of the topic and that there are relatively few experts on any given subject in a small society (and often even in very large ones). By capturing the range of possible variation on the topic and interviewing all known experts, we can ensure the acquisition of information on how that specific cultural domain works. What we cannot know is the range of variation among individuals in the population with respect to that cultural domain. Answering that question falls within the scope of probability sampling.

It is important to determine the number of interviews that should be conducted with each informant as well as the number and composition of the informant pool. Some advocates of qualitative research believe that a single interview is sufficient to capture comprehensive information from individual informants about a cultural domain. We don't agree with this for two reasons: (1) Cultural patterning is portrayed in events and event sequences, activities, settings, and social interactions as well as through the lens of the key informant; and (2) Repeated interviews with the same individuals builds trust and reflective capacity. The rule of thumb some methodologists use is to conduct five interviews with a single respondent/informant over a designated period of time (P. J. Pelto, personal communication), coupled with other forms of ethnographic data collection.

Finally, sampling doesn't only apply to individual respondents. Sampling units can be specific events, event sequences, classroom activities, or observations at scheduled time points. The most important consideration is not whether the sampling unit is an individual, or some other unit in time and space, but on what basis the sampling unit is determined in relation to overall research design and methods.

Until recently, selective sampling was considered a weakness of qualitative research. However, as researchers have learned more about representativeness in populations, and to appreciate the importance of the discovery process (or ongoing inquiry) and local expertise in shedding light on new or evolving cultural domains, they have developed protocols that enable them to carefully select a sample on the basis of cultural expertise that permits generalizing to the whole group (culture, community, ethnic group, social system, etc.). Identifying key informants for gaining understanding of cultural domains and selectively sampling a population to obtain information about a range of views and experiences about that domain are distinctly different enterprises, calling for different sampling approaches.

The new and emerging approaches to ethnographic sampling are well explained by Johnson (1990), who thoroughly explores the similarities and differences between probabilistic sampling used in surveys and experimental designs, compared with the purposive sampling strategies necessary for successful qualitative research. This work is also valuable for models of mixed sampling designs that link qualitatively sampled data with probabilistic samples for surveys.

Snowball Sampling

In snowball sampling, each person interviewed leads the researcher to the next person or persons, based on a designated set of criteria. The result is the continuous accrual of related research respondents. It is an important instance of chain analysis (Diaz et al. 1992). This technique allows the researcher to build a sample of individuals with one or more common characteristics within a large known or unknown universe of individuals, not all of whom may, as a group, share the behavior or cultural element in question. Snowball sampling has been used to study drug subcultures such as cocaine users (Bieleman et al. 1993) in the Netherlands and polydrug users (Medina-Mora et al. 1980) in Mexico. In the latter case, drug users served as case-finding agents, introducing to the researchers a growing sample of other users.

Bieleman et al. (1993) define snowball sampling as a chain starting from the first (index) individual. These individuals are asked to name their acquaintances who have a particular characteristic (drug use, sex partner, etc.) and who will constitute the second wave of interviewees. The same questions asked of the index individuals are asked of the second wave in order to construct the third wave and so on. A critical issue is the degree to which the captured sample is representative of the universe. This is difficult if the universe is unknown, but Frank and Snidjers (1994) have shown the method is excellent for identifying hidden populations and comparing them to larger ones. The method has been successfully applied to individuals engaged in drug use and other illegal activities, homeless people, and school leavers.

Intensive Case Finding—Geographical Sampling

Intensive case finding takes advantage of the common condition that different physical settings offer the opportunity to collect observational or interview data on cultural domains that are important for specific groups. People with similar behaviors tend to be geographically concentrated and are therefore easier to recruit from high concentration locations. Hughes et al. (1982) describe several methods for identifying locations for sampling drug abusers, depending on the type of substances used and characteristics of the drug subculture. In Mexico, Medina-Mora et al. (1980) and Medina-Mora et al. (1982) used this approach to study marijuana and solvent users. They monitored and collected data when these individuals gathered in groups on the street, even though these places were not used as a source of drug supply. Leal et al. (1977) found much more secretive (hidden) forms of inhalant use in a high-risk area in the same city. Children kept an open bottle in their pants pocket and repeatedly soaked their sweater sleeves through discrete jumps. They could then put their sleeves up to their nose and inhale the solvent on their sleeves to get high without most people recognizing that they were doing something unusual or harmful.

In an educational ethnography, Marshall and Rossman (1989:58–63) describe a field entry process in which they first identified settings where activities relevant to their study of educational instruction occurred. Through observation and interviewing they identified events, actors, and artifacts and text coded these domains for five major dimensions of teaching they considered important. The patterned presence or absence of these instructional dimensions with regard to the four observational units (setting, event, actor, and artifact) provided the matrix within which sampling could be carried out to ensure cultural representation.

In each of these cases, the researchers used ethnography to identify the types of drug-use locations. Then they mapped locations and sampled them as intensive case-finding sites. The researchers used their knowledge of the collection points to acquire significant samples of participants. This approach can be applied to any topic where persons can be observed as being engaged in specific activities in a variety of geographically defined areas (such as street corners, playgrounds, malls, sports events, empty lots, lunchrooms, McDonald's restaurants) from which samples can be drawn for interviewing purposes. It can be used to explore any cultural domain in which behaviors and geographic location overlap. Irene Glasser (1996), for example, identified homeless individuals through observations in selected homeless shelters in a northeastern city. The sites themselves may also be considered units of observation and analysis if behavior conducted in them is the topic of study.

Targeted Sampling

Often, you can't identify the universe of units from which to draw a sample. Such populations may be composed of commercial sex workers, homeless youth, undocumented household servants, or school dropouts. In these examples, key parameters—including the need to remain hidden—prevent the use of traditional random sampling procedures. In such cases, targeted sampling (Watters and Biernacki 1989) is an appropriate substitute. Targeted sampling is a systematic technique for creating a proxy sampling framework that ensures that the major divisions or categories of the population being studied are systematically sampled in theoretically correct portions. It uses all of the available secondary data relating to the population to create geographically focused targeted sampling areas. This data may include health information, social service data, ethnographic knowledge of the population, observations, or any secondary data sources that describe some important segment of the target population.

Bieleman et al. (1993) successfully used a new application of this technique to assess the extent and nature of cocaine use in three cities in Holland, Spain, and Italy. Their approach was to deliberately identify respondents whom they had good reason to believe formed a reasonable cross-section of the cocaine subculture (in terms of subgroups and settings where use took place), using all of the secondary data (arrest data, treatment data, baseline ethnographies) available to them. For example, in Barcelona targets were defined by setting, type of use, and economic status: (1) elite: fashion, business, and art world; (2) new urban middle class: professions, jobs linked to night life, middle ranks in the fashion, business and art world; (3) young people; (4) illegal circuits and opiate addicts; and (5) middle and middle-low status. As additional ethnographic data were collected, new groups were identified and added.

Nominative Technique

The nominative approach is a sampling and estimation technique based on information provided by individuals (in a sample) about others whom the respondent knows has a specific attribute or behavior. This approach is often necessary when there is a need to study rare events in a culture. Shelley et al. (1995) used a nominative approach to identify the personal social networks of a known sample of seropositive individuals and proposed ways of using network size to determine amount of HIV in the general population. Johnsen et al. (1995) used similar methods to corroborate the total number of AIDS/HIV-infected persons in the United States. In Hartford, Connecticut, this technique was used to estimate the number of homeless youth in the city (City of Hartford 1994). Key informants working in homeless shelters and social service programs were asked to estimate the number of homeless youth they knew and from that to estimate approximately how many homeless youth were living in the city. All of their estimates fell between 400 and 450 against a census-based estimate of approximately 450. The nominative technique can provide important additional demographic and other information about hidden groups as well as a more accurate estimate of the size of a hidden population.

Methods in Applied Anthropology

There are many resources on methods of ethnographic data collection and analysis. These include Pelto and Pelto's (1978) pioneering work, *Anthropological Research: The Structure of Inquiry*; Bernard's (1994) *Research Methods in Anthropology*; the two-volume series by Werner and Schoepfle (1987) *Systematic Fieldwork*; Agar's *(1986) Speaking of Ethnography*; Weller and Romney's (1988) *Systematic Data Collection*; Strauss's (1985) *Qualitative Analysis for Social Scientists*; and Strauss and Corbin's (1990) *Basics of Qualitative Research*. These works contain descriptions of research design and methods for participant observation and advanced ethnographic data collection. They are complemented by Miles and Huberman's (1994) *Qualitative Data Analysis*. A new synthesis of applied ethnographic methods is the seven-volume *Ethnographer's Toolkit*, authored and edited by J. Schensul and LeCompte (In press).

Many specific ethnographic methods—decision tree modeling, cognitive methods (pile sorts, triad tests, etc.), the long interview, the life history—are described in a continually expanding series of monographs published by Sage Publications. The following sections identify the methods commonly used in applied anthropology, especially educational, medical, and urban anthropology (efforts concerned with improving the status of communities in relation to service systems).

Analysis of Culturally Defined Cognitive Systems

Cognitive anthropologists have developed methods that allow us to explore how people think about and locate meaning in the world around them. As we noted earlier, it is important to consider cognition and behavior since the relationship between them is not always predictable. Change agents often recognize the need to influence both simultaneously or to influence behavior by changing attitudes, beliefs, norms, values, and intentions. In this section, we discuss cognitive research methods that (1) assist in determining the content and limits of cultural domains; (2) help us analyze the structural elements of cultural domains; and (3) portray a domain from a consensual framework.

There is a well-developed set of basic cognitive anthropology techniques that have been used in cross-cultural research. The cultural models methods of Quinn and Holland (1987) are a solid starting point for cultural cognitive research. These provide systematic questions to investigate broad cultural domains, such as models of health conditions. Other ethnographic cognitive methods include systematically administered, semistructured, open-ended (qualitative or ethnographic) interviews analyzed through hierarchical coding and pattern recognition of themes and conceptual linkages (Werner and Schoepfle 1987; Weller and Romney 1988) and systematic data collection techniques (sometimes referred to as elicitation techniques) such as pile sorts and triad tests, borrowed from cognitive psychology and linguistics (see Weller, this volume).

Determining the Content and Limits of Cultural Domains

Free listing is the technique most commonly used to begin the exploration of cognitive domains. The basic format is to ask a set of respondents to list and describe all the things that are part of a particular domain. The ethnographer records and probes unexpected or unfamiliar responses in detail (including new words and phrases or words used in new ways) since these labels provide a window into unknown concepts, beliefs, or behaviors. Free lists provide information and local vernacular that can be used in culturally specific questionnaire construction, written educational materials, or behavioral exercises that are being constructed to meet intervention or health education goals. They also allow us to differentiate between key subdivisions in the populations since the domains can differ significantly by gender, ethnicity, age, and cultural expertise. This gives researchers the ability to assess intra- and intercultural variation within the same geographic region, across the nation, or around the world. Some of the more sophisticated uses of free-listing data treat these nominal or categorical data as variables that can be used in statistical procedures, to provide more extensive explorations of the relationships among informants or among the elements in a cultural domain (see Weller and Romney 1988:9–16).

Techniques similar to free listings, such as exploratory open-ended questions, Spradley's domain analysis techniques (1979), or sentence-completion processes, can also be analyzed using the approaches described for free listings. These rapid-scanning techniques can be used as an individual exercise in a face-to-face interview or in group settings (as a form of focus group). Empiricists tend to use the individual interviewing technique so as to avoid contamination by other informants, while constructivists often use the group interview (including the focus group) to enable observation of negotiated meaning.

Techniques to Define and Analyze
Structural Relationships among Elements
in a Cultural Domain

Research methods in cognitive anthropology that allow a researcher to explore the relationships among the elements of a cultural domain include pile sorts (Bernard et al. 1986; Weller and Romney 1988:20–31), triads tests (Lieberman and Dressler 1977; Weller and Romney 1988:31–37), and sentence frame techniques (Weller and Romney 1988:55–61). Each of these techniques begins where free listings leave off. They start with the elements of a well-defined cultural domain (explored through free listings). The researcher explores the relationships among the key elements of that domain by asking informants to make judgments about the similarities and differences of the items in the domain to one another.

One such technique is a pile sort. A pile sort is a rapid assessment technique that uses visual aides to let informants create either free or constrained (predefined) classifications of elements within a cultural domain. The most common method is to place pictures, real objects, written labels, or combinations of the three on cards. Each card represents one element in the domain being studied. The researcher asks the informant to classify all the elements by stacking the cards into piles defined by one or more common elements. The final groupings represent each individual's classification system for items in the domain. Weller (this volume) describes the pile sort method in detail. Handwerker and Borgatti (this volume) describe multi-dimensional scaling and cluster analysis, two of the methods most commonly used in analyzing pile sort data. Weller and Romney (1988) and Bernard (1994) show how these techniques can be integrated into ethnographic research. The most commonly used computer program for the analysis of pile sort data is ANTHROPAC (Borgatti et al. 1992).

Consensus Modeling

In consensus modeling, an ethnographer can identify a consensus-based description of a cultural domain, while simultaneously assessing an individual informant's expertise in that domain. The following quote from the creators of the technique describes its theoretical base.

> The central idea in our theory is the use of the pattern of agreement or consensus among informants to make inferences about their differential competence in knowledge of the shared information pool constituting culture. We assume that the correspondence between the answers of any two informants is a function of the extent to which each is correlated with the truth. . . . Suppose, for example, that we had a "perfect set" of interview questions (cultural information test) concerning the game of tennis. Suppose

further that we had two sets of informants: tennis players and non-tennis players. We would expect that the tennis players would agree more among themselves as to the answers to questions than would the non-tennis players. Players with complete knowledge about the game would answer questions correctly with identical answers or maximal consensus, while players with little knowledge of the game would not. (Romney et al. 1986:316)

These assumptions about the nature of "cultural truth" and informant accuracy are derived from a probabilistic model of culture. Investigators need to know the accuracy of the information they receive in self-reports from informants, and consensus theory provides one type of answer to these questions.

Consensus theory models of culture are developed through a formalized set of questions about a cultural domain that appropriately explore similarities and differences in shared experience and knowledge on the part of informants. Consensus theory melds ethnographic survey questions with a formal mathematical model based on approaches used by psychometricians in test construction and influenced by signal detection theory and latent structural analysis for deriving cultural truths from informants' statements about their beliefs and knowledge (Romney et al. 1986:316). Culturally correct answers are the ones that most people believe to be true—a normative or consensual framework for their world view.

Consensus theory is designed to work with a set of questions, all in the same format, all on the same topic, and all at the same level of difficulty. The goal, then, is to estimate the best set of culturally appropriate answers to the questions. The formal model (Romney et al. 1986) can accommodate categorical-type responses: single words or short-phrase responses to open-ended questions, or close-ended multiple choice responses (including true/false or yes/no). An informal version of the model can accommodate interval or fully ranked data. For an example of the use of the formal model with yes/no responses, see Weller et al. (1993); for the informal model with ranked responses, see Chavez et al. (1995).

Analysis of Social Structures

Anthropologists and other social scientists have long been interested in the effects of social structure on human survival and social interaction. The anthropological literature is filled with information about the kinship organization, voluntary associations, and formal organizations found in cultures around the world. Modern network analysis is a set of techniques for expanding our knowledge of the effects and dynamics of human social organization. These techniques are used in the study of kin- and nonkin-based networks. (See Scott [1991] and Marsden [1990] for reviews of methods and analytical issues in network analysis.) Increasingly, applied anthropological research has involved the examination of informal and formal human networks.

Research in this area focuses on three kinds of networks: ego-centered networks, specialized interactive partial networks (for example, sex or drug use/risk networks), and full relational networks. Each involves different methods of data collection. Research questions drive the choice of which type of network to investigate and which type of data to collect.

Ethnographic Network Data

Since social networks are the basis for social activity in a community or institutional setting, one effective method for identifying local social networks is through ethnographic interviewing. Interviewers ask respondents to identify clusters, networks, cliques, or other kinds of groups in which individuals are related to one another (see Bott 1957; Mitchell 1969). Questions may also probe membership in groups by virtue of some activity—presence at various types of events or meetings, interactions with others through eating or shopping or other daily tasks, and so on. The characteristics of the networks defined through ethnography can be used to create a typology or classification of the types of social relationships that exist in a culture and the groupings by size, class, gender, ethnicity, income, family, or other demographic characteristics that they represent.

Giordano's (1993) informal ethnographic study of social groupings in an urban high school setting is a good example of ethnographic identification of social networks. By "hanging out" with key teen informants while waiting for permission to do a formal survey in an urban high school, Giordano was able to identify six student networks, defined by location, activities, cultural preferences, and degree of school attachment. She later used the information about these networks as background for a study of female gangs in that school environment. Curtis et al. (1995) used ethnography to define initial networks. They followed up with a formal survey to confirm social ties among network members. Ethnography was used to describe the activities of network members and to contextualize networks in the street drug economy.

Ego-Centered Network Data

Ego-centered network analysis is based on an individual's definition of the individuals connected to him or her by specified social relationships. Attributes of the content of ego-centered networks (size, gender and ethnic composition, etc.), and characteristics of those networks themselves (density, intensity, etc.) can be incorporated into "typical" network profiles, which can then be associated with other psychosocial variables (Trotter et al. 1995a). Ego-centered networks can provide the basis for determining specific influences on ego, which can then be used in interventions. The social support literature examines that subset of ego's networks that provides social supports for a variety of issues from accessing health services or information (S. Schensul and J. Schensul 1982) to managing chronic health problems. Ego network analysis has also been used to understand risk-taking behavior and to provide direction for drug and HIV intervention programs (Trotter et al. 1996).

Partial (Specialized) Networks

In partial networks, individual linkages are traced under specialized exchange-related circumstances (for example, disease or infection, specific risk behaviors, shared group membership). Researchers ask individuals to identify their networks and, within these, to specify which members share the designated characteristics. A random sample of one or more of these network members with designated characteristics is interviewed to determine the validity of ego's responses and the level of reciprocity between ego and various members of the network. These interviews may also produce additional network members for interviewing. Partial networks can be used in interventions when individuals are asked to bring their friends of the same gender, age, and interest group to programs and when friendship networks are the basis for the group intervention. This information has been used successfully in federally funded AIDS intervention studies as the basis for recruitment and intervention grouping (Needle et al. 1995; Trotter et al. 1995a, 1995b, 1995c, 1996).

Full Network (Relational) Data

Ethnographic and ego-centered network approaches provide valuable baseline data for intervention strategies (Trotter et al. 1996), but they don't always provide detailed information about the type, strength, or direction of relationships within networks. This type of data emerges from the analysis of reciprocal relationships among all members of a network. Scott (1991) describes macronetwork data collection, analysis, and use. The collection of data on full or macronetworks is costly and time consuming, so there is continuing interest in the development of techniques to approximate full networks from data on partial networks. Klovdahl (1989) and McGrady et al. (1995) discuss procedures, advantages, and disadvantages of sampling in constructing large macronetworks.

Thicker Description

Applied anthropologists use many other approaches for collecting data. Here, we review several newer approaches, including spatial mapping, group interviews, and rapid assessment procedures.

Sociogeographic (Spatial) Mapping

Anthropologists have always used maps in field research in part, at least, because early fieldwork was often conducted in places where there were no maps. It was important to bound communities and demarcate residential and other structural units in relation to one another. Mapping "the community"—whether a classroom, organization, neighborhood, or village—is still highly recommended. The process of making a community map, for example, helps researchers select a household sample, generate hypotheses about social relationships among households and between households and other social units, and observe changes over time, especially with respect to household/land and other environmental use patterns.

Now, computerized mapping programs and national and state GIS (Geographic Information Systems), allow for relatively quick mapping of virtually any data across space and over time. Geographic mapping of social networks by residence of network members in relation to primary points of interaction in the community (defined through ethnographic observation) can be used to frame the location of interventions based on natural patterns of spatial use.

In a study conducted in the mid-1980s, Schensul and colleagues first mapped the location of new communities (shanty towns) in the northern quarter of Lima. When communities were identified by age, these chloropleth MAPS (three-dimensional maps showing degrees of altitude) demonstrated graphically that communities were arranged by age, with newer invasions located on steepest hillsides, and older, more established ones lower down or in flat valley beds. Using data collected from municipalities, community officials, and health workers, Schensul and his team mapped the presence of elements of infrastructure, social organization, and major pediatric health problems. These relationships were derived from community-level surveys and also displayed in tables and graphs. However, the mapping strategy showed visual evidence of the disintegration of social organization as communities moved from unofficial to official status and accrued public resources and of the associated shift in priority health problems as the social organizational and resource bases of the communities changed. The information presented through map illustrations had an important influence on decisions about allocating health services resources to communities (Schensul et al. 1985).

Similarly, by mapping residential locations over time, the Institute for Community Research was able to show patterns of intraneighborhood, interneighborhood, and intercommunity mobility for each of Hartford's neighborhoods. The demographic data, portrayed visually, were immediately usable by educational policymakers for school-based planning (ICR 1991). These applications are useful for describing the arrangement of social variables in geographic space, for hypothesis testing, and for eliciting cognitive responses to research-driven questions reflected in such data.

Focused Group Interviews

All group interviews yield text data for coding and analysis, which can be treated quantitatively and qualitatively. Most group interviews have a short practical time limit—from one–two hours—and can address a relatively small number of related topics. Focused group interviews may be formal or informal, preorganized or occurring in natural settings, guided to a greater or lesser degree by the anthropologist/facilitator, and more or less open ended. Group interviews can be used for many purposes—for example, to collect information on a cultural domain, to develop listings for pile sorts, to identify the range of variation in opinions or attitudes on a set of topics, to collect simple numerical data on reported experiences, or to react to the results of previously collected data.

The focus group technique appeared in the 1930s as an alternative to direct interviews and became popular as method for qualitative research in marketing (Kozel 1993). More recently, focus groups have been used to study knowledge, attitudes, and beliefs in many social situations (Schensul 1998b). One disadvantage of group interviews is that they are limited to topics that people are willing to discuss in public. Topics considered personal or intimate should be avoided in group interviews or depersonalized.

Even with this limitation, group interviews offer a number of advantages. They can produce a good deal of data in a short time from a larger number of people than would be possible by interviewing key informants. Group interviews tend to produce good "natural language discourse," which allows the researcher to learn the communication patterns in the community rapidly. Morgan (1988) notes that the hallmark of group Interviews is the "explicit use of the group interaction to produce data and insights that would be less accessible without the interaction found in a group" (p. 12).

Group interviews allow the researcher to record and analyze group members' reactions to ideas and to each other. The interviews are normally lively and create back-and-forth discussions between the participants, based on topics and broad questions that are supplied by the researcher, who typically takes the role of facilitator or moderator. The interactions may be recorded on audio or videotape. The verbatim transcripts of the discussions are subsequently analyzed either through qualitative summary or through systematic coding and content analysis. The questions should extract a maximum range of relevant topics. The idea is to foster interaction that explores the participants' feelings in some depth to elicit responses that illuminate participants' personal experiences and their understanding of the cultural context and community conditions that have an impact on the subject under discussion.

Focused group interviews are useful for orienting yourself to a new field of study; for generating hypotheses based on informant's insights; for evaluating different research sites or study populations; for developing individual questions for interview schedules and questionnaires; and for getting participants' interpretations of results from earlier studies (Morgan 1988). An interesting example of the use of this technique was reported by the Community Epidemiology Work Group established by the National Institute on Drug Abuse in a 12-city study conducted to understand an apparent inconsistency coming from statistical information on indicators of price, purity, and seizures of heroin. The available information suggested an increase in heroin use, although there was no evidence of a concomitant increase in new users. Group interviews among known heroin users were directed at exploring changing patterns of use and hidden populations of new users. Although these discussions identified some new user groups, researchers also discovered that previously identified addicts were concerned about contracting HIV and changed their form of heroin use from injecting to snorting. Snorting requires maintaining a higher level of drug consumption, or a higher level of purity of the drug, than other forms of consumption (Kozel 1993).

In 1994, youth participants in ICR's (the Institute for Community Research in Hartford, Connecticut) summer Teen Action Research Institute conducted a study of adolescent sex norms. Young people (13–18 years old) in this group-guided interview process were first asked to list all the sex behaviors they thought were important. Then they were asked to define and discuss the importance of each of the 22 resulting behaviors. This produced text data on sex behaviors and their meaning to these youth and led to consensus on the most salient terms and their meanings. The group interview produced a list of sex behaviors for a pile sort exercise designed to identify sex behavioral norms with a sample of 169 urban adolescents of the target age group (Schensul 1998a).

To ensure that most aspects related to the subject of inquiry have been captured, Khan et al. (1990) suggest that for research on a single issue at least two focus groups should be conducted with respondents from each representational category. Thus, if only four representational variables are considered—such as age (older/younger), sex (male/female), use of an illicit substance (heroin/cocaine), and caste (three exemplary caste groupings)—24 focus groups are required (2 x 2 x 2 x 3 = 24) for each research issue or area. The authors state that if more than one issue is included, the number of focus groups required multiplies accordingly.

Ethnographic Surveys

Ethnographic surveys differ from most surveys in one or both of the following ways. First, ethnographic surveys are based on prior experience in a specific field situation. They may incorporate instruments or questions from other studies, including nationally validated instruments, but their strength is their validity in relation to local culture and the construction and testing of midrange theory. Thus, ethnographic surveys measure constructs known to be relevant to, or understood by, the study population. Second, they are most commonly administered in a face-to-face interview (preferred because it is more intimate). Self-administration is not possible with nonliterate respondents or to those unfamiliar with answering written questions.

Ethnographic surveys make two critical assumptions: (1) that the ethnographer is a neutral party with no obvious change agenda; and (2) that the ethnographer is a person of confidence who will reveal no secrets to others in the community. In traditional ethnography, these assumptions are usually tested extensively by community residents as ethnographers move from participant observation and mapping through in-depth interviewing, elicitation techniques, and finally to the survey. Recently, however, these steps have been shortcut because of constraints in time and funding and/or because the research is being conducted by a team of surveyors or ethnographers who may be interviewing people with whom they have not established relationships of confidentiality. Under these circumstances, the face-to-face ethnographic survey may be more threatening or liable to elicit less valid information than in the past. Thus, validity of self-report is increasingly an issue in ethnographic surveying.

Rapid Ethnographic Assessment

Rapid ethnographic assessment techniques have been developed for situations where there is a strong need for ethnographic data but little time to conduct a full ethnography. These"rapid scanning" techniques are also called rapid ethnographic procedures, rapid rural appraisals, focused ethnographic studies, and brief ethnographies (S.C.M. Scrimshaw 1992; Scrimshaw and Gleason 1992). Most of these techniques share the following characteristics:

1. They are narrowly confined—for example, to one disease category, or one cultural domain.
2. They are problem oriented; they are called for to help decision makers develop programs or make policy.
3. They are participatory; local partners include potential users who, at the same time can provide ethnographic insights otherwise obtained through more time-intensive participant observation and in-depth interviewing.
4. They provide techniques for rapid sampling of representative sectors.
5. They use small sample sizes.
6. They do not pursue intracultural complexity or range of variation; instead they focus on cultural patterning, and on gross differences across sectors of populations and service providers.
7. They use a systems perspective, making sure to collect information from all relevant sectors of the community.
8. They use cognitive techniques to identify and assess cultural domains.
9. They generally do not make use of quantitative sampling or survey techniques

Typical rapid ethnographic assessments are modest in cost and duration. They last from three days to six weeks, depending on time, resources, and previous ethnographic work. The assessments include mapping, brief participant observation in targeted cultural domains and spaces, free listing and pile sorting or other systematic elicitation methods, key informant interviewing, and group interviewing. Critical to focused ethnography is prior determination of all of the important sectors contributing to the problem, from which researchers can draw representative samples of key informants and focus group respondents. This determination can be made either by ethnographers familiar with the setting or by the interdisciplinary/ intersectoral team responsible for the study and its uses.

Although brief ethnography appears simple, it is more difficult and demanding than other forms of ethnographic research or assessment. Challenges include the need to develop an accurate understanding of the problem and its context in a relatively short and cost-effective period of time, the need for systems for transforming the data into satisfactory solutions, and the need to produce socio-culturally acceptable solutions. These three requirements characterize much of applied research, but the protocols for the conduct and utilization of brief eth- nographies are still not widely known and accepted. Thus, both researchers and contractors/clients take risks when using brief ethnographies for programs, and especially for policy-related purposes.

Informant Accuracy

Informant accuracy is a critical issue in ethnographic research. In survey research, data reliability and validity depend on the consistency of self-report data and studies in which survey responses are checked against information known to be correct (laboratory tests, health records, or mechanically measured data). The validity of the responses of ethnographic informants (that is, cultural experts) is assessed by other criteria (Kirk and Miller 1986). Ethnographic field research depends on developing close personal relationships with community members over time. It emphasizes the rapport between the researcher and the respondent. The increasing intimacy of the ethnographer-informant relationship is expected to produce increasingly accurate information, although in some cases cultural values interfere with this process (Blimes 1975; Nachman 1984). Field research offers the potential for repeat interviews with the same respondent during the study period. These interviews, both formal and informal, are opportunities to look for narrative inconsistencies, recheck and verify data, and obtain clarification of previous statements.

Ethnography is heavily based on individual perception, memory, and self-report through life histories, cultural process interviews (Pelto and Pelto 1978), narratives, or stories (Florio 1997) as well as elicitations. Each approach raises questions about the accuracy of recall and the veracity of individual informants. Individuals vary in their level of expertise and in their ability to accurately recall information about the things that have happened to them. Some are highly accurate in describing unique events; others are more accurate in describing repeated events. Some informants have narrowly defined or specialized expertise; others are knowledgeable about a range of cultural domains but their depth of knowledge on any single topic is limited. Sometimes it is important to interview "special" people in a culture; at other times it is best to talk to "typical" or representative samples of people.

The issue of informant accuracy was studied systematically in the 1970s and 1980s (Killworth and Bernard 1976, 1979; Bernard and Killworth 1977; Bernard et al. 1980, 1982; Weller 1984; Romney et al. 1986; Freeman and Romney 1987). These studies show that informant reports of behavior are incorrect about half the time, but that the distortions are highly patterned. That is, self-reports of behavior have high validity at the aggregate level when the sources of distortion are known and taken into account.

The assumption in anthropology is that ethnographic data—reports by informants about putative cultural facts—are reported only when they are confirmed and reconfirmed from multiple sources, thus increasing the potential for validity. Still, the problem of the validity of ethnographic data is a constant theoretical and pragmatic problem, just as it is in quantitative research. People can outright lie, they can be innocently wrong, they can provide partial truths, and they can avoid talking about sensitive subjects. The researcher has to be constantly vigilant to protect against sources of error, and research on the sources of distortion in informant reports remains important.

It is worth remembering, however, that ethnography focuses on broad cultural patterning. While individuals are central in giving information about cultural phenomena, the validity and reliability of individual accounts are less important in ethnography than in survey research. This is because in ethnographic research individual responses can be checked against group responses and against repeated interviews with the same respondent and observations.

We believe that the most effective way to ensure reliability and validity of ethnographic data is to obtain comparable, confirmatory data from multiple sources at different points in time, and through the use of multiple methods. This is the process of "triangulation." Many investigators, however, now consider ethnographic self-reporting as a form of narrative or storytelling in which the individual interviewed is attempting to convey a particular impression or image to the researcher (Marcus and Fischer, 1986). The story itself must be situated historically, contextually, and in the life of the storyteller in order to understand it as data.

Ethnographic Field Teams and
Cross-Site/Cross-National Applied Research

Anthropology has a long but spotty history in the creation of ethnographic field teams and coordinated cross-site research. These efforts have been sporadic because ethnographic work is considered valuable only at times—usually when there's great interest in understanding social phenomena or diseases and environments that are little known and perceived as difficult to gain access to. Ethnographers must comprehend study needs (theory and method), collect relevant data in complex social settings, and use good judgment and social skills. Ethnographic teamwork requires proper and constant management of team members and the data they are collecting. Proper management calls for attention to comparability of interview and observation skills across interviewers, careful group construction of coding systems related to the theoretical framework of the study and the field situation, regular monitoring and feedback with respect to field notes, and careful attention to entering and coding of data. Furthermore, since good field research involves interaction with the data and both deepening and expanding of text codes, continuous analysis of incoming data with the field team is important.

Ethnographic field teams encounter situations comparable to cross-national ethnographic research when team members work in settings marked by differences in ethnic culture. In both instances, meaning systems, contexts, and social interactions may vary, reducing the comparability of coding systems. Investigators who engage in cross-site or cross-national studies need to pay very close attention to the construction of comparable coding categories across settings as well as to the possibility that some phenomena may be unique to each setting.

One solution to the problem of cross-site comparability is to assume that *common* research *methods* will produce *unique cultural responses* in each setting that point to differences as well as possible similarities in approach. One example of this approach is the WHO Acute Respiratory Infection cross-national effort addressing barriers to identification of symptoms of pneumonia in six countries. The overall project is designed to produce earlier identification, reporting and treatment of pneumonia, and to reduce infant mortality (WHO 1993). The project, under the guidance of Gretel Pelto, has generated focused ethnographic methods for problem identification and analysis, and for the creation and use of information in country-specific social marketing and counseling interventions.

The project first developed and refined an approach to focused ethnographic assessment based on individual studies conducted by ethnographers in six countries (Pelto and Pelto 1997). The result is a manual with complete instructions for collecting, tabulating by hand, and analyzing ethnographic data. Those data can be used for country-specific analyses of mothers' perceptions of pneumonia symptoms and their perceptions of barriers to rapid treatment. The second component of the manual is a translation protocol enabling researchers or trainers to use these results to generate key messages, products, and communications strategies that will increase mothers' ability to recognize the symptoms of acute respiratory illness. The translation protocol and intervention strategy (a communications approach) is generic; the inputs and products are specific to each country.

Computer software now gives teams of researchers the ability to systematize text data collection and coding by standardizing categories of information collection. (See Weitzman and Miles [1995] for an assessment of some of the available programs.) These systems facilitate the establishment and ongoing monitoring of interrater reliability scores. They permit ethnographers to use coding systems to refine field observations and interviews. Finally, proper monitoring of data quality can ensure the inclusion of adequate contextual data to permit coders—even those who know little or nothing about the field site—to make accurate coding judgments.

Ethnographic Research and Policy-Making

A standard complaint of policy-oriented researchers and community advocates or lobbyists is that policymakers believe only in the results of large quantitative surveys or demonstration/evaluation studies. It would be naive to believe that this is not the case some of the time. Indeed, some large studies sway public opinion, which then influences what policymakers, funders, and legislators decide. And surveys using representative samples can identify the scope of a problem.

However, policy-making is also influenced by personal interventions with powerful individuals. Anthropologists directly involved in policy-making (such as those in high-ranking positions in national and international bureaucracies) know that having continuous personal communication, well-strategized workshops and technical working groups, consensus groups, and the like can do as much to influence policymakers as large-scale social surveys do. Legislators and policymakers are, in fact, influenced by many factors—constituency size, hearings, testimony, financial contributions, and personal commitments. Policymakers and legislators are also driven by their own, often only partly formulated, social theories and assumptions about social welfare and behavioral change. Most have little time to read. Thus, large, complex presentations, written or oral, qualitative or quantitative, are not likely to be effective.

Anthropologists need to find ways to interact directly or indirectly with policymakers, and to do so on a consistent basis (J. Schensul 1985; Pelto and Schensul 1987). They need to let decision makers know that their ethnographic data identify issues and point to solutions, while their survey data identify the scope of a problem once it has been detected (Weeks and J. Schensul 1993).

Emerging Areas of Applied Theory and Method in Anthropology

A number of new theory and methods combinations have emerged recently in the anthropological literature that show promise for being useful in applied settings. The following section is a brief introduction to some of them.

Symbolism, Language, and Communications

Symbolic anthropology (Geertz 1973) is an important area of theory development, as are current anthropological linguistics research, some postmodernist approaches to health research (for example, Bourgois 1995a, 1995b), critical medical anthropology (Singer and Baer 1995), and cross-cultural health communication research (Trotter 1991).

A number of the midrange theories in psychological anthropology depend on refinements of communication and symbolic interaction for expression and for associated research methods. Some of the current midrange theories from linguistic anthropology include: (1) the theory that grammatical categories are the primary mechanism influencing culturally specific thought patterns (Lucy 1985); (2) the position that the creation of meaning is only emergent and negotiated in interaction and cannot be reduced to individual intent or to grammatical categories (Verschueren 1995); (3) the condition that meaning is constructed through a metalanguage structure ("mentalese") that is an evolutionary byproduct overshadowing the meanings constructed by any particular oral or written language that we might use (Pinker 1994); (4) the proposition that methods for "unpacking" the constituent "footings" or "voices" present in speakers' roles are critical to understanding communication in context, in opposition to the reduction of communication patterns to speaker/sender and receiver/hearer constructions (Trawick 1988); and (5) the theory that speech creates social context and cannot be separated from the notions of "context," "class," and "identity" sufficiently to justify reifying those notions as separate from speech (Goodwin and Duranti 1992).

These midrange propositions are now being applied to communication in cross-cultural contexts and offer a focus for research in medical anthropology and linguistics. To do basic or formative research in these areas, you need to use audio-visual recording techniques that permit complex text coding of speech flow, interpretation of meaning and context variables, and systems of interaction with key informants (see Graham and Farnell, this volume). Basic understanding of communications dynamics is especially critical in organizing, staffing, and conducting small group interventions, which depend on speech to create community and the negotiation of meaning; mass media and social marketing campaigns, which depend on appropriate terminology, context portrayal, and the strategic selection of core messages; network interventions, which depend on approaches to communication that use the most effective and rapid diffusion of information through individuals; and behavioral interventions, which involve the use of counseling techniques to engage and reinforce behavior change in key individuals. Research has been conducted in these areas for many years, but theories and methods still have to be tested properly in applied situations.

Group Research Methods

Anthropologists have always been interested in the behavior of groups. Through participant observation and attendance at public or family events, traditional service or social support organizations, ceremonies, and rituals, most anthropologists have had numerous opportunities to observe different types of groups. This work is not conceptualized as the "capture" of data from groups because it occurs in naturalistic settings, where questions are asked informally. In the search for patterns, through cultural elicitation methods, anthropologists have returned to the sample of single respondents, even when the context is envisioned as much broader. But with increasing emphasis on smaller or larger group interventions or programs and the desire to "shortcut" the identification of cultural patterning, anthropologists and other social scientists have increasingly turned to the focus group to collect data from groups.

The focus group has a long tradition in marketing, but it has a different character in applied ethnography. First, group interviews can be arranged on a continuum from formal to informal, allowing for open, semistructured, and structured interviewing. Second, most elicitation techniques can be used in a group setting by either gathering data from individuals (for example, pile sorts or behavioral items for a Guttman scale) and then discussing the items in a group setting, or by eliciting information, such as free listing for pile sorting, in other settings. Using a group allows you to collect the needed data from group members about the items. Furthermore, you can incorporate both the data collection and the discussion into a theory-driven group intervention so long as the theoretical framework permits open discussion of the issue. Group-based research holds much promise for future use in research, intervention, and advocacy.

Participatory Action Research and Iterative Research Processes

A final area of attention is participatory action research, which calls for adapting research methods for popular use in furthering instrumental goals in the field. Some of the best descriptions of participatory action research are in Scrimshaw and Gleason's (1992:Section III) publication on rapid assessment procedures, especially in the chapters on rapid rural appraisal. Here, social scientists working with rural farmers and agricultural developers have developed innovative methods for using materials, maps, pictures, and products in the field (that is, local elicitation materials) to engage farmers in problem solving through dialogue and information collection and analysis. This produces indigenously identified improvements in farming practices. This technique has also been used as a core intervention strategy in programs of the Institute for Community Research[1] with women (on policy change), youth (on AIDS prevention), preadolescents (on homelessness and alcohol use), men (in economic development), and older adults (on the early identification and reporting of Alzheimer's disease).

Another example of iterative participatory research, in which research methods used in the formative phase were replicated for both education and data-collection purposes during the demonstration intervention stage, comes from sex-risk prevention work in Sri Lanka. There, a team of researchers (Nastasi et al. 1998) conducted ethnographic research with young adults in an urban community. Methods included narratives of sexual experience, free listing of sex behaviors, pile sorts, analysis using multidimensional scaling and cluster analysis, and an ethnographic survey. Narrative data were used to create dilemmas for group problem solving in the intervention phase, and sex terms were used in a group intervention exercise in which individual participants were asked to identify which terms were "sex" and of those, which were "risky sex." The ensuing discussions provided ethnographic data on gender differences in definitions of sex and risk. This assisted in the interpretation of the intervention results and of the data from the ethnographic survey. Publications of the Center for the Study of Organizational Change and Development (Reason and Rowan 1981; Reason 1988) are also at the forefront in delineation of these approaches. We expect to see more careful documentation of these methods, and efforts to evaluate their efficacy—in the collection of valuable ethnographic data and in the promotion of improved health, economic development, and educational practices in field settings.

Summary and Conclusions

We have presented an overview of the theories, informant selection processes, and research methods used in applied anthropology. Many of the methods are common to all cultural anthropology, but some, like rapid assessment, are more commonly used in applied anthropology. All methods must have a strong theoretical foundation that relates to the purpose of an applied project, to the theory of cultural meaning that is intended to guide the project, and to the plan for change being attempted. Applied research methods start with this theory and evolve through the interaction between expressed needs in the field, the literature on the issue, and the deepening research experience of the anthropologists and their partners in the field. The evolution of the theory, by definition, involves the collaboration of "partners in change," for without partners for whom the designated direction of change is centrally meaningful, the research will remain on the shelf. We have argued for consideration of the appropriate selection of individuals who will be able to access data critical to the success of the project. Sometimes such individuals come from the community wishing to initiate cultural change; sometimes they are from the same designated group but from another geographic location; more often than not, they are other anthropologists of different backgrounds who are committed to sharing their research and social skills to improve the quality of life in a community. Each of these individuals can serve an applied rescarch project well.

Once the initial stages of development have occurred, a multifaceted set of research and development methods driven by clearly articulated theory can be put into place. These methods are intended to do two things simultaneously: (1) produce sound data using rigorous research methods that are convincing and can guide change efforts; and (2) maintain close working relationships with the community committed to the change process. Both are necessary. The means should always be consistent with the desired ends to avoid the contradictions that can so easily destroy a project even before it begins. Whenever possible, there should be a full partnership of researchers and interventionists or policymakers (or all three) in all aspects of the research. This is important to ensure full use of the results and to ensure that people who know best how to make and act on decisions to bring about the desired change are also intimately familiar with the research that is intended to guide it.

Remember, though we may try, we cannot control conditions in field situations as we can in clinic or laboratory settings. Ethnographic methods suit field research because they offer researchers and their partners a greater degree of methodological flexibility to respond to new circumstances as they arise. Furthermore, ethnography, while guided by general theoretical principles, gives high value to inductive or localized theory building. Local theory (in interplay with more general theories of change) that is controlled (that is, developed, shared, and understood) by partners in change, is far more likely to result in positive outcomes than theory imposed from above. This is not in opposition to experimental design since we both believe in and have successfully used experimental designs in field situations. Instead, we suggest that anthropologists have much to offer the field of applied social science and interdisciplinary research because we are wedded not to specific designs and instruments, but to inquiry, exploration, and discovery that guides the most effective selection of theory, methods, and data-collection techniques for a given situation.

Finally, as applied anthropologists, we should never forget that in addition to methodological flexibility, the greatest strength of our field is that it provides ethnographers with the methods and tools to understand culturally based needs, values, perceptions, beliefs, knowledge, models, and reasons for behavior—and to use these for designing programs of change. Even with the best intentions of all partners to change, it is only with the use of these tools that a change effort is likely to result in long-term success.

NOTE

We thank Dr. James Wilce, Department of Anthropology, Northern Arizona University, for his quick review of midrange theories that are being applied in linguistic medical anthropology.

1. Projects referred to in order include: Urban Women's Development Project (USOE), Community Action Against Substance Abuse (Connecticut State Department of Mental Health), National Teen Action Research Center and Urban Mothers and Daughters Against Substance Abuse (Center for Substance Abuse Prevention), Men's Economic Development Project (AETNA Foundation), and the Puerto Rican Alzheimer's Education Project (Federal Administration on Aging).

REFERENCES

Agar, Michael. H. 1986. *Speaking of Ethnography*. Qualitative Research Methods Series, Vol. 2. Thousand Oaks, CA: Sage Publications.

Baba, Metta, and Carole Hill, eds. 1996. *The Global Practice of Anthropology*. Studies in Third World Anthropology, No. 58. Dept. of Anthropology, Williamsburg: College of William and Mary.

Bateson, Gregory. 1979. *Mind and Nature: A Necessary Unity*. New York: Dutton.

Bearison, D. J. 1982. New Directions in Studies of Social Interaction and Cognitive Growth. In *Social Cognitive Development in Context*. F. C. Serafica, ed. Pp. 199–221. New York: Guilford Press.

Berger, Peter L., and T. Luckman. 1966. *The Social Construction of Reality: A Treatise in the Sociology of Knowledge*. Garden City, NJ: Doubleday.

Bernard, H. R. 1994. *Research Methods in Anthropology: Qualitative and Quantitative Approaches*, 2d ed. Walnut Creek, CA: AltaMira Press.

Bernard H. R., and P. Killworth. 1977. Informant Accuracy in Social Network Data II. *Human Communication Research 4*:3–18.

Bernard H. R., P. Killworth, and L. Sailer. 1980. Informant Accuracy in Social Network Data IV. *Social Networks 2*:191–218.

Bernard H. R., P. Killworth, and L. Sailer. 1982. Informant Accuracy in Social Network Data V. *Social Science Research 11*:30–66.

Bernard, H. R., Pertti J. Pelto, Oswald Werner, James Boster, and A. Kimball Romney. 1986. The Construction of Primary Data in Cultural Anthropology. *Current Anthropology 27*(4):382–396.

Bieleman, B., A. Diaz, G. Merlo, and C. H. Kaplan. 1993. *Lines Across Europe. Nature and Extent of Cocaine Use in Barcelona, Rotterdam and Turin*. Amsterdam: Academic Publishing Division, Swets & Zeitkinger.

Blimes, J. 1975. Misinformation in Verbal Accounts: Some Fundamental Considerations. *Man 10*:60–71.

Borgatti, S. P., M. Everett, and L. C. Freeman. 1992. UCINET IV, Version 1.0. Columbia, SC: Analytic Technologies.

Bott, Elizabeth. 1957. *Family and Social Network: Roles, Norms and External Relationships in Ordinary Urban Families*. London: Tavistock.

Bourgois, Philippe. 1995a. *In Search of Respect: Selling Crack in El Barrio*. New York: Cambridge University Press.

Bourgois, Philippe. 1995b. Participant Observation Study of Indirect Paraphernalia Sharing/ HIV Risk in a Network of Heroin Injectors. Paper presented at the Scientific Symposium on AIDS Prevention and Drug Abuse. Sponsored by National Institutes on Drug Abuse, and the American Anthropological Association.

Brady, J. P., and E. E. Levitt. 1965. The Scalability of Sexual Experiences. *Psychological Record 15*:275–279.

Bronfenbrenner, Ury. 1977. Toward an Experimental Ecology of Human Development. *American Psychologist 32*:513–531.

Campbell, Donald T., and J. C. Stanley. 1963. *Experimental and Quasi-Experimental Designs for Research*. Chicago: Rand McNally.

Castillo, C. O., and J. H. Geer. 1993. Ambiguous Stimuli: Sex in the Eye of the Beholder. *Archives of Sexual Behavior 22*:131–143.

Chambers, Erve. 1985. Applied Anthropology in the Post-Vietnam Era: Anticipations and Ironies. *Annual Review of Anthropology 16*:309–337.

Chavez, L. R., F. A. Hubbell, J. M. McMullin, R. G. Martinez, and S. I. Mishra. 1995. Structure and Meaning in Models of Breast and Cervical-Cancer Risk-Factors: A Comparison of Perceptions among Latinas, Anglo Women, and Physicians. *Medical Anthropology Quarterly 9*(1):40–74.

City of Hartford, Department of Social Services. 1994. *Homeless Youth in Hartford*. Hartford: City of Hartford.

Clatts, Michael C. 1994. All the King's Horses and All the King's Men: Some Personal Reflections on Ten Years of AIDS Ethnography. *Human Organization 53*(1):93–95.

Cross, William J., Jr. 1990. Race and Ethnicity: Effects on Social Networks. In *Extending Families: The Social Networks of Parents and Their Children*. M. Cochran, M. Larner, D. Riley, L. Gunnarsson, and C. R. Henderson, Jr., eds. Pp. 67–85. New York: Cambridge University Press.

Curtis, R., S. R. Friedman, A. Neaigus, B. Jose, M. Goldstein, and G. Ildefonso. 1995. Street-Level Drug Markets: Network Structure and HIV Risk. *Social Networks* (17): 229–249.

Damon, W. 1983. The Nature of Social-Cognitive Change in the Developing Child. In *The Relationship Between Social and Cognitive Development*. W. S. Overton, ed. Pp. 103–141. Hillsdale, NJ: Lawrence Erlbaum.

DeVos, George, and Lola Romanucci-Ross. 1995. Ethnic Identity: A Psychocultural Perspective. In *Ethnic Identity: Creation, Conflict and Accommodation*, 3d ed. L. Romanucci-Ross and G. DeVos, eds. Pp. 349–379. Walnut Creek, CA: AltaMira Press.

Diaz, A. M. Barruti, and C. Doncel. 1992. *The Lines of Success? Study on the Nature and Extent of Cocaine Use in Barcelona*. Barcelona: Laboratory of Sociology, ICESB.

Dryfoos, Joyce G. 1990. *Adolescents at Risk: Prevalence and Prevention*. New York: Oxford University Press.

Ervin, Alexander. 1996. Collaborative and Participatory Research in Urban Social Planning and Restructuring: Anthropological Experiences from a Medium-Sized Canadian City. *Human Organization 55*(3):324–333.

Fetterman, David M. 1993. *Speaking the Language of Power: Communication, Collaboration and Advocacy (Translating Ethnography into Action)*. Washington, DC: Falmer Press.

Florio, Susan. 1997. To Tell a New Story: Reinventing Narratives of Culture, Identity and Education. *Anthropology and Education Quarterly 28*(2):152–162.

Frank, Ove, and Tom Snijders. 1994. Estimating the Size of Hidden Populations Using Snowball Sampling. *Journal of Official Statistics 10*:53–67.

Freeman, Linton C., and A. Kimball Romney. 1987. Words, Deeds, and Social Structure: A Preliminary Study of the Reliability of Informants. *Human Organization 46*(4): 330–334.

Freire, Paulo. 1995. *Pedagogy of the Oppressed*. New York: Continuum.

Gagnon, J. H., and William Simon. 1987. The Scripting of Oral-Genital Sexual Conduct. *Archives of Sexual Behavior 16*(1):1–25.

Galaskiewicz, J., and S. Wasserman. 1993. Social Network Analysis: Concepts, Methodology, and Directions for the 1990s. *Sociological Methods & Research 22*(1):3–22.

Garro, Linda. 1987. Explaining High Blood Pressure: Variation in Knowledge about Illness. *American Ethnologist 15*:98–119.

Geertz, Clifford. 1973. Thick Description: Toward an Interpretive Theory of Culture. In *The Interpretation of Cultures*. C. Geertz, ed. Pp. 3–30. New York: Basic Books.

Giordano, Patricia. 1993. Personal communication at NIMH-sponsored conference on researching violence in adolescents.

Giroux, H. A. 1981a. *Dialectics and the Development of Curriculum Theory: Ideology, Culture, and the Process of Schooling*. Philadelphia: Temple University Press.

Giroux, H. A. 1981b. *Paulo Freire's Approach to Radical Educational Theory and Practice*. In *Ideology, Culture, and the Process of Schooling*. H. A. Giroux, ed. Pp. 127–142. Philadelphia: Temple University Press.

Gladwin, C. 1989. *Ethnographic Decision Modeling*. Qualitative Research Methods Series, Vol. 19. Thousand Oaks, CA: Sage Publications.

Glaser, B. G., and A. L. Strauss. 1967. *The Discovery of Grounded Theory*. Chicago: Aldine.

Glasser, I. 1996. A Study of Homelessness in Hartford. Department of Anthropology, Eastern Connecticut State University, Willimantic, CT.

Goodwin, C., and A. Duranti. 1992. Rethinking Context: An Introduction. In *Rethinking Context: Language as an Interactive Phenomenon*. A. Duranti and C. Goodwin, eds. Pp. 1–42. Cambridge: Cambridge University Press.

Heath, Shirley B., and M. W. McLaughlin, eds. 1993. *Identity and Inner-City Youth: Beyond Ethnicity and Gender.* New York: Teachers College Press.

Hill, Carole E., ed. 1991. *Training Manual in Applied Medical Anthropology.* Special Publications No. 27. Washington, DC: American Anthropological Association.

Holmberg, Alan. 1954. Participant Intervention in the Field. *Human Organization 14*(1): 23–26.

Holmberg, Alan. 1958. The Research and Development Approach to the Study of Culture Change. *Human Organization 17*(1):12–16.

Holmberg, Alan. 1966. *Vicos: Metodo y práctica de antropología aplicada.* Investigaciones Sociales Serie: Monografías Andinas, No. 5. Lima, Editorial Estudios Andinos, S.A.

Hughes, P. H., G. K. Harvis, U. Khant, M. E. Medina-Mora, V. Navaratnam, V. Poshyachinda, and K. A. Madud. 1982. Ethnographics and Secrecy Patterns among Drug Abusers. *Bulletin on Narcotics 34*:1–14.

Institute for Community Research (ICR). 1993. *Rapid Sociodemographic Assessment Project: 13 Neighborhood Profiles.* Hartford: ICR.

Johnsen, E. C., H. R. Bernard, P. D. Killworth, G. A. Shelley, and C. McCarty. 1995. A Social Network Approach to Corroborating the Number of AIDS/HIV+ Victims in the U.S. *Social Networks 17*:167–187.

Johnson, J. C. 1990. *Selecting Ethnographic Informants.* Qualitative Research Methods Series, Vol. 22. Thousand Oaks, CA: Sage Publications.

Johnson, J. C. 1994. Anthropological Contributions to the Study of Social Networks: A Review. In *Advances in Social Network Analysis.* S. Wasserman and J. Galaskiewicz, eds. Thousand Oaks, CA: Sage Publications.

Jordan, G., and C. Weedon. 1995. *Cultural Politics: Class, Gender, Race and the Postmodern World* (see esp. Part III). Cambridge: Basil Blackwell.

Khan M. E., B. C. Patel, R. S. Hemlatha, and Sandhya Rao. 1990. *Use of Focus Groups in Social and Behavioral Research—Some Methodological Issues. Consultation on Epidemiological and Statistical Methods of Rapid Health Assessment.* Geneva: World Health Organization. E.M./CONS/R.A./90.18.

Killworth, P. D., and H. R. Bernard. 1976. Informant Accuracy in Social Network Data. *Human Organization 35*:269–286.

Killworth P. D., and H. R. Bernard. 1979. Informant Accuracy in Social Network Data III. *Social Networks 2*:19–46.

Kirk, Jerome, and Marc L. Miller. 1986. *Reliability and Validity in Qualitative Research.* Qualitative Research Methods Series, Vol. 1. Thousand Oaks, CA: Sage Publications.

Kleinman, A. 1980. *Patients and Healers in the Context of Culture.* Berkeley: University of California Press.

Klovdahl Alan S. 1989. Urban Social Networks: Some Methodological Problems and Possibilities. In *The Small World.* M. Kochen, ed. Pp. 176–210. Norwood, NJ: Ablex.

Klovdahl, A. S., J. J. Potterat, D. E. Woodhouse, J. B. Muth, S. Q. Muth, and W. W. Darrow. 1994. Social Networks and Infectious Disease: The Colorado Springs Study. *Social Science and Medicine 38*(1):79–88.

Koester, Stephen. 1994. Coping, Running, and Paraphernalia Laws: Context and High Risk Behavior. *Human Organization 53*(3):278–295.

Kozel, N. 1993. Integrating Quantitative and Qualitative Methods in Drug Abuse Surveillance. Paper presented at the 6th Iberoamerican Congress on Alcohol, Tobacco, and Drugs. Mexico City.

Leal, H., L. Mejia, L. Gómez, and Salinas de Vo. 1977. Estudio naturalístico sobre el fenómeno del consumo de inhalantes de niños de la Ciudad de México. In *Inhalación voluntaria de disolventes industriales*. Contreras, ed. Pp. 442–459. Mexico City: Trillas.

Lieberman, D., and W. Dressler. 1977. Bilingualism and Cognition of St. Lucian Disease Terms. *Medical Anthropology 1*:81–110.

Lucy, J. 1985. Whorf's View of the Linguistic Mediation of Thought. In *Semiotic Mediation*. E. Mertz and R. Parmentier, eds. Pp. 73–97. Orlando: Academic Press.

Marcus, G. E., and M.M.J. Fischer. 1986. *Anthropology as Cultural Critique*. Chicago. University of Chicago Press.

Marsden, P. V. 1990. Network Data and Measurement. *Annual Review of Sociology 16*:435–463.

Marshall, C., and G. B. Rossman. 1989. *Designing Qualitative Research*. Thousand Oaks, CA: Sage Publications.

McGrady, F. A., C. Marrow, G. Myers, M. Daniels, M. Vera, C. Mueller, E. Liebow, A. Klovdahl, and R. Lovely. 1995. A Note on Implementation of a Random-Walk Design to Study Adolescent Social Networks. *Social Networks 17*:251–255.

Medina-Mora, M. E., A. Ortiz, C. Caudillo, and S. López. 1982. Inhalación deliberada de los disolventes en un grupo de menores mexicanos. *Revista Salud Mental 5*(1):77–81.

Medina-Mora, M. E., P. Ryan, A. Ortiz, T. Campos, and A. Solis. 1980. A Methodology for Intensive Case-Finding and Monitoring of Drug Use in a Mexican Community. *Bulletin on Narcotics 32*(2):17–26.

Miles, Matthew B., and A. M. Huberman. 1994. *Qualitative Data Analysis: An Expanded Sourcebook*, 2d ed. Thousand Oaks, CA: Sage Publications.

Mitchell, J. C. 1969. The Concept and Use of Social Networks. In *Social Networks in Urban Situations*. J. C. Mitchell, ed. Manchester, England: Manchester University Press.

Morgan, D. L. 1988. *Focus Groups as Qualitative Research*. Qualitative Research Methods Series, Vol. 16. Thousand Oaks, CA: Sage Publications.

Morgan, G., ed. 1983. *Beyond Method: Strategies for Social Research*. Beverly Hills, CA: Sage Publications.

Morgen, Sandra. 1993. *Gender and Anthropology: Critical Reviews for Research and Teaching*. Washington, DC: American Anthropological Association.

Nachman, Steven R. 1984. Lies My Informants Told Me. *Journal of Anthropological Research* 40:536–555.

Nastasi, Bonnie K., Jean J. Schensul, Amarasiri de Silva, Kristen Varjas, K. Tudor Silva, Priyani Ratnayake, and Stephen Schensul. In press. A Community-Based Sexual Risk Prevention Program for Sri Lankan Youth. Influencing Sexual Risk Decison-Making. International Quarterly of Community Health Education.

Needle, Richard H., Susan L. Coyle, Stephen G. Genser, and Robert T. Trotter, II. 1995. Introduction: The Social Network Paradigm. In *Social Networks, Drug Abuse, and HIV Transmission*. R. H. Needle, S. L. Coyle, S. G. Genser, and R. T. Trotter, eds. Pp. 1–2. NIDA Research Monograph 151. Rockville, MD: USDHHS.

Parker, R. G., and J. H. Gagnon. 1995. *Conceiving Sexuality: Approaches to Sex Research in a Postmodern World*. New York: Routledge.

Pelto, Pertti J., and Gretel H. Pelto. 1978. *Anthropological Research: The Structure of Inquiry*, 2d ed. Cambridge: Cambridge University Press.

Pelto, Pertti J., and Gretel H. Pelto. 1997. Studying Knowledge, Culture and Behavior in Applied Medical Anthropology. *Medical Anthropology Quarterly* 11(2):147–163.

Pelto, Pertti J., and Jean J. Schensul. 1987. Toward a Framework for Policy Research in Anthropology. In *Applied Anthropology in America*. E. Eddy and W. L. Partridge, eds. Pp. 505–528. New York: Columbia University Press.

Pinker S. 1994. *The Language Instinct*. New York: William and Morrow.

Quinn, N., and D. Holland. 1987. *Cultural Models in Language and Thought*. New York: Cambridge University Press.

Reason, Peter, ed. 1988. *Human Inquiry in Action: Developments in New Paradigm Research*. London: Sage Publications.

Reason, Peter, and J. Rowan, eds. 1981. *Human Inquiry: A Sourcebook of New Paradigm Research*. Chichester, England: Wiley.

Rogoff, B. 1990. *Apprenticeship in Thinking: Cognitive Development in Social Context*. New York: Oxford University Press.

Romanucci-Ross, Lola, and George DeVos. 1995. *Ethnic Identity: Creation, Conflict and Accommodation*, 3d ed. Walnut Creek, CA: AltaMira Press.

Romney, A. Kimball, W. H. Batchelder, and Susan C. Weller. 1987. Recent Applications of Consensus Theory. *American Behavioral Science* 31(2):163–177.

Romney, A. Kimball, Susan C. Weller, and W. H. Batchelder. 1986. Culture as Con-sensus: A Theory of Cultural and Informant Accuracy. *American Anthropologist* 88(2): 313–338.

Schensul, Jean J. 1985. Systems Consistency in Field Research, Dissemination and Social Change. In *Collaborative Research and Social Policy*. Special Issue of *American Behavioral Scientist*. J. Schensul and G. Stern, eds. Vol. 29(2):186–204.

Schensul, Jean J., D. Donelli-Hess, M. D. Borrero, and M. P. Bhavati. 1987. Urban Comadronas: Maternal and Child Health Research and Policy Formulation in a Puerto Rican Community. In *Collaborative Research and Social Change*. D. Stull and J. Schensul, eds. Pp. 9–32. Boulder: Westview Press.

Schensul, Jean J. 1998a. Community-Based Intervention with Urban Youth. Miniseries edited by B. Nastasi. *Journal of School Psychology*, Vol. 2, in press.

Schensul, Jean J. 1998b. Focused Group Interviews. In *Enhanced Ethnographic Methods*, Ethnographer's Toolkit, Vol. 3. J. Schensul and M. LeCompte, eds. Walnut Creek, CA: AltaMira Press.

Schensul, Jean J. 1998c. Learning about Sexual Meaning and Decision-Making from Urban Youth. In *Cross-Cultural Perspectives of Women's Sexual Decision Making: Implications for Sexual Health Protection at the Community Level*. Special issue of the *International Quarterly of Community Health Education*. M. Idaliz Torres and Margaret Weeks, eds.

Schensul, Jean J., and Marlene Berg. 1997. Using Process Evaluation to Enhance Facilitation Skills in Prevention Staffing. Invited paper in CSAP evaluation conference, Washington, DC.

Schensul, Jean J., Donna Donelli-Hess, Maria D. Borrero, and M. P. Bhavati. 1987. Urban Comadronas: Maternal and Child Health Research and Policy Formulation in a Puerto Rican Community. In *Collaborative Research and Social Change*. D. Stull and J. Schensul, eds. Pp. 9–32. Boulder: Westview Press.

Schensul, Jean J., and Margaret D. LeCompte, eds. In press. The Ethnographer's Toolkit. 7 volumes. Walnut Creek, CA: AltaMira Press.

Schensul, Jean J., and Stephen L. Schensul. 1992. Collaborative Research. In *Handbook on Qualitative Research Methods in Education*. Judith Goetz and Margaret D. LeCompte. Pp. 161–200. New York: Academic Press.

Schensul, Jean J., Miriam Torres, and Terrie Wetle. 1993. *The Latino Alzheimers Education Project: Training Curriculum*. Hartford: Institute for Community Research.

Schensul, Jean J., Steven Truscott, Sandra Sydlo, and David Robinson. 1997. *The National Teen Action Research Center: Concept Paper*. Hartford: Institute for Community Research.

Schensul, Stephen L. 1985. Science, Theory and Application in Anthropology. In *Collaborative Research and Social Policy*. Special issue of *American Behavioral Scientist*. J. Schensul and G. Stern, eds. Vol. 29(2):164–185.

Schensul, Stephen L., and Jean J. Schensul. 1978. Advocacy and Applied Anthropology. In *Social Scientists as Advocates*. G. H. Weber and G. J. McCall, eds. Pp. 121–166. Beverly Hills, CA: Sage Publications.

Schensul, Stephen L., and Jean J. Schensul, 1982. Helping Resource Use in a Puerto Rican Community. *Urban Anthropology 11*(1):59–80.

Schensul, Stephen L., Jean J. Schensul, and Mario Zegarra. 1985. Mapping Community Development and Community Health in Lima's Shantytowns. Paper presented at annual meeting of American Anthropological Association; report to University of Connecticut Research Foundation and Universidad de Cayetano Heredia, Lima, Peru.

Scheper-Hughes, Nancy. 1989. Three Propositions for a Critically Applied Medical Anthropology. *Kroeber Anthropological Society Papers 69–70*:62–77.

Scott, J. 1991. *Social Network Analysis: A Handbook*. London: Sage Publications.

Scrimshaw, Nevin S., and G. R. Gleason, eds. 1992. *RAP: Rapid Assessment Procedures: Qualitative Methodologies for Planning and Evaluation of Health-Related Programs.* Boston: International Nutritional Foundation for Developing Countries (INDFC).

Scrimshaw, Susan, C. M. 1992. The Adaptation of Anthropological Methodologies to Rapid Assessment of Nutrition and Primary Health Care. In *RAP: Rapid Assessment Procedures: Qualitative Methodologies for Planning and Evaluation of Health-Related Programs.* N. S. Scrimshaw and G. R. Gleason, eds. Pp. 25–38. Boston: International Nutritional Foundation for Developing Countries (INDFC).

Shelley G. A., H. R. Bernard, P. D. Killworth, E. Johnsen, and C. McCarty. 1995. Who Knows Your HIV Status? What HIV+ Patients and Their Network Members Know About Each Other. *Social Networks 17*:189–217.

Singer, Merrill, and Hans Baer. 1995. *Critical Medical Anthropology.* Amityville, NY: Baywood Publishing.

Singer, Merrill, Ray Irizarry, and Jean J. Schensul. 1991. Needle Access as an AIDS Prevention Strategy for IV Drug Users: A Research Perspective. *Human Organization 50*(2):142–153.

Spradley, James P. 1979. *The Ethnographic Interview.* New York: Holt, Rinehart and Winston.

Strauss, Anselm L. 1985. *Qualitative Analysis for Social Scientists.* Cambridge: Cambridge University Press.

Strauss, Anselm L., and J. Corbin. 1990. *Basics of Qualitative Research.* Thousand Oaks, CA: Sage Publications.

Stringer, E. T. 1996. *Action Research: A Handbook for Practitioners.* Thousand Oaks, CA: Sage Publications.

Stull, Donald, and Jean J. Schensul. 1987. *Collaborative Research and Social Change.* Boulder: Westview.

Szalay, L. B., A. Inn, J. B. Strohl, and L. C. Wilson. 1993. Perceived Harm, Age, and Drug Use: Perceptual and Motivational Dispositions Affecting Drug Use. *Journal of Drug Education 23*:333–356.

Tax, Sol. 1960. Action Anthropology. In *Documentary History of the Fox Project.* Department of Anthropology, Chicago: University of Chicago.

Trawick, M. 1988. Spirits and Voices in Tamil Songs. *American Ethnologist 15*: 193–215.

Trotter, Robert T., II. 1991. Ethnographic Research Methods for Applied Medical Anthropology. In *Training Manual in Applied Medical Anthropology.* C. E. Hill, ed. Pp. 180–212. American Anthropological Association Special Publications No. 27. Washington, DC: American Anthropological Association.

Trotter, Robert T., II. 1995. Drug Use, AIDS, and Ethnography: Advanced Ethnographic Research Methods Exploring the HIV Epidemic. In *Qualitative Methods in Drug Abuse and HIV Research.* Pp. 38–64. NIDA Monograph Series No. 157. Washington, DC: National Institute on Drug Abuse, NIH.

Trotter, Robert T., II. 1996. Communication and Community Participation in Program Evaluation Processes. In *Advanced Methodological Issues in Culturally Competent Evaluation for Substance Abuse Prevention*. Ada-Helen Bayer, Frances Larry Brisbane, and Amelie Ramirez, eds. Pp. 241–266. CSAP Cultural Competence Series (No. 6). DHHS Publication No. (SMA) 96–3110.

Trotter, Robert T., II. 1997. Anthropological Midrange Theories in Mental Health Research: Selected Theory, Methods and Systematic Approaches to At-Risk Populations. *Ethos* 25(2):259–274.

Trotter, Robert T., II, and James M. Potter. 1993. Pile Sorts, A Cognitive Anthropological Model of Drug and AIDS Risks for Navajo Teenagers: Assessment of a New Evaluation Tool. *Drugs and Society* 7(3/4):23–39.

Trotter, Robert T., II, A. M. Bowen, J. M. Potter, and D. Jiron. 1994. Enfoques ethnográficos y anlisis de las redes sociales, par la creación de programas de prevención del uso de drogas y de MIH, in usarios activos. In *Las addicciones: Hacía un enfoque multi-disciplinario*. A. Rotiz, ed. Pp. 45–53. Mexico City: Secretaría de Salud, Subsecretaría de Coordinación y Desarrollo, Consejo Nacional Contra las Addicciones.

Trotter, Robert T., II, Julie A. Baldwin, and Anne M. Bowen. 1995a. Network Structure and Proxy Network Measures of HIV, Drug and Incarceration Risks for Active Drug Users. *Connections* 18(1):89–104.

Trotter, Robert T., II, Anne M. Bowen, and James M. Potter. 1995b. Network Models for HIV Outreach and Prevention Programs of Drug Users. In *Social Networks, Drug Abuse, and HIV Transmission*. R. H. Needle, S. L. Coyle, S. G. Genser, R. T. Trotter, II, eds. Pp. 144–180. NIDA Research Monograph 151. USDHHS. Rockville, MD: National Institute on Drug Abuse.

Trotter, Robert T., II, Richard B. Rothenberg, and Susan Coyle. 1995c. Drug Abuse and HIV Prevention Research: Expanding Paradigms and Network Contributions to Risk Reduction. *Connections* 18(1):29–46.

Trotter, Robert T., II, Anne M. Bowen, Julie A. Baldwin, and Laurie J. Price. 1996. The Efficacy of Network Based HIV/AIDS Risk Reduction Programs in Midsized Towns in the United States. *Journal of Drug Issues* 26(3):591–606.

Van Willigen, John. 1993. *Applied Anthropology: An Introduction*. Westport, CT: Bergin and Garvey.

Verschueren, J. 1995. The Pragmatic Return to Meaning: Notes on the Dynamics of Communication, Degrees of Salience, and Communicative Transparence. *Journal of Linguistic Anthropology* 5(2):127–156.

Vygotsky, L. S. 1978. *Mind in Society: The Development of Higher Psychological Processes*. Cambridge: Harvard University Press.

Wasserman, Stanley, and K. Faust. 1993. *Social Network Analysis: Methods and Applications*. New York: Cambridge University Press.

Watters, John K., and Peter Biernacki. 1989. Targeted Sampling: Options for the Study of Hidden Populations. *Social Problems* 36(4):17–18.

Weeks, Margaret R., and Jean J. Schensul. 1993. Ethnographic Research on AIDS Risk Behavior and the Making of Policy. In *Speaking the Language of Power: Communication, Collaboration and Advocacy.* D. Fetterman, ed. Pp. 50–69. Washington, DC: Falmer Press.

Weitzman, E. A., and M. B. Miles. 1995. *Computer Programs for Qualitative Data Analysis.* Thousand Oaks, CA: Sage Publications.

Weller, Susan C. 1984. Consistency and Consensus among Informants: Disease Concepts in a Rural Mexican Town. *American Anthropologist 86*(4):966–975.

Weller, Susan C., Lee M. Pachter, Robert. T. Trotter, II, and Roberta D. Baer. 1993. Empacho in Four Latino Groups: A Study of Intra- and Inter-Cultural Variation in Beliefs. *Medical Anthropology 15*:109–136.

Weller, Susan C., A. Kimball Romney, and D. P. Orr. 1986. The Myth of a Sub-Culture of Corporal Punishment. *Human Organization 46*:39–47.

Weller, Susan C., and A. K. Romney. 1988. *Systematic Data Collection.* Qualitative Research Methods Series, Vol. 10. Thousand Oaks, CA: Sage Publications.

Werner, Oswald, and G. M. Schoepfle. 1987. *Systematic Fieldwork: Ethnographic Analysis and Data Management*, Vol. 2. Thousand Oaks, CA: Sage Publications.

Wertsch, J. V. 1991. *Voices of the Mind: A Sociocultural Approach to Mediated Action.* Cambridge: Harvard University Press.

Whyte, William F., ed. 1991. *Participatory Action Research.* Thousand Oaks, CA: Sage Publications.

World Health Organization (WHO). 1993. *Focused Ethnographic Study of Acute Respiratory Infections.* Geneva: WHO/ARI.

Nineteen

Presenting Anthropology to Diverse Audiences

In this chapter I assume that I am mainly addressing cultural anthropologists and that many or most readers will be academics and graduate students. I draw on a career that goes back to 1962, when I was an undergraduate anthropology major at Columbia College of Columbia University and had my first field experience in Arembepe, Bahia, Brazil. I got my Ph.D. from Columbia in 1966, did postdoctoral fieldwork in Madagascar, and in January 1968—direct from Madagascar—joined the faculty of the University of Michigan, where I have remained. During the more than 30 years since then, I have addressed, through writing and speaking, many different audiences. Since 1981, in addition to academic anthropology, I have done applied anthropology, working as a consultant to organizations such as USAID and the World Bank.

This experience is the basis for what follows. I offer several observations and suggestions, not all of which I have adhered to consistently. My aim is to suggest ways of writing and speaking that are appropriate to contexts into which cultural anthropologists enter regularly. I have never worked in a museum, made a film, or collected music in the field. I do have ideas about dos and don'ts in ethnographic film making and museum displays, but I won't say much about those here, leaving such comments for those with more expertise in those areas.

Writing Anthropology

Cultural anthropology is a book field. This means that ethnologists are expected to write books as well as articles. One implication is that if someone wants to get tenure at a major university, he or she needs to have an academic book published (articles, too, preferably). Other subfields of anthropology are or have been article fields. This means that one can get tenure with a series of articles in respected, refereed journals in which manuscripts are submitted independently (rather than being solicited) and sent out for peer review. Linguistic anthropology used to be an article field but has become more of a book field. Biological anthropology is still mainly an article field.

Ideally, the first book should be an academic book (see below) that demonstrates the author's special knowledge and skills at research, analysis, and interpretation. Often, this book is a revision of a doctoral dissertation. When graduate students defend their dissertations, their committee members typically suggest ways of turning the dissertation into a book and/or a series of articles. After the recent Ph.D. anthropologist incorporates at least some of the committee's suggestions, he or she usually submits the revised manuscript to a university press or to a monographs series. Such series often have one or more anthropologists who function as acquiring editors. They may read the manuscript and suggest further revision before sending it out for review. Acquiring editors who are not anthropologists often request a prospectus and sample chapter(s) rather than the entire manuscript. They send these to one or two trusted reviewers for a quick response. If favorable, the manuscript is sent to two or three external reviewers who read the work, recommend for or against publication, and suggest further revisions. Given generally positive reviews, the author and editor work together on a revision plan, and the book eventually goes into production. Such a book is rarely published less than two years after the dissertation defense. Normally, a second printed book, based on a different research project or body of work, is needed (along with articles) for promotion to the rank of professor. These books and articles need to be aimed at an academic audience and to have gone through peer review.

Once these hurdles are passed (or before, in some cases), the anthropologist can consider other forms of writing. Anthropologists mainly write three kinds of books: trade, text, and academic books.

Trade Books

I have never written a trade book, but many anthropologists have. (See Richardson [1990] for an account of a trade book author's experience.) Cultural anthropologists who have been or are successful trade book authors include Margaret Mead, Ruth Benedict, Marvin Harris, and Oscar Lewis. Some anthropologists have agents, who are useful in negotiating trade book contracts—not so necessary or useful for other kinds of books, such as texts. No cultural anthropologist has dominated the trade market as did Mead. One reason for Mead's fame was her use of multimedia—books, magazines, films, television, radio, and public lectures. Another reason was her unique ability to bring lessons from other cultures to bear on discussions of social issues and cultural change in the United States. The range of interesting topics she dealt with also attracted attention: sex, gender, adolescence, sex education, child rearing, and intergenerational relations. Since Mead's passing, biological anthropologists have been more successful in trade publishing than have cultural anthropologists. Examples of biological anthropologists include Ashley Montagu, Richard Leakey, Donald Johanson, and Jane Goodall.

In general, it isn't possible to write a book for more than one audience. You have to identify a group (for example, college students, educated nonspecialists, lay readers) and write for it. A trade book (for example, Marvin Harris's *Cows, Pigs, Wars, and Witches* [1974], or *Cannibals and Kings* [1977]) may find a college audience, but a book written for college students rarely crosses over to the trade market.

Initially, I tried to sell *Assault on Paradise* (1992) as a trade book. But this case study of social change in a Brazilian fishing community was too case specific and too anthropological for a trade audience. It had too much data about issues not of overwhelming interest to the general public, even the educated public. After being rejected by a trade publisher, I offered the manuscript to the publisher of my textbooks. *Assault on Paradise* is used widely as a readable case study of social change. It's appropriate for its audience because it has case material illustrating topics typically covered in introductory anthropology courses, such as race, class, economics, kinship and marriage, religion, culture and personality, and social change. Like other popular case studies (also known as "supplemental texts") used in introductory courses, such as *Nisa* (Shostak 1981) and *Yanomamo* (Chagnon 1992), *Assault* departs somewhat from traditional ethnographic writing, using such literary conventions as a cast of characters that includes the ethnographer(s), first-person narration and occasional dialogue. Some other widely assigned case studies are: *Return to Laughter* (Bowen 1964), *The Harmless People* (Marshall Thomas 1958), *The Forest People* (Turnbull 1964), *The Mountain People* (Turnbull 1971), and *Maps and Dreams* (Brody 1981).

Textbooks

Not everyone can write a textbook. To do one in general (four-field) anthropology one needs a background in all four subfields, and a decreasing number of departments are providing such training. Another option is for the general text to have coauthors with different subdisciplinary backgrounds. But such a book will lack a uniform, coherent voice.

I believe that effective textbooks are based on up-to-date teaching experience. I've taught introductory general anthropology at the University of Michigan for 30 years and still teach it once a year—to 350–500 students. The first edition of my textbook *Anthropology: The Exploration of Human Diversity* (7th ed., 1997a), which covers "four-field anthropology," was published in 1974. That book has been the basis of spin-off texts—*Cultural Anthropology* (1994), *Mirror for Humanity: A Concise Introduction to Cultural Anthropology* (1996), and, most recently, the custom-published text *Cultural Anthropology: The Exploration of Human Diversity* (1997b). Other general anthropology texts, such as those by Carol and Melvin Ember (1993), William Haviland (1996), and Marvin Harris (1997) all have at least a cultural anthropology text as a spinoff.

How does one get to be a textbook writer? Names of potential authors are often sent to a college division acquiring editor by a sales representative after a campus visit. The aspiring author will have to provide an outline, prospectus, and writing samples. Often a sample chapter will be sent out for review if the editor is interested and thinks the book has a market niche. If reviews are positive, a textbook may be born. Most proposals sent to college divisions are rejected. If the acquiring editor deems the book unmarketable, he or she may send it back, suggesting the author try a university press. (Note that even university presses are now focusing increasingly on sales potential.)

Experienced textbook authors also face a review process. Before an edition is revised, the current one is reviewed by several actual and potential users (for example, instructors of introductory cultural anthropology), who make suggestions for revision—usually to add something. Sometimes new chapters are reviewed as a textbook is being written or revised. How does one respond to and use such prepublication reviews? I pay special attention to recurrent comments and criticisms made by more than one reviewer. I also accept suggestions I agree with, even if made by a single reviewer. I generally reject suggestions with which I disagree if they come from a single reviewer (unless my editor convinces me that the reviewer is onto something). Often, reviewers who are specialists want more detail than a textbook needs. If you follow their suggestions, your book will be too advanced for your target audience. As new material and topics are added, texts tend to get too long. If the book is not to become unwieldy, one must cut as well as add; this means constantly rethinking what is basic to the field.

The used-book machine is the engine driving the college textbook market today. Textbook authors are well aware of the economics of the industry. Used-book buying has been centralized and computerized, so books used anywhere in the country can be shipped to a bookstore anywhere else. Students can even shop for used books on the Internet. New book sales are only significant the first year of publication —then the used books kick in. It becomes less and less profitable for publishers to do textbooks, especially when students and instructors have become accustomed to color, modern graphics, and a support package of pedagogical aids. Two- and three-year revision cycles have become common as a way of producing new sales. Fortunately, anthropology has been changing rapidly enough to justify the new editions.

In the used book market, books may be bought back for as little as 10% of the original sales price, then sold to the next student at 75% the price of the book new. Bookstores usually profit more from selling used copies than new books because of the higher markup on used books. The authors and publishers who produce the books get nothing from the resale of their intellectual property.

Doing a successful text means writing for a known target audience—usually first- and second-year college students—taking an introductory course in some field. Fields with multiple texts include general anthropology, cultural anthropology, anthropological archaeology, and biological anthropology. Some smaller fields with introductory texts include survey of world cultures, sociolinguistics, medical anthropology, human evolution, human genetics, Old and New World prehistory, etc. The textbook author should aim for the reading level of the target audience. Writing programs like Grammatik, now part of some word processors, enable you to check reading (grade) level and make suggestions for improving readability, for example, by shortening sentences and eliminating obscure words and passive constructions.

Students are the target audience, but so are the professors who decide which texts to use. Instructors choose textbooks they like and feel comfortable using. Good texts have most of the following features: up-to-date scholarship; accessible prose and interesting writing (texts can be low level but boring); visual appeal; and illustrations that have pedagogical (not just decorative) value. Most texts have interesting boxes and various kinds of study aids (chapter summaries, study questions, suggested reading, study guides). The readable case study (for example, *Nisa, Yanomamo, Assault on Paradise*) and the article anthology (for example, Podolefsky and Brown 1994; Spradley and McCurdy 1994; Angeloni 1996) are also standard parts of introductory curricula in general and cultural anthropology.

Contemporary anthropology teachers continue to present the field as a mirror for humanity: By looking at people in other cultures, we can learn more about ourselves. The centrality of discussions of race, language, culture, and mind is part of the Boasian foundation of U.S. anthropology. Marvin Harris has commented at American Anthropological Association meetings that his introductory textbook (and mine) have their roots in the introductory anthropology course we both took (almost a generation apart) at Columbia University. This course can be traced back to Franz Boas—in Harris's case through Charles Wagley, his teacher; in mine, through Lambros Comitas. The framework of that course (and its transformations at Berkeley, Pennsylvania, and Yale) has remained remarkably constant and continues as the framework for most textbooks in introductory, general, four-field anthropology.

Most introductory anthropology teachers think, even if they don't fully articulate it, that their task is to present certain basics of a reasonably systematic, distinctive, and useful field of study. We introductory (four-field) teachers feel comfortable with what we take to be a basic set of issues and an agreed-on content in (general) anthropology. Because of this, textbook authors have learned—through numerous revisions—that certain chapters have to be included (although they should be as independent of each other as possible, so that instructors can assign them out of order). Some of the key chapters are "Evolution and Genetics," "The Primates," "Hominid Evolution" (often covered in two chapters focusing respectively on earlier and later hominids), "Human Biological Variation," "Culture," "Language," "Economic Organization," "Marriage," "Kinship," and "Religion."

Although particular instructors want new and different features and use textbooks differently, the basic course has remained remarkably stable. The organization and content of the most-used textbooks reveal what anthropology is about. Experimental texts usually don't do very well. To stray too far from the familiar is to be over-innnovative and to risk poor sales. Constant updating is fine, particularly inclusion of new fossil or archeological finds, or discussions of "hot topics" such as gender and ethnicity—but only when those topics are clearly related to anthropology's traditional subject matter. New—"innovative"—chapters should be added with care—anthropologists may be miffed when a chapter is added that they don't see as part of the core (like the chapter on American culture I added to my second edition, which I now include only as an appendix).

Professional (Academic) Books

Academic ("scholarly") books (a.k.a. books that almost no one will read) are usually submitted to a university press. Here again, an acquiring editor is the initial gatekeeper who decides if the manuscript merits a review. Presses often have consulting editors, series editors, or advisory committees to take the first professional look at such submissions. If manuscripts are sent out for review, those reviews are called reader reports. Usually, a manuscript's fate rests with these readers. Anthropologists are notable for their divergent views. (This is true among manuscript and book reviewers as well as in grant proposal reviews—see below.)

Academic books are supposed to make some kind of contribution to "theory," a term that means very different things to different cultural anthropologists. By definition, theory may refer to: (1) "a coherent group of general propositions used as principles of explanation for a class of phenomena" or (2) "the branch of a science or art that deals with its principles or methods, as distinguished from its practice" (Stein 1982:1362). The second sense is the basis of the distinction between "theoretical" (academic) and "applied" (practicing) anthropology.

With respect to the first meaning, a generation ago "ethnological theory" meant an established set of isms: evolutionism, diffusionism, historical particularism, functionalism, structuralism, etc. For many anthropologists today, the fashionable jargon reflects concepts borrowed from literary criticism—words like "contesting," "resistance," "privileging," "grounded," "theorized," "interlocutor," "discourse," "dialogic," "hegemonic," and "subaltern." Examine any recent program of the American Anthropological Association or almost any journal in cultural anthropology. You will find titles like "Contesting Hegemonic Domination: Trade and Barter in Postcolonial India." This title illustrates the most common format for an article or paper title in cultural anthropology, featuring a precolonic phrase. When you write for insiders, you must, to some extent, show that you share the norms and knowledge of the culture of academic anthropology.

Those norms have changed. Fifteen years ago, titles were more straightforward, less playful-literary: "Coffee Production in a Peruvian Valley," "Modes of Production and Anthropology of Labor," and so on. The pattern of Title-colon-Subtitle is now the rule in cultural anthropology. Norms change across the field, but more so in certain venues than in others. If you aim to publish in a particular journal, you should determine its current conventions and make sure your subject, treatment, language, and style are right for that journal. An article that's called "Empowering *Homo erectus:* The Dialogics of Oppression and Resistance in a Lower Paleolithic Population" probably won't fly at the *American Journal of Physical Anthropology.*

Much (though certainly not all) academic writing is bad writing. Deplorably, some professors reward it and perpetuate it among their students. I have worked with graduate students who entered our program as excellent writers and whose writing has subsequently been contaminated by purveyors of jargon, name dropping, and complicated prose that may obscure either simple or complex thoughts. I warn graduate students about this hazard and urge them to "eschew obfuscation."

Although an academic book may appeal mainly to specialists (such as geographic area specialists), it will reach a wider academic audience if you address theoretical, methodological, historical, or comparative issues beyond the specific case and area. In general, an anthropological work should place a case study in a broader context through comparison with material from other areas and/or by showing its relation to theory. A killing review in a major journal might say "This book is of interest only to area specialists" (although this is exactly the audience you want to reach if you are publishing in a journal like *Oceania)*. Academic books aimed at anthropologists should have something to say to as many anthropologists as possible.

As I noted, anthropologist reviewers (of books, articles, and grant proposals) are notoriously divergent in their views. When I served on the NSF cultural anthropology panel, I was shocked by the variability in reviewers' scores and comments for the same proposal. For some proposals, scores ranged from excellent (5) to poor (1). A competent and experienced editor or series editor will help you assess and balance variable reader reports and decide which revisions to make and which suggestions to ignore.

Articles

Refereed Journals

Junior faculty seeking tenure should publish in refereed (peer-reviewed) journals. The major ones for cultural anthropologists include *American Ethnologist, American Anthropologist, Ethnology, Journal of Anthropological Research, Current Anthropology, Cultural Anthropology, Human Organization, Human Ecology,* and the *Journal of the Royal Anthropological Institute,* which has been titled both JRAI and *Man.* Other potential venues include area studies journals, such as the *Journal of Southeast Asian Studies* or *Latin American Research Review.* All these journals share the canons of academic books. They offer variable speed of publication since your manuscript will normally be sent to three readers who have little incentive (other than intrinsic interest) to read it. Usually, the readers' reports, if generally favorable, will require at least minor revisions. The editor's specialty can make him or her more or less receptive to your article. If the editor is in the same field as you and likes your article, he or she may pay less attention to readers, prod them to speed up the review, and decide to publish even if the reviews are mixed. If reviewers aren't prodded, it can take longer to get an article out than a book.

Collections

Many collections originate in conferences and are uneven. Some are solicited, as in the book you are now reading. Generally, such edited volumes are reviewed for academic presses, so they are refereed, but there is less independent effort here (someone you know asks you to contribute) than when you submit a journal article; it wasn't your original idea to begin with. Chapters in books carry less prestige for promotion.

Popular Articles

Cultural anthropologists have not been very successful recently in writing for the larger audience of educated nonspecialists. It is uncommon to see a piece by an anthropologist in *The New York Times Magazine, The New Yorker, Harper's,* or *Atlantic Monthly.* Anthropologists do publish in *Natural History, Psychology Today, Discover,* and *The New York Review of Books.* Since Margaret Mead, however, cultural anthropology has produced no "popularizer" comparable to Stephen Jay Gould, who writes a column for *Natural History;* his columns are then collected to yield paperback trade books. (Given the paucity of anthropologist popularizers, the Anthropology and Media award of the American Anthropological Association often goes to nonanthropologists, such as Gould.) One strategy for popular writing is to use an anthropological approach or perspective derived from studying other cultures to interpret or explain aspects of contemporary American culture, such as fast food, sports, and the media. Another strategy is to focus on a problem affecting a traditional anthropological population (endangered natives or rainforests)—but avoid whining. Suggest solutions, so that readers can get involved, rather than merely throwing up their hands in despair.

Grant Proposals

Grant proposals are vehicles for addressing highly critical colleagues. I have served on the NSF Cultural Anthropology panel and have been awarded grants from NSF, NIMH, and NASA (for satellite imagery and on-the-ground research in areas of increasing deforestation in Madagascar). Based on this experience, I conclude that any grant proposal should answer four key questions:

1. **Why this topic/problem?** Funds, after all, are limited; reviewers and panelists determine which projects are worthy of funding. The grant writer must convince them that the topic is important—more so than other topics being proposed for funding at the same time.
2. **Why this place?** The topic may be important, but why study it in the place proposed? Some topics make sense in certain locales but not others; the grant writer must show the connection. For example, it was easy for me to justify research on the cultural impact of television in Brazil because that country has the world's most watched commercial television network, with national penetration. It would not have made much sense for me to study television in Madagascar, where sets and transmissions reach a limited audience—mainly urban.
3. **Why this person?** With the proliferation of anthropologists, it is not uncommon to come across two people who want to study similar topics in the same country. Especially in that event, but in any case, it is important to identify the special qualifications of the person who proposes to do this research in this place. Relevant here are such background factors as: a history of residing in the country, language training or fluency, pilot research in the proposed project locale, experience elsewhere with the topic or method, etc.
4. **How will the study be done?** Grant proposals in cultural anthropology are notoriously weak in formulation and discussion of methods. Applicants should take the methods section very seriously, particularly sampling design. Books like *Anthropological Research: The Structure of Inquiry* by Pertti and Gretel Pelto (1978) and especially H. Russell Bernard's *Research Methods in Cultural Anthropology* (1994) have allowed anthropology methods courses to burgeon in colleges and universities. (Methods camps and workshops supported by NSF also helped raise our methodological awareness.) But I've heard and read comments by grant program officers and panelists that anthropologists still need to give more serious attention to sampling design. Too many say they're planning to use network sampling or snowball sampling rather than one of the random procedures described in the Bernard and Pelto books. Random sampling designs allow greater inference and are used more widely in the other social sciences.

The reader of a grant proposal (as of an article or book) should know certain things after reading the abstract and a few pages: What's the topic/problem? What's the research plan? What's going to be tested and how? Why is this research important? Where and when will it happen? Is the person proposing it qualified to do it? How will he or she do it? It's amazing how much wheel spinning there often is in the first few pages of grant proposals. The lesson is get moving at once; don't waste the reader's time. (And don't irritate the reader's eyes with a small font or right justification—proven harder to read.) Addressing these questions systematically is especially important when submitting proposals to the more scientifically oriented funding sources, including NSF and NIMH. Knowing your audience means paying attention to the names and missions of particular agencies, such as the National Science Foundation. Not all agencies that fund anthropologists have science as their mandate—but you must always justify your topic, setting, and qualifications and say what you propose to do and how, even if you don't plan to use scientific methods.

Audiences

For *any kind* of presentation, written or oral, know your audience and address it. Before you submit an article to a journal, scope out that journal to see what recent articles are like. Before you give a "job talk," find out all you can about what is being sought and make sure your talk addresses that need. Read the ad and talk to members of the search committee about the topics and issues of interest to them. It's usually not worth your time to apply for positions you don't fit. If an ad calls for an Africanist and you work in the Middle East, don't apply. If the ad says Africanist, give your talk about Africa, not some other place you've worked. And if the ad says economic anthropology, don't give a talk about religion.

Accept your audience. Don't address the audience you'd like to have instead of the one you do have. In writing, it's usually a mistake to try to write for more than one audience. If you do, you probably won't reach either or any of them as well as you will if you are more targeted. Resist the tendency to try to change your audience. If it expects certain styles and conventions, give them that style and those conventions. For example, there is a culture of "giving papers" at meetings among anthropologists, who read their papers. Cultural anthropologists typically read aloud, rather than talking or giving a presentation, using slides or transparencies. A few years ago, I vowed to never again *read* a paper at a AAA meeting because I think read papers are boring and hard to follow. (The vow was culturally inappropriate but hasn't yet caused me grief. However, departing from tradition can be riskier for someone with less lecturing experience or at a more junior level.)

I talk rather than read. I also use this approach—talking with no notes or minimal ones—in my college and graduate teaching. This lecture style requires a good memory, but memories can be trained. How does one lecture without a text or notes? Simply reduce the memory aids you take to class; you'll probably get the hang of it eventually.

One comment I sometimes get from students exposed to this style is that my lectures could be better organized. To address this criticism, I've started using minimalist transparencies—rarely more than two or three—in very large font—for a one and a half hour lecture. The topics I plan to cover are outlined, but I talk, rather than read, about each one in order.

Anthropologists use different techniques to make their presentations at meetings and conferences interesting. My colleague Ruth Behar, a gifted author who has mastered trade book writing and poetry, among other genres, tells me she does read her papers aloud but has learned how to read them dramatically. Anthropologists must pay more attention to delivery at meetings. It's embarrassing to see a novice anthropologist (or even an occasional senior one) rush through a too-long text that's been written for the eyes rather than for the ears.

E-Mail

Specific communicative practices develop in different media. One equalizing feature of cyberspeak (the range of styles and conventions people use when they write messages in cyberspace) is its informality compared with print. Language is neither as fixed nor as precise as it is in writing for print. Cyberwriters aren't as concerned with typos as print writers are. Writing exclusively in capital letters (using the Caps Lock key) is bad form ("shouting"). Lower-case letters are proper, and some people hardly use "caps" at all. Cyberspeak, including e-mail, reflecting an origin in ham radio, has its own abbreviations (BTW—by the way; IMHO—in my humble opinion; how r u?) and combinations of diacritical symbols (emoticons) to express various degrees of pleasure or displeasure.

Use e-mail with care. If you get a message that's at all problematic, don't answer it right away, except perhaps to say "I'll get back to you on this." E-mail often cannot be undone, once a message is sent. Think over your response, ideally for a day.

E-mail makes your writing seem blunter than you may want it to be. You may want to soften it with "pleases," exclamation points, or smiley faces. Again, know your audience—don't write family members or good friends with the same impersonal style you use for university correspondence. Long e-mail messages may be okay between family and friends, but can be irritating in professional e-mail. (BTW—also avoid leaving long voice mail and answering-machine messages. And always repeat your phone number or say it slowly.)

Talking about Anthropology

Most of us probably spend more time presenting anthropology through talking than through writing. Most communication with our colleagues and students is by talking or through e-mail. If you're like me, you'll be constantly explaining the nature, breadth, and value of anthropology in new settings and to diverse audiences—to students, administrators, and colleagues in other departments; to the people whom we study; and in organizations where people have little correct information about the range of anthropological knowledge, methods, perspectives, and general expertise.

Teaching Anthropology

I repeat the advice offered above: Address the audience you have rather than the one you'd like. I failed to do this when I first arrived at the University of Michigan in winter 1968. Immediately before that I had been a graduate student at Columbia University and then had spent 6 months in Paris preparing for 15 months of ensuing fieldwork in Madagascar. I had no previous teaching experience. I started teaching introductory anthropology by discussing issues that had been important to me in graduate school. Many of my topics were way over the heads of the primarily first-year students in the class. I wrote out my lectures and read them aloud, not very dramatically. I didn't know how to be a lecturer or a teacher. In recompense, students routinely greeted my entrance to the auditorium with hisses and boos.

I had the good fortune to teach two courses—economic anthropology and culture and personality—during the ensuing spring-summer session. Each met twice a week for seven weeks; I didn't have time to overprepare or write out my lectures. I had to talk to students and make sure they were getting the main points in the readings. In the fall, I transferred those lessons to the introductory course with good results.

I have regularly taught Anthropology 101 since my first semester at Michigan. The course meets in a large auditorium. I stand on a platform in front of the massed undergraduates. In 13–14 weeks of lecturing I survey the subfields of anthropology. Among the first courses taken at the university, Anthropology 101 carries social science distribution credit. It also satisfies our new Diversity requirement (a course dealing with race and ethnicity). Few students in it plan to major in anthropology, and many will never take another anthropology course. For these reasons, the successful lecturer, like the textbook author, must work hard to keep students' attention. The lecturer in a mammoth class may adapt to the student perception that he or she is not simply a teacher, but something of an entertainer. The combination of large auditorium, huddled masses, and electronic amplification transforms this assembly from a mere class into something like a studio audience.

In response to developments in technology and the media, lectures, like textbooks, have changed. Texts have added colors, and many provide a bundle of accessories, such as transparencies, for classroom use with an overhead projector. I now use transparencies and have modified my lecture style, trying to enhance students' attention, interest, and learning. I subscribed to a newsletter called *The Teaching Professor* (Magna Publications) and have heeded some of its advice for effective teaching—"Don't stand passively at the front of the room and lecture." "Don't let yourself be chained to a chalkboard, lectern, podium, overhead projector, or microphone." "Move around and show your students you own the entire classroom." These lessons led me to adopt the technology of the current media age to instruct today's students. Like a TV talk-show host, I use a remote microphone, which allows me to roam the lecture hall at will. I use two overhead projectors for transparencies, which I produce on my LaserJet printer or get from my textbook's pedagogical package.

Today's students are more diverse (in age and ethnic background, for example) than ever, yet they have grown up in a mass-mediated world, and many are more comfortable with modern technology than we are. For these students and to explicate the culture(s) of the contemporary world, we teach new courses and use new teaching styles, methods, and tools. For example, I regularly teach a course called "Television, Society, and Culture"—mainly for seniors and graduate students in anthropology, American culture, area studies, and communication. The course objectives are: (1) to develop the ability to analyze television (content and impact) using perspectives from cultural anthropology; (2) to consider the social/cultural context of (a) creation, (b) distribution, (c) reception, and (d) impact of TV messages; and (3) to apply the anthropological perspective within a single culture (for example, the United States) and across cultures (for example, Brazil and the United States).

As the world and our ways of understanding it change, new courses proliferate (such as "Ethnography as a Form of Writing," "The Culture of Postmodernity"), replacing old ones with antiquated titles like "Peoples and Cultures of the Soviet Union" or "The Mind of Primitive Man."

Many of us use modern technology in our teaching. Access to a TV set and a VCR (by students and in the classroom) is indispensable to my Television, Society, and Culture course. The students produce their own videos for projects analyzing aspects of television in a cultural context. I also use new technology (computers) in my course on Research Methods (an increasingly important course as anthropolo-gists are forced to learn more about formal methods and statistics in a world of growing numbers). I teach statistics and data analysis, using appropriate hardware and software, including programs and packages for word processing, data entry, spreadsheets, and statistical analysis. We work directly with my datasets, doing quantitative analyses in one minute that would have taken days when I was a graduate student. Changes in technology allow us to ask and answer a trove of new questions.

College Administrators and Academic Colleagues

As a department chair (and drawing, too, on the experience of other anthropology chairs), I am constantly selling my field. Administrators know the reputations, strengths, and weaknesses of departments in their units, but are often unaware of changes in academic fields outside their own, especially a stereotyped one such as anthropology. "Been on any digs lately?" lurks in the minds of most people who hear the word anthropology. It's important for administrators to be aware of anthropology's increasing focus on contemporary issues and societies, including the United States. It's useful for anthropologists to demonstrate the field's relevance to such issues as immigration and diversity based on gender, race, ethnicity, sexual orientation, age, and differential "abledness." The contemporary significance of anthropology is not well known outside the field, which continues to have an anti-quarian reputation. Anthropology's increasing focus on problems and issues reflecting social and cultural diversity adds to its value within the modern college or university, which has an increasingly diverse student body.

We must work to ensure that anthropology's long-time "ownership" of diversity isn't forgotten as colleges and universities increasingly institute requirements for courses on diversity and multiculturalism. At the University of Michigan, I've noticed that many of the people who have been most active in advocating a diver-sity requirement know little about anthropology. We need to get our perspectives and cumulative knowledge across to them. Anthropologists at Michigan worked hard to ensure that Introductory Anthropology and other appropriate anthropology courses be allowed to satisfy the University's recently created diversity requirement. Some people who advocate a diversity requirement only want other *American* voices represented, not voices from around the world—voices that anthropologists have been heeding for years.

Academic colleagues in other fields have varied ideas about what cultural anthropology is and entails. Usually, their notions are favorable but misinformed. Sometimes, we must disabuse colleagues in other departments of certain notions: that cultural anthropology deals exclusively with non-Western societies; that it is necessarily interpretive rather than explanatory; or that anthropologists know little or nothing about survey research and quantitative methods.

It's easy to show links between anthropology and other fields: social work (applied anthropology), natural resources and the environment (ecological anthro-pology), business (anthropology's global focus), economic development (develop-ment anthropology). I have often heard someone in a unit, agency, or organization remark, "People tell me we need an anthropologist." The person making the remark doesn't actually know what anthropologists do. Most people are unaware of anthro-pology's breadth and the diversity of its subject matter. Most think archaeology. The more sophisticated think international. Most are unaware that anthropologists work on social issues and topics related to public policy in the United States.

Anthropologists must confront a series of naive and false impressions about culture, ethnicity, and multiculturalism. Many Americans (even academics and intellectuals) rely on a Disneyesque model of cultural diversity. "It's a Small World" is an attraction at Florida's Walt Disney World and California's Disneyland in which visitors take a boat ride through an exhibit consisting of hundreds of "ethnically correct" dolls from all over the world, dancing and singing "It's a small world after all." The exhibit is a relentlessly commercial welding of globalization, multiculturalism, and postmodernism.

Many nonanthropologists think of culture in terms of curious customs and colorful adornments—clothing, jewelry, hairstyles, dancing—like the dolls at Disney World. This bias toward the exotic and the superstructural (often recreational or musical—a minstrel show view of culture) even shows up in anthropological films. Many ethnographic films start off with music, often drum beats: "Bonga, bonga, bonga, bonga. Here in (supply place name) the people are very religious." The (usually unintended) message is that people in nonindustrial societies spend most of their time wearing colorful clothes, singing, dancing, and practicing religious rituals. This feeds into the current commercial manipulation of culture as exotic superstructure—costumes, jewels, crystals, lost arks, temples of doom, mysterious, inexplicable, and ultimately unserious—to be appreciated, appropriated, and sold in ethnic fairs and oh-so-carefully-quaint boutiques. In their ethnographic accounts— whether spoken, written, or visual—anthropologists can do more to spread the word that culture is something that ordinary people live each day.

The Media

As chair of a large and active department, I receive a monthly report on "media hits" involving our faculty. My university has an excellent News and Information Office, which provides press releases when faculty write or do something deemed newsworthy. Faculty members usually work with the news and information officer assigned to the department to develop and approve a press release. The same office maintains a file of faculty willing to talk about particular subjects. Several faculty members (C. Loring Brace, Lawrence Hirschfeld, Ann Stoler, and Milford Wolpoff) are interviewed regularly by members of the press about issues involving "race." Wolpoff and Brace comment on new fossil discoveries, and I discuss aspects of contemporary U.S. culture. Interviews with the press are usually arranged by the News and Information Office, but some reporters call the department directly and ask that an "expert" be recommended. Unless you are commenting on some kind of "discovery," reporters are generally seeking some Mead-like application of anthropology to events, developments, and trends in American life.

Be careful talking to the press. Reporters often get it wrong, and your more outlandish, spur-of-the-moment comments are likely to find their way into print. On the other hand, if you're too boring or prosaic, you usually won't be quoted. Surprisingly, one of my most carefully done and accurately reported interviews was for the *National Enquirer*—"Anthropologist Tells Why Going to McDonald's Is Like Going to Church"—despite the grabber title. (I noticed that when psychologists are quoted in the *National Enquirer*, they usually get the label "top psychologist." I was disheartened that I was just a run-of-the-mill "anthropologist" telling something.) Many reporters and columnists (as well as TV people) want juicy tidbits—be especially careful what you say on television. Press interviews can become time consuming; you may eventually have to make choices about which venues are worth your time. And you may learn to avoid reporters and columnists who want to pick your brain for ideas they eventually present as their own—without mentioning you.

People in the Field (Local People, Informants)

Grant writing forces us to be selective and specific; we must identify a problem and develop hypotheses and a research design. The trend toward specialization diverts us from old-style holistic ethnography; we must narrow our focus. But what happens when we arrive in the field and people aren't very interested in what we are studying? (This problem may be partially precluded by a preliminary field trip to the area, which I think is essential when a major research project or dissertation research is being planned.) People in the field may work hard to direct us away from the issue we were funded to study and to push us in another direction. Government officials, for example, can deprive us of the research clearance we require to pursue certain subjects.

Brazilians have reacted very differently to successive projects I have done in their country. Three recent ones (since 1983) have involved multisite team research investigating the impact of television (1983–87), the emergence of ecological awareness and environmental risk perception (1991–95), and participatory development in the Northeast (1993–94). Issues that are of substantial interest (and considered highly fundable) in North America may have a much lower priority in other areas—and vice versa. It has been easier for me to find funding for my ecological awareness and global environmental change projects than for the study of television. Academics have tended to look down on mass media and popular culture, so research proposals about aspects of modernity (or postmodernity) must be very carefully done. By contrast, Brazilians at all our fields sites liked the television project much more than the ecological awareness project, which bored them. Finally, rural people in northeastern Brazil were willing to cooperate in our World Bank–funded participatory development project because they thought they might get something out of it.

The people we study enjoy some research projects more than others, and local and national culture influence such preferences, which affect the direction and scope of our fieldwork. My first research project in Madagascar eventually reflected the interests of my Betsileo informants in history and kinship as much as my own initial focus on economy, ecology, and political organization.

The research preferences of local people may be especially evident in places that have been sites of team research and field schools, such as Arembepe, Bahia, Brazil (Kottak 1992), which has had several projects and researchers. Arembepe entered anthropology in 1962 as one of several field sites (in Brazil, Peru, Mexico, and Ecuador) for undergraduate research within the Columbia-Cornell-Harvard-Illinois Summer Field Studies Program in Anthropology. Several researchers, including myself, Isabel Wagley Kottak, David Epstein, Marvin Harris, Niles Eldredge, Janice Perlman, Shepard Forman, Carl Withers, Joseph Kotta, and Peter Gorlin, have done summer fieldwork there or participated in the program as field director or assistant director. I was there in 1962, 1964, and 1965 and have done longitudinal research in Arembepe ever since.

This tradition has been abetted by several of my students who have also worked there. Doug Jones, in perhaps the project Arembepeiros liked most, weighed people and took and showed photographs as he investigated standards of physical attractiveness. Janet Dunn is currently examining the role of various modernization variables, including television, in influencing family planning. As I write this, Christopher O'Leary has just arrived in Arembepe, which he will use (drawing on some of Dunn's sample) as a springboard for a study of Protestant conversion in northeastern Brazil.

The lesson here: You have to sell your anthropology in the field as well as back home. As with development projects (see below), local people are more likely to cooperate with research projects they like (and which are culturally appropriate) than with those that don't interest them.

Another factor that influences our reception in the field is our sponsorship—the agency or agencies that are funding us. Fulbright fellowships, for example, provide useful contacts with U.S. Embassy and USIS officials, which can provide logistical support, especially in national capitals. The anthropologist working as an independent researcher will have a different status and role (and probably more explaining to do in the field) than one who works for an organization like USAID or, especially, the World Bank. When one works for "the Bank," cooperation (or at at least the appearance of it) by government officials and interested local people is virtually guaranteed—because people hope to gain from what the anthropologist is learning. The benefits to be derived from participating in an independent research project are often unclear—so the anthropologist has more selling to do, both with government officials and local people. Independent researchers have to justify their missions to host country officials at various levels and to host country academics who can recommend necessary affiliations. A key obligation of the independent researcher is to remember such people—those who have facilitated our research. Host country academics and students can become our future research collaborators and coauthors. We often have better access to funding sources, which may one day facilitate their research, incomes, or academic careers.

Fieldwork raises another issue of writing for an audience. The researcher may want to use an interview schedule, the cultural appropriateness of which must be determined through pilot research and pretesting. In 1984, we used Arembepe to pretest a basic interview schedule that was eventually used at six other Brazilian field sites (with some necessary local tinkering at each site). One result of pretesting was our discovery that some questions could be discarded because they produced little or no variation. (Note, however, that such questions can still be valuable for comparison across communities or cultures, or over time, as variation may develop.) Pretesting also showed which questions respondents did not understand and which were too complicated. For example, we rejected the advice of an American researcher to use seven-point ordinal scales because rural Brazilians were not accustomed to dealing with such fine distinctions. We used three- or four-category scales instead. The manipulation of a seven-point ordinal scale requires a degree of exposure to print media and testing that exists in contemporary North America but not in rural Brazil. Again, the issue is cultural appropriateness.

Presenting Applied Anthropology

Applied anthropology, recognized by the American Anthropological Association (AAA) as our fifth subdiscipline, focuses on anthropology's role with respect to contemporary human problems. I see applied anthropology (also called practicing anthropology) as the use of anthropological data, perspectives, theory, and methods to identify, assess, and solve social problems. Applied anthropologists serve as social commentators, problem solvers, and policy makers, advisers, and evaluators. We express our policy views in books, journals, and technical reports; through participation in social and political movements; and through professional organizations, such as the Society for Applied Anthropology and the National Association of Practicing Anthropologists (NAPA). NAPA, part of the AAA, is designed to help applied anthropologists refine their skills and market their services. NAPA fosters information sharing among practitioners, publishes materials useful to them, helps train them, and works to support their interests in and outside of academic settings.

An increasing number of anthropologists work for groups that promote, manage, and assess programs aimed at influencing human social conditions. The scope of applied anthropology includes change and development abroad and social problems and policies in North America. Practicing anthropologists work (regularly or occasionally) for nonacademic clients: governments, nongovernmental organizations (NGOs), tribal and ethnic associations, interest groups, businesses, and social-service and educational agencies.

As Karin Tice (1997) observes, practicing anthropologists have to teach their field constantly, because they work in so many contexts in which sociocultural anthropology is unfamiliar. But *we also learn in such settings*. Many of us never imagined as graduate students or young academics that we would eventually do applied anthropology. The world has changed, though, more rapidly and radically than we imagined, and most of our field sites have been affected by global forces. Academic anthropologists are now being invited to consult about the direction of change in nations, regions, even communities where we originally did academic research focusing on theoretical issues. And we accept consultancies for varied reasons: (1) They allow us to return to the field without the paper work and uncertainty of the research grant application process; (2) They let us play a role in advocating, designing, implementing, and evaluating policies involving people we know and care about; (3) Practice enriches theory: applied anthropology offers research opportunities; the linkages and transformations in the modern world system are intrinsically interesting; and (4) We can use the money.

Many scholars have trained themselves in applied anthropology by reading, from personal experience with projects and agencies, and through contact with the people in those agencies who design and implement projects. As consultants, we benefit from our own informal internships. In this role, we may use our eyes and ears, as ethnographers, to study the people, organizations, and institutions involved in social change. Sometimes, especially working full time for such agencies, we feel frustrated. Often we have to argue perspectives and positions unfamiliar to, or challenged by, associates. (This, of course, also happens in academia.) We have to fit into "results-driven," deadline-oriented organizations and confront goals we may regard as unwise. As advocates we argue for our views, but they don't always prevail (see Tice 1997).

My own applied anthropology has mostly been development anthropology. I have consulted as a social analyst in several settings related to economic development. I will draw on my experience to indicate some of the varied roles an anthropologist can play in development organizations.

Presenting Anthropology at the World Bank

I began my work in what is now called development anthropology with an assignment for the World Bank in Madagascar in 1981. (People who work for the World Bank always refer to it as "the Bank," as if there were only one bank in the world.) My work for the Bank started with a phone call from John Malone, representing the Operation Evaluations Department (OED), which evaluates projects after they are officially completed. A development anthropologist who had read my book on Madagascar (Kottak 1980) had referred him to me. Malone told me about a large-scale irrigation project that had gone awry in the Lake Alaotra region of north-central

Madagascar. He mentioned that an accountant often used by the Bank had been sent to Madagascar to evaluate the project, but he had spent his time talking to officials in the national capital, rather than traveling to the field site. The accountant consultant had heard there were social problems at the project site. I suggested some likely reasons for the problems. By the time the phone call was over, I had been invited to go to Madagascar as a short-time consultant for the Bank. Thus began my occasional career as a World Bank consultant.

After a briefing in Washington, I traveled to Madagascar for three weeks in February 1981. Following a procedure I would recommend to any anthropologist in my position, I also arranged to have a local social scientist, Jean-Aimé Rakotoarisoa, appointed as my companion and coinvestigator. (Rakotoarisoa later served as my "counterpart" or *homologue* on a USAID project for which I served as social soundness analyst in 1990). He and I (eventually joined by OED's Malone) traveled to the Lake Alaotra region and spent several days consulting with a series of villagers affected by the project. We discovered some interesting and egregious errors that could have been prevented if anthropologists had been involved in planning and implementing the project and not just called in to find out what had gone wrong once the project was over.

My report on the Lake Alaotra project impressed John Malone sufficiently for him to mention my work to Michael Cernea, the Bank's long-time senior sociologist, who retired in 1996 but who has done more than anyone to ensure that social analysts are employed by the Bank and that social analysis is an important part of project planning. In 1983, Michael and John asked me to examine the Bank's files for a comparative study of the extent and role of social analysis in project planning and implementation and the relation of social analysis input to the sociocultural appropriateness and outcome of the project.

For that 1983–84 study I reviewed materials on 68 completed rural development projects from all over the world. My task included an assessment of the social and cultural factors that had affected those projects, most of which had been designed during the 1960s and early 1970s, when planners had little experience using sociocultural expertise for development planning. (Remember that OED routinely sent accountants to places like Madagascar to evaluate projects in remote parts of the country, which they frequently did not visit.) Most of the projects I examined demonstrated a tendency to stress technical and financial factors and to neglect social issues.

I was also to consider another issue that arises in discussions of development projects—the relationship between sociocultural impact and the measurement and evaluation of project success. Sometimes a contrast is posed between quantitative evaluation in economic terms and qualitative evaluation of cultural impact. Thus, for example, a positive effect on GNP may be accompanied by an adverse effect on the "quality of life." My comparative study of rural development projects revealed no such discrepancy between production goals and sociocultural well-being. On the contrary, I found that social analysis aimed at identifying and designing socio-culturally compatible projects paid off financially. For the 68 rural development projects studied, the average economic rate of return for culturally compatible projects exceeded 19%, much higher than the comparable rate for incompatible ones ojects of less than 9%. (Sociocultural compatibility was evaluated independently of economic rate of return, to avoid any tendency to identify projects as culturally incompatible once they were known to be economic failures.)

I have written about this comparative study in several contexts. First was my 1984 report for the Bank, initially read by Cernea and Malone, as well as a few Bank staff members whom Cernea considered especially sympathetic to social analysis. I refined the report by incorporating suggestions, then gave two presentations at the Bank (one seminar and one large public lecture) detailing the results. Most reactions were favorable or neutral; the main negative reaction came from the Livestock Division, which had the largest percentage of culturally incompatible and failed projects (usually reflecting the tendency to impose ranching models derived from North America, Australia, and New Zealand on people everywhere). The next written version was as a chapter in an edited volume (Kottak 1985), and I revised this chapter for the second edition of the book (Cernea 1991). I felt my findings had reached "the development community" but not anthropologists, so I wrote an essay for the *American Anthropologist* entitled "Culture and Development" (1990), which was aimed at development anthropologists and highlighted the main findings of my comparative study.

Reports written for development agencies have little or no value for tenure and promotion unless and until they are turned into academic studies and published as books or as articles in refereed journals or chapters in refereed books. There is one problem, however, with such publications. Some consultant contracts have a clause banning external dissemination without approval. (I strike out this clause.) The World Bank requests that information gathered for the Bank not be published for three years after the study is complete.

David Mandelbaum (1963:10) believed that studies in applied anthropology "show how theoretical concepts are deployed empirically and how the empirical data feed back into the development of theory." My own experience leaves me with no doubt that theory and practice are intertwined. The fieldwork and comparisons I have done in applied anthropology have consistently fed back on my academic work, providing opportunities, practice, classroom material, and research topics for me and my students—graduate and undergraduate. I like applied anthropology because it offers new and varied opportunities to do research on change. For me, a key role of the *applied* anthropologist is to facilitate "bottom up" social change. Doing so entails going to local people to discover their wants and perceived needs at the very beginning of project planning. One way of gathering such information is to consult or work with anthropologists already familiar with the area. In my work in development anthropology, I have tried to ascertain "locally based demand" by visiting a series of communities and promoting wide public consultation, sometimes organized through town meetings.

In presenting anthropology to development agencies, I have tried to demonstrate the value of social analysis throughout the project cycle: identification (ideally of locally perceived needs), appraisal, preparation and design, implementation, monitoring, feedback, and evaluation—including identification of potentially generalizable lessons learned. My research has supported the value of the routine use of social analysts (foreign and especially native) in designing and implementing policies and programs aimed at social change.

The presentation and implementation of development anthropology itself remains somewhat problematic because of the variety and lack of uniform training in anthropology. A World Bank official once remarked to me "When you hire an economist you know what you're getting; when you hire an anthropologist you have no idea." Outsiders perceive anthropologists as lacking basic, uniform training and being hopelessly idiosyncratic and individualistic. "If one anthropologist leaves," said the same official, "there's no way of telling whether the next one will use the same approach or something completely different." More consistent training of applied anthropologists in academic settings, including major universities that lack applied anthropology foci per se, may be one solution.

Reports for Development Agencies

Documents produced for development organizations go through a long review process in which they may be modified severely. This is done not only to improve them, but also to protect feelings, interests, and reputations—of agency officials and nationals in host countries. The review process varies by agency. At the World Bank, different audiences typically hear and read reports, especially when a country is involved. Analysts must be sensitive about people's turfs and egos, especially in a highly bureaucratized organization like the World Bank. Consultants have to learn the culture of the Bank, and that culture is resistant to change. Bank officials like to hire people who have worked for the Bank previously and thus are familiar with procedures, formats, and expectations.

Reports should read like other Bank reports. During my most recent (1995–96) comparative study for the Bank, I discovered limitations to my presentation of statistical analysis. Pearson's r and multiple regression were no-nos. My too-many tables changed Bank eyes to blank eyes. For people we'd expect to deal well with figures, Bank staff aren't very well trained statistically. The typical Bank format for reporting quantitative findings is through a three- or four-point ordinal scale and percentages. This crude format seems to be easily comprehensible to Bank officials, while I—as a social scientist accustomed to more precise and complex quantitative analysis, including correlation matrices—found it somewhat opaque and confusing. But this kind of writing is part of the culture of the Bank, along with several other conventions. Paragraphs are numbered; zippy prose is taboo. Passive constructions are excellent devices for obscuring responsibility. Key ritual phrases in preparation documents (staff appraisal reports) offer clues that Bank staff doubted that certain project components (usually favored by government) would succeed (for example, "assurances have been made"), but had allowed them to stay anyway.

The canon of cultural appropriateness remains in effect in presenting anthropology within development organizations, businesses, or wherever. To succeed as a consultant, you need to avoid overinnovation. You must know, and not deviate too far from, cultural expectations. It is said that World Bank staff spend so much time traveling and attending meetings that they must hire short-term consultants to read the reports they hire other short-term consultants to write. Development agencies (like businesses) require reports to be prefaced by an executive summary, which lists the main findings and conclusions. This may be all that staff reads. The bulk of the reports are shelved as eventual consultant fodder. (Consulting for the Bank in Recife, Brazil, in June 1993, I was initially delighted to find a copy of Cernea's *Putting People First* (1985) on a prominent shelf in the Bank office library. Then I discovered it was still wrapped in its original cellophane.)

Presenting Anthropology at USAID

As an anthropologist, it should be second nature for you to start by assessing the culture of whatever organization you are working in, long or short term. You must determine and know your audience(s) and address it (them). As an employer, USAID is more problematic than the World Bank. Its personnel lacks the international diversity and financial expertise that are strong features of the Bank, and it does not pay as well. (Salaries and consultant fees are pegged to U.S. congressional salaries.) At the Bank, but especially at USAID in my experience, you not only have to know your audience, you also have to keep it.

One of the most troubling characteristics of development organizations is their personnel instability. People come and go, rotating in and out of "missions." This means that, even if you have a long-term commitment to the country, area, or project, you often have to start over, with someone new. You may have convinced some official that social analysis is valuable and that a project should unfold in a certain way. Then someone else arrives from Washington, and the process repeats. Anthropologists who have worked in Madagascar over the past decade, for example, have seen a succession of USAID officers, at all ranks, including more than six mission heads, rotate in and out. The new directors arrive with ideas of their own, often knowing little or nothing about social science—but sometimes with prior positive or negative experiences with anthropologists and agencies that employ them. So again you reinvent the wheel; you resell the role of anthropology—either in general or for a specific project. Note that this instability applies not only to the major development agencies, but also to the NGOs who are increasingly charged with project implementation. Your relationships are constantly forged anew. And you also may have to persuade politicians and elected representatives about project soundness and proper implementation strategy.

Be True to Your Anthropology

Working mainly among nonanthropologists in various organizations, how does one remain an anthropologist, rather than becoming simply another organization man or woman? There is a real danger that the need to communicate with others within that organization will distance you from an anthropological perspective. The discourse, behavior, and modus operandi of the mix of professionals making up a team tend to converge toward an organizational norm. Anthropologists should be ever mindful of the special potential contribution of their field. Otherwise why are they there? And why did they spend all that tuition money?

REFERENCES

Angeloni, E., ed. 1996. *Annual Editions, Readings in Anthropology, 1995/96*. Guilford, CT: Dushkin.

Bernard, H. R. 1994. *Research Methods in Cultural Anthropology: Qualitative and Quantitative Approaches*, 2d ed. Walnut Creek, CA: AltaMira Press.

Bowen, E. S. 1964. *Return to Laughter*. Garden City, NY: Doubleday.

Brody, H. 1981. *Maps and Dreams*. New York: Pantheon.

Cernea, M. M. 1991. *Putting People First: Sociological Variables in Rural Development*, 2d ed. New York: Oxford University Press.

Chagnon, N. 1992. *Yanomamo: The Fierce People*, 4th ed. New York: Harcourt Brace.

Ember, C., and M. Ember. 1993. *Anthropology*, 7th ed. Englewood Cliffs, NJ: Prentice Hall.

Harris, M. 1974. *Cows, Pigs, Wars, and Witches: The Riddles of Culture*. New York: Random House.

Harris, M. 1977. *Cannibals and Kings: The Origins of Cultures*. New York: Random House.

Harris, M. 1997. *Culture, People, Nature: An Introduction to General Anthropology*, 7th ed. New York: Longman.

Haviland, W. 1996. *Anthropology*, 8th ed. Forth Worth: Harcourt Brace.

Kottak, C. P. 1980. *The Past in the Present: History, Ecology, and Social Organization in Highland Madagascar*. Ann Arbor: University of Michigan Press.

Kottak, C. P. 1985. When People Don't Come First: Some Lessons from Completed Projects. In *Putting People First: Sociological Variables in Rural Development*. M. M. Cernea, ed. Pp. 325–356. New York: Oxford University Press.

Kottak, C. P. 1990. Culture and Economic Development. *American Anthropologist 93*(3): 723–731.

Kottak, C. P. 1992. *Assault on Paradise: Social Change in a Brazilian Village,* 2d ed. New York: McGraw-Hill.

Kottak, C. P. 1994. *Cultural Anthropology,* 6th ed. New York: McGraw-Hill.

Kottak, C. P. 1996. *Mirror for Humanity: A Concise Introduction to Cultural Anthropology.* New York: McGraw-Hill.

Kottak, C. P. 1997a. *Anthropology: The Exploration of Human Diversity,* 7th ed. New York: McGraw-Hill.

Kottak, C. P. 1997b. *Cultural Anthropology: The Exploration of Human Diversity.* New York: McGraw-Hill.

Magna Publications. *The Teaching Professor.* Madison: Magna Publications (newsletter published ten times annually).

Mandelbaum, D. G. 1963. The Transmission of Anthropological Culture. In *The Teaching of Anthropology.* D. G. Mandelbaum, G. W. Lasker, and E. M. Albert, eds. Pp. 1–21. Berkeley: University of California Press.

Pelto, P., and G. Pelto. 1978. *Anthropological Research: The Structure of Inquiry.* New York: Cambridge University Press.

Podolefsky, A., and P. J. Brown, eds. 1994. *Applying Anthropology: An Introductory Reader,* 3rd ed. Mountain View, CA: Mayfield.

Richardson, L. 1990. *Writing Strategies: Reaching Diverse Audiences.* Qualitative Research Methods Series, Vol. 21. Thousand Oaks, CA: Sage Publications.

Shostak, M. 1981. *Nisa: The Life and Words of a !Kung Woman.* Cambridge: Harvard University Press.

Spradley, J., and D. McCurdy, eds. 1994. *Conformity and Conflict: Readings in Cultural Anthropology,* 8th ed. Prospect Heights, IL: Waveland.

Stein, J., gen. ed. 1982. *Random House College Dictionary,* rev. ed. New York: Random House.

Thomas, E. M. 1958. *The Harmless People.* New York: Random House.

Tice, K. 1997. Reflections on Teaching Anthropology for Use in the Public and Private Sector. In *The Teaching of Anthropology: Problems, Issues, Decisions.* C. P. Kottak, J. J. White, R. H. Furlow, and P. C. Rice, eds. Pp. 273–284. Mountain View, CA: Mayfield.

Turnbull, C. 1964. *The Forest People.* New York: Simon and Schuster.

Turnbull, C. 1971. *The Mountain People.* New York: Simon and Schuster.

About the Authors

H. RUSSELL BERNARD (Ph.D., University of Illinois, 1968) is professor of anthropology at the University of Florida. He has taught at Washington State University, West Virginia University, and the University of Florida. He has also taught or done research at the University of Athens, the University of Cologne, the National Museum of Ethnology (Osaka), and Scripps Institution of Oceanography. Bernard works with indigenous people to develop publishing outlets for works in previously nonwritten languages. He does research in social network analysis, particularly on the problem of estimating the size of uncountable populations. His publications include (with Jesús Salinas Pedraza) *Native Ethnography: An Otomí Indian Describes His Culture* (Sage Publications, 1989), *Technology and Social Change* (Waveland Press, 1983, 2d ed., edited with Pertti Pelto), *Research Methods in Anthropology* (AltaMira Press, 1994, 2d ed.). Bernard was editor of *Human Organization* (1976–1981) and the *American Anthropologist* (1981–1989). He is currently the editor of the journal *Cultural Anthropology Methods*.

STEPHEN P. BORGATTI is associate professor of organization studies at the Carroll Graduate School of Management, Boston College. He earned his B.A. (1977) in anthropology from Cornell University and his Ph.D. (1989) in mathematical social science from the University of California, Irvine. His research interests include social networks, semantic structures, and biological perspectives on economic systems. His publications include the following: Elicitation Techniques for Cultural Domain Analysus (in The Ethnographer's Toolkit, J. Schensul and M. LeCompte, eds., Sage Publications, In press), ANTHROPAC 4.0 (Analytic Technologies, 1992), and (with M. G. Evererett and L. C. Freeman) UCINET IV (Version 1.0, Analytic Technologies, 1992). He is currently studying the adoption of organic farming in Finland and the social structure of the wine industry.

CAROLINE B. BRETTELL (Ph.D., Brown University, 1978) is professor and chair of anthropology at Southern Methodist University. Between 1989 and 1994 she served as director of Women's Studies. Her interest in the intersections between anthropology and history began during her postdoctoral research in historical demography at the University of Texas at Austin. She is the author of *Men Who Migrate, Women Who Wait* (Princeton, 1986) and *We Have Already Cried Many Tears* (Waveland, 1995) and co-author of *Painters and Peasants in the 19th Century*. She is editor of *When They Read What We Write: The Politics of Ethnography* (Bergin and Garvey, 1993) and co-editor of *International Migration: The Female Experience* (Rowman and Allenheld, 1986), *Gender in Cross-Cultural Perspective* (Prentice-Hall, 1993, 1997), and *Gender and Health: An International Perspective* (Prentice-Hall, 1996). She is currently working on a book about a nineteenth-century charismatic priest who led a group of French-Canadian migrants to Illinois and is completing revisions on a book about her mother, a Canadian journalist, which will be published in 1999.

BILLIE R. DEWALT has a Ph.D. in anthropology from the University of Connecticut (1975). He is director of the Center for Latin American Studies, professor in the Graduate School of Public and International Affairs, University Center for International Studies Professor, and professor of anthropology at the University of Pittsburgh. His research focuses on natural resources; agricultural-, land tenure-, and food policies; as well as political ecology, economic anthropology, and anthropological theory and methods. He is editor of the Pitt Latin American Series published by the University of Pittsburgh Press. His publications include (co-edited with Pertti Pelto) *Micro and Macro Levels of Analysis in Anthropology: Issues in Theory and Research* (Westview Press, 1985), (co-edited with John Poggie and William Dressler) *Anthropological Research: Process and Application* (State University of New York Press, 1992), and (with Jackson Roper and John Frechione) *Indigenous People and Development in Latin America: A Literature Survey and Recommendations* (World Bank and Center for Latin American Studies, University of Pittsburgh, 1997).

KATHLEEN M. DEWALT (Ph.D., University of Connecticut, 1979) is professor of anthropology and public health at the University of Pittsburgh. She currently serves as the Associate Dean of Arts and Sciences for Graduate Studies and Research. Since 1970, she has done research related to health and nutrition in Mexico, Brazil, Honduras, Ecuador, and rural Kentucky. Her primary research interests are in the impact of economic, agricultural, and health policy on the food security and nutritional status (broadly defined) of children and older adults in rural settings. She is currently involved in two projects in Ecuador. One examines the impact of land reform and agricultural policies since 1950 on the demography, land, and water use and health in a single watershed in northern Ecuador. The other is a study of the impact of income-generating projects on women's social status and child welfare in coastal Ecuador. Among her most recent publications are: Nutrition and the Commercialization of Agriculture: Ten Years Later (*Social Science and Medicine*, 1993), (with William R. Leonard, James P. Stansbury, and M. Katherine McCastor) Growth Differences between Children of Highland and Coastal Ecuador (*American Journal of Physical Anthropology*, 1995), and (with Sara Quandt, Mara Z. Vitolins, and Gun Roos (Meal Patterns of Older Adults in Rural Communities: Life Course Analysis and Implications for Undernutrition (*Journal of Applied Gerontology*, 1997).

CAROL R. EMBER (Ph.D., Harvard University, 1971) is executive director of the Human Relations Area Files, Inc. (HRAF), an international not-for-profit research agency at Yale University that produces annual installments of the electronic Collection of Ethnography and the electronic Collection of Archaeology. She has served as president of the Society for Cross-Cultural Research, serves on the boards of three journals—*Cross-Cultural Research*, *Ethos*, and *Journal of Conflict Resolution*. She has received grants (with Melvin Ember and Bruce Russett) from the National Science Foundation and United States Institute of Peace to support her research on war and interpersonal violence. She has recently received grants (with Robert Munroe and Michael Burton) from NSF to support the Summer Institutes for Comparative Anthropological Research. She has conducted cross-cultural research on variation in family, kinship, and gender roles, and cross-species research on female-male bonding and female sexuality. She is the senior author of *Anthropology* (Prentice Hall, forthcoming 1999) and *Cultural Anthropology* (Prentice Hall, forthcoming 1999), now in their 9th editions. She is currently co-editing the *Encyclopedia of National Cultures* (Macmillan, n.d.).

MELVIN EMBER (Ph.D., Yale University, 1958) is president of the Human Relations Area Files, Inc. and editor of *Cross-Cultural Research*, the official journal of the Society for Cross-Cultural Research. He directed the first NSF Summer Institute in Cross-Cultural Research in 1964 and served as president of the Society for Cross-Cultural Research. He is co-editor of the *Encyclopedia of Cultural Anthropology* (Henry Holt, 1996), *American Immigrant Cultures* (Macmillan 1998), the upcoming *Encyclopedia of Prehistory* (Plenum, forthcoming 1999), and the upcoming *Encyclopedia of National Cultures* (Macmillan, n.d.). His cross-cultural research has been supported by NSF, the National Institute of Mental Health, and the U.S. Institute of Peace and has focused on marital residence, marriage, family and kinship, war and peace, and interpersonal violence. He is co-author (with Burton Pasternak and Carol R. Ember) of *Sex, Gender, and Kinship: A Cross-Cultural Perspective* (Prentice Hall, 1997).

BRENDA FARNELL received her Ph.D. in 1990 from Indiana University, Bloomington, and is currently an assistant professor in the Department of Anthropology, University of Illinois (Urbana-Champaign). Her research interests include linguistic anthropology and movement performance, problems in embodiment and social theory, and endangered Native North American languages. She has done extensive linguistic and ethnographic research on storytelling performance among the Assiniboine of Montana and the Kiowa of Oklahoma, in which the spoken languages are accompanied by Plains Indian Sign Language. Her publications include an ethnography, *Do You See What I Mean: Plains Indian Sign Talk and the Embodiment of Action* (University of Texas Press, 1995) and an award-winning CD-ROM, *WIYUTA: Assiniboine Storytelling with Signs* (University of Texas Press, 1995).

JAMES FERNANDEZ (Ph.D., Northwestern University, 1962) is professor of anthropology at the University of Chicago, where he has taught since 1986. He formerly taught at and was chair at Princeton University, Dartmouth College, and Smith College. He has been a Simon Visiting Professor at the University of Manchester and visiting professor at Uppsala University, the University of Bergen, the University of Barcelona, and the University of Santiago. He has also taught at the Facultad Latino-Americana de las Ciencias Sociales (FLACSO) in Quito. He has been a Fellow at the Center for Advanced Study in the Social Sciences (Stanford) and at the Institute for Advanced Study (Princeton). He is a past president of the Northeast Anthropological Association and of the Society for Humanistic Anthropology. He has written extensively on sign theory and trope theory, on revitalization theory, and on African and southern European ethnology and ethnography. He is the author of *Fang Architectonics* (Temple University Press, 1977), *Bwiti: An Ethnography of the Religious Imagination in Africa* (Princeton University Press, 1982), *Persuasions and Performances* (Indiana University Press, 1986), and *Campos léxicos y vida cultural n'Asturies* (Academia de la Lingua Press, 1996). He has edited *Beyond Metaphor* (Stanford University Press, 1992) and (with Milton Singer) *The Conditions of Reciprocal Understanding* (University of Chicago Press, 1995). He is currently working on the problem of consensus in culture and, with Mary Huber, is editing a collection of articles on anthropological irony. He is a fellow of the American Academic of Arts and Sciences and of the Asturian Academy of the Language.

CAROLYN FLUEHR-LOBBAN is a professor of anthropology and director of General Education at Rhode Island College. She received her B.A. and M.A. from Temple

University and her Ph.D. in Anthropology and African Studies from Northwestern University in 1973. She joined Rhode Island College in 1973 and received the Award for Distinguished Teaching in 1990. Over the last 27 years she has spent 6 years living and conducting research in the Sudan, Egypt, and Tunisia, and has traveled around the world twice teaching anthropology on the University of Pittsburgh's Semester at Sea program. Her research has covered such topics as Islamic law and and society, women's social and legal status in Muslim societies, human rights and cultural relativism, and ethics and anthropological research. She is the author or editor of seven books, including *Islamic Society in Practice* (University Press of Florida, 1994), *Islamic Law and Society in the Sudan* (Frank Cass, Ltd. [London], 1987) (which has been translated into Arabic), and *Ethics and the Profession of Anthropology: Dialogue for a New Era* (University of Pennsylvania Press, 1991). From 1995–1996 she served on the AAA Commission to Review the Statements on Ethics that produced a new comprehensive code of ethics for the discipline. She has chaired the Committee on Human Participants at Rhode Island College and she served on the Ethics Committee of the Middle East Studies Association.

CHRISTINE WARD GAILEY (Ph.D., New School for Social Research, New York, 1981) is professor of anthropology at Northeastern University, Boston. She is author of *Kinship to Kingship: Gender Hierarchy and State Formation* (University of Texas Press, 1987), editor of *The Politics of Culture* and *Creativity and Civilization in Crisis: Anthropological Perspectives* (University Press of Florida, 1992), and co-editor (with Thomas Patterson) of *Power Relations and State Formation* (American Anthropological Association, 1987). Among her articles related to feminist ethnology are Evolutionary Perspectives on Gender Hierarchy (in *Analyzing Gender*, Beth Hess and Myra Ferree, eds., Sage Publications, 1987), "A Good Man is Hard to Find": Overseas Migration and the Decentered Family in the Tongan Islands (*Critique of Anthropology*, 1992), and Women and the Democratization Movement in Tonga: Nation Versus State, Authority Versus Power (*Women's Studies International Forum*, 1996). Her recent research on adoption will appear in *Identities* (1998, forthcoming) and in *Blue-Ribbon Babies and Labors of Love: Race, Class, and Gender in U.S. Adoption Practice* (University of Texas Press, forthcoming).

LAURA R. GRAHAM received her Ph.D. in 1990 from the University of Texas at Austin. She is an associate professor of anthropology at the University of Iowa. Since 1981 Graham has conducted extensive fieldwork among the Xavante Indians of central Brazil. Her research and published work focuses on the ways in which social actors use discourse and forms of expressive performance, including music and narrative to create identity, social organization, and social memory. Most recently, she has been examining Native Amazonians' uses of discourse and forms of expressive performance in national and international arenas. Her published articles include: A Public Sphere in Amazonia? The Depersonalized Collaborative Construction of Discourse in Xavante (*American Ethnologist*, 1993), Dialogic Dreams: Creative Selves Coming into Life in the Flow of Time (*American Ethnologist*, 1994), and (with Beth A. Conklin), The Shifting Middle Ground: Amazonian Indians and Eco-Politics (*American Anthropologist*, 1995). Her book, *Performing Dreams: Discourses of Immortality among the Xavante of Central Brazil* (University of Texas Press, 1995) was the winner of the 1996 Chicago Folklore Prize.

FADWA EL GUINDI is adjunct professor of anthropology at the University of Southern California, where she teaches in the Visual Anthropology Program. She holds a Ph.D. in anthropology from the University of Texas, Austin (1972). Her field research areas include Arab, Nubian, and Zapotec cultures, and Arab-Americans. She recently ended a four-year term as editor of film reviews for the *American Anthropologist* and is past president of the Society for Visual Anthropology, a section of the American Anthropological Association. Her print publications include *The Myth of Ritual: A Native's Ethnography of Life-Crisis Rituals* (University of Arizona Press, 1986). Her visual ethnographies include *El Sebou': Egyptian Birth Ritual*, *El Moulid: Egyptian Religious Festival*, and *Ghurbal*. Her forthcoming book, *Veil: Modesty, Privacy and Resistance*, is a visual, cultural, and textual analysis of the phenomenon of veiling in the Arab East.

W. PENN HANDWERKER (Ph.D., Oregon, 1971) is professor of anthropology at the University of Connecticut, where he directs the program in medical anthropology. He has done field research in West Africa (Liberia), the West Indies (Barbados, Antigua, and St. Lucia), the Russian Far East (Chukotka), and various portions of the United States (Oregon, California's North Coast, Connecticut, and Alaska). He has published in all five fields in anthropology on topics including the origins and evolution of culture, entrepreneurship, rice production, public sector corruption, and the intergenerational implications of gender and intergenerational power differences for violence, sexuality, fertility, and the spread of sexual diseases, as well as research methods for the study of cultural and life experience phenomena. Currently, he is conducting parallel long-term historical studies of the sources and consequences of violence and other health transition phenomena in the West Indies and the Russian and American Arctic. Among his publications are Universal Human Rights and the Problem of Unbounded Cultural Meanings (*American Anthropologist*, 1997), (with Danielle Wozniak) Sampling Strategies for Cultural Data: An Extension of Boas's Answer to Galton's Problem (*Current Anthropology*, 1997), and Why Violence? A Test of Hypotheses Representing Three Discourses on the Roots of Domestic Violence (*Human Organization*, 1998).

ULF HANNERZ (Ph.D., Stockholm University, 1969) is professor of social anthropology at Stockholm University, Sweden. He is a member of the Royal Swedish Academy of Sciences and the American Academy of Arts and Sciences, a former chair of the European Association of Social Anthropologists, and a former editor of the journal *Ethnos*. He has taught at several U.S., European, and Australian universities and has done field research in the United States, West Africa, and the Caribbean. His current research is on globalization and transnational cultural processes, and his most recent project on news media foreign correspondents has involved interviews and observations in Europe, the United States, the Middle East, and South Africa. Among his books are *Exploring the City* (Columbia University Press, 1980), *Cultural Complexity* (Columbia University Press, 1992) and *Transnational Connections* (Routledge, 1996). He is the anthropology editor for the forthcoming *International Encyclopedia of the Social and Behavioral Sciences* (Elsevier), scheduled to appear in 2001.

MICHAEL HERZFELD (D.Phil., Oxford University, 1976) is professor of anthropology at Harvard University, where he has taught since 1991, and curator of European ethnology in the Peabody Museum. Before that, he taught at Vassar College (1978–80) and Indiana University (1980–91). Elected as a Fellow of the American Academy of Arts and Sciences in 1997, he has held visiting appointments in Australia, France, Italy, and the United Kingdom. He is past president of the Modern Greek Studies Association and the Society for the Anthropology of Europe and was formerly editor of *American Ethnologist*. His books include *Anthropology through the Looking-Glass: Critical Ethnography in the Margins of Europe* (Cambridge University Press, 1987), *Cultural Intimacy: Social Poetics in the Nation-State* (Routledge, 1997), and *Portrait of a Greek Imagination: An Ethnographic Biography of Andreas Nenedakis* (University of Chicago Press, 1997). His current major general research interest is the comparison of the forms of historical experience in Greece and Italy.

DOUGLAS W. HOLLAN is professor of anthropology (Ph.D., University of California, San Diego, 1984) and Luckman Distinguished Teacher at UCLA, and a doctoral graduate of the Southern California Psychoanalytic Institute (1997). He is the author of numerous articles on the culture and psychology of the Toraja of Indonesia and is co-author of *Contentment and Suffering: Culture and Experience in Toraja* (Columbia University Press, 1994) and *The Thread of Life: Toraja Reflections on the Life Cycle* (University of Hawaii Press, 1996). He is working on a book on the Toraja that will focus on cultural process and individual variation.

ALLEN JOHNSON is professor of anthropology and psychiatry, and chair of the Latin American Studies Program, at the University of California, Los Angeles. He received his Ph.D. in anthropology at Stanford in 1968 and taught at Columbia University until moving to UCLA in 1975. He has done ethnographic research in a Zapotec village in Oaxaca, Mexico, on a plantation (*fazenda*) in northeastern Brazil, and among the Matsigenka of the Peruvian Amazon. His interests focus on problems in adaptation, both ecologically in terms of food production and health maintenance in tropical ecosystems, and psychologically in terms of cognitive and emotional aspects of coping with natural, social, and cultural stresses. He has published in ecological and psychological anthropology, on methodological issues, and on native and contemporary communities in Latin America. His books include *Quantification in Cultural Anthropology: An Introduction to Research Design* (Stanford University Press, 1978) and (with Timothy Earle) *The Evolution of Human Societies* (Stanford University Press, 1987). His most recent book is (with Douglass Price-Williams) *Oedipus Ubiquitous: The Family Complex in World Folk Literature* (Stanford University Press, 1996), which last year was awarded the Boyer Prize by the Society for Psychological Anthropology. He has just completed a book-length ethnography, *The Matsigenka: In Nature and Culture*, and is beginning a new book based on more than 30 years of research with Brazilian sharecroppers.

JEFFREY C. JOHNSON is a senior scientist at the Institute for Coastal and Marine Resources and professor in the Department of Sociology, Department of Anthropology, and Department of Biostatistics, East Carolina University. He received his Ph.D. in 1981 from the University of California, Irvine, and is working on a long-term research project comparing group dynamics of the winter-over crews at the American South Pole Station with those at the Polish, Russian, Chinese, and Indian Antarctic Stations. He is the author of *Selecting Ethnographic Informants* (Sage Publications, 1990) and is principal investigator and co-director of the National Science Foundation Summer Institute for Research Design in Cultural Anthropology. He has published extensively in anthropological, sociological, and marine journals and was the former editor-in-chief of the *Journal of Quantitative Anthropology*.

CONRAD PHILLIP KOTTAK (Ph.D., Columbia University, 1966) is professor and chair of anthropology at the University of Michigan. He has done fieldwork in Brazil (since 1962), Madagascar (since 1966), and the United States. His general interests are in the processes by which local cultures are incorporated, and resist incorporation, into larger systems. This interest links his earlier work on ecology and state formation in Africa and Madagascar to his more recent research on global change, development, national and international culture, and the mass media. Kottak's ethnographic books include *Assault on Paradise: Social Change in a Brazilian Village* (McGraw-Hill, 1992, 2d ed.; McGraw-Hill, 1999, 3rd ed.), *Prime-Time Society: An Anthropological Analysis of Television and Culture* (Wadsworth,

1990), and *The Past in the Present: History, Ecology and Cultural Variation in Highland Madagascar* (University of Michigan Press, 1980). His textbooks, all published by McGraw-Hill, include: *Anthropology: The Exploration of Human Diversity* (1997, 7th ed.), *Cultural Anthropology* (1994, 4th ed.), and *Mirror for Humanity* (In press, 2d ed.). His most recent book is (with Kathryn A. Kozaitis) *On Being Different: Diversity and Multiculturalism in the North American Mainstream* (McGraw-Hill, In press). His articles have appeared in the *American Anthropologist*, *Journal of Anthropological Research, American Ethnologist, Ethnology, Human Organization, Transaction/Society, Natural History, Psychology Today*, and *General Anthropology*.

ROBERT I. LEVY (M.D., New York University, 1947) is emeritus professor of anthropology at the University of California, San Diego. Before beginning research in anthropology in 1961 he practiced medicine and psychiatry. His first fieldwork (1961–64) was in Piri, a Tahitian village in French Polynesia. From 1973–75 he worked in Bhaktapur, a Hindu city in Nepal's Kathmandu Valley. His main interest has been in the interaction among historical, cultural, social, and material communal forms and the personal understandings and psychological organization of members of those communities, that is, in psychological- or person-centered anthropology. He is the author of *Tahitians, Mind and Experience in the Society Islands* (University of Chicago Press, 1973), *Mesocosm, Hinduism and the Organization of a Traditional Newar City in Nepal* (University of California Press, 1990), and many articles on various aspects of person-centered anthropology and on Tahitian and Newar ethnography.

GERY W. RYAN (Ph.D., University of Florida, 1995) is an assistant professor of anthropology at the University of Missouri, Columbia. He is a co-editor of the journal *Cultural Anthropology Methods* and has written and lectured on qualitative data collection and analysis techniques, ethnographic decision modeling, and response biases in the field. For two years, he was associate director of the Fieldwork and Qualitative Data Laboratory at the UCLA Medical School where he consulted and trained researchers in text analysis. His substantive interests in medical anthropology focus on how laypeople select among treatment alternatives across illnesses and cultures. He has conducted fieldwork in Mexico and Cameroon and has published in *Social Science & Medicine, Human Organization*, and *Archives of Medical Research*.

ROSS SACKETT is assistant professor of anthropology at Rhodes College in Memphis, Tennessee. He is an ecological anthropologist, with a special interest in the evolution of human activity patterns. During the early 1980s, he investigated the time use and metabolic energy expenditure of the Yukpa Indians (Venezuela), work that formed the core of his masters thesis. Since then he has spent six field seasons working with Saraguro Quichua in the southern Ecuadorian Andes examining energy expenditure, the division of labor, and the Saraguro ethnoclassification of activities. In 1996 he was awarded a doctorate in anthropology (University of California, Los Angeles) for his dissertation on the social evolution of labor and leisure. Following his most recent Ecuadorian fieldwork, he has become interested in documenting the rapidly disappearing craft activities once central to the maintenance of Saraguro ethnic identity. Sackett is co-author (with Michael Paolisso) of *Time Allocation of Venezuela* (HRAF Press, 1988) and is currently working on publications based on his dissertation research.

JEAN J. SCHENSUL (Ph.D., University of Minnesota, 1974) is a cultural anthropologist with experience in using ethnographic research methods in applied health and education settings in the United States and internationally. Founder and executive director of the Institute for Community Research, an independent federally and foundation-funded nonprofit research center based in Hartford, Connecticut, she has been involved in the creation of several other applied research centers, including the Hispanic Health Council and the Center for Intersectoral Community Health Studies in Sri Lanka. Her substantive research interests are in the areas of AIDS and substance-abuse prevention, adolescent development, and ethnographically based theories of prevention. Her most recent publications include The Ethnographer's Toolkit (AltaMira Press, 1998)—a seven-book series on applied ethnographic methods, written and edited with Margaret LeCompte and collaborators. Schensul is the immediate past president of the Society for Applied Anthropology and holds appointments as adjunct professor of anthropology at the University of Connecticut and as a senior fellow, Psychology Department, Yale University.

THOMAS SCHWEIZER is professor and chair of cultural and social anthropology at the University of Cologne. He studied anthropology, sociology, and psychology and received his Ph.D. from the University of Cologne in 1975 (dissertation translated as Methodological Problems of Cross-Cultural Comparisons, Human Relations Area Files Press, 1987; originally published in German in 1978). He has taught at the Universities of Bayreuth and Tübingen, and has conducted fieldwork on agrarian and social change in Java/Indonesia. His research interests are in anthropological theory, methods, economy, social organization, social change, and Southeast Asia. His books include *Reisanbau in einem javanischen Dorf* (Cologne and Vienna: Böhlau-Verlag, 1989), *Muster sozialer Ordnung* (Berlin: Reimer Verlag, 1996), and (edited with D. R. White) *Kinship, Networks, and Exchange* (Cambridge University Press, 1998). He has also published papers on his fieldwork and reassessments of ethnographic cases using social network approaches. He is currently writing a book on social networks and ethnography.

ROBERT T. TROTTER, II (Ph.D., Southern Methodist University, 1976) is Regent's Professor of Anthropology at Northern Arizona University, Flagstaff, Arizona. His primary research area is the investigation of cross-cultural barriers to the delivery of health care in multicultural settings. He has studied traditional healing in Mexican American communities; alcohol and drug use in Mexican American, Native American, Anglo American, and African American communities in the United States; and international classifications of disease, migrant health issues, and border health. His current research is in cultural epidemiology and prevention of the spread of HIV infection in active drug-using communities in the United States. He is also assisting in developing the World Health Organization's International Classification of Impairments, Disabilities and Handicaps (ICIDH). He has a long-term interest and expertise in computer-assisted ethnographic research and in the development and use of advanced ethnographic methods for medical anthropological research. He is involved with developing midrange anthropological theory that can be applied in multidisciplinary settings, especially in cognitive anthropology and social network research. Among his recent publications are *Multicultural AIDS Prevention Programs* (editor, The Hayworth Press, 1996) and *Curandisimo: Mexican American Folk Healing* (with Juan Antonio Chavira) (University of Georgia Press, 1997, 2d ed.).

CORAL B. WAYLAND is an assistant professor in the Department of Sociology, Anthropology, and Social Work at the University of North Carolina, Charlotte. She has recently completed her dissertation on child health among the urban poor in the Amazon (Ph.D., University of Pittsburgh, summer of 1998). Her current research examines the gendered nature of medicinal plant use among low-income households in Brazil.

SUSAN C. WELLER is a professor in the Department of Preventive Medicine and Community Health in the Division of Sociomedical Sciences at the University of Texas Medical Branch in Galveston. She received her graduate training in Social Sciences at the University of California, Irvine (Ph.D., 1980) and has taught at the University of California Irvine Medical Center and at the University of Pennsylvania. She is a medical anthropologist and has conducted fieldwork in Guatemala, Mexico, and the United States. Recent projects include a series of cross-cultural comparisons of illness beliefs among Latinos in rural Guatemala, urban Mexico, rural South Texas, and urban Connecticut (with R. Baer, L. Pachter, and R. Trotter). Her research focuses on the description of beliefs and attitudes, including intracultural variation, informant accuracy, and statistical modeling. She also has published two Sage monographs (with A. K. Romney): *Systematic Data Collection* (1988, in the qualitative research methods series) and *Metric Scaling* (1990, in the quantitative methods series).

Author Index

(*n* identifies a note)

Abdullah, M., 466
Abedi, M., 241
Abel, T. F., 58
Abelson, R. P., 604
Aberle, D., 570
Abrahamson, A.A.A., 368, 397
Abu-Lughod, L., 60, 68, *252n8*, 415, 422, 443*n5*
Achinstein, P , 44
Acredolo, L. P., 442*n3*
Adair, J., 479
Adams, J., 515, 521
Adenaike, C., 533*n4*
Adler, P., 262
Agaf, A., 417, 442n3
Agar, M., 13, 14, 41, 48, 68, 131, 137, 259, 271, 272, 608, 620
Ahern, E., 521
Ahern, J., 360*n3*
Aissen, J., 443*n10*
Alarcon, N., 218
Albanese, J. P., 630*n6*
Albert, H., 45, 62
al-Bindari, M, 466
Aldenderfer, M., 563
Alexander, R. M., 307
Allen, K., 279
Alpers, E., 527
Alter, G., 520
Altmann, J., 314, 315, 317, 320
Altork, K., 282
Alvarez, R., 239

Amadiume, I., 210
American Anthropological Association, 273
Amin, S., 466
Andaya, L., 533*n4*
Angell, R., 526
Angeloni, E., 741
Anglin, M., 217
Appadurai, A., 239, 245, 251*n4*, 252n10
Appleby, J., 533*n10*
Arabie, P., 389
Araujo, L., 613
Ardener, E., 105, 418, 424
Arensberg, C. M., 307
Aries, P., 521
Asad, T., 189
Asch, P., 468, 488
Asch, T., 468, 469, 478, 488, 499*n9*
Austin, J. L., 91, 95, 96, 415
Azoulay, L., 462

Baba, M., 691
Babbie, E., 151, 152
Bachelard, G., 112
Backhouse, R. E., 45
Baer, H., 693, 702, 722
Baer, R. D., 398, 400, 402, 711
Bahloul, J., 112
Bailey, F. G., 96
Bailey, R. C., 317
Bakhtin, M. M., 415, 419
Baksh, M., 314, 319–320, 321
Baldwin, J. A., 693, 697, 700, 701, 712, 713

Balierio, M., 570
Balikei, A., 480, 482, 486
Balzer, W., 51, 64, 69, 70, 71, 79n6
Bandhauer, D., 14
Banks, M., 462
Barker, S. F., 44
Barnes, J. A., 186
Barnett, G., 621, 622
Barnett, H., 569
Barnett, M. N., 112
Barnouw, V., 287
Barry, III, H., 661, 670
Bartenieff, I., 459–460, 473
Bartleborth, T., 62, 64, 65
Bartlett, F. C., 601, 604
Basch, L., 240
Basso, E., 417
Basso, K., 415, 421, 438
Batchelder, W. H., 13, 61, 304, 397, 399, 400,
    569, 570, 698, 711, 719
Bateson, G., 461, 472, 476, 483, 698
Bateson, P., 307, 309, 315, 317, 318, 320, 321
Baum, W., 528
Bauman, R., 101, 413, 415, 417, 419–421,
    422n2, 440, 442n1, 442n2
Bearlson, D. J., 699
Bechtel, R. J., 617, 618
Becker, G., 75
Becker, H., 608, 609
Behar, R., 142, 218, 224, 263, 521, 527, 530,
    533n6
Behrens, C., 470
Bell, D., 282
Bell, K., 210, 214
Bellman, B., 479, 480
Belsey, D., 584
Benedict, B., 239
Benedict, R., 287
Bennett, D., 520
Bennetta, J., 479, 480
Benveniste, E., 415, 442n3
Berelson, B., 613
Berg, D. N., 16
Berger, P. L., 699
Berkowitz, S. D., 74, 75
Berlin, B. O., 368, 372
Bernard, H. R., 13, 41, 61, 134, 137, 151,
    152, 262, 270, 272, 284, 302, 307, 315,
    321, 360n3, 379, 499n3, 596, 601, 608,
    614, 623, 697, 707, 710, 719, 745

Bertaux, D., 527
Bertaux-Wiame, I., 527
Besnier, N., 597
Best, J. A., 609
Besteman, C., 528
Betzig, L., 75, 315
Bidney, D., 569
Bieleman, B., 705, 707
Biella, R., 470
Biernacki, P., 707
Biersack, A., 515
Bierstedt, A., 70
Biklen, S., 608
Bingham, A., 566, 587
Birdwell-Pheasant, D., 519
Birdwhistell, R., 459, 473, 477
Bizarro Ujpan, I., 596
Black, M., 115
Blackman, M., 460, 526
Blakely, T., 461
Blalock, Jr., H. M., 667, 668, 678
Blanc, C. S., 240
Blashfield, R. K., 563
Blaug, M., 45
Bleicher, J., 629n2
Blier, S. P., 98
Blimes, J., 718
Bloch, M., 97, 530, 533n10
Blok, A., 533n6
Blount, D., 630n6
Blowsnake, S., 15, 31n1, 596
Boas, F., 46, 135, 174–175, 419, 463, 585, 596
Bock, P. K., 266
Boehm, C., 102
Bogdan, R., 608
Bohannan, L., 244, 520
Bohman, J., 40, 46n3, 66
Bolles, A. L., 216
Bolton, R., 282
Bond, G. C., 90
Bonvillain, N., 221
Boorman, S. A., 389
Booth, R. E., 162–163
Boothe, C., 16
Borenstein, M. H., 314, 315
Borgatti, S., 389, 391, 396, 554, 622, 626
Borgerhoff Mulder, M. B., 321, 323, 324, 327
Bornstein, M. H., 314, 315
Borofsky, R., 53, 72, 104, 518, 533n8
Boruch, R. F., 13

Boster, J. S., 13, 152, 159, 302, 373, 389, 400, 402, 569, 570, 572, 587, 710
Bott, E., 700, 712
Bourdieu, P., 92, 95, 97, 102, 107, 111, 116, 414
Bourgois, P. I., 14, 23, 60, 260–261, 267, 272, 276, 285, 289, 701, 722
Bowen, A. M., 693, 697, 700, 701, 712, 713
Bowen, E. S., 739
Bowen, J., 427
Bowlin, J. R., 56
Boyer, L. B., 13
Boyer, R. M., 13
Bradburn, N. M., 360*n*3, 375
Bradley, C., 630*n*6, 662, 664, 667, 670, 672, 673, 675
Brady, J. P., 700
Brandt, E., 427
Braudel, F., 113
Breedlove, D., 368, 372
Brenneis, D., 415, 418
Brettell, C., 516, 519, 521, 527, 531, 534*n*13
Brewer, B. W., 13
Brewer, D. D., 13, 397
Briggs, C. L., 360*n*3, 413, 415, 417–420, 423, 427, 438, 440, 442*n*1; 442*n*2, 443*n*10
Briggs, J., 279
Brim, J. A., 13, 134, 136, 154
Brislin, R. W., 383
Britt, T., 612
Brodbeck, M., 46*n*3, 52
Brodkin, K., 211, 217, 221, 224
Brody, H., 739
Bronfenbrenner, U., 701
Brouwer, M., 617, 630*n*6
Brown, J. K., 211
Brown, M. B., 396
Brown, P. J., 741
Brown, R., 417, 576
Brumfiel, E., 219, 220
Bruner, E. M., 90, 101
Bruns, G., 629*n*2
Bryant, C., 17
Buchholtz, C., 397
Bucholtz, M., 422
Bullough, V. L., 653
Bunnin, N., 42, 79*n*1
Burke, P., 513
Burris, M. A., 222
Burt, L.B.S., 4432*n*7

Burt, R. S., 375
Burton, D. M., 629*n*2
Burton, M. L., 389, 390, 393, 630*n*6, 661, 654, 655, 662, 664, 667, 670, 672–674, 679, 682*n*3
Bynum, C., 533*n*4, 534*n*18
Byrne, B., 13, 147

Caldarola, V., 460
Calhoun, C., 248
Cameron, G.T., 630*n*6
Campbell, D. T., 13, 139, 147, 148, 150, 152, 155, 550, 555, 658, 667, 668, 692
Campbell, G., 534*n*10
Campbell, J., 215, 379
Campos, T., 705, 706
Cannell, C. F., 360*n*3
Caplan, P., 214, 218, 280–281, 282
Cardador, M. T., 630*n*6
Carey, J. W., 613, 616
Carley, K., 623, 624, 624*n*2
Carlstein, T., 313
Carmines, E. G., 667, 676
Carmone, F. J., 397
Carnap, R., 44
Carneiro, R., 586
Caro, T. M., 321, 323, 324, 327
Carr, E., 533*n*10
Carroll, J., 586
Cashdan, E., 66
Cassell, J., 275, 286
Casson, R., 604
Casteñeda, C., 276
Castillo, C. O., 700
Caton, S., 423
Caudillo, C., 706
Cernea, M. M., 757
Cesara, M., 281, 282
Chafe, W., 418, 601
Chagnon, N., 292*n*7, 469, 470, 739
Chakraborty, G., 630*n*6
Chalfen, R, 486
Chambers, E., 692
Chan, A. R. M., 625
Chance, J., 515, 526, 532*n*2
Chanock, F., 485
Chanoff, D., 261
Chaplin, E., 472
Chapple, E. D., 307
Charmaz, K., 608

Chavez, L. R, 373, 398, 401, 711
Chick, G. E., 386
Chvatal, V., 586
Cicourel, A. V., 411
City of Hartford, Department of Social Services, 708
Clark, C. C., 617, 630n6
Clark, S., 526
Clatts, M. C., 701
Cleveland, W., 559
Clifford, J., 41, 49, 95, 100, 221, 241, 265, 271–272, 443n10
Cline, S., 521
Cobb, W. J., 360n3
Cochran, W. G., 660
Codere, H., 527
Cohen, A., 106, 109, 612
Cohen, C. B., 218
Cohen, J., 616
Cohen, R., 12, 160, 192
Cohn, B., 515, 516, 521, 523, 530
Cohn, C., 221
Colby, B. N., 95, 617, 618, 630n6
Cole, J., 526
Coleman, J. S., 66, 74, 75
Colen, S., 251n7
Collado-Ardon, R., 163–165
Collier, G., 525, 534n17
Collier, J., 221, 469, 471–476, 485
Collier, M., 471–473
Colombres, A., 466, 481
Comaroff, J. (Jean), 514, 515, 523, 526, 531
Comaroff, J. (John), 515, 526, 531
Conaway, M. E., 214
Conkey, M., 219, 220
Conklin, H., 372
Connell, P., 217
Connor, L., 478
Consorte, J. G., 13, 147
Cook, T. D., 13, 136, 139, 147, 148, 150, 152, 555, 667
Corbin, J., 608, 609, 708
Cordell, D., 518, 534n11
Cosmides, L., 576
Counts, D., 215
Cowan, G., 611
Cowan, J. K., 97
Coy, M., 107, 108, 265
Coyle, S., 697, 701, 713
Crabtree, B.F., 613

Craig, R. S., 630n6
Craig, R.T., 630n7
Crain, M. M., 95
Crapazano, V., 526, 527
Crawford, P., 474, 483, 488
Cressey, D. R., 625
Crick, M., 95
Crosbie, P., 554, 555
Cross, Jr., W. J., 700
Cruikshank, J., 529
Csordas, T. J., 109, 361n5
Curtain, J., 596
Curtis, R., 712

Dahlén, T., 242
Damon, W., 699
Danchy, J. J., 355, 357, 360n4
D'Andrade, R., 40, 54, 65, 74, 76, 303, 368, 378, 393, 395–399, 604, 605, 607, 610, 623, 675
Daniels, M., 701, 713
Danielson, W. A., 630n6
Danowski, J., 621
Darnell, R., 421
Darnton, R., 533n4
Das, V., 113, 252n8
Davidson, D., 56
Davies, B., 419
Davis, D., 518
Davis, J., 521
Davis, N., 515, 533n4
deBessa, Y., 377
de Brigard, E., 462, 464, 468, 471, 472, 475, 478, 481, 498n3, 498n4, 499n11
Deese, J., 613
de Jorio, A., 105
Delaney, C., 213
Delbos, G., 107
DeMaillie, R., 532
Dening, G., 514
Denzin, N. K., 14, 141, 624
de Olivares, K., 14
de Ridder, J. A., 630n6
Derrida, J., 49
deSilva, A., 698, 699, 724
Desjarlais, R., 264–265
De Valck, C., 14
Devereaux, G., 360n4
de Vo, S., 706
DeVos, G., 702

DeWalt, B. R., 269, 280, 288, 290, 377–378, 672
DeWalt, K., 269, 279, 290
Dey, I., 609, 613
Diawara, M., 467
Diaz, A., 705, 707
Diaz, A.M.B., 705
Diederich, W., 70, 71
di Leonardo, M., 223
Dilthey, W., 47, 57, 629n2
Dirks, N. B., 49, 515, 523
Ditton, J., 273
Ditton, P., 210
Divale, W. T., 655, 671, 672
Dixon, R. B., 596
Dixon, W. J., 396
Doerfel, M. L., 622
Dohrenwend, B. S., 360n4
Dolgin, J. L., 49, 95
Doncel, C., 705
dosSantos, J., 570
Doucet, L., 618
Dougherty, J.W.D., 107
Douglas, J. D., 360n3
Douglas, M., 91, 99, 111
Douglass, W., 514
Dovring, K., 79n2
Dow, M. M., 679, 682n3
Downing, P., 602
Draper, P., 577
Drass, K., 626
Dresch, P., 90
Dressler, W., 368, 393, 570
Driver, H., 563, 588, 655
Drummond, L., 251n6
Dryfoos, J. C., 701
Du Bois, C. A., 13
Du Bois, J., 13, 415, 418
Dufour, D. L., 315
Dumont, J., 41, 60
Dunaway, D., 528
Dunbar, R.I.M., 314
Dundes, A., 98
Dungy, C. I., 368, 371, 398
Dunlop, I., 482, 483
Dunphy, D. C., 613, 617, 631n10
Duranti, A., 415, 418, 419, 421, 433, 438, 722
Durkheim, E., 111
Duval, R., 554
Duvall, D. C., 629n3

Dworkin, P. H., 398
Dworkin, S. F., 368
Dwyer, K., 281

Earle, T., 65, 73
Eco, H., 119
Edginton, E., 554
Edholm, F., 211
Edmonson, M. S., 596, 601
Edwards, D. B., 243
Edwards, E., 460
Edwards, J. A., 426
Efrom, B., 554
Eggan, F., 655
Eibl-Eisesfeldt, I., 320
Ekman, P., 40
Elder, G., 520
Eley, G., 49
El Guindi, F., 460, 476, 477, 483, 486–490, 493, 497n1, 499n13, 499n14, 499n15, 596
El-Haj, N. A., 90
Ellegard, A., 588
Ellen, R. F., 132, 135
Ellis, J., 412
El Saadawi, N., 216
Ember, C. R., 302, 630n6, 648–650, 652, 655, 662, 664, 665, 667, 670–673, 677, 678, 680, 681, 682n1, 682n2, 740
Ember, M., 153–154, 630n6, 648, 652–655, 657, 665, 670, 671, 675, 677–681, 740
Engelman, L., 396, 397
Engle, P., 302
Ensminger, J., 66, 74
Erickson, E., 361n9
Erikson, F., 439
Errington, F. K., 41, 243
Ervin, A., 693
Escobar, A., 243
Esser, H., 66, 75
Ethnographic Atlas, 659, 662
Etienne, M., 204, 211–213
Evans, G. W., 397
Evans-Pritchard, E. E., 72, 109, 514
Ewick, P., 221

Fabian, J., 251n6
Faia, M. A., 140
Fan, D. P., 618
Fanshel, D., 411, 423
Fararo, T. J., 66, 74

Farnell, B. M., 99, 120n5, 411, 414, 416, 418, 422, 427, 433–439, 443
Farris, J., 460
Faust, K., 74, 75, 386, 396, 700
Feiring, B., 586
Feld, S., 115, 418, 421, 427, 428, 436
Feld, S. C., 630n6
Feldhutter, I, 320
Fenno, R. F., 14
Ferber, A., 459, 485
Ferguson, J., 41, 239
Fernandez, J., 530, 534n19
Fernandez, J. W., 93, 95, 97, 98, 101, 102, 106, 108, 114, 115, 118, 119
Fernandez, R., 285
Fernandez-Kelly, M. P., 217
Ferreira-Pinto, J., 386
Fetterman, D. M., 692
Fielding, N. G., 630n5
Fillenbaum, S., 368
Fink, A., 375
Fink, E. J., 630n6
Fischer, J. L., 668
Fischer, M. M. J., 41, 49, 241, 252n12, 467, 719
Fisher, R., 554
Fishman, J., 417
Fiske, M., 360n3
FitzGerald, G., 397
Flaherty, R., 481
Flannery, K., 219
Fleisher, M., 14
Fleiss, J. L., 630n7
Florio, S., 718
Fluehr-Lobban, C., 21–22, 177, 178, 184, 185, 278, 285–287
Fogelson, R., 524
Folbre, N., 221
Fontana, A., 360n3
Ford, C. S., 651, 673
Fortes, M., 260
Fowler, F. J., 374
Fox. A. A., 418, 436
Fox, R., 49, 443n10, 524
Frake, C. O., 368, 372
Frank, G., 527
Frank, O., 705
Franklin, S., 50, 221, 223
Franz, C. E., 630n6
Franzosi, R., 630n6

Frazer, J. G., Sir, 115
Frechione, J., 290
Freeman, D., 135, 153, 278, 287
Freeman, H. E., 377, 386, 389
Freeman, L. C., 378, 386, 719
Freeman, S., 378, 386, 520
Freidman, J., 246, 251n6
Freire, P., 702
Frey, B. S., 66, 75
Frey, J. H., 360n3
Friedl, E., 209, 211
Friedman, J., 252n9, 518
Friedman, S. R., 712
Friedrich, P., 49, 115, 523, 526
Friendly, M. L., 397
Frykman, J., 530
Fuglesang, N., 244
Furbee, L., 602, 603, 618
Furbee-Losee, L., 596

Gable, E., 90
Gacs, U., 209
Gadamer, H., 48, 50, 57, 58, 61, 67
Gagnon, J. H., 700
Gailey, C., 523
Gailey, C. W., 212, 213, 223
Gal, S., 421
Galaskiewicz, J., 74, 75, 700
Galt, A., 521
Galton, F., 677–679
Gannotti, M., 586
Gantz, W., 630n6
Garcia Canclini, N., 251n6
Gardin, J., 106
Gardner, R., 115
Garfinkel, H., 417
Garrett, A. M., 360n3
Garrison, V., 251n7
Garro, L. C., 157–158, 393, 395, 398, 400
Garsten, C., 242
Garvey, C., 422
Gearing, J., 281, 282, 284
Geer, B., 608, 609
Geer, J. H., 700
Geertz, C., 48, 50, 57, 58, 59, 60, 61, 67, 92, 106, 113, 114, 263, 268, 722
Geier, M., 44
Gelatt, R., 443n7
Geldsetzer, L., 47
Genser, S. G., 701

Gerbner, G., 617, 630*n*6
Gero, Joan, 106, 219
Gessell, A., 472
Gewertz, D. B., 41, 243, 514
Gibbs, R. W., 94
Giddens, A., 102, 414
Gilbert, J. R., 609
Gillett, G., 412, 414, 415
Gilliam, A., 90
Gillman, A., 445
Gilly, M.C., 612, 630*n*6
Ginsburg, F., 221, 223, 245, 486
Giordiano, P., 712
Giroux, H. A., 702
Gladwin, C., 698
Gladwin, T., 13
Glantz, S. A., 630*n*6
Glaser, B. G., 139, 608, 609
Glaser, B. O., 696
Glaser, J. M., 14
Glasersfeld, E. von, 50
Glasser, I., 706
Gleason, G. R., 717, 723
Gmelch, S., 527
Goddard, P. E., 596
Goffman, E., 417, 433
Golde, P., 209
Golder, T. V., 386
Goldin, L. R., 165–166
Goldschmidt, W., 134, 658
Goldstein, L. J., 93
Goldstein, M., 712
Gombrich, E. H., 105
Gómez, L., 706
Gonzalez, M., 222
González Ventura, J., 597
Good, K., 263, 276–277, 281
Goodall, E. W., 443*n*6
Goodenough, W. H., 59, 586, 668
Goodwin, C., 417–419, 421, 422, 433, 438, 473, 722
Goodwin, M., 417, 438
Goody, J., 521, 526, 530
Gorden, R. L., 360*n*3
Gordon, D., 218, 224
Gorfain, P., 90
Görlich, J., 66, 74
Götthard, W., 465
Gottlieb, A., 221
Gottschalk, L. A., 526, 617, 618, 630*n*6

Gough, K., 209
Graburn, N. H. H., 243, 251*n*6
Graff, H., 527
Graham, L. R., 414, 415, 418, 419, 421, 423, 428, 430, 438–441, 442*n*3
Green, P. E., 397
Greenacre, M., 586
Greenson, R. R., 360*n*4
Gregory, J., 518, 534*n*11
Grele, R, 528
Grewal, I., 218
Griaule, M., 461, 485
Griffith, D. C., 161
Grimshaw, A. D., 417
Gross, D. R., 313, 315–317, 320, 324
Gross, L., 486
Grossbart, S., 519
Gruenbaum, E., 215–216
Guba, E. G., 608, 609
Gujarati, D., 576, 583, 586
Gulliver, P. H., 515, 522, 532, 533*n*5, 533*n*6, 534*n*16
Gummeson, E., 14
Gumperz, J. J., 417, 421, 442*n*1, 443*n*5
Gunesekara, A. M., 11
Gunn, J., 480
Gupta, A., 41, 239
Gusterson, H., 249
Guthrie, S., 115

Haddon, A. C., 11
Hage, P., 76, 621
Hall, E., 459
Hall, Kira, 422
Hames, R., 315, 323
Hammel, E., 519, 576
Handelman, D., 90
Handler, R., 90, 413, 417
Handron, D. S., 630*n*6
Handwerker, P., 378, 553–555, 563, 570, 579, 585, 587, 588
Hanks, W. F., 416, 421, 433, 598, 600
Hanley, S., 518, 521
Hannerz, U., 239, 242, 247, 248, 251*n*1, n6
Hansen, K. T., 246, 523, 526, 531
Harary, F., 76, 621
Haraway, D., 220
Harding, S., 206, 208, 215
Hardy, K., 519
Hareven, T., 519, 520

Harman, H., 563
Harpending, H., 577
Harré, R., 56, 412–415, 419, 442*n*3
Harrell, S., 518
Harris, J., 553
Harris, M., 13, 97, 147, 302, 307, 739, 740
Harris, O., 211
Harrison, F., 224
Hartley, J. A., 152, 373, 402, 569, 587
Harvis, G. K., 706
Haskins, L., 519
Hastrup, K., 239
Hatcherson, J., 553
Haug, M. R., 376
Haugen, E., 425
Haviland, J., 416, 418, 423, 433, 440
Haviland, W., 740
Hawkes, K., 315, 320–321
Hawkins, J., 534*n*19
Hayes, J., 629*n*12
Hazan, A. R., 630*n*6
Hearn, J., 14
Heath, C., 418
Heath, S. B., 438, 702
Hegeman, E. B., 14
Heider, K., 461, 464, 482, 486, 497
Hemlatha, R. S., 716
Hempel, C. G., 45*n*2, 46, 46*n*3, 62, 63, 68, 69
Henige, D., 528
Henley, N. M., 368, 393
Henry, J., 13
Henry, L, 534
Herdt, G., 361*n*5
Hermer, C., 461
Hernández Jiménez, A., 596
Herzfeld, M., 90, 92–95, 98, 105, 106, 109–112, 116–119, 602
Hill, C. E. , 691, 702
Hill, J. (James), 480
Hill, J. (Jane), 413, 415, 417, 418
Hill, J. (Johnathan), 104, 533*n*8
Hill, K., 315, 321, 322, 413, 417
Hill, M. A., 396
Hirschman, E. C., 614, 630*n*6
Hitchcock, J., 608
Hockett, C. F., 355, 357, 360*n*4
Hockings, P., 461, 465
Hoehler-Fatton, C., 528
Hoff, L. A., 215, 217
Hogan, D., 519

Hogden, M. T., 111
Holladay, J., 629*n*12
Hollan, D. W., 360*n*1, 361*n*5, 361*n*7
Holland, D., 74, 527, 607, 698, 709
Holliday, L., 221
Hollis, M, 40
Holloway, M., 15
Holmberg, A., 693
Holmes, T. H., 383
Holquist, M., 418
Holstein, J. A., 360*n*3
Holsti, O. R., 613, 618, 628*n*1, 630*n*6, 630*n*7
Holy, L., 261
Homiak. J., 465
Honigmann, J., 12
hooks, b., 278
Hoopes, J., 528
Horwitz, R., 525
Hosmer, D., 586
Howard, J., 11
Howell, N., 284, 518
HRAF, 659
Hrdy, S. B., 220
Hsu, F.L.K., 13
Huang, C., 518, 519
Hubbell, F. A., 373, 398, 401, 711
Huberman, A. M., 152, 608–610, 613, 614, 708
Hubert, L. J., 158, 587
Hudson, A. E., 651, 673
Hughes, E. C., 608, 609
Hughes, P. H., 706
Hugh-Jones, C., 286
Hunt, E. S., 241
Hunt, G., 596
Hunt, L., 533*n*10
Huntington, G. E., 285–286
Hurlbert, S. H., 144, 147
Hurtado, A. M., 315, 321, 322
Husmann, R., 465
Hutchins, E., 386, 605
Hutchinson, J. W., 397
Hutchinson, S. A., 608
Hyman, H. H., 360*n*3
Hymes, D., 412, 416, 421, 423–425, 430, 438, 440, 441, 442*n*1, 442*n*2, 443n5, 594, 598
Hymes, V., 598, 599

Ildefonso, G., 712
Imrich, D. J., 630*n*6

Inder, P. M., 14
Irizarry, R., 701
Ironsmith, M., 148
Irvine, J., 413, 415, 417, 418, 436
Issac, R., 533n4, 533n6
Ives, E. D., 422

Jablonko, A., 465, 471
Jacknis, I., 472, 473
Jackson, J., 270, 271, 272, 278
Jackson, M., 92, 107–109
Jacob, M., 535
Jacobs, S., 209
Jacobson, L., 674
Jaggar, A., 208
Jakobson, R., 93, 95, 97, 415
James, J., 577
Jameson, F., 96
Jang, H., 621
Janik, A., 44
Jaraush, K., 519
Jarrett, R., 222
Jarvella, R. J., 442n3
Jefferson, G., 417
Jeffrey K., 519
Jehn, K. A., 618
Jelinek, C. E., 110
Jenkins, T., 107, 108, 116
Jenrich, R. I., 396
Jhala, J., 467
Jiron, D., 701
Johnsen, E., 707
Johnsen, E. C., 707
Johnson, A., 302, 306, 314, 319, 324, 327, 630n6, 654
Johnson, A. W., 13, 65, 73
Johnson, J. C., 133, 137, 143, 147, 148, 151–153, 159, 161, 166, 167, 374, 386, 572, 587, 700, 703, 705
Johnson, K. E., 13
Johnson, M., 92, 109, 114, 120n5, 606
Johnson, O. R., 319, 324, 327
Johnson-Laird, P. N., 604
Johnston, F. E., 377
Jordan, G., 702
Jorgensen, J. G., 655
Jorgenson, D., 262
Jorgenson, J., 567, 588
Jorion, P., 11, 107
Jose, B., 712

Josselson, H. H., 411

Kaeppler, A., 421
Kagan, J., 377, 386, 389
Kahn, J., 523
Kahn, R. L., 360n3
Kaid, L, 630n6
Kanuha, V., 217
Kaplan, C. H., 705, 707
Kaplan, H., 315, 321
Karim, W. J., 214, 282
Karp, I., 107
Kasakoff, A., 302, 521
Kassis, H., 629n2
Katz, E., 244
Katz, L., 676
Kaufer, D. S., 623, 624
Kaufman, D. R., 207
Kay, M. A., 372
Kay, P. D., 368, 372, 378
Keane, W., 415, 418
Kearney, M. H., 608, 610, 611
Keating, E., 433
Keesing, R., 55, 569
Keiffer, M., 391, 397
Kelle, U., 614, 630n5
Kellogg, S., 515, 523
Kelly, E. F., 617
Kemeney, T., 629n2
Kemnitzer, D. S., 49, 95
Kemper, H.C.G., 310
Kempton, W., 152, 373, 402, 569, 587, 607
Kendal, L., 526
Kendall, M. B., 107
Kendall, P. L., 360n3
Kendon, A., 105, 418, 421, 422, 433, 459, 485
Kennedy, R., 651, 673
Kennedy, S., 630n6
Kertzer, D., 515, 516, 519, 520, 534n13
Khalaf, S. N., 239
Khan, A., 209
Khan, M. E., 716
Khant, U., 706
Kiiski, S., 312, 30n6
Killworth, P. D., 321, 379, 707, 719
Killworth, P.R.P., 14
Kim, B., 71
Kincheloe, J. L., 141
King, G., 13
Kirch, P., 533n9

Kirk, J., 132, 387, 393, 718
Kirkpatrick, J., 415
Kish, L., 553, 660, 678
Kitahara, M., 681
Klapp, O. E., 109, 110
Klass, M., 285
Klein, D., 360n3
Klein, R. E., 377, 381, 382, 386, 389, 391, 397
Klein, W., 442n3
Kleinbaum, D. G., 146, 148, 151
Kleinman, A. M., 113, 245, 698
Kleinman, J., 245
Kleinnijenhuis, J., 630n6
Klovdahl, A. S., 701, 713
Kluckhohn, C., 360n3, 526
Knight, J., 66, 74
Knodel, J., 521
Koester, S., 162–163, 701
Kohli, M., 527
Kolbe, R. H., 630n6
Koloss, H., 465
Kondo, D. K., 41, 60, 107
Kornblum, W., 14, 269
Kortendick, O., 613, 614
Kottak, C. P., 739, 740, 753, 756, 757
Kozel, N., 715, 716
Kracke, W., 361n5
Kraemer, H. C., 680
Krausz, M., 56
Krebs, S., 476, 477
Krech, S., 532n1, 532n3
Krige, E. J., 210
Krige, J. D., 210
Krippendorff, K., 613, 617, 630n6, 630n7
Kristjanson, L. J., 14
Kroeber, A., 12, 15, 17, 46, 102, 251, 530, 588, 596
Kronenfeld, D., 95, 379
Kroskrity, P., 417
Kruskal, J., 393, 394, 396, 563
Kuh, E., 584
Kuhn, T. S., 50
Kuipers, J., 419
Kuipers, T.A.F., 45n2, 64
Kulick, D., 280–281, 282
Kumar, K., 269, 276
Kupper, L. L., 146, 148, 151
Kutschera, F. von, 42, 54, 57, 58, 83
Kuznar, L. A., 40, 140

Laban, R., 474
Labov, W., 411, 423
Labovitz, S., 680
Laderman, C., 436
Laderman, R., 421
Laffal, J., 618, 631n11
Lagacé, R. O., 659
Lajard, J., 462
Lakatos, I., 51
Lakoff, G. K, 92, 109, 114, 606
Lampert, M. D., 426
Lamphere, L., 206, 208–211, 221
Lancaster, J., 220
Lang, H., 40
Lang, J., 13, 147
Langness, L., 526, 527
Laslett, P., 519
Lasorsa, D. I., 630n6
Latsis, S., 45
Lave, J., 107
Lawler, J., 14
Lawrence, D., 112
Lawson, A., 90
Leach, E. R., 72, 100, 260, 261, 267
Leach, J. W., 98
Leacock, E. B., 204, 205, 209–213
Leal, H., 706
Leap, W., 280–282
Leavitt, J., 109
LeCompte, M., 708
Lederman, R., 278
Lee, R. B., 314
Lee, R. M., 284, 630n5
Leggett-Frazier, N.K., 630n6
Leibowitz, L., 220
Lemeshow, S., 586
Lenk, H., 54
Leone, M. P., 106
Leroi-Gourham, A., 485
Lessinger, J., 241
LeVine, R. A., 102, 134, 137
Levine, R. V., 314
Levine, S., 527
Levinson, D., 652, 672, 674
Lévi-Strauss, C., 63, 91, 109, 288
Levitt, E. E., 700
Levy, J., 178
Levy, R. I., 336, 345, 346, 356, 360n2, 361n5, 361n7, 361n10, 361n11
Lewin, E., 217, 223, 280–282

Lewis, C. E., 385
Lewis, I., 514, 520
Lewis, M. A., 385
Lewis, N., 221
Lewis, O., 287, 534n20
Lhermillier, A., 312
Lhermillier, N., 312
Lieberman, D., 368, 393
Liebes, T., 244
Liebow, E., 701, 713
Liem, J., 577
Light, R. J., 630n7
Liikkanen, M., 312
Limón, J. E., 95
Lincoln, Y. S., 14, 141, 608, 609
Linde, C., 527
Lindenberg, S., 66, 75
Linder, D. E., 13
Lindesmith, A.R., 625
Lindsay, E. A., 609
Lindstrom, L., 41
Lindzey, G., 13
Linnekin, J., 523, 534n17
Lins Ribeiro, G., 243
Linz, C., 630n6
Liou, H., 368
List, G., 418, 421
Lobban, R., 285–287, 493
Lock, M., 113
Lockhead, G. R., 397
Löfgren, O., 243, 530
Lofland, J., 698
Lofland, L. H., 608
Loftus, E., 378
Loizos, P., 463, 464, 468, 474, 478, 484, 485, 499n17
Lomax, A., 459–460, 473, 474, 477
Lonkila, M., 608
López, S., 706
Lovely, R., 701, 713
Low, S. M., 112, 377
Lowie, R. H., 46, 135, 596
Luckman, T., 699
Lucy, J., 417, 419, 722
Lumière, L., 462
Lumpkin, J., 302
Lurie, N., 209, 596
Lutz, C., 221, 415
Lutz, K., 274–275, 279
Lykes, M. B., 188

Lynch, K., 519, 520
Lynd, R., 12
Lyotard, J., 49

MacCormack, C., 212
MacDougall, D., 463, 484–486, 497
MacGregor, F., 472, 476
MacMahon, M.K.C., 424, 425, 443n6
MacVean, R. B., 377
Maddox, R., 522
Madud, K. A., 706
Magaña, J. R., 393, 397, 401
Magna Publications, 749
Maitland, F., 513
Malinowski, B., 10, 23, 72, 260, 270, 278, 281, 289
Malkki, L. H., 112, 241
Mandelbaum, D. G., 757
Mandler, J., 603
Mann, K., 521
Mann, N. C., 401
Mannheim, B., 413, 419
Manning, P. K., 624
Manuel, P., 423
Marburger, W., 378
Marchetti, K., 630n6
Marchi, N. de, 45
Marcus, G., 153, 719
Marcus, G. E., 41, 49, 95, 219, 221, 248–250, 251n4, 252n12, 443n10
Marcus, J., 219
Margolis, M. L., 251n7
Marks, D., 462, 466
Markus, G. B., 558
Marrow, C., 701, 713
Marsden, P. V., 711
Marshall, C., 706
Marshall, J., 468, 472
Martin, E., 221
Martin, M. M., 671, 682n2
Martin, P., 307, 309, 315, 317, 318, 320, 321
Martindale, C., 629n2
Martinez, R. G., 373, 398, 401, 711
Martínez, W., 488
Marx, Karl, 94
Maryanski, A., 73
Mascia-Lees, F., 218
Mason, K., 528
Mason, W., 528
Massey, W. C., 655

Mathews, H., 603, 604
Maynes, M., 527
McCarty, C., 707
McCleary, R., 625
McClendon, S., 430
McCracken, G. D., 360n3
McCurdy, D., 741
McDonald, L., 31n2
McDonogh, G., 530
McEwan, P., 554, 555
McGill, R., 559
McGrady, F. A., 701, 713
McIntyre, J., 209
McKenzie, D., 629n2
McKinnon, A., 629n2
McKinnon, L. M., 630n6
McLaren, P. L., 141
McLaughlin, M. W., 702
McMullin, J. M., 373, 398, 401, 711
McNabb, S., 550, 575
McNeill, D., 418
McTavish, D. G., 618
Mead, M., 238, 278, 287, 461, 472, 473, 475, 476, 483, 476, 472, 484
Medick, H., 515
Medina-Mora, M. E., 705, 706
Meeker, M. E., 90
Meister, C., 534n10
Mejia, L., 706
Melbin, M., 155–156
Merleau-Ponty, M., 109
Merlo, G., 705, 707
Merton, R. K., 360n3
Mertz, E., 412
Mervis, C. B., 13
Meskill, J., 521
Messenger, J., 481
Meyer, M. A., 14
Meyers, C. F., 11
Meztger, D., 372
Mezzich, J. E., 396
Miceli, S., 91
Michaelis, A., 470
Michaels, E., 423
Michaelson, A. G., 386
Michalski Turner, D., 286
Milanesi, L, 630n6
Miles, M., 608–610, 613, 614, 626, 627, 630n5
Miles, M. B., 152, 708, 721

Mill, J. S., 16
Miller, D., 252n9
Miller, G., 386, 562
Miller, M. L., 132, 252n9, 368, 386, 387, 718
Miller, W. L., 613
Milligan, G. W., 397
Mintz, J., 528
Mintz, S., 246, 514, 530
Mishra, S. I., 373, 398, 401, 711
Mitchell, J. C., 60
Modell, J., 223
Moerman, M., 417
Mohler, P., 617, 631n9, 631n11
Mole, J., 103
Montoye, H. J., 310
Mooney, C., 554
Moore, C. C., 368, 393, 630n6, 679
Moore, J., 534n10
Moore, R., 368
Moore, S. F., 113
Moran, A. L., 397
Moran, E. F., 135
Moreno, E., 284
Morgan, D. L., 715
Morgan, G., 692, 694
Morgan, L., 223
Morgan, L. H., 12
Morgan, M., 613, 616
Morgen, S., 212, 221, 224, 702
Morgenstern, H., 146, 148, 151
Morin, E., 464
Morphy, H., 252n11
Morrill, W., 520
Morris, R., 463, 481
Morse, J. M., 613
Mosteller, F., 629n2
Moulines, C. U., 51, 69, 70, 71
Moulines, D. U., 64, 68, 69, 70
Mowen, J. C., 630n6
Mueller, C., 701, 713
Mühlhäusler, P., 412–413, 415, 442n3
Muhr, T., 609
Mullin, C., 630n6
Mullings, L., 212
Munroe, R. H., 656, 658
Munroe, R. L., 656, 658
Murdock, G. P., 46, 569, 651, 655, 659–663, 673, 675, 678
Murphy, R. F., 279
Murphy, S., 608, 610, 611

Murphy, W., 417
Murphy, Y., 279
Murray, J. D., 147, 153, 167
Murray, S. O., 282, 283, 284
Murray, T. E., 422
Musgrave, A., 51
Muybridge, E., 462
Myers, F., 252n11
Myers, G., 701, 713

Nachman, S. R., 718
Nader, L., 268, 278, 292n10
Nagel, T., 115
Namboordini, K., 558
Namenrith, J., 631n9, 631n11
Narayan, K., 214, 242
Naroll, R., 12, 134, 183, 287, 288, 653, 659,
   661, 667, 671, 672, 678
Nash, J., 204, 210, 213, 217, 241, 245, 277
Nastasi, B. K., 698, 699, 724
Nattrass, S. H., 386
Navaratnam, V., 706
Neaigus, A., 712
Needham, R., 111
Needle, R. H., 701
Nerlove, S. B., 390
Ness, R. C., 288, 672
Netting, R. McC., 41, 65, 66, 516, 519, 521
Newton, E., 281, 282
Nichter, M., 285, 286
Nichter, N., 285, 286
Niego, S., 400
Niemi, I., 312
Nightingale, F., 16
Nisbet, R. A., 111, 113
Noreen, E. W., 153
Nuckolls, J., 418
Nunnally, J. C., 379, 384, 676

O'Barr, W. M., 246
Oberschall, A., 17
Obeyesekere, G., 27, 72, 104, 361n5, 518,
   521, 533n8
Oboler, R. S., 210
O'Brien, M., 611
Ochberg, R. L., 527
Ochs, E., 422, 424, 443n5
Odland, J., 585
Ogburn, W. F., 17
Ogilvie, D. M., 613, 617, 631n10

Ohnuki-Tierney, E., 515, 525, 530
Okeyo, A. P., 210
O'Leary, T., 671, 682n2
Olien, M., 476
Olivier, D. C., 389
Olwig, K. F., 239
Omori, Y., 465
Omvedt, G., 210
O'Nell, C. W., 163–165
Ong, A., 241
Orans, M., 135, 136, 146, 154
Orr, D. P., 699
Ortiz, A., 705, 706
Ortner, S. B., 49, 211–213, 251n5, 514, 521,
   524, 529, 533n7
Osgood, C. E., 114, 621
O'Toole, J., 577
Otterbein, K. F., 657, 678
Oxman, T. E., 617, 618, 630n6, 631n12
Oxtoby, M. J., 613, 616
Özkök, B., 98

Pachter, L. M., 398, 400, 711
Page, J., 433, 436
Page, Jr., H., 671, 682n2
Paine, R., 96
Paisley, W. J., 630n6
Palmquist, M., 623, 624
Panourgia, N., 142
Panter-Brick, C., 316
Paolisso, M. J., 313
Parish, S. M., 361n5, 361n12
Parker, R. G., 700
Parkin, D., 95
Parmentier, R., 412
Parmentier, R. J., 104, 118
Pasternak, B., 665
Patel, B.C., 716
Patterson, T., 219
Patton, M. Q., 613
Paul, B., 262
Paul, R. A., 13
Paulay, F., 459–460, 473
Paulme, D., 209
Payne, S. L., 360n3
Peacock, J. L., 95, 527
Peacock, N., 317
Pedelty, M., 242
Peebles, C., 106

Pelto, G. H., 13, 132, 134, 143, 151, 270, 524, 569, 696, 708, 718, 720, 745
Pelto, P. J., 12–13, 132, 134, 143, 151, 270, 302, 400, 524, 569, 696, 708, 710, 718, 720, 721, 745
Perlmutter, D. D., 531
Perry, H. S., 14
Peters, E., 90
Peters, V., 609
Peterson, A., 465
Philips, S., 422
Piajet, J., 604
Piault, C., 490
Pica, T., 221
Picchi, D. S., 261, 265, 267
Piché, V., 518, 534n11
Pick, H. L., 442n3
Ping, X. Y., 222
Pinker, S., 722
Pirro, E. B., 618
Pirsig, R. M., 107
Pitkin, D. S., 534n22
Pitt, D. C., 517
Pitt, J., 62, 64
Pittinger, R. E., 355, 357, 360n4
Plakans, A., 515
Plattner, S., 41
Pocius, G. L., 98
Podolefsky, A., 741
Pollanc, R., 133
Poole, W. K., 520
Popper, K., 44, 45n2, 54, 69, 71, 79n1
Porter, T. M., 133
Poshyachinda, V., 706
Postel-Coster, E., 597
Poteat, G. M., 148
Potter, J. M., 693, 698, 701
Potts, R., 630n6
Powers, M. N., 516
Poyer, L., 528
Prados, M., 475
Pratt, M. L., 281
Prendergast, G. L., 629n2
Pressman, J., 417
Preziosi, D., 98
Price, L. J., 607, 695, 697, 700, 713
Price, R., 529, 530
Price-Williams, D., 630n6
Prost, J., 475, 477
Provost, C., 675

Pryor, F. L., 670, 674
Punch, M., 273, 274
Putnam, H., 54

Quandt, S., 279
Quételet, A., 16
Quine, W.V.O., 45, 56, 114
Quinn, N., 74, 76, 161, 210, 373, 605–607, 698, 709

Rabinow, P., 140, 281, 443n10
Radcliffe-Brown, A. R., 46
Radin, P., 15, 419, 443n4, 596
Ragin, C. C., 625
Ragone, H., 206
Rahe, R. H., 383
Ramos, A. R., 142
Rao, S., 716
Rapoport, A., 368
Rapp, R. [Reiter], 208, 209, 212, 221, 223
Rappaport, J., 104
Rappaport, R. A., 72, 91
Rapport, N., 109, 112
Ratnayake, P., 698, 699, 724
Raven, P., 368, 372
Rawls, J., 53
Read, D., 470
Reason, P., 692, 694, 724
Redfield, R., 17, 236, 287
Reed-Danahay, D., 107, 110
Rees, M. W.
Regnault, F., 462, 471
Reinharz, S., 206
Reiter, R. see Rapp, R.
Reitz, K., 679
Reynolds, M., 567
Rice, E. G., 605
Richards, I., 609
Richards, T., 609
Richardson, J., 15, 17, 102, 530
Richardson, L., 738
Richardson, S. A., 360n3
Richie, B., 217
Ricoeur, P., 49, 58, 61
Riemer, J. W., 261, 263
Rietberg, E. M., 630n6
Riley, C., 223
Rivers, W.H.R., 11, 12
Roberts, C. W., 630n6
Roberts, J. M., 386

Roberts, M., 90, 104
Roberts, R., 521
Robertson, R., 251*n*2
Robson, C., 148, 155, 323, 328
Rogaff, B., 699
Rogers, C., 360*n*4
Rogers, S. C., 528
Rohner, E. C., 677
Rohner, R. P., 288, 596, 672, 676, 677
Rohrlich-Leavitt, R., 214
Rollwagen, J., 487, 488, 497, 497*n*1
Romanucci-Ross, L., 702
Romney, A. K., 13, 61, 160, 302, 304, 368,
    370, 375, 378, 386, 389–391, 393, 396,
    397, 399–401, 569, 570, 676, 679, 698,
    699, 708–711, 719
Roos, G., 279
Roper, J. M., 290
Rorty, R., 415
Rosaldo, M., 208, 209, 221, 415, 418
Rosaldo, R., 414, 516, 520
Roseberry, W., 515, 523, 533*n*7
Roseman, M., 427, 428
Rosenau, P. M., 49
Rosenbaum, M., 608, 610, 611
Rosenberg, H. G., 521
Rosenberg, S. D., 617, 618, 630*n*6, 631*n*12
Rosenberger, N., 246
Rosenthal, R., 674, 676
Rosenwald, G. C., 527
Rosnow, R. L., 676
Ross, M. H., 662, 664, 667, 670–674
Rossman, G. B., 706
Roter, D., 630*n*6
Rothenberg, R. B., 697, 701, 713
Rouch, J., 461, 462, 464, 466, 477, 498*n*4
Rouse, R., 240
Rousseliere, G., 482
Rovegno, I., 14
Rowan, J., 724
Roy, R., 467
Royal Anthropological Institute of Great
    Britian and Ireland, 10–11
Rubel, A. J., 163–65
Rubin, G., 213
Rubin, H. J., 360*n*3
Rubin, I. S., 360*n*3
Ruby, J., 463, 468, 469, 473, 480, 481, 486,
    487
Ruebush, II, T. K., 377, 381, 382

Ruggles, S., 531*n*11
Rummel, R., 563
Rummelhart, D. E., 368, 397, 604
Runyan, D., 630*n*6
Rusch, C. D., 368, 393
Russell, B., 533*n*6
Russett, B., 652
Rutman, D., 515
Ryan, G., 614
Ryan, P., 705, 706
Ryder, N., 520
Rynkiewich, M. A., 277

Sabean, D., 521
Sackett, R., 304, 313
Sacks, H., 417
Sacks, K. see Brodkin, K.
Safa, H., 204
Safranski, R., 48
Sahay, K., 466
Sahlins, M., 27, 53, 72, 104, 113, 414,
    514–516, 518, 525, 533*n*8, 533*n*9
Said, E., 466
Sailer, L., 379, 719
Salaff, J., 527
Salinas Pedraza, J., 596, 597, 601
Salmond, A., 92
Salzman, P. C., 90
Samarin, W., 476
Sammons, K., 440
Sampson, S. L., 246
Sanday, P. R., 209, 215, 217
Sandelowski, M., 608, 613
Sanjek, R., 93, 210, 260, 261, 267, 269,
    270–272
Sankoff, G., 398
Sapir, E., 596
Sarason, S. B., 13
Saris, W.H.M., 310
Sartre, J., 94
SAS Institute, Inc., 396
Saussure, F. de, 412
Saville-Troike, M., 421
Scaglion, R., 313, 320, 321
Schama, S., 112
Schank, R. C., 604
Schapera, I., 514
Schegloff, E. A., 417
Schensul, J. J., 698, 699, 701, 708, 712,
    714–716, 721, 724

Schensul, S. L., 692, 696, 698, 699, 712, 714, 724
Scheper-Hughes, N., 53, 277, 286–287, 702
Scherer, J., 460
Scherzer, J., 411, 414, 421, 424, 427, 428, 432, 433, 440
Schiaffino, A., 520, 534n13
Schieffelin, B., 417, 422, 424, 438, 443n5
Schieffelin, E., 514
Schiller, N. G., 240
Schlegel, A., 209
Schleidt, M., 320
Schmid, M., 71
Schnegg, M., 623
Schneider, D., 133
Schneider, D. M., 49, 95
Schneider, J. C., 514, 515, 519, 523, 531, 532, 534n12, 534n24
Schneider, P. T., 514, 515, 519, 523, 531, 532, 534n12
Schneidman, E. S., 617
Schnurr, P. P., 617, 618, 630n6, 631n12
Schoepfle, G. M., 39, 41, 55, 61, 152, 360n3, 708, 709
Schroder, L., 576
Schuessler, K., 563
Schultz, J., 439, 587
Schutz, A., 48, 66
Schwandt, T. A., 140
Schweizer, T., 66, 75, 76, 625
Schwimmer, E., 101
Scott, J., 711, 713
Scott, J. C., 105
Scott, W. A., 630n7
Scrimshaw, N. S., 717, 723
Scrimshaw, S.C.M., 717
Seaman, G., 470
Searle, J. R., 56, 418
Sechrest, L., 134
Seeger, A., 421, 422, 427, 428, 441
Segre, C., 629n2
Seidel, J., 614
Seidman, S., 49, 132, 140, 141
Seligmann, B. Z., 11, 270, 271, 272
Seligmann, C. G., 11
Sewell, W. H., 93
Sexton, J., 596
Shaffer, C.L., 618
Shankman, P., 153
Shapiro, G., 618

Sharpe, P., 218
Shelley, G. A., 707
Sheridan, M., 527
Sherry, Jr., J. F., 14
Sherzer, J., 421, 428–429, 442n2, 600, 601
Shimmin, H. S., 658
Shoemaker, N., 517
Shostak, M., 215, 526, 739
Shryock, A., 90, 104, 236
Shuy, R., 423
Shweder, R. A., 303, 576
Siegel, J. M., 385
Silva, K. T., 698, 699, 724
Silverblatt, I., 205, 212, 523
Silverman, M., 515, 533n5
Silverman, S., 514, 515, 532
Silverstein, M., 412–417, 419, 430, 440
Simmons, L. W., 651, 673
Simon, W., 700
Simonsen, J, 488
Singer, J., 609
Singer, M., 698, 701, 702, 722
Singer, M. B., 118
Singh, K., 466, 467, 498n6
Sipes, R.G., 659, 661
Sjoquist, S., 576
Skinner, W. G., 518
Skocpol, T., 516
Sleath, B., 630n6
Slocum, S., 220
Smith, A. B., 14
Smith, C. D., 14
Smith, C. P., 630n6
Smith, E. A., 74
Smith, K. K., 16
Smith, M. S., 613, 617, 631n10
Smith, T., 386, 389
Smith, V., 243
Sneath, P., 397, 561, 563
Sneed, J. D., 51, 69, 71
Snijders,T., 705
Snow, C. W., 148
Sohier, R., 608
Sokal, R., 397, 561, 563
Solis, A., 705, 706
Solomon, H., 396
Solomon Klass, S., 285
Sorenson, R., 465, 469, 470, 471, 474, 484, 485
Spain, D. H., 13, 134, 136, 154

Spears, N. E., 630*n*6
Sperber, D., 100, 101
Spevack, M., 629*n*2
Spiggle, S., 630*n*6
Spindler, G., 134
Spiro, M. E., 13, 40
Spitulnik, D., 245, 423
Spradley, J., 608, 741
Spradley, J. P., 259, 260, 262, 277, 360*n*3, 367, 372, 709
SPSS, Inc., 381, 397
Stack, C., 207, 210, 268
Stanley, J. C., 550, 555, 692
Stark, F., 101
Steckel, R. H., 534*n*15
Steedly, M. M., 41, 104
Steele, S., 422
Steffire, V. J., 389, 395
Stegmüller, W., 42, 51, 53, 57, 58, 61, 62, 65, 68–70
Stein, H. F., 13
Stein, J., 742
Steiner, C. B., 246
Stephan, E., 397
Stephan, P., 576
Stephen, L., 217–219
Sterk, C., 268
Stewart, K., 111
Stinchcombe, A. L., 131, 145, 156, 165
Stockard, J. E., 528
Stocking, G., 260, 463
Stolcke, V., 528
Stoler, A., 213
Stoller, P., 464
Stoller, R. J., 361*n*5
Stone, L., 379
Stone, P. J., 613, 617, 630*n*6, 631*n*10
Stout, D. B., 649
Strathern, M., 212, 223
Strauss, A. L., 139, 608, 609, 696, 708
Strauss, C., 54, 74, 76, 607, 610
Streeeck, J., 421, 422
Strobel, M., 527
Stromberg, P. G., 56
Struever, N., 98
Struever, S., 471
Studdert-Kennedy, M., 443*n*6
Sturtevant, W. C., 475, 517, 518
Suci, G. J., 114
Sudman, S., 360*n*3, 375

Sullivan, H. S., 360*n*4
Suppes, P., 79*n*5
Susser, I., 222
Svarstad, B., 630*n*6
Swadesh, M., 596
Swann, B., 424
Swanton, J. R., 596
Sykes, B., 214
Szabo, J., 531
Szalai, A., 312, 315, 324

Tagliacozzo, G., 94
Tannebaum, P. H., 114
Tannen, D., 221, 417, 419
Tanner, N., 220
Tanz, C., 422
Tatje, T. A., 675
Taussig, M., 142
Tax, S., 693
Taylor, C., 116, 415
Taylor, C. C., 11
Taylor, D. W., 609
Taylor, L., 460, 525, 526, 528, 534*n*18
Taylor, S. J., 608
Tedesco, J. C., 630*n*6
Tedlock, B., 263–265, 288, 289, 294*n*8
Tedlock, D., 413, 419, 423–426, 440, 443, 596, 599, 600
Templin, P., 488
Tesch, R., 613, 630*n*5
Testa, R., 417
Theimann, S., 680
The Navajo People, 479
Thiam, A., 216
Thibault, P. J., 412
Thirsk, J., 521
Thomas, E. M., 739
Thompson, E., 521
Thompson, P., 528
Tibshirani, R., 554
Tice, K., 755
Tilly, C., 93, 516
Tjon Sie Fat, F. E., 69, 74
Tonkin, E., 262, 263, 534*n*22
Tonkinson, R., 482
Tooby, J., 576
Tooker, E., 11
Torres, M., 698
Toulmin, S., 44
Townsend, L. H., 534*n*21

Traweek, S., 248–249
Trawick, M., 722
Trevor-Roper, H. H., 532n1
Trigger, B., 516, 518, 534n10
Trost, J. E., 612
Trotter, II, R. T., 398, 400, 692, 693, 696–698, 700, 701, 711–713, 722
Truex, G. F., 389
Tsatoulis-Bonnekessen, B., 13
Tsing, A. L., 41
Tsui-James, E. P., 42, 79n1
Tuareg, M., 462, 465
Tucker, G., 618, 631n12
Tukey, J., 554, 559
Tula, M. T., 218
Turke, P., 315
Turnbull, C., 281, 283, 739
Turner, D. M., 285
Turner, J. H., 73
Turner, L. D., 425
Turner, T., 423, 480
Turner, V., 101, 103, 110, 525
Turton, D., 474
Tversky, A., 398
Tyler, S. A., 141
Tylor, E. B., 12, 584, 678

Unger, J., 625
Urban, G., 411–415, 418, 419, 422, 423, 424, 427, 439–441, 442n3, 442n4
Urciuoli, B., 221, 412–417
Urry, J., 136
Ushijima, I., 465
Ushiyama, J., 465

Valentine, L., 438
Van Allen, J., 210
Van de Woestijne, K. P., 14
van Gennep, A., 493
Van Maanen, J., 143, 259
Van Raalte, J. L., 13
Vansina, J., 527, 528, 533n4
Van Willigen, J., 692
Varela, C. R., 414
Varjas, K., 698, 699, 724
Vera, M., 701, 713
Verdery, K., 251n3
Verschueren, J., 722
Vico, Giambattista, 92

Villa Rojas, A., 265–266, 267–268
Vincent, J., 210, 525
Viney, L. L., 618
Visweswaran, Kamala, 224
Vitolins, M. Z., 279
Vogt, E. Z., 106, 471
Vygotsky, L. S., 699

Wagner, D. G., 49
Wagner-Martin, L., 218
Waitzkin, H., 612
Wallace, A.F.C., 113, 523, 569
Wallace, D. L., 629n2
Wallerstein, I., 238.
Walley, C., 216
Wang, C., 222
Warren, C.A.B., 278, 284
Washburn, R. A., 310
Wasserman, S., 74, 75, 386, 396, 700
Waterman, C. A., 238
Watson, J. L., 240
Watson, L. C., 527
Watson, R. S., 106
Watson, T. J., 14
Watson-Franke, M. B., 527
Watson-Gegeo, K. A., 417
Watters, J. K., 707
Waugh, L. R., 97
Wax, M., 186
Weatherford, E., 214
Webb, B., 14, 16
Webb, S., 16
Weber, M., 57
Weber, R. P., 617, 630n6, 631n9, 631n11
Webster's New International Dictionary of the English Language, 89
Weedon, C., 702
Weeks, M. R., 721
Weick, K. E., 14
Weinberg, R., 209
Weiner, A. B., 534n24
Weinstein, P., 368
Weisfeld, G. E., 14
Weisner, T., 614
Weiss, C., 251n7
Weitzman, E. A., 609, 626, 627, 630n5, 721
Welch, W., 432n7
Wellenkamp, J. C., 360n1, 361n5, 361n7
Weller, S. C., 13, 61, 160, 304, 368–371, 375, 377, 378, 381, 382, 385, 386, 389–391,

393, 395–401, 553, 569, 570, 698, 699, 708–711, 719
Wellhouse, K., 221
Wellman, B., 74, 75
Wells, R. V., 534n14
Welsch, R., 584
Welsch, W., 49
Wenger, E., 107
Werner, O. G., 39, 41, 55, 61, 152, 302, 360n3, 618, 629n3, 708, 709, 710
Wertsch, J. V., 699
West, B. A., 527
West, C., 411
West, F., 609
Weston, K., 217, 223
Whitcher, A. L., 148
White, D. R., 11, 76, 630n6, 654, 655, 659, 661, 670, 678, 679, 682n3
White, G. M., 415, 417
White, L., 534n23
Whitehead, H., 213
Whitehead, T., 214
Whiting, B., 308, 315, 316, 317, 656
Whiting, J.W.M., 10, 308, 315, 316, 317, 651, 654, 670, 673, 679
Whorf, B. L., 424
Whyte, K. K., 268, 272, 273
Whyte, M. K., 670, 675
Whyte, W. F., 59, 143, 267, 268, 272, 273, 360n3, 694
Wiget, A., 421, 433
Wilk, R. R., 41
Wilkinson, L., 554
Williams, D., 99, 414, 433, 436, 443n11
Williams, G., 372
Williams, H., 470
Williams, J., 460, 461
Williams, S., 220
Williams, T. R., 137
Willigan, D. J., 519, 520
Willis, P. E., 107
Willson, M., 281, 282
Wilms, D. G., 609
Wilson, D.M.C., 609
Wilson, H. S., 608
Winchester, I., 519
Winsborough, H. H., 520
Winterhalder, B., 74
Wintle, P., 465
Wish, M., 393, 394, 396, 563

Wissler, C., 629n3
Witkowski, S. R., 655
Wodak, R., 604
Wolcott, H. F., 14
Wolf, A., 518, 521
Wolf, A. P., 518, 519
Wolf, E. R., 10, 41, 238, 514, 526, 569, 596
Wolf, G., 465, 470, 486
Wolf, M., 218
Wolfe, A., 241
Woodbury, A., 412, 424, 430, 601
Woodgate, R., 14
Woods, P., 14
Woolard, K., 413, 417
World Health Organization, 720
Worth, S., 459, 462, 479, 486, 487, 498n2
Worth, T., 486
Wozniak, D., 553, 557, 570, 585
Wright, M., 527
Wright, R., 220
Wulff, H., 242
Wylie, A., 219

Yamaguchi, K., 586
Yanagisako, S., 213, 221
Yang, M. M., 41
Yans, M., 527
Yarborough, C., 377
Yasuhiro, O., 486, 488
Yin, Z., 221
Young, J. C., 157–158, 368, 369, 393, 395, 398
Young, K., 211
Yule, G. U., 629n2

Zabusky, S. E., 117, 140, 141
Zaki, E. P., 360n3
Zavella, P., 206
Zegarra, M.
Zeller, R. A., 667, 676
Zepeda, O., 418
Zerger, A., 630n6
Zhang, Y., 162–163
Zihlman, A., 220
Znaniecki, F., 624
Zucker, H., 659, 661
Zuell, C., 617, 631n9, 631n11

Subject Index

The following typographical conventions are used in the index. **Bold** denotes peoples and ethnographic study areas; *italics* denote terms, publication titles, and film titles; *f* denotes a figure; *t* denotes a table.

AAA, *see* American Anthropological Association
academic and applied anthropology, tension between, 177–178
academic anthropologists, 750–751
  as consultants, 755
  lack of positions, 719
action research, *see* advocacy research
active participation, 262–263
activity presence sampling, *see* one-zero sampling
Addams, Jane, 16
advocacy research, 693
aerial photography, 471
Agar, Michael, 620–621
Almolonga (Guatemala), 165–166
ALSCAL, 397
American Anthropological Association (AAA)
  code of ethics, 195–201
  ethics, early statement about, 174
  and informed consent, 185–186
American Bureau of Indian Affairs, 189
  analysis, in person-centered interviews, 355–359
analytic induction, 624–627
  computer software and, 626
  defined, 624–626
  examples, classic, 625
analytic philosophy, 45
  theoretical concepts in, 68–69

Andrew's Fourier Plots, 586
anonymity, of participants, 274
ANTHROPAC computer program, 389, 391, 554, 571–573, 626
Anthropological Society of Washington, 175
anthropologists, European, and informed consent, 186
Anthropologists of Human Movement, 443*n*11
anthropology
  academic reasons for, 738
  and the media, 751–752
  as eclectic, 17
  writing in, 737–747
Antigua (West Indies), 580–582, 585–587
Apple computer company, 242
applied and academic anthropology, tension between, 177–178
applied anthropology, 695
  applications, 695–696
  challenges to, 692
  as different from traditional ethnography, 694–695
  ethnographer responsibilities, 692
  intervention research in, 692–693
  methods, publications, 708
  and midrange cultural theory, 696–697
  partnerships in, 695
  and personal advocacy, 695–696
  presenting, 754–755
  sampling in, 702–708
  scope of, 755

skills needed, 695
theories in, 696–700
uses for, 691
see also applied research
applied research, types of, 692–693
apprenticeship of self, as fieldwork method,
107–108, 264–265
architectonics, 105–106
archival research
and ethnocentrism, 518
sources, 517–518
Archives of Traditional Music, 425
Asch, Timothy, 468–469, 498*n*8–9
Assiniboine, 439
storytelling, 436, 437f
Atlas of World Cultures, 659, 661
attitudinal studies, 366–367
rating scales, use in, 382–385, 393–394

Bailey, R. C., 317–318
balanced-incomplete block designs, *see* paired-
comparisons, balanced-incomplete block
designs; triad studies, balanced-incomplete
block designs
Bali, 596
Balikci, Asen, 480
Barnett, G., 621–622, 622f
Bateson, Gregory, 459, 461, 472, 476
Bedouin, 649
behavior, human, defined, 301
behavioral description, 323–324
structural, 323–324
behavior description, bias in, 304–306, 305t,
306t
behavior measurement
defined, 307
detail in, 311
flow of behavior, 310
quantitative variables, 310
recording strategies, 332–323
temporal resolution, 310
beliefs, cultural, 399
belief studies
as different from classification studies, 398
formulating questions in, 398
Benedict, Ruth, 15
Bernard, H. Russell, 596–597, 601
Besnier, Niko, 597

bias
in behavior description, 304–306, 305t,
306t
in coding, 675
differs from situating oneself, 206
ethnographer, examples of, 287–288
in field notes, 271
gender, in anthropological writings, 305,
306t
heterosexual, in anthropology, 213
homosexual, in anthropology, 213
in interview topics, 341
in participant observation, 287–289, 291
in research, 151
binary variables, 558
binomial test, *see* chi-square test
biological anthropology, and feminist anthropology, 220
Blackfoot, 629*n*3
Bloch, Marc, 530
Blowsnake, Sam, 15, 31*n*1, 596
BMDP, 396, 397
Boas, Franz, 15, 134–136, 598
contributions to the corpus of texts, 596
and ethics, 174–175
and spatial and temporal autocorrelation,
584
and visual anthropology, 459, 473
early fieldwork, 459
reconstruction of culture, 480–481
body language, defined, 443*n*11
book, anthropology, types to author, 738–743
Book of Chilam Balam of Tizimin, The, 596,
601
books
academic, 742–743
audience for, 743
and theory, 742–743
titles for, 743
anthropological trade
audience for, 739
authors of, 738–739
examples of, 739
professional, *see* books, academic
Boolean Tests, 624–627
Booth, Charles, 16
Booth, R. E., 162–163, 163f
bootstrap test, 554, 584
border studies, 239

Boster, J. S., 159–160, 160*f*
box-and-whisker plot, 559
box plots, 552, 559, 560*f*
Brazil, 752–753
brief ethnographies, *see* rapid ethnographic assessment
Brim, J. A., criticisms of Mead, 154–155
Brumfiel, Elizabeth, 220

Cademe, 479–480
Cambridge Anthropological Expedition to the Torres Straits, 462–463
camera direct, 487–488
Carley, Kathleen, 623–624
case-control study, 149t
case histories, *see* narrative accounts
Catholicism, and economics, 165
CATI, *see* computer-assisted telephone interviews
causal understanding, *see* empathic understanding, causal
central tendency measures, 399
Chafe, Wallace, 601–602
Chagnon, Napoleon, 468–469
charting content, in filming, 490–493, 491*f*, 492*f*
Chen Village, 625–626
children, and fieldwork, 284–287
Chinookan, 598
chi-square test, 399, 553
chloropleth MAPS, 714
Chomskian generative linguistics, 412–413
Choreometrics Project (Columbia University), 473–474, 477
Chronbach's alpha, *see* Spearman-Brown Prophesy Formula
chronophotography, 461, 462
clandestine research, *see* secret research
classical content analysis, in sociological text analysis, example, 611–612
classification studies, 367, 386–398
   description of, 386
   reliability, 397–398
   types of analyses, 396–398
   validity, 396–398
   see also paired-comparison, pile-sorting, triad studies
Clifford, James, and postmodern anthropology, 149
close-ended interviews, 349–350

close-ended multiple choice questions, 375
cluster sampling, 566–567
   when to use, 552
Code of Ethics of the American Anthropological Association, 195–201
coders, naive, 674–675
coding
   in cross-cultural research, 671–677
   in ethnographic research, 324–328, 325–326*t*
   problems with, 327–328
   in sociological text analysis, 613–618
   consensual, 619
   deductive coding, 614–615
   example, 614–615
   inductive, 614
   intercoder agreement, 616–617, 630*n*7
   multiple codes, 616–617
   tagging, 615–616
   when to use, 614
COE, *see* Committee on Ethics
coefficient, reliability, *see* reliability coefficient
coefficient alpha, *see* reliability coefficient
coefficient of determination, 561
cognitive anthropology, 76, 708–709
cognitive anthropology technique
   consensus modeling in, 710–711
   in cross-cultural research, 709
cognitive distortion, in person-centered interviews, 347
cognitive maps, 623–624
   example, 623–624, 624*f*
cognitive unconscious, 358
Cohen's Kappa, in sociological text analysis, 616
cohort analysis, 520
cohort study, 149*t*
Colby, B. N., 617–618
Collado-Ardon, R., 163–165, 164*f*
collective rights
   and informed consent, 189
   Western vs. non-Western, 189
colonial ethnography, 466–467
Committee on Ethics (COE) (AAA), 176
Committee to Review the AAA Statement on Ethics, 178
communities open to the world, 237–239
   historical, 238
Community Epidemiology Work Group, 715–716

comparative method, in historical anthropology, 526
complete participation, 263
computer-assisted telephone interviews (CATI), 374
computer software programs, 389, 391, 427, 432f, 443*n*9
computer technology, 167
    and visual anthropology, 470
Comte, Auguste, 43
conceptual-incompatibility hypothesis, 157
concordance, defined, 629*n*2
Conference on Visual Anthropology, 460
confidence interval, 553, 559
confirmation, *see* positive evidence
consensus analysis, *see* cultural consensus analysis
consensus model, *see* cultural consensus analysis
consensus modeling, in cognitive anthropology, 710–711
consensus theory, 698–699
consent, informed, 184–190
content analysis
    history of, 630*n*6
    in sociological text analysis, defined, 611
    traditional, in sociological text analysis, 611–619
continuous monitoring (CM) observation, 315–317
continuous observation, *see* continuous monitoring
continuous recording, *see* continuous monitoring
continuous scan/focal follow, *see* continuous monitoring
controlled comparison, 655–656
    in anthropology, 655–656
    disadvantages of, 655–656
convenience samples, 374
conversational analysis, focus of, 417
Cook, Captain James, 104, 544*n*8
correspondence analysis, 393, 393*f*, 396, 397, 552
"country," in anthropology, 659
Cowan, G., 611–612
Crashing Thunder: An Autobiography of a Winnebago Indian, 15, 31, 596
Crete (Greece), 99–100
critical rationalism, 44

critical theory, 702
Cronbach's alpha, *see* reliability coefficient
cross-cultural comparison, 653–655
    examples, study, 655–656
    primary data, cost of using, 653, 656–657
    types of, 652–653, 681
    validity in, 654
cross-cultural research, 652–653
    available samples, comparison of, 660–663
    basic assumption of, 650
    history of, 651–652
    as interdisciplinary, 652–653
    measurement in, 663–679
    statistical data in, 679–681
cross-cultural studies
    and descriptive/statistical questions, 650
    proliferation of, 652
    and visual anthropology, 473–474
Cross-Cultural Survey, 651–652
cross-historical studies, 653
cross-national research, 653
cross-sectional profile matrix, 558
cross-sectional study, 149*t*
cross-sequential design, 148
cross-site comparability, 719–720
Cuiva (Venezuela), 322
cultural beliefs, 399
cultural boundaries, and social identity, 569
cultural consensus analysis, 399–402, 552, 569–575
    and ANTHROPAC, 571–573
    applications, 400, 569
    data, types of appropriate, 572
    defined, 399–400
    eigenvalue in, 563–565, 564*f*, 573
    and evaluation research, 571
    examples, 569–570, 573–575, 574*f*
    and knowledge, cultural, 570–572
    number of informants needed, 400, 401
    questions, formulating, 400
    see also life experience data
cultural consensus model, *see* cultural consensus analysis
cultural consonance, 570
cultural contexts research, in applied anthropology, 700–702
cultural creativity, and communities open to the world, 238
cultural data, measurable, 550

cultural data analysis
example, 557–563
problems with, 553–554
cultural domain, 368, 570–572
cultural ecological theory, 701
cultural intervention research, in applied
anthropology, 692–693
cultural midrange theory, in applied anthropology, 696–697
cultural poetics, 95–97
criticisms of, 96
cultural relativism, and feminist practice, 215,
223
culture, reconstructing on film, 480–483
culture congruency theory, 698
culture shock, 266, 272
Cuna, 649
cyberspace studies, transnational, 243

Data matrix, 558
deductive nomological explanation, 63–65
deliberate sampling, for heterogeneity, and
external validity, 152
demography, historical, 518–521
descriptive inference, 157–158, 160
descriptive linguistics, and elicitation, 420
descriptive statistics, 552–553
Desjarlais, Robert, 264
determinative understanding, *see* empathic
understanding, determinative
deterministic laws, 63–64
diachronic comparison
defined, 652
problems in using, 656
diachronic data, cost of using in research,
656–657
diaspora studies, transnational, 241
dictionaries, content analysis, 617–618
computer programs, 617
differencing, in Ordinary Least Squares (OLS)
regression, 585
digitized sound, 427, 428*f*
Dilthey, Wilhelm, 47, 48
direct measurement, in cross-cultural research,
when to use, 668–669
direct relationships, 248
direct systematic behavior observation
as compared to other methods, 302–307
cost of, 308, 309
defined, 302

need for, 306–307, 328
sampling methods, 312–322
targets for observation, 313–315
types of information to collect, 309–311
when to use, 308
discourse
in traditional ethnography, 414
transcribing, 424–433, 426*f*, 428f, 429–
430*f*, 431–432*f*
discourse, and the cultural construction of self,
414–415
discourse, spoken
information, collecting in, 420–422
marked, 421–422
recording, mechanical, 422–424
and soundscape, 421–422
unmarked, 421–422
discourse analysis
and collaboration with native speakers, 436,
438–441
computer-assisted, 427–433, 428*f*, 429–
430*f*, 431–432*f*
examples of, 438–441
in historical anthropology, 526
discourse-centered, defined, 411–412
discourse-centered methods
and body movement, 436
challenge to Western notions of discourse,
415–418
and context analysis, 418–419
and culture, 411–413
focus, 413, 441
goal, 414
and sociolinguistics, 413
vs. Chomskian generative linguistics, 412–
413
see also language
discourse-centered researchers, and reflexive
dynamics of discourse, 417–418
disease, and culture, 163–165; *see also* illness,
native conceptions about
disproportionate stratified random sampling,
660, 661
difficulties with, 661
dissimilarity coefficients, 552
distortion of understanding, 347–348
Divale, William, 655
DN, *see* deductive nomological explanation
domain, in cultural anthropology, 368
Doucet, Lorna, 619–620

Douglas, Mary, 112
Driver, Harold, 655
Driver's G, 561, 588*n*1
dummy variables, *see* binary variables
dynamic unconscious, 358

Earth First!, 569
economic anthropology, historical, 41
economic man, *see* rational choice theory
Edison, Thomas, 498*n*2
Efe (Zaire), 317–318
Eggan, Fred, 655–656
ego-centered network analysis, 712–713
eigenvalue, in cultural consensus analysis,
     563–565, 564*f*, 573
einfühlen, 59
elicitation
     in descriptive linguistics, 420
     taxonomic, 372
     in visual anthropology, 475, 477
El Sebou': Egyptian Birth Ritual, 489–496
e-mail, 747
Ember, C. R., 655
Ember, M., 655
embodied meaning of activity, 109–110
emic data, 302
empathic understanding, 57–61, 61, 77, *see*
     also verstehen
     causal, 57
     determinative, 57
     in fieldwork, 58–59
     functional, 58
     genetic, 58
     intentional, 58
     of meanings, 57
     rational, 58
empirical validation, 55
Enniskillen Poor Law, 525
epistemic reasoning, 64
epistemology
     anthropological, problems in, 51–53
     defined, 30–40, 204
     method, defined, 40
     theory, defined, 40
epistemology, feminist, 208–219
error
     measurement, *see* measurement error
     effect of time and place on, 671
     examples, 667
     in measurement, defined, 667

     results of, 672
     sources of, 151, 667
error, coder in cross-cultural research
     minimizing, 675–676
error, ethnographer
     in coding, 674–677
     example, 673
     length of stay in field, effect on, 673
     minimizing, 671
error, informant, in cross-cultural research
     example, 673
     minimizing, 671–674
     by what is not reported, 673–674
error, judgment, *see* judgment error
error, systematic, in measurement, 667
ethics
     and anonymity of informants, 274
     and fictive kinship relationships, 272–276
     general principles of, 190–191
     history of, 174–177
     and implications of friendships in the field,
         274
     and limiting participation by ethnologist,
         276
     as ordinary part of anthropological work,
         173–174
     in participant observation, 263, 272–276,
         280–284, 291
     reference sources about, 193–194
     and sex in the field, 283
Ethics Network (international), 191
ethnobiology, and comparative design, 159–
     160
ethnographer
     as activist, 216, 277
     in coding, 674–677
     example, 673
     and length of stay in field, 672
     minimizing, 671
     by what is not reported, 673–674
Ethnographic Atlas, 659, 660
ethnographic research, generalizations in,
     60–61
ethnographic writing
     experimental, 141
     interpretive, 59–60
     reflexive, 289–291
ethnography
     colonial, *see* colonial ethnography
     as eclectic, 143

lack of consensus of meaning of the word, 143–144
multimethod, 65–166, 166*f*
narrative, 263–264
and poetic wisdom, 113–115
ethnography and cross-cultural research, 648
ethnohistory, 514
different from conventional history, 533
ethnology as memoir, problems with, 218
ethnomusicologists, 428
ethnopoetics, 425–427, 426*f*
etic data, 302
etymology, 89–94, 98
as methodological instrument, 89–94
see also nonverbal etymology
Euclidean distance coefficients, 561
European Space Agency, 117
evaluation research, 571
in applied anthropology, 692
Evans-Pritchard, E. E., 109, 514
evidence
negative, 44–45
positive, 44
evolutionary ecology theory, 75
experimental research designs, 555
experiments
anthropological, rarity of, 146–147
manipulative, 147
mensurative, 147
natural, 147
true, 146
explanandum, 63
explanans, 63
explanation
as complementary to *verstehen*, 65–67
scientific, 62–65, 77
explanatory research, strategies, 138–139*f*
exploratory interviews, 367–368
exploratory research
example of, 160–161*f*
strategies, 138–139*f*
Exposition Ethnographique de l'Afrique Occidentale, 462
external validity, 552–553

Factor analysis, 552, 563–566
falsification, *see* negative evidence
family reconstitution
applications, 519
publications about, 534*n*12

Fang (Gabon), 105–106, 108
female genital mutilation, 216
female-male fieldwork
success of, 279–280
feminism
need for diversification within, 212
and poststructuralism, 213
feminism as a lens for analysis, *see* standpoint theory
feminist anthropology
and activism, 216
and biological anthropology, 220
corrective stage in, 220
and cultural relativism, 215
as interdisciplinary, 221
and life history, 526
as marginalized, 221
feminist empiricism, 208–212
feminist epistemology, 208–219
feminist ethnography, as memoir, 218
feminist linguistics, 221
feminist methods, in archaeology, 219–220
feminist ontology, 205–208
feminist research
correction of male bias, 209
as distinct from research on work, 205
early studies, 209–210
focus and purpose, 219
and gender, 205
and positivism, 206, 212
relationship with anthropology, 203
and women's movement, 209–210
feminist researchers
and accountability, 206
and reflexivity, 206–207, 218
field experiment using systematic research design, 155–156
field notes
and bias, 271
as data and analysis, 271–272
importance of, 270
participants' attitudes toward, 271
and recording technology, 423–424
types of, 270
using computers for, 270
writing, 270
fieldwork
costs in time and resources, 137
parenting and, 284–287
sex and, 280–284

see also participant observation
film
  anthropological, as teaching method, 471
  in archaeology, 471
  research, as different from ethnographic
    film, 470
  theory and methodology, 471
film, ethnographic, 461–470
  analysis of, 473–474
  and collaboration with subjects, 467–468,
    478
  and colonialism, 466–467
  criteria of, 486–487
  criticisms of, 488, 497
  and homogenization of culture, 483
  informant made, 478–480
  list of, 509–510
  by non-Western countries, 466–467,
    498*n*6–7
  reconstructing culture with, 480–483
  as reinforcing stereotypes, 488
  sequence vs. thematic, 468
Film as Ethnography (conference), 497*n*1
filmmaker, and relationship with the filmed,
  488
filmmaking, triadic relations in, 487–488
Fischer, John L., 668
fixed-interval instantaneous sampling, 317–318
fixed-interval sampling, *see* fixed-interval
  instantaneous sampling
Flaherty, Robert, 463, 466
  and visual anthropology, 463, 466, 481–482
focal-animal sampling, *see* continuous monitoring
focal-individual follows, 314
focused ethnographic studies, *see* rapid
  ethnographic assessment
focus groups, 714–716, 723
  example of, 715–716
follows, *see* focal-individual follows
Ford, Clellan S., 651–652
Foundations of Social Anthropology, The, 46
Fourier blob icon analysis, 587
F-ratio, 553, 582, 583
free listing, in cognitive anthropology, 709–
  710
  uses of, 709
Freeman, Derek, and criticism of Margaret
  Mead, 153–155
free-recall listing, 368–372, 369t

freezing structure, in filming, 493–495
French Académie des Sciences, 461–462
French Rural History, 530
frequency, in measurement, 551
frequency distribution, 552
full network data, 713
functional behavioral descriptions, 323–324
functionalism, and participant observation, 261
functional understanding, *see* empathic understanding, functional
funding agencies, 753–754
funding sources
  and ethics, 181
  and Institutional Review Boards, 182–184
Furbee, Louanna, 602–603

Gabon, 105–106, 108
Gadamer, Hans Georg, 48
Galton, Sir Francis, 584–585, 677–678; *see
  also* Galton's Problem
Galton's Problem, 661, 677–679
Garro, L. Y., 157–159, 158*f*
Geertz, Clifford, 149
Gemeinschaft, 247
gender
  in anthropological writings, 305, 306*t*
  changes in meaning of, 213
  and the division of labor, 220, 655
  issues in participant observation, 220
  roles and conversational analysis, 207
  as a social construct, 207
gender and reproduction, 223–224
gender bias
  in research, 220–221
  in writings, anthropological, 305, 306*t*
gender conformity in the field, expected,
  278–279
genealogical method, in historical reconstruction, 520, 521
  application of, 520
General Inquirer computer program, 617
General Social Survey, 375
genetic understanding, *see* empathic understanding, genetic
genital mutilation, female, 216
geographical sampling, 706–707
Geographic Information Systems (GIS), 714
Gesellschaft, 247
GIS, *see* Geographic Information Systems
global feminism vs international solidarity, 216

globalization, and cultural homogenization, 236
going native, *see* pure participation
Goldin, L. R., 165–166, 166*f*
Goldschmidt, Walter, 658
Goodall, Jane, 15
Goodenough, Ward, 668
Gottschalk-Gleser psychological scale, 618
Gould, Stephen Jay, 744
Grammatik computer program, 741
grant proposals, 745–746
graphic theory technique, 396
Griaule, Marcel, 459, 461
grounded theory, in sociological text analysis, 607–611
    applications, 608
    defined, 607–608
    displaying results, 610
    example, 610–611
    mechanics of, 608
    model building, 609
    software programs, 609
    themes in, 608–609
group interviews, 372
group research design, 723
group scans, 314
Guttman scale, 377–378, 586
gynocentrism, *see* feminist empiricism

Haddon, Alfred Cort, 459, 462–463
Handwerker, W. Penn, 563, 588*n*6
Hansen frequency, 321–322
Harvard IV computer program, *see* Harvard Psychosocial Dictionary computer program
Harvard Psychosocial Dictionary computer program, 617
Heidegger, Martin, 48
hermeneutic circle, 47, 61–62, 77
hermeneutics, 43, 76–77
    defined, 47
    impact on anthropology, 48–49
hermeneutic theory, 61–62, 77
Herzfeld, Michael, 602
heterosexual bias in anthropology, 213
heterosexuality, challenge to naturalness of, 213
heteroskedasticity, and residuals, 584
hierarchical clustering, 396–397
high-inference variable, in cross-cultural research, 670

Hill, K. R., 322
Hirschman, E. C., 614–615
historical anthropology
    as an accepted methodology, 514
    applying ethnographic methods of analysis to, 524–526
    beginnings, 514
    comparative method in, 526
    as different from history, 523, 531
    example, 523–524
    discourse analysis in, 526
    documentary sources, 516–518, 524–525
    evaluating archival sources in, 517–518
    ethnocentrism in, 518
    and family history and historical demography, 518–521
    focus of, 532
    and local history, 522
    and material culture, 530–531
    methods used in, 515
    and oral history, 525
    and political economic history, global, 523
    and primary sources, 519, 521, 525–526
    use of documentary sources in, 524–525
    and visual images, 530–531, 531
historical demography, sources for, 519
historical demography and family history, quantitative methods in, 518–521
history and myth, 104
Holmes and Rahe Social Adjustment Rating Scale, 383–384
homosexual bias, in anthropology, 213
HO schema of explanation, *see* deductive nomological explanation
household scan sampling, 314
HRAF, *see* Human Relations Area File
HRAF Collection of Archaeology, 681
HRAF Collection of Ethnography, 652, 659, 661, 662
    advantage of in using in cross-cultural research, 662–663
HRAF Probability Sample, 652, 659, 661
    and use of random sampling, 652, 659, 661
HRAF Quality Control Sample, *see* HRAF Probability Sample
human behavior, 301
Human Genome Diversity Project, 189
humanism
    defined, 40
    in ethnography, 15–16

humanistic vs. scientific methodology, 41
Human Relations Area File (HRAF), 612, 651,
652, 661
Human Studies Film Archives, 465
Hunt, George, 15, 596
Hurtado, A. M., 322
Husserl, Edmund, 47–48
Hymes, Dell, 598–599

Icon Analysis, 586
Identities, 235
identity formation, 343–344
ideographic, defined, 47
IDU, *see* injection drug users
Ifaluk, 278–279
illness, native perceptions about, 157, 163–
165, 400
see also disease and culture
indexicality, notion of, 415, 416
indices, development of from questioning
process, 378
indigenous language text, 596–597
indigenous literature, analysis of, 597
indigenous media, *see* media studies, transnational
indirect measurement, in cross-cultural
research, 669
indirect relationships, 248
individual accounts, *see* narrative accounts
individual rights, Western vs. non-Western,
189
induction, analytic, *see* analytic induction
inductive method, defined, 44
inference, moderate, *see* moderate inference, in
cross-cultural research
inferential data, 553
inferential statistics, 553
informant
accuracy, 718–719
in person-centered interviewing, 335
informants
hiring, 339
maintaining anonymity of, 274,
reactions to fieldwork projects, 752–753
trustworthiness of, 338–340
informed consent, 184–188
and collective rights, 180
problems with, 188–190
and sexual activity, by ethnographer, 184–
188

injection drug users, 162–163
instantaneous and scan sampling, *see* fixed-
interval instantaneous sampling
instantaneous time-sampling, 311
Institute for Community Research, 714, 716,
723–724
Institute of Human Relations (Yale), 651
Institut für den Wisenschaftlichen Film, 465
Institutional Review Board (IRB), 182
intensive case finding, *see* geographical
sampling
intentional understanding, *see* empathic
understanding, intentional
internal validity, 555
International Congress of Anthropological and
Ethnological Studies (IUAES), 497n1
International Journal of American Linguistics,
Native American Text Series, 596
International Phonetic Alphabet (IPA), 425,
443n6
International Phonetic Association, 425
interpretive anthropology, 67–68
goals of, 59
interpretive research strategies, 140
interpretivism, *see* hermeneutics
interrupted time series design, 149t
intersubjectivity, defined, 55
interval scales, 588n2
interview, person-centered, *see* person-
centered interviews
interviewing
challenges to results, 378–379
group, 372
open-ended, 349–350
order of questions, 375
proxy questions in, 376
preliminary steps to, 367
to prevent ambiguity, 378
use of standardized lists in, 366
relevancy of questions in, 375–376
surveys, 376
techniques, 367–396
structured, 373–396
variables, cost, 374
see also person-centered interviews
interview research
defined, 301
as opposed to systematic observation,
302–304

interviews
 close-ended, 349–350
 computers-assisted, 374
 exploratory, 367–368
in vivo coding, *see* text coding
IPA, *see* International Phonetic Alphabet
IRB, *see* Institutional Review Board
IUAES, *see* International Congress of Anthropological and Ethnological Studies

Jaccard's coefficient, 561
jacknife test, 554, 585
Jakobson, Roman, 415, 416
Jang, H-Y, 621–622, 622*f*
Japanese Committee of Film on Man, 465
Jehn, Karen A., 619–620
Johnson, A., 319–320
Johnson, J. C., 159–160, 160*f*
Johnson, O., 319–320
Journal for the Anthropological Study of Human Movement, 433
journals, refereed, 744
judgment errors, 555–556

K, in sociological textual analysis, *see* Cohen's *Kappa*, in sociological text analysis
Kearny, M. H., 610
khelidonisma, 602
kinship, in lesbian families, 213, 217, 223
k-means cluster analysis, 566
KNOWLEDGE score (ANTHROPAC), 571–572
knowledge tests, 366, 379–382
 example, 381–382
Koester, S., 162–163, 163*f*
KR-20, *see* Kuder-Richardson 20
Kroeber, Alfred, 15
Kuder-Richardson 20 (KR-20), 381
Kuhn, Thomas, 50
Kuna chanting, 428, 430, 432*f*
Kwakiutl, 463
Kwakiutl (language), 596
KWIC lists, defined, 629*n*2, 631*n*10

Laban, script, 433–434, 436
Laban Effort-Shape (theory), 474
Labanotation, 433–434, 434*f*, 435*f*
labor, gender division of, 220
La Llorona (morality tale), 603–604

language
 and the notion of indexicality, 415–417
 as performative, 415
 as social action, 412, 413
 traditional methods for study of, 419–420, 442*n*4
 see also discourse-centered methods
language-recording technology, historical, 425
language skills, in transnational studies, 249–250
latent root, *see* eigenvalue
laws
 defined, 46
 deterministic, 63–64
layering, in filming, 489
Leacock, Eleanor
 influence in feminist anthropology, 204–205
 research methods of, 204–205
 research projects of, 204
Leibowitz, Lila, 220
life course method, 519–520
life experience data, measurable, 550, 575–577
 examples, 576–577
 uses, 576
life history
 as controversial, 526
 different from oral history, 526
 life-focused approach in, 527
 publications about, 527
 as reflexive, 526
 story-focused approach in, 527
 validity of, 527
lineage segmentation, 90
linguistic analysis, 419–420
 and elicitation, 419–420
 and text, 419–420
linguistic anthropology
 theories in, 722
 see also discourse-centered methods
linguistic competence, in person-centered interviews, 337–338, 353–354
linguistics
 descriptive, *see* descriptive linguistics
 feminist, 221
linguistics and visual anthropology, 473, 475, 476
loading, in factor analysis, 563
loan words, in text performance analysis, 603

local history
    applications, 522
    see also historical anthropology
logical positivism, 44
logs, for tape recordings, 354
Loizos, Peter, 464
Lomantán (Mexico), 602–603
long-term memory, 303–304
Lowie, Robert, 15
low-inference variable, in cross-cultural research, 670
low-risk research, 184
Lumière brothers, 498n2
Lutz, Catherine, 278–279

Machinguenga (Peru), 319–320
Madagascar, 755–757
Mae Enga, 648–649
Maitland, Frederick, 513
male bias
    in anthropology, 211
    in ethnography, 278
male-female fieldwork
    success of, 279–280
Malinowski, Bronislaw, 10, 135
    and ethnographic filmmaking, 466
    on field notes, 271
    and functional theoretical perspective, 261
    participant observation, pioneer, 260
    and Trobriand Islands, 260
Mandler, Jean, 603–604
manipulative experiments, 147
mapping, sociogeographic, see sociogeographic mapping
Marey, Jules-Etienne, 461–462
marriage, cultural models of, 161–162, 162f, 605–607
Massey, William C., 655
master status, in script theory, 700
mathematical anthropology, 679
Mauss, Marcel, 462
maximum, in measurement, 552, 559
MDS, see multidimensional scaling
Mead, Margaret, 15
    anthropological writings of, 738–739
    in Bali, 596
    criticisms of her fieldwork, 153–155
    on field notes, 271
    in Samoa, 135–136
    and Society for Applied Anthropology, 174

and visual anthropology, 459, 461, 472–473, 476
mean, 558
    defined, 399, 551
meanings, understanding of, see empathic understanding, of meanings
measure, designing, in cross-cultural research, 664
    examples of processes involved in, 665
    minimizing error in, 667–671
    principles of, 664
    scales in, 666–667
    steps to, 664
    word description example in, 666–667
measurement
    in cross-cultural research, 663–679
    in ethnographic research
    defined, 550
    kinds of, 550
measurement, forms, 551
measurement error, 550, 555
measurement unit transforms, 585
median, 559
    defined, 399, 551
media studies, transnational, 243–245
medical anthropology, 157
Melbin, M., 155–156
memoing, in grounded theory, 608
    types of, 609
memory
    of informants, as problematic, 378–379
    long-term, 303–304
    short-term, 303–304
men ethnographers, and violence in the field, 278, 283–284
mensurative experiments, 147
MESA Board, 176
method
    anthropological, problems in, 51–53, 77
    meaning of as a word, 87–94
    in text analysis, 595–596
method and theory, relationship between, 204
methodological debate in anthropology, 40–42
methodological framework, defined, 40, 76
methods, as cross disciplinary, 13–14
Middle East Studies Association, 175–176
midrange cultural theory, in applied anthropology, 696–697
midrange theory, in applied anthropology, 700–701

definition of, 696
migration studies, transnational, 240–241
Mill, John Stuart, 16
Minangkabau (Sumatra), 597
minimum, in measurement, 552, 559
modal beliefs, *see* cultural beliefs
modal frequency, 551
mode, 551
moderate inference, in cross-cultural research, 670
moderate participation, 262
montage
  in ethnographic writing, 141
  as organizing principle, 142
  in visual anthropology, 464–465
Morgan, Lewis Henry, 12
motion film technology
  early attempts to use, 461–463
  and ethnography, 461–470
multicollinearity, 584
multidimensional scaling (MDS), 394, 394f, 396, 552, 567–568, 574f
  applications, 567–568
  maps, 567–568, 568f, 574f
  stress value in, 568
  in text analysis, 619, 622f
multilocale fieldwork, see multisited ethnography
multimethod ethnography, 165–166, 166f
multinational corporations, *see* transnational anthropology of work, multinational corporations
multiple regression analysis
  defined, 555
  example, 577–579
  and path analysis, 579
  uses of, 578–579
multisited ethnography, 247
multisited fieldwork, *see* multisited ethnography
Munroe, R. H., 658
Munroe, R. L., 658
Murdock, George Peter, 29, 651
Muybridge, Eadweard, 462
myth and history, 104
My Tribe syndrome, 188–189

Nadel, Siegfried, F., 46
Ñähñu (Otomí), 601
Nakota, spoken language, 436, 437f

Nanook of the North, 463
NAPA, *see* National Association of Practicing Anthropologists
Naroll, Raoul, 287–289
narrative accounts, 373
narrative ethnography, 263–264
narrative performance, patterns in, 598–602
  comparisons, cultural of, 601–604
  discovery of, 598
  examples, 598–601
National Anthropological Film Center, 460, 465
National Association of Practicing Anthropologists (NAPA), 177–178
National Institute of Ethnological Studies, 465
National Institute on Drug Abuse, 701, 715
National Security Education Program (NSEP), 175–176
nation-state, in anthropology, 659
Native American Text Series of the International Journal of American Linguistics, 596
natural experiments, 147
Navaho, 617–618
  filmmakers, 479
negative case analysis, 609
negative coefficient, 561
negative evidence, 44–45
network analysis, *see* structural analysis
network data, ethnographic, 712
networks, partial, *see* partial networks
New Guinea, 115
New Science, 90, 92
Nichter, Mark, 285
Nichter, Mimi, 285
night, as frontier, 155–156
Nightingale, Florence, 16
Nilotes, 648
Nisa: The Life and Words of a !Kung Woman, 215
nominal data, in behavior measurement, 310
nominal measurement, 679–680
nominal record linkage
  applications of, 519
  defined, 519
  publications about, 534n12
nominative technique, 707–708
nomothetic, defined, 47
nonmetric multidimensional scaling (MDS), 396, 397

nonparticipation, 262
nonprobability sampling methods, and ethnographic informants, 152–153
nonrandom assignment, problems of, 146
nonrandom samples, problems with, 374
nonverbal communication, 265, 267
nonverbal etymology, 105–106
nonverbal signs, 99–101
notes, *see* field notes
Notes and Queries in Anthropology, 10–11
note-taking, 353
    in interviewing process, 353
NSEP, National Security Education Program, 175–176
Nukulaelae (Polynesia), 597
numerical analysis
    applications, 586–587
    defined, 555
    fieldwork, types used in, 550–555
    historical, 584–585
numerical analysis tools, as related to anthropological questions, 556*t*
numerical methods, 549
numerical reasoning, 549, 555
Nupe, 648–649

Objectivity
O'Brien, M., 611–612
observation, pure, *see* pure observation
observational research designs, 149*t*
occupation studies, *see* transnational anthropology of work, occupation studies
Ogburn, William F., 17
OLS, *see* Ordinary Least Squares (OLS) regression
one group posttest only, 149*t*
O'Nell, W., 163–165, 164*f*
one-zero sampling, 321–322
ontology
    defined, 204
    feminist, 205–208
open-ended interviews, 349–350
    sample size, how to determine, 371–372
    when to use, 365
open-ended questions, 375, 709
oral history, 525
    aims of, 528
    applications, 522, 528
    as event-focused, 529–530
    as giving voice to the silent, 528

goals of, 520–530
publications about, 528
range of traditions, 528
and the written record, 529
Orans, Martin, criticism of Margaret Mead, 154–155
ordinal, 551
ordinal-scale measurement, 679–680
Ordinary Least Squares (OLS) regression
    defined, 576
    example, 576, 580–582
    validating findings, 582–586
Other, 40, 42, 140
    in feminist anthropology, 224
    and radical alerity, 55–56
outliers, 559
    defined, 552
Outline of Cultural Materials, 651, 673

Paired-comparisons, 367
    balanced-incomplete block designs, 390
    and correspondence analysis, 393, 393*f*
        vs. pile sorts, 390
    see also triad studies
panel data, 558
Panter-Brick, C., 316
PAR, *see* participatory action research
paralinguistic phenomena
    in narrative performance, 599
    in person-centered interviewing, 357
parameters, 553
parenting in the field, *see* children and fieldwork
Park, Robert, 14
Parsons, Elsie Clews, 15
partial networks, 713
participant camera, 487–488
participant observation
    advantages of, 266
    anonymity, maintaining, 274
    in anthropology, 237
    dangers in, 276–277
    defined, 259–261, 301–302
    degree of participation as problematic, 263
    disadvantages of, 266
    and emotional involvement, 262–263
    ethical concerns of, 263, 272–277, 280–284
    and ethnographer bias, 287–289
    examples of, 162–163, 163f, 165–166, 166*f*
    and field notes, 270–272

gender issues in, 277–280
guidelines, 266–267
historical link to functionalism, 261
importance of, 10, 264–265
as individualistic, 261–262
interdisciplinary use, 13–14
limiting participation of ethnologist, 276–277
as opposed to systematic observation, 304–307
as paradox, 263
and parenting, 284–287
physical involvement in, 262–263
rapport in, 267–270, 283, 284–285
and reflexive writing, 289–291
and the social sciences, 14
see also fieldwork
participatory action research (PAR), 693–694, 723–724
passive-observational studies, *see* experiments, natural
passive voice, to avoid agency and accountability, 93
paternalism
and informed consent, 188–190
path analysis, in multiple regression analysis, 555, 579
Peacock, N., 317–318
Pearson correlation coefficient, 380, 381, 396, 399, 400, 401, 561
and binary data, 588*n*4
in cross-cultural coding, 676
Pearson's r, *see* Pearson correlation coefficient
Pear Story, 601–602, 629*n*4
Pelto, Gretel, 720
percentage, 551
Perceptual Mapping Analysis (in SYSTAT), 586
permutation test, 554, 585
person-centered interviews
analyzing, 355–359
body-centered sociocultural topics, 344
children, inquiries about, 346
closing, 351
cognitive distortion in, 347
and concept of self, 343–344
conducting, 337–355
death, inquiries about, 345
as different from other interviewing methods, 335–336

distortions in, 347–352
emotion, inquiries about, 345
establishing trust with respondent in, 338, 340
expression vs. communication in, 359
health, inquiries about, 345
and identity, 342–343
and linguistic competence, 337–338
morality, inquiries about, 343–344
and motivations of respondents and informants in, 338–340
movement between informant and respondent modes in, 336
number and length of, 352
open-ended interventions in, 349–350
and paralinguistic phenomena, 357
as performing art, 334–335
probes, closed, 349–350
probes, open, 349–350
projective activities, inquiries about, 346
recording, 353–354
religion and the supernatural, inquiries about, 345–346
requirements of ethnographer to perform, 334–335
and respondent/informant ignoring probes, 357
sensitive topics in, 351
sensitivity in, 349
silence, role of, 351
similar to other interviewing methods, 335–336
technique, problems in, 335
topics, 340–342
transcribing, 354–355
and visual phenomena, 358
where to conduct, 340
women as informants, barriers to, 340
perspective, in filming, 489
photo/film elicitation, 475–477
photography
aerial, *see* aerial photography
in scientific archaeology, to reproduce culture, 480
still, uses of, 473, 475, 476
Pichátaro (Mexico), 157–159, 158*f*
PIEF, *see* Program in Ethnographic Filmmaking
pile-sorting, 367
in cognitive anthropology, 710

description of, 386
examples, 386–387, 387*f*
how to collect data using, 389
sample size in, 389
use of ANTHROPAC in, 367, 710
variations in method, 389
when to use, 388
poetic function, 97–98, *see also* cultural
poetics, social poetics
poetics of space, 112
poetic wisdom, 92, 94–95, *see also* social
poetics; cultural poetics
steps to attaining, 118
point estimate, 553
policy-oriented research, 721
policy research, in applied anthropology, 692
political economic history, in historical anthropology, 523–524
polygyny, 671, 673
Popol Vuh, 596
as textual performance, 599–600
Popper, Karl, 44
positive coefficient, 561
positive evidence, 44
positivism, 16–17, 42
classical, 43–44
impact on anthropology, 46, 76
and scientific theory, 68–69
and textual analysis, 395–396
types of, 43–45
Postel-Costner, Els, 597
postmodern influence on anthropology, 49
postmodernism, defined, 43
postmodernism and traditional ethnological
practices, 41
poststructuralism, 213
posttest only nonequivalent groups, 149*t*
power, dynamics of
in anthropological field research, 214–215
in feminist research, 214–215
pretest/posttest nonequivalent groups, 149*t*,
151
prevention research, and ecological theory, 701
primary data, in cross-cultural research
cost of using, 653, 656–657
defined, 652
example, 658
problems with, 658
primary relationships, *see* direct relationships
probabilistic sampling, *see* random sampling

probability, 553
profile data, *see* sentence substitute data
collection
PROFIT, *see* Property-Fitting (PROFIT) in
ANTHROPAC
Program in Ethnographic Filmmaking (PIEF),
460
Project Camelot, 175
Property-Fitting (PROFIT) in ANTHROPAC,
586
proportion, 551
proportionate stratified random sampling, 660
Protestantism, and capitalism, 165
proxy measurement, in cross-cultural research,
670
when to use, 669
proxy questions, 376
psychological anthropology, 361*n*13
publications, methodology, 12–13
Public Culture, 235
pure observation, 262
pure participation, 262

Q AP, *see* Quadratic Assignment Procedures
(QAP) in ANTHROPAC
Quadratic Assignment Procedures (QAP) in
ANTHROPAC, 587
quantile plots, 552
quantiles, defined, 551
quasi-experimental research designs, 149
quasi-experiments, 146*t*
vs. observational studies, 148
quaternary relationships, *see* indirect relationships
question formats, 375, *see also* open–ended
questions, close-ended multiple choice
questions, rating scales
questionnaire design, 373–401
questionnaire design, weakness in, 374–375
questions
general, in interviews, 374–379
proxy, *see* proxy questions
Quételet, Adolphe, 16
Quinn, Naomi, 161–162*f*, 605–607

R 2, *see* coefficient of determination
Radcliffe-Brown, A. R., 46, 513
radical alerity, 55–56, 79*n*4
radical conceptual relativism, *see* radical
alerity

radical constructivism, 43, 50, 55
Radin, Paul, 15, 596
random-interval instantaneous sampling, 318–321
  advantages of, 319–321
  disadvantages of, 320–321
random sampling
  advantages of, 660
  in ethnography, 702–703
  value of, 313–314
  vs. random assignment, 147
rapid ethnographic assessment, 717–718
  challenges in, 718
  characteristics of, 717
rapid ethnographic procedures, *see* rapid ethnographic assessment
rapid rural appraisals, *see* rapid ethnographic assessment
rapport, in participant observation
  building process, 269–270
  example, 268–269
  see participant observation, rapport development
rating scales
  in attitudinal studies, 382–385, 393–394
  creating a new scale, 384–385
  modifying existing materials for, 383–384
  as questioning format, 375
ratio, 551
rational choice theory, 66, 75
rational understanding, *see* empathic understanding, rational
RCA computer program, 626
realism, 54
recording, video, *see* video recording
recording technology
  historical, 423n8
  problems with, 423
recording technology, in fieldwork
  and dynamics of power, 423
  and self-consciousness, 423
  usefulness of, 423–424
reflexivity
  in anthropology, 142
  in feminist anthropology, 206–207, 218
  in film viewing, 282
  in participant observation, 262, 289–291
  and sex in the field, 282
regional comparisons, small-scale, *see* controlled comparison

Regnault, Félix-Louis, 461–462, 463
regression coefficient, 578
relational data, *see* full network data
relative frequency, 665
reliability, test, *see* split-half reliability; test-retest reliability
reliability coefficient, 380
reliability of tests, in interviews, 380–382
reports, for development agencies, 758–759
reproduction, gendering of, 223–224
rereading, of pioneer women anthropologists, 209
research, ethnographic
  explanatory and exploratory, 144–145, 145f
  secret, 179–180
  as social action, 413
research data, ethical use of, 181–182
research design
  components, 134, 144–145
  defined, 132–133
  and funding agencies, 132
  importance of, 133–134, 144
  influence of ethnography on, 143
  limitations of, 145
  purpose of, 145
  systematic, 143–151
research designs
  anthropological, basic, 149t
  experimental, 555
  observational, 149t
  quasi-experimental, 149t, 151
research projects, potential and ethics, 181
residuals, defined, 580
resistance, and communities open to the world, 238
respondent, in person-centered interviewing, defined, 335
Review Boards, 182–184
Ricoeur, Paul, 48
risk-taking behavior, and ego network analysis, 713
ritual space within cultural space, 495–496
Rivers, W.H.R., 11–12
Rorschach test, 13
rotation, 565
Rouch, Jean, 498n4
  and visual anthropology, 464, 467
  colonialism, 466
  contributions to, 464
  use of montage in, 464–465

Royal Anthropological Institute Film Festival, 497*n*1

Royal Anthropological Institute (RAI) of Great Britain and Ireland, 10

Rubel, A. J., 163–165, 164*f*

Ruby, Jay, 460

Sackett, R., 304–306, 305*t*, 306*t*

Sahlins-Obeyesekere debate, 104

Salinas, Jésus, 601

Samoa, 135–136, 153–154

sample
how to choose, 153
cluster, 552–567
deliberate, 152
fixed-interval instantaneous, 317–318
nonprobability, 152–153
nonrandom, 374
one-zero, 321–322
random, 147, 313–314
random-interval instantaneous, 318–321
saturation, 703–704
unbiased, 553
units, 704–705

sample design
influences on, 151
types of, 151

sample size, 612, 613

sampling
in cross-cultural research, 657–653
use of primary data in, 658
defined, 553
in sociological text analysis, 612–618
examples, 612–613

sampling frame, in cross-cultural research, 652, 657, 659, 663

sampling universe, 312

San Blas Kuna chant, as textual performance, 600

Sapir, Edward, 15

SAS, 396

SAVICOM, *see* Society for the Anthropology of Visual Communication

scales
construct validity of, 376–377
content validity of, 376
development by questioning process, 376–378
examples, 377
Guttman, 377–378, 586

scaling, multidimensional, *see* multidimensional scaling (MDS)

scans, *see* group scans

schema
defined, 604
examples of, 605–607

Schwiezer, Thomas, 625–626, 631*n*13

scientific explanation, 62–65, 77

scientific method
actual use of in fieldwork, 134–137
defined, 40
vs. humanistic method, 41

Screening Score for Psychiatric Impairment, 164

scree plot, 564, 564f

script, *see* metaphor

script theory, 699–700

secondary data, in cross-cultural research, 653
defined, 653

secondary relationships, *see* direct relationships

secret research, 179–180, 182

self, concept of, 343–344

Seligmann, Brenda, 11, 648

Seligmann, Charles, 11, 648

semantic anthropology, 95

semantic domain, *see* cultural domain

semantic network analysis, 621

semasiological theory of human actions, 433

sentence substitute data collection, 395–396

sex, in the field
advice to graduate students, 284
ethical question of, 283
historical accounts of, 281
lack of discussion about, 280–281
and reflexivity, 280–281

sexual differences, naturalness questioned, 211

sexuality, as cultural construct, 213

sexual participation, by ethnographer
as data, 283
and exploitation, 283
impact on subsequent researchers, 283
as important to acceptance, 283
and informed consent, 283

SfAA, *see* Society for Applied Anthropology

shapono, 263

Sherzer, Joel, 600

short-term memory, 303–304

Signalyze computer program, 427, 443*n*9

Sign Language, Plains, 436, 437*f*

similarity coefficients, 552

defined, 552
types of, 561
situated knowledge, 215
Six Cultures project, 656
skewing, in measurement, 552
snowball sampling, 705
Social Adjustment Rating Scale, Holmes and
    Rahe, 383–384
social construction theories, 699
social network,
    analysis, 75–76
    theory, 700–701
social poetics, 95, 96–97, 114
    criticisms of, 96
Society for Applied Anthropology (SfAA), 174
Society for the Anthropology of Visual
    Communication (SAVICOM), 460
Society for Visual Anthropology (SVA),
    460–461
sociocognitive theory, 697–698
sociogeographic mapping, 713–714
sociolinguistics, 413, 442n2
sociological analysis of text, 604–607
    methodology, 619
Sorenson, E., 470–471
SoundEdit computer program, 427, 432f,
    443n9
soundscape, 421–422
space, meanings of, 111–112
Spain, D. H., criticisms of Mead, 154–155
spatial autocorrelation, 584, 679
spatial mapping, see sociogeographic mapping
Spearman-Brown Prophesy Formula, 553–554,
    585
    in cross-cultural research, 676
specialized networks, see partial networks
Spencer, Baldwin, 459, 463
split-half reliability, in tests, 380
spot checks, see random-interval instantaneous
    sampling
spot observation, see random-interval instan-
    taneous sampling
Spradley's domain analysis, 709
Sri Lanka, 724
SSPS, see Statistical Package for the Social
    Sciences
Standard Cross-Cultural Sample, 659, 661–662
standard deviation, 552, 559
standard error of estimate, 581–582
Standard Ethnographic Sample, 659, 661, 662

standardized regression coefficients, 579
standpoint theory, 213–215, 217
State Ethnographical Museum of the Estonian
    Soviet Socialist Republic, 465
static-group comparison, 149t, 152, 154, 157
    example, 159–160
statistical inference, 157–158, 160
Statistical Package for the Social Sciences
    (SPSS), Reliability Procedure in, 381
statistical tests, 553
    classical, 553
stem-and-leaf plots, 552, 559, 560f
Stephen, Lynn, 218–219
stratified random sampling, 660
stress value, in multidimensional scaling, 568
structural analysis, 621
    example, 621–622, 622f
structural behavioral descriptions, 323–324
structuralism, 621
structuralist theory concept, 69–71
stucturalist theory of science, 50
structuralist-functionalism, as ahistorical, 514
studies
    classification, 367
    knowledge, 366
studies, attitudinal, see attitudinal studies
subcultural variation, 570
sufficient redundancy, interviewing, in satura-
    tion sampling, 704
Sumner, William Graham, 651
Susser, Ida, study on New York City home-
    less, 222–223
susto, 163–165
SVA, see Society for Visual Anthropology
SVA Film/Video Festival, 460–461
symbolic analysis, defined, 602
symbolic anthropology, 95, 525, 722
symbols
    analysis of, 100–101
    instability of meaning, 98–99
    variation in meaning, permissible, 98–99
symmetrical, in measurement, 552
synchronic comparison, defined, 652
synchronic measurement, 671
SYSTAT computer program, 554, 564, 580
systematic distortion, in person-centered
    interviews, 347
systematic random sampling, 660
systematic research design, 138, 139f, 315–
    322

example of, 155–156
Systems of Consanguinity and Affinity of the
    Human Family, 12

Tagging, in sociological text analysis,
    615–616
Tamang (Nepal), 316
tape recording
    advantages of, 422, 423
    in discourse-centered approach, 422–424
    in person-centered interviews, 348, 353–
        354
    problems in the field, 422–423
targeted sampling, 707
TAT test, 13
taxonomic elicitation, 372
teaching
    methods, 748–749
    use of technology in, 748–749
teamwork, in ethnography, 719–721
    managing, 720
Techniques du corps, 462
technology
    recording, *see* recording technology
    and teaching, 748–749
Tedlock, Dennis, 425–427, 426*f*, 599–600
teleology, 111
telephone interviews, 374
Temascalcingo, 285
temporal autocorrelation, 584
tertiary relationships, *see* indirect relationships
test-retest reliability, 380
tests
    in interviewing, reliability of, 380–382
    statistical, *see* statistical tests
text, in traditional linguistic analysis, 419–
    420
text analysis
    computer-assisted, 627
    guide for research, 627
    reviews of software, sources for, 627*n*5
    use of computers in, 627
text analysis studies
    linguistic tradition, defined, 595
    proliferation of, 628*n*1
    requirements to carry out, 602
    sociological tradition of, defined, 595
    see also classical content analysis, grounded
        theory, indigenous literature, metaphor,
        narrative performance, patterns in,

sampling, in sociological text analysis,
    schema
textbooks, anthropological, 739–742
    audience for, 740–741
    experimental, 742
    features of good, 741
    and used book market, 740–741
    writer, becoming a, 740
text coding, 608–609
text description, in ethnographic research, 323
theory
    in anthropology, 72–76, 73–74
    building, 73–74
    elements, 70–71, 78
    historical, rereading, 72, 78
    uses of, 71–72
theory and method, relationship, 204
theory-blind coders, *see* coders, naive
theory-nets
    in anthropology, 74–76, 78
    in structuralism, 71
thick description, 48
time allocation studies, 314–315, 318–321
time allocation technique, *see* random-interval
    instantaneous sampling
time-point sampling, *see* fixed-interval instan-
    taneous sampling
time-sampling, instantaneous, 311
time-series data, 558
Todas, 12
Torres Straits, 11
tourism studies, transnational, 243
transcribing, tape recordings, 354–355
transcribing audio tapes, 354–355
transcription systems, phonetic, development
    of, 424–425
translocalities studies, transnational, 239
transmigrants, 240
transnational, defined, 237
transnational anthropology
    as collaborative work, with natives, 250
    history of, 236
transnational anthropology of work, 241–242
    multinational corporations, 241–242
    occupation studies, 242
transnationalism, 217–218
transnational studies
    cultural competence of anthropologist,
        249–250
    dispersion vs. intensity, 248–249

length of studies, temporal, 249
size of populations, 248–249
units of study, 246–248
types of, 237–246
triad studies, 367
administering, 390
ANTHROPAC in, 391
balanced-incomplete block designs, 367
creating, 391
and multidimensional scaling, 394, 394*f*
in psychology, 390
tabulating responses, 390–394
types of data used for, 393
vs. pile studies, 390
see also paired comparisons
triangulation, 550, 719
uses of, 575
Trobriand Islands, 260, 278
true experiments, 146
t-tests, 553, 582, 583
Tulle, Marie Trees, 218–219
Turner, Victor, 525
2SLS, *see* Two-Staged Least Squares
Two-Staged Least Squares (2SLS), 585
Tylor, Edward B., 29, 584–585, 677–678
Type I error, in measurement, 667
Type II error, in measurement, 667

U.S. Department of the Army, Project
    Camelot, 175
universal interviewing, in saturation sampling,
    703–704
unobtrusive research, 184
unstandardized regression coefficients, 579
urban ethnography, 14
Uricho (Mexico), 157–159, 158*f*
USAID, 759–760

Validity
challenges to question response, 378–379
defined, 555
external, in quasi-experiments, 152
external threats to, 150, 150*t*, 151
internal threats to, 150, 150*t*
types of, 148–149
universal, in worldwide cross-cultural
    research, 654
value-free science, 17
Vansina, Jan, 527–528

variable
high-inference, *see* high-inference variable,
    in cross-cultural research
low-inference, *see* low-inference variable,
    in cross-cultural research
variables, 550
and indirect and direct measurement, 664
variation, 550, 552
random, 575
Vedda, 11
verisimilitude, 307, 328
verstehen
as complementary to explanation, 65–67
defined, 47
varieties of, 57–58
Vico, Giambattista, 90, 92, 98–99, 109, 111,
    120*n*5
video recording
and discourse-centered methods, 422
problems with, 361*n*14
Vienna Circle, 44, 46
logical positivism of, 17
Vietnam War, and ethics, 176
violence
in the field, 278, 283–284
against men, 278, 283–284
against women, 215–216, 217
visual anthropology
and cross-cultural studies, 473–474
focus, differences between U.S. and
    Europe, 459
founders of, 459
history of, technological, 460
history of, as a discipline, 459, 460–461
methodology, 475–478
elicitation, 475–477
feedback, 477–478
problems in, 483–487
reverse, 467
see also film, ethnographic
visual ethnography, 487
example of, 489–490, 491*f*, 492*f*, 496*f*
visual phenomena, in person-centered inter-
    viewing, 358

Webb, Beatrice, 14
Weber, Max, and value-free social science,
    52–53
weighted least squares, 585

Whiting, Beatrice, 656
Whiting, John, 656
WHO Acute Respiratory Infection, project,
 720
Winnebago (language), 596
Wissler, Clark, 15
within-region comparisons, 655–656
Wolf, Eric, 10, 596
women ethnographers
 and access to the worlds of women, 278,
 340
 and violence in the field, 278, 283–284
women as a homogeneous group, problem
 with, 212
women as informants
 access problems with, 340
 and oral history, 528
word-by-word co-occurence matrix, 622–623
World Bank, 753
 presenting anthropology to, 755–758
World Ethnographic Sample, 659, 662
Worth, Sol, 460, 462
Wozniak, Danielle, 557–563
writing
 articles, 744–745
 importance in fieldwork, 744–745

Xavante, 428–430, 429–430*f*, 439
Ximénez, Francisco, 599

Yanomamo, 142, 263, 276, 281, 615–616
 and ethnographic films, 469
Yolmo, 264–265
Young, J. C., 157–159, 158*f*

Zabusky, Stacia, 117
Zapotec (Mexico), 476, 487
zero-order analysis, 554
Zhang, Y., 162–163, 163*f*
Zuni, 617–618